# STUDIES IN THE BYZANTINE MONETARY ECONOMY

*c.* 300–1450

# STUDIES IN THE BYZANTINE MONETARY ECONOMY *c.* 300–1450

MICHAEL F. HENDY

*Associate Advisor in Numismatics, Dumbarton Oaks Center for Byzantine Studies, Washington, D.C.*
*Lecturer in Numismatics, University of Birmingham*



CAMBRIDGE UNIVERSITY PRESS

CAMBRIDGE

LONDON NEW YORK NEW ROCHELLE

MELBOURNE SYDNEY

CAMBRIDGE UNIVERSITY PRESS
Cambridge, New York, Melbourne, Madrid, Cape Town, Singapore, São Paulo, Delhi

Cambridge University Press
The Edinburgh Building, Cambridge CB2 8RU, UK

Published in the United States of America by Cambridge University Press, New York

www.cambridge.org
Information on this title: www.cambridge.org/9780521247153



First published 1985
This digitally printed version 2008

*A catalogue record for this publication is available from the British Library*

*Library of Congress Catalogue Card Number: 83–2631*

ISBN 978-0-521-24715-3 hardback
ISBN 978-0-521-08852-7 paperback

# CONTENTS

SECTION IV: COINAGE (PRODUCTION)

# PLATES

(between pp. 734 and 735)

# MAPS

# TABLES

# ABBREVIATIONS

| | |
|---|---|
| *BNC* | C. Morrisson, *Catalogue des monnaies byzantines de la Bibliothèque Nationale* (2 vols) |
| CFHB | Corpus Fontium Historiae Byzantinae |
| *CJ* | *Codex Justinianus* |
| CSHB | Corpus Scriptorum Historiae Byzantinae – 'Bonn edn' |
| *CTh.* | *Codex Theodosianus* |
| *DOC* | *Catalogue of the Byzantine Coins in the Dumbarton Oaks Collection and in the Whittemore Collection* (see Bibliography I *s.v.* A. R. Bellinger, P. Grierson and M. F. Hendy) |
| *DOP* | *Dumbarton Oaks Papers* |
| *DOS* | *Dumbarton Oaks Studies* |
| *DOT* | *Dumbarton Oaks Texts* |
| *FHG* | *Fragmenta Historicorum Graecorum* |
| MGH | Monumenta Germaniae Historica:<br>*AA – Auctores Antiquissimi*<br>*Ep. – Epistolae*<br>*SRG: NS – Scriptores Rerum Germanicarum, Nova Series*<br>*SRLang. – Scriptores Rerum Langobardicarum et Italicarum Saec. VI–IX*<br>*SRMerov. – Scriptores Rerum Merovingicarum*<br>*SS – Scriptores* |
| *MIB* | W. R. O. Hahn, *Moneta Imperii Byzantini* (3 vols) |
| *N.Dig.Occ.* | *Notitia Dignitatum Occidentalis* |
| *N.Dig.Or.* | *Notitia Dignitatum Orientalis* |
| *PG* | Patrologiae Cursus Completus, *Patrologia Graeca* |
| *PL* | Patrologiae Cursus Completus, *Patrologia Latina* |
| *PLRE* | *Prosopography of the Later Roman Empire* (2 vols) |
| *PO* | *Patrologia Orientalis* |
| *PSI* | see Bibliography F: *Papiri greci e latini* |
| RHC,*Occ.* | Recueil des Historiens des Croisades, *Historiens Occidentaux* |
| *RIC* | *The Roman Imperial Coinage* (see Bibliography I *s.v.* P. M. Bruun, J. P. C. Kent, J. W. E. Pearce and C. H. V. Sutherland) |
| *Sb.* | *Sammelbuch griechischen Urkunden aus Aegypten* (see Bibliography F) |
| *SPP* | C. Wessely, *Studien zur Palaeographie und Papyruskunde* |

# PREFACE AND ACKNOWLEDGEMENTS

This book has been an unconscionable time in preparation, and one can only hope that it is the better for it. Written over a number of years, in a number of places, various institutions (willingly or unwillingly) bear some responsibility for its existence: the Fitzwilliam Museum, Cambridge; the Barber Institute of Fine Arts and the Department of Mediaeval History, University of Birmingham; and the Dumbarton Oaks Center for Byzantine Studies, Washington, D.C.; to name only the main ones.

In the course of the text, I have attempted to quote, verbatim and extensively, as many of the major primary sources as is possible and as seems relevant. I have done this because a number of them have not previously been rendered into a modern language, or, even if they have been so rendered, are still not readily accessible. I thus hope to have made them accessible to students and amateurs who lack the necessary languages, or the academic facilities, or both. This has meant that, in many cases, and with some trepidation, I have had to do the translating involved myself. In doing so, I have attempted to retain the original form and flavour in as far as it is possible, and particularly where the ponderous, allusive, and elliptical pomposity of imperial legislation is concerned. On the other hand, I have felt little hesitation in changing the moods or tenses of verbs where I have thought it necessary the better to indicate a particular modern sense, or to retain a reasonable linguistic facility.

The extensive quotation of sources has also been undertaken in the belief that, where a source is virtually or entirely self-explanatory, it is better to allow it to remain so, and that it is in any case frequently quite as succinct as a modern paraphrase and commentary.

Technical terms, and crucial phrases, have nevertheless been simply transliterated and included in parenthesis where thought necessary, for the use of scholars.

I genuinely would be most grateful for the correction of egregious errors (particularly where couched in moderate terms), and – as I have doubtless not picked up all the major sources that are available, and that I ought to have done – for the provision of any additions to what I hope to be the emergent canon.

I have generally, at least where easily possible, given Greek personal and family names, and Greek toponymics, in an English or Latinised form (the latter quite often with the modern equivalent, where very different, as is frequently the case with Turkish). This I have done partly for the ease of the more general reader (if any such there be), and partly in reaction to the lunatic excesses of direct, and extremely complex, transliteration, to be seen in at least one still quite recently published book. Where I have broken this general rule, it has tended to be either quoting or directly reporting a mediaeval author, or with a definite aim in mind: for example, whereas I have generally used the forms Macedonia and Cappadocia where the wider geographical sense is to be indicated, I have nevertheless used the forms Makedonia and Kappadokia where a particular administrative circumscription (i.e. a mediaeval theme) is involved.

Footnotes, with regard to the inevitable and omnipresent consideration of expense, have been kept to a minimum, not so much of number, but certainly of length. In general, I have referred either to the original textual source, or to the most modern comprehensive treatment of the subject involved, or to both, only. I have attempted to do the equivalent for the bibliography, which as a body of material is extensive, but in which individual entries have been kept to a minimum. For other reasons entirely, I have been able to take major acount of works published before – sometimes, and always at a stretch, actually in – 1981, only.

I owe particular thanks to my friend and colleague, Chris Wickham, both for much stimulating discussion – whether in the course of conversation, or in that of joint teaching – and for performing the arduous task of reading over the text in typescript and making valuable suggestions with regard to it. If I have not invariably acted upon them, then I bear full responsibility, and for the remaining faults and eccentricities, whether analytical or otherwise, he of course cannot be blamed.

I also owe thanks to my friend Alan McQuillan for advice on various matters of an agricultural or a technological nature.

I owe a number of cardinal references to the kindness of various friends, colleagues, and pupils, and I have attempted to indicate my indebtedness and thanks at the appropriate points in the text. If I have forgotten any, I can only tender my apologies and express my thanks here and now, with the assurance that any such omission was entirely unintentional.

For the final typing of the text and footnotes, I owe thanks to Joyce Kirkpatrick and Diana Glanville-Jones of the School of Hellenic and Roman Studies, University of Birmingham.

For the photography involved in the plates, I owe principal thanks to Eric Taylor of the Barber Institute, University of Birmingham, from the collection of which the great majority of the non-Dumbarton Oaks coins illustrated derive.

I would also like to thank my friends Simon Bendall and John Casey for invaluable help, and particularly for that given at short notice with regard to the plates.

Fox the drawing of the splendid series of maps, I owe thanks to Jean Dowling of the Department of Geography, University of Birmingham.

For being a kind and patient but efficient sub-editor, with an eagle eye for the superfluous comma, I owe thanks to Ann Johnston of the Cambridge University Press.

And lastly, I should particularly like to thank the British Academy, but also the Foundation for the Promotion of Numismatic and Archaeological Research, Basel; and the University of Birmingham; for generous grants in aid of publication, without which the book inevitably would have been far more expensive even than regrettably, and necessarily, it actually is.

*Department of Mediaeval History*
*The University of Birmingham*
*27 October 1982*

# INTRODUCTION

When, now a number of years ago, I commenced work on this book, it was intended as a very different kind of affair from that which it has eventually turned out to be. It was originally intended to be a single volume, of moderate length, on the Byzantine coinage in the wider sense: that is, both as regards chronology and as regards scope. It is now a series of eight studies, on the three main constituent elements in the Byzantine monetary economy: economy and society, finance, and coinage (circulation and production).

From the nature and extent of the three elements mentioned above, it should be obvious that I do not regard the study of an historical monetary economy as consisting of the mere record and analysis of coin hoards and archaeological site-finds (although I hope that eventually both of these will have their own not inconsiderable place), but as something much wider and more inclusive. It is, after all, pointless to analyse coin finds, and to derive 'monetary' or 'economic' conclusions from such analyses, either in total ignorance of the fundamental causative factors behind the production and circulation of a coinage, or on the basis of some superficial or faulty causative and behavioural framework.

In any case, each of the eight resultant studies, or chapters, is more or less self-contained, and the fact that the findings of each, whether implicit or explicit, are not formally and comprehensively interrelated in a concluding synthesis, is quite deliberate. For although many of the particular relationships implied or specified will be outlined, and although the nature and directions of future explorations will be indicated, in a concluding section, thereby at least suggesting the overall shape of the final structure as it seems likely to emerge, this series is, and is intended to be, a preliminary one only, and to be followed by one, or perhaps even two, more. In other words, much remains to be done before the history, dynamics and mode of operation of the Byzantine monetary economy emerges in as full a detail, if in however imperfect a fashion, as it is possible for me to depict and analyse it.

The distinction between original intention and present reality is the result of a number of factors, some personal, others impersonal. But in retrospect, it was certainly premature, and perhaps even naïve, given the existing state of the discipline, to suppose that the Byzantine coinage, in its desired wider sense, could be encapsulated within a single moderate volume. A necessary pre-condition for such an attempt is the existence of a largely defined body of material, and a reasonably limited range of opinions as to its significance. This situation barely obtains in the case of the Byzantine coinage in its narrowest sense, let alone in that of its wider, and, *a fortiori*, its widest, sense.

Byzantinists of all disciplines frequently complain of the lack of surviving evidence, and Byzantine numismatists and historians are no exception to this general rule. To a certain extent, of course, the complaint has foundation. Numismatists, for example, quite justifiably point out the complete lack of the mint documentation that, in most western states, survives however sporadically at first, and increasingly with time. To a certain extent, equally, the complaint lacks justification. While certain types of documentation undoubtedly have failed to survive, others have not, and it therefore behoves the Byzantine numismatist to make the best possible use of what is available, rather than to lament what is not. This may well mean that a number of the questions which numismatists in other fields have traditionally asked and still do ask of their material will, in the case of Byzantine numismatics, turn out to be unanswerable – at least by way of the traditional and currently conceivable methods of enquiry. While these questions should not be entirely neglected, and new methods of enquiry into them should certainly be explored, it is probably more useful, for the moment at least, to award them a lower order of priority than is customary, and to turn instead to different questions for which the surviving material is better suited to providing the answers.

For the numismatist, if for no other scholar, the implied or incipient choice involved is an acute one, presenting imagined or even real difficulties. On the one hand, there exists a series of coins, the chronological and geographical spread of which is virtually if not entirely unparalleled, and the historical information from which – on even a very limited interpretation of the discipline – there is to be gained an amount at least commensurate with that spread. On the other hand, between this and what is in kind a totally different body of evidence there is next to nothing: not only no state archives or mint documents, but no mercantile manuals except western ones which deal with eastern materials only incidentally; no epistolary collections or journals with a consistent numismatic, financial, or economic bias; no account-books (again except for the latest period and even then largely of western origin); and no municipal archives with collections of mercantile regulations and documents.

Because of this accentuated division between coins as such and the other materials which have potential or real bearing upon coins or coinage in a wider sense, the Byzantine numismatist has tended to internalise his discipline: to worry incessantly about problems – again imagined or real – such as the nature and development of imperial dress and regalia, and the propagandist intent behind the issue of coin; the sequence of issues and the identity of mints; even the number of coins going to make up an issue or a series of issues. All these subjects have their own place and significance. This author has himself indulged in several of them, and a concentration upon them is certainly not confined to Byzantine numismatics, being in some cases shared with the ancient branch of the discipline, in some with the western mediaeval, and in some with both and indeed others. Much more than this, however, is needed, and much more, as it happens, is possible.

There have been, it is true, faint signs, more recently, of the evolution of a rather wider consciousness. The existence of such a wider consciousness, or at least of its desirability, has indeed generally been acknowledged, but has all too frequently been the subject of lip-service, or of decorous consignment to the (apparently ever-receding) future, when the state of the discipline shall permit it: 'the Time is not Ripe'.

Nevertheless quite recently, for instance, an attempt has been made to trace in some detail, and to account for, the first phase (*c.* 1040–71) of the increasingly severe and eventually catastrophic debasement of the precious-metal coinages in the eleventh century, in terms that are well outside the normally accepted ones. To be sure, the very attempt is in itself praiseworthy, but the distinction in the degree of success attained as between the measurement and the explanation of the phenomenon well reveals the limitations of the conceptual framework within which even leading numismatists tend to work.

Now, given the establishment of a basic sequence of issues, and of a reasonably accurate and (not unimportant) an appropriately used method of metallurgical analysis, the course of a debasement is capable of being plotted without too much difficulty, and in this particular case, in its main lines at least, it may now be considered to have been successfully effected. But, beyond that, the application of Fisher's Equation (essentially a development, but not the most developed form, of the Quantity Theory of Money) to the phenomenon not only fails to provide a satisfactory explanation for it, but also quite unconsciously begs a number of really fundamental questions as regards the nature and operation of the Byzantine – and for that matter of most ancient and mediaeval – monetary economies.

The assumption implicit in the application of this equation, that is that the Byzantine monetary economy functioned essentially as a modern free and commercially based and oriented one, and that the laws governing the former must immutably, and in detail, have been identical with those that govern the latter, may well appear attractive, the more particularly so as the precious-metal – or, more precisely, the gold – coinage appears in the light of a traditional commodity, and as credit played a relatively minor, and may even have played an absolutely minimal, rôle at all major levels of commerce and finance. It is to be observed, however, that the recent application of strict monetarist policies, which evolve from and rely upon such equations and theories, to several modern economies, has not left many convinced of their entire validity even there.

The reality, paradoxically enough, is in any case likely to have been at once both more simple and more complex. It goes without saying, of course, that the Byzantines knew nothing of Fisher's Equation itself, and in all probability that they were almost equally ignorant of each of its conceptual components. Admittedly, its strict operation amongst the Byzantines is in no way thereby disproved, although such ignorance may well not be entirely insignificant. But, in addition, on all the available evidence, the Byzantine coinage was intended to perform certain very limited functions only, and amongst these functions that of public utility (the provision of a convenient medium of exchange for the private sector of the economy) ranked as very secondary. It was produced according to the current pattern and emphasis of the imperial fiscal administration, in which the structural needs and requirements of that administration were modified by one further identifiable consideration, those of the imperial military forces. It was distributed, at least as far as its precious-metal components were concerned, entirely as the product of state expenditure, in which the principal item was provided by those same military forces. It was therefore distributed according to a very accentuated and fundamentally 'uneconomic' pattern, in which a particular region might well be agriculturally highly exploited, fiscally productive, with a relatively large number of urban concentrations, and a correspondingly numerous and complex population, and yet both lack a mint, because there were present no appreciable military concentrations, and apparently any alternative methods of coin-supply. It was distributed, as far as its base-metal components were concerned, either as state expenditure, or through the medium of technical fiscal practices which, while they may have ensured a considerable volume of production and a greater degree of uniformity of distribution, also involved discrimination against those base-metal components, both on the part of the state (certain), and on that of private citizens (probable, at least where anything else was available for the purposes of storing wealth). In other words, precious- and base-metal coinages were produced and distributed to serve very different functions, not simply that of serving as convenient vehicles for high- and low-value private exchanges.

It is true that the precious-metal components of the coinage were the preferred, even demanded, medium, in the payment of state taxes, but the state itself was apparently normally unconcerned as to their availability, and as to the provision of the means of rendering them readily available. It therefore shows every sign of having been endemically scarce, even in those regions where it would have been much more convenient to the population at large for it to be common.

It is equally true that the normal processes of exchange and trade would have guaranteed that this extraordinarily accentuated pattern of production and distribution was to some extent alleviated as regards circulation and supply. But at the same time it should not be forgotten that this monetary economy, which at the outset was both specialised and superficial, also functioned in a society in which – inevitably – the means of communication were painfully crude and slow; in which the costs of transport, at least in areas that were more than a few miles removed from a navigable river, or from the sea, were extremely high; in which therefore trade in basic products was acutely limited as regards distance, and that in luxury products was equally limited as regards volume; in which the producer was almost invariably the distributor and/or the seller, operating almost equally invariably on a small scale; in which there in any case seems to have been a fundamental distinction in the degree to which coin was available and/or used, both as between rural and urban areas, and as between regions and metropolis; and in which (besides the emperor) a very few secular families and the church as a corporate body owned a very high proportion of the total of available moveable (as well as other) wealth, a very high proportion of this in turn being immobilised in the form of plate in its widest sense, or hoarded in the form of coin.

It is of course true that many or most of these features were not peculiar to Byzantine civilisation, but obtained in most or all large ancient or mediaeval societies. Indeed, in this respect, it might well turn out to be extremely useful to be aware of the nature and operation of a monetary economy in a historically recent, or even present-day, but still primitive or underdeveloped, society. In the case of Byzantium in particular, and indeed that of the gold-based eastern and southern Mediterranean in general, the mechanics and velocity of circulation of the standard, and overwhelmingly the most important, denomination will have been determined not least by the extremely high purchasing power of the nomisma/dinar, whether metallically pure or subjected to a moderate degree of debasement, and – with regard to Byzantium, at least, and over long stretches of time – by the lack of a reasonably flexible system of subordinate denominations. Even when gold was used in private transactions, it seems clear that the sum involved was normally weighed out, the actual weight of the coins necessarily being almost invariably made up or restored to the theoretical one, in itself a most cumbersome physical process.

In the light of all these circumstances separately or in combination, and despite wide-ranging claims to the contrary, it is at least questionable whether the application of Fisher's Equation has much, if any, relevance to the situation, and whether the pre-conditions necessary for its operation in any chronologically and geographically uniform, and in any detailed, fashion existed.

Part of the trouble, of course, is that the Byzantine coinage-system was in its primary characteristics alone an economic phenomenon, and that between it and the economy as a whole there intervened the state, its finances, and its political will and its ability to exploit society and the economy as a whole, as a major – probably the major – secondary determinant factor.

In a civilisation in which the sources of revenue effectively available to the state were only minimally flexible; in which the dominant classes of society had the greatest capacity to evade such financial obligations as the state chose to impose upon them; and in which the significant use of credit in any flexible and systematic sense on the part of the state was simply not possible, it is all too easy to envisage a set of circumstances in which, at a time of general economic expansion and demographic increase, because of the political power that increasingly, and mainly, accrued to the dominant classes as a result of their social and economic position, the state would paradoxically have found it increasingly difficult, and eventually impossible, to extract from those classes and eventually from society as a whole, the revenue that it needed to perform its traditional rôles. At this stage, even in the absence of such complicating factors as imperial extravagance and increased military and civil expenditure (for all of which there is ample evidence), it would have been threatened, perhaps even afflicted, by a classic budgetary deficit. No matter that it might have had reserves to rely on for some while: it provided a classic response to the problem – the debasement of the precious-metal coinages.

What the state could not extract from the dominant classes, it might attempt, of course, to extract from the dependent ones – in other words to 'screw the peasants' – and there is explicit, if slightly later (that is, twelfth-century) evidence, in the shape of the treatise known as the *Palaia kai Nea Logarikē*, which demonstrates that it had attempted to do just that. This was obviously an entirely unsatisfactory solution, or attempted solution, both as regards equity and as regards practicalities: it may well be that the financial short-fall made on the dominant classes was, in the long run, simply not capable of being made up on the dependent ones, and even if it were, the social and economic consequences of the resultant crippling over-taxation of the latter classes, in anything but the short run, might have proved obviously disastrous and self-defeating. It is noticeable that when the state found itself once more in a position to reassert the financial control that it had lost, it speedily did so. The apparent contradiction in the fact that the emperor involved in this reassertion of state control, Alexius I, was a member of one of the leading families of those classes that had earlier escaped control, and was by then systematically allied by blood and marriage to a nexus of other such families, merely emphasises the simple truth that if the individual at the head of the state wished it to perform its traditional rôles – and in many ways Alexius was a very traditional figure – then some appreciable degree of financial control over the dominant classes was a crude necessity.

Other similar models of this kind, none of which need necessarily be represented as, or based upon, a precise mathematical interrelationship, can be constructed without difficulty: this is perhaps merely the most plausible.

These observations are not intended on the one hand to advocate a retreat to the *laager* of internalised numismatics, nor on the other to deprecate the use of modern methods of monetary analysis. Still less are they designed to suggest that the Byzantine coinage and monetary system operated in some mystical way, entirely removed from the observation and empirical knowledge of contemporaries, and equally absolved from behaviour conforming to recently formulated economic laws: the anonymous author of the *De Rebus Bellicis*, describing the effects of Constantine's confiscation of the temple-treasures, seems to have some basic perception of the interrelation of metallic supply and its consequence for the level of appropriate exchanges; both Procopius and John Lydus, describing the effects of Justinian's abandonment of the public post, seem to have an equivalent perception of that and its consequence for the supply of coin; both Theophanes and the patriarch Nicephorus place Constantine V's attempt at gold thesaurisation in correct juxtaposition to the consequent fall in the prices of other commodities; the composition of twelfth-century hoards of billon coins acutely reflects the monetary manipulations of contemporary emperors with regard to their silver-content, and therefore the effective operation – if not necessarily the conscious knowledge – of Gresham's Law.

What they are intended to suggest is that it is on the one hand unacceptable for the numismatist, in accounting for some monetary phenomenon, to connect it with a contemporary 'economic crisis' (for the basic distinction between a financial and an economic crisis is one that is scarcely ever made), the existence of which is asserted through reference to another such assertion, which turns out to be based on a statement in George Ostrogorsky's *History of the Byzantine State* – however distinguished that author, and however valuable that work. But they are also intended to suggest that it is on the other hand equally dangerous, that is dangerous enough to be unacceptable, for the numismatist, in accounting for some other monetary phenomenon, to insert it into a precise mathematical interrelationship evolved in the light of modern monetary theories and conditions. In general, if in no other sense, the result is thereby lent an entirely spurious air of precision and authority, and the nature and mode of operation of the ancient or mediaeval monetary economy involved is effectively never questioned.

Much the same kind of approach and much the same kind of objections to be raised to it are evident in the case of recent attempts to estimate the original size of issues in gold, silver and copper, covering a chronological range extending from the eighth to the fourteenth centuries. The methods in this case are based on a mixture of practical experiment (with modern dies and blanks approximating to those used in ancient Greek silver coinage) and mediaeval mint documentation (mainly regarding English silver pennies), and involve what is essentially a relatively simple exercise in statistical probability. On the assumption that there exists an average number of coins liable to be struck from a single die, and on examination of the number of dies represented, and the degree to which they are repeated, in a sample of surviving coinage, it is theoretically possible to calculate the number of dies originally used for an issue, and therefore the number of coins originally forming that issue. This may sound rather grand and impressive. Unfortunately, even given the assumption that there is indeed such a thing as a meaningful average number of coins liable to be struck from a single ancient or mediaeval die (in itself a controversial issue), and even ignoring the certain physical differences between the size and thickness of Greek, English and many Byzantine coins, and the possible technological differences between modern, mediaeval English and Byzantine dies, there still remains such a large number of probable practical flaws in the logical and methodological sequence as to render it effectively useless in a Byzantine context.

The whole sequence depends upon the calculation of the number of dies involved in a sample of surviving coins being accurate, and on that sample being a random one. It is, however, notorious that examination of a single sample by different scholars commonly yields different results, this being particularly the case where a base-metal coinage is in question, as it is peculiarly liable to disfiguration by corrosion and is in any case likely to have been struck in much greater quantity and with much less care than a precious-metal one. Much more important, however, is the fact that no sample of surviving coins is likely to be entirely random, and it is virtually – probably absolutely – impossible to judge just how select any sample is likely to be, or actually is. This is particularly the case where a precious-metal coinage is in question, as its extremely high purchasing power is likely to have rendered its velocity of circulation extremely low, and a high proportion of it is likely to have circulated over long but varied periods of time sealed up in purses, separately, issue by issue, each only very gradually being broken down, and only very gradually being mixed with others.

It is also notorious that precious-metal coins, at least, tend very strongly to be found in the form of hoards – being very rarely, for example, found singly, in the course of archaeological excavations – and that the contents of a single large hoard, or of several smaller ones, found and broken up in subsequent times, are capable of changing, not to say entirely distorting, the current commonness or rarity of individual issues.

Finally, on this immediate subject, it should be noted that whether it is a base- or a precious-metal coinage that is in question, the smaller the current sample, the greater the margins of eventual error, and that samples are always relatively, and are in most cases absolutely, minute. The result is likely to be – to a greater or lesser, but entirely unknown, degree – a severe underestimate.

Even if, despite all this, it proved possible to evolve an accurate estimate of the number of coins that had originally gone to form an issue or several issues, the knowledge gained – paradoxically enough – would still, at least currently, be of internal and numismatic interest only, for as the size of the Byzantine population amongst which it circulated remains entirely unknown, and beyond the limits even of reasoned guesswork, and as the coinage-using habits of that population have in any case been so little studied, the knowledge would be incapable of being put to effective wider use.

The employment of modern scientific methods without significant recourse to thought about the wider historical background has also tended to characterise the use of various techniques of metallurgical analysis to discover the metallic composition of coins or coin issues. Here, the dichotomy between the two elements is admittedly less accentuated, or at any rate less important. After all, it is very useful indeed to know how the gold-content of the nomisma and the silver-content of the miliaresion declined in the eleventh century, the gold-content of the electrum trachy and the silver-content of the billon one declined in the twelfth, and the gold-content of the hyperpyron declined in the thirteenth and fourteenth, quite independently of any enquiry into contemporary metallurgical knowledge. In these cases, too, the study of contemporary documentary sources, and the analysis of the composition of hoards, indicates the existence and operation, at a fairly short remove, of a popular awareness of many of the major details of what was going on. Nevertheless, for example, when minutely analysing the metallic composition of late third- and early fourth-century billon nummus, there is a marked tendency to assume that everything that is now present in a coin, and in however small proportions, then formed a deliberate admixture, with a sound metallurgical reason behind it. Examination of the few surviving sources having some bearing on the matter, however, suggests that two metals only were recognised as being of formal significance: copper to provide the bulk of the alloy, and silver to provide the required enhanced value for the coin. Examination of ancient, mediaeval western, Persian and Arabic treatises on minerals and metals and their utilisation might well also reveal a generally and distinctly less ordered and logical situation than that now customarily assumed.

The burden of all this, of course, is quite simply that modern scientific methods are liable to be of more than very limited use to the numismatist only where the ancient or mediaeval conceptual, technological and behavioural background is known, or at least its limitations and potentialities appreciated. In other words, the application of modern scientific methods does not absolve the numismatist from the greatest possible effort to discover, in as far as is now possible, how an ancient and/or mediaeval monetary economy actually appeared and worked: ignoring this is likely to result in the evolution of a vast numismatic superstructure with minimal historical foundations, and this unsound edifice currently shows every sign of coming into being, a premature sophistication disguising what is essentially a reversal of the logical order of research.

If these remarks are directed against certain salient trends in the study of Byzantine numismatics, then it has to be admitted that those in that of Byzantine history, which are of a somewhat similar nature, have at least not helped the situation. With certain notable exceptions, Byzantine historians, other than purely political ones (and they are always with us), have tended of recent years to be obsessed either with the concept of 'decline' – how far back in time it, or its roots, can be traced – or with that of 'feudalism' – whether, and if so how, the term can be applied to Byzantine society – or indeed with both, the former frequently being seen as caused by the latter. Allied to these there has tended to be an overwhelming concern with 'foreign [i.e. Latin] domination', particularly with regard to trading concessions, the disadvantages for and decline of the Byzantine mercantile classes, and the losses to imperial revenue. The second and third of these – feudalism and foreign domination – have both tended to be seen as internal and external causative equivalents in the first: decline.

To a great extent, of course, these obsessions derive ultimately from the two major political and intellectual strands or inheritances amongst the scholars involved: marxist historians have tended to dominate the field where questions of social structure, feudalism, the *pronoia* grant, and so on, are concerned; what are pleasantly termed 'bourgeois' ones have tended to dominate that where those of trade and allied subjects such as east–west relations are concerned. Admittedly, this distinction has never been absolute, and in recent years – even during the (somewhat lengthy) gestation period of this book – with some relaxation in the intellectual rigidities of 'official' marxism in most eastern countries, and more particularly with the widespread acceptance and adoption, as respectable and even fashionable, of marxist modes of thought (even if 'deviant' ones) in virtually all western countries, it has tended to become increasingly blurred. This may well be no bad thing, and the resultant synthesis valuable, but the essential distinction survives.

In addition to all this, there has remained constantly in the background the division between the numismatist and the historian that is commonly found elsewhere in the general historical discipline, and that may well be inherent. This division seems to be based on a fear, on the part of the numismatist, of venturing beyond what can be deduced from coinage in its narrowest sense, or even (given the disproportionate position of the amateur collector in the discipline) on a straightforward lack of interest in the possible results of so venturing. The fear is perhaps understandable, but the lack of interest is certainly inexcusable. The study of coins, while justified and necessary, is (or should be) merely a means to an end, and that end is the contribution they can make, or can thereby be made to make, towards the study of the civilisation that produced and used them. Now coins by themselves tend to impart information of a very particular and restricted nature only, although – given the fragmentary nature of the surviving evidence – even that is not to be despised. Nevertheless, it is in attempting to answer a more general type of question – such as why, when and where coins were, or were likely to be, struck; the functions that they were intended to, and did, perform; how, and by whom, they were used; and their relationship to contemporary concepts of wealth, and to the financial system and the economic structure of the state – that information of wider interest, and of more general use, tends to come to light. To fail to explore the full potential of coins is therefore simply to indulge in bad numismatics.

That being said, however, there remains one most important *caveat*. Which is that the numismatist should be aware not only of the potential, but also of the limitations, of his subject, and it is precisely here that the division between numismatist and historian is likely to occur and evolve. For information derived from coins, and of a perfectly legitimate historical status, has on occasion been neglected, or even consciously ignored, by the historian, because, in pressing the claims of his material too far at other times, the numismatist has discredited his discipline.

From the other side, the tendency has been for the historian to assume the numismatist to be interested only in numismatic details of an internal nature, and of a minor import, and (as pointed out above, with some justification) to be distinctly unimpressed whenever the latter has ventured outside those details – while at the same time remaining somewhat nervous of techniques that he considers arcane, yet of potential bearing upon his subject. It may be objected that, in taking a particular numismatist, or numismatists, as representative of the discipline, or as reflecting the antiquarian basis of the discipline itself, the historian merely betrays his own professional inadequacy. But even historians are human in respect of simple prejudice and, however justified the theory of the objection, numismatists would be well advised to take account of the practical effect of their conclusions in this respect.

In any case, the effect of these several tendencies and divisions – current tendencies in the study of numismatics, inherited divisions in the study of history, and a general division between numismatists and historians – has been little short of disastrous for the study of the Byzantine monetary economy as a whole. Numismatists have duly tended to internalise their discipline; marxist historians, while rejecting (probably justifiably) the concept of a 'trade-based' economy, have also tended to ignore (probably unjustifiably) the study of coins and coinage, as forming an extension and antiquarian adjunct of that concept; and 'bourgeois' historians, while in most cases accepting (probably unjustifiably) the concept of a 'trade-based' economy, have therefore also – and paradoxically – tended to neglect (probably unjustifiably) the study of coins and coinage, considering it merely to confirm, in an antiquarian way, what is already known and capable of being independently verified. Both types of historians therefore tend to avoid numismatics, and numismatists and historians alike all tend to avoid the monetary economy.

And yet it is precisely on the question of the general nature and functioning of the monetary economy that the Byzantinist possesses an immense advantage over other mediaevalists. For the Byzantine empire comprised territorially, over much of its history, holdings in two peninsulas, the Balkan and Anatolian, each with a very accentuated physical structure and with all the concomitant characteristics deriving from that, and it survived, with an unique degree of historical continuity, and in however varying a territorial form, for over a millennium. The Byzantinist is thus assured of a certain degree of territorial uniformity, but equally of a basic geographical diversity, and of a high degree of historical continuity, over an extended period of time. Upon this foundation, he is in a position to superimpose the information to be gleaned from a body of straightforward numismatic materials – the coins – the unique nature of which has already been mentioned. In addition to an almost continuous sequence of hoard evidence, there is, increasingly, a body of evidence deriving from the investigation of archaeological sites – some of which is on a relatively massive scale. The Byzantinist also has increasingly at his disposal an extremely important body of sphragistic materials – and also a number of administrative treatises and texts to flesh these out. For the early period, he has a superb collection of epigraphic materials, and for the early and middle periods, an extensive and wide-ranging sequence of legal codifications, thus permitting the evolution – amongst other things – of an extremely important prosopographical tool. Again for the early period, he has a huge corpus of papyrological materials, which cannot be discarded entirely on the grounds of its overwhelmingly Egyptian provenance, and therefore of its supposedly atypical nature. For the middle and later period, there also exists an increasing number of – with time – increasingly detailed monastic chartularies.

In addition to all this, the Byzantinist possesses a superb sequence of chronicles and narrative histories extending, virtually continuously, from one end of Byzantine history to the other. It is true that many of these histories have one major and obvious defect in common: that they were written in Constantinople, by Constantinopolitan-educated and/or based authors, for a limited Constantinopolitan audience. This inevitably tends to result in quite severe problems of conceptual interpretation: what has been well described as the 'distorting mirror' effect. Yet even here, many of them also have one major advantage: that they were written by emperors, by members of the imperial house, or by senior figures in the imperial court or administration – in other words, not only by ecclesiastics, whether metropolitan or regional (although the former, at least, also figure notably), but also by an educated laity with at least a theoretical, and often a widely exercised, access to secular sources other than their own personal experience or hearsay. It is also true that many of these histories have not received modern editing, and still have to be consulted in nineteenth-century or even earlier editions. This is frequently the subject of complaint, the strong implication being that nothing can really be done until the situation has been rectified: once again, the Principle of Unripe Time. But Byzantium has in no way a monopoly of this situation, and yet progress is made elsewhere, for example in the western early mediaeval field. The doctrine of the establishment of a pure text as a pre-condition for serious work (a pre-condition that is never fulfilled, as each generation finds reason for dissatisfaction with a text), strongly resembles, and is probably derived from, the dead hand of classical studies of a now (fortunately) almost extinct type. It may be suggested that the sooner the doctrine expires in Byzantine studies the better: with some few exceptions, it is most unlikely that many fundamental historical discoveries will derive from such re-editing, the price of the results in any case being now frequently so high as to render them available in specialist libraries only, thus at least in part nullifying their undoubtedly greater convenience, and ironically representing to some extent a reversion to the mediaeval situation.

It may thus again be suggested that what the Byzantinist interested in the study of coinage and money lacks in some aspects of his material is compensated, or is more than compensated, for in what is available in others.

This series of preliminary studies, then, represents an attempt to take as full an advantage as is possible of these many and varied sources of information, or at least of as many of them as seem currently necessary, in laying down what are intended to be the foundations for the further and more detailed study of the Byzantine monetary economy. It thus proceeds from the very general, the basic geography of settlement and society, to the very particular, the coinage itself, with the three elements involved forming a pyramid: settlement and society being the base, and coinage the apex.

It may be thought that I have wandered far from the customary or even proper preserve of the numismatist, in discussing such questions as erosion, predominant forms of land-use, and twelfth- and thirteenth-century frontiers – and so, perhaps, I have. But the nature of the basic resources of the economy, the areas in which these resources were concentrated, the methods by which – and the degree to which – they were exploited, and the effect that the possession, gain or loss of these areas might or did have upon the finances of the state, and upon its ability to carry out its traditional functions, are all questions of perfectly legitimate concern even to the numismatist in a narrow sense, let alone to the numismatic scholar interested in a rather wider context. And if questions like this have not so far been treated in any detail, or treated in a satisfactory fashion, by the historian, then there is nothing for it but for the numismatist to attempt to do it for him.

There is indeed an impeccable case in logic, and of a more directly numismatic nature, for extending the scope of the enquiry so as to encompass such topics as mentioned above. As also implied or mentioned above, it is quite clear that the late Roman and Byzantine coinage was, in a very direct sense, a fiscal instrument, that is, pertaining to the revenue and expenditure of the state. It is equally clear that the state obtained the vast bulk of its revenue from land and its exploitation, the precise balance between land and other sources of revenue obviously being likely to have varied over the course of its history. The nature of the land involved, and both the degree to which and the way in which it was exploited, all become of even more direct relevance to the issue in hand than is implied by this connected sequence of general statements when it is also realised that the accentuated physical structure of the land together with its concomitant characteristics are likely to have entailed equally accentuated patterns of coin-use amongst the public: it is scarcely likely that a pattern of coin-use characterising the coastal plain of Anatolia will have been repeated on the central plateau of that peninsula; and it is scarcely more likely that a pattern of coin-use obtaining in a town or city of some relative size – wherever it may have been – will have also penetrated very far into its dependent territory.

For all these reasons, the broad scope that has been adopted in this enquiry into the Byzantine monetary economy becomes desirable or even necessary.

It may also be thought that the whole project is over-ambitious. But at least for the strictly numismatic element, the time is in fact particularly propitious. The recent past has seen the publication of catalogues of the greater parts of two major collections of Byzantine coins: those in Dumbarton Oaks in Washington, and in the Bibliothèque Nationale in Paris. In addition to these, the publication of a 'systematic' classification and arrangement of the series in the German language has also commenced. The attribution, classification and arrangement of Byzantine coins has not reached its ultimate with these publications: they will doubtless be superseded in due course, just as they have themselves superseded publications (such as that of the collection of the British Museum in London, and the Ratto sale catalogue) that have long been published. They do nevertheless provide, for the first time, what has every appearance of being a broadly representative assemblage of the series, arranged with a logical consistency, suggesting that the basic structure of the original whole has now been established. This should in itself bring closer, perhaps even inaugurate, the stage at which the study of Byzantine coins can be usefully supplemented and extended by the study of Byzantine coinage, and even by that of the Byzantine monetary economy.

The project therefore may well be ambitious, but it should not – in theory at least – be over-ambitious. This, of course, in no way guarantees the actual success of the particular enterprise, which will in any case be the subject of criticism and correction by others and of constant revision by myself.

Two particular criticisms that I do anticipate are that, on the one hand, I have paid insufficient attention to the many hagiographical writings and *vitae* that are available, and that, on the other, I have paid overmuch attention to the monetary figures that are found from time to time in casual contexts and sources. Both features are quite deliberate, although in point of fact I have neither rigorously excluded hagiographical sources, nor have I placed particular reliance on any single monetary figure.

It is frequently supposed that the occasional mention of coins, coinage, or monetary transactions in hagiographical sources denotes the existence and operation of a monetary economy. This, in any modern sense (that in which it is normally quite carelessly used), is inevitably suspect. But in any case, individually, such mentions mean very little: many or most are of such a general nature as to have no particular context or application. For example, they normally indicate nothing of the commonness or rarity of the coins involved; or of the ease or difficulty with which they were obtained; or of the methods by which they were obtained. Even collectively, they are of little or no greater value or application: all the other forms of evidence suggest that the availability and use of coin was subject to such wide extremes of variation according to time, place and particular circumstances as to render any generalisation derived from what one might term crudely the totting up of particular hagiographical cases to be virtually meaningless. This is not to suppose that such mentions cannot, or will never, be of use, but much more work needs to be carried out on the question of when, where, by whom, and for whom, such sources were written, and on the problems inherent in their utilisation, before they can at all usefully be employed in this way. Whatever the solutions, they are unlikely to be simple, or capable of general application. They cannot, in any case, be compared in reliability or significance with the relatively extensive and detailed accounts of monetary behaviour that are occasionally to be found in imperial laws or narrative histories, where such accounts have a particular context, and where they are capable of insertion into a structure capable of independent verification. For all these reasons, I have tended to utilise hagiographical sources only where their evidence can be shown to conform with that of other kinds of sources: in other words, in a basically passive and supportive rôle, rather than in an active and assertive one.

The unreliability of mediaeval figures, whether military or monetary, is notorious, and indeed almost universally acknowledged amongst historians, with perhaps the partial exception of Byzantinists, amongst whom at least one scholar has argued for the reliability of a particular figure on the grounds that it is so precise and odd as to be unlikely simply to have been made up. I would in fact argue for the absolute reliability of very few indeed of the individual figures that I have quoted. Those given by Justinian for the salaries of the various officials dealt with in his legislation are, except where obviously textually corrupt, exceptions to this general rule. Those given by Constantine Porphyrogenitus for the costs of the Cretan expeditions of 911/12 and 949 are also to be counted as exceptions, for Constantine was in an excellent position to obtain the official accounts from which they do indeed appear to have been derived. Occasionally, figures can be cross-checked, and where found coincident are likely to be correct (except, of course, where both are clearly derived from a common secondary source). The figure given by Nicetas Choniates for the compensation awarded the Venetians as a result of the confiscations of 1171 is actually also given in official Byzantine–Venetian sources, and again Nicetas was in an excellent position to have or to obtain the information. The figures given by Ramon Muntaner for the pay-scales of the members of the Catalan expedition of 1303–5 are, when multiplied out, virtually identical with the global ones given by George Pachymeres. And so on.

On several occasions the authors who give the figures claim to be relying on official sources, but it is difficult to be sure whether invariably they indeed were, or whether mainly at least one is here in the presence of a literary *topos*. Even so, the accumulation of a sequence of individually unverifiable figures for a particular class of function, whether it be the reserves amassed by individual emperors, the costs of military expeditions, the building and decoration of churches, or the revenue and expenditure of monasteries, can be collectively of interest and significance when compared with, say, a similar sequence composed of figures for provincial revenues or private fortunes. At the very least, each individual figure ought, when evolved, to have been subject to what one might call 'a threshold of expectation or plausibility', however elastic that threshold might be at any particular time, and however much it might change over a period of time. What one is obtaining here, therefore, is a range of figures which may demonstrate some tendency to change over a period of time, but in which any component figure that jars egregiously, either over the range as a whole, or within a particular chronological section of the range, and which cannot be confirmed or explained independently, is automatically suspect. In other words, what is important is not the individual figures, but the general pattern.

As it happens, to take two examples only, the figures for imperial reserves, and those for the costs of military expeditions, are almost all acceptable within their own range. That given by Nicetas for the Italian expedition of 1155/6 does seem high, but may include the considerable political expenditure that is known to have been involved. What emerges unambiguously from a comparison between the two ranges is that in the case of any large or even relatively large expedition on the scale of the Vandal expedition of 468, the Italian expedition of 1155/6, or the Catalan (i.e. anti-Ottoman) expedition of 1303–5, the funds spent must have equalled or even surpassed a whole year's imperial revenue. Lesser expeditions, not involving the full resources of the empire, cost correspondingly less, but even here comparison shows that they must have been extremely burdensome. From the outsider's point of view it may be supposed that a disproportionate amount of scholarly effort has to be put into proving what should, in any case, be basic and considered obvious, and this may indeed be so – except that in practice it does not seem to have been either much commented upon, or by many considered obvious.

Two further criticisms that I also anticipate are that I have failed to use the available physical evidence – particularly the coins, whether casual single finds or hoards, or site-finds – when dealing with such matters as monetary circulation, and that I have not drawn a sufficiently sharp distinction between the various periods into which Byzantine history is customarily divided, when following through the various basic topics treated in the course of the work. Again, both features are deliberate, although again I have neither ignored the physical evidence where it has appeared necessary to an individual case, nor have I by any means automatically assumed that evidence for one period is necessarily valid for another. What I have attempted to do in this series of preliminary studies is, in as far as it is possible, to set up a basic and independent structure, within which the physical evidence (much of which possesses very severe evidential limitations) is capable of being assessed and analysed, and against which the various bands or phases of continuity or discontinuity are capable of being defined and synthesised. These latter aims remain to be realised in a further series of studies.

Finally, it seems to have become accepted that numismatic works dealing with the Byzantine empire should commence with the reign of Anastasius I (491–518) and, more particularly, with the reform of the copper coinage initiated by his *comes sacrarum largitionum* John the Paphlagonian in 498. The choice of this point of departure is generally accompanied by an acknowledgement of its arbitrary nature, for while Anastasius or his *comes* undoubtedly did carry through reforms both in the coinage system in particular and in the fiscal system in general, the overall structure of neither thereby underwent fundamental change. The dilemma therefore remains: where to start?

It has increasingly come to seem to the author that, while it is entirely proper for a catalogue of Byzantine coins to commence with the Anastasian reform – if only on the grounds that a start has to be made somewhere, or that an earlier date would involve the inclusion of a vast extra mass of material, or that it did at least mark a visually obvious change – there is much less excuse for a treatment of the coinage or monetary economy doing likewise. It will be stressed in the seventh chapter of this book that the production of coinage was influenced above all by the needs and organisational structure of contemporary fiscal administration. If the question arises as to when the fiscal administration typifying the early Byzantine empire took shape, or at least becomes evident to modern scholarship, then there really can be no other answer than during the reign of Diocletian (284–305). It should be noted, incidentally, that on this kind of consideration, the foundation and dedication of Constantinople by Constantine I (306–37) assumes a position of secondary importance only: it was for long not the sole eastern capital, and was for even longer administratively anomalous – more anomalous, indeed, than Rome itself.

The alternative to the implications of this last major point seems the drastic one of considering the empire to have evolved into a form that is recognisably 'Byzantine' only as a result of the upheavals marking the seventh century. The case for such a division is, on the face of it, a strong one, for the empire that emerged into the relative light of the eighth and ninth centuries was undeniably a very different one from that which had disappeared into the certain darkness of the seventh. Why, then, take the reign of Diocletian as the point of departure rather than that, say, of Leo III (717–41)? There is no completely satisfactory answer. The reigns of these two emperors do indeed appear less arbitrary choices than most or all the others, for it is arguable that both marked a change, or perhaps rather the culmination of a series of changes, in the east, in a way that the division of the empire between Arcadius (395–408) and Honorius (395–423) in 395/6, or the gradual disintegration of the western half of the empire in the fifth century, did not. The situation is, naturally, not quite so simple: just as features of the reigns of Gallienus or Aurelian are now as a matter of *chic* seen as pre-figuring those of the reign of Diocletian, so there are good reasons for believing features of the reign of Heraclius (610–41) to have pre-figured those of the reign of Leo III. Having abandoned the choice of the reign of Anastasius on the grounds of its arbitrary nature, one is then apparently confronted with a similar choice between those of Diocletian and Leo III.

There is, however, an important difference: which is that they do in fact provide almost equally viable points of departure, and in such circumstances the personal preference of the author may perhaps be permitted decisive weight. To commence with the reign of Leo III would be to forgo the use of earlier primary sources that, despite the changes mentioned above, still appear to have validity for, and relevance to, the later period. It would also be to omit the greater part of one of the most fascinating of all Byzantine numismatic phenomena: the process by which the coinage system and pattern of coin production reflecting the economic conditions and fiscal structure typical of the late Roman and early Byzantine period evolved into those typical of the developed Byzantine empire. The responsibility for which process is to be divided, as it happens, between Heraclius and Leo III.

The reign of Diocletian will therefore form the point of departure for this book. Coverage of the earlier period will perhaps be spasmodic, and will certainly be weighted towards the east, but the attempt will at least have been made. The attempt will itself have been made immeasurably easier by the still relatively or even very recent publication of several of the appropriate volumes of *Roman Imperial Coinage*. Whether it will be considered to have proved a worthwhile experiment, and to have resulted in a novel perspective, remains to be seen.

SECTION I

# ECONOMY AND SOCIETY

# CHAPTER 1

# THE LAND

## (I) THE MODERN SITUATION

### *A. The Balkans*

The Balkan Peninsula is dominated by mountain systems which, if they are of only moderate height (none attains 3,000 m), nevertheless comprise some two-thirds of its surface area. The most extensive of these systems, that which has the Dinaric Alps and Pindus Mountains as two of its principal elements, forms a vast wedge extending some 1,500 km down through modern Yugoslavia and Greece and possessing a north-west to south-east axis. A second system, that of the Balkan Mountains, forms a large arc extending from the Carpathian Alps, crossing the River Danube at the Iron Gate, and continuing into modern Bulgaria along a west to east axis. Between these a third system, that of the Rhodope Mountains, forms a somewhat similar but more southerly and much less extensive arc. The area in which these three systems come closest to intersecting, the western central Balkans (Macedonia), is inevitably one of extreme structural fragmentation and complexity. (Map 1)

Because of the existence of a north-west to south-east mountain barrier, few major rivers, in the northern half of the peninsula at least, flow westwards into the Adriatic Sea. They tend rather to flow eastwards, north-eastwards, or even directly northwards, into the Danube, and hence into the Black Sea. Such are the Rivers Drava, Sava, Bosna, Drina, Morava and Iskur. This tendency is not, however, an absolute one: in the north the Rivers Neretva and Drin do flow into the Adriatic, and in the south exceptions grow more frequent, the Rivers Devoll, Arakhthos, Akheloos and Alfios all flowing either into the Adriatic or into the Ionian Sea. On the other hand, although these rivers tend to have a steep gradient, none has either the volume or the length of those of the Danubian system. Rivers in the southern half of the peninsula as a whole tend to flow eastwards, south-eastwards, or even directly southwards, into the Aegean Sea. Such are the Rivers Pinios, Aliakmon, Vardar, Strimon and Nestos. The River Maritsa, while conforming to this tendency, also represents a complicating factor in first flowing more or less directly

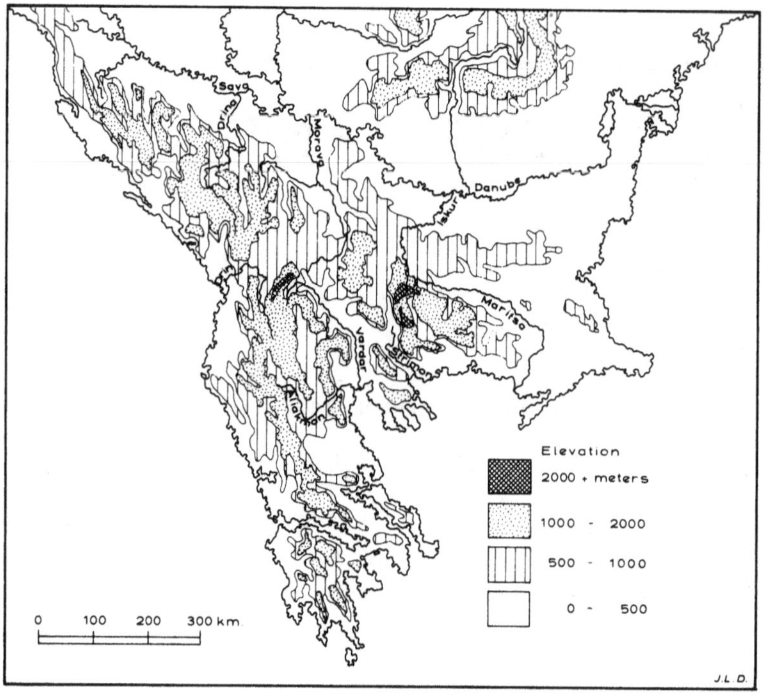


Map 1 The Balkans: physical structure

eastwards between the Balkans and the Rhodope and then turning due south at the eastern termination of the latter having met up with the River Tundzha, and meeting up also with the River Ergene, before flowing into the Aegean. (Map 1)

With mountain systems taking up such a large proportion of the surface area of the peninsula, plains – whether at high or low altitudes – are correspondingly restricted in extent. The only plain of really considerable size, the Danubian, is divided into two parts by the arc of the Balkans. The first of these, for the purposes of this chapter at least, accounts for the area between the Danube itself and the Sava. The second accounts for the often rather hilly area between the Danube and the west to east axis of the Balkans, and includes the Dobrogea, now incorporated into modern Romania. Of considerably smaller but still not wholly inconsiderable size, the Thracian (Maritsa) Plain accounts for the area between the Balkans and the Rhodope, and after the eastern termination of the latter extends southwards to the Aegean. Other than these, most of the rivers mentioned above have their own minor plains, and some combine so as to produce somewhat larger ones: the Strimon and Maritsa (including, between them, the Nestos) define a narrow strip of territory between the Rhodope and the Aegean that represents an area of reasonably continuous plain; the Vardar and Aliakmon combine to produce another plain (the Macedonian), while the Pinios has its own (the Thessalian). Of the rivers flowing

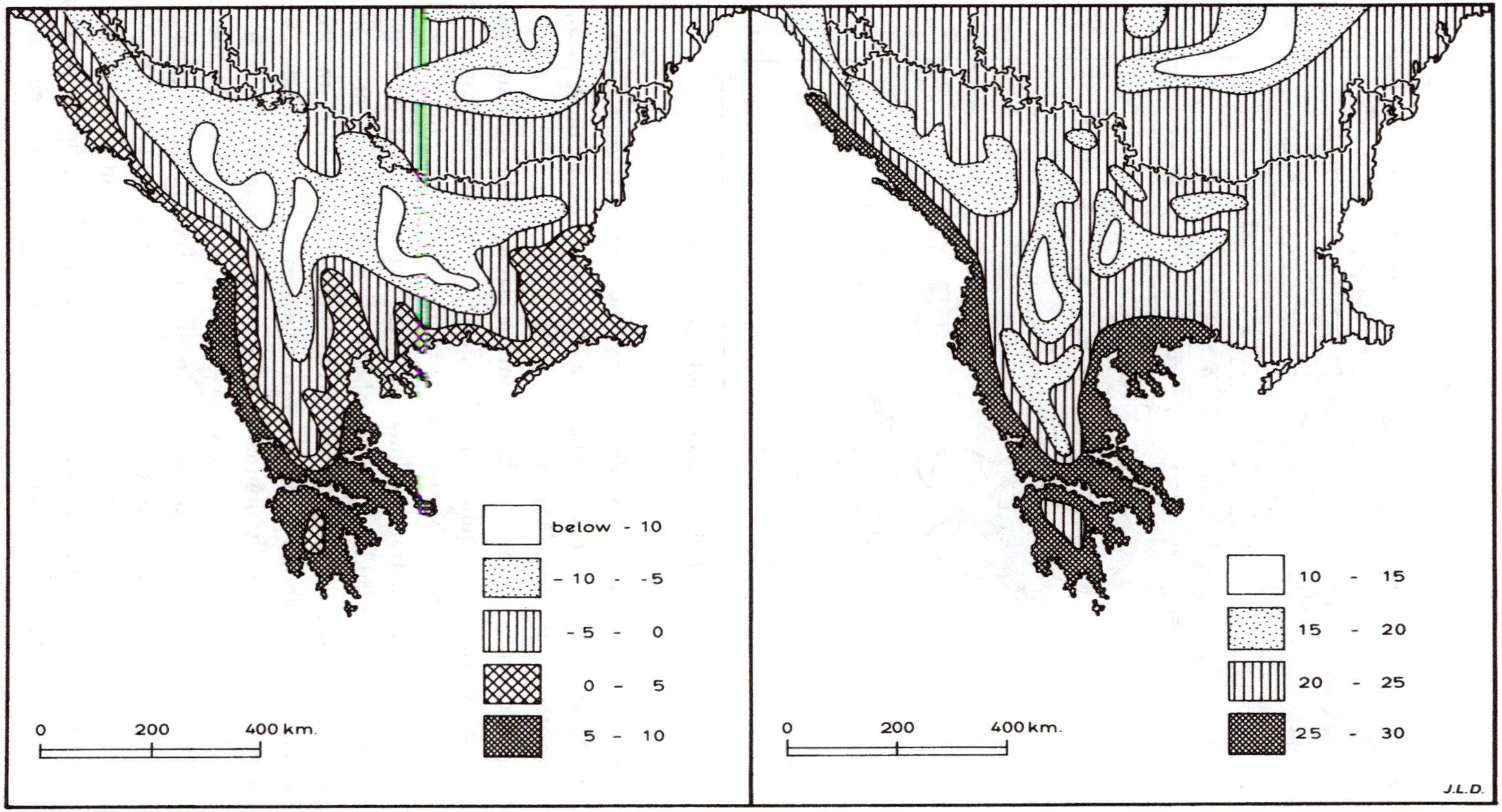


Map 2 The Balkans: (a) January temperature; (b) July temperature (degrees Centigrade)

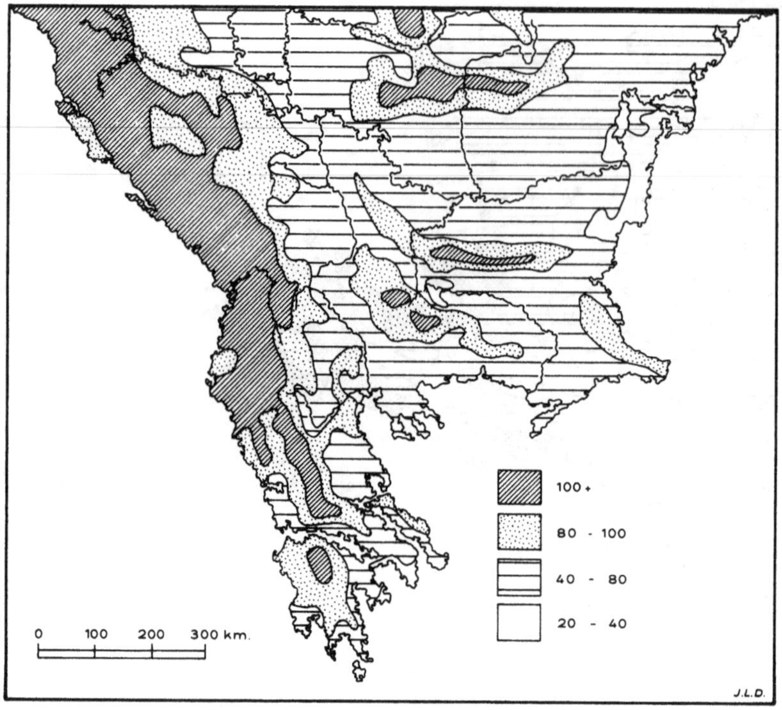


Map 3 The Balkans: mean annual precipitation (cm)

into the Adriatic, the Drin and Devoll define a narrow strip of territory between the mountains and the sea that represents a further area of reasonably continuous plain, while the Alfios dominates yet another. (Map 1)

The climate of the peninsula varies widely, from the classic Mediterranean type to the classic Continental, often within quite small distances. In general, the existence of the north-west to south-east mountain barrier and the approximately west to east axis of the Rhodope ensures that the Mediterranean climate is quite sharply confined to the coastlands and to their immediate hinterland, a Continental one being more typical of the interior. The sheltering action of the Balkans and the early eastern termination of the Rhodope provide the single major exception to this pattern: that area south of the Balkans which extends uninterruptedly or virtually uninterruptedly to the Aegean enjoys a transitional Mediterranean climate. This is very obvious, for example, with regard to temperatures. (Maps 2a, b). The pattern of precipitation in the peninsula is also clearly dominated by the existence of the north-west to south-east mountain barrier: although its steep western slopes which give directly onto the Adriatic and Ionian Seas receive in excess of 1,000 mm of rain per annum, most localities receiving well in excess of that figure, areas in the interior (with the exception of the Balkans and the Rhodope which receive almost as much [800–1,000 mm], or as much, as the western slopes), and even those giving directly

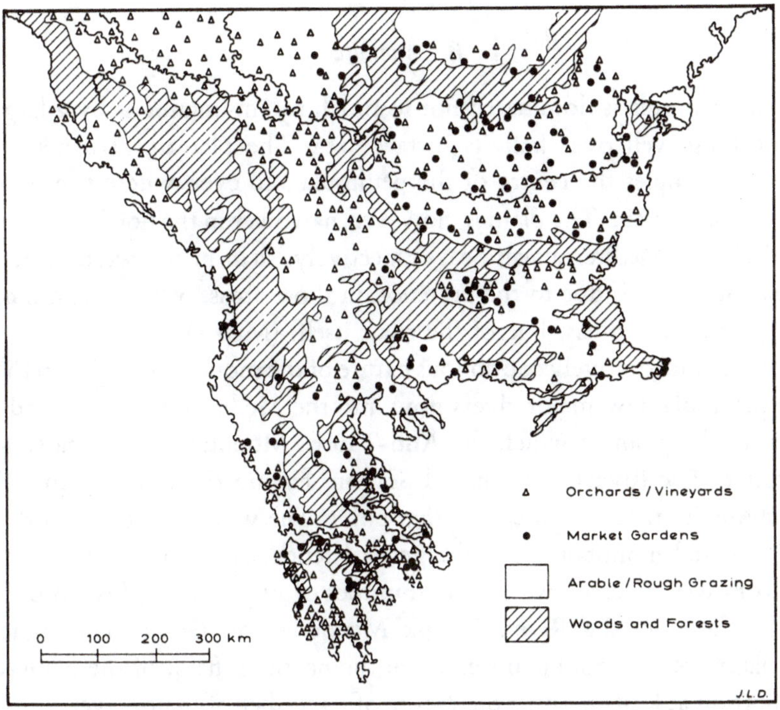


Map 4 The Balkans: natural vegetation, land-use (modern)

onto the Aegean and Black Seas, receive between 400 mm and 800 mm only. (Map 3)

It is in this physical and climatic context that the pattern of vegetation and land-use in the peninsula is to be seen. The vast wedge of the north-west to south-east mountain barrier is represented by a more or less coterminous extent of woodland and forest, interspersed with meadows, permanent grassland, rough grazing land, and bare rock or land incapable of agricultural use. The woodland and forest consists largely of conifers and oak, the former at higher altitudes, the latter at lower ones, but frequently involves little more than scrub-pine and scrub-oak. Arable land is rare in any quantity. The same pattern – a massive preponderance of woodland and virtual lack of arable land – also holds good for the Balkans and the Rhodope. Arable land, and land suitable for orchards, vineyards, olive groves or market-gardening, is in fact very heavily concentrated in the areas of plain mentioned above: the two parts of the Danubian Plain, the Thracian, Macedonian and Thessalian Plains, and the plains of the Maritsa-Strimon, Alfios, and so on. These areas, and a relatively few others of restricted extent which are less arable than given over to orchards, vineyards, olive groves, or market-gardening, such as the plains of the Arakhthos and Akheloos, the southern shore of the Corinthian Gulf, the valley of the Evrotas, the shore of the Argolic Gulf, and certain areas in Attica and Boeotia, account for virtually the entirety of such land in the peninsula. (Map 4)

## B. Anatolia

The Anatolian peninsula is dominated not so much by mountains as by a large elevated plateau comprising well over half its surface area. The plateau, at a height of some 1,000–2,000 m, occupies the centre of the peninsula and everywhere rises rapidly from the peripheral coastal plain. The plain is, however, narrower in the north and south, giving on to the Black and Mediterranean Seas respectively, than in the west, which gives on to the Aegean Sea. This is due to the presence, in those areas, of mountain ranges which closely follow the west to east line of the coast itself. (Map 5)

Because of the comparatively continuous nature of the mountain ranges on the southern flank of the peninsula, few major rivers flow into the Mediterranean Sea, and none into that sea west of the point at which the Anti-Taurus Mountains sweep north-eastwards into the interior. The Rivers Ceyhan and Seyhan, having risen in the Anti-Taurus, do flow into the Mediterranean, but east of that point. The west to east axis of the northern and southern coastal mountains, and the general tendency for altitude in the peninsula to increase from west to east ensure that a number of major rivers flow into the Aegean Sea. Chief of these are the Rivers Büyük Menderes and Gediz. The somewhat less continuous nature of the mountain ranges on the northern flank of the peninsula (or on its western portion at least) permits the escape of a number of major rivers into the Black Sea, chief of which are the Rivers Sakarya, Kızılırmak, and Yeşilırmak. The last of these, and its main tributary the Kelkit Çayı, in particular, flows a considerable distance westwards before managing to break through the mountains to the sea. Similarly, the Çoruh flows a considerable distance eastwards before escaping to the sea. The peninsula possesses, in addition, a number of rivers of lesser length and volume than those already mentioned, but still of considerable size. Among these are the Gök Su and Ak Su which flow into the Mediterranean, Küçük Menderes and Bakır which flow into the Aegean, Simav which flows into the Sea of Marmara, and Filyos which flows into the Black Sea. (Map 5)

With the central plateau and its peripheral mountain ranges taking up such a large area, the coastal plains and river valleys form some 10%, and land under 500 m some 18%, only, of the total surface area of the peninsula. As in the Balkans, most of the rivers mentioned above have their own plains and some combine so as to produce rather larger ones. The Ceyhan and Seyhan combine to produce the Cilician Plain, and the Ak Su and Köprü to produce the Antalya (Pamphylian) Plain. Of the others, the Menderes, Gediz, Simav, Sakarya, Kızılırmak and Yeşilırmak have the largest plains. (Map 5)

Again as in the Balkans, the climate varies widely, depending mainly on the altitude and relative geographical position of the areas involved. The high altitude of the central plateau and the sheltering action of the northern and southern coastal mountains combine to ensure that the plateau has an extreme seasonal variation in temperature and is arid:

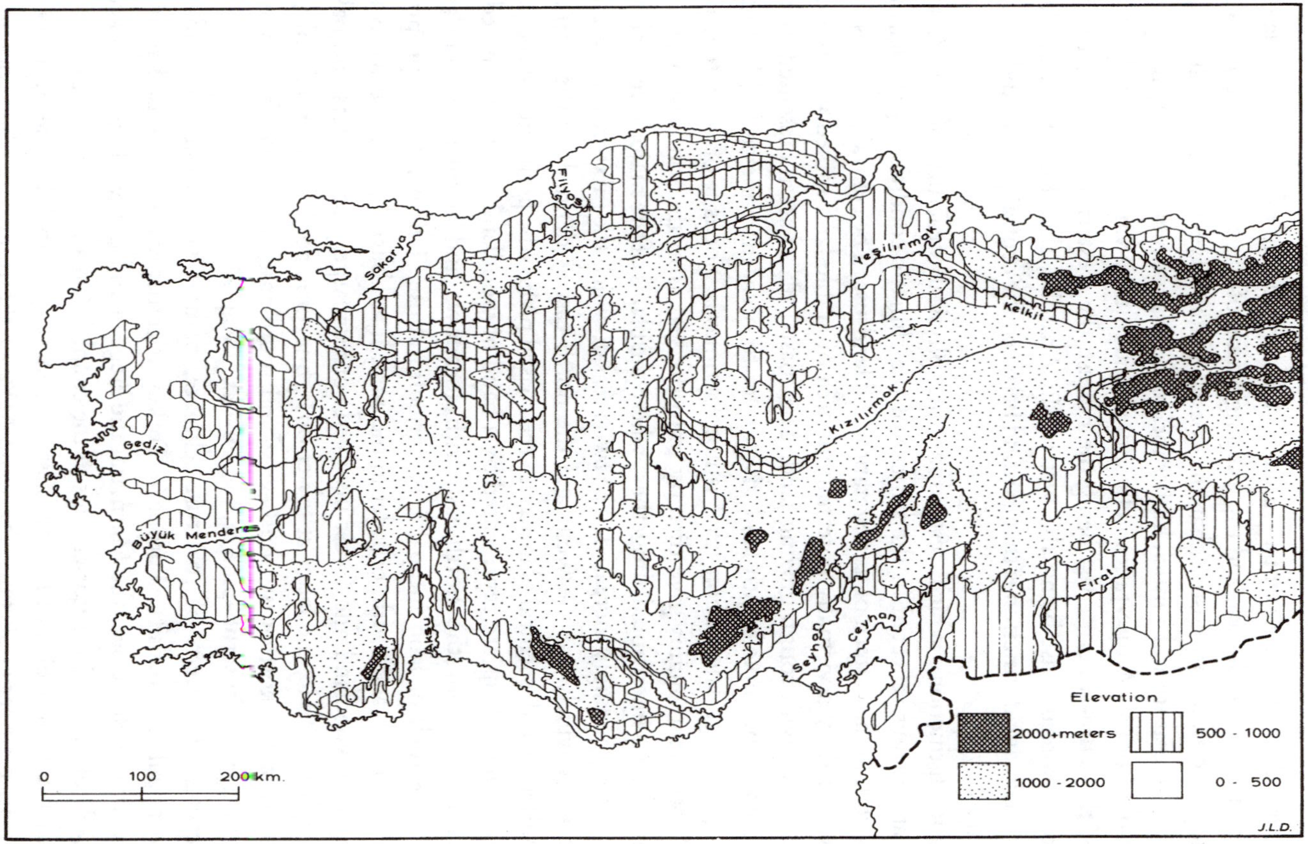


Map 5 Anatolia: physical structure

that it has, in other words, a steppe climate. The low altitude of the coastal plains, the moderating influence of the sea, and the trapping action of the coastal mountains on their seaward slopes combine to ensure that the coastal plains have a much smaller seasonal variation in temperature and a much higher incidence of precipitation. They have, in fact, a classic or transitional Mediterranean climate, although they vary considerably amongst themselves, the south-eastern coast being the hottest, the western coast being the driest, and the north-eastern coast being the wettest. In Anatolia, therefore, the essential and very marked climatic distinction is that existing between the central plateau and the coastal plains. (Maps 6, 7)

This basic distinction, which rests upon the physical structure of the Anatolian peninsula, and is thus reflected in the variety of the climatic conditions prevalent there, is also to be seen in the pattern of its vegetation and land-use. The central plateau is treeless and is represented by a virtually coterminous area of arable land mixed in more or less equal proportions with rough grazing land. The coastal plains are represented by a thin ribbon of arable land mixed with land given over to orchards, vineyards, olive groves, or market-gardening. The ribbon itself is not continuous, nor is it of consistent width: where the coastal mountains give directly onto the sea, as in the south-western corner of the peninsula, it is interrupted altogether; where the plains of the major rivers intervene, its width is correspondingly increased. The two areas in which the mixture is most marked and occurs most widely are the west, and the north-east as defined by the Yeşilırmak and Çoruh. Between the central plateau and the coastal plains, the perimeter of the plateau and the coastal mountains are represented by a band of woodland and forest mixed with rough grazing land – in the north-east with meadows and permanent grassland as well – and bare rock or land incapable of agricultural use. This band is, appropriately, narrower in the north and south, broader in the west. It tends to appear at between 350 m and 450 m. The woodland and forest involved consists largely of conifers and oak, the former at higher altitude, the latter at lower ones, but some 20% of the total only, with concentrations in the north-east, south-west and south-east, is suitable for timber, the remainder being mainly scrub-pine and scrub-oak. (Map 8)

The accentuated pattern of structure, climate, natural vegetation and land-use is reflected in population density. European Turkey together with the coastal plains and river valleys of the Black Sea, the Marmara, the Aegean and the Mediterranean account for some 38% of the total territorial mass of the country (on a more generous interpretation than that used above), but nevertheless contain 54% of its inhabitants. The central plateau and its peripheries account for some 62% of the total mass, but contain 46% only of its inhabitants. A simplified diagram of areas containing higher than the national average of population density is particularly dramatic. (Map 9)

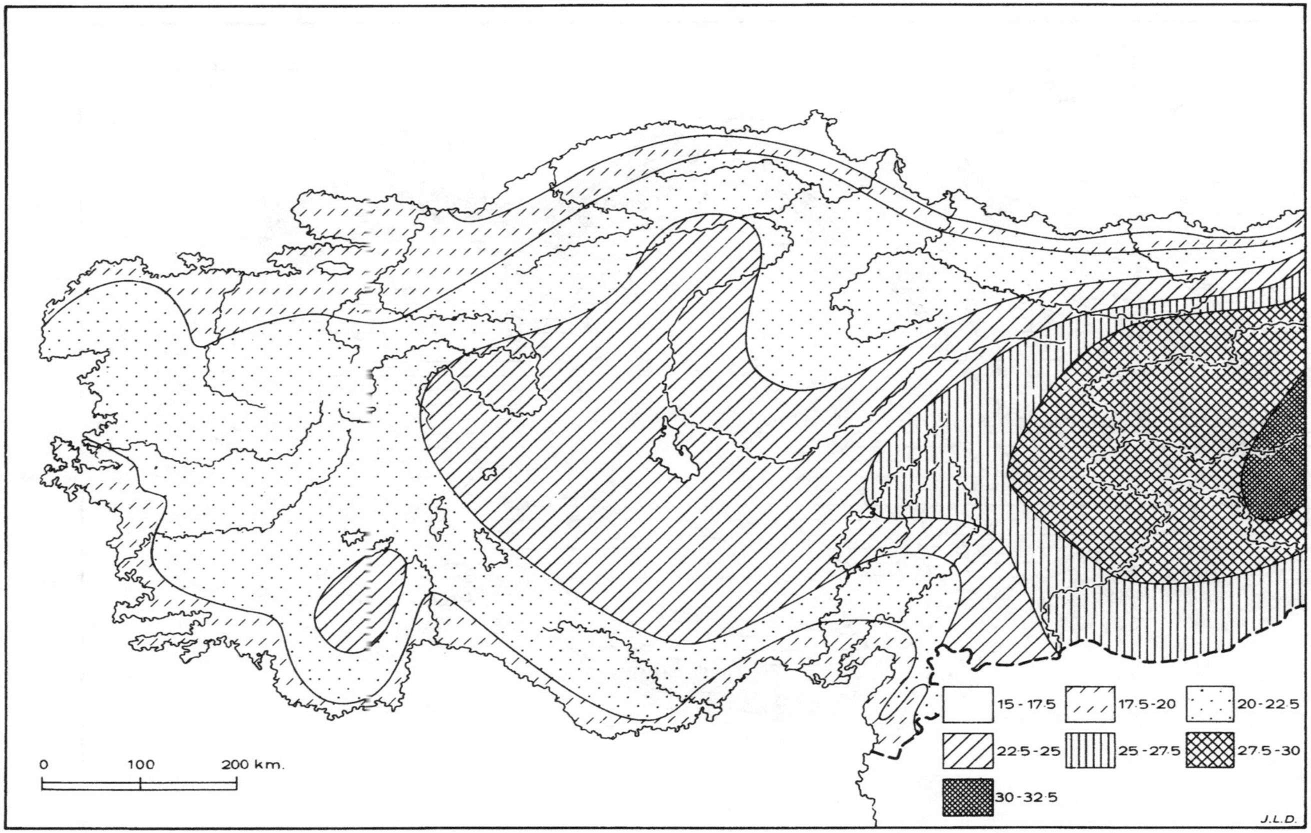


Map 6 Anatolia: average temperature range (degrees Centigrade)

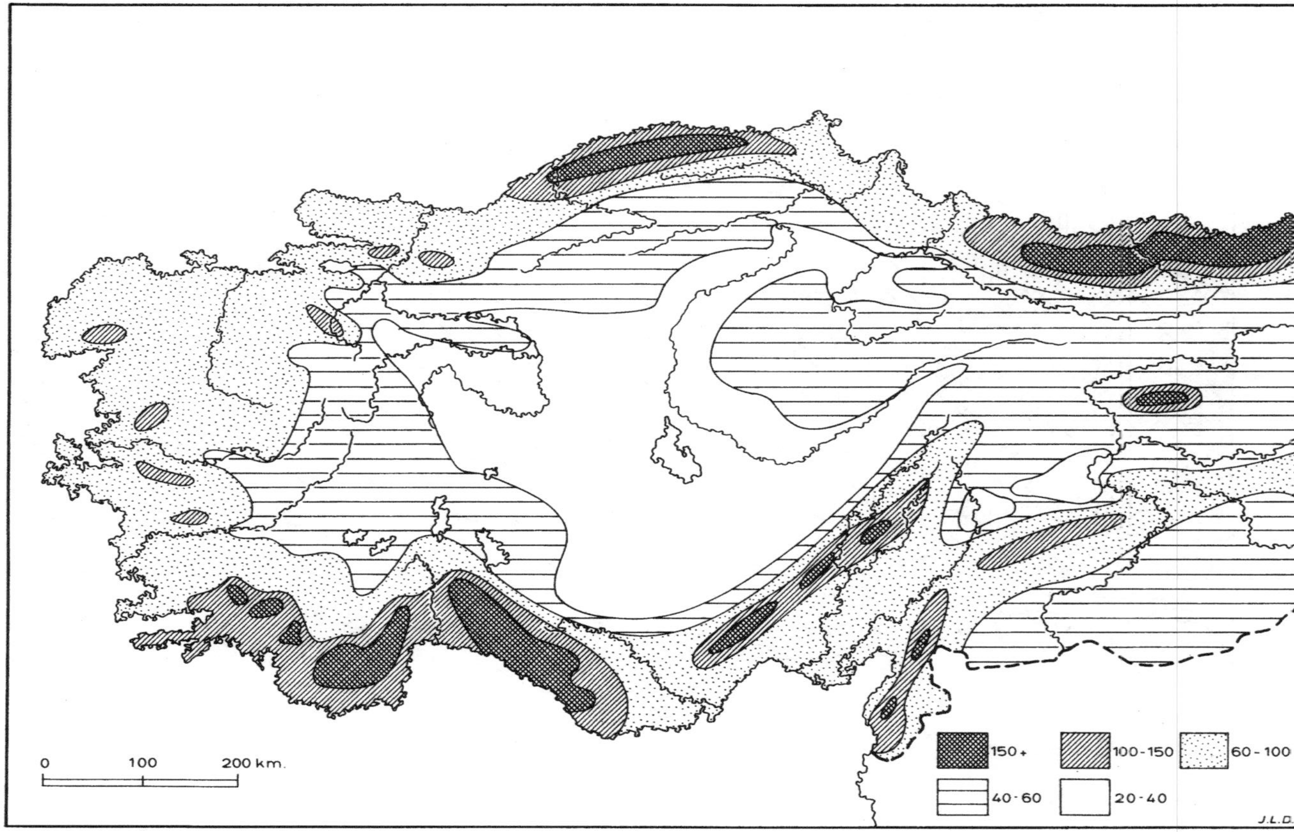


Map 7 Anatolia: mean annual precipitation (cm)

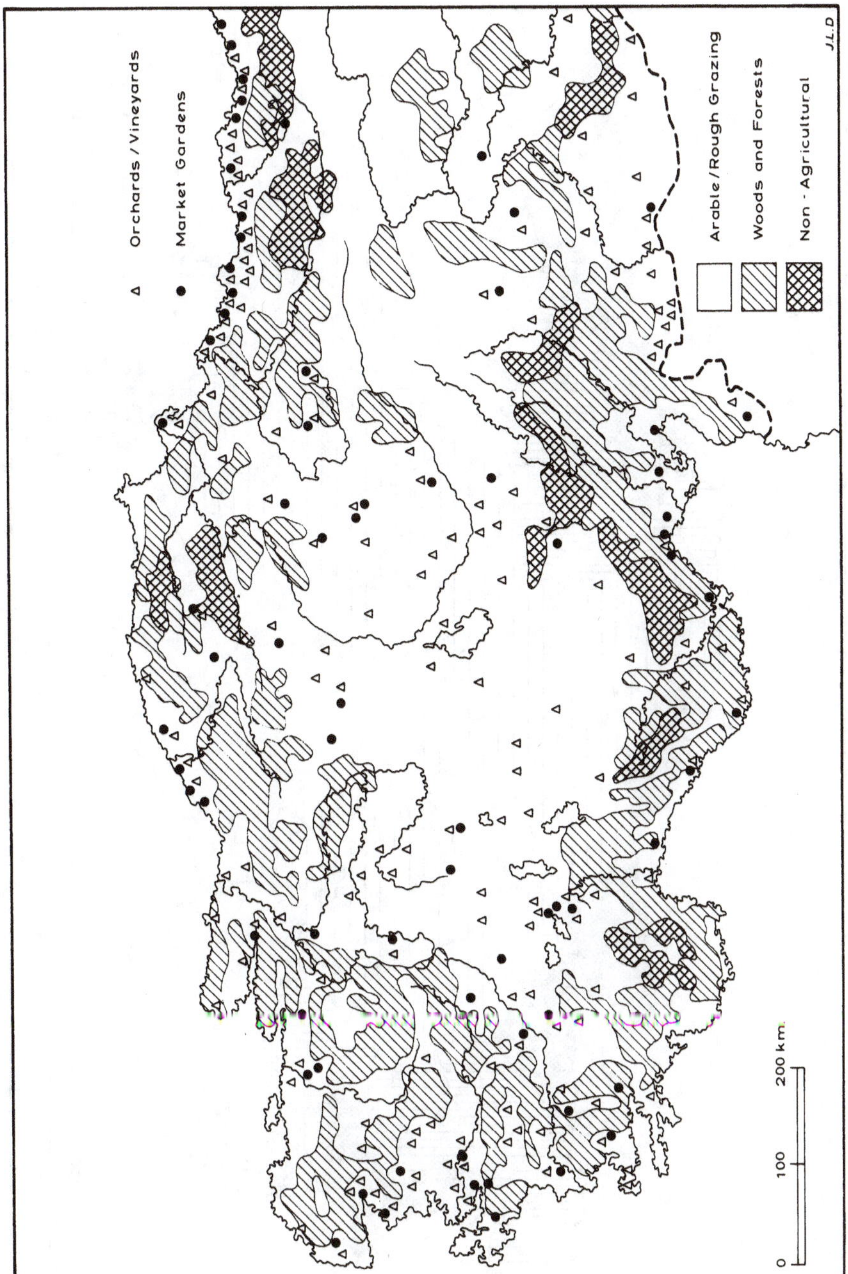


Map 8 Anatolia: natural vegetation, land-use (modern)

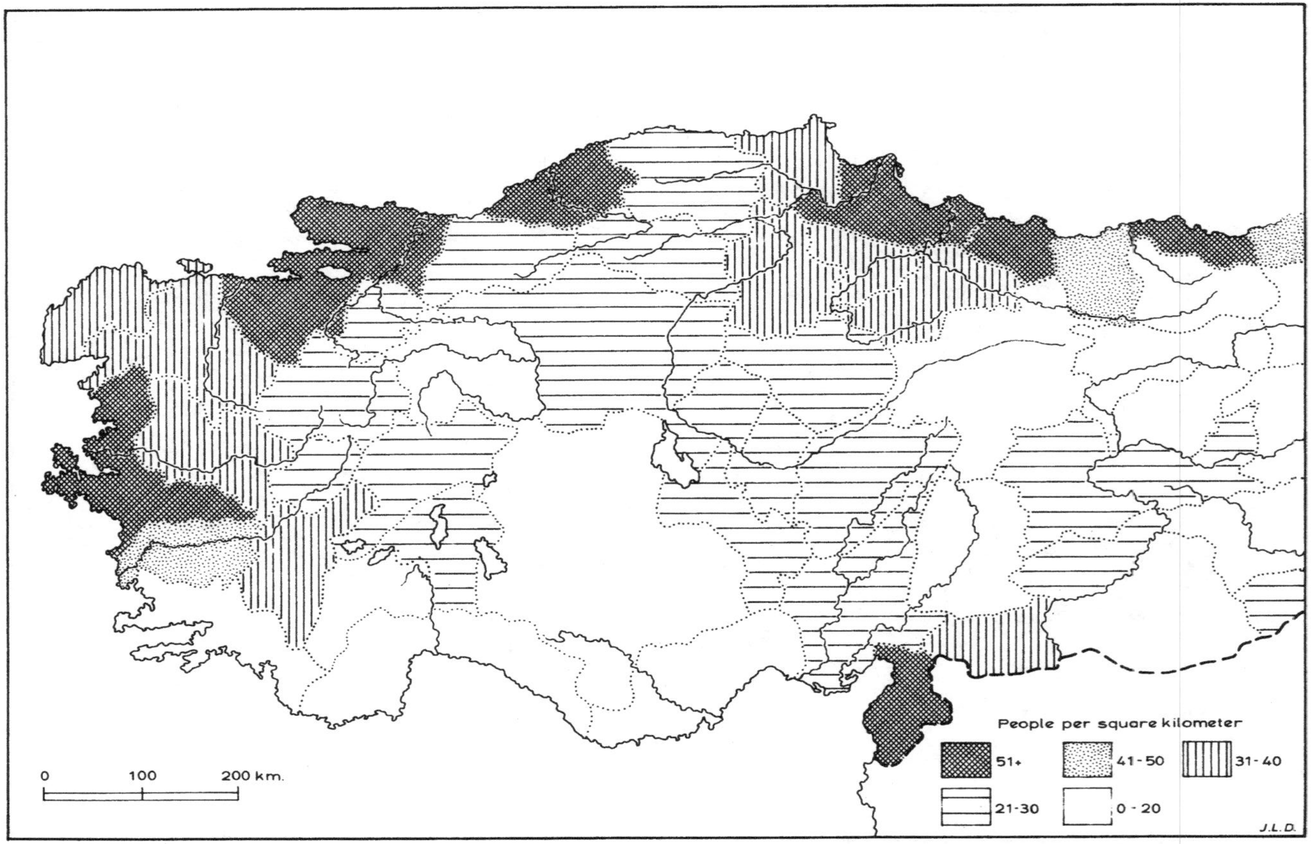


Map 9 Anatolia: arithmetic mean density of population (modern)

## *C. The islands*

Besides the Balkan and Anatolian peninsulas, certain islands should be taken into account as having remained more or less consistently in imperial hands over the period *c.* 300–1250. Cyprus, Crete and the Ionian and Aegean Islands all fall into this category.

The island of Cyprus is divided structurally into four sectors, each of which is aligned along a more or less west to east axis, generally mountainous ones alternating with generally flat ones. The most northerly of these sectors is a narrow one formed by the Kyrenia Mountains. These are succeeded on their southern side by a broader and largely low-lying and alluvial plain (the Mesaoria). The plain is succeeded in its turn by the Troodos Mountains, and they in theirs by a descending series of elevated plateaux terminating in a narrow strip of coastal plain. Plains and plateaux thus account for something like half of the total surface area of the island. The climate is a classic Mediterranean one, the pattern of precipitation reflecting a basic division into mountainous and flat areas, the latter occasionally being afflicted with periods of drought. The pattern of vegetation and land-use reflects the same basic division, the Kyrenia and Troodos Mountains being represented by bands of woodland and forest (again, largely scrub-pine and scrub-oak) mixed with rough grazing land, the plains and plateaux being represented by bands of arable land mixed – particularly in the south – with land given over to orchards, vineyards, olive groves, or market-gardening.

The island of Crete is dominated throughout the whole of its west to east axis by a mountain range that achieves higher altitudes in three massifs. Its climate is a classic Mediterranean one, except for that of the south-eastern corner which is intermediate between a Mediterranean and a semi-desert one. Precipitation is heavy on the massifs only and is much reduced elsewhere. The pattern of vegetation and land-use is one of a mixture of rough pasture land and – especially in the foothills of the mountain range and in the sporadic and very narrow stretches of coastal plain – land given over to orchards, vineyards, olive groves and market-gardening. Arable land, in other words, is extremely rare.

The main Ionian Islands (Corfu, Leucas, Cephallenia and Zacynthos) all have a rugged physical structure, a Mediterranean climate with a high incidence of precipitation, and a high proportion of land given over to orchards, vineyards, olive groves and market-gardening. The main Aegean islands (Lesbos, Chios, Samos and Rhodes) are somewhat less rugged than the Ionian Islands and, although they have the same general type of climate, have a considerably lower incidence of precipitation. A high proportion of their land is given over to orchards, vineyards, olive groves and market gardening, although Rhodes also has a relatively high proportion of arable land.

### D. Observations

The principal fact emerging from this survey is that the predominant physical and climatic characteristics of the Balkan and Anatolian peninsulas, and of the various islands, ensure that the predominant pattern of vegetation and land-use is one of woodland and forest and of rough grazing land. A high proportion of the woodland and forest is of low quality, and therefore only capable of limited exploitation for timber. The rough grazing land is only capable of extensive exploitation: that is, by nomadic herds of sheep and goats – and even then frequently during the summer months only. The corollary is that arable land is scarce, and arable land of high quality extremely scarce.

The central plateau of Anatolia serves as a classic illustration of this latter fact. In that large area, as mentioned above, the climate is steppe-like, precipitation is sparse, and the predominant combination of land-use is now rough grazing land with arable land in more or less equal proportions. The rough grazing land is of poor quality and fit only for extensive exploitation, and since it is combined with arable land the implication must be that the arable land is of equally poor quality. The point is confirmed by a consideration of the development of land-use in Turkey since 1927. In that year, the area occupied by meadows, permanent grassland and rough grazing land (and mainly by the last) formed 60% of the total. In 1960 it formed only 37%, representing a decrease of 23%. In 1927 the area occupied by arable land formed only 9% of the total. In 1960 it formed 30%, representing an increase of 21%. Over the same period variations in other forms of land-use involved relatively minor percentages, and it is therefore clear that the increase in arable land has been achieved overwhelmingly by conversion from rough grazing land. The present position, in which some 40% of the main Turkish cereal crop, wheat, is produced on central Anatolian arable land, is therefore a relatively new one and, moreover, rendered possible only by the extensive exploitation of poor quality land. This latter has been brought about, to a very considerable degree at least, by the governmental establishment of high minimum prices for cereal crops.[1]

[1] For the Balkan and Anatolian materials quoted above, see the various national entries in: Committee for the World Atlas of Agriculture (ed.), *The World Atlas of Agriculture* I. These include: M. Milivoievic and J. Roglić, 'Yugoslavia', at pp. 512–27; G. Favaretti, 'Albania', at pp. 21–6; C. Dragonas and N. Olympitis, 'Greece', at pp. 191–207; D. Davidescu, M. Stancu and C. Papacostea, 'Rumania', at pp. 343–67; I. Zahariev, T. Jordanov and B. Raichev, 'Bulgaria', at pp. 57–69; and Z. Gökalp Mülâyim, 'Turkey', at pp. 423–37. For the Balkans in general, see also P.-Y. Péchoux and M. Sivignon, *Les Balkans*, pp. 11–24; and for Turkey in general, see also J. C. Dewdney, *Turkey*. For Turkey in Asia Minor in the early twentieth century, see also the excellent conspectus in: Admiralty (Naval Staff Intelligence Division), *C.B. 847 A: A Handbook of Asia Minor* I, *General*.

## (II) THE MEDIAEVAL SITUATION (FERTILITY AND INFERTILITY)

The question inevitably arises as to what degree the situation revealed in this survey resembles that obtaining during the late Roman and Byzantine period. There is, amongst Byzantinists at least, a widespread, if tacit, assumption that the situation is now in some quite fundamental way worse than it was then, and although few would care to be too specific as to the cause of this deterioration, there is little doubt that many (Greeks & Slavs aside) would lay it at the door of the post-Byzantine – inevitably Turkish – régime. Both assumption and blame are in the main quite unfounded. It should in the first place be observed that the major elements involved – characteristics of, and relationships between, topography and climate – are of a kind that is not normally susceptible to radical change on a limited time scale. Features of vegetation and land-use are admittedly rather more open to such change on such a time scale, and indeed one recent example has been noted in the preceding section. The general point is nevertheless very simply made, with regard to both the Balkans and Anatolia, by reference to the major authors who travelled overland with the First, Second, and Third Crusades, and who provided eye-witness descriptions – however brief and unsystematic – of the regions through which they passed.

### *A. The Balkans*

According to the anonymous author of the *Gesta Francorum*,[2] Bohemund and his companions in 1096 landed in the regions of Bulgaria (*Bulgariae partes*) where they found a superabundance of corn, wine and bodily nourishments (*nimiam abundantiam frumenti et vini et alimentorum corporis*). Anna Comnena makes it clear[3] that they landed at Boousa (presumably at the mouth of the River Voioussa) and Khimara, both in the Drin–Devoll Plain. From there,[4] they descended the valley of Andronopolis (i.e. Dryinopolis, Argyrokastro), where they collected themselves together, and passing through a region of superabundance (*nimiam plentitudinem*), from village to village, town to town, and fortress to fortress, they arrived at Kastoria where they spent Christmas. By way of Pelagonia (i.e. Monastir), they cross the Vardar and arrived at Serra (i.e. Serres) where they spent Lent. Again, by way of Rusa (Rousia, probably Keşan), they then entered a certain valley full of all supplies suitable for bodily nourishment (*vallem quamdam plenam omnibus bonis quae corporalibus nutrimentis sunt congrua*), where they spent Easter. For whatever reasons, Bohemund seems deliberately to have avoided landing at Dyrrhachium (i.e. Dürres) or Avlona, so taking the classic route – the Via Egnatia – through to

[2] Anonymous, *Gesta Francorum et Aliorum Hierosolimitanorum* I.iv–II.v; ed. R. Hill, pp. 7–8.
[3] Anna Comnena, *Alexiad* X.8.1; ed. B. Leib, II, p. 215.
[4] Anonymous, *Gesta Francorum* I.iv–II.v; ed. Hill, pp. 8–11.

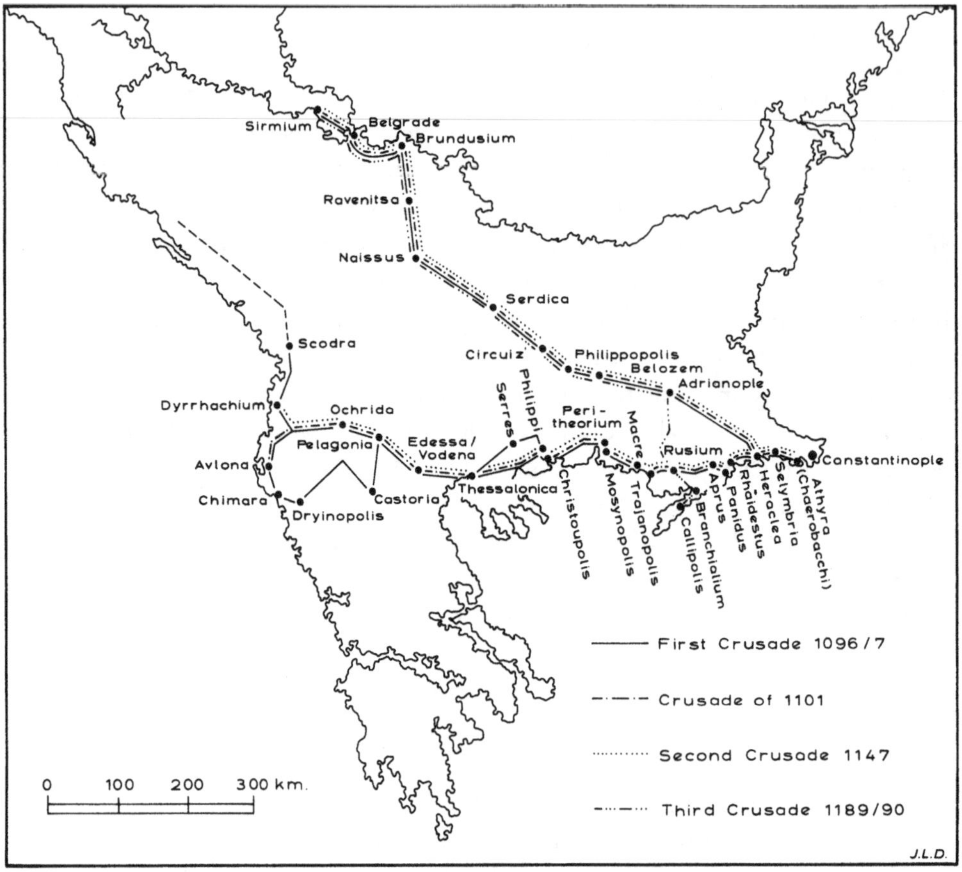


Map 10 The Balkans: crusading routes

Thessalonica and Constantinople by way of Ochrida, and instead, having taken a more circuitous southerly route, to have joined up with the Via Egnatia at Pelagonia only. Although it takes advantage of the Drin–Devoll, Vardar–Aliakmon, Strimon–Maritsa and Thracian Plains, the route is not an easy one throughout, for the Pindus Mountains have to be crossed early on. Even so, whether because of the resources provided by the route itself, or because of those provided by imperial agents, Bohemund seems to have had little difficulty in obtaining provisions, except at Kastoria, the inhabitants of which were hostile and refused to sell. (Map 10)

According to Fulcher of Chartres,[5] Stephen of Blois, Robert of Normandy and their companions, in 1097, landed at Dyrrhachium and took the Via Egnatia by way of Lucretia (i.e. Okhrid) and Philippi. Between Dyrrhachium and Ochrida they found themselves

[5] Fulcher of Chartres, *Historia Iherosolymitana Gesta Francorum Iherusalem Peregrinantium ab Anno Domini MXCV usque ad Annum MCXXVII* VIII; RHC, *Occ.* III.1, p. 330.

travelling through precipitous mountains and places with few inhabitants (*per montium praerupta et loca satis deserta*) or surrounded by great mountains with no inhabitants at all (*montes vasti nobis undique praeerant, in quibus nemo incola parebat*). (Map 10)

According to Raymond of Aguilers,[6] Raymond of Toulouse and his companions had a not dissimilar experience. They entered Sclavonia (i.e. Dalmatia) in 1096, and found it a deserted, roadless and mountainous land (*tellus deserta, et invia, et montuosa*) where they saw neither bird nor beast for three weeks. Its inhabitants, who had fled their villages and fortresses, were so savage and uncultivated (*agrestes et rudes*) that they would neither sell provisions nor provide a guide, and instead turned to harassment. They were in Sclavonia for nearly forty days, during which they encountered mist in some places that was so thick that they had to feel their way (!), eventually arriving at Scodra (i.e. Shköder) where they came to some arrangement regarding the sale of provisions – an arrangement that, however, did not render them immune from harassment. They eventually arrived at Dyrrhachium and took the Via Egnatia through to Thessalonica and Constantinople, from then on apparently having less trouble with provisions at least. Anna Comnena calls,[7] as indeed it still is called, the wild area (*topos*) common to the accounts of both Fulcher and Raymond the *Zygos*, and describes it as mountainous (*okhthōdēs*), full of ravines (*kharadrōdēs*), forested (*synērephēs*), and little trodden (*mikrou abatos*). (Map 10)

According to Odo of Deuil,[8] the French members of the Second Crusade in 1147 entered Bulgaria at Belgrada (i.e. Beograd) and, after reaching Brundusium (i.e. Braničevo), encountered a five days' journey of wooded meadowland or pastured woodland (*pratum nemorosum vel nemus pabulosum*) before reaching Nit (Naissus, i.e. Niš). This abounded in supplies (*bona*) which grew of their own accord, and it would have been suitable for other things had it had inhabitants to cultivate it (*coloni*). It was neither flat nor rugged with mountains, but lay amongst hills that were suitable for vines and cereals (*vinae et segetes*) and was watered by the clearest of streams and springs. It is nevertheless, despite this favourable appraisal, again later described as deserted (*deserta*). From Niš onwards, to the contrary, by way of Hesternit (i.e. Sofiya), Philippopolis (i.e. Plovdiv), and Adrianopolis (i.e. Edirne), and as far as Constantinople itself, lay a wide, rich and pleasant plain (*lata, diva, et iocunda planities*), bordered by mountains and studded with towns and fortresses (*villis et castellis*), and abounding in all supplies (*omnibusque bonis*). This is again later described as a most beautiful and rich land which, without interruption, extends as far as Constantinople (*terra pulcherrima et opulentissima quae sine interruptione protenditur usque Constantinopolim*) (Map 10). The same basic distinction as observed by Odo is implied by the anonymous author (the so-called Ansbert) of the *Historia de*

[6] Raymond of Aguilers, *Historia Francorum qui Ceperunt Iherusalem* I–II; RHC, *Occ.* III.1, pp. 235–8.

[7] Anna Comnena, *Alexiad* IX.1; ed. Leib, II, p. 156. See also: N. G. L. Hammond, *Epirus. The Geography, the Ancient Remains, the History and the Topography of Epirus and Adjacent Areas*, p. 11.

[8] Odo of Deuil, *De Profectione Ludovici VII in Orientem* II–III; ed. V. G. Berry, pp. 30, 32, 40.

*Expeditione Friderici Imperatoris*,[9] according to whom the German members of the Third Crusade in 1189 reached Brandiez through woodland (*silvestria*). They then entered the extremely lengthy forest of Bulgaria (*silva longissima Bulgariae*) and eventually, having reached Straliz (i.e. Sofiya) and then the furthest and strongest passes of Bulgaria (*clusae ultimae et firmissimae Bulgariae*), presumably referring to the Trajan's Gate area, they entered the plains (*campestria*) of 'Greece', where they found a level region abundant in vineyards and all supplies (*terra plana vinetis et omnibus bonis habundans*) called Circvviz. This latter must represent the town of Pazardzhik or somewhere in its close vicinity, for it is there that the transition from pass to plain (the Thracian Plain proper) takes place. Much the same distinction had already been described by Albert of Aix[10] who, although not providing an eye-witness account of the First Crusade, nevertheless seems to have used reliable sources. (Map 10)

The situation seems to have been as follows. The vast and mountainous north-west to south-east axis of the peninsula was for the most part lightly populated and roadless. Only in the southern section of the axis do these conditions seem to have been alleviated somewhat, if the author of the *Gesta Francorum* is to be believed. Much of the interior, and in particular the part of it stretching from Beograd down to Niš, was under forest, and even where conditions were more favourable – as in what was obviously the Morava Valley – the lack of population and hence cultivation remained. The forest nature of the area (*khōra*) around Niš is suggested by the twelfth-century Byzantine name for it: *Dendra*.[11] The area of the Danube seems to have been in a very similar condition: certainly, according to Cinnamus,[12] the plains (*pediades*) in the region of the river were entirely deserted and uninhabited as from old (*erēmai pantapasi kai aoikētai ek palaiou*), and were the haunt of wildlife (*zōa*) that provided good hunting only. Acropolites also implies[13] livestock to be typical of the area. It was from Niš, or perhaps and more particularly from Pazardzhik, onwards, in other words in the Thracian Plain, that population, cultivation and urban concentrations became significantly denser, the extremely fertile area of lower Thrace coming in for specific mention. Similarly, the Macedonian Plain is described[14] by the author of the twelfth-century satire *Timarion* as a place (*topos*) quite worth depicting: for farmers, bringing all manner of seed to birth and fruition (*geōrgois pantoiōn spermatōn anadotikos hama kai telesiourgos*), the region (*khōra*) being free of stones and scrub, and mostly smooth (*alithos... kai athamnos kai homalē es ta malista*), and so on.*

* I owe this reference to the kindness of Meg Alexiou.

9 Anonymous ('Ansbert'), *Historia de Expeditione Friderici Imperatoris*; MGH, *SRG: NS* v, pp. 27–71.

10 Albert of Aix, *Historia Hierosolymitana* I.6–14; RHC, *Occ.* IV, pp. 274–83.

11 B. Radojčić, 'La région de la Dendra de la Serbie au XII^e siècle', *Balkan Studies* 11 (1970), pp. 249–60.

12 John Cinnamus, *Epitome* III.3; ed. A. Meineke (Bonn edn), p. 93.

13 George Acropolites, *Historia* XI; ed. A. Heisenberg and P. Wirth (Teubner), in *Georgii Acropolitae Opera* I, at p. 18.

14 Anonymous (Pseudo-Lucian), *Timarion*; ed. R. Romano, p. 52. See also below, pp. 50, 51–2, 53, 57.

The evidence of the crusading chroniclers is confirmed by that of William of Tyre,[15] who visited the Serbian borderlands in 1168. This author, one of the most enlightened and reliable in mediaeval historiography, describes the area as mountainous, cut off by woodlands, and difficult of access (*regio montuosa, et nemoribus obsita, difficiles habens aditus*). He describes the population as crude (*incultus*) and as ignorant of agriculture (*agriculturae ignarus*), but the territories involved as full of flocks and herds, and as richly abounding in milk, cheese, butter, and meats, and in honey and wax (*gregibus et armentis copiosi, lacte, caseo, butyro, carnibus, melle, et cera uberius abundantes*). This description of a basically pastoral, rather than an agricultural, economy for the area is confirmed by its known exports. The same author adds the fascinating information that it had been the policy of the Byzantines to keep the area deserted, and that they still did not permit settlers to enter it, or it to be cultivated (*etiam hodie non permittunt habitatores introire, nec excoli regionum*), commenting that Epirus up to four days' journey from Dyrrhachium was similarly treated, and that they applied this policy in their outlying territories, and particularly in those which abutted onto foreign kingdoms and through which access to them might be had (*in ulterioribus provinciis et maxime quae regnis exteris collimitant et per quos ad eos acceditur*). The implications of this policy, involving the deliberate creation and maintenance of deserted and wild borderlands to act as barriers, are clearly radical, are well exemplified in Alexius I's treatment of the Zygos, and are presumably to be applied both to other areas in the Balkans, for example to the Danube, and to Anatolia.[16]

The primary divisions as they can be seen today certainly, and many of the secondary distinctions that they entailed probably, were then already present, as indeed they must long have been. They can, for example, even be shown to have been closely reflected in the variations in the average daily mileage attained by several of the crusading armies.[17] Certain relatively recent modifications obviously have to be taken into account: the Morava Valley, for example, is now well populated and cultivated, and this has entailed the disappearance of much of the 'Bulgarian Forest'. The great potential of the area seen by Odo, in other words, has now been realised, or rather has been permitted to be realised. Much the same is true of the Danube Plain.

15 William of Tyre, *Historia Rerum in Partibus Transmarinis Gestarum a Tempore Successorum Mahumeth usque ad Annum Domini MCLXXXIV* xx.4; RHC, *Occ.* I.2, pp. 946–7.

16 On Byzantine borders in general, see: D. Obolensky, 'Byzantine Frontier Zones and Cultural Exchanges', *XIV[e] Congrès International des Études Byzantines, Bucarest 6–12 septembre 1971, Rapports* II, pp. 91–101. See also above, pp. 36–8; below, pp. 83, 124, 126.

17 J. W. Nesbitt, 'The Rate of March of Crusading Armies in Europe: A Study and Computation', *Traditio* 19 (1963), pp. 167–81.

### B. Anatolia

The exercise may be repeated for Anatolia. According to the author of the *Gesta Francorum*,[18] the First Crusade in 1097, after defeating the Selçuks in the vicinity of Dorylaeum (i.e. Eskişehir), pursued them through a deserted, waterless, and uninhabitable land (*per deserta, et inaquosam et inhabitabilem terram*), in which the crusaders suffered greatly from hunger and thirst, for they found there nothing at all except thorny vegetation (*spicae*). It was as the crusaders approached Iconium (i.e. Konya) only that they once more began to reach a prosperous land, full of bodily nourishment and all delightful supplies (*terra optima, plena corporalibus alimentis et deliciis omnibusque bonis*). At Iconium they were warned to supply themselves well with water on account of its great scarcity (*maxima penuria*) for a day's journey from the city. The evidence of the *Gesta* seems confirmed by that of the *Annales Palidenses*,[19] according to which the German members of the Second Crusade in 1147, having arrived in what was presumably somewhere in the region of Dorylaeum, were obliged to spend two or three days crossing a desert (*desertum*), finding shepherds' tents and flocks of sheep (*tabernacula pastorum et greges ovium*) only. They were then obliged to spend a further fourteen days crossing a horrible wilderness (*horribilis eremus*), which was a place of horror and a waste of solitude (*locum horroris et vaste solitudinis*), suffering from the barrenness of the land (*a sterilitate terrae*). Eventually they were defeated, apparently shortly before or after reaching Philomelium (i.e. Akşehir), and fled back to Nicaea (i.e. İznik). (Map 11)

According to Albert of Aix,[20] the Lombard and the French members of the crusade of 1101 decided to rescue Bohemund from where he was held in captivity (at Neocaesarea, i.e. Niksar). They therefore travelled by way of Nicomedia (i.e. İzmit), Ancyra (i.e. Ankara), and Gangra (i.e. Çankırı), and then further on towards Amasia (i.e. Amasya) when, so it is claimed, they were led away from the road, through lonely and roadless deserts and arid places (*per deserta et invia et solitudines locaque arida*). Eventually it was decided to turn back, but even so they were obliged to spend fifteen days in the solitudes and uninhabitable places of horror, in the roughest of mountains, finding no one, neither man nor beast (*in solitudines, et loca inhabitabilia et horroris, per montana asperrima, ubi nichil reperientes, non hominem, non pecudem*). Even those who had money could buy no food (*esca*), for there was simply none to be had. Only those who had brought supplies from Nicomedia or Cibotus were in a fortunate position. Their exact route remains uncertain, although the mountains involved were presumably the Köroğlu/Ilgaz Dağları, and one group, consisting of a thousand foot, ended up foraging in the vicinity of Castamenon (i.e. Kastamonu), where it found unripe barley (*ordeum sed nondum maturum/immaturum*

[18] Anonymous, *Gesta Francorum* IV.X; ed. Hill, p. 23.

[19] *Annales Palidenses*, s.a. 1147; MGH, *SS* XVI, p. 83.

[20] Albert of Aix, *Historia Hierosolymitana* VIII.4–24; RHC, *Occ.* IV, pp. 561–74. See also: Anna Comnena, *Alexiad* XI.8. 1–5; ed. Leib, III, pp. 36–9.

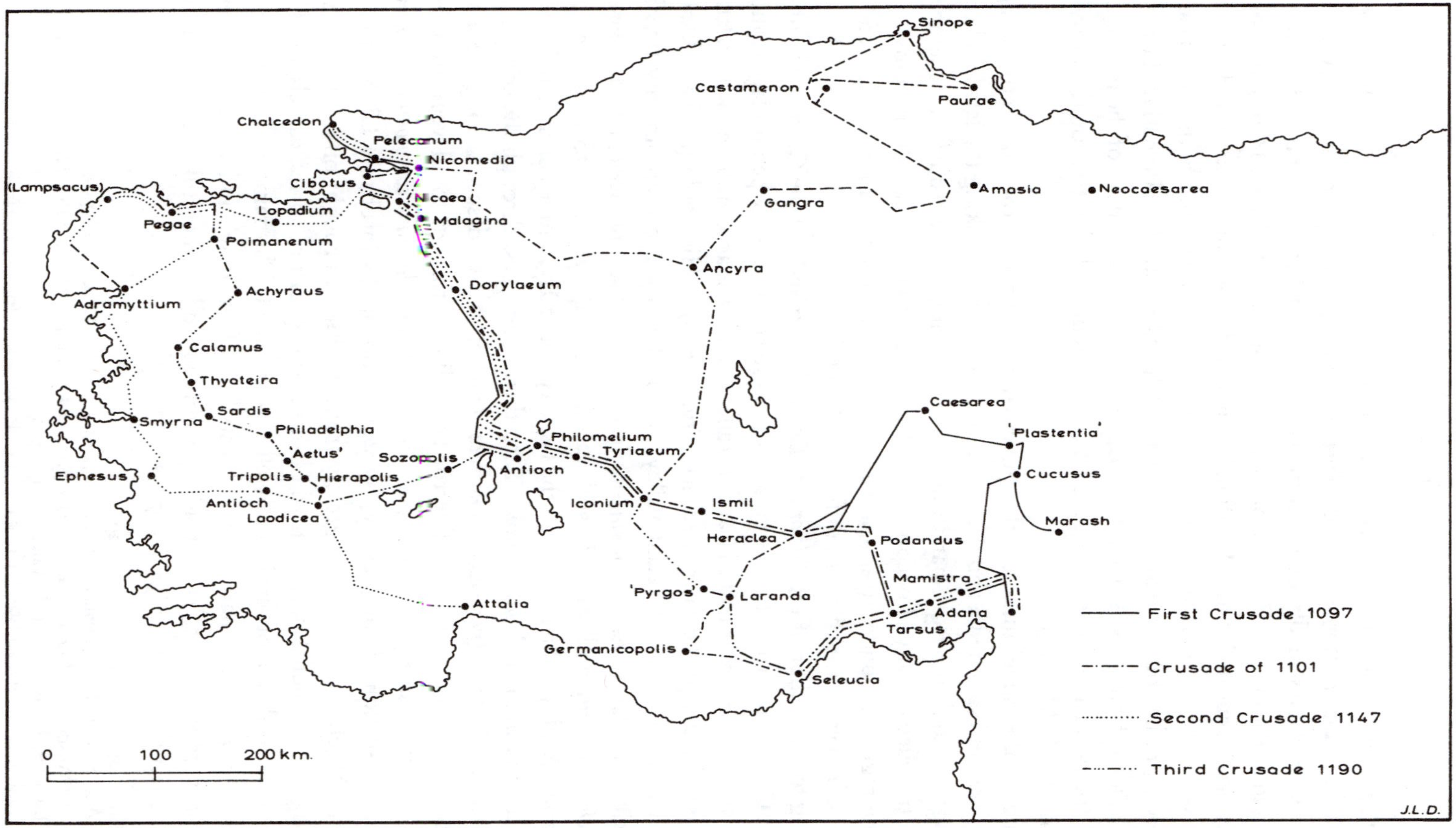


Map 11 Anatolia: crusading routes

*hordeum*). The army as a whole, having overcome the narrow and difficult passes of Paphlagonia (*angustae et laboriosae fauces Flaganiae*), and having approached a level plain (*planities campestris*), was finally defeated in the vicinity of Maresch, and fled to Sinope (i.e. Sinop) and to Paurae (i.e. Bafra), from where it made its way back to Constantinople. Maresch has been identified with Mersifon, but it seems much more likely to denote the river and town of Araç, the river being a tributary of the Filyos, and both being nearer, somewhat west, rather than much further east, of Kastamonu. An alternative, but even less probable, identification is Amasia itself. Again, the waterless nature of the terrain and the lack of forage in the vicinity of Ancyra had presented difficulties for the army of Mu'tasim in 838.[21] (Map 11)

According to the same author,[22] the Nivernais members of the same crusade also travelled by way of Nicomedia and Ancyra, but then instead of taking the left-hand road into Paphlagonia, took the right-hand one towards Iconium. The Aquitanian members, by contrast, travelled by way of Nicomedia to Nicaea, through the beautiful meadowlands in which the region abounded (*per amoena prata, quibus haec abundat regio*). The road to Iconium was, however, much more difficult. (Map 11)

According to the author of the *Historia de Expeditione Friderici*,[23] the German members of the Third Crusade in 1190, after keeping to the western edge of the peninsula, advanced inland by way of the Hermus and Maeander Valleys. This was accomplished with relative speed and ease. Having passed the ruined city (*diruta civitas*) of Hierapolis (i.e. Pamukkale), they crossed through a very pleasant valley, rich in liquorice, cardamom, myrtle, figs and other kinds of plants (*per vallem amoenissimam, liquoericia, cardomomo, myrto, ficulneis, et aliis speciebus opimam*), and reached Laodicea (i.e. Denizli), which lies towards the head of the Maeander Valley, which was then the last city under Byzantine control, and where they found a good market (*bonum forum*). They then had to pass through the completely deserted places of Turkey (*per desertissima loca Turciae*) and to descend alongside a salt lake (the Acı Tuz Gölü) in a land of terror and salinity, foreign to all vegetation and human comfort (*in terram horroris et salsuginis, omni viriditate et humana commoditate alienam*). Throughout this section of the journey, by way of Sozopolis (probably Uluborlu) and Philomelium/Akşehir, they suffered greatly from weakness, brought on by hunger and thirst, finding the occasional flock or herd of sheep, goats, cattle, horses, camels, or asses, or only the occasional area of fertile and well-watered land. This same area, that around Choma, had already been remarked upon for its lack of pasturage and water by Nicetas Choniates in 1176,[24] and it had already possibly included the still current Turkish toponym Dazkırı ('bare steppe') by 1178.[25]

[21] A. A. Vasiliev, *Byzance et les Arabes* I, p. 298.

[22] Albert of Aix, *Historia Hierosolymitana* VIII. 26–33, 37–40; RHC, *Occ.*IV, pp. 575–8, 580–2.

[23] Anonymous ('Ansbert'), *Historia de Expeditione Friderici Imperatoris*; MGH, *SRG:NS* V, pp. 72–90.

[24] Nicetas Choniates, *Historia*; ed. J.-L. van Dieten, I, p. 179.

[25] Nicetas Choniates, *Historia*; ed. van Dieten, I, p. 195. P. Wittek, 'Von der byzantinischen zur türkischen Toponymie', *Byzantion* 10 (1935), pp. 26–7 (n.2). But see below, p. 130.

Again, it was only as they approached Iconium that they came across royal gardens, with a great abundance of pasture and water (*hortum et viridarium regium multam habundantiam graminis et aquarum invenimus*). These gardens (*kēpoi*), an unusual feature for this area, taking maximum advantage of the presence of a large stretch of alluvium, and implied or mentioned by the authors of both the *Gesta Francorum* and the *Historia de Expeditione Friderici*, are also mentioned, along with the ditches (*taphrheumata*) and channels (*diōrhykhai*) which irrigated them, and upon which they depended, by Choniates.[26]

Thereafter, by way of Laranda (i.e. Karaman), they made for Seleucia (i.e. Silifke), with considerably less trouble as regards the terrain and the supplies derived from it, at least (Map 11).

The principal elements of the main crusading descriptions summarised in the preceding paragraphs are immediately recognisable: the crusading armies began to experience consistent difficulties with the terrain and its supplies at particular points and thereafter, and these points still represent the same divisions that they then did and must long have done. Eskişehir/Dorylaeum (792 m) lies towards the north-western edge of the central plateau of Anatolia, which the crusaders would have had to cross in order to reach Konya/Iconium (1,027 m). It effectively represents the limit of the comparatively fertile and well-watered terrain that characterises the coastal plain and major river-valleys and that is therefore comparatively intensely populated and cultivated. It gives way very soon to the steppe-like nature of the plateau (of which thorn-scrub is still a predominant feature in many areas). The fertile and well-watered area in the region of İzmit/Nicomedia and İznik/Nicaea still contrasts sharply, not only with the broken and semi-arid nature of much of the region of Çankırı/Gangra (730 m) and northwards, but even with the appreciably less extreme one of that of Kastamonu/Castamenon (790 m). Denizli/Laodicea (450 m) lies towards the south-western edge of the plateau, which the crusaders would again have had to penetrate to reach Konya/Iconium. Equally, it marks the division between the coast and river-valleys and the plateau, and it shortly gives way to steppe (of which extensive grazing is still a predominant feature).

The same division was understood and can be traced in the description provided by Odo of Deuil. According to that author,[27] the French members of the Second Crusade, on reaching Nicomedia, or actually rather Nicaea, had a choice of three routes to Antioch. The first was basically that which had been taken by the First Crusade and by the Aquitanian part of the Crusade of 1101. The second followed the coast, and although it was more peaceful and better supplied (*pacatior...et abundantior*) than the first, was also much longer and cut across the courses of too many rivers. Eventually, a third, rather similar to that which was later taken by the Third Crusade, was chosen. Having followed the western coast of the peninsula, and having camped in the very fertile valley (*vallis*

[26] Nicetas Choniates, *Historia*; ed. van Dieten, I, pp. 413–14.

[27] Odo of Deuil, *De Profectione Ludovici VII in Orientem* V–VII; ed. Berry, pp. 88–128.

*praedives*) of Decervion, probably representing Celbianum, the region of the Caÿster (i.e. Küçük Menderes), near Ephesus (i.e. Selçuk), where they spent Christmas, the crusaders advanced inland by way of the Maeander Valley and reached Laodicea which they found purposely emptied of all supplies (*quibusque utilitatibus*). This they counted a disaster, for they knew that between there and Satellia (Attalia, i.e. Antalya), they would find no provisions anywhere else (*victualia...alibi*). The area between Antalya/Attalia and Antioch, that is the southern coast, was reportedly roadless (*invia*) and constant in barrenness (*egestas*). (Map 11)

The division is also implied by the pattern of occurrence of thirteenth-century Selçuk hans. (Map 12)

## (III) THE MEDIAEVAL SITUATION (AGRICULTURE AND PASTORALISM)

### A. *Agriculture*

The same broad distinctions in land-use as exist today may also be traced back to an early period, if not directly, then by way of the basic products of the land, whether agricultural or pastoral. Prior to the First World War – prior, that is, to general agricultural mechanisation and use of artificial fertilisers, to the mechanisation of water-supply and irrigation, and to the widespread evolution of governmentally established minimum prices of crops and agricultural subsidies of whatever kind – the main areas of arable land, mainly producing cereal crops, were, as far as the Balkans were concerned, the Danubian Plain, the Thracian Plain, the Thessalian Plain (i.e. that of the Pinios), and the Macedonian Plain (that of the Vardar–Aliakmon). Of these, the Danubian Plain – or that portion of it lying between the Danube and the Balkan Mountains but excluding the Dobrogea – produced more than half of the wheat and maize grown in Bulgaria, the chief regional port and centre for exportation being Varna.[28] The Dobrogea was not then, in general, given over to arable and cereal-producing, although its chief regional port and the largest Rumanian centre for exportation was Constanţa.[29]

The Thracian Plain – with Pazardzhik as its westernmost limit, and elsewhere delimited by the Balkan Mountains on the north, the Black Sea on the east, and the Aegean and Marmara Seas on the south – was also of considerable importance, although quantification, even of a most rudimentary kind, is impossible as it was then already shared between Bulgaria and Turkey. The chief regional port and centre of exportation at the western end of the plain was Bourgas on the Black Sea, and those at the southern end were Enos on the Aegean dealing with the Maritsa trade through Edirne, and Rodosto on the Marmara, dealing with the trade of lower Thrace.[30]

[28] Admiralty, *I.D. 1155: A Handbook of Bulgaria*, pp. 106–7, 114.
[29] Admiralty, *I.D. 1204: A Handbook of Roumania*, pp. 140–2, 160–3.
[30] Admiralty, *A Handbook of Bulgaria*, pp. 109, 110–12, 113; *idem*, *ID. 1129: A Handbook of Turkey in Europe*, pp. 148–53, 181–3.

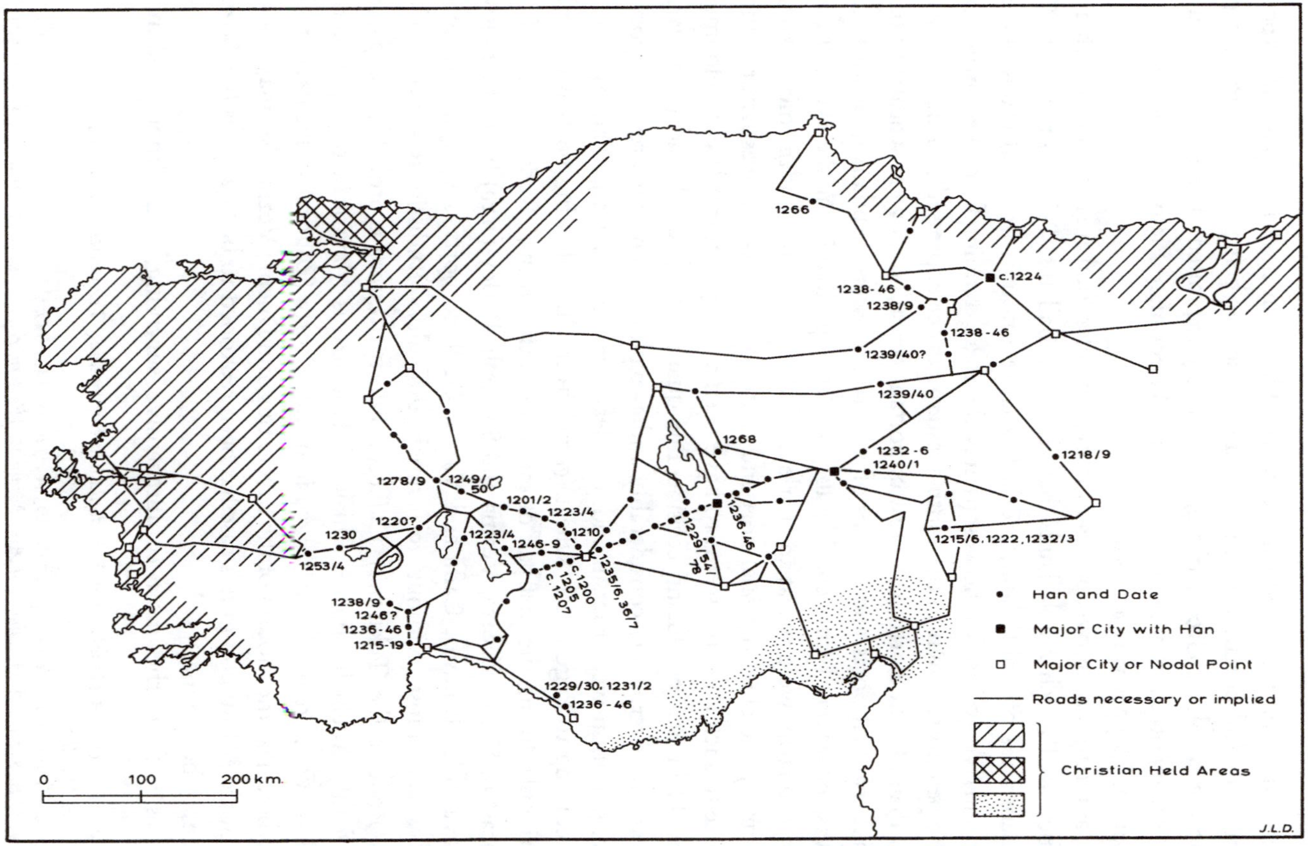


Map 12 Anatolia: thirteenth-century Selçuk hans (after Erdmann)

The Thessalian Plain was producing considerable quantities of cereals and exporting some, although its full potential was not being realised, it being reckoned to be capable of supplying the whole of Greece if more intensively exploited. The chief regional port and centre of exportation was Volo.[31] The Macedonian Plain was being similarly under-exploited. Its port was Thessaloniki.[32]

Anatolia, as mentioned above, possesses an even smaller total area of plain, and therefore of at least potentially rich arable land, than does the Balkans. Prior to the First World War, the main areas of arable land, producing large amounts of cereal crops, were the coastal plain and river-valleys of the west (that is, the area extending from the north-western corner of the peninsula down to the south-western corner expressed as a single unit) and the Cilician Plain. In the north, the most important cereal crops were wheat and barley, and the chief regional ports and centres of exportation were Mudanya, Bandırma, and İzmit. It was, however, being considerably under-exploited.[33] In the west, the most important cereal crops were wheat and barley, of which the latter was the more exported. Overwhelmingly the chief regional port and centre of exportation was İzmir, although its dominance to such a degree seems to have been a comparatively late development.[34] The Cilician Plain was producing considerable quantities of cereal, and particularly of wheat. It was, however, being considerably under-exploited. The chief regional ports and centres of exportation were Mersin and, to a lesser extent, Ayas and Karataş.[35]

Now, according to Pegolotti,[36] wheat (*grano*) from the following ports was available in Constantinople during the first half of the fourteenth century: Rudistio, Caffa, Lifetti, Asilo, Maocastro, Varna, Zaorra, Vezina and Sinopoli. Barley (*orzo*) from the following ports was available: Rodisto, Caffa and Varna. Of these ports, several are identifiable immediately, and most without too much difficulty. Rudistio/Rodisto is clearly Rhaedestus/Rodosto (i.e. Tekirdağ); Caffa is Feodosiya; Lifetti is probably Yevpatoriya; Asilo is probably Anchialus (i.e. Ankhialo); Maocastro is Mavrocastro (i.e. Akkerman, Cetatea Albă); Varna remains unchanged in name; Zaorra (Zagora) seems likely to have been somewhere near the mouths of the Rivers Bug and Dnepr; Vezina (Vicina) is possibly Păcuiul lui Soare;[37] Sinopoli in this case has been reckoned to be Sozopolis (i.e. Sozopol) but may simply be Sinope.[38]

The list as such is the most comprehensive surviving, and although individual

[31] Admiralty, *I.D. 1114: A Handbook of Macedonia and Surrounding Territories*, pp. 33, 493.

[32] Admiralty, *A Handbook of Macedonia*, pp. 34–5, 478–83.

[33] V. Cuinet, *La Turquie d'Asie* IV, pp. 47–8, 103–6, 320–5, 343, 347–52.

[34] Admiralty, *C.B. 847 B: A Handbook of Asia Minor* II, *Western Asia Minor*, pp. 102–12, 123–4, 573–8.

[35] Admiralty, *C.B. 847 D 2: A Handbook of Asia Minor* IV.2, *Cilicia, Antitaurus, and North Syria*, pp. 45–6, 693–4, 707, 713–15. Cuinet, *La Turquie d'Asie* II, 13–14, 21, 25.

[36] Francesco Balducci Pegolotti, *La Pratica della Mercatura*; ed. A. Evans, p. 42. Because mediaeval terminology for grains and livestock varies, the terms used in the texts are given as well as the translation.

[37] P. Diaconu, 'Păcuiul lui Soare–Vicina', *Byzantina* 8 (1976), pp. 407–47.

[38] Pegolotti, *La Pratica della Mercatura*; ed. Evans, p. 405; see below, pp. 47, 50.

Table 1. *Constantinopolitan grain sources after Pegolotti*

| Ports | Hinterlands |
|---|---|
| Varna | Danubian Plain |
| Vicina | Danubian Plain |
| Rodosto | Thracian Plain (Marmara) |
| Anchialus | Thracian Plain (Black Sea) |
| Sozopolis | Thracian Plain (Black Sea) |
| Mavrocastro | South Russian Plain |
| Zagora | South Russian Plain |
| Caffa | Crimea |
| Lifetti | Crimea |

documents and sources of the period add somewhat to its total of ports, the general balance remains intact.[39] If the ports included in the list are lined up against the hinterlands they may be assumed to have served, the pattern emerges as in Table 1.

The virtually exclusive dependence of the capital upon cereals supplied by the Black Sea and Marmara ports during this period is immediately apparent. Several of the ports involved are also identical with those that were to be predominant later: Rodosto and Varna were still instrumental in serving their respective hinterlands during the period prior to the First World War. Anchialus and Sozopolis had by then been superseded by nearby Bourgas (i.e. Develtus), but the functions of the latter were the same. The basic continuity expressed or implied by these examples of identity or near-identity is confirmed on examination of the situation obtaining during the intervening period, that of the Ottoman empire.[40] The degree of dependence involved is exemplified by what is known to have happened on two occasions when the capital was deprived of a proportion of its cereals from the Black Sea ports. Between 1305 and 1307, the Bulgarian tsar Todor Svetoslav occupied the Thracian ports on the Black Sea and put a stop to their export of cereals. The capital, at the same time deprived of its grain (*sitos*) from the Thracian ports on the Marmara by the Catalans, faced famine. One of the stipulations of the peace treaty finally ratified by Svetoslav and Andronicus II in 1307 was that grain (*sitos*) should once more be supplied to the capital from Sozopolis.[41] In 1343, due to disturbances in the South

[39] W. Heyd, *Histoire du commerce du Levant au moyen-âge* II, p. 177. G. I. Brătianu, *Études byzantines d'histoire économique et sociale*, pp. 157–68. J. Chrysostomides, 'Venetian Commercial Privileges under the Palaeologi', *Studi Veneziani* 12 (1970), pp. 312–27. For the later trade in wheat, see now also: A. Laiou-Thomadakis, 'The Byzantine Economy in the Mediterranean Trade System; Thirteenth–Fifteenth Centuries', *DOP* 34/5 (1980/1), pp. 183–5, 214–15, 218–20. The main areas of production remained the same as previously.

[40] Brătianu, *Études byzantines*, pp. 168–77.

[41] George Pachymeres, *De Michaele et Andronico Palaeologis*, *De And.* VII.27; ed. I. Bekker (Bonn edn), II, pp. 628–9.

Russian Plain, the capital was deprived of its grain (*sitos*) from the ports of the Sea of Azov and the neighbouring rivers, and again faced famine.[42]

Granted the fact of dependence at that period, it may well be enquired whether the situation was recent or of long standing, for on the face of it, at least, it seems all too probable that the relatively restricted area which the capital was then drawing upon (or was then able to draw upon) reflected merely the reduced territorial extent and political interests of the contemporary empire. Certainly as late as 1187, when the revolt of Alexius Branas against Isaac II had attracted the support of both the eastern and the western sections (*lēxeis*) of the empire, the usurper had been able to prevent grain shipping (*nēa sitagōgon*) from reaching the capital, thus bringing about a famine in the City.[43] As the Bulgarians were by then in control of the Danube Plain, and as the usurper was in control of the greater part of the empire itself, but not of the sea-routes to the capital; it would seem to follow that the city was not then heavily dependent upon foreign or Black Sea grain, but still dependent rather upon its own – probably mainly sub-Balkan and Aegean – supply.[44] The contrast with the fourteenth-century situation is thus considerable.

In attempting to provide an answer to this problem it seems clear that a primary distinction should be preserved between the Thracian Plain on the one hand, and the South Russian Plain and Crimea on the other, the position of the Danubian Plain remaining largely indeterminate. Evidence for the exploitation of the cereal-bearing capacities of the Thracian Plain and for the predominant position of Rodosto in the exploitation of cereals from the southern end of the plain can be traced back as far as the seventh century.[45] Evidence for the exportation of cereals from the ports of southern Russia and the Crimea can, to the contrary, be traced back no further than the twelfth.[46] Exploitation of the Danubian Plain, apparently prohibited and probably non-existent as late as the twelfth century, seems to have been basically a thirteenth- and even more a fourteenth-century phenomenon.[47]

The alternative sources of cereals that were necessarily drawn upon when the capital was deprived of its South Russian and Crimean grain in 1343 serve to indicate another potentially major source of supply. According to Gregoras[48] the grain needed on this occasion came from: 'Ionia and Phrygia, and indeed Bithynia and whatever distant land

42 Nicephorus Gregoras, *Historia Byzantina* XIII.12; ed. L. Schopen (Bonn edn), II, pp. 686–7.

43 Nicetas Choniates, *Historia*; ed. van Dieten, I, p. 381.

44 See below, pp. 50, 51–2, 53, 174, 559.

45 Brătianu, *Études byzantines*, pp. 141–57. J. L. Teall, 'The Grain Supply of the Byzantine Empire, 330–1025', *DOP* 13 (1959), pp. 117–18, 123–4.

46 Teall, 'The Grain Supply of the Byzantine Empire', pp. 118–19. See also below, pp. 49–50.

47 Teall, 'The Grain Supply of the Byzantine Empire', pp. 118–19. See also above, p. 38, below, p. 279 and n. 145.

48 See above, n. 42.

that Persian (i.e. Turkish) hands cultivate.' The areas specifically mentioned comprise the coastal plain and river-valleys of western Anatolia – in other words, precisely those areas that were still important prior to the First World War. Their exploitation for cereals is mentioned or implied as far back as the eighth century,[49] and they had still been able to export grain (*sitos*) to the Selçuk state, under famine conditions, in the thirteenth.[50] According to Pegolotti,[51] Altoluogo (Ephesus, Hagios Theologos, i.e. Selçuk) acted as a centre for the exportation of wheat (*grano*), and by implication Ania (Anaea, i.e. Kadi-Kalesi) and Palattia (Palatia, i.e. Balat, Milet) as well. Focie (Phocaea, i.e. Eski or Yeni Foça) is also known to have acted as a centre for the exportation of grain (*frumentum*).[52] Of these, Altoluogo will have served the Caÿster Valley, Ania and Palatia the Maeander Valley, and Focie the Hermus (i.e. Gediz) Valley. Smyrna will have served its own immediate area as well as, to some extent, the others. Grain, together with wine and oil, are the characteristic concerns of the mainly thirteenth-century documentation of the monastery of Lembos, in the vicinity of Smyrna.[53]

Bithynia was not only fertile, it was also the Anatolian area most proximate to the capital, and therefore guaranteed enhanced economic activity. Grain, wine and oil are all mentioned as products in casual contexts.[54] It was specifically from the region of Nicaea that the imperial baggage-train had been supplied with old wine (*oinos palaios*) and oil (*elaion*) when setting out on an expedition.[55] It was to the ports of Nicomedia and Pylae that livestock, mainly from the interior, was driven for embarkation to the capital.[56]

The area of Anatolian exploitation is probably extended somewhat, and the lack of South Russian and Crimean exploitation confirmed, by a remark of Constantine Porphyrogenitus:[57] 'If crops (*gennēmata*) do not pass across from Aminsos (Amisus, i.e. Samsun), from Paphlagonia, from the Boukellarioi, and from the flanks (*plagia*) of the Armeniakoi, the people of Cherson cannot live.' Assuming the word *gennēmata* to refer to, or to include, the grain (*sitos*) as well as the wine (*oinos*) implied in an immediately preceding remark, it is indeed further evidence for the exportation of Anatolian cereals. It is noticeable that Constantine refers to the 'flanks' of the theme of Armeniakon which in the circumstances can only refer to its coastal areas (rather than, that is, to its interior),

49 Teall, 'The Grain Supply of the Byzantine Empire', pp. 125–6.

50 See below, p. 283.

51 Pegolotti, *La Pratica della Mercatura*; ed. Evans, p. 104.

52 Chrysostomides, 'Venetian Commercial Privileges under the Palaeologi', pp. 321, 331–3 (no. 3).

53 H. Ahrweiler, 'L'histoire et la géographie de la région de Smyrne entre les deux occupations turques (1081–1317) particulièrement au XIII^e^ siècle', *Travaux et Mémoires* I (1965), p. 18.

54 S. Vryonis, *The Decline of Medieval Hellenism in Asia Minor and the Process of Islamization from the Eleventh through the Fifteenth Century*, pp. 11–12.

55 Constantine Porphyrogenitus, *De Caerimoniis* (*Aulae Byzantinae*), *Appendix ad Librum Primum*; ed. J. Reiske (Bonn edn), p. 491. For the baggage-train, see below, pp. 272–5, 304–15.

56 See below, pp. 55, 558, 562–4.

57 Constantine Porphyrogenitus, *De Administrando Imperio* LIII; ed. G. Moravcsik and R. J. H. Jenkins, p. 286.

Amisus/Samsun being the regional port. Sinope also seems likely to have been involved in the export of grain (*sitos*).[58] Cherson, on the other hand, seems already to have lacked bread (*panis*) and to have been importing grain (*frumentum*), along with wine and oil, from Pontic areas (*Ponticae partes*) in the mid seventh century, although there is a single but inconclusive reference to the reverse situation, that is to ships bearing goods (*ta eidē*) coming from the regions of the Laz and from Bosporus and the Chersonese (*epi te tēs Lazōn khōras kai Bosporou kai Khersonēsou*), in the late sixth.[59]

The essential difference between land-use and agricultural produce on the Pontic coast and in the interior is strikingly illustrated by the circumstances in which the ambassadors of Edward I of England to the Mongol *ilhan* found themselves in 1292. On the coast they were able to purchase cereals, wine and olive-oil, their bread-bill amounting to some 5–10% of their daily expenditure. In the interior they were able to purchase meat and little else, their bread-bill amounting to some 55% of their expenditure.[60]

The Pamphylian Plain, or more particularly that part of it adjacent to Attalia, was, according to William of Tyre,[61] potentially rich (*opimus*) but actually lying useless (*infructuosus*) because of constant Turkish attacks, crops (*fruges*) having to be brought in from outside. The lack of grain seems confirmed by Odo of Deuil,[62] who mentions that the French contingent of the Second Crusade could not obtain it (*annona*) there at any price. Earlier evidence[63] does no more than suggest that this may not always have been the case, but later Pegolotti[64] mentions Setalia as a centre for the exportation of both wheat (*grano*) and barley (*orzo*), and by implication Candelloro (i.e. Calonorus/Alanya or Celenderis/Gilindire to the east) as well. As Calonorus had been used as an official grain-port as early as 949, the former identification seems the more likely.[65] The position of the Cilician Plain remains largely indeterminate.

The Thessalian and Macedonian Plains, unlike the Pamphylian, both seem to have been exploited for the production of wheat (*pyros*) during the twelfth century,[66] and the exploitation of the former at least can be traced back as far as the seventh.[67] The generally fertile, well-watered and exploited state of both plains had, indeed, already been affirmed by Procopius[68] in the sixth. The Morea and Greece (probably representing the theme

[58] *Vita Sancti Phocae*; ed. K. van der Vorst, in *Analecta Bollandiana* 30 (1911), at p. 289.

[59] Martin I (pope), *Epistulae* XVI, XVII; *PL* LXXXVII, cols 202–4. Tiberius II Constantine, Novel XI (CLXIII) (575: *Peri Kouphismōn Dēmosiōn*). I. Zepos and P. Zepos, *Ius Graeco-Romanum* I (*Novellae et Aureae Bullae post Iustinianum*), pp. 18–19. For Pontic wine, oil, and grain (in that order of importance), see also: A. A. M. Bryer, 'The Estates of the Empire of Trebizond', *Arkheion Pontou* 35 (1978), pp. 376–9.

[60] A. A. M. Bryer, 'Greeks and Türkmens: The Pontic Exception', *DOP* 29 (1975), pp. 119–20.

[61] William of Tyre, *Historia Rerum* XVI.26; RHC, *Occ.* I.2, pp. 750–1.

[62] Odo of Deuil, *De Profectione Ludovici VII in Orientem* VII; ed. Berry, pp. 128, 130.

[63] Teall, 'The Grain Supply of the Byzantine Empire', p. 126. See also below, p. 139.

[64] Pegolotti, *La Pratica della Mercatura*; ed. Evans, pp. 58, 92, 104.

[65] See below, p. 58.

[66] See below, pp. 51–2

[67] Teall, 'The Grain Supply of the Byzantine Empire', pp. 121–2.

[68] Procopius, *De Aedificiis* IV.3. 6–8, 27–8; ed. J. Haury (Teubner), IV, pp. 113, 115.

of Hellas-Peloponnesos) were also used as a source for the supply of grain (*sitos*) on at least one occasion in the eleventh century.[69]

Prior to the seventh century and the loss of Egypt to the Arabs, Constantinople was supplied overwhelmingly with grain from that country, a fact which tends to mask other potential or actual sources of supply. But, according to Procopius,[70] when on one occasion, in 545, the annual grain fleet (*sitagōgos stolos*) arrived at the capital with insufficient quantities, Peter Barsymes who was then prefect of the East was obliged to obtain grain by means of compulsory purchase (*synōnē*) from Bithynia, Phrygia and Thrace. The sellers were faced with the necessity of transporting the grain involved down to the coast for shipments to the capital, a task that was performed only with great difficulty (*ponō pollō*), doubtless due to the high cost of transport which the same author implies elsewhere. Rome is known to have been supplied, on one late fourth-century occasion at least, with grain from Macedonia.[71] The areas involved, in other words, seem to have been those which were later to become standard as sources of supply.[72]

Pegolotti[73] designated the following wines by their places of origin: *vino di Romania, vino di Cipri, vino di Creti* and *di Candia, vino da Rodi*(?), *vino di Triglia, vino di Malvagia, vino di Stiva*. Of the wines themselves, all occur in contexts which imply that they were or were likely to be exported. Of the places, the identity of Triglia alone presents a problem and is probably to be found in Tirilya on the southern shore of the Marmara; Malvagia is still generally reckoned to be Monemvasia in the south-eastern Morea, but may be Malvesino in Crete; Stiva is Thebes. The list of places acting as centres for the exportation of wine is again capable of expansion,[74] but even as it stands suggests the main areas that were involved: Greece and the islands.

The broad distinctions in land-use in the southern Balkans in the twelfth century, at least, were recognised and defined by Michael Choniates, as archbishop of Athens (1175–1204), in the following passage:[75]

For what do you [in Constantinople] lack? Not the wheat-bearing plains (*pyrophoroi pediades*) of Macedonia, Thrace and Thessaly, which are farmed by us [provincials]; nor the wines of Euboia, Ptelion, Chios and Rhodes, which are pressed by us; nor the fine garments (*ampekhonai*) which are woven by our Theban and Corinthian fingers; nor all of the moneys (*khrēmata*) which, just as many rivers flow into one sea, flow into the Queen City [i.e. Constantinople].

The passage is of considerable interest, not only as evidence for the resentment which the overwhelming financial and economic dominance of the metropolis was then capable

[69] See below, p. 145.

[70] Procopius, *Historia Arcana* XXII.17–20; ed. J. Haury (Teubner), III, p. 137. See also below, pp. 295–6, 555–9.

[71] Symmachus, *Epistulae* III.55; MGH, *AA* VI.1, p. 88.

[72] See above, pp. 44–6.

[73] Pegolotti, *La Pratica della Mercatura*; ed. Evans, pp. 85, 118, 433–4 ('Glossary and Index of Commodities').

[74] E.g. above, pp. 35, 38, 49, below, pp. 559, 588–9 and n. 160.

[75] Michael Choniates, *Epistolai* L; ed. S. Lampros, II, p. 83.

of arousing even in a Constantinopolitan resident of long standing turned provincial archbishop – a resentment which was to lead to representatives of the metropolitan aristocracy being jeered by the local peasants (*agroikoi kai agelaioi*) when, as refugees, they landed at Selymbria after the fall of the City to the Fourth Crusade[76] – but also for the very clear threefold distinction and definition of the main cereal-producing, wine-producing, and manufactured luxury-producing areas and centres of the contemporary southern Balkans. In mentioning Thrace, it seems likely that Choniates had in mind that part lying between the Rhodope and the Aegean (i.e. the Strimon–Maritsa Plain), and that stretching eastwards to the Marmara, and in mentioning Macedonia, the Vardar–Aliakmon Plain.

This same distinction between the mainly cereal-producing and the mainly wine- (and indeed oil-) producing areas of the empire is also implied in the developing pattern and balance of Venetian trade and territorial possession in Romania.

Prior to 1204, Venice had no territorial possessions (except certain cities of the Dalmatian coast) in Romania, and it is generally recognised that – despite the apparently open-ended terms of Veneto-Byzantine treaties – she was forbidden, or at any rate failed to exploit, access to the Black Sea.[77] During the twelfth century the evidence suggests that Corinth, Halmyrus (Armiro, i.e. Almiros), Thebes and Sparta (Lacedemonia, i.e. Sparti) were the chief regional ports of call, and that oil was the chief commodity traded.[78] The importance of the olive, and the great quantities of the oil derived from it, in the Maina and the region of Coron in the southern Morea, was commented upon by both Constantine Porphyrogenitus in the tenth century, and by the author of Benedict of Peterborough who had reports of the area in 1191.[79] In view of the analysis made above, ports of call and commodity were thus entirely compatible.

After 1204, Venice had both considerable territorial possessions in Romania and access to the Black Sea, but although cereals thereupon came to form a much more significant commodity of her trade,[80] this was clearly due less to her acquisition of territory and more to her gaining of access to the Black Sea. The point is that the major direct, or virtually direct, Venetian territorial possessions were confined to Crete and Negropont (Negroponte, i.e. Evvoia), and that neither of these islands, with their high proportion of mountains and correspondingly low proportion of plains, and with their high proportion of forests and rough grazing land, is or was suitable for the large-scale production of cereals.[81] True, under Venetian domination and colonial exploitation, Crete

[76] Nicetas Choniates, *Historia*; ed. van Dieten, I, p. 593.

[77] M. E. Martin, 'The First Venetians in the Black Sea', *Arkheion Pontou* 35 (1978), pp. 111–22.

[78] M. E. Martin, 'Venice and the Byzantine Empire before the Fourth Crusade', pp. 94–5, 98–9.

[79] Constantine Porphyrogenitus, *De Administrando Imperio* L; ed. Moravcsik and Jenkins, p. 236. Benedict of Peterborough, *Gesta Regis Ricardi*, s.a. 1191; ed. Stubbs, II, p. 199.

[80] E.g. Chrysostomides, 'Venetian Commercial Privileges under the Palaeologi', pp. 312–27.

[81] Above, p. 33; F. Thiriet, *La Romanie vénitienne au moyen âge*, pp. 107–8.

was made to produce and export cereals, but as compared with Venice's other sources of cereals this was evidently on a very restrained scale.[82] The production and exportation of wine, on the other hand, was on a much more notable scale.[83] Contemporary Negropont was seemingly more important for its strategic and commercial position than for its agricultural products, and its cereals seem mainly to have been derived from the Thessalian and Macedonian Plains.[84]

Much the same balance (fruit, livestock) is visible in Edrisi's account of the islands of Crete, Negropont, Astipalia, Samos and Naxos.[85]

Examination of the twelfth-century section of the archive of the monastery of St John the Theologian on Patmos reveals, in general terms, the economic basis of the island, and its dependencies Lipso and Leros, also to have rested to a minimal degree only upon the exploitation of arable land – which in any case was in short supply – and to a much larger degree upon the cultivation of the vine, olive, and various kinds of fruit, with the rearing and exploitation of livestock – particularly sheep and goats – also playing an important rôle.[86]

The main conclusions and implications to be drawn from this survey so far are therefore the following. The physical structures and hence the climate and natural vegetation of, and land-use in, the Balkan and Anatolian Peninsulas are all markedly extreme. The Balkans are dominated by mountains which go to make up a high proportion of their total area, and plains are therefore correspondingly restricted in extent. This preponderance of mountains ensures that a high proportion of the total area is accounted for by forest, rough grazing land and bare rock, and that this proportion heavily outweighs that accounted for by cultivable land and more particularly by arable land. The position of the main mountain ranges ensures that a Mediterranean climate is confined largely to the coastlands, a Continental one being more typical of the interior. Anatolia is dominated by a basic distinction between the narrow and low-lying plains of its periphery and the great elevated plateau of its interior, the two being marked off from each other by mountain ranges, except in the west, where a number of river-valleys also effectively extend the characteristics of the periphery some way into the interior. Physical structure is again reflected in climate, natural vegetation and land-use. The climate of the periphery is Mediterranean, that of the interior extreme Continental, resulting in a prevalence of steppe-like conditions. Until comparatively recently, overwhelmingly the greater part of the total of cultivable and more particularly of arable land was to be found in the periphery, rough grazing land being equally overwhelmingly predominant in the interior.

[82] Thiriet, *La Romanie vénitienne*, pp. 317–19, 326–7.

[83] *Ibid.* pp. 320–1.

[84] *Ibid.* pp. 337–41.

[85] Edrisi, *Geography* IV.4, V.4; ed. P. A. Jaubert, II, pp. 126–8, 296.

[86] P. Karlin-Hayter, 'Notes sur les archives de Patmos comme source pour la démographie et l'économie de l'île', *Byzantinische Forschungen* 5 (1977), pp. 198–207.

Inevitably, the basic features of Balkan and Anatolian physical structure and climate, natural vegetation and land-use obtaining today are those that were to be found during the late Roman and Byzantine period. For instance, the situation of the crusading armies as they passed through central Anatolia will doubtless have been exacerbated, with regard to the terrain and the supplies to be gained from it, by the inclemency of the seasons, whether summer or winter; by incessant harassment by Turks, whether Selçuk or Türkmen (*Bedewini*, *agrestes Turci*, etc.); by the adoption of a 'scorched earth' policy, whether this entailed the actual burning of crops or the gathering of livestock in order to drive them before the armies, so as to deprive the latter of supplies and fodder; by the destruction or filling-in of cisterns or wells; by the evacuation of the population and the removal of its possessions; and so on. But these were not the fundamental causes of their difficulties, which the descriptions suggest to have been rather the infertile, unpopulated and uncultivated terrain, the arid climate, and the sparse natural vegetation. These characteristics then commenced more or less at the same points as they now do, and were and are typical of the interior areas through which the crusaders had to pass. The confusion is nevertheless a long-standing one. Fulcher of Chartres, for instance, was prepared to account[87] for the shortage of bread and foodstuffs (*panis et cibaria*) encountered by the First Crusade between Pisidian Antioch (i.e. Yalvaç) and Iconium not by the nature of the terrain and climate (*nam Romaniam quae terra est optima et valde fertilis bonorum omnium*) but by Turkish devastation (*invenimus nimis a Turcis vastatum et depopulatum*).

### B. *Pastoralism*

The predominant use of the great central plateau of Anatolia for the extensive grazing of flocks and herds until comparatively recently was therefore an inevitable consequence of its physical structure, climate and natural vegetation. It was also of long standing. Galatia, Lycaonia, eastern Phrygia and western Cappadocia were, even in the earlier Roman period, cold, bare or virtually treeless (*axylon*), and lacking in water.[88] Parts of central Cappadocia were, in the later Roman period, waterless and devoid of vegetation.[89] The Gauls who had settled in what consequently came to be called Galatia in the third century B.C. were apparently pastoralists rather than agriculturalists, and Amyntas, one of their later kings, is reported to have owned three hundred flocks of sheep in Lycaonia. All the regions mentioned above were well known, in the earlier Roman period, for their pastoral products.[90] Cappadocia, in the late Roman and early Byzantine period, was the

[87] Fulcher of Chartres, *Historia Iherosolymitana* XIII; RHC, *Occ.* III.1, p. 336.

[88] T. R. S. Broughton, 'Roman Asia Minor', in T. Frank (ed.), *An Economic Survey of Ancient Rome* IV, at p. 607.

[89] See below, p. 99.

[90] Broughton, 'Roman Asia Minor', at pp. 617–20. For the modern and mediaeval pastoral régime, see: S. Payne, 'Kill-off Patterns in Sheep and Goats: The Mandibles from Aşvan Kale', *Anatolian Studies* 23 (1973), pp. 281–303. See also below, p. 60 n. 120 (deforestation), and p. 144 n. 249 (agricultural régime).

scene of a relatively high concentration of separately administered areas (*regiones*) that were probably imperial estates (the *domus divina per Cappadociam*), and was also well known for its production of horses, the two features probably not being unconnected.[91] The adjacent theme of Lykandos could be described as suitable for stock-raising (*kourotrophos*), horse-grazing (*hippobotos*), and all kinds of cattle-fattening (i.e. as *boskēma*) in the tenth century.[92]

It had been to regions beyond the Sangarios (*pera tou Sangariou*), presumably to Paphlagonia and Phrygia, that *The Book of the Prefect* had insisted that meat-dealers (*makelarioi*) repair to meet those outside sheep-dealers (*exothen probatarioi*) driving their herds (*agelai*) towards Nicomedia for sale.[93] Later, the author of the satire *Timarion* characterises Paphlagonians as dealing in pigs and pig-meat (*khoiremporos / en makellō... meta khoreiou kreatos*), and earlier, it was in the region of Lagania (Anastasiopolis), in adjacent Galatia, that St Luke the Stylite had tended pigs.[94] Much of this livestock ended up, after a journey which may well have been very considerable, not only at Nicomedia, but also at Pylae which, according to Leo of Synnada,[95] was full of pigs (*khoiroi*), asses (*onoi*), oxen (*boes*), horses (*hippoi*) and sheep (*probata*), all of which was bound for the capital.

The Selçuk Turks who penetrated Anatolia in the eleventh century, and whose several jurisdictions were confined to the central plateau and the east for the entire twelfth century, and were somewhat less so confined only for much of the thirteenth, were originally – like the earlier Gauls – pastoralists rather than agriculturalists, and this balance, however muted, remained characteristic of the developed Selçuk state even in the thirteenth century.[96] When, in 1147, the German members of the Second Crusade had arrived on the plateau, presumably somewhere in the region of Dorylaeum, they came across shepherds' tents and flocks.[97] When, in 1175, Manuel I had rebuilt Dorylaeum, he found there some 2,000 Persian (Turkish) nomads: these disliked the prospect of being forced to leave the plains (*pedia*) where their herds of goats and cattle (*aipolia kai boukolia*) were accustomed to graze.[98] Similarly, when in the mid twelfth century, a martial bishop of Chonae (i.e. Honaz), who was also a relative of the Choniates brothers, had accompanied an army on a raid on Charax (probably Çardak),[99] which was further up

91 A. H. M. Jones, *The Later Roman Empire 284–602: A Social, Economic, and Administrative Survey*, pp. 425–7; II, pp. 713, 768–9.

92 Constantine Porphyrogenitus, *De Thematibus* XII; ed. A. Pertusi, p. 75.

93 'Leo VI', *To Eparkhikon Biblion* XV.3; ed. J. Nicole, p. 50.

94 Anonymous, *Timarion*; ed. Romano, pp. 89, 92. *Vita Sancti Lucae Stylitae*; ed. A. Vogt, in *Analecta Bollandiana* 28 (1909), at p. 21.

95 Leo of Synnada, *Epistolai* LIV; ed. Darrouzès, at p. 209.

96 C. Cahen, *Pre-Ottoman Turkey: A General Survey of the Material and Spiritual Culture and History c. 1071–1330*, pp. 157–60.

97 See above, p. 40.

98 John Cinnamus, *Epitome* VII.2; ed. A. Meineke (Bonn edn), p. 295. Nicetas Choniates, *Historia*; ed. van Dieten, I, p. 176. See also below, pp. 126–7 and n. 171.

99 See below, p. 130 and n. 189.

towards the plateau and then in Turkish hands, he returned with spoils (*laphyra*) which seem largely to have been composed of thick-fleeced sheep (*oïes pēgesimalloi*),[100] and when, later in the same century (1190), the German members of the Third Crusade had penetrated much the same area, they found there little more than the occasional flock or herd.[101] Even earlier in the twelfth century (1146), it had been in very much this area (the headwaters of the Maeander) that the emperor Manuel himself unexpectedly had come across Turkish tents (*skēnai*), together with their owners' horses (*hippoi*), while out hunting.[102] In the thirteenth century the Nicaean borderers seem also to have been known for their wealth in livestock (*thremmata*).[103]

With the loss of the plateau in the late eleventh century, the empire will have lost, amongst other things, access – or at least direct access – to its characteristic products. The consequences of this loss of access are perhaps seen in an incident reported by Anna Comnena.[104] Shortly before (or in) 1112, Alexius I ordered Manuel Butumites to attempt to bribe the subordinate counts of the prince of Antioch with: 'much money of all kinds, and of every form, effigy and quality (*khrēmata polla kai pantodapa, kai apo pasēs ideas kai eikonomismatos pantodapōn poiotētōn*)'. The money was lodged in the palace (*episkopē*) of the bishop of Tripolis (i.e. Tarabulus) for safe keeping. The attempt at bribery having failed, Butumites eventually bought horses of Damascene, Edessan and even Arabian blood with the money, and returned to the emperor. This incident seems confirmed by an earlier one.[105] When, in 1090, Robert of Flanders sent Alexius 500 selected horsemen, and a present of a further 150 selected horses, the emperor also purchased any mounts that the horsemen had spare. By the fourteenth century, on the other hand, the Venetians were making official and annual purchases of horses, which had quite possibly been driven down from the interior, from the (now Turkish) Anatolian ports, and were using them for military purposes in Crete.[106]

### C. *Observations*

Virtually all the distinctions involved in the preceding sections of this chapter: those of physical structure, climate, and predominant products, are mentioned or implied in the treatise known as the *Expositio Totius Mundi et Gentium*, by an uncertain but certainly mid fourth-century author.[107] Here, a clear distinction is drawn between the central areas

100 Nicetas Choniates, *Historia*; ed. van Dieten, I, p. 197.
101 See above, p. 42.
102 John Cinnamus, *Epitome* II.9; Bonn edn, pp. 59–60.
103 George Pachymeres, *De Michaele et Andronico Palaeologis, De Mich.* I.5; Bonn edn, I, p. 18.
104 Anna Comnena, *Alexiad* XIV.2.6, 7, 14; ed. Leib, III, pp. 148, 149–50, 154.
105 Anna Comnena, *Alexiad* VII.7.4; ed. Leib, II, pp. 109–10. F.-L. Ganshof, 'Robert le Frison et Alexis Comnène', *Byzantion* 31 (1961), pp. 71–2.
106 Thiriet, *La Romanie vénitienne*, p. 335.
107 Anonymous, *Expositio Totius Mundi et Gentium* XXXIX–XLIX (Anatolia), L–LIII, LVII (the Balkans), LXIII–LXIV (the Islands); ed. J. Rougé pp. 176–84, 185–90, 204–8. On the work itself, see now (with refs): J. H. Oliver, 'Achaia, Greece, and Laconia', *Greek, Roman, and Byzantine Studies* 21 (1980), pp. 75–81.

(*media terrena*) and the coastal lands (*partes propinquantes mari*) of Anatolia. The former are enumerated as consisting of Cappadocia, Galatia, Phrygia, Armenia Minor, Paphlagonia and Pontus (in its older and wider sense), and the latter as consisting of Cilicia, Isauria, Pamphylia, Lycia, Caria, Asia, Hellespontus and Bithynia (that is, in correct clockwise sequence). Cappadocia is described as having great frosts (*frigora maxima*), Galatia as being self-sufficient (*sibi sufficiens*), and the region as a whole as producing men, animals, skins and clothing. The coastal lands are variously described as fertile (*frugifera*), or self-sufficient, as having numerous, great, or admirable cities (*civitates innumerabiles, maximae, admirabiles*), and as producing wines (*vina*), oil (*oleum*), wheat (*frumentum*), barley (*oridia*), spelt (*alica*) (?), and so on.

It is therefore again to be emphasised that such distinctions fundamentally have nothing whatsoever to do with the presence or absence of Turks.

In the case of the Balkans, Thracia, Macedonia and Thessalia are singled out as rich in crops (*dives in fructibus*), as abounding in all things (*abundans omnia*), and as producing much wheat, respectively. Achaia, Graecia and Laconia are described as small, infertile and lacking in self-sufficiency, because of their mountainous nature, and as producing a little oil and attic honey (*mel*) only. Dalmatia is singled out for its wood, suitable for building material (*ligna tectis utilia*). The only cities mentioned as notable are Thessalonica, Athens, Corinth and Salona. These peripheral areas are treated separately from the central ones of Moesia and Dacia, which are self-sufficient, but have great frosts, and only one notable city, that of Naissus.

Of the main islands, to Cyprus are attributed woods (*ligna*), as well as everything necessary to building the ship (*navem conficere*); and to Lemnos and Crete, wine.

Nevertheless, neither the degree of distinction between the products of the central plateau and those of the coastal plain, nor the uniformity of products within the plateau itself, should be exaggerated. Doubtless, the rôle of mixed farming should not be minimised: animal husbandry certainly took place on the plain, particularly in the hills that bordered the river-valleys; and arable farming equally certainly took place on the plateau, particularly in sheltered positions such as river-valleys. It is the overall balance between the two, and the nature of the predominant surplus, that are in question. In the eighth century, the wealth of Philaretus of Amnia, in northern Paphlagonia, was reckoned primarily in terms of livestock (oxen, horses and mules), but he also owned estates which were at least partly devoted to arable.[108] In the eleventh century much the same balance is found in accounts of the regions of Synnada, in Phrygia Salutaris, and of Euchaita, in western Helenopontus.[109] In the tenth century, the main sources for the supply of mules and horses for the imperial baggage-train seem to have been Asia and (less surprisingly, perhaps) Phrygia, up to and including Malagina.[110] At the same time, the

[108] See below, pp. 208–9.

[109] See below, pp. 139–41.

[110] See below, pp. 311–12, 610–12.

main sources for the supply of cereal products (barley/*kritharion*, wheat/*sitos*, biscuit/*paxamation* and flour/*areurion*) for at least one military expedition (that of 949 against Crete) seem to have been not only the themes of Thrakesion and Kibyrrhaioton (which might be expected), but also that of Anatolikon (which might not).[111] Again, a description of the estate (*oikoproasteion*) of Baris, part of the *episkepsis tōn Alōpekōn*, in the region of Miletus–Priene, given by Michael VII to the *prōtoproedros* Andronicus Ducas in 1073, mentions the existence there of a 'sowing (*kataspora*)', consisting of 260 *modioi* of wheat (*sitos*) and 150 *modioi* of barley (*krithē*), and of a 'store' (*parathesis*) consisting of 124 *modioi* of wheat and 60 *modioi* of barley.[112] These figures might be taken as reflecting an approximate wheat:barley relationship of 2:1 for the immediate area, at least, and so they may actually be. But the figures for the cereal products supplied to the expedition mentioned above are: Thrakesion – 20,000 measures of barley to 40,000 measures of wheat, biscuit and flour; and Kibyrrhaioton and Anatolikon – 20,000 measures of barley to 60,000 measures of biscuit, wheat and flour. In other words, much the same. The two sets of figures, having such different origins and bases, are quite probably simply not comparable. (Map 13)

## APPENDIX

# THE PROBLEM OF EROSION

### *A. The problem*

Despite all the evidence demonstrating that the major features of physical structure, climate and land-use obtaining in the mediaeval Balkans and Anatolia were essentially the same as those obtaining until very recently, and often until the present day, it should nevertheless be acknowledged that certain of the relatively minor changes that are conceivable as having occurred on the limited time scale involved are also quite capable of having possessed not inconsiderable implications.

For example, the erosion of surface material at higher altitudes, its transportation and its eventual deposition at lower altitudes (water normally being the chief instrument and medium involved) form a process that is by no means peculiar to the Mediterranean countries. Nor is the process a new one there: Plato recognised its operation, causes and implications, with regard to Greece at least,[113] and the scale of the problem that it

[111] Constantine Porphyrogenitus, *De Caerimoniis* II.44; Bonn edn, pp. 658–9.

[112] F. Miklosich and J. Müller (eds), *Acta et Diplomata Graeca Medii Aevi Sacra et Profana* VI, p. 6. See also below, pp. 68, 106, 133–4.

[113] Plato, *Critias* CX–CXI; ed. R. G. Bury (Loeb), pp. 270, 272, 274.

currently represents, whether potentially or actually, is officially admitted in the large-scale programmes of preventive or curative action being undertaken against it by a number of Mediterranean governments. Its effect is also actually visible, of course, in the landscape. The Mediterranean countries must in any case be counted amongst those that are, by their pedology, topography and climate, naturally the most susceptible to erosion: their topsoils are generally light and shallow; their mountain- and hill-slopes are generally steep; and their rainfall-pattern is generally heavily accentuated – with a mild and wet winter, a hot and virtually dry summer which yet is liable to be punctuated by short periods of heavy rain, and a spring and autumn that tend to form mere interludes between the other two seasons.

There also seems little doubt but that in these countries the problem is being, and probably long has been, aggravated by human agencies. The fact of the progressive destruction of their natural vegetation, whether by deforestation or depasturage, seems beyond reasonable doubt, although its rate and extent are naturally unquantifiable. The systematic exploitation of the timber resources of the Anatolian peninsula was, for instance, already well under way quite early on in the Roman period. The regions particularly well known for their timber in the Roman period were: Pontus, Paphlagonia, Bithynia and the Troad; Lycia and Pamphylia; and Cilicia. In other words, the regions that are still well known for these resources. The main objects of this exploitation seem to have been military and industrial, the requirements of naval construction being overwhelmingly predominant.[114]

The exploitation of Anatolian timber resources in the late Roman and Byzantine period is much less well documented, but it has been maintained that both the main regions of operation and the main objects involved were the same. This is based largely, but by no means entirely, upon conjecture.[115] It was, for example, to Lycia and Cilicia that Libanius sent for timber for uncertain but undoubtedly private purposes,[116] and it was from Paphlagonia, Lycia and Cilicia that Turks and Arabs derived timber for naval construction.[117] According to Procopius,[118] Justinian had cut down all the trees (*ta...dendra...apanta*) in certain areas of eastern Pontus so as to oblige a troublesome local tribe, the Tzani, to integrate with the surrounding peoples. The object was in this instance purely political, and as such unusual, possibly unique. More recently, the conversion of woodland and forest into pasture or arable land and an increase in the numbers of the

[114] Broughton, 'Roman Asia Minor', at pp. 616–17.

[115] M. Lombard, 'Un problème cartographié: le bois dans la Méditerranée musulmane (VII^e^–XI^e^ siècles)', *Annales (Ec. Soc. Civ.)* 14 (1959), pp. 234–54. A. M. Fahmy, *Muslim Sea-Power in the Eastern Mediterranean from the Seventh to the Tenth Century* A.D., p. 79.

[116] J. H. W. G. Liebeschuetz, *Antioch: City and Imperial Administration in the Later Roman Empire*, pp. 45–6.

[117] C. Cahen, 'Ibn Sa'īd sur l'Asie Mineure seldjuquide', rep. in *idem*, *Turcobyzantina et Oriens Christianus*, as article no. XI (Turcobyzantina), pp. 42, 49. See also *idem*, *Pre-Ottoman Turkey*, pp. 281–2.

[118] Procopius, *De Aedificiis* III.6.11; ed. Haury (Teubner), IV, p. 97.

domestic goat have both at various times had to be officially, but not very effectively, discouraged.[119]

The inevitable result of all this has been a decrease in the extent of the Anatolian forest-cover: although the main regions of concentration have remained the same as in antiquity, there is some evidence that at least one of what may have been the less important and more peripheral regions disappeared in Roman times, and that several others have done so since.[120]

Exploitation of the timber resources of the island of Cyprus seems to have had a similar history and result. There, the demands of naval construction, metal production and direct land clearance had effected a reduction in the forest coverage of the plains that was noticeable even in the Roman period, and the conflict between goat-grazing and forestry has been as acute as in Anatolia.[121] Even so, the timber resources of Cyprus were thought worthy of mention by Edrisi in the twelfth century.[122] Again, exploitation of the resources of the coast of Dalmatia and its hinterland may well have resulted in or contributed to the deforestation of the region,[123] and much the same has been suggested of nearby Epirus and Macedonia, and indeed of more distant areas of the Mediterranean.[124]

Alongside of the systematic exploitation of the timber resources of these areas there went a parallel one of pasturage and arable farming. Its extent is, again, impossible to quantify at any period, but in Anatolia, at least, the evidence for an increase in the number of private estates, in the number and activity of cities, and in the general prosperity of the region, during the second half of the first and in the second century, suggests that it must have increased more or less commensurately during that period.[125] In Greece the situation was different, for there was less potential for such an increase there, but the evidence for an increase in prosperity over the immediately preceding period, at least, seems decisive.[126]

The general geological effects of deforestation and depasturage are well known. With

119 W. C. Brice, 'The Turkish Colonization of Anatolia', *Bulletin of the John Rylands Library* 38 (1955–6), pp. 37–8. Mülâyim, 'Turkey', in *The World Atlas of Agriculture* I, at p. 430.

120 Brice, 'The Turkish Colonization of Anatolia', p. 34; A. J. Toynbee, *Constantine Porphyrogenitus and his World*, p. 112. For a particular history of deforestation in eastern Anatolia, the more general application of which remains entirely problematic, see G. H. Willcox, 'A History of Deforestation as indicated by Charcoal Analysis of Four Sites in Eastern Anatolia', *Anatolian Studies* 24 (1974), pp. 117–33 (based on the Elâzığ *vilayet*). For the remainder of the geographical, ecological and agricultural horizons of the area, see above, p. 54 n. 90 (pastoral régime), and below, p. 144 n. 249 (agricultural régime).

121 G. Hill, *A History of Cyprus* I, pp. 7, 10, 156, 174. Lombard, 'Le bois dans la Méditerranée musulmane', pp. 234–54. A. H. Unwin, *Goat-Grazing and Forestry in Cyprus.*

122 Edrisi, *Geography* V.5; trans. Jaubert, II, p. 130.

123 J. J. Wilkes, *Dalmatia*, pp. 201, 238, 267, 408.

124 Hammond, *Epirus*, p. 19; *idem*, *A History of Macedonia* I, *Historical Geography and Prehistory*, p. 14. C. Vita-Finzi, *The Mediterranean Valleys, Geological Changes in Historical Times*, pp. 107–8.

125 Broughton, 'Roman Asia Minor', at pp. 666, 794–7.

126 J. A. O. Larsen, 'Roman Greece', in T. Frank (ed.), *An Economic Survey of Ancient Rome* IV, at pp. 465–83.

the removal of protective vegetation, soil is exposed to the full rigours of the local climate: its absorption of rainfall is decreased and run-off is therefore proportionally increased, at the same time frequently being concentrated by such man-made features as plough-furrows, wheel-ruts, and so on. Erosion is inevitably accelerated and where, as in the Mediterranean countries, the pedology, topography and climate of an area render it particularly susceptible to erosion in any case, the situation can only be that much worse. It may be even further worsened by a climatic shift leading to a further accentuation of the local pattern of seasonal rainfall.[127]

### *B. The process*

The basic elements of the process as a whole were, interestingly and significantly enough, known to ancient authors. Plato, in the passage mentioned above,[128] remarks on the loss of soil, deforestation and desiccation of Greece, strongly hinting also at an accentuation of the pattern of seasonal rainfall. Pausanias,[129] writing in the middle of the second century A.D., is much more specific and detailed. He reckons that the reason why the Echinadian Islands had not already been made into mainland (*epeiros*) by the Akheloos (the river flowing into the sea over against the islands) was that the Aetolian people had been driven from their houses and their whole land desolated. Because the land remained uncultivated (*asporos*), the Akheloos was not transporting as much mud (*ilys*) as it otherwise would have done. He offers as proof of his contention the fact that the Maiandros (i.e. the Büyük Menderes), flowing through the lands of Phrygia and Caria which were ploughed up each year, had in no time at all turned into mainland the sea which had formerly existed between the cities of Priene and Miletus. It has also been pointed out[130] that many of the Roman dams of Tripolitania were constructed as much for the purposes of soil-retention as for those of water-retention, involving a practical application of the theoretical knowledge.

Over the last 50,000 years or so, erosion in the Mediterranean countries has alternated between two basic and distinctive patterns. The one has involved rivers cutting down their beds and depositing eroded material down-valley towards or at their mouths, or – to a degree ever more diffuse with distance – at sea. The other has involved rivers building up their beds and – because they have tended to flood or change course, or both, more frequently – depositing eroded material in a more extensive fashion, that is up-valley as well as down towards their mouths and onwards.

Within the period in question two phases of cutting down have alternated with two

[127] E.g. Vita-Finzi, *The Mediterranean Valleys*, pp. 108–10.

[128] See above, p. 58 and n. 113.

[129] Pausanias, *Description of Greece* VIII.24.11; ed. W. H. S. Jones (Loeb), IV, pp. 18, 20.

[130] Vita-Finzi, *The Mediterranean Valleys*, pp. 14–28.

of building up.[131] A preliminary phase of building up, which seems to have characterised the period c.50,000 years before the present, left its mark in the alluvial deposits that are now to be seen as terraces at the sides of many valleys. This was followed by a phase of cutting down which seems to have lasted from c.10,000 years before the present until a date relatively early on in the Christian era. This in turn gave way to a renewed but shorter and somewhat less effective phase of building up that seems, in Italy at least, to have come to an end already by the sixteenth century. It left its mark in the alluvial deposits that now provide the broad, smooth floors of many valleys. It was succeeded by the renewed phase of cutting down that still obtains.[132] The basic cause or causes behind this sequence of alternating phases remains uncertain, but seems most likely to have been climatic.[133]

The progress made by Anatolian rivers in depositing eroded material down-valley towards or at their mouths, a process common to both the patterns of erosion described in the preceding paragraph, is reasonably well documented. According to Strabo,[134] writing at the end of the first century B.C. or at the beginning of the first century A.D., the city of Ephesus had for some time already been having trouble with silt (*khous*) which had been brought down by the Caÿster (Küçük Menderes) and deposited in its harbour, and the process continued and can be traced throughout the ancient and mediaeval periods. Similarly,[135] the ancient city of Troy had long been cut off from the sea by the alluvial deposit (*proskhōma*) brought down and deposited by the Skamandros (Menderes) and Simoeis. Again,[136] so much silt was being brought down from Cataonia and the plains (*pedia*) of Cilicia to the sea, by the Pyramus (Ceyhan), that a prophecy had grown up which predicted the joining of Cilicia to Cyprus. Finally,[137] the city of Priene, formerly on the sea, had already been stranded by some 8 km (i.e. 40 *stadia*) of alluvial deposit brought down and deposited by the Maeander (Büyük Menderes). According to Pausanias,[138] Priene and Miletus, formerly separated by the mouth of the Maeander, had by this time been joined by the mud brought down and deposited by the river. All these cities are at present many kilometers from the coast, and the process, of course, continues: İzmir was, for instance, threatened by the Gediz with the fate of the cities at the mouth of the Maeander until the former river was diverted to a new course as late as 1886.[139]

[131] *Ibid.* pp. 7–88.

[132] *Ibid.* pp. 91–102.

[133] *Ibid.* pp. 103–15.

[134] Strabo, *Geography* XIV.1.24; ed. H. L. Jones (Loeb), VI.pp.228, 230. For the subsequent periods, see: C. Foss, *Ephesus after Antiquity: A Late Antique, Byzantine and Turkish City*, pp. 185–7 (Appendix 3: 'The Silting of the Harbor of Ephesus').

[135] Strabo, *Geography* XIII.1.36; ed. Jones (Loeb), VI, pp. 72, 74.

[136] Strabo, *Geography* I.3.7; ed. Jones (Loeb), pp. 192, 194.

[137] Strabo, *Geography* XII.8.17; ed. Jones (Loeb), V, pp. 512, 514.

[138] See above, p. 61, n. 129.

[139] D. Magie, *Roman Rule in Asia Minor to the End of the Third Century after Christ* II, pp. 785 (n. 13), 882–3 (n. 79), 888 (n. 89), 893–4 (n. 100). Admiralty, *A Handbook of Asia Minor* II, pp. 68, 574–5.

Elsewhere, the great deltas of the Kızılırmak and Yeşilırmak consist almost entirely of shifting alluvial deposits.

Literary sources also describe the processes up-valley that combined to produce the situation described in the preceding paragraph. Strabo remarks[140] that the Maeander changed its bed (*rheithron*) frequently, and that its bends were being eroded or swept away (*perikrousthōsin hoi ankōnes*). A law of Theodosius II,[141] dated 440 and addressed to Cyrus, then praetorian prefect of the East and consul designate, is concerned with the ownership of land liable to constant erosion by rivers and with that of land (*adluvio*) formed elsewhere from it. Its terms were specifically not to apply to land affected by the Nile alone, suggesting that eastern regions other than Egypt were being faced with the problem.

It is, however, Procopius who provides the most extensive and telling information on the contemporary situation. The chapter of that author's *De Aedificiis* dealing with the building activities of Justinian in Anatolia are taken up, to a considerable degree, with descriptions of the havoc and devastation then being wrought by the rivers of the peninsula, and of the emperor's efforts to repair it and bring them back under control.

The River Drakon (Kırk Geçid) which flowed into the Propontis (i.e. Sea of Marmara) near Helenopolis (i.e. Yalova), obstructed by a dense forest and expanse of reeds that had formed at its mouth, backed up and flooded, spreading out over the surrounding area and doing immense damage. Justinian had the forest cleared and the reeds cut so as to allow the river a clear passage through to the sea.[142]

The River Cydnus (Tarsus) which flowed onto the Cilician Plain through the city of Tarsus, and into the Mediterranean, and which hitherto had caused no great trouble, suddenly flooded owing to a combination of melting snows and heavy rains and caused immense destruction in the city. Justinian had another bed (*koitē*) prepared above the city and a portion of the river diverted into it so that only the remainder actually flowed through the city.[143] It was nevertheless presumably the river that was eventually responsible for covering the city with deposits up to 7 m deep, and for the city now being some 13 km further away from the coast than in the ancient period.[144]

The minor River Skirtos, which similarly flowed through the city of Edessa (i.e. Urfa), also suddenly flooded, owing to heavy rains, and caused immense destruction and loss of life in the city. Justinian had another course (*poreia*) circumventing the city prepared for the river, so that when it was swollen a portion only actually flowed through the city.[145]

140 Strabo, *Geography* XII.8.19; ed. Jones (Loeb), V, p. 516.

141 Theodosius II, Novel XX (*De Adluvionibus et Paludibus*).

142 Procopius, *De Aedificiis* V.2.6–13; ed. Haury (Teubner), IV, pp. 152–3.

143 Procopius, *De Aedificiis* V.5. 14–20; ed. Haury (Teubner), IV, pp. 160–2. *Idem, Historia Arcana* XVIII. 40; ed. Haury (Teubner), III, pp. 118–19.

144 Magie, *Roman Rule in Asia Minor* II, pp. 1146–8 (n. 28).

145 Procopius, *De Aedificiis* II.7.1–10; ed. Haury (Teubner), IV, pp. 66–7. *Idem, Historia Arcana* XVIII.38; ed. Haury (Teubner), III, p. 118.

Again, the seasonal torrent called Onopniktes (possibly that which was also called Parmenios) more than once swept down from the mountains, over the walls and into the city of Theopolis (Antioch, i.e. Antakya) causing immense damage. Justinian had a dam with sluice-gates built, so as to protect the walls and city.[146]

Finally, a road through a mountain-pass not far from Theopolis, which was probably that through the Beilan Pass over the Amanus Mountains, was washed away by heavy rains. Justinian had it recut and restored.[147]

Of the five examples of Justinian's building activities in Anatolia and the adjacent region to its east and south-east quoted in the preceding paragraphs, four were rendered necessary by the climate acting through rivers. But these represent only the most spectacular of the total described in the appropriate chapter of the *De Aedificiis*. The fifth chapter, that dealing with Anatolia, is full of floods, of bridges being carried away because their foundations had been eroded, of fortification-walls being threatened, both by rivers, and of swamps being formed. It is consequently full also of bridges and protective dams being constructed and of causeways being laid. The fourth chapter, that dealing with the Balkans, and the sixth, that dealing largely with Africa, are by contrast free of such spectacular examples, and relatively or completely free, even of such secondary ones.

It is of course difficult, if not impossible, to discern whether this distinction is an accurate reflection of a contemporary reality,[148] or due merely to coincidence or to some idiosyncrasy of the author or of imperial policy. In this context it should not be forgotten that the Alfios has, at some uncertain stage since 575, covered the city of Olympia with deposits up to a depth of 6 m.[149]

The distinction is nevertheless heightened by the fact that the two major south Balkan rivers mentioned in terms other than the purely casual, the Rekhios (possibly the Vardar) and the Peneios (Pinios), are both described as 'exceedingly gentle' or 'gentle' (*mala prosēnōs, prosēnēs*).[150] The distinction is also emphasised on examination of the numerous examples of natural disasters mentioned or described in the *Vita* of Theodore of Sycaeum (d. 613) in north-western Anatolia. Floods by the local rivers, the Sagaris (Sangarius, i.e. the Sakarya) and its tributaries the Siberis and Skopas, are the commonest of such disasters in the work, vicious and unseasonal storms, including hailstorms, being perhaps the next commonest. The gradual erosion of much of the local arable land (*sporimos gē*) by the Siberis, and a change in its bed (*koitē*), provide material for one of the edifying tales of the *Vita*. A similar situation regarding the Skopas provides material for another.[151]

146 Procopius, *De Aedificiis* II.10.15–18; ed. Haury (Teubner), IV, pp. 78–9. G. Downey, 'Procopius on Antioch: A Study of Method in the "De Aedificiis"', *Byzantion* 14 (1939), pp. 366, 371–8.

147 Procopius, *De Aedificiis* V.5.1–3; ed. Haury (Teubner), IV, pp. 158–9.

148 See, for example, Vita-Finzi, *The Mediterranean Valleys*, pp. 81–2.

149 *Ibid.* pp. 78–80.

150 Procopius, *De Aedificiis* IV.3.6–8, 27–8; ed. Haury (Teubner), IV, pp. 113, 115.

151 *Vita Sancti Theodori Syceotae* XLV, LIII; ed. A.-J. Festugière, pp. 40, 46.

Constant mention and description of the storms and swollen rivers, streams and seasonal torrents encountered by the French members of the Second Crusade in the course of their march from Nicaea to Attalia by way of Smyrna (i.e. İzmir) during the winter months of 1147/8 gives some impression of the ferocity of the Anatolian climate and of the potential of Anatolian water-courses for eroding and transporting material.[152]

The distinction, assuming it to have existed, does not seem to have been permanent, however: Anna Comnena[153] (of all authors!) gives a classic description of the process of a river building up its bed and the consequences, in remarking that it is the case with all the greatest rivers that, when a reasonable height of alluvial deposit (*anastēma proskhōseōs*) has been built up, they flow onto lower ground in changing their first bed (*koitē*) and leaving their old passage (*parados*) empty of liquid and deprived of water while filling the one which they currently flow through with abundant water. She then goes on to mention[154] that Alexius, while still a general of Nicephorus III and on campaign against the usurper Nicephorus Basilacius, had pitched camp between two such passages of the Vardarios (Vardar), the one being an old river cutting (*kharadra*), the other the recently made course (*poreia*), so as to utilise their defensive possibilities. The old passage (*diodos*) by that stage had come to form a ravine (*pharanx*) owing to the channeling action of the water (*ek tēs tou rheumatos epirrhoias*).

That the Balkans were then at least no less liable than Anatolia to vicious and unseasonal storms resulting in flash-flooding emerges from two separate incidents reported as having occurred during the course of the Second Crusade.

Odo of Deuil reports[155] that when the French contingent reached the Droa (i.e. Drava) they found it to have one sloping bank (*ripa proclivis*) and one steep (*ripa ardua*), like a balk (*scamnum*), with the result that it tended to overflow (*effluere*) with even a light rain (*modica pluvia*). When joined with the neighbouring swamps (*paludes*) it tended to flood (*submergere*) even quite distant places. It had only recently and suddenly inundated the camp of the German contingent. This and other rivers of the same area tend still to exhibit the same habits.[156]

Otto of Freising reports[157] that the German contingent, having loitered for several days in the extremely fertile areas of lower Thrace (*in locis fertilissimis per inferiorem Traciam*), chose a luxuriantly vegetated valley (*vallis viriditate laeta*), conspicuous for the stream (*amniculus*) flowing down its centre, and near to the town of Cherevach (Khoirobakkhoi) not far from Selymbria (i.e. Silivri), in which to pitch their tents on 7 September 1147. A very small cloud (*nubecula parva*) appeared in the sky and produced

[152] Odo of Deuil, *De Profectione Ludovici VII in Orientem* VI, VII; ed. Berry, pp. 104–40.
[153] Anna Comnena, *Alexiad* I.7.3; ed. Leib, I, p. 30.
[154] Anna Comnena, *Alexiad* I.7.4; ed. Leib, I, p. 30.
[155] Odo of Deuil, *De Profectione Ludovici VII in Orientem* II; ed. Berry, p. 30.
[156] Milivoievic and Roglić, 'Yugoslavia', in *The World Atlas of Agriculture* I, at p. 512.
[157] Otto of Freising, *Gesta Friderici Imperatoris* I.57; ed. G. Waitz, pp. 65–7.

gentle rain (*imber mitis*). This suddenly developed into a violent storm of rain and wind (*pluviarum ventorumque impetuosus turbo*) which caused the stream first to rise (*intumuere*) and then to flood (*inundare*), overwhelming virtually the entire contingent, throwing it into the utmost confusion, and drowning many of its members. The disaster was evidently on a large and memorable scale, for it is also reported both by other Latin sources and by Byzantine ones.[158] Khoirobakkhoi and its rivers (*potamoi*), which were apparently normally fordable and which were called Melas and Athyras, are mentioned in the account of Alexius I's campaign of 1091 against the Patzinaks by Anna Comnena.[159]

## C. *Observations*

Although the physical structure of the Balkan and Anatolian Peninsulas remains, inevitably given the limited time scale involved, much the same as it was during the later Roman and Byzantine period, it does therefore differ insofar as it has been continually subject to at least one phenomenon that has brought about a number of minor physical changes which in sum potentially do have significant agricultural and therefore fiscal implications. The phenomenon is that of the combined process of the erosion of soil at one place and its deposition at another, processes to which the Balkans and Anatolia, together with most of the Mediterranean area, are particularly susceptible.

Now, to the extent that soil has been eroded from a great number of places, generally at higher altitudes, the phenomenon possesses negative implications: those places will have become, in other words, decreasingly cultivable and fertile. But, to the extent that soil has also been deposited in a smaller number of places (i.e. has been concentrated), generally at lower altitudes, the phenomenon also possesses positive implications: some of those places will have owed their very existence to the phenomenon, while others will have become increasingly cultivable and fertile through it. However, these positive implications are merely potential, and become actual only to the extent that the newly formed or fertilised places are exploited, and given that such places are liable to occur in river-valleys or towards or at river-mouths, this distinction is a crucial one. For alluvial valley-floors, and more particularly alluvial plains and deltas, are in their natural state almost always marshy, and frequently malarial. To drain them and thus to permit their full exploitation requires considerable resources of money, man-power and technology.[160]

In an area such as the Balkans and Anatolia, that is dominated by mountains and an elevated plateau respectively, and in which a high proportion of arable land, and a very

158 Latin: Odo of Deuil, *De Profectione Ludovici VII in Orientem* III; ed. Berry, pp. 46–8. *Annales Herbipolenses*, s.a. 1147; MGH, *SS* XVI, p. 4. Byzantine: Cinnamus, *Epitome* II.14; Bonn edn, pp. 73–4. Nicetas Choniates, *Historia*; ed. van Dieten, I, pp. 64–5.

159 Anna Comnena, *Alexiad* VIII.1.5; ed. Leib, II, p. 130.

160 Vita-Finzi, *The Mediterranean Valleys*, pp. 116–20.

high proportion indeed of good-quality arable land, is to be found in river-valleys and plains and deltas – precisely those places that are liable to have been formed out of, or improved by, water-borne alluvium – the implications of all this are clearly considerable. For the evidence suggests that in this area the draining and full exploitation of these places is very largely a late nineteenth- and twentieth-century feature. Prior to the First World War, in the southern Balkans, large stretches of the Macedonian and Strimon–Maritsa Plains were marshy,[161] and certain stretches of the southern end of the Thracian Plain were in a similar condition.[162] In Anatolia, large stretches of the Cilician Plain were marshy,[163] and stretches of the Pamphylian Plain were also in a similar condition.[164] The lower stretches and mouths of most of the large rivers of the west – the Trojan Menderes, Bakır, Gediz, Küçük Menderes and Büyük Menderes – were also under marsh.[165] In Greece, large areas of land have been drained and reclaimed, but this was a process that commenced as late as 1882–6 with the draining of Lake Kopaïs and that only became intensive in 1925.[166] Much the same must be true of other countries in the same area.

The degree of alluviation which Anatolia has undergone, much of it since classical times, was in fact recognised and systematically described as long ago as 1862. (Travellers to individual sites, whether earlier or later, not infrequently mention the phenomenon.) The rivers of Cilicia, Pamphylia, Lycia, the west coast, the Troad, and Paphlagonia and the Pontus are all described as having contributed to the process. The tendency towards the formation of marshland in these areas is also noted and described: the alluvial plain of Cilicia is described as consisting largely of marshland, and so are the alluvial deltas of the Kızılırmak and Yeşilırmak.[167]

To suppose that the conditions outlined in the preceding paragraphs were radically different from those obtaining in the Byzantine period or at any particular time in that period would be merely perverse and beyond all bounds of plausibility. The particular evidence for this statement is not good, and is indeed almost entirely negative, but the general evidence suggests that Anastasius and Justinian were the last emperors to possess both the resources and the will to undertake extensive civil projects of the required nature, in any systematic sense. In addition, whereas each prefecture of the late Roman and early Byzantine period possessed its own *scrinium operum* with responsibility for its public works,[168] the central administration at least of the middle and later Byzantine periods seems to have lacked a unit with a specific responsibility for public works, for nothing

[161] Admiralty, *A Handbook of Macedonia*, pp. 35, 39, 40.
[162] Admiralty, *A Handbook of Turkey in Europe*, pp. 148, 149.
[163] Admiralty, *A Handbook of Asia Minor* IV.2, pp. 19, 33–4.
[164] Admiralty, *A Handbook of Asia Minor* III.3, p. 32.
[165] Admiralty, *A Handbook of Asia Minor* II, pp. 56, 67, 68, 69, 72.
[166] Dragonas and Olympitis, 'Greece', in *The World Atlas of Agriculture* I, at pp. 195–7.
[167] C. F. M. Texier, *Asie Mineure: description géographique, historique et archéologique*, pp. 16–25.
[168] See below, p. 411, Jones, *Later Roman Empire* I, pp. 449–50, 461–2; II, pp. 589–90.

of the kind appears, or even is hinted at, in any of the lists of ranks and offices of the period. Again, at the earlier period the cities held formal responsibility for their own public works, and possessed the administrative structure and (at least in theory) the financial means to carry out that responsibility.[169] This system had shown signs of disintegrating by the fifth century, if not before, but at the later period there is no sign at all of any such reponsibility, let alone the capacities for implementing it. The later thematic *stratēgos* seems to have been responsible for such public works in his own area as were likely to affect the military capacities of that area (for example, the maintenance and upkeep of roads, bridges and fortresses), but no others.[170] Systematic responsibility and capacities seem to have collapsed.

The conclusion therefore can only be that while the Byzantine empire suffered the negative consequences of continued and widespread erosion, it never actually enjoyed the potentially positive ones of deposition – or that it enjoyed them to a limited degree only. The scale of the loss to agricultural productivity, and therefore eventually to state finances that is implied, is of course impossible to gauge, but it was probably appreciable, and may even have been fundamental.

Lest the last statement seem exaggerated, it is finally worth noting that one section of an estate (*proasteion*) called Mandraklou, one of several estates given by Michael VII to Andronicus Ducas in 1073, forming a much larger entity, the *episkepsis tōn Alōpekōn*, and situated to either side of the Maeander towards its mouth at Miletus–Priene, had been reduced from 285 *modioi* down to 36 *modioi* in extent. The explanation given for this reduction is that the river (*sc.* the Maeander) had 'destroyed' the remaining land to either side (*tēn de loipēn gēn apōlesen ho potamos peran peran*). Another section of the same estate consisted of 212½ *modioi*, without the cultivation of the land that had been 'carried off' by the river and had become marshland (*aneu tēs hypergou gēs tēs apospatheisēs para tou potamou kai genomenēs myrikotopou*) consisting of 371 *modioi*. In dealing with other estates in the same entity, mention is made of the 'old river (*palaios potamos*)', and the 'great river (*megas potamos*)', which may well imply that the Maeander was still shifting its bed from time to time.[171*]

In the Balkans much the same seems to have been true of the Vardar, for estates there, in the second half of the fourteenth century, are delimited either by the course of the (contemporary) Vardar, or by that of the 'old Vardar (*palaios Vardarios*)'. This distinction presumably represents a continuation of the process earlier described by Anna Comnena.[172]

* I owe this reference to the kindness of Alan Harvey.

169 Jones, *Later Roman Empire* II, pp. 724–37.

170 Toynbee, *Constantine Porphyrogenitus and his World*, pp. 178–9.

171 Miklosich and Müller, *Acta et Diplomata Graeca Medii Aevi* VI, pp. 10, 12, 13.

172 P. Schreiner, 'Zwei unedierte Praktika aus der zweiten Hälfte des 14. Jahrhunderts', *Jahrbuch der Österreichischen Byzantinistik* 19 (1970), pp. 34–5; see above, p. 65.

CHAPTER 2

# THE BASIC GEOGRAPHY OF SETTLEMENT AND SOCIETY

## (I) GENERAL: THE DISTRIBUTION OF CITIES

It is against this background, composed of elements such as physical structure, climate, natural vegetation and land-use which are very largely natural and unchanging, that the general pattern and development of settlement and communications in the Balkan and Anatolian Peninsulas during the later Roman and Byzantine periods should be seen. A further element of major significance, that is the political and administrative history of the various regions that go to make up the two peninsulas, which almost by definition did change and on occasion in a manner which ignored or defied some or all of the natural elements listed above, should also be taken into account. The interaction of these several elements brought into existence, and occasionally maintained, a number of sharp contrasts within each peninsula, as well as a number between them.

A map based upon the *Synecdemus* of Hierocles, modified where necessary on the evidence of the appropriate *Notitiae Episcopatuum* and Conciliar Lists, and drawn up so as to illustrate the distribution of cities in the Balkans and Anatolia in the mid fifth century, exhibits a number of interesting and significant features.[1] (Map 14)

The extremely conservative practice of recognising existing communities when a region was annexed and of rarely making fundamental changes thereafter, which had been adhered to by the Roman state throughout, meant that even at this date the distribution of cities largely reflected that which had already existed when each region had come under Roman rule.[2] This practice accounts, in the historically most immediate sense at least, for the most obvious disparities in the density of the distribution of cities within both the Balkans and Anatolia.

In the Balkans, prior to the annexation by the Roman state, Moesia and inner Thrace had been inhabited by large tribal communities living scattered in villages, and it was

[1] A. H. M. Jones, *Cities of the Eastern Roman Provinces*, pp. 514–21 (Appendix 3: 'Hierocles and Georgius'), 522–41 (Appendix 4: 'Tables'); *idem*, *Later Roman Empire*, map 5 ('Distribution of cities in the middle of the fifth century').

[2] Jones, *Later Roman Empire* II, pp. 715–16.

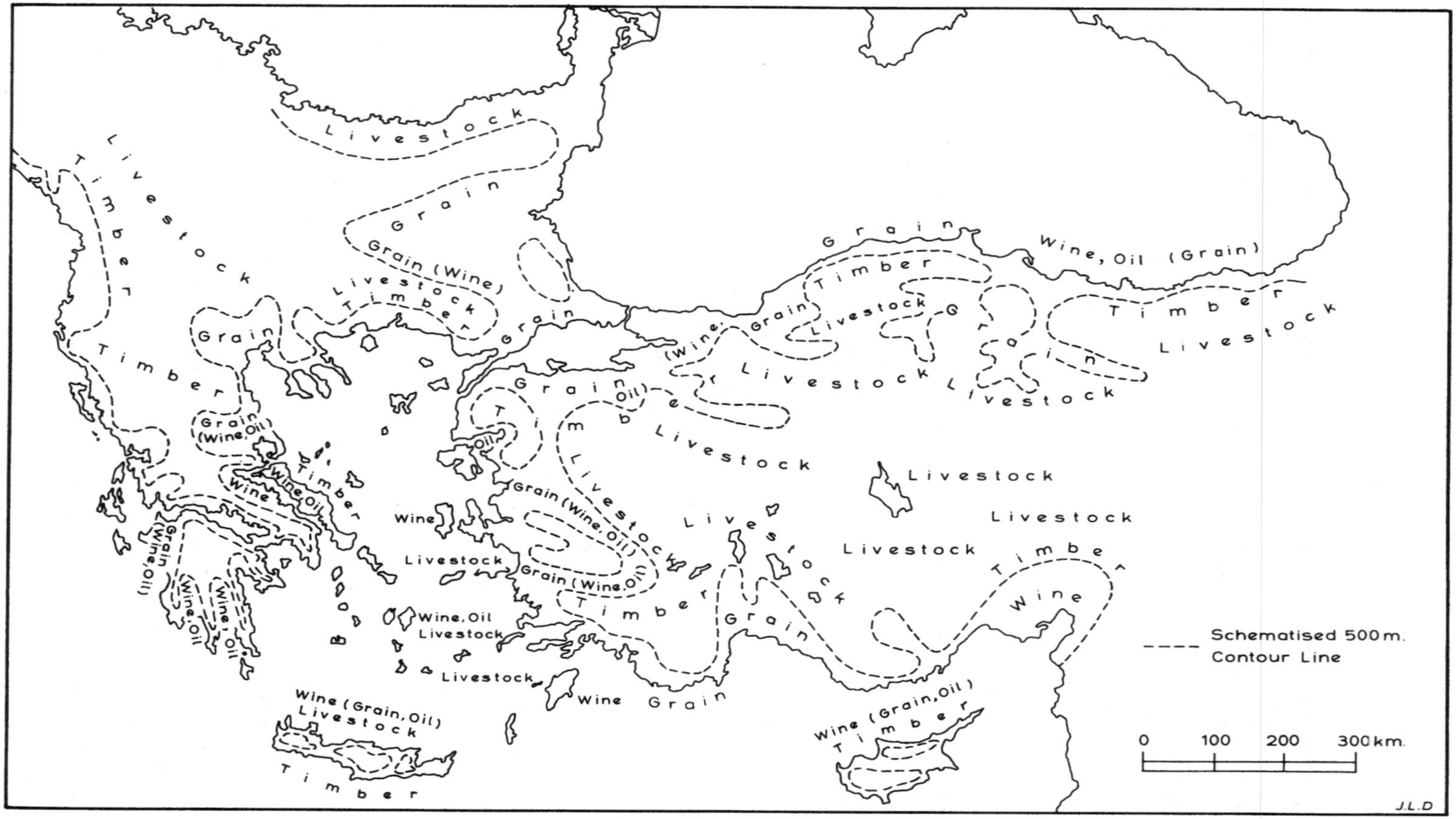


Map 13 The Balkans and Anatolia: basic agricultural/pastoral divisions and products (to *c.* 1300)

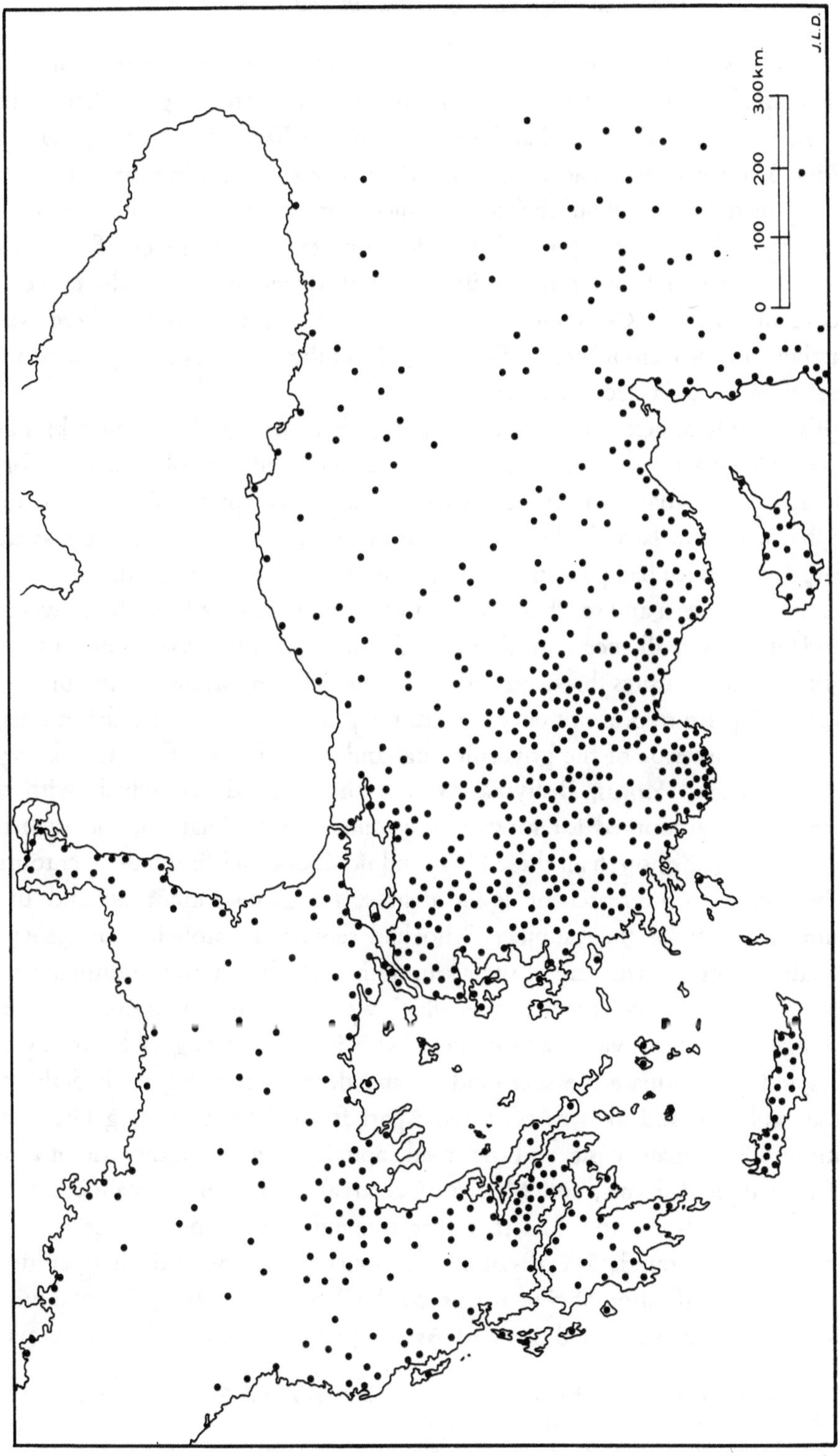


Map 14 The Balkans and Anatolia: distribution of cities, *c.* 450 (after Jones)

on the Thracian coast only, to the south and east (i.e. on the Aegean, Marmara and Black Seas), that a number of Greek cities had been founded. At the same stage of their histories Macedonia and Greece, on the other hand, had long been urbanised, and contained several hundred cities. The result was that, in spite of some changes in the interim, the essential distinction remained. (The total number of cities incorporated in the later dioceses of Dacia and Thrace increased somewhat through the development of a number of cities along the Danube, most of which was military in origin; as a concomitant of the choice first of Nicomedia and then of Constantinople as the main imperial capital, there was an increased activity in their environs; while the total number of cities incorporated in the later diocese of Macedonia decreased somewhat.)[3]

In Anatolia, prior to annexation, Asia had earlier formed part of the Seleucid kingdom, and more recently virtually the whole of the Attalid one. The control which the former had exercised over its Anatolian territories had always been spasmodic and had rarely been close; that which the latter had exercised was in any case of relatively recent standing on such a large scale. Both had paid lip-service, at least, to the theory that the pre-existing Greek cities of the western and southern coasts and their immediate hinterlands were free and independent states in alliance with them. Both had founded or re-founded a number of cities in the interior, on sites that were either strategically important, or notably fertile, or both. Both had permitted, if not encouraged, the gradual adoption by the indigenous communities of the interior of the governmental and social forms of the Greek city.[4]

Prior to annexation, Pontus, Bithynia, Galatia and Cappadocia, which with their various dependencies accounted for most of the remainder of Anatolia, had each been ruled by its own king. Although all these kings and no doubt their immediate entourages had been hellenised to a greater or lesser degree, the same cannot be said of the overwhelming majority of their subjects who had remained untouched by hellenism. Neither the administrative structure of their kingdoms, which although rudimentary was heavily centralised, nor the social structure – which was dominated by a nobility, whether secular or religious, owning vast tracts of land with fortified strongholds serving both as residences and to dominate the surrounding and dependent villages – had therefore favoured the evolution and growth of cities. Apart from the pre-existing Greek cities of the Pontic and Bithynian coasts, and the royal capitals – Amasia in the case of Pontus, Nicomedia in that of Bithynia, and Mazaca (Caesarea) in that of Cappadocia, Galatia then lacking a major city – cities had therefore remained exceptional.[5] The result was that, despite the direct foundation of colonies and cities, and the indirect operation of a policy favouring the adoption of civic forms, by the Roman emperors, the total number of cities incorporated in the later diocese of Asiana (which represented, approximately,

[3] Jones, *Cities of the Eastern Roman Provinces*, pp. 1–27; *idem*, *Later Roman Empire* II, pp. 716–17.
[4] Magie, *Roman Rule in Asia Minor* I, pp. 3–33, 53–146.
[5] *Ibid.* I, pp. 179–82, 304–11, 454–9, 491–4.

the former Seleucid territory) remained high, if somewhat reduced from its zenith, while that incorporated in Pontica (which represented, equally approximately, the kingdoms) remained low.[6]

The low density of cities in the inner Balkans and in northern and eastern Anatolia is confirmed by the evidence of the *Itinerarium Burdigalense*, the record of a pilgrim travelling from Bordeaux to Jerusalem in 333. Between Sirmium and Constantinople, the pilgrim records[7] 39 *mutationes*, 22 *mansiones* (both being local stations of the public post), and nine cities only. To these figures there should probably be added several more *mutationes* and *mansiones*, and certainly the city of Adrianople. But even so, of a modified total of ten cities, five (Bassianae, Singidunum, Aureus Mons, Margus and Viminacium) occur during the relatively short stretch of road along the Danube, and clearly possess a mainly military basis. The remaining five (Naissus, Serdica, Philippopolis, Adrianopolis and Heraclea) have to suffice for the much longer stretch of road across the Balkans. Between Chalcedon and Tarsus, the pilgrim records[8] 27 *mutationes*, 20 *mansiones*, and only eight cities (Nicomedia, Nicaea, Iuliopolis, Ancyra, Aspona, Colonia [Archelais], Tyana and Faustinopolis). Had he taken a more southerly and westerly route, the total of cities could not but have been far higher. (Maps 10–11, 14, 15, 17, 19–23)

Before attempting to draw any more detailed conclusions from the distribution of cities at this period, or to make any comparisons with that at other periods, two points should first be noted.

The first of these points is that any formal list of the cities existing at this period which is based on contemporary sources will almost inevitably tend to underestimate the number of communities which might be classed as cities at the present time. The reason for this tendency lies in the nature of the Greco-Roman *polis/civitas* itself. Formal possession of the title and status of a city depended upon the possession of a particular form of governmental and social structure, and only secondarily upon the fulfilment of certain economic functions, the possession of certain public facilities and provision of services, and the possession of a certain physical plan and size. A community might quite well, in theory, conform to most or all of these secondary requirements and still not possess, at least immediately, the civic title and status. It is true that, for various reasons largely of their own, the Hellenistic, Roman and Byzantine states encouraged the adoption of the primary requirements by such communities as possessed some or all of the secondary ones, so that they might then confer the title and status upon them. It seems even to be the case that the title and status was often coveted. But on the other hand, encouragement seems likely to have been indirect or at least unsystematic, and conferment

[6] Jones, *Cities of the Eastern Roman Provinces*, pp. 28–214; *idem*, *Later Roman Empire* II, pp. 717–18.

[7] Anonymous, *Itinerarium Burdigalense*, 563–71; ed. Cuntz, pp. 89–91.

[8] *Ibid.* 571–9; ed. Cuntz, pp. 91–3. For the actual course of this section of the road, see now: D. French, *Roman Roads and Milestones of Asia Minor* I, *The Pilgrim's Road*.

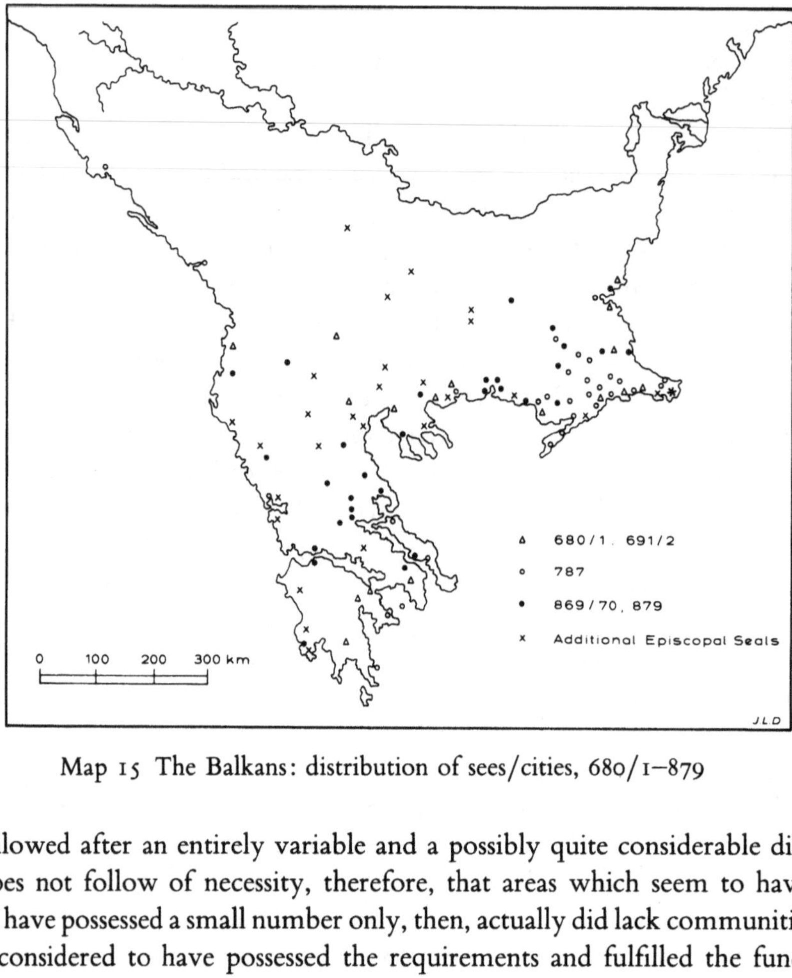


Map 15 The Balkans: distribution of sees/cities, 680/1–879

to have followed after an entirely variable and a possibly quite considerable distance in time. It does not follow of necessity, therefore, that areas which seem to have lacked cities, or to have possessed a small number only, then, actually did lack communities which would be considered to have possessed the requirements and fulfilled the functions of a city at the present time.[9]

The second of these points derives essentially from the first, and is that, whereas areas seemingly lacking in cities were not necessarily actually lacking in communities of some size and complexity and were not unexploited economically, areas abounding in cities were necessarily relatively highly exploited economically and – given that – agriculturally, for the ancient (as doubtless the mediaeval) city was in the vast majority of cases heavily dependent upon the exploitation of the surrounding land.[10]

[9] For the late Roman and early Byzantine state and the creation of cities: A.H.M.Jones, *The Greek City from Alexander to Justinian*, pp. 85–94. As an apparent exception, the case of Orcistus, elevated to formal city rank in *c.* 325, but claiming to have long possessed virtually all the other necessary attributes: *idem*, *The Cities of the Eastern Roman Provinces*, pp. 67–8.

[10] E.g. M. I. Finley, *The Ancient Economy*, pp. 123–49; K. Hopkins, *Conquerors and Slaves*, pp. 15–19; Jones, *Later Roman Empire* I, p. 714, II, pp. 769–70, 856, 871–2. There is every reason to believe the same of all but a very few Byzantine cities. See for example, Lampsacus, which in 1219 apparently possessed an adult male population of 163, agricultural classifications accounting for 113: G. L. F. Tafel and G. M.

The low density of cities in the dioceses of Dacia and (inner) Thrace in the Balkans, and in that of Pontica in Anatolia, therefore, cannot in itself be considered a reliable indication of a lack of communities in and exploitation of those areas. On the other hand, the fact that both Dacia and Thrace had been exposed to barbarian devastation from the third century onwards, that Thrace was unable to meet its fiscal requirements in the late fifth century,[11] and that certain of its Danubian provinces had to be supported by maritime ones outside the diocese in the mid sixth century,[12] does suggest that it is a reliable indication. The fact that Pontica included a high proportion of the central plateau which, because of the character of its climate and its land, was generally far more suited to extensive grazing than to arable farming, tree- or fruit-farming, or viticulture,[13] and was therefore in any case far less capable of supporting a high density of population and communities, again suggests that it is nevertheless a reliable indication. (Map 13)

Within the dioceses of Macedonia and Asiana, the distribution of cities also varied considerably in density. With regard to the first, a blank area extending in an approximately north-west to south-west direction clearly defines the spine of the Pindus Range, while a large area of comparatively high density in the north-east equally defines the Macedonian Plain. A further somewhat smaller area of comparatively high density to the south defines the Thessalian Plain, while yet another small area of high density in the extreme south-east defines the Boeotian Plain. Procopius' mention of the fertile, well-watered and intensively exploited character of the Macedonian and Thessalian Plains[14] thus tends to confirm the evidence of the map, and so does Symmachus' implication of the export of Macedonian grain.[15] With regard to the second, two large areas of low density lying towards the interior define the regions of Lycaonia and Phrygia, the first of which belongs entirely to the central plateau, the second partially. Two smaller and less obvious areas of low density in the north-west and south-west define or relate to the Mysian and Bithynian Highlands and the Lycian Taurus respectively. (Maps 1, 5)

The essential distinction in the distribution of cities existing between the dioceses of Asiana and Pontica was, as implied above, not only a political and structural but also a climatic one. Comparison of the maps of distribution and structure on the one hand with those of average temperature range, annual precipitation, snow cover, frost occurrence, and so on, amply demonstrates the close coincidence.[16]

It is unfortunately much more difficult, even impossible, to draw up a map illustrating the distribution of cities in the Balkans and Anatolia at a date significantly later than

Thomas (eds), *Urkunden zur älteren Handels-und Staatsgeschichte der Republik Venedig*. II, pp. 208–9. M. J. Angold, *A Byzantine Government in Exile, Government and Society under the Laskarids of Nicaea (1204–1261)*, pp. 109–10. See also below, pp. 173–5.

11 See below, p. 397.

12 See below, pp. 404, 645–6, 651–4.

13 See above, pp. 26–8, 40–4, 54–6, 57; below, pp. 100–4.

14 See above, p. 50 n. 68.

15 See above, p. 51 n. 71.

16 Maps 6, 7; A. Tanoğlu, S. Erinç, and E. Tümertekin, *Türkiye Atlası*, maps 18, 40. See also below, pp. 90–100.

the fifth century which possesses the same authority and degree of exhaustiveness as that drawn up for the fifth century. The problem is basically one of sources. No later equivalent of the *Synecdemus* seems to have existed, or at least survives.

The *Notitiae Episcopatuum*, which are in most cases only very approximately dated, bear a very uncertain relationship to contemporary reality, and given their highly formalised nature and largely ceremonial object, and their undoubted antiquarian propensities, do not and cannot possess the same authority where they cannot be independently and consistently checked and controlled by other evidence. Recent work on them has tended only to confirm their unreliable, and indeed positively deceptive, nature. By the time that they can be shown to be gradually admitting and revealing the existence of a situation that had plainly long obtained, other sources of evidence have revealed it in detail.[17]

There remain the Conciliar Lists: registers, that is, of those bishops who were present at, or of those who subscribed to, or both, the various later ecumenical councils. These have their own limitations: they are frequently badly preserved and for the most part have not received modern editing; the later in date, the less explicit the actual signatures and the less strictly ordered the regional groupings and precedence within them; they are inevitably nowhere near exhaustive. The second of these limitations means that, where a name is shared by two or more sees, it becomes increasingly difficult to decide which see is involved. The third arises from the fact that they are registers only of those bishops present at, or subscribing to, the councils, and that they therefore do not take account of those who – for whatever reasons – were unable to attend the councils, or of those who were unable or unwilling to sign their acts.

Use of both the *Notitiae* and the Lists involves the generally – but by no means entirely – valid assumption, for the immediate purpose at least, of an equation between secular city and ecclesiastical see.[18] Use of both, equally, is subject to the very severe limitation that the sites of a large number of cities or sees remain entirely unknown or so uncertain as to be useless for the purpose. Finally, in the case even of the Lists, there is always present the alarming possibility that a proportion, at least, of the bishops who are represented in them, themselves represented, as absentees, cities or sees that effectively no longer existed. Although there are occasional indications that this situation was not entirely unknown,[19] the number of occasions on which bishops can be attested as actually resident in their cities or sees – for example through epistolary collections and

[17] Vryonis, *The Decline of Medieval Hellenism in Asia Minor*, pp. 302–10.

[18] Jones, *Cities of the Eastern Roman Provinces*, pp. 519–20. G. Ostrogorsky, 'Byzantine Cities in the Early Middle Ages', *DOP* 13 (1959), pp. 52–3; Vryonis, *The Decline of Medieval Hellenism in Asia Minor*, pp. 26–7.

[19] Ostrogorsky, 'Byzantine Cities in the Early Middle Ages', p. 58. See also below, pp. 79–80 (Stobi and Lacedaemonia); J. F. Haldon, and H. Kennedy, 'The Arab–Byzantine Frontiers in the Eighth and Ninth Centuries: Military Organisation and Society in the Borderlands', *Zbornik Radova Vizantoloshkog Instituta* 19 (1980), p. 95 n. 57 (Tyana, and possibly Ciscissus). Noticeably, all of these were in areas that were either outside imperial territory, or constantly under dispute.

references[20] – is so overwhelmingly greater as to ensure that this was the predominant pattern, both chronologically and geographically, however much the subject of complaint.

Finally, it should be observed that, even given the existence of an equation between city and see, and the effective local residence of the bishop, maps based upon the result may reveal a lack of cities/sees in some areas, and concentrations of them in others, but cannot reveal directly anything of the particular nature or structure of either city or see.

Nevertheless, and despite these several limitations, a series of maps based on the registers of those bishops who were present at or who subscribed to the later ecumenical councils, and drawn up so as to illustrate the distribution of their sees in the Balkans and Anatolia, reveals a number of consistent – and therefore probably significant – features. The councils involved are the Sixth Ecumenical Council, held in Constantinople in 680/1, together with the Quinisext Council, held in Constantinople in 691/2; the Seventh Ecumenical Council, held in Nicaea in 787; and the Anti-Photian Synod, held in Constantinople in 869–70, together with the Photian Synod, held in Constantinople in 879. The three groups are thus conveniently staggered at approximately hundred-year intervals.

The registers themselves reveal steadily increasing numbers of episcopal participants or subscribers. Thus, the councils of 680/1 and 691/2 involved some 174 and 211 bishops respectively; the council of 787 some 365; and the synods of 869/70 and 879 some 100 and 380 respectively. These are all minimal figures, and other sources suggest that totals may well have been somewhat – perhaps even considerably – higher.[21]

Strong confirmation of the validity of the registers for the purpose in hand is to be found in an index of surviving episcopal seals arranged according to the sees involved. The registers, of course, cover a somewhat narrower chronological range than the seals, which extend on into the twelfth century at least. Nevertheless, in the Balkans, the pattern established by the registers is amplified, but not fundamentally altered, by the evidence of the seals; in Anatolia, even the degree of amplification is minimal.[22] (Maps 15, 22)

[20] E.g. (to name only those represented in this book): Michael of Athens (see above, pp. 51–2); Leo of Synnada (see below, pp. 138–40); John of Euchaita (see below, pp. 140–2); Eustathius of Thessalonica (see below, pp. 114, 133); John of Neopatras (see below, p. 240). Further examples, whether earlier or later, abound.

[21] Ostrogorsky, 'Byzantine Cities in the Early Middle Ages', pp. 54–60. J. Darrouzès, 'Listes épiscopales du concile de Nicée (787)', *Revue des Études Byzantines* 33 (1975), p. 61.

[22] G. Zacos and A. Veglery, *Byzantine Lead Seals* I.3, pp. 1869–75 (Index iv). V. Laurent, *Le corpus des sceaux de l'empire byzantin* V.1, pp. 775–8 (Index i), V.2, pp. 490–6 (Index i.3), V.3, pp. 312–16 (Index i.3).

## (II) THE BALKANS

### A. The distribution of cities

In the Balkans, the distribution of sees contrasts sharply with that of cities obtaining in the fifth century and is itself clearly subject to development. The sees represented at the councils of 680/1[23] and 691/2[24] are extremely few in number and, moreover, confined – with a single major exception (Stobi) alone – to the coastal areas. The main concentration occurs in Thrace, whether on the Black Sea, the Marmora, or the Aegean, but another occurs in Attica and the eastern Peloponnese. The sees newly represented at the council of 787[25] show a distinct tendency to extend inland into eastern Thrace as defined by the Rhodope on the one hand and by the Istranja Mountains on the other. Those newly represented at the synods of 869/70[26] and 879[27] confirm this finding and show an equally distinct one to extend into the area between the Rhodope and the Aegean, central Greece and the western Peloponnese. Those represented by seals confirm the general pattern established by the registers, while themselves also sharing a distinct tendency to extend into central Greece and the inner Balkans. (Map 15)

Proportionally by far the greater increase in the number of sees occurs in the Balkans, as opposed to Anatolia, and there seems no doubt but that this whole development and its particular pattern represent a more or less straightforward reflection of contemporary political events.

It should not be forgotten that when, in 688/9, Justinian II mounted a military expedition against the Slavs and Bulgars, he made a sally as far as Thessalonica, and captured many Slavs whom he ordered to be settled in the theme of Opsikion, but while returning was ambushed by the Bulgars in a narrow part of the pass (*en tō stenō tēs kleisouras*, i.e. in the narrow plain between the Rhodope and the Aegean) and lost much of his army. Similarly, when in 708/9 he mounted another expedition against the Bulgars, he penetrated as far as Anchialus with a fleet and army, but was again ambushed by the Bulgars, again losing men, horses and wagons (presumably of the baggage-train). The clear implication of the events of these expeditions is that the empire held all or much of the Thracian coast-land as far as Thessalonica in the west and as far as Anchialus in the north, but that it held even these precariously, and that its hold did not extend far inland.[28]

[23] G. D. Mansi, *Sacrorum Conciliorum Nova et Amplissima Collectio* XI, cols 611–18, 626–30, 639–54, 667–82, 687–94, etc. [24] *Ibid.* XI, cols 987–1006.

[25] *Ibid.* XII, cols 994–9, 1086–1111, 1146–54; XIII, cols 133–52, 365–73, 380–97. See now: Darrouzès, 'Listes épiscopales du concile de Nicée (787)', pp. 62–76.

[26] Mansi, *Sacrorum Conciliorum Nova et Amplissima Collectio* XVI, cols 81–2, 96–7, 134–5, 143–4, 157–9, 189–95, etc. [27] *Ibid.* XVII, cols 373–8.

[28] Theophanes, *Chronographia*; ed. C. de Boor, I, pp. 364, 376. See also: G. Ostrogorsky, *History of the Byzantine State*, p. 130 (and n. 3); A. N. Stratos, *Byzantium in the Seventh Century* V (*Justinian, Leontius*

It is well established that the city of Thessalonica itself, during the course of the sixth, seventh and eighth centuries, was surrounded by settlements of Slav tribes, with which relations seem normally to have been neutral or even cordial, but with which they were occasionally hostile, leading on the one hand to emperors mounting expeditions against them (that of 688/9 being only the best recorded), and on the other to the tribes actually laying siege to the city.[29]

It is equally well established, although not without a varying degree of Greek chauvinist dissent, that much of northern and central Greece, and even the Peloponnese, during the sixth, seventh and eighth centuries, was invaded and settled possibly by Avar and certainly by Slav tribes, and later by Bulgar ones. The concurrence of contemporary documentary and literary sources, Hellenic and Slavonic place-names, archaeological findings, and coin-hoards, on this question, is overwhelming: the empire certainly held the coastal section of the Macedonian Plain, Athens and Attica, Corinth, Argos and the Argolid, and the eastern section of the Peloponnese, only. It may have held the coastal section of the Thessalian Plain, Boeotia and Euboea in addition. Much of the previous population, or of certain classes amongst that population, retired to the islands off the (Adriatic or Aegean) coasts, or (as in the case of Patras), emigrated to Italy.[30]

It is therefore against this devastating background that the Conciliar Lists of 680/1 and 691/2 have to be seen. Eighteen Balkan sees only are represented: Mesembria, Sozopolis, Bizye, Uzuse, Selymbria, Heraclea, Panium, Aenus, Philippi, Amphipolis, Thessalonica, Stobi, Edessa, Athens, Corinth, Argos, Lacedaemonia and Dyrrhachium. Of these, Uzuse is not readily identifiable, and the remainder form a very distinctive pattern, virtually entirely in conformity with that which might have been expected on the other grounds already outlined. The two exceptions to this conformity are the sees of Stobi and Lacedaemonia (i.e. Sparti), and here it may merely be that bishops in exile (the former at Thessalonica, the latter at Monemvasia), or acting as suffragans elsewhere, or both, are involved:[31] certainly, even Monemvasia remained continuously under

*and Tiberius, 685–711*), pp. 16–18 (a discussion on the mistaken premise that Justinian was operating far more to the north than he possibly could have done).

29 The subject is complex and controversial. On the first attacks on Thessalonica, see for example: Toynbee, *Constantine Porphyrogenitus and his World*, pp. 528–35; P. Lemerle, *Les plus anciens recueils des miracles de saint Démétrius et la pénétration des slaves dans les Balkans* II, *Commentaire*, pp. 49–65 (first major attack 586); S. Vryonis, 'The Evolution of Slavic Society and the Slavic Invasions of Greece: The First Major Attack on Thessaloniki, A.D. 597', *Hesperia* 50 (1981), pp. 378–90.

30 Toynbee, *Constantine Porphyrogenitus and his World*, pp. 619–51 (Annex 3: 'The Slav Völkerwanderung South of the Danube' (useful and unbiased)); J. Herrin, 'Aspects of the Process of Hellenization in the Early Middle Ages', *The Annual of the British School of Archaeology at Athens* 68 (1973), pp. 114–18 (emigration). See now: M. W. Weithmann, *Die Slavische Bevölkerung auf der Griechischen Halbinsel: Ein Beitrag zur Historischen Ethnographie Südosteuropas*, and S. Vryonis 'Review Essay' (of Weithmann, *op. cit.*), in *Balkan Studies*, 22 (1981), at pp. 405–39.

31 See above, p. 76 and n. 19; R.-J. Lilie, '"Thrakien" und "Thrakesion". Zur byzantinischen Provinzorganisation am Ende des 7. Jahrhunderts', *Jahrbuch der Österreichischen Byzantinistik* 26 (1977), p. 43 (and n. 159).

Byzantine control, although in 723–8 Willibald, the future bishop of Eichstätt, could describe it as being 'in a Slavonic land (*in Slawinia terra*)'.[32]

The reign of Constantine V (741–75) seems to have marked a military and political turning-point. In 763, the Byzantine forces massively defeated the Bulgars under their khan Teletz at Anchialus, as a result of a pincer-movement, troops having been moved southwards from the Danube, where they had been landed by a fleet, and northwards from Thrace. During the same reign, although the Aegean islands, along with Monobasia (i.e. Monemvasia) and the Greek remnants (i.e. Hellas, the *katōtika merē*), still represented the limits of imperial control in the area, nevertheless a systematic (and forcible) recolonisation of Thrace, mainly with recently reconquered eastern Anatolian heterodox, and its ensured protection through the foundation of fortresses (*kastra*), are both also reported.[33]

In 783, the empress Irene sent the patrician Stauracius with a large army against the Slavs, and he, passing through Thessalonica and Hellas, subjected and made the whole region tributary to the empire. He also entered the Peloponnese, and led off many captives and much spoil into the empire. The clear contrast between Stauracius' subjection of areas in central Greece and his mere plundering in the Peloponnese is undoubtedly significant.[34]

In 784, Irene and her son Constantine (VI), again with a large army, passed through Thrace, reached Berrhoe, and ordered it restored. They then proceeded as far as Philippopolis, and on their return journey ordered Anchialus restored.[35]

In 809/10 the limit of Byzantine power seems to have been Serdica.[36]

The same background is therefore still present in essence when the list of 787 is considered. The number of Balkan sees represented has by now more than doubled, but the overwhelming bulk of new sees lies in lower Thrace, and only relatively few in Greece proper. Of the former, some or all may well represent Constantine V's measures, and of the latter, Oreus and Porthmus in Euboea, along with the possible addition of Larissa in Thessaly, may represent some, or all, of the gains due to Stauracius' expedition. Aegina, Troezen and Monemvasia all represent areas that were already in Byzantine hands in 680/91; and Nicopolis, and Decatera and Salona, in Epirus and Dalmatia respectively, probably also represent isolated enclaves continuously in Byzantine hands.[37]

A schematic map of Balkan territory under some kind of regular Byzantine administration over the period 680/91–787 therefore reveals drastic change between the two terminal dates in Thrace alone (Map 16).[38] Here, with the additional information

32 *Vita Willibaldi Episcopi Eichstetensis*; MGH, *SS* xv. 1, p. 93.

33 Theophanes, *Chronographia*; ed. de Boor, I, pp. 422–3, 429, 433, 447.

34 *Ibid.* pp. 456–7. P. Lemerle, 'La Chronique improprement dite de Monemvasie: le contexte historique et légendaire', *Revue des Études Byzantines* 21 (1963), p. 28.

35 Theophanes, *Chronographia*; ed. de Boor, I, p. 457.

36 *Ibid.* p. 485.

37 Wilkes, *Dalmatia*, pp. 435–7.

38 Cf. the two maps in Lilie, '"Thrakien" und "Thrakesion"', pp. 39, 44, and also that in Toynbee, *Constantine Porphyrogenitus and his World* (map 1: 'Greece in the seventh century A.D.').

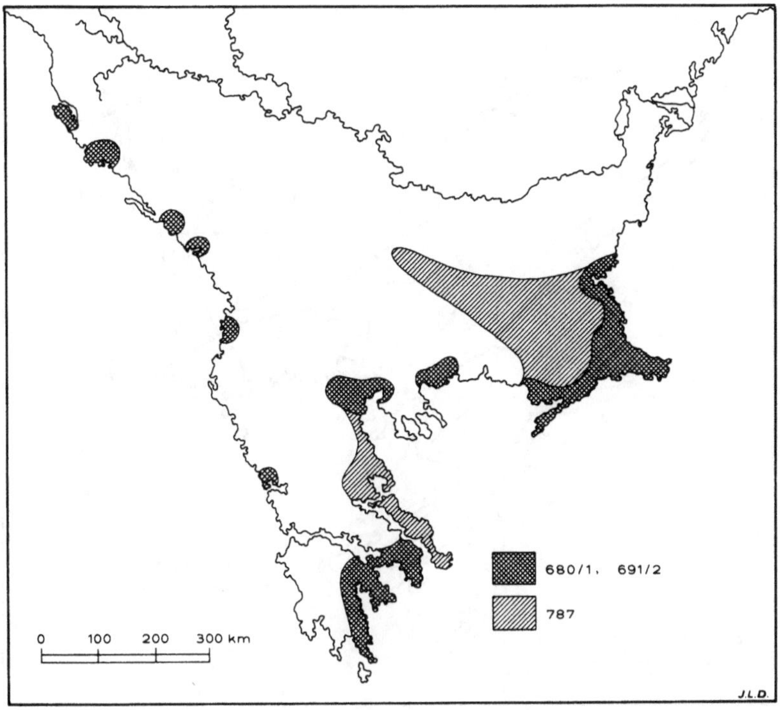


Map 16 The Balkans: imperial territory, *c.* 680/1–787

of the sources mentioned above, the main thrust of Byzantine strategy is clear: control of the Thracian plain along the line of the classic trans-Balkan route up through Adrianople and Philippopolis as far as Serdica. It is presumably no coincidence that, between Adrianople and Heraclea, preceded long previously by *mansio Virgoles* (Bergula = Arcadiopolis) and *mansio Drizupara*, not less than three stations of the public post represented in the *Itinerarium Burdigalense* (333) (*mansio Nicae*, *mutatio Urisio*, and *mansio Tunorullo*[39]), which had not previously been represented by sees,[40] are nevertheless so represented as Nicaea, Brysis and Tzurullum, in 787. The same may well be true of the classic sub-Balkan route, the Via Egnatia, where the line between Heraclea and Trajanopolis probably conceals several of the new sees: *mansio Registo* had long been Rhaedestus, but *mansio Sirogellis* should be identical with Garella, and *mansio Gipsila* is certainly identical with Cypsella.[41] It is indeed very noticeable that a map of the communications-system of the Balkans demonstrates a very high proportion of the sees/cities to have been on the relatively few arterial roads and major routes. (Map 17)

[39] Anonymous, *Itinerarium Burdigalense*, 569; ed. Cuntz, p. 90.

[40] Jones, *Cities of the Eastern Roman Provinces*, p. 524 (table 2).

[41] Anonymous, *Itinerarium Burdigalense*, 601–2; ed. Cuntz, p. 99. Jones, *Cities of the Eastern Roman Provinces*, pp. 524–5 (tables 2, 5).

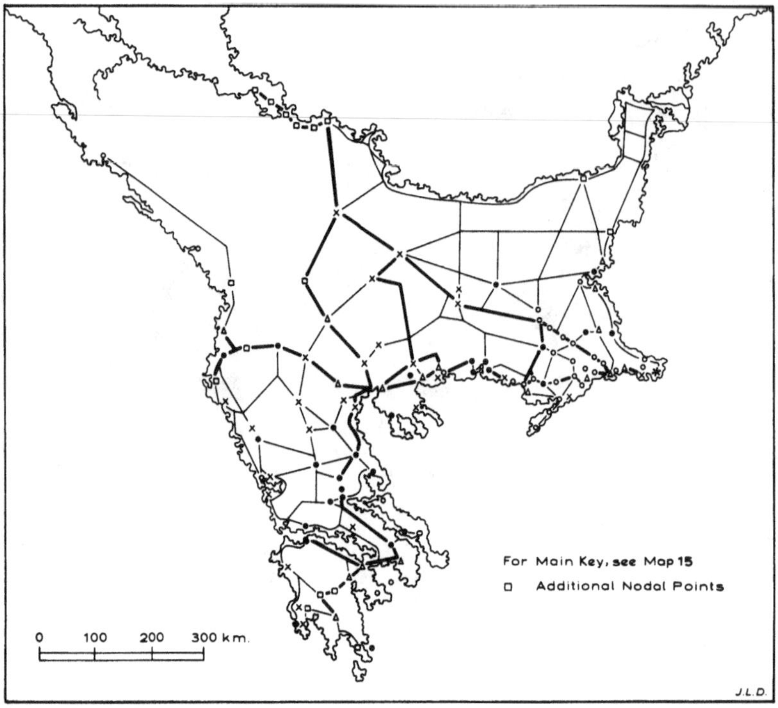


Map 17 The Balkans: communications

In the early ninth century, two major events occurred in quick succession that were drastically to affect the pattern of sees. In 805, the Peloponnese was brought back under Byzantine control, resettled, given a new ecclesiastical structure, and subjected to a process of rehellenisation.[42] In 809/10, the emperor Nicephorus I ordered Christian colonists to be brought from each theme to the *Sklaviniai*, having sold off their belongings.[43] It is possible that the colonisation of Slav areas mentioned here was limited to the recently recovered Peloponnese, but it seems virtually certain that a much wider-ranging measure and more extensive areas were involved.[44]

In 811, Nicephorus was defeated and killed in the Balkan Mountains by the Bulgars under their khan Krum (803–14), and his several briefly reigning successors were also defeated by the same enemy on a number of occasions.[45] The devastation that ensued was appalling: it included the destruction of Develtus, Mesembria and Adrianople, and the abandonment of Anchialus, Berrhoe and Philippopolis, all in upper or middle Thrace.

[42] Lemerle, 'La Chronique improprement dite de Monemvasie', pp. 16–40. Herrin, 'Aspects of the Process of Hellenization', pp. 113–26. A. Bon, *Le Péloponnèse byzantin jusqu'en 1204*, pp. 43–8.

[43] Theophanes, *Chronographia*; ed. de Boor, I, p. 486.

[44] Lemerle, 'Le Chronique improprement dite de Monemvasie', pp. 28–9. Bon, *Le Péloponnèse byzantin*, p. 47.

[45] See below, pp. 272–3.

It also included the destruction of Arcadiopolis, Selymbria, Daonium, Rhaedestus and Aprus, all in lower Thrace.[46]

Despite this, the elaborate treaty that was arranged in 815/16 between Leo V and Krum's successor Omurtag (814–31), – which was to last thirty years and which was given definition by the construction of the ditch and rampart called the Great Fence – was surprisingly generous to the Byzantines: the frontier was advanced southwards, but the Black Sea ports, Adrianople, Philippopolis and Serdica, were all apparently (or at least formally) left in Byzantine hands; some arrangement was also arrived at concerning the Slav tribes that both Byzantines and Bulgars had under their loose control.[47]

The treaty was subject to rectification, whether informal or formal, on several occasions during its long life: under Malamir (831–6), Serdica seems to have fallen into Bulgar hands; and under Boris (852–89), the Black Sea ports together with a strip of Thracian territory seem to have been ceded to the Bulgars.[48] Under Boris, some arrangement seems also to have been arrived at concerning territory in the western Balkans (i.e. Macedonia), and this seems to have resulted in the empire recognising the acquisition, by the Bulgars, of the whole region around Mount Grammus, and Lakes Ochrida and Prespa.[49]

Against this background, the Lists of 869/79 reveal a changed pattern of sees that makes some sense. The presence of sees such as Patras and Methone in the western Peloponnese clearly testifies to the empire's recovery of that area. The presence of sees such as Larissa, Demetrias, Pharsalus, Zetunium, Ezerum, Trikkala and Neopatras in the Thessalian plain, and those such as Peritheorium, Xanthia, Pora, Mosynopolis and Macre in the narrow plain between the rivers Nestus and Hebrus (Maritsa), very strongly suggests that these areas may have been two of the *Sklaviniai* colonised under Nicephorus. Certainly, both areas had been settled by Slavs: Larissa alone had previously and doubtfully appeared in Thessaly in *c.* 800; and the intervening region of the Strymon was the scene of their activities as early as 678 and as late as 821.[50] At last, Thebes also puts in an appearance (869), and so does Naupactus (879).

Now, according to the *Continuation of Theophanes*,[51] the empress Theodora (842–56) had ceded to the Bulgars the deserted territory from Sidera as far as Develtus (*erēmēn ousan apo tēs Sidēras akhri tēs Develtou*) and, whatever the precise topographical interpretation of this phrase, the Black Sea ports, devastated by Krum, should have been included.[52] Sure enough, in 869, the only see appearing which might have been included

[46] S. Runciman, *A History of the First Bulgarian Empire*, pp. 56–67.

[47] *Ibid.* pp. 71–4.

[48] *Ibid.* pp. 87, 90–1.

[49] *Ibid.* p. 104.

[50] Teall, 'The Grain Supply of the Byzantine Empire', pp. 121–3. A. P. Avramea, *Hē Vyzantinē Thessalia mekhri tou 1204* (table 2, at end). R.-J. Lilie, *Die byzantinische Reaktion auf die Ausbreitung der Araber: Studien zur Strukturwandlung des byzantinischen Staates im 7. und 8. Jhdt.*, p. 215 (and n. 44).

[51] *Continuation of Theophanes* IV; ed. I. Bekker (Bonn edn), p. 165.

[52] See above, and p. 82.

in this region is that of Berra which, as it appears with Tzurullum and Heraclea, is presumably Thracian Berrhoe and not Macedonian Berrhoia. Yet, in 879, Mesembria, Anchialus and Develtus all appear, as does Achrida (Ochrida) which, as it appears in that form and not as Achridos, is presumably the Macedonian city and not the Rhodopean region. Thus, for the first time, the list of Balkan sees represented at a council does not closely coincide with the actual frontier of the empire.

The reason for this, and what must have happened, seems clear. Obviously after the conversion of Boris in 864, and presumably between 869 and 879, the Black Sea ports, which had all previously been sees, had had bishops appointed to them, and these, although the ports were now in Bulgarian territory, can only have been Byzantine appointments. This, of course, although historically understandable, technically infringed the rights of the papacy which, established in 866 but rejected in 870, were the cause of so much acrimony in Papal–Byzantine relations.[53] It seems equally clear that, at some stage, a Byzantine bishop had been appointed also to Ochrida, which was again in Bulgarian territory, and which was later to be the scene of much missionary activity, and eventually the seat of the Bulgarian patriarchate.[54] These measures can only have served further to irritate Papal–Byzantine relations.

The final stratum to be added to the map of the distribution of sees in the Balkans is that represented by surviving episcopal seals. This stratum demonstrates a strong tendency to spread, however thinly, into northern Greece and the inner Balkans, therefore presumably betraying not simply a geographical distinctiveness, but also a chronological one, the phenomenon as a whole necessarily post-dating the Byzantine recovery of those areas in the early eleventh century.

The resultant map, with all its imperfections, demonstrates the pattern of distribution to have been a highly accentuated one, with the vast majority of sees (and therefore presumably of cities) to have been concentrated within what is probably considerably less than half the total surface area of the peninsula. Whole stretches of territory in Dalmatia (which was in any case only loosely attached to the empire at the best of times), in the plain between the Danube and the Balkan Mountains, and in the Pindus Mountains, remain devoid of sees and cities. With regard to each of these areas, the crusading and Byzantine historians whose works have been quoted as evidence of their unpopulated nature should be remembered: the two totally different sources of evidence support each other.[55] The mountainous centre of the Peloponnese and the Rhodope also remain bare. The concentrations of sees are equally dramatic: overwhelmingly the largest and densest of these is that in lower Thrace, wedged between the Rhodope and Istranja Mountains. Again, with regard to this, the evidence of the crusading historians, contrasting

[53] F. Dvornik, *The Photian Schism: History and Legend*, pp. 113–215.

[54] F. Dvornik, *Byzantine Missions among the Slavs: SS. Constantine-Cyril and Methodius*, pp. 248–9, 254–5.

[55] See above, pp. 35–9.

the deserted nature of the upper stretches of the trans-Balkan route with the populous, fertile and well-citied nature of the lower stretches in consistent combination, should also be remembered.[56] Other and much smaller concentrations occur: right along the narrow ribbon of plain between the Rhodope and Aegean, in Macedonia, in Thessaly, along the western coast of the Peloponnese, and around the Ambracian Gulf.

The phenomenon is not, of course, purely one of Byzantine policy or physical structure, for this latter, at least, inevitably had implications for climate, natural vegetation and land-use. It seems that the concentration of sees/cities occurs overwhelmingly in areas that possessed a classic or transitional Mediterranean climate, that were low-lying, and that possessed a certain flexibility in the choice of crops, and more particularly a suitability for cereal cultivation. Where not all of these apparent pre-requisites are met, sees/cities very quickly become sparse.[57] (Maps 1–4)

### *B. The distribution of magnates*

A map based on a list of eleventh-century Balkan landed magnates, derived largely from casual sources, and drawn up so as to illustrate their regional origins, or their ownership of estates, or both, where they are recorded, demonstrates an overwhelming proportion, approximately three-quarters of the total (36), to have originated or to have owned estates in the four areas of Macedonia (13), the Peloponnese (5), Thrace (4) and Thessaly (4). It is of course difficult to be sure when, say, Macedonia is involved, whether the theme of that name or the rather wider traditional area is intended, for the two are in this case not identical. The evidence seems to suggest, however, that it is the thematic definition which is at least generally being followed. Other much smaller and less dense concentrations occur in Attica (3), Boeotia (2), Crete (2), and even Constantinople (3).[58] (Map 18)

The methodology involved, necessarily relying as it does upon the rare and largely casual occurrence of such magnates' names, origins and ownership of estates, is admittedly an extremely crude one, but the results are so overwhelming in their proportions as to suggest it to be essentially sound.

What is significant is that the major concentrations of magnates are essentially identical with major concentrations of sees/cities, and with major concentrations of land that by structure, climate, natural vegetation and land-use, are also well defined and consistent.[59] (Maps 1–4, 14–17)

A map based on twelfth-century evidence, and drawn up in an attempt to illustrate

[56] See above, pp. 35–9.

[57] See above, pp. 69, 72, 75.

[58] S. Vryonis, 'The Internal History of Byzantium during the "Time of Troubles" (1057–81)', pp. 395–6 (n. 118). See also below, pp. 131–2, 136–8.

[59] See above, pp. 21–5, 35–9, 69–75.

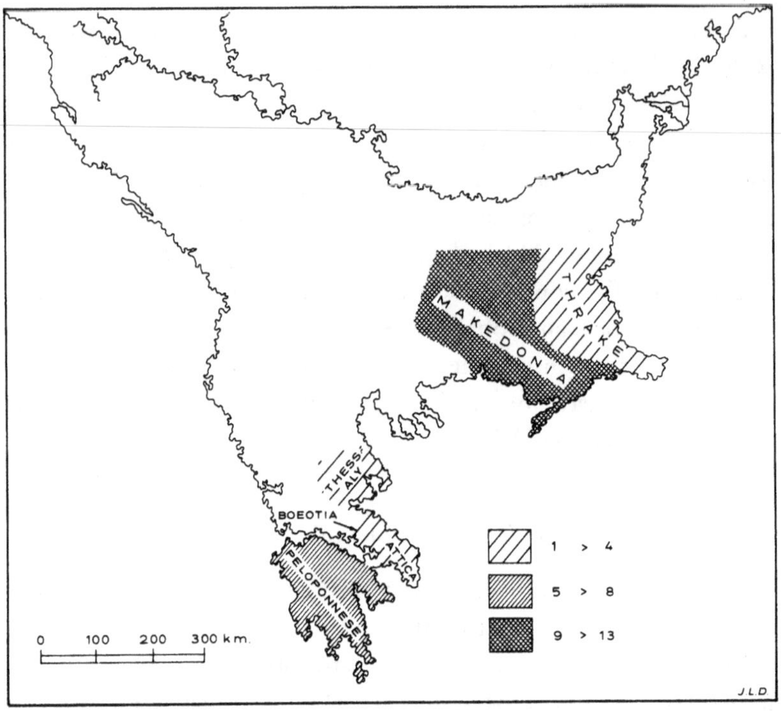


Map 18 The Balkans: magnates' origins and estates (to *c.* 1100)

a rather more complex situation, nevertheless shows concordant results. It was during the later eleventh and twelfth centuries that, with the advent of the Comnenian dynasty – and the growing consciousness of imperial descent by blood or relationship by marriage, precise status and proximity to the throne being indicated by the granting of titles of a quasi-imperial nature, all of which resulted in the evolution of what was essentially an imperial clan – it was considered necessary or desirable to provide for dependent members of the clan through a share in the revenues of the state. This could be achieved in three major ways: by the grant to the dependant of the right to collect state taxation over a defined area, by the direct grant of state revenues, and by the direct grant of state lands. In the twelfth century it seems to have been the first of these that was favoured. The following represents an attempt to draw up a preliminary list of such major grants (frequently, but not entirely satisfactorily, termed 'appanages') for the Balkans (Map 19).[60]

[60] For the full names of the authors and the full titles of the works listed below, see the Bibliographies (below, from p. 670). To this list there should probably be added (8 bis): To Maria Tzousmene (daughter of John II, wife of John Roger (8)), reg. Hierissus; refs: Bompaire, *Actes de Xéropotamou*, no. 8, pp. 67–71.

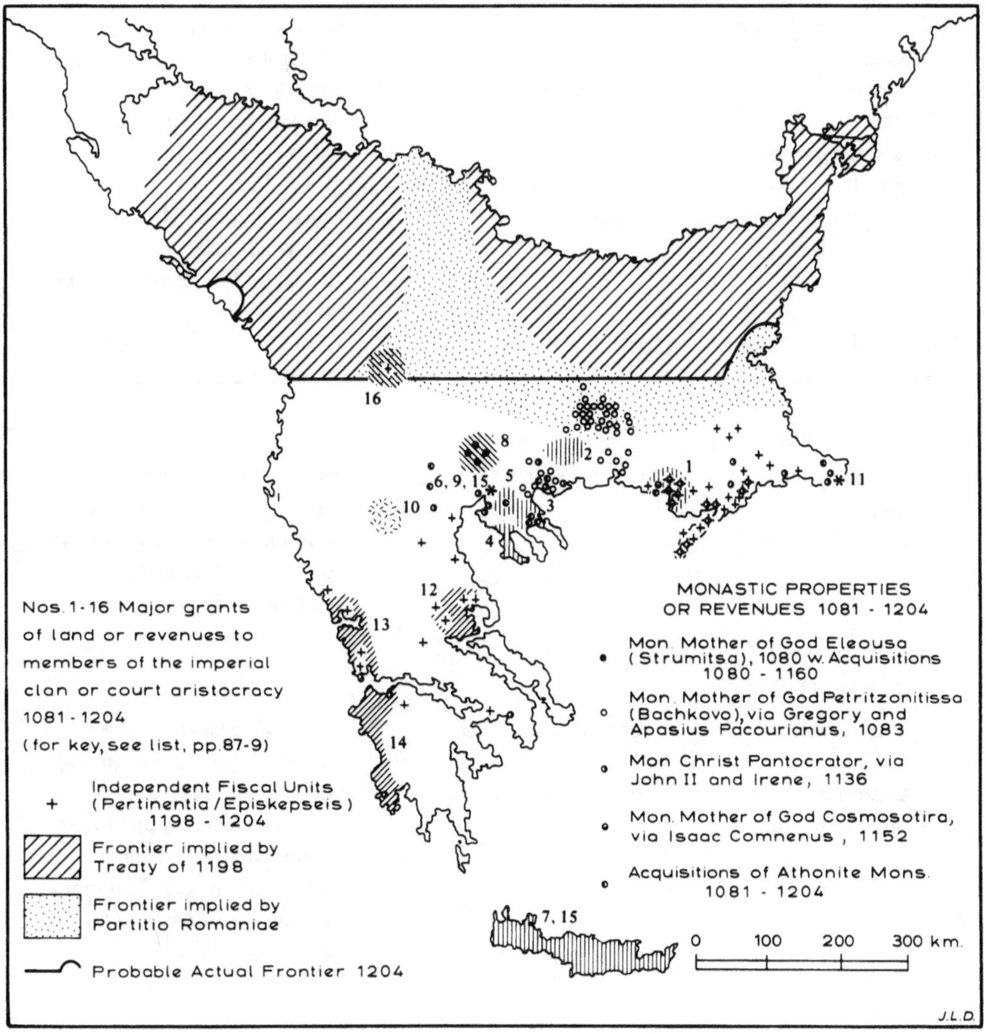


Map 19 The Balkans: imperial, aristocratic and monastic estates (to 1204)

## ALEXIUS I (1081–1118)

| | | |
|---|---|---|
| 1. To Isaac Comnenus (son) | reg. Trajanopolis, Aenus | Petit, in *Izvestiya Russkago Arkheologicheskago Instituta v Konstantinopole* 13 (1908), at pp. 52–3. |
| 2. To Gregory Pacourianus (*megas domestikos*) | reg. Smolena (?) | Petit, in *Vizantiĭskiĭ Vremennik* 11 (1904), Suppl. 1, at pp. 55–6; Ahrweiler, *Byzance et la mer*, p. 213; cf. Lemerle, *Cinq études sur le XI siècle byzantin*, p. 156. |

| | | |
|---|---|---|
| 3. To Nicephorus Comnenus (brother) (?) | reg. Hierissus | Bompaire, *Actes de Xéropotamou*, no. 7, pp. 64–7. |
| 4. To Adrian Comnenus (brother) | reg. Cassandrea | Lemerle *et al.*, *Actes de Lavra* I, no. 46, pp. 247–51. |
| 5. To Isaac Comnenus (brother) | reg. Peristera, Thessalonica | *ibid.* no. 51, pp. 269–71. |
| 6. To Nicephorus Melissenus (brother-in-law) | Thessalonica | Anna Comnena, *Alexiad* II.8.3; ed. Leib, I, p. 89. Zonaras, *Epit.* XVIII.21.11–13; Bonn edn, III, p. 732. |
| 7. To Nicephorus Diogenes (porphyrogenitus) | is. Crete | Anna Comnena, *Alexiad* IX.6.3; ed. Leib, II, p. 173 |

JOHN II (1118–43)

| | | |
|---|---|---|
| 8. To John-Roger (son-in-law) | reg. Strumitsa | Petit, in *Izvestiya Russkago Arkheologicheskago Instituta v Konstantinopole* 6 (1900), at pp. 36–46. Ferjančić, in *Zbornik Radova* 12 (1970), at pp. 193–201. |

MANUEL I (1143–80)

| | | |
|---|---|---|
| 9. To John-Renier (son-in-law) | Thessalonica | Brand, *Byzantium Confronts the West*, pp. 19, 319 (n. 12) |
| 10. To Andronicus Comnenus (cousin) | reg. Castoria | Nicetas Choniates, *Historia*; ed. van Dieten, I, pp. 101–2. Cinnamus, *Epitome* III.16; Bonn edn, p. 124. Maksimović, in *Zbornik Radova* 14/15 (1973), at p. 115. |

ISAAC II (1185–95)

| | | |
|---|---|---|
| 11. To Alexius Angelus (brother) | Constantinople, Port of Bucoleon | Aubrey of Trois-Fontaines, *Chronica*; MGH, *SS* XXIII, p. 870. Brand, *Byzantium Confronts the West*, pp. 111, 345 (n. 83). |

ALEXIUS III (1195–1203)

| | | |
|---|---|---|
| 12. To Euphrosyne Ducaena (wife) | reg. Thessaly | Tafel and Thomas, *Urkunden* I, p. 487. |
| 13. To sebastocrators and caesars (unnamed), daughters (prob. Irene and Anna), and wife (Euphrosyne Ducaena) | reg. Nicopolis | Tafel and Thomas, *Urkunden* I, p. 264. |

| | | |
|---|---|---|
| 14. To Irene Ducaena (daughter) | reg. Patras, Modon (shared w. Branas and Cantacuzene families) | *ibid.* pp. 469–70. |
| ALEXIUS IV (1203–4) | | |
| 15. To Boniface of Montferrat | is. Crete, Thessalonica (?) | *ibid.* pp. 512–15. |
| ALEXIUS I OR JOHN II (?) | | |
| 16. To Alexius (son of Theodora porphyrogenita, the daughter of Alexius I) (?) | reg. Scopia (inc. Nerezi) (?) | Kondakov, *Makedoniya*, p. 174; Tafel and Thomas, *Urkunden* I, pp. 261–2 |

It is generally recognised that the fiscal term *episkepsis* is applied, during the twelfth and thirteenth centuries, to an estate that to a greater or lesser extent possessed an independent administrative status, and therefore at least in the main to an estate belonging to the state, or over which rights were exercised by members of the imperial clan or of the court aristocracy, by grant from the state. The most complete list of such *episkepseis*, which were numerous, and which were termed *pertinentia* in the Latin, is that obtained by combining the territorial descriptions in the Veneto-Byzantine Treaty of 1198 and the *Partitio Romaniae* of 1204,[61] both of which seem to have been based on cadastral documents of some kind.[62] (Map 19)

In the course of the late eleventh and twelfth centuries a number of great imperial or aristocratic monasteries were founded, the *typika* of some of which survive and contain descriptions of the properties left to them by their founders. Three such *typika*, involving as they do mainly Balkan properties, are of particular relevance and significance: that of the Mother of God Petritzonitissa at Bachkovo, founded by the *sebastos* Gregory Pacourianus in 1083;[63] that of Christ Pantocrator in Constantinople, founded by John II and his wife Irene in 1136;[64] and that of the Mother of God Cosmosotira at Pherae, founded by the *sebastokratōr* Isaac Comnenus in 1152.[65] All three of these as it happens

[61] Tafel and Thomas, *Urkunden* I, pp. 258–72 (1198), pp. 464–93 (1204). A. Carile, 'Partitio Terrarum Imperii Romanie', *Studi Veneziani* 7 (1965), pp. 217–22.

[62] N. Oikonomides, 'La décomposition de l'empire byzantin à la veille de 1204 et les origines de l'empire de Nicée: à propos de la "Partitio Romaniae"', *XV^e Congrès International d'Études Byzantines, Athènes 1976, Rapports et Co-rapports* I, pp. 11–12.

[63] Ed. L. Petit, in 'Typikon de Grégoire Pacourianos pour le monastère de Pétritzos (Bačkovo) en Bulgarie', *Vizantiĭskiĭ Vremennik* 11 (1904), Supp. I, at pp. 10–14, 55–6 (text). P. Lemerle, 'Le typikon de Grégoire Pakourianos (décembre 1083)', in *Cinq études sur le XI^e siècle byzantin*, at pp. 175–81 (topographical commentary and map).

[64] P. Gautier, 'Le typikon du Christ Sauveur Pantocrator', *Revue des Études Byzantines* 32 (1974), pp. 114–24.

[65] Ed. L. Petit, in 'Typikon du monastère de la Kosmosotira près d'Aenos (1152)', *Izvestiya Russkago Arkheologicheskago Instituta v Konstantinopole* 13 (1908), at pp. 52–3.

involve properties that had originally belonged to the state and were being transferred into private hands, whether directly or indirectly, together with a considerable or even complete fiscal immunity. (Map 19)

Over the same period of time, the contents of monastic archives, frequently recording the acquisition, sale or exchange of properties, also become fuller. Of these the Athonite archives are, of course, the most notable, in particular that of the Lavra. Not all are relevant in containing twelfth-century material in the form of acquisitions, but several are.[66] Also known are the acquisitions of the monastery of the Mother of God Eleousa, founded by the monk Manuel, bishop of Strumitsa, at Strumitsa in 1080.[67] These properties, too, had originally belonged to the state, were transferred into private hands, and were fiscally immune.

The map resulting from the combination of all these separate elements (Map 19), as already mentioned,[68] demonstrates features that are in entire concordance with those of the previous ones: all the great 'appanages' (with the possible and partial exception of that granted out to Alexius, the son of Theodora Comnena), the overwhelming majority of *episkepseis*, and of monastic properties and acquisitions, involve the same very limited areas as do the maps of sees/cities and of magnates. These are themselves all very much in concordance with the tenor of the contemporary descriptions given by crusading and Byzantine historians, and indeed with that of the observations made by William of Tyre.[69]

## (III) ANATOLIA

### A. *The distribution of cities*

In Anatolia, the later distribution of sees resembles strongly that of cities obtaining in the fifth century, and itself remains essentially static throughout, reflecting a continuity of political control that is lacking in the Balkans. This is perhaps less evident in the map based upon the councils of 680/1 and 691/2 than in those based upon the council of 787 and the synods of 869/70 and 879, but this is surely due more to the reduced number of sees represented in the two earliest councils than to anything else. It seems clear that the reduced representation was itself due to the disturbed conditions prevalent in Anatolia

[66] P. Lemerle, *Actes de Kutlumus* (= Archives de l'Athos II). J. Bompaire, *Actes de Xéropotamou* (= Archives de l'Athos III). N. Oikonomides, *Actes de Dionysiou* (= Archives de l'Athos IV). P. Lemerle, A. Guillou, and N. Svoronos, *Actes de Lavra* I (= Archives de l'Athos V). J. Lefort, *Actes d'Esphigménou* (= Archives de l'Athos VI). D. Papachryssanthou, *Actes du Prôtaton* (= Archives de l'Athos VII). Earlier publications, involving documents from the monasteries of Chilandar, Pantocrator, Philotheou, Xenophon and Zographou (refs: Lemerle *et al.*, *Actes de Lavra* I, p. vii), are uniformly unhelpful in this respect.

[67] L. Petit, 'Le Monastère de Notre-Dame de Pitié en Macédoine', *Izvestiya Russkago Arkheologicheskago Instituta v Konstantinopole* 6 (1900–1), pp. 6–13, 25–68.

[68] See above, p. 85.

[69] See above, pp. 35–9.

at the time, the four-year long first Arab siege of Constantinople (674–8) then being still a recent event. Indeed, the *Acta* of the council of 691/2 expressed the hope that clerics (*klērikoi*) resident in the capital under the pretext of barbarian invasion (*prophasei barbarikēs epidromēs*) may return to their posts with the restoration of settled conditions.[70] Although the particular factor will have tended to boost attendance, it seems reasonable to suppose that other – and indeed more – clerics were detained by local conditions, which will have tended actually to reduce overall attendance. The only other appreciable difference between the maps is the disappearance of the Cilician sees between 680/91 and 787, reflecting their loss to the Arabs at the beginning of the eighth century. (Maps 20–2)

Because of the somewhat different principle upon which the later maps, as contrasted with the fifth-century one, were constructed (sees of very uncertain identity or site were simply omitted and not placed haphazardly within the putative or even appropriate province), the later maps exhibit a greater degree of sensitivity to the existence of relatively minor internal distinctions. This is even more the case with a single map combining the evidence of the later ones and that of the seals. The combined map (Map 23), while confirming the general tenor of the later ones, permits the full complexity of the factors behind the distribution of contemporary cities or sees to be seen or deduced. It thus emerges that, although the distribution of cities or sees can be explained immediately in terms of particular historical events, developments or policies, nevertheless the primary parameters within which these operated were of a structural or climatic nature, or a mixture of both, and in any case doubtless possessed significant implications in the spheres of land-use and agriculture.

The combined map in fact demonstrates the pattern of distribution to have been a highly accentuated one. The cities or sees involved formed a relatively small number of concentrations, of a greater or lesser extent or density, or both, which were separated off from each other by stretches of open (or virtually open) land, frequently of vast extent.

The first of these concentrations (1), as great as any in extent, and greater than almost all in density, involves the land delineated by the Bakır Çayı in the north and the Dalaman Çayı in the south, extending with decreasing width from the Aegean eastwards towards the interior. In historical territorial and administrative terms it includes the late Roman and early Byzantine provinces of Asia & Lydia together with the northern part of Caria. It is thus effectively co-extensive with the coastal plain and the river-valleys of the west extending, by way of a relatively gentle gradient, approximately up as far as the 500 m contour-line. (Maps 5, 23)

The second (2) is smaller in extent but as great in density, involving a broad arc of land tending to block off the first from the interior and particularly in the north, even to enclose it. In historical territorial and administrative terms it includes the late Roman and early Byzantine province of Phrygia Pacatiana and the western parts of Phrygia

[70] Mansi, *Sacrorum Conciliorum Nova et Amplissima Collectio* XI, col. 951.

Map 20 Anatolia: distribution of sees/cities, 680/1, 691/2

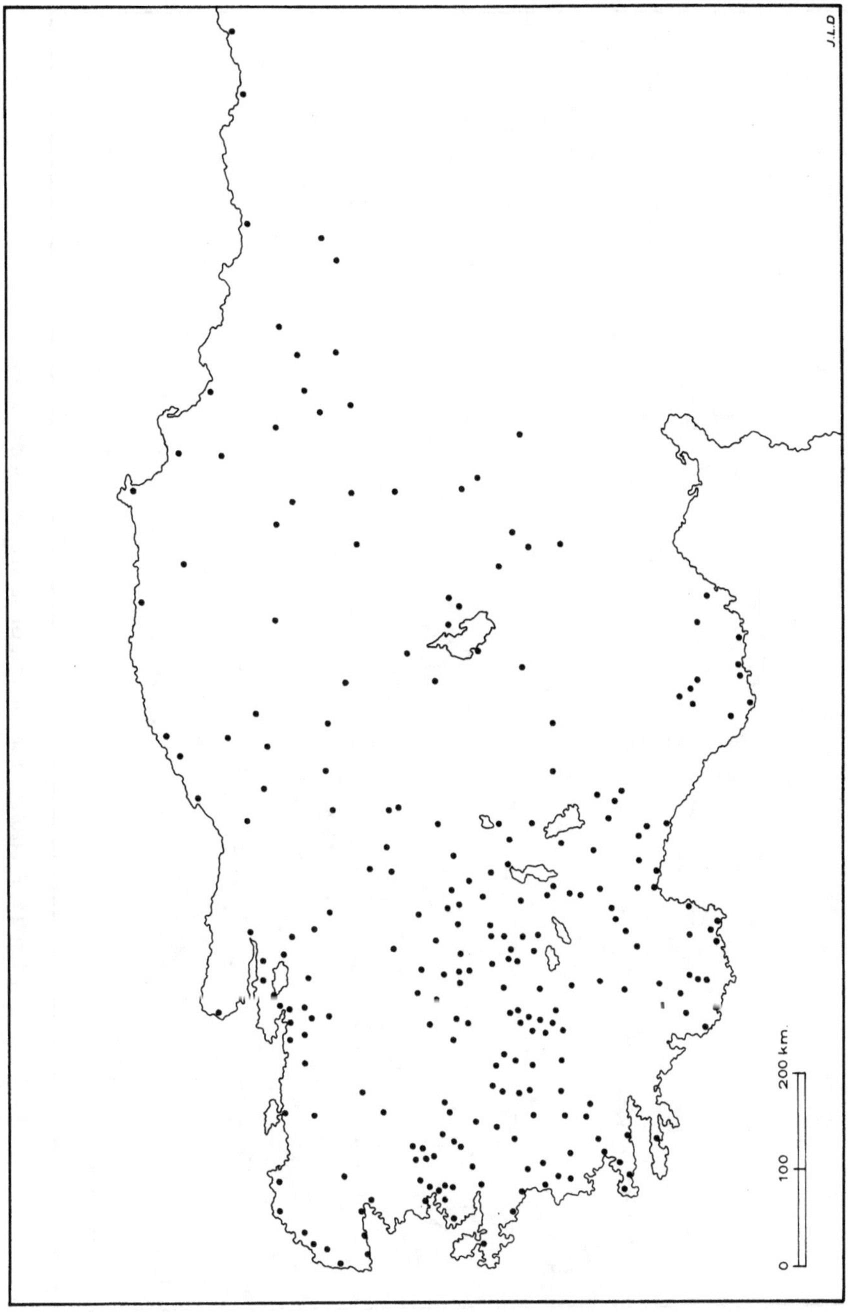


Map 21 Anatolia: distribution of sees/cities, 787

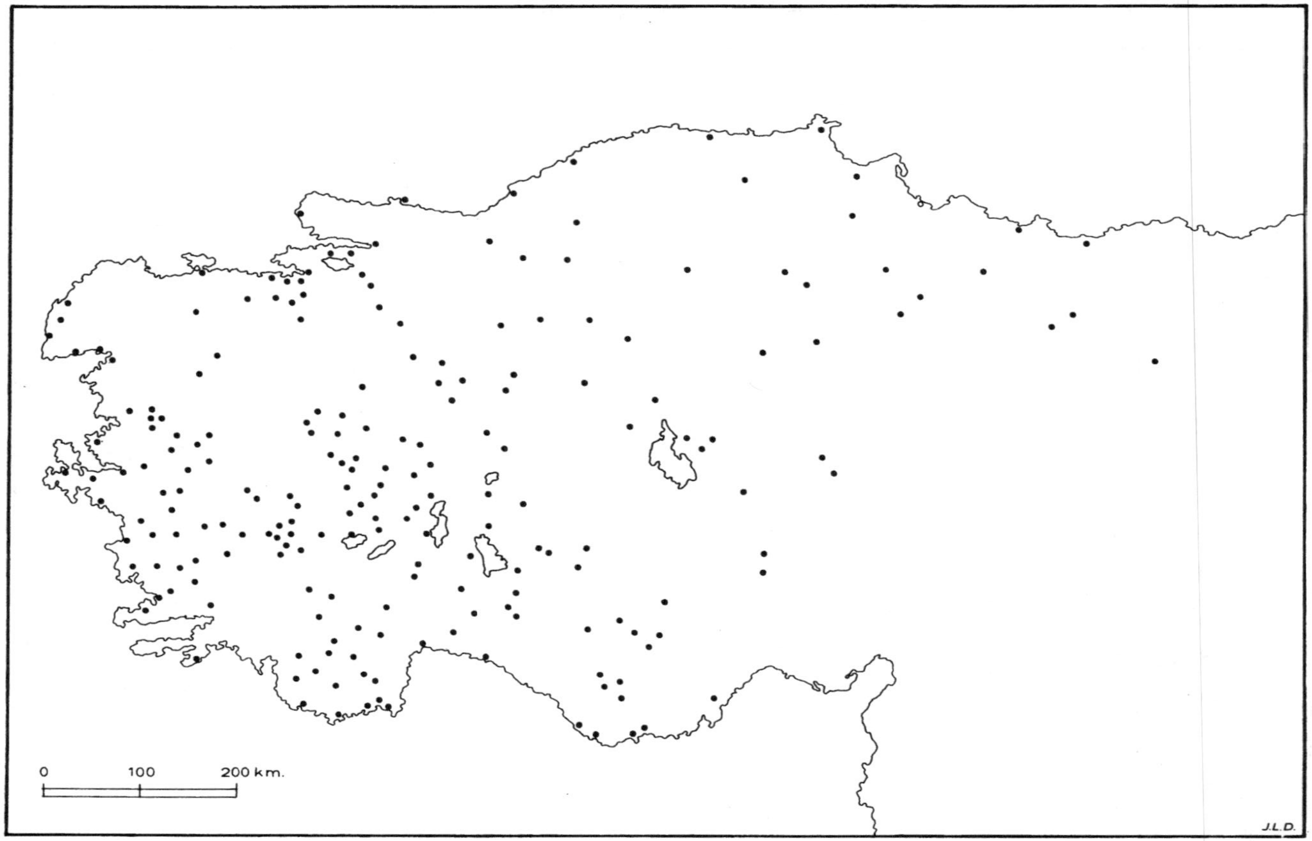


Map 22 Anatolia: distribution of sees/cities, 869/70, 879

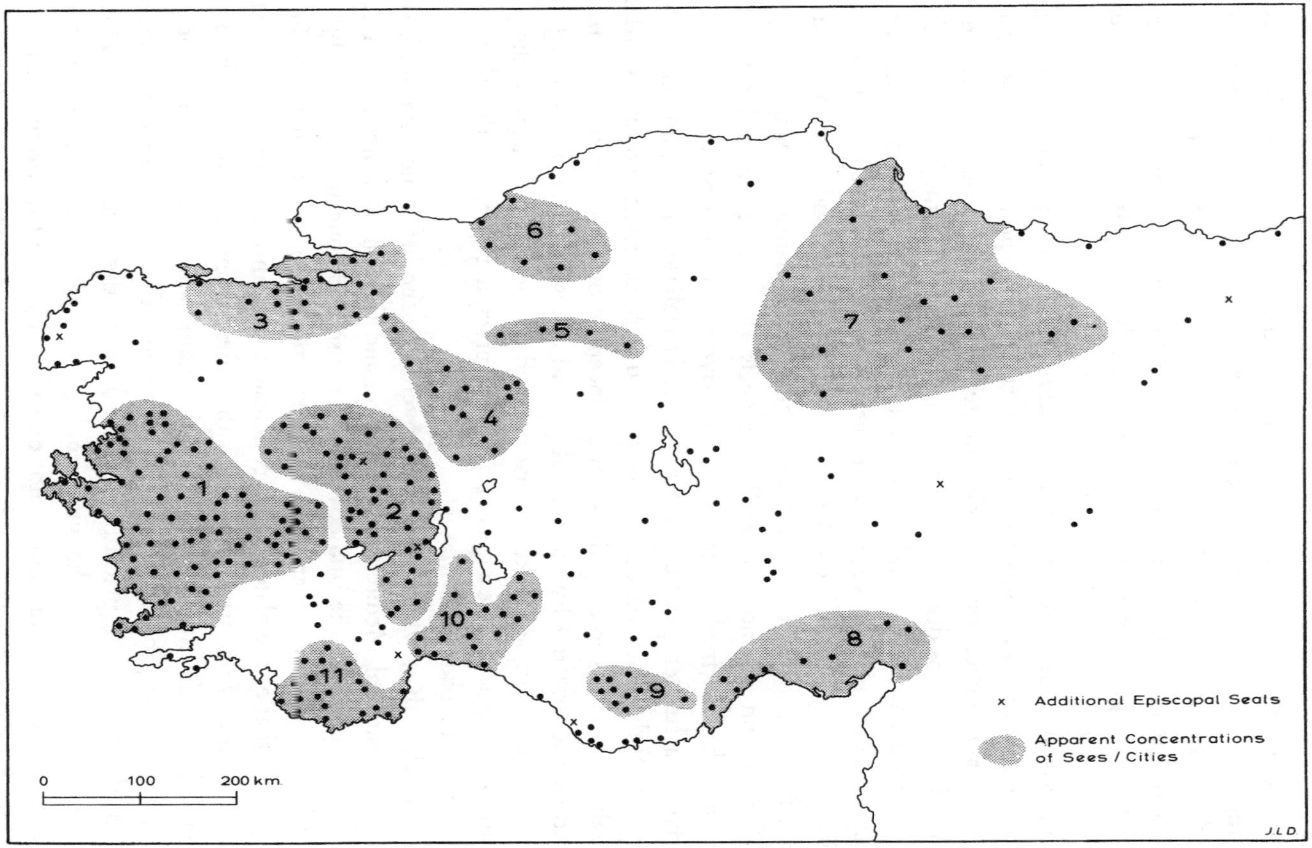


Map 23 Anatolia: distribution of sees/cities, 680/1–879

Salutaris (in the north) and Pisidia (in the south). It thus mainly covers the transitional ground rising, by way of a relatively steep gradient, up towards the central plateau, including the headwaters of the Gediz and the Büyük Menderes and their various tributaries, and extending from the 500 m contour-line approximately up as far as the 1,000 m one, although in certain areas – particularly towards its eastern limits – it somewhat exceeds the latter. (Maps 5, 23)

The distinction in distance from the coast, relative gradient and absolute height between the land covered by the two concentrations described in the preceding paragraphs must have had significant implications for their climate, land-use and agriculture. Examination of a series of climatic maps drawn up on a seasonal basis reveals the land covered by the bulk of both the first and the second concentrations to fall within the same single bracket over against the central plateau as regards the average temperature range, and mean annual precipitation (Maps 6, 7), and the land covered by the second concentration to be intermediate between that covered by the first and by the plateau as regards the number of days of frost and of snow-cover.[71] It reveals the land covered by the second concentration to be intermediate between that covered by the first and by the central plateau as regards actual temperatures in January, and to fall within the same single bracket as that covered by the first over against the plateau as regards temperatures in March.[72] It also reveals the land covered by the second concentration to be intermediate between that covered by the first and by the central plateau as regards precipitation in January, to fall within the same single bracket as that covered by the first over against the plateau in March, and actually to receive a greater degree of precipitation than either that covered by the first or by the plateau in May.[73]

It thus seems clear that, whereas the land covered by the first concentration is subject to a classic or transitional Mediterranean climate, and the central plateau to an equally straightforward steppe one, the land covered by the second concentration is subject to a climate which, while basically that of the first, nevertheless betrays distinct modifications in the direction of that of the plateau. The conclusion is, admittedly, not a surprising one: the physical structure of the areas involved is thus merely reflected climatically. Perhaps the most generally significant fact revealed by the examination is that in no major respect and in any case over no prolonged period of time does the land covered by the second concentration share with the plateau the full rigour of the latter's climate. This is of particular significance as regards the winter and spring seasons: on the one hand the land covered by the second concentration is not entirely subject to the prolonged periods of severe sub-zero temperatures, frost and snow-cover that characterise the climate of the plateau in winter; and on the other it is subject to the higher incidence of precipitation

[71] Tanoğlu *et al.*, *Türkiye Atlası*, maps 18, 40. For the general distinctions of climate, see above pp. 26–32.
[72] Tanoğlu *et al.*, *Türkiye Atlası*, maps 19, 20.
[73] *Ibid.* maps 26–8.

that characterises the climate of the land covered by the first concentration in winter and spring. To be sure, the climatic situation is not uniform throughout the land covered by the second concentration: with increasing distance inland and altitude the prevailing climate increasingly resembles and eventually merges with that of the plateau, and this itself has and doubtless had implications for land-use and agriculture. The point is driven home by a description, by the metropolitan of Synnada, Leo, of the conditions prevalent in his see, which will be quoted and discussed shortly.[74]

The third of these concentrations (3) involves the land delimited by the Simav Çayı to the west and the Sakarya to the east, extending virtually right along the coast of the Marmara but never very far back into the interior. In historical territorial and administrative terms it includes most of the late Roman and early Byzantine province of Bithynia. It is thus effectively co-extensive with the coastal plain, being blocked off from the interior by the Bithynian Highlands, and most if not all of it is contained within the 500 m contour-line. (Maps 5, 23)

The fourth (4) involves a large, somewhat pear-shaped, stretch of land, on a north-west to south-east axis, with its narrower end reaching back towards the third, and its broader one extending forward far into the central plateau. In historical territorial and administrative terms it includes much of the later Roman and early Byzantine province of Galatia Salutaris together with the north-eastern part of Phrygia Salutaris. It is thus effectively co-extensive with the great inland basin through which the headwaters of the Sakarya and its tributary the Porsuk Çayı both flow, and much of it lies between the 500 m and 1,000 m contour-lines (Maps 5, 23).

The relationship between the land covered by the third and fourth concentrations, and between that covered by both and the central plateau, parallels quite closely that between the land covered by the first and second concentrations, and between that covered by both and the plateau, as far as physical structure is concerned. The relationship is rather less obviously parallel as far as climate is concerned, the land covered by the fourth concentration being far less open to the Mediterranean climate of the coast and correspondingly more open to the steppe one of the plateau than is the land covered by the second. Even so, some minor and partial degree of alleviation of the full rigours of the climate of the plateau can be detected, particularly as regards actual temperatures in the period January to March.[75] The basic parallelism nevertheless holds good where land-use and agriculture are concerned.

The sixth of these concentrations (6) forms a somewhat ovoid stretch of land with one of its narrower ends abutting onto the coast and the other extending forward into the interior. In historical territorial and administrative terms it includes by far the greater part of the late Roman and early Byzantine (or, more accurately, pre-Justinianic) province

[74] See below, pp. 138–40.

[75] Tanoğlu *et al.*, *Türkiye Atlası*, maps 19, 20.

of Honorias. It is thus effectively co-extensive with the plain of the Filyos at its lower end, and with the basin through which that river and its various tributaries flow at its upper end. Much of the former lies below the 500 m contour-line, and much of the latter between the 500 m and 1,000 m contour-line (Maps 5, 23). Although its upper end, at least, pertains to the central plateau as regards average temperature range (Map 6), the number of days of frost and snow-cover, and even precipitation (Map 7), it is nevertheless spared the lowest temperatures of the period January to March.[76]

The seventh (7) forms a huge, somewhat triangular, stretch of land, lying on an approximately west to east axis, and having two of its sides defined by the great sweep of the Kızılırmak and its tributary the Delice Irmak, and its third by the Kelkit Çayı and Pontic Mountains. In historical territorial and administrative terms it includes the late Roman and early Byzantine (or, more accurately, pre-Justinianic) province of Helenopontus, together with a part of Pontus Polemoniacus and smaller parts of Armenia Prima and Cappadocia Prima. It is thus effectively co-extensive with the exceedingly broken land through which the Kızılırmak and Yeşilırmak and their various tributaries make their way, eventually, to the sea. Much of it lies between the 500 m and 1,000 m contour-lines (Maps 5, 23), and as regards average temperature range (Map 6) and actual temperatures it is spared the full rigours of the climate of the plateau, particularly those of the winter months.[77] Like the second concentration, it actually receives a greater degree of precipitation than much of the plain, or the plateau, in May.[78]

The sixth and seventh concentrations are less easily classifiable than the first to fourth as regards the predominant features of their physical structure, climate, and so on. Each includes both coastal plain and land that is transitional between plain and central plateau, and each therefore has a less uniform and distinctive set of dependent characteristics. The point is again driven home by descriptions, by the metropolitan of Euchaita, John Mauropus, in a series of letters and sermons, of the conditions prevalent in his see, which will again be quoted and discussed shortly.[79]

The eighth of these concentrations (8) forms a swathe of land at the extreme north-eastern head of the Mediterranean and in the south-eastern corner of the Anatolian peninsula, extending inland shallowly only in its western section and much more deeply in its eastern one. In historical territorial and administrative terms it includes the late Roman and early Byzantine provinces of Cilicia Prima or Tracheia, and Cilicia Secunda or Pedias, together with a small fragment of Isauria. It is thus virtually co-extensive with the Cilician Plain and most if not all of it is contained within the 500 m contour line (Maps 5, 23). Climatically it belongs to the Mediterranean in much the same way and to the same marked extent as the land covered by the first and third concentrations (Maps 6, 7).[80]

[76] *Ibid.* maps 18, 40, 19, 20.
[77] *Ibid.* maps 19, 20.
[78] *Ibid.* map 28.
[79] See below, pp. 140–2.
[80] Tanoğlu *et al.*, *Türkiye Atlası*, maps 18, 19–24, 26–31, 40.

The tenth (10) involves an irregular block of land towards the south-western corner of the peninsula. In historical territorial and administrative terms it includes much of the late Roman and early Byzantine province of Pamphylia together with parts of Pisidia. It includes the basins of the Aksu and Köprü, much of it being contained within the 500 m contour-line and most within the 1,000 m line (Maps 5, 23), and climatically it belongs to the Mediterranean (Maps 6, 7).[81]

The eleventh (11) involves a block of land forming a promontory at the south-western corner of the peninsula. In historical territorial and administrative terms it is virtually co-extensive with the late Roman and early Byzantine province of Lycia. Unlike the other concentrations it thus includes a relatively low proportion of the land below 500 m and a relatively high one of land above 1,000 m (the Lycian Taurus) (Maps 5, 23). Climatically, however, it again belongs essentially to the Mediterranean (Maps 6, 7).[82]

Other smaller, less dense, or less well-defined, concentrations, the fifth and ninth in particular, remain as yet unmentioned. The former (5) represents the line of the main road up through the basin of the Sakarya and Porsuk Çayı and on towards Ankara. It also represents the classic route of the *Itinerarium Burdigalense*, and – as in the Balkans, so in Anatolia – the public post seems to have played a significant rôle in the appearance of new sees. The *mansiones* of Agannia (Lagania = Anastasiopolis), Mnizus, Parnassus, Anathiango (Nazianzus) and Sasima along this route are all, with the exception of the last, regularly represented as sees from the second half of the fourth, and from the fifth century, onwards. Paradoxically, it is in respect of the last, Sasima (i.e. Gölcük-Hasköy) that there survives an unflattering description by Gregory of Nazianzen:

> There is a certain post-station (*stathmos*) [the *mansio Sasima* of the *Itinerarium*] at the mid-point of the highway (*leophoros*) through Cappadocia, where it divides into three (*eis trissen hodon*); waterless (*anhydros*), and devoid of vegetation (*akhlous*); a not entirely free, terribly squalid and mean, little village (*komydrion*); with dust (*konis*) everywhere, noise, carriages (*harmata*), lamentations, groans, tax-collectors (*praktores*), tortures and fetters; a population (*laos*) of total strangers (*xenoi*) and vagabonds (*planomenoi*). And this was our church (*ekklēsia*) of Sasima.
>
> (Gregory of Nazianzen, *Carmina* II.I; *PG* XXXVII, 1059–60)

It is true, of course, that Gregory's consecration to the see of Sasima was the result of ecclesiastical politics rather than of legal necessities or pastoral requirements, but even so, the description, however negative in some respects, also conveys an impression of rude vigour, a floating population, and a certain size and varied social and economic basis, thus independently confirming other very approximately contemporary sources.[83] It is

[81] See above, n. 80.

[82] See above, n. 80.

[83] See below, pp. 294–6, 603–7 (economic and monetary functions), 331–2 (provision of standard weights and measures, and of centres of tax-payment). See also below, pp. 311, 610–12 (later: provision of pack-animals for the imperial baggage-train).

therefore presumably significant that a map representing the communications-system of Anatolia demonstrates a high proportion of those sees/cities on the central plateau and in its peripheral areas, which are not included in the major concentrations, nevertheless to be on arterial roads and major routes (Map 24).

The last concentration to be discussed (9) represents the Isaurian decapolis, and is more or less co-extensive with the valley and basin of the Göksu. Most of it lies below the 1,000 m contour-line and, despite its small size, has its own climate, particularly as regards actual temperatures in the winter months.[84]

From this analysis of the distribution of cities, with particular regard to Anatolia over the period *c.* 450–*c.* 900, a number of points emerge. In the first place, as already mentioned, it seems clear that the general pattern of distribution already evident at the beginning of the period in question remained essentially unchanged at the end. The overwhelming majority of cities was concentrated within less than half of the total surface area of the peninsula. This concentration involved the coastal plain and river-valleys and in general land at altitudes of up to approximately 1,000 m, major extensions into the central plateau occurring only where features of physical structure, such as river-valleys and basins, permitted. The largest of these extensions inevitably and in turn entailed modifications, to a greater or lesser degree, in the climate, natural vegetation and pattern of land-use otherwise prevailing on the plateau. Even now, a close connection exists between the former pattern for the distribution of cities, and the present pattern for the concentration of fields, in Anatolia.[85] The close connection between the pattern of distribution and the presence or rather the availability of alluvial deposits also becomes apparent on examination of the geology of the area.[86]

### B. *The distribution of magnates*

The question inevitably arises as to what extent this particular and accentuated pattern of distribution lasted further on into the Byzantine period. It is unfortunately incapable of being answered in any systematic sense owing to the lack of appropriate sources. Two items of evidence of a very different and indeed largely negative type do nevertheless suggest the continuing existence of the pattern in the eleventh and twelfth centuries.

A map based on a list of eleventh-century Anatolian landed magnates, and drawn up so as to illustrate their regional origins by themes, and by concentrated estates, where they are recorded, demonstrates over three-fifths of the total (47) to have originated in the three themes of Anatolikon (13), Kappadokia (10) and Paphlagonia (7). None at all

[84] See above, p. 98, n. 80.
[85] Tanoğlu *et al.*, *Türkiye Atlası*, map 68.
[86] *Ibid.* map 4.

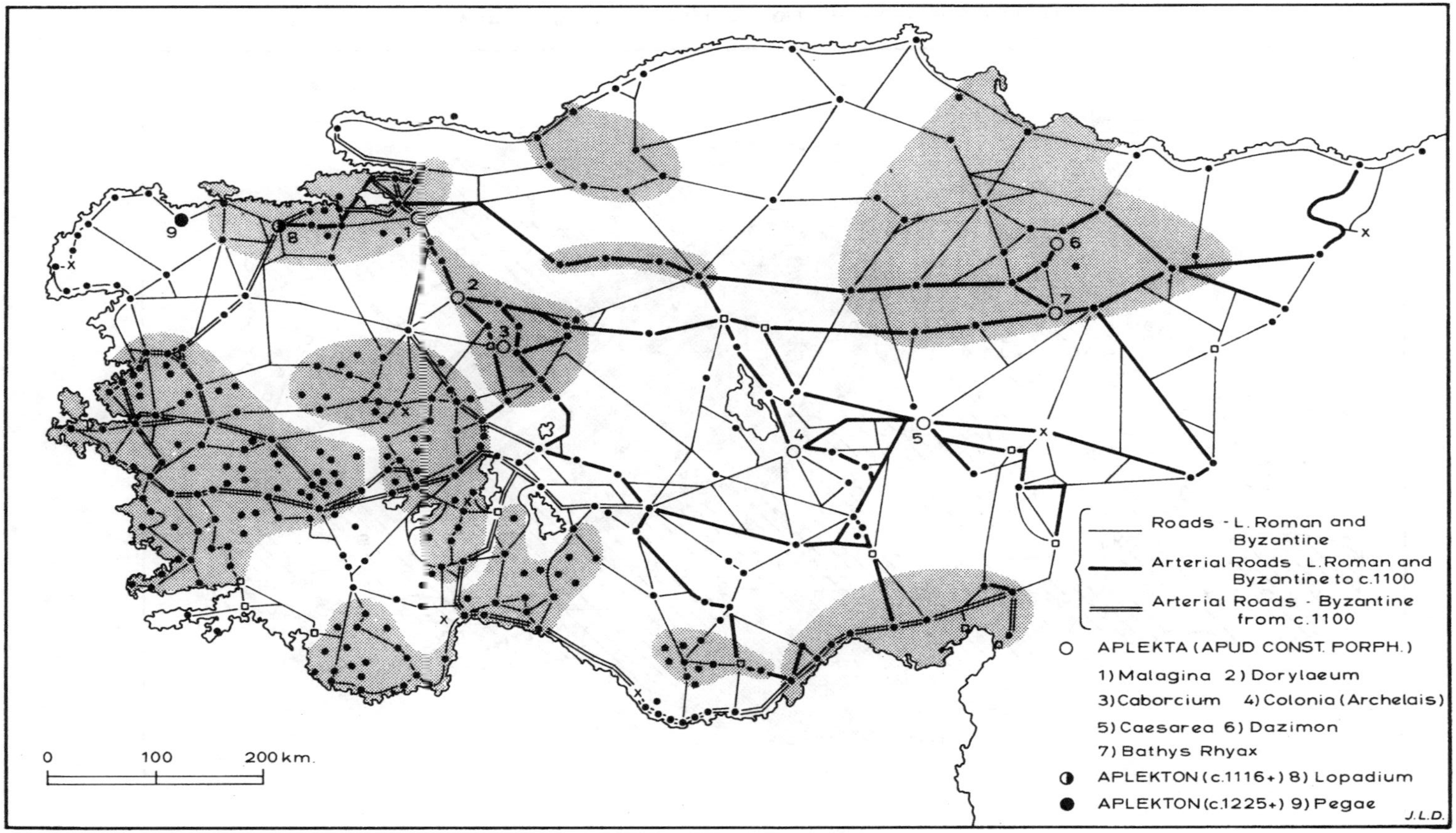


Map 24 Anatolia: communications

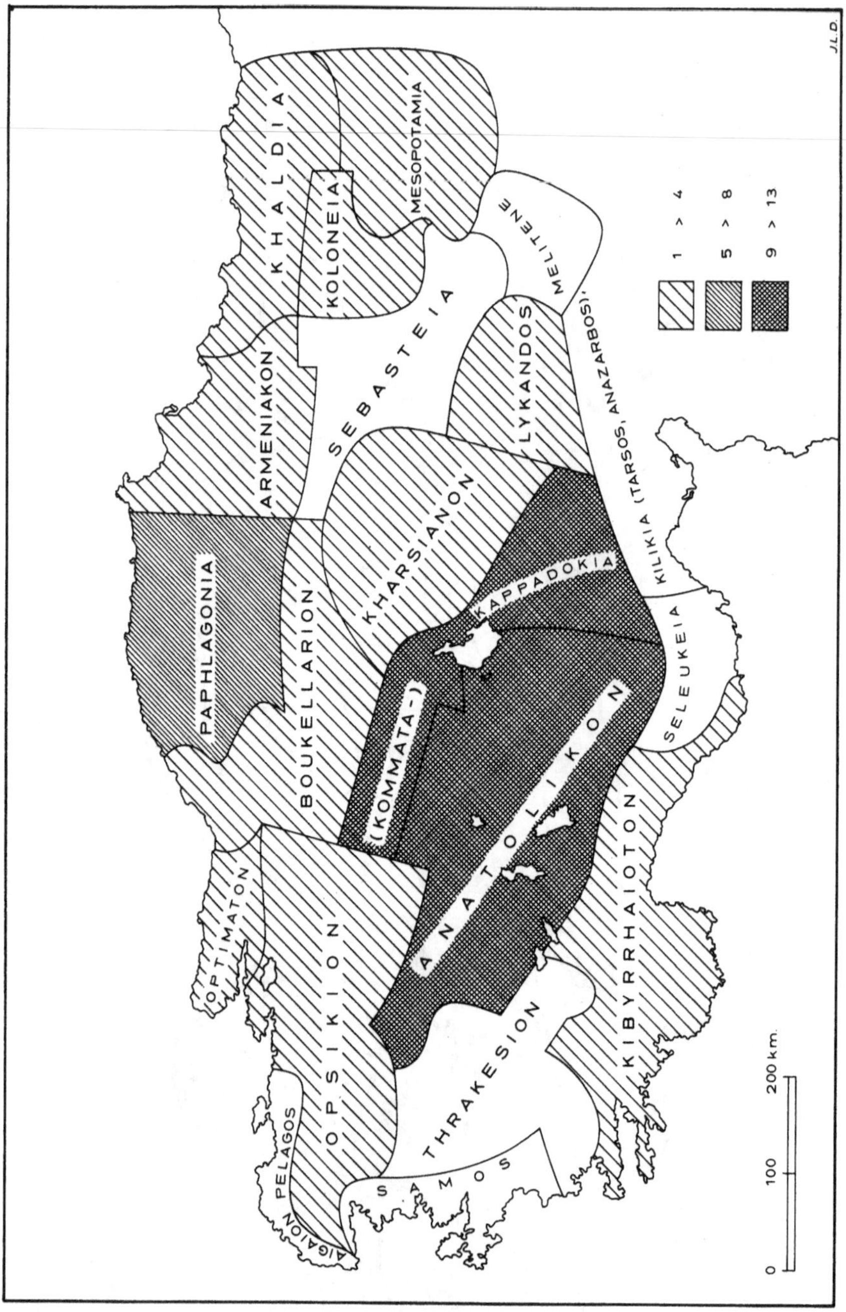


Map 25 Anatolia: magnates' origins and estates (to *c.* 1100)

originated in the six themes of Samos, Thrakesion, Seleukeia, Kilikia, Sebasteia and Melitene (Map 25).[87]

The methodology utilised, with its necessary reliance upon casual sources is, as already noted, an admittedly extremely crude one, but the results again suggest it to be essentially sound in the particular case at least. For a comparison of this map with those illustrating the distribution of sees/cities demonstrates the majority of magnates to have originated in precisely those themes that were most lacking in cities, and few to have originated in those that were most abundant in them (Maps 23, 25). The identity of the themes with, apparently, the greatest number of magnates, and the evident tendency for magnates and cities to exclude each other, suggest, of course, the nature of the land held by the magnates, the use to which it must have been put, and therefore their major source of income. The land covered by Anatolikon, Kappadokia and Paphlagonia involves parts of Phrygia, Galatia, Lycaonia and Pisidia, as well as Cappadocia and Paphlagonia, and the basic distinction implied is thus again that between coastal plain and central plateau, and between agriculturalism and pastoralism. Eustathius Maleinus, who is commonly taken as having been a fairly representative member of a magnate family which (like its much earlier equivalents) owned vast tracts of land – up to 115 km in extent – in the theme of Boukellarion, and equivalent tracts in that of Kharsianon, and who was confined to the capital and had his estates expropriated by Basil II when that emperor became aware of their extent, was thus in a very real way the successor of Amyntas of Galatia.[88] The Phocas family, which owned similar tracts of Kappodokia, and which was related to the Maleini, similarly attracted the notice of Basil II, and seems to have been of like status but even longer standing.[89]

In view of the localisation identified or outlined above, it can only be held significant that it had been the excesses of the local magnates (*potentes/dynatoi*), their agents (*conductores/epitropeuontes*) and dependents (*clientes/doryphoroi*) – and particularly their illegal acquisition of imperial and private lands, herds of horses, and revenues – in precisely

87 Vryonis, 'The Internal History of Byzantium during the "Time of Troubles" (1057–81)', pp. 390–1; *idem*, *The Decline of Medieval Hellenism in Asia Minor*, p. 25 (n. 132). For Boukellarion, see below. See also below, pp. 610–12 (*Ouranus in Thrakesion*).

88 Eustathius and the Maleini: John Scylitzes, *Synopsis Historiarum*; ed. H. Thurn, p. 340. George Cedrenus, *Historiarum Compendium*; ed. I. Bekker (Bonn edn), II, p. 438. Basil II, Novel XXIX (996); Zepoi, *Ius Graeco-Romanum* I, pp. 264–5 (n. 24). E. Honigmann, 'Un itinéraire arabe à travers le Pont', *Annuaire de l'Institut de Philologie et d'Histoire Orientales et Slaves* 4 (1936), pp. 263, 268–71. Maleinus–Phocas relationship: R. Morris, 'The Powerful and the Poor in Tenth-century Byzantium: Law and Reality', *Past and Present* 73 (Nov. 1976), p. 16. Earlier examples of widely scattered estates: see below, pp. 202 (west), 203 (east). See also below pp. 206–7 (Danelis), 208–9 (Philaretus). On the Maleini, see also: S. Stavrakas, 'The Byzantine Provincial Élite: A Study in Social Relationships during the Ninth and Tenth Centuries', pp. 28–33.

89 Phocae: H. Grégoire, 'Notes épigraphiques VII – Melias le magistre', *Byzantion* 8 (1933), pp. 79–88. N. Adontz and H. Grégoire, 'Nicéphore au col roide', *Byzantion* 8 (1933), pp. 203–12. H. Grégoire, 'Notes de géographie byzantine', *Byzantion* 10 (1935), pp. 251–6. Basil II, Novel XXIX (see above, n. 88). See now: I. Djurić, 'Poroditsa Phoka', *Zbornik Radova Vizantoloshkog Instituta* 17 (1976), pp. 189–296.

those areas (the provinces of Cappadocia, Paphlagonia and Helenopontus), that had been one of the explicitly-mentioned causes of the Justinianic administrative reorganisation of those areas.[90] Noticeably, Pisidia and Lycaonia had been included in the same phase of reorganisation,[91] and so had Phrygia Pacatania and Galatia Prima.[92] Although Isauria, Caria and the Armenias had also been included,[93] the presence of the first can be accounted for by a long-standing tendency to mountain-banditry and disorder, that of the second by absorption into the *Quaestura Exercitus*, and that of the third as part of a wider programme to reduce the power of the Armenian magnates.[94] With the exclusion of these three rather special cases, the territorial coincidence becomes remarkable (Maps 25, 26).

It seems equally significant that the large swathe of land on the south and east of Anatolia, comprising the themes of Seleukeia, Kilikia, Sebasteia and Melitene, and showing surprisingly little evidence of magnates, includes a high proportion of land only relatively recently recovered from, or cleared of, the Arabs. When Melitene had been recovered in 934, it had been converted promptly into an imperial estate (*kouratoreion*); Tarsus, when recovered in 965, along with parts of Seleukeia, seems to have been similarly treated; and so does Antioch, recovered in 969; and other, perhaps somewhat less impressive, examples could be quoted, such as Mesopotamia, and Artach near and east of Antioch.[95] The land was thus simply not allowed to fall into magnate hands.

An apparent exception to this last observation is provided by the two vast estates around Anazarbus and Podandus (therefore partly in Kilikia, partly in Kappadokia) that were found by John I to belong to the *parakoimōmenos* and imperial eunuch Basil. Parts of these estates had been recovered from the Arabs by Nicephorus II, parts by John himself functioning as *domestikos tōn skholōn*, and parts by other individuals. All had been acquired by the eunuch. But although these estates were vast, it should be noticed that most originally seem to have been public possessions (*dēmosia ktēmata*), and subsequently only to have been devolved through imperial grant. Both the Cilician estate, elsewhere called *Longias* or *Longinias*, and the Cappadocian one, similarly called *Drizion* or *Drizēs*, in any case appear to have been identical with the imperial *episkepseis* in those places. Basil himself, for obvious reasons, cannot be counted as more than a 'once-off', non-dynastic,

[90] See below, pp. 178, 179.

[91] See below, p. 178.

[92] See below, p. 180.

[93] See below, pp. 178, 179, 404.

[94] Isauria: Jones, *Later Roman Empire* I, pp. 25, 116, 192. E. Stein, *Histoire du bas-empire* II, pp. 82–4. Caria: see below, p. 404. Armenia: Stein, *Histoire du bas-empire* II, pp. 470–2.

[95] N. Oikonomides, *Les listes de préséance byzantines des IX^e et X^e siècles*, pp. 356 (Melitene), 355 (Tarsus), 363 (Artach); *idem*, 'L'organisation de la frontière orientale de Byzance aux X^e–XI^e siècles et le taktikon de l'Escorial', *XIV^e Congrès International des Études Byzantines, Bucarest 6–12 septembre 1971*, *Rapports* II, pp. 78 (Melitene), 77 (Tarsus, Artach), 88 (Antioch, Mesopotamia). For Seleukeia: private correspondence between W. B. R. Saunders and G. Zacos (to the former of whom I owe the information).

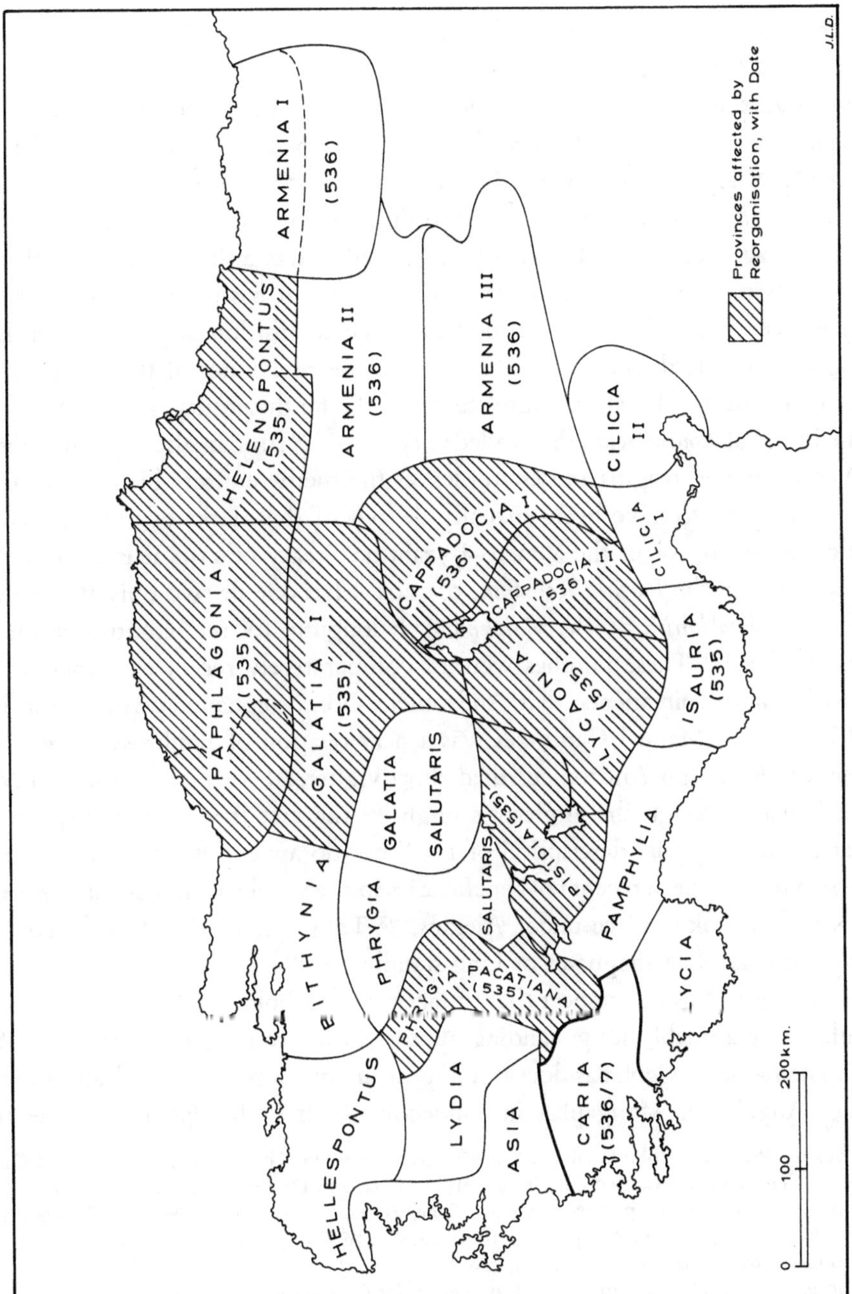


Map 26 Anatolia: Justinianic administrative reorganisation (535–7)

magnate, the estates involved presumably reverting to the state on his subsequent disgrace. The observation, then, effectively stands.[96]

In view of all this, it is extremely curious that no less than two of the laws directed against the magnates are devoted not to the lands of the plateau but to those of the coastal plain and river-valleys. Constantine VII's Novel VI of 947[97] was provoked by the abuses of the *dynatoi kai hyperekhontes* with regard to the illegal acquisition of land in the theme of Thrakesion, and Romanus II's Novel XVI of 962[98] was also concerned with similar problems involving the lands of *stratiōtai* in that theme. It has been supposed[99] that this coincidence is an effective measure of the large-scale acquisition of property on the part of the magnates in the theme of Thrakesion, but the remainder of the evidence points uniformly in a contrary direction. Admittedly, in the tenth century, Lydia had possessed at least an imperial *kouratoreia*: that called *Trykhinai*.[100] But in the eleventh, the map (Map 25) of magnates' origins and estates leaves the theme entirely blank. And again in the twelfth, it seems to have been virtually devoid of the marks of imperial, court or aristocratic possession, for in the Veneto-Byzantine Treaty of 1198 it is entirely devoid of *episkepseis*, and in the *Partitio Romaniae* of 1204 it has one or two only (the *pertinentia Sampson et [T]ama[la]chii = Ta Malakhiou*) belonging to the Contostephanus and Camytzes families.[101] These families were of comparatively recent eminence, and it is unlikely to be mere coincidence that Andronicus Contostephanus was a son-in-law of Alexius III, and that Manuel Camytzes was a near relation of Euphrosyne, wife of the same emperor. Although Andronicus died shortly after Alexius' accession, and Manuel rebelled half way through the emperor's reign,[102] the fact that their family-names do not appear in the territorial description of 1198, but do appear in that of 1204, strongly suggests them to have been recent co-beneficiaries in the wholesale hand-out of state lands that seems to have taken place under Alexius.[103] They cannot therefore be considered as examples of Anatolian magnates of long standing.

It is interesting in this last respect that in fact the land-holdings of none of the known local families of reasonably long standing appears in the territorial descriptions of 1198 and 1204. The name of Cephalas does not appear in connection with Adramyttium, nor do those of Angelus or Mangaphas in connection with Philadelphia, nor does that of

[96] Anazarbus and Podandus: John Scylitzes, *Synopsis Historiarum*; ed. Thurn, pp. 311–12. George Cedrenus, *Historiarum Compendium*; Bonn edn, II, pp. 414–15. Longias and Drizion: Leo the Deacon, *Historia* X.11; ed. C. B. Hase (Bonn edn), p. 176. Scylitzes, *Synopsis, ed. cit.* p. 268. *Episkepseis*: G. Schlumberger, *Sigillographie de l'empire byzantin*, pp. 315 (Podandus), 276 (Longias). See also: W. M. Ramsay, *The Historical Geography of Asia Minor*, pp. 348, 449.

[97] Constantine (VII) Porphyrogenitus, Novel VI; Zepoi, *Ius Graeco-Romanum* I, pp. 214–17.

[98] Romanus II, Novel XVI; Zepoi, *Ius Graeco-Romanum* I, pp. 243–4.

[99] E.g. Toynbee, *Constantine Porphyrogenitus and his World*, p. 159 n. 1.

[100] See below, p. 313.

[101] See below, pp. 133, 134.

[102] C. M. Brand, *Byzantium Confronts the West 1180–1204*, pp. 119–20, 133.

[103] Particularly in the Balkans: see above, pp. 88–9, and Map 19.

Asidenus in connection with the lower Maeander, nor that of Maurozomes in connection with the middle or upper Maeander. The point presumably is that Constantine Angelus who made the family's fortune by marrying Theodora, the youngest daughter of Alexius I, was, in origin at least, not a member of the court aristocracy, and that Theodore Mangaphas, Sabbas Asidenus, and perhaps even Manuel Maurozomes, were still not members of that aristocracy in 1204. The occurrence of the *episkepsis* is therefore strictly the mark of state ownership or of an appanage or franchise held by a member of the imperial clan or court aristocracy (whether lay or ecclesiastical), and not necessarily the only mark of large-scale land-owning as such. Nevertheless, evidence for the region of Smyrna suggests that, at the beginning of the thirteenth century, the bulk of the land was held by local owners, and that this was on a relatively restrained scale, the great extension of aristocratic land-owning being an understandable phenomenon of the second or even third decades of the century.[104]

The inherent problem posed for the imperial government by the existence of a powerful landed aristocracy, whether civil or military, in Anatolia was therefore not only not new, but was even of long standing. Justinian, in dealing with what seems to have been an essentially civil phenomenon, had been prepared to meet the problem head-on, in those areas most prone to it (the central plateau), and to attempt an administrative solution. The emperors of the tenth to twelfth centuries, in dealing with what was an essentially military phenomenon, because of the intervening militarisation of society, were reduced to preventing its spread to newly recovered territory and the coastal plain. They were, moreover, deprived of the possibility of an administrative solution, for by then the military had already monopolised regional administration. They therefore instead legislated on matters of land-acquisition and -holding.

The evidence provided by the distribution of magnates is confirmed by the other source of information: descriptions of crusader journeys. The maps illustrating the distribution of sees/cities (Maps 20–3) consistently demonstrate the first and second concentrations to have been separated off from the third by a broad band of apparently open land lying on an approximately west to east axis; this band defines the Mysian and Bithynian Highlands. It remained open in the twelfth century, for Odo of Deuil remarks[105] that while travelling between Lupar (Lopadium/Uluabat) and Demetrias (Adramyttium, i.e. Edremit), apparently by way of the coast-road along the Dardanelles, the majority of French members of the Second Crusade wandered off the road into certain valleys (*concava*) and, finding themselves obstructed by mountain-crags (*scopuli montium*), it was not until the third day that they came across a village with peasants (*villula habens rusticos*), one of whom they obliged to lead them towards Adramyttium. Many of their pack

[104] Angold, *A Byzantine Government in Exile*, pp. 60–79, 121–43.

[105] Odo of Deuil, *De Profectione Ludovici VII in Orientem* VI; ed. Berry, pp. 102–6.

animals meanwhile had died and their loads been lost to the forest-dwellers (*Graeci silvestres*). The minority of members, who had taken the direct route across the Mysian Highlands, a wide road but meagrely supplied, had nevertheless made much better time. It was only after they had all passed Adramyttium that they began to come across cities once again. The author of the *Historia de Expeditione Friderici Imperatoris*[106] remarks that, after having crossed the straits from Europe, at Kallipolis (i.e. Gelibolu), into Asia, presumably at Lampsacus (i.e. Lâpseki), and while travelling – again apparently by way of the coast-road – towards Pegae (probably Biga), the German members of the Third Crusade encountered three days of mountainous and rough roads (*montuosae et asperae viae*). Beyond Calamus, on the way to Thyateira, they encountered further mountains (Map 11).

The same maps (20–3) again consistently demonstrate the first concentration to have been separated off from the tenth and eleventh by a further broad band of apparently open land lying on an approximately south-west to north-east axis. This band, or part of it at least, is related to the Lycian Taurus. It was, however, already open in the mid fifth century, being then occupied by the Patrimonial and the Milyadic lands (*khōria Patrimonialia* and *khōria Milyadika*), apparently two bodies of imperial estates which had remained without a city structure,[107] and it remained open in the twelfth century, for Odo of Deuil remarks[108] that when the crusaders reached Laodicea and found it emptied of supplies they counted it a disaster, for they knew that between there and Attalia no provisions could be found anywhere else. The road, by way of Themisonium, Eriza (i.e. Dere Köy), Cibyra (i.e. Horzom Armutlu), Lagbe and Isinda (i.e. Korkuteli), passes through the Milyadic Lands and over the mountains, valleys and forests of Lycia. The extremely mountainous nature of coastal Lycia between Attalia and the west of Patara, and its use as a haven for pirates in the late twelfth century, is constantly commented upon by the author of Benedict of Peterborough.[109]

### C. *The twelfth and thirteenth centuries*

The physical structure and pattern of urban settlement in Anatolia goes a long way towards explaining the speed and depth of penetration of the various invasions of the peninsula: those of the Persians in the seventh century, of the Arabs in the seventh to ninth centuries, and of the Selçuks in the eleventh century. Quite simply, once the frontier – whether natural or man-made or both – had been breached, there was then very little to prevent a speedy advance towards the urban concentrations of the west and

106 Anonymous ('Ansbert'), *Historia de Expeditione Friderici Imperatoris*; MGH, *SRG:NS* v, pp. 72–3.

107 Jones, *Cities of the Eastern Roman Provinces*, pp. 75–6.

108 Odo of Deuil, *De Profectione Ludovici VII in Orientem* VI–VII; ed. Berry, pp. 112–28.

109 See below, p. 114.

the coasts, other than the few cities of the plateau, which were in any case capable of being by-passed with relative ease and impunity, and which, in any prolonged invasion, could be forced into submission or taken later, if necessary. This latter seems to have been the pattern for the great Arab raid of 715–18, at least, and was certainly the pattern for the Selçuk invasions and subsequent occupation.[110]

The structure and pattern was, potentially at least, also a factor that could operate in favour of the Byzantines. The fact that the plateau is even now sometimes impassable in winter, that it is and was so arid in summer, and that it is and was so lightly inhabited and exploited, would have meant that overwintering by an enemy was likely to be unattractive, and that water and foodstuffs were scarce even in the campaigning season. Settlement (except perhaps to nomads and/or pastoralists) would therefore have been difficult, and supply-lines (except to self-sufficient, or mobile, and in any case lightly-armed, troops) would have been dangerously extended. These factors, forming a natural complement to the conscious policy later operated in the Balkans at least, would have impeded Persians, and perhaps even Arabs, but would positively have favoured Turks.[111]

It is indeed the political division of the peninsula between Byzantines and Selçuks during the twelfth and thirteenth centuries that once again strikingly demonstrates the fundamental structural distinction between the coastal plain and central plateau, with all its inherent climatic and other implications.

In attempting a reconstruction of the political situation and representing it in map form, too much weight has hitherto been placed on the (frequently tacit) assumption that whatever is recorded as having been recovered by the Byzantines as a result, say, of the Crusade of 1101, remained Byzantine throughout the period in question, in default of specific evidence to the contrary. The assumption has only to be formulated to appear absurd, and yet it must underline any reconstruction which, for instance, includes Ancyra and Amorium within the imperial frontiers. What has hitherto tended to emerge is therefore a very exaggeratedly maximal, and at the same time essentially static, representation of the situation. What is needed is, rather, a more flexible reconstruction, in which a number of different but relevant elements are represented, in which each element can be accorded appropriate weight, and in which a degree of movement is capable of being depicted.

A composite map along these lines, attempting to depict the twelfth-century situation,

110 Persians: Stratos, *Byzantium in the Seventh Century* I (*602–634*) pp. 103–17, 135–44, 151–240, and C. Foss, 'The Persians in Asia Minor and the End of Antiquity', *English Historical Review* 90 (1975), pp. 721–8. Arabs: Lilie, *Die byzantinische Reaktion auf die Ausbreitung der Araber*, pp. 122–33 (in period 715–18); Haldon and Kennedy, 'The Arab–Byzantine Frontier in the Eighth and Ninth Centuries', pp. 106–16 (general). Selçuks: Cahen, *Pre-Ottoman Turkey*, pp. 26–30, 66–84, and Vryonis, *The Decline of Medieval Hellenism in Asia Minor*, pp. 80–113.

111 The point is perhaps best illustrated in the case of the Arabs, see: Lilie, *Die byzantinische Reaktion auf die Ausbreitung der Araber*, maps facing pp. 188, 287, 336, with accompanying text. The central plateau was both the main later centre of military conflict, and economically the least vital area for the empire.

including the imperial fortification or refortification of cities and imperial campaigns, distinguishing between cities that were normally Byzantine, those that were normally Selçuk, and those that were more or less continuously in dispute, and depicting the main areas and direction of Turkish attacks, gives what is in many ways a much more accurate impression of the situation. (Map 27)

The classification of fortifications reign by reign demonstrates both the implementation and the basic aims of imperial military policy. A concentration on the coastal areas is common to the fortifications of all the Comnenian emperors: those of Alexius I are virtually confined to the coast itself; those of John II include Achyraus (i.e. Balıkesir) and Laodicea/Denizli; and those of Manuel I include Dorylaeum/Eskişehir and Sublaeum (possibly identical with Choma/Angelocastrum, i.e. Homa). Each reign thus represents a separate stage in the progressive recovery of a whole section of the peninsula,[112] a fact which seems to have been realised at the time, for Eustathius of Thessalonica compares the three Comneni to waves of the sea: 'And the first of these three waves [i.e. Alexius] swept the confused litter of Hagar [i.e. the Turks] from the sea; the second [i.e. John] separated them off even further from it; and the third [i.e. Manuel] obliterated them and encroached not only on the sea but also on the land, so that in our day it is a matter of difficulty for those who work by the sea to see the face of a son of Ishmael.'[113]

A similar classification of campaign routes confirms the effective extent and limits of the Byzantine territorial recovery: the classic routes across the plateau were never taken, and those routes encroaching appreciably upon it were rarely taken, even when the Pontus or Cilicia was the goal. Rather, a distinct shift is evident, so as to take as much advantage as possible of routes that kept to the coastal plain and river-valleys. One apparent exception to this in fact proves the rule. When Cilicia was the goal of a campaign, the customary route taken was that up the Hermus/Maeander valleys, over the lakes, down into Lycia or Isauria, and along the coast. The only campaign that utilised the apparently more direct route between Laodicea and Attalia was that formed by the French section of the Second Crusade, and that met with utter disaster. The point is that, although much closer to the coast and shorter in distance, it is also much more vulnerable, owing to the rough and enclosed nature of the prevalent terrain, the Lycian Taurus.

An equivalent categorisation of cities according to the nature of their predominant political affinities over the period demonstrates that, from Trebizond right round to (Isaurian) Antioch, Byzantine cities were virtually confined to the thin ribbon of coastal plain, with the sole major exception of the west, where occupation of the great river-valleys permitted a greater degree of penetration. Conversely, Selçuk cities were confined to the plateau. Between these two a broad band of cities that changed hands or were under more

[112] H. Ahrweiler, 'Les forteresses construites en Asie Mineure face à l'invasion seldjoucide', in *Akten des XI. internationalen Byzantinistenkongresses, München 1958*, at pp. 182–9.

[113] Eustathius of Thessalonica, *Orationes* III; ed. W. Regel and N. Novossadsky, at p. 29.

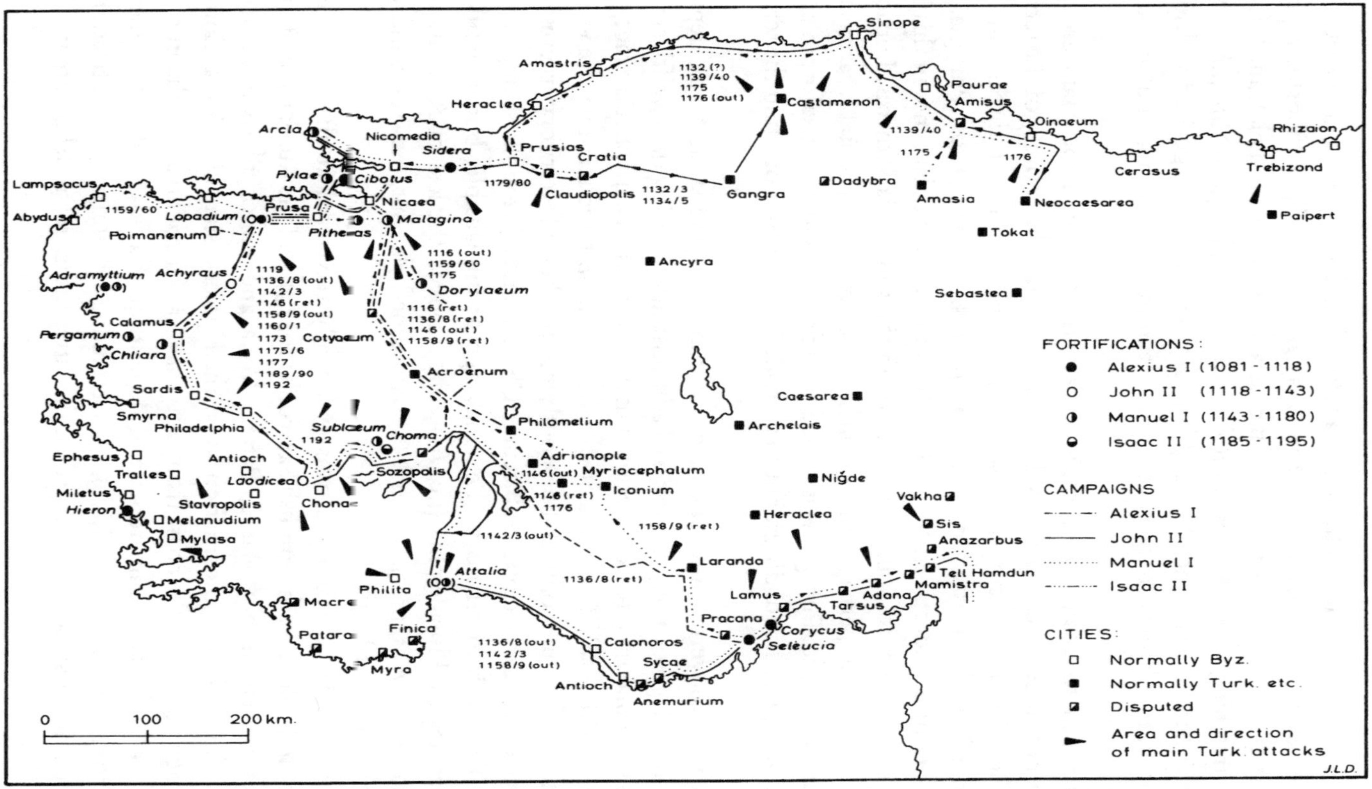


Map 27 Anatolia: imperial fortifications, campaign-routes and cities, *c.* 1116–1204

or less continuous dispute, and including Dadybra (i.e. İskilip), Cratia (i.e. Gerede), Claudiopolis (i.e. Bolu), Cotyaeum (i.e. Kütahya) and Sozopolis/Uluborlu, represent what is effectively the transitional land between coastal plain and central plateau. A further group of cities stretching from Anemurium (i.e. Anamur) through to Sis (i.e. Kozan), representing Little Armenia and the Cilician Plain, are necessarily categorised as disputed, but the main parties involved were of course not Byzantines and Selçuks, but Byzantines and Armenians.

Finally, an attempt to depict, in however schematic a fashion, the main areas and directions of Turkish attacks demonstrates that, while virtually the entirety of the territory recovered by the Comnenian emperors was under some degree of threat, the main pressure was northwards, westwards and southwards, from out of Phrygia. The fortification programme undertaken by the Comneni makes particular sense in this light: from Malagina in the north to Sublaeum–Choma in the south, via Pithecas, Lopadium, Achyraus and Laodicea, and perhaps others which, while not precisely datable, are as likely to be Comnenian as Lascarid, Phrygia was ringed with fortified cities in an effort to protect not only their immediate surroundings, but to provide a barrier in protecting the territory behind them.

When this map is converted into one of more traditional and static form, depicting territory under some degree of regular imperial administration during the twelfth century, what emerges is still a maximal representation, but nevertheless on a much less exaggerated scale than is normal (Map 28). The limits of Byzantine-administered territory are virtually coincident with the 500 m contour-line, outlying patches of territory representing Dadybra, Dorylaeum, Cotyaeum, Sublaeum–Choma and Sozopolis being entirely surrounded by Turkish-held territory. This may appear implausible, but it should not be forgotten that nearby Philadelphia (i.e. Alaşehir) survived the loss of Anatolia in the early fourteenth century as precisely such a Byzantine-held outpost, surrounded by Turkish-held territory, until 1390.

There is no real evidence that Lycia was ever really recovered at all. Two western pilgrims to Syria and Palestine, the English Saewulf (1102/3), and the Russian abbot Daniel (1106/7), between them imply Macre, Patara, Myra and Finica all to have been in Christian hands, but offer no information as to their precise status.[114] Anna Comnena remarks on the devastation of the coast from Smyrna to as far round as Attalia in *c.* 1108, and this may well be the approximate date of deposition of a hoard of gold hyperpyra of Alexius I from Macre (i.e. Fethiye).[115] Certainly, no imperial fortifications or campaigns in the immediate area are recorded, the latter rather seem deliberately to have

[114] Saewulf, *Relatio de Peregrinatione ad Hierosolymam et Terram Sanctam*; ed. W. R. B. Brownlow, p. 51. Daniel, *Pilgrimage in the Holy Land*, trans. C. W. Wilson, pp. 6–7.

[115] M. F. Hendy, 'Seventeen Twelfth- and Thirteenth-century Hoards', *Coin Hoards* 6 (1981), no. 231, pp. 67–8.

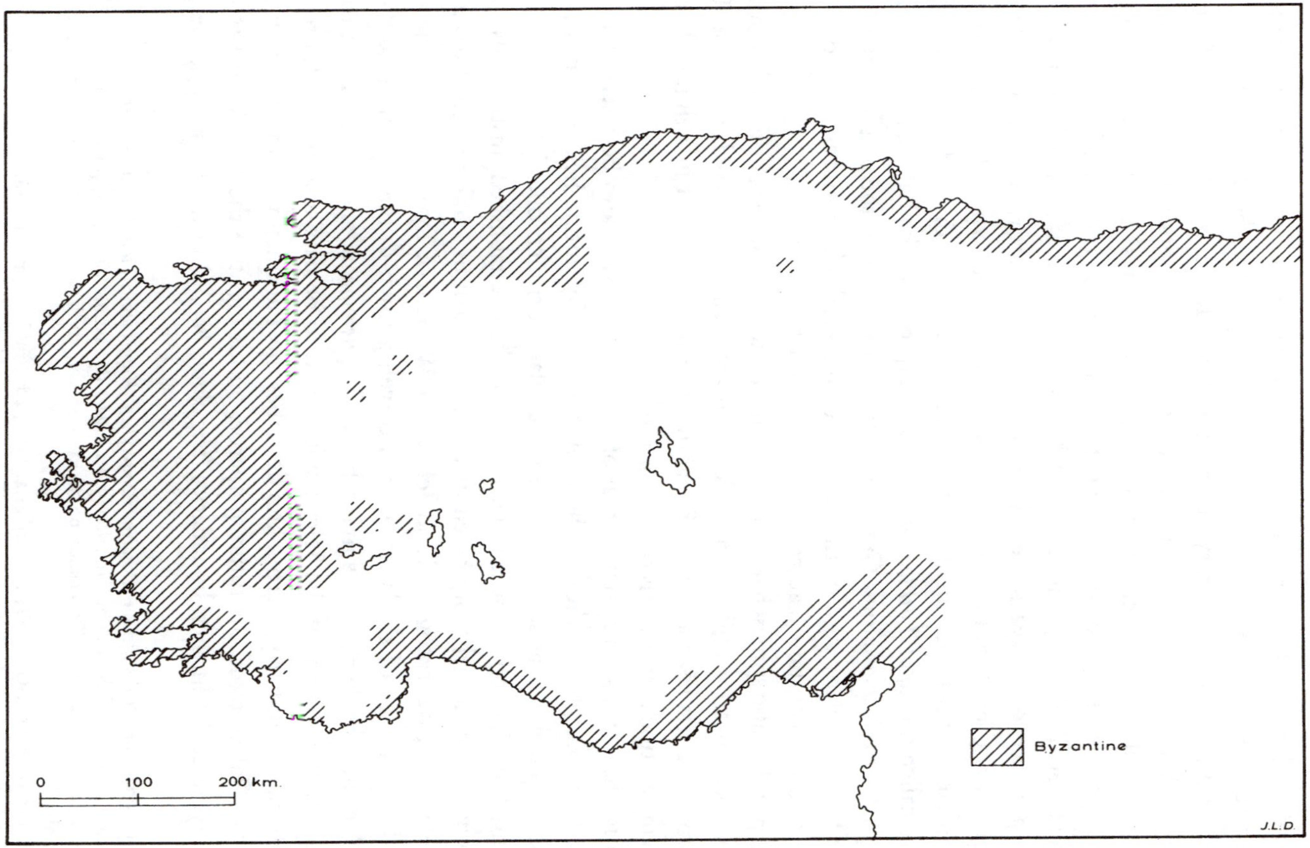


Map 28 Anatolia: imperial territory, *c.* 1116–1204 (maximal position)

avoided it, and the history of the French section of the Second Crusade – under continual attack right across the area – suggests that it was not Byzantine-held in 1147.

Other than this, a Greek funerary inscription from Myra is dated 1118,[116] and a metropolitan of Myra attended synodal meetings in Constantinople during the period 1166–70.[117] It should also be remembered that Eustathius was the accepted candidate for the metropolitanate of Myra in *c.* 1174, before being transferred to his actual metropolitanate of Thessalonica in *c.* 1175.[118] None of these facts need, of necessity, indicate the presence of a Byzantine administration in the area; indeed, Benedict of Peterborough, in also mentioning Finica, Myra and Patara, describes the whole coast as a haven for pirates in 1191, and mentions that imperial territory divided off from Selçuk at a mountain called the *caput Turkiae*, west of Patara (probably the Baba Dağ [1,975 m]): *et exinde incipit Rumania quae dicitur Graecia.*[119] On the other hand, the presence of pirates is not in itself an automatic sign of the absence of imperial administration, as collusion between the two is a constant feature of the late twelfth century.[120]

West, and possibly also somewhat north, of Attalia, the furthest Byzantine-held outpost seems to have been nearby Philita, briefly lost and apparently recovered in *c.* 1160. East of the city, more or less regularly held Byzantine territory stretched in a thin ribbon as far as (Isaurian) Antioch, and occasionally on into Cilicia.[121]

The map is, then, a maximal representation, but it may well also be a seasonal one, for it is clear that, except sporadically, the main threat to Byzantine-held areas came not from regular Selçuk forces as such, but from irregular Türkmen ones.[122]

The essential distinction between Turks, with their established institutions, and Türkmen, with their loosely organised patriarchal tribalism, and indeed altogether different mode of life, was recognised and defined by William of Tyre.[123] The positioning and potential for damage of the latter were also well known to the Byzantine authors. Cinnamus identifies the Türkmen as living by thefts (*klemmata*), and implies them to be normally outside the control of the Selçuk sultan, and to be particularly harmful to the land of the Romans. Similarly, Acropolites describes the Türkmen who met up with and robbed Michael Palaeologus, the future emperor, on his flight to the Selçuks in 1256/7, as: 'a nation lying at the furthest boundaries (*tois akrois horiois*) of the Persians [*sc.* Selçuk

[116] H. Rott, *Kleinasiatische Denkmäler aus Pisidien, Pamphylien, Kappadokien, und Lykien*, p. 340.

[117] J. Darrouzès, 'Listes synodales et notitiae', *Revue des Études Byzantines* 28 (1970), pp. 78, 79.

[118] S. Kyriakidis, *La Espugnazione di Tessalonica*, pp. xxxviii–xxxix, xlviii (see Bibliography under 'Eustathius of Thessalonica').

[119] Benedict of Peterborough, *Gesta Regis Ricardi*, s.a. 1191; ed. Stubbs, II, pp. 195–8.

[120] Brand, *Byzantium Confronts the West*, pp. 211–14, 220–1. H. Ahrweiler, *Byzance et la mer*, pp. 228–92.

[121] John Cinnamus, *Epitome* IV, 24; Bonn edn, pp. 198–201.

[122] On the nature and predominant rôle of the Türkmen: Vryonis, *The Decline of Mediaeval Hellenism in Asia Minor*, pp. 258–85; *idem*, 'Nomadization and Islamization in Asia Minor', *DOP* 29 (1975), pp. 41–71. See also above, p. 50 n. 60.

[123] William of Tyre, *Historia Rerum* I.7; RHC, *Occ.* I.1, pp. 21–5.

Turks], which holds an implacable hatred towards the Romans, and which delights in plundering them and glories in taking spoils from them in battle'.[124]

The essential of Türkmen existence was a pastoral nomadism or transhumance (the precise degree of 'nomadism' involved doubtless varying with time and place), involving a seasonal migration between high summer-pastures (*yayla*) and low winter-quarters (*kışla*): this alternation could involve movement over relatively short distances within a natural area that nevertheless provided the requisite climatic and ecological changes; or it could involve movement over rather longer ones between such areas in pursuit of the same object. It was when this alternation involved movement between areas that the inherent problems became acute, for a situation that might in any case have possessed a severe enough potential for friction tended to become a straight conflict between the Muslim pastoral nomad, acting (or purporting to act) as a fighter for the faith (*gazi*), and the Christian sedentary agriculturalist, in the frontier area (*uc*) where their interests clashed.

The main evidence for early Turkish settlement in Anatolia, the (somewhat later) presence of toponyms deriving from the names of the Oğuz tribes that provided the human material of the earlier invasions, shows heavy concentrations on the broken or transitional lands of Paphlagonia, Phrygia and Lycia, rather than on either the coastal plain (held by the Byzantines) or on the central plateau (subject to too wide extremes of climate). A somewhat similar point of departure, the presence of the toponym *kışla* and its derivatives, reveals a similar pattern with, noticeably, something of a movement downwards, away from the centre of these lands, and towards the coastal plain or river-valleys.[125] Closer examination of a particular area, the axis of which is provided by the Pisidian lakes (the *yayla*) and the Pamphylian plain (the *kışla*), reveals much the same pattern of toponymic survival, and much the same kind of alternation, by the modern, partly settled *yürük*, downwards to the winter-quarters in October and upwards to the summer-pastures in May, the distances involved being up to 150 km in extent. Again, much the same is observable in the area around Konya and elsewhere.[126]

The essentials of Türkmen existence were also clearly well known to both the Greek and Latin (and other) authors of the period. Cinnamus, for instance, in a classic passage, remarks that – probably in 1124, and noticeably in winter (*kheimōnos*) – John II attacked the Anatolian Turks, taking many captive and converting them. He continues: 'For they were as yet unversed in agricultural matters (*geēponikois enēskēmenoi ergois*), gulping milk (*gala*) and devouring meats (*krea*), in the Scythian [*sc.* Patzinak] fashion, and as they were

[124] John Cinnamus, *Epitome* v.3; Bonn edn, pp. 207–8. George Acropolites, *Historia* LXV; ed. Heisenberg and Wirth (Teubner), p. 136.

[125] X. de Planhol, *Les fondements géographiques de l'histoire de l'islam*, pp. 220–9, 236–7.

[126] X. de Planhol, *De la plaine pamphylienne aux lacs pisidiens, nomadisme et vie paysanne*, pp. 103–6 (fig. 11), 195–9 (fig. 14).

always encamped scattered over the plain (*aei sporades te ana to pedion eskēnēmenoi*), they were very readily accessible to those who wished to attack them.' William of Tyre is even more specific and detailed.[127]

There seems equally little doubt but that the seasonal alternation involved, along regular and defined routes, was established at a very early date. It is strikingly enunciated in the work of the early fourteenth-century poet Yunus Emre: 'We went down into Rum, we wintered, we wrought much good and evil. Spring came, we returned, praise be to Allah.'[128] It is very noticeable that it was in winter that the French section of the Second Crusade began to suffer Turkish attacks in areas in which they might not have been expected to occur otherwise. The first occurred on 24 December (1147), in the very rich valley of Decervium just outside Ephesus, and a number of others occurred during the next several days, as the army proceeded up the Maeander.[129] Lycia was swarming with Turks, and even when the French arrived at Attalia on about 20 January (1148), they found it closely invested by them.[130] Again, it was in winter, probably in February/March 1180, that the Turks laid siege to Claudiopolis, forcing Manuel I to rise from his sickbed and disperse them, and conversely it had been in the winters of 1159/60 and 1160/1 that Manuel had chosen to attack the Phrygian Turks in the vicinities of Dorylaeum and Philadelphia respectively.[131] Other, similar, instances are known, and the whole forms a clear and consistent pattern.[132]

Such seasonal alternations even received a formal imperial response, particularly after 1204, when emperors were forced to exist outside the capital. It has been convincingly suggested[133] that the frequent visits by the Trapezuntine emperor Alexius III (1349–90) to the city of Limnia (near Çarşamba) in the western Pontus, at the month of the Iris/Yeşil Irmak, which tended to occur between October and May, were connected with the winter-grazing habits of the local Türkmen. It may equally well be that the regular winterings of the Nicaean emperors at Nymphaeum (i.e. Kemalpaşa), established from a very early date,[134] have less to do with minor advantages of health or climate,[135] and more to do with the necessity of protecting the Hermus and Maeander valleys, which together formed the agricultural basis of their state, from the winter incursions of the local Türkmen.

[127] John Cinnamus, *Epitome* I.4; Bonn edn, p. 9. William of Tyre, above, p. 114 n. 123.

[128] X. de Planhol, *Les fondements géographiques de l'histoire de l'islam*, p. 224.

[129] Odo of Deuil, *De Profectione Ludovici VII in Orientem* VI; ed. Berry, pp. 108–14.

[130] *Ibid.* VI–VII; ed. Berry, pp. 114–30.

[131] Nicetas Choniates, *Historia*; ed. van Dieten, I, pp. 197–8. Brand, *Byzantium Confronts the West*, pp. 24, 321 (n. 24).

[132] See below, pp. 117, 129–30.

[133] Bryer, 'Greeks and Türkmens: The Pontic Exception', pp. 128–30. These dates were of course common to pastoralism over a wide chronological and geographical area; for example, for ancient Italy, see: J. M. Frayn, *Subsistence Farming in Roman Italy*, p. 49.

[134] See below, pp. 443–5.

[135] So George Acropolites, *Historia* XLI; ed. Heisenberg and Wirth, p. 68.

An accurate map of Byzantine-held territory in Anatolia during the twelfth century should, then, take account of both the summer and winter seasons, when the situation may have differed quite sensibly. The modern concept of a 'frontier', always suspect in an ancient or mediaeval context, would of course be rendered virtually meaningless in such terms. To a certain degree, a symbiotic relationship between the two forms of life should have been possible. Muslim nomadic pastoralists were in their summer-pastures from May until October, which was very much when Christian sedentary agriculturalists were harvesting and replanting. The latter – but not their young winter crops – should have been relatively safe behind their city walls when the former returned to their winter-quarters.[136] It was probably in 1196, and was certainly during the winter – because of the atrocious seasonal cold (*to tēs hōras... anēkeston*) that is mentioned – that the young Keyhusrev, on arriving by night before the city of Antioch (on the Maeander), mistook the sounds of festivities inside, on the occasion of a local marriage, for the signals (*synthēmata*) of an imperial army, and promptly retired.[137] Matters of this kind did not, of course, always turn out so fortunately, but evidence, whether mediaeval or relatively modern, of a symbiosis, even along relatively formal lines, is not entirely lacking: for example, William of Tyre reports[138] that Attalia, while remaining Byzantine, paid tribute to the Turks 'so as to have a trade in the necessaries of life with the enemy (*per hoc necessariorum cum hostibus habens commercium*)'.

It should be noted that the nomads' grazing of the agriculturalists' winter cereals may not only not have been harmful, but may even have been of some benefit, as at this stage the grazed single shoot tends merely to multiply, through the process known as 'tillering'. Winter grazing is also of possible benefit to the agriculturalist where arrangements for manuring are involved.*

The programme of recovery, and then of the protection of what had been recovered, as undertaken by the three Comnenian emperors, was effective and long-lasting, even if somewhat neglected by their two Angelan successors,[139] and even if less dramatic than the chaos and destruction which had preceded it, which accounts for it being accorded less space than is justified in modern works on the period and subject.[140]

A map based on the information provided by the territorial descriptions in the Veneto–Byzantine Treaty of 1198 and in the *Partitio Romaniae* of 1204 involves a minimal

* I owe these points to the kindness of Alan McQuillan.

136 W. Eberhard, 'Nomads and Farmers in Southeastern Turkey, Problems of Settlement', *Oriens* 6 (1953), pp. 35–8.

137 Nicetas Choniates, *Historia*; ed. van Dieten, I, pp. 494, 495.

138 William of Tyre, *Historia Rerum* XVI, 26; RHC, *Occ.* I.2, p. 751. See also Odo of Deuil, *De Profectione Ludovici VII in Orientem* VI–VII; ed. Berry, pp. 108–26 (Maeander). Bryer, 'Greeks and Türkmens: The Pontic Exception', pp. 122–4, 130–2 (Pontus).

139 But see, for example: H. Ahrweiler, 'Choma-Aggélokastron', *Revue des Études Byzantines* 24 (1966), pp. 278–83 (reconstruction of Choma-Angelocastrum by Isaac II in the face of Türkmen).

140 E.g. Vryonis, *The Decline of Medieval Hellenism in Asia Minor*, pp. 103–42, 143–223.

representation of the situation at the very end of the century, and as such acts as a useful complement to the slightly earlier maximal one (Map 29). Much the same general pattern is evident, subject to a few relatively minor specific changes. Dorylaeum and Sublaeum were to be dismantled according to the terms of the treaty concluded between Manuel I and Kılıç Arslan II after the battle of Myriocephalum (1176); the latter was duly dismantled, the former not, but it seems clear that the Byzantines were unable to retain it.[141] Sozopolis and Cotyaeum fell into Turkish hands in 1182.[142] Dadybra fell into the same in 1196.[143] Certainly, Dorylaeum/Eskişehir, Cotyaeum/Kütahya and Sozopolis/Uluborlu are all mentioned in the division of Selçuk territories by Kılıç Arslan in favour of his sons and nearest relations in *c.* 1190.[144] The *Partitio* mentions Prusias (i.e. Düzce), but neither that source nor the Veneto–Byzantine Treaty of 1198 mentions Claudiopolis/Bolu or Cratia/Gerede, presumably indicating their fall into Turkish hands. Again, neither source mentions Lycia or the Lycian cities, tending to confirm the earlier evidence that the area had never been recovered. The last quarter of the century had therefore witnessed a regression of relatively minor proportions, involving the steady falling-away of outlying patches of territory, with perhaps the sole exception of Choma-Angelocastrum, which are duly reflected in the map.[145]

Maps drawn up for the thirteenth century equivalent to those drawn up for the twelfth show a further territorial regression, but again on a relatively minor scale (Maps 30, 31). With the loss of Sinope in the north (1214), and of Attalia in the south (1207), the Selçuks definitively broke through the coastal ribbon of Byzantine-held territory in two places.[146] On the other hand, Theodore I is known to have fortified or refortified Heraclea Pontica, Nicaea and Prusa, and John III to have fortified or refortified Pergamum, Smyrna, Magnesia, Nymphaeum, Tripolis, and probably others, as he appears to have possessed and implemented an extensive and co-ordinated building- and fortification-programme, as well as a financial and economic one.[147]

The geographical pattern shows an interesting and significant shift in balance as between the two emperors, although Theodore had to some extent already anticipated

[141] Nicetas Choniates, *Historia*; ed. van Dieten, I, pp. 189, 192. See also below, p. 152.

[142] *Ibid.* p. 262.

[143] *Ibid.* pp. 474–5.

[144] *Ibid.* pp. 520–1. Cahen, *Pre-Ottoman Turkey*, p. 111.

[145] Tafel and Thomas, *Urkunden* I, p. 475. Carile, 'Partitio Terrarum Imperii Romanie', pp. 217, 235–6. For Choma-Angelocastrum, see above, n. 139.

[146] Sinope: Bryer, 'Greeks and Türkmens: The Pontic Exception', pp. 116 n. 5, 123 n. 27. Attalia: J. Hoffman, *Rudimente von Territorialstaaten im byzantinischen Reich (1071–1210)*, pp. 69–71.

[147] Angold, *A Byzantine Government in Exile*, pp. 98 (Heraclea), 99 (Nicaea, Prusa), 100 (Tripolis), 110 (Smyrna), 111 (Nymphaeum). C. Foss, 'Late Byzantine Fortifications in Lydia', *Jahrbuch der Österreichischen Byzantinistik* 28 (1979), p. 307 (Magnesia). Many of the Lydian fortresses described by Foss, and dated by him to the Lascarid period, are not at all precisely datable, and may well rather belong – in origin at least – to the Comnenian one. E.g., see below, p. 131, for Manuel and the theme of Neokastra. See below, p. 283, for John's financial policies.

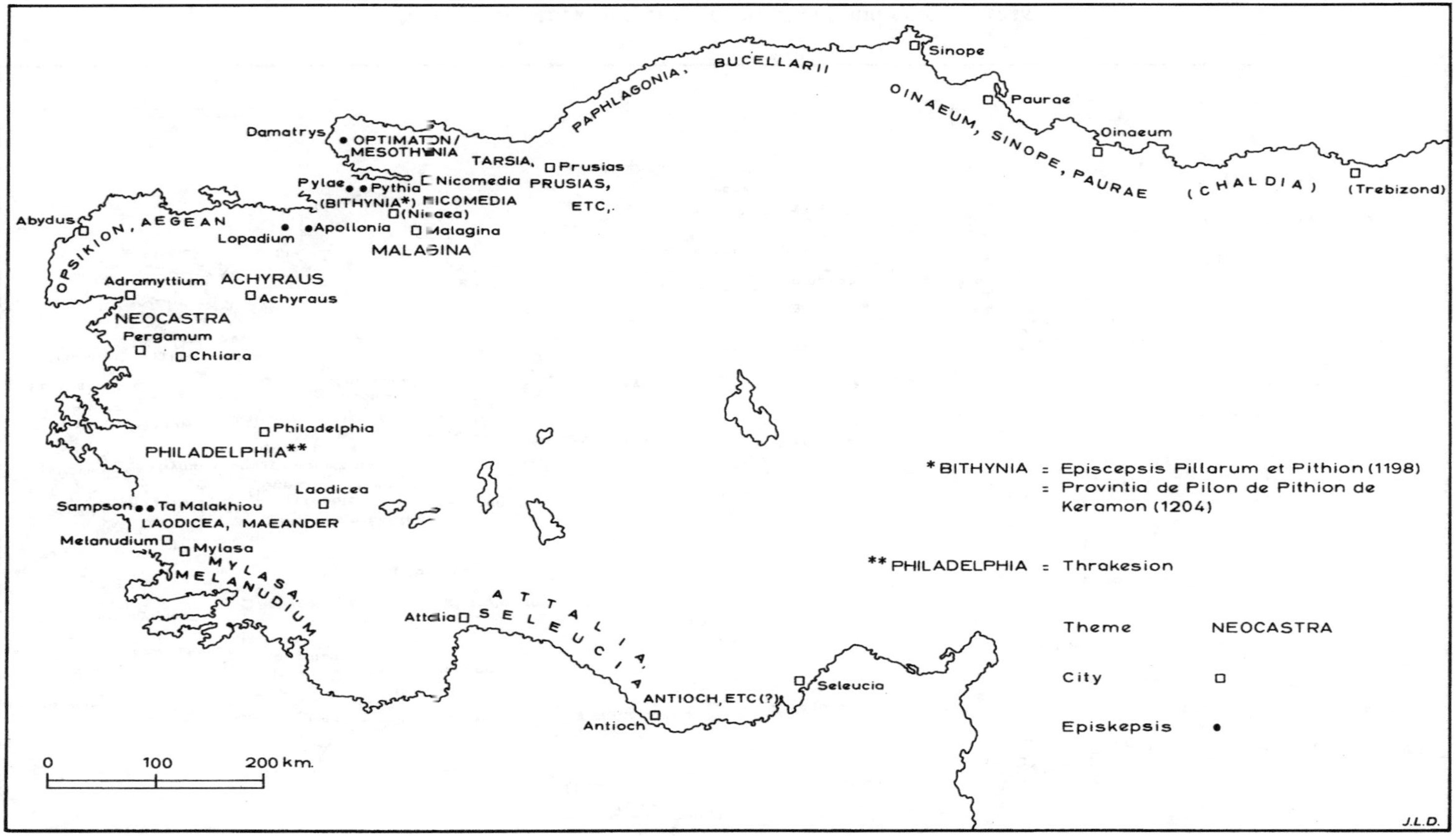


Map 29 Anatolia: imperial territory, 1198, 1204 (minimal position)

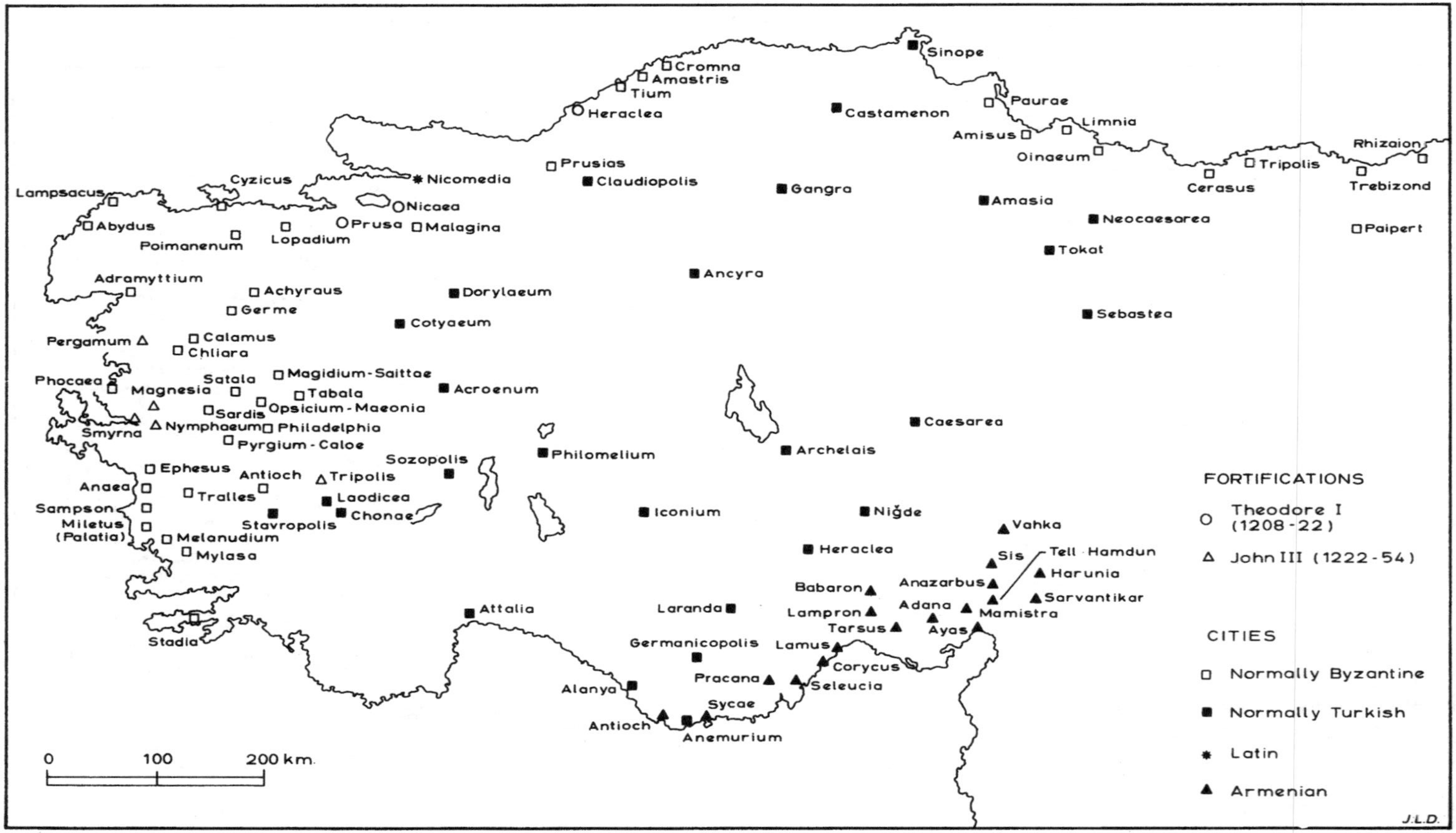


Map 30 Anatolia: imperial fortifications and cities, *c.* 1225–61

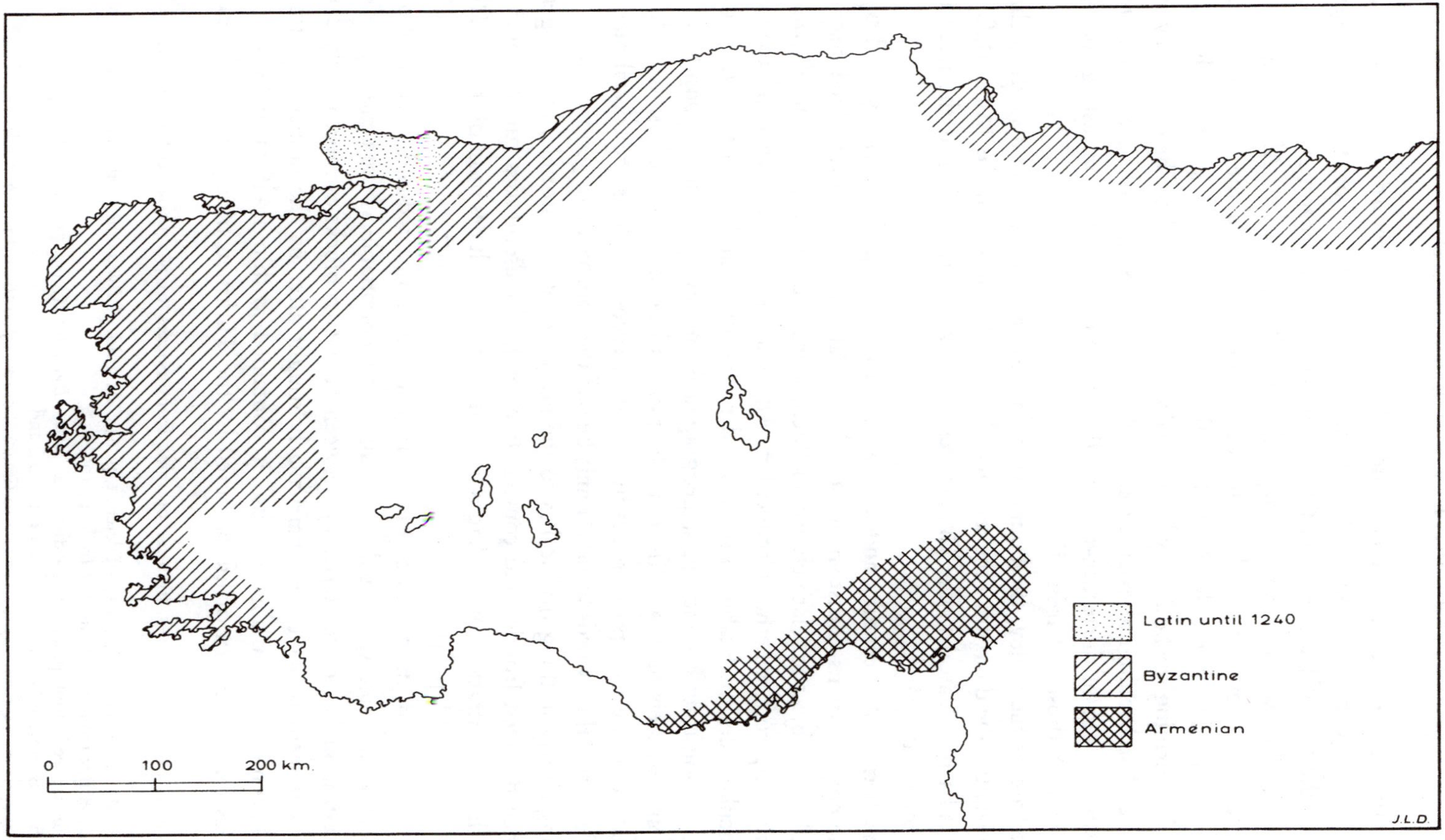


Map 31 Anatolia: imperial territory, *c.* 1225–61

the weighting to the south evident under John.[148] The refortification of Tripolis, recorded, along with Hierapolis, as still ruined in 1190, was an obvious and necessary response to the loss of Laodicea and Chonae to Manuel Maurozomes and subsequently to the Turks, a loss which was never more than briefly rectified.[149] Along with the loss of Laodicea and Chonae probably went that of all or most of the south bank of the Maeander: certainly, at the head of the valley, the river itself seems to have been recognised as forming the boundary between Byzantine- and Selçuk-held territory at this period,[150] and archaeological excavations at Aphrodisias (Stauropolis, i.e. Geyre) reveal no numismatic signs of thirteenth-century Byzantine occupation, contrasting sharply in this respect with those at Sardis.[151]

At the base of the valley, the boundary seems to have turned southwards, including within Byzantine-held territory the region of Mylasa–Melanudium (i.e. Milas–Bafa), and that of Stadia (i.e. Datça) in the Cnidan peninsula, and terminating at the river Indus (i.e. Dalaman Çayı).[152]

For the period of a century and a half (*c.* 1116–*c.* 1260), the territory held by the Byzantine empire (or its Christian offshoots) in Anatolia therefore remained essentially constant, being subject to relatively minor fluctuations. The fortification-programmes of the various emperors, whether Comnenian, Angelan, or Lascarid, whether attributable to a particular ruler or datable to the general period only, and whether in Asia, Lydia, or Ionia, demonstrate a conceptual, geographical and even technical consistence that clearly points to their having fulfilled a common and unchanging defensive need.[153]

The nature of the land protected is immediately recognisable as the coastal plain and river-valleys, in other words as land lying below the approximate 500 m contour-line, there being clearly nothing mystical as to the precise choice of altitude, but the general coincidence between frontier and contour-line renders it useful as a rule of thumb. In terms of the concentrations of sees/cities defined above, it includes most of the first, third, sixth and eighth. (Map 23)

The territory held (in the sense of being regularly administered and sedentarily based) by the Selçuk sultanate was equally constant and recognisable as the central plateau. It was the transitional or mixed territory between these two blocks of more clearly defined territory that seem to have been particularly sought after by the nomadic pastoralists termed Türkmen, presumably because it contained within itself virtually complete possibilities for the pattern of life favoured by the Türkmen tribes – that of a seasonal

148 See below, pp. 443–4, 444–5 (transfer of mint from Nicaea to Magnesia; custom of wintering in Thrakesion).

149 Nicetas Choniates, *Historia*; ed. van Dieten, I, p. 638. Angold, *A Byzantine Government in Exile*, p. 100.

150 Angold, *A Byzantine Government in Exile*, p. 100.

151 Aphrodisias: see below, p. 439, n. Sardis: G. E. Bates, *Byzantine Coins*, pp. 141–5.

152 Angold, *A Byzantine Government in Exile*, p. 100, and n. 30.

153 See above, p. 110 (Comneni), p. 117 n. 139 (Isaac); below, pp. 126–7, 131 (Manuel).

migration between summer pastures and winter-quarters. In territorial terms this favoured territory comprised Phrygia and Paphlagonia in particular, and in those of concentrations of sees/cities the second, fourth and seventh. It is doubtless significant that virtually nothing is known of the cities of these concentrations, which of course included both Synnada and Euchaita,[154] during the twelfth century, and even during much of the thirteenth, and even the survival-rate of Greek toponyms is significantly lower here than elsewhere.[155] A nomadic pastoralism of the kind practised by the Türkmen simply did not require, and indeed might be positively hampered by, sedentary agriculturalism. In other words, although it might be capable of tolerating the seasonal pattern of the plain with its autumn sowing and early summer harvesting, it might well be antagonistic (to the point of destruction) to that of the transitional land with its tendency towards a spring sowing and autumn harvesting – the two busiest and most crucial periods of the agricultural year occurring there precisely when the Türkmen expected to be in occupation.

The existence of an essentially static territorial division between Byzantines and Selçuks, and the intermediate position, nature and rôle of the Türkmen, can now be seen to form an interesting and complex pattern, however submerged in a welter of geographical and historical detail, but it is difficult to be sure that then its existence was appreciated, let alone formally sanctioned. The various statements by Cinnamus, Choniates and the several crusading chroniclers suggest that the position, nature and rôle of the Türkmen was indeed appreciated.[156] Whether the pattern as a co-ordinated whole was recognised or formalised is much more difficult to decide: the pattern established by the major imperial military campaigns of the period nevertheless suggests that perhaps it was.

In 1116, Alexius I decided to undertake a campaign 'as far as Iconium (*mekhri tou Ikoniou*)', for: 'it was there that the sultanate of Kılıç Arslan [I] divided off (*keithi gar to soultanikion tō Klitziasthlan, apomemeristo*)'.[157] Having waited for the appropriate campaigning season (the autumn[158]), the emperor set out along the road through Dorylaeum and advanced as far as Santabaris (i.e. Bardakçı), sending out detachments against Amorium (i.e. Ümraniye), and Cedrea (i.e. Bayat) and Polybotus (i.e. Bolvadın).[159] Having arrived at Cedrea himself, the emperor was pressed to take Polybotus and advance as far as Iconium (i.e. to keep to his original decision) but finding the country in front of him burned,[160] and therefore fearing for supplies, he decided to leave the decision to God by means of a curious device. The question was whether

154 See below, pp. 138–42.
155 W. M. Ramsay, *The Cities and Bishoprics of Phrygia* I, p. 30.
156 Vryonis, 'Nomadization and Islamization in Asia Minor', pp. 48–50, 52–6.
157 Anna Comnena, *Alexiad* XV.1.1; ed. Leib, III, p. 187.
158 See below, p. 130.
159 Anna Comnena, *Alexiad* XV.3.6–4.1; ed. Leib, III, pp. 197–200.
160 See below, pp. 142–5.

he should take the road to Iconium, or should campaign against the Turks around Philomelium/Akşehir. The decision was taken for the campaign against Philomelium.[161] The real question was whether he should advance along the same road simply as far as Philomelium or right up as far as Iconium.

The decision having been made, the emperor duly advanced along the road, took Mesanacta (i.e. Ortaköy) on the Lake of the Forty Martyrs (i.e. Akşehir Gölü), and finally took Philomelium by assault, sending out flying columns against all the small towns (*kōmopoleis*) lying around Iconium. These flying columns released a number of prisoners of war (*doryalōtoi*) from the Turks and were themselves accompanied back to the emperor, apparently spontaneously, by numbers of local inhabitants (*autokhthones*) taking the opportunity of fleeing Turkish rule. The result was that when the emperor began his return journey he was accompanied by large numbers of refugees who needed protection on the march.[162] (Map 27)

The emperor, for the return journey, intended to march by way of Ampoun (i.e. Ambanaz), in other words choosing the more westerly Cotyaeum route back to Bithynia, rather than the more easterly Dorylaeum one by which he had advanced. A fierce battle took place, in which the imperial forces emerged victorious. Overtures of peace were made by the Turks and accepted by the emperor, the sultan and emperor meeting on the plain (*pedias*) between Augustopolis (i.e. Sülmenli) and Acroenum (i.e. Afyonkarahisar). The emperor stated that if the Turks were to submit to the Roman empire (*tē basileia Rhōmaiōn hypeikein*), and to cease making attacks (*ekdromai*) against Christians, they would henceforth enjoy favour and honour and live freely (*anetōs*) in the regions set aside for them (*en tais apotetagmenais hymin khōrais*), and where they had formerly resided before the accession of Romanus IV and the defeat and capture of that emperor at the hands of Alp Arslan. The sultan and his satraps agreed to do this, and the two sides then parted: the emperor to Constantinople; the sultan towards Iconium.[163] (Map 27)

Anna's account of the campaign reveals curious contradictions: on the one hand, the basic chronology and facts are consistent and plausible, and the account as a whole is therefore presumably accurate; on the other, the terms of the emperor's statement to the sultan are neither compatible with the rest of the account nor plausible in themselves, and therefore presumably cannot be accurate. The account admittedly commences with a slip: the reigning sultan is named as Kılıç Arslan (I), whereas he was already dead (1107) and his successor Şahinşâh (1107–16) established, but the slip is rectified further on. The statement that the sultanate 'divided off' at Iconium is a curious one, for its effective boundaries were far to the west and north of that city; it could, on the other hand, mean

[161] Anna Comnena, *Alexiad* xv.4.2–5; ed. Leib, III, pp. 200–1.
[162] *Ibid.* xv.4.7–9; ed. Leib, III, pp. 202–4.
[163] *Ibid.* xv.6.3–6; ed. Leib, III, pp. 207–10.

that that is where its formally recognised boundaries were in 1116. If they were so recognised, it still remains entirely obscure as to when they were first so recognised, presumably in the context of a treaty.

Alexius' caution in deciding between Philomelium and Iconium as the limit of his campaign, his evacuation of the inhabitants of the small towns between the two cities, and indeed the whole tenor of the campaign itself, demonstrate it not to have been intended as a definitive solution to the Turkish invasion, but rather to have involved the recognition of the permanent realities of the Turkish occupation. To nullify or reverse the results of the battle of Manzikert would have required at least another battle on that scale and with that degree of decisiveness, but it is quite clear not only that the battle on the plain before Acroenum was not on the scale required, but that the imperial victory that resulted from it, although handsome, was in no way annihilating. Alexius' subsequent withdrawal behind his own frontiers confirms this interpretation.

The actual terms of the agreement between emperor and sultan are irrecoverable: they may well have involved an acknowledgement of a formal Byzantine suzerainty on the part of the Turks, as on several previous occasions, and they almost certainly involved some territorial definition or adjustment, again as on previous occasions, but beyond that all remains entirely speculative.

What, then, does Anna's version of Alexius' statement to Şahinşâh represent, and why was it included in the text? It should not be forgotten that, whatever his own assessment and intentions, Alexius may well have been under some considerable pressure to achieve a definitive solution to the whole Turkish problem. Near Cedrea lay a number of villages (*polikhnia*) that had formerly belonged to the famous Burtzes, and it was his son Bardas whom Alexius sent against the Turks gathered there.[164] This reminder of aristocratic dispossession must have been a common feature of the campaign, particularly as the army advanced further into what had been the theme of Anatolikon,[165] and it may well explain Alexius' anxiety to leave the decision (apparent or real) whether to proceed no further than Philomelium, or to proceed right on up to Iconium, to the Almighty. Anna's version of the statement would have been precisely what such dispossessed magnates would have liked to hear. It would also have furthered the glory of her father Alexius, and embarrassed his son John, and his grandson Manuel, for – despite their own considerable achievements – a situation that was to be desired, and apparently had been agreed upon, patently had not come about.[166]

In 1146, Manuel I, in response to the loss of Pracana (probably Alakapı, between Köselerli and Gülnar) in particular, and a continuing state of hostilities in general, decided to undertake a campaign against Masud (1116–55), who had challenged him to battle

[164] *Ibid.* xv.4.2; ed. Leib, III, p. 200.
[165] See above, pp. 100, 103.
[166] See above, pp. 110, 112, Maps 27–9.

at Philomelium. The emperor apparently advanced by way of the Cotyaeum route, for he met the Turkish advance forces near Acroenum and defeated them there, whereupon the sultan withdrew his main forces from Philomelium and retreated towards Iconium. The emperor took Philomelium by assault and burned it, releasing a number of prisoners who had been detained there. The emperor, not having found the sultan at Philomelium as promised, advanced towards Iconium, by way of Gaïta (i.e. Akait) and Adrianople (i.e. Adaras), at one of which (the account is evidently confused), he met and defeated the main Turkish forces. The sultan fled to Iconium and, after a brief stay, to the fortress of Caballa (probably a fortress on Gevele Dağ) a short distance from the city. The emperor, following, defeated the Turks again, at Caballa, but having examined the strength of Iconium itself and having decided it to be impregnable, and having heard of the approach of the Second Crusade, decided to withdraw.[167] The withdrawal, accomplished with some difficulty, apparently took place through the pass called Tzibrelitzemani and then by way of Lake Sclerus/Pousgouse (i.e. Beyşehir Gölü) and the headwaters of the Maeander. On arrival in Bithynia he constructed, or rather reconstructed, the fortress (*phrourion*) of Pylae for the prisoners that he had released at Philomelium.[168] (Map 27)

The repeated apparent, but unstated, significance of Philomelium in this campaign, as in the previous, should be noted. Taken by the German members of the Third Crusade in 1190, it was repopulated by Keyhusrev in about 1196, with Greek captives taken on a raid on Caria (probably Aphrodisias/Stauropolis) and Tantalus (probably nearby, on the Dandal Su). These were given land, seed for sowing, and a guarantee of five years' immunity from taxation, to keep them on their new site.[169] It may well be that the Byzantines had been attempting to apply a policy, that of maintaining empty borderlands to act as barriers, which is attested for the contemporary Balkans.[170]

Again, although too much weight perhaps should not be placed upon the somewhat quixotic nature of the challenge that was offered and accepted, and that dictated the opening phases of the campaign, there is no indication that the campaign as a whole was seen as providing the opportunity for more than a temporary and partial settlement of the matters outstanding between Manuel and Masud.

Finally, in 1175/6, Manuel again turned his attention to the Turkish problem. The campaign opened in 1175 with the refortification of Dorylaeum and Sublaeum. The former had not been in Byzantine hands for some time, and was in a destroyed state: the emperor first found it necessary to expel numbers of nomads (i.e. Türkmen) encamped around it. The latter had apparently collapsed through age (*khronō*), but was again not

[167] John Cinnamus, *Epitome* II.5–6; Bonn edn, pp. 38–45.

[168] *Ibid.* II.6–9; Bonn edn, pp. 45–63. For Tzibrelitzemani, see also below, pp. 146–54; and for Pylae, see also below, pp. 133–4.

[169] Third Crusade: below, pp. 147–8. Keyhusrev: Nicetas Choniates, *Historia*; ed. van Dieten, I, pp. 494–5. For an even earlier example of the same pattern (Alexius I in 1098): Anna Comnena, *Alexiad* XI.6.1, 4; ed. Leib, III, pp. 27, 29.

[170] See above, p. 139.

in an area regularly held by imperial forces. At the same time, an army under Michael Gabras was sent against Amasia, but returned unsuccessful.[171] (Map 27)

The second phase of the campaign, which took place in September 1176, involved the collection of enormous quantities of supplies, including oxen (*boes*) and over three thousand wagons (*hamaxai*), in Thrace, and of a huge army, including both Latin and Cuman elements. The expedition (*strateuma*) was reportedly sufficiently large to have been capable of obliterating the Turks, uprooting the walls of Iconium, and taking the sultan himself, so that his neck might be trampled underfoot at the throne of the victorious emperor. The smaller section of this army, under Andronicus Vatatzes, was sent against Neocaesarea, while the larger, under the emperor himself, advanced through Laodicea, Chonae, Choma and Celaenae (Apamea, i.e. Dinar), towards Myriocephalum, an old and deserted fortress.

Kılıç Arslan (II) (1155–92) had been alarmed from the refortification of Dorylaeum and Sublaeum onwards, and had sent at least two embassies with offers of peace and concessions. To the second of these, which apparently reached Manuel well after he had left Maeander and entered Turkish territory, the emperor – against the advice of his more senior counsellors, and in conformity with that of his less experienced relatives by blood (*ex aimatos*) – boasted that he would give his reply at Iconium. But the sultan had also received considerable reinforcement, and as the imperial army, strung out over ten miles because of the difficulties of the terrain, was traversing the pass called Tzybritze at Myriocephalum, it was cut in sections and severely mauled, with the loss of the entire baggage- and siege-trains. Morale was not improved by the sight of the head of Andronicus Vatatzes, whose army had been destroyed, being paraded about on the end of a Turkish spear. At this stage, the imperial army having spent the night virtually surrounded, the sultan sent a messenger called Gabras, obviously of Byzantine descent, and probably the *vezir* Hasan ibn Gavras, offering what have been seen as surprisingly generous terms: certainly the dismantling of Dorylaeum and Sublaeum, and possibly the payment of an indemnity or annual subsidy. The terms were duly accepted, a truce signed (although the terms were fully carried out by neither side), and the imperial army retired, still harassed by Türkmen (over whom Kılıç Arslan claimed – probably truthfully – to have no control), along the same route as that by which it had advanced.[172] (Map 27)

A number of significant questions arise from the events of this much-described and relatively well-documented campaign. The first of these concerns the actual location of Myriocephalum and the pass called Tzybritze. It is customarily assumed[173] that the battle

[171] John Cinnamus, *Epitome* VII.1–3, Bonn edn, pp. 293–8. Nicetas Choniates, *Historia*; ed. van Dieten, I, pp. 176–7.

[172] For the latest treatment of this campaign: R.-J. Lilie, 'Die Schlacht von Myriokephalon (1176)', *Revue des Études Byzantines* 35 (1977), pp. 257–75. This does not, however, deal with the site of the battle.

[173] E.g. W. M. Ramsay, *The Historical Geography of Asia Minor*, p. 136 (but cf. p. 359); *idem*, *The Cities and Bishoprics of Phrygia* I, pp. 224–5 (but cf. pp. 346–7); *idem*, *Studies in the History and Art of the Eastern Provinces of the Roman Empire*, pp. 235–8.

took place either towards the headwaters of the Maeander, or not far from the head of the double lake called Limnae (i.e. Hoyran/Eğridir Gölü). The Syriac, Greek and Latin evidence is, however, consistent in placing it a long way to the south-east, and much nearer Iconium, and it seems worthwhile treating the question in greater detail in an appendix to this chapter.[174]

The second of these questions is the extent to which the Byzantine army was destroyed or survived the disaster as an organised force. According to Choniates[175] the vanguard, under John and Andronicus, the sons of Constantine Angelus, survived virtually intact, as did the section that followed it in the pass, under Constantine Macroducas and Andronicus Lapardas. As this latter section was itself followed by the wings it seems likely to have formed the main body of the army. The right wing under Baldwin, who was himself killed, seems to have been at least severely mauled. The fate of the left wing, under Theodore Maurozomes, remains uncertain, although its commander seems to have survived.[176] It is agreed by all the sources that the main and most spectacular loss was that of the entire baggage- and siege-trains, including the draught animals and the attendants: given the known contents of the baggage-train, and the crucial nature for the whole enterprise of the siege-train, a concentration upon them may well have been deliberate.[177] Manuel himself claims to have rallied and saved the bodyguard.[178] The rearguard, under Andronicus Contostephanus, seems to have been at least severely mauled, although again its commander survived.[179] The slaughter nevertheless seems to have been extensive on both sides, and its appearance was doubtless accentuated by the extremely confined nature of the terrain. It is pointless to attempt a numerical or even a proportional assessment of losses, but it would seem reasonable to suppose that somewhat over half the total of effectives came through relatively unscathed, and that somewhat under half was subject to losses that were, to a greater or lesser degree, extensive.

That the imperial army survived, reduced in size and badly shaken in morale, but nevertheless as a considerable fighting-force, is the only real way of explaining the generous nature of the terms offered by Kılıç Arslan. It should also be remembered that, with the relocation of the site of the battle, the imperial army was much nearer Iconium than generally has been realised, and that now it was on the Iconium side of the pass. It is in the light of this combination, and the evidently severe losses to his own forces, and not merely in that of his being advised by persons who had previously been in receipt of Byzantine moneys (*khrēmata*), as suggested by Choniates,[180] that the sultan's apparent generosity is to be understood. Indeed, Michael the Syrian suggests[181] that it was not

174 See below, pp. 146–54.

175 See below, p. 151.

176 Brand, *Byzantium Confronts the West*, pp. 59, 61.

177 See below, pp. 151, 152, 272–5, 304–15.

178 See below, pp. 149, 151, 152.

179 See below, p. 151.

180 Nicetas Choniates, *Historia*; ed. van Dieten, I, p. 244.

181 Michael the Syrian, *Chronicle* xx.5; ed. Chabot, III, p. 371.

only the Byzantines, but also the sultan himself, who took fright at the outcome of the battle.

Given a decision, on whatever precise grounds, in favour of generosity, the major element in the terms offered (the dismantling of Dorylaeum and Sublaeum) suggests the employment of considerable political acumen. On the one hand, both had been in ruins when rebuilt in 1175,[182] and neither was in an area that had been under regular Byzantine administration for some time (Map 27). What was being demanded from the Byzantines was therefore essentially the restoration of the *status quo ante bellum*. On the other hand, the people most incommoded by the rebuilding of the two cities were themselves not those under regular Selçuk administration, but the Türkmen, whose transitional territory they deeply penetrated, and with whose seasonal nomadic alternations they decisively interfered, as no doubt they were meant to.[183] Through the dismantling of the two cities, Kılıç Arslan therefore was taking little that was of crucial interest to the Byzantines, keeping nothing that was of crucial interest to himself, but giving back what was of crucial interest to the Türkmen, over whom he or his agents claimed to have no control, and whose reaction to a truce he must have feared. Indeed, some of the Turks called the sultan a traitor in any case, and as it was the Türkmen who harassed the returning imperial army, it seems likely that it was they who did so.[184]

The loss of international prestige on the part of Manuel, after a virtually unbroken run of military successes extending back to the commencement of the reign, is unquestionable, considerable, and reflected in both eastern and western sources. The more direct military and political results are best considered under short- and long-term headings.

The short-term results of the battle, particularly once Kılıç Arslan understood that Manuel did not intend to abide by the terms of the truce, and to dismantle Dorylaeum as well as Sublaeum, were inevitably an increase in Turkish military activity. An army of 24,000 strong, under an *atabeg* (*atapakos*), attacked the coastal and Maeander cities and took Tralles (i.e. Aydın) and Antioch (i.e. Karapınar), as well as several other forts (*erymata*). The devastation seems to have been considerable, but no political annexation seems to have resulted. Indeed the army was subsequently defeated, virtually destroyed, and the *atabeg* killed, by a force sent against it by Manuel under John Vatatzes, Constantine (Macro)ducas and Michael Aspietes.[185]

Two points should be noted in connection with this campaign and counter-campaign: in the first place that it took place in winter, suggesting that the *atabeg* may have been commanding a largely Türkmen force;[186] and in the second place that it was precisely

182 See above, pp. 126–7, below, p. 153.
183 See above, pp. 55–6, 114–17, 122–3.
184 Michael the Syrian, *Chronicle* xx.5; ed. Chabot, III, p. 372.
185 Nicetas Choniates, *Historia*; ed. van Dieten, I, pp. 192–5.
186 Ramsay, *The Cities and Bishoprics of Phrygia* I.1, pp. 175–7.

a section of the army composed of the eastern (i.e. Anatolian) regiments (*stratia ek tōn eōōn stratelogoumenōn tagmatōn*) under Constantine Macroducas, that was amongst those sections of the army that escaped virtually unscathed at Myriocephalum,[187] suggesting that the military capacities of the region had not been seriously affected.

In the following year (1177), Manuel himself found it necessary to campaign against the Türkmen encamped in Lacerium (possibly Dazkırı or the Baklan Ovası) and Panasium (i.e. the Banaz Ovası) (*kata tōn en Lakeriō kai Panasiō kataskēnountōn Persōn*).[188] Possibly in the year following that (1178), the military operations under Andronicus Angelus and Manuel Cantacuzene, again at the head of the best part of the eastern regiments (*tōn eōōn tagmatōn*), were in the region of Charax (probably Çardak, where there is an early Selçuk *han* [Map 12]) and Lampe and Graos Gala.[189] All these campaigns, and others of a similar nature, have the appearance of being winter ones, and against Türkmen in their low winter-quarters, in areas contiguous to or impingeing on regularly administered Byzantine territory.[190]

It thus appears that imperial offensive campaigns, against regularly defended sites, took place in the autumn, because of the relatively temperate nature of the season, while imperial defensive campaigns, against mobile raiders, took place in winter, because of the nomadic nature of the Türkmen.

The long-term results of the battle are frequently said to have included the final disappearance of any hope of recovering Anatolia and expelling the Turks.[191] This is highly questionable, if for no other reason than that there is no good evidence that such a hope ever formed a serious or consistent element in imperial policy. Whatever Anna Comnena or Nicetas Choniates[192] may say about imperial claims or hopes, the public actions and policies of the emperors of whom they are writing belie them. For all the huge army that Manuel collected together in 1176, and for all his boasting that he would dictate terms at Iconium, there is no evidence that those terms would have involved the extinction of the sultanate of Rum. Indeed, the major aim of the operations of the preceding year, which were clearly intended as a prelude, had involved the refortification of two cities whose unmistakable function was to be to act as focal points in the control of the local Türkmen.

Imperial policy in Anatolia as pursued by Alexius, John and Manuel, and as seen in their fortifications, campaigns and diplomatic dealings, therefore suggests that not only

[187] See below, pp. 149, 151.

[188] Nicetas Choniates, *Historia*; ed. van Dieten, I, p. 195. Ramsay, *The Cities and Bishoprics of Phrygia* I.I, pp. 21, 238–9. But see above, p. 42.

[189] Nicetas Choniates, *Historia*; ed. van Dieten, I, pp. 195–6. See also: Wittek, 'Von der byzantinischen zur türkischen Toponymie', pp. 26–7 n. 2.

[190] See above, pp. 115–17, 122–3.

[191] E.g. Vryonis, *The Decline of Medieval Hellenism in Asia Minor*, p. 125. Brand, *Byzantium Confronts the West*, p. 16.

[192] See above, pp. 124, 127.

was their recovery of the peninsula limited, but that also it was intentionally limited to certain areas and certain aims.

The paradigm of Comnenian policies in Anatolia is that emerging from Choniates' account of Manuel's treatment of the three cities of Chliara (reg. Soma, Kırkağaç), Pergamum (i.e. Bergama), and Adramyttium (i.e. Edremit), and his creation of the theme of Neokastra, between 1162 and 1173:[193]

> The Asian cities (*poleis*) of Chliara, Pergamum and Adramyttium were suffering badly from the Turks, for the surrounding regions (*perioikides khōrai*) were formerly inhabited in a scattered fashion [i.e. were *asynoikistoi*], and as their people lived in villages (*kōmedōn*), they lay open to invasion by enemies (*eis pronomēn tois polemiois*). He [Manuel] therefore strengthened them with walls (*teikhesi*), and scattered the nearby plains that were fit for horsemanship with strong fortresses (*phrouriois... erymnois*). And so these small towns (*polikhnia*) abounded with a plentiful supply of inhabitants and of the things that are necessary to daily life, becoming superior to many very prosperous cities. For the fields (*agroi*), being cultivated, brought forth an abundance of crops (*euphorian karpōn*), and the gardener's hand planted there every kind of fruit-giving tree, so that (according to David) the desert was changed into pools of water, and what was formerly deserted became habitable.... So these fortresses, having been assigned a name of their own – for they are called Neokastra – have their own governor (*harmostēn*) brought out from Byzantium, and gather annual revenues (*etēsia... kermata*) for the imperial treasury (*eis to basileion tamieion*).
>
> (Nicetas Choniates, *Historia*; ed. van Dieten, I, p. 150)

Choniates' account may well, of course, be somewhat exaggerated in the speed and completeness with which such a policy brought results, whether financial or otherwise, but it is within this limited context, and not within that of an ever-expanding empire and an ever-diminishing Turkish presence, that the Comnenian recovery of Anatolia should be assessed. Nor should the Comnenian achievement be regarded as a mere prelude to the establishment of the Lascarid state, with all the undertones of parachronistic approval for a small-scale and enclosed economic and military self-sufficiency that generally accompany such an assessment.

## (IV) GENERAL: COMPARISONS

It should now readily be apparent that, in one of the aspects of the basic patterns of settlement discussed above, the Balkan and Anatolian peninsulas shared common features, while in the other they were diametrically opposed.

It is in the distribution of cities that the two peninsulas shared features: in both, physical structure and its dependent and concomitant phenomena dictated a very accentuated pattern. Concentrations of cities were confined to the low-lying areas towards the peripheries of the peninsulas, and in both cases it was to those areas that the frontiers

[193] Ahrweiler, 'L'histoire et la géographie de la région de Smyrne', p. 133.

retreated – in the Balkans in the face of the nascent Serbian and Bulgarian national states in the late twelfth century, and in Anatolia in the face of Turkish (whether Selçuk or Türkmen) penetration in the late eleventh century.

It is equally in the distribution of magnates that the two peninsulas differed fundamentally. In the Balkans, magnates tended very markedly to originate or to own estates, or both, in areas that were virtually coincidental with the concentrations of cities. In Anatolia, they very markedly tended to originate or own estates in areas that were virtually devoid of concentrations of cities. In other words, in the one cities and magnates were coincidental, in the other they were mutually exclusive.

The reason for this distinction remains uncertain. It might, on the face of it, be supposed that the reason was basically a political one: that the very limited extent of the territory held by the empire in the Balkans for much of the period between the seventh and eleventh centuries had dictated the emergence of the two elements coincidentally, while the much more extensive nature of the empire's holdings in Anatolia over the same period had permitted their emergence exclusively. There may even be some truth in this, but it cannot nevertheless be the whole truth, for the distinction seems both to have pre-dated the period involved and also to have lasted unabated well on into a period when the political reason posited no longer obtained, and was in fact reversed. For, in the twelfth century, in the Balkans, where imperial territory had increased greatly, the 'appanages' granted out to members of the imperial family and household, the widespread presence of *episkepseis*, and the donations made to the great monasteries, all tended to occur in that area in which both cities and magnates were already concentrated, while in Anatolia, where imperial territory had diminished greatly, the retained or recovered areas remained virtually free of them.

According to Cinnamus,[194] John II, towards the end of his reign, had it in mind that Cilicia with Antioch and Attalia, and the island of Cyprus, should be given away as a possession (*eis klēron apodōsesthai*) to his youngest son Manuel. Assuming the accuracy of the claim, several points arise. The territorial combination implies, as already suggested,[195] that Lycia had never been recovered from the Turks, and that the largely coastal territory from Attalia round to Antioch therefore formed a separate enclave, the nearest – but equally isolated – imperial territory being Cyprus, the two components being both historically and stategically related. The scale of the proposed 'appanage', however, would have been fundamentally different from the others that have been and are to be discussed, and the terms of the account suggest the combination to have been intended to function as an effectively separate state, somewhat along the lines of the later Morea. But, of course, the intention was never implemented. (Maps 28–9)

It has been suggested[196] that Cyprus (regarded for the purposes of argument as an

[194] John Cinnamus, *Epitome* I.10; Bonn edn, p. 23.

[195] See above, pp. 112–14.

[196] Ahrweiler, *Byzance et la mer*, p. 218 n. 4.

Anatolian province) was also granted out by Manuel I to his cousin Andronicus Comnenus, in *c.* 1166, as an 'appanage'. But this is not strictly accurate. According to Cinnamus,[197] Manuel indeed gave Andronicus a plentiful sum in gold (*aphthonon khrysion*) and, so that the latter could indulge in heavy expenses (*aphthona analōmata*), the emperor also gave him the revenues of Cyprus (i.e. *kai Kypron autō phorologeisthai edōken*). According to Choniates,[198] the emperor gave him the revenues (*dasmologia*) of Cyprus to use in expenditure (*dapanai*). But all this was in the rather extraordinary context of sending him to Cilicia as governor to terminate the Armenian revolt under Thoros there. For this, both men and money in quantity would have been needed, and Cyprus, the annual revenues of which seem to have amounted to about 50,000 hyperpyra, was again the nearest imperial territory.[199]

It has also been suggested[200] that Paphlagonia was granted out by Manuel to the same Andronicus, late in his reign, as an 'appanage'. This suggestion is based on much better grounds than the previous two. According to Eustathius of Thessalonica,[201] Manuel, in return for Andronicus' submission and recognition of his son Alexius (II's) rights, gave Andronicus the land of the Paphlagonians (*tēn tōn Paphlagonōn...gēn*), in which to be military commander (i.e. *stratopedarkhein*), and from which to receive a profit (*kerdos*). Choniates adds[202] that Andronicus was sent to Oenaeum (i.e. Ünye), in some form of enforced but gilded exile. Now, Oenaeum was not in the theme of Paphlagonia as such, but in that of Oenaeum, Sinope and Paurae (Map 29), and so either Eustathius was using Paphlagonia in a very general sense, or Andronicus' jurisdiction was wider than a single theme. The former seems the more probable. In any case, it seems clear that Manuel did give Andronicus an unprecedentedly extensive appanage of the type under discussion, but it should also be noted that it is the only really extensive example known for Anatolia during the twelfth century, and that it was again given under exceptional circumstances: the need to send Andronicus into effective exile, while at the same time providing him with handsome means of support in return for concessions over the rights of succession.

Other than this, the only other formal and institutionalised signs of imperial, court or aristocratic possession are the few *episkepseis* mentioned in the Veneto–Byzantine treaty of 1198 (Damatrys, Pylae and Pythia, and Lopadium and Apollonia) and the *Partitio* of 1204 (Sampson and Ta Malakhiou, belonging to the Contostephanus and Camytzes families).[203] (Map 29)

Now of these *episkepseis* that of Damatrys seems to have represented an imperial

[197] John Cinnamus, *Epitome* VI.1; Bonn edn, p. 250.

[198] Nicetas Choniates, *Historia*; ed. van Dieten, I, p. 138.

[199] See below, p. 173.

[200] Ahrweiler, *Byzance et la mer*, p. 218 n. 4.

[201] Eustathius of Thessalonica, *De Capta Thessalonica Liber*; ed. S. Kyriakidis, p. 28.

[202] Nicetas Choniates, *Historia*; ed. van Dieten, I, p. 227.

[203] For 1198: Tafel and Thomas, *Urkunden* I, p. 269–71. For 1204: *ibid.* I, pp. 478, 479. Carile, 'Partitio Terrarum Imperii Romanie', pp. 218, 241–2, 246–7.

hunting-preserve (*khōra*); that of Pylae and Pythia probably represented the estate (*ktēsedion*) which had been acquired by Manuel, through exchange with a monastery, for the refugees from Philomelium; and that of Lopadium and Apollonia probably represented the area frequently referred to as being simply on the Rhyndacus, which had been fortified by either Alexius I or by John II, and which Comnenian emperors clearly all used as a fortified military encampment (i.e. as an *aplēkton*).[204] Both Pylae and Lopadium had earlier been the sites of state hostelries (*xenodokheia*), attesting both their significance in the arterial road-network, and the presence of state-owned land.[205]

The *episkepseis* of Sampson and Ta Malakhiou probably represented properties that had been granted to the families involved still quite recently in 1204.[206] The suspicion, however, arises that land in this region was peculiarly liable to be granted out in this way. The *praktikon* of 1073 through which Michael VII grants out a number of *proasteia* to Andronicus Ducas, and which apparently mentions other *episkepseis* (Miletus, Alopekai), has to do with precisely this region.[207] It is in fact all too probable that the two *episkepseis* involved in 1073 and 1204 were actually identical, merely appearing under different names on the two occasions. If this were indeed the case, then the geographical name Sampson would be the equivalent of Miletus, the land involved presumably stretching across the Maeander from one to the other. Ta Malakhiou, presumably denoting the presence of fish or a fishery (*malakhios*), then would be the equivalent of Alopekai, presumably denoting the presence of foxes (*alōpēkai*) or just conceivably of salt-pans (*halopēgia*) or their workers (*halopēgioi*). In such marshy areas, the presence of any or all of these would be probable or certain.

After 1204, a local dynast, Sabbas Asidenus, held Sampson, perhaps as a consequence of the disgrace of the Camytzes family, but a Nicephorus Contostephanus still held land in the vicinity of Miletus.[208]

In any event, the fact that the five Anatolian *episkepseis* of 1198 and 1204 can each be identified and explained so readily from independent sources implies that the list is either complete, or at least is essentially so, and thus merely confirms and emphasises the distinction between the Balkans and Anatolia in this respect.

It would, of course, be quite absurd to claim that the great monasteries did not own

[204] Damatrys: John Cinnamus, *Epitome* VI.6; Bonn edn, p. 266. Pylae and Pythia: see above, n. 168. Lopadium and Apollonia: John Cinnamus, *Epitome* II.5; Bonn edn, p. 38 (John II) – but see Anna Comnena, *Alexiad* XV.1.3, 5, and 2.5; ed. Leib, III, pp. 188, 190, 193 (Alexius I). *Aplēkton*: Map 24 (in the thirteenth century, Lopadium (*ap.* 8) seems to have been replaced by Pegae (*ap.* 9), presumably because of the latter's proximity to the Hellespont and the Balkan provinces, where most military activity then took place). In the eleventh century, there had also been a palace at Damatrys: George Cedrenus, *Historiarum Compendium*; Bonn edn II, p. 634.

[205] Pylae: Philotheus, *Klētorologion*; ed. Oikonomides, in *Les listes de préséance*, at p. 123. Lopadium: Zacos and Veglery, *Byzantine Lead Seals* I.2, pp. 1016 (no. 1779), 1091 (no. 1938), 1353 (no. 2495).

[206] See above, p. 106.

[207] See above, p. 68.

[208] Angold, *A Byzantine Government in Exile*, pp. 61–2.

land in Anatolia: for example, in the period subsequent to 1204, the appreciable possessions of the (now Latin) Great Church and Constantinopolitan monasteries, in the region of Smyrna, were confiscated by Theodore I, some of them subsequently being redistributed, whether in the form of military *pronoiai*, or in that of donations to local monasteries.[209] Nevertheless, the same sharp distinction as observed when dealing with 'appanages', and with *episkepseis*, again emerges on examination of the list of donations made by John II to the Pantocrator Monastery in 1136.[210] Such donations, wherever certainly located, almost exclusively involve Balkan properties. The single exception to this, even then a relatively minor one, involves a small group of sub-metropolitan monasteries, located on the Anatolian shore of the Bosphorus or the Marmara, which was given to serve as daughter-houses.[211]

It might be argued that the evidence for this distinction between the Balkan and Anatolian peninsulas was deficient as regards one, or perhaps even two, of these elements: that the lack of appanages in Anatolia is due to the insufficiency of the evidence only; that the lack of *episkepseis* was due to a fiscal technicality or to some difference in terminology; or that the evidence of the Pantocrator *typikon*, however impressive its list of donations, is unrepresentative. But the consistency of the evidence as regards all three elements is not lightly to be ignored or discarded, all the more so given that the themes of Thrakesion and Samos – which account for much of the twelfth-century territory under discussion – were unmarked by the expansionism of the powerful in the eleventh century (Map 25), and given the existence of the novels dealing with the abuses and illegal acquisitions of the powerful in the former theme, dating from 962 and 947.[212] What seems to be emerging is a previously unsuspected, but consciously and consistently pursued, determination on the part of the imperial government to preserve its fiscal position not only in the areas recovered from the Arabs in Cilicia and eastern Anatolia, but also (and on a much longer term) in the theme of Thrakesion in particular and possibly in western Anatolia in general.[213]

It is not suggested, and it should not be supposed, that, because the novels in question concerned or were addressed to officials in the theme of Thrakesion, their terms were necessarily intended to apply to that theme only, but it is suggested, and it can be supposed, that the novels are evidence of a particular governmental determination with regard to the theme. This determination was not only conscious and consistent (Michael VII and Alexius III representing momentary lapses), but also, on the whole, successful.

Again, it is not suggested that no member of the powerful, whether lay or ecclesiastical,

[209] H. Ahrweiler, 'La politique agraire des empereurs de Nicée', *Byzantion* 28 (1958), pp. 55–7; *idem*, 'L'histoire et la géographie de la région de Smyrne', pp. 99–100.

[210] See above, p. 89 and n. 64, and Map 19.

[211] Gautier, 'Le typikon du Christ Sauveur Pantocrator', pp. 69–73, 122–3.

[212] See above, pp. 100, 103, 106.

[213] See above, pp. 104, 106.

ever acquired or owned land in Thrakesion or western Anatolia, but it is suggested that such acquisitions and ownership were neither granted nor encouraged, and that their independent status was not formalised or institutionalised in the same way and on the same scale as they were in the Balkans and central Anatolia.

The reason behind this apparent governmental restraint, involving both itself and its dependants, with regard to Thrakesion and western Anatolia, remains even more obscured than the existence of the phenomenon itself. There may have been some basic historical factor involved, and this kind of explanation seems inherently the most plausible, or it may simply be that the government recognised this region to form the largest single fertile and densely populated, and therefore fiscally productive, block of territory which had remained continuously in imperial hands, and that it was therefore determined to maintain its fiscal hold over the area. Certainly, any suggestion that, in the twelfth century, the region was fundamentally less secure and/or desirable than the Balkans seems generally unconvincing and belied by the particular evidence.

Each of the two peninsulas therefore seems to have had two very basic divisions within it. In the case of the Balkans, the division was between the northern and southern halves: the northern, despite certain areas of fertile land, remaining relatively lightly populated, and therefore lightly exploited economically; the southern containing areas that were not only fertile, but also relatively densely populated, and therefore heavily exploited economically. In the case of Anatolia, the division was between the central plateau and the coastal plain plus the river-valleys, the plateau being inevitably relatively lightly populated and therefore lightly exploited economically. In fact, a combination of physical structure and its dependent and concomitant phenomena consistently favoured, on the plateau, the emergence of a social and economic pattern, involving the tenure by a relatively small number of individuals or families of great estates, consisting mainly of ranch-like land and devoted mainly to the extensive grazing of livestock. The coastal plain and river-valleys were, in their fertile and relatively densely populated and economically heavily exploited nature, very similar to the southern Balkans. In this case, physical structure and its dependent factors may well not naturally have favoured, and may well even have impeded, the evolution of a social and economic pattern characterised by great estates, similar to that obtaining on the plateau.

These basic divisions may well have been reflected in the professional occupations of their respective dominant classes. It has been observed that, while the family-names of the military aristocracy of the eleventh and twelfth centuries tend to derive from offices or, more important, toponymically, from small regions, villages and fortresses in the central plateau of Anatolia, those of the contemporary civil aristocracy tend to derive from professions or, toponymically, from the various quarters of Constantinople or cities in the coastal areas of Anatolia and Greece, or from the islands. Even more pertinently, it has been observed that, during the same period, some 52% of families of the military aristocracy originated in the Caucasus or in central Anatolia, some 19% from Macedonia or Bulgaria, and some 25% from outside the empire. In contrast, some 63% of families of the civil aristocracy originated in the capital, the islands and the coastal areas of Anatolia and Greece, some 10% from Macedonia or Bulgaria, and some 7% from outside the empire.[214]

The contrast is a very marked one, and conforms well with the divisions outlined above: the military aristocracy seems securely identified with the unurbanised, lightly populated and lightly exploited areas of the empire; the civil aristocracy seems equally identified with the urbanised, densely populated and heavily exploited areas. The one predominated in Anatolia, the other in the Balkans.

This basic division between the eastern and western halves of the empire, involving not only simple geography, but also a way of life, and even a profession, may well lie at the root of Attaliates' disparaging remark[215] comparing the emperor Nicephorus III (Botaniates) with the usurper Nicephorus Bryennius: 'For the emperor is an aristocratic product of the East, while he [*sc.* the usurper] is western and low-born in comparison (*...ek tēs heōas eupatridēs ho basileus pephyken, autos d'hesperios kai dysgenēs esti kata synkrisin*).' However unsatisfactory the emperor might be, or prove, and however illustrious and however much land the usurper might own, there is here the full force of the contempt held by the great rancher (or by his supporter) for the small dirt-farmer.

Again, Psellus scathingly identifies[216] Leo Tornices, rebel against Constantine IX (Monomachus), who was ultimately of Armenian descent, but a resident of Adrianople, as oozing 'Macedonian arrogance (*Makedonikē megalaukhia*)' and, more significantly, the 'Macedonian party (*Makedonikē meris*)' supporting him as 'being accustomed not to military simplicity but to civilian ribaldry (*ou stratēgikēs apheleias alla politikēs bōmolokhias ontes ethades*)'. The eastern army was to be used against that of the west (*tēs heōas, tes hesperas, stratopedon*).

To the contrary, Psellus treats[217] Isaac Comnenus, rebel against Michael VI (Bringas), who was ultimately of Macedonian descent but possessed estates in Anatolia, very differently, along with his fellow conspirators who were mostly or all of Anatolian origin. Michael used western forces (*ek tēs hesperas dynameis*) against eastern ones (*tois heōis tagmasin*).

There were, of course, personal reasons why the author should have been against Leo

214 A. P. Kazhdan, *Sotsial'n'ĭi Sostav Gospodstvuiushchego Klassa Vizantĭi XI–XII vv.*, tables 6, 7, pp. 195, 204, and accompanying text; I. Sorlin, 'Bulletin byzantino-slave: publications soviétiques sur le XIe siècle', *Travaux et Mémoires* 6 (1976), p. 374, and nn. 28, 29.

215 Michael Attaliates, *Historia*; ed. I. Bekker (Bonn edn), p. 288.

216 Michael Psellus, *Chronographia* VI.99, 103, 104, 110; ed. E. Renauld, II, pp. 14, 17, 18, 22.

217 Michael Psellus, *Chronographia* VII.4–43; ed. Renauld, II, pp. 85–110, esp. at pp. 89–91.

and for Constantine, and for Isaac and against Michael, but the evidence nevertheless seems suggestive, and supported by a certain amount of independent, if sporadic, material.[218]

This same basic division will then also have underlain the general hostility between the military (*stratiōtikon*) and civilian (*politikon*) factions of the dominant class and their long-standing competition for supremacy, which are implied or even admitted by Psellus and which, however complex and blurred, cannot be entirely ignored or discarded by modern scholars; the constant comment or complaint of various authors that the emperors of the second half of the eleventh century favoured the members of the lower classes (*hoi banausoi*), those of the market-place (*hoi tēs agoras*) and the senate (*synklētos*); and the final reaction that resulted in the supremacy of the Comnenian dynasty, the formation of an imperial clan of birth and rank, and the pursuit by that dynasty and clan of a clearly anti-senatorial policy, leading ultimately to the triumph of family over state.[219]

The deep contempt in which a member of the regional military aristocracy might hold the Constantinopolitan civil bureaucracy is best and most explicitly enunciated in the well-known advice given[220] by Cecaumenus: 'Do not wish to be a man of affairs [i.e. a civilian administrator], for you cannot be both the general and a clown (*Mē thele einai politikos, ou gar dynasai stratēgos kai mimos tugkhanein*).'

The Selçuk invasions, by destroying the military faction, or rather ensuring its at least partial transfer from a Byzantine into a Turkish context, also ensured that the pattern of government, and the relationship of government to the rest of society, which were to mark the twelfth century, were very different from those that had marked the eleventh.

## APPENDIX I

## ANATOLIA – THE CASES OF SYNNADA AND EUCHAITA

Two major sources, the first datable to *c.* 1000, the second to *c.* 1050, possess a direct bearing on the subject under discussion and, as being detailed, contemporary and first-hand, are deserving of quotation and discussion in their own right.

Leo, metropolitan of Synnada, in a letter to the emperor Basil II, describes the

218 S. Vryonis, 'Byzantium: The Social Basis of Decline in the Eleventh Century', *Greek, Roman, and Byzantine Studies* 2 (1959), pp. 161–2. D. I. Polemis, *The Doukai, a Contribution to Byzantine Prosopography*, p. 9 and n. 1. See also: W. E. Kaegi, 'Regionalism in the Balkan Armies of the Byzantine Empire', in *Actes du IIe Congrès International des Études du Sud-est Européen* (Athens, 7–13 mai 1970), II: *Histoire*, at pp. 397–405.

219 Lemerle, *Cinq études sur le XIe siècle byzantin*, pp. 258, 294–5 (*stratiōtikon/politikon*), 287–93 (*synklētikoi, banausoi*, etc.), 297–300 (advent of Comneni). See also: S. Vryonis, 'Byzantine Dēmokratia and the Guilds in the Eleventh Century', *DOP* 17 (1963), pp. 302–14, and below, pp. 570–87.

220 Cecaumenus, *Stratēgikon* LVIII; ed. B. Wassiliewsky and J. Jernstedt, p. 20 (cf. XXIII, XXIV, pp. 8–9).

conditions prevalent in one of the easternmost cities of the second concentration of sees/cities, on the edge of the plateau and formerly in Phrygia Salutaris, in the following terms:

For we do not produce olive-oil (*elaion*), which is a feature common to all who inhabit the theme of Anatolikon. The place does not normally produce wine (*oinos*), owing to the height and speedy [growing/harvesting] nature of the place (*hypsēlēs kai takhinēs lakhousa tēs theseōs*). We use *zarzakon*, which is treated dung (*kopros*), a despicable and stinking substance, instead of wood (*xylon*) [for fuel]. We have everything else, whether for the use of the sick or healthy, brought in from the theme of Thrakesion, or from Attalia, or from the capital itself...For the area of Synnada is not wheat-bearing (*sitophoros*), but barley-bearing (*krithophoros*) only. I describe only such things as are true and real.

(Leo of Synnada, *Epistolai* XLIII; ed. Darrouzès, in *Epistoliers byzantins*, at pp.198–9. For an exhaustive commentary: Robert in *Journal des Savants* 1961, pp. 115–66)

The conditions described or implied are all ones that might have been expected on the basis of both the modern and the mediaeval and ancient evidence: the lack of trees; the presence of livestock, the dung of which was noticeably used for heating rather than for fertilisation; the inability to grow the olive and, normally at least, the vine; the reliance on barley, a cereal hardier than but generally reckoned inferior to wheat; the necessity, for the wealthy at least, of importing many of the normal requirements of life from Thrakesion (Ionia, Lydia and Caria), or Attalia (Pamphylia), or Constantinople, largely that is from the land covered by the first concentration.

Even at the present time the olive will not grow, and the vine is not normally grown, in the vicinity of Şuhut (*c.*1150 m), the successor of Synnada and on the same site. According to Strabo,[221] Synnada had formerly been able to produce the olive, but the information may well be corrupt or even have been erroneous. Certainly, even if the natural olive-line has retreated downwards somewhat, it seems unlikely to have extended so high in comparatively recent historical times. In any case, according to Symeon Seth,[222] in the eleventh century, olive-trees (*elaiai*) did not grow further than 300 stadia (about 60 km) from the sea – ultimately, of course, a function of altitude – which would certainly exclude Synnada. Trees in general are rare and stunted, except in the immediate vicinity of the village itself – and they are far too valuable to be used for fuel. Dung-cakes, termed *tezek*, are therefore prepared and used instead. The same conditions prevail in the remainder of the area which formed eastern Phrygia, and are common throughout that which formed Phrygia as a whole. They are also virtually standard throughout the plateau.[223]

221 Strabo, *Geography* XII.8.14; ed. Jones (Loeb), V, p. 506.

222 Symeon Seth, *Syntagma de Alimentorum Facultatibus*; ed. B. Langkavel, p. 75.

223 L. Robert, 'Les Kordakia de Nicée, le combustible de Synnada, et les poissons-scies. Sur des lettres d'un métropolite de Phrygie au Xe siècle. Philologie et réalités I', *Journal des Savants* 1961, pp. 115–37; de Planhol, *De la plaine pamphylienne aux lacs pisidiens*, pp. 50, 145–6. For the preparation and rôle of *tezek*

In one respect only may Leo seem to have erred: wheat is now quite commonly grown. But this contradiction is probably more apparent than real, and the wheat involved may well be one of the modern hardier varieties, its use having been encouraged by modern governmental policy.[224]

Details regarding conditions in the cities of the next peripheral concentration, the fourth, are lacking. The land, like that of any of these concentrations at a similar altitude, and at a similar remove from the coastal plain, tends to suffer, and presumably long has tended to suffer, from an aridity that progresses more or less *pari passu* with altitude and distance from the coast. The point is well driven home, by implication at least, by a comparison of the terms in which John Cinnamus describes the situation of Dorylaeum (i.e. Eskişehir), at the coastal end of the concentration, with those in which the emperor Constantine (I) describes that of Orcistus (i.e. Alikel), at the plateau end. Cinnamus is full of praise for both the temperate climate and the well-watered nature of Dorylaeum, and the splendid fertility of its surrounding plains;[225] Constantine confines himself to describing the well-watered nature of Orcistus (apparently a matter of note, but it, too, was on a river), and its convenience as a road-junction (it had been classed as a *vicus*, and possessed a *mansio*).[226] It was, apparently, not least on account of the water, that the citizens of nearby Nacolia (i.e. Seyitgazi) had insisted that the Orcistans be annexed to them. The waterless nature of the vicinity of nearby Amorium (i.e. Ümraniye) had already caused considerable difficulties for the Arab army of caliph Mu'tasim in 838,[227] and the similar difficulties later encountered by the First and Second Crusades have already been quoted.[228] The name of one of the few cities in this general area, Anydroi Pyrgoi, also suggests a notable aridity.[229]

John Mauropus, the metropolitan of Euchaita, in a series of letters and sermons, describes the conditions prevalent in one of the westernmost cities of the seventh concentration, formerly in the province of Helenopontus, in terms which usefully complement those used by Leo of Synnada:

But furthermore on such matters, much of the region (*khōra*) is desert (*erēmia*), uninhabited (*aoikētos*), unpleasant (*akharis*), treeless (*adendros*), devoid of vegetation (*akhloos*), without wood (*axylos*), and without shade (*askios*); wholly wild and entirely uncared for (*agriotētos holē kai akēdias mestē*); much lacking both in estimation and reputation. As regards a crop of grain (*apo karpou*

in nineteenth-century Armenia: R. Curzon, *Armenia*, pp. 110–14. For the latest word on *tezek*: L. Robert, *À travers l'Asie Mineure*, pp. 155, 276, 286, 348. As for its calorific qualities, one need only remember the old Turkish story, the punch-line of which begins: *Tezek boktur*....

224 Mülayîm, 'Turkey', in *The World Atlas of Agriculture* I, at p. 431 (establishment of high minimum prices for cereals).

225 John Cinnamus, *Epitome* VII.2; Bonn edn, pp. 294–5.

226 H. Dessau, *Inscriptiones Latinae Selectae* II, pp. 526–7, no. 6091.

227 Tabarī, in Vasiliev, *Byzance et les Arabes* I, at p. 309.

228 See above, p. 40.

229 Ramsay, *The Historical Geography of Asia Minor*, pp. 198, 345–6.

*sitou*), this is possible only with the greatest of troubles (*kan syn pollois kai touto kamatois*) – in which the region abounds – and as regards wine and oil (*oinou de kai elaiou*), similarly, and this produces an absolute wretchedness of poverty and want (*aporian kai endian*).

(John Mauropus, *Opera* CLXIII; ed. Lagarde, p. 88.)

At much the same time, Mauropus can refer, in an expansive mood, to the various signs and forms of wealth present amongst his congregation; whether in gold (*khrysos*) and silver (*argyros*), or other concentrated forms; or in crops (*karpoi*), fertile and well-watered land (*khōra*), herds of fattened cattle (*boskēmatōn agelai*), and so on.[230] Or, in a similar mood, he can refer to the fair (*panēgyris*) that was held annually on the feast of Saint Theodore (Tyro), the patron of the city, although the wares available seem mainly to have been the products of local villages (*kōmai*): crops (*karpoi*), or livestock (*zōoi*), whether lambs (*arnoi*) or calves (*moskhoi*) and their herds.[231] Elsewhere, he can indeed refer to isolation and to difficulties of communication.[232]

The salient points of the main passage are, in fact, remarkably similar to those provided by Leo of Synnada and concerning a not totally dissimilar region: a lack, or near lack, of olive-oil, of wine, and of trees and wood; a lack, or near lack, possibly of cereals altogether, more probably of wheat only, if John Mauropus is using the term *sitos* in the same particular sense as Leo of Synnada. Equally, in the secondary passages, a concentration upon livestock seems evident, and if Mauropus' description of the local fair and its wares is accurate in balance, then he too, together with his social and economic peers, will also have had to import many of what they would have regarded as the normal requirements of life from areas that were capable of a greater variety.

For the problem involved is fundamentally not that of a low level of manpower and production, a high level of taxation and a lack of opportunity for investment,[233] although these features, which were universal, must have been present, and cannot have helped the situation. The problem is, or was until the introduction of modern methods of agriculture and transportation, inherent in the land, its climate and natural vegetation, and the consequently limited uses to which the land could be put. The olive cannot at all recently have grown in the vicinity of Avkat/Mecitözü, the successor of Euchaita and on the same site; the vine is rare; and so are trees in any quantity and of any quality. Arable land will have been scarce, and will have tended to have been of poor quality: it is quite probable that barley alone was capable of being grown on it. The only areas in which these constraints will not have operated, or will have been somewhat alleviated, will have been the river-valleys, towards the upper end of one of which Avkat/Euchaita indeed stands. The prosperity involved in such a city will nevertheless have been a very

230 John Mauropus, *Opera* CLXXXIV; ed. P. de Lagarde, p. 160.

231 *Ibid.* CLXXX; ed. Lagarde, p. 135.

232 *Ibid.* CLXIV; ed. Lagarde, pp. 88–9.

233 N. Svoronos, 'Remarques sur les structures économiques de l'empire byzantin au XI^e siècle', *Travaux et Mémoires* 6 (1976), pp. 51–63, particularly at p. 63.

restricted and localised one, the more particularly so given its distance from the sea, or from a navigable river, and its not having been on one of the great arterial roads. The contradictions in Mauropus' descriptions are therefore apparent ones only, and not real.

What the distinction between plain and plateau involved, however, was not only the relatively narrow one involving the possibility of growing wheat on the former and the necessity of relying on barley on the latter, but probably also a much wider one, involving the possibility of planting a variety of cereals in the autumn, with a good chance of their surviving the winter in their young state, or of planting the same, or others, in the spring, on the plain; and the necessity of planting a much more restricted range of cereals, in the spring only, on the plateau.

It is very noticeable that, when the Fourth Crusade reached the Dardanelles and put in at Abydus (near Çanakkale) on or about 1 June 1203, it took wheat (*blez*) from the fields, because it was harvest-time (*moisons*) there.[234] When it reached Chalcedon (i.e. Kadiköy) on 24 June, the sheaves of harvested wheat (*moies des blez qui estoient messoné*) were already standing in the fields there.[235] An October/November sowing seems to have been the practice in the Chalcidice and, according to fourteenth-century evidence, the possibility of a May/June harvest extended into lower Thrace at least as far as Didymoteichum.[236]

These dates would all be normal for the Mediterranean world.[237] To the contrary, the Crusade of 1101 had an altogether different experience. Now, the Crusade reached Ancyra/Ankara immediately before the feast of St John Baptist (24 June), travelled to Gangra/Çankırı, and then spent fifteen days wandering before part of it emerged before Castamenon/Kastamonu. Therefore, this last cannot have occurred before mid-July, and probably occurred well into the second half of that month. It found there, significantly enough, barley, and of course it was still unripe,[238] despite Leo of Synnada's claim that such areas were speedy-growing/harvesting. What Leo meant by this phrase was

234 Geoffrey of Villehardouin, *La conquête de Constantinople* CXXVI; ed. E. Faral, I, p. 128.

235 *Ibid.* CXXXV; ed. Faral, I, p. 136.

236 A. E. Laiou-Thomadakis, *Peasant Society in the Late Byzantine Empire*, p. 27; C. Asdracha, *La région des Rhodopes aux XIII^e et XIV^e siècles: étude de géographie historique*, pp. 192–3, 202. For the climatic/agricultural régime in eastern Macedonia in general, and in the regions of Chalcidice and the Strymon in particular, see: J. W. Nesbitt, 'Mechanisms of Agricultural Production on Estates of the Byzantine Praktika', pp. 3–84. Michael Psellus actually mentions 11 and 13 November as the best time for the sowing (*pros ton sporon*) of wheat, for then many rainstorms (*ombroi*) descend, both the earth and nature supporting germination (*ta speiromena*). June is the best time for harvesting. He also mentions that wheat (*sitos*) is best cultivated on low-lying land and plains (*eis bathgeōn gēn kai pediada*), barley (*krithē*) on middle-bearing land (*eis tēn meseōs ekhousan*), and pulses (*ospria*) on light-bearing land (*eis tēn leptoteran*). See: Psellus, *Peri Geōrgikōn*; ed. J.-F. Boissonade, in *Anecdota Graeca*, I, at pp. 242–3. The main problem with this work is that much of it is lifted straight from the classical *Geoponica* – not that such lifting necessarily invalidates the points made. See: J. L. Teall, 'The Byzantine Agricultural Tradition', *DOP* 25 (1971), pp. 39–44.

237 E. C. Semple, *The Geography of the Mediterranean Region, its Relation to Ancient History*, pp. 382–3. K. D. White, *Roman Farming*, p. 173.

238 See above, pp. 40, 42.

presumably that crops had to be sown and harvested in spring and autumn, and that the climate was conducive to particularly fast maturation.[239]

When the German members of the Third Crusade reached the head of the lakes called Limnae (i.e. Hoyran/Eğridir Gölü) on 2 May 1190, because of the cold they found there no standing corn or grass, implying that the former at least had either not yet been sown, or that it was as yet insufficiently advanced to provide fodder, let alone grain. The contrast with the situation obtaining at Hierapolis only a few days earlier is thus very marked.[240]

Conversely, when, in 1116, after a wait of three months at Lopadium (i.e. Uluabat), because of the lack of water (*anhydria*) and the unbearable heat (*alea aphorētos*) in the area through which he intended to pass, Alexius I advanced through Dorylaeum/Eskişehir into the region of Polybotus/Bolvadın, and towards Iconium/Konya, the Turks put to flame all the arable or corn lands (*arourai*) and the plains (*pediades*), so as not to leave food (*trophē*) for the invading men and horses. This advance took place after the autumn equinox, and therefore probably in late September, implying that some at least of the local cereals were still standing and had not been harvested.[241]

The distinction, then, seems clear: the inhabitants of the plain (Abydus, Chalcedon) had chosen to plant their wheat in the autumn, as was again normal in the Mediterranean world;[242] those of the mixed or transitional land (Castamenon, Polybotus, etc.) had perforce planted their barley in the spring. The former harvested in May/June, the latter in September/October. A similar distinction, basically dependent upon rapidly increasing height between coast and mountain, seems to have been practised in the Pontus.[243] It, of course, represents an extreme, and doubtless various intermediate situations obtained in the appropriate transitional lands. Similarly, eleventh-century evidence suggests that, in the inner (north-western) Balkans, between Niš and Sofia, harvesting was possible between 2 and 12 July.[244]

If the second, fourth and seventh concentrations shared these limitations, then so, presumably, did the fifth, and there is indeed some slight indication that this may have been the case. The *Vita* of St Theodore of Sycaeum mentions[245] that the village of Mazamia, in the territory of Mnizus – a city which is probably to be located at the modern Ilıca, and which was well within the land covered by the fifth concentration – was infested with locusts in the month of June. This infestation consumed the village's crop of grain

[239] A point confirmed for the modern period by E. Chaput, *Phrygie: exploration archéologique* I, *Géologie et géographie physique*, p. 101. For the ancient *trimestre*, or three-month wheat, said to have been appropriate to high, cold, areas, and involving a spring sowing, see: N. Jasny, *The Wheats of Classical Antiquity*, pp. 71–6, 88–9.

[240] See above, p. 42, below, p. 147.

[241] Anna Comnena, *Alexiad* XV.1.5, 3.5, 5.3; ed. Leib, III, pp. 190, 197, 200.

[242] Semple, *The Geography of the Mediterranean Region*, pp. 382–3. White, *Roman Farming*, pp. 173, 180.

[243] Bryer, 'The Estates of the Empire of Trebizond', p. 400.

[244] Albert of Aix, *Historia Hierosolymitana* I.12; RHC, *Occ.* IV, pp. 281–2.

[245] *Vita Sancti Theodori Syceotae* XXXVI; ed. Festugière, p. 32.

and vines (*ton te tou therous kai tēs ampelou karpon*). It seems likely that this would have happened (or, given the context, would have been considered plausible) only if the grain was still then unharvested and, moreover, still unripe. The *Vita* also suggests,[246] in another incident, that pure bread (*artos katharos*), presumably white (i.e. wheaten) bread, was considered a luxury in the area.

It is noticeable that the land occupied by the second and seventh concentrations is that which, although mixed or transitional between plain and plateau, and therefore tending towards aridity, nevertheless receives briefly a greater degree of precipitation, however exiguous in absolute terms, than either, in late spring (May). In many places on the plateau itself, spring precipitation is actually greater than either autumn or winter.[247]

It is also noticeable that the average number of days with snow-cover in the mixed or transitional areas, and over much of the plateau, does not exceed 10–20 days in the case of the former, and 20–30 days in that of the latter. As the average number of frost-days in these two areas is 75–100 days and 100–125 respectively, and as the frosts involved are quite capable of exceeding −10 °C or even −20°, it seems quite probable that the one would have been insufficient to protect standing crops from the other.[248*]

These factors, of course, would almost certainly have encouraged, might in extreme conditions even have dictated, a spring sowing, in any case. Indeed, for all these reasons, barley is still peculiarly suited to the central plateau, and it is still difficult – and with height becomes virtually impossible – to maintain an autumn sowing, a spring sowing and autumn harvesting being the norm there.[249] As a particular example: in the nineteenth-century *sancak* of Sivas, the normal sowing season lasted until May, and the harvesting one stretched from late August to October.[250]

The situation, on land so inherently tending towards aridity, with so brief and slight an advantage as regards precipitation, and with so insufficient a winter protection, would even so at very best have remained extremely precarious. A farmer on the plain could, if he possessed the wherewithal, and his autumn sowing had failed, count on sowing again in the early spring with at least some hope of success. A farmer on mixed or transitional

* I owe this reference to the kindness of Bob (R. E. F.) Smith.

246 *Ibid.* xv; ed. Festugière, p. 13.

247 Tanoğlu *et al.*, *Türkiye Atlası*, maps 28, 49.

248 *Ibid.* maps 40, 18. On the general problem, with particular reference to the climatically not dissimilar USSR, see: N. I. Vavilov, *The Origin, Variation, Immunity, and Breeding of Cultivated Plants*, pp. 282–5.

249 N. I. Vavilov, *World Resources of Cereals, Leguminous Seed Crops and Flax, and their Utilization in Plant Breeding*, pp. 99, 105. For the modern, or recent, agricultural régime in Turkey, see: J. F. Kolars, *Tradition, Season, and Change in a Turkish Village* (based on the Antalya *vilayet*). For the modern, and potential historical, régime, see: M. Wagstaff, 'Physical Geography and Settlements'; G. Hillman, 'Agricultural Resources and Settlement in the Aşvan Region', 'Agricultural Productivity and Past Population Potential at Aşvan', and 'Crop Husbandry and Food Production: Modern Basis for the Interpretation of Plant Remains', all in *Anatolian Studies* 23 (1973), at pp. 197–215, 217–24, 225–40, 241–4 (based on the Elâzıg *vilayet*). See also above, p. 54 n. 90 (pastoral régime), and p. 60 n. 120 (deforestation).

250 Cuinet, *La Turquie d'Asie* I, pp. 674–5.

land had no such flexibility (however effectively limited it may have been for the lowland farmer): he would go under unless he possessed the wherewithal to survive for a whole year and then to sow again in the spring; or was large enough a land-owner to possess scattered holdings, some of which might not have been affected; or was in any case not mainly dependent upon an agricultural base (when he could, at least within limits, move his livestock). *A fortiori* a farmer on the plateau in this situation. The large land-owner was thus naturally favoured over the small, and the pastoralist over the agriculturalist.

There is some small indication that the mixed or transitional land, together with the plateau land, did indeed tend to form a unit in any climatic/agricultural perturbation. According to Cedrenus,[251] in 1032 the themes of Kappadokia, Paphlagonia and Armeniakon, along with the region of Honorias (part of the theme of Boukellarion), and presumably, although unmentioned, the intervening themes and parts of Boukellarion, Kharsianon and Sebasteia, were struck by the classic combination of famine and pestilence (*limos kai loimos*). The land involved includes the whole of the central northern and the eastern central parts of the peninsula, therefore much of the mixed or transitional land and much of the plateau land, represented by the sixth and seventh concentrations. The precise cause of the trouble is not mentioned, but was presumably ultimately climatic in origin. The inhabitants began to leave in order to live. The emperor Romanus III, aware of the migration (*apanastasis*), compelled them to return home (*hypostrephein oikade katenagkaze*), giving them gold and the other necessities for life (*pros to zēn anagkaia*). Zonaras[252] confirms the account, and adds that the east was infested with locusts at the same time, so the migration was presumably westwards.

Again, according to Cedrenus,[253] in 1035 there was a six-month long drought (*aukhmos*), and in 1036, presumably as a result, the themes of Thrake and Makedonia, Strymon and Thessalonike, and right on up to Thessaly, were struck by famine. This couples together most of the autumn-wheat growing lands of the outer Balkans, and shows them not always to have escaped, whatever their flexibility. The Morea and Greece were apparently the only such lands to escape on this occasion. The general point nevertheless remains a valid one.

[251] George Cedrenus, *Historiarum Compendium*; Bonn edn, II, p. 499.
[252] John Zonaras, *Annales* XVII.12.14–15; ed. T. Büttner-Wobst (Bonn edn), III, p. 580.
[253] George Cedrenus, *Historiarum Compendium*; Bonn edn, II, pp. 516, 518.

## APPENDIX II

# ANATOLIA – MYRIOCEPHALUM AND THE PASS TZYBRITZE

According to Michael the Syrian,[254] the disaster took place one day's march only from Iconium. Nicetas Choniates is much less precise: he gives[255] Manuel's route as Laodicea, Chonae (Colossae), Lampe and Celaenae, and then goes on to remark that, from there, he proceeded to Choma and Myriocephalum. Now, this is admittedly curious, for in order to get from Celaenae to Choma (i.e. from Dinar to Homa) he would have had to retrace his steps, moving away from Iconium, and it may well be this that has caused the trouble in locating Myriocephalum, and in supporting the assumption that it lay somewhere on the slopes above the Hermus and Maeander valleys, in other words, in west-central Phrygia. The latter part of this route should, therefore, be regarded with some reserve and perhaps even with some suspicion.

Choniates also remarks,[256] however, that Myriocephalum was in the pass called Tzybritze. Manuel himself, in his letter to Henry II of England, claims[257] the pass to have been called Cybrilcymani by the Turks, and this is obviously identical with Cinnamus':[258] 'region difficult of access and exit, not only to men drawn up in order of battle, but even to those travelling in small groups', which was marked by ravines (*pharanga*) and which was called Tzibrelitzemani in Turkish; which Manuel I had had to negotiate in 1146; and which he places well removed from Roman territory, between Iconium and Lake Sclerus (Pousgouse, i.e. Beyşehir Gölü), implying that plains lay between the end of the pass and the lake, and suggesting with some exaggeration that there was a day's journey or even less between the city and the lake.

Tzybritze, Cybrilcymani and Tzibrelitzemani therefore represent the same pass, and the two reasonably specific sources for its location place it consistently: at one day's march from Iconium, and between that city and Lake Sclerus. William of Tyre generally agrees[259] with the more specific evidence in remarking that the disaster took place in the neighbourhood of Iconium (*circa Iconium*), which any Phrygian site could not be. All this almost inevitably makes the pass one of those due west of the city, at the bottom of the Sultan Dağları. Cinnamus, moreover, was in a particularly good position to know precisely where the pass was located, for there is good internal evidence in his writings for his having been an eyewitness to the campaign of 1176.[260]

254 Michael the Syrian, *Chronicle* xx.5; ed. Chabot, III, p. 371.

255 Nicetas Choniates, *Historia*; ed. van Dieten, I, p. 178.

256 *Ibid.* I, p. 179. See also below, p. 153.

257 Manuel I Comnenus, *apud* Roger of Hoveden, *Chronica*; ed. W. Stubbs, II, p. 103.

258 John Cinnamus, *Epitome* II. 7; Bonn edn, p. 47. See also below, p. 152.

259 William of Tyre, *Historia Rerum* XXI.12; RHC, *Occ.* I.2, p. 1024.

260 C. M. Brand, *Deeds of John and Manuel Comnenus*, pp. 3–4.

The Latin sources for the German section of the Third Crusade, which passed through the area and actually took Iconium in 1190, are also extremely pertinent to the question. According to the anonymous author of the *Historia de Expeditione Friderici*,[261] the crusade passed Sozopolis/Uluborlu on 30 April and arrived at Philomelium/Akşehir on 7 May. Meanwhile, on 3 May, 30,000 Turks gathered in a certain very narrow pass (*in quadam arctissima clausura*), which the crusade was to traverse, and in which the emperor Manuel with a very large army was destroyed, so that they might perform the same office for Frederick and his army. Frederick, forewarned by the Holy Spirit, turned in another direction (*aliorsum tetendit*), and the army was led by a certain captive Turk, who had promised to lead them out of the land of solitude (*terra solitudinis*) into a richer one (*in terram uberiorem*), over a very rough and very high mountain (*mons asperrimus et altissimus*), in a journey that was fit only for goats (*solis ibicibus pervium*). It was as a result of this journey that Frederick and the army reached Philomelium.

According to the *Historia Peregrinorum*,[262] the crusade passed Sozopolis and, after a two days' march through a region that was empty of all pleasantness and in which nothing grew (*per regionem ab omni amenitate vacuam et inmunem*), found itself again attacked by Turks as it was about to advance between a certain lake and nearby mountains (*inter quendam lacum et montes contiguos*). It was at this stage that, by divine intervention, a recently captured Turk was found who was prepared to lead the crusade out of these deserted and roadless places (*locis desertis et inviis*) and, by a shorter road (*via compendiosiore*), into the plains of Turkey (*ad Turcie campestria*). The Turk warned the crusaders that if they took the road to the right (*ad dextram*), inevitable death and destruction awaited them, for they would enter a region that was sterile, waterless and roadless (*terram... sterilem, inaquosam et inviam*), and where numberless thousands of Turks awaited them. He offered instead to lead them to the left (*ad levam*), by means of a difficult but secure road (*viam... difficilem sed securam*), so that by the following night they would be in the plains of Turkey where there was a sufficiency of water and a flat route from city to city as far as Iconium. This offer was accepted, and they arrived, after some difficulty, before Philomelium.

The *Epistola de Morte Friderici Imperatoris*[263] remarks that, on 2 May, the crusaders were again attacked by a great number of Turks in a certain narrow passage (*in angusto quodam transitu*); that, because of the cold, they found no standing corn or grass (*propter frigiditatem segetem et herbam non invenimus*); and that, forced by necessity, they turned away from the imperial road (*a via regia*) which the emperor Manuel was accustomed to use, because it was deserted and very long towards Iconium (*deserta et longissima versus*

[261] Anonymous ('Ansbert'), *Historia de Expeditione Friderici Imperatoris*; MGH, *SRG:NS*. v, pp. 77–8. On this section of the crusade, see now: E. Eickhoff, *Friedrich Barbarossa im Orient: Kreuzzug und Tod Friedrichs I*, pp. 113–18, and map 6 at end ('Von Den Mäanderquellen nach Lykaonien 29.4–17.5.1190'), but the route chosen and depicted is clearly incorrect.

[262] Anonymous, *Historia Peregrinorum*; MGH, *SRG:NS* v, pp. 157–9.

[263] Anonymous, *Epistola de Morte Friderici Imperatoris*; MGH, *SRG:NS* v, pp. 174–5.

*Yconium*) and entirely closed in by mountains (*tota montibus clausa*) and turned towards the left (*ad sinistram*). On 3 May the crusaders took to a very rough mountain and narrow road (*per montes asperrimos et viam angustissimam*), and despite great difficulty descended into the plain (*planities*) of Philomelium on the same day.

The situation, from the combined evidence of these Latin sources, is perfectly clear. If the crusade passed Sozopolis/Uluborlu on 30 April, then it would indeed have arrived at a lake, the Limnae/Hoyran and Eğridir Gölü, on 2/3 May. At the head of those lakes the road passes between Toklu Tepe and the Çam Ormanı, and the lakes, by way of a very narrow passage, obviously where the crusade was attacked, and into a small plain called the Hoyran Ovası, at the far end of which stands a village called Kumdanlı. At Kumdanlı the road divides, or in the early twentieth century did divide, into two main branches. The left-hand branch continues in an east south-easterly direction to Pisidian Antioch/Yalvaç, where there is, or then was, a choice of two passes over the Sultan Dağları at their most accentuated and into the plain of Philomelium/Akşehir. Both passes are capable of being described as very rough, very high and very narrow: the more northerly is the rougher but also the shorter, there being only 21 miles between Yalvaç and Akşehir; the less rough is the longer, there being some 34 miles between the two towns.[264] The right-hand branch continues in a south-easterly direction down the eastern side of Lake Sclerus/Beyşehir Gölü, and is mainly over the relatively wide plain between the mountains and lakes.[265]

It was quite clearly this choice of roads which faced the crusaders after passing the head of the Limnae, and it is equally clear that they chose the left branch to Antioch, and probably the shorter but rougher pass over the mountains into the plain of Philomelium.

But what of the right branch? The very narrow pass in which Manuel and his very large army were destroyed is obviously that of Myriocephalum/Tzybritze, and it has also been assumed that the pass was very near the head of the Limnae, where the choice between the left and right branches was made. But none of the three sources actually says this, nor does any of them indeed imply it. The *Historia de Expeditione* says that the Turks occupied the pass and that, for whatever reason, the crusaders turned in another direction (i.e. to the left). The *Historia Peregrinorum* says that the road to the right led to death and destruction because of natural conditions and waiting Turks. The *Epistola* says that the road to the right was deserted, long, and closed in by mountains. It does add, moreover, that it was the imperial road by which the emperor Manuel was accustomed to go (*ire solebat*). Now this can only have been something of an exaggeration, for Manuel can only have been along it on one certain occasion, that is on his return

264 Admiralty (Naval Staff, Intelligence Division), *C.B. 847C(2): A Handbook of Asia Minor* III.2, *The Central Plateau West of the Kyzyl Irmak*, pp. 48, 192 (Route 27), 191 (Route 26).

265 Admiralty, *A Handbook of Asia Minor* III.2, pp. 172–9 (Route 22, Yonuzlar–Gundanly).

journey from Iconium in 1146, and on two possible other occasions, that is on the assumption that he used it for his outward and return journeys in 1176.

As mentioned above, the road continues in a south-easterly direction down the eastern side of Lake Sclerus/Beyşehir Gölü, and then a left-hand branch veers almost east round the bottom end of the Sultan Dağları, for it is indeed the road to Iconium. For virtually all of the distance between Kumdanlı and Yunuslar the road is through the open plain, with occasional undulating hills. Then, just past Yunuslar, it reaches Barsak Dere Boğazı – 'the Pass through the Valley of the Gut' – between the three mountain masses of Aladağ, Erenler Dağ, and Loras Dağ, forming a barrier to the way through to Iconium. Here, then, after having been deserted and very long, finally it is entirely closed in by mountains.

Now, any plausible candidate for identification as the pass of Myriocephalum/Tzybritze should have at least three features. Two of these are natural: it should have some characteristic allowing it to be described as myriad- (i.e. many-)headed (*Myriokephalon*); and it should have another allowing it to be described as an enclosed meadow or plain (*Çivrilçimeni/Cybrilcymani/Tzibrelitzemani*).[266] The third of these is man-made: it should be on a known ancient or mediaeval route. With these in mind, it seems worthwhile considering a late nineteenth-century itinerary (Table 2) describing the section of the Konya–Dinar road lying between Kızılviran and Yunuslar, that is the Barsak Dere Boğazı and its approaches.[267] Now, in the first place, there is no doubt that this is a Roman route: Yunuslar is probably Pappa-Tiberiopolis, and Kızılviran is possibly Sinianda, in addition to which there is of course the particular evidence of the Roman milestone mentioned* in the itinerary. It is also a Selçuk route, having at least one early *han* along it (Map 12).

Manuel's army had apparently adopted, at least while crossing the plain, a classic formation. In the pass, too, John and Andronicus, the sons of Constantine Angelus, leading the household forces (*meta tōn oikeiōn taxeōn*), formed the vanguard; Constantine Macroducas (apparently leading the eastern regiments) and Andronicus Lapardas (in that case presumably leading the western regiments), both probably forming the main body of the army, followed on; Baldwin the emperor's brother-in-law, possibly leading Latin mercenary forces, formed the right wing; Theodore Maurozomes led the left; then followed the hardware and baggage of the army (*ta skeuophora kai to oiketikon* [*tou strateumatos*]), including the wagons for the siege-engines (*helepoleis*); after that came the emperor himself with the élite guard (*epilekton*); Andronicus Contostephanus led the rearguard (i.e. was *opisthophylax*).[268]

[266] W. Tomaschek, *Zur historischen Topographie von Kleinasien im Mittelalter* I, *Die Küstengebiete und der Wege der Kreuzfahrer*, p. 101.

[267] Admiralty, *A Handbook of Asia Minor* III.2, p. 172 (Route 22, Kyzylviran–Yonuzlar).

[268] Nicetas Choniates, *Historia*; ed. van Dieten, I, pp. 180, 189.

Table 2. *Itinerary from Kızılviran to Yunuslar (the Barsak Dere Boğazı and approaches)*

| Time in hours (intermediate) h. | m. | Remarks, salient features, etc. |
|---|---|---|
| | 0 | Hills on either side draw closer★. Below the road, a brook. |
| | 10 | Old Turkish cemetery r. |
| | 5 | Enter defile. To r. and l. dwarf pines on flanks of hills. |
| | 20 | A yaila to l. |
| | 20 | Enter a small bare plain★. |
| | 20 | To r., at some distance, among wooded hills, a rock with ancient ruins, called Assar Kalesi★. Still follow chaussée with telegraph. Direction N.W. Descend course of small stream★. |
| | 15 | To l. a mountain with many small peaks★; to r. a small hill covered with scrub★. |
| | 40 | Enter Baghyrsak Dere, a defile with stream; many windings. |
| | 15 | The defile narrows. |
| | 15 | A mill to l. A few minutes farther a stone bridge. Cross the stream. Sandy road. Direction S.W. To l. low hills. |
| | 30 | To r. a Roman milestone belonging to a Roman road from Yalovach to Konia, following the same course as the present★. |
| | 5 | Yonuzlar village among trees. |

The distance between Kızılviran and Yunuslar, on the ground, is approximately 15 miles or 24 kilometers, and the time taken between the two, on horseback, is approximately $4\frac{3}{4}$ hours. The route as a whole is on a S.E.–N.W. axis.

The emperor had, however, neglected to take the normal military precautions for the pass: he had removed to a place of safety neither the baggage- nor the siege-train; and he had not attempted to clear the Turks from the surrounding mountain-valleys with light-armed troops, so as to facilitate the passage of the army. In fact, he behaved exactly as if he had been out on the plain – and this despite the fact that he had heard, as he was to see, that the Turks had occupied the heights, with every kind of weapon, and with every intention of barring his way.[269]

Because of the terrain, and because of this neglect, the army, with between three and five thousand wagons in the baggage- and siege-trains, stretched out over ten miles, with

[269] *Ibid.* I, p. 180.

the vanguard having lost contact with the rearguard, and with no single element of the extended army being able to move freely to the support of another.[270]

According to Nicetas Choniates,[271] when the Turkish attack finally came, the sons of Constantine Angelus plus Macroducas and Lapardas, that is the vanguard plus the main body, came through without harm. Baldwin was himself killed, and the soldiers of the right wing broken. Andronicus Contostephanus and the soldiers of the rearguard, and the emperor himself, were unable to help, or even to retreat or to move to the side, because the wagons of the baggage- and siege-trains, which had been in the middle of the extended army, were thrown into total confusion when both the oxen that pulled them and their attendants became the objects of Turkish arrows, completely blocking the narrow passage: the wagons could neither go forward, nor (not least because of their doubtlessly wide turning-circle) turn back. It soon became a matter of every man for himself, including the emperor.

The vanguard and the main body, having overcome the difficult passage without harm, made camp, seizing the security afforded by a nearby hill. Elsewhere, the confusion was immense, and the slaughter on both sides frightful, some kind of dust-storm adding difficulties of visibility to those already present. An attempt was made to utilise a nearby hill as a refuge, but many perished not having noticed the intervening presence of a ravine, into which they inevitably fell. Eventually, having partially redeemed his previous neglect by acts of personal heroism, the emperor caught up with the vanguard, and was subsequently joined by Andronicus Contostephanus and others of the high nobility (*tōn dynamenōn mega*).

The army, regrouped after a fashion by companions, companies and battalions, but demoralised by fear, spent a miserable night in the camp on the hill. The Turks who surrounded it encouraged the Turkish forces on the imperial side to come over to them and to leave the camp, for at dawn it was to be completely annihilated. The emperor himself shared in the general demoralisation and, at an impromptu council of war, was only with difficulty dissuaded from secret flight.

According to Choniates,[272] hostilities did recommence at dawn, but it was at this stage that Kılıç Arslan sent Gabras with presents and offers of peace on generous terms. These were, of course, accepted and duly signed. The emperor wished to return by a different route, and not to retrace his steps, so as to avoid the site of the battle. But the guides (*hoi de tēs hodou hēgemones*) insisted upon leading him back that way, so that he should see the pitiful sight with his own eyes. The ravines were level, the hollows were heaped up, and the plains were covered, with the dead. Many of the bodies had had their scalp and penis removed so as to render Byzantine and Turk indistinguishable, for many had fallen in either army.

270 Manuel Comnenus, *apud* Roger of Hoveden, *Chronica*; ed. Stubbs, II, p. 103.

271 Nicetas Choniates, *Historia*: ed. van Dieten, I, pp. 180–7.

272 *Ibid.* I, pp. 188–92.

The returning imperial army, or rather the stragglers from it, and particularly the wounded and non-combatants, was constantly harassed by Türkmen furious at losing their intended prey and plunder, this despite the (relatively effective) efforts of the emperor to protect the rear.

At Chonac, where enemy territory evidently ceased, the emperor gave a silver stater (i.e. presumably an electrum trachy) to each of the wounded for medical expenses, and proceeded to Philadelphia where he paused for rest for several days. From there he sent on messengers to those in Constantinople, to announce what had happened, calling himself a Romanus Diogenes, for that emperor had lost the greater part of his army in battle with the Turks, and had himself been made prisoner, whereas he, Manuel, had made a truce with the sultan, he had a solemnly-signed piece of paper to prove it (!), and he had obtained it through fear and trembling (*sc.* on the part of the sultan). He had nevertheless proceeded to the dismantling of Sublaeum, as the sultan expected, but not to that of Dorylaeum. This last inevitably caused the sultan to complain and, when the complaint was not met, to break the truce.

Manuel's own letter to Henry II of England[273] is essentially in accordance with Nicetas' account, but nowhere admits blame for what happened, and stresses his own heroic actions in holding off Turkish attacks so as to allow the rearguard to extract itself from the pass and join the main body of the army, and in defending the camp on the nearby hill. It does, nevertheless, admit to a severe loss of personnel, including relatives, and of the entire siege-train, it being the latter which caused him to give up all thought of effecting anything against Iconium itself.

According to Michael the Syrian,[274] the disaster took place only a day's march from Iconium; most of the damage done to the imperial army was caused by the Türkmen; mainly the damage involved the loss of the baggage-train, including gold, the imperial chapel, crosses, all kinds of other things, and foodstuffs, and the siege-train. It was these last two losses that caused the emperor to seek peace from the sultan. The emperor later recovered what was apparently the imperial processional cross, itself containing a piece of the true cross,[275] through the payment of an indemnity in gold.[276]

The basic question remaining is whether, given the historical and topographical information available, the disaster can be proven to have taken place in the context of the Barsak Dere Boğazı.

Choniates, perhaps significantly echoing Cinnamus, states[277] that Kılıc Arslan occupied in advance the difficult ground called the passes of Tzybritze (*tas dyskhōrias hai*

[273] Manuel Comnenus, *apud* Roger of Hoveden, *Chronica*; ed. Stubbs, II, pp. 102–4. A. A. Vasiliev, 'Manuel Comnenus and Henry Plantagenet', *Byzantinische Zeitschrift* 29 (1929/30), pp. 237–40 (Eng. trans.).

[274] Michael the Syrian, *Chronicle* XX.5; ed. Chabot, III, pp. 370–2.

[275] M. F. Hendy, *DOC* IV.

[276] See also below, pp. 265, 275.

[277] Nicetas Choniates, *Historia*; ed. van Dieten, I, pp. 179–80; above, p. 127.

*kleisōreiai tou Tzybritzē katanomazontai*), and that he permitted the imperial army to pass Myriocephalum, which was where he had stationed his forces so as to oppose the Byzantine advance. Myriocephalum itself he has already described[278] as an old and deserted fortress, and gives what is clearly a parachronistically fanciful derivation for the name. Tzybritze itself he describes in the following terms:

> For this place is a rectangular glen (*epimēkēs aulōn*), having a superfluity of mountains (*orōn hyperbolas*), which on the northern side having descended gradually and with a gentle gradient forms hills (*gēlopha*) and towards the east is hollowed out into ravines (*pharangas*), while on the other side it forms a face of forward-bending rocks (*protomas proneuōn petrōn*) which rise up suddenly into precipitous cliffs (*krēmnōdeis*) all around.

This is very clearly what can be described as an enclosed meadow or plain (*çivrilçimeni/cybrilcymani/tzibrelitzemani*). The pass was at least to some extent wooded, and a river or stream (*potamos*) ran through it, although both are admittedly true of most passes.[279]

The extended imperial army would have entered the defile proper shortly after leaving Pappa-Tiberiopolis/Yunuslar (i.e. reversing the order given in the itinerary). It would clearly have been in the interest of Kılıç Arslan not to attack at once, but to wait until the whole army was well inside the pass. The sources say or imply that this is indeed what happened. If the army was indeed strung out over anywhere near ten miles (about nine modern miles or fourteen kilometres), then by the time the wings, the baggage- and siege-trains, the emperor and bodyguard, and the rearguard were well inside the defile proper, the vanguard and the main body of the army will have been virtually clear of the other end of the pass. This again is what the sources say or imply.

Now, as the vanguard left the defile proper, it will have observed on its left (i.e. on the north side of the pass) a small hill*, probably that which was utilised as an attempted refuge, and on its right (i.e. on the south side) a mountain with many small peaks*, surely the eponymous *myriai kephalai*. A little further on it will have noted on its left, at some distance, among wooded hills, a dominant rock with ruins*, presumably *Phrourion Myriokephalon/Asar Kalesi*. It is quite clear that Nicetas had only the vaguest idea as to its date and nature, nor is the Turkish name any more informative. It seems nevertheless to be at least mediaeval and possibly ancient.[280] Both in the defile itself, and at this stage, it will have noted the existence of a stream*, and that it was on its left (i.e. north) side that there were hills, and on its right (i.e. south) side that there were mountains. Again a little further on, it will have entered a small, bare (and presumably sunken or enclosed) plain*, *epimēkēs aulōn/çivrilçimeni*. The Turkish name implies the presence of grass, but the difference may be seasonal, or the result of a real change.

278 *Ibid.* I, p. 178.

279 *Ibid.* I, pp. 184, 185.

280 W. M. Ramsay, 'Pisidia and the Lycaonian Frontier', *Annual of the British School at Athens* 9 (1902/3), p. 255.

It was presumably at about this stage that the Turkish attack occurred: in this case, the vanguard will have been virtually clear of the pass; the main body will have been between the small bare plain and the defile proper; and the two wings, the baggage- and siege-trains, the emperor and bodyguard, and the rearguard, will still all have been in the defile – the winding gut – itself.

The vanguard and the main body of the army, virtually unscathed, will therefore have made its camp on one of the hills near the head of the pass*, and were joined there eventually by those of the remainder who had managed to extricate themselves from the gut, and to fight their way through. At this stage, the army will, ironically, have been some thirty or forty kilometres, on horseback only some eight hours, from Iconium.[281]

Michael the Syrian is therefore essentially correct in locating the disaster only one day's march from Iconium; Cinnamus is correct in locating Tzibrelitzemani between that city and Lake Sclerus; William of Tyre is correct in locating the disaster in the neighbourhood of the city; and the crusading sources are correct in locating Manuel's defeat along the right-hand branch of the road at the head of the Limnae. Tzybritze, Cybrilcymani and Tzibrelitzemani all denote one and the same pass, and that pass, in which Myriocephalum lay, and where the disaster took place, is identical with Barsak Dere Boğazı – 'The Pass through the Valley of the Gut'.

The result is to relocate precisely the site of the battle of Myriocephalum some 200 kilometres to the south-east of its previous approximate site. This obviously has a number of major repercussions. (Map 27)

The revised site clearly, however, has to be checked out on the ground at the earliest available opportunity.

[281] Ramsay, *Studies in the History and Art of the Eastern Provinces of the Roman Empire*, p. 242.

SECTION II

# FINANCE

# CHAPTER 3

# THE BUDGET

## (I) GENERAL

It is axiomatic that, in the vast majority of cases, the largest single source of public revenue available to an ancient or mediaeval state was one based on the product of the land lying within its territorial boundaries. It is also axiomatic that, similarly, by far the largest object of public expenditure in such a state was the single one consisting of its military forces and, *a fortiori*, the composite one consisting of its military forces, civil service and public works. Although there is no absolute proof of either axiom as regards the later Roman and Byzantine empire, there is nevertheless every reason to believe both to have been conformed to.

Although, as pointed out in the preceding paragraph, there is no absolute proof as to the validity of either axiom, nevertheless there do exist a number of extremely suggestive indications as to their validity. It has been calculated[1] that, in the fifth and sixth centuries, the revenue derived from land and agriculture amounted to something like twenty times that derived from trade and industry. The precise figures of 95% (land) and 5% (trade) are doubtless open to dispute, but their order is likely to be correct.

According to Gregoras,[2] Andronicus II's attempt at fiscal reform in *c.* 1321 resulted in the imperial revenue amounting to a million hyperpyra a year, and, according to the same author,[3] the Latins (i.e. Genoese) of Galata were receiving an annual revenue (obviously deriving largely from customs-dues), in *c.* 1348, of 200,000 hyperpyra, while Constantinople itself was receiving 30,000 only. These figures suggest that other sources of revenue (presumably principally land) might have provided something of the order of 80% of imperial revenue, and trade some 20% – had the empire been in a position to exploit trade to the full, which, of course, now it was not. But this was, in any case, subsequent to a long-standing and fundamental reduction in the empire's territorial bases – total, in the case of Anatolia, partial, but severe, in that of the Balkans – and the part played by land would have weakened in the face of that played by trade.

[1] Jones, *Later Roman Empire* I, p. 465; II, pp. 869–72. [2] See below, p. 161.

[3] Nicephorus Gregoras, *Historia Byzantina* XVII.I; Bonn edn, II, pp. 841–2.

Similarly, calculations for a contemporary microcosm of the empire, the so-called empire of Trebizond, suggest that some 70 or 80% of imperial revenue may have derived from land, and some 20 or 30% from trade.[4] This, again, involved a state with a minor territorial base, but with a whole string of (mainly small) trading ports.

The fact that, in the twelfth century, the entire annual trade of a major Italian trading city, and *a fortiori* that the entire possessions or at least the best part of the possessions, of a complete Latin colony or trading-quarter, might amount to no more than the monetary fortunes of one or two Byzantine ecclesiastical or lay magnates, suggests the same pattern to have obtained during the intervening period.[5]

In the tenth century, the crucial interdependence of the empire's main source of revenue, and its main object of expenditure, is well expressed by Leo VI in an original section of his *Taktika*:[6] 'For there are two occupations (*epitēdeumata*) that We consider most necessary (*lian anagkaia*) to the stability and permanence of the nation (*pros ethnous systasin kai diamonēn*): agriculture (*geōrgikē*), which supports and increases the soldiers (*stratiōtai*); and military service (*stratiōtikē*), which maintains and protects the farmers (*geōrgoi*). And We consider these two occupations to take precedence over all the others.' The same considerations are apparent elsewhere.[7]

In the fourth century, the relationship between army and taxation is constantly alluded to, and military expenditure is specifically identified as one of the principal causes of harm to the state by the anonymous author of the treatise *De Rebus Bellicis*.[8] Having provided chapters on the reduction of largesse (I: *De Inhibenda Largitate*); the fraudulence of the mint and its correction (III: *De Fraude et Correctione Monetae*); the dishonesty of governors (IV: *De Iudicum Pravitate*); he continues with a chapter, entitled 'Concerning the Diminution of Military Expenditure (V: *De Relevando Militari Sumptu*)', which commences: 'Having described, as we have seen, the injuries to the state deserving to be removed by imperial foresight, let us now turn to the enormous expenditure on military forces (*ad enormia militum alimenta ratione*), which should be stopped in a not dissimilar fashion, for it is from this cause that the collection of revenue afflicts the whole system of tributary payment (*quorum causa totius tributariae functionis laborat illatio*).'

In the sixth century, the same point is made even more specifically by another anonymous author of a treatise on military matters,[9] who remarks that: 'Financial expertise (*to khrēmatikon*) is now accumulated on account of other affairs of public utility (*koinōphela pragmata*), such as ship-building (*naupēgia*) and wall-making (*teikhopoiïa*), and above all through expenditure on the soldiers (*dia ta analōmata tōn stratiōtōn*): for in this way each year most of the public revenues (*dēmosiōn eisodōn...ta pleista*) are consumed.'

[4] Bryer, 'The Estates of the Empire of Trebizond', pp. 370–1.

[5] See below, pp. 201–6, 590–7.

[6] Leo VI, *Taktika* XI.11; ed. J.-P. Migne, in *PG* CVII at col. 796.

[7] Refs: Toynbee, *Constantine Porphyrogenitus and his World*, p. 33.

[8] Anonymous, *De Rebus Bellicis*; ed. R. Ireland, p. 7.

[9] Anonymous, *Peri Stratēgikēs* II.4; ed. H. Köchly and W. Rüstow, p. 46.

In the eleventh century, the point is again made, if only negatively, when Psellus,[10] in characterising Constantine X, remarks that his policies of financial retrenchment and political appeasement were geared to ensuring that the greater part of available funds were not consumed by military expenditure (*hina mēte ta pleiō katanaliskoi tois stratiōtais*).

In the sixth century, Corippus compared[11] the treasury to a stomach through which all the limbs were fed (*cognoscite fiscum ventris habere locum, per quem omnia membra cibantur*), the empty stomach entailing the failure of everything (*fuerit si venter inanis, omnia deficiunt*...). In the eleventh, Psellus considered[12] that to render full the imperial treasury (*plēreis te tous basileious poiein thēsaurous*), and to consider such funds as destined for the military (*kai stratiōtika tauta hēgeisthai ta khrēmata*), were two of the major duties facing an emperor. The former, as will be seen in the chapter succeeding this,[13] is a recurrent theme in imperial finance.

Very little that is specific is known of the basic methods behind the construction of the imperial budget, although what little is known or can be deduced suggests them to have been capable of practical complexity without the possibility of conceptual sophistication – the fundamental parameters being provided by the severe limitations both of contemporary technology and the state of financial and economic knowledge.

As it happens, rather more is known of the basic budgetary methods of particular institutions within the state, which do appear to give some sort of microcosmographic picture of the larger unit. For example, the *typikon* drawn up by Gregory Pacourianus, *megas domestikos* of the West under Alexius I, for his monastery of the Virgin *Petritzonitissa* at Bachkovo, and dated 1083, reveals the following pattern.

Revenues from the monastic estates in the themes of Philippopolis (i.e. Makedonia), Voleron and Thessalonike were all collected in by September. From the total of the revenues, certain sums were put aside, in the keeping of the abbot, for the regular and statutory heads of monastic expenditure for the following year, including distributions made on the occasion of the annual commemorations of the founder and his near relations that occurred throughout the year, and monastic salaries which were disbursed on Easter Sunday. From the remainder of these revenues, a sum of up to 10 lbs gold (i.e. 720 nomismata) was put aside, in the keeping of the treasurer, for the satisfaction of the occasional needs of the monastery for the following year. The final remainder, or surplus, if any, was given over to the purchase of an estate, to remain under monastic control. Monastic revenues were collected by agents who rendered their accounts to the treasurer

[10] Michael Psellus, *Chronographia*, Constantine X, XVII; ed. Renauld, II, p. 146. Cf. also Isaac I, LIX; *ed. cit.* II, p. 119: *tais te dēmosiois syneisphoreis ouk eis stratiōtikas syntaxeis apokhrōmenōn, all'eis politikas kharitas kai lamprotētas*... (of Isaac's predecessors). These are only the most specific examples, others exist: see, for example, below (n. 12).

[11] Corippus, *In Laudem Iustini Augusti Minoris* II; ed. Averil Cameron, p. 55.

[12] Michael Psellus, *Chronographia*, Romanus III, XV; ed. Renauld, I, p. 43.

[13] See below, pp. 224–7.

twice in the course of the year, in September and at Easter, and who, having provided satisfaction, were given quittance.[14]

Now, it is quite clear that this pattern is, to a very considerable degree, a conscious imitation of the imperial one. The imperial financial year, the *indictio*, ran from 1 September to 31 August; tax-payments could be, or were, made semi-annually, in September and March; and imperial salaries, or *rhogai*, were paid out in Holy Week.[15] There are some indications that at an earlier period accounts had been rendered every four months,[16] and there are indications that at a later period payments were similarly made every four months.[17] But it is also very noticeable that it must have been between 15 February (the day after Quinquagesima Sunday) and 1 April (Maundy Thursday) 1081 that a tax-collector called Byzantios, who was carrying a purse of gold deriving from tax-revenues (*eispraxeis*), and who was on his way to the City to deliver the gold to the imperial bed-chamber (*koitōn*), was hijacked by the caesar John Ducas, who was himself on his way to join the Comnenian faction in Thrace, then in revolt against Nicephorus III.[18] Alexius and his companions had fled the City on 15 February, and re-entered it on 1 April, Alexius presumably being crowned emperor on 4 April (Easter Sunday).[19] Byzantios had presumably met up with John Ducas sometime in March, and it is obviously tempting to suppose that he was on his way into the City not only to deliver the gold, but also to render his accounts, and in both cases to meet a deadline of March or Easter Sunday.

For it would clearly, in any case, have been a very great convenience to have had a March/Eastertide delivery and rendering. The indictional year (1 Sept.–31 Aug.) was clearly geared to the Mediterranean climate, according to which cereals were harvested in late May/early June.[20] Land-owners could sell off their surplus in return for coin in which to fulfil their tax-liabilities subsequently, and still meet a deadline of 1 September.[21] Other crops (such as grapes, olives and other fruits), and more particularly cereals in areas subjected to a continental climate, would have been harvested in September/October – in the case of olives, even later.[22] Land-owners would then have found it impossible to sell off crops in return for coin and meet a September deadline, and – given the rigours of winter – might well have found it necessary to wait until spring, when a March/Eastertide delivery and rendering would have come into its own.

[14] Petit, 'Typikon de Grégoire Pacourianos', pp. 1–63. P. Lemerle, 'Le typikon de Grégoire Pakourianos', in *Cinq études sur le XI^e siècle byzantin*, at pp. 113–91. M. F. Hendy, 'The Gornoslav Hoard, the Emperor Frederick I, and the Monastery of Bachkovo', in C. N. L. Brooke, J. G. Pollard, B. H. I. H. Stewart and T. R. Volk (eds), *Studies in Numismatic Method: Essays Presented to Philip Grierson*, at pp. 179–91.

[15] The semi-annual (Sept./Mar.) payment of taxes/rents occurs in both the public and private sectors. Refs: C. M. Brand, 'Two Byzantine Treatises on Taxation', *Traditio* 25 (1969), p. 43; Laiou-Thomadakis, *Peasant Society in the Late Byzantine Empire*, p. 181. For the payment of *rhogai*, see below, pp. 191–2 and n. 187.

[16] See below, pp. 388, 459–60. [17] See below, pp. 222–3. [18] See below, p. 227.

[19] Anna Comnena, *Alexiad* II.4.9, 10.4; ed. Leib, I, pp. 74–5, 94. V. Grumel, *Traité d'études byzantines* I, *La chronologie*, pp. 256, 312. See also below, pp. 582–3. [20] See above, p. 142.

[21] See below, pp. 295–6 and n. 208, 298 and n. 213, 386 and n. 58. [22] See above, pp. 142–3.

## (II) ANDRONICUS II

In any case, it is in the light of this imitation of imperial practice that the only contemporary account of the imperial budget and its principal elements which survives in any degree of detail – that recorded by Gregoras as having been intended by Andronicus II as part of his attempt at fiscal reform in *c.* 1321, but which was never actually put into effect because of the various internal and external disturbances of the time – should be seen. The terms of this account are as follows:

And so, in a short time only, and despite the constant diminution being undergone by the dominion of the Romans, the nomismata entering the imperial treasury (*ta to basilikon eisagomena tameion nomismata*), from the hands of the revenue- and tax-collectors (*argyrologoi kai phorologoi*), so increased as to amount to a million a year. Out of which, the senior emperor [i.e. Andronicus II] intended to maintain twenty ships on a permanent footing against enemies on the seas and in coastal areas, a land army of a thousand cavalrymen on a permanent footing in Bithynia, and of two thousand on the same footing in Thrace and Macedonia. He intended the moneys (*khrēmata*) remaining over to be used up in expenses (*dapanai*) for ambassadors arriving from wherever at whatever time, in annual payments (*khorēgia*) to surrounding peoples, and in the myriad other expenses deriving from imperial affairs.

(Nicephorus Gregoras, *Historia* VIII.6; Bonn edn, I, pp. 317–18)

Much the same methods and concerns are evident in the budgetary settlement recorded by Cantacuzene in somewhat less detailed terms as having been arrived at between himself (John VI) and John V, in 1354:

Of the moneys (*khrēmata*) collected annually through public taxes (*dēmosioi phoroi*), as much as was needed for the payment of the military (*pros te to misthophorikon tēs strateias*), the equipment of ships (*tōn triēreōn paraskeuēn*), and the other heads of public administration (*dēmosiai dioikēseis*), should be spent by the treasurers (*prytaneioi*), as customarily. What remained over beyond this requirement (*khreia*) should be shared out between the emperors equally, to provide for the expenses (*analōmata*) of their households (*oikiai*).

(John Cantacuzene, *Historiarum Lib. IV* IV.40; Bonn edn, III, pp. 291–2)

The strong generic similarity between the reconstructed budget of the monastery of Bachkovo and the two accounts of the imperial budget provided by Gregoras and Cantacuzene should be immediately obvious: there is an annual revenue, presumably collected by 1 September, or at least by Easter, out of which there needed to be set aside a sum for certain specific and regular purposes, and a sum for contingency purposes, for the ensuing year. The possibility of a surplus, which is itself to be devoted to specific purposes, is provided for. The same implications are to be drawn from the account given by Psellus of Michael VII's financial skills: what was involved was a knowledge of current revenue, and current expenditure, and the exercise of certain technical skills such as the composition of the coinage and the use of the touchstone.[23] There is no suggestion, in any of these cases, of the possibility of utilising credit as some kind of buffer for any disequilibrium that might occur between revenue and expenditure. Nor is it likely that any such possibility existed in any systematic sense: there was no profession or social class that could, or if it could, would, offer such facilities;[24] in default of a reserve from which the difference could be made up,[25] recourse would have to be made to one or more of a number of the crude and short-term expedients that are outlined in the next chapter of this book.[26]

The main item of cash expenditure in the budget of the monastery of Bachkovo was that of 761 nomismata for monastic salaries, compared with that of 720 nomismata for contingencies, and that of 222 nomismata for commemorations and distributions.[27] Salaries thus accounted for some 45% of the total cash budget.

The main concern in both descriptions of the imperial budget is naval and military salaries. If Andronicus II intended to maintain 20 ships and 3,000 horsemen on a permanent footing, some very approximate calculations can be made.

In the Veneto-Byzantine Treaty of 1187, the complement of a galley (*gallea*) was reckoned as 140 rowers (*romatores* = *remigatores*?).[28] It is not clear whether this number includes non-commissioned officers and officers, but the impression is gained that it does not. Even so, the full complement is unlikely to have exceeded 160 men, and such a figure accords quite well with others of the high mediaeval period.[29] In the Genoese-Byzantine Treaty of Nymphaeum of 1261, the full complement is reckoned as 154 men, including 46 officers and non-commissioned officers, and the basic pay of an ordinary seaman (*voguerius*) is reckoned as 1 hyperpyron 18 keratia per month, or 21 hyperpyra per year, and that of the various other offices and functions at various rates around an approximate median of 3 hyperpyra per month or 36 hyperpyra per year.[30] At such figures and rates each ship will have cost 310 hyperpyra per month, and 3,720 hyperpyra per year, in salaries, and 20 ships will therefore have cost 74,400 hyperpyra per year.

In 1272, the basic pay of a salaried *stratiōtēs*, presumably a cavalryman, was reckoned as being up to either 24 or 36 hyperpyra per year.[31] It has been supposed[32] that the difference is one not of rank but of nature, the former involving salaried soldiers, the

[23] See below, pp. 241–2.
[24] See below, pp. 238–41.
[25] See below, pp. 224–7.
[26] See below, pp. 228–37.
[27] Hendy, 'The Gornoslav Hoard', at pp. 184–8. See also below, p. 215 and Table 5.
[28] Tafel and Thomas, *Urkunden* I, pp. 196–7.
[29] C. Manfroni, *Storia della Marina Italiana dalle Invasioni Barbariche al Trattato di Ninfeo*, pp. 449–65. Constantine Porphyrogenitus reckons that a *dromōn* holds 300 men – 230 *ploïmoi* (sailors) and 70 *polemistai* (marines, soldiers), but this figure of 230 for the crew seems out of kilter with at least the later ones: *De Caerimoniis* II.45; Bonn edn, p. 670.
[30] Zepoi, *Ius Graeco-Romanum* I, p. 493. H. Antoniadis-Bibicou, *Études d'histoire maritime de Byzance: à propos du 'thème des Caravisiens'*, p. 144.
[31] A. Heisenberg, *Aus der Geschichte und Literatur der Palaiologenzeit*, p. 40.
[32] *Ibid.* pp. 70–2. G. Ostrogorsky, *Pour l'historie de la féodalité byzantine*, pp. 70–2.

latter involving holders of grants in *pronoia*, but the text gives no warrant for such a distinction. Shortly after 1261, the normal upper limit of a grant in *pronoia* appears to have been fixed (on the Anatolian frontiers at least) at 40 hyperpyra per year, and there is some cumulative later evidence (1334/5, 1344, etc.) which suggests that this limit may earlier have obtained in Europe as well.[33] In any event, at an approximate median rate of 30 hyperpyra per year, 3,000 cavalrymen will have cost 90,000 hyperpyra in salaries per year.

The naval and military standing forces proposed by Andronicus II in *c.* 1321 might, then, have cost something of the order of 165,000 hyperpyra in salaries per year. This assumes, of course, that the rates for seamen had remained stable between 1261 and *c.* 1321, and that those for cavalrymen had remained stable between 1272 and *c.* 1321. Now in 1261 the hyperpyron had stood at 16 carats fine; in 1272 it stood still at 15 carats fine; but in *c.* 1321 it stood only at 11/12 carats fine.[34] It is therefore all too probable that rates had risen during the intervening period to take account of debasement. Certainly, other sums mentioned in near-contemporary and casual contexts – 100,000 hyperpyra per year to defend the islands in 1340, and 50,000 hyperpyra for the expedition against Thessaly in 1321[35] – give a rather more burdensome impression.

With regard to the implications of the last statement, a recently evolved alternative rate for military salaries would put the annual salary of a *stratiōtēs* at 70–80 hyperpyra after *c.* 1321.[36] In this case, at a median rate of 75 hyperpyra per year, 3,000 cavalrymen will have cost 225,000 hyperpyra in salaries per year, and at a proportionally increased rate 20 ships will have cost 186,000 hyperpyra in salaries per year, giving an annual total of 411,000 hyperpyra. It ought to be observed, however, that these higher figures would make perfectly good sense if they represented silver hyperpyra, and not (notional) gold ones, the former being worth half the latter. This would bring the rate back down to a more normal 35–40 (gold) hyperpyra.[37]

As to the other items specifically mentioned in the two accounts, near-contemporary casual sources give the occasional figure. Annual payments to surrounding peoples could well be heavy: in 1333, the government agreed to pay the Ottomans 120,000 hyperpyra per year to preserve the few remaining imperial possessions in Anatolia.[38] So could the expenses of the imperial households: in 1322 it was agreed to grant the co-emperor

[33] George Pachymeres, *De Michaele et Andronico Palaeologis, De Mich.* I.5; Bonn edn, I, p. 18. Ostrogorsky, *Pour l'histoire de la féodalité byzantine*, pp. 122, 150–2 (grants worth 40 hyp.). See also: Schreiner, 'Zwei unedierte Praktika', pp. 37–9 (late 14th-c. grant worth 40 + 40 = 80 hyp.), and Laiou-Thomadakis, *Peasant Society*, p. 5 n. 3.

[34] See below, pp. 527–8 and Table 23.

[35] See below, p. 223.

[36] Laiou-Thomadakis, *Peasant Society*, p. 5.

[37] See below, pp. 539–40 and Table 25. But see also above, n. 33: the grants still seem to be in basic units of 40 hyp., and the particular grant (of 80 hyp.) is merely a multiple. The later situation is, however, clearly a residual one only. For the Palaeologan army and its financing see, in the last instance: N. Oikonomides, 'A propos des armées des premiers Paléologues et des compagnies de soldats', *Travaux et Mémoires* 8 (1981), pp. 353–5.

[38] See below, p. 266.

Andronicus III 36,000 hyperpyra per year for the expenses of his household and his wife.[39] The expenses of Andronicus II's own household are likely to have been very much higher.

What neither of the accounts mentions are the large sums that at this period, at least, tended to impinge on the imperial budget as a direct consequence of granting out quasi-imperial titles to nearer relations by blood or marriage: it may well be that a co-emperor rated some 80,000 hyperpyra per year; an emperor/despot some 60,000; a despot some 50,000; a sebastocrator some 40,000; and a caesar some 30,000.[40] An empress may have rated some 30,000 hyperpyra per year, and even a deposed emperor between 20,000 and 24,000.[41] This scale may be an exaggerated one, and is in any case likely to have included payments to military dependents as well as the civilian household, but it is not unlikely to be of the correct order.

It should be noted that the military forces proposed by Andronicus, at least as described by Gregoras, do not include infantry, of which – proportionally – there would have had to have been considerable numbers. Indeed, Justinianic figures[42] suggest that the total of military expenditure might well have been virtually doubled by such an inclusion. If this were to have been the case, then military salaries will have formed something between 35% and 80% of the annual imperial revenue, depending upon which of the two figures evolved above is the more accurate, although for the reason also given above, the former seems the more plausible. Such a wide range of possible estimates is of course scarcely satisfactory, but well illustrates the severe limitations within which it is necessary to operate.

As to the actual or possible sources of revenue at this period, the statement by Gregoras that Galata and Constantinople were yielding revenues of 200,000 and 30,000 hyperpyra respectively has already been noted.[43] Cantacuzene states that the island of Chios was yielding a revenue of 120,000 hyperpyra, and as it possessed a virtual monopoly of the highly-priced commodity, mastic, the figure may not be as exaggerated as otherwise it might look.[44]

## (III) JUSTINIAN I

### *A. Africa and the west*

Unfortunately, virtually nothing worthy of any great degree of confidence is known of the total of imperial revenue or expenditure, and little more of the individual elements that went to make up the imperial budget, during the later Roman and early and middle Byzantine periods. This, of course, has not prevented estimates and comparisons being made, and will not do so in the future – indeed, such exercises have their values, if only

[39] See below, pp. 205–6. [40] See below, p. 205. [41] See below, p. 206.
[42] See below, p. 166. [43] See above, p. 157.
[44] John Cantacuzene, *Historiarum Libri IV* II.12; Bonn edn, I, p. 380.

that of imparting some idea of the range of possibilities and probabilities. It must, however, be acknowledged that none of them possesses a status higher than more or less informed guesswork, and that in the likely default of evidence of a totally different order this will inevitably remain the case. The most convincing range is still that provided by the estimates of Stein on the lower side and of Andréadès on the higher: the former reckons the total budget as being in the region of 7–8 million solidi; the latter reckons it as being in the region of 10–13 million nomismata, both principally with reference to the period *c.* 300–600.[45]

Justinian's schedule for the restored prefecture of Africa (534) mentions that the prefect himself was to be paid 100 lb gold annually, his advisers (*consiliarii*) 20 lb, his secretaries (*cancellarii*) 7 lb, and his *officium*, consisting of 396 members, 4,172 solidi, making a total of 13,316 solidi. The four *consulares* and three *praesides* of the provincial tier of administration (there was no diocesan) were apparently each to be paid 448 solidi annually, and their *officia* (each consisting of 50 members) 160 solidi, making a total of 4,256 solidi. The combined civil total would therefore have amounted to 17,572 solidi distributed between about 750 officials.[46] This is not a large sum, but then it was not upon their salaries that such officials mainly relied, rather upon the perquisites that accompanied their offices and functions.

The annual salary of the *magister militum per Africam* remains unknown, for the military commander there when Justinian's schedule was drawn up was Belisarius, who was then still technically *magister militum per Orientem* and who presumably drew his salary as such, but the five *duces* at his disposition were each to be paid 1,582 solidi (to include personal staff), and their *officia*, each consisting of 40 members, 674½ solidi, making a total of 11,282½ solidi.[47] This sum not unexpectedly reveals a considerably higher rate of pay for subordinate military officials than for equivalent civil ones.

Now if, as seems not entirely improbable, the magister's annual salary was somewhere in the region of the 100 lb paid his colleague, the prefect, and his personal staff's salaries were somewhere in the region of the 27 lb paid the prefect's personal staff, and if the magister's *officium* consisted of 300 members[48] who were paid an annual sum bearing much the same ratio to that paid the ducal *officia* as the annual sum paid the prefect's

[45] E. Stein, *Studien zur Geschichte des byzantinischen Reiches*, pp. 141–60. A. M. Andréadès, 'Le montant du budget de l'empire byzantin', *Revue des Études Grecques* 34 (1921), pp. 20–56. Stein subsequently defended his figures in a review of Andréadès' article, in *Byzantinische Zeitschrift* 24 (1923/4), at pp. 377–87. Cf., on the very high side: A. Segrè, 'Essays on Byzantine Economic History I, The *Annona Civica* and the *Annona Militaris*', *Byzantion* 16(I) (1942/3), pp. 435–8 (30–60 million sol. for Diocletian and Constantine, 15 million sol. for Justinian). Not the least of the problems involved is the definition of budget and revenue. Below, 'budget' is taken as meaning the central state budget, and 'revenue' the sums that might have entered, or did enter, the Constantinopolitan (and in the earlier period, the prefectural) treasuries. The distinctions involved are perhaps formal ones only, but are certainly necessary.

[46] *CJ* I.27(i).21–39. Various other civil officials (*medici*, *grammatici*, *oratores*), who were subsidised by the state (*CJ* I.27(i).40–1), form negligible additions.

[47] *CJ* I.27(ii).20–34.

[48] Theodosius II, Novel VII.4 (441).

*officium* bore to that paid the consular *officia*, then the annual salaries of magister, personal staff and *officium* may have amounted to somewhere in the region of 24,000 solidi. The combined military total would then have amounted to about 35,000 solidi distributed between 500 officials, and the global total for the regular civil and military bureaucracy of the African prefecture would have amounted to about 53,000 solidi or somewhat under 7 kentenaria distributed between about 1,250 officials.

The precise strength of the regular army in Africa remains uncertain. According to Procopius,[49] Belisarius invaded the country with a regular army that had originally consisted of 15,000 men, including 10,000 infantry and 5,000 cavalry. Although this force was depleted by disease, combat and transfer, it was also reinforced on occasion, and it seems not improbable that it was intended to form the permanent regular establishment. According to the same author,[50] the army in Italy consisted of 12,000 men in 542 and, according to Agathias,[51] the same army – which had, apparently, been reinforced by as many as 30,000 men under Narses in 552 – consisted of 18,000 men in 554.

The two Italian figures relating to what might be termed more normal circumstances suggest that 15,000 is at least a reasonable African one. At the minimum rate of basic pay (one *annona* per man adaerated for five solidi), 10,000 infantry would have cost 50,000 solidi annually, and at a similar rate (one *annona* and one *capitus* per man, the latter being adaerated for four solidi), 5,000 cavalry would have cost 45,000 solidi annually, making a total of 95,000 solidi. Neither of these items takes account of the existence of long-serving ordinary soldiers receiving rates of basic pay above the minimum, or of non-commissioned officers, or indeed of commissioned officers. The first (*semissales*) received one and a half *annona*, the second (*circitores* on up to *primicerii*) received between two and five *annonae*; *ducenarii*, *numerarii*, and *primicerii* also received one and a half or two *capitus*.[52] Commissioned officers obviously received even more. Nor do these items take account of allowances paid out for uniforms, arms, and so on.[53] Even so, it seems improbable that the additional expenditure represented by rates of basic pay above the minimum, and by allowances, would have increased the total sum spent on the regular establishment by more than half, in other words beyond 142,000 solidi or somewhat under 20 kentenaria.

In addition to the regular establishment, Justinian intended to recreate the African section of the *limitanei*, the static frontier force engaged in cultivation as well as defence, and to pay it a *stipendium* of some kind.[54] Neither the extent to which the first intention

49 Procopius, *De Bello Vandalico* I.11; ed. J. Haury (Teubner), I, p. 361. It should be noted that this figure, and the following ones, even if accurate, may involve effectives only, but that there is no way of knowing whether this is the case or not, let alone of calculating what the relative proportions or numbers of effectives and support staff, etc., might have been.

50 Procopius, *De Bello Gothico* III.3; ed. J. Haury (Teubner), II, p. 309.

51 Agathias, *Historiarum Libri V* II.4; ed. R. Keydell, p. 45. Stein, *Histoire du bas-empire* II, p. 600.

52 *CJ* I.27(ii).20–34.

53 *CTh.* VII.6.4 (396), VII.6.5 (423). Jones, *Later Roman Empire* II, pp. 670–1.

54 *CJ* I.27(ii).7–9.

was realised nor the size of the *stipendium* that was to be paid are known, although *limitanei* as a class seem to have been paid less well than regular soldiers and in practice less regularly.[55]

Despite this considerable military lacuna and the complete lack of information regarding the third major element in the budget, that of public works – which is likely to have been a large one for the first few years of the restoration at least – it is nevertheless of interest to be able to be reasonably confident that the cost of the African civil service and military bureaucracy amounted to somewhere in the region of 53,000 solidi, and that the cost of the regular military establishment did not exceed 142,000 solidi, making a probable total of about 195,000 solidi or somewhat over 27 kentenaria. On this basis it would seem probable that the budget itself did not exceed double that amount, that is 390,000 solidi or somewhat over 54 kentenaria. What proportion of this was collected in and paid out in kind, and what in gold, there is no means of knowing, although Justinian's schedule gives the impression that payment in gold (or at least in cash) was the norm as far as the civil service and military bureaucracy were concerned.

As it happens, the material for a very approximate independent check exists. It is known[56] that the annual revenues derived from two of the six provinces of the African diocese, Numidia and Mauretania Sitifensis, amounted to 120,000 solidi, paid partly in kind, partly in gold, prior to 445. Territorially these two provinces covered only about a quarter of the diocesan total, owing to the small size of Sitifensis. It would therefore seem probable that the revenues deriving from the African diocese amounted to somewhere in the region of 480,000 (4 × 120,000) solidi, or somewhat under 67 kentenaria. Although the Justinianic prefecture included the isolated enclave of Septem (the bare remnant of Mauretania Tingitana) and the islands of Corsica and Sardinia, which the Valentinianic diocese had not, the intervening period had seen the loss of some of Mauretania Sitifensis and much of Mauretania Caesariensis to the Berbers, and since the latter loss, at least, was never really made good, it was not included in the prefecture. It seems improbable that the prefecture's territorial gains should have outweighed the diocese's losses, and the difference implied by a maximum budget of 390,000 solidi for the prefecture and a revenue of about 480,000 solidi for the diocese is therefore not in itself an implausible one.

Even if the sum of 390,000 solidi for the maximum budget of the African prefecture is of the correct order only, and this is really the most that should and can be expected of it, then it is difficult to envisage the combined budgets of the African, Italian and Illyrian prefectures as having amounted to much over 1 million solidi, if indeed they exceeded that sum at all. Neither the Italian nor the Illyrian prefecture included whole provinces noted for their fertility and agricultural productivity as did the African. That Italy was

[55] Jones, *Later Roman Empire* II, pp. 653, 661–2.

[56] See below, p. 173.

in any case in a worse state than Africa, and that Illyricum was in a worse state than either, is indeed directly affirmed by Procopius.[57] The two dioceses of the Italian prefecture were the scene of more or less continuous warfare between the Byzantines and Ostrogoths between 535 and 554 and then, before they had had time to recover, were invaded by the Lombards from 568 onwards. The more northerly of the two dioceses of the Illyrian prefecture, that of Dacia, had been exposed to constant raids and invasion by various barbarian tribes from the second century onwards. For what it is worth, the gold coinages of both these prefectures are consistently less common than that of the African, and that of what remained of the Italian prefecture was debased in material from the seventh century onwards, while that of the African prefecture retained a relative purity.[58] The evidence suggests that neither the Italian nor the Illyrian prefecture can have been fiscally very productive and that both were less so than the African.

## B. *The east*

Evidence for the budget of the eastern prefecture is in some ways even less satisfactory than for that of the African prefecture. No schedule of salaries survives for the former as it does for the latter, although several of Justinian's novels effecting administrative changes do contain pertinent information, and several interesting – if ultimately unverifiable – figures for large elements of its revenue do exist.

Now, if the figure given by Agathias for the strength of the Justinianic army (150,000 men[59]) is deprived of its African section (15,000 men[60]), its Italian section (12/18,000 men, an average of 15,000 men[61]), and its Illyrian section (15,000 men?[62]), then its eastern section ought to have had a strength of around 105,000 men. At the same basic proportion of infantry to cavalry as observed in the case of the African section (2:1[63]), this eastern section would have been composed of some 70,000 infantry and 35,000 cavalry. At the same basic minimum rates of pay as used in Africa,[64] 70,000 infantry would have cost 350,000 solidi annually, and 35,000 cavalry would have cost 315,000 solidi annually, making an annual total of 665,000 solidi. Again, this figure does not take into account the existence of long-serving ordinary soldiers, non-commissioned officers and commissioned officers, or of allowances for uniforms, arms, and so on, but – applying

57 Procopius, *Historia Arcana* XVIII.5–9 (Africa), 13–15 (Italy), 16–21 (Illyricum); ed. Haury (Teubner), III, pp. 111–15. The terms are clearly exaggerated, and so (as usual) is the attribution of entire blame to Justinian, but the general phenomenon, and the relative order of devastation, need not be doubted.

58 Grierson, *DOC* II.1, pp. 43, 46, 48, 49, 51.

59 See below, p. 176

60 See above, p. 166; Jones, *Later Roman Empire* II, p. 685.

61 See above, p. 166; Jones, *Later Roman Empire* II, p. 685.

62 Marcellinus Comes, *Chronicon*, s.a. 499; MGH, *AA* XI, p. 95. Procopius, *De Bello Gothico* III.29.3; ed. Haury (Teubner), II, p. 423 (548). Jones, *Later Roman Empire* II, p. 685.

63 See above, p. 166.

64 See above, p. 166.

the same multiplying factor as used in the case of the African section ($\frac{1}{2}$[65]) – it seems improbable that the sum spent on the regular eastern establishment would have exceeded 997,500 solidi.

According to Procopius,[66] those performing military services or handling documents (*hoi hoplizomenoi ē grammata diakheirizontes*) on behalf of the emperor and his officials (*arkhai*) in Constantinople, that is presumably the members of the military and civilian *officia* there, had a steady order of promotion through seniority, from the bottom right on up to the top. To those of this dignity there had been assigned from of old a sum of money of such a size that they collected over 100 kentenaria or 720,000 solidi every year. Justinian deprived them of nearly all of this, and so poverty afflicted first them and then spread through the rest who had previously shared their benefits.

It is unfortunately not entirely clear what the real sense of the passage is. Certainly, as it stands, the sum of 720,000 solidi is most unlikely to represent the total annual salaries of the departmental heads alone, for even a praetorian prefect rated only 7,200 solidi, and members of the *officia* – whether metropolitan or provincial, military or civilian – were notoriously ill-paid.[67] It is therefore tempting to assume that the sum represents (if it represents anything real) the total annual salaries of the entire metropolitan bureaucracy, both military and civilian, possibly including also the palatine guards.

The prefecture of the East was at this date composed of about 50 provinces, each normally having its own *praeses* or *consularis*, personal staff and *officium*. The administrative legislation of Justinian[68] suggests that a *praeses*, personal staff and *officium* might have been paid on average some 600 solidi annually. The total annual salaries of the provincial representation of the prefecture are therefore likely to have amounted to somewhere in the region of 35,000 solidi. Even if it is assumed that the provincial representation of the prefecture was precisely reflected in that of the two *comitivae*,[69] and in that of the army, the total for the regular civil and military provincial bureaucracy of the eastern prefecture is therefore unlikely to have much exceeded 140,000 solidi (the civil bureaucracy was worse paid than the military).

The prefecture of the East was at this date also composed of five dioceses, and although the diocesan tier of administration seems to have been abandoned, at least temporarily, under Justinian, it is perhaps worthwhile taking it into account. Certainly even if it was abandoned, tax assessment and payment are unlikely to have been reduced appropriately, and indeed sums saved on the diocesan administration appear to have been required for the increased remuneration of the provincial one.[70] Assuming the annual salaries of a

65 See above, p. 166.

66 Procopius, *Historia Arcana* XXIV.30–3; ed. Haury (Teubner), III, pp. 151–2.

67 See above, pp. 165–6; below, p. 181; Jones, *Later Roman Empire* II, pp. 590–1, 594.

68 See below, pp. 178–80.

69 For the distinction between the praetorian prefecture and the *comitivae sacrarum largitionum* and *rerum privatarum*, see below, pp. 371–2.

70 See below, pp. 178–80.

diocesan vicar, personal staff and *officium* to have been approximately equivalent to those of Justinian's remodelled *dux et Augustalis Alexandriae* plus his staff and *officium*, that is, 4,240 solidi,[71] the total annual salaries of the diocesan representation of the prefecture are likely to have amounted to somewhere in the region of 21,200 solidi. Again, even if it is assumed that this was repeated for the *comitivae* and the army,[72] the total for the regular civil and military diocesan bureaucracy of the eastern prefecture is therefore unlikely to have much exceeded 84,800 solidi.

In addition, the government was at this date of course still responsible for the provisioning of the metropolitan populace by means of free issues of grain. According to Edict XIII (8) of Justinian, the wheat yielded by Egypt (overwhelmingly the main regular source of supply) and transported to Constantinople amounted to 8 million units. It has been observed[73] that these units must have been *artabae*. At one official rate of adaeration (one solidus per ten *artabae*[74]), this would have amounted to 800,000 solidi.

The budget of the eastern prefecture is therefore likely to have included the major items listed in Table 3.

As in the case of the African prefecture, the part played by a further major element in the budget, that of public works – and it is likely to have been a large part, given Justinian's building propensities – remains entirely unknown. Similarly, the part played by yet another element, the provision of normal (i.e. not accessional or quinquennial) largesse, remains unknown, although a considerable proportion of that may have been debited not to the prefecture, but to the *largitiones*. It would seem probable, however, that the budget itself did not normally much exceed double the amount of its cash portion (i.e. excluding the issues of grain), that is 3,884,600 solidi or just under 540 kentenaria.

Again, the possible material for a very approximate independent check exists. According to Procopius,[75] during the nine years of Justin I's reign (518–27) 4,000 kentenaria were brought into the imperial household. This has been taken as implying an annual gold revenue of somewhat over 440 kentenaria or 3,200,000 solidi,[76] but the sum was apparently brought in unlawfully (*oudeni nomō*) and was presumably to some extent, however minor, abnormal. On the other hand, it conforms very well with the cash portion of the budget, 1,942,300 solidi, with a handsome allowance made for public works, a further one for occasional largesse,[77] and a much less handsome one made for unlawfulness.

[71] See below, p. 179.

[72] See below, pp. 373–8 and Map 32 (*com.*).

[73] Jones, *Later Roman Empire* I, p. 463.

[74] A. C. Johnson and L. C. West, *Byzantine Egypt: Economic Studies*, pp. 176–8. J.-M. Carrié, 'Le rôle économique de l'armée dans l'Égypte romaine', in *Armées et fiscalité dans le monde antique*, at p. 386, utilises an adaeration rate of 1 sol. per 12 art. and therefore arrives at a cash equivalent of 666,666 sol. Both are equally possible: 1 sol. per 10 art. has the merit of resulting in a conveniently round figure.

[75] Procopius, *Historia Arcana* XIX.8; ed. Haury (Teubner), III, p. 121.

[76] Jones, *Later Roman Empire* I, p. 463.

[77] See below, pp. 192–201.

Table 3. *Major items in the budget of the eastern prefecture under Justinian*

| Items | Expenditure | |
|---|---|---|
| Army | 997,500 | |
| (Metropolitan populace) | (800,000) | |
| Metropolitan bureaucracy | 720,000 | including equivalent comitival and military tiers of administration |
| Diocesan bureaucracy | 84,800 | |
| Provincial bureaucracy | 140,000 | |
| Total | 2,742,300 sol. | |

To look at the picture in another light: if the annual gold revenue of the eastern prefecture really was something like 3,000,000 solidi (i.e. making an allowance of some 200,000 solidi for unlawfulness), and to that is added the 800,000 solidi for adaerated issues of grain, and 216,000 solidi for the proceeds of the *aerikon* tax instituted by Justinian,[78] a total of 4,016,000 solidi is reached.

It is in fact difficult to avoid the conclusion that the budget and revenue of the eastern prefecture stood somewhere quite close to 4 million solidi, whether somewhat below or (more probably) somewhat above that level. Actual revenue, for example, may have been somewhat, but is unlikely to have been fundamentally, higher, if a regular surplus was built into the budget. If it is true that Anastasius accumulated some 23,000,000 solidi in the course of a twenty-seven year reign (491–518), this surplus could have represented as much as a million solidi a year, resulting in a revenue of 5,000,000 solidi. Even with the addition of Africa, Italy and Illyricum, the total imperial budget and revenue is thus most unlikely to have exceeded 5 or 6 million (i.e. 4 + 1 or 5 + 1 million) solidi.[79]

### C. *Observations*

A number of interesting and significant points follow on from these conclusions. The financial position of the prefectures of Africa, Italy and Illyricum, *vis-à-vis* that of the East, was almost absurdly weak. The budget of Africa alone amounted to barely a tenth of that of the east (on the basis of a budget of 4 million solidi for the latter), and the budgets of Africa, Italy and Illyricum combined amounted to barely a quarter of that of the east. In the long term (that is not forgetting the acquisition of the immediate contents of the Vandal and Ostrogothic treasuries), and as a source of surplus revenue, Justinian's reconquest was a dead loss.

[78] See below, pp. 237–8.

[79] The estimate being, in other words, much more in concordance with that of Stein, rather than with that of Andréadès. See above, p. 165. For Anastasius, see below, p. 224.

The position of the metropolis *vis-à-vis* the remainder of the prefecture of the East is also an interesting one, for its population and bureaucracy consumed three-eighths of the prefecture's budget.

The position of Egypt *vis-à-vis* the metropolis, the remainder of the prefecture and the other prefectures is perhaps just as interesting, for it not only provided the metropolis with 800,000 solidi in grain, but the prefecture as a whole with an actual gold revenue that seems to have amounted to not all that much less.[80] In other words, it not only provided the prefecture with about three-eighths of its budget, but alone could have supported the metropolis. As a single diocese, it outweighed the three other prefectures. Its loss first to the Persians and then to the Arabs must have been truly disastrous, and emphasises the very minor nature of what remained of the empire. Indeed, the general position of Egypt in imperial finances, and by implication the financial impact of the loss of its resources, were remembered as late as the twelfth century, when Cinnamus remarks[81] that, formerly, it had furnished annually a great wealth of tribute (*mega... khrēma dasmou... etēsion*), and that it was principally with the aim of regaining these many talents (*polytalantoi*) that Manuel I combined with the Latins in a campaign against the country in 1169.

Again, the proportion of the budget of the eastern prefecture taken up by military expenditure stands at around 25%. The figure includes the army as a whole and does not take account of its administration. If the military are awarded a quarter share (i.e. along with the prefecture and the two *comitivae*) of the three tiers of administration (i.e. metropolitan, diocesan and provincial), then the figure rises to around 35%.

Finally, it should be noted that if the imperial revenue stood at very approximately 5/6 million (pure) solidi in the sixth century, and at approximately 1 million (half-pure) hyperpyra in the fourteenth, then the revenue is very likely to have stood somewhere between these two effective limits during the long intervening period. Variations were doubtless dependent not simply upon the physical extent of the empire at any given time, but also upon the potential and actual economic states of the territory involved, as well as upon the determination and capacity of the state itself to extract revenue from it. But given the inelasticity of the empire's principal sources of revenue, figures for this intervening period (however detailed and however apparently sophisticatedly evolved) that are fundamentally outside these limits therefore have much in them to be explained.

With these points in mind, it is worth noting that the latest independently evolved estimates for the annual imperial revenue of the middle Byzantine period would put it at somewhere in the region of 1,700,000 nomismata in the years 780–802, and in that of 3,300,000 nomismata in the years 842–56. In the latter case a surplus of some 500,000 nomismata is involved. These figures in fact sit quite well between those evolved above

[80] Jones, *Later Roman Empire* I, p. 463.

[81] John Cinnamus, *Epitome* VI.9; Bonn edn, p. 278.

for the sixth and the fourteenth centuries, whereas one, say, of 6,000,000 nomismata would not.[82]

### (IV) ITEMS OF REGULAR REVENUE AND EXPENDITURE

#### A. *Provinces and cities (revenue)*

Other sporadic and partial figures are available. Novel XIII (pr. 5) of Valentinian III, dated 445, permits the reliable calculation that before then the North African provinces of Numidia and Mauretania Sitifensis had been yielding annual revenues of 78,400 and 41,600 solidi, or somewhat under 11 and 6 kentenaria respectively.[83] A good deal later, according to Arnold of Lübeck,[84] the island of Cyprus had been yielding an annual revenue of 7 kentenaria or somewhat over 50,000 hyperpyra in the late twelfth century and, according to John of Brompton,[85] the island of Corfu had been yielding 15 kentenaria or somewhat over 100,000 hyperpyra at much the same time. As it happens, the Cypriot figure is entirely consonant with that of 300,000 bisanti in the early thirteenth century given by one of the continuators of William of Tyre, utilising the value of 4 carati (i.e. $\frac{1}{6}$ perpero) for the early *bisante di Cipri* implied by Pegolotti.[86] Now, when these last two figures are compared with the earlier North African ones, and indeed with the later Chiot one of 120,000 hyperpyra,[87] they do not seem wildly exaggerated, but when they are compared with each other the unlikelihood of Cyprus yielding only half the revenue of Corfu immediately becomes apparent: either the figures represent different things, the Cypriot one the eventual surplus of revenue over expenditure, the Corfiot one the total revenue, or one or both figures are incorrect.

Sporadic figures for even smaller territorial entities and individual taxes are also available. According to Benjamin of Tudela,[88] the city of Constantinople was said to have been yielding a daily revenue of 20,000 hyperpyra, amounting to 7,300,000 hyperpyra or somewhat over 1,000 kentenaria annually, in the mid twelfth century. But according to Gregoras,[89] Byzantine Constantinople and Genoese Galata combined were yielding an annual customs revenue of only 230,000 hyperpyra or somewhat over 30 kentenaria in the mid fourteenth century. Even given the disturbances of the later period such a catastrophic decline is unlikely. The earlier figure is almost certainly wildly

[82] W. T. Treadgold, *The Byzantine State Finances in the Eighth and Ninth Centuries*. I owe a view of this work, prior to publication, to the kindness of the author.

[83] Jones, *Later Roman Empire* I, pp. 462–3.

[84] Arnold of Lübeck, *Chronica Slavorum* IV.16; MGH, *SS* XXI, p. 178.

[85] John of Brompton, *Chronicon*; ed. R. Twysden, col. 1219.

[86] William of Tyre, *Historia Rerum (Cont.)*; RHC, *Occ.* II.1, p. 191. Pegolotti, *La Pratica della Mercatura*, ed. Evans, p. 288.

[87] See above, p. 164.

[88] Benjamin of Tudela, *Itinerary*; trans. A. Sharf, in *Byzantine Jewry from Justinian to the Fourth Crusade*, at p. 136 (and p. 158 n. 4).

[89] See above, p. 157.

exaggerated, unless, as is possible, the correct reading involves an annual revenue of 20,000 hyperpyra, in which case it is equally certainly too low: a local tax, appropriately termed *topikē*, and apparently deriving from rights over fishing (i.e. *tēs aleutikēs*), alone amounted to either about 10,000 or 12,000 hyperpyra annually, in the fourteenth century.[90] Western estimates of Constantinopolitan wealth are not uncommonly fabulous.

One of the main local taxes of Alexandria, termed *exagogion*, which was devoted to several major items of municipal expenditure such as the public baths, brought in an annual revenue of 1,469 solidi during the period from Anastasius to Justinian.[91]

According to Joshua the Stylite,[92] the city of Edessa was paying 140 lb gold or just over 10,000 solidi once in four years in *khrysargyron* as a contribution towards the quinquennial donative when the tax was abolished by Anastasius (491–518). Edessa was of some strategic, and should have been of some economic, importance yet it was paying a sum of only 35 lb or just over 2,500 solidi, in annual terms, in answer to what was universally regarded as a very severe tax. The point seems to some degree confirmed by the fact that, according to Cedrenus,[93] the same city, which had retained its importance into the eleventh century, was then yielding an annual revenue of 50 lb gold or 3,600 nomismata.

According to Theophanes,[94] the annual fair (*panēgyrion*) of Ephesus was yielding at least 100 lb gold or 7,200 nomismata in *kōmerkion*, a tax levied on imports, exports and commercial transactions, in the late eighth century; according to the Arabic author Ibn Ḥauḳal,[95] the city of Attalia was yielding between 3 kentenaria (21,600 nomismata) and 30,000 nomismata, and the city of Trebizond under 10 kentenaria or 72,000 nomismata, both apparently in *kommerkion*, in the tenth century; and according to Attaliates,[96] the city of Selymbria was yielding at least 60 lb or 4,320 nomismata, again apparently in *kommerkion*, in the late eleventh century. It should, however, be noted that Attalia and Trebizond were apparently being used as official ports of entry for Anatolian commerce – at least with regard to Arabic merchants and merchandise – during the period in question, which may explain the relatively high sums yielded. Selymbria, too, was the site of a state warehouse (*phoundax*), part of an attempt to set up a state monopoly (*monopōlion*) of Thracian cereals (wheat [*sitos*] and barley [*orgē*]), during the period involved.[97]

[90] Nicephorus Gregoras, *Historia Byzantina* IX.7; Bonn edn, I, p. 428 (about 10,000). John Cantacuzene, *Historiarum Libri IV* II.1; Bonn edn, I, p. 311 (12,000). K.-P. Matschke, 'Situation, Organisation, und Aktion der Fischer von Konstantinopel und Umgebung in der byzantinischen Spätzeit', *Byzantinobulgarica* 6 (1980), pp. 281–98.

[91] Justinian, Edict XIII.15 (probably 538/9: see below, p. 179 n. 133).

[92] Joshua the Stylite, *Chronicle* XXXI; ed. trans. W. Wright, p. 22.

[93] George Cedrenus, *Historiarum Compendium*; Bonn edn, II, p. 502.

[94] Theophanes, *Chronographia*; ed. de Boor, I, p. 469.

[95] Ibn Ḥauḳal, *Liber Imaginis Terrae*; ed. J. H. Kramers, I, pp. 192–3; trans. M. Canard in Vasiliev, *Byzance et les arabes* II.2, at pp. 414–15, 416–17.

[96] Michael Attaliates, *Historia*; Bonn edn, pp. 203–4.

[97] Ibn Ḥauḳal, *Liber Imaginis Terrae*; ed. Kramers, I, p. 192; trans. Canard, in Vasiliev, *Byzance et les arabes* II.2, at p. 414. Michael Attaliates, *Historia*; Bonn edn, pp. 201–4.

On the whole, with the exception of the twelfth-century figures for Constantinople, which are patently unreliable, and with the possible exception of the tenth- and eleventh-century figures for ports of entry, which are probably exceptional, the evidence tends to conform to an already expected pattern: revenues derived from essentially urban contexts, and therefore particularly from trade, are relatively insignificant when compared with those derived from land. The point seems confirmed by the fact that, in 1219, the city of Lampsacus paid to the Venetian state an annual total of 1,671¼ hyperpyra, or somewhat over 23 lb gold, partly in cash (1,361¼ hyp.), and partly in compulsory services (*angareia*) commuted for cash (310 hyp.).[98]

### B. *The accessional and quinquennial donatives (revenue and expenditure)*

The accessional and quinquennial donatives of the later Roman and early Byzantine periods were, of course, paid for out of special taxation: *aurum coronarium*, a theoretically voluntary offering levied on the curial class; *aurum oblaticium*, a similar offering levied on the senatorial class; and the *collatio lustralis* or *khrysargyron*, levied on those making their living by buying and selling or charging fees, and who were obviously in the main urban-based.[99]

A few figures relating to this taxation survive. According to Libanius,[100] some cities (or rather their *curiales*) had offered crowns (*stephanoi*) of 1,000 or 2,000, or even more solidi (whether in the form of an actual crown, or, more commonly, in that of cash), as *aurum coronarium*, until Julian placed an upper limit of 70 solidi upon such offerings. According to Symmachus,[101] the Roman senate was informed that it was expected to offer 1,600 lb gold, or 115,200 solidi, as *aurum oblaticium* on the occasion of Valentinian II's *decennalia* in 384/5, and it seems probable that the same body offered 30 kentenaria or 216,000 solidi on the occasion of Tiberius II's accession in 578.[102] The Constantinopolitan senate offered 3,000 lb silver on the occasion of Leo I's accession in 457.[103] The city of Edessa was offering 140 lb gold, or just over 10,000 solidi, as *collatio lustralis* under Anastasius.[104]

What is significant about the figures for *aurum coronarium* and the *collatio lustralis* is that an admittedly small number of nevertheless always relatively, and often absolutely, wealthy *curiales* were expected to produce appreciably less than an admittedly much larger

[98] See above, pp. 74–5 n. 10.

[99] Jones, *Later Roman Empire* I, pp. 430, 464–5 (*aur. cor.*), 430–1, 464–5 (*aur. obl.*), 431–2, 465 (*coll. lust.*). See now also C. E. King, 'The *Sacrae Largitiones*: Revenues, Expenditure, and the Production of Coin', in C. E. King (ed.), *Imperial Revenue, Expenditure, and Monetary Policy, in the Fourth Century A.D.*, at pp. 147–8 (*aur. cor.*), 147 (*oblatio senatoria* = *aur. obl.*), 146 (*coll. lust.*).

[100] Libanius, *Orationes* XVIII.193; ed. R. Foerster (Teubner), II, pp. 320–1.

[101] Symmachus, *Relationes* XIII; MGH, *AA* VI.1, p. 290.

[102] See below, pp. 407–8.

[103] See below, p. 408.

[104] See above, p. 174.

number of relatively, and often absolutely, poor artisans, merchants and members of the professions. What is significant about those for *aurum oblaticium* is that, while they are huge in comparison with the others, the sums involved are nevertheless minute in comparison with those for senatorial revenues and fortunes. Even the larger of the two amounts to less than the annual cash revenue of a single major Roman senatorial household.[105]

It is of course impossible to be certain of the accuracy of such figures, but the definite impression is gained that, although the major source of wealth may have been land, it was nevertheless effectively less harshly taxed than trade, and that the least severely taxed amongst the land-owners were precisely those who were in a position to contribute most: the senators.[106]

What is also significant about the figures for the Roman senatorial *aurum oblaticium* is that the senate was apparently expected to pay on the same scale in 578 as it had done in 384/5, for 3,000 lb gold as a contribution towards an accessional donative of nine solidi would be almost exactly proportional to the 1,600 lb paid as a contribution towards a quinquennial one of five solidi. The senate quite simply cannot have been either as numerous or as wealthy at the later date as it had been at the earlier, and what had then been a derisory sum might well have become a crushing burden.[107]

What is also significant about the figure for the Constantinopolitan senatorial *aurum oblaticium* is the comparison between it and the Roman one: the figures had clearly been very carefully chosen – 3,000 lb silver in the case of the former, 3,000 lb gold in that of the latter – demonstrating the theoretical equivalent status of the two bodies, while inevitably accepting, in the most ingenious of ways, the initial financial and economic inferiority of the former.[108]

According to John Lydus,[109] the Roman army consisted of 389,704 men, and the navy of 45,562, making a total of 435,266 men, during the reign of Diocletian (284–305). The origins of these figures are unknown, as is the period of the reign to which they were supposed to have applied, but they at least seem not unreasonable.[110] Again, according to the sixth-century historian Agathias,[111] the Roman army had consisted of 645,000 men under the former emperors, but had been allowed to decrease to 150,000 by the end of the reign of Justinian (565). Again, the origins of these figures are unknown, as is the period to which the former was supposed to have applied, but the fourth century

105 See below, pp. 201–2.

106 Jones, *Later Roman Empire* II, pp. 536–42.

107 See below, pp. 407–8. This might well have been, of course, a major factor in changing the way in which senatorial membership and status eventually came to be regarded.

108 See below, p. 408.

109 John Lydus, *Liber de Mensibus* I.27; ed. R. Wuensch (Teubner), p. 13. For a more sceptical view of this, and the following figures, than is customarily adopted, see now: R. MacMullen, 'How Big was the Roman Imperial Army?', *Klio* 62 (1980), pp. 451–60, esp. pp. 455–60. The points made are generally valid but, equally, unhelpful.

111 Agathias, *Historiarum Libri V* v.13; ed. Keydell, p. 180.

has been suggested, and calculations based on the *Notitia Dignitatum* seem to give approximately concordant results.[112] The latter figure seems remarkably low, but it has been suggested that it excludes the *limitanei*, members of the static frontier force whom, according to Procopius,[113] Justinian had deprived of the name of soldier.[114]

Even if these figures are only of the right order, they nevertheless permit some interesting calculations to be made. It has been reckoned, on good evidence, that the regular annual *stipendium et donativum* of an ordinary legionary amounted to some 11,800 denarii in 299/300. That of an ordinary auxiliary may have amounted to considerably less, and that of an officer to considerably more.[115] Nevertheless, taking the figure 12,000 as a round average, it emerges that the annual cash expenditure on military salaries may have amounted to something of the order of 5,220 million denarii, or 416 million billon nummi of 12½ denarii apiece.[116]

It is known that the customary donative on the occasion of an imperial accession amounted to five solidi and a pound of silver per man. This sum is first recorded for Julian in 360, and is also known for Leo I in 457, Leo II in 473, Anastasius I in 491, and Justin I in 518; it was clearly traditional, being probably Diocletianic and possibly even earlier. The amount recorded for Tiberius II in 578, nine solidi and no silver, probably represents the equivalent, and is perhaps to be regarded as evidence for the eastern scarcity of silver coinage at the time.[117]

If the Diocletianic army consisted of approximately 435,000 men and the traditional sum had already been established, then an accessional donative will have amounted to a total of something of the order of 4,350,000 aurei, or some 725 kentenaria, in terms of gold. If the fourth-century army consisted of 645,000 men then the donative will have totalled 6,450,000 solidi, or somewhat under 900 kentenaria, in the same terms. If the Justinianic army consisted of 150,000 men then the donative will have totalled 1,500,000 solidi, or somewhat over 200 kentenaria.[118]

It is also known that the customary quinquennial donative amounted to five solidi per man. This sum is recorded by both Zachariah of Mitylene and Procopius, and is at least strongly implied by Cassiodorus:[119] it was again probably traditional. Given the same

[112] Jones, *Later Roman Empire* II, pp. 680–4.

[113] Procopius, *Historia Arcana* XXIV.13; ed. Haury (Teubner), III, p. 149.

[114] Jones, *Later Roman Empire* II, p. 684, III, p. 211 (n. 176).

[115] R. P. Duncan-Jones, 'Pay and Numbers in Diocletian's Army', *Chiron* 8 (1978), pp. 544–5, 549–51. The (papyrological) evidence may be good, but it is not entirely uncontroversial: Duncan-Jones' figures are intended as corrections to the earlier ones of T. C. Skeat and A. H. M. Jones – see esp. pp. 556–60 (Appendix 2: 'Existing Interpretations of the Beatty Figures').

[116] See below, p. 458, Table 15.

[117] See below, pp. 468, 475–6, 481.

[118] These figures to a certain extent depend, of course, on the exchange-rate between gold and silver operating at any given time: but official rates were inflexible – generally 4 or 5 solidi to the pound of silver (i.e. 1:18 or 1:14.4, the latter being the more common). See below, p. 481 and Table 16.

[119] Zachariah of Mitylene, *Chronicle* VII.8; trans. F. J. Hamilton and E. W. Brooks, p. 172. Procopius, *Historia Arcana* XXIV.27–9; ed. Haury (Teubner), III, p. 151. Cassiodorus, *Variorum Libri XII.* V.16; MGH, *AA* XII, p. 152. For Zachariah, see also below, pp. 189–90.

numerical strengths as used above, the quinquennial donative will have totalled 2,175,000 aurei or somewhat over 360 kentenaria under Diocletian, 3,225,000 solidi or somewhat under 450 kentenaria during the fourth century, and 750,000 solidi or somewhat over 100 kentenaria under Justinian. It should however be noted that, according to Procopius,[120] Justinian allowed the quinquennial donative to lapse, although, as regards the field armies at least, this seems unlikely.

### C. *The civil administration* (*expenditure*)

In 535, the two provinces of Helenopontus and Pontus Polemoniacus were amalgamated, the governor of the resultant single province being termed *moderator Helenoponti* and receiving both military and civil authority and the combined salaries of the two former governors. The salary of the *moderator* therefore amounted to 725 solidi, that of his juridical advisor (*assessor*) to 72, and that of his *officium* to 447⅓.[121] In the same year, the two provinces of Honorias and Paphlagonia were amalgamated in the same way, the governor of the resultant province being termed *praetor Paphlagoniae*. The salary of the *praetor* again amounted to 725 solidi, that of his *assessor* to 72, and that of his *officium* consisting of 100 members to 447⅓.[122] (Map 26)

In 535, the offices of military count and provincial governor of Pisidia were combined in the person of a *praetor* who was allotted the combined salary of 800 solidi, his *assessor* receiving 72 solidi and his *officium* of 100 members 5 lb gold or 360 solidi.[123] In the same year, precisely the same was done with the military and provincial offices of Lycaonia,[124] and with those of Isauria[125] where, however, they were combined in the person of a *comes*. (Map 26)

Also in 535, the two vicariates of the Long Wall established by Anastasius, one being a military vicariate of the *magistri militum*, the other a civil vicariate of the praetorian prefects, were combined in the person of a *praetor* who was allotted a salary of 800 solidi, his *assessor* receiving 72 solidi and his *officium* of 100 members 5 lb gold or 360 solidi.[126]

In the same year, the provincial governors of Arabia and Phoenice Libanensis received the title of *moderator*, and with it an increased salary. The former was paid 15 lb gold or 1,080 solidi, his *assessor* 2 lb or 144 solidi, and his *officium* the same.[127] The latter was paid 10 lb gold or 720 solidi.[128]

In 536, the provincial governor of Palaestina Prima received the title of *proconsul* and

[120] Procopius, *Historia Arcana* XXIV.27–9; ed. Haury (Teubner), p. 151. But cf. Jones, *Later Roman Empire* I, pp. 284–5.

[121] Justinian, Novel XXVIII, 1–3.

[122] Justinian, Novel XXIX.1–2.

[123] Justinian, Novel XXIV.1, and *notitia*.

[124] Justinian, Novel XXV.1, and *notitia*.

[125] Justinian, Novel XXVII.1, and *notitia*.

[126] Justinian, Novel XXVI.1–2, and *notitia*.

[127] Justinian, Novel CII.1–2.

[128] Justinian, Edict IV.1.

with it an increased salary of 22 lb gold or 1,584 solidi, to be divided between himself, his *consiliarius* and his *officium*, as he wished.[129] In the same year the private financial office of *comes domorum*, which had previously been at the disposition of the *praeopsitus sacri cubiculi*, who had in turn inherited it from the *comes rei privatae*,[130] was combined with that of provincial governor of Cappadocia Prima in the person of a *proconsul*, who was also given military authority. The *proconsul* was allotted a salary of 20 lb gold or 1,440 solidi, and his *assessor* 2 lb or 144 solidi.[131] (Map 26)

Also in 536, the administration of Armenia underwent a number of changes. One of these was that the province of Armenia Secunda was renumbered Tertia and its governor given the title of *comes* with military and civil authority. His annual salary was fixed at 700 solidi, that of his *assessor* at 72, and that of his *officium* at 360.[132] (Map 26)

A short while later, probably in 538/9,[133] the administration of Egypt underwent a complex series of changes. The office of *praefectus Augustalis*, which had hitherto involved a civil authority over the whole of the Egyptian diocese, was amalgamated with that of *dux Aegypti*, which had involved a military authority over the provinces of Aegyptus Prima and Aegyptus Secunda. The resultant office of *dux et Augustalis* involved a combined military and civil authority, but over the two Aegypti only. The salary of the *praefectus Augustalis*, which had amounted to 50 *annonae* and 50 *capitus* and which presumably represented the sum of 400 solidi when adaerated (i.e. reckoned in cash), was increased to 40 lb gold or 2,880 solidi for the *dux et Augustalis*. That of the new Augustalis' *assessores* was fixed at 5 lb or 360 solidi, and that of his *officium* at 1,000 solidi or somewhat under 14 lb. This latter sum represented an increase of two-thirds and was clearly intended to take account of the increased size of the augustal *officium* which, through the amalgamation of the former civil and military *officia*, had come to consist of 600 members.

The remaining parts of the Egyptian diocese seem to have been similarly treated. The civil governors of the two Theban provinces, Thebais Inferior and Thebais Superior, were placed under the authority of the *dux Thebaidis*, who was also given the title of *dux et Augustalis*. The civil governor of Libya Inferior was placed under the authority of the *dux Libyci limitis* (*sc. Libyae Inferioris*) whose basic annual salary, which seems to have amounted to 50 *annonae* and 50 *capitus* adaerated for 400 solidi, was confirmed. The salary of the ducal *officium* is given as 187½ solidi, but that of the forty-strong *officium* of the

129 Justinian, Novel CIII.1.

130 Jones, *Later Roman Empire* I, pp. 425–6.

131 Justinian, Novel XXX.1, 6.

132 Justinian, Novel XXXI.1, 3.

133 R. Rémondon, 'L'édit XIII de Justinien a-t-il été promulgué en 539?', *Chronique d'Égypte* 30/59 (1955), pp. 112–21; *contra*, for example, G. Malz, 'The Date of Justinian's Edict XIII', *Byzantion* 16 (1942/3), pp. 135–41. The basic argument of whether Edict XIII dates from 538/9 or from 553/4 seems to have been conducted at a remarkably low and internalised level: it is inherently almost certain that it should be subsumed under the various eastern reorganisational measures of 535–9 (see above), and any supposed connection with the *Constitutio Pragmatica* (554) reorganising Italy after Narses' victory there would be entirely fortuitous, and is in fact entirely spurious.

other *dux Libyae* (*sc. Pentapoleōs*) is independently known to have amounted to 40 *annonae* and 40 *capitus*, and on this basis it has been suggested that a figure of 387½ would be more appropriate.[134]

Finally, the salaries attached to two metropolitan offices are known. The office of *praetor populi*, created in 535 with the intention of providing a more efficient supervision of the capital than that hitherto provided by the *praefectus vigilum*, rated an annual salary of 10 lb gold or 720 solidi, to be shared between the *praetor* and his *assessor*.[135] The office of *quaestor*, created in 539 with the intention of providing a supervision over visitors to the capital, rated an annual salary of 10 lb or 720 solidi. Its *consiliarius* rated 100 solidi and its *ministrantes* (i.e. *officium*) 330 solidi.[136]

The series of measures outlined above has been seen as possessing a long-term administrative significance, for it was combined with the abolition of the three diocesan vicariates of Pontica, Asiana and Oriens, and the transfer of their authority, *officia* and salaries to the provincial governors of Galatia Prima, Phrygia Pacatiana and Syria Prima respectively. These governors were to hold the title of *comes* and the rank of *spectabilis* with both a military and civil jurisdiction.[137] The effect of these combined measures was to leave no administrative tier between the prefectural and the provincial, a number of officials in the latter possessing both a military and civil jurisdiction. This has been seen as something in the way of a prefiguration of the thematic system, but any formal connection is unlikely, for the abolition of the vicariates at least was a temporary measure only.[138] (Map 26)

The series of figures deriving from the laws giving force to these measures is, however, of some interest, for it demonstrates the basic annual salaries of all but a few of the more prestigious or important of the new regional officials to have amounted to between 700 and 800 solidi, or approximately 10 and 11 lb gold. This was itself an improvement on the pay scale of the normal *praeses* or *consularis* which seems to have been in the region of 300–400 solidi or approximately 4–6 lb gold. This improved range is comparable with the later figures given for the salaries of the lowest rank of later thematic *stratēgoi*, the 'naval' one: the *proconsules Palaestinae* and *Cappadociae* together with the *dux et Augustalis Alexandriae* alone received salaries comparable with those of the higher ranking *stratēgoi*.[139]

The impression that is therefore gained is that earlier regional officials tended to be

[134] Justinian, Edict XIII.1–4 (Egypt); Ed. XIII.23 (Thebaid); Ed. XIII.18–19 (Libya Inf.), cf. Valentinian III, Novel XIII.5; *Supplementum Epigraphicum Graecum* IX, n. 356, pp. 67–70 (Libya Pent.). Salary of Libyan *officium*: Jones, *Later Roman Empire* II, p. 598.

[135] Justinian, Novel XIII.3.

[136] Justinian, Novel LXXX.8.

[137] Justinian, Novel VIII.2, 3, 5 (535). See also: Jones, *Later Roman Empire* I, pp. 280–3 (gen. admin. measures); pp. 280–1 (ab. of vicariates); below, pp. 397–8 (ab. of vic. of Thrace).

[138] Jones, *Later Roman Empire* I, p. 294.

[139] The improved range of salaries will generally have represented at least a doubling of the old. See above, p. 179 (*proconsules*), *loc. cit.* (*dux*); below, pp. 182, 184 (*stratēgoi*).

somewhat worse paid (as regards their basic salaries, at least) than later ones with an approximately equivalent function and status. This impression seems confirmed by the fact that, according to Nicetas Choniates,[140] Andronicus I paid public officials and their dependants better than had been customary, hoping thereby to mitigate their avarice and venality, and gave them 40 lb and even 80 lb of silver coins, presumably electrum trachea, and therefore between 13 and 26 lb gold at the current rate of exchange. This, then, was better, but presumably not fundamentally better, than was customary.

On the other hand, it is not clear whether these later officials had to pay their own personal staff and *officia* from these better salaries, or whether such dependants were paid separately. Certainly, the earlier dependants were vilely paid: regional *assessores* might rate 72, 100, or even 144 solidi per year, on the improved Justinianic scales, but members of an *officium* might find themselves only three or four solidi to the better after the share-out envisaged on the same scales. The massive extent and ingenious nature of the rapacity exercised by the dependants of the *megas doux* and *praitor* of Hellas–Peloponnesos in the late twelfth century, as reported (possibly with some exaggeration) by Michael Choniates, might be taken as suggesting that they were paid very little, if at all, although of course rapacity is not the prerogative of the ill-paid.[141]

And in any case, as already remarked in dealing with Justinian's African administration, it was not upon their salaries that these dependants relied, but on the institutionalised perquisites and fees that accompanied their offices and functions. The disparity between actual income and official salary might well be enormous, and in this respect it is worth remembering that when John Lydus, clearly a favourite of Zoticus, briefly (511–12) prefect of the East under Anastasius, was appointed an *exceptor* in the lower ranks of his patron's *officium*, he made not less than 1,000 solidi in a little over a year, by acting 'moderately (*sōphronōs*)'. This sum clearly represented the informal element of his income, for even when, shortly after, he was chosen as first *chartularius* (of three) by the *adiutores* of the *ab actis* within the same *officium* – a premature and handsome promotion – he was awarded an annual salary of only 24 solidi. But even this was exceptional: his two colleagues, unlike him, were old, had purchased their posts, and served free.[142]

### D. *The later army and civil administration* (*expenditure*)

Rather less is known of numbers and the salary structure of the later Byzantine army, where the very considerable differences between tagmatic and thematic forces have to

[140] Nicetas Choniates, *Historia*; ed. van Dieten, I, pp. 325, 330.

[141] J. Herrin, 'Realities of Byzantine Provincial Government: Hellas and Peloponnesos, 1180–1205', *DOP* 29 (1975), pp. 267–9, 270–6, 282.

[142] John Lydus, *De Magistratibus Populi Romani* III.27; ed. R. Wuensch (Teubner), p. 114. Fees: Jones, *Later Roman Empire* I, pp. 353–4, 467–8, 496–9, II, pp. 568–9, 603–5 – all *officia*, palatine, metropolitan and regional, civil and military, had their own scales and occasions. See also below, p. 187 and n. 164, for later examples and occasions.

be taken into account. Two ninth/tenth-century Arabic sources (Ibn Khurradadhbīh and Kudāma) reckon the contemporary Byzantine army to have consisted of 120,000 men, and the Asian section of that army alone to have consisted of 70,000 men. Another (Ya'ḳūbī) reckons the total cavalry force to have consisted of 40,000 men which, when multiplied out at the previously-used ratio of cavalry to infantry (1:2), works out at precisely 120,000 men.[143]

If these figures, and the interpretation implied by them, have any validity at all, then the Asian army might have consisted of some 25,000 cavalry and 50,000 infantry, while the European army might have consisted of some 15,000 cavalry and 30,000 infantry. This is, however, not the only possible interpretation of the figures, and in any case, as mentioned above, account has to be taken of the tagmatic or professional army mostly in the capital, as well as the thematic army or militia in the regions.[144]

Ibn Khurradadhbīh claims ordinary thematic soldiers to have been paid between 12 and 18 nomismata per annum, but elsewhere claims recruits to have been paid first a single nomisma per annum and then one extra for every year of service on up to the twelfth. The same source claims the *stratēgos* to have been paid between 40 and 36 lb gold per annum, and subordinate *tourmarkhai* 24 lb, *meriarkhai* 12 lb, *komites* 6 lb, and *kentarkhoi* and *dekarkhai* 1 lb. Actual payment was made every three years or more.[145]

[143] The Arabic totals are arrived at by adding together the numerical strengths allotted the individual units (*tagmata*, *themata*, and so on). The first two sources are cited in the most recent and sensible general survey of the problem – that of Toynbee, in *Constantine Porphyrogenitus and his World*, at pp. 286–9 – and the third in J. F. Haldon, *Byzantine Praetorians: An Administrative, Institutional and Social Survey of the Opsikion and Tagmata, c. 580– 900*. I owe a view of this latter work, prior to publication, to the kindness of the author. Neither Ibn Khurradadhbīh nor Kūdama define the status of the forces they give figures for, while Ya'ḳūbī specifically refers to cavalry. If the first two included infantry (the certain existence of which is then and now generally ignored) then all three would make good sense. But this proposition may well be merely the result of a modern hope for consistency, and it may equally well be that one or more of the figures is simply incorrect. Whether the infantry would in any case have been paid, and if so how often and how much, remains entirely obscure.

[144] The Asian and European figures evolved above are, of course, 'pattern' ones, depending on a rigid 1:2 ratio between cavalry and infantry, only. On the other hand, they do at least have the merit of actually working. Most alternative interpretations assume either that the Arab figures are incorrect (i.e. that they are much too high), or that they represent theoretical strengths (i.e. that effective strengths were much lower). The inclusion of infantry by no means solves all the problems, but most discussions have taken place in the context of an entirely – or virtually entirely – cavalry army, which, however important the mid-Byzantine cavalry-arm, is absurd. The problem involved is well illustrated by Toynbee, who acknowledges the necessary existence of the infantry (*Constantine Porphyrogenitus and his World*, pp. 282–4), but who then goes on to discuss actual numerical strengths entirely in terms of the cavalry (*op. cit.*, pp. 286–9). For the *tagmata*: J. F. Haldon, 'Kudāma ibn Dj'afar and the Garrison of Constantinople', *Byzantion* 48 (1978), pp. 78–90 (assuming the Arabic figures to be basically confused and/or conflated); and W. T. Treadgold, 'Notes on the Numbers and Organization of the Ninth-Century Byzantine Army', *Greek, Roman and Byzantine Studies* 21 (1980), pp. 269–88 (assuming the Arabic figures to be basically explicable and correct).

[145] The passage was first cited and discussed by H. Gelzer, in *Die Genesis der byzantinischen Themenverfassung*, at pp. 114–15. It has subsequently been taken up on several occasions: see, for example, J. B. Bury, in *History of the Eastern Roman Empire from the Fall of Irene to the Accession of Basil I (802–867)*, at p. 226 n.2;

Soldiers, whether tagmatic or thematic, and indeed seamen, in any case also received what appear to have been additional salaries (*rhogai*) while actually on campaign. The official accounts for the (unsuccessful) imperial expeditions against Arab-held Crete in 911 and 949 survive in the *De Caerimoniis* of Constantine Porphyrogenitus,[146] and it is quite clear that such payments will have added very considerably to regular costs, although it seems equally clear that some at least of the additional costs were met out of the proceeds of *ad hoc* levies, whether in cash or in kind, upon thematic units that were uninvolved or that did not wish to be involved.[147]

Much has been made of these and similar figures, and it has been claimed[148] that the military budget of the Anatolian themes must have amounted to between 690,300 and 1,260,000 nomismata per year, and that expenditure on this scale can have occurred only within the context of a vital urban society and monetary economy. The first of these claims alone is of relevance to this chapter, the second being more appropriately discussed elsewhere in this book.

The claim is based on several of the figures quoted above, and Theophanes' information that the *rhoga* of the *kleisoura* or theme of Strymon, captured by the Bulgarians in 809, amounted to 1,100 lb gold, and that that of Armeniakon, captured by the Arabs in 811, amounted to 1300 lb.[149] These last figures, which at first sight seem not unreasonable in themselves, and which compare not too implausibly given the different status of the two themes involved, are then subjected to calculations based upon Constantine Porphyrogenitus' list of *stratēgoi* and their *rhogai*, and a total is evolved. The possible fundamental error in these calculations (assuming the accuracy of the rest of the information used) lies in the supposition that Theophanes' figures represent annual payments, whereas the Arab source mentions that thematic *rhogai* were paid every three

and more recently, Antoniadis-Bibicou, *Études d'histoire maritime de Byzance*, at p. 141 table 1. The detailed rank/*rhoga* equations above are those adopted by Antoniadis-Bibicou, but only because until recently they were the latest detailed ones. Even more recently, however, Treadgold (see above, n. 82) regards the sums from 40 lb down to 6 lb as appropriate to *stratēgoi* and *kleisourarkhai*; 3 lb down to 1 lb as appropriate to *tourmarkhai*, *droungarioi* and *komites*; and 18 and 12 nom. as appropriate to *kentarkhoi* and *dekarkhai*. This latest set of equations has some merit, as it is difficult to believe – particularly in view of Const. Porph.'s figures for *stratēgoi* (see below, n. 151) – that subordinates such as *tourmarkhai* received a sum as high as 24 lb. On the other hand, neither set is based on more than guesswork. Bury's suggestion, based on a comparison of Ibn Khurradadhbīh's and Const. Porph.'s range of figures, that payments had decreased the meanwhile, grants the Arab figures too high a degree of accuracy.

146 See below, pp. 222 and nn. 6, 7.

147 See, for example, the case of the theme of Peloponnesos which, under Romanus I, rather than form part of an expeditionary force destined for Italy, bought itself out through the payment of 1,000 horses equipped with horsecloths and bridles (*hipparia 1,000 estrōmena kai khalinōmena*), and a kentenarion in cash (*logarion*): Constantine Porphyrogenitus, *De Administrando Imperio* LI, LII; ed. Moravcsik and Jenkins, p. 256. Bon, *Le Péloponnèse byzantin*, p. 115. In view of the numbers involved, the price seems steep, and at this stage was perhaps punitively so.

148 S. Vryonis, 'An Attic Hoard of Byzantine Gold Coins (668–741) from the Thomas Whittemore Collection, and the Numismatic Evidence for the Urban History of Byzantium', *Zbornik Radova Vizantoloshkog Instituta* 8.1 (1963), pp. 298–9.

149 See below, p. 429.

years or more, and Constantine himself notes[150] that the themes had formerly been paid every four years (*kata tessara etē*), in annual groups of three, the composition of each group evidently depending upon the *rhoga* of the *stratēgos* and the status of the theme. During the reign of Leo VI (886–912) the themes of Anatolikon, Armeniakon and Thrakesion, the *stratēgoi* of all of which received 40 lb gold per year, were thus paid in the first year; those of Opsikion, Boukellarion and Kappadokia, the *komēs* and *stratēgos* of the first two of which received 30 lb, and the *stratēgos* of the third 20 lb, were paid in the second; those of Kharsianon, Koloneia and Paphlagonia, the *stratēgoi* of all of which received 20 lb, were paid in the third; and those of Thrake (20 lb), Makedonia (30 lb) and Khaldia (10 + 10 lb from the *kommerkion* tax) were paid in the fourth.[151] This order exactly reproduces that of the list of precedence in the *Klētorologion* of Philotheus (899).[152]

The question therefore arises as to whether thematic *rhogai* were reckoned annually, but actually paid quadrennially, or whether they were both reckoned and paid quadrennially. There is no obvious reason why the former should have been the case, except on the further supposition that the statutory or effective tenure of a thematic *stratēgos* was four years, *stratēgoi* of each group of three themes assuming and relinquishing their appointments simultaneously, the incoming *stratēgoi* also accompanying the annually reckoned *rhogai*. There is no specific evidence for the operation of such a rota, although there is some suggestion that *stratēgoi* may have accompanied *rhogai*.[153] But even if such a rota did operate, the *stratēgoi* involved may have accompanied quadrennially reckoned *rhogai*.

Theophanes' figures (assuming their accuracy) may therefore quite well represent *rhogai* both reckoned and paid on a quadrennial basis, which (accepting the methodology outlined above) would bring down the average annual military budget for the main Anatolian themes to somewhere within the range 172,500 to 315,000 nomismata, or somewhat under 24 to somewhat under 44 kentenaria.

For the rest there is a partial, confused and generally suspect (because in some cases demonstrably faulty) list of the *rhogai* of mostly palatine officials given by a western visitor to Constantinople, Liutprand, bishop of Cremona, writing in the mid tenth century. According to Liutprand,[154] the *rhaiktōr* (an official whose regular functions remain uncertain), the *domestikos tōn skholōn* (the commander of the imperial army) and the *droungarios tōn ploïmōn* (the commander of the imperial fleet), the last two of whom were equal in rank and therefore received equal payment, all received *rhogai* so large that these officials were obliged to carry them off on their shoulders, or to receive assistance in dragging them off, at the annual ceremony of distribution (*dianomē*) during the week

[150] Constantine Porphyrogenitus, *De Caerimoniis* I (*Appendix*); Bonn edn, pp. 493–4.
[151] Constantine Porphyrogenitus, *De Caerimoniis* I (*Appendix*), II.50; Bonn edn, pp. 494, 696–7.
[152] Philotheus, *Klētorologion*; ed. Oikonomides, p. 101.
[153] See below, p. 191.
[154] See below, p. 191.

Table 4. *Ranks and* rhogai *in the eleventh century (after Lemerle)*

| Rank | *Rhoga* |
|---|---|
| *kouropalatēs* | 32 lb |
| (*proedros*) | (28 lb) |
| *magistros* | 16 lb |
| (*vestarkhēs*) | (14 lb) |
| (*vestēs*) | (12 lb) |
| *anthypatos* | 8 lb |
| *patrikios* | 4 lb |
| *hypatos** | 2 lb* |
| *prōtospatharios** | 1 lb* |
| *spatharokandidatos** | $\frac{1}{2}$ lb* |
| *spatharios** | 12 nom.* |

preceding Palm Sunday. Officials with the rank of *magistros* received 24 lb gold or 1,728 nomismata, and those with the rank of *patrikios* 12 lb or 864 nomismata. Each also received a number of *skaramangia* or ceremonial tunics, the number varying according to rank. Officials of lower rank received between 7 and 1 lb gold or 504 and 72 nomismata, and some even less, but because those lower ranks and smaller *rhogai* are listed separately, the former numbering fewer than the latter and being in any case incomplete and incorrectly graded, no direct and reliable correlation can be established: it is indeed quite possible that none was intended.

The latest systematic contribution to the subject of the size and nature of contemporary *rhogai*[155] would propose the tentative scale for the later part of the eleventh century given in Table 4.

Of these items, the ranks and suggested *rhogai* in parentheses represent historically recent additions to the scale, and those accompanied by an asterisk are the ones for which there is explicit documentary evidence for their having been valid for the later eleventh century. Indeed, the *rhoga* appropriate to the rank of *prōtospatharios* (1 lb gold) is attested in several sources from the ninth century onwards.

Unfortunately, while of some interest in themselves and recorded here for that reason, these figures are capable of extremely limited application only. In the first place, the total number of holders of few or none of these ranks is known and therefore no sub-totals can be established. In the second, it is quite clear that, although an official would possess a rank or *rhoga* by virtue of his office, both could be bought for a capital sum during

[155] P. Lemerle, '"Rhoga" et rente d'état aux X$^{e}$–XI$^{e}$ siècles', *Revue des Études Byzantines* 25 (1967), pp. 77–100, esp. p. 94; cf. H. Antoniadis-Bibicou, 'Démographie, salaires et prix à Byzance au XI$^{e}$ siècle', *Annales* (*Ec. Soc. Civ.*) 27 (1972), pp. 223, 224 n. 33 (*kouropalatēs* = 40 lb, *magistros* = 20 lb, *anthypatos* = 10 lb, *patrikios* = 9 lb).

the period under discussion. The rank could be bought with or without the appropriate *rhoga*, and with or without increments. The rank of *prōtospatharios* is known to have cost 12 or even 18 lb gold, and that of *spatharios* to have cost 5 lb gold – but with the *rhoga* they are known to have cost an additional 4 lb gold. Michael Psellus seems to have paid 20 lb gold for a *prōtospatharaton* with *rhoga* in the eleventh century. Similarly, the position of attendant at the imperial table (*eis to trapezion*) is known to have cost 6 lb gold, and to have rated a *rhoga* of 10 nomismata. And so on.[156]

The classic case of the purchase of such a rank involves the aged and very wealthy cleric Ktenas, a member of the chapter of the New Church under Leo VI. Ktenas, although (as a cleric) theoretically ineligible to hold the rank, nevertheless desperately desired the position of *prōtospatharios*, along with its ceremonial rights and its annual *rhoga* of one pound of gold. He therefore persuaded the patrician Samonas, who was then *parakoimōmenos*, to intercede with the emperor on his behalf, and offered the high sum of 40 lb gold for the purchase. The emperor refused to make a cleric *prōtospatharios*. Ktenas promptly increased the sum and offered a pair of ear-rings (*skholarikia*) valued at 10 lb, and a silver table (*trapeziou asēmin*), gilded and inscribed with animals, and also valued at 10 lb, in addition. The emperor, persuaded by Samonas, accepted the total of 60 lb, and granted Ktenas the rank. However, Constantine Porphyrogenitus, who reports the incident at some length, concludes by remarking with some apparent relish that Ktenas lived two years longer, and then died having received only a *rhoga* of one pound for each of the years.[157]

The incident was quite clearly an atypical one, although quite how atypical it is impossible to say. Constantine's conclusion nevertheless distinctly implies that not the least important feature of the whole incident was the (presumably atypically) handsome profit which the state made on the purchase.

It seems clear that the possibility of purchasing such ranks and *rhogai* goes back at least into the sixth century, and possibly even earlier. According to Procopius,[158] Justinian (inevitably) had regularised the situation as regards the *scholae*, at least, by creating 2,000 new positions in that body, the holders of which were termed supernumeraries (*hyperarithmoi*), but he had subsequently dismissed them without compensation. The tenth-century equivalent seems to have been membership of the *megalē* or *mesē hetaireia*, or the *pharganoi* or *Khazaroi*.[159]

Such posts were transferable: Justinianic legislation dealt with what should happen when their holders went bankrupt;[160] and Psellus even included one in a dowry.[161]

[156] Constantine Porphyrogenitus, *De Caerimoniis* II.49; Bonn edn, pp. 692–4 (ranks and *rhogai*); below, p. 216 (Michael Psellus).

[157] Constantine Porphyrogenitus, *De Administrando Imperio* L; ed. Moravcsik and Jenkins, p. 244.

[158] Procopius, *Historia Arcana* XXIV. 18–20; ed. Haury (Teubner), III, pp. 149–50.

[159] Constantine Porphyrogenitus, *De Caerimoniis* II.49; Bonn edn, p. 693.

[160] See below, pp. 244–5.

[161] See below, p. 216.

What the purchase of such posts represented as an annual revenue to the imperial government remains entirely unclear. If Justinian's 2,000 supernumeraries each paid anywhere near the sum in excess of 2,000 solidi that the post of *domesticus praesentalis* is known to have cost,[162] then that will have represented some 4 million solidi over several years as the posts were filled. But a creation and profit on this scale was a once-only affair, and subsequent regular purchases as such posts fell vacant will have represented a much less considerable sum.

In any event, although it might well happen, as it was doubtless intended to, that the state made a profit on such transactions, it is clear that many or all of the later holders of these posts received not only a *rhoga*, but also additional – if smaller – sums on the occasion of the ancient feast termed *Broumalia*, and on those of imperial coronations and their anniversaries, just as their earlier predecessors had doubtless done.[163] Later officials also relied on the perquisites that accompanied their posts, again as their earlier predecessors had done.[164]

The second half of the eleventh century saw the increasingly indiscriminate granting out of the membership of the various honorary *offikia* as a reward or favour, rather than as the result of real service or purchase. This meant that the total of the *rhogai* involved not only exceeded that of the service performed or of the revenue gained, but also became a serious burden on the treasury, eventually, when combined with other concomitant factors, leading to financial chaos.[165]

### E. *The payment of salaries and donatives (processes and descriptions)*

The details of the process by which the annual cash *stipendium* and *donativum* of the fourth century (the former, at least, possibly paid in base-metal coin) was distributed to the army remain undocumented. The details of that by which the accessional and quinquennial *donativa* of the same century and that following, evidently paid in precious-metal coin, were distributed are, however, known. In 365, Venustus, a member (*apparitor*) of the *largitiones* owing allegiance to Valens, who had been sent to Nicomedia to distribute personally a gold *stipendium* to the military in the east, was forced to take refuge in Cyzicus (where there was apparently also a regional *thesaurus*), in an attempt to evade capture by the usurper Procopius.[166] It has plausibly been suggested that this *stipendium* represented Valens' accessional donative.[167] In 370, the *tribunus et notarius* Palladius was

162 See below, p. 244.

163 *Broumalia*, etc.: below, p. 197. Philotheus, *Klētorologion*; ed. Oikonomides, pp. 225–31.

164 Cf. Justinian, Novel VIII, *Notitia*. Philotheus, *Klētorologion*; ed. Oikonomides, pp. 89–99, 231–5. Constantine Porphyrogenitus, *De Caerimoniis* II.53, 55; Bonn edn, pp. 787–9, 798–806.

165 See below, pp. 235, 570–80.

166 Ammianus Marcellinus, *Historia* XXVI.8.6; ed. V. Gardthausen (Teubner), II, p. 84. Serenianus, then *comes domesticorum*, was sent *ad thesauros tuendos* there (8.7). For regional *thesauri*, see below, pp. 383–5 and Table 9.

167 Jones, *Later Roman Empire* II, p. 624.

sent out to Africa to distribute a *stipendium* to the military there.[168] This may have represented Valentinian's first quinquennial donative. In 500, the *tribunus notariorum* Paulus was sent into Illyricum to distribute a *donativum* to the military there: it certainly represented Anastasius' second quinquennial donative, his first (called by the technical name *augustaticum*) having been distributed in 496.[169]

It seems clear, therefore, that the distribution of these donatives which, unlike the annual adaerated *annonae*, were the sole responsibility of the *largitiones*, was customarily entrusted to officials (seemingly tribunes) sent out from the imperial *comitatus* with that specific purpose in mind. They presumably either transported with them the bullion or coin involved, or made use of that stocked in the regional *thesauri*.[170]

It seems equally clear that distribution was frequently somewhat late, despite the obvious political and propagandist advantages to be gained from promptness.[171] The one documented exception is provided by Procopius, who seems to have been in a position to despatch 'gold coins designed with the face of the new emperor [*sc.* with his own face] (*aurei nummi effigiati in vultum novi principis*)' to at least some military units in an attempt to gain their loyalty.[172] The possibly would-be usurper Rufinus stands accused of having even anticipated production, if not distribution, of such coins.[173] On the other hand, it has been suggested that the gold *stipendium* distributed in Gaul in 355 represented the tricennial donative of Constantius II that theoretically fell due in 353.[174] If the *stipendium* that Venustus was distributing in 365 really did represent Valens' accessional donative then it was a year late; and if that which Palladius was sent out to distribute in 370 represented Valentinian's quinquennial donative it was at least a year late.

When an imperial college consisting of several members was in existence, it seems probable that their various quinquennial celebrations, including the collection of taxes and the distribution of donatives, might be combined, no doubt for reasons of convenience and economy. The Theodosian house seems even to have arranged its imperial elevations (which would inevitably have entailed donatives) to coincide with quinquennial

168 Ammianus Marcellinus, *Historia* XXVIII.6.12; ed. Gardthausen (Teubner), II, p. 156.

169 Marcellinus Comes, *Chronicon*, ss.aa. 496, 500; MGH, *AA* XI, pp. 94, 95.

170 See below, pp. 383–5 and Table 9.

171 Jones, *Later Roman Empire* II, p. 624 (payments for each member of an imperial college); but see below, n. 175 (payments consolidated by the Theodosian college). It seems likely that the earlier annual *stipendium et donativa*, the former of which was certainly paid in base metal coin, and the latter of which in any case involved small sums, will have tended to have commemorated each member, while accessional and quinquennial *donativa*, which were certainly paid in precious metal, and which involved considerable sums, will have tended to have been consolidated.

172 Ammianus Marcellinus, *Historia* XXVI.7.11; ed. Gardthausen (Teubner), p. 81.

173 M. F. Hendy, 'Aspects of Coin Production and Fiscal Administration in the Late Roman and Early Byzantine Period', *Numismatic Chronicle* 12[7] (1972), p. 129 n. 5.

174 Ammianus Marcellinus, *Historia* XV.6.3; ed. Gardthausen (Teubner), I, p. 61. Jones, *Later Roman Empire* III, p. 189 n. 2.

celebrations (and therefore donatives) that were due in any case, presumably for similar reasons.[175]

A highly-coloured account of what may have been the collection of taxation for the accessional donative of the usurper Magnus Maximus (383–8) appears in a panegyric on Theodosius by Pacatus; it was apparently delivered in 389, in the presence of that emperor and the (Roman) senate:*

Clad in the purple, he himself [*sc.* Maximus] stood at the scales (*ad lances*) and, pale and staring, watched the movements of the weights (*momenta ponderum*) and the oscillations of the balances (*nutus trutinarum*). Meanwhile, there were brought and weighed out the spoils of the provinces, the belongings of exiles and the goods of the slain: here, gold taken from the hands of women; there, *bullae* torn from the necks of children; and there, silver drenched with the blood of its masters. Everywhere, coins (*pecuniae*) were counted up, chests (*fisci*) were filled up, moneys (*aera*) were heaped up, and vessels (*vasa*) were cut up. To the observer, the scene would have appeared not as the residence of an emperor, but as the lair of a brigand.

(Pacatus, *Panegyricus Theodosio Augusto Dictus* XXVI; in Galletier (ed.), *Panégyriques Latins* III, XII(2), at p. 93).

The scene as envisaged and described is striking enough, but of course is quite preposterous. It does occur, however, almost immediately after a reference to the death of Gratian and the victory of Maximus, and therefore may well have been meant to carry the implication of oppressive fiscality for the accessional donative. In any case, it was, ironically, very much at this time (387) that the collection of taxation for the decennial and quinquennial donative for Theodosius and Arcadius provided the basic excuse for a serious outbreak of popular unrest at Antioch. As mentioned above, it seems to have been the urban populace that was the hardest hit in such occasions.[176]

As it happens, a detailed description of the actual distribution of a quinquennial donative that occurred during the reign of Anastasius survives in the *Chronicle* of Zachariah of Mitylene:

And on the 29th the king [Anastasius] assembled all the commanders of the forces and all the officers of the scholarians [imperial guard] and the patricians, and he said to them, 'According to my regular custom I wish to give a donative (*donativum*).' For so it had been his practice to give it once in five years ever since he became king, at the same time requiring oaths from all the Romans to the effect that they would not act treacherously against the kingdom. But on this occasion he required them to take the oath in the following manner: A copy of the gospel being placed for them, they went in and received the five denarii [solidi] each, and they swore as follows, 'By this law of God and by the words which are written in it, we will contend with

* I owe this reference to the kindness of John Casey.

175 Hendy, 'Aspects of Coin Production and Fiscal Administration', pp. 137–8, 139.

176 R. Browning, 'The Riot of A.D. 387 in Antioch', *Journal of Roman Studies* 42 (1952), pp. 13–20, esp. pp. 14–15.

all our might for the true faith and for the kingdom, and we will not act treacherously either against the truth or the king.' In this manner, indeed, he required them to take the oath, because he heard that Macedonius [patriarch of Constantinople] was trying to raise a rebellion against him.

On the 30th of July the king gave a largesse (*rhoga*) to the whole army.

(Zachariah of Mitylene, *Chronicle* VII.8; trans. Hamilton, Brooks, p. 172)

The donative seems to have been Anastasius' fourth quinquennial one, which should have taken place in 511, since it was immediately followed by Macedonius' arrest and exile. It may have been anomalous to some extent: the form of the oath (the imperial *votum* that was an essential part of the ceremony) seems to have been unusual, perhaps in including a reference to the 'true faith' and the 'truth' as well as to the empire and emperor; and it in any case involved palatine troops rather than regional ones. It may nevertheless be regarded as essentially the same as those which must have taken place elsewhere in the empire.

It seems reasonable to conjecture that the distribution of the annual adaerated *annonae* would have been largely the responsibility of the prefecture and its subordinate administrative tiers, and this conjecture seems confirmed by the fact that, according to Synesius,[177] it was a certain decurion (*bouleutēs*) of Alexandria who brought out gold to the military in the Pentapolis. It may well be that the ceremony at which annual *stipendia* or adaerated *annonae* were actually distributed resembled that described above for, according to Gregory of Nazianzen,[178] when the day of an imperial largesse (*dōreas basilikēs hēmera*) came round, whether it was the regular annual (*etēsias*) one or specially instituted for the purpose, Julian, as emperor, took the opportunity of combining it with a pagan sacrifice. This, and the incidental description of the military drawn up according to dignity (*axia*) and rank (*taxis*), with gold and incense both at hand, receipt of the one depending upon sacrifice of the other, suggests a pagan (and, of course, the original) version of the Christianised quinquennial ceremony. The ceremonial distribution of provincial *rhogai* in the presence of the local military commander is also implied by the terms of a letter of pope Gregory I to the emperor Maurice dated 595.[179]

Some civilian palatine officials, at least, seem also to have received their salaries or largesse from the hands of the emperor himself.[180] It was the indecent eagerness to receive their gold in their bare cupped hands displayed by certain of the *agentes in rebus* at some kind of ceremonial distribution held in the *consistorium* that prompted Julian to remark that they knew how to take, but not how to receive.[181]

Details of the process by which the *rhoga* of the seventh century and later, evidently

[177] Synesius, *Epistolai* XVIII; *PG* LXVI, col. 1353: *bouleutēs...khrysion hōs hymas nomēn stratiōtais komizonta.*

[178] Gregory of Nazianzen, *Orationes* IV (= *Contra Julianum* I) 82–4; *PG* XXXV, cols 608–12.

[179] Gregory I, *Epistolae* V.30; MGH, *Ep.* I, pp. 310–11: *Rogae quoque militum ita per praedictum confamulum meum scribonem praesente quoque glorioso Casto magistro militum factae sunt.*

[180] See also below, pp. 191–2 and n. 187, for the later period.

[181] Ammianus Marcellinus, *Historia* XVI.5.11; ed. Gardthausen (Teubner), I, p. 83.

paid at least mainly in terms of gold coin, was distributed to the army remain, once again, undocumented. The *rhoga* of the tagmatic army and navy was presumably always paid from Constantinople. It might be expected on general grounds that the *rhogai* of the eastern thematic forces would be paid from Constantinople while those of the western ones would be paid from local funds, just as the *rhogai* of thematic *stratēgoi* are known to have been paid.[182] Certainly, it was on precisely such a mission (the distribution (*dianomē*) of allowances (*sitēresia*) in the theme of Anatolikon) that Nicephorus Bryennius and John Opsaras were sent out in 1057, and that ended in the blinding of Bryennius, who was also the thematic *stratēgos*, on the suspicion of treason, because he insisted on distributing more of the imperial gold (*basilikon khrysion*) than he had been ordered to.[183]

Although no details of the payment of the later regional armies are known, a detailed description of the actual distribution of *rhogai* to certain military and civil officials of the period, who seem to have been largely, but by no means entirely, palatine, does nevertheless survive in the *Antapodosis* of Liutprand of Cremona:

In the week before the Feast of *Vaiophoron*, which we call the Feast of Palms, the emperor makes a distribution of gold nomismata to the military and to various officials, each receiving the sum appropriate to his office. Because he wished to interest me, the emperor commanded me to attend this distribution. It took place after this fashion. A table ten cubits long and four wide had been brought in, which table carried nomismata tied up in purses, as many as were owed each person, the amount being written on the outside of the purses. The recipients then entered at the command of somebody who read out the list of names according to the dignity of the officials involved. The first of these officials is termed the *rector domus* (*rhaiktōr*), and his nomismata together with four *skaramangia* (ceremonial tunics) were placed not in his hands but upon his shoulders. Next were the officials termed *ho domestikos tōn skholōn* and *ho droungarios tōn ploïmōn*, the one of whom commands the military, the other the navy. These, because they were of an equal dignity, received an equal number of nomismata and *skaramangia* which, on account of their bulk, they were unable to carry off even upon their shoulders, but dragged off behind them with the aid of others. After these there were admitted the *magistroi*, to the number of twenty-four, who each received the number of pounds of gold nomismata equal to their total of twenty-four, together with two *skaramangia*. Then after these followed the order of patricians, and they were given twelve pounds of nomismata together with a single *skaramangion*. As I do not know the number of patricians, but only what each was given, I do not know the total amount involved. After these an immense crowd was summoned: *prōtospatharioi*, *spatharioi*, *spatharokandidatoi*, *koitōnitai*, *manglavitai*, *prōtokaraboi*; of whom some received seven pounds, others six, five, four, three, two, or one pound, according to the degree of their dignity. I do not wish you to suppose that this was effected in a single day, for it was begun at six o'clock, and continued until ten o'clock, on the fifth day of the week, and was completed – as far as the emperor was concerned – on the sixth and seventh days. For those who received less than a pound are paid not by the emperor, but by the *parakoimōmenos*, over the entire week which precedes Easter.

(Liutprand of Cremona, *Antapodosis* VI.10;
ed. Becker, pp. 157–8)

[182] See below pp. 648–54.

[183] George Cedrenus, *Historiarum Compendium*; Bonn edn, II, pp. 621–2.

According to Cedrenus,[184] and Yahya of Antioch,[185] it was directly after such a distribution (*dianomē*) to the senators (*synklētikoi*), on Maundy Thursday, 11 April 1034, that Romanus III met his death in suspicious circumstances.[186] A distribution to the whole senate (*pasa hē synklētos*), actually on Palm Sunday, 1 April 1078, by Nicephorus III, is to be inferred from Attaliates, and on this occasion the continuing custom of summoning the recipients by name and dignity (*axia*) is confirmed by the fact that the *prōtovestiarios* responsible actually lost his voice because of the huge numbers involved.[187] During the course of the eleventh century, between 1058 and 1079, the responsibility for the payment of these senatorial *rhogai* seems to have been transferred from the *eidikon* to the *sakellion*.[188]

The capture of thematic *rhogai* by the enemy is recorded on two ninth-century occasions, as mentioned above: on each of these, a Lenten or Eastertide distribution is clearly implied, and the custom is known to have spread into the private sector, presumably through conscious imitation.[189]

## (v) ITEMS AND DESCRIPTIONS OF OCCASIONAL LARGESSE

### *A. The consulship*

Tenure of the consulship was expensive enough for private individuals, even in the east where they were aided by the state: it might necessitate the expenditure of very considerable sums by emperors and caesars, and even by their relatives. According to Olympiodorus of Thebes,[190] Flavius Constantius must have spent at least 40 kentenaria or 288,000 solidi on his first consulship, celebrated in 414. According to Procopius,[191] the office customarily required the expenditure of 20 kentenaria or 144,000 solidi on the part of private individuals, although a considerable proportion was paid by the state, and according to Marcellinus Comes,[192] Justinian (as nephew of the reigning emperor, Justin) spent precisely twice that – 288,000 solidi or 40 kentenaria – on his first consulship,

[184] George Cedrenus, *Historiarum Compendium*; Bonn edn, II, p. 505.

[185] Yahya of Antioch, trans. J. H. Forsyth, in 'The Byzantine-Arab Chronicle (938–1034) of Yaḥyā b. Saʿīd al-Anṭākī', p. 337.

[186] P. Grierson, *DOC* III.2, p. 711.

[187] Michael Attaliates, *Historia*; Bonn edn, p. 275. On the other hand, if circumstances dictated, the date of the annual distribution could be advanced. Such an advance is specifically implied once only, but as Holy Week must frequently have formed part of the campaigning season, it should not have been uncommon (see below, pp. 229 n. 52, and 579 and n. 71).

[188] N. Oikonomides, 'L'évolution de l'organisation administrative de l'empire byzantin au XI$^{e}$ siècle (1025–1118)', *Travaux et Mémoires* 6 (1976), pp. 135, 137. The *eidikon* had undoubtedly long been a repository of imperial wealth, but it is by no means certain that the *sakellion* still was. It may well be that the *sakellarios* ended up responsible for the payments, but it does not follow that his own department actually housed the funds involved, which may have been taken from elsewhere – for instance, one of the *vestiaria*. Note the presence of the *prōtovestiarios* in 1078 above.

[189] See below, pp. 215 Table 5, 429.

[190] Olympiodorus of Thebes, *Fragmenta* XXIII; ed. K. Müller, IV, at p. 62.

[191] Procopius, *Historia Arcana* XXVI.12–13; ed. Haury (Teubner), III, p. 159.

[192] Marcellinus Comes, *Chronicon*, s.a. 521; MGH, *AA* XI, pp. 101–2.

celebrated with admittedly exceptional magnificence in 521.[193] According to John of Ephesus,[194] Tiberius II spent 7,200 lb gold or 518,400 solidi, besides silver and silk, on largesse during his first year as emperor. If the sum is anywhere near accurate then it will presumably have included the expenses of his consulship, which he is known to have assumed in traditional fashion on 1 January following his accession (late September 578), but will have excluded those of his accessional donative, which he is also known to have given.[195] Maurice broke with tradition by failing to assume the consulship until 25 December of the year following his accession (mid August 582), thereby holding it for one week only and ensuring that, although he distributed the customary largesse, he avoided or minimised expenditure on games. This was clearly done to relieve the treasury, left in a depleted state by Tiberius, and confirms the significant scale of such expenditure.[196]

The distribution of largesse to both the senators and to the palatine guards, as well as to the people, on the occasion of Justin II's consular celebrations in 566 is described in some detail by Corippus.[197] The senators were summoned to the imperial presence individually, their names being called from a register (*ab albo*). Extending their right hands they received the imperial gift of gold and then retired. The palatine guards were summoned in a similar fashion by rank, school and company (*ordinibus propriis...perque scholas turmasque*).

Although the major item of expenditure involved in the consulship seems to have been the customary series of games, nevertheless the equally customary gifts to the senators and guards, and the scatterings (*sparsiones*) of largesse to the people, will have taken up a not inconsiderable amount of money, particularly where an emperor or a member of the imperial house was concerned.[198] In the east, at least, the quality and quantity of the largesse involved in such *sparsiones*, and the number of occasions during a consulate on which they were permitted, where private individuals were concerned, were all subject to an increasing degree of regulation. The laws going to make up this degree of regulation, in defining what was permitted and what was not permitted to a private individual as consul – or indeed as the holder of another magistracy – also provide a good deal of information as to what was confined to an emperor, or to a member of the imperial house, as consul. The earliest known of these laws is one of Theodosius I preserved in the *Codex Theodosianus*,[199] the terms of which are as follows:

Emperors Valentinian [II], Theodosius and Arcadius, Augusti, to the Senate

It shall not be permitted for a private individual to distribute a pure silk garment (*holoserica vestis*) as largesse at any performance of the games. We also confirm by this law that, ordinary

193 But cf. the figures for (western) praetorian games: below, p. 202.

194 John of Ephesus, *Ecclesiastical History* III.14; trans. R. P. Smith, pp. 189–90.

195 See below, p. 481.

196 Theophanes, *Chronographia*; ed. de Boor, I, p. 253. Theophylact Simocatta, *Historiae* I.12.12–13; ed. C. de Boor (Teubner), p. 64.

197 Corippus, *In Laudem Iustini Augusti* IV; ed. Averil Cameron, pp. 73–84, esp. pp. 75, 76, 77, 78.

198 See below, p. 200.

199 *CTh.* XV.9.1.

consuls excepted, absolutely no one else shall have the right of giving away a gift in gold (*aurea sportula*), or a diptych in ivory (*diptycha ex ebore*). When public ceremonies are enacted, silver coin (*argenteus nummus*) shall be used for gifts, and another material for diptychs. Nor is it permitted to expend [*sc.* in this manner] a silver coin larger than that which is customarily formed when a pound of silver is divided into sixty pieces of coin. And We permit those who wish to give a smaller one to do so not only freely, but even honourably.

Given 25 July at Heraclea in the consulships of Richomeres and Clearchus [384].

The law is a comparatively straightforward one, although the text as it stands seems to lack at least one other section that was later carried over into the *Codex Justinianus.*[200] The senate involved was presumably the Constantinopolitan one, for Theodosius was indeed at Heraclea during the months of June and July of the year 384.[201]

A law of Marcian addressed to Sporacius, *comes domesticorum* and consul for the year 452 (and therefore presumably datable to that year), subsequently withdrew even from ordinary consuls the right of scattering largesse in their processions, and commanded them instead to pay what was probably the approximately equivalent sum into the fund for the repair of aqueducts.[202] This law seems to have remained in force, technically at least, until the issue of Novel CV of Justinian in which it is indeed several times mentioned. Novel CV is dated 536/7 and is addressed to Strategius, then *comes sacrarum largitionum*, ex-consul and patrician, copies having been sent equally to John (the Cappadocian), then praetorian prefect of the East for the second time, and to Longinus, then *praefectus urbis*. *Caput* 2.1, that section specifically dealing with the subject in hand, reads as follows:

And so We better regulate the consular scattering of largesse to the people in these seven processions (*proodoi, processiones*), just as the law of Marcian of Blessed Memory states. This law forbade entirely the exercise of munificence, but We amend it, acting at the suggestion of the individual who has the honour of holding the consulship. Now if the holder does not wish to scatter (*rhiptein, spargere*) anything We do not compel him to do so, and if he wishes to restore the situation and to honour the people with gifts of money (*ex argyrou dōrois*) We do not forbid him to do so. Nevertheless We command him not to scatter gold, whether small in form or – and more particularly – large, whether of medium size either struck or simply weighed, but to scatter silver only, just as We have commanded above. For to scatter gold is reserved for the emperor, since it is to him alone that the summit of fortune has given the capacity to despise gold. Silver, which is considered most precious directly after gold, is a suitable largesse for other consuls. Therefore We command them to scatter largesse in what are called *miliarēsia* (*en te tois kaloumenois miliarēsiois*) and *mēla* and *kaukia* and *tetragōnia* and so on. For the smaller the objects that are scattered, the greater is the number of recipients...

The general sense of that section of the law quoted is straightforward enough, although the particular meaning of several of the terms in the penultimate sentence have occasioned

[200] *CJ*. I.16.1.

[201] O. Seeck, *Regesten der Kaiser und Päpste für die Jahre 311 bis 476 n. Chr.*, p. 265.

[202] *CJ* XII.3.2. See also below, p. 200.

discussion. It seems possible, if in the light of other evidence improbable, that the text originally mentioned *miliaria* (not miliaresia) as well as *mēla*, *kaukia* and *tetragōnia*, and that all these terms represent the various vessels holding the coins that were to be scattered, rather than the coins or objects that were to be scattered, as is more plausibly supposed.[203] The holder of the consulship who is mentioned as having suggested the amendment of Marcian's law is likely to have been John the Cappadocian, consul in 538.[204] At any rate, it is clear that whereas John Lydus[205] primarily associates the scattering of miliaresia (i.e. silver coins) with the consulship, Corippus,[206] in describing the ceremonial of an imperial consulship (that of Justin II in 566), mentions the golden rain (*aureus imber*) to be scattered to the people, and the silver vessels filled with gold (*fulvo plena...argentea vasa metallo*) that were distributed to the senators and guards.

The latter author, in also mentioning old silver renewed into various shapes and objects, marked with inscriptions and engraved with designs (*vetus argentum formas speciesque novatum in varias, pressum titulis sculptumque figuris*), together with the known variety of surviving objects distributed on such occasions, renders it most likely that Justinian's law also refers to such objects.[207]

In much the same way, therefore, as the consulship eventually became confined to the emperor himself, so the privilege of scattering largesse in gold was first confined to the ordinary consuls in general, and finally to the emperor in particular. The distribution of silk garments, also an imperial privilege of the later period, had suffered a similar limitation very early on.[208]

## B. Other items and occasions

The accessional and quinquennial donatives, and the largesses and expenses of the consulship, must have accounted for a high proportion of state expenditure expressed in the form of regular or at least institutionalised bounties; but the other occasions on which, and frequency with which, imperial munificence was exercised, the forms that it took and materials which it involved, not to mention the variety of social classes and individuals

[203] So A. Maricq, 'Noms de monnaies ou noms de vases dans la "Nov. Just." 105, 2?', *Byzantion* 20 (1950), pp. 317–26. But see below, 207.

[204] Stein, *Histoire du bas-empire* II, pp. 461–2.

[205] John Lydus, *De Mensibus* IV.9; ed. Wuensch (Teubner), pp. 73–4. The one documented, clear, and possibly significant exception to what previously may have been a customary limitation of silver to private consuls, had been Belisarius, consul in 535 – who distributed gold on two occasions: Alan Cameron and D. Schauer, 'The Last Consul: Basilius and his Diptych', *Journal of Roman Studies* 72 (1982), p. 141.

[206] See above, p. 193 n. 197.

[207] See above, p. 193, n. 197. For the objects involved: R. MacMullen, 'The Emperor's Largesses', *Latomus* 21 (1962), pp. 159–66, and R. Delmaire, 'La caisse des largesses sacrées et l'armée au bas-empire', in *Armées et fiscalité dans le monde antique*, at pp. 312–15.

[208] For particular examples, see above, p. 191; below, pp. 210, 213, 229.

upon which it was lavished, probably ensured that their total was not of a fundamentally different order from that of the more regular and institutionalised bounties.[209]

With the discontinuation of the regular donatives and the cessation of extensive expenditure on the consulship, both of which probably occurred during the seventh century, the state and indeed the tax-payer will have been relieved of a very considerable burden. True, the emperor still exercised munificence, particularly in the form of largesse (still, significantly, termed *hypateia*). He might do this in Easter Week, perhaps on a regular basis, as Irene did in 799 from a golden chariot drawn by four white horses led by patricians,[210] or on Christmas Day, combined with a family baptism, as Basil I and Eudocia did in or about 867 in a similar fashion.[211] He might take advantage of his accession combined with the news of a military victory, as Basil and Eudocia with their sons Constantine and Leo did in 867,[212] or the dedication of a church, as Basil again did in 880.[213] He might respond to the occasion of a hard winter and/or famine, as Romanus I did in 927/8;[214] of an earthquake, combined with a family death, as Romanus III did in 1032;[215] or of a severe fire, as Isaac II (1185–95) did in his turn.[216] The occasions could be multiplied indefinitely.[217]

Certain feasts and ceremonies entailed the distribution of largesse to various officials: that occurring on the feast termed *Broumalia* involving gold coin has already been mentioned; those on the Vigil of the Feast of St Elias, the Vigil of Palm Sunday and Palm Sunday itself involved little crosses made of silver (*stauria argyra mikra*), of which at least one probable example survives.[218] By the second half of the thirteenth century, the distribution on Palm Sunday had been augmented, more probably replaced, by one of silver and copper nomismata, tied together in *epikompia*, and thrown to the people in the course of a procession. But whether this was a regular event remains uncertain.[219]

Imperial coronations and promotions entailed the distribution of largesse to the people,

209 See above, n. 207; below, pp. 200–1.

210 Theophanes, *Chronographia*; ed. de Boor, I, p. 474.

211 Leo Grammaticus, *Chronographia*; ed. I. Bekker (Bonn edn), p. 254.

212 *Continuation of Theophanes* V.29; Bonn edn, p. 256.

213 Leo Grammaticus, *Chronographia*; Bonn edn, p. 258.

214 *Continuation of Theophanes* VI.27; Bonn edn, pp. 417–18. Symeon the Magister, *Annales, De Constantino Porphyrogenito et Romano Lacapeno* XXXVIII; ed. I. Bekker (Bonn edn), pp. 743–4. The *Continuation* could be read as saying that the total sum involved was 12,000 nom.; Symeon states quite specifically that the sum was 12,000 nom. per month, for 120 days (or a total of 48,000 nom.). Symeon, whose account is the tighter, should be preferred.

215 George Cedrenus, *Historiarum Compendium*; Bonn edn, II, p. 500.

216 Nicetas Choniates, *Historia*; ed. van Dieten, I, p. 445.

217 For two distributions, under Michael IV and John III, each on the occasion of a terminal imperial illness, see below, p. 234 and n. 82.

218 Constantine Porphyrogenitus, *De Caerimoniis* I.19, 31, 32; Bonn edn, pp. 115, 170, 173. Philotheus, *Klētorologion*; ed. Oikonomides, p. 215. For the surviving cross (refs): M. C. Ross, *Catalogue of the Byzantine and Early Mediaeval Antiquities in the Dumbarton Oaks Collection* II, pp. 73–4 (no. 97).

219 George Pachymeres, *De Michaele et Andronico Palaeologis, De Mich.* IV.18; Bonn edn, I, pp. 293–4.

and their anniversaries a distribution to officials at least.[220] Even a casual imperial visit to the Great Church necessitated the giving of gifts of gold coin to the clergy and patriarch,[221] and an imperial military campaign involved the transport of whole sacks (*sakkia*) of gold nomismata and silver miliaresia, not only for pay and expenses, but also for distribution to those who had distinguished themselves.[222]

On most of the above occasions, it seems likely that the necessary sums would have been provided from public funds, and indeed on one occasion when they were not to be had from that source, it is recorded that the emperor (Basil) obtained them: 'not from public funds (*ouk ek tōn dēmosiōn*), for there were none, but from the private ones (*all'ek tōn oikeiōn*)'. Presumably the two *vestiaria* are meant.[223]

The size of such distributions tended on the one hand to increase and on the other to become increasingly formalised. During the reign of Leo VI the *Broumalia* of each of the rulers had been celebrated separately, and each had rated an hierarchically appropriate size: an *apokombion* of 20 lb for Leo, as the senior emperor; one of 10 lb for Alexander, as junior; and one of 8 lb for Zoë, as augusta. Constantine VII consolidated the celebrations, and increased the *apokombion* to 50 lb gold.[224]

The gifts of gold coin to the patriarch were similarly arranged: of the total of 10 lb gold, the senior emperor gave the most (all, if he were the sole emperor), the juniors lesser but equal amounts; if there were two emperors other than the senior, the former would have given two sums of three pounds, the latter one of four pounds; if there were three emperors other than the senior, the former would have given three sums of two pounds, the latter still one of four pounds, and so on. Each presumably gave a single *apokombion*.[225]

220 Coronation rite: Anonymous (Pseudo-Codinus), *De Officiis* VII; ed. J. Verpeaux, pp. 255, 271. Particular examples – Tiberius II and Anastasia (augusta) in 578: Theophanes, *Chronographia*; ed. de Boor, I, pp. 249, 250. Phocas in 602: Theophylact Simocatta, *Historiae* VIII.10; ed. de Boor and Wirth (Teubner), p. 303. Maria (augusta, wife of Leo III) in 718: Theophanes, *Chronographia*; *ed. cit.* I, p. 400. Sons of Constantine V in 769: Theophanes, *Chronographia*; *ed. cit.* I, pp. 443–4. Michael I and Procopia in 811: Theophanes, *Chronographia*; *ed. cit.* I, pp. 493–4. Bardas (caesar) in 856: Leo Grammaticus, *Chronographia*; Bonn edn, p. 238. Andronicus III in 1325: John Cantacuzene, *Historiarum Libri IV* I.41; Bonn edn, I, p. 203. Manuel II in 1391: Anonymous, *Laurentianus* VIII.17; ed. Verpeaux in *De Officiis*, at pp. 360–1. This is a selection of only the most explicit and/or obvious examples, and others could be found without difficulty: e.g. Manuel I in 1143 – see below, pp. 198–9.

221 See below, and p. 198.

222 See below, pp. 272–4, 309.

223 *Continuation of Theophanes* V.29; Bonn edn, pp. 256–7. The *Continuation* also mentions that the sources of Basil's eventual generosity were (a) the many treasure-troves found at the time and (b) the imperial ceremonial apparatus sent to the foundry by his predecessor. See below, pp. 225, 228, 229.

224 Philotheus, *Klētorologion*; ed. Oikonomides, pp. 223, 225. Constantine Porphyrogenitus, *De Caerimoniis* II.16–18; Bonn edn, pp. 601, 606–7. The relevant sums seem, on these occasions, to have been provided by the *oikeiakon vestiarion* – the *prōtovestiarios* is mentioned as being in attendance and handing to the emperor an *apokombion* of 200/500 miliaresia.

225 Constantine Porphyrogenitus, *De Caerimoniis* I.1; Bonn edn, pp. 18–19. For a reconstruction of, and commentary upon, the *scholium* including the detailed breakdown, see: Const. Porph. *De Caer.*; ed. A. Vogt, I (text), p. 14, I (commentary), pp. 64–6. It is impossible to be certain, on these occasions, which

An imperial visit to the Great Church on the occasion of one of the great feasts of the Christian Year necessarily entailed even larger gifts to the patriarch and clergy: Theophilus is known to have given a kentenarion at Christmas and on Palm Sunday, while Manuel I deposited a purse of gold (*khrysou desmon*), presumably representing a kentenarion, at the Church on the occasion of his visit at Christmas 1150.[226] Again, the gift of a kentenarion is known to have provided one of the principal ceremonies of Holy Saturday. This is implied to have been, or was, in existence by the ninth or tenth century, but had been discontinued by the fourteenth.[227]

This kind of donation clearly goes back some considerable way: Justin II gave gifts (*dona*) to the Great Church, enriching it with an immense offering (*immenso...munere*), after praying there at the inauguration of his consulship on 1 January 566.[228]

According to Cinnamus,[229] Manuel seems, typically, to have combined virtually all these options at the very commencement of his reign. Having distributed gifts to, and dismissed, the military forces with which he had returned to Constantinople, he then gave two hyperpyra to each metropolitan household (*oikion*) and, when crowned, left a kentenarion of gold upon the altar of the Great Church, following this up with an annual grant of two kentenaria to its clergy. The last, as events turned out, was to be paid in the nomisma called the second (*to deuteron*), clearly implying the electrum trachy, the implication being confirmed by Choniates, according to whom[230] the grant was of 200 *menai* of silver coins (*argyrea kermata*). It was thus equivalent to $66\frac{2}{3}$ lb gold at the current rate of exchange.

Now certain elements in this exercise of munificence were of a purely customary nature: the gift of a kentenarion (or 50 lb in the case of a junior emperor) to the Great Church on the occasion of an imperial coronation can be traced back as far as the late ninth century,[231] and Manuel himself repeated the exercise when he married and crowned as augusta Maria of Antioch in 1161.[232] The gifts to the military forces may have been

department provided the relevant sums: the *argyros* ('cashier' – an otherwise unknown official unless, as seems probable, the term is a synonym) and the *praipositos* (*sc. sacri cubiculi*) were both in attendance, but it is by no means clear, at this stage, that the *praipositos* still headed a department which possessed the actual care (as opposed to effective disposal) of funds. Most probably the sums were provided by the *oikeiakon vestiarion* (see above, p. 197 n. 224; below, n. 227, 199 n. 235).

226 Theophilus: *Continuation of Theophanes* III.15–16; Bonn edn, pp. 106–7. Manuel: Michael the Rhetor, *Oratio ad Manuelem Imperatorem* X; ed. W. V. E. Regel, in *Fontes Rerum Byzantinarum*, I, pp. xx, 168. See also below, p. 199 (gift of a kentenarion by Michael I and Theophylact at Christmas 811).

227 Philotheus, *Klētorologion*; ed. Oikonomides, p. 199 (where the gift is not actually mentioned). Constantine Porphyrogenitus, *De Caerimoniis* I.1; Bonn edn, pp. 33, 34. Anonymous, *De Officiis* IV; ed. Verpeaux, pp. 237–8. According to Const. Porph., a *koubikoularios* (who carried the kentenarion, and who was perhaps termed *argyros* for the occasion?), and the *praipositos*, were both in attendance; but according to the *De Officiis* the sum had actually come *apo tou bestiariou*, again presumably the *oikeiakon vestiarion*.

228 Corippus, *In Laudem Iustini Augusti* IV; ed. Averil Cameron, p. 82.

229 John Cinnamus, *Epitome* II. 2; Bonn edn, pp. 32–3.

230 Nicetas Choniates, *Historia*; ed. van Dieten, I, p. 49.

231 Philotheus, *Klētorologion*; ed. Oikonomides, p. 98.

232 John Cinnamus, *Epitome* V.4; Bonn edn, p. 211.

of a similar nature.[233] According to Theophanes,[234] Michael I, when crowned in 811, had made a gift of 50 lb gold to the patriarch, 25 lb to the clergy, and various other gifts to the senate and military forces; when he crowned his son Theophylact, the sums had been 25 lb for the patriarch, and (presumably because it was also Christmas) 100 lb to the clergy. According to Constantine Porphyrogenitus,[235] Leo I, when crowned in 457, had made a gift to the church, apparently consisting of valuables (*keimēlia*) and gold (*khrysion*), but this had been only as much as he wished (*haper boulētheiē*). Again, as Constantine actually implies, such gifts had increased in size, and had eventually been formalised.

On the other hand, the distribution to metropolitan households seems to have been something over and above the customary coronation *hypateia*, and the annual grant to the clergy of the Great Church presumably augmented, rather than replaced, both the gifts that have already been mentioned, and the previous grant of 80 lb gold made by Romanus III.[236] This had itself replaced a previous grant of 40 lb.[237]

It is true, of course, that Manuel's position, which involved the passing over of his elder brother Isaac's claims to the throne, can scarcely have appeared secure at the time, and therefore that it may well have been thought politic to conciliate popular opinion by acts of conspicuous generosity. Nonetheless, these acts set the tone for the entire reign.[238] In addition to everything else, Manuel was apparently capable of spending huge sums on precious stones. He wore a huge pendant ruby to impress Kılıç Arslan II in 1162, and it may well have been this which was used at the coronation of Baldwin I in 1204, having reportedly cost him 62,000 marks, probably amounting to some 300,000 hyperpyra.[239] The price may well be fantastical, however,

These instances of later imperial largesses obviously form a sample only of the total number of occasions on which some kind of distribution might be made or might be expected: others can be found without difficulty, and the total both of occasions and of expenditure was doubtless considerable.

Figures of this kind of expenditure are, of course, rare. The distribution of alms during the hard winter of 927/8, undertaken by Romanus I, which has been mentioned above, apparently cost 48,000 nomismata.[240] According to Zonaras, the same emperor cancelled

233 Philotheus, *Klētorologion*; ed. Oikonomides, p. 98.

234 Theophanes, *Chronographia*; ed. de Boor, I, pp. 493–4.

235 Constantine Porphyrogenitus, *De Caerimoniis* I.91; Bonn edn, pp. 413 (Church of St John (Studium): *hoia bouletai*), 415 (Great Church: *haper boulētheiē*). The relevant sums seem, on this occasion, to have been provided by the *privata* – the *komēs tōn pribatōn* is mentioned as being in attendance. Later, the *oikeiakon vestiarion* would presumably have been responsible (see above, p. 197 n. 224, p. 198 n. 227).

236 George Cedrenus, *Historiarum Compendium*; Bonn edn, II, p. 486.

237 Nicholas Mysticus, *Epistolae* LXXII; ed. R. J. H. Jenkins and L. G. Westerink, pp. 318, 320.

238 See below, pp. 222, 227, 265, 270, 271 and n. 95.

239 John Cinnamus, *Epitome* V.3; Bonn edn, p. 206. Robert of Clari, *La conquête de Constantinople* XCVI; ed. P. Lauer, p. 95.

240 See above, p. 196 n. 214.

the debts of metropolitan households, having the relevant documents burned and costing the state nineteen kentenaria or somewhat over 136,000 nomismata. The story is repeated by Cedrenus.[241] According to Nicetas Choniates,[242] Isaac II – who is by general consent acknowledged to have been a spendthrift – distributed five kentenaria in gold or 36,000 hyperpyra to the people in the course of a ten-year reign, but this probably represented the less significant portion of his total largesse. The annual figure implied is not, as it happens, an implausible one, for Marcian, by a law of 452, had forbidden[243] ordinary consuls to scatter gold amongst the crowd during their consulships, commanding instead that they should pay the sum of 100 lb gold or 7,200 solidi into the fund for the repair of aqueducts. Zeno had dictated[244] the same of honorary consuls. This sum was, then, the probably approximate equivalent of the consular *sparsiones*.

No model of state revenue and expenditure – whether for the early period or the late – can be considered viable without some account, however brief, having been taken of the exercise of imperial *philanthropia*, an exercise that involved the expenditure of considerable sums, whether in the form of coin, or kind, or even land, on any number of philanthropic causes, the extent and goals of such expenditure obviously varying with the reigning emperor and, frequently, his closer relatives.[245]

An overwhelming impression of what this could mean is to be gained from the Roman *Liber Pontificalis*,[246] recording the donations made by Constantine to the Roman churches and their dependencies. Huge quantities of gold, silver and jewels are represented, almost all in the form of furniture and plate. Land is represented on an equal scale.

Total figures for this kind of expenditure are, once again, difficult to come by, but, according to John Lydus,[247] 4,000 lb gold were expended on the construction of Hagia Sophia during the short administration of Phocas as prefect of the East (532) alone, and, according to Procopius,[248] the sanctuary of the same church contained 40,000 lb silver, the equivalent of 200,000 solidi at a gold:silver ratio of 1:14.4.[249] Repairs to the dome and western arch, damaged by earthquake in 989, seem to have cost at least 10 kentenaria.[250]

Other figures for Hagia Sophia have a less reliable appearance: those of 3,200 kentenaria for the building itself, together with other sums for its elements and furniture, while not

[241] John Zonaras, *Annales* XVI.20; Bonn edn, III, p. 478. George Cedrenus, *Historiarum Compendium*; Bonn edn, II, p. 318.

[242] Nicetas Choniates, *Historia*; ed. van Dieten, I, p. 445.

[243] See above, p. 194.

[244] *CJ* XII.3.3.

[245] D. Constantelos, *Byzantine Philanthropy and Social Welfare*, esp. chapter 8 ('Philanthropy and the Byzantine State'), pp. 111–36.

[246] *Liber Pontificalis* XXXIIII (Sylvester); ed. L. Duchesne, I, pp. 170–87.

[247] John Lydus, *De Magistratibus Populi Romani* III.76; ed. R. Wuensch (Teubner), pp. 169–70.

[248] Procopius, *De Aedificiis* I.1.65; ed. J. Haury and G. Wirth (Teubner), p. 15.

[249] The commonest fourth-/fifth-century ratio: see below, pp. 480–1 and Table 16.

[250] George Cedrenus, *Historiarum Compendium*; Bonn edn, II, p. 438. C. A. Mango, *Materials for the Study of the Mosaics of St. Sophia at Istanbul*, pp. 77–8.

in themselves totally unbelievable, have the disadvantage of commencing with the precise sum recorded as having been left by Anastasius as a reserve.[251] It is difficult to believe that the two were not connected in the popular mind. That of 12,653 kentenaria, while mysteriously precise, is totally unbelievable.[252]

In 526/7, after a disastrous earthquake had devastated Antioch, Justin I sent a total of 4,500 lb gold to the city to aid in the reconstruction, and particularly that of its public works and buildings.[253]

Such impressions and figures are, however, entirely exceptional. Much more within the normal (but still upper) range of imperial generosity are the two sums of two kentenaria or 14,400 solidi given by the empresses Eudoxia and Eudocia to found a church and hostel in Gaza, and to restore the public baths in Antioch, respectively, in the fifth century. Eudoxia also gave a further 1,000 solidi and plate (*skeuē*).[254] An annual income of 1,850 solidi was granted to a hospital of 100 beds that Justinian intended to have built in Jerusalem in the sixth century. Income and number of beds were both subsequently doubled.[255] The annual expenditure of the metropolitan monastery of the Pantocrator, founded and endowed by John II and his wife Irene in 1136, amounted to some 2,600 hyperpyra, besides considerable quantities of bread, grain, wine, oil and firewood, implying a much larger endowment.[256] As a matter of private comparison, 14,400 solidi for the foundation of a major church would appear to have been quite normal,[257] and the annual expenditure of the monastery of Bachkovo, founded and endowed by Gregory Pacourianus in 1083, may have amounted to up to some 1,700 nomismata, besides products in kind.[258] The net annual revenue of the Athonite monastery of the Lavra in 1089 may have amounted to some 1,600–2,000 nomismata.[259]

## (VI) PRIVATE WEALTH

### A. Overall figures

The figures quoted in the preceding sections of this chapter no doubt seem large, but it should be remembered that, according to Olympiodorus of Thebes,[260] many Roman households of the first rank received an annual cash revenue of around 40 kentenaria or

[251] Refs: G. Dagron and C. Morrisson, 'Le *Kentènarion* dans les sources byzantines', *Revue Numismatique* 17[6] (1975), p. 157. For Anastasius, see below, p. 224.

[252] Refs: Dagron and Morrisson, 'Le *Kentènarion* dans les sources byzantines', p. 147.

[253] John Malalas, *Chronographia* XVII; Bonn edn, p. 422, 424.

[254] *Vita Sancti Porphyrii Gazae* LIII; ed. H. Grégoire and M.-A. Kugener, p. 44. Evagrius, *Ecclesiastical History* I.20; ed. J. Bidez and L. Parmentier, p. 29.

[255] *Vita Sancti Sabae* LXXIII; ed. E. Schwartz, p. 177.

[256] Gautier, 'Le typikon du Christ Sauveur Pantocrator', pp. 12–21.

[257] See below, pp. 245–6.

[258] Refs: see above p. 160 n. 14. Lemerle (pp. 189–90) and Hendy (pp. 184–6) utilise somewhat different sub-totals, but the results are within the same order of magnitude.

[259] N. Svoronos, 'Remarques sur les structures économiques de l'empire byzantin au XIe siècle', p. 61.

[260] Olympiodorus of Thebes, *Fragmenta* XLIV; ed. Müller, IV, at p. 67.

some 288,000 solidi. And this was excluding revenues in kind which might amount to a third as much again if sold. Households of lesser rank received between 15 and 10 kentenaria or 108,000 and 72,000 solidi. According to Gerontius,[261] when two main branches of the *gens Valeria* were united by the marriage of Pinianus and Melania in 397, their combined annual revenues amounted to 120,000 units, presumably solidi, making somewhat under 17 kentenaria. These derived from properties in Italy, Sicily, Africa, Spain and Britain. Again according to Olympiodorus,[262] the entire fortune of Heraclian, the rebellious *comes Africae*, which was confiscated and spent on the first consulship of Flavius Constantius in 414, amounted to 20 kentenaria in gold and a further 2,000 lb gold in kind, making a total of 288,000 solidi. But this was evidently less than had been expected. Similarly, Probus is said[263] to have spent 12 kentenaria or 86,400 solidi on his praetorian games held in 424/5, Symmachus (of moderate wealth) to have spent 20 kentenaria or 144,000 solidi on his son's praetorian games held in 401, and Maximus (one of the wealthy) to have spent 40 kentenaria or 288,000 solidi on his son's games held in *c.* 411.

These huge revenues and fortunes, and these huge sums spent on magistracies and the functions and duties deriving from them, did not necessarily, however, imply the accumulation of equivalent amounts of surplus liquidity, and this despite the fact that, according to the anonymous author of the *De Rebus Bellicis*,[264] the private houses of powerful citizens (*potentes*) were filled (*repletae*) with gold, a claim supported by the nature and quality of many surviving artefacts in the precious metals. On the other hand, the praetorship, for example, was allotted and announced up to ten years in advance, one probable reason for this being to permit the accumulation of the requisite funds.[265] Again, when Pinianus and Melania began to sell off their property in order to devote the proceeds to charitable purposes, they accepted gold from some purchasers, silver from others, and bonds (*cautiones*) from yet others: 'Because the property was great, and the purchasers were unable to pay the prices involved at one go, although it was the great and noble who were buying (*Quoniam magna erat substantia et non sufficiebant emptores in semel persolvere pretia, etiam cum magni et nobiles essent qui emerent*).'[266]

The figures, in any case, relate to the great western families and their members, and easterners seem neither to have possessed the same resources nor to have indulged in

[261] *Vita Sanctae Melaniae Junioris* I.10, 11, 15, 19; ed. H. Delehaye, in *Analecta Bollandiana* 8 (1889), at pp. 27, 31, 34 (Latin), and in *AB* 22 (1903), at pp. 14, 17, 19 (Greek); *PLRE* I, pp. 702 (Pinianus 2), 593 (Melania 2).

[262] Olympiodorus of Thebes, *Fragmenta* XXIII; ed. Müller, IV, at p. 62. *PLRE* II, pp. 539–40 (Heraclianus 3), 321–5 (Fl. Constantius 17).

[263] Olympiodorus of Thebes, *Fragmenta* XLIV; ed. Müller, IV, at pp. 67–8; *PLRE* II, p. 910 (Probus 2), *PLRE* I, pp. 865–70 (Symmachus 4), *PLRE* II, pp. 749–51 (Maximus 22: the Maximus referred to will have been the otherwise unknown father of this one, the later emperor Petronius Maximus).

[264] Anonymous, *De Rebus Bellicis* II; ed. Ireland, p. 5.

[265] Jones, *Later Roman Empire* II, p. 540.

[266] *Vita Sanctae Melaniae Junioris* I.15; ed. Delehaye, at p. 32 (Latin).

expenditure on so massive a scale. It has been calculated[267] that the annual cash revenue of a Roman household of lesser rank would have represented the entire capital of a Constantinopolitan household of the first rank, and it has also been observed[268] that the sums spent on praetorian games in Rome were on a fundamentally different scale from those spent on the equivalent in Constantinople: these latter, noticeably expressed in terms of silver, never amounted to more than 1,000 lb, representing somewhat under 70 lb gold or some 5,000 solidi, at a gold:silver ratio of 1:14.4.[269] Again, whereas the Roman senate paid its *aurum oblaticium* in the form of 3,000 lb gold, the Constantinopolitan one paid its offering in the form of 3,000 lb silver – approximately one fourteenth only of the other sum.[270]

There were, nevertheless, a few exceptions to this general rule. The widow Olympias, closely related to leading imperial officials, is said to have been worth 10,000 lb gold and 20,000 lb silver, or somewhat under 820,000 solidi, in the early fifth century: she also, like Pinianus and Melania, owned widely separated property, in Thrace, Bithynia, Galatia and Cappadocia Prima, as well as in Constantinople.[271] Juliana Anicia, the builder of the metropolitan church of St Polyeuctus, married to an eastern official, Aerobindus, but, as daughter of the emperor Olybrius, related to the great western senatorial family, was presumably her even grander equivalent in the early sixth century.[272] Belisarius, on regaining imperial favour, is said to have had restored to him a portion of his confiscated fortune amounting to 30 kentenaria or 216,000 solidi in the sixth century, and Theodosius, the adopted son of Belisarius and Antonina, supposedly purloined, from the conquered palaces of Carthage and Ravenna, 100 kentenaria or 720,000 solidi, and made that sum the basis of his fortune.[273]

Eunuchs, because of their position, frequently managed to accumulate great wealth in a short time: Theodore, *castrensis sacri palatii* under Justinian, seems to have possessed between 15 and 20 kentenaria, or 108 and 144 thousand solidi, in gold, as well as plate, clothes, and slaves. On the other hand, their peculiarly exposed situation rendered them particularly liable to disgrace and confiscation.[274]

Beside these sums, ecclesiastical revenues and fortunes of the period tend to appear relatively moderate: Constantine donated lands to the Roman church which yielded well over 400 lb gold;[275] Leo III confiscated the lands of the church in Sicily and Calabria

[267] Jones, *Later Roman Empire* II, pp. 554–5.
[268] *Ibid.* pp. 538–9.
[269] See below, pp. 480–1 and Table 16.
[270] See below, pp. 407–8.
[271] *Vita Sanctae Olympiadis* IV; ed. H. Delehaye, in *Analecta Bollandiana* 15 (1896), at p. 413; *PLRE* I, pp. 642–3 (Olympias 2).
[272] *PLRE* II, pp. 635–6 (Anicia Iuliana 3), 143–4 (Fl. Areobindus 1).
[273] Procopius, *Historia Arcana* IV.31; ed. Haury (Teubner), III, p. 29 (Belisarius); I.33, *ed. cit.* p. 11 (Theodosius).
[274] *Vita Theodori Castrensis*; ed. E. W. Brooks, at pp. 202–4. Eunuchs: Jones, *Later Roman Empire* II, pp. 566–71; K. Hopkins, 'The Political Power of Eunuchs', in *Conquerors and Slaves*, at pp. 172–96; R. Guilland, 'Les eunuques dans l'empire byzantin', (*Revue des*) *Études Byzantines* 1 (1943), pp. 197–238. See also above, pp. 104, 106, for Basil the *parakoimōmenos*.
[275] See above, p. 200.

which apparently yielded $3\frac{1}{2}$ kentenaria or 25,200 solidi.[276] In the sixth century, the annual revenue of the Ravennate church amounted to 12,000 solidi;[277] in the seventh century the lands of the church in Sicily yielded 31,000 solidi, plus much in kind, of which 16,000 actually went to the church itself;[278] between the two dates the Ravennate church was able to lend an exarch 600 lb gold or 43,200 solidi.[279] On the other hand, when John the Almsgiver was made patriarch of Alexandria in 610, he found 80 kentenaria or 576,000 solidi, which apparently represented the accumulated fortune of the see.[280]

Even after the drastic territorial diminution of the empire at the hands of the Arabs, great fortunes are still found. According to Cedrenus,[281] the *nobilissimus* Constantine, brother of Michael IV and chief advisor to Michael V during his short reign (1041–2), was subsequently found to have amassed a fortune of 53 kentenaria or 387,600 nomismata. As he had apparently misappropriated much of this from public funds (*ta dēmosia khrēmata*), it cannot be considered typical, although it compares interestingly with Theodosius' earlier (and similarly purloined) fortune. Again, according to Cedrenus,[282] archbishop Theophanes of Thessalonica was able to amass a fortune of 33 kentenaria or 237,600 nomismata, and patriarch Alexius of Constantinople one of 25 kentenaria or 180,000 nomismata, in 1038 and 1043 respectively. The former, in claiming to the emperor Michael IV that he had only some 2,000 nomismata to hand in ready cash, and, presumably, in expecting to be believed, does not suggest the degree of liquidity normally available to an eleventh-century ecclesiastical magnate to have been fundamentally different from that available to a fifth-century lay one.[283]

Even after the further diminution of the empire at the hands of the Selçuks and Latins, the situation remained the same. According to Cantacuzene,[284] the moveable fortune of the *prōtovestiarios* Andronicus Palaeologus amounted to at least 72,000 hyperpyra in 1328. This, which came to light during the course of the civil war, consisted of three major deposits: one contained a hoard of his wife's ornaments (*kosmoi gynaikeioi*) worth 20,000 hyperpyra; and of the other two deposits (*kibōtoi*), one, in a great copper vase (*angeion ek khalkou*), contained 12,000 hyperpyra in cash; and the other, belts (*zōnai*) and cups (*ekpōmata*) of gold (*ek khrysou*), silver bullion (*argyros asēmos*), and more of his wife's ornaments, worth 40,000 hyperpyra. According to the same author,[285] the moveable

[276] Theophanes, *Chronographia*; ed. de Boor, I, p. 410.

[277] Agnellus, *Liber Pontificalis Ecclesiae Ravennatis* LX; MGH, *SRLang.*, p. 319.

[278] Agnellus, *Liber Pontificalis Ecclesiae Ravennatis* CXI; MGH, *SRLang.*, p. 350. Of the 31,000 sol., 15,000 went to the *palatium Constantinopolitanum*, 16,000 to the Ravennate *archivum* (= Gk. *arkheion*). But this did not include 50,000 modii of wheat (*triticum*), and other revenues in kind. The Constantinopolitan (and palatine) destination of the 15,000 sol. presumably arose from the fact that the island was then under direct palatine jurisdiction (see below, pp. 404–5).

[279] See below, p. 231.

[280] *Vita Sancti Ioannis Eleemosynarii* XLV; ed. H. Gelzer, pp. 92–3.

[281] George Cedrenus, *Historiarum Compendium*; Bonn edn, II, p. 541.

[282] George Cedrenus, *Historiarum Compendium*; Bonn edn, II, pp. 518, 550.

[283] See above, p. 202.

[284] John Cantacuzene, *Historiarum Libri IV* I.55; Bonn edn, I, pp. 278–9.

[285] See below, p. 241.

fortune of the wealthy parvenu Patrikiotes amounted to 140,000 hyperpyra in 1341. This consisted of 100,000 hyperpyra in cash, and a further 40,000 hyperpyra in utensils and plate (*epipla kai skeuē*) of gold and silver.

At this later period, large annual revenues tended to be granted out by the state to the holders of the many quasi-imperial titles who were also generally nearer imperial relations by blood or marriage. The practice was first systematised by Alexius I and, although some emperors seem to have been more extravagant than others in this respect, subsequently became normative.

The annual revenues (*oikonomiai*) left to Constantine the porphyrogenitus, the younger son of Michael VIII, by his father, in 1282, amounted to 60,000 hyperpyra, and the latter had reportedly intended 100,000 hyperpyra, but had been prevented by death. Such revenues, of course, were derived ultimately, possibly even directly, from public funds. Even so, Constantine's fortune in cash and kind was thought worthy of remark when it was confiscated by Andronicus II, his brother, not long afterwards. His property (*pronoiai*) consisted of herds (*agelai*), stores of all kinds (*apothēkai pantoiōn eidōn*), and gold (*khrysos*) – the latter partly in coined money (*en nomismasi kekkomenon*), and partly in worked cups (*en ekpōmasin eirgasmenon*). It also included silver (*argyros*) and costumes of all kinds (*pepla pantodapa*).[286]

There are some slight grounds for supposing the annual revenues thought appropriate to a caesar, at much the same date (1304), to have amounted to 30,000 hyperpyra. For, according to Pachymeres,[287] Andronicus II sent to Roger de Flor, the Catalan leader, the insignia of a caesar (*kaisaros symbola*), a chrysobull (presumably conferring or confirming the rank), and 30,000 hyperpyra (the annual revenues of the rank?). Constantine had held a curious and anomalous status below that of emperor but above that of despot, Roger held the regular rank of caesar. It is therefore tempting to assume the order of rank and revenue to have been: emperor/despot 60,000; despot 50,000; sebastocrator 40,000; caesar 30,000; but this is obviously incapable of proof. In any case, such revenues were presumably applied to 'active' holders of such ranks only.

At any rate, the junior emperor Andronicus III was given an annual revenue of 36,000 hyperpyra out of public funds (*ek tōn dēmosiōn khrēmatōn*) in 1322, but this was for the expenses of his household (*oikia*) (6,000 hyp.?) and wife (30,000 hyp.?) only, and the money needed for the payment of his military (*misthophorou strateias khrēmata*) was counted as separate. Noticeably, the whole arrangement was confirmed by a chrysobull.[288] The fact that, four years and four months later, Andronicus was claiming to be owed 350,000 hyperpyra shows that his total expenditure was indeed far higher, and again tempts the assumption that the total annual revenue agreed had been 80,000 although again it is

[286] George Pachymeres, *De Michaele et Andronico Palaeologis, De And.* II, 19; Bonn edn, II, pp. 157, 161.
[287] *Ibid.* VI.17; Bonn edn, II, p. 508.
[288] John Cantacuzene, *Historiarum Libri IV* I.34, 48; Bonn edn, I, pp. 167, 236–7.

incapable of proof. This would have meant that 45% of his revenue was being allotted to his household, and 55% to the payment of his military. The proportions are not at all improbable in the light of the general burden of the evidence.[289]

The ex-empress Constance of Hohenstaufen, widow of John III, claimed (not very convincingly) an annual revenue from three Anatolian cities amounting to 30,000 hyperpyra in *c.* 1316. Again, the claim – noticeably equivalent to the revenues suggested for a caesar – was based upon a supposed chrysobull.[290]

Finally, even the emperor Andronicus II was given the annual revenue of the Constantinopolitan fisheries, amounting to about 10,000 or 12,000 hyperpyra, and as much again from the imperial treasury (*basilikon tamieion*), for his own support (*diatrophē*) and that of his dependents, after his deposition in 1328.[291]

## *B. Casual descriptions*

Descriptions of wealth in general are sporadic throughout, and those with any degree of system or exhaustiveness are decidedly rare. They do, however, exist, and are perhaps best divided into three categories: casual descriptions in historical sources, testamentary descriptions and inventories, and fictional descriptions in literary sources.

The *Continuation of Theophanes* records[292] the various possessions of, and gifts made by, the widow Danelis, who had befriended Basil I long before he became emperor, who continued the friendship subsequently, and who finally died during the reign of Leo VI. The fact that the *Continuation* pays such attention to the details of these possessions and gifts suggests their very unusual, perhaps unique, nature and size. Danelis apparently owned some kind of weaving establishment, or establishments, at or near Patras in the Peloponnesus, and also not a small part of the peninsula itself.

She seems to have made two major gifts to Basil. The first, before he became emperor, consisted of a considerable amount of gold (*khrysos hikanos*); thirty trained slaves (*andrapoda pros hypēresian*), and great riches in clothing and goods (*en himatismō kai diaphorois eidesi*). The second, after he became emperor, and on an appropriately enhanced scale, consisted of 500 domestic servants (*oiketika prosōpa*), of which 100 were eunuchs; 100 women weavers (*gynaikes skiastriai*); 500 items of various kinds of woven wares (*sidonia, linomalotaria, amalia*, etc.); and a considerable amount of precious plate (*skeuē*), in gold and silver, and of various kinds.

But in addition to this, she had the Nea, a church founded by Basil, laid with huge and especially manufactured thick-piled prayer-rugs (*nakotapētai...apo tēs euchēs*), and

[289] *Ibid.* 1.48; Bonn edn, I, pp. 237, 239; see also above, pp. 158–9, 162, 164, 172.

[290] Refs: A. E. Laiou(-Thomadakis), *Constantinople and the Latins: The Foreign Policy of Andronicus II, 1282–1328*, p. 178 n. 75.

[291] See above, p. 174.

[292] *Continuation of Theophanes* V. 11, 73–7; Bonn edn, pp. 226–8, 316–21.

made annual gifts to the emperor. And she is also known to have furnished and endowed the Monastery of St Diomedes with rich gifts (*anathēmata polytela*), including books, other valuables (*keimēlia*), magnificent costumes (*esthēmata*) for ceremonies that glittered with stones (*lithoi*), great properties (*ktēmata*), considerable revenues (*prosoda*), and so on.

And yet, when she died, and despite her overwhelming liberality, her possessions remained apparently undiminished. There were found, by the *prōtospatharios* Zenobius who liquidated her estate on behalf of the emperor: great quantities of gold in coin (*khrysos en nomismasi pampoly*), and another superabundance in silver and gold clothing (*periousia en te argyrōmasi kai khrysōmasin esthēti*), in copper (*khalkō*), in slaves (*andrapodois*), and in livestock (*ktēnesi*), all on a scale surpassing private wealth (*idiōtikon...plouton*) and more appropriate to that of monarchs (*tyrannikōn*). As the number of her domestic slaves (*oiketika...andrapoda*) was simply too large to be coped with (and was indeed seemingly unique), by imperial order 3,000 of them were freed and transferred to the theme of Lagobardia as colonists (*eis apoikian*). In addition to everything else, the emperor found himself the heir, in his own right of possession (*eis idion klēron*), to eighty estates (*proasteia*).

The phenomenon was quite clearly an extraordinary one, even if the possibility of exaggeration is taken into account, and how such a vast accumulation of wealth could have occurred in an area that, only a half-century previously, had still been very much a frontier one, and at least partially depopulated, remains totally unexplained by the *Continuation*, and has also attracted remarkably little attention in modern scholarship. The clue to the solution is probably to be found in Danelis' name itself, possibly a graecised form of the Slavonic Danilo/Danila, suggesting her to have been descended from the Slav colonisers of the peninsula, although even prior to that period Patras noticeably had acted as a centre for the manufacture and export of clothing and textiles, as it still does: a remarkable record of continuity.[293]

John Cantacuzene's description[294] of his own and his mother's wealth, most of it confiscated by the loyalist régime on his proclamation as emperor, is of equal interest, and possibly represented something like an equal accumulation to that of Danelis, despite the great disparity in date.

In general terms the family wealth is described as consisting of gold, silver, livestock (*boskēmata*) and crops (*karpoi*). When loyalist agents entered the family palace (*basileia*) in Constantinople, they found there, and confiscated (*edēmosiōsan*), great wealth (*pleistēn*

[293] Danelis: S. Runciman, 'The Widow Danelis', in K. Varvaressos (ed.), *Études dédiées à la mémoire d'André M. Andréadès*, at pp. 425–31. This proposed Slav descent is not disproved by the fact of the Slav revolt in the area under Nicephorus I, after the suppression of which the former rebels were placed under the jurisdiction of the metropolitan church of Patras. Presumably only limited elements were involved – Bon, *Le Péloponnèse byzantin*, p. 43 and n. 3. Patras: Larsen, 'Roman Greece', pp. 471, 472, 484–5. The industry was based on flax, and, noticeably, a high proportion of its operatives were women (hence, presumably, Danelis' *gynaikes skiastriai*).

[294] John Cantacuzene, *Historiarum Libri IV* III.24, 27, 30; Bonn edn, II, pp. 148–9, 164–5.

*ousan*). This was in the form of silver and gold, precious stones (*lithoi polyteloi*) and pearls (*margaroi*), wheat (*pyrrhoi*) and barley (*krithai*), and other crops (*karpoi*). In a house (*oikia*) nearby, they found other heaps (*pyramides*) of crops that were even greater. As to numbers, the plate (*skeuē*) consisted of over two hundred pieces in silver alone. The family properties in Thrace provided for many herds (*agelai pollai*) of fattened oxen (*boskēmatoi boes*) totalling 5,000 that were out to pasture (*nomades*), and 1,000 yoke (*zeugē*) that were for farming purposes (*pros tas geōrgias*), 2,500 brood-mares also out to pasture, 50,000 pigs (*sybōsia*) in herds, 70,000 sheep, and unbelievable stocks of crops (*karpoi*) of incalculable worth (*khrēma*). Even so, the family fortress (*phrourion*) of Empythium, on the Hebrus (Maritsa) and not far from Didymotichum, which Cantacuzene himself had restored at a great expenditure of wealth (*pollai khrēmatōn dapanai*) and which housed his treasury (*tamieion*), was never taken.[295]

Again, this huge accumulation of wealth had occurred in just about a century, for the area which clearly provided the main concentration of estates had been in Latin or Bulgarian hands until *c.* 1240. Even so, the phenomenon is not quite as remarkable as that involving Danelis, for the Cantacuzene family had long belonged to the great landed aristocracy and to the court, John himself having long been *megas domestikos* before his proclamation.

The details of the description given by Cantacuzene of his own wealth are themselves closely comparable to the somewhat less extensive allusions made by Theodore Metochites to his wealth, largely accumulated as *megas logothetēs* and *mesazon* to Andronicus II.[296]

Beside these two accounts, that of the property of Philaretus, contained in the *Vita* of the saint, is both of somewhat less interest and on a less dramatic scale. Within these limitations it is nevertheless still of relevance:

> There was a man in the region (*khōra*) of the Paphlagonians by the name of Philaretus, and this man, well-born (*eugenēs*) amongst those from the regions of Pontus and Galatia, was the son of the *hyparkhos* George, called *Pheronymos*. He was exceedingly wealthy (*plousios*) and owned many livestock (*ktēnē polla*): 600 oxen, 100 yoke of oxen, 800 horses that were out to pasture (*nomades*), 80 saddle-horses and mules (*tēs promoselas*), 12,000 sheep, 48 estates abounding in great lands (*proastia de pollēs gēs peplēromena*), all of them distinct (*monotata*), very fertile (*hōraia*), and worth a great deal (*pollēs timēs axia*). For, over against each of them, a spring (*pēgē*), gushing forth from a height (*koryphē*), gave the possibility of fulfilling the water-needs of each in abundance. And he also owned many domestic servants (*oiketai*), and a very great deal of property (*ktēmata*).
>
> (*Vita Sancti Philareti*; ed. M.-H. Fourmy and M. Leroy, in *Byzantion* 9 (1934), at pp. 113, 115)

The account is perhaps less valuable because it is obviously, but to an unknown extent, idealised. It was, however, written by his grandson Nicetas, in 821/2, only twenty years

[295] *Ibid.* III.30; Bonn edn, II, p. 184. Nicephorus Gregoras, *Historia Byzantina* XIV.5; Bonn edn, II, p. 708.

[296] Refs: I. Ševčenko, 'Society and Intellectual Life in the Fourteenth Century', *XIV^e Congrès International des Études Byzantines, Bucarest 6–12 septembre 1971, Rapports* I, p. 28.

after his death on 1 December 792. At the very least, therefore, it represents a near contemporary concept of considerable wealth, and having been written by a descendant from the same region (that of Amnia, near Gangra), at most it represents something quite close to accuracy.[297] Even given the latter, however, it is totally illegitimate to deduce detailed agricultural statistics from the figures, and totally unwarranted to make detailed social comparisons between Danelis and Philaretus.[298]

The three descriptions of wealth summarised or quoted above, the first dealing with a provincial 'industrialist' and landowner of the ninth century, the second with a landed aristocrat and courtier of the fourteenth, and the third with a provincial landowner of the eighth, all have one relevant feature in common. Wealth admittedly consists of gold and silver, but also of other valuables such as precious stones and pearls, of clothing and stuffs, of servants and slaves, of crops and livestock, and ultimately, of course, of land.

Constantine the porphyrogenitus had what appears to have been a largely cash income, but his accumulated wealth is described in similar terms. Even when the classification is restricted to precious metals and valuables, as in the case of the *prōtovestiarios* Andronicus, the place occupied by cash remains low, 16.6%, and that occupied by kind remains high, 83.4%. Archbishop Theophanes claimed to possess no more than 30 lb gold, or 2,160 nomismata in cash, and presumably expected to be believed.[299] Only the parvenu Patrikiotes, who had made his career and fortune in taxation,[300] stands out in contrast, 60% in cash, and 40% in kind. The contrast is presumably a significant one.

## C. *Testamentary descriptions*

Very much the same impression is to be gained from testamentary description of wealth. A number of these survive, but three seem particularly relevant, as concerning middle- and high-ranking members of the military aristocracy, the most important and influential section of the dominant class. The three descriptions involved are those of the wealth of the *kouropalatēs* Symbatius Pacourianus, dated 1093; of that of his wife Kale, dated 1098; and of that of the *hypatos* Eustathius Boïlas, dated 1059.[301]

Symbatius Pacourianus describes[302] his wealth (*periousia*) and substance (*hypostasis*) as consisting of coin (*nomismata*), products in kind (*eidoi genēmatōn*), and the remainder (*ta*

[297] J. W. Nesbitt, 'The Life of St. Philaretos (702–792) and its Significance for Byzantine Agriculture', *The Greek Orthodox Theological Review* 14.2 (1969), pp. 150–8.

[298] *Contra* H. Evert-Kappesowa, 'Une grande propriété fonçière du VIII^e s. à Byzance', *Byzantinoslavica* 24 (1963), pp. 32–40. [299] See below, p. 240. [300] See below, p. 241.

[301] Commentaries – Pacouriani: P. Tivchev and G. Tsankova-Petkova, 'Au sujet des relations féodales dans les territoires bulgares sous la domination byzantine à la fin du XI^e et pendant la première moitié du XII^e siècle', *Byzantinobulgarica* 2 (1966), pp. 109–23. Boïlas: Lemerle, in *Cinq études sur le XI^e siècle byzantin*, at pp. 58–63.

[302] Text: I. Iverites, 'Ek tou arkheiou tēs en Hagio Orei Hieras Monēs tōn Ivērōn: Vyzantinai diathēkai', *Orthodoxia* 60 (Dec. 1930), pp. 614–18.

*loipa*). He owned at least four estates (*proasteia*) in the theme of Makedonia, of which one was an imperial gift; slaves (*anthrōpoi*); flocks and herds (*sphakta kai agelada*), of which horses, whether geldings (*eunoukha aloga*), or mares (*phorbadia*), and pigs (*khoiroi*), are specifically mentioned; clothing, of which tunics (*himatia*) of various kinds, and a cloak (*kabadion*), are specifically mentioned, one of the former items being an imperial gift. Crops (*genēma*) are also mentioned. A major legacy was his golden saddle and harness (*khrysoun selokhalinon*), and also mentioned is the interesting fact that the fifty pounds in coin (*dia kharagmatos*), which he had received in dowry (*proika*) for his wife, had been used in the purchase of various items of silver plate (*argyreia skeuē diaphora*).

Kale, his wife, is considerably more forthcoming in her various legacies. She describes[303] her wealth (*ousia*) as consisting of struck gold coin (*kharagma khrysion*), stuffs (*blatia*), bullion (*asēma*), livestock (*zōa*), and the remaining kinds of moveables (*loipa kinētōn eidoi*). Her major legacies in coin were: 7,000 gold nomismata to the Athonite monastery of Iberon; 54 lb in struck coin (*dia kharagmatos*) to the *proedros* Sergius, her brother-in-law; and 30¾ lb in coin to the nun Helena. Assuming the same basic denomination to have been involved in all three cases, somewhat over 13,000 nomismata will have been in the form of cash.

However, her jewellery and plate were at least on a similar scale. To the Athonite monastery of the Lavra she left, for instance: 'My armlet with a clasp (*brakhionion...to* kleiston), in gold, and worth [or weighing] two pounds; 12 nomismata (*hexagia*); and my tunic in yellow velvet[?] (*to himation...to hexamiton to kitrinon*); my great coffer (*katzion*), with a cover (*skepaston*), in silver; the great vase (*stamnion*) in silver; the cast basin (*kherniboxeuton*) in silver; the great wine-cup (*oinanthorion*), made after the saracen fashion (*sarakinikon*), with two handles (*diotion*), gilded (*diakhryson*), and with a cover; the other gilded container (*kaneion*); and the two new silk cushions (*tyloproskephala*).' The plate was to be sold and the proceeds realised.

The pattern of her personal legacies is an interesting one: to her nearer relatives she tended to leave her most valuable effects in jewellery, plate, or clothing, each item being specifically described; to monks and nuns her books or icons; to her many named servants or slaves (*anthrōpoi, doulai*) a mixture of clothing and coin, if female, and of livestock and coin, if male. These last are, appropriately, on a smaller scale: two or three items of clothing (tunics, cloaks, and so on); two or three animals (horses, oxen, and so on); a half-pound or pound of trachea (probably electrum, possibly billon, and in either case frequently termed 'new'). To her unnamed servants or slaves she left grain (*sitos*) and wine (*oinos*), and two pigs (*khoiroi*) and two sheep (*sphakta*) each. A good deal of care and hierarchical thought is thus apparent.

[303] Text: I. Iverites, 'Ek tou arkheiou tēs en Hagio Orei Hieras Monēs tōn Ivērōn: Vyzantinai diathēkai (synekheia)', *Orthodoxia* 66 (June 1931), pp. 364–71.

Eustathius Boïlas describes[304] his wealth as consisting of moveables, that is both self-moveables and easily moveables (*kinēta kai autokinēta kai eukinēta*), and in particular of slaves (*psykharia*), bullion (*asēmia*), stuffs (*blatia*) and livestock (*ktēna*). He also owned immoveable properties (*akinēta*) consisting of eleven estates (*ktēmata kai proasteia*), several of which are described as *monidia*, presumably identical with Philaretus' *monotata*, and probably referring to their independent fiscal status (that is, they were probably *idiosystata*), all of which were in Armenia.

His main aim seems to have been the provision of dowries for his two daughters Irene and Maria, and to this end they were each provided with thirty pounds. These two sums were, however, made up not, as far as can be seen, from coin at all, but from shares in the various estates and from the list of moveables. His son-in-law, Michael, similarly received, instead of (*anti*) five pounds, a village (*khōrion*). The church of St Barbara received 200 modioi of grain (*sitos*) and 1,000 litrai of wine (*oinos*). The church of the Mother of God received an half share in an estate. At some stage he had built, furnished and endowed the latter church, and a complete list of its furnishings is included: these must have represented an appreciable proportion of his total wealth, for a small selection of the plate (*skeuē*) alone had cost 300 nomismata, the rest of the plate, the cloths, ceremonial costumes, icons and about ninety books being excluded from that price. As for the rest, a female slave (*doulē*) had cost 400 nomismata, a price so high as to remain inexplicable – at least in any 'respectable' sense.

The only legacies regularly made in coin as such were small ones, of between three and ten nomismata, accompanying small plots of land (*zeugotopia*, *boidotopia*), which he made to his various household servants (*oiketika prosōpa*), and the only relatively large one, that of two or even three pounds, was that which he made to his powerful neighbours, the Apocapes brothers, for their accepting to be executors of his will. The latter was presumably merely politic. Other sums in coin are rare, and of no great prize.

The relative importance of the rôles played by coined money and by other forms of wealth is, in the case of the Pacourianus wills, difficult to assess. Certainly there are only three legacies that are of any great size, but their total (13,000 nomismata) is nevertheless considerable. The fact that Symbatius had spent Kale's dowry of 3,600 nomismata on items of plate, and had presumably made further acquisitions subsequently, and the sheer scale of the plate, jewellery, and clothing, even so suggests that the value of the coined money will at least have been equalled, and may well have been far exceeded, by that of other moveables. The balance between the various kinds of moveables and that of immoveables remains completely obscure. The relative importance of cash and of other wealth is, in the case of the Boïlas will, much easier to assess. There, the former seems to have played a minimal rôle only.

[304] Text: Lemerle, in *Cinq études sur le XIe siècle byzantin*, at pp. 20–9.

A rather later testamentary description, involving the wealth of another member of the same class, the *megas stratopedarkhēs* Demetrius Tzamblakon, is also extant.[305] The document is datable to 1366/7 and describes the wealth of an individual who owned land in the region of Serres and Christoupolis. It is somewhat shorter and rather less informative than the preceding ones, but includes all the customary forms of wealth: properties, houses and their belongings, servants, livestock, garments, personal effects, and pieces of plate and jewellery. Bonds and goods are not infrequently valued in monetary terms, but actual cash (which nevertheless includes *hyperpyra argyra*) is restrained in its appearance.[306]

### *D. Gregory Pacourianus and the Bachkovo Typikon*

All these descriptions and inventories are, however, overwhelmed in detail, if not in every case in absolute size, by the description and inventory of the wealth donated by the *sebastos* Gregory Pacourianus to his newly-founded monastery of the Mother of God at Batzokoba (i.e. Bachkovo) near Philippopolis (i.e. Plovdiv), and contained in his *typikon* for the monastery dated 1083.[307]

Gregory Pacourianus, of an illustrious Georgian family, had been *doux* of Kars, possibly *stratēgos* or *doux* of Smolena, and *doux* of Theodosiopolis (at least, possibly in that order), and finally *megas domestikos* of the West, dying in *c.* 1086. It is just possible that he had also been *stratēgos* of Samos at some stage. He had, obviously because of the prevalent political situation, transferred his economic base from Anatolia, where he had originally owned land in the regions of Ani and Taik and (possibly later) in the theme of Armeniakon, to the Balkans, where he had been granted estates by at least three emperors – Michael VII, Nicephorus III and Alexius I. His Balkan estates lay in three distinct and widely separated geographical concentrations: at the mouth of the Strymon (reg. Kaisaropolis-Khrysoupolis), which he had inherited from his brother, the *magistros* Apasius; in the district of Philippopolis (reg. Stenimakhos–Batzokoba), which was by far the largest; and in the district of Mosynopolis (reg. Peritheorion–Xantheia).[308] (Map 19)

In passing, Pacourianus describes[309] the fortune of his brother Apasius as having

[305] G. I. Theocharides, 'Eine Vermächtnisurkunde des Gross-Stratopedarchen Demetrios Tzamblakon', in P. Wirth (ed.), *Polychronion: Festschrift Franz Dölger zum 75. Geburtstag*, at pp. 489–91.

[306] For *hyperpyra argyra*, see below, p. 544.

[307] Text, summary, and commentary: see above, p. 160 n. 14. For an inventory of the treasury of another monastery – that of St John on Patmos – acquired by gradual accumulation rather than by single gift, see now: C. Astruc, 'L'inventaire dressé en septembre 1200 du trésor et de la bibliothèque de Patmos, édition diplomatique', *Travaux et Mémoires* 8 (1981), pp. 15–30.

[308] Career: Lemerle, in *Cinq études sur le XIe siècle byzantin*, at pp. 164–74. But see also Ahrweiler, *Byzance et la mer*, p. 213 (suggesting that Pacourianus had been granted an 'appanage' in the region of Smolena – as in Map 19 above), and R. Browning, 'Literacy in the Byzantine World', *Byzantine and Modern Greek Studies* 4 (1978), p. 43 (suggesting that he may have been identical with a Pacourianus who was *patrikios* and *stratēgos* of Samos). Estates: Lemerle, at pp. 175–83.

[309] Petit, 'Typikon de Grégoire Pacourianus', p. 13.

generally consisted of property (*ktēmata*) and wealth (*khrēmata*), and more particularly of coin (*nomismata*) and all sorts of uncoined wealth (*pantoia khrēmata asimia*); of clothing (*himatismos*) and every other sort of goods in kind (*eidoi*); and of livestock (*tetrapoda*) – finally remarking that, through the favour of God, he had been: 'entirely wealthy and lacking in nothing in all sorts of goods in kind (*pantē plousios kai pantoiōn eidōn adialeiptos*)'.

Pacourianus is, understandably, considerably more detailed in describing his own wealth. Even in more general terms it is described[310] as consisting of property (*ktēmata*) which included: his own teams of oxen (i.e. *despotika zeugaria*); peasants (*paroikoi*) with their own livestock (*zōa*) of every sort; land (*gē*) of every sort, both mountain and plain, mountain-pastures (*planēnai*) and ordinary pastures (*nomadiaiai*), arable land (*gē arosimos*) and vineyards (*gē ampelōnōn*); trees (*phyta*) of every sort, both fruit-bearing (*karpima*) and non fruit-bearing (*akarpa*); mills (*mylika ergastēria*), both water-driven (*hydrokinēta*) and animal-driven (*zōokinēta*); marshes (*limnai*), together with the surrounding dry lands (*khersaiai gaiai*); fortresses (*kastra*), together with every sort of building (*oikodomēmaton*) and every sort of thing (*pragma*) inside them, with the revenues (*prosodoi*) of the immoveables (*akinēta*), moveables (*kinēta*), and self-moveables (*autokinēta*) from both inside and outside them.

In addition to all this, it included precious manufactured objects (*morphōmata timia*): likenesses (*apeikonismata*) of Christ and the saints; precious crosses (*stauroi*) with relics of the true cross in them: and Gospel-books (*euangelia*) both in Greek and in Georgian. In the case of many of these objects they had been decorated, at great expense (*pany analōmasi*), with various stones (*diaphoroi lithoi*), pearls (*margaroi*) and cast metal (*khymeusis*). It included, similarly, items of plate (*skeuē*): covered goblets (*diskopotēria*) and multiple lamp-holders (*polykandēla*) in silver and of various kinds; single lamp-holders (*kandēlai*) of all kinds; most precious imperial tunics (*himatia basilika timalphestata*) given by the emperor Alexius, and similar very precious (*polytima*) ones given by that emperor and by his brother the *sebastokrator* Isaac. These, described elsewhere[311] as: 'for use with a breastplate, and of deep purple (*epilorika oxykastora*)', had been given as rewards for particular acts or services.[312] They were set aside (*anakeimena*), presumably on some kind of display, in the nave of the monastic church. But there were also included: other very precious tunics of an undecorated variety (*barytima himatia arrhapha*) and various other items of plate of all kinds with ornamentation and very suitable for church use (*pros kosmon te kai euprepeian tēs ekklēsias*); portable wooden boards (*pinakes xylinai*) painted with the portraits of various saints (i.e. portable icons); multiple candle-holders in copper, and large handbasins. And so on.

The full list of properties involved,[313] and of the legal documents of various kinds proving their title, some of which were conserved at the Great Church in

310 *Ibid.* pp. 13–14.

311 *Ibid.* p. 53.

312 See above, pp. 193–4, 195.

313 Petit, 'Typikon de Grégoire Pacourianus', pp. 10–13.

Constantinople,[314] some at the monastery itself,[315] together with the full list of precious moveables involved,[316] and of livestock,[317] all provide impressive totals. These totals involve 29 estates of various kinds, including 12 *khōria*, 9 *agridia*, 6 *kastra*, and 2 *proasteia*, and 8 religious establishments, including 2 *monai*, 4 *hesykhasteria*, 1 *metokhion*, and 1 *aulē*.[318] They involve more than 92 documents of various kinds (*khrysoboulloi*, *pittakia*, etc.) at the Great Church, and more than 50 at the monastery.[319] They also involve 36 icons and 3 crosses, 13 liturgical objects, 31 books, 29 pieces of costume, 55 items mainly for lighting purposes, and 24 items for various other purposes.[320] They finally involve 110 male horses and mares (*aloga arrhenika te kai phorbadia*) with their young (*polaria*); 15 male and female asses (*onika arrhenika te kai thēle*) with their young, 4 buffaloes for milking (*boubalia amelgadia*), 2 heifers (*moskharia*), 47 pairs (*zeugaria*) of working oxen (*boes kamateroi*) for all the property (*ktēmata*) of the monastery, 72 cows and bulls (*ageladia kai tauria*), 238 sheep for milking (*probata amelgadia*), 94 rams (*kriaria*), and 52 goats (*aiges*).[321]

The reason for the apparent failure of cash to form part of the donation remains unclear, all the more so as Pacourianus mentions[322] that he had left his wealth (*khrēmata*) and coin (*nomismata*) on deposit (*parakatathēkes logō*) with his brother Apasius while he was acting in Anatolia as duke of Theodosiopolis. This fortune, represented by the deposit, and by the revenues (*prosodoi*) subsequently deriving from his properties (*ktēmata*) of various kinds (*pronoiai*, *dioikēseis*), consisted – in its cash portion at least – of 'old money of Romanus [III], the trachy of [Constantine IX] Monomachus, of [Constantine X] Ducas, of "sceptre" type, and also of Michael [VII, Ducas] (*palaion logarion rhōmanaton, trakhy monomakhaton, doukaton, te kai skēptraton, pros de kai mikhaēlaton*)'.[323]

It is true that Pacourianus also mentions that, on his return from the east, after the death of his brother, he was able to recover none of this, but he should have had no difficulty in accumulating cash from subsequent revenues. Possibly the bulk of any such accumulation had been exhausted in what must have been the very considerable expenditure involved in the construction of the church and monastery, possibly Pacourianus had reserved his cash fortune for his own use. With regard to the first of these explanations, Pacourianus himself mentions[324] the great trouble and extraordinary expenditure (*dapanēmatōn hyperbolē*) involved.

At any rate, although the lists in the *typikon* are not testamentary ones, and there is

314 *Ibid.* p. 54.
315 *Ibid.* pp. 55–6.
316 *Ibid.* pp. 52–4.
317 *Ibid.* p. 54.
318 Totals: Lemerle, *Cinq études sur le XI^e siècle byzantin*, at p. 181.
319 Totals: *ibid.* at pp. 154–7.
320 Totals: *ibid.* at p. 153.
321 Totals: *ibid.* at p. 153.
322 Petit, 'Typikon de Grégoire Pacourianus', p. 13.
323 Refs: Grierson, *DOC* II.1, pp. 53, 58–9 (*Rhōmanaton*), 59 (*Monomakhaton*), 59–60 (*Doukaton*), 60 (*Skēptraton*), 60–1 (*Mikhaēlaton*). Hendy, *DOS* XII, pp. 29–31 (*Trakhy*).
324 Petit, 'Typikon de Grégoire Pacourianus', p. 9.

Table 5. *Items of monastic expenditure in Easter Week (the Bachkovo* Typikon/*Gornoslav Hoard)*

| Items | Expenditure (hyperpyra) | Occasions |
|---|---|---|
| *Rhogai* | | |
| *Kathēgoumenos* | 36 | Easter Sunday |
| 15 monks at 20 histamena | 300 | |
| 15 monks at 15 histamena | 225 | |
| 20 monks at 10 histamena | 200 | |
| Total | 761 | |
| Commemoration of Pacourianus' father (distribution) | 24 | Maundy Thursday |
| Total | 785 | |
| Banker's charge (for changing) | 1 | Maundy Thursday |
| Grand total | 786 | |

therefore no absolute assurance that the whole of Pacourianus' fortune is there described, there is some reason to suppose that they represent the very great bulk of that fortune.[325]

It is worth noting, in this context, that the Gornoslav Hoard of 786 hyperpyra of the emperors Alexius I to Isaac II,[326] buried after 1185, almost certainly represents a body of coin put by out of the monastic revenues for 1189, and intended for paying out in 1190, but lost in the disturbances arising out of the passage of the Third Crusade in 1189/90.[327] The modern village of Gornoslov lies some 9 km only away from Bachkovo, on land certainly then owned by the monastery, the three estates of Topolnitza (Topolovo), Tzerbena (Cherven) and Dobrostanos (Dobrostan) forming a neat triangle around it: it may even be identical with the estate of Gelloba.[328] The sum will have been made up as listed in Table 5.

The colossal discrepancy between the size of the fortune of Pacourianus, *megas domestikos* under Alexius I, and that of the fortune of Cantacuzene, *megas domestikos* under Andronicus III, may well be apparent rather than real. The documentation is very different indeed in kind. Pacourianus, in the formal and legal context of a monastic *typikon*, could scarcely describe other than his own directly held property: in fact he specifically draws a distinction between his own teams of oxen and peasants with their own livestock. Cantacuzene, whose figures are in any case very obviously at least rounded out, in the

325 Lemerle, *Cinq études sur le XIe siècle byzantin*, at p. 175.

326 Hendy, *DOS* XII, pp. 343–4.

327 Hendy, 'The Gornoslav Hoard', pp. 179–91.

328 Lemerle, *Cinq études sur le XIe siècle byzantin*, at pp. 176–7. See also map in Hendy, 'The Gornoslav Hoard', p. 182.

entirely casual context of his own history, may well have included both his personal property and that of his dependent peasants. Even if a shift in favour of the land-owner and at the expense of the peasant, whether formal or informal, had meanwhile taken place, this particular comparison would not be a valid one.

What does seem to be of possible significance is the concentration on livestock evident in Cantacuzene's description. Whether this really implies a movement away from agriculturalism towards pastoralism in an area naturally favouring the former, but encouraged by a great magnate, nevertheless remains doubtful. Although a similar shift seems to have taken place in another, and rather similar, area, that is Thessaly, at much the same time, it is quite possible that outside factors (the supremacy of pastoralist Vlachs) were involved in the case of Thessaly, and that Cantacuzene simply found a description based on livestock more convenient or more effective in that of Thrace.[329]

## *E. Dowries*

Dowries themselves could vary very widely, not only in size, as is obvious, but also in general composition, and in the particular proportion of cash involved. Pacourianus apparently received his wife's dowry entirely in cash, Boïlas apparently intended his daughters' dowries to be in other forms of valuables and property, to the entire exclusion of cash. Somewhere in between these two extremes lies the dowry (*meros proikos*) provided by Michael Psellus for his adopted daughter: of a total value of fifty pounds, ten were in the form of coined gold (*kekharagmenou khrysiou*), twenty in that of various articles in kind (*eidesi diaphorois*), and the remaining twenty in that of the dignity of *prōtospatharios* (i.e. a *prōtospatharaton*), which yielded not only status but also an annual *rhoga* of 72 nomismata.[330] In this case, the cash still amounts to a mere 20% of the total value, and conversely it is well worth noting that something that conveyed status, as well as income (the *prōtospatharaton*), amounts to 40% of the total.

Similarly, between these two extremes, if on a much smaller scale, lies the dowry described by a Jewish physician, a Byzantine subject, and a resident in Seleucia (i.e. Silifke), in 1137:

> Dowries in this country [*sc.* the Byzantine Empire] are very expensive. I gave my son-in-law, R. Samuel, son of R. Moses, son of R. Samuel, the Longobard merchant, the following: 324 pieces of gold; a pound of silver; a brocade robe; two silk robes; two woollen garments; two Greek pounds of ornaments; a silken purse; four tunics; two cotton robes; ten long and short turbans; a bed with a canopy; a round cupboard, decorated with paintings; a copper ewer, wash basin and dipper; rings of gold and silver; blankets; servants; altogether two hundred dinars.
>
> (trans. Goitein in *Speculum* 39 (1964), at p. 299)

[329] Thessaly (and perhaps Thrace also): Angold, *A Byzantine Government in Exile*, pp. 107, 284.

[330] Michael Psellus, *Dikastikē Apophasis*; ed. K. N. Sathas, in *Mesaiōnikē Bibliothēkē* v, at p. 205. R. Guilland, 'Un compte-rendu de procès par Psellos', *Byzantinoslavica* 20 (1959), pp. 210–11. For the *rhoga*, see above, p. 185 and Table 4.

The pound of silver was presumably in bullion form, and therefore would have been included in the second total of 200 dinars (*sc.* nomismata). The total value of the dowry would therefore have stood at 524 nomismata, of which 324 (which is $4\frac{1}{2}$ lb), or 62%, was in cash.

But this last example can in no way be considered as providing some kind of norm, even where directly comparable material is concerned. A much smaller dowry, consisting of an otherwise very similar collection of items, and paid by a Jewish inhabitant of Mastaura (i.e. Nazilli), in 1022, includes no cash at all, although its total value ($35\frac{1}{3}$ dinars) was reckoned in terms of it.[331]

Finally, fictional descriptions of wealth in literary sources have their own value, for, however exaggerated they may be, they should at least in theory relate to a concept of wealth prevalent at a particular time and place, and in a particular society. In fact, the best known, and perhaps the most exhaustive of such fictional descriptions, those contained in the epic *Digenes Akrites*, conform remarkably closely to what has already been observed in the cases of the other categories of descriptions, relating as they do to the concept of wealth prevalent during the ninth to twelfth centuries, in the Anatolian border-lands, amongst the military aristocracy.

The intended dowry of Eudocia, daughter of the *stratēgos* Ducas, and wife of Digenes, is described by the *stratēgos* as:

> 20 kentenaria of old (*palaia*) nomismata, put aside and held back in her beloved name, for the occasion; a *vestiarion* [i.e. a store or place of storage], worth 500 pounds, in silver plate (*argyraia skeuē*); many immoveable properties (*ktēmata akinēta*), numbering thirty-six, with their revenues (*eisodoi*); 70 female servants together with her mother's house, which is notable to see and most precious; similarly, her mother's superb ornaments (*kosmia*), including her famous crown (*stephanos*), which is an admirable work made up out of gold and most precious stones (*ek khrysou, lithōn timiotatōn*); and with all these, the livestock (*zōa*) to be found there, 400 first-class animals, and 80 grooms; 14 cooks and as many bakers; 150 other slaves (*psykharia*).
>
> (*Digenes Akrites*, ed. trans. Mavrogordato, p. 116)

The *stratēgos* gave in any case: 12 black horses (*hippoi*), 12 fine mares (*pharia*), 12 selected mules (*moulai*) with saddles and harnesses of encrusted silver (*sellokhalinoi argyroi kai khymeutoi*), 12 household servants and gold-belted grooms, hunting animals and their attendants, two encrusted icons of St Theodore, a gold-stitched tent (*tenda khrysokentēton*) with its accompanying equipment of silk and silver, arms, and so on. Others gave: pearls, gold, stones and precious silks (*blattia*) in reddish-purple (*oxea*), turbans (*phakeōlia*), a cloak (*kabbaddē*), eunuch attendants, and so on.[332]

The list could be continued, to no useful purpose. Doubtless, many of the particular

[331] J. Starr, *The Jews in the Byzantine Empire, 641–1204*, no. 130, pp. 187–90. The total actually does not include a share in a house, which is not valued.

[332] *Digenes Akrites* IV; ed. I. N. Mavrogordato, pp. 128, 130.

numbers or quantities in it are fantastical, or have their own literary rationale. But what is striking is the resemblance of the general terms in which wealth is expressed in the epic, to those expressed in the other categories, the resemblance extending even to a number of rarely met technical terms.

What is equally striking is the extremely close similarity between the nature and expression of private wealth in general, and that of imperial wealth, whether that distributed to foreign allies or potential allies as bribes, or to enemies as tribute, or that transported in the imperial baggage-train as a necessary pre-condition for imperial comfort and as an exemplar of imperial splendour.

## *F. Observations*

The possession of coined money was, then, only one way in which the possession of wealth could be, or actually was, expressed. There was certainly no necessary or even direct equation between the two. Procopius describes[333] the unheard-of wealth (*ploutos*) of the Arians which, he claims, was equalled neither by that of the whole senate (*hē synklētos boulē xympasa*), nor by that of any other great section (*megistē moira*) of the Roman state, as consisting of valuables (*keimēlia*) of gold and silver, and treasures (*synkeimena*) of precious stones, that were unspeakable and uncountable, houses (*oikiai*) and villages (*kōmai*) in great numbers, and much land in all parts of the world (*khōra pollē pantakhothi tēs gēs*), and indeed every other kind of wealth that has an existence and that has a name amongst mankind. The accuracy of the passage is immaterial to the question in hand, its significance lying in the terms in which all this wealth is described, amongst which coinage fails to appear.

In effect, coinage was restricted in potential, and therefore in actual use. For this there are a number of pertinent explanations. In many areas it might be difficult to come by: the two apparently accentuated examples of its failure to appear in major descriptions involve Paphlagonia (Philaretus) and Armenia (Boïlas), and this may be no coincidence, for the difficulty of obtaining coinage in Paphlagonia is mentioned, quite independently, elsewhere.[334] This does not necessarily mean that in areas where it might be expected to be more readily available, it was so, for although there was apparently no shortage in Macedonia (the Pacouriani), there certainly had been in a rather similar area, western Asia Minor.[335] And even if it were readily available, it was not necessarily desirable beyond a certain measure. It could not be gainfully employed or invested in any large quantity in a society where trade, industry and credit played a very restricted rôle. Indeed, a virtual lack of such investment is a most noticeable feature of the descriptions and inventories above. Psellus' investment in a dignity is scarcely significant as an exception,

[333] Procopius, *Historia Arcana* XI. 17–18; ed. Haury (Teubner), III, p. 73.
[334] See below, p. 298. [335] See below, pp. 295–6.

given the minimal capital and yield involved.[336] Pacourianus' instruction as to what should be done with any surpluses (*hyperperisseumata*) of monastic revenue was specifically and significantly that it should be used in the purchase of a property (*eis agoran ktēmatos*) which was to remain subject to the monastery.[337]

Coinage was thus relatively little used, even amongst the greatest possessors of wealth, members of the landed aristocracy, who clearly aimed rather at self-sufficiency (*autarkeia*).[338] It did not easily and obviously express either status or even the possession of wealth itself – in other words, it could not be used, worn, or otherwise publicly and successfully exhibited.

Members of the landed aristocracy nevertheless obviously cared deeply about the precious-metal moveables that formed a large portion of their total wealth. When Zeno, grandson of the former western emperor Anthemius, was sent into effective exile as governor of Egypt, having loaded a ship with the most precious items of his wealth (*khrēmatōn to ploion tōn timiōtatōn explēsamenos*), he made ready to embark. The wealth involved consisted of an uncountable weight of silver (*stathmos te argyrou anarithmētos*), and gold plate decorated with pearls and emeralds (*khrysōmata margarois te kai smaragdois kallōpisthenta*) and with other such precious stones (*lithois allois toioutois*). The precious cargo was supposedly (and inevitably) removed by a fraudulent stratagem of Justinian and Theodora, and the ship put to the flame, to give the impression that both cargo and ship had been destroyed. Zeno died, apparently shortly after.[339] When Andronicus Palaeologus, the *prōtovestiarios*, had lost many of his livestock (*boskēmata polla*), his moveable fortune and finally the fortress of Prilep, he too died shortly after.[340] When George Palaeologus fled the City in 1081, to take part in the revolt of the Comneni against Nicephorus III, he went first to the sanctuary of the Mother of God at Blachernae, where he had had stored (*enkeimene*) all his wealth in moveables (*khrēmata/en kinētois...periousia*). This he had packed on the backs of the monastic baggage-animals (*hypozygia*) and took with him.[341]

The number of possible kinds of actual receptacles used as safe-deposits for moveable valuables was of course virtually limitless with regard to material and shape: linen sacks or purses, wood or iron coffers, and copper or pottery vases are all recorded, whether by way of documentary sources or by that of archaeological finds.[342]

The use of monasteries as virtual safe-deposits for valuables was in itself, however, also

336 See above, pp. 185–6 and Table 4; below, pp. 244, 246.

337 Petit, 'Typikon de Grégoire Pacourianus', p. 46.

338 See below, pp. 565–8.

339 Procopius, *Historia Arcana* XII.1–3; ed. Haury (Teubner), III, p. 77.

340 John Cantacuzene, *Historiarum Libri IV* I.54–6; Bonn edn, I, pp. 275–85.

341 Anna Comnena, *Alexiad* II.6.3; ed. Leib, I, p. 81.

342 C. Morrisson, 'La découverte des trésors à l'époque byzantine: théorie et pratique de l'*euresis thesaurou*', *Travaux et Mémoires* 8 (1981), pp. 322–5. See also, in this book, above, p. 204, below, pp. 274, 309, 341–3.

apparently not uncommon. Nicephoritzes, the eunuch favourite of Michael VII and *logothetēs tou dromou*, utilised the suburban monastery of the Hebdomon as a repository (*kentron kai tameion*) for the belongings (*ktēseis*) which he had accumulated.[343] When the survivors of the Latin massacres fled the City in 1182 their first action was to raid the monasteries on the Princes' Islands and the Sea of Marmara. From these they are said to have extracted huge quantities of gold, silver, jewels and silks (*infinitae auri, argenti, gemmarum et holosericorum... copiae*). The reason for the extraordinary wealth gained from them was that: 'For besides the immense riches (*divitiae innumerae*) and infinite treasures (*thesauri infiniti*) of these monasteries, which they had collected over many years, many Constantinopolitan citizens had deposited there huge weights of gold and other forms of wealth (*ingentia ibidem deposuerant auri et caeterarum gazarum pondera*).'[344] The significance of this statement, in view of what has been said in the preceding paragraphs, should be obvious.

343 Michael Attaliates, *Historia*; Bonn edn, p. 201.

344 William of Tyre, *Historia Rerum* XXII.13; RHC, *Occ.* I.2, pp. 1085–6.

# CHAPTER 4

# THE LIMITING FACTORS

## (I) EXTRAORDINARY EXPENDITURE

### *A. Military expeditions*

Extraordinary expenditure, particularly that on military expeditions, had always formed what might now seem a disproportionate strain on imperial finances, because of the inelasticity of the empire's principal sources of revenue and the conservative nature of its social structure which never permitted the development of a substantial capacity for, and a sophisticated system of, state credit.

The cost of the great and unsuccessful naval expedition undertaken by Leo I against the Vandals in 468 is relatively well documented. According to Candidus,[1] the expedition cost the prefectural reserve 47,000 lb gold or 3,384,000 solidi, the comitival (i.e. that of the *komēs tōn thēsaurōn* or *comes largitionum*) 17,000 lb or 1,224,000 solidi, totalling 64,000 lb or 4,608,000 solidi, and in addition a further 700,000 lb silver or 2,722,160 solidi assuming a gold: silver ratio of 1:18, making a grand total of 7,330,160 solidi, part also being paid by the western emperor Anthemius. According to John Lydus,[2] it cost 63,000 lb gold or 4,680,000 solidi, and 700,000 lb silver or 2,722,160 solidi assuming an identical gold: silver ratio, totalling 7,402,160 solidi. According to Priscus and Procopius[3] it cost 1,300 kentenaria or 9,360,000 solidi.

Both the sums involved and the figures for shipping and manpower differ according to the source, but John Lydus – who had been on the strength of the *officium* of the prefecture of the East – was perhaps in the best position to know, and moreover the sum quoted by him virtually agrees with the detailed breakdown quoted by the earlier Candidus. What is also interesting is the relative size of the prefectural and comitival contributions, which supports the suggestion that the prefecture by now represented a far more important instrument of revenue and expenditure than did the *comitivae*.

[1] Candidus, *Fragmenta*; ed. K. Müller, IV, at p. 137.

[2] John Lydus, *De Magistratibus* III.43; ed. Wuensch (Teubner), p. 133.

[3] Priscus, *Fragmenta* XLII; ed. K. Müller, IV, at p. 110. Procopius, *De Bello Vandalico* I.6.2; ed. Haury (Teubner), I, p. 335.

According to the patriarch Nicephorus,[4] Heraclius Constantine was able to set aside 50,200 nomismata, plus a further 16,000, making a total of 66,200 nomismata, in 641, to be used by his son Constans II and his supporters to gain military support in the event of a *coup d'état* by Martina and her sons.

According to Theophanes,[5] the Bulgarian khan Tervel, in an attempt to dethrone Leo III in 718, furnished the ex-emperor Anastasius (II) with an army (*stratos*) and 50 kentenaria or 360,000 nomismata. The latter was presumably expected to defray the cost both of military and more general expenditure.

According to official information quoted by Constantine Porphyrogenitus,[6] the unsuccessful naval expedition undertaken by Leo VI against the Arabs of Crete in 911–12, which consisted of 177 ships (including *dromōnes* and *pamphyloi*) and 51,164 men (including tagmatic, thematic and mercenary units), cost 28 kentenaria, 27 lb, 66 nomismata, or 203,610 nomismata.

According to information of the same status also quoted by Constantine,[7] the equally unsuccessful expedition undertaken by himself against the same enemy in 949 consisted of 132 ships of various kinds, of which the imperial fleet supplied approximately three-quarters, the thematic fleet the remainder. The imperial fleet and the military it transported cost 1,691 lb, 53 nomismata, in gold, and 73 lb, 22 nomismata, 4 miliaresia, in silver, making a total of 127,083 nomismata, 4 miliaresia.

According to Nicetas Choniates,[8] the unsuccessful expedition undertaken by Manuel I against the Sicilian Normans in 1155–6, presumably including the very considerable and long-standing political expenditure involved, cost 300 kentenaria or 2,160,000 hyperpyra. If this figure is anywhere near correct, then the only comparison is with that for the earlier Vandal expedition.

According to the same author,[9] Isaac II sent out 40 kentenaria or 288,000 hyperpyra to the military forces defending the empire against the Normans in 1185, and[10] he paid out 15 kentenaria in gold and 60 in silver to the expedition he intended to lead against the Vlachs and Bulgarians in 1195. Assuming these last two sums to have involved gold hyperpyra and electrum trachea, respectively, they will have totalled some 216,000 hyperpyra at the then current rate of exchange.

The composition of the Catalan mercenary *companya* hired by Andronicus II in 1303 for service against the Ottomans, and the conditions under which it was hired, are variously reported in the Byzantine and Catalan sources. It seems most likely that the

[4] Nicephorus, *Breviarium*; ed. I. Bekker (Bonn edn), p. 33.

[5] Theophanes, *Chronographia*; ed. de Boor, I, p. 400.

[6] Constantine Porphyrogenitus, *De Caerimoniis* II.44; Bonn edn, pp. 651–60. Antoniadis-Bibicou, *Études d'histoire maritime de Byzance*, pp. 92–3, 142–3.

[7] Constantine Porphyrogenitus, *De Caerimoniis* II.45; Bonn edn, pp. 664–78. Antoniadis-Bibicou, *Études d'histoire maritime de Byzance*, pp. 94, 143–4.

[8] Nicetas Choniates, *Historia*; ed. van Dieten, I, pp. 96–7.

[9] *Ibid.* p. 357.

[10] *Ibid.* p. 447.

company originally consisted of 1,500 cavalry, 4,000 infantry, and 1,000 other foot soldiers, and that it was to be paid in advance, every four months, at a monthly rate of three ounces of hyperpyra per cavalryman and two ounces per foot soldier. The main body of cavalry would then have cost 18,000 ounces or 108,000 hyperpyra, and the main body of infantry 32,000 ounces or 192,000 hyperpyra, making a total of 50,000 ounces or 300,000 hyperpyra, every four months.

Both the rates of pay and the total involved are far in excess of those attained by or expended upon contemporary Byzantine military forces.[11] That this composition and these conditions, collated from the various Byzantine and Catalan sources, are nevertheless approximately correct at least seems confirmed by the evidence of Pachymeres,[12] who mentions that Roger de Flor, the Catalan leader, was demanding 300,000 hyperpyra from Andronicus in late 1304. This sum would, then, have represented four months' arrears.[13] The emperor claimed to have paid nearly a million (presumably actually 900,000) hyperpyra at this stage.[14]

According to Cantacuzene,[15] Andronicus II sent out 50,000 hyperpyra with the expedition against the Catalans in the duchy of Athens that had been entrusted to his command as *megas domestikos* in 1321, and finally, according to the same source,[16] Andronicus III awarded the governorship (*arkhē*) of the islands, together with 100,000 hyperpyra from their annual revenues (*etēsioi phoroi*), towards the cost of the fleet against the Turks entrusted to the *parakoimōmenos* Alexius Apocaucus in 1340.

The effect of extraordinary expenditure on this scale was, in the case of the Vandal and Ottoman expeditions at least, catastrophic. On each of these occasions a sum that probably exceeded a whole year's revenue was necessarily written off. The state of virtual bankruptcy that followed the failure of the Vandal expedition, depriving the empire of whatever financial flexibility it might have had, is described in some detail by John Lydus,[17] according to whom it brought the empire to the verge of disintegration. The state of the actual bankruptcy soon caused by payments to the Catalans is described by both Pachymeres and Gregoras from the Byzantine side and Muntaner from the Catalan. Although Andronicus appears to have started out with some cash in reserve at least, and was therefore able to make two four-monthly payments – the first in late 1303, the second in early 1304 – in full and without too much difficulty, the third – which was already in arrears when being demanded by Roger de Flor in late 1304 – was never paid in full

[11] See above, pp. 162–3.

[12] George Pachymeres, *De Michaele et Andronico Palaeologis, De And.* VI.7; Bonn edn, II, pp. 491–2.

[13] For the most recent discussion of the subject until now, involving figures differing slightly from those utilised above, see: Laiou(-Thomadakis), *Constantinople and the Latins*, pp. 185–7.

[14] George Pachymeres, *De Michaele et Andronico Palaeologis, De And.* IV.14; Bonn edn, II, p. 502.

[15] John Cantacuzene, *Historiarum Libri IV* I.18; Bonn edn, I, pp. 87–8.

[16] *Ibid.* II.38; Bonn edn, I, p. 540.

[17] John Lydus, *De Magistratibus* III.44; ed. Wuensch (Teubner), pp. 133–4.

and yet still caused financial disaster. The emperor was obliged to run through almost the entire gamut of expedients designed to make any available cash go further and to raise extra cash in haste: the cessation of payments to his own officials and military forces, the debasement of the gold and silver coinages, and the imposition of extra taxation.[18]

## *B. The reserve*

It was obviously in part the possibility of having to meet this kind of expenditure that caused certain of the more prudent rulers to build up a reserve. This must have been very considerably facilitated, at least, by the transfer from taxation in kind to taxation in coin in the course of the fourth and fifth centuries.

The size of a number of these reserves is recorded. According to John Lydus,[19] Theodosius II and Marcian had managed to accumulate over 100,000 lb gold or 7,200,000 solidi, and this at a time when large sums were being paid out annually, as tribute and bribes, to the Huns. According to Procopius,[20] who claims to be relying on official information, Anastasius had managed to accumulate the enormous sum of 3,200 kentenaria or no less than 23,040,000 solidi. The claim to official information is not in itself implausible, as Procopius may well have been acquainted with the works or even the person of John Lydus at the praetorian prefecture.[21] Even the Ostrogothic queen Amalasuntha had a reserve of 400 kentenaria or 2,880,000 solidi at her disposal.[22]

According to the *Continuation of Theophanes*,[23] the empress Theodora on yielding up power in 855/6 claimed to the senate that she and her late husband, the emperor Theophilus, had managed to accumulate 1,090 kentenaria in gold (*khrysou*) and 3 in silver (*argyriou*). The sum in gold would have amounted to 7,848,000 nomismata, that in silver to some 21,600 nomismata or 259,200 miliaresia assuming a relationship of 1:12 between the nomisma and the miliaresion, making a total of some 7,869,600 nomismata. Of this,

18 Laiou(-Thomadakis), *Constantinople and the Latins*, pp. 187–90; see also below, pp. 228, 230, 230–1, 238, 530–1.

19 John Lydus, *De Magistratibus* III.43; ed. Wuensch (Teubner), p. 132.

20 Procopius, *Historia Arcana* XIX.7; ed. Haury (Teubner), III, p. 121.

21 See below, p. 295.

22 Procopius, *De Bello Gothico* I.2.26; ed. Haury (Teubner), II, p. 14.

23 *Continuation of Theophanes* IV.20; Bonn edn, pp. 171–2. The sum as it stands makes sense only if it is assumed that the three kentenaria of silver were three gold kentenaria in value but silver miliaresia in actual form, thus: 3 × 7,200 nom. = 21,600 nom., and probably 12 × 21,600 nom. = 259,000 mil. See also: Joseph Genesius, *Regum Libri IV* IV.11; ed. A. Lesmueller-Werner and H. Thurn, p. 64, where the editorial restoration of the sum as 1,090 kentenaria in gold, and 3,*000* kentenaria in silver is clearly incorrect. It is superficially tempting to assume that the apparently enormous discrepancy between the sum in gold and that in silver is the result of textual corruption. This is theoretically possible, but actually improbable: the point surely is that the gold nomisma was not only the standard denomination but also, as a full-bodied coin, a reliable store of wealth; to the contrary, the silver miliaresion may have formed a useful subordinate denomination, but because it was in theory a ceremonial, and was in fact a partly fiduciary, one, only, it was (even for the state that produced it) not necessarily a reliable store of wealth. See below, p. 505.

it is reckoned[24] that Theophilus had accumulated 970 kentenaria in struck gold (*kekharagmenou khrysou*), besides the silver in bullion and coin (*argyrou tou te asēmou kai episēmou*), and that Theodora had added a further 30 kentenaria, making up 1,000 kentenaria, obviously a rounded-out figure, possibly to the detriment of Theodora.

When Basil I came to power in 867, he found only 3 kentenaria and nine sacks of miliaresia in the treasury, but there was also available the various items of ceremonial apparatus, worth some 200 kentenaria and stored in the *eidikon*, which Michael III, his predecessor, had sent to be melted down, and he himself managed to recover (at the rate of 50%) 300 kentenaria from the people on whom it had been squandered by the same predecessor. This makes a total of 503 kentenaria or somewhat over 3,600,000 nomismata.[25]

According to Michael Psellus,[26] Basil II had managed to accumulate 200,000 'talents', presumably pounds, and in that case 14,400,000 nomismata. Zonaras repeats[27] the same figure, and both mention that special underground spiral vaults had to be constructed to accumulate the reserve. Again, even the Bulgarian tsars had a reserve of 100 kentenaria or 720,000 nomismata at their disposal.[28]

According to Nicetas Choniates,[29] the metropolitan mob, on breaking into the Great Palace at the time of the deposition of Andronicus I in 1185, found there 12 kentenaria in gold, 30 kentenaria in silver, and 200 kentenaria in copper coin, besides much that was not in the form of coin, all stored in the *khrysioplysioi*. Assuming these sums to have involved gold hyperpyra and electrum and billon trachea respectively, they would have totalled some 170,000 hyperpyra at the then current rates of exchange. The *khrysioplysioi* or *khrysoplysiai* (literally 'places for the washing of gold') seem, for Nicetas at least, to have been identical with the *khōneia* ('foundry') apparently related to the mint there.[30] Again, according to Nicholas Mesarites,[31] when the mob broke into the same palace and looted the treasury and mint, at the time of the attempted usurpation of John Comnenus in 1201, gold flowed out 'just like the flow of a river (*katha tis potamos rheon*)' Finally, according to Choniates,[32] when Alexius III fled the City by ship in 1203, he was able to take with him 10 kentenaria or 72,000 hyperpyra besides imperial ornaments (*kosmoi basilikoi*). The last two sums, of course, represent partial ones only: the casual contents of the palace at a particular time, the second being merely what remained in it after almost a month's siege by the Latins.

[24] *Continuation of Theophanes* v.27; Bonn edn, p. 253.

[25] *Ibid.* iv.21, v.27–9; Bonn edn, pp. 173, 253, 255–7.

[26] Michael Psellus, *Chronographia* i.31; ed. Renauld, i, p. 19.

[27] John Zonaras, *Annales* xvii.8.23–6; Bonn edn, iii, pp. 561–2.

[28] See below, p. 281.

[29] Nicetas Choniates, *Historia*; ed. van Dieten, i, p. 347.

[30] E. Miller, 'Fragment inédit de Nicétas Choniate relatif à un fait numismatique', *Revue Numismatique* 11[2] (1866), pp. 3–12. See also below, pp. 230, 259–60, 427 n. 245.

[31] A. Heisenberg, *Nikolaos Mesarites: die Palastrevolution des Johannes Komnenos*, pp. 25–6.

[32] Nicetas Choniates, *Historia*; ed. van Dieten, i, p. 547.

The building up of a reserve might evidently, perhaps if gone about too thoroughly or too hastily, have a noticeable effect on the general level of prices, for both Theophanes[33] and the patriarch Nicephorus[34] report that what seems to have been just such an action on the part of Constantine V led to a decrease in the price of goods, forcing farmers to sell off their products cheaply. The absolute size of this reserve is unrecorded, although, according to Cedrenus,[35] Constantine had put by 500 kentenaria or 3,600,000 nomismata, in a certain place, to the account (*logō*) of his five younger sons, the caesars (Nicephorus and Christopher), and the *nobilissimi* (Nicetas, Anthemius and Eudocimus), when he died in 775. This sum, which presumably formed a part of the reserve, was promptly appropriated by his eldest son and successor, Leo IV: the total must have been a good deal larger, and therefore, particularly in view of the date, very considerable indeed.*

The unfortunate corollary of all this was, of course, that prudent rulers tended to be followed by spendthrift ones. Theodosius' and Marcian's reserve was squandered by Leo on the Vandal expedition; Anastasius' by Justinian on military ventures and building programmes; Constantine's by Leo IV on propitiating the populace and securing the coronation of his son; Theodora's and Theophilus' by Michael III on pursuits that are best not thought too much about; and Basil's by Constantine IX and Zoë on pretty well anything that one might care to think about.[36]

The tensions that such abrupt changes of policy as those mentioned above might cause are amusingly exemplified in a (probably apocryphal) story recorded by John of Ephesus:[37] Justin II and Sophia had accumulated a reserve the size of which is not known, but which was evidently considerable; Tiberius II, both as caesar under Justin, and subsequently as emperor in his own right, was notoriously extravagant.[38] Eventually, Sophia's patience broke, and she complained bitterly: 'All that we [*sc.* Justin and she] by great industry and care have gathered and stored up, you are scattering to the winds as with a fan.' Tiberius was unrepentant and replied: 'What you collected by iniquity and plunder and rapine, I am doing my best that not a fragment of it may remain in my palace.' He had previously remarked: 'What good is all this gold hoarded up here, while the whole world is choked with hunger?' Whether precisely accurate, or entirely fictional, or indeed something in between, the attitudes depicted represent an oscillation

* I owe this reference to the kindness of Warren Treadgold.

33 See below, pp. 298–9.

34 See below, pp. 298–9. See also pp. 665–6.

35 George Cedrenus, *Historiarum Compendium*; Bonn edn, II, p. 18.

36 Leo: see above, p. 221. Justinian: John Lydus, *De Magistratibus* III.51; ed. Wuensch (Teubner), p. 14 and Procopius, *Historia Arcana* VIII.4–9, XIX.4–10; ed. Haury (Teubner), III, pp. 51, 120–2. Leo IV: Theophanes, *Chronographia*; ed. de Boor, I, pp. 449–50. Michael III: *Continuation of Theophanes* IV.21; Bonn edn, pp. 172–3. Constantine IX and Zoë: Michael Psellus, *Chronographia* VI; ed. Renauld, I, pp. 117–54, II, pp. 1–71 (virtually *passim*).

37 John of Ephesus, *Ecclesiastical History* III.11, 14; trans. Smith, pp. 187, 190.

38 Refs: H. N. Turtledove, 'The Immediate Successors of Justinian', pp. 375–84.

found throughout Byzantine history: Choniates reports[39] that John II heaped up an accumulation of wealth, collecting it together just like gravel (*eis sōreias ta khrēmata epestoibase, kai hōs kakhlēkas auta synagēokhen*), while Manuel I squandered it in an ocean of generosities, and an abyss of alms (*thalassa philodōrias, eleous abyssos*), until on maturing he restrained himself.

## (II) INTERNAL AND EXTERNAL DISRUPTION

The disruptive effect that incessant usurpations must have had upon the revenue is well illustrated by an incident, single but presumably not untypical, that occurred during the revolt of Alexius Comnenus against Nicephorus III and that is recorded in some detail by Anna Comnena.[40] The caesar John Ducas, on his way to join the Comnenian faction at Tzurulum in Thrace, happened to meet up with a certain Byzantios who was carrying a large purse of gold (*khrysou balantion hikanon*). It emerged that this gold formed the proceeds of taxation and that Byzantios was conveying it to the imperial bed-chamber (*pros ton koitōna*). Ducas promptly relieved the unfortunate Byzantios of the gold which therefore never reached its intended destination. The payment of taxation or tribute into the 'God-guarded' bed-chamber (*theophylaktos koitōn*) was quite normal, and can be traced at least as far back as the tenth century.[41]

According to Genesius,[42] Thomas the Slav had already done much the same as the caesar during his revolt against Michael II, and according to Scylitzes[43] so had Bardas Sclerus during his revolt against Basil II. According to Gregoras,[44] Andronicus III was later to carry out a systematic policy of relieving Thracian tax-collectors of the money they had collected, during his revolt against Andronicus II.

Matters did not always turn out in quite such a way, of course: when the Norman fleet, returning from a raid on the Bosphorus in 1149, by chance met up with and attacked the Byzantine ships escorting the public revenue collected on Crete (*to dēmosion Krētēthen ekomizon nomisma*) back to Constantinople, it was soundly defeated.[45]

The disruptive effect that both civil disturbance and foreign invasion might have upon the production of coin and therefore, presumably, upon the revenue had already been graphically demonstrated during the latter part of the reign of Phocas and the earlier part of that of Heraclius. Then, as a result of both these factors, the metropolitan mint had

39 Nicetas Choniates, *Historia*; ed. van Dieten, I, pp. 59–60.

40 Anna Comnena, *Alexiad* II.6.6–7; ed. Lieb, I, pp. 82–3.

41 Constantine Porphyrogenitus, *De Administrando Imperio* L; ed. Moravcsik and Jenkins, p. 234 (payment of tribute by Peloponnesian Slavs). For the twelfth century, see the *Palaia kai Nea Logarikē*: Zepoi, *Ius Graeco-Romanum* I, p. 329 (payment of the land-tax).

42 Joseph Genesius, *Regum Libri IV* II.2; ed. Lesmueller-Werner and Thurn, p. 23.

43 John Scylitzes, *Synopsis Historiarum*; ed. Thurn, p. 316.

44 Nicephorus Gregoras, *Historia Byzantina* VIII.6; Bonn edn, I, p. 319.

45 John Cinnamus, *Epitome* III.5; Bonn edn, p. 101.

been reduced from operating on a ten-*officina* (A–I) basis for its production of gold coin to operating on a two-*officina* (E, I) one. The contraction was virtually precisely coterminous with the disruption.[46]

## (III) SOURCES OF READY CASH

### A. Available options

Faced with a deficit, an impending deficit, or a sheer lack of ready cash, there were a number of things an emperor might do. Although it has been assumed[47] that problems of this kind might be solved by means of relatively sophisticated manipulations perhaps more appropriate to a modern economic context, the evidence of the sources suggests that, in effect, the range of solutions available was extremely limited, and that the solutions actually attempted were invariably of a simple, even crude, nature.

The opportune discovery of a treasure-trove might, of course, make a difference. This might not seem an entirely serious proposition, but, according to the *Continuation of Theophanes*,[48] the favour shown to the poor by Basil I, during the course of his reign, in the form of largesse, was caused or facilitated by the discovery of many underground treasures (*pollous tōn hypo gēn thēsaurōn*). The Byzantines clearly had a highly developed sense of the supernatural prerequisites necessary to make such finds, and the government oscillated between lenient legislation on the subject designed to encourage their declaration, and confiscatory measures designed to alleviate its own budgetary needs.[49]

The simplest normal solution, however, was to cut down or cease expenditure on what was almost certainly the main single item in the imperial budget: civil and military *rhogai*. The former is known to have been done by Heraclius, who cut *rhogai* by half, and by Isaac I; the latter by Nicephorus III, by Alexius I, by Andronicus II, who resorted to the expedient several times during the course of his reign, and by John V, who even received a formal letter of complaint on the subject.[50] Alexius may have discontinued definitively the payment of annual *rhogai* (*etēsias doseis*) to those holding certain classes of

[46] Grierson, *DOC* II.1, pp. 156–7 (Phocas, Class IV (607–10)), 244–6 (Heraclius, Class I (610–13)), 247–9 (Her., Class IIA (613–*c.* 616)). The phenomenon is still just noticeable for Class IIB (*c.* 616–*c.* 625), but is no longer so for Class IIC (*c.* 626–9).

[47] C. M. Cipolla, 'Currency Depreciation in Medieval Europe', *Economic History Review* 15² (1962/3), pp. 414–15.

[48] *Continuation of Theophanes* V.29; Bonn edn, pp. 256–7.

[49] Morrisson, 'La découverte des trésors à l'époque byzantine', p. 321–43. See now also: *idem*, 'Découverte de trésors à l'époque byzantine et monnaies inconnues: les *pentalaimia*', *Bulletin de la Société Française de Numismatique* 37 (1982), pp. 150–2.

[50] Heraclius: see below, p. 494. Isaac I: 'John Scylitzes' (*Scylitzes Continuatus*); ed. I. Bekker (Bonn edn), p. 642. Nicephorus III: see below, p. 235. Alexius I: John Zonaras, *Annales* XVIII.21.14; Bonn edn, III, p. 733. Andronicus II: George Pachymeres, *De Michaele et Andronico Palaeologis, De And.* V.13, VI.8; Bonn edn, II, pp. 397, 493. John V: Demetrius Cydones, *Epistulae* LXX; ed. R.-J. Loenertz, p. 102.

civil/senatorial dignities (*axiai*), but this remains uncertain, and is on the whole unlikely.[51] Romanus IV seems to have been obliged to pay *rhogai* in gold and silk, rather than in gold only, when his supplies of the former proved insufficient.[52] The government of Constantine VII is known to have ceased the payment even of ecclesiastical *rhogai*, and that of Nicephorus II to have cut both secular and ecclesiastical ones.[53]

Scarcely less simple a solution was the melting down of imperial ceremonial apparatus or metalware for conversion into coin, a measure implicitly condoned by the fourteenth-century writer the *magistros* Thomas.[54] This is one known to have been adopted (but not carried out) by Michael III to the tune of 200 kentenaria or 1,440,000 nomismata, and by Michael IX as co-emperor of Andronicus II (who did carry it out). The despoliation of former emperors' tombs to the tune of 70 kentenaria in silver and some gold was a variation practised by Alexius III, although he had apparently been preceded by Alexius I (with regard to the tomb of the empress Zoë). A similar expedient, involving the melting down of the antique statuary with which the City was adorned, with the same end in mind, is known to have been resorted to by Marcian, Heraclius, Alexius I, and the Latins of the Fourth Crusade.[55] Avitus had a number of the statues with which Rome was adorned melted down and their copper sold off of to gain gold for the treasury (*basilikoi tameioi*), and Constans II seems to have resorted to a similar, but perhaps even more comprehensive, measure.[56]

51 Lemerle, '"Rhoga" et rente d'état', pp. 97–9, and Oikonomides, 'L'évolution de l'organisation administrative de l'empire byzantin', p. 127. The fact that a number of the twelfth-century treaties between the empire and the Italian trading-states mention the gift or continuation of such ranks and *rhogai* suggests that they had at least not been entirely discontinued. It is of course true that the ranks involved were the higher ones, and that the former lower end of the scale may simply have dropped out.

52 'John Scylitzes' (*Scylitzes Continuatus*); Bonn edn, pp. 688–9. It should be noted that Romanus made the annual distribution (of *rhogai*) to both the army and the senate (*tō te stratō kai tē synklētō*) on the day before the Feast of Orthodoxy (the first Sunday in Lent), which seems early (see above, pp. 191–2), but this was before setting out on his fatal campaign against the Selçuks (1071), so the distribution had probably been deliberately advanced. In any case, Easter was particularly late in 1071 (24 April): Grumel, *La chronologie*, p. 255.

53 Constantine VII: Nicholas Mysticus, *Epistolae* LXXII, CLXXXIII; ed. Jenkins and Westerink, pp. 320, 514. Nicephorus II: John Zonaras, *Annales* XVI.25.16; Bonn edn, III, pp. 504–5.

54 Thomas Magistros, *Peri Basileias* XXI; *PG* CXLV, col. 481.

55 Michael III: *Continuation of Theophanes* IV.21, V.29; Bonn edn, pp. 173, 257. Although this melting down was apparently not effected, or at least completed, by Michael, it was by his successor Basil: for the coin, the *senzaton*, supposedly first struck from the resultant metal, see Grierson, *DOC* III.1, p. 46, III.2, p. 476. Michael IX: George Pachymeres, *De Michaele et Andronico Palaeologis, De And.* V.28; Bonn edn, II, pp. 446–7. Alexius III: Nicetas Choniates, *Historia*; ed. van Dieten, I, pp. 478–9. Alexius I: Anna Comnena, *Alexiad* VI.3.3; ed. Leib, II, p. 46. Marcian and Heraclius: *Scriptores Originum Constantinopolitanarum, Parastaseis Syntomoi Khronikai* XIII, XLII; ed. T. Preger (Teubner), I, pp. 7, 20–1. Alexius I: see below, p. 516. Latins: see below, p. 521. The proceeds of Heraclius' measure, allegedly worth 24 lbs silver, were despatched to the pay-chest (*tamieion*) of a reconnaissance-force (*skoulkaton* = prob. Lat. [*au*]scultatum), or *skoulkatameion*, then operating in the Pontus. On this last, see now: W. E. Kaegi, 'Two Studies in the Continuity of Late Roman and Byzantine Military Institutions', *Byzantinische Forschungen* 8 (1982), pp. 90–8 – not all of whose detailed conclusions are however to be accepted.

56 Avitus: John of Antioch, *Fragmenta* CCII; ed. K. Müller, IV, at p. 616. Constans II: *Liber Pontificalis* LXXVIII (Vitalian); ed. Duchesne, I, p. 343: *omnia quae erant in aere ad ornatum civitatis deposuit; sed et ecclesiae sanctae Mariae ad martyres* [*sc.* the Pantheon] *quae de tigulis aereis erant discoperuit*.... See also below, p. 261.

Alternatively, imperial possessions, and particularly the regalia, might be mortgaged, or even sold off, in return for cash. Isaac II is known to have mortgaged silverware (*argyrea skeuē*) from the imperial treasury (*ek tōn basilikōn tamieiōn*) to the Church on this basis – and then to have resumed possession of it without payment.[57] The baronage of the Latin empire mortgaged the relic known as the Crown of Thorns to the Venetian merchant Nicolo Quirino during the absence of Baldwin II in the west, and that notoriously impoverished emperor, having sold the lead from the palace roof, was reduced to mortgaging his son and heir to the Venetian Ferro brothers, after his return to Constantinople.[58] Among the many financial sacrifices that Andronicus II was obliged to undergo was the selling off of heirlooms (*keimēlia* – presumably items of regalia) deriving from former emperors. The empress Anna, as regent for John V, reverted to mortgaging the current imperial regalia, this time to a Venetian syndicate of merchants. The return of this was the subject of prolonged negotiation, and in fact seems never to have been carried out.[59] By the middle of the fourteenth century there can have been little left to melt down, sell, or pawn, and at the coronation festivities of John VI the jewels of the imperial regalia consisted for the most part of coloured glass, and the plate of pewter or pottery.[60]

Faced with exceptionally severe financial difficulties, an emperor might appeal for relief to his relatives and supporters, who stood to lose from the replacement of his régime by another, or – particularly when the cause of the difficulties was an external one – to the public at large, which stood to lose from the replacement of his régime by a foreign one.

The first of these alternatives was resorted to by Alexius I who, absent from the capital, appealed to his mother Anna Dalassena and his brother Isaac Comnenus, both of whom he had left behind, to procure him money. They began by collecting whatever they themselves possessed in gold and silver, and sending it along to the imperial foundry (*basilikē khōneia*). They then collected gold and silver from supporters.[61]

The second was resorted to by Alexius III, who appealed to the entire metropolitan population, including the senate, the clergy, and artisans, and members of the professions. It was only when his appeal was refused that he turned to the desperate method described above.[62] Andronicus II seems to have repeated the exercise with, apparently, rather

[57] Nicetas Choniates, *Historia*; ed. van Dieten, I, pp. 383–4.

[58] R. L. Wolff, 'Mortgage and Redemption of an Emperor's Son: Castile and the Latin Empire of Constantinople', *Speculum* 29 (1954), pp. 45–84.

[59] T. Bertelè, 'I gioielli della corona bizantina dati in pegno alla Repubblica veneta nel sec. XIV e Mastino II della Scala', in *Studi in Onore Amintore Fanfani* II, *Medioevo*, at pp. 89–117. J. W. Barker, *Manuel II Palaeologus (1391–1425): A Study in Late Byzantine Statesmanship*, pp. 443–5 (*Appendix* I: 'The Pawning of the Byzantine Crown Jewels to Venice').

[60] Nicephorus Gregoras, *Historia Byzantina* XV.11; Bonn edn, II, pp. 788–9.

[61] Anna Comnena, *Alexiad* V.2.1; ed. Leib, II, p. 10. See also above, n. 30.

[62] Nicetas Choniates, *Historia*; ed. van Dieten, I, p. 478.

greater – but still insufficient – success.[63] John VI similarly appealed to the representatives of the entire metropolitan population, including the merchants, artisans and lower classes, together with the military and monastic and secular clergy. It was again only when refused, interestingly enough at the instigation of members of the lower classes and the money-changers (*ek tōn en ergastēriois emporeuomenōn argyramoibōn*), that he turned to extraordinary taxation.[64]

Appeal is historically, of course, only one step removed from constraint, and the confiscation of property (particularly that of former, current, or potential opponents) in order to alleviate financial difficulties had a history so long as to render it almost traditional before late Roman and Byzantine rulers ever came to and continued it. Much less frequent, and much less respectable, was the outright confiscation, extraordinary taxation, or forced loan, of ecclesiastical property. The precedent for this had been set by Constantine himself, when he confiscated the treasures accumulated in the pagan temples.[65] It was, however, not taken up in any systematic way until Heraclius, having taken over ecclesiastical property in the form of a loan, proceeded to seize the equipment of the Great Church.[66]

It emerges, from a casual reference in a letter of pope Gregory I dated 599, that the exarch of Italy had borrowed the sum of six centenaria from the church of Ravenna to pay the allowances of the military (*cotidiana militum*), and that little had so far been repaid.[67] But the precise details of the loan – including whether it was voluntary or forced – remain entirely obscure.

The government of Constantine VII resorted to several such measures,[68] and those of Michael III, Isaac I and Michael VII all stand accused of having laid hands on ecclesiastical property.[69] Alexius I did much the same (although he later denounced his own action and forbade future recourse to it), and so did Alexius IV, Alexius Apocaucus on behalf of John V, John V himself, Manuel II and Constantine XI.[70] Alexius I certainly,

63 George Pachymeres, *De Michaele et Andronico Palaeologis*, *De And.* VII.4; Bonn, II, p. 576.

64 John Cantacuzene, *Historiarum Libri IV* IV.5–6, 12; Bonn edn, III, pp. 33–42, 80–1. Nevertheless, 50,000 hyperpyra seem to have been collected as a result.

65 See below, pp. 284–5.

66 See below, p. 495.

67 Gregory I, *Epistolae* IX.240; MGH, *Ep.* II, pp. 234–5. The sums involved had been: *in cimiliarchio Ravennatis ecclesiae...commendati*. The *cimiliarchium* (= Gr. *keimēliarkhion*) was clearly the same as the *archivum* mentioned above (p. 204 n. 278), that is, the treasury.

68 Nicholas Mysticus, *Epistolai* LXXIII (levying of an *ad hoc* tax termed *kokkos*), XCII (collection of a *posotēta khrysiou*); ed. Jenkins and Westerink, pp. 320, 322, 354, 356. See also *ed.cit.* pp. xxiii–xxiv, and above, p. 229 (cessation of eccl. *rhogai*).

69 Michael III: *Continuation of Theophanes* V.27; Bonn edn, p. 254. Isaac I and Michael VII: 'John Scylitzes' (*Scylitzes Continuatus*); Bonn edn, pp. 642–3, 726.

70 Alexius I: Anna Comnena, *Alexiad* V.2.2–6, VI.3.2–5; ed. Leib, II, pp. 10–13, 46–8. Alexius IV: Nicetas Choniates, *Historia*; ed. van Dieten, I, pp. 551–2. Alexius Apocaucus: Nicephorus Gregoras, *Historia Byzantina* XIII.8; Bonn edn, II, p. 665, and I. Ševčenko, 'Nicolas Cabasilas' "Anti-zealot" Discourse: A Reinterpretation', *DOP* 11 (1957), pp. 165–70 (quoting Cydones and Cabasilas). John V and Manuel II: refs in Ševčenko, 'Society and Intellectual Life in the Fourteenth Century', p. 81. Alexius I's confiscations

and Constantine XI possibly, made use of a clause in canon law permitting the alienation of ecclesiastical property to redeem prisoners of war.[71]

Isaac II seems to have indulged in the despoliation of the church on a grand and shameless scale, for, according to Choniates,[72] in addition to resorting to the subterfuge that has been mentioned above, he also purloined sacred metalware (*ta hiera skeuē*) from actual churches, to use it at his own tables (*trapezai*). Amongst the pieces involved, some were from emperors' tombs and fashioned out of precious stones and pure gold (*ek lithōn timalphōn kai khrysiou apephthou eskeuasmena*), and others, from the churches themselves, were basins (*kherniba*) which had been used in the holy mysteries. He even took precious ornaments (*kosmoi polyteleis*) from crosses and book-covers, and had them made into collar-pieces and necklaces or torques (*perideraia kai streptoi*), and other elements of imperial costumes (*basilikai stolai*).

In resorting to the subterfuge, there is no doubt that he had been responding to immediate financial needs, but in these other cases there is no evidence that this was so. When reproached for his actions, he merely replied that emperors were permitted to do anything, and that between God and emperor there was no great difference, giving as an example a supposed action of Constantine I. In other words, he was merely abusing what he regarded as being his rights.[73]

The other major possibility in the range of solutions available lay in the manipulation of the coinage, which basically involved ensuring that such metal as a ruler did possess went further in future than it had done previously and would have done otherwise. This desirable end might be achieved (for however short a time) by one of two principal means: lightening the weight of the coinage, or alloying its material, or indeed both, but in any case preferably while maintaining its former face value.

The fiscal basis of such manipulations comes over quite clearly in any examination of the history of the coinage itself, and is explicitly confirmed by the sources. The first two reductions in the weight of the Diocletianic billon nummus, and the similar reduction that converted the Diocletianic 'aureus' into the 'solidus', all occurred while Constantine was confined to Britain and Gaul yet was incurring the increased expenditure necessary to build up and maintain his military forces for use against Maxentius.[74] The first two

('the affair of Leo of Chalcedon'), however muted by Anna, have created a considerable literature – in the last instance, see: P. Gautier, 'Le synode des Blachernes (fin 1094), étude prosopographique', *Revue des Études Byzantines* 29 (1971), pp. 213–84 (with essential refs on pp. 213–16). Alexius apparently attempted a second confiscation in 1086/7 – Gautier, *op cit.* p. 214. It should be noted that G. T. Dennis, 'Nicholas Cabasilas Chamaëtos and his Discourse on Abuses committed against Sacred Things', *Byzantine Studies/Études Byzantines* 5 (1978), pp. 80–7, proposing Cabasilas' *Discourse* to be generally, rather than particularly, directed, even if successful, does not exonerate Apocaucus, in view of Gregoras' particular evidence.

[71] This is made explicit by Anna: *Alexiad* v.2.2; ed. Leib, II, pp. 10–11. It may well be what is referred to by Leonard of Chios: see below, p. 545. For Justinian's law on the subject, see below, p. 260 and n. 16.

[72] See above, p. 230. Nicetas Choniates, *Historia*; ed. van Dieten, I, p. 443.

[73] *Ibid.* p. 444. For a comparison with John III's attitude to such things, see below, p. 271.

[74] See below, pp. 462–3, 466.

reductions in the weight of the still recently reformed billon coinage of Constans and Constantius II occurred while the latter was incurring the increased expenditure of his campaign against Magnentius.[75] Several of the variations in the weight of the copper follis during the reign of Heraclius may be connected fairly intimately with contemporary military vicissitudes.[76] The two instances of the inception of a light weight gold coinage both occur in reigns marked by their military efforts: those of Justinian I and Nicephorus II.[77] It seems clear, as mentioned above, that any extraordinary military effort imposed a heavy strain on the financial resources of the empire, and that this strain was likely to be reflected in a fairly immediate and direct way in its coinage.[78]

The pattern of the eleventh-century debasement and reform of the gold coinage also strongly suggests it to have had a fiscal basis. The detailed course of the debasement remains to be described in the eighth chapter of this book,[79] but the significant points seem to be that debasement was initiated by Michael IV; that the rate of debasement was greatest between the reign of Michael VII and the first decade of the reign of Alexius I; and that debasement was then quite suddenly halted and the purity of the gold coinage restored to something approaching its former level.

Now, in the first place, this pattern is not that of a general economic decline and recovery as still occasionally suggested.[80] If the coinage of the period were to be seen as reflecting something as vague as the general economic climate, it would be necessary to suppose that climate to have undergone a quite astonishing, indeed most implausible, degree of change, in what was essentially a very short space of time. In fact, the entire chronological framework within which the pattern was worked out is one dominated by political and military events, and it is therefore much more plausible to see the pattern as a financial expression of the consequences of these events. It is, in other words, much more plausible to see drastic alterations in the weight or metallic quality of the late Roman and Byzantine coinages in as short a space of time as this as tending to reflect not general economic, but particular fiscal, phenomena. Such a view has at least the merit of conforming to what is known of the earlier example of catastrophic debasement – that of the third century – and to the clear conclusions that are to be drawn from the material collected elsewhere in this book.

The fiscal régime of Michael IV seems to have been characterised by lavish expenditure on the one hand, and by harsh taxation on the other. The latter was presumably the consequence of the former. Because of his long-standing and steadily-worsening illness, which he considered to be a form of divine punishment for his sins, the reign was marked by the foundation of a number of churches, monasteries and charitable institutions, the

[75] See below, p. 469. [76] See below, pp. 498–9. [77] See below, pp. 492–3, 507–8.

[78] For a comparison of military expenditure, state revenue, and the reserve, see above, pp. 161–72, 221–4, 224–7. [79] See below, pp. 508–10, 511, 513.

[80] E.g. J. D. Breckenridge in *American Journal of Archaeology* 74 (1970), at p. 314 (review of Hendy, *DOS* XII).

church of the *Anargyroi* and the hostel of the *Ptokhotrophion* being among the metropolitan examples of such foundations.[81] It was also marked by the lavish distribution of alms: two nomismata to every priest in the empire, one to every monk, and one nomisma four miliaresia to every newly baptised child, being one instance of such distributions.[82] Presumably to pay for expenditure on this scale, Michael, or rather his brother John the *orphanotrophos*, was forced to impose what appears to have been harsher taxation than was normal: it was, for instance, an attempt to change over from taxation in kind to taxation in coin that drove the Bulgarians into revolt and the state into yet further expenditure.[83]

Faced with a deficit, or an impending deficit, in the balance of his annual revenue and expenditure (which would have been on an account separate from that of any reserve he might have had), as Michael may well have been, an emperor had all the solutions outlined above available to him. With the immense force of tradition behind them it is probable that, except in sheer desperation, most emperors other than Michael would not have chosen the last of these solutions, that of debasement. But he was, for his period, something of an exception, and was of humble origins. More than that, according to Scylitzes, he had been engaged in the money-changing profession (*argyramoibē epistēmē*) before his elevation, and had then indulged in debasement.[84] The former statement is presumably accurate, the latter may be libellous, but it is surely the case that any prejudice against debasement that most other emperors might have had would have been less, or even lacking, in Michael.

The distinction between the public resources (*dēmosiai...aphormai*) contributed by the populace – that is the public revenues – and the imperial treasures (*anaktorōn...tameia*) – that is the imperial reserve – was perfectly well understood by Psellus, who is also

[81] For the two particular foundations: Michael Psellus, *Chronographia* IV.31, 36; ed. Renauld, I, pp. 71–2, 74–5. For a useful study of what such foundations might have meant financially: Lemerle, *Cinq études sur le XIe siècle byzantin*, at pp. 273–83 (St George *Tropaiophoros* founded by Constantine IX), 283–5 (*Orphanotropheion* founded by Alexius I). But see also above, Map 19 (donation of estates to the Mon. of the Pantocrator by John II). On the Mangana, see now also: N. Oikonomides, 'St George of Mangana, Maria Skleraina, and the "Malyj Sion" of Novgorod', *DOP* 34/5 (1980/1), pp. 239–46.

[82] John Scylitzes, *Synopsis Historiarum*; ed. Thurn, p. 405. The only directly comparable general largesse seems to have been that given by John III, in circumstances very similar to those in which Michael found himself. This is said to have involved the distribution of 36 *tōn akibdēlōn nomismatōn* to each of the poor, and mules laden (with gold presumably) to the churches and monasteries. If *akibdēlon* is to be taken in its strict sense of 'unalloyed', then this is merely a reflection of the status enjoyed by John's relatively pure coinage (*c.* 16 carats) in the fourteenth century. George Pachymeres, *De Michaele et Andronico Palaeologis, De Mich.* I.24; Bonn edn, I, p. 70. But see also above, p. 198 (Manuel I's gift of 2 hyperpyra to each metropolitan household).

[83] See below, p. 297.

[84] John Scylitzes, *Synopsis Historiarum*; ed. Thurn, p. 390. What he actually says is that Michael 'alloyed the silver coins [i.e. miliaresia] – *kai ta argyria ekibdēleuon*'. The charge is repeated, as usual almost word for word, by George Cedrenus (*Historiarum Compendium*; Bonn edn, II, p. 504).

absolutely consistent in attributing the financial ruin of the state to the insensate and multifarious extravagance of the successors of Basil II.[85]

The period that saw the greatest rate of debasement, that covering the reigns of Michael VII, Nicephorus III and the first decade of the reign of Alexius I (i.e. 1071–91), was also a period that saw a whole series of political and military disasters, including incessant usurpations and revolts; the effective escape of the lay and ecclesiastical 'powerful' (*dynatoi*) from central financial control; the loss of virtually the whole of Asia Minor to the Selçuks; the Norman invasion of the western Balkans; the Patzinak invasion of the northern Balkans; and Selçuk piracy in the Aegean. It was brought to an end only with the expulsion of the Normans (1085), the annihilation of the Patzinaks (1091), and the repulse of the most immediate pirate threat (1091). The latter events implied a return to some sort of political and military stability and, significantly, were almost immediately followed by the reform of the coinage (1092), by a restructing of the metropolitan financial administration (before 1094), and by a radical overhaul of the system of taxation that entailed the restoration of central financial control (1106–9).[86]

The existence of an intimate connection between contemporary political and military events, finance and coinage is confirmed by Nicephorus Bryennius while describing the policies of Nicephorus III:

> He [Nicephorus] did not grant the highest honours to the most notable among the aristocracy, the military, or members of the senatorial class, or to those showing some favour towards him, but to all those who asked for them. He did the same with what the Romans called *offikia*, so that as a consequence expenditure (*exodoi*) exceeded revenue (*eisodoi*) by several times. And so, for this reason, within a short space of time, money (*khrēmata*) was lacking, the nomisma was debased, and the gifts (*dōreai*) of money attached by the emperor to such honours and offices were brought to an end. For the influx of money which derived from Asia and which went to supply the treasury ceased because the whole of Asia fell into the possession of the Turks, and since that deriving from Europe also decreased drastically, because of its ill-use by earlier emperors, the imperial treasury (*basilikoi tameioi*) found itself in the greatest want of money.
>
> (Nicephorus Bryennius, *Historiarum Libri IV* IV.1; ed. P. Gautier, pp. 257, 259)

[85] Michael Psellus, *Chronographia* VII.59; ed. Renauld, II, p. 119. Psellus (in discussing Basil II) is also perfectly well aware of the necessity for a ruler to ensure that revenues exceeded expenditures, and thereby to amass a reserve: *kai ton ekeithen plouton eis ta basileia eisenenkōn, polyplasious te tas epigonomenas eisodous tōn apogignomenōn pepoiēkōs, tōn enteuthen apiōn thēsaurous amythētous khrēmaton kataleloipei tō adelphō Konstantinō* (*Chronographia* VII.52; *ed.cit.* p. 115).

[86] Debasement: below, pp. 508–10. Reform: below, pp. 514–16. Restructuring: below, pp. 432–4. Overhaul: Hendy, *DOS* XII, pp. 50–64. On this last subject (basically the *Palaia kai Nea Logarikē*), see now also: C. Morrisson, 'La Logarikè: réforme monétaire et réforme fiscale sous Alexis Ier Comnène', *Travaux et Mémoires* 7 (1979), pp. 419–64. This provides a virtually complete translation and detailed commentary, although a number of the monetary/numismatic conclusions are unacceptable.

It seems quite clear that, as for Psellus, so for Bryennius, the debasement of the nomisma was a natural consequence of the budgetary imbalance that arose out of increased expenditure on the one hand, and a decreasing revenue on the other. The former was undoubtedly due in large part to the indiscriminate extravagance of the reigning emperor, also described in some detail by Attaliates,[87] while the latter was the inevitable financial consequence of military defeat and political chaos.

To suppose the first phase of the eleventh-century monetary debasement to have formed some kind of *dévaluation d'expansion*, with its implication of complex financial insight and pre-emptive application of policy, as opposed to the second phase having been a *dévaluation de crise*, which – however it might be dressed up – was essentially the forced result of a budgetary imbalance,[88] is to credit the Byzantine state, or rather its administrative personnel, with a conceptual level for which there is no evidence, and indeed which they cannot possibly have achieved. Such a supposition also fails to take into account the existence and nature, and the causes and effects, of the succeeding monetary reform. A contrast between the two phases there may have been, but it was one of degree and not of nature.

The second phase of general monetary debasement, that covering the second half of the thirteenth century and the first half of the fourteenth, seems to have been caused by factors similar to those that had caused the first. Pachymeres' well-known passage describing the course of the second phase clearly identifies a high level of expenditure, however necessary it may have been politically, as the primary cause of the debasement of the gold coinage,[89] and Muntaner's classic description of a virtually entire cycle of debasement implies as much for the silver.[90] The frequent occasions on which the emperors of the period are known to have been obliged to have recourse to the various expedients for raising extra cash confirm the diagnosis.

An accurate assessment of the causes of this second phase of debasement has itself been

[87] Michael Attaliates, *Historia*; Bonn edn, pp. 273–6. The descriptions of Psellus, Bryennius and Attaliates are in absolute accordance with one another, providing a nexus of opinion and information that should not lightly be discarded.

[88] The two phrases are taken immediately from Lemerle, *Cinq études sur le XI$^e$ siècle byzantin*, pp. 285–7, 307–9, but both of his definitions are derived from C. Morrisson, 'La dévaluation de la monnaie byzantine au XI$^e$ siècle: essai d'interprétation', *Travaux et Mémoires* 6 (1976), pp. 3–48, esp. pp. 17–24, where a 'monetarist' interpretation of the whole phenomenon is attempted (see above, e.g. p. 3). It must be emphasised that Lemerle's conclusion: 'Le résultat est une économie cassée. Byzance ne s'en relèvera jamais', although apparently authoritative, is certainly simplistic and is probably untenable: his case fails to distinguish between state finances and the general economy, and it relies on a false (i.e. trade-based) model of the economy itself. If a 'monetarist' element in the phenomenon is to be sought, then one might do worse than to take a look at Basil II's reserve of over 14 million nomismata and its fate: if the accumulation of a reserve by Constantine V caused a noticeable *fall* in the prices of goods (see above, pp. 298–9), then the disbursement of the reserve accumulated by Basil ought to have caused a noticeable *rise* in the price of goods (both movements being in terms of gold). This should have taken place whether or not the gold coinage was debased.

[89] See below, p. 527.

[90] See below, p. 531.

rendered more difficult by the complicating intervention of a further and separate phenomenon: the Byzantine transfer from a gold-based to a silver-based coinage during the second half of the fourteenth century.[91] It may be suggested that whereas the debasement was due to a combination of factors that were largely local and fiscal – in essentials a necessarily high level of expenditure and a static or insufficiently flexible revenue – the transfer from gold to silver was due to general economic factors operating within a much wider geographical framework that involved the entire Mediterranean basin at a minimum.[92]

## B. *Unavailable options*

It is as interesting and as significant to note several of the solutions that were available only with difficulty, or that were completely unavailable, to an emperor faced with a deficit or with a similar problem.

It might be considered a matter of relative ease to have raised extra revenue, whether in kind or in cash, through the normal methods of taxation, and, within certain limits, this could indeed be done. The later Roman and early Byzantine indiction varied from year to year, or was in theory at least capable of such variation, as the government calculated that its need dictated, and if in any year its calculations proved inadequate then it made supplementary ones and collected a superindiction.[93] But calculations and collection both took time, the latter in particular, owing to the primitive methods of, and facilities for, communications and transport, and much in any case must have depended upon the season of the year.[94]

If, as seems certain, land and agriculture were overwhelmingly the principal sources of revenue, the government would have been, if not precluded from taxing urban society (it imposed on it, for example, the *collatio lustralis* and the *commercium*), then precluded from extracting significant contributions from it.[95] It would have been, in other words, unable to extract from the section of society that was the most monetised of all and the least subject to the problems of transport and the seasons, the amount of ready cash that it frequently lacked and occasionally desperately needed.[96]

It is surely significant that, for all the known financial pressures of the reign of Justinian, and despite the known professional ingenuity of several of his senior financial officials, one major addition only was made to the list of taxes. This was John of Cappadocia's *aērikon*, a tax of uncertain nature but which seems likely to have been a supplement to the land-tax at this stage and which, according to Procopius,[97] netted the respectable

[91] See below, pp. 530–5, 536–46.

[92] See below, pp. 546–7.

[93] Jones, *Later Roman Empire* I, pp. 450–3.

[94] See below, pp. 555–9.

[95] *Collatio lustralis*: see above, pp. 175–6. *Kommerkion*: see above, p. 174. See also below, pp. 590–602.

[96] See above, pp. 223–4.

[97] Procopius, *Historia Arcana* XXI.1–2; ed. Haury (Teubner), III, pp. 128–9.

but by no means very remarkable sum of 30 kentenaria or 216,000 solidi. The budget seems rather to have been balanced by the more efficient collection of existing taxes and by various economies.[98]

The radical reform or overhaul of the system of taxation was in fact rare in the late Roman and Byzantine empires, once again, it may be suspected, largely because the principal sources of revenue being so constant in nature, opportunities for alteration or diversification were extremely limited. Diocletian and Constantine, Nicephorus I, Alexius I, and possibly Andronicus II, are virtually the only emperors who, on present evidence, may be considered to have performed either operation, although Anastasius, Leo III, and several of the tenth-century emperors – notably Romanus I and Basil II – may be credited with adjustments of some significance.

The main taxes of the middle Byzantine period therefore still seem to have been the land-tax, in however modified a form and with however many supplements, and the *kapnikon* or hearth-tax which was levied on certain classes of peasant tenantry, and there is no good reason to believe that this general balance ever altered in any fundamental sense – although with the loss of territory from the last quarter of the thirteenth century onwards it might have done, had not the remaining sources of revenue been in Genoese hands. The effective later equivalents of the superindiction seem likely to be found in various *ad hoc* taxes such as the *dikeraton* and perhaps the *hexafollon* of Leo III, the *kokkos* of Constantine VII, the *alamanikon* of Alexius III which was intended to total 16 kentenaria or 115,200 hyperpyra but of which a proportion only needed to be collected, and the *sitokrithon* of Andronicus II which was collected and perhaps partly paid out in kind. These theoretically *ad hoc* taxes inevitably tended to become institutionalised.[99]

Again, it might be considered a matter of ease for an emperor to have floated a loan on the banking or merchant communities. The nature and rôle of late Roman and Byzantine bankers, and the regulations that governed their activities, will be described and briefly discussed in the next section of, and in an appendix to, this chapter,[100] and at this stage it is sufficient to note that the available evidence suggests neither community to have been capable of advancing credit systematically, and on a scale that would have permitted it a significant rôle in state finance.

According to Corippus,[101] in 565, there were numbers of individuals who had lent Justinian money, at his orders (i.e. *iubenti domino*), and against bonds (*syngrapha*, *cauta*).

[98] Jones, *Later Roman Empire* I, p. 284.

[99] *Dikeraton*: Theophanes, *Chronographia*; ed. de Boor, I, p. 412 (at the rate of 1 miliaresion to the nomisma, and as a *dikeraton* therefore one twelfth). *Hexafollon*: Zepoi, *Ius Graeco-Romanum* I, p. 328. *Kokkos*: see above, p. 231 n. 68. *Alamanikon*: Nicetas Choniates, *Historia*; ed. van Dieten, I, p. 478 (50 kent. had originally been demanded). *Sitokrithon*: George Pachymeres, *De Michaele et Andronico Palaeologis*, *De And.* VI.7–8; Bonn edn, II, pp. 492–3 (at the rate of 6 *modioi* of wheat, and 4 of barley, to the *zeugarion*). *Dikeraton* and *hexafollon* were still being collected as late as the twelfth century, when the *Palaia kai Nea Logarikē* was redacted.

[100] See below, pp. 242–51, 251–3.

[101] Corippus, *In Laudem Iustini Augusti* II; ed. Averil Cameron, pp. 58–9.

Justin II immediately paid off his debts and reclaimed his bonds (*debita persolvit...cauta recepit*), and the whole is worked up into a splendid scene in the hippodrome (*et totus fuso circus resplenduit auro*). It has been supposed[102] that bankers and merchants were heavily involved in this credit, and public business (*publica commercia*) is indeed alluded to in this respect. But the allusion is no more specific than that, and details of the identity of the creditors, the size of the sums involved, and the degree of normality of the phenomenon, all remain unknown. The fact that the debts were paid off immediately, and from the imperial private treasury (*thesauri privati*), does not suggest them to have been that great, or even to have been that necessary, being perhaps more appropriate to deliberately unpaid bills, and the whole scene is in any case described in highly rhetorical terms. The cancellation of tax-arrears, whether periodic or conducted as an exercise in public relations, is of course an entirely more normative phenomenon.[103]

According to the Syriac chronicler Bar Hebraeus,[104] Basil II requested a loan from three merchants of Melitene, the sons of Abu Imran. This, apparently amounting to 100 kentenaria, he was granted, and duly repaid. But the figure is widely out of kilter with the rest of what is known of the financial capacities of the Byzantine mercantile classes, although perhaps more appropriate to their Arab and Jewish equivalents (and it may well be no coincidence that Melitene had been recovered from the Arabs still relatively recently), and can therefore only be regarded with suspicion.[105]

Finally, it is noticeable that when, eventually, Byzantine emperors did turn to bankers, or merchants, or both, to ease their financial difficulties, it was to western ones, despite the continuing existence of their Byzantine colleagues, and the same appears to have been true of Trapezuntine emperors too.[106]

The only classes with sufficient capital to have played the necessary rôle in any systematic and large-scale sense were the lay and ecclesiastical aristocracies, and in that case – given the aristocratic origins of much of the surviving evidence – one might have expected some allusion to it, had it existed. There is, indeed, one known instance of an exarch of Italy obtaining a loan from the Ravennate church, but the precise details of the loan are obscure, and the contemporary political situation was so disturbed and anomalous that it remains quite impossible to decide how typical the phenomenon was.[107] The one instance of an emperor requesting of a loan from a member of these classes in

102 *Ibid.* at pp. 176–7. As the editor rightly points out, the whole passage is something of a *topos*, and certainly exaggerated. But it surely follows from this that it would be unwise to draw from it too many particular conclusions.

103 Jones, *Later Roman Empire* I, pp. 466–7. The late Roman and early Byzantine instances seem to have been designed to benefit the state more than the individual. The practice seems to have become rarer (or is at least less frequently attested), but see for example above, pp. 199–200 (Romanus I).

104 Bar Hebraeus, *Chronography*; ed. trans. E. A. T. W. Budge, I, p. 178.

105 See below, p. 245.

106 See for example above, p. 230 (Baldwin II and the regent Anna). For the Trapezuntine emperors: A. A. M. Bryer, 'The Society and Institutions of the Empire of Trebizond', I, p. 139 (imperial involvement with Genoa).

107 See above, p. 231.

comparatively normal political circumstances, however, suggests the unusual nature of the request itself.

According to Cedrenus,[108] Michael IV, while staying at Thessalonica during a famine, requested archbishop Theophanes to pay his clerics their legitimate allowances (*sitēresia*). The archbishop proving obdurate, the emperor decided both to circumvent and emphasise his avarice by sending along several imperial officials to request the loan of a kentenarion while gold was being conveyed from Constantinople. The archbishop denied possessing more than thirty pounds of gold, and it was only upon his death, which followed shortly, that he was found to have amassed no less than 33 kentenaria. It is incidentally of some considerable interest as a measure of normal liquidity to know that it might be thought plausible for the holder of the richest see in the empire after those of the capital itself, and perhaps of Antioch, to claim to possess 30 lb of gold, or just over 2,000 nomismata only, in ready cash. An additional element of plausibility is added to the claim by the fact that, according to John Apocaucus,[109] the revenue (*apaitēsis*) of the whole of his see of Naupactus amounted to no more than 180 hyperpyra in the second decade of the thirteenth century, and this pattern seems not to have been untypical of the period.[110]

Of two private individuals who did place their military or financial resources at the disposal of the state or its representatives in times of need, it is known for certain that neither was of aristocratic origin.

Maurex, an inhabitant of Pontic Heraclea acquainted with maritime matters (*kata thalattan*), from which he had drawn a considerable fortune (*ploutos pleistos*) and a crowd of servants and a military following (*doulōn plēthos kai tōn allōn hypēretountōn peri ta stratiōtika*), placed his troops at the disposal of Alexius Comnenus whilst the latter was still a general of Michael VII.[111] On the other hand, at about the same stage of his career

[108] George Cedrenus, *Historiarum Compendium*; Bonn edn, II, pp. 518–19.

[109] S. Petrides, 'Jean Apokaukos, lettres et autres documents inédits', *Izvestiya Russkago Arkheologicheskago Instituta v Konstantinopole* 14 (1909), p. 11.

[110] C. A. Mango, *Byzantium: The Empire of New Rome*, p. 49. The author concludes that the later church hierarchy had been sharply affected by urban decline, and the contrast that he implicitly draws with the earlier situation (*op. cit.* pp. 36–9), seems to demonstrate just this. But much of the earlier evidence is based on the great patriarchates, and wealthy patriarchates and metropolitanates are to be found in the later period too – see the cases of Alexius of Constantinople and Theophanes of Thessalonica (above, p. 204). More probably there was always a great contrast between a few wealthy sees and the remainder, thereby accurately reflecting the general structure of society. It may be, of course, that the relative proportions between the two groups changed with time, with sees of great wealth becoming not only absolutely, but also relatively, fewer, as against those of moderate or little wealth. The position is doubtless complicated by the severance of the other three eastern patriarchates from the empire, by the transfer of the Balkans from Roman to Constantinopolitan jurisdiction, and the partly consequent rise of Constantinople and Thessalonica.

[111] Nicephorus Bryennius, *Historiarum Libri IV* II.26, 27; ed. P. Gautier, pp. 197, 199. This Maurex may, or may not, be identical with a Michael Maurex whose career seems to have covered most of the second half of the eleventh century (*c.* 1050–84). See: W. Seibt, *Die byzantinischen Bleisiegel in Österreich* I, *Kaiserhof*, no. 58, pp. 168–71. On the whole, the identity seems unlikely: both were undoubtedly connected with the sea, but Maurex seems to have been a private person who had made a fortune from it, and Michael Maurex seems to have been an imperial official with a long and distinguished record of service on it. The two are clearly not entirely incompatible, but the apparent discrepancy should at least lend caution.

Alexius was able, with the greatest of difficulty only, to persuade the citizens of Amasia to make a monetary contribution towards a course of action reflecting the interest and immediate needs of the state.[112] He also seems to have had to offer the citizens of Ancyra and its region a full reimbursement with interest (*panta syn tokō*) to persuade them to contribute to the ransoming of his brother Isaac from the Turks.[113]

Patrikiotes, who had long concerned himself with matters of taxation (*peri apographas*) from which he had made his fortune, placed his financial resources at the disposal of John Cantacuzene whilst he was *megas domestikos* to the empress Anna as regent for John V. The sum involved amounted to 100,000 hyperpyra in coin, and a further 40,000 in gold and silver garments and plate (*epipla te kai skeuē*).[114]

It is, however, quite clear that in neither of these cases was there any question of a formal loan, although both individuals obviously hoped to gain ultimately, and it is equally clear – from the attention paid to both episodes – that they were considered exceptional. The public at large, whether metropolitan or provincial, aristocratic or of lesser status, seems to have been fairly consistently incapable of aiding, or disinclined to aid, the state or its agents in this respect.

The lack of systematic credit in state finance seems confirmed by its omission from Psellus' laudatory description of Michael VII's financial knowledge and skills:

> He [Michael] understood every detail of finance (*synteleia*) exactly: its organisation (*syntaxis*) and management (*prytaneia*); how much the treasury (*ta dēmosia*) paid to each person and how much each paid back to the treasury; the production (*exergasia*) of coins and the equilibrium of a balance (*stathmēs isorrhopia*); excesses and deficiencies of weight (*hai rhopai kai ta leimmata*), how the touchstone (*khrysitēs*) worked; and how many measures of pure material (*kathara hylē*) each of the pieces of stamped gold (*khrysos kharaktēros*) contained.
>
> (Psellus, *Chronographia* VII.2; ed. Renauld, II, p. 173)

The clear impression is given that state finance involved the budgeting for, and acquisition of, a neutral or positive balance of revenue over expenditure, and the exercise of certain other technical skills. There is no suggestion, despite the circumstances of the time, which would have made it appropriate, that it involved credit.

It was presumably for this reason that the sources pay so much attention to the physical state of the imperial treasury, the emptiness of which is directly equated with imperial

112 Anna Comnena, *Alexiad* I.2.2–3, 3; ed. Leib, I, pp. 12–15. Alexius persuaded the Amasians to buy the renegade Norman Roussel from the Turks, on the promise of reimbursement from the emperor Michael. They were – perhaps with some excuse – sceptical, and were only finally persuaded by a ruse: the pretended blinding of Roussel.

113 Nicephorus Bryennius, *Historiarum Libri IV* II.8; ed. Gautier, pp. 155, 157. This ransom was one of many thousands of gold nomismata (*timēs khrysiou khiliadōn sykhnōn*). Isaac's military career apparently cost his family dear: see below, p. 267.

114 John Cantacuzene, *Historiarum Libri IV* III.8; Bonn edn, II, pp. 58–64. On Patrikiotes, see in the last instance: E. Lappa-Zizikas, 'Un chrysobulle inconnu en faveur du monastère des Saints-Anargyres de Kosmidion', *Travaux et Mémoires* 8 (1981), p. 262.

bankruptcy. Two examples may perhaps suffice. Anna Comnena remarks[115] that the treasury had been needlessly emptied by the former emperor, Nicephorus III, to such an extent that its gates were no longer closed and that they were left open to all comers because of its exhaustion. Gregoras remarks[116] that the treasury was found in so exhausted a condition by John VI that it contained nothing except air, dust and Epicurean atoms. Even allowing for an appreciable element of literary exaggeration, the equation seems clear enough.

## (IV) THE BANKING COMMUNITY

The profession of banking was carried on by two main classes of people during the late Roman and Byzantine period: the money-changers (*trapezitai* or *collectarii*) and the silversmiths (*argyropratai* or *argentarii*). Neither the terms used nor the division of function implied by them seem to have been at all consistently applied or observed, and there existed, in addition, any number of other terms that might be used.[117] The division seems nevertheless to have been at least formally correct, for each class is known later to have formed a separate guild (*somateion* or *systēma, collegium* or *corpus*), at Constantinople.[118]

The social status of neither class seems to have been very high. In 436, Theodosius II ruled that, if any person engaged in business, whether he be a money-changer (*trapezites*) or a seller of precious stones, silver (*argenti...venditor*), or clothing, a dealer attached to a customs depot (i.e. an *apothecarius*), or a seller of other merchandise attached to whatever workshop (*ergasterium*), were to be found to have obtained a position in any of the provincial *officia*, he was to be removed from it and degraded to his former status: 'So that in this way every honour and position of public service (*militia*) may be isolated from contagion.'[119] In 528–9 Justinian ruled: 'We debar from all positions of public service those who have charge over some workshop, whether in this mother-city [i.e. Constantinople], or in the provinces, with the exception of those sellers of silver (*argenti distractores*) who do business in this mother-city.'[120]

The two laws reveal that it had become common for *trapezitai* and *argyropratai* alike, as well as other dealers, to purchase a position of public service that, although probably a sinecure, nevertheless carried with it a certain social status, legal privileges, and an annual salary.[121] They also reveal the metropolitan *argyropratai* to have been recognised as

[115] Anna Comnena, *Alexiad* V.1.4; ed. Leib, II, p. 9.

[116] Nicephorus Gregoras, *Historia Byzantina* XV.12; Bonn edn, II, p. 790.

[117] E.g. R. Bogaert, *Banques et banquiers dans les cités grecques*, pp. 37–60 (useful, despite the limitations of geography and chronology). A nice example of the tendency to blurr definitions is to be had from a later metrological writer (F. Hultsch, *Metrologicorum Scriptorum Reliquiae* I, p. 307): '*Kollektarios*. The money-changer, that is the banker who exchanges the small coin against silver, the silversmith (*Kollektarios. Ho argyramoibos ētoi ho kerma anti argyrou allassomenos trapezitēs, ho argyropratēs*).'

[118] See below, pp. 251–3. The division is also at least implicit elsewhere: see, for example, below, p. 245 and n. 140.

[119] *CJ* XII.57.12.

[120] *CJ* XII.34.1–4.

[121] See above, pp. 185–7.

forming something of a special case and as worthy of exception from the general debarment.

The efficiency of this debarment may, as usual, be questioned: according to Procopius,[122] Peter Barsymes was a Syrian by origin and a money-changer (*argyramoibos*) by profession, yet he obtained membership of the *officium* of the prefecture of the East, became principal financial adviser to Justinian during the latter part of his reign, and ended up having been twice *comes sacrarum largitionum* and twice prefect of the East.[123] There is, even so, no evidence that, in pursuing his public career in defiance of the laws, he was aided (except, perhaps, in the purchase of his first *militia*) by financial resources gained while in his earlier profession. Similarly, in a Ravennate document of *c.* 600,[124] one Armatus signs brazenly as *v(ir) d(evotus), schol(aris), et (coll)ectarius*, which would seem to indicate that, whether for reasons of time or place, the debarment was no longer operative. In the eleventh century, one former money-changer (*argyramoibos*) even became emperor (Michael IV).[125] In the later twelfth century, certain money-changers (*kollybistai*) were able to afford the title of *sebastos* (no longer very high).[126]

As a profession, *argyropratai* and money-lenders (*sēmadarioi*) in general were, not unnaturally, unpopular: according to Theophanes,[127] the empress Sophia summoned them in 567 and confiscated their agreements to, and pledges of, debt (*hai homologiai tōn khreōstountōn kai ta sēmadia*), restoring them to the debtors, which was accounted a praiseworthy act by the whole city. That they were nevertheless actually recognised as having a certain professional standing seems clear from John of Ephesus, according to whom[128] the silversmiths and bankers – together with the lawyers and doctors – were the objects of Tiberius II's largesse. Similarly, the fact that the *De Caerimoniis*[129] can mention 'the *argyropratai* and all those involved in business affairs (*argyropratai kai pantes pragmateutai*)' suggests that they stood at or near the head of the business professions in status and reputation. The point presumably is that while the *argyropratai* may have been

122 Procopius, *Historia Arcana* XXII.3–5; ed. Haury (Teubner), III, p. 134.

123 Jones, *Later Roman Empire* I, p. 295.

124 J.-O. Tjäder, *Die nichtliterarischen lateinischen Papyri Italiens aus der Zeit 445–700* I, *Papyri 1–28*, pp. 344–52 (no. 20).

125 See above, p. 234.

126 Nicetas Choniates, *Historia*; ed. van Dieten, I, p. 484. The passage couples together: *hoi en triodois kai agorais kai kollybistai kai pratai tōn othonōn*, as well as Scythians and Syrians – a general rag-bag of prejudicial descriptions, rather like John of Ephesus' Jews, Samaritans and heretics, below. For a similar set of imperial/aristocratic prejudices against the urban mercantile and/or administrative classes, see above, pp. 235, 242, and below, p. 247 and n. 154. See also below, pp. 570–82, 582–7.

127 Theophanes, *Chronographia*; ed. de Boor, I, p. 242.

128 John of Ephesus, *Ecclesiastical History* III.11; trans. Smith, p. 186. The order in which the professions are said to have been called: lawyers, doctors, silversmiths, and bankers is presumably a reflection of their relative standing, and (with the exception of the doctors, who are not included) also represents the order present in *The Book of the Prefect*: *taboullarioi, argyropratai, trapezitai.*

129 Constantine Porphyrogenitus, *De Caerimoniis* I (*Appendix*); Bonn edn, p. 498. The passage continues: *kai pan systēma*, so it was clearly a question of the guilds.

capable of being classed along with the lawyers and doctors, and may have ranked first amongst the business professions, the status of none of these was very high.

It has been supposed,[130] on the basis of a further passage in John of Ephesus,[131] that Jews, Samaritans and heretics were heavily represented in the profession, but the connection is not an absolute one, and the classification is so traditional as to render the point quite inconclusive. As a profession, it was the money-changers, acting together with members of the lower classes, that refused John VI's appeal to the metropolitan population for funds.[132]

*Trapezitai* seem generally to have been outranked by *argyropratai*. It is the latter only who are represented by lead seals of the sixth to eighth centuries.[133] In late sixth-century Egypt, *trapezitai* seem to have ranked as *eudokimotatoi* (i.e. *viri honesti* or *devoti*), *argyropratai* as *lamprotatoi* (i.e. *viri clarissimi*); and in contemporary Italy, *collectarii* also generally seem to have ranked as *honesti* or *devoti*, and *argentarii* as *clarissimi*.[134] Again, these titles had by then ceased to mean much.[135]

The financial resources available to the generality of neither class seem, in any case, to have been very considerable. True, as a profession concentrated in one locality, they represented a significant and vulnerable accumulation of wealth. According to Sozomen,[136] the Goth Gainas intended to plunder the metropolitan *argyropōloi* at the turn of the fourth century, but was unable to do as, pre-warned by rumour, they had withdrawn the readily moveable wealth (*prokheiron plouton*) and cash (*argyron*) from their tables (*trapezai*).

True, also, that the *militiae* which their individual representatives seem to have been intent on purchasing required the outlay of a certain amount of money: membership of the *sacra scrinia* is known to have cost 250 solidi in 443–4; the position of *domesticus praesentalis* is known to have cost something in excess of 2,000 solidi in 519; and the scale seems to have been very similar to that still operating in the tenth century.[137] On the other hand, Justinian's rulings on what should be done with such *militiae* when the *argyropratai* who had purchased them went bankrupt, give the distinct impression that a purchase, or purchases, of this kind might involve a large proportion of the total

130 Turtledove, 'The Immediate Successors of Justinian', pp. 346, 349–50. See also Nicetas Choniates, above.

131 John of Ephesus, *Ecclesiastical History* III, 31; trans. Smith, p. 216.

132 See above, p. 231.

133 Zacos and Veglery, *Byzantine Lead Seals* I.1, pp. 380 no. 315, 457 no. 513, 592–3 no. 828, 650 no. 962, 697 no. 1078; I.2, pp. 1218–19 nos. 2209 A–B.

134 Egypt: see below, pp. 350, 351. Italy: Tjäder, *Die nichtliterarischen lateinischen Papyri Italiens* I, pp. 218–24 (no. 6), 244–52 (no. 20) (*collectarii*), pp. 198–216 (*argentarii*); G. Marini, *I Papiri Diplomatici*, pp. 131 (no. 84), 174 (no. 114). Of those *argentarii* appearing in the papyri and whose rank is known, only Theodore (Tjäder, *op. cit.* p. 214), and Flavius Severus and Julianus (Marini, *op. cit.* pp. 131, 174) rank merely as *viri honesti*. See also: A. Guillou, *Régionalisme et indépendance dans l'empire byzantin au VII^e^ siècle*, pp. 80–1.

135 Jones, *Later Roman Empire* II, p. 529.

136 Sozomen, *Historia Ecclesiastica* VIII.4; ed. J.-P. Migne, in *PG* LXVII, at col. 1524.

137 *Sacra scrinia*: *CJ* XII.19.7. *Domesticus praesentalis*: *CJ* II.7.25. Tenth century: see above, pp. 185–6.

resources available to any one *argyropratēs*.[138] This does not suggest the possession of a very great deal of money, and the capacity to play a significant rôle in state finance, an assessment that seems as valid for the generality of fourth-century *trapezitai* at Antioch as for the generality of sixth-century *argyropratai* at Constantinople.[139]

Again, other provincial guilds, their individual members, and even their corporate and personal benefactions, are known, those of Ephesus forming a good example, and the benefactions involving a proconsular statue and a domed mausoleum at the Tomb of the Seven Sleepers, respectively. But even so, the provincial evidence does not necessarily contradict the metropolitan.[140]

Occasional exceptions or apparent exceptions, in addition to the Ephesian examples, can, of course, always be found: Andronicus, an Antiochene *argyropratēs* married to the daughter of another, was sufficiently wealthy to be able to donate money for the foundation of hospitals and hostels in the sixth century;[141] the metropolitan *argyropratēs* Marcellus was sufficiently wealthy to be able to part with 50 lb gold or 3,600 nomismata to further an assassination attempt in which his colleagues Isaac and Vitus, all of them being seemingly connected with the household of the patrician Belisarius, were apparently involved, also in the sixth;[142] the metropolitan money-changer (*kollybistēs*) Kalomodios, who had made a great deal of money (*khrēmasin*...*pollois*) out of long and arduous travels for the purpose of commerce (*kat' emporian*), was sufficiently wealthy to be considered worth fleecing by certain of the court nobility (i.e. those *peri ton basilea*) in the late twelfth century.[143] None of these exceptions need, in fact, to have been of more than relatively moderate means, particularly in comparison with members of the great aristocratic houses of the day, and they would, in this respect, only be conforming to what is known of other sections of the contemporary mercantile class.[144]

On the other hand, Julianus, apparently a Ravennate *argentarius*, who was responsible for the building and decoration of the churches of S. Vitale (at a cost of 26,000 solidi or somewhat under 4 kentenaria), and S. Apollinare in Classe, as well as others, in the sixth century, really does seem to have been of a very different order of wealth. But even so, the word *argentarius* could quite well represent not Julianus' profession, but part of his name, and it is not even certain that the funds involved derived from his own private

138 *CJ* VIII.13.27 (528). Justinian, Novel CXXXVI.2 (535).

139 Liebeschuetz, *Antioch: City and Imperial Administration in the Later Roman Empire*, pp. 87–8.

140 Foss, *Ephesus after Antiquity*, p. 8. For another provincial guild and individual members (both *argyropratai* and *trapezitai*) at Corycus, see: E. Patlagean, *Pauvreté économique et pauvreté sociale à Byzance 4^e–7^e siècles*, pp. 158, 162 (7e).

141 Ed. L. Clugnet, 'L'orfèvre Andronicus et son épouse Athanasie', in 'Vie et récits de l'abbé Daniel, de Scété (VI^e siècle) (Suite) (I)', in *Revue de l'Orient Chrétien* 5 (1900), at pp. 370–87.

142 Theophanes, *Chronographia*; ed. de Boor, I, p. 237–8.

143 Nicetas Choniates, *Historia*; ed. van Dieten, I, pp. 523–4.

144 Jones, *Later Roman Empire* II, pp. 864–72. A. M. Andréadès, 'De la monnaie et de la puissance d'achat des métaux précieux dans l'empire byzantin', *Byzantion* I (1924), pp. 108–13.

wealth rather than, through his agency, from official ecclesiastical or state wealth.[145] As a matter of eastern comparison, however, the patrician Sphoracius spent 3 kentenaria or 21,600 nomismata on the building and decoration of the metropolitan church of St Theodore in the fifth century,[146] and the *megas logothetēs* George Acropolites, who spent a sum well in excess of 17,000 hyperpyra on the clearing and restoration of the metropolitan church of the *Anastasis* in the thirteenth century, seems thereby to have seriously overstrained his resources.[147] Building-costs seem, on the face of it, to have been distinctly lower in the west, where the rebuilt cathedral church of Narbonne, possibly not nearly as richly decorated as the others, seems to have cost something – but probably not overmuch – in excess of 2,450 solidi, the bulk being contributed by the praetorian prefect of the Gauls, Marcellus, in 441–5.[148]

Despite these examples, it may strongly be suspected that the norm, both of social status and of scale of operation, is represented by one Flavius Anastasius, another metropolitan *argyropratēs* who, having obtained – presumably purchased – the minor *militia* of attendant at the imperial table (*kastresianos tēs theias trapezēs*), probably for something in the region of 6 lb gold or 432 nomismata, is found lending the sum of 20 nomismata of pure gold and good weight (*ombryza eustathma*) to Flavius Victor and Flavius Apollos, two Egyptian visitors to Constantinople, for four months at the legal rate of 8%, repayable to Thomas, Anastasius' man in the customs depot (*apothēkē*) at Alexandria, in 541.[149]

Later on, in the fifteenth century, Constantinopolitan bankers seem to have operated, singly or in association, in much the same way and on much the same scale as resident Latin ones, and there is just the slightest suggestion that some kind of public bank or exchange, related to the mint, existed. It does seem clear, however, that nothing along the lines of the great Italian banking-houses ever evolved.[150]

145 Agnellus, *Liber Pontificalis Ecclesiae Ravennatis* LVII, LIX, LXIII, LXVII; MGH, *SRLang.*, pp. 318, 322, 330. On Julianus, see: F. W. Deichmann, 'Giuliano Argentario', *Felix Ravenna* 5³ (56) (1951), pp. 5–26. Deichmann insists on Julianus' private status, on not very convincing grounds (*op. cit.* pp. 9–10), and apparently favours an identification with the *Ioulianos u(ir) h(onestus) argentarios* who is known from a Ravennate papyrus of 539–46 (*op. cit.* pp. 10–11; Marini, *I Papyri Diplomatici*, p. 174), at the same time rejecting the word *argentarius* as part of Julianus' name (*op. cit.* p. 9). But it ought to be observed that in none of the inscriptions, and the passages from Agnellus, through which Julianus is known, is he termed either *v.h.*, or *v.c.*, *argentarius*, which would render it certain that this was his profession rather than his name, and that if he really is the Ioulianos of the papyrus, then *vir honestus* is a surprisingly low status for so wealthy and influential a personage (see above, n. 134).

146 Anonymi, *Scriptores Originum Constantinopolitanarum*, *Patria Kōnstantinoupoleōs* III, 30; ed. Preger (Teubner), II, p. 225.

147 H. Delehaye, 'Constantini Acropolitae, hagiographi byzantini, epistularum manipulus', *Analecta Bollandiana* 51 (1933), pp. 279–84.

148 E. Diehl, *Inscriptiones Latinae Christianae Veteres* I, pp. 353–4, no. 1806; *PLRE* II, p. 712 (Marcellus 2).

149 *P. Cairo* 67126. For the probable cost of the *militia*. see above, p. 186 (purchase of the office of *epi tēs trapezēs*). For the *basilikē trapeza*, see, in the last instance: W. Seibt, 'Über das Verhältnis von *kēnarios* bzw. *domestikos tēs trapezēs* zu den anderen Funktionären der *basilikē trapeza* in mittelbyzantinischer Zeit', *Byzantinische Zeitschrift* 72 (1979), pp. 34–8.

150 N. Oikonomides, *Hommes d'affaires grecs et latins à Constantinople (XIIIe–XVe siècles)*, pp. 63–8.

Members of the upper classes are known to have turned their hand to money-lending on occasion, examples being known for both the fourth and the fourteenth centuries, but the available evidence suggests their capital to have originated in land, and money-lending to have been a subsequent venture only.[151] Members of the clergy seem to have done the same in the fifth and twelfth centuries, but there is again no reason to believe their capital to have originated in a fundamentally different way.[152] Honorius, indeed, forbade[153] the nobles (*nobiliores natalibus*), office-holders (*honorum luce conspicui*), and the wealthy by inheritance (*patrimonio ditiores*) to indulge in trade (*mercimonium*), which was harmful to cities and their inhabitants and merchants, as a general principle. Theophilus' indignation[154] at his own wife, the augusta Theodora, having placed him in a position where he might be considered to have been playing the shipowner (*nauklēros*), indulging in trade (i.e. as an *emporos*), is well known. The attitude was clearly deeply ingrained.[155] Great fortunes simply were not made from trade or money-lending as such, and the only plausible exceptions to this general rule were bankers who were also involved in the collection of state taxation, or attached to a great household.[156]

In Constantinople, both *trapezitai* and *argyropratai* were obliged to site their workshops

[151] Fourth century: Liebeschuetz, *Antioch: City and Imperial Administration in the Later Roman Empire*, p. 87. Fourteenth century: Demetrius Cydones, *Ad Ioannem Palaeologum Oratio* XXI; ed. R.-J. Loenertz, p. 21, and Nicholas Cabasilas, *Logos kata Tokizontōn*; ed. J.-P. Migne, in *PG* CL, at cols 733, 741, 745. See also: Ševčenko, 'Society and Intellectual Life in the Fourteenth Century', p. 90.

[152] Fifth century: Sidonius Apollinaris, *Epistulae* I.18; ed. P. Mohr (Teubner), p. 18: *faenerantur clerici... negotiatores militant monachi negotiantur*. The passage forms part of the amusing and obviously exaggerated description of Ravenna (*sitiunt vivi natant sepulti*), but it might help explain Julianus Argentarius (*faenerantur clerici*), and it is certainly borne out by *argentarii* and others such as *monetarii* with official ranks and offices (*negotiatores militant*): see above, pp. 242–3, 244–5; below, pp. 350–1. For a later and eastern banker, who was also a cleric, see: Zacos and Veglery, *Byzantine Lead Seals* I.1, p. 650 no. 962 (*Paulos, diakonos kai argyropratēs*). Twelfth century: Eustathius of Thessalonica, *De Emendanda Vita Monachica* CXXII; ed. G. L. F. Tafel, p. 243. See also: Mango, *Byzantium, the Empire of New Rome*, pp. 119–20. For *zygostatai*/clerics, see below, p. 317 n. 12.

[153] *CJ* IV.63.3 (408/9). The law was taken over into the *Basilika* (LVI.1.21), which talks *tēs olethrias tōn en tais polesin emporeias*.

[154] *Continuation of Theophanes* III.4; Bonn edn, pp. 88–9. Joseph Genesius, *Regum Libri IV* III.20; ed. Lesmueller-Werner and Thurn, p. 53. The episode is slightly differently reported in the two sources, the *Continuation* being the more detailed but perhaps the less informative. It is implied that the ship involved, which Theophilus ordered burned, and which belonged to Theodora, was carrying basic foodstuffs (*sitou ē oinou ē tinos allou tōn kat' oikon analiskomenōn*). The further implication is that the ship having put into the (imperial) port of Boucoleon, the intention was to sell off its cargo having avoided (prefectural) taxation or regulation. The episode thus well illustrates a number of things, of which the most important are the imperial/aristocratic attitude to entrepreneurship, and the insistence upon state control over the economy.

[155] The contrast with the west, or at least with Italy, at this very period, is beautifully illustrated by the will of the doge Giustiniano Partecipazio, of Venice, drawn up in 829, that is during the reign of Michael II and Theophilus himself. There, although much of the doge's fortune is bound up in houses and land, precious metals and spices, and other similar things, much (in the form of *laborantes solidi*) is also invested in commercial ventures overseas. This last would be inconceivable in the case of a member of the Byzantine dominant class (although Partecipazio, as doge, had been granted the imperial dignity of *hypatos*). The will is conveniently translated and commented upon by R. S. Lopez and I. W. Raymond, in *Medieval Trade in the Mediterranean World*, at pp. 38–41.

[156] See above, p. 245, below, pp. 344, 350–1.

in a particular location: the first apparently in the Forum of Constantine; the second in that part of the main street, the *Mesē*, which led from that forum down towards the Great Palace.[157]

According to the *Chronicon Paschale*,[158] the whole portico of the *argyropratai*, the palace of Symmachus the ex-ordinary consul, and the church of St Aquilina, up to the vaults of the other portico of the Forum of Constantine, were burnt down in the Nika Riot of 532.[159] The portico was presumably rebuilt, for *The Book of the Prefect* still required the *argyropratai* to site their workshops in the *Mesē* in the tenth century, and other evidence suggests the same for the eleventh.[160] According to Nicetas Choniates[161] the Selçuk sultan Kılıç-Arslan II was unable to cross the forum without being mocked by the money-changers of the place (i.e. the *argyrokopioi agoraioi*) who rattled the iron parts of their tables (*ta tōn trapezōn...sidēria*) at him when he was on a visit to Manuel I in 1162.

Finally, according to Robert of Clari,[162] one of the marvels of Constantinople was a pair of large seated bronze statues, feminine in form, one of which held out its arm towards the west. These statues were to be found: 'In front of the exchange (*devant le cange*) which used to be very rich there, for the rich money-changers (*cangeeur*) who had before them great piles of bezants and precious stones used to be there before the capture of the City [by the crusaders], but there were not so many of them after its capture.' According to Nicetas Choniates,[163] a statue of Athena which held out its arm towards the west was destroyed by the mob in 1203 because it was thought to be beckoning to the crusaders. The statue was to be found: 'In the Forum of Constantine'.[164] The diminution of activity so insouciantly mentioned by Robert of Clari is scarcely surprising, for even before the final capture of the City in 1204, the Constantinian forum and all that was within it (*hē Konstantineois agora kai ta metaxy panta*) had been devastated by the great fire of August 1203.[165] As late as 1436–9 there seems to have been some building or area formally reserved both for the mint, and an exchange, or bank (*bancho*), although its site remains unknown.[166]

According to *The Book of the Prefect*,[167] metropolitan money-changers and their dependants operating in the open spaces and streets (*en tais plateiais kai rhymais*) outside the permitted area were termed *sakkoularioi* and regarded as illegal in the tenth century.

157 R. Janin, *Constantinople byzantine*, pp. 95, 96 and maps 1, 5.

158 *Chronicon Paschale*; ed. B. G. Niebuhr (Bonn edn), I, p. 623.

159 Cf. Theophanes, *Chronographia*; ed. de Boor, I, p. 184.

160 Tenth century: see below, p. 252. Eleventh century: Vryonis, 'Byzantine *Dēmokratia* and the Guilds in the Eleventh Century', p. 305.

161 Nicetas Choniates, *Historia*; ed. van Dieten, I, p. 120.

162 Robert of Clari, *La conquête de Constantinople* XCI; ed. Lauer, pp. 88–9.

163 Nicetas Choniates, *Historia*; ed. van Dieten, I, pp. 558–9.

164 For the whole episode, see: R. J. H. Jenkins, 'The Bronze Athena at Byzantium', *Journal of Hellenic Studies* 67 (1947), pp. 31–3 (where the reference in Robert of Clari is nevertheless missed).

165 Nicetas Choniates, *Historia*; ed. van Dieten, I, p. 555. For other refs, see: Brand, *Byzantium Confronts the West*, p. 379 n. 34.

166 See below, p. 545.

167 See below, p. 253.

On the other hand, the Venetian quarter of the city, at least, had its own money-changers' tables (*tabulae nummulariorum*) in the twelfth.[168]

In Rome the situation seems to have been much the same: there the *argentarii* are known, from both documentary and physical evidence, to have been concentrated in the Forum and its environs.[169] The state of the city and its *argentarii* eventually became so bad, however, that in 600 pope Gregory I was forced to intervene to prevent John, who owned the last stall (*statio*) there, from going out of business.[170] In Antioch, too, a mention by Malalas of the silversmiths' workshops (*ta argyropratia*), in what appears to be a directionally collective sense, at least suggests the possibility of a similar arrangement there.[171] A similar mention of the same, by Theophanes, tends to confirm the point.[172]

The major item of professional equipment required by the money-changer was still, as it had always been, the table (*mensa, tabula, trapeza*) from which, of course, the profession took its name. Odo of Deuil, a French member of the Second Crusade, writes[173] of the metropolitan money-changers: 'And so we crossed over [the Bosphorus], and food-ships with money-changers (*cambitores*) aboard followed us. And they [the money-changers] spread out their treasures on the shore, their tables (*tabulae*) gleaming with gold and weighed down with silver vessels which they had bought from us.' These tables seem to have been of some particular form: this certainly involved at least iron fittings to them, and an accounting or reckoning design on them, the latter presumably being in some kind of chequerboard or grid pattern.[174]

The ecclesiastical writer John Cassian describes the money-changers (*trapezitae*) as:

> Those whose highest skill and science it is to distinguish which is the purest gold (which is also commonly called *obrizum*), and which has been less refined by the fire; to remain undeceived, through the exercise of a most practised discernment, by the copper and base denarius if it should happen to imitate the precious nomisma under the colour of gleaming gold; to not only recognise, judiciously, the nomismata of tyrants from the portraits they carry, but – with an

168 Tafel and Thomas, *Urkunden* I, p. 111: *loca...octo numulariorum tabule* (near the hospital of St Marcian); *loca tabularum duarum numulariorum* (near the monastery called Mili). The hospital was presumably the *xenōn* or *xenodokheion* of St Irene, founded by Marcian (R. Janin, *La géographie ecclésiastique de l'empire byzantin* I.3, p. 571). The monastery seemingly remains unknown.

169 Pauly-Wissowa, *Real-Encyclopädie* II, cols 706–11, ss.vv. *argentaria basilica* and *argentarii*. For the physical evidence (coins supposedly fused onto the floor by the heat of the fire of 410), see: M. Grant, *The Roman Forum*, p. 144.

170 Gregory I, *Epistulae* XI.16; MGH, *Ep.* II, pp. 277–8.

171 John Malalas, *Chronographia* XVI; Bonn edn, p. 395.

172 Theophanes, *Chronographia*; ed. de Boor, I, p. 150. *Contra* Liebeschuetz, *Antioch: City and Imperial Administration in the Later Roman Empire*, pp. 56–7.

173 Odo of Deuil, *De Profectione Ludovici VII in Orientem* IV; ed. Berry, pp. 72, 74.

174 See above, p. 248 (iron fittings), below, p. 252 (grid pattern: the tables are termed *abakioi*). For a sixth-century miniature representation of a money-changer, his table, and his abacus, see: Patlagean, *Pauvreté économique et pauvreté social à Byzance*, pl. 20 (from the Rossano Gospels). For contemporary balances and weights, see: *op. cit.* pls. 21–3 (although none of these were necessarily used for precious metals). For two undoubted coin- (or precious-metal) weights, see below, Pl. 3.7, *8*.

even greater degree of perception – to discern those which, although stamped with the portrait of a legitimate emperor, were struck unlawfully; and finally, through the decision of the balance (*trutina*), to carefully examine whether any among them are of less than the legitimate weight.

(John Cassian, *Collationes* 1.20; ed. E. Pichery, I, pp. 101–2)

The official regulations governing the appointment and functioning of later metropolitan *trapezitai* and *argyropratai* form two complete chapters of *The Book of the Prefect*, and are treated in an appendix to this chapter.[175]

The implication that one of the functions of money-changers was to withdraw from circulation the nomismata of usurpers is an interesting one in the light of repeated imperial legislation that a nomisma should be considered valid as long as it bore an imperial portrait and was of full weight and metallic quality.[176] As it happens, the portraits of most of the major usurpers of the fourth century, and of at least one of those of the fifth, must have been recognisable with comparative ease: both Eugenius and John, in the west, and Procopius, in the east, wore beards, a feature that they shared with Julian alone amongst the legitimate emperors. Magnentius, too, must have been recognisable without great difficulty: his portrait is almost invariably a bare-headed one – lacking, that is, the diadem of those of other emperors – a feature that it shares, however, with those of caesars. The withdrawal from pre-circulation store, rather than from circulation itself, of what should have been an appreciable issue of metropolitan base-metal coinage in the name of Magnus Maximus has also plausibly been held to account for the rarity of that issue today.[177]

The details of a further, and probably much more significant, mechanism, which the state operated through the money-changers, so as to affect the composition of the circulating medium, are revealed by Symmachus who, as prefect of the City (*sc.* of Rome) in 384–5, addressed a letter to Valentinian II in the following terms:

The guild of money-changers (*corpus collectariorum*) is under an obligation to sell solidi, of which the public service demands great numbers, and the established price (*statutum pretium*) of which the *arca vinaria* furnishes. Upon this class of person the Divine Brother of Your Own Divinity [i.e. Gratian] decided there ought to be conferred, through the fluctuating baseness of a small profit (*taxatio exigua*), as much per solidus as the principles of justice then demanded, my Lords and Emperors. But by degrees the force of this divine solution was broken by the enormously increasing [price of] gold, and since the solidus is [now] reckoned at a higher tariff (*maior summa*) on the open market (*in foro venalium rerum*), lower prices (*pretia minora*) are paid out to the money-changers (*nummularii*). On account of the present reckoning (*ratio praesens*) they, who even now are unequal to the sustaining of such a burden, therefore seek from Your Eternity a just increase in the established price (*definitio*). This is the cause of the complaint, which the reliability of the minutes will make known more fully to Your Divine Perception. If You find this kind

[175] See below, pp. 251–3.

[176] See below, pp. 302–3, 363–6.

[177] R. A. G. Carson, P. V. Hill and J. P. C. Kent, *Late Roman Bronze Coinage, A.D. 324–498*, p. 43.

of petition worthy of approval, I beg that this party too, by a decision of Your Clemency, may be granted a health-giving solution.

(Symmachus, *Relationes* XXIX; MGH, *AA* VI.I, pp. 303–4)

The situation, in brief, seems to have been this. The Roman guild of money-changers was under an obligation to sell such solidi as it acquired from the public to the state. The state paid for them in base-metal coinage from the *arca vinaria* which received such coinage from the sale of artificially cheap wine. The emperor Gratian had regulated part of the process, fixing the price at which the money-changers sold their solidi to the state, and allowing them a small profit on the exchange dependent upon the variable market price at which they acquired the solidi from the public. However, a large rise in the market price of solidi had resulted in a situation whereby, under Valentinian, the state was paying less to the money-changers for solidi than they were paying to acquire the solidi from the public. The loss to the money-changers that this involved could only be remedied by increasing the price the state paid them, and it was precisely this that the petition sought. Valentinian's reply to Symmachus is unknown, but it is difficult to see how it can have been anything other than affirmative.[178]

Once again, what this mechanism involved was a discrimination by the state against its own base-metal coinage in favour of its precious-metal one, and consequently an exaggeratedly high rate for the passage of small change through administrative hands. It bears a close generic relationship to the forced purchase of gold in the fourth century, and to the practices termed *kharagma* and *strophē* which certainly existed in the eleventh century, may have originated at a much earlier period, and in that case presumably derived from the same tradition.[179]

APPENDIX

## THE BOOK OF THE PREFECT II, III (ON BANKING)

### *II. Concerning silversmiths* (*Peri Argyropratōn*; ed. Nicole, pp. 22–4)

(i) We decree that *argyropratai* are permitted, when called upon to do so by anyone, to purchase those things which are appropriate to them: that is, gold, silver, pearls and precious stones (*khryson, argyron, margaritas, lithous timious*). They are not permitted to buy copper (*khalkon*), or articles woven from linen (*ek linōn hyphasmata*), or other kinds of goods (*eidē*) which concern others [i.e. other dealers] rather than they themselves. But if they wish to buy such things for their own domestic need (*pros khreian oikeian*), they are not forbidden to do so by this regulation.

178 *Arca vinaria*: Jones, *Later Roman Empire* II, pp. 691, 704–5.

179 Forced purchase of gold: see below, pp. 285, 457, 465. *Kharagma* and *strophē*: see below, pp. 285–9.

(ii) It does not behove them to under-value articles for sale (i.e. *ta pipraskomena*), or to over-value them, to the injury of those who are selling, but it behoves them to value them according to their just valuation (*kata tēn dikaian autōn apotimisin*). If one of them does act fraudulently (*kata dolon*) in this way, he is to pay his own valuation of the articles to the seller.

(iii) The *argyropratai*, according to an old custom (*kata ton palaion typon*), on days set aside for the market (*en tois tetagmenais hēmerais tou phorou*), are obliged to remain in their own workshops (*en tois ergastērios autōn*), with the *stētores* (= Lat. *statores*), that is the guardians of their reckoning-tables (*ēgoun ephestridōn tois abakiois autōn*), and with nomismata and miliaresia set out before them, so that if any article appropriate to an *argyropratēs* (*argyropratikon eidos*) is to be sold off, they can buy it up.

(iv) If anyone amongst the *argyropratai* discovers that a female citizen (*p*[*r*]*atria*) is offering for sale goods in gold or silver, pearls or precious stones (*eidē khrysa ē argyra*...*eite margaritas ē lithous timious*), he is obliged to warn the prefect [*sc.* of the City] of the fact, so that they shall not be exported to the foreign nations (*ina mē tois ethnesi parapempōntai*).

(v) He who commits a fraud with [*sc.* adulterates] bullion (*eis asēmion*), and who works it up and sells it (*ex autou ergazomenos kai pipraskōn*), shall have his hand cut off.

(vi) If anyone from outside (*ton exōthen*) [*sc.* a non-resident] should come for the sale of gold or silver, whether worked or unworked (*eirgasmenon eite anergaston*), he is to be examined as to whence he derived it, and is to be drawn to the attention of the president [*sc.* of the guild], so that thefts (*ta kloipimaia*) can be detected.

(vii) Whichsoever *argyropratēs* is detected purchasing a sacred vessel (*hieron*), whether in pieces or whether intact, and without displaying it to the prefect, shall be rendered liable to confiscation, along with its seller.

(viii) We decree it forbidden for a goldsmith (*khrysokhoos*), whether slave or free (*doulos ē eleutheros*), to purchase more than a single pound of bullion, whether unworked or worked, for the purpose of working it up (*eis ergasian*).

(ix) If anyone buys more than a pound of bullion for the purpose of working it up, and does not instantly warn the president of the goldsmiths of the fact, then if a slave he is liable to confiscation, if free he is to be subjected to a flogging and the fine (*zēmia*) of a pound [*sc.* of gold].

(x) A slave intending to set up a silversmith's workshop (*ergastērion argyropratikon*) shall be under the guarantee of his own master (*oikeois despotēs*), who must be [sufficiently] prosperous (*euporos*); if a free person is involved, he shall be under the guarantee of five persons (*prosōpa*), naturally placed under the same caution as he whom they have put forward.

(xi) We decree it forbidden for a goldsmith to have the right to work gold and silver in his own household (*oikos*), [and anywhere] but in the workshops of [the street called] the *Mesē*; nor is anyone to be put forward as a goldsmith without the knowledge of the prefect.

(xii) The silversmiths ought not to absent themselves for the purpose of making a valuation without the knowledge of the prefect, nor are those making a valuation to engage in quarrels with one another; if any of them are detected engaged in such practices they shall be flogged, shaved and removed from the list of members (*tou katalogou*).

### *III. Concerning money-changers* (*Peri Trapezitōn*; ed. Nicole, pp. 25–8)

(i) The person intending to be put forward as a *trapezitēs* must be guaranteed by worthy and experienced men (*par' entimōn kai khrēsimōn andrōn*) who will testify that he will not act contrary to the regulations (i.e. *para ta diatetagmena*); that is, that he will not file (*xeein*), or clip down (*temnein*), or counterfeit (*parakharattein*), nomismata or miliaresia; that he will not permit a personal slave (*doulon idion*) to stand in for him at his table (*en tē trapezē*) for the purpose of business (*tēn pragmateian*) if, by chance, he should be engaged by reason of some obligatory services (*douleiai*), lest matters pertaining to the profession (*tekhnē*) should be harmed by him [i.e. the slave]. If anyone is found acting in such a way, he shall be liable to the punishment of the cutting off of a hand.

(ii) The money-changers (*katallaktai*) ought to warn the prefect of the *sakkoularioi* [i.e. illegal money-changers] standing in the open spaces and streets (*en tais plateiais kai rhymais*), lest anything inequitable (i.e. *para to eikos*) be done by them. If any of them knowingly fail to give warning, they shall lay themselves open to the said punishment.

(iii) The money-changers should not distinguish against (i.e. *mē diairheitōsan*) the unadulterated and not illegally struck miliaresion having the imperial stamp (*to miliarision to akibdēlon ton basilikon ekhon kharaktēra kai mē parakekommenon*), but should accept equally for each one twenty-four *oboloi* [*sc.* folleis]; that holding any other status (i.e. *to de allōs pōs ekhon*) should be valued according to its quality (*kata tēn toutou...poiotēta*). Those not doing this are to be flogged, shaved and rendered liable to confiscation.

(iv) Each of the *trapezitai* ought to possess two servants (*hypēretoumenoi*) for the accumulation of coins (*eis tēn episōrheusin tōn noumiōn*), and guaranteed by him, so that if either of them is detected acting contrary to the regulations he, the guarantor (*prostēsamenos*), is rendered liable to the aforesaid punishments along with them.

(v) The money-changer who receives an illegally struck ([*para*]*kekommenon*) nomisma or miliaresion without warning the prefect of the fact and of its possessor shall be flogged, shaved and exiled.

(vi) The *trapezitai* ought not to give their dependents cash, that is coin (*logarion eite noumion*), so that they can stand in open spaces and streets and make a profit (*kerdos*) out of it [*sc.* act as *sakkoularioi*]; nor ought they to absent themselves for the purpose of duty (*khorēgia*), whether an imperial obligatory service or a money-changing one (*eite basilikēs douleias ean tas trapezas*). If any of them are detected doing such things they shall be flogged, shaved, and rendered liable to confiscation.

SECTION III

# COINAGE (CIRCULATION)

# CHAPTER 5

# SUPPLY

## (I) CONTROL OF OUTWARD FLOWS

### *A. The legislation*

Monetarily speaking, the late Roman and – for much of its history at least – the Byzantine empire effectively operated a closed economy. For gold certainly, and silver very probably, this was a matter of law. For copper it seems to have been a matter of practice: because coinage in that metal was almost uniformly of a fiduciary nature, it was normally pointless to export it beyond the imperial frontiers, where its value dropped immediately to that of its bullion content.

The first known step towards the formal establishment of a closed economy of this kind is to be found in a law preserved in the *Codex Justinianus*:[1]

The same Augusti [Valentinian I and Valens], and Gratian Augustus, to Tatianus, *Comes Sacrarum Largitionum*

> Not only shall gold not be supplied to the barbarians, but even if it is found amongst them it shall be removed by means of subtle ingenuity (*subtili ingenio*). If, henceforth, gold is supplied by merchants (*mercatores*) to the barbarians, either for sale (*pro mancipiis*) or in exchange for whatever kind of commodities (*species*), they shall suffer not just a fine but an even heavier punishment. And if a governor (*iudex*) does not confiscate such gold as is found, he is immediately party to the concealment of a criminal act.

The law is certainly an eastern one, for (Flavius Eutolmius) Tatianus is known to have been *comes sacrarum largitionum* in the east in 374–80,[2] and it should therefore be dated 374–5. Its provisions were repeated in the *Basilika* of Leo VI[3] and, although this may not be considered as providing reliable evidence for their actual application in the tenth century, their appearance in the contemporary *The Book of the Prefect*[4] does, nevertheless, provide such evidence:

[1] *CJ* IV.63.2.

[2] *PLRE* I, pp. 876–8 (Tatianus 5).

[3] Leo VI, *Basilika* LVI.1.20.

[4] 'Leo VI', *To Eparkhikon Biblion* II.4; see also above, p. 252.

If anyone amongst the *argyropratai* discovers that a female citizen is offering for sale goods in gold or silver, jewels or precious stones, he is obliged to warn the prefect [*sc.* of the City] of the fact, so that they shall not be exported to the foreign nations.

*The Book of the Prefect* as a body of regulations for the metropolitan guilds seems to have had some application as late as the mid twelfth century.[5]

An apparent exception to these provisions is that the Byzantine authorities should collect the *kommerkion* on gold, silver, brocade, unworked silk, precious stones, jewels, pearls and fine (worked) silk being exported from the empire into the Hamdanid emirate of Aleppo. The Muslim authorities collected that on other forms of merchandise. But the treaty of 969, of which this is a clause, marked the virtual incorporation by the empire of that state into its own territory (it had, for example, to pay a capitation tax of 1 dinar, a clear sign of abandoned sovereignty), and the situation cannot therefore be considered to have been normal.[6]

Certainly, the experience of Liutprand of Cremona who, in 968, and despite his status as an ambassador, was deprived of the most precious purple cloths (*pretiosissimae purpurae*) that he had bought in Constantinople, by vindictive officials of Nicephorus II, because no imperial permission (*imperatorius sermo/imperialis promissio*) had been given for the export of the cloaks (*pallia*) involved, because they were forbidden goods (*prohibita/kōlyomena*), and were certainly not sealed with lead (*plumbo signata*), suggests that normally care was taken to enforce restrictive provisions.[7] Liutprand's use of the term *kōlyomena* for such restricted goods in this, one of the more spectacularly vituperative passages in his account, merely confirms its authenticity, for the term is a technical one and, in the form *kekōlymena*, is frequently used as such when dealing with restricted silks and dyes in the appropriate sections of *The Book of the Prefect*.[8]

Occasionally, an example of what seems to be the application of such provisions, or at least of the attitude that led to their promulgation, is met with. According to Procopius,[9] Justinian forbade the ransoming of a certain John, son of Basilius, of Edessa by his grandmother for 2,000 lb silver (approximately 10,500 nomismata at a gold:silver ratio of 1:14.4): 'So that the wealth of the Romans (*ho Rhomaiōn ploutos*) should not be exported to the barbarians [i.e. the Persians]'. According to Nicetas Choniates,[10]

[5] Manuel I, Novel LV (1148); Zepoi, in *Ius Graeco-Romanum* I, at p. 375. *Contra* the implications of E. Frances, 'La disparition des corporations byzantines', in *Actes du XII^e Congrès International d'Études Byzantines, Ochrid 10–16 septembre 1961* II, at pp. 93–101. The article is even more badly than usual vitiated by modern political/intellectual considerations. See also below, pp. 584–5.

[6] M. Canard, *Histoire de la dynastie des H'amdanides de Jazīra et de Syrie*, pp. 833, 835.

[7] Liutprand of Cremona, *Legatio Constantinopolitana* LIIII–LVI; ed. I. Bekker, pp. 204–6.

[8] 'Leo VI', *To Eparkhikon Biblion* IV, VI, VIII; ed. Nicole, pp. 26–38.

[9] Procopius, *Historia Arcana* XII.8–9; ed. Haury (Teubner), III, p. 78.

[10] Nicetas Choniates, *Historia*; ed. van Dieten, I, p. 533. The sum involved was apparently considered moderate, as Alexius had meanwhile confiscated far more of Manuel's property, consisting of silver and

Alexius III effectively refused the ransoming of Manuel Camytzes the *prōtostratōr* from the Bulgarians for two kentenaria (i.e. 14,400 hyperpyra), but this was probably for personal reasons.

The confidence towards foreign nations engendered by these provisions is perhaps best seen in the well-known remark made by one of the officials of Nicephorus II to Liutprand of Cremona: 'With the money in which we are strong we shall summon all nations against you and break you like a clay pot which, once broken, cannot be put together.' Later, Psellus was to remark that the two main factors preserving Roman rule (*hēgemonia*) were the system of dignities, and wealth (*axiōmatōn phēmi kai khrēmatōn*), adding that judiciousness in their distribution formed a third.[11]

The first known major breach – but still a partial one only – of this formal tradition is to be found in a clause of the Treaty of Nymphaeum,[12] signed between Michael VIII and the Genoese in 1261:

> Also that every merchant of Genoa and its district shall have the freedom to produce, work on and export, from any part of Our empire, any kind of merchandise, with the exception of gold and silver – unless it be according to Our imperial will. They shall, however, be free to export and carry away gold yperperi and Turchiferi [presumably Tartar or Selçuk dinars or dirhems] at their own will.

The precise significance of the distinction made between the export of uncoined and coined precious metal remains obscure. It may be suspected, however, that the state by this stage at least was charging a fee of some kind for minting, and that it was therefore merely protecting a source of revenue. Pegolotti fails to mention such a charge in the Constantinopolitan section of his *Pratica della Mercatura*,[13] but this omission should not be regarded as conclusive evidence against its existence, for his information on the subject seems unsystematic in other cases. Certainly, the (presumably imperial) gold-foundry (*khrysepsēteion*), which seems to have been closely connected to or identical with the mint, existed, and was at least thought capable of drawing a revenue (*eisodon*) from its activities, at the time of the Latin empire, for Michael VIII demanded half of that revenue, albeit in a not entirely serious context. Again, the fourteenth-century mathematical writer, Nicholas Rhabdas, includes an hypothetical problem involving someone who possesses two lots of *exagia* (i.e. hyperpyra) of different purities (21 and 15 carats), and who wishes to have them worked up into *exagia* of an alloy of 18 carats (i.e. *tēn tou kramatos kataskeuēn*

gold plate, silken woven stuffs and precious garments (*tōn argyreōn kai khryseōn skeuōn tōn sērikōn te nēmatōn kai tōn periphanōn esthēmatōn*).

11 Liutprand of Cremona, *Legatio Constantinopolitana* LIII; ed. Bekker, p. 204. Michael Psellus, *Chronographia* VI.29; ed. Renauld, I, p. 132.

12 Zepoi, *Ius Graeco-Romanum* I, at p. 494.

13 Pegolotti, *La Pratica della Mercatura*; ed. Evans, pp. 32–54.

*tōn ana 18 kokkiōn to exagion* . . .), by the imperial gold-workshop (*to basilikon khrysourgion*). Assuming that anything like this kind of operation was indeed then quite feasible, as very much earlier it had been, a fee would undoubtedly have been charged.[14]

The operation of the imperial mint on a private basis, as suggested by these two pieces of evidence, is possibly to be seen in its products, the coins themselves, not only in the cases of thirteenth-century Magnesia and Thessalonica, but even in that of twelfth-century Constantinople. The practice was possibly even earlier in origin, and it also seems possible that it is to be traced on into the fifteenth century.[15]

## B. *The exceptions* (c. *400–600*)

It is quite clear that the state never intended itself to be bound by these laws and regulations and that, as the clause of the Treaty of Nymphaeum quoted above implies, it could waive their application to private individuals at will. The ransoming of prisoners of war was, for instance, one occasion upon which they were customarily so waived: then, even the alienation of ecclesiastical property was both permitted and, as in the case of a bishop of Sirmium, anticipated.[16] Some of these ransoms, whether individual or collective, could be large. Anastasius seems to have paid a total of 2,000 lb gold to procure peace and to ransom his nephew Hypatius from the rebel Vitalian and his Hunnic mercenaries in 515, the high price presumably reflecting Hypatius' status, and Justinian is said to have paid 10,000 nomismata to ransom the general Constantiolus from the Bulgars, in 529.[17]

According to Marcellinus Comes, Anastasius sent 1,000 lb gold, via the praetorian prefect of Illyricum, to ransom prisoners taken by the Getae in 517.[18] According to Procopius, Hierapolis paid 2,000 lb in silver to buy off Chosroes I in 540. Berrhoea

[14] George Acropolites, *Historia* LXXVIII; ed. Heisenberg and Wirth, p. 163. P. Tannery, 'Notice sur les deux lettres arithmétiques de Nicolas Rhabdas (texte grec et traduction)', in *Mémoires Scientifiques* IV, *Sciences exactes chez les byzantins*, at p. 154. Earlier example: see below, pp. 389–90. Contemporary (non-imperial) example: see below, pp. 547–8.

[15] Hendy *DOC* IV. For the fifteenth century: S. Bendall, work in progress on a hoard from Çorlu (Tzurulum), consisting mainly of silver of John VIII and Manuel II.

[16] E.g. *CJ* I.2.21 (529): *Nam si necessitas fuerit in redemptione captivorum, tunc et venditionem praefatarum rerum divinarum et hypothecam et pignorationem fieri concedimus, cum non absurdum est animas hominum quibuscumque causis vel vestimentis praeferri.* Cf. Justinian, Novels VII.8 (535), LXV.1 (538), CXX.10 (544). These clauses obviously merely codified current practice. The case of the bishop of Sirmium who, fearing capture by the Huns, handed over the golden dishes (*phialai khrysai*) of his see to someone whom he hoped, falsely, would use them for his own (or, secondly, his citizens') redemption, is a well-known one. Priscus, *Fragmenta* VIII; ed. Müller, IV, at pp. 84–5. See also: P. Grierson, 'Commerce in the Dark Ages: A Critique of the Evidence', *Transactions of the Royal Historical Society* $9^5$ (1959), p. 135.

[17] Hypatius: Marcellinus Comes, *Chronicon*, s.a. 515; MGH, *AA* XI, p. 99. Constantiolus: John Malalas, *Chronographia* XVIII; Bonn edn, p. 438 (*nomismata myria*). Theophanes, *Chronographia*; ed. de Boor, I, p. 218 (*khilia nomismata*). It is difficult to see how this discrepancy arose, assuming it not to be quite fortuitous, but clearly Malalas is to be preferred: 10,000 solidi for a senior general would have been respectable, 1,000 an insult.

[18] Marcellinus Comes, *Chronicon*, s.a. 517; MGH, *AA* XI, p. 100.

(assessed at 4,000 lb in silver) paid 2,000 lb but was sacked in any case. Apamaea paid 1,000 lb in silver and so did Dara. Antioch, assessed at ten kentenaria in gold in the course of the same campaign, was sacked instead. Chalcis paid two kentenaria in gold, and so did Edessa.[19] Candidus, bishop of Sergiopolis, was able to ransom 12,000 citizens of Sura for two kentenaria in gold,[20] and a citizen of Edessa would have been able to ransom her grandson for 2,000 lb in silver had not the emperor forbidden it.[21]

The state was itself, however, and admittedly of necessity, also prepared to pay out large sums to foreign nations. In *c.* 422 the eastern government agreed to pay the Huns an annual subsidy of 350 lb gold; in *c.* 437 this was increased to 700 lb and in *c.* 447 to 2,100 lb. On the last of these occasions it also agreed to pay a block sum of 6,000 lb, partly in settlement of arrears.[22] In 473 it agreed to pay the Goths an annual subsidy of 2,000 lb gold.[23]

Meanwhile, in 408, the western government had agreed to pay the Visigoths a subsidy of 4000 lb gold,[24] and in 409 the Roman senate had agreed to pay them 5,000 lb gold and 30,000 lb silver, as well as 4,000 silk tunics (*sērikoi khitōnes*), 3,000 scarlet-dyed skins (*kokkobaphē dermata*), and 3,000 lb pepper (*peperi*). In order to raise the latter sum, it was found necessary to strip off the ornaments (*kosmoi*) adorning certain statues (*agalmata*), and even to melt down certain gold and silver statues, including that of *Virtus*.[25] At much the same time a certain Marinianus was forced to ransom his son Maximilianus for 30,000 solidi.[26]

In 532 the government agreed to pay the Persians a subsidy of 11,000 lb gold;[27] in 545 it agreed to pay them 20 kentenaria;[28] and, in 551, 26 kentenaria.[29] In 561 it agreed

[19] Procopius, *De Bello Persico* II.6.24; ed. Haury (Teubner), I, p. 177 (Hierapolis). *Op. cit.* II.7.5–6; *ed. cit.* p. 178 (Berrhoea). *Op. cit.* II.11.3; *ed. cit.* p. 198 (Apamaea). *Op. cit.* II.14.28; *ed. cit.* p. 213 (Dara). *Op. cit.* II.8.4; *ed. cit.* p. 184 (Antioch). *Op. cit.* II.12.2; *ed. cit.* p. 204 (Chalcis). *Op. cit.* II.12.34; *ed. cit.* p. 209 (Edessa).

[20] Procopius, *De Bello Persico* II.5.29; ed. Haury (Teubner), I, p. 172. The rate, just over a solidus per head, seems to have been about average where large numbers were concerned, although considerably lower ones are known (Maurice negotiated with the Avars for the redemption of over 12,000 soldiers, at about 4 keratia per head), and so are much higher ones: Grierson, 'Commerce in the Dark Ages', pp. 134–5, and p. 135 n. 1; see also below, n. 22.

[21] See above, p. 258.

[22] Priscus, *Fragmenta* I, V; ed. Müller, IV, pp. 72, 74. On the chronology, see now: B. Croke, 'Anatolius and Nomus: Envoys to Attila', *Byzantinoslavica* 42 (1981), pp. 159–70. The going rate for ordinary and individual Roman captives at this stage seems to have been 8 (p. 72) or 12 (p. 74) solidi, which is high and presumably punitive (see above, n. 20).

[23] Malchus, *Fragmenta* II; ed. K. Müller, IV, p. 114.

[24] Zosimus, *Historia Nova* V.29. 9; ed. L. Mendelssohn (Teubner), p. 254.

[25] *Ibid.* V.41.4–7; ed. Mendelssohn (Teubner), pp. 270–1.

[26] *Ibid.* V.45.4; ed. Mendelssohn (Teubner), pp. 274–5. *PLRE* I, pp. 559–60 (Marinianus 2), II, p. 741 (Maximilianus 3). The relationship is a putative one only.

[27] Procopius, *De Bello Persico* I.22.3; ed. Haury (Teubner), I, p. 115.

[28] *Ibid.* II.28.10; ed. Haury (Teubner), I, p. 283.

[29] Procopius, *De Bello Gothico* IV.15.3–4; ed. Haury (Teubner), II, p. 566.

to pay 30,000 solidi annually, the first seven instalments to be paid in a block sum that would therefore have amounted to almost 3,000 lb gold.[30] In 574 it agreed to pay 45,000 solidi, and, in 575, 30,000 solidi annually for three years.[31]

In *c.* 574 the government had also agreed to pay the Avars an annual subsidy of 80,000 solidi;[32] in 584 this was increased to 100,000 solidi; and in 599 to 120,000 solidi.[33]

Early in the reign of Tiberius II (probably in 579 or 580) the government had returned 30 kentenaria to Italy, instructing that it should be used either to hire Lombards for service in the east or to bribe the Franks to attack the Lombards.[34] Early in the reign of Maurice (probably in 584) the Franks duly received a bribe of 50,000 solidi to attack the Lombards.[35] In 605, on the other hand, the government agreed to pay subsidies to the Lombards themselves to procure peace: on this occasion the sum agreed was the relatively minor one of 12,000 solidi,[36] but in 616/19 it agreed to pay 5 kentenaria annually and, in 631/2, 3 kentenaria annually.[37]

These examples form only a sample of the total number of occasions on which the late Roman government showed itself prepared to pay out large sums to foreign nations: others could be found without difficulty. Not all the money involved will actually have been paid, or, if paid, will have left the empire, but a high proportion of it will have done so, and doubtless will have left its mark in the form of the solidi that now come to light in the appropriate areas. A series of solidi that is now found mainly in the Baltic islands of Scandinavia has been convincingly connected with the wandering career of the Ostrogoths, from their first subsidised settlement in Pannonia under Marcian to the destruction of their Italian kingdom under Justinian, with which career the series is chronologically virtually coterminous and to which, by geographical origin, it is virtually identical.[38] It seems reasonable to suppose the existence of a similar connection in the case of many of the solidi, frequently light-weight ones, that are now found in western Europe, particularly in the region of the Rhine, and in Russia, particularly in the region of the Dnieper.[39] The Franks, Lombards and Avars are obvious candidates for such a connection.

Trade has been put forward as an explanation for the existence of both the Scandinavian and the western European series; but the evidence – including on the one hand the known

[30] Menander Protector, *Fragmenta* XI; ed. K. Müller, IV, pp. 208–9.

[31] *Ibid.* XXXVIII, XXXIX; ed. Müller, IV, pp. 240, 241.

[32] *Ibid.* XLVIII, LXIII; ed. Müller, IV, pp. 252–3, 263–4.

[33] Theophylact Simocatta, *Historiae* I.3.7 (80,000), 13 (80,000 + 20,000), VII.15.14 (100,000 + 20,000); ed. de Boor, pp. 45, 46, 273. The steps seem regular at 20,000 solidi.

[34] See below, pp. 407–9.

[35] Gregory of Tours, *Historia Francorum* VI.42; MGH, *SRMerov.* I, p. 314.

[36] Paul the Deacon, *Historia Langobardorum* IV.32; MGH, *SRLang.*, p. 127.

[37] Anonymous, *Continuatio Havniensis Prosperi*; MGH, *AA* IX, p. 339. Fredegar, *Chronicarum Libri IV* IV.69; MGH, *SRMerov.* II, p. 155.

[38] J. M. Fagerlie, *Late Roman and Byzantine Solidi found in Sweden and Denmark*, pp. 163–74.

[39] H. L. Adelson, *Light Weight Solidi and Byzantine Trade during the Sixth and Seventh Centuries*, pp. 78–103.

strict control of trans-frontier trade in general and the absolute legal barrier to trade of this kind involving gold, and on the other the frequency and size of the official political payments of whatever kind, the gifts, and the ransoms, and so on, that are known to have crossed the frontier – favours the proposition that it was not trade but these other factors that brought the two series into existence.[40]

It is a well-known fact that late Roman medallions in precious metals are now found more frequently in areas that were then contiguous to, or even well outside, the imperial frontiers than in those that were then inside them, and it has therefore long been accepted that many of them must originally have formed part of imperial political payments or gifts to barbarians.[41] The connection is formally established by a passage in Gregory of Tours' *Historia Francorum*.[42] According to Gregory, in 581 the ambassadors that king Chilperic had sent to the emperor Tiberius II three years before (presumably on the latter's accession) returned, not without great loss and difficulty. They brought with them imperial gifts, some of the more spectacular of which Chilperic evidently showed off to Gregory:

> He showed me the gold coins which the emperor had sent, each of which weighed one pound and had on one side a portrait depicting the emperor, and an inscription in a circle: TIBERII CONSTANTINI PERPETUI AUGUSTI, and on the other side a quadriga containing a passenger, and the inscription: GLORIA ROMANORUM. (Pls. 1–3)

As it happens, no medallions of this emperor and weight survive, but medallions of Tiberius' successor Maurice, probably originally weighing one ounce, do. The reverse design of these is indeed a quadriga containing a figure of the emperor. (Pl. 2, 8)[43]

In attempting to assess the effect of these payments on imperial finances, and on the supply of precious metals available to the empire, a sense of proportion should be preserved. Until the last quarter of the sixth century the eastern government had rarely been faced with more than one major and actively hostile enemy at a time, for any length of time: it was from that date only that it found itself obliged to make frequent and often annual payments to more than one. It is very much at this period that the first unmistakable signs of financial strain occur: the reign of Maurice in particular was marked by persistent attempts at serious military economies, and it was indeed these that caused the emperor's downfall.[44]

Theodosius II seems to have had no great difficulty in raising the sums required for the heaviest payments to the Huns[45] and, at the same time, playing what was no doubt

[40] Grierson, 'Commerce in the Dark Ages', pp. 123–40.

[41] E. Babelon, 'La trouvaille de Helleville (Manche) en 1780', *Revue Numismatique* 10[4] (1906), pp. 185–9.

[42] Gregory of Tours, *Historia Francorum* VI.2; MGH, *SRMerov*. I, pp. 266–7.

[43] Bellinger, *DOC* I, p. 294 (Medallion, 6 Solidi).

[44] Jones, *Later Roman Empire* I, pp. 314–15.

[45] *Ibid*. pp. 206–7.

the major rôle in accumulating a reserve of over 100,000 lb gold.[46] None of these payments is, in any case, to be compared with the minimum estimate for the cost of the Vandal expedition of 468;[47] none is to be compared with the minimum estimate for the total imperial budget;[48] and few are even to be compared with the yield of one of the budget's constituent taxes.[49] It seems far more likely that such payments normally had a far greater positive effect upon the disintegrating finances of the barbarian kingdoms,[50] or upon the rudimentary finances of the nomadic or semi-nomadic tribes, than they had a negative one upon the relatively sound finances of the eastern Roman state.

By the same token, it seems unlikely that they had any serious or prolonged effect on the supply of precious metals available to the empire. The longest lived of the annual subsidies mentioned above were those of the Huns, which was first agreed to in *c.* 442 and was discontinued in 450, and to the Avars, which first assumed serious proportions in *c.* 574 and was apparently still being paid in 617, although it presumably ceased after their defeat in 626.[51] Subsidies to the Persians, which first assumed serious proportions in 532 but which tended to be spasmodic if relatively frequent, ceased to be necessary after 591. Those to the Lombards never assumed the proportions of those paid out to more immediately dangerous enemies. It should also not be forgotten that, throughout the period in question, and despite the trans-frontier payments that it was itself making, the state continued to operate its policy of prohibiting the private export of precious metals while encouraging their import. Quite a high proportion of what had been exported officially will thus very probably have been re-imported privately, in return for other luxury or manufactured goods.

## C. *The exceptions* (c. *600–1450*)

The payment of subsidies by the state to foreign nations was, obviously, not a phenomenon confined to the late Roman and early Byzantine period. During the seventh century, the Persians were replaced by the Arabs as the main recipients of such subsidies in the east, while the Avars were replaced by the Bulgars in the west. In 781, the Byzantine government agreed to pay the Arabs a subsidy of 70,000 nomismata annually, or twice annually, for three years and, in 806, one of 30,000 or 50,000

[46] See above, p. 224.
[47] See above, p. 221.
[48] See above, pp. 164–71.
[49] The *aērikon*: see above, pp. 237–8.
[50] See, for example: J. P. C. Kent, 'Gold Standards of the Merovingian Coinage, A.D. 580–700', in E. T. Hall and D. M. Metcalf (ed.), *Methods of Chemical and Metallurgical Investigation of Ancient Coinage*, at pp. 72–3 (a sharp increase in the fineness of the Merovingian gold coinage under Dagobert I is here equated with the acquisition of some 200,000 Visigothic solidi in *c.* 631).
[51] Theophanes, *Chronographia*; ed. de Boor, I, pp. 301–2.

nomismata, annually.[52] In *c.* 924, it agreed to pay the western Arabs a subsidy of 22,000 nomismata annually, a sum soon afterwards reduced to 11,000 nomismata.[53]

Reliable figures for subsidies to the Bulgars are lacking, but during certain reigns – such as those of Constantine IV, Constantine VI and his several successors, Leo VI, and the early part at least of that of Constantine VII – they must have represented considerable sums. As late as 966, the government subsidised the Russians to the tune of 15 kentenaria gold on condition that they attacked the Bulgarians.[54]

In 1083, the Byzantine government agreed to pay a subsidy of 144,000 nomismata 'in worked silver and Romanata of the old quality (*dia te eirgasmenou argyrou kai Rhōmanatou palaias poiotētos*)', with the promise of more, to Henry IV of Germany in order to secure his help against the Sicilian Normans. Payment of the subsidy may well have had an appreciable effect on the designs of the contemporary German coinage.[55] In 1170, it seems to have offered to pay 56,000 hyperpyra to the Genoese to procure an alliance against Frederick I, although the Genoese later claimed actually to have refused 28,000 only.[56] In 1176, it seems to have agreed to pay 100,000 hyperpyra and as many silver pieces (presumably electrum trachea), a total of somewhat under 135,000 hyperpyra at the then current rate of exchange, to procure peace after the battle of Myriocephalum.[57] In 1189/90, it sent 4 kentenaria in silver pieces (presumably electrum trachea), or somewhat under 10,000 hyperpyra at the then current rate of exchange, to Frederick I of Germany to buy off that emperor's hostility as he passed through the Balkans on crusade.[58] In 1196, it agreed to pay Henry VI of Germany and Sicily 16 kentenaria although, as it happened, not more than a portion of the sum was collected, and none needed to be despatched.[59] In 1203, after the flight of Alexius III with the contents of the palace and part of the regalia,[60] and on the very eve of the conquest of the City by the Fourth Crusade, the government was able – by resorting to desperate measures – to

[52] F. Dölger, *Regesten der Kaiserurkunden des oströmischen Reiches von 565–1453* I.1, pp. 41, 45. M. A. Shaban, *Islamic History, a New Interpretation* II (*A.D.750–1055*), p. 25.

[53] George Cedrenus, *Historiarum Compendium*; Bonn edn, II, pp. 355, 357. For another subsidy to the western Arabs in *c.* 957/8, see: S. M. Stern, 'An Embassy of the Byzantine Emperor to the Fatimid Caliph Al-Mu'izz', *Byzantion* 20 (1950), pp. 239–58. The description of the gifts which accompanied the subsidy (gold and silver vessels inlaid with jewels, embroidery, silk, nard, and so on) conforms closely to the norm for such occasions (see below, pp. 268–71).

[54] Leo the Deacon, *Historiae* IV.6; Bonn edn, p. 63.

[55] Anna Comnena, *Alexiad* III.10.4; ed. Leib, I, p. 134. W. R. O. Hahn, 'Regensburger Denare mit dem Bildniss Kaiser Heinrich IV. im byzantinischen Stil als Schlussmünzen in nordischen Schatzfunden', in R. Zeitler (ed.), *Les pays du nord et Byzance (Scandinavie et Byzance), Actes du colloque nordique et internationale de byzantinologie tenu à Upsal 20–22 avril 1979*, at pp. 117–24.

[56] Obert, *Oberti Cancellarii Annales, a. 1164–1173*, ss.aa. 1170, 1172; MGH, *SS* XVIII, pp. 86, 91.

[57] Refs: Vryonis, *The Decline of Medieval Hellenism in Asia Minor*, p. 125, n. 234.

[58] Nicetas Choniates, *Historia*; ed. van Dieten, I, p. 411. The cash was accompanied by precious gold-woven stuffs (*periphanē nēmata khrysoüphē*).

[59] See above, p. 238 (the *alamanikon*).

[60] See above, p. 225.

pay the crusaders the equivalent of 100,000 marks in silver, half of what was owed and probably amounting to some 500,000 hyperpyra.[61]

The first two reigns of the restored empire witnessed considerable payments to foreign powers. Michael VIII, whose payments to westerners are remarked upon by Pachymeres, may well have despatched at least 30,000 ounces or 180,000 hyperpyra to the Hohenstaufen in Aragon in order to encourage their intervention against the Angevins in Sicily in *c.* 1279/80, and Andronicus II is known to have despatched sums that were certainly well in excess of 10,000 hyperpyra to Italy in order to encourage various diplomatic schemes, and in particular to provide for his son Theodore, the marquess of Montferrat, in 1318.[62]

During the fourteenth century, the most regular recipients of such subsidies were the Venetians. Between 1342/3 and 1423/4 the imperial government repeatedly committed itself to paying them sums ranging from 40,000 ducats downwards, in response to demands made under the pretext of the repayment of loans, damages, or services. Many of these sums could not be, or were not, paid, but some undoubtedly were, whether in part or in entirety.[63]

Subsequently, and finally, the Venetians were replaced by the Ottoman Turks. This process began as early as 1333, when the imperial government agreed to pay the latter 120,000 hyperpyra annually to retain the remaining imperial possessions in Mesothynia, between Nicomedia and the capital.[64] In 1379 and 1424, the government agreed to pay them annual subsidies of 30,000 *khrysinoi* (possibly hyperpyra but more probably ducats), and 300,000 aspra (silver), respectively. These last two sums are very approximate equivalents.[65]

Mercenaries, too, continued to be paid: perhaps not on the scale of the federate tribes of the earlier period, but certainly and similarly on one that was sufficient to attract notice or leave traces in those areas in which the mercenaries involved had originated, and to which they often eventually returned with their accumulated wealth. A whole series of Danish silver pennies with designs imitating those of eleventh-century Byzantine gold nomismata and silver miliaresia has been closely connected with the return of Harold

[61] Refs: Brand, *Byzantium Confronts the West, 1180–1204*, pp. 245–6, 378 n. 29. See also above, p. 231 (Alexius IV).

[62] Michael VIII: refs in S. Runciman, *The Sicilian Vespers*, pp. 206–8, 317. Andronicus II: refs in Laiou (-Thomadakis), *Constantinople and the Latins*, pp. 265–6.

[63] P. Wirth, 'Das Ende der römisch-byzantinischen Goldwährung', *Jahrbuch für Numismatik und Geldgeschichte* 25 (1975), pp. 113–22.

[64] R.-J. Loenertz, 'La chronique brève de 1352, texte, traduction et commentaire, deuxième partie: de 1328 à 1341', *Orientalia Christiana Periodica* 30 (1964), p. 40.

[65] O. Iliescu, 'Le montant du tribut payé par Byzance à l'empire ottoman en 1379 et 1424', *Revue des Études Sud-est Européennes* 9 (1971), pp. 427–32. Iliescu supposes the *khrysinoi* to be hyperpyra, which is possible, but at this date ducats are rather more likely: see below, pp. 536–46.

Hardrada to Scandinavia after a period of service (*c.* 1034–43) in the Varangian guard.[66] The wealth that he returned with is said to have been greater than ever before seen in northern Europe, and so heavy that twelve young men could scarcely lift it.[67] Its size and weight were clearly exceptional, and it had apparently been built up out of misappropriated booty as well as his salary, for the highest dignity that he had obtained was that of *spatharokandidatos* which rated an annual *rhoga* of $\frac{1}{2}$ lb gold only.[68] Nevertheless, the considerable scale of wealth that such payments might involve has already been noted with regard to Catalan mercenaries in the early fourteenth century.[69]

Ransoms, too, continued to be exacted and paid. According to the Arabic sources,[70] that promised by Romanus IV on his own behalf after his capture by Alp Arslan in 1071 amounted to a million and a half nomismata. This was of course not only exceptional, but was also never paid. When a *doux* of Edessa was captured in 1066, 20,000 nomismata were exacted for him, and when Isaac Comnenus, the *doux* of Antioch, was captured (for the second time) during the reign of Michael VII, 20,000 nomismata were exacted for him.[71] When Gregory Maurocatacalon was captured during the reign of Alexius I, 40,000 nomismata were exacted for him, and when Constantine Gabras, the *doux* of Khaldia, was captured during the same reign, 30,000 dinars (presumably nomismata) were exacted for him.[72] Finally, when Manuel Camytzes, the *prōtostratōr*, was captured during the reign of Alexius III, two kentenaria were demanded (but never paid) for him.[73]

Over the late Roman and Byzantine period as a whole there were, of course, any number of other occasions when the state made payments that, to a greater or lesser degree, were likely to result in the trans-frontier movement of precious metals. Some of these were regular, such as the (relatively small) gifts made annually to various states and churches, or to their officials, or to both, frequently in the form of imperial *rhogai*, which

66 P. Grierson, 'Harold Hardrada and Byzantine Coin Types in Denmark', *Byzantinische Forschungen* I (1966), pp. 124–38; M. F. Hendy, 'Michael IV and Harold Hardrada', *Numismatic Chronicle* 10⁷ (1970), pp. 187–97. See also now: C. Morrisson, 'Le rôle des Varanges dans la transmission de la monnaie byzantine en Scandinavie', in R. Zeitler (ed.), *Les Pays du Nord et Byzance* (*Scandinavie et Byzance, Actes du colloque nordique et internationale de byzantinologie tenu à Upsal 20–22 avril 1979*), at pp. 131–40.

67 Snorri Sturluson, *Heimskringla: The Saga of Harald Sigurtharson* XVI, XXIV; trans. L. M. Hollander, at pp. 590, 595–6. Adam of Bremen, *Gesta Hammaburgensis Ecclesiae Pontificum* III.51, *scholium* LXXXIV; MGH, *SS* VII, p. 356. The *scholium* clearly errs, however, in supposing Harold's wealth to have fallen intact into the hands of William of Normandy.

68 Snorri Sturluson, *Heimskringla: The Saga of Harald Sigurtharson* XIII; trans. Hollander at p. 587. Cecaumenus, *Logos Nouthetētikos pros Basilea* CCXLVI; ed. B. Wassiliewsky and V. Jernstedt, p. 97. For the *rhoga*: see above, p. 185 and Table 4.

69 See above, pp. 205, 222–3, below, pp. 531–2.

70 C. Cahen, 'La campagne de Mantzikert d'après les sources musulmanes', *Byzantion* 9 (1934), p. 637. An annual subsidy of 60,000 nomismata was also promised.

71 Bar Hebraeus, *Chronography*; trans. Budge, pp. 217–18. Nicephorus Bryennius, *Historiarum Libri IV* II.29; ed. Gautier, p. 207.

72 Anna Comnena, *Alexiad* VII.2.3; ed. Leib, II, p. 89. Bar Hebraeus, *Chronography*; trans. Budge, p. 249.

73 See above, p. 258–9.

are a constant feature of twelfth-century treaties with western mercantile powers. Some were only occasional, such as the gifts made and expenses paid to ambassadors from or to foreign nations.[74] According to Procopius,[75] Justinian had lavished 10 kentenaria in this fashion upon an ambassador from Ctesiphon, while, according to the *Continuation of Theophanes*,[76] Theophilus lavished 4 kentenaria upon his own ambassador to Baghdad. This latter was done so that he would be able to scatter (*speirein*) gold like sand (*ammos*). The rest of the equipment with which he was provided was on a similar scale. What with this, and the counter-extravagance that it called forth on the part of the caliph, the embassy caused a sensation.

The composition and size of the gifts and bribes involved in such embassies were always very carefully considered, and normally geared to achieve the maximum effect for the minimum expenditure. According to Constantine Porphyrogenitus, the gifts and bribes entrusted to the *prōtospatharios* Epiphanius, sent on a military expedition to the theme of Lagobardia in 935, and intended for the king of Italy, Hugh of Provence, and his dependants, in order to induce Hugh to intervene against the princes of Capua, Benevento and Salerno, and the Lombard rebels, were as follows:

1 kentenarion in cash (*logarion kentēnarion*); 10 *esōphoria* [presumably under-garments, possibly *kolobia*];[77]· 1 chalice of onyx (*potērion onykhitou*); 17 pieces of glassware [of an uncertain kind] (*hyelia kleopt.*); 30 sacks of incense (*thymiama thylakia*); and 500 measures of fragrant oil (*aleipta*). For each of the same king's [*sc.* Hugh's] seven counts, 2 *esōphoria*; for the same king's six bishops, 6 all-yellow *skaramangia*. To the account of the same king's count and marquess who is neighbour to the theme of Lagobardia, 5 [ordinary, i.e. purple?] *skaramangia*, [plus] one of all-yellow, one of all-red, one of all-blue, and one of all-white – a total of 9 *skaramangia*; 4 *esōphoria*, and 3 *esōphoria* of lesser value (*leptozēla*) – a total of 7; 3 pieces of gilded silverware (*argyra diakhrysa*).

(Constantine Porphyrogenitus, *De Caerimoniis* II.44; Bonn edn, I, pp. 661–2)

The complex composition of these gifts and bribes was, to judge from other casual and partial accounts, not unrepresentative, although it is clear that, as regards actual quality and size, Hugh ranked low.[78]

Along with the gifts and bribes, Epiphanius was given,[79] to the account of expenditure on the same expedition (*logō exodou tou autou taxeidiou*): 6 *skaramangia* of various colours and patterns (*diaphorōn khroiōn kai exempliōn*); 30 *esōphoria oktalia* (presumably of purple of that tint which *The Book of the Prefect* terms *oktapōlon* and regards as 'forbidden';[80]

[74] *Rhogai*: see above, p. 185 and Table 4. Gifts and expenses: Toynbee, *Constantine Porphyrogenitus and his World*, pp. 498–509.

[75] Procopius, *De Bello Persico* II.28.44; ed. Haury (Teubner), I, p. 289.

[76] *Continuation of Theophanes* III.9; Bonn edn, pp. 96–8.

[77] See below, pp. 307–8.

[78] For cash comparisons, see above, pp. 264–6. For gifts, see below, pp. 269–71.

[79] Constantine Porphyrogenitus, *De Caerimoniis* II.44; Bonn edn, p. 662.

[80] See above, p. 258, below, p. 310 n.

20 *lōrōta* (presumably garments resembling, or pertaining to, the *lōros*, or possibly consisting of leather, or having thongs);[81] 20 genuine purple (*alēthina*) garments. These were presumably for unexpected expenditure, whether they were to be used in their stated form or converted into cash, and were possibly designed to keep the export of precious metals to a minimum, in accordance with contemporary law. Epiphanius spent (*exodiasen*): 2 *skaramangia*, 17 *esōphoria*, 12 *lōrōta* and 14 *alēthina*. On his return he duly refunded (*eisekomizen*) the remainder: 4 *skaramangia*, 13 *esōphoria*, 8 *lōrōta* and 6 *alēthina*. Of such items, and careful accounting, were Byzantine diplomacy and warfare made.

The composition of such gifts also remained remarkably constant over the centuries. According to Anna Comnena,[82] the gifts sent by Alexius I to the German emperor Henry IV in 1083 consisted not only of cash and 100 cloths (*blattia*), but also a pectoral of gold decorated with seed-pearls (*enkolpion khrysoun meta margaritariōn*), a gilded reliquary (*thēkē diakhrysos*) with individually identified relics, a sardonyx cup (*kaukion sardonyhkion*), a crystal goblet (*empotēs kryos*), a thunderbolt (*astropelekion*) wrapped (or contained) in gold, and extract of balsam. According to Pachymeres,[83] the gifts entrusted to the various lay and ecclesiastical representatives to present to the pope Gregory X, on the occasion of the Council of Lyons in 1278, consisted of: costumes (*stolai*), golden icons (*katakhrysa eikonismata*), blends of precious incenses (*syntheta polytima thymiamata*), and an altar-cloth in gold-woven reddish-purple decorated with pearls (*endytē ek khrysopastou oxeias dia margarōn*). The last had evidently come from the Great Church, there having been no time to manufacture another. All, as it happens, were lost in a shipwreck.

Certain of the items utilised with regard to the Christian west were, of course, inappropriate with regard to the Muslim east, and adjustments were accordingly made. According to Abdel-'Azīz bin Yūsuf,[84] a secretary at the Buyid court, the gifts and bribes sent by Basil II to the emir 'Aḍuḍ al-Daulah in 983, and intended to induce the latter to renew a truce, consisted of: 'two hundred imperial costumes, gold and silver ornaments, white falcons, excellent mules, speedy horses, and other things of that kind' * According to Ibn al-Zubair,[85] who appears to have been a Fatimid civil servant responsible for the reception of foreign embassies, the gifts and bribes sent by Constantine IX to the caliph al-Mustansir in 1045, and also intended to induce the latter to renew

* I owe these Arabic references to the kindness of Wesam Farag.

81 See below, pp. 308, 310.

82 Anna Comnena, *Alexiad* III.10.7; ed. Leib, I, p. 135. For the cash, see above, p. 265.

83 George Pachymeres, *De Michaele et Andronico Palaeologis, De Mich.* V.17; Bonn edn, I, pp. 384–5.

84 W. A. Farag, 'Byzantium and its Muslim Neighbours during the Reign of Basil II (976–1025)', p. 97. The items involved, were, as customarily (see below, n. 87), enumerated in the imperial letter that accompanied the embassy.

85 Ibn al-Zubair, *Kitāb al-Dhakā'ir wa al-Tuḥaf*; ed. M. Ḥamīdallāh, pp. 74–7. For a summary description of these, and other embassies, deriving from ibn al-Zubair, see: M. Canard, 'Les sources arabes de l'histoire byzantine aux confins des X^e et XI^e siècles', *Revue des Études Byzantines* 19 (1961), pp. 289–91. The *magrīs lutfan* seem, on the face of it, to be identical with Constantine Porphyrogenitus' *vestomiliarēsia*: see below, p. 412 n. 175.

a truce, amounted to the unprecedented sum of 30 kentenaria or 216,000 nomismata – equivalent to 300,000 dinars – and comprised 150 mules and horses, each with an embroidered cloth equipage, another 50 mules, each carrying a pair of silk-covered chests containing gold vessels, 1,000 silk costumes, belts embroidered in gold, turbans similarly embroidered, and 300 curtains and handkerchiefs. The train was led by 200 freed Muslim prisoners, presumably one to an animal. Again, an embassy sent apparently by the same emperor to the same caliph in 1052 was entrusted with Turkish slaves, exotic birds, trained bears, hunting-dogs, and many chests containing uncertain (but presumably precious) items, together with 1,700 *magrīs lutfan* as used in the emperor's treasury (*khazanah* = store-place = *vestiarion*?), sealed with lead, and each worth 7 dinars. These possibly represented sealed purses of miliaresia, straight from the mint. At the same time, it was entrusted with gold crosses encrusted with precious stones and each weighing one kentenarion, gold trays similarly encrusted, and *polykandēla* with gold chains, all of which were intended for the Church of the Holy Sepulchre. The same tradition of imperial generosity was continued by John II, who intended to present the Church with a lampstand (*lykhnia*) worked up from 20 lb gold.[86]

The items entrusted to such embassies apparently tended to be listed and described in painstaking detail (presumably partly for the sake of prestige, partly for that of safety) in the imperial letter that also accompanied them, as they certainly were in the case of an embassy sent by Romanus I, Stephen and Constantine VII to caliph al-Raḍi in 938.[87]

Later, when it became accepted for imperial brides, or brides related to the imperial family, to be given in marriage to foreign rulers, their dowries might involve considerable sums. When Theophano, married to the German emperor Otto II in 972, arrived in the west, she came accompanied by a considerable dowry, and so did Eudocia Comnena when she married Odo Frangipane in 1170.[88] According to William of Tyre,[89] the dowry and marriage expenses of Theodora Comnena, married with admittedly exceptional splendour to Baldwin III of Jersusalem in 1158, amounted to 150,000 hyperpyra, not only in gold (100,000 + 10,000 hyp.), but also in gems, silks, and so on (40,000 hyp.).

The visit of a foreign ruler might also occasion the expenditure of considerable sums: the gifts made to Olga of Russia and her suite in 957, for which there exist official accounts, involved over a million miliaresia, presumably taking into account the Russian taste for silver;[90] those made to Baldwin III in 1159, which were said to have amounted to 22,000

[86] John Cinnamus, *Epitome* I.10; Bonn edn, p. 25.

[87] Ibn al-Zubair, *Kitāb al-Dhakā'ir wa al-Tuḥaf*; ed. Ḥamīdallāh, pp. 60–65. See also above, n. 84.

[88] Theophano: refs in K. Leyser, 'The Tenth Century in Byzantine–Western Relationships', in D. Baker (ed.), *Relations between East and West in the Middle Ages*, at pp. 43, 60 (nn. 86, 87). Eudocia: refs in Brand, *Byzantium Confronts the West, 1180–1204*, pp. 20, 320 n. 16.

[89] William of Tyre, *Historia Rerum* XVIII.22; RHC, *Occ.* I.2, pp. 857–8.

[90] Constantine Porphyrogenitus, *De Caerimoniis* II.15; Bonn edn, pp. 597–8.

hyperpyra, besides silver, silks and vessels of precious metal, and those made to Amalric I in 1171, were probably in no way inferior in gold, silver, and so on.[91]

That expenditure of this kind and on this scale might be used as a deliberate expression of financial power, in order to impress visitors, is obvious. That it was indeed so used by Alexius I is admitted by no less a person than Anna Comnena, with reference to Bohemund in 1097.[92] That it was so used by Manuel I is stated by Nicetas Choniates with reference to Kılıç-Arslan II in 1161.[93] Something similar seems also to have happened in the case of Baldwin III.[94] On each of these occasions, a whole roomful of gold and silver coins, vessels, cloths and jewels was given away with a deliberate air of insouciance (although doubtless subjected to meticulous accounting), and an equally deliberate intent, on the part of the donor, to dazzle and overwhelm the recipient with the magnitude and magnificence of the gift.[95]

A similar, if somewhat more restrained, concept lay behind the expression, by John III, of the disapproval of his son wearing golden garments while out hunting that is recorded by Pachymeres.[96] For such gold-embroidered and silk (*khrysosēma kai sērika*) garments represented the blood of the Romans (*aima Rhomaiōn*), and as such were to be worn only in the presence of foreign embassies to manifest Roman wealth (*ploutos*): the wealth of the emperors was thus to be counted as the wealth of their subjects (*ho gar basileōn ploutos ploutos tōn hypēkoōn logizetai*).[97] The consciousness of Roman wealth and its political uses was by then of long standing, even if of already limited future.

[91] William of Tyre, *Historia Rerum* XVIII.24, XX.22–4; RHC, *Occ.* I.2, pp. 861–3, 980–7. S. Der Nersessian, 'The Armenian Chronicle of the Constable Smpad or of the "Royal Historian"', *DOP* 13 (1959), p. 147. Smpad noticeably claims that Manuel prepared a royal palace which he filled with all kinds of gold and silver vessels, and furniture, 'as is customary', and then gave the whole to Baldwin.

[92] Anna Comnena, *Alexiad* X.11.5–6; ed. Leib, II, p. 233: *pantoion eidos khrēmaton,... kai amphiōn kharagmatos te khrysiou kai argyrou kai tes kātoterō hylēs tosouton plērōsas to oikēma....*

[93] Nicetas Choniates, *Historia*; ed. van Dieten, I, 120–1: *Ēn de tauta khrysos te kai argyros kekommenos eis nomisma kai tryphōsa esthēs argyrea te ekpōmata kai Thērikleia khrysea kai othonai tōn ex hyperēphanou hyphēs alloi te kosmoi exairetoi....*

[94] See above, n. 91.

[95] '*Tauta soi tēn sēmeron apokharizetai apanta ho basileus*' (a palace functionary to Bohemund); '*Philotimoumai se toutois pasi...hina kai toumon eideiēs philodōron te ama kai megalodōron kai hosōn esti kyrios khrēmaton ho tosois hena dōroumenos*' (the emperor Manuel to Kılıç Arslan). Such generosity did not, needless to say, always have the result intended: Choniates (*ed. cit.* pp. 124–5) claims that soon after the events described, Kılıç Arslan boasted that the more injuries he did (to the Byzantines), the more hand-outs (*nemomena*) he could expect (from the emperor). The tensions inherent in the available alternatives – those of subsidising or of making war upon the enemy – were, however, in no way confined to the reign of Manuel. It seems clear that Procopius (in his *Historia Arcana*) considered Justinian to have inclined too much in favour of the subsidy, while it seems equally clear that Corippus (in his *In Laudem Iustini Augusti*) considered Justin to have abandoned it in favour of war. Much later, the same kind of tension, if less explicit, is apparent in the two main accounts of the conflicts between the Andronici, Gregoras favouring the old Andronicus II, Cantacuzene the young Andronicus III.

[96] George Pachymeres, *De Michaele et Andronico Palaeologis, De Mich.* I.14; Bonn edn, I, pp. 38–9.

[97] Cf. Thomas Magistros, above, p. 229.

An enlightened attitude such as John III's cannot have been representative of those of the generality of Byzantine emperors, to judge from their conduct, although whether they would have agreed entirely with Isaac II who, when reproached for his use of sacred metalware effectively purloined from the churches at his own tables, replied that emperors were permitted to do anything, and that between God and emperor there was no great difference, seems very doubtful.[98]

### D. *The imperial baggage-train*

Yet others of these occasions, because catastrophic, were very rare only. The complex organisation, composition and massive contents (including, for example, a portion at least of the private vestiarion (*oikeiakon vestiarion*), bed-chamber (*koitōn*) and the *eidikon*) of the imperial baggage-train, as used in military campaigns, are described exhaustively by Constantine Porphyrogenitus. The full list is nothing short of prodigious, and as such will be dealt with in an appendix to this chapter.[99]

Part of this baggage-train had presumably been lost by Valens to the Goths in 378, thus accounting for the modern occurrence of gold ingots marked with the appropriate official stamps in areas that were then outside the imperial frontiers.[100] Admittedly, however, the bulk of it seems to have escaped on this occasion, for, according to Ammianus Marcellinus,[101] Valens had possessed the foresight to leave his treasury (*thesauri*), and the imperial regalia (*principalis fortunae insignia*), within the walls of Adrianople itself, the remainder of the baggage (*impedimenta et sarcinae*) being left outside. The treasury and regalia, at least, remained untaken, although the knowledge of their presence added ferocity to the subsequent unsuccessful Gothic attack on the city. They were afterwards withdrawn, piecemeal, westwards through Philippopolis to Serdica, or southwards into Macedonia.[102]

The baggage-train was apparently lost by Justinian II to the Bulgars in 708/9, and was certainly lost by Constantine VI to them in 792 for they are described as having gained possession of the baggage-train (*touldon*), money (*khrēmata*), horses (*hippoi*), and the tent (*kortē*) with all the imperial apparatus (*meta pasēs tēs basilikēs hypourgias*).[103] It was lost by Nicephorus I again to the Bulgars in 811, for they are reported to have attacked the imperial tent (*skēnē*), although the imperial clothing (*esthēs basilikē*) had already been lost to them through the defection of one of the emperor's domestic servants.[104] It was

[98] See above, p. 232.

[99] See below, pp. 304–15. See also: Toynbee, *Constantine Porphyrogenitus and his World*, pp. 195–8.

[100] See below, p. 385, n. 51. See also Pl. 3, 9–10.

[101] Ammianus Marcellinus, *Rerum Gestarum Libri* XXXI.12.10; ed. Gardthausen, II, p. 263.

[102] *Ibid.* XXXI.16.2; ed. Gardthausen, II, p. 275.

[103] Theophanes, *Chronographia*; ed. de Boor, I, p. 468.

[104] *Ibid.* pp. 490, 491. The servant managed to make off with 100 lb gold, as well as with the clothing. See also below, p. 280 and n. 151.

lost by Michael I yet again to them in 813, for they took as booty the baggage-train (*touldon*) and such things.[105]

Described by Arabic sources as consisting of mules and camels loaded with the imperial regalia (tent, crown and vestments), cash, gold and silver vessels, and rich stuffs, the baggage-train was apparently lost by Romanus III to the Arabs in 1030.[106] From the Byzantine side, Psellus[107] admits the loss of the imperial tent (*basilikē skēnē*) and its contents, which were of a huge value equal to those of actual palaces (*pollō tōn nun anaktorōn antimetron*), consisting of necklaces or torques (*streptoi*), diadems (*tainiai*), stones and pearls (*lithoi kai margaritides*), and so on. Similarly described by Arabic sources as consisting of mules and wagons loaded with the imperial regalia (tent, throne and vestments), cash (supposedly to the order of one million nomismata), jewels, arms, and so on, it was certainly lost by Romanus IV to the Selçuk Turks in 1071.[108] Again, from the Byzantine side, Bryennius[109] admits the loss of the entire camp (*stratopedon*), with the imperial tent (*hē skēnē hē basileios*), the money (*khrēmata*), and the finest items of the imperial regalia (*basilika parasēma*), including a famous pearl (*margaros*) called 'the orphan'. Some of the booty deriving from the capture of the imperial tent (*skēnē*) and camp (*kharax*) was later recovered by John II during his Syrian campaign of 1138. It included a cross to be held in the hand (*stauros eis kheiras*), obviously a sceptre cruciger, and a table (*trapeza*). The cross was apparently spectacular: according to Choniates,[110] it was carved out of ruby, or a ruby-like stone (*lykhnitē lithō kekolammenos*); the description is confirmed by Cinnamus,[111] according to whom it had come down from the emperor Constantine, and fell into Arab hands by unknown means. The table was reportedly of a like quality.

Meanwhile, the imperial tent and whole baggage-train (*hē basilikē skēnē kai apasa hē skeuē*) had been lost by Alexius I to the Normans in 1081, and some of the sections of hanging (*temakhia...parapetasmatōn*) used to furnish the imperial chamber (*aulē*), left behind owing to a lack of baggage-animals (*hypozygia*), had been lost by John II himself to the Hungarians in 1129/30.[112]

[105] Theophanes, *Chronographia*; ed. de Boor, I, pp. 501–2.

[106] Canard, 'Les sources arabes de l'histoire byzantine', p. 308. John Zonaras, *Annales* XVII.11.22; Bonn edn, III, pp. 577–8. What seems to have been Romanus' *khlamys*, sown with pearls, and decorated with golden crosses studded with rubies, appears to have passed into the Fatimid treasury as a result of their capture of Aleppo in 1037/8 (Canard, *op. cit.* p. 291).

[107] Michael Psellus, *Chronographia* III.10; ed. Renauld, I, p. 38.

[108] Cahen, 'La campagne de Mantzikert d'après les sources musulmanes', pp. 630, 636, 638–9. Romanus apparently also lost the great processional cross that preceded the emperor and which was sent by Alp Arslan to the Abbasid caliph at Baghdad (*op. cit.* p. 639). For this cross, see: Hendy, *DOC* IV; above, p. 152 (Manuel I loses it to the Turks); below, p. 275 (Isaac II loses it to the Bulgars).

[109] Nicephorus Bryennius, *Historiarum Libri IV* I.17; ed. Gautier, p. 119.

[110] Nicetas Choniates, *Historia*; ed. van Dieten, I, pp. 30–1.

[111] John Cinnamus, *Epitome* I.8; Bonn edn, p. 20.

[112] Anna Comnena, *Alexiad* IV.7.1, V.1.1; ed. Leib, I, p. 163, II, p. 7. John Cinnamus, *Epitome* I.5; Bonn edn, p. 13.

Again similarly described, but by this stage including the *vestiarion* proper (*basilikon/ koinon tamieion*), the distinction between imperial (state) wealth and imperial (private) wealth having disappeared in the interim, the baggage-train was almost lost by Michael VIII to the Mongols and Bulgars in 1265.[113]

During the later period, at least, junior emperors seem to have rated a baggage-train that was similar in scale to those of their seniors, for, according to Gregoras,[114] when the army of Michael IX, co-emperor to Andronicus II, was defeated by a motley band of Turks in 1310, they came into possession of the imperial money (*ta basilika...khrēmata*), secured in purses (*en desmois*), and such of the imperial regalia (*ta basilika parasēma*) as was found in his tent (*skēnē*). This latter included the imperial diadem (*basilikē kalyptra*), ornamented, as customarily, with stones and with chains of pearls (i.e. with pendilia) (*kekosmēmenē synēthōs tō te lithō kai tais tōn margarōn seirais*). The Turkish leader, one Halil, put the diadem on his own head, and made mocking and ironic remarks about the emperor. Usurpers, of course, aped their more regular colleagues. According to Benedict of Peterborough,[115] when the camp of Isaac Comnenus, the Cypriot usurper, was unexpectedly attacked by the army of Richard I of England in 1191, the former fled naked, leaving behind his treasures (*thesauri*), horses and arms, his most beautiful tents (*tentoria*), and the imperial standard (*vexillum imperiale*), woven throughout in gold (*per totum auro contextum*).

It may also be deduced that the baggage-train had been lost by Manuel I to the Turks in 1176. Both Nicetas Choniates and Manuel himself, as well as others, describe it in the customary terms.[116] Choniates subsequently vividly describes[117] the emperor contemplating the chests (*thēsaurophylaktai*) and purses (*thylakoi*) of struck coin (*nomismata kekkomenon*), in gold and silver (i.e. electrum), that had been ripped open, emptied onto the ground and plundered by the Persians (i.e. Turks), in the rout of his army.

A similar situation obtains with regard to the baggage-train lost by Isaac II to the Bulgars in 1190. Choniates records and describes[118] the defeat of the army on that occasion without referring to the loss of the baggage-train as such, although elsewhere[119] he implies that that taken on another campaign included the imperial tent (*skēnē basileios*), the gilded bed (*klinē khrysopastos*), the imperial couch (*skimpous basilikos*), and gold-woven garments (*peploi khrysoüpheis*). Acropolites, however, remarks in addition[120] that the

113 See below, p. 440.

114 Nicephorus Gregoras, *Historia Byzantina* VII.9; Bonn edn, I, p. 258.

115 Benedict of Peterborough, *Gesta Regis Ricardi*, s.a. 1191; ed. Stubbs, II, p. 164.

116 See above, pp. 149–51, 152.

117 Nicetas Choniates, *Historia*; ed. van Dieten, I, p. 186.

118 *Ibid.* pp. 429–30. The baggage-train (*ta skeuophora*) is mentioned, in the course of the battle, but not its ultimate fate.

119 Nicetas Choniates, *Epanagnōstikon eis ton Patriarkhēn kai tēn Synodon*; ed. K. N. Sathas, in *Mesaiōnikē Bibliothēkē* I, at pp. 80–1 (Arabic numerotation).

120 George Acropolites, *Historia* XI; ed. Heisenberg and Wirth, pp. 19–20.

Bulgars took much plunder (*leia pollē*), including some of the most valuable objects from the imperial regalia (*ek tōn basilikōn parasēmōn*) – the *pyramides* of the emperor (probably diadems), personal dishes (*phialai*), money in plenty (*khrēma eis plēthos*), and the imperial *stauros* (probably a processional cross, its centre containing several relics).[121] The plunder involved was apparently sufficiently spectacular to be considered worthy of keeping and regular display, even to subsequent Byzantine ambassadors,[122] although it seems eventually to have been recovered by the Byzantines when tsar Ivan III fled Turnovo with it, and presumably handed it over to them, in 1280.[123*]

The private *vestiarion*, or a portion of it, apparently also accompanied the emperor on naval journeys or expeditions, for its head, the *prōtovestiarios*, was always in attendence on such occasions in the tenth century.[124] It must have been the imperial galley carrying this *vestiarion* that fell into Venetian hands off Corfu in 1149. For through their capture of the ship they gained access to imperial ceremonial objects such as gold-woven garments (*peploi khrysoüpheis*), purple hangings or carpets (*alourgoi tapētai*), and a crown (*stephanos*), in which they proceeded to dress up a negro and accord him imperial honours in a glorious parody of imperial ceremonial. This parody seems likely to have been hilarious, and certainly verged upon the blasphemous. Manuel, of course, never forgave them.[125]

It was presumably the imperial galley in which Alexius III fled to Develtus in 1203, taking with him what may have been this *vestiarion* – including ten kentenaria in cash as well as imperial ornaments (*kosmoi basilikoi*) of precious stones (*lithoi timalphes*) and translucent pearls (*margaroi diaphanes*).[126] On the other hand, these seem rather more likely to have come from the *vestiarion* proper, still housed in the Great Palace, for a treasure containing crowns, which had belonged to former emperors, jewels of gold, silk cloths, imperial robes, precious stones, and so on, was found when the crusaders broke into the Blachernae Palace in 1204.[127] This seems more likely to have represented the private *vestiarion*.

Finally, it is known that the *vestiarion* proper, for the reason given above, accompanied the emperor on naval journeys or expeditions, in a ship commanded by its head, the *prokathēmenos*, in the fourteenth century.[128]

* I owe these 'Bulgarian' references to the kindness of Ruth Macrides.

121 *Pyramides, stauros*: Hendy, *DOC* IV.

122 Theodore Scutariotes, *Synopsis Khronikē*; ed. K. N. Sathas in *Mesaiōnikē Bibliothēkē* VII, at pp. 547–8.

123 George Pachymeres, *De Michaele et Andronico Palaeologis, De Mich.* VI.9; Bonn edn, I, pp. 448–9.

124 Constantine Porphyrogenitus, *De Administrando Imperio* LI; ed. Moravcsik and Jenkins, p. 246. Oikonomides, *Les listes de préséance byzantines*, p. 305.

125 Nicetas Choniates, *Historia*; ed. van Dieten, I, p. 86.

126 See above, p. 225.

127 Robert of Clari, *La conquête de Constantinople* LXXXIII; ed. Lauer, pp. 83–4.

128 See below, p. 440.

### *E. The* Topography *of Cosmas and its evidence*

It is in the light of the state's continuing prohibition of the private export of precious metals that two well-known passages in the *Christian Topography* of the sixth-century monk and former merchant Cosmas 'Indicopleustes' should be considered.

The first of these passages[129] takes the form of a general statement:

There is another mark of the power of the Romans, which God has given them. I mean that it is in their nomisma that every nation conducts its commerce, and that it is acceptable (*dekton*) in every place from one end of the earth to the other. This nomisma is admired by all men and all nations, for in no other nation does such a thing exist.

The second[130] takes the form of a somewhat lengthy tale:

There was once a merchant of ours called Sopatros, known to have died thirty-five years ago, who reached the island of Taprobane [Ceylon] in the course of business, a ship from Persia by chance anchoring at the same time. Now, the men from Adoulis [an Axumite port on the west coast of the Red Sea], with whom Sopatros was, disembarked along with the men from Persia, with whom there also was an aged Persian. Then, according to custom, the chief men and customs-officers (*telōnai*) having received them, led them to the king. The king, having received them in turn, and having received their homage, ordered them to be seated. He then asked, 'How are your countries and how do they fare?' They replied, 'Well'. Subsequently, in the middle of the conversation, the king asked, 'Which of your kings is the greater and more powerful?' The Persian, seizing the opportunity, replied, 'Ours is the more powerful, the greater, and the richer, and is the King of Kings; whatever he wishes, he does.' But Sopatros merely sat. The king then asked, 'Have you nothing to say, Roman?' Sopatros replied, 'What have I to say, when he has said so much? But if you wish to learn the truth, you have both kings present here; examine each and you will see which is the more magnificent and the more powerful.' The king, surprised at what he had heard, asked, 'How can I have both kings present here?' Sopatros replied, 'You have the coins (*monetai*) of both, the nomisma of the one, and the drachma, that is, the miliaresion, of the other; examine the image of each and you will see the truth.' The king approved and, nodding his assent, ordered both to be produced. Now the nomisma was of the purest gold (*obryzon*), was brilliant (*lampron*), and was a thing of beauty (*eumorphon*), for such pieces are picked out (*eklekta*) for export to the island. But the miliaresion, to put it in a word, was of silver, and, suffice it to say, not to be compared with the gold coin. The king turned them this way and that and, having examined both, praised the nomisma highly, remarking that the Romans were indeed magnificent, powerful, and wise... Sopatros himself, and those who accompanied him from Adoulis to the island, related these things, and – so they said – the Persian was extremely vexed at what had happened.

The two passages obviously raise several relevant points. The first of these concerns Cosmas' claim that every nation conducted its commerce in the Byzantine nomisma, a claim which – even allowing for an element of exaggeration – implies the presence of

[129] Cosmas Indicopleustes, *Christian Topography* II; ed. E. O. Winstedt, p. 81.
[130] *Ibid.* XI; ed. Winstedt, pp. 323–4.

a considerable amount of imperial gold coinage outside the imperial frontiers. It need not be supposed, however, that this presence resulted from the free private export of the metal: illegal export, with or without official knowledge or connivance, was, as the novel of Valentinian I, Valens and Gratian implies, always a possibility, and much of the metal exported by the state itself, in whatever form and on whatever pretext, must in any case have ended up eventually in foreign private hands.

The second of these points concerns Sopatros' claim that fine examples of the nomisma were picked out for export to Ceylon. This is no more decisive than the first, for it is to be noted that Sopatros embarked not from an imperial port, but from Adoulis, an Axumite one where imperial laws and regulations would have had no force. It has indeed been argued[131] that embarkation from Axumite ports was normal for Byzantine merchants trading eastwards at this period, direct trade being virtually non-existent. It is also to be noted that most of the late Roman and early Byzantine coins now found in southern India and Ceylon are in fact not of precious but of base metal.[132] This contrasts with the situation as regards earlier Roman coins, is in itself most unusual, and – since these coins form the one group found outside the frontiers that is unlikely to have resulted from political payments but is likely to have resulted from trade – is surely significant.

The accuracy and even the basic veracity of Sopatros' story is also subverted by the occurrence of a similar one in the *Natural History* of Pliny.[133] On this occasion an unnamed freedman of Annius Plocamus, who had a contract with the treasury to collect the tax (*vectigal*) from the Red Sea, was driven to Ceylon by gales and was entertained there by the local king. The latter was struck above all by the fact that the denarii found on his guest were of equal weight (*paris pondere*), although the portraits on them showed them to have been struck by several different emperors (i.e. they showed *diversae imagines*). This episode apparently resulted in the sending of a Ceylonese embassy to Rome during the reign of Claudius (41–54). The existence, approximate dating and locale of operation of Plocamus are all confirmed by the extraordinary discovery of a double (Greek and Latin) graffito naming a certain Lysas as one of his freedmen, dated A.D. 6, on the road to Berenice, an imperial port on the west coast of the Red Sea.[134] The strong suspicion that the Byzantine story is, however indirectly, merely an updated and elaborated version of the Roman original immediately arises, although it remains quite unverifiable.

It is in a similar sceptical light that the claim of an undatable and unattributable Arabic

[131] K. Hannestad, 'Les relations de Byzance avec la Transcaucasie et l'Asie centrale aux 5ᵉ et 6ᵉ siècles', *Byzantion* 25–7 (1955–7), pp. 425–7, 455.

[132] E. H. Warmington, *The Commerce between the Roman Empire and India*, pp. 120–4, 140, 394f.

[133] Pliny, *Natural History* VI.84–5; ed. H. Rackham (Loeb), II, pp. 400, 402.

[134] D. Meredith, 'Annius Plocamus: Two Inscriptions from the Berenice Road', *Journal of Roman Studies* 43 (1953), pp. 38–40.

text,[135] dealing with commercial affairs, and sometimes attributed to Gahiz, that utensils in gold and silver, dinars in pure gold (*gaysarani*), brocades, and so on, were imported from the land of the Byzantines, should be seen. The claim of Svyatoslav of Russia[136] that, rather than live at Kiev, he would prefer Pereyslavets on the Danube, for gold, silks, and so on from Greece were available there, may well refer to imperial gifts, of which he was already in receipt. In all these cases, the possibility of illegal export should also not be lightly disregarded.

### F. Observations

The evidence, then, would seem to suggest that, until the thirteenth century, the political frontiers of the empire formed a more or less effective barrier to the private export of precious metals, and that such precious-metal objects of provable late Roman or Byzantine origin as are now found in abnormally large quantities in areas that were then outside the frontiers are likely to have resulted, ultimately, from political payments of some kind.

It is for this reason that, for instance, a theory seeking to account for the rarity of silver hexagrams from towards the end of the reign of Constantine IV onwards by postulating a scarcity of silver in the empire caused by its export, in exchange for gold, across the frontier into the Abbasid caliphate, in order to take advantage of differing gold:silver ratios,[137] is bound to be regarded with considerable suspicion. Apart from begging the question of whether contemporary Byzantine–Arab trade was really on a scale capable of bringing about so relatively sudden a scarcity as this,[138] the theory fails – as the earlier ones involving solidi found in western Europe and Russia also fail – to take account of the relevant imperial legislation. The novel of Valentinian I, Valens and Gratian admittedly mentions gold and omits silver, but then so did the more or less contemporary legislation on the form in which money-taxes were to be collected, although silver nevertheless seems to have been equally affected.[139] *The Book of the Prefect* mentions both gold and silver, and so does the Treaty of Nymphaeum. A treaty of 1111 also treats both metals alike.[140]

A similar rarity of silver coinage from the beginning of the fifth century to the introduction of the hexagram at the beginning of the sixth has been accounted for by postulating the existence, over this period, of an insufficiently flexible and therefore eventually unfavourable official gold:silver ratio within the empire itself.[141] It may well be that the rarity of later hexagrams is susceptible to a similar, internal, explanation.

135 C. Pellat, 'Ǧaḥiẓiana, I, le *Kitāb al-Tabaṣṣur bi-l-tiǧāra* attribué à Ǧāḥiẓ', *Arabica* 1 (1954), p. 159 (14).

136 *The Russian Primary Chronicle*, s.a. 969; trans. S. H. Cross and O. P. Sherbowitz-Wetzor, p. 86.

137 P. Grierson, 'The Monetary Reforms of 'Abd al-Malik', *Journal of the Economic and Social History of the Orient* 3 (1960), pp. 257–64.

138 See, for example, above, pp. 157–8, below, pp. 582–90, 590–601.

139 See below, pp. 387–91.

140 See above, pp. 258, 259, below p. 283.

141 See below, pp. 451 and n. 11, 465, 480–2, 494.

This is not necessarily to suppose that the Byzantine empire operated, or indeed was able to operate, as a completely insulated economic unit: it had probably, paradoxically, been easier to insulate the late Roman and early Byzantine empire, when it controlled virtually the entire Mediterranean basin and possessed a far more sophisticated civilisation than did most of the areas that surrounded it, than it was to insulate the developed Byzantine empire when it formed only one of a number of Mediterranean states and possessed a civilisation that was only marginally, if at all, more sophisticated than those of several of the surrounding states. It seems clear, for instance, that – although at least one internal factor added a degree of complexity to the situation[142] – the empire shared in the so-called 'silver famine' that afflicted the Muslim world from Asia to North Africa and Spain during the eleventh, twelfth and thirteenth centuries:[143] after *c.* 1000, issues of Byzantine silver coinage too became increasingly sporadic and seem to have declined in scale.[144] It was, even so, less afflicted than the Muslim world, for its monetary silver never disappeared entirely, whether the metal was to be found in the form of essentially silver miliaresia or in that of electrum and billon trachea. The reason for its being less afflicted remains uncertain. Possibly its geographical position, between Muslim areas that were heavily afflicted and the Christian west which seems to have remained unaffected, helped. Equally possibly, the continuing enforcement of its traditional policy *vis-à-vis* the precious metals resulted in the retention of a portion, at least, of its supply of silver.

With the relaxation of this traditional policy, probably during the thirteenth century, the empire will have lain open to the normal flow of precious metals. To take one example only: the appearance of a relatively large number of hoards of fourteenth-century gold hyperpyra in Bulgaria, and particularly at the eastern, coastal, end of the Danubian plain, seems to reflect an increasing agricultural exploitation of the region consequent upon the termination of the Byzantine veto; the exportation of the resultant surplus into the empire, particularly by Venetian merchants; and its exchange for gold.[145] In its reintroduction of a large-scale silver coinage, possibly in 1295; in the disappearance of its gold coinage during the first half of the fourteenth century; and in its eventual definitive transfer to a silver-based currency during the second half of the same century; the empire was thus merely conforming to the dictates of the then prevailing flow of precious metals.[146]

142 The immobilisation of quantities of silver as the alloying material in the debasement of the gold coinage. See below, pp. 509–11.

143 A. M. Watson, 'Back to Gold – and Silver', *Economic History Review* 20² (1967), pp. 2–5.

144 Grierson, *DOC* III.2, pp. 611–12.

145 The main numismatic references are to be found in: D. M. Metcalf, *Coinage in South-eastern Europe, 820–1396*, pp. 130–2 ('7.Nicaean Gold Coinage in the Balkans'), 280–4 ('3.The Black Sea Trade: Byzantine Gold Coinage in Bulgaria and the Dobrogea'). To this should be added: S. Avdev, 'Secheni li ca perperi vuv Varna i Mesembriya prez XIV vek', *Numizmatika* 3 (1979), pp. 7–14. For the trade in cereals, see: Chrysostomides, 'Venetian Commercial Privileges under the Palaeologi', pp. 316–27; and, in the last instance, M. Balard, 'L'activité économique des ports du bas-Danube au XIV^e siècle', *Travaux et Mémoires* 8 (1981), pp. 40, 43. See also above, pp. 44–8. For the probable Byzantine veto upon the exploitation of the area (until *c.* 1200), see above, p. 39.

146 Watson, 'Back to Gold – and Silver', pp. 5–34.

### (II) OCCASIONAL INWARD FLOWS

Over much of the later period, with the notable exception of the very latest one of all (that extending from the beginning of the fourteenth century onwards), the frequency and scale of official trans-frontier payments diminished considerably. There are, for instance, no later parallels to the relatively concentrated – and, towards the end, actually simultaneous – payment of subsidies, first to the Huns, then to the Persians and Avars, that had marked the fifth and sixth centuries. In conformity with the considerably reduced frequency of trans-frontier payments of the middle and later Byzantine period, the number of contemporary Byzantine coins found outside the frontiers shows a sharp diminution when compared with those of the earlier period: even in Russia, where one might expect otherwise, Byzantine coins are rare, whether absolutely, or when compared with western or Arabic issues.[147] Moreover, later payments were sometimes partly, on occasion wholly, balanced by tributary payments made by the Arabs to the Byzantines. To take two examples only: during the later part of the reign of Constantine IV and the earlier part of that of Justinian II, the Arabs were paying at the very considerable rate of 365,000 dinars annually.[148] That they were able to do so, of course, arose largely out of their having inherited a sophisticated fiscal system in those areas that they had conquered from the Byzantines. This was a fact recognised by the Byzantines themselves.[149]

Later, in 969, the Hamdanid government of Aleppo was forced to pay a capitation tax of one dinar on each of its citizens, and an annual tribute of 700,000 dirhems (= 43,755 dinars). In 981 the tribute was renegotiated at 400,000 dirhems (= 20,000 dinars), and in 986 it was confirmed at that figure.[150]

During the ninth and tenth centuries, and the first half of the eleventh, in particular, the Byzantine government also happened upon the occasional windfall. When Nicephorus I took the Bulgaran capital, Pliska, in 811, he found there the royal treasury (*ta tamieia*): this he may have put under seal with the intention of appropriating it, or may have distributed to his troops, although whether its contents remained in Byzantine hands at all after his subsequent defeat and death must remain very doubtful.[151] When Basil II

[147] The general point is made by P. Grierson, 'Coinage and Money in the Byzantine Empire, 498–*c*. 1090', in *Settimane di studio del Centro italiano di studi sull'alto medioevo* VIII, *Moneta e scambi nell'alto medioevo*, at pp. 448–53. There does not seem to be much point in documenting in detail what is essentially a lack of evidence, particularly when it is compared with the earlier period. For Russia, however, the references are now conveniently collected in T. S. Noonan, 'The Circulation of Byzantine Coins in Kievan Rus', *Byzantine Studies/Études Byzantines* 7 (1980), pp. 143–81.

[148] Dölger, *Regesten* I.1, p. 31.

[149] Theophanes, *Chronographia*; ed. de Boor, I, p. 376 (description of Walid's attempt to arabicise the Syrian financial bureaux, which were still staffed by Greek Christians).

[150] Canard, *Histoire de la dynastie des H'amdanides*, pp. 833, 850–1, 853. See also above, p. 258.

[151] Theophanes, *Chronographia*; ed. de Boor, I, p. 490. I. Duichev, 'La chronique byzantine de l'an 811', *Travaux et Mémoires* I (1965), pp. 210–16. Theophanes claims that the treasure was put under seal (*sphragidai*); the chronicle that it was divided amongst the troops (*ērxato diamerizein tō laō autou en*

took the Bulgarian capital Eilisson (which, from its position, according to Anna Comnena, dominated the whole plain of Dyrrhachium) in 1018, he found there the royal treasury, containing items of regalia and 100 kentenaria in coined gold (*khrysos episēmos*), some of which – but surely not, as suggested, all – he distributed to his troops as salary (*eis rhogas*).[152]

These two instances can, of course, be paralleled by Belisarius' earlier acquisition of the contents of the Vandal royal treasury on behalf of Justinian in 534;[153] by his acquisition of those of the Ostrogothic royal treasury in 540;[154] or by Heraclius' acquisition of a large part of the Sassanian royal treasury in 628,[155] although much of the last had to be burned. On the other hand the victorious campaigns of John Curcuas, Nicephorus Phocas, John Tzimiskes, Basil II and George Maniaces, in the east, must also have netted very considerable sums, in booty and from the ransoming of prisoners, over an extended period of time. In the fourteenth century, at least, the emperor received a fifth part (*pentamoiria*) of any booty (*koursos*) taken, and in the eleventh, foreign booty is specifically mentioned as having formed a major element in the reserve amassed by Basil II.[156]

*katagraphē*). The two are clearly not incompatible. The last words should doubtless be translated as 'on the (military) rolls', and demonstrate clearly that what the chronicle had in mind was a ceremonial and traditional distribution of *rhogai*. The mention of *khalkon* amongst the items found in the treasury leads Duichev (*op. cit.* pp. 228–9) to suppose, tentatively, the existence of an indigenous copper coinage. This is certainly incorrect, and is otherwise totally unrecorded in any way. It could have been Byzantine copper coinage, but the singular fact that the chronicle fails to record the finding of gold or silver makes it overwhelmingly more likely that *khalkon* should be translated as 'metal' – doubtless precious metal – a possibility that Duichev recognises, only to reject.

152 George Cedrenus, *Historiarum Compendium*; Bonn edn, II, p. 468: *Eilisson to phrourion, mētropolis ousa tēs pasēs Boulgarias kai ta khrēmata apotethauristo.* Anna Comnena (*Alexiad* XII.9.5–7; ed. Leib, III, pp. 83–4) is silent on its former history, but is in no doubt as to its strength and strategic position: *Ho de Elissos meteōron esti polikhnion kai pantē dysalōton....* The description of the treasure is entirely normal: *khrēmata polla kai stemmata ek margarōn kai khrysoüpheis esthētas kai khrysou episēmou kentēnaria hekaton.* The fact that the sentence then continues: *halina panta eis rhogas enekōse tēs peri auton stratias*, suggests that Basil put on the same kind of show as Nicephorus evidently had.

153 Procopius, *De Bello Vandalico* II.9.4–5; ed. Haury (Teubner), I, pp. 456–7. The treasure was obviously remarkable, containing as it did not only the Vandalic elements, but also Roman ones deriving from the sack of Rome by Gaiseric, and even Jewish ones deriving (through Rome) ultimately from the sack of Jerusalem by Titus.

154 Procopius, *De Bello Gothico* II.29.37, III.1.1–3; ed. Haury, II, pp. 288, 297–8. See also above, p. 224, for its contents, which do not seem to have excited the same admiration as those of the Vandal treasure.

155 Theophanes, *Chronographia*; ed. de Boor, I, pp. 321–2. The treasure, as might be expected, seems to have been as remarkable as the Vandal one, and is described as consisting of spices of all kinds, metal bullion, silk tunics, carpets (*nakotapēta*) and hangings, and so on.

156 Booty: Anonymous, *De Officiis* VI; ed. Verpeaux, p. 251. Ransoms: Toynbee, *Constantine Porphyrogenitus and his World*, pp. 390–3. Basil II: Michael Psellus, *Chronographia* I.31; ed. Renauld, p. 19 – noticeably, the property of those who had rebelled against him, which had then been sequestrated, is also mentioned. At an earlier date, the state had received a sixth part of any booty taken, and this itself seems to have replaced a tenth part. For the general situation, see: A. Dain, 'Le partage du butin de guerre d'après les traités juridiques et militaires', in *Actes du VI^e Congrès International d'Études Byzantines, Paris 27 juillet–2 août 1948* I, at pp. 347–54. For the particular situation see: Haldon, *op. cit.* above, p. 182 n. 143.

Even the twelfth century was not without its windfalls: the compensation for property and money seized by Manuel I from such Venetian citizens as were found on imperial territory in 1171 was later officially reckoned as amounting to 15 kentenaria.[157] It may well be that this action on Manuel's part had a politically negative result in the bitterness and distrust that it engendered, but it may equally well be considered as having been financially worthwhile. For the sum seems to have represented somewhat less than a third of the total that had been involved, and although most of the money was indeed handed over in compensation by Manuel's successors, this was done in small and irregular instalments only.[158] Much later Andronicus II was driven to confiscating Venetian property and money from the metropolitan colony to the value of 80,000 hyperpyra – although by this stage, of course, the situation was entirely different.[159]

The undoubted growth in the volume of trade with western mercantile powers during the eleventh and twelfth centuries may even have improved the situation somewhat, although the degree to which it was capable of doing this should not be exaggerated.[160] A clause in the treaty of 992 between Basil II and Constantine VIII on the one side, and the Venetians on the other, stipulates that Venetian merchants should in future pay a *kommerkion* of two nomismata per ship on arrival at Abydus and fifteen on departure, making a total of seventeen nomismata rather than more than thirty as previously.[161] One possible interpretation of the greatly differing rates for arrival and departure is that the balance of trade was heavily in favour of the empire, which is entirely plausible in view of what is known of the primary nature of western exports on the one hand, and the luxury – chiefly manufactured – nature of many Byzantine exports on the other.[162] If this interpretation is correct, then Venetian merchants will have had to make up the difference involved in precious metals, whether in coin or in ingot form.

There is also some evidence not only that the private export of precious metals was still prohibited in the twelfth century, but that their import, in ingot form at least, by foreigners was being positively encouraged. This, of course, would have been very much in conformity with the principle enunciated in the original novel of Valentinian I, Valens and Gratian.[163] A clause in the treaty of 1111 between Alexius I and the Pisans stipulates

[157] Nicetas Choniates, *Historia*; ed. van Dieten, I, pp. 174, 538. Tafel and Thomas, *Urkunden* I, p. 207 (14+1 centenaria).

[158] Refs: Brand, *Byzantium Confronts the West*, pp. 196–200, 366 (n. 5). At the rate of compensation actually mentioned (Brand, *op. cit.* p. 197), the entire sum would have amounted to some 48 kentenaria or some 345,000 hyperpyra. Brand is, of course, incorrect on the supposedly nugatory nature of the contemporary hyperpyron – see below, pp. 514, 517.

[159] George Pachymeres, *De Michaele et Andronico Palaeologis, De And.* III.19; Bonn edn, II, p. 242. Other refs: Laiou(-Thomadakis), *Constantinople and the Latins*, p. 105 n. 81.

[160] See below, pp. 590–602

[161] Tafel and Thomas, *Urkunden* I, pp. 36–9. See also: Martin, 'Venice and the Byzantine Empire before the Fourth Crusade', pp. 33, 36–7.

[162] See, for example: M. F. Hendy, 'Byzantium 1081–1204: An Economic Reappraisal', *Transactions of the Royal Historical Society* 20[5] (1970), pp. 49–50.

[163] See above, p. 257.

that: 'You [i.e. the Pisans] shall pay no *kommerkion* whatsoever on gold (*khrysaphion*) and silver bullion (*asēmion*) imported from your land.'[164]

Very much the same consciousness and mode of operation is evident in Gregoras' account[165] of the mighty famine and great dearth of necessary supplies (*limos iskhyros kai spanis megistē tōn khreiōdōn*) that afflicted the Selçuk sultanate during the reign of John III, and probably in *c.* 1234. Then, all the roads were full of Turks leaving and entering Roman territory, and the whole of Turkish wealth (*pas ho tōn Tourkōn ploutos*) ended up effortlessly in Roman hands, whether in the form of silver and gold, or in that of woven objects (*hosos en argyrō kai khrysō, hosos en hyphasmasi*), and in fact in the form of every kind of ware (*eidos*) that was intricate, very pleasant and precious. Thus (Turkish) wealth of great value (*pollon axia*) was offered for the sale of a little (Roman) grain (*sitos*), and a fowl (*ornis*), an ox (*bous*), or a goat (*eriphos*), became objects of great value. In this way, Roman households (*oikoi*) suddenly acquired an abundance of barbarian wealth, and the imperial treasury (*ta basilika tameia*) also filled up, and became weighed down with an abundance of wealth. It was from the sale of eggs produced by his flocks of fowls, and from the wealth thus acquired, that the emperor had a crown (*stephanos*) fashioned for the empress. This, adorned with very precious stones and pearls, he termed 'the egg-crown (*oatos*)'. On the other hand, when the same emperor saw that Roman wealth (*Rhomaïkos ploutos*) was being fruitlessly spent (*matēn kenoumenon*) upon the garments of foreign nations (*es ta ex allodapōn ethnōn endymata*), whether silk ones from Syria and Mesopotamia or well-woven ones from Italy, he issued a law (*dogma*) forbidding his subjects to wear them, under the threat of personal and family disgrace: they should wear only what Roman land grew, and what Roman hands fashioned.

These two instances of John III's actions, together with his known attitude to the imperial use of embroidered and silk garments, representing the 'blood of the Romans', and to be worn only as a formal expression of 'Roman wealth', strongly suggest his possession – and indeed implementation – of a conscious and co-ordinated financial and economic programme, however rudimentary it may have been. What, if anything, was unusual or novel in this, however, was his possession of a programme, and not the nature of the individual elements of that programme, each of which can be paralleled without difficulty.

[164] J. Müller, *Documenti sulle relazioni delle città toscane coll' Oriente Christiano e coi Turchi*, pp. 44 (Greek), 53 (Latin).

[165] Nicephorus Gregoras, *Historia Byzantina* II.6; Bonn edn, I, pp. 42–4.

## (III) INTERNAL AVAILABILITY

### A. The gold coinage: Beginnings and mechanisms

It seems clear that, although the conditions essential to the existence of a viable gold coinage were brought into being by Diocletian in his restoration of political stability, his administrative and financial reforms, and his restandardisation of the weight of the 'aureus', the successful provision of such a coinage was in large part the work of Constantine. In this provision, that emperor's introduction of the 'solidus' was probably a factor of marginal significance only: introduced early in the reign, at a time of financial exigence and monetary manipulation, its lower standard of weight was merely somewhat more convenient in matters of account and calculation than that of its predecessor.[166]

Far more significant are likely to have been three further factors: his acquisition of his defeated rivals' accumulated reserves (certainly that of Maxentius in 312, and presumably that of Licinius in 324); his confiscation of the treasures immobilised in the pagan temples, probably late in the reign and possibly in 331; and his institution of new taxes in precious metals, such as the *collatio glebalis* – levied annually on the senatorial class – and the *collatio lustralis* or *khrysargyron*. By this double action he (probably quite coincidentally) both immediately secured a large addition to the supply of precious metals available to the government and, on its having been expended, went some way towards ensuring its eventual continual recirculation. The gradual commutation of taxation in kind by his successors, in however unsystematic a fashion in the majority of cases, will have accentuated this cycle. Significantly enough, a marked increase in the use of gold in Egypt is indicated by the evidence of papyri from the middle of the century onwards. The process may also be seen, in a very general way, in the increasing relative ease with which it is now possible to procure solidi of the various fourth-century emperors: it is easier to procure a late solidus of Constantine than an early one; it is even easier to procure a solidus of Constantius II; and yet easier to procure one of Valentinian I or Valens.[167]

The significance of Constantine's confiscation of the temple treasures was appreciated

[166] See below, pp. 371–8 (administrative reforms), 449 ('aureus'), 466 ('solidus').

[167] Maxentius: Julian, *Orationes* II.8.B; ed. W. C. Wright (Loeb), I, p. 20. Julian, in praising Constantine, very interestingly remarks that Maxentius' greed (*aplēstia*) had acted like a drought (*aukhmos*), so that there was a severe lack of money (*pollē aporia khrēmatōn*), whilst in the recesses of the palace (*ta basileia*) wealth (*ploutos*) had been amassed. Constantine unbarred the door (of the palace) and suddenly released all the wealth. Julian cannot, of course, be regarded as more than an indirect source, and within the conventions of the panegyric hyperbole rules. He is therefore not a little suspect. But his account of the effects of imperial hoarding on the supply of coin agrees very well with those of Nicephorus and Theophanes (see below, pp. 298–9). Temple treasures: Anonymous, *De Rebus Bellicis* (see below, p. 285). Other refs: Jones, *Later Roman Empire* I, p. 92, III, p. 13 n. 33. C. R. Whittaker, 'Inflation and the Economy in the Fourth Century A.D.', in King (ed.), *Imperial Revenue, Expenditure and Monetary Policy in the Fourth Century A.D.*, at p. 5, regards Julian as contradicting himself as between Maxentius and the temple treasures, but this is too severe. New taxes: see above, p. 175. Commutation: see below, pp. 294–6.

by the anonymous author of the fourth-century treatise *De Rebus Bellicis*, who reports it in the following terms:

It was in the time of Constantine that extravagant largesse (*profusa largitio*) assigned gold instead of copper – which previously was considered of great value (*magni pretii*) – to transactions of low value (*vilibus commerciis*). The source of this greed is thought to have emerged in this way. When the gold and silver and the great quantity of precious stones (*aurum argentumque et lapidum pretiosorum magna vis*) stored up in the temples from ancient times reached the public, it kindled every man's desire for giving and possessing. And although the expenditure (*erogatio*) of copper itself – which, as we have stated, had been stamped with the faces of kings (*regum... vultu signatum*) – was considered already vast and burdensome, nevertheless, from a certain blindness, there ensued an earnestness for the more extravagant expenditure of gold which is considered more precious.

(Anonymous, *De Rebus Bellicis* II;
ed. Ireland, p. 5)

As has been more than once pointed out, the anonymous author's economic theory is crude, even confused.[168] The central fact of this section of his account – the increased use of gold from the time of Constantine onwards – does nevertheless seem accurate, and the explanation provided for that fact – the confiscation and entry into circulation of the temple treasures – is nevertheless entirely plausible.

The late Roman state of the fourth century had, in any case, its own much more direct method of acquiring the additional gold that it needed but had failed to bring in through regular taxation: a papyrus dated 300 reveals that it was then the practice of Diocletian's government to make forced purchases of gold outright, and sets a maximum price of 60,000 denarii per pound, again suggesting that payment was being made in base-metal coinage. A few years later the price had risen to 100,000 denarii per pound.[169] At these prices the state would have been paying out 4,800 billon nummi per pound of gold in 300, and 4,000 nummi per pound a few years later.[170] If it was paying out in the copper denominations of even smaller value, then the number of coins put into circulation by this method would obviously have been that much greater.

## *B. The base-metal coinage: Mechanisms*

The production, possibly, and the putting into circulation, certainly, of base-metal coinage seem likely to have been influenced substantially – at certain periods of late Roman and Byzantine history at least – not only by those factors that have been described or implied already, but also by a further factor inherent in a discrepancy existing between the financial

[168] E.g. L. Tondo, 'Il *De Rebus Bellicis* e la politica monetaria', *Rivista Italiana di Numismatica* $23^6$ (78) (1976), pp. 201–7.

[169] See below, pp. 457, 465.

[170] See below, p. 458, Table 15.

demands made by the state upon tax-payers, and the limitations placed upon the tax-payers' capacity to meet those demands by the denominational structure of the coinage.

The essence of this situation is revealed by a late twelfth-century treatise known as the *Palaia kai Nea Logarikē* which describes a series of reforms in the reckoning and collection of certain taxes undertaken by Alexius I between the years 1106 and 1109.[171] The taxes involved are those termed *parakolouthēmata*: the *dikeraton*, *hexafollon*, *synētheia* and *elatikon*, all of which were ancillary to the basic land-tax, the *dēmosios kanōn* or simply *kanōn*. The first two had always gone to the profit of the state, the last two had originally gone to the profit of the tax-collector, and to that of the state only later.

This distinction in origin had entailed another in reckoning and collection, for it is clear that when, prior to the reforms of 1106–9, the sum of the *kanōn*, *dikeraton* and *hexafollon* had amounted to two-thirds of a nomismata and upwards, or to a whole nomisma or a whole number of nomismata and two-thirds of a nomisma and upwards, then it had been the rule for the tax-collector to demand a whole nomisma or the next whole number of nomismata from the tax-payer. This practice was termed *kharagma*. The tax-collector had then returned the difference to the tax-payer in the form of small change. This practice was termed *strophē* or *antistrophē*. For example, if the sum of the *kanōn*, *dikeraton* and *hexafollon* had amounted to $1\frac{2}{3}$ nomisma, then two whole nomismata would have been demanded as *kharagma*, and one-third nomisma in small change returned as *strophē*.[172] For sums amounting to between a whole nomisma or a whole number of nomismata and two-thirds of a nomisma it seems probable that the tax-collector would have preferred payment in the second of the precious metals, silver, rather than in base metal. Even subsequent to the reforms of 1106–9, the basic land-tax, now divided into two parts, the *kharagma* and the *lepta psēphia*, theoretically should have been collected partly in precious-metal coin (*dia kharagmatos*) and partly in base-metal, i.e. copper coin (*dia noumiōn khalkōn*), while the *parakolouthēmata* should have been collected entirely in copper coin. But it is clear that, when it came to actual collection, the sums reckoned in terms of copper coin were commuted for billon, i.e. part silver, coin, at favourable rates.[173]

What these practices effectively involved in fiscal terms was the forced purchase of gold (in the form of whole nomismata) in return for copper (in the form of small change). What they quite clearly must have involved in terms of coinage was either an exaggeratedly high rate for the passage of small change through administrative hands as the state used whatever it had acquired, perhaps by means of other taxes, perhaps by purchase, to return *strophē* to the tax-payer, or the production of an exaggeratedly large amount of small change for the same purpose, or indeed a combination of both. The possible scale of the phenomenon becomes clear when it is considered that the state would

[171] Refs: see above, p. 235 n. 86.

[172] Hendy, *DOS* XII, pp. 51, 60–1.

[173] Hendy, *DOS* XII, pp. 58, 64.

have required ninety-six copper folleis in order to return a *strophē* of one third of a nomisma to the tax-payer. It is indeed quite conceivable that, to operate a system of this kind at all effectively, a tax-collector would have needed to have been already well supplied with small change (presumably direct from the appropriate mint) when he commenced his task in the district allotted him.

The Hohenstaufen and Angevin kings of Sicily seem to have operated a rather similar system whereby each regional justiciar was obliged to purchase on behalf of the state, within his own region and according to an annual assessment, a certain amount of gold, in return for which he paid out billon denarii.[174] This similarity, in view of the Byzantine origin or derivation of a number of features of Sicilian administration, may well not have been coincidental.

The adoption by the contemporary mint of Magnesia of an annual set of signa for its gold hyperpyra and of designs for its electrum and billon trachea; the probable adoption by the mint of Thessalonica of an annual set of designs for its billon trachea; and the adoption by the fourteenth-century mint of Constantinople of sporadic indictional dating for its billon trachea and copper tetartera: all demonstrate the connection implied above to be at least a not implausible one.[175]

The extraordinarily common and consistent overstriking of the base-metal, and particularly of the copper, coinage that is practised at various periods of Byzantine history would also be explained by a mechanism operating on such a basis. The assumption would be that each time a piece of base-metal coin passed through governmental hands, it was cycled through the mint, and there overstruck, rather than being melted down and entirely re-manufactured, as the precious-metal coinage tended to be. In a situation where this cycling was in any case artificially enhanced, such overstriking might well occur a number of times over a relatively short period.[176]

The date at which the practices termed *kharagma* and *strophē* first came into operation remains unknown. They were certainly already in existence by the middle of the eleventh century.[177] They are, however, not mentioned in the so-called *Ashburner Treatise* on

[174] E.g. N. Barone, 'La cedola per l'imposta ordinata dal Re Carlo I d'Angiò nel 1276 per la circolazione della nuova moneta di denari in Terra d'Otranto', in *Studi di Storia Napoletana in Onore di Michelangelo Schipa*, at pp. 127–39.

[175] Magnesia, Thessalonica: Hendy, *DOC* IV. Constantinople: T. Bertelè and C. Morrisson, *Numismatique byzantine*, pp. 123–36 (Appendix I: 'La date par l'indiction sur quelques monnaies des Paléologues'). It is also likely that at least much of the later Latin series of trachea attributable to Constantinople is also of an annual nature by type: Hendy, *DOC* IV.

[176] The most frequent examples of such overstriking derive from the late sixth and early seventh centuries, and from the tenth and eleventh centuries, but they are only somewhat less common from several other periods, and are perhaps entirely absent from none. See: Grierson, *DOC* II.1, pp. 218–19, III.2, pp. 635–9. Gold and silver is much less frequently overstruck, but even here, quite large-scale particular exceptions are known – e.g. Grierson, *DOC* III.1, p. 456 (Solidi, Class I, of Theodora, Michael III and Thecla, probably struck in haste in 842/3); below, p. 501 (miliaresia overstruck on dirhems).

[177] N. G. Svoronos, 'Recherches sur le cadastre byzantin et la fiscalité aux XI^e et XII^e siècles: le cadastre de Thèbes', *Bulletin de Correspondance Hellénique* 83 (1959), pp. 1–77, 86–9. Many of Svoronos' observations

taxation, which is probably of tenth-century date.[178] Their omission in that treatise should not, on the other hand, owing to its nature and brevity, be taken as conclusive evidence for their non-existence during that century. On general principles it might seem probable that their application to sums amounting to between two-thirds of a nomisma and the whole pre-supposes the existence, or possibly the still recent existence of the tremissis, at their moment of origin. Since the reign that saw the effective discontinuation of the denomination also saw the institution of one, and perhaps both, of the *parakolouthēmata* of which they took cognisance, it is clearly tempting to suppose that all of the elements involved were at least approximately contemporaneous and were therefore features of the reign of Leo III, or of those of his immediate successors.[179]

It is, as implied above, difficult to see how, in a state such as the late Roman and Byzantine which placed so high a priority upon the acquisition of precious metal through its taxation system, practices such as the *kharagma* and *strophē* could have been avoided. Indeed, on that basis they were inherent, for even at its most flexible the denominational structure of the gold coinage took effective account of the whole nomisma, the tremissis and the semissis only, and if tax payments were preferred in, or even limited to, gold coin, then the only sums other than those involving the whole nomisma or whole nomismata that could have been paid in that metal without some intermediate mechanism were those of one-third, one-half, two-thirds, or five-sixths of the nomisma, or their various multiples or multiple combinations.[180] With silver coin as a supplement or an alternative to gold, the situation might have been eased, but not rectified entirely.[181]

The institution of a series of light-weight solidi weighing 20 and 22 siliquae rather than a full 24 siliquae under Justinian, its continuation by his successors, and the addition of solidi weighing 23 siliquae under Maurice, seems very unlikely to be connected with this situation.[182] Had it been so connected, one would not have expected the existence of a solidus of 20 siliquae, attainable by the combination of one semissis and one tremissis, but one would have expected the existence of a solidus of 21 siliquae, not attainable by any such combination. It is conceivable that such solidi were occasionally used in such

upon the numismatic or monetary aspects of the Theban cadaster, and of the *Palaia kai Nea Logarikē*, have since been superseded by the studies of Hendy and Morrisson (see above, p. 235 n. 86), but his contribution to the study of Byzantine finance and taxation in this article remains a fundamental one.

178 Text: F. Dölger, *Beiträge zur Geschichte der byzantinischen Finanzverwaltung besonders des 10. und 11. Jahrhunderts*, pp. 113–23. Date: Ostrogorsky, *History of the Byzantine State*, p. 216 n. 3.

179 Discontinuation of tremissis: see below, p. 502. Institution of *dikeraton* and *hexafollon*: see above, p. 238.

180 Coins of $\frac{1}{4}$ nomisma are known for the seventh century, and of $\frac{1}{6}$ nomisma for the sixth and seventh centuries, but neither class can ever have formed a significant element in the circulating medium. See: Grierson, *DOC* II.1, pp. 10–11. A number of additional specimens have since come to light, but fail to alter the general pattern.

181 And in any case, a silver coinage was for long periods itself uncommon – for example during the fifth and sixth centuries, and during the eleventh. See below, pp. 468, 476, 511.

182 See below, pp. 492–3.

a situation, but the geographical pattern of their occurrence suggests that this was not their *raison d'être*, and their apparent internal rarity suggests that in any case they would have been of very limited use in this respect.[183]

## C. *The textual evidence* (c. *300–600*)

Circulation, of course, is likely to have been affected not so much by where coinage was produced as by where it was paid out and, in this connection, the dominance of fiscal and military factors in the production and distribution of coin should imply the existence of a highly accentuated pattern of circulation. Evidence for the existence of such a pattern does, in fact, exist.

The original Diocletianic pattern of coin production seems to have entailed the provision of a single main mint for each major fiscal unit, but although this pattern prevailed absolutely in the east it was rather less dominant in the west. There, although Britain, Gaul, Africa and Urbs Roma were each provided with a single mint, Gaul and Italy ended up with two mints each, and the Five Provinces and Spain with none. It has been pointed out that these exceptions were dictated by the presence or absence of heavy military concentrations in the fiscal units involved. In *c.* 307, the mint of Carthage was moved to Ostia and, in *c.* 313, to Arles. These movements both seem to have been dictated by political considerations. The result was that the diocese of Africa lacked a mint throughout by far the greater part of the fourth century.[184] It did, however, contain a relatively moderate number of military units, and its provinces of Mauretania (Caesariensis and Sitifensis), Numidia, Africa (Proconsularis) and Byzacena – but not that of Tripolitania – did contain a large number of cities, many of which were admittedly, very small.[185]

How, then, was the diocese of Africa supplied with coinage? The local military will, presumably, have been paid their annual *stipendia et donativa* in base-metal coinage. They will, presumably, also have been paid their accessional and quinquennial *donativa* in precious-metal coinage sent out from the *comitatus*.[186] The civil bureaucracy will have been paid, although to what extent in kind and to what in coinage remains uncertain.

183 Nor, by extension, is it likely to be connected with officially dictated fluctuations between the gold: copper ratio (so Hahn, *MIB* I, pp. 25–7, II, pp. 14–17, followed by Morrisson, in *Revue Numismatique* 16$^6$ (1974), at pp. 187–9, and again, but noticeably with much less enthusiasm, in *op. cit.* 17$^6$ (1975), at p. 198 (reviews of Hahn, *MIB* I, and II, respectively)). Next to nothing that is direct is known of such fluctuations, and the indirect nature of the evidence permits only circular argument (cf. below, pp. 477–8). Besides, the continued issue of such light-weight solidi over one hundred and fifty years, much of the period witnessing metrological chaos in the copper coinage, brought about by military and political events, renders any such consistent explanation simply improbable (see pp. 498–9).

184 See below, pp. 380–1, 385–6.

185 Military: Jones, *Later Roman Empire* I, pp. 59, 196–7. Cities: *ibid.* II, p. 715–16, and map 5 ('Distribution of cities in the middle of the fifth century').

186 See above, pp. 187–90 (acc. and quinq. *donativa*); below, pp. 458–9 (annual *stipendia et donativa*).

Other than this, some base-metal coinage may have entered the diocese by means of technical fiscal practices,[187] and some by the normal processes of trade.[188] There is, however, no evidence for any other systematic method or source of supply.

If the reconstruction attempted above is anywhere near accurate, then the level of liquidity within the diocese of Africa should have been quite exceptionally low, and it is with this consideration in mind that a law preserved in the *Codex Justinianus*[189] may perhaps best be understood:

The same Augusti [Valentinian I and Valens] to Oricus, *Praeses Tripolitaniae*

> The owners of estates should accept what the land produces [i.e. crops], and should not demand coin (*pecunia*), which the peasants (*rustici*) do not dare to hope for, unless the custom of the estate requires this.

The law has been dated from its context to 366. The addressee, Oricus, is otherwise unknown, and since a certain Ruricius is known to have been *praeses Tripolitaniae* during the years *c.* 364–8, it has been suggested[190] that his name should be restored as such.

It would obviously have been helpful to know the detailed circumstances surrounding the issue of the law, and the precise status that the law was intended to possess. It does at least seem reasonable to assume, from its heading, that the law was issued in response to a request for a ruling on the part of the *praeses*, and, because it was carried over into the *Codex Justinianus*, that it was intended to be of general application when issued, and was still, even if in theory only, of general application when the *Codex* was drawn up.

The precise significance to be attributed to the law must also remain uncertain. Again, it does at least seem reasonable to accept, from the identity of the addressee, either that the owners of Tripolitanian estates might have been more pressing than those elsewhere to convert their rents from kind to money, or that the level of liquidity in Tripolitania might have been lower than elsewhere, or indeed that both situations might have held good. There is some slight evidence that the second of these situations, a lower level of liquidity than elsewhere, did actually hold good, for rents in money – whether partly or wholly – do seem to have been rather commoner outside Africa.[191] Two Constantinian laws preserved in the *Codex Theodosianus* dealing with the counterfeiting of base-metal coinage are also addressed to African officials.[192] Whether the problem was even more acute in Tripolitania than in the rest of Africa remains entirely obscure, although on

187 Such as the direct forced purchase of gold (below, pp. 457, 465), or some such indirect means as the *kharagma* and *strophē* (above, pp. 285–8) or their predecessors.

188 See for example below, pp. 291–3.

189 *CJ* XI.48.5.

190 *PLRE* I, pp. 654 (Oricus), 786 (Ruricius).

191 Jones, *Later Roman Empire* II, pp. 803–5.

192 See below, pp. 324–5. This may simply be a reflection of the known over-representation of African laws and officials in the *Codex* (Jones, *Later Roman Empire* I, pp. 474–5), but in the light of the other evidence it may be of genuine significance.

general grounds this would not seem improbable, for the province had fewer cities than the others and was geographically the furthest removed from a mint.

It is with the possible existence of an exceptionally low level of liquidity within the diocese of Africa in mind that a further, approximately contemporary, law, preserved in the *Codex Theodosianus*,[193] should be considered:

IF ANYONE SHOULD MELT DOWN OR (*VEL*) TRANSPORT COINS FOR THE PURPOSE OF TRADING THEM OR (*AUT*) HANDLE FORBIDDEN COINS

Emperor Constantius Augustus and Julian Caesar, to Rufinus, Praetorian Prefect

Whoever is found either (*vel*) melting down or (*vel*) transporting coins (*pecuniae*) to different regions in order to sell them (*vendendi causa*) let him come under the sentence of sacrilege and suffer capital punishment. For We order ports and various shores where there is customarily easy access to ships, and minor roads, to be guarded by suitable officials and appointees established by governors (*praesides*) and others possessed of authority, so that having learned the truth the governors of provinces (*provinciarum rectores*) may punish the guilty according to the laws. Their bureaux (*officia*) shall also be under extreme peril. (1) No one amongst the traders (*negotiatores*) is to carry on his animals more than a thousand folles in coins established in public use (*pecuniae in usu publico constitutae*) for the purpose of expenses (*gratia sumptuum*). And if anyone should be discovered carrying a greater amount, his property shall be forfeited to the control of the treasury (*fiscus*), and he himself banished. (2) For We order that merchants (*mercatores*) should not carry every kind of coin in their ships, and in fact We permit only such coins as are established in public use to be so carried, and similarly only such goods (*species*) as are customarily carried to different regions by merchants to be bought. But it shall be entirely unlawful for anybody to buy or handle forbidden coins (*pecuniae vetitae*), because it is proper for the price of a thing to be in coins established in public use and not in merchandise (*merces*). [And finally it is Our pleasure that if by any chance any coin (*nummus*) other than that continuing in public use shall be found in the possession of any merchant, it should be forfeited to the control of the treasury with all the property of the offender.] And if ships do by chance come with merchandise to whatever province then it shall be sold with all the customary freedom, with the exception of the coins which they call *maiorinae* or (*vel*) *centenionales communes* by usual custom or (*vel*) others which they know to be forbidden.

Received 8 March at Constantina in the consulships of Constantius Augustus (for the eighth time) and Julian Caesar [356].

[193] *CTh.* IX.23.1. This law has attracted a considerable secondary literature. See, in the last instance: J.-P. Callu, 'Rôle et distribution des espèces de bronze de 348 à 392', in King (ed.), *Imperial Revenue, Expenditure and Monetary Policy in the Fourth Century A.D.*, pp. 44–5, 47–8, 68. Callu (who cites his own preceding work on the subject only) accepts that the law basically concerns trade in coin between Arles and Africa and Spain, and also that the *pecuniae vetitae* of the law are issues of Magnentius. However, he then goes on to assume that because of 'inflation' the face value of the large coin had become less than its intrinsic value, and that it therefore passed at a premium: the emperor's reaction was therefore to demonetise the coin. In order to achieve this sense he has to assume that the *vel* between *maiorinae* and *centenionales* is conjunctive. He also has to admit that the hoard of evidence, on which he normally places so much emphasis, does not actually correspond with his assumption of demonetisation, and the coins continued to be hoarded. In other words, the interpretation proposed below still seems the most consistent and satisfactory.

The law, a somewhat confused one, raises a number of problems, including the basic ones of the identity of the addressee and both the date and the place at which it was received. One possible solution[194] is that the law is in fact a conflation of two, the earlier text of which was addressed to an unknown praetorian prefect, probably of Gaul, and that it was received on 8 March 356 at Arles (Constantina). The phrase 'And finally... the offender' (in square brackets) should, in this case, be omitted from this text and transferred elsewhere.[195] On the other hand, the fact that (Vulcacius) Rufinus was indeed praetorian prefect in Gaul in 354,[196] apparently being replaced by (C. Ceionius Rufius) Volusianus by 1 January 355,[197] strongly suggests the law to have been somewhat less drastically altered than the above solution proposes.

The proposition that the postscript to the law originally read: '...*Constantio A. VII et Constantio C. III Conss.*' (i.e. 354), and that it was only subsequently emended to: '*Constantio A. VIII et Iuliano C. Conss*'. (356), so as to take account of the disgrace and execution of Gallus in 354, is not in itself an implausible one, for Constantius was indeed in Arles, and Rufinus was indeed prefect, in 354. On the other hand, so radical an emendation, on no evidence beyond the circumstantial, seems little short of cavalier. In any case, whether 354, or 356, or thereabouts, the intent of the law was probably identical.[198]

Whatever the solution, as the heading to the law indicates, its general aims were three-fold: to forbid the melting down of coin, the transport of coin for speculative sale, and the use of forbidden coin.

Of these aims, the first had already been the subject of a law of 349[199] and, perhaps for this reason, receives very little attention. The second is the subject of a much greater degree of attention. It may be deduced from the text that merchants had been transporting coin, on a scale sufficient to attract the notice of the authorities, for the purposes of speculation. This presumably involved taking coin, or one kind of coin, from an area in which it was relatively common, and therefore cheap in terms of goods or other kinds of coin, to an area in which it was scarce, and therefore dear. There, presumably, it had been sold at a premium. The authorities' reaction to the situation was to station officials at strategic points to enforce a limit on the amount of coin that merchants were permitted to take from one place to another. This limit, of 1,000 folles, implies that what was being transported was base-metal rather than precious-metal coin, for the sum expressed in gold or silver would still have been very large, while expressed in billon or copper, or as

194 P. Grierson, 'The Roman Law of Counterfeiting', in R. A. G. Carson (ed.), *Essays in Roman Coinage Presented to Harold Mattingly*, at pp. 260–1.

195 *CTh.* IX.21.10 (*Rufino, p.po.*, 393), see below, p. 325.

196 *PLRE* I, pp. 782–3 (Vulcacius Rufinus 25).

197 *PLRE* I, pp. 978–80 (C. Ceionius Rufius Volusianus *signo* Lampadius 5).

198 E.g. Callu, 'Rôle et distribution des espèces de bronze de 348 à 392', p. 56 n. 67.

199 See below, p. 470.

individual coins, it would have been that much smaller and therefore more plausible as a limit.[200] The speculative transport that was being legislated against seems to have included within its scope certain classes of coin already termed 'forbidden', and the third aim of the law was to forbid not only their limited transport but their continued use under any circumstances whatsoever.

The two subsidiary problems arising from the law concern the origin and destination of the coin that was being speculatively transported, and the identity of the 'forbidden' coins.

As in the case of the previous law, it would obviously have been helpful to know the circumstances surrounding the issue of this one. On general grounds it is not impossible that it was issued in response to a request for a ruling on the part of the prefect, and one particular consideration suggests that this may indeed have been so. This is that the law mentions both transport by land and transport by sea – but then subsequently pays less attention to the former than to the latter.

Now Arles itself, while not on the open sea, stood at the head of the Rhone Delta and was one of the chief ports of Gaul. The implication therefore seems to be that the transport in question originated at Arles. But what, then, was its destination? Surely those neighbouring areas which, because they lacked heavy military concentrations and therefore mints, probably had an exceptionally low level of liquidity. In the case of transport by land, probably Spain; in that of transport by sea, probably Spain, or Africa, or both. The existence of such transport might well be held to explain the relatively large numbers of coins of the mint of Arles in North African, and more particularly in Spanish, hoards.[201]

The situation would in fact bear a curious resemblance to a thirteenth-century one, in which – despite legislation – enormous quantities of silver coin were shipped from the Christian ports of southern France to the Muslim ones of Spain and northern Africa.[202]

The law concludes with the sentence: 'And if ships do by chance come with merchandise to whatever province, then it shall be sold with all the customary freedom, with the exception of the coins which they call *maiorinae* or (*vel*) *centenionales communes* by usual custom or (*vel*) others which they know to be forbidden.' The term *maiorina* is clearly a vulgar or technical one, presumably deriving from the comparative adjective *maior* and referring to the relatively large size of the coin involved. The coin itself is known, from a law of 349,[203] to have contained both silver and copper. The centenionalis may be deduced, from a law of 395,[204] as having been a relatively small coin. The most natural interpretation is that the maiorina is to be identified with the large billon coin, and the

[200] See below, pp. 339–41.

[201] Callu, 'Rôle et distribution des espèces de bronze de 348 à 392', pp. 48–9.

[202] Watson, 'Back to Gold – and Silver', pp. 11–14.

[203] See below, p. 470.

[204] See below, pp. 474–5.

centenionalis with the small copper coin, of the reformed coinage system of 348.[205] The former had already suffered a debasement of its material and a lightening of its weight, and the latter had already ceased to be struck, by 356.

The question arises as to whether, as frequently supposed, the intention of the law's concluding sentence was to demonetise, or to confirm the demonetisation of, these coins. The answer depends, to a considerable extent, on the punctuation supplied: does the phrase 'which they know to be forbidden' apply to maiorinae, centenionales, and others, or to the last alone? The structure of the Latin text, (*pecunias*) *quas more solito maiorinas vel centenionales communes appellant vel ceteras quas vetitas esse cognoscunt*, with its repetition of the relative pronoun and of the present indicative form of the verb, surely suggests the latter. The second half of the sentence should, then, read: 'with the exception of the coins which they call *maiorinae* or *centenionales communes* by usual custom, or others which they know to be forbidden'. The word 'or' (*vel*) is thus used throughout in a disjunctive sense. This is as might be expected, for it is on the face of it unlikely, for example, that in the concluding sentence, *vel* is in the first case conjunctive and in the second disjunctive.

Again, the development of the text as a whole surely supports this interpretation. The concluding sentence clearly acts as a summary of the main provisions of the law: merchandise is thus to be sold with all the customary freedom, with the exception of maiorinae and centenionales (which as current coins are to be transported and used in limited quantities only) and 'forbidden' coins (which as demonetised coins are to be neither transported, nor sold, nor handled, under any circumstances).

Finally, both the date and the place of receipt of the law suggest the identity of the 'forbidden' coins. They were those of the Gallic usurper Magnentius, who had been finally defeated less than three years before (summer 353), and whose issues would otherwise have formed a considerable element in the circulating medium. It is known from John Cassian[206] that one of the functions of money-changers was to withdraw from circulation the coinage of usurpers. The law should be taken as further evidence of this attitude.

It should not be supposed, however, that a level of liquidity fundamentally higher than the one already implied necessarily prevailed even in areas (other than in large and densely populated urban areas) that were apparently well served by mints. In this respect, an episode occurring during the earlier part of the reign of Justinian is significant and instructive.

The systematic commutation of taxation in kind to taxation in coin, and therefore to precious-metal coin, particularly gold, in the eastern half of the empire, seems to have been the work of Anastasius. Up until his time, the transport of taxes in kind from where they had been grown, or had been collected, to where they were needed for whatever reason, but principally for the payment of the military, had been one of the major official functions of the slow section (*cursus clabularis*) of the public post (*cursus publicus*).

[205] See below, pp. 470, 474–5.

[206] See above, pp. 249–50.

Subsequently, the transport of taxes in coin from where they had been collected to the imperial *comitatus*, by this stage a static metropolitan residence, will have become an increasing official function of the fast section (*cursus velox*) of the post.[207]

The systematic commutation of taxation meant that the maintenance of the *cursus clabularis* in particular, which was expensive, became less necessary to the state, and that it was liable to be curtailed or even abandoned in any search for economies: its vestigial official functions might be performed adequately by hired facilities. During the earlier part of the reign of Justinian, John the Cappadocian, then praetorian prefect of the East, carried through a number of economies, amongst which was the drastic curtailment of the *cursus publicus* throughout his prefecture, and its complete abandonment in the diocese of Asiana. What then happened is described both by John Lydus, and by Procopius, in the following terms:

For he [John the Cappadocian] considered the service (*hypēresia*) provided by the public post (*dēmosioi hippoi*) to be excessive, not being able to see – being more stone-blind than Niobe herself – the use of the institution. So the prefect, without the knowledge of the emperor, for the latter would not have permitted the public to be incommoded, abolished that aspect of the state as well. As a consequence, the unsold crops (*eidoi apratoi*) rotted on the estates, and it happened that Asiana was virtually destroyed, the land-owner being ruined when gold was exacted by the tax-collectors instead of kind (*anti tōn eidōn*), for he was neither able to sell the crops because he was far removed from the sea, nor was he permitted – as formerly – to use them up in taxation (*tō dēmosiō*). In addition to this there followed a change in the disposition of the military forces stationed in the area, effected by the state in accordance with necessity. Because of this coincidence, with the harvest (*karpoi*) remaining in the fields, and with taxation changed into gold, the harvest was ploughed back into the earth each year.

(John Lydus, *De Magistratibus* III.61; ed. Wuensch (Teubner), pp. 151–2)

Besides, land-owners in every region, and particularly those whose land happened to be in inland areas, enjoyed great prosperity because of this system [the public post]: for every year they sold the surplus of their harvest (*karpoi*) to the state to provide food for the horses and grooms [*sc.* of the post], and they made a great deal of money (*megala khrēmata*). And so, in this way, it happened both that the state always received the taxes (*phoroi*) due from each person, and that those who paid [the taxes] received [their money] back immediately. In addition, the needs of the state were satisfied.

(Procopius, *Historia Arcana* XXX.5–7; ed. Haury (Teubner), III, pp. 181–2)

And the land-owners, with their harvest rotting and lying useless, remain continuously profitless.

(*Ibid.* XXX.11; *ed. cit.* p. 183)

The two accounts substantially confirm and complement one another, indeed do so in terms that strongly suggest them to be closely connected, whether directly or indirectly, and clearly describe a crisis which they may have exaggerated to some extent, but which nevertheless must have been of considerable proportions.

[207] *Cursus publicus*: Jones, *Later Roman Empire* II, pp. 830–4. See also below, pp. 603–13

The commutation of taxation was evidently feasible without further arrangement in some areas, but to the extent that the state provided – through the presence and functioning of one of its own organs – merely the requisite degree of liquidity, in many others. The possibilities for, bulk, and costs of private transport were clearly such that the produce of estates more than a relatively short distance from the coast, or from a navigable river, could not be sold – without immense physical difficulty and prohibitive financial loss – for the cash in which commuted taxes were to be paid, without some form of government intervention. This took the form of purchase, whether to satisfy the needs of the public post or of the military forces. It therefore depended not upon an awareness of, or a concern for, the convenience of the land-owner, but upon the application of administrative or military policies that arose out of an entirely different set of considerations.

The existence of much the same cycle as described above had already been implied in the early fourth century, when Lactantius identifies its basic components during the reign of Galerius, and when specific papyrological evidence illustrates its operation at much the same time. It was clearly normative.[208] Cappadocian land-owners are reported to have been in a somewhat similar helpless condition to that of their colleagues in Asiana, later in the fourth century, in the following well-known passage from Gregory of Nazianzen, describing a famine in the region of Caesarea:

There was a famine (*limos*), it was the worst within living memories, and the city was hard-pressed, for there was neither aid from anywhere, nor was there a remedy for the evil. Now, the coastlands (*paraliai*) bear such scarcities (*endeiai*) with no difficulty, giving of their own and receiving [i.e. exporting their own products and importing others in exchange] by sea (*para tēs thalassēs*). But for us who live inland (*tois d'hēpeirōtais hēmin*), both a surplus is unprofitable (*kai to peritteuon anonēton*), and a need is unsatisfiable (*kai to endeon anepinoēton*), not having the means to export what does exist (*ta onta*), or to import what does not exist (*ta ouk onta*).

(Gregory of Nazianzen, *Orationes* XLIII.34; *PG* XXXVI, cols 541, 544)

[208] Lactantius, *De Mortibus Persecutorum* XXXI.2, 5; ed. J. Moreau, I, pp. 113, 114: *(Et ut) qui iam dudum provinciis afflixerat auri argentique indictionibus factis, quae promiserat redderet, etiam in nomine vicennalium secure altera afflixit... Quid vestis omnis generis? Quid aurum? Quid argentum? Nonne haec necesse est ex venditis fructibus comparari? Unde igitur haec, o dementissime tyranne, praestabo, cum omnes fructus auferas?* The *vicennalia* involved were those of Galerius. *P.Cair. Isidor.* 89: A group of five men, one of them Aurelius Isidorus, acknowledges receipt of 15 talents as the price of 100 artabas of beans (payment to be in advance of delivery). The following declaration then occurs: *Hoper argyrion ekhōrēsen eis synonēn khry[siou kai] asēm[ou hy]per tēs eautōn ktēseōs eis tēn theia[n epi]bolēn, kai eperōtēth(entes) hōmolog(ēsan).* The date is 308. It looks as if *argyrion* here means 'cash' rather than 'silver' (as translated), and that the consortium had sold their beans for billon or copper coins to buy gold and silver bullion to pay the tax. See also below, p. 298 n. 213.

## D. *The textual evidence (c. 600–1450)*

The scale of the difficulties that commutation, at least, might cause the land-owner is hinted at by Cedrenus in his description of one of the major causes of the Bulgarian revolt of 1040–1, during the reign of Michael IV, and the financial direction of his brother John the *orphanotrophos*:

> For the emperor Basil [II], when he had subdued the Bulgarians, wishing neither any innovations to be made nor practices to be changed, ordered that under his own rule things should remain the same, and that they were to be done just as they had been under Samuel [the former Bulgarian tsar]. And so the Bulgarian who owned a yoke of oxen was to pay the state a measure (*modios*) of wheat (*sitos*), as much of millet (*kenkhros*), and a measure (*stamnos*) of wine (*oinos*). But [John] the *orphanotrophos* ordered nomismata to be paid instead of kind (*anti tōn eidōn*). With the locals not bearing this entirely patiently, and having discovered the convenient and well-timed appearance of Deljan [the leader of the Bulgarian revolt], they rid themselves of Roman domination and returned to their former state.
>
> (George Cedrenus, *Historiarum Compendium*; Bonn edn, II, p. 530)

The difficulties faced by the Balkan land-owners in the eleventh century no doubt were greater than those faced by the Anatolian ones in the sixth; when Bulgaria was finally recovered in 1018 it had not formed part of a state regularly issuing coinage for over four hundred years, and it is doubtful whether the two decades between recovery and revolt had sufficed to effect any great change in its basic financial and economic structure. In the mid sixth century, on the other hand, Asiana had a virtually continuous tradition of monetary production and use extending back not only to the beginnings of Roman rule but to those of coinage itself. That despite this, and its relatively developed economy, the commutation of taxation followed by the abandonment of the public post and the movement of military forces should entail a crisis of considerable proportions, suggests the existence of a monetary economy of a very specialised and indeed precarious nature only.

Documentary and literary evidence for the later period is scarcer even than that for the earlier. It is frequently supposed[209] that the persistence of prices or juridical penalties in terms of coin is a guarantee of the continuation of a monetary economy – whatever that may mean in view of the conditions revealed above. Fines, at least, tend to be relatively large, and, in any case, are neither exacted nor paid every day, and even when expressed in monetary terms they need not necessarily be paid in actual coin. Indeed, one of the codes frequently quoted on this subject, the *Nomos Geōrgikos*, generally dated to the late seventh or early eighth century,[210] would rather seem to indicate a virtual

[209] E.g. Ostrogorsky, 'Byzantine Cities in the Early Middle Ages', pp. 63–5.

[210] W. Ashburner, 'The Farmer's Law', *Journal of Hellenic Studies* 30 (1910), pp. 85–108. For the nature and date of the *Nomos Geōrgikos*, see, in the last instance: N. G. Svoronos, 'Notes sur l'origine et la date du code rural', *Travaux et Mémoires* 8 (1981), pp. 487–500.

lack of coin in rural areas of the time: of its eighty-five headings, most involving penalties or fines, only two involve a specific monetary sum (12 folleis).[211]

Particular study, for example of thirteenth-century documents relating to western Anatolia, in any case tends to suggest the submerged existence of a much more ambiguous situation, which actually comes to light only from time to time, in which taxation might well be both defined in terms of coin and paid in it, but in which other prices could well be defined in terms of coin but paid wholly or partly in kind, or even both defined in terms of kind and paid in it. The existence of such a situation, perhaps in a more extreme form, known and openly acknowledged for the early mediaeval west, should occasion no surprise for the east.[212]

According to Pachymeres, the (probably punitive) reassessment (*exisōsis*) of the tax-yields of the Anatolian regions of Boukellarion, Maryandena (i.e. Optimaton) and Paphlagonia, at the order of Michael VIII, and the consequent demands for increased payments to the public treasury (*koinon tamieion*), the reserves (*ta tethēsaurismena*) of which had been exhausted, on the part of his financial agents, were at least partly responsible for provoking a serious crisis in those regions:

> And so it happened to both the Paphlagonians, and to those who were even more distant, that at the time they suffered through the levying of taxes. For although the land particularly easily yielded useful things [*sc.* crops], it only sparsely yielded coinage (*nomismata*), which resulted in pressing needs (*ta anagkaia*) for all the farmers. For the tax-headings having been reckoned in terms of gold and silver coins (*kephalaioumenōn goun tōn telōn epi nomismasi khrysiou kai argyriou*), they were driven to give their stock [i.e. *to tethen*, presumably reserves of coin] out of necessity.
>
> (Pachymeres, *De Michaele et Andronico Palaeologis*, *De Mich.* III.22; Bonn edn, I, pp. 221–2)

As it happens, and despite the somewhat indeterminate details of the account, it does serve to confirm and elaborate the details of earlier accounts, given by both the patriarch Nicephorus and the chronicler Theophanes, of what happened when the emperor Constantine V attempted to build up a reserve:[213]

211 Ashburner, 'The Farmer's Law', pp. 100 (cap. xxii), 105 (cap. lxii). Ostrogorsky's similar claim that the *Nomos Geōrgikos* 'often speaks of the daily wage of village laborers, communal herdsmen and guards' ('Byzantine Cities in the Early Middle Ages', p. 64), is equally specious: it does so on four occasions only (including one of the instances quoted above) – Ashburner, *op. cit.* pp. 100 (cap. xxii), 101 (cap. xxv), 102 (caps xxxiii, xxxiv). The term used is *misthos*, which is not necessarily a monetary one, but even if it were given a monetary value it need not necessarily be paid in coin.

212 Angold, *A Byzantine Government in Exile*, p. 107 and n. 90. C. M. Cipolla, *Money, Prices and Civilization in the Mediterranean World*, pp. 3–12.

213 See above, p. 284 n. 167, for the somewhat suspect passage of Julian on Maxentius. Theodoret also mentions a local lack of gold (*spanis khrysiou*) and a cessation of purchasing (i.e. *tōn ōniōn errhimenōn*), with nobody offering for the fresh or dried crops (*hygrois...xērois...karpois*), the inhabitants having rather borrowed (*daneisamenoi*) five, ten, or twenty, gold coins, stripping the local soldiery, so as to be able to send gold to Neon the *arkhōn* (Theodoret, *Epistolai* XXXVII; ed. Y. Azéma, I, p. 102). The precise cause and nature of the situation are left unclear.

For Constantine, the lover of gold and hater of Christ, showed himself a new Midas, and hoarded all the gold (*kai ton khryson apanta apothēsaurizei*). And so it came about that the tax-payers (*phorologoumenoi*) were so pressed in the collection of taxes (*phoroi*) that the fruits of the earth (*tēs gēs karpēmata*) and the crops (*gennēmata*) were sold off cheaply (*euōnōs*), so that sixty modioi of wheat (*sitos*) were bought up for a nomisma, and seventy of barley (*krithē*), and for the most part they were sold off at an altogether smaller price. This was termed an abundance of the earth (*euphoria tēs gēs*) and a thriving state of affairs (*pragmatōn euthēnia*) by the ignorant, but a work of tyranny and avarice (*philokhrēmatia*), and an evil of inhumanity, by those who know better.

(Nicephorus, *Breviarium*; Bonn edn, p. 85)

He [Constantine] caused goods (*ta eidē*) to abound in the City [*sc.* Constantinople], at this time. For, becoming a new Midas, he hoarded gold (*ton khryson apethēsaurise*), and ruined the farmers (*geōrgoi*), for through the collection of taxes men were forced to sell off cheaply the supplies (*khorēgiai*) that derive from God.

(Theophanes, *Chronographia*; ed. de Boor, I, p. 443)

Much later, George Gemistus Plethon, with reference to the fifteenth-century Morea, complains that most taxes were paid in coin (*nomismati*) and not in kind (*khrēmasi*). In future they should be paid not in coin, for this had led to long-standing and extreme difficulties of collection (*khalepōtatai...eispraxeis*) for both payers and receivers (*eispherousi kai...eisprattousi*), but in kind. Elsewhere, he proposes the same solution to obviate the absurdity of utilising foreign, bad, and copper-coloured coins (*tois xenikois toutois kai hama ponērois khalkeiois khrōmenous*), presumably mainly Latin billon ones. The basic problem in making use of the information provided in the two treatises addressed to Manuel II is that they are so permeated by Platonic ideals and even phrases that it is even more than usually difficult to judge what in them represents mere literary *topos*, and what contemporary reality.[214]

### E. Regional distinctions

If the political frontiers of the empire defined the general area within which the late Roman and Byzantine coinage may be considered as having circulated to some extent normally, then internal political or administrative boundaries might also define, or at least play the major rôle in defining, particular areas within which the production or circulation of the coinage might vary.

That internal political boundaries, which came into existence when the government of the empire was divided – with or without the agreement of the various parties involved – between a number of rulers, might affect the production or circulation of the coinage, seems obvious, and indeed a number of instances of this kind of situation will later be mentioned.[215]

[214] George Gemistus Plethon, *Orationes* I.7, 11, 21; ed. J.-P. Migne, in *PG* CLX, at cols 825, 829, 837.

[215] See below, pp. 453–4, 466, 470–1, 471–2, 468.

That internal administrative boundaries, which could exist whether the government of the empire was united or divided, might have much the same effect, is perhaps less immediately obvious, but is nonetheless the case. The classic instance of such a situation is that which characterised the fourth to seventh centuries when production varied according to the administrative status of the mints involved: in the first place whether the mints were comitatensian or palatine on the one hand, or regional on the other;[216] in the second whether they were eastern or western.[217] During the sixth century the production of a significant silver coinage was confined to the western palatine mints of Carthage and Ravenna, the eastern ones of Thessalonica and Constantinople producing little or none.[218] During the seventh century the opposite situation obtained, the production of silver being virtually confined to Constantinople, the western mints producing little or none.[219] The difference may well have reflected varying gold:silver ratios within the several prefectures.[220]

Again, the extent of the Heraclian reform which resulted in the centralisation of production in the east, but which was clearly not intended to apply to production in the west, was defined by administrative and, in particular, prefectural boundaries.[221] A similar situation prevailed during the twelfth century, when the absence of regional mints in the Asian provinces contrasted with their presence in the European ones, a contrast which seems to have reflected the differing administrative structure of the two regions.[222] Within the European provinces themselves, a distinction between the base-metal denomination prevalent in an area approximating to Greece, and that prevalent in Bulgaria, also seems to have been defined by administrative and particularly thematic boundaries.[223]

All the accounts reproduced or mentioned above agree in their essentials. The imposition of extra taxes, or of extraordinarily severely collected taxes, or both, specifically or by implication in cash, presumably gold and silver, caused a fairly immediate and noticeable shortage of coin that resulted in its being bought at a premium in return for commensurately cheapened agricultural products. This clearly tended to favour the capital, where taxation was probably less severe and coin more readily available, at the expense of the regions, where the opposite obtained. Once again, the suggestion is of a monetary economy of a very limited kind only.

The evidence therefore suggests the existence of extreme variations in the degree of liquidity prevailing in the different sectors of society. No doubt that prevailing in large and densely populated urban areas was relatively, even absolutely, high. During the earlier period, at least, a number of the largest of these areas contained, or occasionally contained,

216 See below, pp. 378–86, 386–94.

217 See below, p. 468.

218 See below, pp. 399–401, and Table 11.

219 See below, pp. 494–5, cf. Pl. 22, 4.

220 See below, pp. 484–6.

221 See below, pp. 417–19, and Table 12.

222 See below, pp. 430–2.

223 See below, pp. 435–7, and Map 36.

an imperial court. Even if they did not, they and many of the smaller ones contained the headquarters of a regional tier of civil or military administration, or both. Yet others contained a garrison. Virtually all of those areas in the first category, and several of those in the second, also contained a mint.[224]

Private trade, of whatever kind, and on whatever scale, will no doubt have caused the movement of a certain amount of coin from one urban area to another, while governmental purchase and trade generated movement from each urban area into its rural hinterland. The extent of the hinterland regularly served by trade should not, however, be exaggerated, since it will have been more or less coterminous with the maximum distance which a peasant and the animal he used for transport might cover in a day. It will thus have involved an area within a radius not greatly exceeding ten kilometres from each urban area. Technical fiscal practices will also have played their part. It may nevertheless be suspected that the level of liquidity prevailing in rural areas, with the exception of those in the immediate vicinity of a city or major road, was generally low. In some, it seems, the level was exceptionally low. At this very basic level, the late Roman and Byzantine economy may well have been less monetised than, say, the Anglo-Saxon economy, and was almost certainly less so than the late Saxon or Norman one.[225]

A particular example of the distinction between urban and rural coin-use and liquidity is provided by Antioch in the fourth century. In the city itself, coin was quite clearly widely used in payments for services and in commercial transactions, although even here social considerations might dictate the settlement of certain debts in kind. But even official *annonae* were frequently paid out in adaerated form. In its hinterland the position is less clear: the *annona* was collected in kind; land-rents might take the form of share-cropping; even the peasant who had brought his produce into the city for sale might return to the country with little cash, having exchanged it for urban wares. In other words, coin was at least not widely necessary, and may have been little used.[226]

[224] It would clearly be of interest, and possibly of significance, to attempt a comparative classification of the nature of sites and of the coin series which derive from them. The major drawback at the moment is that attention has inevitably focussed upon the great urban centres of antiquity, the fact that they also had a late antique and Byzantine history being frequently fortuitous (and until recently positively disregarded). A certain amount of work has recently been done on frontier sites (particularly in those modern countries bordering on the Danube), but vast geographical areas and numerous types of sites remain virtually unexplored. In this kind of classification bodies of chance, single, losses rate much more highly than hoards, however valuable those may be in other ways: it cannot be repeated too often that appreciable numbers of hoards from a given area do not necessarily reflect a plentiful supply of coin in that area.

[225] This is not necessarily to suppose that the fundamental bases of the late Roman and Byzantine coinages were very different from those of the Anglo-Saxon and Norman ones. One may well suspect, for example, that the much-vaunted plentitude of mints in Anglo-Saxon and Norman England had much less to do with 'trade', and much more to do with the necessity of exchanging coins in accordance with the regular or semi-regular *renovationes monetae* that seem to have prevailed. The *renovatio monetae* was, of course, basically a fiscal mechanism. Even the enforced exchange of foreign coin for the indigenous at entry ports is of course equally a fiscal mechanism, although it may take advantage of, and even reflect, trade.

[226] Liebschuetz, *Antioch: City and Imperial Administration in the Later Roman Empire*, pp. 83–92.

A clear distinction between the metropolis and the regions, at least with regard to the treatment of coin, is revealed by the experience of the French members of the Second Crusade in 1147. According to Odo of Deuil,[227] on their entry into imperial territory at Belgrada (i.e. Beograd) and Brundusium (i.e. Braničevo), the crusaders first encountered the copper coin (*cuprea moneta*) called *staminas* (i.e. the billon trachy), for each of which they were forced to hand over five denarii (i.e. pennies), an exchange (*concambium*) which, so they claimed, represented a loss. In the capital, both in front of the palace (*ante palatium*) and amongst the tents outside the walls, for one trachy they gave less than two denarii. But, again, once they had travelled three days beyond the capital, for one trachy they had to give five or six denarii. The German members of the Third Crusade in 1189 also seem to have had trouble with the exchange-rate of the staminum.[228]

The precise cause of this distinction remains uncertain. It has been suggested[229] that in the regions the exchange-rate of the billon trachy was based upon its full and official value of $\frac{1}{48}$ gold hyperpyron, while in the metropolis it was based upon its bullion value alone, for the trachy was, to a considerable extent, a fiduciary coin.[230] The Germans seem merely to have been confused by the co-existence in circulation of both old (*vetera*) trachea and new (*nova*) trachea, the one having a higher silver content, the other a lower.[231] These explanations still seem the most plausible, although others are doubtless possible. It is the existence of the distinction, however, which is significant, the explanation behind it being of less interest, at least in the present context.

In any case, the essentially precarious nature of the supply of precious-metal coin, even in urban areas – possibly in Constantinople itself – let alone rural ones, and the accentuated effects of what were probably unconsidered actions on the part of individual emperors upon that supply, seems confirmed by the terms of Novel LII of Leo VI:[232]

The same emperor [Leo VI] to the same Stylianus [Zautzes]

> If the nerves of affairs (*pragmata*) provide the basis for them, and if the stability of the state is assured by those affairs, then the ancients did well in holding want (*endeia*) to be a disease and a cause of injury, and consequently in determining that all kinds of nomisma, even if they went back to former or ancient emperors, should hold the same value. But, having suffered I do not know quite what from this good practice, subsequent holders of the imperial office decided that this state of affairs should not remain unchanged, and, because they begrudged the plenty (*euporia*) of their subjects, they made redundant (*apoliteuton*) coin (*nomisma*) bearing the shape (*morphē*) of [any] one of their predecessors, and made current (*politeuton*) only that bearing their own. They decided not to recognise the new state of affairs deriving from this,

[227] Odo of Deuil, *De Profectione Ludovici VII in Orientem* III, IV; ed. Berry, pp. 40, 66.

[228] Anonymous ('Ansbert'), *Historia de Expeditione Friderici Imperatoris*; MGH, *SRG:NS* V, p. 66.

[229] Hendy, *DOS* XII, p. 21.

[230] M. F. Hendy and J. A. Charles, 'The Production Techniques, Silver Content and Circulation History of the Twelfth-century Byzantine Trachy', *Archaeometry* 11 (1970), p. 18. Hendy, *DOS* XII, p. 21.

[231] Hendy and Charles, 'The Production Techniques', pp. 18, 19. *DOS* XII, p. 231.

[232] P. Noailles and A. Dain, *Les novelles de Léon VI le Sage*, pp. 199, 201.

nor the damage (*blabē*) which resulted for everyone – and particularly for the poor, who most needed aid and protection. For the great number of merchants (*emporoi*), and of those living by their hands (*ek kheirōn*), and the whole of the farming class (*geōrgikon genos*), were put to the greatest degree of difficulty and need, not possessing the means of acquiring, in any other way, the necessities of life, when what previously had been the basis of their support [*sc.* coin] disappeared. Therefore, as We do not approve of the innovations of these more recent [emperors], but follow the foresight of earlier ones, We decree – imitating their philanthropy and statesmanlike wisdom – that every kind (*pan eidos*) of nomisma possessing an unaltered shape, unadulterated material, and good weight (*aparapoiēton tēn morphēn ekhon kai tēn hylēn akibdēlon kai tēn holkēn teleion*), whether it be of an earlier [emperor] or of a more recent one, is to be both equally valued and current (*di' isou kai timasthai kai politeuesthai*). The penalty for those daring to hold this decree in contempt shall be flogging, shaving of the hair down to the skin, and, in addition, a fine of three pounds of gold.

The precise circumstances surrounding the issue of this novel, together with the nature and status of a number of its terms, remain uncertain because of their tantalising allusiveness and lack of particular content. This characteristic they of course share with those of other novels. It remains unclear whether the emperor had in mind a single instance, or the more general practice, of what he was complaining, or indeed whether he merely desired to reaffirm a long-standing principle, and considered it necessary to provide that reaffirmation with some kind of explanation or justificatory backing.

Nevertheless, it does seem likely that one now unidentifiable instance, at least, at whatever chronological remove, and a degree of actual experience as to its result, can alone explain issue and content. It seems clear that it is the gold coin, the nomisma, that is in question throughout, but whether at any stage all earlier nomismata could have been simply and unilaterally demonetised without provoking a much more general disorder than that envisaged here seems most unlikely. Some selective demonetisation, perhaps of the nomismata of a particular emperor, or group of emperors, with their handing over to the authorities being enforced, with or without a reimbursement, in the former case perhaps at a discount, is much more likely to be involved. The motivation behind such a demonetisation may conceivably have been either political or religious, or both, iconoclast or iconodule emperors being obvious vehicles of such feelings, but that of a general malevolence towards imperial subjects seems unlikely, partly because it is unnecessary, partly because it stands in the midst of a long tradition of such accusations.[233] But whatever action and motivation is represented, the results – a want of coin, leading to widespread difficulties in exchange, particularly amongst those classes least capable of flexibility in this respect, whether urban or rural – do seem clear.

It is noticeable that *The Book of the Prefect*, which apparently achieved its first formal redaction at approximately the same time, in its chapter of regulations concerning

[233] See, for example, Lactantius on Diocletian, below, p. 373; and Procopius on Justinian, above, pp. 219, 295. The two cases are clearly extreme, but more moderate ones are not difficult to find.

linen-dealers (*othōniopratai*), forbids[234] them to hoard coins (i.e. *mē thēsaurizetōsan ta noumia*) against a time of want (*eis kairon endeias*) – probably, but not necessarily, of coins – and instructs them to hand over to the money-changers (*trapezitai*) instead.

In addition to the issue of the novel, and the regulation, the rarity of nomismata in the name of Leo VI, particularly obvious in a reign of twenty-six years (886–912), has been seen[235] as a further, negative, measure, encouraging or rendering necessary the unprejudiced circulation of the nomismata of earlier emperors, but this connection remains conjectural.

## APPENDIX

### *Treatise on Imperial Expeditions (Hypothesis tōn Basilikōn Taxeidiōn)*

According to the *Appendix* attached to the first section of Constantine Porphyrogenitus' *De Caerimoniis*, the imperial baggage-train when on campaign required the services of a total of some 1,086 pack-animals (*sagmaria*), including mules (*molaria*) and horses (*hipparia*). Grand total, totals and sub-totals do not always coincide exactly, but are generally so near as to provide a considerable degree of confidence in the whole.

This grand total involves those animals devoted to the effects and personnel of the personal and immediate imperial services, and includes those of the native and foreign (and partly ceremonial) guard (the *hetaireia*), but excludes those of the vast majority of the effective members of such expeditions, whether metropolitan or provincial.

Of this grand total, the imperial provisioning (*basilikē hypourgia*) required the services of 80 mules and 62 horses; the imperial tent (*basilikē kortē*) those of 50 mules and 43 horses; the private imperial wardrobe (*oikeiakon basilikon vestiarion*) those of 30 mules and 15 horses; and the repository known as the *eidikon* those of 40 mules and 15 horses. These figures result in a sub-total of 335 pack-animals, including 200 mules and 135 horses. As for the rest, the 200 members of the native *hetaireia* required the services of 100 mules and 24 horses, the 100 of the foreign one (i.e. *tōn ethnikōn*) those of 50 mules and 100 horses, resulting in a further sub-total of 274 pack-animals, including 150 mules and 124 horses. The combined total amounts to 609 pack-animals, including 350 mules and 259 horses. The balance is made up in mules and horses held in reserve and/or used for various other purposes.[236]

[234] 'Leo VI', *To Eparkhikon Biblion* IX.5; ed. Nicole, p. 40.
[235] Grierson, *DOC* III.2, pp. 509–10.
[236] Constantine Porphyrogenitus, *De Caerimoniis* I (*Appendix*); Bonn edn, pp. 478–81.

The *epi tēs trapezēs*, the *domestikos tēs hypourgias*, and the *oikeiakos basilikos kellarios* (all officials involved in the service, provisioning or equipment of the imperial table)[237] had the services of 80 mules, for the purpose of transporting the provisioning (*hypourgia*) and the plate (*asēmion*) of the imperial table (*tēs basilikēs trapezēs*). They also had the charge of cash (*logarion*) taken from the *eidikon* for expenditure to the account of seasoning for food (*eis exodon logō artysias*).

The provisioning seems to have been massive in quantity and complex in nature. It included, for example, skins (*askia*) of wine (*oinarin*) of various grades (i.e. *basilikon/despotikon, magistron, patrikion*), smaller skins (*skortzidia* = Lat. *scortea*) of olive-oil (*elaion*) of imperial grade (*despotikon*), beans (*phasoulin*), rice (*orizin*), pistachios (*pistakin*), almonds (*amygdalon*), and lentils (*phakēn*). The remaining edibles (*brosima*), including perishables such as animal fats (*lardēn, apoktin*), cheeses (*tyrin*), salted fish (*opsaria pasta*), and meats (*sphakta*), and livestock such as sheep with their lambs (*probata hyparna*), and cows with their calves (*ageladia hypomoskha*), together with local (*enkhorion*) wine, and so on, were provided by *prōtonotarioi*, presumably the thematic ones, as the baggage-train passed through each theme. Finally, it included vessels (*angeia*) for keeping local wine, oil and pulses (*ospria*) in; four portable ovens (*phournoi*); nets for keeping birds, presumably fowls, in (*diktya pros to apokleiein ta ornea*); and wooden troughs (*kaukopinakia*) for them to drink from.[238]

The *minsouratōr* (= Lat. *mensurator*), the official in charge of the imperial tent (*kortē*) and its equipment,[239] had the services of 50 mules for the purposes of transport. Two *kortai*, presumably large affairs to serve for public and ceremonial occasions,* and a couple of *tentai*, presumably smaller ones to serve as private quarters, were involved while the emperor was within the frontier (i.e. *eis Rhomanian*), so that one pair (*zygē*) – that is one *kortē* and one *tenta* – together with half the equipment, could be sent on ahead to the next camping-ground (*aplēkton*), and so that the emperor would find all ready and prepared when he arrived.

The equipment included folding benches (*skamnia systelta*), each to sit three persons; folding tables (*trapezia systelta*), of the same length as the benches; a sufficient number of table-cloths (*mesalia* = Lat. *me[n]salia*) and table-napkins (*mandilia*); piled prayer-rugs

* Gr. *kortē* must derive ultimately from Lat. *cohors*, and is probably a re-constituted nominative via some such inflected form as the genitive *co[ho]rtis/kortēs*. Denoting an enclosed space, or court, it is perhaps best translated in this context as 'marquee'. I owe these suggestions, and a number of other similar ones, incorporated into this appendix, to the kindness of Meg Alexiou and Katerina Krikos-Davis, but it is only fair to add that on a number of occasions I have disregarded their advice. The precise meaning of a number of these technical terms remains at best uncertain, at worst entirely obscure. In the latter case, I have left them as they stand. The treatment is in any case not intended as at all definitive: it is basically a summary of the whole, and I am perfectly well aware that a number of the particular translations made – for example those pertaining to carpets and mats – will be regarded as tendentious.

237 Oikonomides, *Les listes de préséance byzantines*, pp. 305–6, 339; see also above, p. 246 n. 149.

238 Constantine Porphyrogenitus, *De Caerimoniis* I (*Appendix*); Bonn edn, pp. 463–4.

239 Oikonomides, *Les listes de préséance byzantines*, p. 306.

for low-reclining on (*epeukhia fountata ta eis khamokoumba* [= *khamai* + Lat. *accumbere*] *energounta*); double-bordered, thick and downy, felt mats (*pilōta diblattia pakhea kai ptena*), for low-reclining on; other blue-linen-warp mats, having their woollen pile combed up, and being of thirty pounds (value or weight) (*pilota linobeneta ekhonta malon kteniston ana litrōn 30*), for invited friends; and coarse-woven mats (*kilikia*), for low-reclining on, for the majority of invited friends. The prayer-rugs and double-bordered mats, certainly, and the others, possibly, were actually provided not from the equipment of the *minsouratōr*, but from the load (*apo tēs phortōseōs*) of the private imperial *vestiarion*.[240]

As the emperor crossed the frontier he left the benches, tables and surplus tents (including one *kortē*) with the local *prōtonotarios* to be stored (*eis apotithēsin*). The equipment also included, however, a 'Turkish' (probably Magyar) bath (*loutron Tourkikon*), called in 'Scythian' (i.e. Turkic) a *çerge* (= tent) with a leather cistern (*meta kinsternēs dermatinēs*), which was for travelling (*apo adēmiou*); twelve cooking-vessels (*koukoumia* = Lat. *cucumae*) of three measures each; twelve heaters (*pyromakhia*) on account of the bath; tiles (*bisala* = Lat. *bessalia*) for the furnace (*eis to kaminion*); folding beds (*krabbatia systelta*); and a chapel (*ekklēsia*) with its sacred vessels (*meta hierōn*). The sacred vessels were actually provided by the *primikērios tou* (*oikeiakou*) *vestiariou*.[241]

The *oikeiakon basilikon vestiarion*, presumably under the control of its head the *protovestiarios*, and certainly under that of his deputy the *primikērios*,[242] had the services of 30 mules for the purposes of transport, their burden being made up from the *vestiarion* itself and from the bed-chamber (*koitōn*). All the imperial clothing (*amphiasis*) and the remaining equipment (*exoplisis*) involved was packed into chests (*skeuaria*) made from purple-dyed leather (*di' alēthinōn tomariōn*), and tinned iron bands (*sidērōn ganōtōn*), with polished leather (*khartalamiōn*) handles for easier carriage.

The equipment included eight silver coolers with their covers (*psykhristaria argyra meta endymatōn*), for vine-flower water (*eis oinanthēn*), for rose-water (*rhodostagma*), and for ordinary water (*neron*); two silver water-containers (*bedouria...eis neron*); various skin containers (*askodablai*) both small and big; four large coolers, pot-shaped (*dikēn magarikōn*) and of tinned copper (*khalka ganōta*) for water; two tinned copper water containers; the sacred vessels for the chapel actually carried by the *minsouratōr*;[243] books (*biblia*) – liturgical, on strategy, on mechanics (with sections on siege-engines [*helepoleis*], missile-making [*belopoiïka*], and other subjects germane to war and siege-craft [*polemous kai kastromakhias*]), historical (Polyaenus and Syrianus), the *Oneirokritikon* (by Artemidorus, on the interpretation of dreams), on omens, on good and bad weather-conditions and storms, rain, lightning and thunder, and gusts of wind – and in addition to these a

240 See below, p. 307.
241 Constantine Porphyrogenitus, *De Caerimoniis* I (*Appendix*); Bonn edn, pp. 465–6.
242 Oikonomides, *Les listes de préséance byzantines*, p. 305.
243 See above.

thunder-chart (*brontologion*) and an earthquake-chart (*seismologion*), and others, such as are used by sailors (*pleustikoi*).

It included piled prayer-rugs for low-reclining on, so that friends could take their repose, and which (as previously noted when dealing with the *minsouratōr*) were actually provided from the *vestiarion*; *thēriakē* and *hēnitzin* and other antidotes (*antipharmaka*), both compound and simple (*skeuasta kai monoeidē*), for those who had been poisoned; containers (*pandektai*) with all kinds of oils and remedies (*elaiōn kai boēthēmatōn*), and with all kinds of salves, ointments, and creams (*emplastrōn kai aloiphōn kai alēmmatōn*), and other medicaments (*iatrikōn eidōn*), and with herbs (*botanōn*) and everything else necessary for the treatment (*therapeia*) of men and animals.

It also included cast-silver bowls with their covers (*sitlolekana argyra kai epikhytaria meta endymatōn*) on account of the emperor, and tinned bronze ones (*asprokhalka kai ganōta*) on account of nobles and well-born refugees (*logō arkhontōn kai eugenōn prosphygōn*); double-bordered, thick and downy, mats on account of the emperor for low-reclining on;[244] two saddles for processions (*sellia...tēs proeleuseōs*); saddles of 'chamber-pot' type (*tou koukoumiliou* = Lat. *cucumella*, presumably enclosed with a high raised support, or crupper, before and behind), gilded and chased all over in a hatch-work pattern (*holokana diakhrysa kopta*), and having fitments (*epistrōmata ekhonta*); other fitments to cover up the chafing of use (*tēn kopēn tēs khreias*); two more such enclosed saddles in silver (*argyrokatakleista*) on account of well-born refugees; imperial cups (*kaukia*) of 'goblet' type (*khalinzia*, dim. *khalina* = bridle, bit, something held in the mouth) on account of the friends invited by the emperor; two imperial swords (*spathia*), one for processions, one for the road (*tēs hodou*); one dagger (*paramērion*); fragrant oil (*aleipta*); various incenses (*kapnismata*); ordinary incense (*thymiama*); mastic (*mastikhēn*); frankincense (*libanon*); sugar (*sakhar*); saffron (*krokon*); musk (*moskhon*); amber (*ampar*); aloe-wood, both moist and dry (*xylaloēn hygran kai xēran*); genuine cinnamon, both of first and second quality (*kinnamōmon alēthinon prōton kai deuteron*); cinnamon-wood (*xylokinnamōmon* – presumably cinnamon-bark, i.e. cassia); other spices (*myrismata*); various kinds of woven wares (*sendes, linōmalōtaria, sabana, sindonia, branaiai*), ending up with napkins of inferior quality (*mandilia katōtika*).[245]

Under the title of undecorated woven wares (*arrhaphia*, i.e. without things sewn on[246]) to be sent as presents (*logō xeniōn*) to foreigners,[247] the list continues with *skaramangia* of various colours and patterns (*diaphorōn khroiōn kai exempliōn*) – all-white, all-yellow, and all-blue; short-sleeved garments (*kolobia*) of great value (*megalozēla*) as worn in the

[244] See above, p. 306.

[245] Constantine Porphyrogenitus, *De Caerimoniis* I (*Appendix*); Bonn edn, pp. 466–9.

[246] R. Guilland, 'Sur quelques termes du *Livre des Cérémonies* de Constantin VII Porphyrogénète', *Revue des Études Grecques*, 62 (1949), pp. 328–33.

[247] The list that follows is remarkably similar to that of the presents made to Hugh of Provence: see above, pp. 268–9.

(imperial) household (i.e. *ek tōn kat'oikous*); under-garments (*esōphoria*) of medium value (*mesozēla*) and of lesser value (*leptozēla*) as worn in the household; under-garments of lesser value of various colours and patterns as worn in the household, including off-white (*aspromynaia*) and all-pure-and-wholesome-white (*diygantaria aspra kai iasta*) ones; *lōrōta* of a triple-weave (*trimita*) both in wholly-genuine (*holovēra*) white and in a collection of various colours (*analekta diaphorōn khroiōn*).[248]

Under the title of decorated woven wares (*errhammena*, i.e. with things sewn on[249]), the list continues with decorated tunics (*himatia*), the collar-pieces being separated (*diskhista maniakata*)[250] from the *skaramangia* themselves of different colours and patterns and made up with double borders (*amphiesmena apo diblattiōn*[251]); and for these (*skaramangia*) the separated collar-pieces, of medium value, and made up with double borders; yet other short-sleeved garments as worn in the household; and for these the separated collar-pieces, of medium value, and plain (*lita*); hose (*toubia*) for all these, the most select (*prokritōtera*) being made up with double borders of eagles (*aetōn*) and imperial symbols (*basilikiōn*), those of second quality with vine-palm (*bdelliōn*) motifs; laces or bands (*sphinktouria*) (to match each tunic[252]); short military tunics (*thalassai*),[253] and cloaks (*abdia* = Ar. *abdayeh*), both thick-woven (*platylōra*) and thin-woven (*masourota* = Ar. *masura*), the one being made up with double borders, the other plain; suits of under-vests and -breeches (*hypokamisobrakia*) of various qualities (*diaphorōn poiotētōn*); gowns of purple of the first, second and third qualities (*epirrhiptaria oxea prōta kai deutera kai trita*); belts (*zōstria*) of purple of various kinds, and of imitation purple (*pseudoxea*) at 1 nomisma 4 miliaresia, 1 nomisma, and 8 miliaresia, apiece; and pairs of travelling boots (*hypodēmata adēmina zygai*) of various kinds. All these were for well-born refugees and for sending to well-born and great foreigners (*megaloi ethnikoi*). Other tunics, of medium value, as worn in the household, and the select and faultless (*prokrita kai kathara*) specimens of which were made up with triple borders (*triblattion*[254]) and double borders of purple, and of double borders of eagles, imperial symbols and vine-palm motifs, were both kept separate along with the batons (*persikia*[255]) for thematic *stratēgoi* and *kleisourarkhai*. So, apparently, were yet

[248] Constantine Porphyrogenitus, *De Caerimoniis* I (*Appendix*); Bonn edn, p. 469.

[249] Guilland, 'Sur quelques termes du *Livre des Cérémonies*', pp. 328–33.

[250] Hendy, *DOC* IV.

[251] Guilland, 'Sur quelques termes du *Livre des Cérémonies*', pp. 339–48.

[252] See below, p. 310.

[253] For the *aetos* and *thalassa*: Hendy, *DOC* IV.

[254] Guilland, 'Sur quelques termes du *Livre des Cérémonies*', pp. 339–48.

[255] *Contra* Guilland, 'Sur quelques termes du *Livre des Cérémonies*', pp. 348–50. This seems to be one of the few occasions where, right at the end of the article, Guilland is simply incorrect. There may well be, almost certainly is, a difference between the adjectival *persikos/ē/on* and *ta persikia*. The latter, in the *De Caerimoniis*, accompany the *stauros* and other ceremonial objects in being carried before the emperor in processions. One may guess that *ta persikia* and so on were objects like the sword, pen-box, cup, napkin and similar things that are known from the blazons of Mamluk royal emirs, denoting the household offices that such emirs occupied, and which, held by the officers, may well have actually accompanied or preceded the sultan on ceremonial occasions. Such objects (particularly the sword) are also known to have accompanied the

other tunics, as worn in the household, of lesser value and second quality, plain, with separated collar-pieces, and for thematic *tourmarkhai* and the remaining refugees and nobles. All of these woven wares, undecorated and decorated, were packed into chests, or into *boulgidia* (= Celt./Lat. *bulgae*), that is double saddle-bags (*disakkia*), for transport.[256]

This list of equipment continues with further items of plate and allied objects: a tinder-box with tinder (*pyrekbolon meta hiskas*); 3 silver lamp-holders (*kandēlai*) and 3 copper – one for the bed-chamber and one for the bath-room (i.e. *koukoumilin*), and the other for the dressing-room (i.e. *parakoitōnarion*). These lamp-holders were apparently somewhat complex in form, the bowl (*lakkos*) of each having a depth (*bathos*) of two spans, being covered over above its surface with gauze-like copper leaves (*hypo petalōn khalkōn koskinōtōn*) (because of the wind and smoke[257]). Nearby these lamp-holders there should be three lamps (*kēroulia*), and lanterns (*phanaria*) again with copper gauzes. Also included were two small clocks (*hōrologia*) for the night-quarters (*dia ta nyktereumata*), one of silver to stand in the bed-chamber, and the other of copper to stand where the chamberlains (*koitōnitai*) were in attendance. Finally included were 4 solid gold salvers (*skoutellia* [= Lat. *scutellae*] *holokhrysa*); 2 solid gold measuring-jugs (*minsourakia* [= Lat. *mensurae*]); and 2 solid gold cups (*orthomilia*). These were to serve when foreigners were dining with the emperor, and were included in the load of the *vestiarion*, while the every-day plate of the imperial table was included in the load of the provisioning.[258]

The cash for the expenditure of the army (*eis exodon tou phossatou*), for rewarding those who had distinguished themselves in battle (*eis philophronēsin tōn agōnizomenōn en polemois*), for nobles, and for the remaining expenses, consisting of sacks of nomismata and of miliaresia (*kentēnaria, miliarēsia, sakkia*), and intended to be given to the guards of the schools (*tois phylassousi skholariois*) in the imperial enclosure (*eis tēn basilikēn phinan* [= Lat. *finis*]), to the imperial pages (*agourois*), to the members of the imperial bodyguard, and to others, to whom the emperor wished to pay honour (*eusebeia*), whether once a week or every two weeks, was taken up by the *sakellarios* and the *eidikos* and included in their loads.[259]

The *eidikon*, under the control of its head, the *eidikos*, had the services of 40 (not 46) mules for the purposes of transport, their burden being made up from the *eidikon* itself and from the bed-chamber. From the latter were taken the sacks of nomismata and

Ottoman sultans. It would be surprising if the institution were a Mamluk innovation, and it almost certainly derives from Ayubid and/or Fatimid precedents, and quite possibly from 'Persian' (i.e. Mesopotamian Arab or ultimately even Sassanian) ones. Meanwhile, I have preferred the ambiguous translation 'batons'. See: Hendy, *DOC* IV.

[256] Constantine Porphyrogenitus, *De Caerimoniis* I (*Appendix*); Bonn edn, pp. 469–71.

[257] See below, p. 310.

[258] See above, pp. 305–6.

[259] Constantine Porphyrogenitus, *De Caerimoniis* I (*Appendix*); Bonn edn, p. 471.

miliaresia as has already been noted when dealing with the *vestiarion*. The remainder of the equipment involved also reads very much like that appropriate to the *vestiarion*: tunics by purchase on the open market (*ex agoras apo tou phorou*), of the tenth, ninth, eighth, seventh and sixth grades (*dekalia, ennalia, oktalia, heptalia, hexalia*);* *lōrōta* of Egyptian silk (*lōrōta metaxōta aigyptika*) and genuine domestic ones (*alēthina enthadia*) – all these for sending to foreigners as presents.

The list continues similarly, with yet other tunics by purchase, decorated, with separate collar-pieces, and of tenth down to sixth grades; *lōrōta* of Egyptian silk, genuine domestic ones, and genuine domestic ones of green cotton (*bambakera...prasina*); belts of various values (*timōn*) and qualities; laces or bands to match each tunic (*ekastou himatiou pros analogian*); suits of under-vests and -breeches of various values and qualities; gowns of various values and qualities; hose to match each tunic; boots of various values and qualities; towels with their accompaniments (*sabana meta ton akolouthiōn autōn*), of the first, second and third qualities; tinder-boxes with tinder; 2 lanterns with copper gauzes; 2 copper lamp-holders for the imperial baggage (*pentzimenta* = Lat. *impedimenta*); gauze-like copper leaves to cover over the bowls of the lamp-holders because of the wind and smoke (*dia ton anemon kai ton kapnon*). Nearby these lamp-holders there should be 2 candles (*phatlia* = Ar. *fatīl*), 2 lamps, and a copper lantern, for necessary gettings-up in the night (*dia tas anakyptousas khreias tē nykti*), the last clearly involving a euphemism for the loo.

The list concludes with 300 lamps of 2 ounces apiece, and 300 candles of a pound apiece, of which the *droungarios* (*sc. tēs viglēs* = *vigil* = of the watch) each evening, on his round (*eis kerketon* = Lat. *ad circitum*), should take one, and, after he has entered the themes, two or three, if required by the force (*bia*) of the wind; and finally with 300 sheaves of parchment (*khartia tomaria*).[260]

The presence of the *epi tēs trapezēs*, the *minsouratōr*, the *prōtovestiarios*, and the *phylax*, and of various other members of the imperial household-service (*kai loipōn tōn diakonountōn oikeiōs tē basilikē hypēresia*), each with his own tent (*skēnē*), grouped regularly around the imperial one, in the camp (*kharax*) of an imperial military expedition

* Termed *dekapōla, oktapōla*, and *hexapōla*, respectively, in *The Book of the Prefect*, which also adds *dōdekapōla*. The suffix *pōlon* must derive from the verb *pōleō* and therefore should involve some notion of sale or price. *The Book of the Prefect* several times specifically restricts the sale of tunics of more than ten nomismata in value (*hyper/epekeina deka nomismata timōmena*), and it is therefore tempting to regard the grading *dōdekapōlon–hexapōlon* as immediately denoting the price in nomismata, and not, for example, the shade or quality (derived from the number of dippings) of dye. Most or all of the items involved were, however, of a purple tint (*porphyraerion*), and it is therefore by no means impossible that shade or quality provided the ultimate consideration. Noticeably, the similar tunics listed in the load of the *vestiarion* are not described as having been obtained by purchase (presumably having been manufactured in imperial workshops), and are therefore not subject to the grading. Interestingly *The Book of the Prefect* also implies the operation of a right of purchase on the open market on the part (*pros khorēgian*) of the *idikon*. See: 'Leo VI', *To Eparkhikon Biblion* IV (*Peri tōn Bestiopratōn*), VIII (*Peri Sērikariōn*); ed. Nicole, pp. 26–8, 35–8.

260 *Ibid.* pp. 473–4.

(*strateuma*), is confirmed by the anonymous author of the tenth-century treatise *De Re Militari*, and therefore itself appears to have been absolutely regular.[261]

The fact that Constantine includes the *eidikon*, and the anonymous source the *phylax*, in their lists clearly implies that the two were effectively equivalent repositories, if not actually synonymous. Certainly, there is some evidence that the two were similar in content, but by the eleventh century, at least, officials of *eidikon* and *phylax* could be listed separately in the same document.[262]

The mounting of an imperial expedition, signalled – at least from the time of Basil I – by the suspension of a breastplate, sword and shield (*lōrikon, kai spathion, kai skoutarion*) from the Brazen Gate of the Palace, clearly involved the emergence and mastery of an immense series of complex logistical problems including funding and provisioning,[263] and not least the construction and organisation of the imperial baggage-train. The pack-animals required seem to have derived from two main sources, both of which were the product of a levy. The logothete of the flocks (*logothetēs tōn agelōn*)[264] was obliged to produce a just distribution and exposition (*dikaian dianomēn te kai ekthesin*) of the requirement, for the post-stations (*mētata*) of Asia and Phrygia, according to the capacity and strength (*kata tēn iskhyn te kai dynamin*) of each, so that the prescribed order of each and the number of animals owed should have been definitely and entirely decided upon beforehand. These *mētata* provided a total of 200 mules at 15 nomismata apiece, and 200 horses at 12 nomismata apiece, making a grand total of 5,400 (not 5,424) nomismata, or 75 (not 76) lb.[265]

In addition to the levy on the *mētata*, a further one was imposed upon various officials of the imperial stables, and more generally upon the holders of the more senior imperial offices, both military and civil. Even the higher clergy were not exempt. Although the obligations involved go under the description of 'customary' (*synētheiai*), which might seem to denote a degree of freedom of will, there is, as usual, little reason to doubt their effectively mandatory nature.

The officials of the imperial stables (*arkhontes ton basilikōn stablōn*) owed a total of 12 mules and 12 horses, which, at the same rates as above, equal 324 nomismata, or 4 lb 36 (not 26) nomismata, which, when added to the grand total above, comes to 79 lb 36 nomismata (not 80 lb 26 nom.).

261 Anonymous, *De Re Militari* 1; ed. R. Vári (Teubner), p. 5.

262 P. Gautier, 'La Diataxis de Michel Attaliate', *Revue des Études Byzantines* 39 (1981), pp. 107 (*kai tōn ephorōn tōn basilikōn kourat*[*o*]*r*[*eiōn*], *eid*[*ikōn*],... *tōn epi tou theiou hēmōn tameiou tou Phyl*[*akos*]...), 121 (repeat). For the relationship between *eidikon* and *phylax* see, in the last instance: R. Guilland, 'Les logothètes: études sur l'histoire administrative de l'empire byzantin', *Revue des Études Byzantines* 29 (1971), pp. 88–9. But the whole question of metropolitan repositories and their derivation needs to be re-examined.

263 See above, pp. 305–10.

264 Oikonomides, *Les listes de préséance byzantines*, p. 338.

265 Constantine Porphyrogenitus, *De Caerimoniis* 1 (*Appendix*); Bonn end, pp. 458–9. The *mētata* are here clearly the descendents of the former *mutationes*, etc. On this, see below, pp. 610–12.

The *logothetēs tōn agelōn* was to deliver the 200 mules and 200 horses extracted from the *mētata* to Malagina (i.e. reg. Osmaneli-Vezirhan), where they were to be received by the count and the inner actuary of the stable (*ho komēs tou stablou kai ho esō khartoularios tou stablou*).[266] Malagina seems to have been the site of the great central imperial stables,[267] as well as being an *aplēkton*.[268] The animals were to be five, six and seven year-olds, and were not to be blemished in the leg (i.e. *mē ekhonta spēlōmata eis tēn psyan*). These officials were to have the 400 animals branded on either side of the shoulder with the imperial seal (*basilikē boulla*), so that this notice and sealing (*ekthesis kai boullōsis*) should be apparent in the future. All the horses were to be castrated for geldings so as to be prepared for military service. The *logothetēs* was to bring the 200 pack-animals (i.e. the mules) already saddled (*sesagmatōmena*), having coverings (*endymata*) in their packs (*en tais stratourais* = Lat. *stratus/stratura*) – patch-work horse-cloths (*kentoukla* = Lat. *centunculus*), with ropes (*sōkaria*, presumably for fastening) loaded away; they were to be shod, wearing their own shoes and harnesses (*kekaligōmena, epipheromena kai selinaia, hama kai tōn kapistriōn autōn*).

Nor were all these sufficient for the imperial service (*hypēresia*), so once in the course of the campaign (*en gar tō kairō tou phossatou prosapax*) the thematic *stratēgoi* 'gave' mules to the emperor: the *stratēgoi* of Anatolikon, Armeniakon, Thrakesion, Opsikion and Boukellarion, 3 mules each; the remaining *stratēgoi* of the east and west, 2 mules each. The *stratēgos* of Seleukeia, however, together with several metropolitan and tagmatic officers, from the *domestikos tōn skholōn* and the *droungarios tou ploïmou*, down to the *domestikos tōn optimatōn*, gave only a single animal apiece. The whole amounted to 58 mules.[269]

Neither the more senior civil officials of the metropolis, nor their subordinates (*ophphikialioi*) in the bureaux (*sekreta*), were exempt from the levy; a long list of officials, bureaux and assessments, beginning with the *hyparkhos* (*tēs poleōs*) at a single animal, ending with the *sekreton tou vestiariou* (*sc.* of the public *vestiarion*) at 2 animals, and amounting to 25 mules, then follows.[270] This brings the total of both series given as presents (*xenalia*) to 83 (58 + 25) mules.

The higher clergy were also liable: the metropolitans for 52 already-loaded mules, and the fifty-two archbishops for another 52 mules. These 104 animals were to be already saddled and shod: the *komēs* and *khartoularios* of the stable were to receive them, and to brand them with the imperial seal, as in the case of the remainder.[271]

The total of animals provided in these two ways, that is through the *logothetēs* of the flocks from the *mētata*, and through presents, thus amounted to 587 (400 + 83 + 104) (not

[266] Oikonomides, *Les listes de préséance byzantines*, pp. 338–9.
[267] Ramsay, *The Historical Geography of Asia Minor*, pp. 202–6.
[268] See above, Map 24.
[269] Constantine Porphyrogenitus, *De Caerimoniis* I (*Appendix*); Bonn edn, pp. 459–60.
[270] *Ibid.* pp. 460–1.
[271] *Ibid.* p. 461.

585). But, in addition, the monasteries provided 100 horses, which were driven before the emperor, to the right and left. These were to be castrated for geldings, but they were not to be branded, so that whenever the emperor wished to give one away, he could order it to be given from amongst them: similarly, they could be put to the needs of the army.[272]

The *komēs* and *khartoularios* of the stable received 3 lb (gold) from the *eidikon* for expenditure (*eis exodon*). They also received the requisite number of imperial packs and horse-cloths (*kaballokilikia*) from the imperial estate (*kouratoreia*) in Lydia appropriately called Trykhinai (*trykhinē* = ragged) for the imperial store (*kellarion*). They received the 200 saddle- and shoe-sets (*sagmatopasmagadia* = *sagma* + Turk. *başmak*) provided once in the course of the campaign by the *mētata*, and the further 104 sets provided once, making a total of 304. They purchased the remainder (*anaplērōsis*) of the 587 (not 585) sets, making it necessary for there to be bought and collected together 283 (not 281) packs and saddles.

They needed to buy smooth and napless cloths (*rasika amalia*), to dye them genuine purple, and to make (*sc.* out of them) 150 saddle-cloths (*sagismata*) and brocades (*borkadia*): 100 to the account of the horses driven before the emperor; 30 to the account of the imperial saddles (*sellaria*); and 20 to the account of the horses given away as presents. They similarly received 150 rations (*tagistra*) from the store laid by in the imperial stable (*ek tou kellariou tou basilikou apothetou tou stablou*); 180 hides (*byrsaria*) out of which to make harness; containers on account of cedar-oil (*hexakanthēla logō kedraias*), and skins for wine and vinegar (*oxos*) on account of the diseases of the animals (*logō tōn periodiōn tōn alogōn*); and axes and pick-axes (*axinorygia*), broad-bladed spades (*platyliskia*), and strong shovels (*ptyaria stibara*) with *potzoi*.

They received 50 lb iron (*sidēron*) from the imperial *vestiarion* (presumably the private one) on account of horse-shoes, and from which they were also to make 150 light-weight bits (*massēmata*); from the hides they were to produce reins (*rhetina* = Lat. *retinacula*), and plain headpieces (*kapitzalia hapla*); from the hemp (*kanabis*) which they received from the same *vestiarion* they were to fashion ropes.[273]

A late Roman or Byzantine emperor on the move must have provided one of the more extraordinary, even bizarre, sights of ancient or mediaeval civilisation. The organisation of the baggage-train was, as seen above, a matter of extraordinary complexity, and its sheer size must have been very considerable: Manuel I, in his letter to Henry II of England, describing the campaign of 1176,[274] claims that the imperial army, including siege- and baggage-trains, because of the entire narrowness and difficulty of the road, stretched out over 10 miles (*exercitu . . . propter viae omnino angustiam et difficultatem, usque ad decem milliaria*

[272] *Ibid.* pp. 461–2. Cf. the rather similar levy made upon the theme of Peloponnesos under Romanus I: metropolitans, bishops and monasteries were all included (Constantine Porphyrogenitus, *De Administrando Imperio* LII; ed. Moravcsik and Jenkins, p. 256).

[273] Constantine Porphyrogenitus, *De Caerimoniis* I (*Appendix*); Bonn edn, pp. 462–3.

[274] See above, pp. 150–1.

*extenso*...). Manuel's general description of the campaign is borne out by those of others,[275] who claim the two trains to have consisted of between three and five thousand wagons, so the figures provided may involve no great degree of exaggeration.

The sheer scale of accumulated wealth involved must also have been huge: if an Arabic source can claim,[276] with anywhere near accuracy, that the 200 mules and horses – and more particularly the 50 mules carrying pairs of chests containing gold vessels, silk costumes, belts, turbans and handkerchiefs – sent by Constantine IX to al-Mustansir in 1045 were worth 216,000 nomismata, then the imperial baggage-train must have been worth proportionally more. The other Arabic source's claim[277] that the cash captured in 1071 amounted to one million nomismata, and that the treasures accumulated by the local inhabitants on that occasion were still identifiable nearly a century later[278] should therefore not be discarded lightly. The huge scale of wealth involved is indeed generally commented upon, on several occasions, with regard to the expeditions of both John II and Manuel I, by William of Tyre.[279]

The effect that the capture, or possible capture, of the baggage-train might have upon enemy and emperor alike therefore seems to have been significant: certainly, the Gothic attack upon Adrianople in 378 was given added impetus by the knowledge of its presence there;[280] a fundamental shift in imperial financial policy – from generosity to avarice – apparently resulted from its capture near Aleppo in 1030;[281] the Selçuk attack upon the army winding through the pass Tzybritze in 1176 seems to have had plunder as one of its principal aims, and it may well have been the plunder taken on that occasion, or the subsequent tribute exacted, or both, that permitted the issue of the first known Selçuk gold coinage, dated to the following year.[282] Similarly, it may well have been the plunder taken by the Normans from Alexius I's baggage-train in 1081, in the form of current Thessalonican trachea, that explains the clearly derivative nature of Roger II's ducat, first issued in 1140: the coins had meanwhile been immobilised in some Norman treasury.[283]

Finally, it seems clear that the through passage of the baggage-train was not something to be looked forward to, either by the population at large or by the thematic officials, and this latter despite the feasts, entertainments and presents that they were likely to be involved in. In an advisory treatise to an emperor, possibly Alexius I, an eleventh-century military author, probably Cecaumenus, advises in favour of a traditional and peripatetic

[275] See above, p. 127, 152.

[276] See above, pp. 269–70.

[277] See above, p. 273.

[278] See above, p. 273 and nn. 106, 108.

[279] William of Tyre, *Historia Rerum* XIV.24, XV.19; RHC, *Occ.* I.I, pp. 642 (1137: *in curribus et equis, thesauris numerum et pondus et mensuram nescientibus*...), 688 (1142: *in curribus et equis, in thesauris infinitis*...). For Manuel, see above, pp. 152, 274 (at Myriocephalum), 270–1 (gifts to Baldwin III).

[280] See above, p. 272.

[281] See above, p. 373.

[282] See above, p. 265. I. and C. Artuk, *İstanbul Arkeoloji Müzeleri Teşhirdeki İslâmî Sikkeler Kataloğu* I, p. 350, no. 1060 – gold dinar dated A.H. 573 (= A.D. 1177, 30 June onwards).

[283] Hendy, 'Michael IV and Harold Hardrada', p. 197. For the capture of the baggage-train, see above, p. 273.

form of imperial life, and against the recently evolved stationary one based upon Constantinople and the palace. Amongst the several arguments adduced against the peripatetic form (admittedly only to be discarded), the damage done to, and the pressure put upon, the regions by the passage of emperor, dependants, officials and army, loom large.[284] Given that a thematic *prōtonotarios* was required to produce, for the needs of the imperial table and entertainments (*maïoumadai!*), 100 sheep with their lambs, 500 goats, 50 cows, 200 fowls and 100 geese, and in view of the numberless other problems of provision and accommodation that are likely to have arisen, all this is unsurprising.[285]

[284] Cecaumenus, *Logos Nouthetētikos pros Basilea* CCLIX; ed. Wassiliewsky and Jernstedt, pp. 103–4.

[285] Constantine Porphyrogenitus, *De Caerimoniis* I (*Appendix*); Bonn edn, p. 487.

# CHAPTER 6

# SUPERVISION

## (I) GENERAL

Once in circulation the gold coinage, in particular, was subject to strict supervision, being on the one hand peculiarly liable to attack because it was composed of the most valuable metal available and therefore was capable of yielding the greatest degree of profit to those who were prepared to risk tampering with it, and being on the other of crucial importance to the state which had increasingly based its finances upon it.

The general case against tampering with the coinage is well enunciated by Cassiodorus in his *formula* for the appointment of a *procurator monetae*:[1] 'Yet it is necessary for complete integrity to be sought in the case of the coinage, on which Our face is impressed, and which is also ascertained to be of general utility (*ubi et vultus noster imprimitur et generalis utilitas invenitur*).'

The most obvious (and evidently the commonest) method of tampering with the gold coinage was to pare or clip it down, and this is mentioned in private documents of both the fourth century (an attempt to arrange a meeting to clip down coinage [*to logarin perikoptein*]),[2] and the thirteenth (a sum of clippings of hyperpyra [*taiaturis iperperorum*]).[3] According to Procopius,[4] the logothete Alexander was nicknamed 'the scissors (*to psalidion*)', from the skill with which he clipped down nomismata without altering their appearance, in the sixth century, and, according to *The Book of the Prefect*,[5] metropolitan *trapezitai* were not: 'to file (*xeein*), or clip down (*temnein*), or counterfeit (*parakharattein*) nomismata or miliaresia' in the tenth. The latter source[6] in addition forbids perfumers (*myrepsoi*) to roughen or scratch (*trakhynein*) coins that they have collected together or

[1] Cassiodorus, *Variae* VII.32; MGH, *AA* XII, p. 219.

[2] *P. Fay.* 134. Eudaemon asks Longinus to come to him and bring with him the *hyalos*, apparently a hard crystalline stone of some kind, so that they can clip, or rather cut down, coins; the session to be rounded off with some Mareotic wine. One of the more extraordinary papyri.

[3] G. I. Brătianu, *Recherches sur Vicina et Cetatea Albă*, no. xxxiii, p. 170.

[4] Procopius, *De Bello Gothico* III.1.28–31; ed. Haury (Teubner), II, p. 302. *Historia Arcana* XXVI.29; *ed. cit.* III, p. 163.

[5] See above, p. 253.

[6] 'Leo VI', *To Eparkhikon Biblion* X.4; ed. Nicole, p. 43.

hoarded (i.e. *ta episynagomena noumia*), presumably referring to the scratches or marks of identification or certification that are quite commonly found on precious-metal coins of this and later periods.[7]

The practice of clipping, at least, was dealt with from early on, in the first place by inflicting savage penalties upon those convicted of it,[8] and in the second by instituting a body of officials whose primary function was to adjudicate in the disputes that arose from it. The law instituting this body of officials is preserved in the *Codex Theodosianus*:[9]

> Emperor Julian Augustus to Mamertinus, Praetorian Prefect
>
> The buying and selling of solidi (*emptio venditioque solidorum*) is impeded if anyone clips down or diminishes or – to use the word proper to such avarice – nibbles them away (*eos excidunt aut deminuunt aut...adrodunt*), for some persons refuse them as light or inadequate (*leves vel debiles*). It therefore pleases Us to appoint a *zygostatēs* [weigher], as the Greek word terms him, in each city (*civitas*), who on account of his faithfulness and industry will neither deceive nor be deceived, so that if a dispute shall have arisen between a seller and a buyer of solidi, it may be settled according to his judgement and reliability.
>
> Given 23 April at Salona in the consulships of Julian Augustus (for the fourth time) and Sallustius [363].

The law is a comparatively straightforward one: (Claudius) Mamertinus was praetorian prefect in Italy, Africa and Illyricum in 363;[10] Julian, however, was in the east at the time,[11] and it is clear that the law must have been received or posted at Salona, and not given there.

The intention of the law was honourable, but the result was unfortunate, for during the fifth and sixth centuries, at least, the *dēmosioi zygostatai* seem both to have extended their competence – to include, for example, banking (at least one *kollektarios kai zygostatēs* is known) and the sealing of purses – and to have become a byword for corruption.[12] By the ninth century their primitive function seems to have been performed by a single, palatine, official, for the Uspenski *Taktikon* (842–3), the *Klēterologion* of Philotheus (899), and the Escurial *Taktikon* (971–5), all mention an official termed *ho zygostatēs* (that is,

[7] E.g. T. Gerassimov, 'Byzantinische Goldmünzen mit Graphiten', *Byzantinobulgarica* 5 (1978), pp. 123–46 (AV, Alexius I to Anna and John V). J. Harris, 'A Gold Hoard from Corinth', *American Journal of Archaeology* 43 (1939), pp. 272–3 (AV, Manuel I). S. Bendall and D. Sellwood, 'The Method of Striking Scyphate Coins using Two Obverse Dies', *Numismatic Chronicle* 18⁷ (1978), p. 104 (El./AR, Theodore I). One can only assume that the marks were made by owners and/or by bankers – some are clearly abbreviated names, others are merely symbols.

[8] *CTh*. IX.22.1. See also below, pp. 322–3.

[9] *CTh*. XII.7.2. (= *CJ* X.73.2, but much altered).

[10] *PLRE* I, pp. 540–1 (Claudius Mamertinus 2).

[11] Seeck, *Regesten der Kaiser und Päpste*, p. 212.

[12] *P. Michael*. 35. Victor is *eudok(imotatos) k. kai z*. See also above, pp. 244 (status), below, 344 and n. 164, 345 (corruption). For Leontius *pres(byteros) kai zyg(ostatēs)*, and Jacob *arkh(ōn) kai zyg(ostatēs)*, both apparently being Jewish rather than Christian officials, see: L. Robert, 'Inscriptions grecques de Sidè en Pamphylie (époque impériale et bas-empire)', *Revue de Philologie* 31³ (1957), no. 69, pp. 36–47. For priests who were also bankers, see above, p. 247 n. 152.

they use the singular). The *Klētorologion* places him, along with *metrētai* (presumably officials concerned with measures), under the authority of the *khartoularios tou sakelliou*, and gives him the rank of *spatharios*.[13] He owed a single mule towards the imperial baggage-train.[14] The even earlier functioning of this single official may well be implied by the existence of the lead seal of a *basilikos* (i.e. not *dēmosios*) *zygostatēs*, dated to the seventh century.[15]

The clipping down of gold and, to a lesser extent, silver coins was not necessarily, however, always the preserve of the individual acting on a private and illegal basis. From time to time the state found itelf publicly adopting a practice that it normally prohibited. This, of course, tended to occur only when particular fiscal or monetary circumstances dictated. The clipping down of fourth- and early fifth-century silver coins in Britain has been assumed to have been a private reaction to an increasing scarcity and appreciating value of silver in the island following its severance from the empire in or about 410. The phenomenon is undoubted, the assumption unsatisfactory: there is no reason to believe that the scarcity and value of silver would naturally have become enhanced in relation to those of gold in these circumstances, yet gold coins do not seem to have suffered in the same way. It seems far more plausible to assume the phenomenon to have been a reaction (whether private or public) to some governmental adjustment in the relative values of silver and gold, and this might have occurred for any number of reasons, by no means all of which would have borne a close relation to natural market forces.[16]

Again, the clipping down of approximately half of a single issue of silver miliaresia, apparently by the state, in the late tenth century seems likely to have represented the same kind of fiscal manipulation as that responsible for the issue of the light-weight tetarteron.[17] The clipping down of earlier billon trachea, once more by the state, in the late twelfth century seems to have been a reaction to the revaluation and then the progressive debasement of the denomination during the second half of that century, which eventually left the bullion value of such earlier trachea as remained in circulation higher than the face value of later ones.[18] A somewhat similar phenomenon affecting the

[13] Oikonomides, *Les listes de préséance byzantines*, pp. 61 (Usp.); 121, 153, 233 (Phil.); 273 (Esc.).

[14] Constantine Porphyrogenitus, *De Caerimoniis* I (*Appendix*); Bonn edn, p. 461. See also above, p. 312.

[15] Zacos and Veglery, *Byzantine Lead Seals* I.3, p. 1610, no. 2803.

[16] On clipped 'siliquae', see: J. W. E. Pearce, 'Notes on the Terling and other Silver Hoards found in Britain', *Numismatic Chronicle*, $13^{5}$ (1933), pp. 170–81, and in the last instance: C. E. King, 'A Hoard of Clipped Siliquae in the Preston Museum', *Numismatic Chronicle* $21^{7}$ (1981), pp. 40–64 (concludes that the clipping was deliberate, to two or more standards, and (therefore) official). On the term 'siliqua' as a probable misnomer, see below, p. 467.

[17] See below, pp. 507–8.

[18] Hendy, *DOS* XII, pp. 20–3, 158–61, 179–81. *Idem*, *DOC* IV. Hendy and Charles, 'The Production Techniques, Silver Content and Circulation History of the Twelfth-century Byzantine Trachy', pp. 13–20. Other refs: Metcalf, *Coinage in South-eastern Europe 820–1396*, pp. 111, 116; *idem*, 'Silver and Tin in the Byzantine Trachy Coinages, ca. 1160–1261', *Revue Belge de Numismatique* 123 (1977), pp. 115–18, 120, 121–3. Metcalf's case, that these clipped trachea formed an 'austerity' or 'expediency' coinage,

electrum trachea of the period possibly represents a parallel reaction to a like problem.[19] The pre-circulation clipping down of a whole issue of billon trachea by the Constantinopolitan Latin authorities towards the middle of the thirteenth century forms perhaps the most complete and obvious example of the practice, although the particular reasons behind it remain obscure.[20]

The state might, from time to time, demonetise or even demonetise and withdraw from circulation particular denominations or issues of coin. A law of Constantius II[21] refers to certain issues of coin as 'forbidden' (i.e. to *pecuniae vetitae*), although the grounds for refusing them currency seem to have been more political than financial.[22] The *trapezitai* are again known to have been involved in the consequences of this kind of refusal.[23] On the other hand, a law of Honorius[24] forbids the exchange of the decargyrus coin, and a law of Valens[25] not only withdraws a whole denomination from use and circulation (*de usu...et conversatione*) but also orders it to be delivered to the *largitiones*. It is reported[26] that Theodosius forbade the use of coins (*noummia*) of Julian for public purposes, but the report is a late one, and the supposed grounds for the action unclear, although possibly iconographical and religious, which would be plausible enough. The report may in any case represent a misattributed but genuine measure of Valens.[27] A law of Leo VI mentions[28] that certain of that emperor's relatively recent, but unnamed, predecessors had made redundant (it uses the word *apoliteuton*) the nomismata of their own predecessors. Use of the word nomismata implies, at this date, that gold coinage was involved, but it seems unlikely that this could, or would, have been simply demonetised and deprived of value. It seems rather more likely that it was called in and exchanged at a discount.

In any case, the composition of later coin-hoards seem to show the results of such processes: the heavy copper folles of Justinian's twelfth to fifteenth regnal years do not

issued – already clipped – at the same time as their unclipped equivalents, and therefore over a prolonged period of time, is flat contrary to the massive burden of the numismatic evidence, is historically quite unsupported and indeed most improbable, is supported by scientific evidence that is at best marginal, and is, in the end, a most unfortunate nonsense. See also below, p. 520 n. 358.

19 *Contra* N. Kapamadji and C. Morrisson, 'Trachéa d'electrum légers de Jean II et Manuel I^er^ Comnène', *Bulletin de la Société Française de Numismatique* 27 (1972), pp. 163–6. The authors conclude that these very rare clipped trachea, known mainly from a single hoard, are in fact officially produced halves of the units with the same obverse and reverse types. This is most improbable.

20 Hendy, *DOC* IV (Type W). For an unclipped specimen, see below, Pl. 32, 4.

21 *CTh.* IX.23.1. See also above, p. 291.

22 See above, p. 294.

23 See above, pp. 249–50.

24 *CTh.* IX.23.2. See also below, pp. 474–5.

25 *CTh.* XI.21.1. See also below, pp. 472–3.

26 Anonymi, *Scriptores Originum Constantinopolitanarum: Parastaseis Syntomoi Khronikai* XLVI; ed Preger, I, pp. 52–3.

27 The law of Valens cited above would most of all have affected Julian's large billon coins with a representation of a bull, a pagan symbol, offensive to the Christians. See below, pp. 471, 472–3.

28 Leo VI, Novel LII. See also above, pp. 302–3.

turn up in hoards of the later sixth or the seventh century; the debased gold coinage of the late eleventh century does not turn up in hoards of the twelfth century; and the billon trachea of Alexius I, John II and the earlier part of the reign of Manuel I do not turn up in hoards of the later twelfth century.[29]

Private individuals might, it is true, take a hand in the process: a law of Constantius II[30] forbids metalworkers to 'purify' (*purgare*) the billon maiorina coin by separating off its silver from its copper, and the phenomenon was no doubt not confined either to the fourth century or to metalworkers.

## (II) FORGERY

### A. *The* Codex Theodosianus: *Gold*

The strict supervision excercised by the state and its agents over the coinage extended, as might be expected, to the prevention of counterfeiting by way of the detection and punishment of the counterfeiters. It is difficult to assess the scale of the problem involved. Patent forgeries of the precious-metal coinages, at least, are uncommon in hoards. Their base-metal equivalents seem equally uncommon in hoards, although they are noticeably more common in site-finds. On the other hand, the fact that a complete title (XXI) of the ninth book of the *Codex Theodosianus* is devoted to laws against counterfeiting suggests that the problem was, or was thought to be, a serious one. The fact that a section (iii) of the anonymous treatise *De Rebus Bellicis* is given over to advocating a measure designed to render counterfeiting impossible serves to strengthen the suggestion. It is also difficult to interpret satisfactorily the terms and sense of some of the laws involved for, although it is clear that a number of significant general distinctions were observed – or were

[29] Justinian: A. Spaer, 'The Rafah Hoard: Byzantine Sixth-century Folles', *Numismatic Chronicle* 18[7] (1978), p. 66 (with refs to other similar hoards). Eleventh century: Hendy, *DOS* XII, pp. 343–4 (Gornoslav), 371–2 (Nicosia), 372–3 (Novo Selo), 401 (Zgurli); and a number of other hoards could be cited. Alexius I, etc.: Hendy, *DOS* XII, pp. 158–61, 170–1. The position with regard to the eleventh century seems misunderstood by both Morrisson, 'La Logarikè: réforme monétaire et réforme fiscale sous Alexis Ier Comnène', p. 449 n. 37, and (to a lesser extent) by Metcalf, *Coinage in South-eastern Europe 820–1396*, p. 105 n. 3. Both authors document several hoards containing both pre-reform and post-reform precious-meal elements, leading them to exaggerate the length of time after 1092 (the reform) that the two circulated together. The whole point of the hoards they quote in their support is that they all contain large proportions of pre- and small proportions of post-reform elements, while the great bulk of hoards from the twelfth century contain all, or virtually all, post-reform elements only. This, and other evidence (Hendy, *DOS* XII, pp. 92, 96) suggests that the period of co-existence was short, and the withdrawal of pre-reform elements quite speedy and thorough. For the Fethiye Hoard, buried in *c.* 1108, which already seems to have contained post-reform elements only, see: Hendy, 'Seventeen Twelfth- and Thirteenth-century Byzantine Hoards', pp. 67–8 (no. 231). For a truly mixed hoard, that from Safranbolu, buried in *c.* 1132/5: Hendy, *op. cit.* pp. 69–70 (no. 232). Noticeably it did *not* contain the most debased issues of all, and this seems true of several similar hoards: refs in D. M. Metcalf, *Coinage in South-eastern Europe, 820–1396*, p. 108 and nn. 16, 17.

[30] *CTh.* IX.21.6. See also below, p. 470.

understood – in the original laws, it is equally clear that they were not always observed or understood by the compilers, and still less by the interpreters, of the *Codex*. It also seems probable that a number of laws and their dates were conflated by the compilers.

Although the latest treatment of this whole question[31] has done much to clarify the situation, it cannot, even so, be regarded as definitive. Nevertheless, the general situation seems to have been as follows. A primary distinction between the counterfeiting of gold coinage and that of base-metal coinage was observed or understood throughout, and is exemplified in the different scale of the punishment meted out to those convicted of the respective acts. This distinction in the legal status of gold coin on the one hand, and of base-metal coin on the other, while not entirely novel, paralleled a similar distinction in the contemporary production and governmental use of coin in those metals that remains to be described in the seventh chapter of this book.[32]

The problem as defined, and the solution as proposed, by the anonymous author of the fourth-century treatise *De Rebus Bellicis*, is as follows:

> Amongst the injuries to the state that are not to be borne is the fact that the form of solidi (*solidorum figura*), corrupted (*depravata*) by the fraudulent acts of some persons, disturbs the population in various ways, and diminishes the portrait of imperial majesty (*regiae maiestatis imago*), when they [*sc.* the solidi] are refused through the fault of the mint (*moneta*). For the unscrupulous cunning of the buyer of such a solidus, and the ruinous need of the seller, have introduced a certain difficulty into transactions (*contractus*) themselves, so that honesty in such matters is no longer possible. Wherefore Your Majesty's correction is to be applied in this matter, as in all, in such a way that the workmen of the mint (*opifices monetae*), collected from every quarter, should be assembled together upon one island, so as to benefit the monetary uses of solidi (*nummariis et solidorum usibus profuturi*). I mean that, as they are permanently forbidden any association with the neighbouring land, the freedom of mingling, which is the opportunity for fraud, should not impugn the integrity of a public service. For in this way, with the support of isolation, complete faith in the mint will be assured, there being no place for fraud where there is no opportunity for trade (*nec erit fraudi locus ubi nulla est mercis occasio*). Now, so that the nature of any further issue (*qualitas futurae discussionis*) should be clear, I have appended, in the illustration provided, the types and size (*formae et magnitudo*) of both the copper and the gold coinage (*tam aereae quam aureae figurationis*).
>
> (Anonymous, *De Rebus Bellicis* III; ed. Ireland, p. 6)

The problem and the solution are both couched in what are perhaps somewhat simplistic terms. On the other hand, if the suggested outside dates for the composition of the treatise (366–75), and more particularly the years 368/9, are correct, and it really was addressed to Valentinian I or Valens, then it does at the very least confirm that the problem was, or was thought to be, a real and pressing one, at precisely the same time (366–9) as the procedural reforms of Valentinian and Valens in the collection of taxation

31 Grierson, 'The Roman Law of Counterfeiting', in R. A. G. Carson and C. H. V. Sutherland (eds), *Essays in Roman Coinage Presented to Harold Mattingly*, at pp. 140–61.

32 See below, pp. 378–94. But see also above, pp. 285–7 (*kharagma* and *strophē*) and pp. 250–1 (*collectarii* purchasing solidi).

and the production of coin which are described in the seventh chapter of this book were under way. It does indeed suggest more. For it is quite clear that the main thrust of these reforms was towards the drastic centralisation of the production of the gold and silver coinage upon the imperal *comitatus*.[33] This did not go as far as isolating such production on an island, but the principle was very similar. It has been suggested[34] that the treatise was intercepted and pigeon-holed by some civil servant, without reaching the emperor for whom it was intended. This may well have been the case; but, as the method by which and the level at which policy was formulated remain quite unclear, it is by no means necessary to suppose that this would have precluded the treatise from effective influence. The fact that several of the coin-types provided are undoubtedly pagan (and western) in nature; that the concentration upon military devices may demonstrate an awareness of imperial (and western) interests; and that the treatise formed part of the *Codex Spirensis*, along with a number of documents of mainly contemporary and mainly topographical and administrative relevance, including the (undoubtedly western) *Notitia Dignitatum*; all render it probable that it had formed part of some official file originating from nearby Trier. These considerations, which do not seem to have been emphasised in the latest treatment of its origin, seem quite as significant as the sparse and largely neutral information gleaned from the text itself and taken as indicating an eastern origin.[35]

The earliest law preserved in the *Codex Theodosianus* specifically dealing with the counterfeiting of gold coin is one of Constantius II:[36]

Emperor Constantius Augustus to Leontius, Praetorian Prefect

> A reward having been offered to informers, let every counterfeiter of solidi (*solidorum adulter*) that can be found, or that is exposed by any man, be immediately and without any delay delivered over to burning by the flames.

Given 18 February at Antioch in the consulships of Placidus and Romulus [343].

The law, although otherwise straightforward, for (Flavius Domitius) Leontius was praetorian prefect in the East in 343,[37] and Constantius was at Antioch then,[38] lacks a

[33] See below, pp. 387–91.

[34] E. A. Thompson, *A Roman Reformer and Inventor, being a new Text of the Treatise* De Rebus Bellicis, p. 6.

[35] Coin types: R. M. Reece, 'The Anonymous: A Numismatic Commentary', in M. W. C. Hassall (ed.), *De Rebus Bellicis*, at pp. 59–66 (throws doubts upon the significance of the coin-types). Imperial interests: J. F. Matthews, *Western Aristocracies and Imperial Court A.D. 364–425*, pp. 49–50 (attempts a 'rehabilitation' of Valentinian, and shows him to have been interested in devising new types of military equipment). *Codex Spirensis*: Thompson, *A Roman Reformer and Inventor*, pp. 6–17 (the only ancient exception amongst its contents is the *Altercatio Hadriani et Epicteti* (a civil servant's light reading?) and the only later work is Dicuil, *De Mensura Orbis Terrae* (put in for the sake of completeness?)). Origin: Alan Cameron, 'The Date of the Anonymous *De Rebus Bellicis*', in Hassall, *op. cit.* at pp. 1–7 (concludes the *De Rebus Bellicis* to have been an eastern document).

[36] *CTh.* IX.21.5.

[37] *PLRE* I, pp. 502–3 (Fl. Domitius Leontius 20).

[38] Seeck, *Regesten der Kaiser und Päpste*, p. 192.

phrase dealing with the clipping down of solidi or the passing of counterfeit solidi in a sale – acts for which the same punishment is prescribed – which was transferred to another law by the compilers of the *Codex*.[39]

Despite the brutally explicit terms of the law, it has been supposed that for much of the fourth century subsequent to its issue the death penalty was not normally imposed upon counterfeiters of the gold coinage, and that counterfeiting of this description was not considered a capital crime.[40] This supposition rests upon the fact that the Easter amnesties of 367(?), 368 and 380 preserved in the *Codex Theodosianus*,[41] while excluding those convicted of any of the five classic capital crimes of treason, sorcery, murder, adultery, or rape, from their provisions, make no reference to those convicted of counterfeiting. It is from 381 only onwards that such amnesties expressly exclude counterfeiters (*adulteratores monetae*, *falsae monetae rei*),[42] and this should represent the point at which it became normal for the death penalty to be imposed upon the counterfeiters of the gold coinage, and counterfeiting of this description came to be considered a capital crime.

Although no actual cases of conviction and punishment capable of providing a solution to the problem in hand are known, nevertheless the supposition is an unlikely one. A law of Constantine[43] prescribes burning or some other form of capital punishment for those convicted, not of counterfeiting solidi, but simply of valuing them at different rates, and a law of Valens[44] specifically prescribes capital punishment for counterfeiters (*adulteratores monetae*). It has been observed, frequently and accurately, that the repetition of legislation seeking to discourage, or to prohibit, a particular practice simply reflects the failure of earlier legislation on the subject, and that it forms, therefore, evidence for the effective continuation of that practice, rather than for its cessation. This observation appertains, however, not to the legislator's intentions, but to his inability – for whatever reason – to enforce those intentions. In this case, the legislator's intentions – that counterfeiting the gold coinage should be considered a capital crime – had already been implied, or had already been specifically expressed, on at least three separate occasions before 381.

The question nevertheless remains as to why it was from that year onwards, only, that those convicted of such counterfeiting were specifically excluded from the Easter amnesty. The answer surely lies in the fact that before 381 the amnesty involved merely a brief and economical formula, and afterwards a lengthier and more verbose one. Before 381

39 *CTh.* IX.22.1; below, pp. 363–4. Grierson, 'The Roman Law of Counterfeiting', at pp. 258–9, 259–60.

40 Grierson, 'The Roman Law of Counterfeiting', at pp. 249–51.

41 *CTh.* IX.38.3, 4; *Constitutiones Sirmondianae* VII.

42 *CTh.* IX.38.6 (381), 7 (384), 8 (385); *Constitutiones Sirmondianae* VIII (386). Cf. Justinian, *Constitutio Pragmatica* (*App.* vii) XX (554): *De Mutatione Solidorum id est Monetae.*

43 *CTh.* IX.22.1. See also below, pp. 363–4; Grierson, 'The Roman Law of Counterfeiting', at pp. 259–60.

44 *CTh.* XI.21.1. See also below, pp. 472–3.

it thus seems probable that counterfeiting was included under the general heading of treason (*maiestas*), which regularly appears in the list of capital crimes excluded from the amnesty, whereas afterwards it achieved reference in its own right. The equation of counterfeiting with treason was, however, by no means abandoned, and was indeed emphasised by the terms of a further law preserved in the *Codex Theodosianus*:[45]

Emperors Valentinian [II], Theodosius and Arcadius, Augusti, to Tatianus, Most Dear to Us, Greeting

Those convicted of counterfeiting (*falsae monetae rei*), whom they commonly call *paracharactae*, are held liable to the charge of treason.

Given 27 June at Constantinople in the consulships of Timasius and Promotus [389].

The law is almost certainly an eastern one, for (Flavius Eutolmius) Tatianus was praetorian prefect in the East in 389.[46] On the other hand, because Theodosius was in the west then,[47] it has been proposed that the text of the law should be emended to read 'posted' rather than 'given' at Constantinople.[48] Such an emendation is in fact unnecessary, and it seems simpler, and more plausible, to assume that it, and other similar laws of approximately the same date, emanated from Arcadius whom Theodosius had left behind in Constantinople under the tutelage of Tatian.

## *B. The* Codex Theodosianus*: Other metals*

Counterfeiting the base-metal coinage was considered a less serious offence. Two laws of Constantine preserved in the *Codex Theodosianus* deal with counterfeiting of this description. The earlier[49] is dated 319,[50] and is addressed to (Locrius) Verinus, who was then vicar in Africa.[51] In it, Constantine ruled that those convicted of making counterfeit coins (*adulterina numismata*) should be punished according to their sex and legal status. A decurion, or the son of a decurion, should be banished perpetually and the disposition of his property referred to the emperor. A plebeian should be subjected to forced labour perpetually and his property confiscated. A slave should be subjected to the supreme penalty.

The later law[52] is dated 326 and addressed to Tertullus, proconsul of Africa.[53] In it, the emperor ruled that if anyone were to be convicted of making a coin (*nummus*) by means of false casting (*falsa fusio*), he should forfeit his property to the treasury (*fiscus*) and himself be punished with a severity prescribed by the law. It seems clear that the intention of the law of 326 was to increase the rigour of the provision in the law of 319

[45] *CTh.* IX.21.9.
[46] *PLRE* I, pp. 876–8 (Fl. Eutolmius Tatianus 5).
[47] Seeck, *Regesten der Kaiser und Päpste*, pp. 275, 277.
[48] Grierson, 'The Roman Law of Counterfeiting', at p. 259.
[49] *CTh.* IX.21.1.
[50] Grierson, 'The Roman Law of Counterfeiting', at pp. 257–8.
[51] *PLRE* I, pp. 951–2 (Locrius Verinus 2).
[52] *CTh.* IX.21.3.
[53] *PLRE* I, p. 882 (Tertullus 1).

concerning the disposition of property. Confiscation was in future to be automatic rather than dependent upon the emperor's decision. The reason for increasing this rigour is a somewhat subdued one: 'so that such a zeal for striking coin should be confined to Our mints (*ut in monetis tantum nostris cudendae pecuniae studium frequentetur*)'.

That the situation remained the same, and that counterfeiting the base-metal coinage was considered a less serious offence as late as the end of the fourth century, may be inferred from the terms of a yet further law preserved in the *Codex Theodosianus*:[54]

> The same Augusti [Valentinian II, Theodosius and Arcadius] to Rufinus, Praetorian Prefect
> If anyone should arrogate to himself the right to strike copper (*super cudendo aere...facultas*), either through some law (*rescribtum*), or even through an annotation (*adnotatio*) of Ours, not only shall he lose the fruit of his petition [for the right], but he shall also receive the punishment which he deserves.
> Given 12 July at Constantinople in the consulships of Theodosius Augustus (for the third time) and Abundantius [393].

The law, although once again otherwise straightforward, lacks a phrase prohibiting the private possession of coin other than that continuing in public use, which was transferred to another law by the compilers of the *Codex*.[55]

The most plausible inference to be drawn from these terms is that a petition requesting the right to strike copper coin had been submitted by a private individual, and that, as a result of whatever means – whether corruption, or inadvertence, or both (corruption on the part of petitioner and officials, inadvertence on the part of the ruler, is an obviously possible combination) – the petition had first been granted, then subsequently discovered, and now was being indignantly nullified. That this could have happened has been doubted,[56] but would not be at all historically unparalleled.[57] Because such a right could, in the first place, have been granted through corruption or inadvertence only, the obvious solution was to regard the coins produced as counterfeit, and the producers as subject to the normal laws against counterfeiting. These laws were doubtless still the two Constantinian ones mentioned above, and the concluding phrase 'the punishment which he deserves' will then have referred to the punishment (confiscation and so on) prescribed by them. If the phrase 'And finally it is Our pleasure that if by chance any coin other than that continuing in public use shall be found in the possession of any merchant, it should be forfeited to the control of the treasury with all the property of the offender' is really to be transferred from *CTh.* IX.23.1 to this law,[58] then a Constantinian reference must be accepted as inevitable.

Counterfeiting the base-metal coinage was considered, on the other hand, a rather more

[54] *CTh.* IX.21.10.
[55] *CTh.* IX.23.1. See also above, pp. 291–2; Grierson, 'The Roman Law of Counterfeiting', at pp. 260–1.
[56] Grierson, 'The Roman Law of Counterfeiting', at pp. 252–3 and n. 2.
[57] On this; K. Hopkins, 'Rules of Evidence', *Journal of Roman Studies* 68 (1978), p. 181.
[58] See above, p. 292.

serious offence when performed by *monetarii* (officials or employees of the mint) than when performed by private individuals, and the punishment inflicted was that much more severe. Like the *zygostatai*, the *monetarii* seem to have been notorious for taking advantage of the opportunity for corruption accorded them by their profession.[59] Again, two laws of Constantine deal with the situation. The earlier[60] is dated 321, was apparently posted at Rome, and is addressed to a certain Januarinus, who is described as *agens vicariam praefecturam* in a law[61] posted at Rome in the previous year, and who was probably vicar of the prefect of the city.[62] In it, the emperor ruled that because many *monetarii* were engaged in the production of counterfeit coinage (*adulterina moneta*), all should recognise the necessity of seeking them out to be handed over to the courts, so that under torture they might reveal their accomplices. Informers were to be rewarded by granting them a degree of immunity dependent upon their fiscal status if freemen, and by granting them Roman citizenship if slaves. Owners of estates or houses in which the crime had been committed were, if they had been aware of the proceedings, to incur banishment and the confiscation of all their property, and if they had been unaware, the confiscation of the estate or house in which the crime had actually been committed. Accomplices amongst the staff of the estate, or in the household, involved were to incur capital punishment along with the criminals themselves. Officials (*milites*) who allowed anyone on such a charge to escape were also to incur capital punishment. Private individuals involved were to be denied the right of appeal, and officials or dignitaries (*promoti*) were to have their name and rank (*gradus*) referred to the emperor. The emperor finally ruled that, if the owner of an estate or house discovered that the crime was being committed on his property and revealed the fact immediately to the authorities, the property should not be forfeit.

The later law[63] is apparently dated 329 and is addressed to a certain Helpidius, who may have been identical with the official of the same name who had been vicar of the suburbicarian diocese in 321–4.[64] In it the emperor drew a distinction between owners who, although resident in the immediate vicinity of the property on which counterfeiting had taken place, nevertheless remained unaware of it, and those who resided at a distance. The former remained liable to the loss of property, the latter were exempted. Widows were also exempted, as long as they had been unaware, and so were pupils under the age of puberty even if they had been aware, on the grounds that they would not have understood what they had seen. Tutors resident in the vicinity, on the other hand, were held liable to the loss of property that their pupils would otherwise have suffered, on the grounds that they should have been aware of what went on on their pupils' property. With these emendations, the provisions of the earlier law were to stand.

59 See, for example, above, pp. 321–2.
60 *CTh.* IX.21.2.
61 *CTh.* IX.34.3.
62 Grierson, 'The Roman Law of Counterfeiting', at p. 258, *contra PLRE* I, p. 453 (Ianuarinus I).
63 *CTh.* IX.21.4.
64 *PLRE* I, p. 413 (Helipidius I).

The position of the silver coinage as a result of all this legislation against counterfeiting (in which it failed nevertheless to achieve a mention) is unclear. It has been supposed[65] that it remained covered by the provisions of the Sullan *lex Cornelia de falsis*, in so far as it dealt with counterfeiting, and by those of subsequent summaries and interpretations of that law. This is not at all impossible, but does on balance seem unlikely. It seems more likely that, from the second half of the fourth century onwards at least, silver coinage had been considered as an adjunct of the gold. In much the same way, legislation regulating the collection of taxation in gold and the production of gold coinage had in effect included silver and silver coinage although the latter was not mentioned, and legislation prohibiting the export of gold by private individuals had taken a similar form and had had a similar effect.[66]

### C. *The* Codex Justinianus *and later legislation*

The legislation of the fourth-century emperors against counterfeiting, as assembled by the compilers of the *Codex Theodosianus*, was carried over, in a yet more abbreviated and conflated form, into the *Codex Justinianus*. *Titulus* XXIV of the ninth book of that *Codex* consists of three composite laws against counterfeiting which represent the three major distinctions detectable in its predecessor. *CJ* IX.24.2 consists of a conflation of *CTh.* IX.21.3 and *CTh.* IX.21.5, with an interpolation from *CTh.* IX.21.9 equating counterfeiting with treason, and was clearly intended to apply to counterfeiters of the gold coinage; *CJ* IX.24.3 consists of a direct repetition of *CTh.* IX.21.10 and therefore applied to counterfeiters of the base-metal coinage; *CJ* IX.24.1 consists of a conflation of *CTh.* IX.21.2 and *CTh.* IX.21.4, somewhat modified, and therefore applied to *monetarii* turned counterfeiters and their accomplices, and to the owners of the property on which the crime had been committed.

The legislation of the later emperors against counterfeiting, as found in the various legal collections and sources of the eighth to fourteenth centuries, is a good deal less complex and flexible even than that in the *Codex Justinianus*, both as regards the circumstances envisaged, and the punishments exacted.[67] The earliest of these legal collections, the *Ekloga*, published in 726 or 741,[68] states baldly:[69] 'Counterfeiters of coin (*parakharaktai monētas*) shall have their hands cut off.' The *Prokheiron*, published between 870 and 879, elaborates somewhat:[70] 'The maker of counterfeit coin (*plastē monita*) shall

[65] Grierson, 'The Roman Law of Counterfeiting', at pp. 242–7, 251.

[66] See below, pp. 387–91 (production), above, pp. 257–8 (export).

[67] R. S. Lopez, 'Harmenopoulos and the Downfall of the Bezant', in *Tomos Kōnstantinou Harmenopoulou*, at pp. 111–25.

[68] Ostrogorsky, *History of the Byzantine State*, p. 152 n. 5.

[69] *Ekloga* XVII.18; Zepoi, *Ius Graeco-Romanum* II, p. 55.

[70] *Prokheiros Nomos* XXXIX. 14; Zepoi, *Ius Graeco-Romanum* II. p. 217.

have his hand cut off, together with his accomplices. And the person in charge of the land on which the counterfeit coin is made, whether he be a farmer, a steward, a householder, or someone belonging to a workshop (*ergastēriakos*), is a party to the crime and as such shall have his hand cut off.' The virtually contemporary *Epanagōgē*, which seems to have been published between 879 and 886, reports the entire formula in precisely the same words.[71]

The *Basilika*, on the other hand, while prescribing the same punishment for the counterfeiter himself and his accomplices, specifically alleviates it in the case of the owner (*despotēs*) of the land on which the counterfeiting had taken place, he being liable to banishment and general confiscation if he had known of it, and to confiscation of the actual land if he had not. The person in charge of the land remained liable to the full punishment.[72] It seems clear, from the way in which the terms of this and other similar laws[73] are couched, that this alleviation was due as much (or more) to a more extensive and closer adherence to the terms of the earlier laws preserved in the *Codex Justinianus* as to pressure successfully exerted in favour of the land-owner.

In addition to these collections, which were official, a number of others, which were to varying degrees unofficial, repeat the contemporary formula and punishment.[74] The same punishment is to be found in *The Book of the Prefect* for mistreating the coinage and similar crimes,[75] and the same formula and punishment in the *Hexabiblos* of Constantine Harmenopoulos[76] in the fourteenth century, although it is clear that by then the Latin-derived word *monēta* was no longer generally understood.[77]

It has been supposed[78] that the transfer from the relatively complex and flexible legislation of the later Roman and early Byzantine period to the simplicity of that of the middle and later Byzantine period was effected by an unrecorded law of Heraclius, permitting reception of the simplified form by the Germanic peoples and its recognition, at least, by the Arabs. This supposition is however based on no specific evidence, is unlikely, and moreover takes little or no account of the possible evolution and eventual recognition of widespread customary law at the expense of formal law.

71 *Epanagōgē* XL.17; Zepoi, *Ius Graeco-Romanum* II, p. 361.

72 *Basilika* LX.60.1.

73 E.g. *Basilika* LX.41.8, 9; LX.60.2.

74 *Ecologa Privata Aucta* XVII, 44; Zepoi, *Ius Graeco-Romanum* VI, p. 45. *Ecloga ad Prochiron Mutata* XVIII.28; *ed. cit.* VI, p. 265. *Synopsis Basilicorum* M.XVIII; *ed. cit.* V, p. 435.

75 See above, pp. 252, 253.

76 Constantine Harmenopoulus, *Hexabiblos* VI.14.3; ed. G. E. Heimbach, p. 772.

77 *Ibid.* VI.14.4; ed. Heimbach, p. 772: '*Monēta* is so called archetypally from the *sphragistērion* or *boullōtērion*, with which the design (*typos*) of the coins is struck onto them.' Lopez' deduction from this ('Harmenopoulos and the Downfall of the Bezant', at p. 122), that the law was no longer enforced, is untenable: Harmenopoulus is merely indulging in a piece of typically Byzantine learned antiquarianism – and equally typically is getting it wrong.

78 R. S. Lopez, 'Byzantine Law in the Seventh Century, and its Reception by the Germans and Arabs', *Byzantion* 16 (1942/3), pp. 445–61.

## (III) WEIGHTS AND MEASURES

### *A. The earlier period* (c. *300–600*)

The precious-metal coinages, which were mostly struck *al pezzo* (that is, each piece to a particular weight) rather than *al marco* (that is, a number of pieces to a larger weight), naturally tended to circulate and pass by weight rather than by tale, great care being expended by state and private individuals alike in ensuring the authenticity and standard nature of the weight and metallic quality of each piece involved in a transaction, or in assessing the degree to which any piece was faulty in either or both of the latter respects, so that it might be valued at an appropriately reduced rate. This will no doubt have been one of the major functions of the tax-collector on the one hand, and was very probably the major function of bankers and *zygostatai* on the other. The extraordinary care that was taken in transactions which involved large sums of money is well illustrated in a document of 1081, recording the sale of an estate by one Athonite monastery to another (!), for: 'twenty-four pounds of hyperpyra nomismata (?), whole and lacking nothing, to be deposited and counted out, from your hands into our hands (*eis* [*nomismata*] [*hyper*]*p*[*y*]*ra litras eikosi-tessaras; sōas kai anellipeis, katablētheisas kai aparithmētheisas, apo kheirōn hymōn eis kheiras hēmōn*)'.[79]★

The opportunities for corruption that the process afforded were nevertheless considerable, and their exercise even by officials led to the enactment of a remarkably detailed piece of legislation by Constantine, the terms of which are once more preserved in the *Codex Theodosianus*:[80]

Emperor Constantine, Augustus, to Eufrasius, *Rationalis Trium Provinciarum*

> If anyone wishes to pay [taxes] in solidi (*solidos appendere*), he shall pay seven [six] solidi of refined gold (*auri cocti*), each of four scruples (*quaternorum scripulorum*), and stamped with Our features (*nostris vultibus figurati*), for every ounce, and, naturally, fourteen [twelve] for two ounces. In this fashion he shall pay the entire amount (*omnis summa*) of what is owed. The same reckoning (*eadem ratio*) is to be observed if anyone should pay in bullion (*materia*), so it shall appear that he has given solidi. Now, when gold is paid, it shall be received with level pans (*aequa lance*) and equal weights (*libramentis paribus*), in such a fashion, naturally, that the end of the cord (*summitas lini*) [i.e. the cord from which the balance was suspended] is held with two fingers, the remaining three being free and extended towards the tax-receiver (*susceptor*) so as not to depress the weights (*pondera*) by restraining either of the pans suspended from the tongue (*examen*) of the balance, but so as to permit the level and equal movement of the balance (*stater*). And so on.

Posted 19 July in the consulships of Paulinus and Julianus [325].

★ I owe this reference to the kindness of Archie Dunn.

[79] Lemerle *et al.*, *Actes de Lavra* I, no. 42, p. 233. The document, which despite the signatures of metropolitan personnel is apparently of provincial origin, actually reads: *apo kheirōn hēmōn eis kheiras hēmōn* – which one would have thought unwise in a document of this kind.

[80] *CTh.* XII.7.1.

The law, which is straightforward in its address and postscript, has been accorded a significance out of all proportion to its content. It seems clear, in the first place, that the text as it stands is an emended version of the original which equated six solidi with an ounce and twelve with two ounces, rather than with seven and fourteen. The emendation is a sixth-century Visigothic or Merovingian one, designed to take account of the reduction in the weight of the solidus from 24 to 21 or 20 siliquae that had occurred in the contemporary barbarian west.[81] The law is therefore not to be considered as evidence for the imposition of a premium in the case of payment by solidi, but even less is it to be considered as evidence for the extraction of a profit in the case of payment by bullion.[82] On the contrary, it is clear evidence for the otherwise universal and absolute identity of solidi with bullion. It was carried over, in a much abbreviated form, into the *Codex Justinianus*.[83] A similar practice to that described, the depression of the pan (*lanx*) of the balance, with the thumb (*pollice*), but with a more generous intent and on a happier occasion – the public paying off of Justinian's debts by Justin II – is mentioned by Corippus.[84]

As implied above, the base-metal coinages, which were mostly struck *al marco* and which tended to be of a fiduciary nature, were subject to a far less careful handling. Michael Psellus remarks:[85] 'By weight, such things as gold, silver and lead; by number [i.e. by tale], small change (*noummoi leptoi*); and by measure, wine', clearly distinguishing the treatments accorded the two coinages. Later, Pegolotti remarks[86] that, in Constantinople and in Pera, all mercantile cash-transactions took place in gold hyperpyra by weight (*a peso di bilance*), although it is true that the weight (as well as the alloy) of the hyperpyron was by then very unstable.

The supervision exercised by the state over the precious-metal coinages and their circulation extended, unsurprisingly, to the provision of standard weights. This was felt necessary, and may well have been so, throughout: a law of Honorius preserved in the

81 This solution was first proposed by Mommsen – refs: Adelson, *Light Weight Solidi and Byzantine Trade during the Sixth and Seventh Centuries*, pp. 11–12 n. 22. The recent discovery of the precious-metal portion of Diocletian's *Edictum de Maximis*, in which gold coin and bars are directly equated, renders it more or less incontestable.

82 Premium: J. P. C. Kent, 'Gold Coinage in the Later Roman Empire', in R. A. G. Carson and C. H. V. Sutherland (eds), *Essays in Roman Coinage Presented to Harold Mattingly*, at p. 199. Profit: P. M. Bruun, 'A Law Concerning Tax Payment in Gold and the Constantinian Solidus', in *Congresso internazionale di Numismatica, Roma 11–16 settembre 1961* II, *Atti*, at pp. 387–98. It can only be said that the standardisation of weights, and the monetary policies, attributed to Constantine and Licinius in this latter article, fall well within the rubric of the remark made below, on p. 337. See, in the last instance: J. Guey, 'Code théodosien, XII.7.1 (19 juillet 325): Le "surhaussement" du Solidus; balance et technique d'une pesée fiscale', *Bulletin de la Société Française de Numismatique* 34 (1979), pp. 610–11; J.-P. Callu, 'Dénombrement et pesée: le sou théodosien', *ibid.* pp. 611–12.

83 *CJ* X.73.1.

84 Corippus, *In Laudem Iustini Augusti* II; ed. Averil Cameron, p. 59.

85 Michael Psellus, *Synopsis tōn Nomōn*; *PG* CXXII, col. 956.

86 Pegolotti, *La Pratica della Mercatura*; ed. Evans, p. 40.

*Codex Theodosianus*[87] mentions the possession by certain tax-receivers (*susceptores*) of measures and weights (*mensurae atque pondera*) that were heavier than they should have been; *The Book of the Prefect*,[88] on the other hand, implies the possession by certain metropolitan grocers (*saldamarioi*) of weights (*hexagia*) that were lighter than they should have been. Both series of weights resulted, in their different ways, in an illegal profit for the owners.

Until well into the fourth century responsibility for the supervision and provision of standard weights and measures had been left in the hands of the appropriate curial officials (the *aediles/agoronomoi*) of each city.[89] During that century the responsibility was increasingly appropriated by the state.

The earliest law preserved in the *Codex Theodosianus* dealing with the supervision of weights is the one of Julian[90] appointing a *zygostatēs* in each city.

The earliest law dealing with the provision of weights is one of Theodosius I:[91]

The same Augusti [Gratian, Valentinian II and Theodosius I] to Postumianus, Praetorian Prefect
Measures and weights (*mensurae et pondera*) shall be placed publicly in each station (*statio*) [*sc.* of the public post], so as to deprive those desirous of committing fraud of the power of doing so.
Given 3 October in the consulships of Merobaudes (for the second time) and Saturninus [383].

A short while later only, a second law, the text of which is somewhat more explicit in its allocation of culpability and its proposed remedy, was issued by the same emperor:[92]

Emperors Valentinian [II], Theodosius [I] and Arcadius, Augusti, to Cynegius, Praetorian Prefect
We command measures (*modii*) of bronze or stone, and liquid measures (*sextarii*), and weights (*pondera*), to be placed in each station (*mansio*) and city (*civitas*), so that each tax-payer (*tributarius*), with the established measures of all articles beneath his eyes, shall know what he ought to give the tax-receiver. As a result, if any tax-receiver should suppose that he may exceed the norm of established measures, liquid measures, or weights, he shall know himself liable to a suitable punishment...
Given 28 November at Constantinople in the consulships of Honorius, Most Noble Youth, and Evodius, *Vir Clarissimus* [386].

Both laws, as it happens, are eastern ones, for Postumianus and (Maturnus) Cynegius were both praetorian prefects in the East at the requisite times,[93] but this should not be taken as implying that the problems involved were more acute there than in the west: not only does the law of Honorius mentioned above appertain to the west, for its addressee, Caecilianus, was praetorian prefect in Italy then,[94] and it was actually given

87 *CTh.* XI.8.3 (409).
88 'Leo VI', *To Eparkhikon Biblion* XIII, 5; ed. Nicole, p. 48.
89 Jones, *The Greek City from Alexander to Justinian*, pp. 216, 255.
90 See above, pp. 317–18.
91 *CTh.* XII.6.19.
92 *CTh.* XXI.6.21.
93 *PLRE* I, pp. 718 (Postumianus 2), 235–6 (Maternus Cynegius 3).
94 *PLRE* II, pp. 244–6 (Caecilianus 1).

at Ravenna where Honorius was at the time,[95] but a novel of Valentinian III[96] also mentions the provision of weights (*exagia*) to avert fraud. Later, Cassiodorus twice refers to fraudulent practices involving balances and weights on the part of tax-collectors (*conductores, exigentes*), once involving Ostrogothic Italy, and once Visigothic Spain, and pope Gregory I devotes a whole section of a letter to forbidding the use of unjust weights (*iniusta pondera*) on the part of papal agents on the Sicilian estates of the church.[97]

The second law of Theodosius I mentioned above was carried over, virtually unaltered, into the *Codex Justinianus*.[98] Despite this, which might be thought to have guaranteed its continuing validity, only a relatively short while later it was found necessary – or was felt necessary, at least – to issue a yet further, and even more explicit, regulation on the subject. *Caput* 15 of Novel CXXVIII of Justinian, dated 545 and addressed to Peter (Barsymes), then praetorian prefect of the East for the first time,[99] reads as follows:

> We command those who exact public taxes (*publica tributa*) to use just weights and measures (*iusta pondera et mensurae*), so that they may not injure Our tax-payers (*tributarii*) in this respect. If, nevertheless, tax-payers (*collatores*) do feel themselves injured, whether in matters of weighing, or in those of measuring, they have permission to receive the measures and weights of commodities (*species*) from the Most Glorious Prefects, and the weights of gold, silver and other metals (*reliqua metalla*) from the Most Glorious *Comes Sacrarum Largitionum* of the time. And these measures and weights are to be preserved in the most holy church of each city (*civitas*), so that both the collection of revenues (*fiscalium illatio*) and military and other expenses (*militares et aliae expensae*) may take place according to them, without inconvenience to the tax-payers.

The shift of emphasis, of which the Justinianic law represented the culmination, is an interesting and significant one. In 383, the first Theodosian law had required standard weights and measures to be placed in each post-station. In 386, the second Theodosian law had reiterated this requirement and extended it to cover each city as well – without, however, stipulating where in each the standards were to be preserved. The inclusion of this second law in the *Codex Justinianus* at least implies that the requirement was still in force when the *Codex* was drawn up. But between the publication of the *Codex* (534) and the issue of the Justinianic law (545) the public post had been very severely curtailed by John the Cappadocian:[100] the requirement had thereupon become redundant in so far as the post-stations were concerned, and the Justinianic law noticeably simply omitted them from consideration while still taking the cities into consideration.

The rôle which the Justinianic law accorded the church for the first time is also not without interest and significance, and is confirmed by heading 19 of the *Constitutio Pragmatica* (*App*. vii), dated 554, and addressed to Narses and Antiochus, then *praepositus*

[95] Seeck, *Regesten*, pp. 316, 318.

[96] Novel XVI. See also below, pp.364–5.

[97] Cassiodorus, *Variae* II.25 (*canonicos solidos non ordine traditos, sed sub iniquo pondere...proiectos* (Italy)), V.39 (*assem publicum per gravamina ponderum premere dicuntur patrimonia possessorum*); MGH, *AA* XII, pp. 60, 165. Gregory I, *Epistolae* I.42; MGH, *Ep*. I, pp. 62–4.

[98] *CJ* X.72.9.

[99] For Peter Barsymes, see above, p. 243.

[100] See above, pp. 294–5.

*sacri cubiculi* and praetorian prefect of Italy respectively, by which Justinian regulated the affairs of reconquered Italy:

CONCERNING MEASURES AND WEIGHTS

And so that no occasion for defrauding or injuring the provinces shall arise, We command commodities (*species*) or coins (*pecuniae*) to be given or received in those measures or weights which Our Piety has delivered into the presence of the Most Blessed Pope or of the Most Distinguished Senate.

Its rôle is also confirmed by the fact that one of the first acts of John the Almsgiver, on his consecration as patriarch of Alexandria in 610, was to promulgate a public edict (*dēmosion prostagma*) forbidding the use of a weight (*stathmion*), or a measure (*metron*), or a balance (*kampanos, zygos*), not conforming to the standard.[101]

The Justinianic law further reveals the authorities for the normal issuance of standard weights to have been the various (i.e. praetorian and urban) prefectures where weights and measures of commodities were concerned, and the *comitiva sacrarum largitionum* where weights of metals – including coins – were concerned. The latter situation is confirmed by such early and explicit coin-weights as survive, a number of which bear not only an imperial portrait or portraits, but also the title and name of a particular *comes*. It is presumably no coincidence that weights of Julian and of the Theodosian house are relatively common, for the first had instituted the *zygostatai*, and it was under the second that such weights were first required to be widely distributed and preserved. One solidus-weight (*exagium solidi*) of Julian even bears the design of a hand holding a balance in much the same fashion as that earlier dictated by Constantine.[102] (Pl. 3, 7–8)

A reference by Theoderic, preserved in Cassiodorus' *Variae*,[103] to 'Our bedchamber pound (*libra cubiculi nostri*)' suggests that care of the standard (in the strictest sense of the term) was then the responsibility of that institution. The same reference implies (i.e. *quae vobis in praesenti data est*) that replicas were distributed to the provinces. A curious passage in Constantine Porphyrogenitus' *De Thematibus*[104] suggests that certain silver and inscribed measures (*argyra...anaglypha...minsouria*) of the earlier period, at least, were then kept in the imperial *vestiarion* (*en tō basilikō vestiariō*), presumably the private one, which was closely related to the bedchamber (*koitōn*),[105] but the precise significance of this remains unclear.

101 *Vita Sancti Joannis Eleemosynarii* III; ed. Gelzer, pp. 9–10.

102 Provision of weights and measures: E. Michon, 'Le "modius" de Ponte Puñide (Espagne)', *Mémoires de la Société Nationale des Antiquaires de France* 4[8] (1914), pp. 214–312. Julian: N. Dürr, *Catalogue de la Collection Lucien Naville, au Cabinet de Numismatique du Musée d'Art et d'Histoire de Genève*, p. 20, no. 278. For a somewhat similar, but earlier, Alexandrian tetradrachm: L. H. Cope, 'The Chemical Composition of a Tetradrachm of Probus with a Reverse Type illustrating Codex Theodosianus XII, VII, 1', *Numismatic Chronicle* 15[7] (1975), pp. 187–90.

103 See above, p. 332, n. 97.

104 Constantine Porphyrogenitus, *De Thematibus* XV; ed. Pertusi, pp. 61–2.

105 See above, pp. 306–9, esp. 309.

## B. *The later period* (c. *600–1450*)

The situation as regards the provision of standard weights and measures during the Byzantine period is much less well documented. The Justinianic law was carried over, virtually unaltered, into the *Basilika*,[106] but its relevance to the contemporary situation at that stage remains uncertain. It is known, from a number of references in *The Book of the Prefect*,[107] that the *eparkhos tēs poleōs* – no doubt as deriving directly from the earlier *praefectus urbi* – provided members of certain of the metropolitan guilds not only with weights or measures (*stathmia ē metra*), but also with balances (*kampanoi*, *zygia*, *bolia*), marked with his seal (i.e. *tē tou eparkhou esphragismena boullē*). The weights apparently included coin-weights (*hexagia*).[108] Their use was obligatory and was enforced by the supervisory activities of subordinate officials termed *boullōtai* ('inspectors of seals').[109] Novel XXVIII of Andronicus II, dated 1316,[110] implies the current existence of taxes on balances and various weights and measures, or more probably, as will emerge, on their use.[111]

It is known, from a document dated 1107[112] recording the donation by doge Ordellaffo Falier of the Constantinopolitan church of St Acindynus to the patriarch of Grado Giovanni Gradenigo, that the church then contained a number of balances, and standard weights and measures. The church was, in other words, donated along with its balances (*staterae*), weights (*pondera*), and measures (*metra*) whether for oil or wine. It was, moreover, forbidden for anyone else (i.e. anyone else in the Venetian colony) to possess such balances or standards. The reason for the grant of this monopoly of balances and standards emerges from a second document, dated 1172,[113] revealing the lease in 1169 by the patriarch Enrico Dandolo of the revenues from the Constantinopolitan property of the patriarchate to Romano Mairano, for a period of six years at 500 lb *denarii veronensium* per year. A large proportion of the revenues concerned evidently derived from balances and standards – doubtless those in St Acindynus.

The position is further clarified by two additional documents[114] concerning the church of St George in Rodosto. The first document, dated 1145, records the grant by doge Pietro Polani of a monopoly of balances, weights and measures in the Venetian colony in Rodosto to the church of St George there which was a dependency of the church of

[106] *Basilika* LVI.18.13.

[107] 'Leo VI', *To Eparkhikon Biblion* VI.4, XI.9, XII.9, XIII.2, XIX.4; ed. Nicole, pp. 32, 45, 47, 48, 56.

[108] *Ibid.* XIII.5; ed. Nicole, p. 48.

[109] *Ibid.* VIII.3, ed. Nicole, p. 37. Philotheus, *Klētorologion*; ed. Oikonomides, p. 13.

[110] Andronicus II, Novel XXVIII; Zepoi, *Ius Graeco-Romanum* I, pp. 538–41 (concessions to the Monemvasiots).

[111] See below, pp. 352–3; cf. H. Antoniadis-Biblicou, *Recherches sur les douanes à Byzance*, pp. 136–9.

[112] Tafel and Thomas, *Urkunden* I, pp. 67–74.

[113] R. Morozzo della Rocca and A. Lombardo, *Documenti del commercio veneziano nei secoli XI–XIII* I, no. CCXLV, pp. 238–9.

[114] Tafel and Thomas, *Urkunden* I, pp. 103–5, 107–9.

S. Giorgio Maggiore in Venice. The second, dated 1147, confirms the grant of the monopoly and gives details of the fees which were charged on the use of the balances and standards and which were paid to the prior of St George: two *stamines* (i.e. billon trachea) in the case of Venetians, four in that of Byzantines; but above a certain weight extra was charged in the *tetartero* (i.e. tetarteron).

At much the same date (1160, 1162, 1180, 1197) it is known that the Constantinopolitan church of SS. Peter and Nicholas also contained balances (*staterae*), weights (*pesae*) and measures (*metra, mensurae*); that they were normally reserved for the use of the Pisan colony, members of which paid half a *staminum* per hundredweight, others paying a whole *staminum*; and that, having first been paid to the Pisan state, these fees were later paid to the Pisan church of S. Maria Maggiore.[115]

A number of points of interest and possible significance arise from these documents and from the situation that they reveal. In 1107, on its transfer from dogal to patriarchal possession, the church of St Acindynus already possessed its own balances and standards. What were these standards, for how long had they been in the church, and why were they there? Unfortunately, none of these three questions is open to a definitive answer, although in two cases the circumstantial evidence indicates provisional ones.

The only unequivocally specific weight or measure mentioned in the documents referring to the Constantinopolitan church is the *rubus*, which was a weight, appears in documents emanating from or dealing with other areas of the Mediterranean, and may have been of Arabic origin. It was, in other words, an 'unofficial' weight of wide usage and was therefore neither specifically Byzantine nor specifically Latin.[116] Similarly, the only specific weight or measure mentioned in the documents referring to the church in Rodosto is the *modius*, a measure of even wider usage and variety. The evidence is obviously inconclusive and the question simply not open to a solution of whatever kind.

The questions of how long the balances and standards had been in the church, and why they were there, seem on the one hand more important, and on the other not only closely related but also more open to solutions. The church itself had been granted to the Venetians by Alexius I in the treaty of 1082/4(?).[117] The balances and standards went unmentioned in that treaty, and remained so in all its twelfth-century renewals and extensions. Indeed, the earliest reference in a regular treaty to the Venetians possessing their own balances and standards, in the Byzantine empire, is that of Michael VIII in the treaty of 1265.[118] A reference occurring in the treaty of 1234 between the Venetians

115 Müller, *Documenti*, pp. 8, 10, 18–19, 70.

116 E. Schilbach, *Byzantinische Metrologie*, p. 207.

117 Text: Tafel and Thomas, *Urkunden* I, pp. 51–4. The precise dating of this treaty, a matter of no great moment in itself, has given rise to a considerable secondary literature which is not really germane to the present problem. However, in the last instance: O. Tůma, 'The Dating of Alexius's Chrysobull to the Venetians: 1082, 1084, or 1092?', *Byzantinoslavica* 42 (1981), pp. 171–85 (contains refs to previous works, favours 1084, but is in no way conclusive).

118 Tafel and Thomas, *Urkunden* III, pp. 66–77 (Greek), 77–89 (Latin).

and the caesar Leo Gabalas, lord of Rhodes, is scarcely to be considered as the product of regular circumstances.[119] This date seems unusually late: in somewhat similar circumstances the Venetian possession of balances and standards in the kingdom of Jerusalem appears to have been granted by Baldwin I in 1111, and was certainly either confirmed or granted by the *Pactum Warmundi* of 1123, and by Baldwin II in 1125.[120]

The documents referring to the churches in Constantinople, and to that in Rodosto, reveal a further unusual element in the situation: the physical attachment of balances and standards to individual churches in the empire rather than to the local Italian community or, indeed, to that community as a whole. True, the ultimate ownership of balances and standards in Tyre briefly devolved upon the church of S. Marco in Venice in 1175, but this came about only with the temporary donation to that church, by doge Sebastiano Ziani, of virtually the whole third part of Tyre with its concomitant privileges that had been granted to doge Domenico Michiele in the *Pactum Warmundi*, and by Baldwin II, in 1123–5.[121]

Both of the anomalous elements mentioned above would be explicable if it were assumed that when the church of St Acindynus was granted to Venice in 1082/4(?) it already contained balances and standards – presumably in conformity with the Justinianic legislation on the subject.[122] The same assumption would have to be made in the case of St George in Rodosto, and possibly in that of SS. Peter and Nicholas in Constantinople. It is worth noting, in this context, that the major item in this legislation had been carried over, virtually unaltered, into the *Basilika*,[123] although in itself this may not be considered as providing reliable evidence for its actual application in the tenth century. Each of these churches would, then, have been granted, along with the balances and standards that they contained, from the very beginning.

If it were further assumed that at some uncertain stage, the late Roman or Byzantine state had realised the use of such balances and standards to be a potential source of revenue, then it would also follow that the fees charged on their use by the Venetian state and subsequently (in a monopoly situation) by the patriarchate of Grado and the church of S. Giorgio Maggiore, and by the Pisan state, and the archbishopric of Pisa, are likely to have been merely a continuation of those that had been charged previously by the Byzantine state and that are known to have continued to be charged by that state on into the fourteenth century. Certainly, at least one fee, more probably for the act of weighing than for the use of balances and standards, is known from a very early stage.[124] In other words, the phenomenon, although known primarily from western sources and although including its early extension to the kingdom of Jerusalem, would have been

119 Tafel and Thomas, *Urkunden* II, pp. 319–22.

120 *Ibid.* I, pp. 75, 84–9, 90–4.

121 *Ibid.* I, pp. 167–71, 88, 92.

122 See above, pp. 332–3.

123 Justinian, Novel CXXVIII.15 = *Basilika* LVI.18.13 = *Synopsis Basilicorum* t. VII.24 (Zepoi, *Ius Graeco-Romanum* V, pp. 525–6).

124 See below, pp. 351–3.

ultimately of Byzantine origin. Noticeably, the approximately contemporary situation in Egypt seems to have been very different, suggesting that it was probably not of Arabic origin.[125]

## (IV) THE LATE ROMAN AND BYZANTINE POUND

Although the weight of the Roman and Byzantine pound might in theory be determinable by any one of three principal methods, in practice reliance has to be placed for the most part upon the surviving 'archaeological' material – that is, either upon standard weights (whether or not specifically marked with their value), or upon coins that are known to have borne some fixed relation to the pound. A number of estimates have been evolved on this basis, many of them involving the possession of anything between one and five decimal figures. From these estimates the Roman and Byzantine knowledge and operation of a number of complex and sophisticated monetary manoeuvres have been deduced. The degree of precision involved is in fact only to a minor degree less of a fantasy than the manoeuvres deduced.[126]

The evolution of an estimate of the weight of the Roman and Byzantine pound pretending to any great degree of precision is open to several major sources of potential error. The authority to be accorded most standard weights (and none, as far as is known, is 'standard' in the strictest sense of the term) and many coins is uncertain. Some weights bear not only a mark identifying their intended value, but also one identifying the issuing authority; most bear only the former; many bear neither. Those explicitly used as coin-weights are likely to have been originally more precise representations of the standard, for they are likely to have been used for weighing precious-metal coins. On the other hand, most weights – even coin-weights – and many coins consist of base metals or alloys (lead, iron, copper or bronze). These are elements or alloys peculiarly liable to corrosion, which may involve a gain or, particularly where the objects have been cleaned, a loss in weight. Some weights, in addition, have lost the inlay with which they were originally decorated. Most base-metal coins in any case are unlikely to have been struck with any great degree of attention to individual weights. Only glass and stone weights and gold coins have any real claim to be regarded as reliable. The last – except those that never saw circulation, a condition applicable to very few – are liable to have suffered a variable, and to a considerable extent unpredictable, degree of loss of weight through circulation.[127]

125 H. Rabie, *The Financial System of Egypt*, A.H. *564–741*/A.D. *1169–1341*, p. 117.

126 For this, and much of what immediately follows, see: P. Grierson, 'The President's Address, Session 1963–1964, Weight and Coinage', in *Numismatic Chronicle* 4[7] (1964), at pp. i–xvii (at the end of vol.), particularly at pp. xi–xiv. It seems pointless to document such attempts to estimate the weight of the pound to so great a degree of accuracy: they are simply not to be believed.

127 See below, pp. 345, 345–6, 348, 361–3.

Two further complicating factors should necessarily be taken into account: the degree of precision of which ancient and mediaeval balances were capable; and the difficulties of maintaining a single standard of weight in an empire of considerable territorial extent over a long period of time. The two are, of course, not unconnected: a considerable use and reliance upon the precision of the balance is implied if a number of mints have to be supplied with replicas of at least the standard pound, and if *zygostatai*, post-stations and cities all have to be supplied with weights and measures. As early as 384, the mention by Symmachus[128] of pounds weight according to the urban (*sc.* Roman) standards (*urbanis ponderibus conferendae*), which was also a weighing according to a more generous balance (*trutinae largioris examine*) presumably than the imperial norm, very strongly implies the existence and use of variant standards.

If little is known in detail of the precision of which balances were capable, rather more is known of the difficulty of maintaining a standard of weight over a period of time. For the evidence of the tabulated weights of nomismata suggests that the weight of the pound itself had already declined by the ninth century, and that it began to decline even more rapidly from the thirteenth century onwards.[129] As it happens, the evidence is confirmed by the one estimate of the weight of the pound dependent not upon the archaeological evidence, but upon the comparison of a meticulous set of fourteenth-century Byzantine figures with an absolutely contemporaneous Venetian one. This comparison suggests that, from a Roman level of some 324/5 g, the Byzantine pound had declined to about 304 g.[130]

## (v) SEALED AND LOOSE COIN

### *A. General*

Because, in principle, the gold coins involved in a transaction had first to be examined and weighed, which might well be a lengthy process, larger sums of money tended to circulate, and to be handled, in sealed purses bearing the number or weight or both of the pieces they contained on their outside. A purse of coin was termed generally in the Greek a *balantion* (i.e. something fastened or secured) or perhaps an *apodesmos* (something tied), and a sealed purse evidently an *apokombion/epikombion* (something buckled) or – even more explictly and probably colloquially – a *sphragis* ('seal'). In the Latin, a purse was termed a *sacculum*, and a sealed purse a *sacculum signatum*. In the Greek, loose coin was termed *apolyton kharagma* and, in the Latin, sealed coin *pecunia clusa* or *obsignata.*[131]

[128] Symmachus, *Relationes* XIII; MGH, *AA* VI.1, p. 290. For the occasion and sum involved, see above, p. 175.

[129] Schilbach, *Byzantinische Metrologie*, pp. 164–8.

[130] See below, p. 539 n. 459.

[131] Hendy, *DOS* XII, pp. 303–9. Add: Philotheus, *Klētorologion*; ed. Oikonomides, pp. 95, 181, 217, 223/5, 231 (*apokombia* of 8 lb; 1 nom.; 3 lb; $1\frac{1}{3}$ nom.; 20/10/8 lb, etc.). It should be noted that an *apokombion*

On the surviving evidence, the history of the sealed purse is a long and somewhat complex one. The *sacculum signatum* and *pecunia obsignata* were both already known to the jurists of the third century, and presumably then involved either silver denarii or gold aurei. A mosaic from Smirat in North Africa depicting purses, identified in the accompaning inscription as *sacci*, with ꝏ (= 1,000) marked on their outside and involving denarii, has been dated to this period.[132] With the catastrophic debasement of the silver coinage during the second half of the third century, a shift seems to have taken place. On the one hand, the general practice of sealing up into purses such precious-metal coinage as might have remained in circulation presumably continued. On the other, the drastically reduced value of the contemporary silver coinage, the increasing scarcity of the gold coinage, and the virtual absence of denominations of medium value must have ensured that transactions involving anything other than minimal sums became absurdly cumbersome.[133] This defect seems to have been remedied, in part at least, by the evolution of purses containing standard numbers of small- (or relatively small-) value coins, the purses therefore holding larger total values as units in terms of the by now largely notional denarius. Such seems to have been the origin of the *follis*.[134]

The combined evidence of the Greek, Latin and Syriac versions of Epiphanius' *De Mensuris et Ponderibus* implies that, by the fourth century, two such *folles* were in existence and use. The Syriac version, the most detailed and comprehensible, reads as follows.[135]

The *follis* is also called the purse, because it is a multiple: for it is $2\frac{1}{2}$ silver (coins) which is 250 denarii. Two *lepta* are a *follis* according to the copper coinage, but not according to the silver coinage. This also was of silver. And, moreover, even at the present time the Romans make use of this number, 125 pieces of silver in number being considered among the Romans as heaped up together to make one purse, because the profusion of the quantity of the silver pieces fills the bag. For as the talent contains 125 *librae* by number, so also in the case of the *follis* 125 silver (denarii) complete the number.

of $1\frac{1}{3}$, if (as implied) in gold, dictates the existence (even if for ceremonial purposes only) of the tremissis/trimision. Add also for the earlier period: Patlagean, *Pauvreté économique et pauvreté sociale*, p. 366 (purses of indeterminate size, of 500 solidi, and of 100 lbs).

132 A. Beschaouch, 'La mosaïque de chasse à l'amphithéâtre découverte à Smirat en Tunisie', *Comptes Rendus de l'Académie des Inscriptions et Belles-Lettres* 1966, pp. 140–5.

133 I know of no contemporary evidence to support this claim, but it cannot have been otherwise.

134 The *follis* has also given rise to a large secondary literature, of which the most recent and most general examples are: A. H. M. Jones, 'The Origin and Early History of the *Follis*', *Journal of Roman Studies* 49 (1959), pp. 34–8. L. Ruggini, 'A proposito del *follis* nel IV secolo', *Atti della Accademia Nazionale dei Lincei, Rendiconti* 16[8] (1961), pp. 306–19 (a reply to Jones). J.-P. Callu, *La politique monétaire des empereurs romains de 238 à 311*, pp. 362–7. For the Rabbinic literature: D. Sperber, *Roman Palestine 200–400, Money and Prices*, pp. 47–54, 64–6 – but Sperber's curious notion that a *follis* (purse) contained coin blanks, as opposed to struck coins, must be rejected. The basic problems are that much of the evidence, particularly as used by Callu and Sperber, is not closely datable, and that in any case a good deal of the above has been overtaken by the epigraphic discoveries made at Aezani and Aprodisias (see below, pp. 450–9 and Table 15). Until the significance of this has been digested, and some kind of consensus reached, precise reconstructions remain personal and hypothetical.

135 Epiphanius, *De Mensuris et Ponderibus* LIII; ed. J. E. Dean, pp. 61–3.

And, again, it is called the *follis* because of the interpretation 'bag' and in *lepta* it lumps up 125 *lepta* of silver in one coin (name) so as to be called individually a *follis*, being mentioned by this name 'bag'.

When this is reckoned in talents the number is carried up to 125 *librae*, but when in *folles* they are composed of 125 (denarii) of silver.

The Greek version states that the *follis* was also called a *balantion* and distinguishes between a *follis* reckoned in denarii (i.e. *kata ton dēnarismon*) and one reckoned in silver (*kata ton argyrismon*), equating the former with 2½ or two silver coins (*argyra*) and 250 denarii.[136] It elsewhere states that the *follis* contained 125 silver coins (*argyria*) and that among the Romans it was called a *thylakos*.[137] The Latin version adds little, identifying the *follis/ballantion* as a *sacculus*, equating it with 2½ silver coins (*argentei*), and stating that it was so called from the weight and number of the denarii that it contained (*secundum denariorum pondus ac numerum*) not from the value of the metal (i.e. *non secundum metalli meritum*).[138]

The evidence of Epiphanius therefore, confused as it is in its various versions, implies the existence of two *folles*, one worth 2½ or two silver coins or 250 denarii, but actually containing copper coins, the other containing 125 silver coins. Now, as it happens, 2½ Diocletianic argentei would have been worth precisely 250 denarii, and could have been made up, prior to the retariffing of 301, by 20 billon nummi, and subsequent to the retariffing by 10 nummi. As it also happens, 125 silver coins, at the same period, would have been worth 12,500 denarii, and there is in fact independent evidence for the existence of a *follis* worth that amount: a mosaic from the Piazza Armerina in Sicily depicts purses with ✱XIIᴔ (= 12,500 denarii) marked on their outside, and a mosaic from Cherchell in North Africa repeats the theme;[139] an official papyrus source dated 300 also mentions a sum in silver bullion (*asēmon*) and *folleis* of money (*argyrion*) that permits the probable equation of the *follis* with 12,500 denarii.[140]

There is abundant evidence suggesting that the *follis* expressed in copper coins sank rapidly in value with the declining weight and debasement of the base-metal coinages repeatedly marking the fourth century, although the *follis* expressed in silver coins seems to have maintained its value. Eventually, as Isidore of Seville remarks:[141] 'Folles are so

[136] F. Hultsch, *Metrologicorum Scriptorum Reliquiae* I, pp. 267 (xlix), 144–5 (n. 4).

[137] *Ibid.* I, p. 269 (xvii).

[138] *Ibid.* II, p. 105 (xl).

[139] Piazza Armerina: G. V. Gentili, *La villa Erculia di Piazza Armerina: i mosaici figurati*, *Pl. 41*. Cherchell: ref. in Callu, *La politique monétaire des empereurs romains*, p. 365 n. 1.

[140] *P. Beatty Panop.* 2, pp. 104, 106, ll. 301–4: 50 lb silver bullion (*asēmon*) and 4 folleis cash (*argyrion*), the latter apparently making 33 talents 500 denarii, or 50,000 denarii, from which it follows that 1 *follis* = 12,500 denarii. See the perceptive commentary by Skeat on p. 152. A *follis* of 12,500 denarii is inherently likely to have contained 125 argentei of 100 d. each, rather than 1,000 nummi of 12.5 d. each, for the latter would have represented an inconvenient bulk (see below, pp. 451–8). On the other hand, the silver cash is reckoned in denarii, and not (as the bullion was) by weight, because it was quite appreciably overhauled at this period (see below, pp. 353 n. 179, 450–1).

[141] Isidore of Seville, *Etymologiarum sive Originum Libri XX* XVI.18.11; ed. W. M. Lindsay, II.

called from the purse (*sacculum*) within which they are enclosed, that which is contained having been named from the container.' The stage at which this development occurred remains uncertain, the earliest certainly dated and explicit use of the name in its developed sense occurring in Marcellinus Comes' account of the Anastasian reform of 498.[142] There is, however, no real reason for believing that this sense was then new, and there is, indeed, good reason for believing it to have been already current in the early fifth century (when a cape is priced at about 500 *folles*, and a large fish at 300), and probably as far back as 356(?), and perhaps even further.[143]

The practice of sealing up into purses sums of precious-metal coinage is detectable, by means of admittedly occasional documentary references and mosaic or pictorial representations, throughout the late Roman and Byzantine period. The sums involved vary greatly in size, from 2,000 pieces down to twenty, both of these examples presumably involving gold nomismata. On the occasion of ceremonial distributions or coronations even smaller sums – a single nomisma; $1\frac{1}{3}$ nomisma; three nomismata, three silver coins, and three copper coins – are known to have been involved, although equally these cannot be regarded as having been typical.

The surviving evidence suggests that, during the earlier period at least, the authority to seal up and mark purses rested with the state in its various institutions and officials – the mints, the *zygostatai*, the *khrysōnes*, and so on: a private individual might, for example, take a sum of money along to a *zygostatēs* or *khrysōnes* to receive his seal.[144] With the subsequent disappearance of several of these officials, it is readily conceivable that the authority may have devolved – if it had not done so already – upon the *trapezitai* and *argyropratai*, and even upon private individuals of sufficient standing.[145]

The continuing existence and use of purses of coin, whether consisting of base or of precious metal, during the late Roman and Byzantine period, is occasionally also demonstrated or implied by the physical shape or by the composition of surviving coin hoards. The physical shape of a number of fourth-century hoards reveals base metal coin,

[142] See below, p. 476.

[143] The same sense is almost certainly present in the almost contemporary Tablettes Albertini (493) – see below, p. 480. For the early fifth century: Augustine of Hippo, *De Civitate Dei* XXII.8.9; ed. J.-P. Migne in *PL* XLI, at col. 766. H. Adelson, in 'The Monetary Deterioration in the Fifth Century', in A. Kindler (ed.), *The Patterns of Monetary Development in Phoenicia and Palestine in Antiquity*, at p. 271, reckons from this, and another passage in Augustine, that the follis stood at less than 1,000 to the solidus, that Florentius' *casula* (see above) would have cost 500 folles made up, but the wool 300 folles (equivalent to the large fish) only. These estimates, if not taken too absolutely, seem reasonable. For 356(?): *CTh.* IX.23.1 – see above, pp. 291–3. Callu, in 'Rôle et distribution des espèces de bronze de 348 à 392', p. 57n. 75, reckons that use of the term follis to denote a single coin was already prevalent in the mid fourth century, and may well be correct. See also: *idem*, '"Pensa" et "Follis" sur une inscription d'Afrique', *Antiquités Africaines* 15 (1980), pp. 273–83. One does not have to accept Callu's detailed calculations in order to accept the general point. For what seems to be a related expression (*denariorum folles singulares*), see: *idem*, '"Follis Singularis" (à propos d'une inscription de Ghirza, Tripolitaine)', *Mélanges de l'École Française de Rome* 71 (1959), pp. 321–37.

[144] *P. Oxy.* 1886. Hendy, *DOS* XII, pp. 304–5.

[145] As in the Arabic world: see below, pp. 361–3.

at least, frequently to have been bound up into rolls, the container presumably having been the intestine suggested by the primitive meaning of the word *follis* itself.[146] The practice can be traced on into the sixth century at least,[147] although one purse at least of a more normal shape is known for the seventh century.[148]

Hoards containing heavy concentrations of coins struck from the same pair, or from a limited number only, of dies, or containing coins entirely or largely struck in a single *officina*, probably tend to have derived at no great distance from bodies of coins despatched from the mint in purses. A number of such hoards are known, prominent examples being the Casa delle Vestali hoard, which contained 397 solidi, including 345 of Anthemius of which 334 were all struck from the same pair of dies;[149] the İzmit hoard which contained 55 solidi including 47 of Zeno of which most were struck in the ninth officina (Θ);[150] the Lagbe hoard which contained 102 nomismata including 35 of a single type of Theophilus which were heavily die-linked;[151] the Suedinenie hoard which contained 21 or more billon trachea including 20 of John II of which all were struck in the same '*officina*';[152] and the Kaloyanovets hoard which contained 884 billon trachea including 238 of Isaac II which were of an extremely concentrated and characteristic composition, having been composed of two purses of 100 and 50+50 coins from two '*officinae*', and 40 loose coins, making up 240 trachea or precisely two hyperpyra, at the current rate of exchange.[153]

Hoards which seem to have been made up to a specific amount, whether up to a particular number of pounds or up to a round number of nomismata or whatever, probably also represent purses. The three classic hoards of this type are those from Aydın (II), apparently deposited under Heraclius; from Lagbe, apparently deposited under Theophilus; and from Banya, apparently deposited under Isaac II. The first contained

146 Callu, *La politique monétaire des empereurs romains*, pp. 362–3 n. 4.

147 P. Grierson, 'The Monetary Reforms of Anastasius and their Economic Consequences', in A. Kindler (ed.), *The Patterns of Monetary Development in Phoenicia and Palestine in Antiquity*, at p. 290 n. 16 (involves the discovery of folles in rolls – private information from Philip Grierson).

148 H. W. Bell, *Sardis* XI, *Coins*, pp. viii–ix (involves 216 folles which had been contained in a purse, the impression of its fabric being visible in the corrosion of many of the coins). This is not an uncommon phenomenon – several of the finds from the metropolitan site of Saraçhane (see below, p. 425 n.) were of a similar character, and the author has seen a number of other examples. The Sardis hoard was itself of a decidedly peculiar composition: Justin II (5 pieces), Maurice (6), Phocas (2), Heraclius (203); total, 216 pieces. The Heraclian coins were all of years 1 (610/11) to 5 (614/15). Given the number of coins involved (216, a very duodecimal figure – 3 × 72), and the unusually concentrated chronology (early Heraclius) it looks very much as if the purse had been made up of a particular figure (216 × 40 n. = 8,640 n.). It is quite possible that this then represented one solidus (see below, pp. 477–8). In any case, the purse was presumably buried on the occasion of a Persian attack (C. Foss, *Byzantine and Turkish Sardis*, pp. 53–6).

149 G. Boni, 'Roma: nuove scoperte nella città e nel suburbio', *Notizie degli Scavi* 1899, pp. 327–30.

150 İ. Ebcioğlu, 'İzmit Definesi', *İstanbul Arkeoloji Müzeleri Yıllığı* 13–14 (1966–7), pp. 166–74.

151 E. T. Newell, *The Byzantine Hoard of Lagbe*, pp. 18–22, nos 67–101.

152 Hendy, *DOS* XII, pp. 177, 386–7.

153 Hendy, *DOS* XII, pp. 176–7, 350–1; *idem*, *DOC* IV. D. M. Metcalf (in *Hamburger Beiträge zur Numismatik* 24/6 (1970/2), at pp. 371–2 – review of Hendy, *DOS* XII), on this hoard, is now completely worthless.

216 nomismata and seems to have been intended to make up three pounds ($3 \times 72 = 216$).[154] The second contained 102 nomismata, as noted elsewhere in this chapter, and seems likely to have been intended to make up the weight of 100 nomismata, involving a deficiency of 2%. It included, as also noted, 35 coins of a single type of Theophilus and in addition one coin of another type of the same emperor, making up a parcel of 36 coins or one half-pound.[155] The third contained 36 electrum trachea, or again one half-pound, and included 35 coins of Isaac II and one – a contemporary forgery – of Manuel I.[156] The Oxarve (Gotland) hoard seems likely to have included a body of 100 silver miliaresia, of which 2 were of Romanus III and 98 of Constantine IX.[157] A hoard from Aphrodisias contained 100 copper Alexandrian 12-nummus pieces of the emperors Justinian to Maurice.[158]

The existence and use of such purses goes far towards explaining another phenomenon evident from the eleventh century onwards: the availability of bodies of coin of a particular type or variety long after that type or variety had ceased to be minted and, it might have been supposed, had ceased to form a recognisable element in the circulating medium. With the debasements of the eleventh and of the thirteenth and fourteenth centuries, and even with the stable but denominationally complex coinage of the twelfth, it would also clearly have become more necessary to distinguish between the various types or varieties of coin, for variant metallic qualities and therefore market values might well have been involved.

This increased necessity is reflected in the contemporary custom of giving to each type or variety of coin a distinctive name which was derived either from its shape or metallic quality, or from the emperor who had issued it, or from some feature of its design, or indeed from a combination of several of these factors.[159] Once isolated, a body of a particular type or variety of coin would very probably have been sealed up into a purse, and might well have continued to circulate as such, according to its appropriate metallic quality and market value. It would have been such a practice that resulted in, for example, four pounds of 'gold *stavrata* nomismata of Monomachus (*nomismata khrysa stavrata tou Monomachou*)' still forming a distinctive block of currency as late as 1143, almost a century after the death of Constantine IX, their issuer.[160] The same would account for quantities

[154] P. Grierson, 'Two Byzantine Coin Hoards of the Seventh and Eighth Centuries at Dumbarton Oaks,' *DOP* 19 (1965), pp. 207–19.

[155] See above, p. 342, below, p. 363.

[156] Hendy, *DOS* XII, pp. 327–8.

[157] Ref.: Grierson, 'Harold Hardrada and Byzantine Coin Types in Denmark', pp. 129–30.

[158] See below, p. 439 (n.).

[159] Coin names: Grierson, *DOC* III.1, pp. 44–62. Hendy, *DOS* XII, pp. 26–38, 225–6, 250–6. V. Laurent 'Bulletin de numismatique byzantine (1940–1949)', *Revue des Études Byzantines* 9 (1951), pp. 199–206 (much outdated, but still with some useful references). For the complex *staurohagiodēmētraton*, see below, p. 513 and n. 323.

[160] A. I. Papadopoulos-Kerameus, *Noctes Petropolitanae, Sbornik vizantiĭskikh tekstov XII–XIII vekov*, pp. 62–3. For the coin: Grierson, *DOC* III.2, pp. 740–1 (Class III).

of hyperpyra of John III (1222–54) having been available in the fourteenth century, when they were classified by Pegolotti.[161]

Bodies of coin circulating in this fashion would have resembled closely the contemporary or somewhat later Italian *fiorini di suggello*, the various metallic qualities and market values of which were denoted by the colour of the wax used to seal up the purses that contained them. The resemblance is presumably not coincidental.[162]

The practice, although obviously immensely convenient, inevitably lent itself to corruption. An official papyrus source dated 300 forbids officials to give *trapezeitai* what was evidently some kind of fee under the pretext of *ballantia* (*prophasei ballantiōn*), and *trapezeitai* to charge or receive it from tax-payers.[163] The source's terms are too vague to permit a detailed reconstruction of what had been happening, but they are suggestive in the light of later evidence. A further papyrus source, datable to the late fifth or early sixth century, forms the petition of one Aurelius Joseph, who had taken a certain sum in gold (*phaneron khrysion*) along to the public *zygostatēs* Anastasius for a purpose that is unfortunatly now lost in the papyrus. Having handed over this sum he received Anastasius' seal (*sphragis*). But when the seal was loosened, and the sum discharged, it apparently showed a loss of 52 keratia. Aurelius Joseph was therefore seeking restitution from Anastasius' heir.[164] Once again, the source is too briefly allusive, and in any case too fragmentary, to permit a detailed reconstruction of what had happened, but is again suggestive in the light of later evidence.

### B. *Justinian's Edict* XI (*Part 1*)

Edict XI of Justinian, dated 559 and addressed to Peter (Barsymes), then praetorian prefect of the East for the second time, is fortunately almost entirely devoted to describing and attempting to eradicate the kind of corruption represented in the two earlier documents. The edict, the terms of which have been discussed with unconvincing results on a number of occasions,[165] is headed as follows:

[161] See below, pp. 367, 527 Table 23 and n. 392.

[162] Giovanni di Antonio da Uzzano, *La Pratica della Mercatura*; ed. G. F. Pagnini della Ventura, p. 152, conveniently translated in Lopez and Raymond, *Medieval Trade in the Mediterranean World*, pp. 149–50.

[163] *P. Beatty Panop.* 2, ll. 93, 94, 97.

[164] *P. Oxy.* 1886. Hendy, *DOS* XII, pp. 304–5, 306. For another early fifth-century case of corruption involving *balantia*, counting, weighing and sealing, see now J.-P. Callu, 'Dénombrement et pesée: le sou theodosien', *Bulletin de la Société Française de Numismatique* 34 (1979), p. 611. The case, quoted from Synesius, by implication also involves a *zygostatēs*.

[165] E.g. C. Diehl, 'Une crise monétaire au VI$^{e}$ siècle', *Revue des Études Grecques* 32 (1919), pp. 158–66. A. C. Johnson and L. C. West, *Currency in Roman and Byzantine Egypt*, pp. 187–91. S. Vryonis, 'Two Numismatic Items from the Thomas Whittemore Collection', *Byzantinische Forschungen* 3 (1968), pp. 229–34. It was, curiously enough, and as will be seen below, the earliest of these treatments, that of Diehl, which, in appreciating the wider problems involved, came nearest to solving the problem. Where Diehl missed the solution was in supposing that there were officially produced defective solidi in circulation, and not seeing that the whole phenomenon was basically a matter of accountancy.

So that in future the *zygostatai* and *khrysōnes* amongst the Egyptians shall have no licence to demand anything under the name of *obryza* (*hyper obryzēs*), but that gold marked there (*to kharattomenon ekeise khrysion*) shall exactly resemble that in this Great City [Constantinople], they shall place their seals (*sphragidai*) on it according to the weight preserved in the coined money (*kata ton sōzomenon en tō kharagmati stathmon*).

In the preface, the emperor states that he intends to suppress a charge, which had earlier been unknown, but which was now termed *obryza* among the Egyptians, and which had reached such a level that nine gold coins were being given for it in every pound, to the detriment both of the state and of transactions generally – particularly in Alexandria.

In *caput* 1, the emperor commands that gold should be treated in the Egyptian diocese according to the old practice, even if during the meantime it had become deficient in what was called the *apolyton kharagma* amongst the Alexandrians, so that no one should have the power to demand anything under the name of the evilly conceived *obryza*. Gold used in Egypt should be so reckoned in transactions as to accord with the fashion in which it was marked in Constantinople. These commands should be enforced by the current *augoustalios* in Alexandria and his subordinates.

In *caput* 2, the emperor observes that, since the instigators of corruption are the *zygostatai* and *khrysōnes*, they are to be placed under caution by the officials under whose disposition they operate so that they render service in transactions in the *apolyton kharagma* and, if at any time it should be necessary for them to seal, they inscribe only as great an amount as the true weight of the gold they seal up. They are not to inscribe more than the true weight of the gold they seal up as, through corrupt practice, they have done until the present. The emperor then proceeds to fix the punishments for infringing his commands – capital punishment and the confiscation of property – and to state that the *zygostatai* and *khrysōnes* must forward all the necessary gold, both to the *augoustalios* in Alexandria and those who in future exercise control over the customary revenues, and to the current and future *alabarkhēs* and *praipositos tōn theiōn thēsaurōn* (i.e. *praepositus sacrorum thesaurorum*), without exacting any sum at all under the name of *obryza*.

In *caput* 3, the emperor entrusts the enforcement of his commands to the appropriate current official (the *augoustalios*) and his successors and to their subordinates, so that if anyone from the bureau of the *alabarkhēs* or of the *praipositos*, or anyone from his own bureau or among the merchants, should receive a sum under the name of *obryza* or include it in his reckoning, he might suffer capital punishment and the confiscation of property. The fee was thus to be totally suppressed and eradicated.

Edict XI which concerns Egypt, and a vast number of other documents actually from Egypt, of both a public and private nature, and in either case of an apparently bizarre complexity as regards the monetary terminology and accounting methods used in them, are comprehensible only within the context of the production and circulation of a standard gold coinage dependent virtually entirely upon weight for its value, the problems inevitably consequent upon this, and the solutions evolved.

All late Roman, and all except the latest and most debased Byzantine, gold coinage was struck *al pezzo*, and each coin will therefore have been examined for its actual conformity to its theoretical standard of weight at some stage of production. The major practical limitations of this general principle will have been those formed by the human imperfections of the mint personnel and the organisational system they operated, and by the technical imperfections of the balances and standard weights they employed.

From the moment this coinage was put into circulation, unless immediately immobilised by hoarding, each constituent coin will have begun inevitably and irreversibly to lose weight through wear. Some coins will have lost extra weight through human tampering: by being pared, clipped, or filed down. Now, since the rate of wear is more or less constant for each denomination, the degree of loss suffered by each coin within that denomination should be more or less directly proportional to the amount of time for which it has circulated. But even if this is realised (whether or not it is understood), it is difficult to convert the realisation into action where a coinage that is largely undated and – except within quite wide limits – often undatable is concerned.

Although the relatively high rate at which the late Roman and Byzantine coinage was extracted from circulation and cycled, by way of the fiscal system, through the mint will have acted towards maintaining its general level of weight, nevertheless a coin population of considerable variation as regards individual weight will inevitably have evolved: very few coins in it will have been above-standard in this respect (it will have been precisely these that will have been liable to be tampered with); few even will have been equal to the standard; the majority will have been, to some varying and unpredictable degree, below-standard.[166]

In this kind of situation, a number of elements or factors are to be observed, or are liable to emerge. The chief of these are: the theoretical weight standard of the coins involved, the actual weight of the same, the difference between the two figures, the process of rectifying the difference, the fees charged for performing the process.

## C. *The* dēmosios zygos, *and the* idiōtikos zygos *and* khrysokhoïkos stathmos

In Egypt where, as elsewhere in the empire, the standard coin was the gold nomisma theoretically weighing 24 keratia and equalling a *hexagion*, the theoretical weight standard was expressed by the *dēmosios zygos* ('public standard'), payments made according to it being made *dēmosiō zygō*.

Alongside of the *dēmosios zygos* there occur a number of what appear to be variant weight standards. It is the relation of these to the public one, and ultimately their precise nature and purpose, that has occasioned considerable discussion.

[166] P. Grierson, 'The President's Address, Session 1962–3, Coin Wear and the Frequency Table', in *Numismatic Chronicle* 3[7] (1963), at pp. i–xvi (at end of vol.).

At Oxyrhynchus, the commonest of these standards is the *idiōtikos zygos* ('private standard'), payments made according to it being made *idiōtikō zygō*. The numerical relation of the public standard to the private is established easily enough. It has been observed[167] that the conversion of a sum in the public standard to the equivalent in the private one may be achieved by adding 2 keratia per nomisma to the former.

At Aphrodito, the place of the *idiōtikos zygos* seems to be taken by the *khrysokhoïkos stathmos* ('goldsmiths' standard'), payments made according to it being made *khrysokhoïkō stathmō*. Again, the numerical relation of the public standard to the goldsmiths' is established easily enough. In a set of accounts recording the expenditure of the *komes* Ammonios, 4 nomismata *z(ygō dēmosiō)* are equated with 5 nomismata minus 14 keratia (apparently 4 nom. 10 ker.),[168] the conversion being achieved by adding 2 keratia for each of the eventual 5 nomismata. In another set of accounts it is recorded that Ammonios' steward (*hypodektēs*) Apollos had received 2 nomismata minus 3½ keratia *khr(ysokhoïkō stathmō)* for wool(?) bought by the priest Hermios, and that he had spent 1 nomisma minus 3½ keratia *z(ygō dēmosiō)* on the church of Romanos and 1 nomisma minus 2 keratia *khr(ysokhoïkō stathmō)* on Kollouthos.[169] His revenue thus apparently amounted to 44½ keratia (*khr.*), and his expenditure apparently to 20½ keratia (*z.*) and 22 keratia (*khr.*). Assuming that the account was intended to balance, it will do so again only if 2 keratia are added to the sum expressed in the *zygos dēmosios*.[170]

It is to be noted that, where a sum *dēmosiō zygō* is equated with another *idiōtikō zygō* or *khrysokhoïkō stathmō*, the former is apparently the smaller, the latter apparently the larger. The clue as to what was happening is to be found in yet another set of accounts recording revenues paid to Ammonios' *hypodektēs* (this time unnamed). In this set the following entry occurs: '1 nomisma minus 1 keration, amounting to 21 keratia at 22 keratia to the nomisma (*no(misma) 1 p(ara keratiou) 1, gi(netai) k(eratia) 21 a(po keratiōn 22 tou nomismatos)*).'[171] The entry is, of course, partially restored, but whether implicitly as in its first part, or explicitly as in its second, the nomisma is reckoned at 22 keratia rather than the normal 24. If this reckoning is adopted for the sums expressed *khrysokhoïkō stathmō* quoted above, then the accounts balance without further trouble: thus, 4 nomismata *z.* (or 96 keratia) equal 5 nomismata minus 14 keratia (actually 4 nom. 8 ker.) *khr.* (or 96 keratia); and 2 nomismata minus 3½ keratia *khr.* (or 40½ keratia) equal 1 nomisma minus 3½ keratia *z.* (or 20½ keratia) plus 1 nomisma minus 2 keratia *khr.* (or 20 keratia).

A rather similar formula is occasionally employed to achieve the same effect. *P.Michael.* 40 (mid sixth century) refers indifferently to a sum as: '10 gold nomismata',

[167] Johnson and West, *Currency in Roman and Byzantine Egypt*, pp. 140–1.

[168] *P. Cairo* 67139, fol. v, rect., l. 26.

[169] *P. Cairo* 67139, fol. vi, rect., ll. 2–3.

[170] Johnson and West, *Currency in Roman and Byzantine Egypt*, pp. 148–9.

[171] *P. Cairo* 67138, fol. i, rect., 2.

or as: '10 standard imperial gold nomismata by tale, each minus two keratia by the goldsmiths' standard of the same village of Aphrodito (...*khrysou despotikōn dokimōn nomismatiōn deka ton arithmon ekastou para keratia dyo tō khrysokhoïkō stathmō tēs autēs kōmēs Aphroditēs*).' *P.Michael.* 43 (526) refers similarly to a sum as: '18 nomismatia', or as: '18 gold nomismatia, each minus two keratia by the goldsmiths' standard of the same village of Aphrodito (*khrysou nomismatia deka oktō ekaston para keratia dyo khrysokhoïkō stathmō tēs autēs kōmēs Aphroditēs*)'. *P.Michael.* 45 (540) refers again to a sum as: '3 imperial gold nomismatia of good weight, each minus two keratia (*khrysou despotikou eustathma nomismatia tria ekaston para keratia dyo*).'

The first sum is also quoted as 10 gold nomismatia minus 20 keratia; the second as 18 gold nomismatia minus 36 keratia by the goldsmiths' standard; and the third as 3 gold nomismatia minus 6 keratia by the goldsmiths' standard.

Now, it is clear that a gold nomisma cannot both be standard and of good weight, and yet also weigh two keratia less than the standard or good weight. It is equally clear that even if such gold nomismata were deficient in weight, they would not invariably be deficient by two keratia.

What both the *idiōtikos zygos* and the *khrysokhoïkos stathmos* therefore effectively involved was discounting the nomisma expressed *dēmosiō zygō* (= 24 keratia) by two keratia per nomisma (= 22 keratia) and what this in turn might mean in matter of payment by tale (assuming, as was certainly the case, that normal gold nomismata were employed) was that, for every 72 nomismata of liability, some 78½ were actually handed over. The gold pound was thus effectively being discounted by some 6½ nomismata.

The reasoning behind this discounting is not difficult to deduce. Given that most coins were actually to some degree below their theoretical weight standard, officials and those involved in the various technical processes attendant upon monetary transactions, and even private individuals, might recover the difference inevitably existing between the theoretical weight of the number of coins required to fulfil a payment and the actual weight of the same number of coins by means of two principal methods: either they could insist that additional coins sufficient to make up the difference in a particular payment be supplied; or they could impose upon the coinage a general discount sufficient to make up the difference in the majority of payments or indeed in all normal payments. The former method, of course involved an absolute amount which nevertheless varied from payment to payment. The latter involved an element of calculation: no one – whether official or private individual – was going to impose a discount which, because it was insufficient to make up the difference in at least the majority of payments, resulted in his consistently being left with a deficit; he might well, on the other hand, impose a discount which, because it more than made up the difference in the majority of payments, resulted in his consistently being left with a surplus. It is quite clearly in this latter method that the evolution of the discounts expressed in the *idiōtikos zygos* and *khrysokhoïkos stathmos* are to be sought.

The papyrus sources are fortunately, if on rare occasions only, more explicit in using involved formulae to describe the same problem and solutions as outlined above. *P.Oxy.*1971, datable to the late fifth or the sixth century, mentions 'seven gold nomismatia by tale (*arithmia*), or six nomismatia and one and one-quarter keration of good weight in the public standard (*eustathma*...*dēmos*[*iō*] *zyg*[*ō*]), which is your ounce and another one and one-quarter keration in the public standard, amounting to the sum of 7 gold nom. or 6 nom. $1\frac{1}{4}$ ker. of good weight in the public standard'. The difference between the theoretical weight of the seven nomismata and their actual weight (= 6 nom. $1\frac{1}{4}$ ker.) is in this case reckoned at $22\frac{3}{4}$ or $3\frac{1}{4}$ keratia per nomisma. If this were to have been converted into a general discount it would have meant that, for every 72 nomismata of liability, some $83\frac{1}{4}$ were actually handed over. The gold pound would thus have been effectively discounted by some $11\frac{1}{4}$ nomismata.

*P.Lond.* 483, from Apollinopolis Magna and dated 616, mentions 'one and two-thirds gold nomismata, with the discount (*synallagē*) making them (i.e. *ta poiounta*) thirty-six and one-half keratia in the goldsmiths' standard'. The straightforward meaning of the word *synallagē* is 'interchange', whether in a social or commercial sense. In this particular case there is little doubt but that the word is being used in a technical fashion, and the translation 'discount' is the only one that is appropriate in the general context. The calculation is a comparatively straightforward one: at a discount of two keratia per nomisma, a rate for the *idiōtikos zygos* and *khrysokhoïkos stathmos* observed above, $1\frac{2}{3}$ nomisma actually equals $36\frac{2}{3}$ keratia, but since the scribe evidently preferred to calculate in fractions no smaller than one-half keration he wrote $36\frac{1}{2}$ keratia, the nearest appropriate sum.

At Aphrodito at least, during the earlier part of the Arab period, yet another formula was utilised to denote the difference between the theoretical and actual weight of coins. *P. Lond.* 1412 dated 699–705, *P. Lond.* 1413 dated 716–21, and *P. Lond.* 1414 of uncertain but approximately contemporary date, all record sums in nomismata and keratia under two headings, *arithmia* and *ekho*(*mena*). It seems clear that entries under the former heading – which, with rare exceptions only, are also the larger – represent the theoretical weights of sums reckoned by tale, and that those under the latter represent the actual weights of those sums. This is in any case, of course, the solution indicated by the terms themselves: *nomismata arithmia* are nomismata by number, and *nomismata ekhomena* are apparently nomismata possessing an actual weight. The difference between the two entries commonly, but by no means invariably, works out to be (or, more likely, to be reckoned at) two keratia per nomisma – again, the rate observed above to have existed between the *idiōtikos zygos* and *khrysokhoïkos stathmos*, and the *dēmosios zygos*, suggesting either an effective identity with, or at least a derivation from, that system. The same terminology and system, with a variant difference, seem also to have operated at contemporary (705–15) Apollonos Ano.[172]

The imposition of a general discount upon the coinage was not a phenomenon that was confined to Egypt, although, in the nature of things, evidence for an imposition of this kind is much more prolific there than elsewhere. Nearby Gaza seems to have possessed its own standard, the *zygos tōn Gazeōn* or *Gazēs*, payments in it being made *zygō tōn Gazeōn* or *Gazēs*. These payments seem invariably to involve a number of nomismata minus an equal number of keratia, thus: 7 nom. minus 7 ker. (562), 4 nom. minus 4 ker. (570), and 9 nom. minus 9 ker. (605). The pattern is, of course, very similar to that already mentioned for Aphrodito, and implies that the nomisma was being reckoned at 23 keratia (rather than 22) and that the gold pound was effectively being discounted by some 3 nomismata (rather than some $6\frac{1}{2}$).[173] According to a letter of pope Gregory I,[174] dated 591, for every 72 solidi of liability $73\frac{1}{2}$ were actually being handed over on certain of the Sicilian estates of the church. The solidus was thus effectively being reckoned at $23\frac{1}{2}$ keratia and the gold pound being discounted by $1\frac{1}{2}$ solidus.

## D. *Obryza* and *analōma*

It seems clear, however, that these general discounts were designed not merely to recover the difference between the theoretical and actual weights of coins (and even to leave those imposing them with a surplus), but also to include a formal fee, or fees, charged on the service, or services, provided in recovering the difference.

At Oxyrhynchus, and presumably elsewhere, the main element in the discount was that termed *obryza*. *P. Oxy.* 126, dated 572, mentions '$22\frac{1}{2}$ keratia in gold which, with *obryza*, make up twenty-four keratia in the public standard (*obryziaka eis dēmosiō keratia eikosi tessara*)'. *P. Oxy.* 144, dated 580, acknowledges the receipt, through John the most honest (*eudokimotatos*) *trapezitēs*, of '1,440 gold nomismata in *obryzon kharagma* and 720 nomismata in *apolyton Aigyption kharagma* in the Alexandrian standard (*zygō Alex-*[*andreias*]), and forty-five nomismata under the name of *obryza* and the restoration of the same (*hyper obryzēs kai apokatastatikōn autōn*), amounting to 2,205 gold nomismata.'

[172] E.g. *P. Apollonos Ano* 82 (703–15): 691 *arithmia nomismata* = 653 nom. 10 ker. *ekhomena nomismata*, the difference being $1\frac{1}{3}$ ker. per nom. The total of 889 nom. was contained in 8 different *apokombia*, all of *arithmia nomismata*, and the conversion to *ekhomena nomismata* is made in a single calculation at the end. It therefore follows that the *ekhomenon* formula is no more 'real' than the other discounts.

[173] *P. Ness.* 21 (562), 26 (570), 46 (605). See also *P. Ness.* 27 (570–1): 2 nom. minus 2 ker.; 28 (post 572): 4 nom. prob. minus 4 ker.; 44 (598): 1 nom. minus 1 ker. *P. Ness.* 46 also has 6 nom. minus 6 ker. and 3 nom. minus 3 ker. (i.e. a total of 9 nom. minus 9 ker.), and the formula is somewhat more elaborate: *khrysina despotịḳạ ombryzạ tetragrammiaia protia dokima toṇ ạrithmon ennea zygō Gazēs khr*[(*ysou*)] *n*[*o*(*m*.)] *9 p̣*(*ara*) *ḳ*(*eratia*) *9*. Thus once again, the distinction is between nomismata reckoned by tale and those reckoned by discount.

[174] See above, p. 332 n. 97.

It then announces the correspondent to be prepared to take the sum to Alexandria, to pay it to John and Simeonios the most famous (*lamprotatoi*) *argyropratai*, and to bring back written receipts (*grammata*) from the most illustrious agent (*apokrisiarios*) Theodore. The *trapezitēs* and the *argyropratai* mentioned in this document seem either to have been officials, or to have been acting on behalf of the state, their functions perhaps being similar to those of the earlier *trapezeitai* met with above.[175]

The charge for *obryza* in the first of the documents quoted in the preceding paragraph is a straightforward 1½ keration per nomisma, or one-sixteenth. That in the second is less obvious, and both the general sense of the document, and ultimately the specific interpretation placed upon the items of monetary terminology used in it, are clearly crucial to its elucidation. The document involves three sums in gold coin: 1,440 nomismata in *obryzon kharagma*; 720 in *apolyton kharagma*; and 45 *hyper obryzēs kai apokatastatikōn autōn*. Of these sums, the first two although disparate (and amounting to 20 lb and 10 lb, respectively) are at least of the same order, while the third is very much smaller than either. Again, the first two are described as forming distinct classes of *kharagma*, while the third is described merely as consisting of a number of nomismata 'under the name of *obryza* and the restoration of the same'. Now, the second half of this latter phrase, 'the restoration of the same', being in the plural in the Greek, cannot refer to the *obryza* of the first half, and indeed can only refer to the nomismata of either the second or the third sums. The implication is, surely, that when the 45 nomismata of the third sum are added as *obryza* to the 720 of the second, they restore the latter to the status of the first – from *apolyton kharagma*, that is, to *obryzon kharagma*. A charge of 45 nomismata on 720 represents a rate of 1½ keration per nomisma, and since this is identical with that occurring in the first of the documents quoted above the implication derived is clearly the correct one.

An identical rate also occurs in *P. Oxy.* 1907, datable to the seventh century, where 692 nomismata with *obryza* (*obryz(iaka)*) are equated with 735 nomismata 6 keratia (*eis Alex(andreias)*). Finally, what is apparently an identical rate occurs in *P. Michael.* 35, which is datable to the sixth or seventh century, and which less specifically mentions '1 gold nomismation at 22½ keratia, amounting to *1 khry. no. ei(s) k. 22½*.'

It seems clear, therefore, from the terms in which these documents are expressed, that the main element in the discount, generally termed *obryza*, was that which was designed specifically to recover (or 'restore') the difference between the theoretical and actual weights of coins.

At Oxyrhynchus, the largest fee, apparently for weighing the coins involved in a transaction, termed *rhopē* ('weight'), customarily amounted to ½ keration per nomisma, and there sums are frequently described as either *ektos rhopēs* (i.e. excluding the fee) or *syn rhopē* (including it).[176] It is in the circumstances clearly tempting to see the origins,

175 See above, p. 344.

176 Johnson and West, *Currency in Roman and Byzantine Egypt*, pp. 133, 141–3.

at least, of the *idiōtikos zygos* and *khrysokhoïkos stathmos* – both of which, as noted above, involved an effective discount of two keratia per nomisma – as the combination or consolidation of charges of $1\frac{1}{2}$ keration per nomisma *hyper obryzēs* and $\frac{1}{2}$ keration per nomisma *hyper rhopēs*. A possible indication that these were indeed the origins of the two general discounts is to be found in a group of earlier documents, most or all of which probably emanate from Antinoöpolis or Hermopolis. *P.Flor.* 95, dated 375, records sums in the following form: 'so many imperial (*despotika*) four-gramme (*tetragrammiaia*) gold nomismatia, amounting to so many – an identical number – gold nomismatia including the defined *obryza* and *analōma* (*meta tēs horistheisēs ombryzēs kai tou analōmatos*')'. *P.Lips.* 62, dated 384/5, utilises virtually the same formula. *P.Lips.* 61, also dated 375, on the other hand utilises a somewhat more specific one in recording 'seventy-two gold nomismatia by tale (*arithmō*), each without weighing and *obryza* and *analōma* (*aneu stathmou kai ombryzēs kai analōmatos*)'. The basic distinction in this group of documents is thus that existing between nomismata reckoned by tale and without extra charges, and those reckoned by weight and with them.

Now, in the three documents quoted in the preceding paragraph, the charge termed *obryza* is found coupled with an element termed *analōma*, and from its position and the manner in which it is used this latter name has every appearance of being applied to a further charge of some kind. This is in any case the interpretation suggested by the straightforward meaning of the word itself: 'expense' or 'cost'. *P.Oxy.* 1919, datable to the seventh century, records a payment of '103 nomismata $9\frac{1}{4}$ keratia *obryza* [or *obryziaka*], and $68\frac{3}{4}$ keratia which is 2 nomismata $7\frac{3}{4}$ keratia [recte $20\frac{3}{4}$ keratia] under the name of *analōma* on the same as customary (*hyper analōmatos autōn ex ethous*), amounting to 106 nomismata 6 keratia in the public standard.'

The entry gives rise to two principal questions: the status of the sum reckoned in the nomismata and keratia and described as *obryza* or *obryziaka*; and the nature – that is, the rate and composition – of the charge termed *analōma*. With regard to the former, it is in the first place quite clear that *obryza* cannot be translated simply as 'gold', and the sum therefore cannot have consisted simply of a fixed number of gold nomismata, semisia and trimisia, or similar, for no fraction of the nomisma such as $9\frac{1}{4}$ keratia either existed or could have been made up. The sum, in other words, cannot have been reckoned by tale: like that in *P.Oxy.* 144 it must have been a sum that had already been 'restored' to a particular weight by the payment of *obryza*, and indeed the final equation is expressed *dēmosiō zygō*.

With regard to the latter question – the nature of the charge termed *analōma* – it has been suggested[177] that, in this case at least, it represented a combination of $\frac{1}{2}$ keration per whole nomisma (= $51\frac{1}{2}$ ker.) *hyper rhopēs*, and $\frac{1}{6}$ keration per nomisma (= $17\frac{1}{6}$ ker.) *hyper parallelismou zygōn*. This seems reasonable enough, although the extra fee termed

[177] Johnson and West, *Currency in Roman and Byzantine Egypt*, pp. 118, 141.

*parallelismos zygōn* ('balancing (or equalling) up of weights') is normally levied at a rate of $\frac{1}{8}$ keration per nomisma, and it is the *parallelismos Alexandreias* that is levied at $\frac{1}{6}$ keration.[178] In addition, such a combination should have resulted in a total of $68\frac{2}{3}$ keratia rather than $68\frac{3}{4}$.

The situation in sum appears to be that, at an early date, the charge termed *obryza* is found coupled with that termed *analōma* in documentary sources; that, later, *analōma* seems to have had as its principal element the fee termed *rhopē*; that, together, *obryza* and *analōma* – or the principal element of the latter at least – would normally have amounted to two keratia per nomisma; and that, again later, the general discounts termed *idiōtikos zygos* and *khrysokhoïkos stathmos* both also involved two keratia per nomisma. The case for the discounts having originated, at least, in a combination or consolidation of the two charges is therefore a circumstantial one only, but a powerful one nevertheless. There is, finally, the not irrelevant consideration that, yet later, *nomismata arithmia* seem commonly to have been discounted against *nomismata ekhomena* at a rate of two keratia per nomisma. The terminology involved was in all three cases different, the methodology used slightly so, but the result was essentially the same.

### E. *Justinian's Edict* XI *(Part 2)*

It is, then, within this context, complex enough but simplified for the purposes of a relatively brief discussion even so, that the terms of Justinian's Edict XI are therefore to be understood. The identity and nature of the charge termed *obryza* which the emperor declares himself to be in the process of suppressing now seems clear. His assertion that the charge had earlier been unknown on the other hand seems mistaken, for what seems to have been the same or a very similar charge is found as early as the later part of the fourth century. It may have existed in essence at an even earlier stage, for what seems to have been a similar charge, termed *katharsis* ('purification') and amounting to approximately one-eighteenth (which would have been equivalent to $1\frac{1}{3}$ keration per nomisma), appears in a document dated 306.[179] In that case, its ultimate origins may have been even earlier, and it should certainly be related to the *hai kath'* formula and the *katharon* classification to be examined later in this chapter.[180]

The emperor's further assertion that the charge now amounted to 9 nomismata in the pound, or 3 keratia per nomisma, cannot be verified specifically, but it is by no means improbable.[181] Although at Oxyrhynchus the customary rate seems to have been $1\frac{1}{2}$

[178] Johnson and West, *Currency in Roman and Byzantine Egypt*, pp. 143–4.

[179] *P. Oxy.* 1653; Johnson and West, *Currency in Roman and Byzantine Egypt*, pp. 128–9. The document records an extra levy of uncoined silver (*asēmou*), and of gold (*khrysou*), in coin (*holokottinois*) – again, possibly a reflection of the contemporary overvalued nature of coined silver, and of the identity of coined and bullion gold (see above, p. 340 n. 140; below, pp. 450–1).

[180] See below, pp. 356–60.

[181] See below, p. 363.

keration per nomisma, at Antaeopolis it seems to have been one keration per nomisma only, while at Heracleopolis it may have been as much as $2\frac{1}{4}$ keratia per nomisma. It was in other words, as indeed might be expected, capable of a certain degree of variation according to the time, the place, and doubtless the circumstances.[182] It may well have been that, at a rate as high as 3 keratia per nomisma, the public would have been unwilling – would have refused if possible – to enter into monetary transactions, to the detriment of both official and private affairs. There is indeed some evidence of a reluctance to incur such charges in private affairs.[183]

Under the first heading of the Edict, Justinian commands that gold (coinage) should be treated in the old fashion in Egypt, even if meanwhile it had become deficient (he uses the verb *parephtheirein*) in the *apolyton kharagma*, and that there should be no demand for *obryza*. Gold should be so reckoned there as to accord with the fashion in which it was marked (he uses the verb *kharassein*) in Constantinople. Under the second, the emperor elaborates: the *zygostatai* and *khrysōnes*, the instigators of the corruption involved, are to render service in transactions in the *apolyton kharagma* and, if required to seal (he uses the verb *sphragizein*), they are to inscribe (he uses the verb *epigraphein*) only the true weight of the gold they seal up, not more than the true weight as formerly.

With the previous discussion and Justinian's description and commands in mind, the true outlines of the situation that had led to the issue of the edict begin to emerge. *Apolyton kharagma* (as deriving from the verb *apolyein*) is, surely, coinage that has been loosened, released, or discharged from something. The term applies, quite simply, to loose, independently circulating, pieces of coin. Such pieces, as already noted, inevitably lose weight (i.e. become deficient) through wear. On the other hand, the size of such an individual or collective deficiency, and therefore that of the compensation or 'restoration' to be made, was ascertainable by weighing the coin involved against the appropriate standard weight or weights. Trouble was liable to arise when, rather than perform the operation as often as coin changed hands, officials began to impose general discounts or charges on loose coin that were in theory sufficient to cover the deficiency and its 'restoration' but were in practice designed to leave them with a surplus. Such a charge was *obryza*.

Once the imposition of such discounts or charges became an accepted practice, the way lay open to major abuse: the obvious temptation was for officials within any given locality to combine so as to bring about a monopoly situation and to discount, or charge,

182 Variation by place is implied by the phrase: *pros tēn synallagēn tēs autēs kōmēs* in *P. Cairo* 67127 (Aphrodito, 544). See also *P. Michael.* 40, 43 (above p. 348). Clearly, if a discount or whatever could be reckoned by a village-name, the implication is that other reckonings in other villages differed. See also: Johnson and West, *Currency in Roman and Byzantine Egypt*, pp. 132–3, 151 n. 13. See also above, p. 350 (Gaza).

183 *P. Oxy.* 1915 (*c.* 560). See also Johnson and West, *Currency in Roman and Byzantine Egypt*, pp. 145–6 and n. 8. The discounts in this document, involving both the *dēmosios zygos* and the *idiōtikos zygos*, and *arithmia nomismata*, seem unusually large. Cf. *P. Oxy.* 1971.

at as high a rate as possible. Alexandrian officials had apparently pitched the rate so high that it was having a deterrent effect, and it was noticeably at this point only that the state, in the person of the emperor himself, intervened. Not that the terms of the resultant edict were any more effective, in the long term at least, than they normally were in such cases, for officials patently continued to charge *obryza*, as in *P.Oxy*. 144 (580). That the Alexandrians may have been peculiarly prone to excesses of this kind seems confirmed by an incident in the *Vita* of John the Almsgiver, patriarch of Alexandria 610–19.[184]

As already implied in the preceding paragraph, a major disadvantage of weighing and 'restoring' the loose coins in a transaction was that, once the operation had been performed and the coins had changed hands, they would normally have been intermingled with, and thereby have become indistinguishable from, any other loose coins that the recipient might have happened to have. Even in the unlikely event of their losing no further weight through wear they would therefore again have become liable to discounts, charges and fees. One way of avoiding such problems was for the coins to be taken to a competent official for sealing up into a purse. They thus became immune from individual loss, collective loss in weight, and liability to further exactions, and – as such and termed *obryzon kharagma* – may well have continued to circulate. In addition, the donor could have them weighed, 'restored', and sealed up in one locality and – all fees paid – sent to the recipient in another.

An *apokombion* of this kind would have been made up to the weight of a particular number of *hexagia* and presumably would have had that number marked or inscribed on its outside. It would, in normal circumstances, have contained rather more nomismata than the number of *hexagia* to which it was made up and with which it was marked, the difference once again being accounted for by the deficiency in the weight of the nomismata which would have had to have been 'restored'. Only if the coins involved were fresh from the mint, or had been immobilised by hoarding, or had been painstakingly culled from the coin population, is the situation likely to have been otherwise.

The *apokombion*, on the other hand, would not itself have weighed the equivalent of the particular number of *hexagia*, the difference this time being that between the gross weight of the coins inside, plus the purse and the seal, and the net weight of the contents alone. This meant that, without loosening the seal and discharging the purse's contents, thus vitiating much of the point of the exercise, the true weight of its contents could not be at all accurately verified. The potential for abuse was thus considerable. The crucial factor in the whole operation was, of course, the honesty of the official involved in sealing the purse, and since – during the late Roman and early Byzantine period at least – the

[184] The specific charge of discounting is made by Justinian in his phrase (cap. 3): *en tois synallagmasin hyper obryzēs lambanontes ē hypologizomenoi* – 'extorting or discounting [or deducting] under the name of *obryza* in interchanges [or exchanges]'. For John the Almsgiver, see above, p. 333.

official was as likely as not to be the local *zygostatēs* or *khrysōnēs*, trouble was almost bound to arise. Justinian implies that these officials had been exploiting precisely the weak point just mentioned: he accuses them, in other words, of having marked (*sc.* on the outside of the *apokombion*) more than the true weight of the coins that they had sealed up. They had presumably been pocketing the difference in addition to whatever profit they had made from discounts, or charges, and fees.

As late as the eleventh century, Cecaumenus, in advising the poor man (*ptōkhos*) on his way to wealth, recommends him[185] not to cut corners by way of some highly profitable practice (*tekhnē polykerdē*), and therefore, for instance, not to counterfeit and clip down nomismata, and label and affix a seal to them, and such things (*parakharassein kai psalizein ta nomismata kai pharsographein kai boulas episphragizein kai ta toutois homoia*), clearly thereby providing a later reference to the same practice.

In order to suppress these two sources of corruption – the charging of *obryza* and the fraudulent sealing of *apokombia* – Justinian commands Egyptian practice to be brought into line with the Constantinopolitan. That performed, in other words, under the virtually direct supervision of the central offices of state. With regard to the first, the implication is that, rather than impose a general charge, officials should weigh the coins involved in each transaction and should make the appropriate 'restoration', and no more. With regard to the second, that they should inscribe the true net weight of the coins sealed up in an *apokombion* on its outside, and no more.

### F. *The earlier evidence: the* hai kath' *formula,* prosdiagraphomenon *and* rhuparai drakhmai

The conservative nature of Egyptian accounting practices and terminology is notorious, and it is therefore of considerable interest, and of quite possible significance, to find several of the distinctive features observed in the preceding discussion to have existed in the late Roman and early Byzantine period already to have been closely paralleled by others existing at a much earlier date. It would in most of these cases be difficult to prove at all conclusively that a later practice or term derived from an earlier and similar one, although such a derivation might be not at all improbable in itself, the difficulty in establishing the connection lying rather in the paucity of evidence from a section of the intervening period – and in particular, of course, from the second half of the third century. Three of these earlier features nevertheless deserve particular attention: the *hai kath'* formula (previously the so-called *hai kai* one), the *prosdiagraphomenon*, and payments made in *rhuparai drakhmai* and so on.[186]

The *hai kath*(*arai?*) ('clean' or 'spotless') formula is quite commonly found in tax-receipts

[185] Cecaumenus, *Stratēgikon* CXXII; ed. Wassiliewsky and Jernstedt, p. 51.

[186] The major refs for the following are now to be found in: J. Day and C. W. Keyes, *Tax Documents from Theadelphia*, p. 285, and J. C. Shelton, *A Tax List from Karanis* (*P. Cair. Mich.* 359) II, pp. 25–8.

from certain districts in Upper Egypt, and very rarely only in those from elsewhere. In these receipts the formula is used to connect and equate larger sums with smaller ones, the difference between the two most commonly amounting to one-sixteenth. It seems clear, and on two occasions at least it is expressly mentioned, that the difference represents a *prosdiagraphomenon* (i.e. 'something defined in addition') or supplementary charge.[187]

Payments in *rhuparai drakhmai*, *rhuparoi oboloi*, and *rhuparon argyrion* are commonly found in tax-receipts from both Upper Egypt and the Fayum. The straightforward meaning of *rhuparos* is 'dirty' or 'foul'.[188]

It has been noticed that the two features are related, if in a negative fashion only. Districts that use the *hai kath'* formula do not record payments in *rhuparai drakhmai* and so on, and *vice versa*. This suggests that, in some way, both derive from or reflect a single phenomenon, as indeed might be expected from the opposition inherent in their meaning. They are also, however, related in a more positive fashion: although at least one earlier example is known (11/10 B.C.), the *prosdiagraphomenon* seems to have been introduced as a common feature about A.D. 15, and payments in *rhuparai drakhmai* and so on commence at very much the same date.[189]

The clue as to what was happening lies in the monetary history of the preceding period. When Octavian took possession of Egypt in 30 B.C. he found there a coinage system based upon two metals: silver, expressed in terms of the stater or tetradrachm, didrachm and drachm, and – probably even more important – copper, expressed in two copper denominations of marked but now still largely unknown relative values. The silver was in fact much debased and was already essentially billon. Although Octavian maintained, and as Augustus developed, the copper or bronze sector of the coinage system, he issued no further billon. Tiberius at first continued this policy, and it was not until his seventh year (A.D. 19/20) that he recommenced issues of tetradrachms in that alloy. Although these seem to have been of considerable size, those of his later years seem to have been much smaller. Caligula (A.D. 37–41) seems to have issued no Egyptian coinage at all. Claudius recommenced issues in billon in his second year (A.D. 41/2) and continued them into his sixth (A.D. 45/6). These seem to have been of reasonable size, but another hiatus, lasting a decade, then intervened before Nero recommenced issues, in considerable quantity, in his third year (A.D. 56/7), and then continued them without serious interruption until his death in A.D. 68. Other issues of didrachms and drachms, datable to the reigns of Claudius and Nero, seem to have been experimental, and in any case minute.[190]

187 Johnson and West, *Currency in Roman and Byzantine Egypt*, pp. 26–9.

188 *Ibid.* pp. 30–42.

189 *Ibid.* pp. 26–7, 37. See now: A. Gara, *Prosdiagraphomena e circolazione monetaria*, pp. 50 (table 1), 51–2 (table 2) (*katharos*); 53–4 (table 3) (*rhuparos*); 55 (table 4), 56 (table 6) (*prosdiagraphomenon*). For the 11/10 B.C. instance: *ibid.* p. 22. The only one of these several elements that has a long history prior to the period in question is the term *katharos*, which has a clear Ptolemaic origin.

190 J. G. Milne, *Catalogue of Alexandrian Coins*, pp. xix–xx.

The consequence was that, for fifty years, between 30 B.C. and A.D. 19/20, no billon coinage was issued in Egypt, and no extraneous silver coinage seems to have been imported into the country in any systematic sense. By the second decade of the first century, the majority of billon coins remaining over from the Ptolemaic régime and still circulating normally must have been in a sorry state: on the one hand they must have been severely reduced in number through conscious withdrawal from circulation and the normal rate of loss, and on the other they must have suffered an appreciable loss in weight through wear. Moreover, it seems unlikely that the large-scale billon issues of A.D. 19/20 and the sporadic and small-scale issues of the succeeding period could have radically altered the situation. Only the continuous and large-scale issues of A.D. 56/7 and after seem likely to have been able to do that.

In these circumstances two reactions might be expected, and both can in fact be documented. On the one hand the billon coinage, because of its increasing scarcity, should have come to command a premium over the copper or bronze coinage, which had probably been commoner in the first place, and which had been issued both by Augustus and by his successors with somewhat greater regularity.[191] This premium might well have been confined to the open market, for the state – which probably preferred or demanded the payment of money or most of its taxes in billon in any case – need not have been concerned with how difficult it was for the private individual to fulfil his tax obligation. The state need have become concerned, and have taken compensatory steps, only when it became so difficult as to be virtually or absolutely impossible for the private individual to fulfil these obligations. Although the existence of a slight premium of silver or billon coinage over copper or bronze was not in itself a novelty, being already found in Egypt under the Ptolemaic régime, and indeed being found quite widely outside at a later date, systematic evidence for a considerable one emerges during the reign of Claudius, which is approximately when it might have been expected to emerge.[192] Significantly enough, direct evidence for its existence – the reckoning of the billon tetradrachm not at 24 but at 27, 28, or even 29, obols – is largely but not entirely confined to private documents.[193]

Nevertheless, that the state did on occasion recognise and even utilise the premium is demonstrated, for example, by tax documents such as *P.Mich.* 4, where two parallel entries, one constructed on the basis of a rate of 6 obols to the drachm, the other, its equivalent, on the basis of 29 obols to the tetradrachm, occur.[194] Other similar documents, such as *P.Cair.Mich.* 359, utilise single entries constructed on the basis of

[191] *Ibid.* pp. xix–xx.

[192] F. Heichelheim, *Wirtschaftliche Schwankungen der Zeit von Alexander bis Augustus*, pp. 26–8. R. H. Pierce, 'Notes on Obols and Agios in Demotic Papyri'. *Journal of Egyptian Archaeology* 51 (1965), pp. 155–9.

[193] Johnson and West, *Currency in Roman and Byzantine Egypt*, pp. 7–12.

[194] H. C. Youtie, 'A Problem in Graeco-Roman Bookkeeping', *Zeitschrift für Papyrologie und Epigraphik* 15 (1974), pp. 117–41.

a rate of 29 obols to the tetradrachm alone.[195] Such evidence suggests either that the state was collecting taxes in copper, but was insisting on charging the premium, or that it was insisting on collecting taxes in billon at the premium rate. The latter seems much the more likely, but such an insistence would not necessarily appear in reasonably formal documentation.

An explanation of the premium purely on the grounds of the greater convenience involved in handling and transporting billon coins rather than copper ones appears too simplistic, although the consideration may not have been entirely absent.[196] And in any case, a state preference for precious-metal coins over base-metal ones is almost universal – witness, for example, the later practice termed *kharagma* – although it did not always go to the same lengths to enforce it. Similarly, an explanation on the grounds of a formal revaluation of the Ptolemaic tetradrachm from 24 to 28 obols, and the establishment of a fixed relationship between the tetradrachm and the denarius of 1 : 1, appears extremely unconvincing: the evidence is either non-existent or, where it exists, negative.[197]

On the other hand the state, in collecting its taxes in billon, eventually might well have become concerned at the degree to which the actual amount of metal brought in by these taxes increasingly fell short of the theoretical amount, the falling short again being due to the increasingly worn state of the billon coinage. It might equally well have refused to take cognisance of the fact that, even if in a worn state, the billon coinage was so scarce as to command a considerable premium over the copper or bronze coinage on the open market: what it desired was a given amount of precious metal, and not an enhanced amount of, or value for, the base metal against which it tended to discriminate. In these circumstances, an attempt to 'restore' the deficiency would have been a natural reaction, and it may be suggested that it is in just such an attempt that the origins of the supplementary charge mentioned above are to be found.

The worn state of the billon coinage also suggests that it was in this that payments in *rhuparai drakhmai* and so on were being made. The relationship between the *hai kath'* formula and such payments then emerges: the *hai kath'* formula equates a larger sum, in *rhuparai drakhmai*, or whatever, representing an actual payment, and including the *prosdiagraphomenon*, with a smaller sum, representing the notional, in effect discounted, value ascribed to that sum. The recent discovery of a somewhat more elaborate version of the *hai kath'* formula ((*drakhmai*) v, *hai k*(*ath'*) x, *pros*(*diagraphomenon*) y, making as stated z) goes far towards confirming this.[198] Both, significantly enough, occur in records of taxation alone, that is, in official documents and not in private ones. Both, it is true,

195 Shelton, *A Tax List from Karanis* II, pp. 7–18.

196 V. B. Schuman, 'The Basis of Accounting Practices in the Karanis Tax Rolls', *Aegyptus* 32 (1952), p. 251.

197 Gara, *Prosdiagraphomena e circolazione monetaria*, pp. 21–95. But see: E. Christiansen, in *Journal of Roman Studies* 69 (1979), at p. 205 (review of Gara, *Prosdiagraphomena*).

198 Shelton, *A Tax List from Karanis* II, p. 28.

lasted on into a period when worn coins must have formed a less characteristic proportion of the circulating medium,[199] but once the imposition of a supplement and the existence of such features had become accepted they would have been difficult to eradicate. Indeed, because of the consistent presence of an annual dating by regnal year on the Alexandrian coinage, it would have been particularly susceptible to treatment of this kind. It is quite possible that, eventually, a situation evolved where coinage of the current year alone was accepted as being *katharon*, the remainder being deemed *rhuparon*.[200]

While it is certainly of some general interest to find several of the distinctive features of the late Roman and early Byzantine period to have been foreshadowed by others existing at a much earlier date, the phenomenon might quite plausibly be considered as having been the product merely of a common reaction to similar circumstances were it not for the occurrence of one example, at least, of identical nomenclature. In a general sense, if in no other, the *hai kath'* formula bears a methodological similarity to the later *arithmia/ekhomena* system, and the most common rate of the *prosdiagraphomenon* – one-sixteenth – is identical with that at Oxyrhynchus for the later charge termed *obryza*. Even the terms involved in the last two – *prosdiagraphomenon* and *apokatastatikon* – are similar in concept and nature. On the other hand, the *rhuparai drakhmai* and so on of the earlier period seem actually to have given way to the *rhupara nomismata* of the later. Their occurrence is, admittedly, somewhat different: whereas the former occur in official documents only, the latter occur in both official and private documents.[201] The mention of a sum of 40 nomismata *rhupara obryziaka* in one document[202] datable to the sixth or seventh centuries suggests, as might be expected, that they were liable to *obryza*. The equation of $\frac{1}{2}$ *rhuparon* nomisma with $8\frac{5}{8}$ keratia, and of 114 *rhupara* nomismata with 81 nomismata $22\frac{1}{2}$ keratia in the Alexandrian standard in another document[203] datable to the sixth or seventh centuries implies that the charge or discount represented was particularly heavy: $6\frac{3}{4}$ keratia per nomisma, equivalent to over 20 nomismata in the pound, and well above the level that prompted Justinian to issue Edict XI against *obryza*. It is in fact difficult to believe that the coins involved were really so deficient as to warrant a 'restoration' of this size, and this and other similar documents probably reflect merely the imposition of a general discount or charge of quite scandalous proportions in the Fayum.

199 J. G. Milne, 'The Currency of Egypt under the Romans to the Time of Diocletian', *Annals of Archaeology and Anthropology* 7 (1914–16), pp. 64–6.
200 Cf. *O. Strass.* 280 (A.D. 134).
201 Johnson and West, *Currency in Roman and Byzantine Egypt*, pp. 151–3.
202 *P. Klein. Form.* 1138.
203 *SPP* XX, 231.

## *G. The later evidence: The Cairo* Geniza

The degree of attention that has been paid to the problems outlined above, and to the solutions evolved, may appear excessive, but the problems must have been real and continuing ones even if the solutions varied from one period to another, or even from one area to another within a single period. The problems must also have been universal ones. The overwhelming position attained by the Egyptian evidence, to a considerable degree the product of climatic conditions, is inevitable: other evidence now simply does not exist, or if it does represents only a minute fraction of that available from Egypt.

As it happens, evidence from Egypt, albeit of a somewhat later date, also provides the most detailed illustration of some of these problems, and to a lesser extent of their solution, that is yet available. The massive evidence surviving from the Cairo *Geniza*, and dating mainly from the tenth to thirteenth centuries, demonstrates the circulation of sealed purses containing gold dinars to have been entirely normal, and there is no reason to suppose that the situation differed in any fundamental respect from that obtaining during the earlier period.[204] The formal connection is established by a document (in Greek) dated 708:[205] 'For that which is in gold I have sent, through the said Moagaritos, under the seal (*hypo tēn sphragida*) of our most renowned lord and governor (*symboulos*) 'Abdallāh.'*

These later purses were sealed up on the one hand by some office of state or official or semi-official bank, or on the other by some private individual, generally a merchant. A letter from Tunisia, datable to the first half of the eleventh century, conveniently reveals details of the contents of six such purses, each sent to Egypt in a different ship. These details, and some of the figures to be drawn from them, may be tabulated as in Table 6.[206]

It is quite clear that such purses tended to be made up to the theoretical weight of a given round number of dinars, identical with the weight of the same number of *mithkals*

* I owe this reference to the kindness of John Nesbitt.

204 Or, for that matter, from that obtaining during the later period. For *fiorini di suggello*, see above, p. 344, and for the Ottoman situation, see: Sperber, *Roman Palestine 200–400, Money and Prices*, p. 207 n. 1.

205 *P. Apollonos Ano* 2. It is worth noting, at this stage, that when the Arab dinar proper emerged at the end of the seventh century, it incorporated a slight reduction from the solidus-standard that had by then long been traditional, weighing 22 rather than 24 keratia. Two main explanations have been advanced to explain this reduction: that the new standard represented the average weight of the Byzantine solidi which had remained in circulation and which had therefore become aged and deficient; and that it represented a weight more appropriate to the Arab version of the keration – the *qīrāt* or *kharrubāh* – of which it weighed 20. See: Grierson, 'The Monetary Reforms of 'Abd al-Malik', pp. 248–60. The two explanations are not, of course, entirely incompatible. In any case, the common practice of discounting the solidus, on the basis – however fictional – of weight, the discount not uncommonly being 2 keratia, and resulting in the solidus being treated as weighing 22 keratia, may form an element which also has to be taken into account.

206 S. D. Goitein, *A Mediterranean Society* I, *Economic Foundations*, pp. 231–4. See also *idem*, *Letters of Medieval Jewish Traders*, pp. 140–1 (mention of purses containing: 20 *Shaykhiyya* dinars worth 18⅓, 44 *Ḥasanī* dinars weighing 43, 56 large dinars and 20 *Ḥākimī rubā'īs* [quarters] weighing 60, from Egypt, *c.* 1060–70).

Table 6. *Contents of sealed purses from the Cairo* Geniza

| 1 | 2 | 3 | 4 |
|---|---|---|---|
| No. of dinars | Weight of dinars | % deficiency | Equivalent in nomismata (approx.) |
| $308\frac{1}{4}$ | 300 | 2.7 | 2 nom. in lb |
| $153\frac{1}{2}$ | $149\frac{7}{8}$ | 2.3 | $1\frac{2}{3}$ " " " |
| $300\frac{3}{4}$ | 300 | 0.2 | — |
| $255\frac{1}{2}$ | $249\frac{5}{6}$ | 2.2 | $1\frac{1}{2}$ nom. in lb |
| 122 | $119\frac{3}{8}$ | 2.2 | $1\frac{1}{2}$ " " " |
| $154\frac{1}{4}$ | $150\frac{1}{12}$ | 2.7 | 2 " " " |
| 50 | $44\frac{7}{8}$ | 10.3 | $7\frac{1}{2}$ " " " |

(the Arab equivalent of the *hexagion/exagium*) (col. 2). It is equally clear that, because of the difference between the actual and theoretical weights of most dinars, the number of coins actually needed to make up such a theoretical weight or number of *mithkals* was consistently, but to a varying degree, greater than that weight or number (col. 1). Because dinars and their quarters only actually existed as current coins it was nevertheless frequently difficult or even impossible to make up exactly the required theoretical weight or number of *mithkals*: $149\frac{7}{8}$ was presumably the nearest to 150 that could be managed, $249\frac{5}{6}$ the nearest to 250, $119\frac{3}{8}$ the nearest to 120, $150\frac{1}{12}$ the nearest to 150, and $44\frac{7}{8}$ the nearest to 45 (col. 2).

The difference between the number of coins used and the weight they made, or attempted to make up, reflects a deficiency that must have been to some considerable degree caused by loss in weight through wear. The figures for this deficiency, calculated both as a percentage (col. 3), and as so many nomismata in the pound (col. 4), are of some interest, although a possible tendency to use the least deficient or worn coins available may mean that they are somewhat lower than they might otherwise have been. The deficiency might be as small as 0.2%, which cannot be given an equivalent in nomismata or in fractions of the nomisma actually represented by current coins. It might be as large as 10.3%, which is equivalent to $7\frac{1}{2}$ nomismata in the pound, as in another letter, datable to the middle of the eleventh century, and also included in the tabulation. In the former case it can only be assumed that coin fresh from the mint or culled from the coin population was involved, in the latter that coin suffering from an abnormal degree of wear or mutilation was involved: both, in other words, were exceptional.

To judge from the remainder of the six purses, the normal deficiency – if such it may be termed – varied from 2.2%, equivalent to $1\frac{1}{2}$ nomisma in the pound, to 2.7%, equivalent to 2 nomismata in the pound, with a concentration towards the lower figure.

This range, however, may at most be taken as a reflection of the state of the circulating medium at a particular time in a particular place. Obviously, other purses, drawn from the circulating medium at different times in different places, might be expected to yield variant figures. Two Tunisian purses of approximately the same date as those mentioned above give figures of 7.6%, equivalent to $5\frac{1}{2}$ nomismata in the pound, and 1.7%, equivalent to $1\frac{1}{3}$ nomisma in the pound. A Libyan purse, again of approximately the same date, gives a figure of 5.8%, equivalent to $4\frac{1}{3}$ nomismata in the pound.

For all the possible sources of error in their evolution, and the limited extent of their potential application, the figures in the preceding paragraph do permit two interesting points at least to be made. In the first place, with one exception only, they somewhat exceed the figure of 1%–$1\frac{1}{2}$% that has been suggested as a reasonable allowance for wear in arriving at the theoretical weights of gold or heavy silver coinages. On the other hand, this should not be unexpected, for the figure was evolved using selected museum material and hoards of virtually uncirculated material, and in fact it has not been suggested that it should be applied to anything else.[207] The mid Byzantine hoard from Lagbe, which seems originally to have involved several bodies of coin in one purse, probably shows a deficiency of 2%, but this is by no means certain.[208]

In the second place, the figures imply that the charges of 1 keration per nomisma or 3 nomismata in the pound for *obryza* at Antaeopolis, and of $1\frac{1}{2}$ keration per nomisma or $4\frac{1}{2}$ nomismata in the pound for the same at Oxyrhynchus, would indeed consistently have left those charging them with a surplus, but perhaps not with an overwhelmingly large one. On the other hand, the possible charge of $2\frac{1}{4}$ keratia per nomisma or $6\frac{3}{4}$ nomismata in the pound for *obryza* at Heracleopolis, and that of 3 keratia per nomisma or 9 nomismata in the pound for the same claimed by Justinian for Alexandria, would have been high and scandalously high respectively.

## (VI) 'IRRATIONALITY'

In addition to everything else, the late Roman and Byzantine state, in its supervision of the coinage, still had an element of sheer irrationality to contend with. One form that this irrationality might take was to discount the solidus, not because of its metallic quality or its weight, but because of its module or some feature of its design. A discount of this kind was the subject of an early law of Constantine, the terms of which are preserved in the *Codex Theodosianus*:[209]

207 Grierson, 'Weight and Coinage', pp. xiii–xiv.

208 See above, pp. 342, 343.

209 *CTh.* IX.22.1.

### IF ANYONE SHOULD CUT OFF THE OUTSIDE EDGE OF A SOLIDUS OR SHOULD SUBSTITUTE A FALSE ONE IN A SALE

Emperor Constantine Augustus to Leontius, Praetorian Prefect

All solidi on which Our face and venerability (*nostri vultus ac veneratio*) is to be found are to be valued and sold at one price (*uno pretio aestimandi sunt atque vendendi*), however diverse the extent of the image (*formae mensura*). For that which is spread out with a larger representation of Our face (*maiore habitu faciei*) is not worth more, and that which is contracted with a smaller portrait (*angustiore expressione*) is not to be thought worth less, when the same weight is present (*cum pondus idem existat*). And if anyone should suppose otherwise he is to be capitally punished either by being handed over to the flames or by some other death-carrying punishment. [And indeed he that should nibble away the extent of the outside edge (*mensuram circuli exterioris adroserit*) of a solidus, so as to diminish the total of its weight (*ut ponderis minuat quantitatem*), or should replace a stamped solidus with a false imitation in a sale (*vel figuratum solidum adultera imitatione in vendendo subiecerit*), is to suffer in the same fashion.]

Given 26 July in the consulships of Gallicanus and Bassus [317].

The law has long been the subject of discussion, for the name of the apparent addressee does not accord with the date on which it was supposedly given. The addressee was in all probability (Flavius Domitius) Leontius who is known to have been praetorian prefect in the East in 340–4.[210] The year in which it was given seems to have been 317. The most convincing explanation of the discrepancy[211] is that the law is in fact a conflation of two, the earlier text of which was addressed to an unknown person, and that it was indeed given on 26 July 317. The phrase 'And indeed he that should nibble away...in the same fashion' (in square brackets) should be omitted from this text and transferred elsewhere.[212]

The sense of the earlier text is nevertheless quite clear: solidi of small module and with a correspondingly smaller portrait of the emperor were being discounted against those of large module with a larger portrait, even if the former were of full weight and in that respect identical with the latter. A tendency for both the module and the relative size of the portrait to increase over the years is in fact a noticeable factor of the Constantinian solidus[213] and it was clearly this that had given rise to the practice which Constantine, quite reasonably, but with characteristic savagery, proceeded to legislate against.

It seems to have been the existence of a somewhat similar practice that prompted the issue of a law of Valentinian III,[214] the terms of which have also been preserved:

210 *PLRE* I, pp. 502–3 (Fl. Domitius Leontius 20).

211 Grierson, 'The Roman Law of Counterfeiting', pp. 259–60.

212 *CTh.* IX.21.5 (343); see above, pp. 322–3.

213 M. R. Alföldi, *Die constantinische Goldprägung*, p. 9. See also below, Pl. 5.

214 Valentinian III, Edict XVI.

## CONCERNING THE PRICE OF A SOLIDUS AND SO THAT NO ONE SHOULD REFUSE AN INTACT SOLIDUS

Emperors Theodosius [II] and Valentinian [III], Augusti, to the Roman People

A repeated complaint of rash behaviour has reached Us, Citizens, that to the abuse of Our relations solidi marked with their names are being refused by all buyers (*insigniti solidi eorum nominibus ab omni emptore recusentur*): which We cannot suffer to go long unpunished. Therefore let it be universally known through this edict that capital punishment awaits him who believes a gold solidus of full weight (*integri ponderis*) in the names either of My father the lord Theodosius [II], or of Our sacred female relations, or of former emperors, to be refused or valued at a lower price. Moreover the Illustrious Prefect of the City [*sc.* of Rome] and his bureau shall be subject to the expenditure of two pounds of gold if anyone should be proved to have contravened this statute.

1. By this command we wish the following to be observed in perpetuity: that a solidus should never be sold for less than seven thousand nummi when bought from a money-changer for seven thousand two hundred (*ne umquam intra septem milia nummorum solidus distrahatur emptus a collectario septem milibus ducentis*). For the uniformity of price shall protect both the favourable position of the seller and the established prices of all saleable goods (*Aequabilitas enim pretii et commodum venditoris et omnium rerum venalium statuta custodiet*).

2. And so that fraud shall be removed entirely with regard to weights also, standards (*exagia*) shall be given out by Us, and these must be preserved without fraud under threat of the above-mentioned penalty.

And in the Sacred Hand: *It shall be published to Our Most Beloved Roman People*. And to the side: *Given 18 January at Rome in the consulship of Valentinian Augustus* (*for the sixth time*) [*and Nomus*: 445].

The law is a straightforward one, both as regards its date and place of issue and its sense. Solidi in the name of Theodosius II, or in the names of the various female members of the imperial house (Aelia Pulcheria and Aelia Eudocia, the sister and wife respectively of Theodosius, and Galla Placidia, Justa Grata Honoria and Licinia Eudoxia, the mother, sister and wife, respectively, of Valentinian), or in the names of former emperors, were being refused or discounted against those in the name of Valentinian himself, again even if they were of full weight. The phenomenon, if the strong implications of two laws preserved in the *Codex Justinianus* are to be believed, was not a new one. The earlier of these two laws[215] reads as follows:

Emperors Valentinian [I] and Valens, Augusti, to Germanianus, Praetorian Prefect

We command solidi shaped in the venerability of former emperors (*solidi veterum principum veneratione formati*) to be given and received by buyers and sellers (*ab ementibus et distrahentibus*) in such a way as to provoke absolutely no dissension, as long as they are of the required weight (*debiti ponderis*) and honest material (*speciei probae*). It should be universally known that if anyone should act otherwise he shall be heavily punished.

It has been suggested that the law originally formed a single one with what are now

[215] *CJ* XI.11.1.

two other separate ones preserved in the *Codex Theodosianus*[216] and that it was therefore addressed to the Germanianus who is known to have been *comes sacrarum largitionum* in the west between 365 and 367.[217] It would in that case have been dated 8 January 367 and have been given at Rheims.

The terms of the later law[218] are as follows:

> Emperors Gratian, Valentinian [II] and Theodosius [I], Augusti, to Arintheus, Praetorian Prefect
> Your Authority should make it universally known, through the posting of this edict, that the price demanded for all solidi of refined gold should be uniform (*obryziacorum omnium solidorum uniforme pretium*...), and that capital punishment will be inflicted upon anyone who should treat the commands of Our Majesty with contumely through the blindness of greed, or who should reckon as cheaper (*viliores*) the eternal faces (*aeternales vultus*) [*sc.* of former emperors] in the pursuit of fraud.

The addressee of the law, Arintheus, may have been either *comes sacrarum largitionum* or praetorian prefect, in the latter case in the East, probably in 379.[219]

A similar concern, no doubt in response to a similar situation, is to be seen behind Justinian's command, in *caput* 20 of the *Constitutio Pragmatica* (*App.* vii), that solidi stamped with the shape of (earlier) Roman emperors (*solidi [veterum] Romanorum principum forma signati*) should be allowed to circulate in every province (*per omnes provincias ambulare*) without any loss in exchange-rate (*sine permutationis dispendio*). It is possible that something similar is true of Novel LII of Leo VI.[220]

The practice whereby coins of the reigning emperor only were regarded as being standard, and whereby those of his relations or predecessors were subjected to some kind of discount, irrespective of their weight and fineness, forms, in its way, the counterpart of the several Egyptian systems of discounting or charging against old coin that already have been discussed.[221] In both cases, the problems created by the existence in circulation of aged (and therefore variably worn and light) coin must have been real and universal. What was irrational was the imposition of a general discount or charge that took no account of the condition of individual coins, or of that of any group of coins. This was also unacceptable to the state – whether on the grounds of disrespect to imperial relations or predecessors (primarily), or on those of inconvenience caused in its own, or in private, transactions (secondarily, and probably in that order).

Similar instances of sheer irrationality are difficult to detect during the later period, although this is more probably due to the nature of the sources available than to the disappearance of the quality itself from the handling of coin. Nevertheless, and despite the existence of legislation to the contrary, the evidence suggests that new coin, if only informally and sporadically, continued to command a premium over old coin, even if

[216] *CTh.* X.19.4; XII.6.13.

[217] *PLRE* I, p. 391 (Germanianus I).

[218] *CJ* XI.11.3.

[219] *PLRE*, I, p. 104 (Arintheus).

[220] But unlikely, see above, pp. 302–4.

[221] See above, pp. 344–60.

the latter were still of standard weight. Twelfth-century documents, for instance, quite commonly distinguish between precious-metal (i.e. gold or electrum) coins described as 'most valued (*protimōmenon*)', 'most preferred (*protimitaion*)', or 'new (*kainourgion*)', and that described as 'old (*palaion*)'. While there seems no doubt that both 'new' and 'old' could on occasion describe the same desired quality of coin (i.e. that of standard weight), for coin is described as *palaiokainourgion* in several documents, it seems probable that a premium or discount was sometimes involved.[222] And, as will later be implied, the existence of 'heavy (*grievi*)' perperi, in the fifteenth century, presupposes a similar if more justifiable distinction.[223]

According to Pegolotti,[224] certain classes of hyperpyra of John III, distinguishable by slight differences in their design or by their signa, possessed a gold-content that also varied slightly (i.e. by as small an amount as a fraction of a carat) from class to class. The claim is an impressive one, not the least because the general accuracy of Pegolotti's list of other hyperpyra and their gold-contents is verifiable from other sources, and because the official use of differences in design to denote changes in metal-content is a common feature of the later Byzantine period.[225] The practice may be seen in operation as late as the reign of Michael VIII.[226] It is quite clear, however, that Pegolotti had little knowledge of, and almost totally failed to comprehend, the designs and iconography of the hyperpyra that he was attempting to describe and differentiate between, and there is therefore no guarantee at all that the slight differences in design and the signa illustrated by him were originally and consistently intended to fulfil the particular distinguishing function which he, by implication at least, assigned to them. The precise nature and significance of the signa remain, as yet, uncertain, but it seems probable that they represent, primarily at least, some organisational factor in the production of the coins that they occur upon. It is by no means impossible that, because of this, the abandonment of one signum in favour of another coincided frequently with a chronological and therefore occasionally with a significant qualitative division in the coinage, but the latter at least would have been purely or largely a matter of coincidence. Such signa can therefore at best be described as approximate popular guides to the gold-content of the hyperpyra concerned.

Instances of this nature should, in any case, be considered separately from those in which the imposition of a premium or discount was given a formal and legal backing. This

[222] Hendy, *DOS* XII, pp. 31–8; cf. Goitein, *A Mediterranean Society* I, *Economic Foundations*, pp. 236–7. *Palaiokainourgion*: Morozzo della Rocca and Lombardo, *Documenti del commercio veneziano* I, pp. 134, no. 135 (1159) (*perperos auri paleoskenurgios bonos pensantes*); 136, no. 137 (1159) (*perperos auri palekenurgos pensantes*); 150, no. 151 (1161) (*perperos auri paleos kenurgos pensantes*); 151, no. 152 (1161) (*perperos paleos auri kenurgos pensantes*). The formula seems to have been quite briefly in fashion mid-century.

[223] See below, pp. 537–40.

[224] Pegolotti, *La Pratica della Mercatura*; ed. Evans, pp. 288–9. Hendy, *DOS* XII, pp. 250–6. See also below, p. 527, Table 23 and n. 392.

[225] E.g. for Constantine IX: Grierson, *DOC* III.2, pp. 734–6.

[226] Hendy, *DOS* XII, p. 263; see also below, p. 527.

certainly occurred on one occasion, perhaps on two. Nicephorus II attempted to ensure in this way that his own tetartera, light by two keratia, circulated at the same rate as histamena of full weight.[227] Leo VI claims[228] that certain of his predecessors had demonetised the coinage of their own predecessors. He restates the traditional doctrine that authentic coins of standard weight and so on should be accepted at the same rate, whatever their age. It seems likely that Leo's predecessors had merely called in their own predecessors' coinage, perhaps exchanging it at a discount.[229]

[227] M. F. Hendy, 'Light Weight Solidi, Tetartera, and The Book of the Prefect', *Byzantinische Zeitschrift* 65 (1972), pp. 70–1.

[228] See above, p. 302.

[229] See above, p. 303.

SECTION IV

# COINAGE (PRODUCTION)

# CHAPTER 7

# ADMINISTRATIVE BASIS

## (I) 284–*c*. 400 (GENERAL)

### *A. Diocletian: Fiscal administration*

The physical production of coin was, throughout the later Roman and Byzantine period, an integral function of one of the several major fiscal institutions of the empire, and it is therefore to the organisational structure and development of those institutions that attention has first to be paid.[1]

The fiscal administration of the later Roman and early Byzantine period was dominated by three institutions: the praetorian prefecture (*praefectura praetorio*), and the palatine ministries (*comitivae*) of the *sacrae largitiones* ('sacred largesses') and *res privata* (perhaps best translated as 'privy purse').[2] These institutions were theoretically, and for much of the period effectively, separate and independent, and although their nomenclature together with that of some of their officers, and the balance between them, were both subject to adjustment and development, the pattern and emphasis of their organisational structure remained comparatively stable.

Of these three institutions, all instruments of both revenue and expenditure, the praetorian prefecture, deprived almost entirely of military competence and reduced to

[1] The first several sections of this chapter are based largely, but not entirely, upon a set of three articles by this author (in chronological order of the subject treated): 'Mint and Fiscal Administration under Diocletian, his Colleagues, and his Successors, A.D. 305–24', *Journal of Roman Studies* 62 (1972), pp. 75–82; 'Aspects of Coin Production and Fiscal Administration in the Late Roman and Early Byzantine Period', *Numismatic Chronicle* 12[7] (1972), pp. 117–39; 'On the Administrative Basis of the Byzantine Coinage *c*. 400–*c*. 900 and the Reforms of Heraclius', *University of Birmingham Historical Journal* 12 (1970), pp. 129–54. These articles should be consulted for a number of further references and more detailed arguments.

[2] Jones, *Later Roman Empire* I, pp. 411–27 (*res privata*), 427–48 (*sacrae largitiones*), 448–62 (*praefectura praetorio*). On the *privata*, see now: F. Millar, 'The *Privata* from Diocletian to Heraclius: Documentary Evidence', in King (ed.), *Imperial Revenue, Expenditure and Monetary Policy in the Fourth Century* A.D., at pp. 125–40. On the *largitiones*, see now: King, 'The *Sacrae Largitiones*: Revenues, Expenditure and the Production of Coin', at pp. 141–73. In the early fourth century, at least, the distinction between *privata* and *largitiones* remains somewhat blurred, and it appears that both then and even somewhat later, the *rationalis* (*summ. rei*) exercised a degree of authority over the *magister* (*rei priv.*). The general point of separation and independence nevertheless remains a valid one. For the *largitones* see also above, p. 195 n. 207.

fiscal and juridical functions by Constantine, was the most significant and indeed increasingly predominant. Given its recent history and remaining functions this was probably inevitable. The precise course of events remains uncertain, but in general it seems clear that as the coinage system, in terms of which the government had first calculated its fiscal needs and then collected and spent its revenue, had depreciated and finally disintegrated during the second half of the third century, so there had developed a consequent and marked tendency to transfer to a fiscal system based upon assessment, revenue and expenditure in kind. By the reign of Aurelian, certainly by that of Diocletian, taxes in coin which had previously provided the bulk of governmental revenue can then have amounted to very little in real terms, and it was one of the achievements of Diocletian to bring to completion and to systematise the transfer to a fiscal system based upon taxation in kind. It seems equally clear that the functions involved in, and resulting from, this transfer had devolved largely upon the praetorian prefecture, and that this institution now not only estimated the annual needs of the military forces, civil service and public works of the empire, but also calculated the rate of taxation necessary to satisfy those needs, and controlled the process of collecting the resulting *indictio* through its own local officers.

For much of the earlier Roman imperial period, and until the transfer to a fiscal system based upon taxation in kind, the most significant of the fiscal institutions had been the *res summa*, as it was still termed during the first half of the fourth century, or the *comitiva largitionum* or *comitiva sacrarum largitionum*, as it subsequently became termed. The gradual revival of taxation in coin that began during the reign of Constantine, that depended upon the restabilised precious metals rather than the still unstable base alloys and metals, and that largely benefited the *largitiones*, will doubtless have gone some way towards restoring the position of the *largitiones vis-à-vis* the praetorian prefecture. But several of the more important of the new or newly systematised taxes in coin – such as the *aurum coronarium* levied on cities, the *aurum oblaticium* levied on senators, and the *collatio lustralis* or *khrysargyron* levied on those making their living by buying and selling or charging fees – were normally of quinquennial incidence only. Other sources of revenue, such as rents, were capable of only minimal flexibility. Most, if not all, seem normally to have been collected not by the *largitiones*' own local officers (who in theory at least performed a merely supervisory rôle in this respect), but by those of the praetorian prefecture. And when taxation in kind began generally to be commuted for coin once more, by the process termed *adaeratio*, during the first half of the fifth century in the west and the second half of the same century in the east, any advantage that may have accrued to the *largitiones* will again have been lost. By the sixth century, with the abolition of its largest single source of revenue, the *collatio lustralis*, during the reign of Anastasius, the functions of the *largitiones* seem to have been residual, and its position *vis-à-vis* the praetorian prefecture one of virtual dependence.

The praetorian prefecture and both *comitivae* each possessed an extensive regional structure, the two main tiers of which – provincial and diocesan – were largely, but not entirely, coincident in their territorial divisions. The regional structure of all three institutions was the object of a radical reorganisation and a considerable degree of innovation during the reign of Diocletian, whose administrative policies are described by Lactantius[3] in the following terms: 'And, so that the terror should be generalised, the provinces (*provinciae*) were also cut into fragments: many governors (*praesides*) and more bureaux (*officia*) crushed each region, indeed almost each city, and similarly many *rationales, magistri* and *vicarii* of the prefects.'

Each detail of Lactantius' description is capable of independent confirmation, although the motive lying behind the whole was doubtless not a generalisation of terror but a tightening of administration. As a result of fragmentation, the number of provinces and therefore of governors and their bureaux was, for instance, approximately doubled during this period and that immediately following.[4] It is nevertheless in the creation of what appears to have been an entirely new tier of regional administration, the diocesan, that Diocletian's reforms seem to bear direct relevance to the subject of this chapter.

The precise date and method of the creation of the diocesan vicariate of the praetorian prefecture, each territorial division or diocese (*diocesis* or *dioikēsis*) consisting of a number of provinces and being directed by a vicar or official acting on behalf of the prefects (i.e. a *vicarius* or, more fully, an *agens vices praefectorum praetorio*),[5] remains uncertain. The *Laterculus Veronensis*, a list of provinces and dioceses datable by general agreement to within two decades of Diocletian's abdication,[6] includes the following twelve dioceses: Britanniae, Galliae, Viennensis, Hispaniae, Africa, Italia, Pannoniae, Moesiae, Thracia, Asiana, Pontica and Oriens.[7] Of these, the Italian diocese seems, from a very early stage if not from its creation, to have been divided unofficially into two: Italia proper, consisting of the north and the Alpine regions, and Urbs Roma (Suburbicaria), consisting of the south and the islands of Sicily, Sardinia and Corsica.[8] At this stage there were thus effectively thirteen dioceses (Map 32).

Even without Lactantius' description, the attribution of the diocesan vicariate to Diocletian would nevertheless be assured, for during his reign vicars begin to put in an increasingly frequent appearance. The earliest known seems to be Septimius Valentio,

[3] Lactantius, *De Mortibus Persecutorum* VII.4; ed. Moreau, I, p. 85.

[4] Jones, *Later Roman Empire* I, pp. 42–3, map I, 'The Severan Provinces and the Dioceses and Provinces of the Verona List'. See also below, n. 6.

[5] Michon, 'Le "modius" de Ponte Puñide (Espagne)', pp. 244–99.

[6] A. H. M. Jones, 'The Date and Value of the Verona List', *Journal of Roman Studies* 44 (1954), pp. 21–9. A number of additions and corrections have been made to this article, and Jones's date and findings could no doubt be refined or even revised, but in neither case significantly. See also: A. Chastagnol, *La préfecture urbaine à Rome sous le bas-empire*, pp. 3–4 (dates the *Laterculus* 303–6).

[7] *Laterculus Veronensis*; ed. O. Seeck, pp. 247–53.

[8] Jones, *Later Roman Empire* I, p. 47.

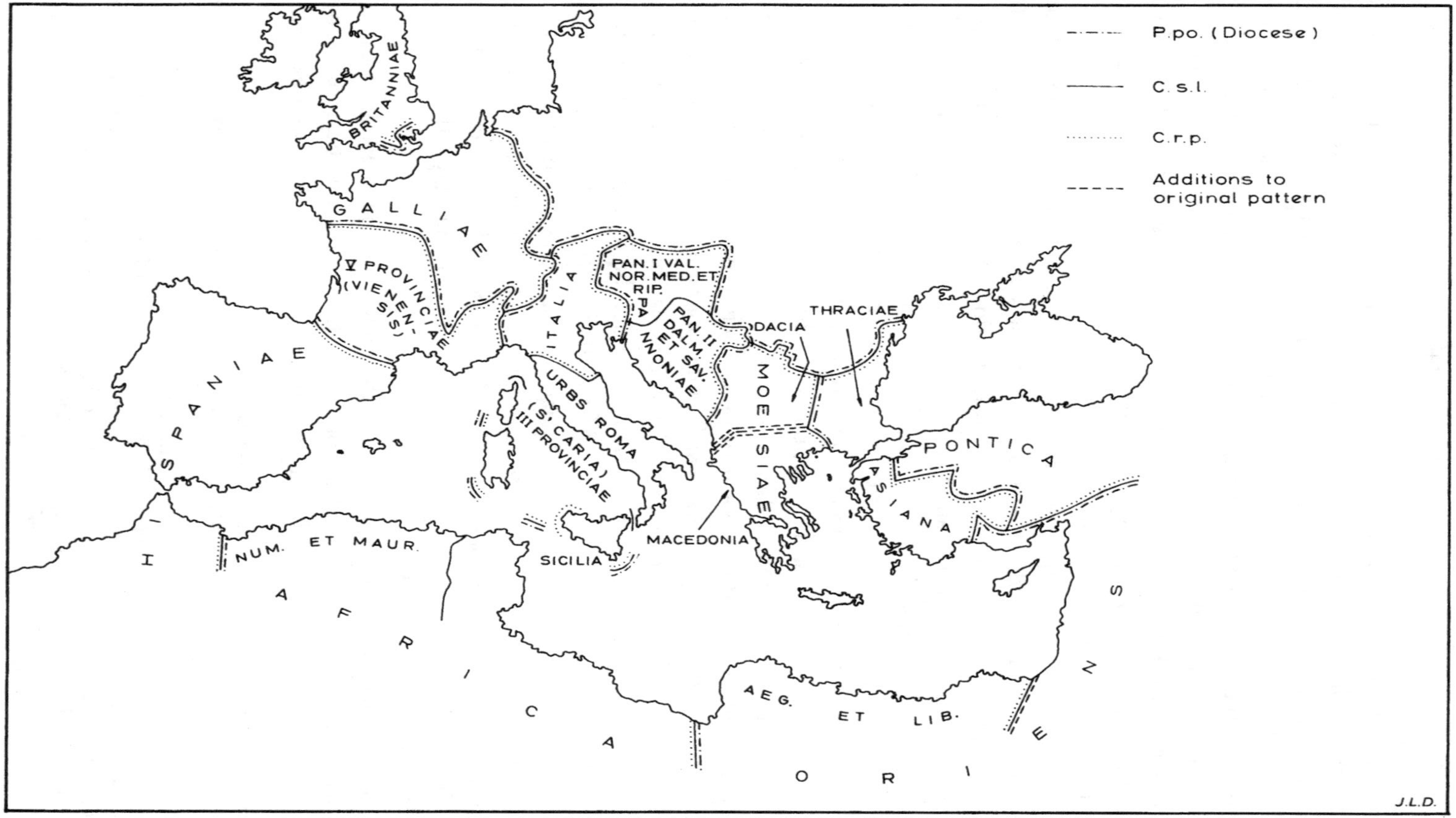


Map 32 The empire: major fiscal units, *c.* 300–450

recorded in 293–6, who may have been an early *vicarius urbis Romae*.[9] Aurelius Agricolanus, recorded in 298, was very probably an early *vicarius Hispaniarum*.[10] Aemilius Rusticianus, also recorded in 298, may have been an early *vicarius Orientis*.[11] Valerius Alexander, recorded in 303 and again in 306–8, was very probably an early *vicarius Africae*.[12] Sossianus Hierocles, also recorded in 303, was then already *ex vicario* of an unknown diocese which he had directed at some stage between 293 and 303.[13]

The position is somewhat complicated by the fact that several much earlier officials acting on behalf of the prefects are known, but these seem to have been unsystematic and temporary appointments only and to have lacked a defined territorial jurisdiction. It is also unfortunately the case that none of the Diocletianic officials mentioned above are assigned a territorial jurisdiction by the sources that mention them. But this is not infrequently so even at a much later date when the diocesan vicariate is known to have been long in existence, and the combined evidence of Lactantius' description and the *Laterculus Veronensis* suggests that most or all of the Diocletianic officials in question are nevertheless likely to have been diocesan vicars.

The crucial figure among the Diocletianic officials is clearly Septimius Valentio, termed *v(ir) p(erfectissimus) a(gens) v(ices) praeff(ectorum) praett(orio) cc(larissimorum) vv(irorum)* on an inscription found at Rome and datable by the fourth consulship of Maximian to 293–6. It has been suggested that this official was merely another of the temporary appointees mentioned above and not a diocesan vicar. This supposition is based on the claim that

[9] *Inscriptiones Latinae Selectae* 619. *PLRE* I, p. 937. M. Christol, 'Effort de guerre et ateliers monétaires de la périphérie au III$^e$ s. ap. J.-C.: l'atelier de Cologne sous Valérien et Gallien', in *Armées et fiscalité dans le monde antique*, at pp. 248–9 and n. 1, closely following Chastagnol, supposes that Septimius Valentio was merely a vicar of two praetorian prefects resident at Rome, and performing largely residual functions such as the command of the praetorian cohorts. But Chastagnol's views on the development of the *vicarius praefecturae urbis/urbis Romae* in any case surely suffer from constitutional and administrative over-elaboration. For an unconsciously telling summary of these views, see: A. Chastagnol, 'L'administration du diocèse italien au bas-empire', *Historia* 11 (1963), p. 353.

[10] *Acta sancti Marcelli* III; ed. H. Delehaye, at pp. 261–2: *Fortunatus praeses [sc. Gallaeciae] dixit: ...et ipse transmitteris ad dominum meum Aurelium Agricolanum agentem vicem praefectorum praetorio....* Despite the evident corruptions of the text, the relationship between Fortunatus and Agricolanus is precisely that of *praeses* and *vicarius*. See also *PLRE* I, pp. 370 (Astasius Fortunatus 2), 31 (Aurelius Agricolanus 2).

[11] *P. Oxy.* 1469: *Aimiliō Roustikianō tō ḍiạṣẹṃ(otatō) diadekho(menō) ta merē tōn exokhōtatōn eparkhōn.... PLRE* I, p. 787 (Aemilius Rusticianus 1).

[12] *L'Année Épigraphique* 20$^6$ (1942–3), p. 171, no. 81: *ex praecepto Val·Alexandri·v(iri) p(erfectissimi)·agent(is)-·vic(es)·praeff(ectorum)·praet(orio)*. *Inscriptions of Roman Tripolitania*, pp. 131–2, no. 464: *Val(erius) Alexander v(ir) p(erfectissimus) a(gens) v(ices) praef(ectorum) praet(orio)*. *PLRE* I, p. 44 (Valerius Alexander 20). See also below, pp. 380–1 (possibly identical with L. Dom. Alexander).

[13] Lactantius, *De Mortibus Persecutorum* XVI.4; ed. Moreau, I, p. 94: *...in Hieroclem ex vicario praesidem.... PLRE* I, p. 432 (Sossianus Hierocles 4). As regards the particular date at which the diocesan vicariate was initiated, the years 297/8 are sometimes suggested, but it is odd that in this case *two* probable vicars, Agricolanus and Rusticianus, from regions as widely separated as Spain and Egypt, should suddenly appear in precisely that year: a slightly earlier date would appear somewhat more plausible. In addition, of course, even if Valentio (293/6) were proven to be merely a vicar of the prefects at Rome (see above, n. 9), that would not in itself prove the initiation of the diocesan system to have taken place in 297/8, merely that this was then the earliest known date for it.

the division of Italy into a number of provinces under *correctores* of consular rank – a division which is itself supposed to have pre-dated the creation of the Italian diocese(s) – cannot be proved to have taken place before *c.* 298. But Titus Flavius Postumius Titianus can be shown to have been *corr(ector) Italiae reg(ionis) Transpadanae* and *corr(ector) Campaniae* before his proconsulship of Africa in 295–6 and his ordinary consulship in 301. The dates proposed for these correctorships, both of which already involve the division of Italy, are 291/2 and 292/3 respectively.[14] There is therefore no conclusive evidence against Septimius Valentio having performed the effective functions of *vicarius Urbis Romae* (whether or not with that precise title) as early as 293–6.

According to Lactantius' description, *vicarii* of the prefects were accompanied by *rationales (rei summae)* and *magistri (rei privatae)*, and it seems clear that the creation of a diocesan vicariate for the prefecture was indeed accompanied or followed shortly by that of an equivalent tier of regional administration for the *res summa* and *res privata*. For a complete list of the officials belonging to this equivalent tier, and the territorial divisions that they directed, recourse must be had to the entries for the *comites sacrarum largitionum* and *rerum privatarum* in the *Notitia Dignitatum*. This document is by general agreement of composite nature and origin, but datable as a whole to the first quarter of the fifth century. The administrative arrangements that it describes are nevertheless in many cases of long standing and in some traceable as far back as the Diocletianic or Constantinian periods.

The *Notitia* records the following *rationales summarum* for the west:[15] Pannonia Secunda with Dalmatia and Savia; Pannonia Prima with Valeria, plus Noricum Mediterraneum and Ripense; Italia; Urbs Roma; Tres Provinciae (Sicilia, Sardinia, Corsica); Africa; Numidia; Hispaniae; Quinque Provinciae (i.e. Viennensis); Galliae; Britanniae. It records a *comes largitionum* in each diocese (*per omnes dioceses*) for the east.[16] A number of these territorial divisions are traceable back into the first half of the fourth century,[17] and it seems likely that the group as a whole is Diocletianic.[18] (Map 32)

[14] *PLRE* I, pp. 219–20 (T. Flavius Postumius Titianus 9). Before leaving this subject, it is worth noting that of late it has again become fashionable to deny Diocletian any real degree of originality or coherence in his administrative policies, whether in the division of provinces or in the creation of a diocesan vicariate. This dogmatic return to the position crystallised by Seston some forty years ago is as simplistic as an insistence upon absolute systematisation and contemporaneity in Diocletian's organisational acts. But if two caesars are appointed in 293 (whether on precisely the same day is immaterial), the diocesan vicariate is at least well started into the course of its development in 293/6 (or 297/8 for that matter), the mint structure is undergoing considerable reorganisation between 292/3 and 298/9 (and betraying a diocesan pattern, however muted, at the same time), and the coinage is reformed in 294/6, then – given the difficulties inherent in any such massive restructuring in an ancient or mediaeval society – to deny any system or coherence is merely ludicrous and perverse.

[15] *Notitia Dignitatum Occidentalis* XI.10–20; ed. O. Seeck, p. 149.

[16] *Notitia Dignitatum Orientalis* XIII.5; ed. Seeck, p. 35.

[17] *PLRE* I, pp. 1066–7.

[18] The observations made regarding the inception of the diocesan structure of the prefecture (see above, n. 14) are more or less applicable to the *largitiones*. While one does not have the same amount of early

The *Notitia* records the following *rationales rei privatae*, as they were by then termed rather than *magistri*, for the west:[19] Illyricum (i.e. Pannonia); Italia; Urbs Roma; Sicilia; Africa; Hispaniae; Galliae; Quinque Provinciae (i.e. Viennensis); Britanniae. Of these it has been suggested that Sicilia was a late addition.[20] It fails to record the distribution of *rationales rerum privatarum* for the east,[21] but there is no reason to believe that this generally failed to reflect the diocesan pattern evident in the west. Several of these divisions are, again, traceable back into the fourth century, and it once more seems likely that the group as a whole is Diocletianic.[22] (Map 32)

The administrative structure can be seen already operating in Egypt at a date still quite early on in Diocletian's reign. There, the old province had been divided into two – Lower Egypt which continued to be ruled by the *praefectus Aegypti*, and the Thebaid which had come to be ruled by a *praeses* (*hēgoumenos*) – by September 298. At some uncertain stage, possibly the same as that at which the other division took place, Libya was also split off.

But, despite this fragmentation, the regional *rationalis rei summae* (*katholikos*) had not only retained his authority over the whole of the area covered by the old province, but had even been given powers formerly belonging to the prefect. A regional *magister rei privatae* (*magistros tēs priouatēs*), with the same extensive jurisdiction as the *rationalis*, is also first recorded in September 298.[23]

To the extent that Egypt possessed both its own *rationalis* and its own *magister* long before becoming a separate diocese by being split off from Oriens, it occupied a somewhat anomalous position. It has been suggested, however, that the prefect retained a residual measure of authority over the *praesides* of the fragments into which the old province had been divided – a suggestion which, if valid (and it has been contested), would reduce the degree of anomaly by placing him in an intermediate position above a normal *praeses*, if still below a *vicarius*.[24]

The *Notitia* accords the Egyptian representative of the *largitiones* the somewhat anachronistic title of *comes et rationalis summarum* rather than that of *comes largitionum* accorded his eastern colleagues,[25] and the representative of the *res privata* is known to have retained the title of *magistros* after it had been discarded elsewhere in favour of that of *rationalis*.[26]

prosopographical evidence in the latter case, one does have the clear testimony of Lactantius (see above, p. 373), and that of the mint-pattern (see below, p. 379, Table 7, and Maps 32, 33).

19 *N. Dig. Occ.* XII.6–15; ed. Seeck, pp. 154–5.

20 Jones, *Later Roman Empire* I, p. 413.

21 *N. Dig. Or.* XIV.4; ed. Seeck, p. 37.

22 *PLRE* I, p. 1063. See also above, nn. 14, 18.

23 *P. Beatty Panop.* I, ll. 205, 227, 339–40 (Pomponius Domnus: *PLRE* I, p. 267).

24 C. Vandersleyen, *Chronologie des préfets d'Égypte de 284 à 395*, pp. 110–14; contested by J. Lallemand, *L'administration civile d'Égypte de l'avènement de Dioclétien à la création du diocèse (284–382)*, pp. 59–60.

25 *N. Dig. Or.* XII.12; ed. Seeck, p. 36.

26 Athanasius, *Apologia ad Constantium Imperatorem* X; ed. J.-P. Migne, in *PG* XXV, at col. 608: *hōn ho men katholikos, ho de magistros ēn ekei* (Rufinus and Stephanus: *PLRE* I, pp. 774, 852).

The policies of Diocletian had therefore resulted in the creation of an entirely new and, in so far as each of the major fiscal institutions was represented, a three-fold tier of regional fiscal administration, that is, central, diocesan and provincial. It is against the background of these policies and their results that various adjustments in the pattern of coin production taking place over the period *c.* 291–*c.* 298/9 should be seen.

### *B. Diocletian: Mints*

At the beginning of the reign of Diocletian the following seven mints (*monetae*) had been in operation: Lyons, Rome, Ticinum, Siscia, Cyzicus, Antioch and Tripolis. In addition Alexandria had continued to produce a series of coins, the origin of which is to be found as far back as the Ptolemaic period, and which consequently bore little or no relation to those produced at other imperial mints. The basic pattern of coin production was that which had achieved its final form during the reign of Aurelian.[27] The years *c.* 291–*c.* 298/9 saw a number of adjustments, as a result of which Diocletian's reformed coinage was the product of fourteen main mints. These are tabulated below, together with the diocese or equivalent fiscal unit in which they were situated (Table 7). Asterisks generally denote mints added during the years *c.* 292/3–*c.* 298/9, and in these cases the date of their inception is also included.[28]

Of the mints tabulated above, London was established not by Diocletian or his colleagues but by the usurper Carausius in *c.* 286, and as a result of the temporary secession of the British and some Gallic provinces from central control; it came under central control only with the recovery of those provinces from Carausius' successor Allectus in 296. Alexandria was brought into conformity with other imperial mints in *c.* 294/6.

The Diocletianic pattern of coin production was brought into being not only by the inception of new mints but also by the closure of old or already established ones. Carausius and Allectus had established three, possibly four, mints: London, probably Colchester, Boulogne or Rouen, and possibly another.[29] London was the only one of these to survive the resumption of central control by any length of time. Tripolis struck a fair amount of pre-reform coinage for both Diocletian and Maximian, but failed to participate in the reform itself, or even to strike for the Caesars Constantius and Galerius after their creation in March 293. A date somewhere between 290 and 293 has therefore been suggested for

[27] P. H. Webb, *RIC* v.1, pp. 256–62, v.2, pp. 212–19.

[28] C. H. V. Sutherland, *RIC* vi, pp. 5–6. To a certain, rather minor, extent, these datings depend on the date of Diocletian's reform of the coinage, taken by Sutherland to be 294 – but this may need some modification: see below, p. 449 n. 4.

[29] R. A. G. Carson, 'The Sequence-marks on the Coinage of Carausius and Allectus', in R. A. G. Carson (ed.), *Mints, Dies and Currency*, at pp. 57–65. In the last instance, see: P. J. Casey, 'Carausius and Allectus – Rulers in Gaul?', *Britannia* 8 (1977), pp. 283–301, and B. Beaujard and H. Huvelin, 'A propos de l'atelier monétaire rouennais de Carausius', *Bulletin de la Société Française de Numismatique* 33 (1978), pp. 360–7.

Table 7. *Major fiscal units and mints under Diocletian (Maps 32, 33)*

| | Diocese or equivalent fiscal unit | Mint | Date of inception, etc. |
|---|---|---|---|
| Partes occidentis (Maximian, Constantius) | Britanniae | London* | (See text) |
| | Galliae | Trier*, Lyons | *c.* 293 |
| | Viennensis | — | |
| | Hispaniae | — | |
| | Africa | Carthage* | *c.* 296 |
| | Italia { Italia | Aquileia*, Ticinum | *c.* 294 |
| | Italia { Urbs Roma | Rome | |
| Partes orientis (Diocletian, Galerius) | Pannoniae | Siscia | |
| | Moesiae | Thessalonica* | *c.* 298/9 |
| | Thracia | Heraclea* | *c.* 292/3(?) |
| | Pontica | Nicomedia* | *c.* 294/5 |
| | Asiana | Cyzicus | |
| | Oriens { Oriens | Antioch | |
| | Oriens { Aegyptus | Alexandria* | (See text) |

its closure.[30] It would not be surprising if there were some connection between the closure of Tripolis and the opening of the mint of Heraclea.

The result of these various adjustments was that the pattern of coin production subsequently exhibited a clear tendency to reflect the pattern of contemporary fiscal administration, and in particular that regional tier of it – the diocesan, directed by *vicarii*, *rationales* and *magistri* – which was seemingly being brought into being at much the same time. It remains uncertain as to whether this parallel was the result of conscious policy or merely the result of convenience working within the framework of the fiscal administration. That the pattern of coin production arose not only out of the inception of new mints but the closure of old ones – giving the whole an air of deliberation – might be taken as supporting the first possibility. That the resulting parallel was, as it were, an imperfect one – not the precise correlation of one mint to a diocese or equivalent fiscal unit – might be taken as supporting the second. What does seem certain is that this parallel would not have occurred had the diocesan tier of administration not already been in existence, or at least been in the process of being brought into existence, when the adjustments were made.

If the primary factor involved in the pattern of coin production is to be found in the pattern of fiscal administration, then a secondary factor will go far towards explaining exceptions to the proposed parallel. Two diocesan units, Galliae and Italia, both possessed two mints, while two further, Viennensis and Hispaniae, both entirely lacked them. The

[30] Webb, *RIC* v.2, p. 218.

connection seems clear: Gaul and Italy (or rather the Raetian provinces of the latter) both included frontier areas and the heavy military concentrations necessary to defend them; the Five Provinces and Spain, on the other hand, both included a number of the wealthiest but at the same time least heavily defended areas in the western half of the empire.[31]

To the extent that these features meant that the parallel between mint and unit of fiscal administration was less clear in the west than in the east where the correlation was (given the anomalous position of Egypt) an exact one, they might also be taken as implying the less thorough application of a conscious policy. The existence of the mint of Lyons, which duplicated Trier in the diocese of Galliae, was for example prolonged: that of Tripolis, which would have duplicated Antioch in the diocese of Oriens, was on the other hand terminated. The two factors represented by the general pattern of fiscal administration and by particular political or military needs are nevertheless those that will be found to recur constantly and in fact to dominate the production of coin throughout the later Roman and at least through much of the Byzantine period.

## C. Constantine and later developments

Between the abdication of Diocletian and the end of the fourth century, neither the pattern of fiscal administration nor that of coin production underwent more than minor adjustment. Between *c.* 321 and 327 the diocese of Moesiae was divided into two, Dacia and Macedonia, for at the earlier date Caius Caelius Saturninus was *vicarius Moesiarum*,[32] while at the later Acacius was *comes Macedoniae*,[33] the Constantinian *comites provinciarum* being a diocesan phenomenon and their functions not differing significantly from those of vicars. In the long term the only survivor of these *comites* was the *comes Orientis*, the probable first of whom, Flavius Felicianus, was appointed in 335.[34] The Moesian mint of Thessalonica automatically fell to Macedonia, and Dacia simply remained without one. At a later date Egypt became a separate diocese by being split off from Oriens, its first *praefectus Augustalis*, like the *comes Orientis* the approximate equivalent of a vicar, apparently being Flavius Eutolmius Tatianus who was appointed in 367.[35] (Map 32)

In *c.* 307 the mint of Carthage was closed, and when the revolt of Lucius Domitius Alexander against Maxentius broke out in Africa during the following year it is clear – from the consistently poor quality of the coinage produced by the reopened mint – that the services of a regular staff were then no longer available.[36] According to Aurelius Victor,[37]

[31] Jones, *Later Roman Empire* III, pp. 379 (table 13: Gaul), 378 (table 12: Raetia), 377 (table 11: Spain, etc.). Lactantius, *De Mortibus Persecutorum* VIII.3; ed. Moreau, I, p. 86: *opulentissimae provinciae, vel Africa vel Hispania....*

[32] *PLRE* I, p. 806 (C. Caelius Saturninus 9).

[33] *PLRE* I, p. 6 (Acacius 3, 4(?)).

[34] *PLRE* I, pp. 330–1 (Fl. Felicianus 5).

[35] *PLRE* I, pp. 876–8 (Fl. Eutolmius Tatianus 9).

[36] Sutherland, *RIC* VI, pp. 419–21. P. Salama, 'Recherches numismatiques sur l'usurpateur africain L. Domitius Alexander', in *Actes du 8ème Congrès International de Numismatique, New York – Washington septembre 1973*, at pp. 365–9. See also below, Pl. 7, 5.

[37] Aurelius Victor, *Liber de Caesaribus* XL.17; ed. F. Pichlmayr and R. Gruendel (Teubner), p. 123.

Domitius Alexander was 'ruling on behalf of the prefect among the Africans (*apud Poenos pro praefecto gerens*)', or was, in other words, *vicarius Africae*. This is confirmed by Zosimus,[38] who adds that Maxentius, prior to the revolt, and doubting the loyalty of the army in Africa, had demanded Alexander's son as hostage. Maxentius' closure of the mint of Carthage and the removal of its staff is surely further evidence of this distrust: it was noticeably not reopened and restaffed on his recovery of Africa in 310.

In *c.* 308/9 a mint, seemingly at least largely composed of the staff withdrawn from Carthage during the previous year, was opened at Ostia in the diocese of Urbs Roma.[39] At first sight this has the appearance of duplicating the mint of Rome. The *Notitia*, however, divides the diocese into two, Urbs Roma and Tres Provinciae (Sicilia, Sardinia, Corsica), for the purposes of the *largitiones*.[40] This division is known to have existed as early as 325, when Eufrasius was already *rationalis trium provinciarum*,[41] and may well explain both the siting and functions of the mint of Ostia. For whereas the mint of Rome would have been well placed to supply the mainland regions under the *rationalis summarum urbis Romae*, that of Ostia would have been equally well placed to supply or to share in supplying the islands of Sicily, Sardinia and Corsica, under the *rationalis summarum trium provinciarum* and indeed even Africa after its recovery in 310.[42] (Map 33)

In *c.* 313, following Constantine's defeat of Maxentius and his conquest of Italy, the mint of Ostia was itself closed. During the course of the same year a mint was opened at Arles in the diocese of Viennensis: it has, unsurprisingly, been found to have been at least largely composed of the staff withdrawn from Ostia.[43] Its location at Arles proved permanent. (Map 33)

In *c.* 325, following Constantine's final defeat of Licinius and his conquest of the east, the mint of London was closed, and in *c.* 326 that of Ticinum. These closures have been very plausibly connected with a redeployment of mint staff anticipatory to, or as a consequence of, the opening of a mint at Constantinople in *c.* 326.[44]

In *c.* 327 the pattern of mints and fiscal units therefore stood as follows: Trier and Lyons (Galliae), Arles (Viennensis), Aquileia (Italia), Rome (Urbs Roma), Siscia (Pannoniae), Thessalonica (Macedonia), Heraclea (Thracia), Cyzicus (Asiana), Nicomedia (Pontica), Antioch (Oriens), Alexandria (Aegyptus). The city of Constantinople stood outside the normal pattern of regional administration to an extent even greater than Rome. It had

38 Zosimus, *Historia Nova* II.12; ed. Mendelssohn, p. 70: *Alexandros…topon epikhein tois hyparkhois tēs aulēs in Libyē*.

39 Sutherland, *RIC* VI, pp. 393–7. See also below, Pl. 7, 6.

40 *N. Dig. Occ.* XI.13, 14; ed. Seeck, 149.

41 *PLRE* I, p. 299 (Euphraxius).

42 Callu, *La politique monétaire des empereurs romains*, p. 455. P. Salama, 'Les trésors maxentiens de Tripolitaine', *Libya Antiqua* 3–4 (1966–7), pp. 21–7.

43 Bruun, *RIC* VII, p. 227. See also: L. H. Cope, 'Die-module Measurements, and the Sequence of Constantine's Reformed Folles Issues of Spring A.D. 310 and of early A.D. 313', *Schweizer Münzblätter* 77 (Feb. 1970), pp. 56–8. See also below, Pl. 7, 8.

44 Bruun, *RIC* VII, pp. 19, 96, 355, 359, 562–3.

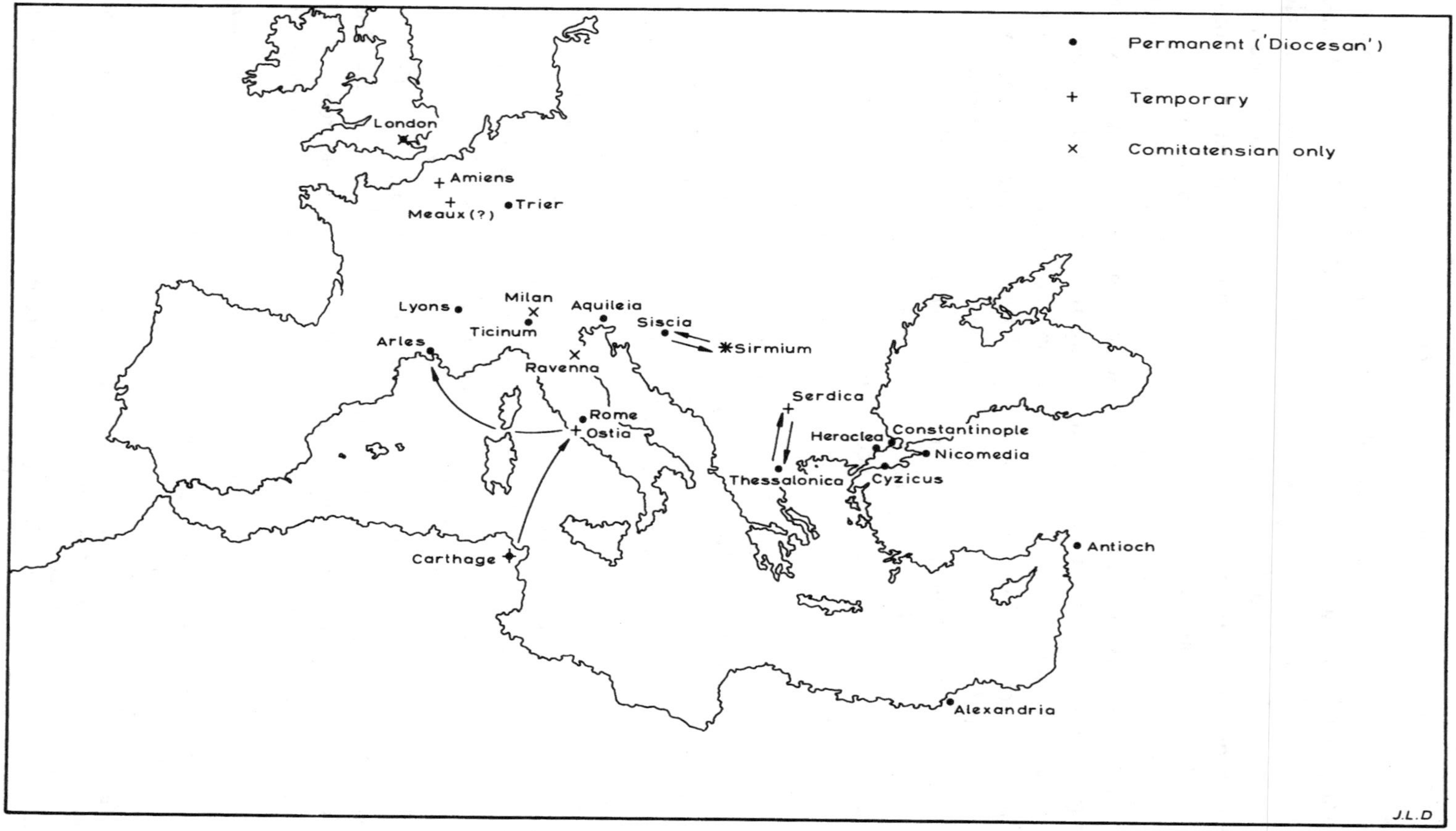


Map 33 The empire: mints, *c.* 300–450

Table 8. Procuratores monetarum *in the* Notitia Dignitatum

| Official | Diocese |
|---|---|
| Procurator monetae Siscianae | (d. Pannoniarum) |
| Procurator monetae Aquileiensis | (d. Italiae) |
| Procurator monetae urbis Romae | (d. Urbis Romae) |
| Procurator monetae Lugdunensis | (d. Galliarum) |
| Procurator monetae Arelatensis | (d. Septem Provinciarum [i.e. Viennensis]) |
| Procurator monetae Triberorum | (d. Galliarum) |

been superimposed upon the Diocletianic system and, for example, did not stand at the head of a diocesan unit. It did, however, act as the main or later as the only eastern imperial residence and focus of administration, and its mint therefore came to occupy an increasingly predominant position. The dioceses of Britanniae, Hispaniae and Africa, in the west, and Dacia, in the east, remained without mints. (Maps 32, 33)

This same pattern of mints survived on into the fifth century and is that recorded in the *Notitia*. That document places six mint procurators (*procuratores monetarum*) at the disposition of the western *comes sacrarum largitionum* as in Table 8.[45]

The *Notitia*, being a western document, does not enumerate the *procuratores monetarum* at the disposition of the eastern *comes sacrarum largitionum*,[46] but the coins themselves and other sporadic documentation show the eastern mints to have been identical with those in operation in *c.* 327.[47] (Maps 32, 33)

Mints, or at least the main and more regular ones, were accompanied – for obvious reasons of convenience – by treasuries (*thesauri*) with stocks of metal, whether in coined or bullion form. The *Notitia* places the following heads of treasuries (*praepositi thesaurorum*) at the disposition of the western *comes sacrarum largitionum*, *thesauri* that were, or might originally have been, paired with *monetae* being marked with an asterisk in Table 9.[48]

The precise stage at which this set of *thesauri* was brought into being remains uncertain, but comparison with that of *monetae* suggests it to have been an early and probably an essentially Diocletianic feature. It seems clear that although by no means all treasuries

[45] *N. Dig. Occ.* XI.39–44; ed. Seeck, p. 150.

[46] *N. Dig. Or.* XIII.18; ed. Seeck, p. 36.

[47] Refs: Hendy, 'Aspects of Coin Production and Fiscal Administration in the Late Roman and Early Byzantine Period', p. 119 n. 3; add John Malalas, *Chronographia* XII; Bonn edn, p. 308 (Antioch: [*Dioklētianos*] *ektise de kai en Antiokheia monētan, hōste kharassesthai ekei nomismata· ēn gar hē autē monēta apo seismou katastrapheisa*). See now also: J.-P. Callu, 'Sozomène, v. 15 et la corporation des monétaires', *Bulletin de la Société Française de Numismatique* 27 (1972), pp. 271–3 (Cyzicus). H.-G. Pflaum, 'Un procurateur de la monnaie de Thessalonique', *Bulletin de la Société Française de Numismatique* 27 (1972), pp. 315–16 (Thessalonica).

[48] *N. Dig. Occ.* XI.23–37; ed. Seeck, pp. 149–50.

Table 9. Praepositi thesaurorum *in the* Notitia Dignitatum

| Official and province | Region |
|---|---|
| Praepositus thesaurorum Salonitanorum, Dalmatiae<br>Praepositus thesaurorum Siscianorum, Saviae*<br>Praepositus thesaurorum Sabarensium, Pannoniae primae | per Illyricum |
| Praepositus thesaurorum Aquileiensium, Venetiae*<br>Praepositus thesaurorum Mediolanensium, Liguriae*<br>Praepositus thesaurorum urbis Romae*<br>Praepositus thesaurorum Augustae Vindelicensis, Raetiae secundae | per Italiam |
| Praepositus thesaurorum Lugdunensium*<br>Praepositus thesaurorum Arelatensium*<br>Praepositus thesaurorum Remorum<br>Praepositus thesaurorum Triberorum* | per Galliam |
| Praepositus thesaurorum Augustensium* | in Britannis |

will have coincided with early mints, each early mint will nevertheless have readily coincided with a treasury. London (Augusta) will thus have lost its mint in *c.* 325 but will have retained its treasury. If the mint of Ticinum was ever paired with a treasury, that at nearby Milan (itself earlier the site of a mint) seems an obvious candidate. The treasury at Arles seems to have antedated the opening of a mint there in *c.* 313 for, according to Lactantius, the old Maximian, attempting a coup there against Constantine in 309, 'suddenly assumed the purple, laid hold of the treasury (*thesauros*), and gave the customary largesse'.[49] It may well be that, if the *res summa* was confronted with the problem of what to do with the mint of Ostia after the defeat of Maxentius, and yet, in view of the recent episode involving Domitius Alexander, was reluctant to restore it to its original site at Carthage, its pairing with the hitherto mintless treasury at Arles may have seemed an obvious solution. It is, finally, tempting to assume that the treasury at Salona was originally connected with the Diocletianic palace there.

It also seems clear that dioceses notably lacking mints lacked treasuries too, for neither Africa nor Spain is mentioned in the list. The Diocletianic mint of Carthage had been withdrawn by Maxentius, apparently as an act of political precaution, in *c.* 307. It seems a reasonable supposition that the treasury which presumably accompanied it was also withdrawn then. Spain had never possessed a mint: it may never have possessed a treasury either.

The *Notitia* does not enumerate the *praepositi thesaurorum* at the disposition of the eastern *comes sacrarum largitionum*,[50] but presumably each mint was accompanied by a treasury,

[49] Lactantius, *De Mortibus Persecutorum* XXIX.5; ed. Moreau, I, p. 111.

[50] *N. Dig. Or.* XIII.10; ed. Seeck, p. 36.

as those at Cyzicus and Alexandria certainly were and others are known from casual sources, at Philippopolis and Nicaea, for instance.[51]

For well over a century the large-scale and comparatively regular production of coin had been confined to a pattern of mints of which two features, its constant composition and its reflection of the pattern of regional fiscal administration, were characteristic. Mints had on occasion been created outside this pattern, but in that case tended neither to exhibit the quality of permanence nor to bear any clear relation to the pattern of administration, their temporary existence frequently having some obvious and specific military or political basis.

A mint probably representing Iantinum (Meaux, Galliae) seems to have operated very briefly during the period *c.* 291–3, and in this case will presumably have been connected with Maximian's contemporary campaigns against Carausius. Subsequently, it may well have provided the basis of the mint of Trier.[52] The mint of Serdica (Moesiae), operative between *c.* 303/4 and *c.* 308, seems to have been merely the mint of Thessalonica moved temporarily northwards. Its existence has been connected with Diocletian's movement westwards and northwards, possibly via Thessalonica and Serdica, to Rome, for the celebration of his *vicennalia* in November 303.[53] The mint of Ambianum (Amiens, Galliae), operative between *c.* 350 and *c.* 353, owed its existence to the usurper Magnentius whose birthplace it was,[54] and to whose tenure of power its activity was virtually confined.[55] The mint of Sirmium (Pannoniae), operative between *c.* 351 and *c.* 364–7, seems to have owed its existence in the first place to the needs and tactical foresight of Constantius II who detached an *officina* from the mint of Siscia, shortly before the *officinae* remaining in that city fell to Magnentius, in order to make use of it himself.[56] The mint of Carthage, briefly operative at an unknown date in the late fourth or early fifth century,

[51] Cyzicus: see above, p. 187. Alexandria: see above, p. 345. Philippopolis and Nicaea: Jones, *Later Roman Empire* I, p. 429. Yet others must have existed in the east, and their sites may probably be deduced from surviving artefacts. For example, gold and silver ingots, the former of which seem to have derived from the battle of Adrianople (378) and/or its aftermath (see above, p. 272), bear the stamps of Sirmium, Naissus and Thessalonica, probably denoting the presence of *thesauri* (whether temporary, as in the case of Sirmium, or permanent, as in those of Naissus[?] and Thessalonica), in those cities. See: O. Iliescu, 'Nouvelles informations relatives aux lingots romains d'or trouvés en Transylvanie', *Revue des Études Sud-est Européennes* 3 (1965), pp. 269–81. F. Baratte, 'Quelques remarques à propos des lingots d'or et d'argent du bas-empire', in V. Kondić (ed.), *Frappe et ateliers monétaires dans l'antiquité et moyen âge*, at pp. 63–71. I. Youroukova, 'L'activité de l'atelier d'orfèvre à Niš au IV$^{e}$ s. à la lumière d'une nouvelle trouvaille en Bulgarie', *ibid.* at pp. 73–8. Later artefacts (items of plate) add Antioch, and, after the Justinianic reconquest, Carthage. See: E. C. Dodd, *DOS* VII, pp. 248 (no. 89), 251 (no. 90) (Antioch); 256 (no. 93) (Carthage). For silver ingots, see also below, p. 391 n. 77.

[52] On this mint, see: F. Loriot, 'Les aurei de Dioclétien et Maximien à la marque IAN', *Bulletin de la Société Française de Numismatique* 36 (1981), pp. 88–92. P. Bastien, 'The Iantinum Mint', *American Numismatic Society Museum Notes* 25 (1980), pp. 77–85.

[53] Sutherland, *RIC* VI, pp. 486–500.

[54] J. Bidez, 'Amiens, ville natale de l'empereur Magnence', *Revue des Études Anciennes* 27 (1925), pp. 312–18.

[55] J. P. C. Kent, *RIC* VIII, pp. 119–20.

[56] Kent, *RIC* VIII, pp. 382–3.

may have owed its ephemeral existence to *comites* Gildo, Heraclian, or Boniface, all of whom were in some state of contumacy with regard to the western administration during that period. Hoard evidence, however, seems to suggest a somewhat later date.[57] (Map 33)

### (II) 284–*c*. 400 (PRECIOUS METALS: THE COMITATENSIAN MINT)

A second major theme in the production of coinage during the late third and fourth centuries involves a distinction in the coining of base metal on the one hand and of precious metal on the other, a distinction that becomes increasingly evident as the fourth century proceeds.

The precise norm for the production of coinage in base metal at the regional mints mentioned in the preceding section of this chapter remains uncertain: whether it tended to be conducted at a relatively uniform rate, or whether in spasmodic bursts of intense activity punctuated by periods of relative idleness. If, as now seems likely, production was geared primarily to the satisfaction of administrative needs, then something in the way of a cyclical pattern is likely to have resulted. To the extent that administrative needs are likely to have been dominated by payments to the military – known to have been in the form of an annual *stipendium* and *donativum*, however residual, at this period – then this cycle seems likely to have had at least a theoretical annual basis, and probably in practice a four-monthly one. On the other hand, the crop–tax relationship seems to have dictated an annual, and basically summer, cycle.[58] With the production of coinage in precious metal there is less need to construct a hypothetical model, for that cycle was to a considerable degree quinquennially based, and clearly related to the quinquennial donative that formed the most significant monetary contribution to a military income and towards the payment of which the proceeds of several taxes were specifically directed.[59] The quinquennial cycle commenced with the accession of an emperor, an event itself commemorated by a donative. Responsibility for the payment of both the annual stipend and donative in base metal and the accessional and quinquennial donatives in precious metal lay with the *res summa* or *largitiones*.[60]

By the middle of the fourth century the simultaneous and widespread production of precious-metal coinage at regional mints had become formalised and virtually confined to the accessional or quinquennial issues that, it seems reasonable to assume, marked the

[57] Carson, Hill and Kent, *Late Roman Bronze Coinage*, A.D. *324–498*, p. 58. But see C. Morrisson, 'Numismatique byzantine', in École Pratique des Hautes Études, IV$^{e}$ Section, *Annuaire* 1974/5, at pp. 461–2, pointing out that the hoard evidence favours a date in the second third of the fifth century.

[58] *Stipendium* and *donativum*: Jones, *Later Roman Empire* II, pp. 623–4; but see above, p. 177, for an approximate revised total. Crop-tax: Milne, *Catalogue of Alexandrian Coins*, p. xix.

[59] Jones, *Later Roman Empire* II, p. 624; see also above, p. 175.

[60] Jones, *Later Roman Empire* II, p. 624; see also above, pp. 187–8.

taxation and donatives appropriate to such occasions. The mints of Trier, Lyons, Arles, Aquileia, Rome, Siscia, Thessalonica, Nicomedia, Cyzicus and Antioch, for instance, participated in the production of such coinage for the tricennial celebrations of Constantius II in 352/3. Those of Trier, Lyons, Arles, Aquileia, Rome, Thessalonica, Heraclea, Cyzicus, Nicomedia and Antioch all participated for the accessional celebrations of Valentinian I and Valens in 364. Sirmium, as a temporary mint, participated in 352, duplicating Siscia in the same diocese; of the two, Sirmium alone participated in 364, despite the greater total of mints involved.[61] Alexandria participated at neither date, and in fact had not done so since 313/14.[62] This tendency to concentrate the production of precious metal at one mint in a diocese containing more than one mint is also noticeable in the diocese of Galliae, where Lyons struck no precious metal at all before 336, and Amiens similarly struck none during the course of its admittedly short life.[63]

The state of affairs whereby regional mints might play a significant rôle in the production of precious-metal coinage, if increasingly on a restricted number of occasions only, was brought to an end as a result of a series of procedural reforms enacted by Valentinian I and Valens during the years 366–9. The reasons behind this series of reforms, and one of the earliest formal steps in it, are preserved in the form of a law in the *Codex Theodosianus*. *CTh*. XII.6.12 (cf. XII.6.13 (367)) reads:

The same Augusti [Valentinian I and Valens] to Rufinus, Praetorian Prefect

> There must be no question but that, as We have already commanded, solidi collected on whatever account should be restored to a solid mass (*massa*) of refined gold (*obryza*).[64] And this is to be the case with all revenue (*inlationes*), so that the opportunity for fraud on the part of members of the *largitiones* (*largitionales*), escorts (*prosecutores*), and tax-collectors (*allectores*), shall be blocked. For the governor of a province (*provinciae rector*) is easily able to compensate for loss those who fulfil the necessary payment by means of two or three solidi if, after the solidi of a large number of individuals have been received separately, by name, and – as We have mentioned earlier – of the quality demanded, all that is owed is melted down into a mass. Naturally, if the same contempt for those receiving the tax as existed formerly is found, and a supply of refined gold which cannot be unsatisfactory is brought along, then he who calumniates it and rejects what is discovered to be a source of honest payment shall be placed under suitable punishment. But first the mass of refined gold that has been rejected is to be

[61] Kent, *RIC* VIII, and J. W. E. Pearce, *RIC* IX, under appropriate mint headings.

[62] Bruun, *RIC* VII, p. 702. Although a minimal silver coinage was struck in the names of the sons of Constantine, no further gold was struck until the reign of Justin II: Kent, *RIC* VIII, pp. 538–9 (silver); see below, p. 404 n. 137, and Pl. 22, 9 (gold).

[63] Bruun, *RIC* VII, p. 141. Kent, *RIC* VIII, pp. 121–4.

[64] For the definition of *obryza*: Isidore of Seville, *Etymologiarum sive Originum Libri XX* XVI.18.2; ed. Lindsay, II: *Obryzum aurum dictum quod obradiet splendore*, who continues with a splendidly learned, and entirely false, etymology. John Cassian: see above, p. 249. Use of the verb *obradiare* with reference to coinage is rare, but for example occurs in the highly vernacular *Tablettes Albertini* as *aurei obbrediaci ponderi pleni* – where, however, it perversely seems to apply to copper coins. See: P. Grierson, 'The *Tablettes Albertini* and the Value of the *Solidus* in the Fifth and Sixth Centuries A.D.', *Journal of Roman Studies* 49 (1959), p. 73.

sent to the current residence (*comitatus*) of Our Clemency, so that We may see on what grounds it was rejected.
Given 10 November in the consulships of Gratian, Most Noble Youth, and Dagalaifus [366].

The law is certainly a western one, for (Vulcacius) Rufinus is known to have been prefect in Italy, Illyricum and Africa in 366.[65] The gold ingots obtained from the melting down of solidi, of which a number are known (Pl. 3, 9–10), received the stamp of the official responsible for their testing.[66] What then happened, or should have happened, is revealed by two further and somewhat later laws in the *Codex Theodosianus*. *CTh*. I.10.7 (cf. VIII.8.5 [395]) reads:

The same Augusti [Arcadius and Honorius] to Limenius, *Comes Sacrarum Largitionum*
We consider that the practice of sending out two members of the palatine staff (*palatini*) into each province every year (*indictio*), and of constraining each assistant (*adiutor*) with a fine of a pound of gold if he neglects the provisions of Our law or sends out unsuitable people, must be observed. It must be the particular care of these members of the palatine staff to send back reports (*notoria*) complaining of the negligence of governors (*iudices*) if the situation demands it, on their own responsibility, so that their inactivity may not go unpunished. It is also appropriate for governors to report the names of those whom they detect attending to their own gain rather than to the public service: and they should know that their four-monthly accounts (*breves quadrimenstruos*) are to be sent up to the palatine bureau (*officium*), and that the gold which has been collected is to be sent up to the *sacrae largitiones* without any delay.
Given 27 February at Milan in the consulships of Vincentius and Fravitta [401].

*CTh*. X.24.3 (cf. XII.8.1 (409)) reads:

The same Augusti [Gratian, Valentinian II and Theodosius I] to Palladius, *Magister Officiorum*
The gold that has been paid promptly by the provincials is being consumed by speculation (*nundinatio*). Therefore perpetrators of such depredations should know that if they can be detected and reported they shall suffer the supreme penalty, unless at the end of their journey they should announce that the gold received from the provincial bureau has been delivered to the *sacrae largitiones*. In addition, if the gold which could have been delivered at the completion of their journey is found to have been detained for more than ten days, either by escorts or by members of the palatine staff, then they should know they are liable for a payment amounting to two per cent of the whole.
Posted 30 November at Beirut in the consulships of Eucherius and Syagrius [381].

The law is certainly an eastern one, but Palladius was *comes sacrarum largitionum* in July 381, and *magister officiorum* in March 382. Its contents are more appropriate to the former office, and it is therefore possible that it was originally addressed to Palladius as *comes*.[67]

What happened to the gold ingots obtained from the melting down of solidi, once stamped and, despite the best efforts of escorts and members of the palatine staff sent out into the provinces to collect them, by use of the express division of the public post,[68]

[65] *PLRE* I, pp. 782–3 (Vulcacius Rufinus 25).

[66] See above, p. 385 n. 51.

[67] *PLRE* I, p. 660 (Palladius 12).

[68] See above, pp. 294–5 and n. 207

Table 10. *Comitatensian* officium *of the* Comitiva Sacrarum Largitionum

| | |
|---|---|
| Scrinium auri massae | (Scrinium auri ad responsum?) |
| Scrinium ab argento | Scrinium a miliarensibus |
| — | Scrinium ad pecunias |
| Aurifices solidorum | |
| (Sculptores et ceteri artifices?) | |

eventually delivered to the *sacrae largitiones*, is revealed by an examination of the internal structure of its bureau. Information on this subject derives mainly from a law of Theodosius I, dated 384 and preserved in the *Codex Justinianus*,[69] and from the appropriate entries in the *Notitia*.[70]

The sub-departments (*scrinia*) of the comitatensian *officium* of the *comitiva sacrarum largitionum* given in Table 10 seem to be the relevant ones.

Gold in ingot form was presumably received into the *scrinium auri massae*. When required, such ingots would presumably have been sent through to the manufacturers of solidi (*aurifices solidorum*) who would have struck them into coin, perhaps using dies cut by the engravers (*scalptores*). The resulting coin would presumably have been lodged temporarily with the *scrinium auri ad responsum*, the title of which suggests that it may have been its function eventually to return or deliver the coin to the appropriate authorities.

At much the same time as the measures of 366/7 mentioned above a further one, no doubt part of the same programme but involving gold in private ownership, was also enacted:[71]

Emperors Valentinian [I], Valens and Gratian, Augusti, to Archelaus, *Comes Sacrarum Largitionum*

> You should know that whatever gold belonging to private individuals you find stamped (*figuratum*) in public mints (*monetae publicae*) is all to be forfeit to Our *largitiones*, for that individual has indeed judged himself worthy of condemnation who considers that his own gold should be brought to the fiscal mints (*monetae fiscales*) without coercion and of his own accord.

Given 11 March at Marcianopolis in the consulships of Valentinian, Most Noble Youth, and Victor [369].

A short while later this drastic policy was revised and somewhat relaxed:[72]

[69] *CJ* XII.23.7 = the corrupt *CTh.* VI.30.7.

[70] *N. Dig. Occ.* XI.92–3, 95–7; ed. Seeck, p. 153. *N. Dig. Or.* XIII.26–7, 29–31; *ed. cit.* p. 36. The definition of functions in Table 10 and below differs somewhat from that to be found in King, 'The *Sacrae Largitiones*: Revenues, Expenditure and the Production of Coin', at pp. 143–6.

[71] *CTh.* IX.21.7.

[72] *CTh.* IX.21.8.

The same Augusti [Valentinian I, Valens and Gratian] to Tatianus, *Comes Sacrarum Largitionum*

By a decision of Our customary moderation, We mitigate Our earlier sentence by which We commanded all gold said to have been brought by private individuals to the mint for stamping to be forfeit to the profit of the treasury (*fiscus*), and We command that, instead of the whole sum which is entered up in the accounts (*breves*), preventive measures having been abandoned, two ounces in the pound shall be contributed.

Given 21 May at Antioch in the consulships of Gratian, Augustus (for the third time), and Equitius [374].

The combination of these measures and the evident capacity of the comitival *officium* to function both as an independent *thesaurus* and *moneta* has long been recognised as having significant repercussions for the production of gold coinage. It ensured that, because all gold collected in taxation was first reduced to ingot form and then sent up to the *officium* at the *comitatus*, and because the *officium* itself possessed the staff required to reconvert the ingots into coin, the production of gold coinage will have become effectively confined to the *officium*.[73] The absolute prohibition on the coining of private gold at *monetae publicae* or *fiscales*, which can only be identified with the regional mints, and the later imposition of a prohibitive charge of two ounces in the pound, or one-sixth, for such coining, will only have emphasised this effective monopoly. It is not until the twelfth, or even the thirteenth century that this latter policy can be shown to have been definitively abandoned.[74]

Confirmation of the effects claimed for these measures is to be found not only in the general cessation of gold coins at mints other than that currently occupied by the *comitatus*, but probably also on the coinage itself, for certain Constantinopolitan solidi seemingly produced for the quinquennial celebrations of Valentinian I and Valens in 368/9 bear the marks $\frac{\text{O|B}}{\text{COMTM}*}$. OB is clearly an abbreviation of the term *obryza* found in the texts quoted above, and it has been suggested that COMT is an abbreviation of the term *comitatus*, or some derivative, the whole possibly standing for something along the lines of COM(*i*)T(*atensis*) M(*oneta*) or 'comitatensian coinage'.[75] The western equivalent is probably to be found in the appearance of the mark TROB on gold coinage from the mint of Trier.[76]

It seems probable that these measures also applied to silver, for a general cessation of simultaneous and widespread coining at regional mints is observable in this case too. Silver in ingot form, of which a number of examples are also known, would have been received into the *scrinium ab argento* of the comitival *officium* and, when required, sent through to the *aurifices* for coining. It would then have been lodged with the *scrinium a miliarensibus*

[73] A phenomenon first observed by Elmer, and followed by Kent (refs: Kent, 'Gold Coinage in the Later Roman Empire', at p. 198 and n. 3). It now seems generally accepted, and only the details, and the rare exceptions to the rule, remain debated.

[74] See above, pp. 259–60.

[75] Pearce, *RIC* IX, p. 217, nos. 26a, b.

[76] Pearce, *RIC* IX, p. 15, nos 11a, b.

to await delivery. From about this time the western silver coinage tends to include the letters PS in its mint-marks, and it has been suggested that this is an abbreviation for refined silver (*pusulatum*).[77]

It also seems probable that copper, which was of no great value, particularly in its bullion form, and which was in any case little struck by the comitatensian mint, will not have needed a particular *scrinium* responsible for its reception, but that the few issues of billon or copper coin that were issued by the mint were lodged with the *scrinium ad pecunias* to await delivery.[78]

The production of the precious-metal objects that are also known to have been the responsibility of the *officium* and its staff was presumably performed not by the *aurifices solidorum*, but by the *aurifices specierum*.[79]

Although regional mints before the Valentinianic reforms of 366–9 play a significant rôle in the production of precious-metal coinage, that rôle was, as already mentioned, heavily influenced by an accessional and quinquennial cycle of expenditure. Not all expenditure was so conveniently cycled, however, and there is no reason to believe that an emperor's need for such coinage on a much more commonplace basis had decreased, even had that need been expressed only in the form of the largesse that was constantly expected of him; there is, on the contrary, good reason for believing that such largesse actually increased during the fourth century.[80] But he was still, in addition, and on any number of occasions, faced with the kind of expenditure that was neither quinquennial nor commonplace: military campaigns, for example, whether prosecuted against barbarians, his erstwhile colleagues, or mere usurpers, will have occasioned great expenditure in cash, and in the circumstances necessarily in precious-metal coinage.

It is against this background that the origins of the mint on the strength of the comitival *officium* should probably be sought. It has been suggested that this mint was itself one of the by-products of the Valentinianic reforms[81] but, while its existence in any formal sense has been denied for the Diocletianic period,[82] plausible, if effectively exaggerated, claims have been made for the Constantinian.[83]

The major difficulty in the way of any attempt to define the origin of the comitatensian mint, its precise nature and mode of operation at any given time, and the implications of its existence for regional mints, arises out of the fact that too few issues of coinage

[77] K. S. Painter, 'A Late-Roman Silver Ingot from Kent', *Antiquaries Journal* 52 (1972), pp. 84–92. See also above, p. 385 n. 51. For the definition of *pusulatum*: below, p. 450 (*De argento hoc est pusula primi...*).

[78] For the usage *pecunia* = copper coin: Augustine, *Sermones* CXXVII.3; ed. J.-P. Migne, in *PL* XXVIII, at col. 707: *aurum, vel argentum, vel pecuniam, vel fructus aliquos pecorum aut frugum.* See also Isidore of Seville, *Etymologiarum sive Originum Libri XX* XVI.18.5; ed. Lindsay, II: *Nam prius aerea pecunia in usu fuit, post argentea, deinde aurea subsecuta est, sed ab ea qua coepit, et nomen retinuit. Unde et aerarium dictum, quia prius aes tantum in usu fuit, et ipsud solum recondebatur, auro argentoque nondum signato.* For the *scrinium ad pecunias* producing copper at Thessalonica, see also below, pp. 400–1.

[79] *CJ* XII.23.7(8).

[80] See: MacMullen, 'The Emperor's Largesses', p. 166.

[81] Kent, 'Gold Coinage in the Later Roman Empire', at p. 200.

[82] Sutherland, *RIC* VI, pp. 54–5.

[83] Bruun, *RIC* VII, pp. 13–18.

are sufficiently closely datable, and that too little is known of imperial, and therefore comitatensian, movements, for its products to be isolated on other than rare occasions. It is only when the emperor and his *comitatus*, or at least the fiscal components of the latter, were resident at a centre where the services of a regional mint were not readily available that its products became distinguishable beyond doubt. A number of such occasions are known.

Between 317 and 324, and particularly between 320 and 324, while preparing his final campaign against Licinius, Constantine spent much of his time in the Pannonian and Moesian dioceses, and particularly at either Sirmium or Serdica. In *c.* 320 a mint was opened at Sirmium and operated there until its closure in *c.* 325/6.[84] (Pl. 5, 15)

For a short time in 352–3, while on campaign against Magnentius, Constantius II was resident at Milan. In *c.* 352 a mint was opened there and was certainly among those striking coinage celebrating Constantius' *tricennalia* in 352/3. It apparently closed shortly afterwards.[85]

For almost a year in 364–5, having been proclaimed emperor in the east on the death of Jovian, and having left his brother Valens as his eastern colleague, Valentinian I was resident at Milan. In *c.* 364 a mint was again opened there and was certainly among those striking coinage celebrating the emperors' accession in 364. It also struck a small coinage celebrating an imperial consulate. This could have been either the first of Valentinian and Valens in 365 or the second of the same emperors in 368. As no coins in the name of Gratian (proclaimed emperor in 367) are known, the first seems much more likely. It again apparently closed shortly afterwards.[86] (Map 33)

The most remarkable general feature of the coinages produced by the mints of Sirmium and Milan on these three occasions is that they are very heavily concentrated on precious metal: on gold with just a little silver and billon in the case of the former; on gold alone in that of the latter.

This was a feature that was to remain unaltered by the Valentinianic reforms of 366–9. The mint of Sirmium was reopened for the production of gold and perhaps just a little silver on the occasion of Gratian's precautionary presence there in 378–9, after the death of Valens.[87] Closed shortly afterwards, it was again reopened, for the production of gold alone, on the occasion of Theodosius' campaign against Eugenius in 394–5, and again closed shortly afterwards.[88]

84 Seeck, *Regesten der Kaiser und Päpste*, pp. 165–73. Bruun, *RIC* VII, pp. 462–77.

85 Seeck, *Regesten der Kaiser und Päpste*, p. 199. Kent, *RIC* VIII, pp. 232–3 (where the bulk of the gold coinage is assigned to Constantius' second residence, 354–7 – Seeck, *op. cit.* pp. 200–3).

86 Seeck, *Regesten der Kaiser und Päpste*, pp. 218, 220, 222, 224, 226. Pearce, *RIC* IX, pp. 75–6 – but cf. O. Ulrich-Bansa, *Moneta Mediolanensis (352–498)*, pp. 26–30.

87 Seeck, *Regesten der Kaiser und Päpste*, p. 250. Pearce, *RIC* IX, pp. 159–60. See below, Pl. 8, 16.

88 Seeck, *Regesten der Kaiser und Päpste*, p. 284. Pearce, *RIC* IX, pp. 160–2. Hendy, 'Aspects of Coin Production and Fiscal Administration in the Late Roman and Early Byzantine Period', pp. 138–9 n. 5. For the very latest issues of Sirmium – commencing with a quite anomalous silver coinage struck by Theoderic in the

The later history of the mint of Milan is somewhat more complicated, for the city became the imperial residence on a number of occasions and for greatly varying periods of time. It is therefore less easy to connect its operation with particular occasions of residence. Like Sirmium, however, it struck in gold, or in gold and silver, alone.[89] In *c.* 402/3 Milan was closed and not reopened until late in the reign of Valentinian III (425–55). At much the same time a mint was opened at Ravenna, the products of which – like those of Sirmium and Milan – were confined to gold and silver. There seems no doubt that the closure of Milan and the opening of Ravenna reflects Honorius' definitive move from the former to the latter city in 402.[90]

The brief revival of the mint of London for the production of gold and silver only has been connected with the presence of Magnus Maximus at two stages of his reign (383–8), which certainly began in Britain.[91] (Map 33)

The numismatic evidence therefore suggests that the comitatensian mint had already achieved at least some degree of formal embodiment by the reign of Constantine. Whether it was a specifically Constantinian creation seems much more doubtful: the momentary production of gold alone possibly at Meaux in *c.* 291–3, for Maximian, and certainly at Serdica in *c.* 313–14, for Licinius, suggests the operation of something very similar.[92] Whatever the solution to that problem, the later existence of the comitatensian mint is emphasised, paradoxically, by the complete omission of the sites used by it, and it alone, at Sirmium, Milan and Ravenna, from the list of western *monetae* in the *Notitia*. Its staff are doubtless included in that document, but undifferentiated, within the *officium* of the *comes sacrarum largitionum*. Its concentration on the production of precious metal, and gold in particular, a feature that might have been expected in view of the terms of the Valentinianic reforms of 366–9, explains why the only undoubted mint staff within the *officium* listed in the *Codex Justinianus* are the *aurifices solidorum*. If silver or, very rarely, billon or copper were needed, then it was doubtless produced by those same *aurifices*[93] who took their name merely from their predominant product.

names of Anastasius and Justin I, and continuing well on into the sixth century under Cunimund and the Gepids, who struck in the names of Justinian and Justin II – see: F. Stefan, *Die Münzstätte Sirmium unter den Ostgoten und Gepiden* (Halle (Saale), 1925). The Ostrogothic issues are conveniently described in W. R. O. Hahn, *MIB* I, pp. 86–7, II, p. 31. For Theodosius, see below, Pl. 8, 20.

89 Pearce, *RIC* IX, pp. 76–84. See, for example, below, Pl. 8, 18–19.

90 Seeck, *Regesten der Kaiser und Päpste*, p. 304. Ulrich-Bansa, *Moneta Mediolanensis (352–498)*, pp. 201, 217. Hendy, 'Aspects of Coin Production and Fiscal Administration in the Late Roman and Early Byzantine Period', p. 123 n. 3.

91 Pearce, *RIC* IX, pp. 1–2. Hendy, 'Aspects of Coin Production and Fiscal Administration in the Late Roman and Early Byzantine Period', p. 122. See now: P. J. Casey, 'Magnus Maximus in Britain', in P. J. Casey (ed.), *The End of Roman Britain: Papers arising from a Conference, Durham 1978*, at pp. 66–79. See below, Pl. 8, 17.

92 Bruun, *RIC* VII, pp. 478–80. See below, Pl. 4, 9.

93 E.g. Carson, Hill and Kent, *Late Roman Bronze Coinage* A.D. *324–498*, p. 58, for copper at Milan and Ravenna.

The comitatensian mint's precise mode of operation is difficult to recover and very probably varied according to circumstances. On a number of occasions during the second half of the fourth century an emperor was required – generally by an emergency of some kind – to mount an expedition involving his own presence, and therefore that of his *comitatus*, at several cities possessing regional mints within a relatively short space of time. When similar issues of precious-metal coin are found at all or a number of these mints, and no others, and the exact date of the expedition as provided by documentary sources is found to lie within the approximate date provided by the coins, then some fairly direct connection between the two may reasonably be assumed.

Gratian's expedition of 378–9 mentioned above resulted in issues not only from Sirmium, but also from Aquileia, Milan and Trier, while Theodosius' subsequent prolonged residence in 379–80 resulted in similar issues from Thessalonica.[94] Theodosius' expedition of 387–91 against Magnus Maximus resulted in issues from Thessalonica, Aquileia, Milan and Rome, while Valentinian II's presence on the same expedition resulted in a distinctive series of parallel issues from Thessalonica, Aquileia and Milan.[95] The years 380–7 had seen an extraordinary situation in which Gratian and then Magnus Maximus in the west, Valentinian II who was subject to the direction of Gratian in the centre, and Theodosius in the east, had all produced distinctive issues: Gratian and Magnus Maximus at Trier, Aquileia and Milan; Valentinian at Aquileia, Milan and Thessalonica; and Theodosius at Constantinople.[96] Theodosius' expedition of 394–5 mentioned above resulted in issues from Thessalonica, Sirmium, perhaps Aquileia, and Milan.[97]

On most of the expeditions mentioned above the evidence suggests the comitatensian mint to have consisted of a skeleton staff only: probably of a selection of its clerical members and *aurifices*. It also seems not have utilised the services of its own *scalptores* but either those of the nearest regional mint or those of the mint on which it was actually currently based. The one known exception to both these norms is the Theodosian expedition of 394–5, which involved the eventual transfer of the entire comitatensian mint staff, *scalptores* included, to Sirmium, which held a conveniently central position on the borders of the two Illyrian dioceses.

The existence of coins struck at different regional mints but from the same obverse dies, and of coins struck at different mints but from the same reverse dies with the mint-mark appropriately recut, suggests that, once engraved, dies were in any case regarded as appertaining to the *comitatus* rather than to the regional mints.[98]

[94] Hendy, 'Aspects of Coin Production and Fiscal Administration in the Late Roman and Early Byzantine Period', p. 126.

[95] Hendy, 'Aspects of Coin Production and Fiscal Administration in the Late Roman and Early Byzantine Period', pp. 127–8, 137–9.

[96] Pearce, *RIC* IX, under appropriate mint headings. Hendy, 'Aspects of Coin Production and Fiscal Administration in the Late Roman and Early Byzantine Period', p. 139.

[97] *Ibid.* pp. 128–9.

[98] *Ibid.* pp. 129–30.

## (III) *c.* 400–610

### *A. Disintegration in the west*

The pattern of coin production obtaining during the latter part of the fourth century, whereby the base-metal coinage was issued by the long-established regional mints, and the precious-metal by the comitatensian, whether from a site of its own, or from one provided by the regional mint on which it currently happened to be based, survived on into the fifth century. In the west, other than in Italy, it then disintegrated more or less in parallel with the empire itself,[99] although after an appreciable hiatus the mint of Lyons then went on to issue a consistent coinage in gold, silver and copper, in the names of the eastern emperors Anastasius, Justin I and Justinian but with the monograms of the local Burgundian kings Gundobald (473–516), Sigismund (516–24) and Gundomar II (524–34). The gold coinage of this type was of good style, full weight and, apparently, high metallic quality.

The scene, even so, had already been set for debasement by Novel VII (14) of the emperor Majorian, dated 458. This had ordered that 'henceforward no tax-collector (*exactor*) shall refuse a solidus of full weight (*integri ponderis*) on the pretext of false disapproval, with the exception of the Gallic one, the gold of which is reckoned at a lesser price (*cuius aurum minore aestimatione taxatur*)'.[100]

In view of the high metallic quality of the Burgundian gold coinage it is probably significant that the *Leges Burgundionum*[101] include a law prohibiting the acceptance of four classes of gold coin on the grounds of their inferior quality. Among these four classes are the Visigothic, the debasement of which from the reign of Alaric II (484–507) is confirmed by a letter of Avitus, bishop of Vienne, dated 509.[102]

A continuing imperial discrimination against Merovingian solidi is indicated by a letter

99 Carson, Hill and Kent, *Late Roman Bronze Coinage*, A.D. *324–498*, under appropriate mint headings, for the copper. No systematic coverage yet exists, in advance of the appearance of *RIC* X, for the gold and silver.

100 Burgundians: P. Le Gentilhomme, 'Le monnayage et la circulation monétaire dans les royaumes barbares en occident (V$^{e}$–VIII$^{e}$ siècle)', *Revue Numismatique* 7$^{5}$ (1943), pp. 92–5. D. M. Metcalf and F. Schweizer, 'Milliprobe Analyses of some Visigothic, Suevic, and other Gold Coins of the Early Middle Ages', *Archaeometry* 12 (1970), p. 176. Novel VII: in the last instance, E. Demougeot, 'A propos des *solidi gallici* du V$^{e}$ siècle après J.-C. (résumé)', *Bulletin de la Société Française de Numismatique* 38 (1983), pp. 269–70.

101 *Leges Burgundionum, Constitutiones Extravagantes* XXI.7; MGH, *Leges* II.1, pp. 120–1: *De monetis solidorum [iubemus] custodire, ut omne aurum, quodcumque pensaverit, accipiatur praeter quattuor tantum monetas, hoc est: Valentiani, Genavensis prioris et Gotici, qui a tempore Alarici regis adaerati sunt, et Adaricianos.* The precise identification of these four classes remains controversial. See, in the last instance: W. A. Oddy, 'The *Moneta Genavensis* of the *Lex Burgundionum*', *Revue Numismatique* 22$^{6}$ (1980), pp. 131–5 – but see also the comments by J. Lafaurie, pp. 136–7. For the other classes, see: J. Lafaurie, 'Monnaies décriées dans le second appendice de la Lex Burgundionum', *Bulletin de la Société Française de Numismatique* 31 (1976), pp. 73–5.

102 Avitus of Vienne, *Epistulae* LXXXVII; MGH, *AA* VI.2, pp. 96–7: ...*cui corruptam potius quam confectam auri nondum fornace decocti crederes inesse mixturam: vel illam certe, quam nuperrime rex Getarum secuturae praesagam ruinae monetis publicis adulterium firmantem mandaverat.*

of pope Gregory I,[103] dated 595, mentioning 'Gallic solidi, which cannot be spent in our land (*qui in terra nostra expendi non possunt*)'. This discrimination seems rather more likely to have been based upon the inferior quality of the contemporary Merovingian coinage than upon the occasional appearance on it of the names or portraits of various Merovingian rulers – an appearance which, for instance, is known already to have caused Procopius pain.[104]

The increasing decentralisation of production is a well-known feature of the later Merovingian and Visigothic coinages and was no doubt a major factor in their crude design and execution, erratic weight and inferior metallic quality. The escape of moneyers from state control into that of private individuals, which seems to have been facilitated by this decentralisation in Visigothic territories, was in fact a development of which the Ostrogothic king Theoderic had already had cause to complain.[105]

In Italy, where the structure of comitatensian and regional administration had been preserved virtually intact, Odovacer continued the pattern of coin production that he had inherited from his imperial predecessors.[106] After an initial period, however, his Ostrogothic successor Theoderic concentrated the production of precious-metal coinage on Rome, rather than on Milan or Ravenna (his main residence), and he was followed in this policy by his own successors.[107] Rome was also the mint from which Theoderic's

[103] Gregory I, *Epistulae* VI.10; MGH, *Ep.* I, p. 389. Cf. Kent, 'Gold Standards of the Merovingian Coinage, A.D. 580–700', at pp. 69–74.

[104] Procopius, *De Bello Gothico* III.33.5–6; ed. Haury (Teubner), II, pp. 442–3: *nomisma de khrysoun ek tōn en Gallois metallōn*[*!*] *pepoiēntai, ou tou Rhōmaiōn autokratoros, hēper eithistai, kharaktēra enthemenoi tō statēri toutō, alla tēn spheteran autōn eikona*.... Procopius goes on to say that even the Persian king, although he strikes silver coin, does not go so far as to strike gold, being unable to enforce its circulation. Cf. Metcalf and Schweizer, 'Milliprobe Analyses of some Visigothic, Suevic, and other Gold Coins of the Early Middle Ages', pp. 182–3 (nos. 0.183–4). Neither of Procopius' subordinate points, the existence of gold-mines in Gaul, and the non-existence of Sassanian gold coins, is accurate.

[105] Cassiodorus, *Variae* V.39; MGH, *AA* XII, p. 165: *Monetarios autem, quos specialiter in usum publicum constat inventos, in privatorum didicimus transisse compendium.* The letter is the same as that in which he complains about the fraudulent use of weights (see above, p. 332). On the status of rather later Merovingian moneyers there is always the well-known, and quite fascinating *Vita Sancti Eligii* (MGH, *SRMerov.* IV, pp. 669–742). On the career and work of this moneyer-saint, see, in the last instance: J. Lafaurie, 'Eligius monetarius', *Revue Numismatique* 19⁶ (1977), pp. 111–51. It emerges that although many of the Merovingian technical and fiscal practices derived – as might be expected – from the late Roman, even the workmanship of the saint is now not above suspicion, playing, as he did, a leading rôle in the Merovingian debasement.

[106] The coinage of Odovacer and his Ostrogothic successors remains as yet without an entirely satisfactory systematic modern treatment. W. Wroth, *Catalogue of the Coins of the Vandals, Ostrogoths and Lombards... in the British Museum* (1911) remains the most extensive body of material available in English. F. F. Kraus, *Die Münzen Odovacers und des Ostgotenreiches in Italien* (1928), occupies much the same position in German. The beginnings of a more modern classification, particularly with regard to the difficult problems of mint-identification, are to be found in J. P. C. Kent, 'The Coinage of Theodoric in the Names of Anastasius and Justin I', in R. A. G. Carson (ed.), *Mints, Dies and Currency*, at pp. 67–74. The Ostrogoths are also included in W. R. O. Hahn, *MIB* I, pp. 75–91, but although this is a useful treatment, it is not a definitive one. Meanwhile, for Odovacer: Wroth, *op. cit.* pp. 43–5; Kraus, *op. cit.* pp. 52–8.

[107] Wroth, *Catalogue of the Coins of the Vandals, Ostrogoths and Lombards... in the British Museum*, pp. 46–59, etc. Kraus, *Die Münzen Odovacers und des Ostgotenreiches in Italien*, pp. 82–99, etc. Hahn, *MIB* I, pp. 80–4

reformed copper coinage of folles and fractions was first and mainly issued, and it seems clear that his policy was a consistent one and dictated by his desire to conciliate the senate of that city.[108]

### *B. Continuity in the east*

In the east, on the other hand, alterations were understandably minimal throughout. The regional mints of Thessalonica, Heraclea, Nicomedia, Cyzicus, Antioch and Alexandria, all continued the production of base-metal coinage at least into the reign of Leo I, and most of them probably into that of Zeno.[109] It is nevertheless probable that the rate of production was by then on a reduced scale, and that this eventually entailed an hiatus at some mints, although the minute size and wretched manufacture of the contemporary nummus renders the matter difficult to judge. The suggestion of an hiatus is however supported by the fact that the reformed copper coinage of Anastasius was the product of Nicomedia and Antioch only, although that of Justin I was once more the product of Thessalonica, Nicomedia, Cyzicus, Antioch and Alexandria.[110]

Of the mints in operation under Leo only Heraclea, which had never been prolific, was not still in operation under Anastasius or Justin, and had in fact closed permanently. The precise stage at which this closure occurred remains uncertain, but it is known from a law of Anastasius dated 491[111] that, owing to barbarian devastations, the annual indiction of the Thracian diocese was failing to meet the requirements of the military, and it is also known from the diocesan vicariate's failure to appear in Justinian's Novel VIII of 535 that the vicariate itself had been withdrawn by that year. It has been suggested that this withdrawal took place in 497 when Anastasius instituted the vicariates of the Long Wall.[112] Certainly a law of Zeno dated 485–6[113] still mentions a *scrinium Thracicum*

(AV), 85–7 (AR), 88–90 (Æ). The transfer of emphasis from Ravenna to Rome was first defined by Kent, 'The Coinage of Theodoric in the Names of Anastasius and Justin I', p. 73. Under the later kings, Baduila and Theia, whose power-base was centred upon the upper Lombard Plain, the emphasis inevitably shifted, and was eventually confined, to Ticinum.

108 See below, pp. 486–90.

109 Carson, Hill and Kent, *Late Roman Bronze Coinage*, A.D. *324–498*, under appropriate mint headings. H. L. Adelson and G. L. Kustas, *A Bronze Hoard of the Period of Zeno I*, p. 41. D. R. Walker, 'A Copper Coinage for Leontius I', *Numismatic Circular* 75 (1967), pp. 264–6. C. Brenot, 'Un bronze de Zénon de l'atelier d'Antioche', *Bulletin de la Société Française de Numismatique* 23 (1968), pp. 323–4.

110 Bellinger, *DOC* I, pp. 3, 34. The modern English-, French- and German-language catalogues of Byzantine coins all commence with Anastasius, and each may from now on be consulted. For reasons simply of space and convenience, I have cited the English-language catalogue (Bellinger, Grierson and Hendy, *DOC* I–IV) only, unless the French-language one (C. Morrisson, *BNC* I, II), or the German-language one (Hahn, *MIB* I–III), adds substantially new, or apparently more correct, information on the subject in hand. Equally, I have cited any of them that I substantially disagree with. For a more specific criticism of Hahn's methodology, see below, p. 404 and n. 137.

111 *CJ* X.27.10.

112 Jones, *Later Roman Empire* III, p. 56 n. 60. On the Long Wall, see in the last instance: B. Croke, 'The Date of the "Anastasian Long Wall" in Thrace', *Greek, Roman, and Byzantine Studies* 23 (1982), pp. 59–78.

113 *CJ* XII.49.10.

in the *officium* of the praetorian prefecture of the East, but when John Lydus came to write his *De Magistratibus Populi Romani* in the sixth decade of the sixth century its functions were being performed by the *skrinion Poleōs*, the sub-department properly dealing with the City itself.[114] It therefore seems a plausible enough supposition that a similar move was then made with regard to the regional staff of the *largitiones*, entailing the closure of the Heraclean mint.

With the accession of Arcadius in 395 the eastern emperors, and therefore their *comitatus* and comitatensian mint, ceased to travel in any serious sense and became virtually confined to Constantinople and its environs. The comitatensian mint thereupon became, in practice as well as in name, a palatine one. The single exception to the consequent Constantinopolitan monopoly of precious-metal coinage not immediately explicable by anomalous circumstances – as in the case of the solidi produced at Antioch for the usurper Leontius (484–8),[115] and those produced at the same mint for the emperor Zeno, possibly during the metropolitan usurpation of Basiliscus (475–6)[116] – involves a sporadic series of Thessalonican solidi and tremisses extending from the early fifth century down to Tiberius II and possibly even later.[117] There are good reasons for believing this exception to have possessed a formal administrative basis but, while noting the general point, it will be convenient to hold detailed discussion over for the moment. (Pl. 20, 1–5)

## C. *Justinian: The prefectures*

The reconquest by Justinian of Africa from the Vandals and of Italy from the Ostrogoths necessitated various adjustments to the structure of imperial regional administration. These adjustments naturally took account of one of the major developments of the second half of the fourth and the fifth century: the increasing dominance of the praetorian prefecture. The importance of the prefecture had remained unaffected, and its dominance may even have been partly caused, by its division into a number of defined territorial circumscriptions or regional praetorian prefectures, the boundaries of which had been progressively less liable to modification. This last tendency had eventually reached the point of crystallisation in the arrangements adopted for the partition of the empire between Arcadius and Honorius in 395/6. At that partition, the eastern half had been divided into two regional

[114] John Lydus, *De Magistratibus* III.5; ed. Wuensch (Teubner), p. 91.

[115] J. Tolstoi, *Monnaies byzantines* I, pp. 68–9.

[116] British Museum collection – see below, Pl. 12, 12.

[117] Refs: Kent, 'Gold Coinage in the Later Roman Empire', p. 203 and n. 3 (Honorius, Theodosius II). Tolstoi, *Monnaies byzantines* I, pp. 97, 98–9 (Marcian), 122–3 (Leo I), 162 (Basiliscus). J. Lallemand, 'Sou d'or de Zénon frappé à Thessalonique', *Bulletin du Cercle d'Études Numismatiques* I (1964), pp. 49–51 (Zeno). From Anastasius to Heraclius, the series is best followed in Bellinger, *DOC* I; Grierson, *DOC* II.1; and Hahn, *MIB* I–III; under appropriate mint/metal headings. The most complete series is Hahn's. For the later part of the series, see now also W. R. O. Hahn, 'New Light on the Thessalonican *Moneta Auri* in the Second Half of the Sixth Century', *Numismatic Chronicle* 21⁷ (1981), pp. 178–82.

prefectures: Illyricum, comprising the two dioceses of Dacia and Macedonia; and the East, comprising the five dioceses of Thracia, Pontica, Asiana, Oriens and Aegyptus. Of these, the East, with its varied economic resources and vast extent, its relatively complex and urbanised society, and the praesental character of its *officium*, inevitably assumed a position of overwhelming importance when compared with Illyricum. This position remained unaffected when Justinian, rather than recreate the great central prefecture of Italy with Illyricum and Africa, instead created separate prefectures for Africa in 534, lacking a diocesan structure but including the Balearics and Corsica and Sardinia,[118] and for Italy in 537, comprising the two dioceses of Italia and Urbs Roma.[119]

As might be expected, the production of coinage within the prefectures of Illyricum and the East remained unaffected by the adjustments described above; that within the new prefectures of Africa and Italy, with one significant exception, continued the pattern that had prevailed under the Vandal and Ostrogothic kings. In Africa, the mint at Carthage, itself a Vandal creation, therefore continued the production of gold, silver and copper.[120] In Italy, where the regional mint of Aquileia had closed permanently at the beginning of the fifth century,[121] and the comitatensian one of Milan at the beginning of the sixth,[122] the mint of Rome continued to produce gold and copper,[123] and that of Ravenna produced gold, silver and copper.[124] To the extent that none of the African or Italian mints was ever visited by emperor, *comitatus*, or comitatensian mint, their production of precious-metal coinages appears to have infringed the palatine monopoly still adhered to (the Thessalonican infringement mentioned above being excepted) in the east. A more precise consideration of the pattern of production in Italy, however, leads to an administrative explanation capable of application to both western and eastern infringements and supported by independent evidence. (Pls. 20, 14–21, 4; 21, 11–22, 3)

The Italian gold coinage of Justinian forms two distinct groups, that of his nearer successors only one. Of the two Justinianic groups one, occasionally bearing the explicit mint-mark ROMOB, continues the characteristics seen on the coinage of his Ostrogothic predecessors that is now also attributed to Rome. The other anticipates the characteristics seen in the coinage of his successors that is customarily attributed to Ravenna. The implication seems clear: at some stage of Justinian's reign the production of gold was transferred from Rome, where it had been concentrated by the Ostrogoths, to Ravenna, where it effectively was to be confined by his successors. What therefore has to be

118 *CJ* I.27.I.

119 Procopius, *De Bello Gothico* I.20.20; ed. Haury (Teubner), II, p. 104. Jones, *Later Roman Empire* I, p. 313.

120 Bellinger, *DOC* I, pp. 158–70.

121 Carson, Hill and Kent, *Late Roman Bronze Coinage*, A.D. *324–498*, pp. 65, 75.

122 Kent, 'The Coinage of Theodoric in the Names of Anastasius and Justin I', pp. 67–72 – Theoderic struck gold and silver at Milan in the name of Anastasius only (and therefore up to 518 at the latest). See also: Hahn, *MIB* I, pp. 80–4, 85–7.

123 Bellinger, *DOC* I, pp. 173–9.

124 Bellinger, *DOC* I, pp. 179–86.

explained is the production of gold coinages at the mints of Thessalonica, Carthage and Ravenna. The factor common to all three mints is, of course, that the cities which contained them also contained the headquarters of the regional prefectures in which they stood: Thessalonica the headquarters of the prefecture of Illyricum, Carthage that of the prefecture of Africa, Ravenna that of the prefecture of Italy.[125]

Two pieces of evidence nevertheless suggest that, while the prefectures may have been permitted to infringe the palatine monopoly of gold coining in fact, the fiction of such a monopoly was carefully preserved. When the Carthaginian mint began to issue gold coin after the reconquest of Africa, the *officinae* responsible seem generally to have numbered themselves eleven and twelve (IA and IB),[126] and a Ravennate papyrus dated 572 mentions the presence in that city of a number of *palatini sacrarum largitionum*, including one *v(ir) d(evotissimus) pal(atinus) s(a)c(rarum) l(argitionum) et monitarius auri.*[127] In the first case the *officinae* concerned seem to have been considered merely as extensions of the ten (A–I) into which the palatine mint was divided. In the second the mint staff are explicitly considered as *palatini* – belonging, that is, to the metropolitan palace. What seems to have happened is that mint staff producing gold coinage at prefectural headquarters had either been seconded from the palatine *officium* for that specific purpose, or were at least considered fictively to have been so seconded. By means of this administrative device a palatine monopoly that would otherwise have been seen to be irretrievably infringed was to some extent preserved.

A further piece of evidence, involving the products of the mint of Thessalonica, also suggests the preservation of a sharp distinction between the production of the precious- and base-metal coinages. The sporadic series of fifth- and sixth-century gold solidi attributable to this mint has already been mentioned.[128] The production of a copper coinage seems, however, to have been entirely interrupted during the fifth century.[129] When it hesitantly recommenced under Justin I,[130] the folleis involved bore the mint-mark THЄSSOB.[131] This was, of course, entirely irregular, the form normally being specifically reserved for the gold coinage. The implication is, therefore, that at first it was the *aurifices solidorum* who also produced the new copper coinage, the operatives formerly producing a copper coinage having meanwhile been made redundant. (Pl. 14, 5)

When the full production of a copper coinage recommenced under Justinian, the anomalous denominations involved bore a normal mint-mark ( **TЄS** *vel sim.*) and the letters **SAP** or simply **AP** in the field, the **S** also forming part of the denominational numeral **IS** (= I6).[132] All kinds of fanciful suggestions such as *a(rkhaia) rh(opē)*, or

[125] Hendy, 'Aspects of Coin Production and Fiscal Administration in the Late Roman and Early Byzantine Period', p. 136 n. 1; *idem*, 'On the Administrative Basis of the Byzantine Coinage *c.* 400–*c.* 900 and the Reforms of Heraclius', pp. 142–5.
[126] Bellinger, *DOC* 1, pp. 158–9.
[127] Marini, *I Papiri Diplomatici*, no. 120, p. 185.
[128] See above, p. 398 n. 117.
[129] See above, p. 397 n. 109.
[130] See above, p. 397 n. 110.
[131] Bellinger, *DOC* 1, pp. 46–7.
[132] Bellinger, *DOC* 1, pp. 104–8. D. M. Metcalf, *The Copper Coinage of Thessalonica under Justinian I*, pp. 35–46.

*a(ntiquo) p(ondere)*, or even *a(rca) p(raefectoria) I(llyrici)*, have been made as to the meaning of these letters, most of them ignoring the normal presence of the letter S, or emphasising the very rare and additional presence of other letters such as Ψ or I.[133] Reference to a weight standard on the copper coinage as required by the former is unlikely, although not unparalleled on the gold, silver and billon ones,[134] and there is no evidence at all that the production of coinage of whatever kind, as required by the latter, had been transferred from the *sacrae largitiones* to the praetorian prefecture. What was involved was quite simply, and given the context quite properly, a transfer of responsibility between sub-departments of the *largitiones* – from the *aurifices solidorum*, responsible for the precious-metal coinage, to the *s(crinium) a(d) p(ecunias)*, or more simply *a(d) p(ecunias)*, now once again responsible for the base-metal one.[135] (Pls. 14, 5; 20, 6–9)

In *c.* 565 the list of dioceses or major fiscal units, more regular mints, and their normal products, was therefore as in Table 11.

Two recent attempts to alter this pattern of production, the one to do so fundamentally, the other substantially, at this date and during the immediately subsequent period in the east, and more particularly in the west, totally and largely, respectively, fail to convince. Neither of these attempts is at all adequately supported by reasoning, and while the pattern of production as at present understood may well need adjustment or some degree of rectification, particularly with regard to the confused situation obtaining in the west, a

Table 11. *Major fiscal units, mints and normal products under Justinian (Maps 34, 35)*

| Diocese or fiscal unit | | Mint | Products |
|---|---|---|---|
| Ppo. Italiae | Italia | Ravenna | AV, AR, Æ |
| | Urbs Roma | Rome | Æ |
| Ppo. Africae | Africa | Carthage | AV, AR, Æ |
| Ppo. Illyrici | Dacia | — | — |
| | Macedonia | Thessalonica | AV, Æ |
| Ppo. Orientis | Thracia | — | — |
| | Constantinople | Constantinople | AV,[136] Æ |
| | Pontica | Nicomedia | Æ |
| | Asiana | Cyzicus | Æ |
| | Oriens | Antioch | Æ |
| | Aegyptus | Alexandria | Æ |

133 Metcalf, *The Copper Coinage of Thessalonica under Justinian I*, pp. 15–19.

134 Gold: see below, pp. 449, 466; silver: see below, pp. 449, 468; billon: see below, pp. 463, 469.

135 See above, p. 391 and n. 78.

136 It seems likely that, whereas the AR products of Ravenna and Carthage formed a significant proportion of their total production of coin, those of Constantinople were of a ceremonial nature only: they have therefore not been included in the table.

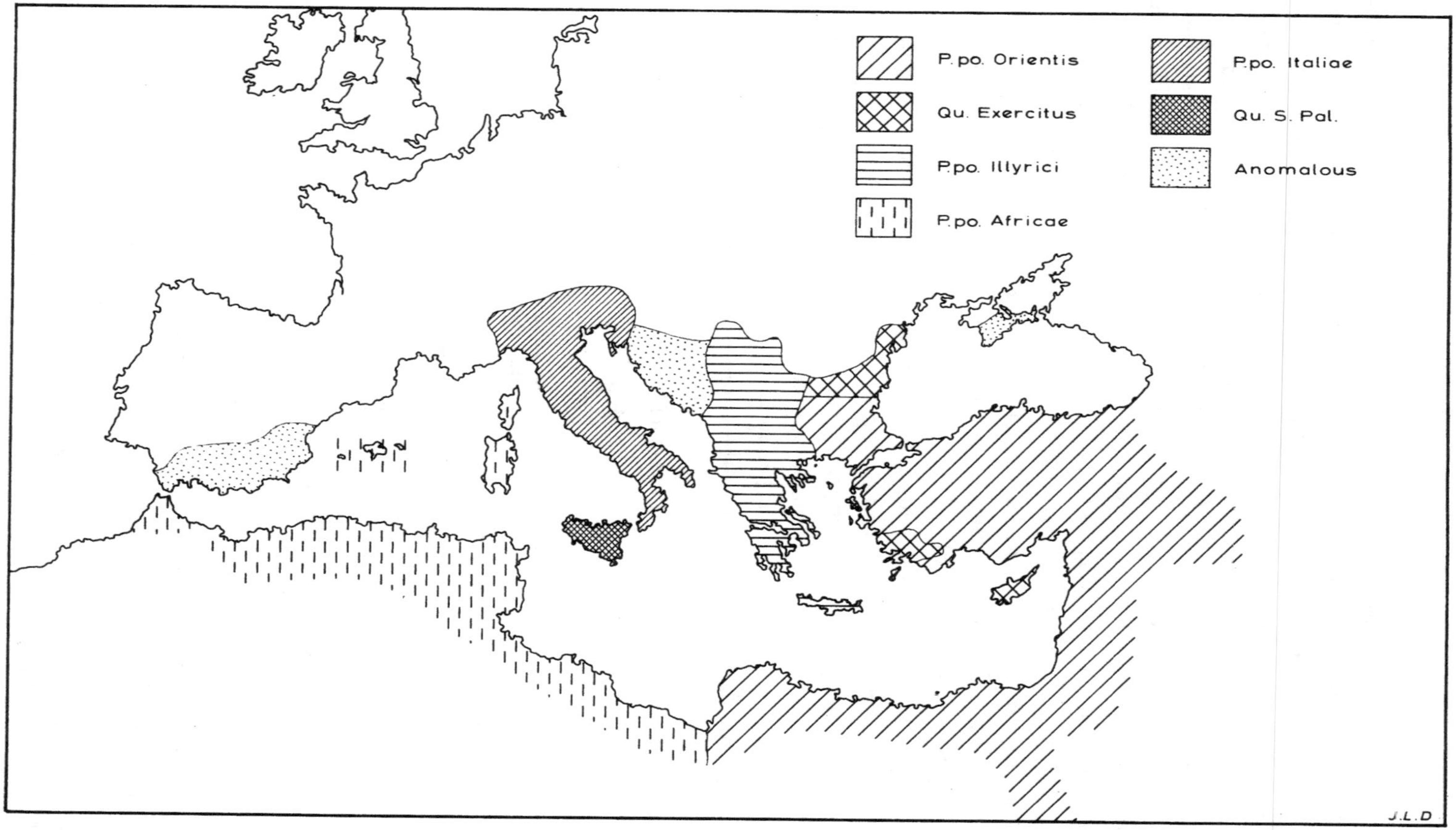


Map 34 The empire: major administrative units, *c.* 527–628/9

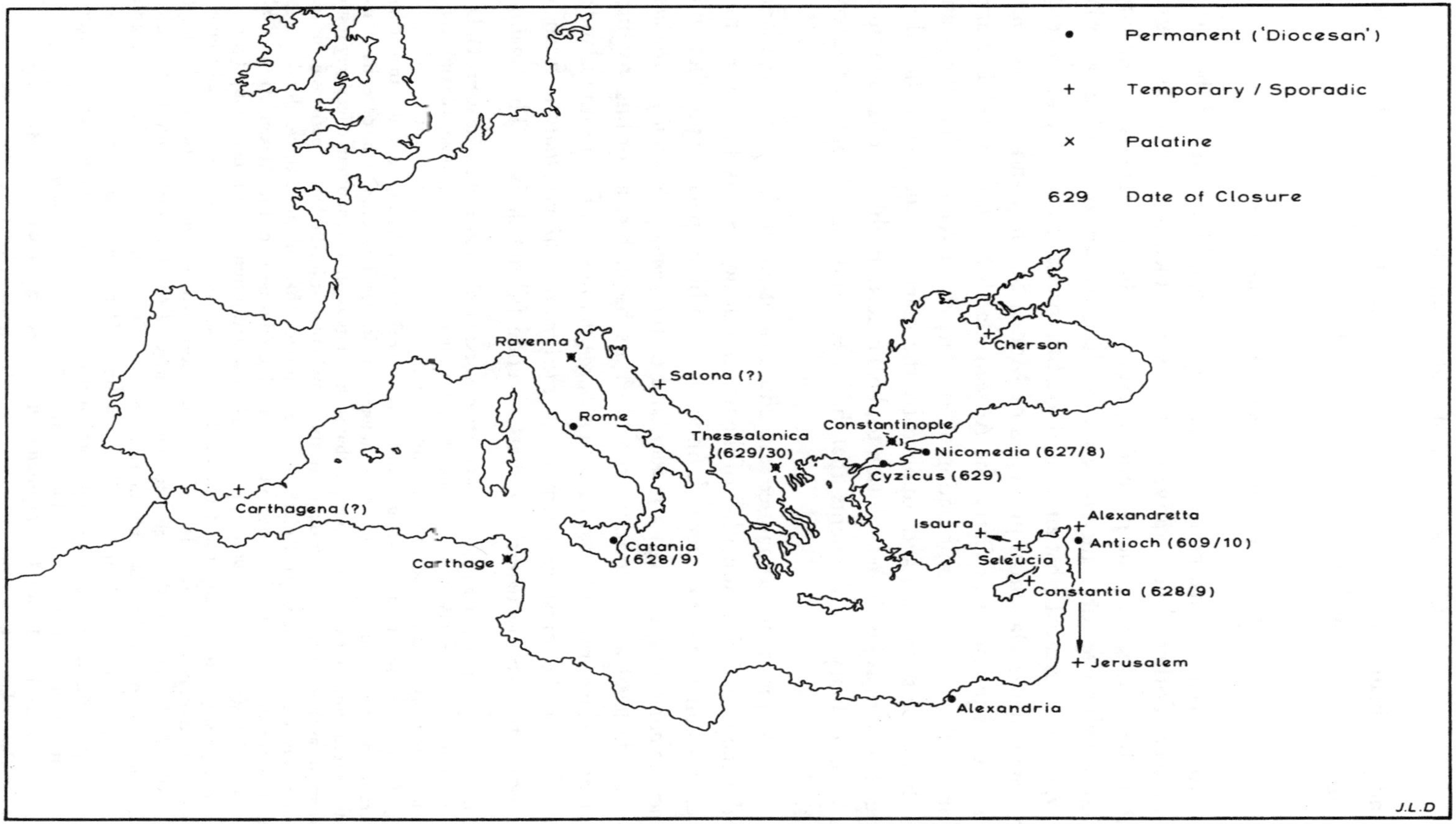


Map 35 The empire: mints, *c.* 527–628/9

virtually indiscriminate proliferation of mints and their products is in the present state of knowledge premature, and is indeed historically unlikely.[137]

### D. *Justinian: Anomalous administrative units*

In addition to the four regional prefectures of Italy, Africa, Illyricum and the East, there existed a number of other administrative units, most of which were creations of Justinian. As several of these units were the piecemeal results of the reconquests of that emperor they tended to exhibit features, including mints, that were to some degree anomalous.

In 536/7, Justinian created what amounted to a fifth prefecture in the *quaestura exercitus*, which consisted of the Danubian provinces of Moesia Secunda and Scythia combined with the maritime provinces of Caria, the Aegean islands and Cyprus.[138] The apparent explanation of this curious combination is that it was intended that the Danubian provinces should be supported and supplied by the maritime ones.[139] It should thus in some respects be seen as Justinian's solution to the Thracian problem of fiscal insufficiency in the face of military requirements that had been enunciated, but not solved, by Anastasius.

When, in 537, Justinian reorganised the administration of Sicily,[140] the island was placed under the jurisdiction of neither of the neighbouring prefects, but 'as if something of a property peculiar to the emperors', under the combined palatine jurisdiction of the *quaestor sacri palatii* acting through a *praetor*, and of the *comes patrimonii per Italiam*. The one provided its legal administration, the other its fiscal, for, according to Justinian: 'ancient custom places the public finances (*publicae functiones*) of that same island under the jurisdiction of the most excellent *comes sacri patrimonii per Italiam*, from whose authority both its taxation (*exactio*) and its revenue (*illatio*) derive'. The *comitiva* was

137 It must be said, at the outset, that in no way do the two works involved share the same status. Of D. Ricotti Prina's *La monetazione aurea delle zecche minori bizantine dal VI al IX secolo* (Rome, 1972), it can be said only, and regrettably, that it is not, and has not generally been accepted as, a work of scholarship. Of Hahn's *MIB* I–III, it must be said that it is not only a work of scholarship, but also that it has made considerable advances in our knowledge of the material and its classification. On the other hand, its critical apparatus is frequently so exiguous as to mean that such things as mint attributions effectively rest on little more than the author's *fiat*, and this is demonstrably nowhere near infallible. It is perhaps in his treatment of the precious-metal coinages, particularly the western ones, that one must above all take issue. Three particular examples may suffice. The existence of a small gold issue at, or for, Alexandria (mm. **ΑΛΞΟΒ**), has long been known (Bellinger, *DOC* I, p. 250). Hahn's attribution of a further group (mm. **CONOB**, *MIB* II, pp. 39–40) is barely supported (although it follows Morrison, *BNC* I, p. 126); indeed some specimens look frankly barbarous. His attribution of gold to Rome under Maurice and Phocas (*MIB* II, pp. 64, 78) is equally tenuous (although it follows Bellinger, *DOC* I, p. 368). With the confusion of the seventh century such examples become more numerous: for example, the attribution of gold to an uncertain mint, possibly either Rome or Alexandria, under Heraclius (*MIB* III, pp. 95–6), demonstrates how apparently whimsical some of his choices are. It may well be that a number of the seventh-century western groups involved are not imperial at all. **ΑΛΞΟΒ**: see below, Pl. 22, 9.

138 Justinian, Novel XLI. John Lydus, *De Magistratibus* II.28–9; ed. Wuensch, pp. 83–5.

139 Jones, *Later Roman Empire* I, p. 280.

140 Justinian, Novel CIV.

apparently an office of Ostrogothic origin, as was its Sicilian jurisdiction,[141] although the special position of the island within the *res privata* is traceable as far back as the *Notitia*.[142] (Map 32)

The province of Dalmatia, reconquered from the Ostrogoths between 535 and 538 and, like Sicily, previously under the jurisdiction of the *comes patrimonii*, seems to have been administered subsequently as an independent unit, before being absorbed into the prefecture of Illyricum by 592.[143]

The areas in southern Spain reconquered from the Visigoths from 552 onwards seem to have been administered by the military, for *magistri militum* and *duces* only are known for them.[144] The imperial possessions in the Crimea – centred on Cherson and, from the reign of Justinian, Bosporus – may have been similarly administered, although Cherson itself, at least, was in the hands of its own city officials.[145] (Map 34)

Of these five administrative units, at least three possessed Justinianic mints. A small issue of copper multiple nummi has been plausibly attributed to a mint in Dalmatia, possibly at Salona where specimens have been found.[146] Salona had, of course, not previously possessed a mint, but the province was the scene of considerable military activity in 549–52 under Germanus and Narses, and, as already mentioned,[147] the *Notitia* records the presence of a regional treasury in the city itself. A Spanish mint, possibly at Carthagena, produced a small and sporadic series of gold tremisses, of which examples are currently known for Justinian, Justin II, Maurice, Phocas, and Heraclius, under the last of whom in *c.* 624 the last Byzantine areas were lost to the Visigoths under Suinthila.[148] The mint of Cherson produced small issues of multiple nummi under Justin I(?), Justinian, Maurice and Heraclius.[149] (Pl. 22, 16–20)

141 Jones, *Later Roman Empire* I, p. 255. 142 See above, p. 377.

143 Jones, *Later Roman Empire* I, p. 255. Stein, *Histoire du bas-empire* II, pp. 801–2.

144 P. Goubert, 'L'administration de l'Espagne byzantine, I, les gouverneurs de l'Espagne byzantine', (*Revue des*) *Études Byzantines* 3 (1945), pp. 127–42; *idem*, 'Administration de l'Espagne byzantine, II (suite), les provinces, les capitales, les villes, les diocèses', (*Revue des*) *Études Byzantines* 4 (1946), pp. 70–110. E. A. Thompson, *The Goths in Spain*, pp. 320–34 (Appendix: 'The Byzantine Province').

145 A. A. Vasiliev, *The Goths in the Crimea*, pp. 70–6.

146 Bellinger, *DOC* I, pp. 187–9.

147 See above, p. 384. It should also be noted that Julius Nepos, the western emperor, had retired to Dalmatia – and presumably to Salona, which seems to have been his power-base – upon his ejection from Italy in 475. A nominal precious-metal coinage seems to have been struck by Odovacer for him in Italy between 476 and his death by assassination in 480. Nepos was presumably actually in charge of Dalmatia itself. See: J. P. C. Kent, 'Julius Nepos and the Fall of the Western Empire', in *Corolla Memoriae Erich Swoboda Dedicata*, at pp. 146–50. See also below, Pl. 11, 13 and 18.

148 Bellinger, *DOC* I, pp. 193 (Justinian), 375 (Maurice). Grierson, *DOC* II.1, pp. 206 (Phocas), 382 (Heraclius). See also: Hahn, *MIB* II, p. 41 (Justin II).

149 Bellinger, *DOC* I, pp. 109 (Justinian), 373–5 (Maurice). Grierson, *DOC* II.1, p. 381 (Heraclius). For Justin I, see: Hahn, *MIB* I, p. 44. The last group certainly has Russian provenances, which favour its mint-attribution, but it might look better under Justin II than under Justin I, so that it would both post-date Justinian's measures and fill in the hiatus beween Justinian and Maurice. It should be noted that imperial activity under Justin I with regard to Bosporus was unsuccessful (Vasiliev, *The Goths in the Crimea*, p. 70).

It is just possible that it was the *quaestura exercitus* that was responsible for the production of a consistent but highly anomalous series of copper multiple nummi extending from at least the reign of Justin II to that of Maurice Tiberius, and seemingly imitating issues of the mints of Constantinople, Nicomedia, Cyzicus, Antioch, Thessalonica and (very curiously) Rome. Certain issues of Justinian himself, including one dated 540/1, may perhaps commence the series. The origins of this series remains unknown, and the precise mechanisms that would have had to have operated for its production are currently difficult to envisage, but it is noticeable that the mints involved – with the admitted exception of Rome, if the identification is correct – are those in regions abutting onto the *quaestura*.[150] (Maps 34, 35)

## E. Later developments: The exarchates and Sicily

The pattern of coin production which Justinian had inherited from his predecessors and which he slightly modified to take account, within the framework dictated by administrative developments, of the problems raised by his reconquests, remained undisturbed in its essentials for the rest of the sixth century. An interesting and possibly significant extension to it nevertheless did occur between 581 and 583. Until that date the African prefecture had produced a gold coinage that seems to have been sporadic and of small volume, and that is today distinguishable from the metropolitan only with difficulty. During the eighth regnal year of Tiberius II and the fifteenth indiction (Dec. 581–Aug. 582) it produced the first of what was to be a much more regular and highly individual series of indictionally dated solidi. During the same regnal year the Italian prefecture began to produce what seems to have been intended as a series of regnally dated solidi.[151] During the first regnal year of Maurice Tiberius (Aug. 582–Aug. 583),

150 The series has long been recognised, but its 'codification' is the work of Hahn: *MIB* II, pp. 49–51 (Justin II), 58 (Tiberius II), 74 (Maurice). But see the remarks of Morrisson in *Revue Numismatique* 17[6] (1975), at pp. 197–8 (review of MIB II), who would connect the series with another (not very similar) one, in the name, or with the types, of Heraclius. One does, nevertheless, wonder whether the earlier series might not be connected with two earlier groups from the reign of Justinian – one consisting of folles and half-folles, dated 540/1–542/3, and attributed by Bellinger (*DOC* I, pp. 171–2) to Constantine in Numidia, a mistake that has generally been admitted; the other consisting of half- and quarter-folles, dated 552/3, and attributed (*DOC* I, pp. 186–7) to Perugia, equally an undoubted mistake. The second of these has been connected by Morrisson (*BNC* I, p. 59) with the Italian campaign of Narses in 552–3, but this would by no means preclude the involvement of the *quaestura exercitus*. In any case, Hahn's description of the later series as in some sense 'military' demonstrates an awareness of the probabilities. See below, p. 411 n. 169, for the *arca* of the *quaest. exerc.*

151 Carthage: P. D. Whitting, 'A Seventh-century Hoard at Carthage', *Numismatic Chronicle* 6[7] (1966), pp. 226, 230, no. B 37. Bellinger, *DOC* I, pp. 353–5. *Contra* Hahn (*MIB* II, p. 54), there is absolutely no reason to believe that the few other known solidi of Tiberius were dated: those of Justin II were certainly not. Ravenna: Bellinger, *DOC* I, p. 289. Hendy, 'On the Administrative Basis of the Byzantine Coinage *c.* 400–*c.* 900 and the Reforms of Heraclius', p. 145 n. 81. Hahn, *MIB* II, p. 54. Again, *contra* Hahn (*op. cit.* p. 54), there is no reason to believe that other solidi were dated.

at the latest, a mint was established at Catania in Sicily, the administrative independence of which island has already been noted, which began to produce probably a gold, and certainly a copper, coinage.[152] These three events clearly denote the application of a marked and consistent policy, and it seems worth considering the possible significance of this policy in a wider context. (Pls. 19, 8; 20, 16; 22, 21)

Following the reconquest of Africa and Italy, the civil administration of these two areas had been confined to their respective praetorian prefects, the military to *magistri militum*. In matters of precedence, a prefect still outranked a *magister* although, where working colleagues, each – as representing a different function – was equal to and independent of the other. In practice, the chronically unsettled state of affairs in the new prefectures, and particularly in Italy after the Lombard invasion of 568, meant that the *magister* inevitably tended to acquire power and influence at the expense of the prefect. At some uncertain stage the existence and direction of this tendency was recognised by the appointment of a military official, generally termed *patricius et exarchus* or similar, who not only headed the military administration with extended powers, but also exercised effective control over the civil.[153] The precise nature and chronology of the evolution or creation of the exarchates of Africa and Italy remains uncertain: even Narses could be quite informally termed *koubikoularios kai exarkhos Rhōmaiōn* by Malalas; but an exarch of Italy is first otherwise mentioned in 584, and an exarch of Africa in 591, both still unfortunately in the entirely casual context of papal letters.[154]

It has generally been assumed, on no explicit evidence, that the first appointments to both exarchates were the work of Maurice. This may have been so, but the ground had at least been well prepared beforehand.

In *c.* 579 the patrician (*axioma basileōs patēr*) Pamphronius appeared at Constantinople having been sent from the Old Rome (*ek tēs presbyteras Rhomēs*) with thirty *kentenaria*

[152] The copper coinage, consisting of quarter- and eighth-folles, of which the former is dated, certainly dates at least from 582/3 (*DOC* I, pp. 304–7). There do exist, however, specimens of an eighth in the name of Tiberius II. These are condemned by Grierson (*DOC* II. 1, p. 44 n. 66) as forgeries, but are accepted by Hahn (*MIB* II, p. 58) as genuine. If the latter is correct, the mint would have been established very late in Tiberius' reign, and probably in 581/2, precisely paralleling events in Carthage and Ravenna. The definition of the gold products of what is probably the same mint (i.e. of Catania) is the work of Hahn (*MIB* II, pp. 63–4). As pointed out by Morrisson in *Revue Numismatique* $17^6$ (1975), at p. 197 (review of *MIB* II), Hahn knew neither of the provenances which would have proved his point, nor of specimens earlier than 601/2, whereas they can now apparently be traced back to 584/5, and even earlier ones may well come to light. Hahn's even more recent denial of the existence of these earlier coins ('More about the Minor Byzantine Gold Mints from Tiberius II to Heraclius', *Numismatic Circular* 87 (1979), p. 553) is merely peevish.

[153] C. Diehl, *Études sur l'administration byzantine dans l'exarchat de Ravenne (568–751)*, pp. 157–84; *idem*, *L'Afrique byzantine: histoire de la domination byzantine en Afrique (533–709)* II, pp. 484–92. Despite their considerable age (1888, 1896), neither of these books has ever really been superseded.

[154] John Malalas, *Chronographia* XVIII; Bonn edn, p. 486. Pelagius II, *Epistolae* I; ed. J.-P. Migne, in *PL* LXXII, at cols 703–5 (*Et exarchus scribit* – Italy). Gregory I, *Epistolae* I.59; MGH, *Ep.* I, pp. 82–3 (*Gennadio patricio et exarcho Africae*).

(3,000 lb) of gold and a request for aid against the Lombards. Tiberius II, distracted by eastern as well as western wars, was unable to send military aid but instead returned the gold, instructing that it should be used either to hire Lombards for service in his eastern wars, thus removing them from the Italian scene, or to bribe the Franks to attack the Lombards.[155]

It has commonly been assumed that Pamphronius' appearance occurred no later than 577 or 578, and this assumption receives some support from the fact that the only source for the event, Menander the Protector, refers to Tiberius as *kaisar*, the title that he held from December 574 until September 578, rather than as *basileus* or *autokratōr*, the titles that might be expected subsequently. On the other hand, it has been pointed out that the obvious occasion to have resulted in the sending of a sum as large as 3,000 lb gold from Rome to Constantinople is the accession of Tiberius as emperor, which would have resulted in the Roman senate sending its customary *aurum oblaticium*.[156] This point in turn receives convincing support from the fact that 3,000 lb gold as a contribution towards a military donative of nine solidi is almost exactly proportional to the 1,600 lb gold which is known to have been sent by the senate as a contribution towards a donative of only five solidi on the occasion of Valentinian II's *decennalia* in 384/5.[157]

The point is rendered more or less incontestable by the fact that 3,000 lb, but in silver, was evidently the contribution expected as *aurum oblaticium* from the Constantinopolitan senate. This emerges from an account of the coronation of Leo I, in 457.[158] The sum was offered by the senators (*synklētikoi*), through the prefect of the City (*eparkhos tēs poleōs*), to the newly crowned emperor, in the form of a written promise (*pittakion*), for there had obviously been no time to collect it. Its identification as *aurum oblaticium* seems assured, and no better example of the imitation of the Roman senate on the part of the Constantinopolitan one, in a financial sense, could be desired. The size of such contributions obviously tended to become formalised, and eventually to become regarded as normative and thus to be imitated.[159]

If, as now seems certain, the 3,000 lb gold was a senatorial *aurum oblaticium*, it would seem to follow that Pamphronius' appearance occurred later than is customarily assumed. Tiberius became emperor in late September 578, sole emperor in early October 578. The news of his accession could not have arrived at Rome until very late in 578, and more probably did not arrive until early in 579. In either case, an appreciable amount of time would then have elapsed while the senatorial offering was collected and before it could be despatched to Constantinople. Pamphronius, its escort, therefore could not have appeared in that city before mid 579.

155 Menander Protector, *Fragmenta* XLIX; ed. Müller, IV, p. 253.
156 Jones, *Later Roman Empire* I, p. 308.
157 See above, p. 175.
158 Constantine Porphyrogenitus, *De Caerimoniis* I.91; Bonn edn, I, p. 415.
159 See above, pp. 197–9.

Tiberius' response to Pamphronius' request was evidently considered unsatisfactory by the Romans, for a short while later, probably in 580, what seems to have been a full scale embassy, composed of representatives of both the senate and the pope, appeared with much the same request.[160] Tiberius was unable to accede fully to the request for the same reason as before, but did send such military forces as he could spare and supplemented these with the bribery of Lombard leaders – with some effect, for a number defected to the imperial side.[161] The date of this apparently second embassy seems fixed by the fact that it was evidently the same as that on which Pelagius II sent the deacon Gregory, later pope, as *apocrisiarius*, probably amongst other things to explain the circumstances of his own election, which had taken place without imperial permission in late November 579.[162]

The application of the consistent policy described above to African, Italian and Sicilian mints between 581 and 583, that is in 581/2 and 582/3, thus falls neatly between the Roman embassies of 579 and 580, and the first mention of an Italian exarch in 584.

It is difficult not to see some connection, however indirect, on the one hand between the embassies and the appointment of an exarch, whatever the precise details and implications of that event, and on the other between the policy applied to the mints and the events bracketing it chronologically. It is even conceivable that the return of the senatorial *aurum oblaticium* in 579 was intended to signal the effective financial independence of the prefecture. Something, at any rate, was 'going on'. For whatever else has arisen and will continue to arise from this chapter, it does seem that major adjustments to minting patterns or practices are likely to have resulted from, and to have reflected, parallel adjustments in fiscal administration, and it does seem likely that the creation of the exarchates, formally a declaration of military supremacy, but inevitably involving a wider degree of general independence, will have entailed just some such adjustments.

## (IV) 610–*c.* 800

### *A. Fiscal administration*

The administrative structure of the developed Byzantine state of the ninth and tenth centuries differed fundamentally, in pattern and emphasis, from that which had characterised the later Roman and early Byzantine state of the fourth to sixth centuries. The precise nature and chronology of the process of change or evolution that must have operated during the seventh or eighth century, or both, in order to bring this difference

[160] It is of course tempting, in view of the fragmentary nature of the evidence, to assume that the two embassies of 579/80 were in fact one and the same.

[161] Menander Protector, *Fragmenta* LXII; ed. Müller, IV, p. 263.

[162] *Liber Pontificalis* LXV (Pelagius II); ed. Duchesne, I, p. 309. *Vita Sancti Gregorii Magni* VII; ed. J.-P. Migne, in *PL* LXXV, at col. 44.

into being, unfortunately remains obscure and indeed even the subject of controversy. The controversy itself is of a class familiar enough in historical studies: whether institutions or practices are to be considered as the responsibility of a single person – and therefore as created at a given moment in time – or whether they are to be seen as the eventual result of an evolutionary development. Its cause is no less familiar: a lack of pertinent evidence. The documentary sources of massive size and varied character surviving from the earlier period have permitted the thorough study and detailed reconstruction of its administrative system. Those surviving from the later period, while scarcely comparable in size or scope, have allowed the recovery of the main features and even some details of its administration. Those of the intervening period have simply failed to survive, and its administrative history therefore remains almost entirely a matter of inference and hence controversy.

The fiscal administration of the developed Byzantine state was dominated by a number of independent palatine bureaux (*sekreta*). Of these *sekreta*, all instruments of both revenue and expenditure, the most important seem to have been the general (*genikon*) and the military (*stratiōtikon*), presided over by auditors (*logothetai*); the treasury (*sakellion*) and the wardrobe (*vestiarion*), presided over by actuaries (*khartoularioi*); and the special (*eidikon*) presided over by an official commonly termed *ho eidikos*, and later termed *logothetēs*.[163] A general supervision over the *sekreta* was exercised by the treasurer (*sakellarios*), who was represented in each *sekreton* by a secretary (*notarios*) of his own.[164] It has been plausibly suggested that when the *sakellarios* – at first merely the head of the appropriate *sekreton* – gained the right of supervision over the other *sekreta*, he left the normal direction of his former charge to the *khartoularios*. The stage at which this occurred nevertheless remains uncertain: both the sixth and eighth centuries have been proposed, although the former seems generally improbable, except perhaps for its very close, for Callinicus, while ranking as *patricius* and acting as *praepositus sacri cubiculi*, still seems to have preserved the primitive function of the office in 'keeping the holy valuables of the imperial *sacellum* (*Augusti servans pia gaza sacelli*)' as late as 565/6, although of course the description may be formulaic. On the other hand, pope Gregory I claimed to be acting

[163] Perhaps still the best general account of the administrative system of the middle Byzantine period, although now outmoded in a number of particular aspects, is J. B. Bury, *The Imperial Administrative System in the Ninth Century*. The most useful modern general work of reference is Oikonomides, *Les listes de préséance byzantines*. For the financial *sekreta*: Bury, *op. cit.* pp. 78–105; Oikonomides, *op. cit.* pp. 312–19. It should perhaps be emphasised that while most late Romanists now accept the overwhelming dominance of the praetorian prefecture in imperial finance, this situation does not seem yet to have filtered through to many Byzantinists, who still have a curious obsession with the count of the sacred largesses. For example, Oikonomides (*op. cit.* p. 312) equates the *sakellarios* with the *c.s.l*, while R. Guilland ('Les logothètes, études sur l'histoire administrative de l'empire byzantin', *Revue des Études Byzantines* 29 (1971), p. 11) equates the *logothetēs tou genikou* with the *c.s.l.* Neither is correct. This is actually important, as until the relative positions of *praefectura* and *comitiva* are understood, the correct derivations of many of the later financial offices will not be properly comprehended.

[164] Philotheus, *Klētorologion*; ed. Oikonomides, p. 113.

as imperial *sacellarius* in paying the daily expenses of his local military as early as 595, suggesting by then a distinct shift in function.[165]

It seems clear that the origins of the *sekreta* are to be found mainly in the extensive *officium* of the former prefecture of the East, and to a lesser extent in those of the sacred bedchamber (*sacrum cubiculum*), and the two palatine *comitivae* (the *sacrae largitiones* and *res privata*).

The *officium* of the prefecture of the East had consisted of a number of *scrinia*. There had existed *scrinia* representing each of the prefecture's constituent dioceses, and another representing the City. A permanent exception to this pattern had been provided by Egypt, which had apparently continued to be represented by the *scrinium* for Oriens after it had become a separate diocese in 367, and a late exception had been provided by Thrace, which seems to have been represented by the *scrinium* for the City after its diocesan vicariate had been withdrawn in 497. There had also existed *scrinia* for public works and for armaments.[166] Two further sub-departments, one dealing with military affairs and hence termed *ton stratiōtikon*, the other dealing with the purchase of corn, had evidently possessed the form, but not the title, of *scrinia*.[167] Each regional prefecture, and the *quaestura exercitus*, had possessed a *scrinium* representing the chest (i.e. a *scrinium arcae*) or gold (i.e. a *scrinium auri*). That at Thessalonica (i.e. of the Illyrian prefecture), termed *arca auri* on a stamped ingot of the fourth century, appears to have been headed by a *curator*.[168] The size and complexity of the eastern *officium* had apparently, however, necessitated the formation of two separate banks: the general (*genikē trapeza*) and the special (*idikē trapeza*).[169] Quite what this distinction involved remains obscure, but it seems probable

[165] E. Stein, 'Untersuchungen zum Staatsrecht des Bas-Empire', *Zeitschrift der Savigny-Stiftung für Rechtsgeschichte, Röm Abt.* 41 (1920), pp. 240–51. Bury, *The Imperial Administrative System*, pp. 84–6. For 565/6: Corippus, *In Laudem Iustini Augusti* IV; ed. Averil Cameron, p. 83. For 595: see below, p. 423 n. 223. The relatively junior nature of the office of *sacellarius*, again during the reign of Justin II, is emphasised by I. Ševčenko, 'The Inscription of Justin II's time on the Mevlevihane (Rhesion) Gate at Istanbul', *Zbornik Radova Vizantoloshkog Instituta* 12 (1970), pp. 4–7. It may be suspected that Bury's candidates for early *sakellarioi* were performing *ad hoc* functions, principally the payment of the military, which later became regularised. It seems that the most rapid increase in these officers' functions and power came with the late sixth and early seventh centuries.

[166] Jones, *Later Roman Empire* I, pp. 449–50. Thrace; see above, pp. 397–8.

[167] Jones, *Later Roman Empire* I, p. 450.

[168] *Ibid.* p. 450. Thessalonica: Iliescu, 'Nouvelles informations relatives aux lingots romains d'or, trouvés en Transylvanie', p. 274: *cur(ator) thes(auri) s(acri) in arc(a) aur(i) ob(ryza)*.

[169] Jones, *Later Roman Empire* I, p. 450. The most complete list of the treasuries occurs in Justin II, Novel I (3–4) (566); Zepoi, *Ius Graeco-Romanum* I, p. 2: *eite tēn genikēn, eite tēn idikēn trapezan tēs sēs endoxotētos tauta hora, ē tēn arkhēn tōn para illyriois hierōn pratiōriōn, ē tou endoxotatou ioustinianou eparkhou tōn epi mysias kai skythias stratiōtikōn katalagōn, ē kai tōn theiōn hēmōn thēsaurōn, ē tou hierōtatou hēmōn tamieiou, ē tou theiou patrimōniou, ē tou megaloprepestatou kouratōros tōn oikiōn*. The *thēsauroi* and *tamieion* were presumably those of the *c.s.l.* and *c.r.p.* respectively. It is perhaps worth noting at this point that the usage *thēsauroi* = *largitiones* (see, for example, above, p. 221), may have briefly impinged even upon the coinage. Certain solidi of Justin II and Tiberius II (578), of Tiberius himself (578–82), and of Maurice (582–602), have a reverse inscription ending ΘS. This was taken by Bellinger (*DOC* I, pp. 263, 281–2, 336–7) as indicating *Th(eoupoli)s*, i.e. the mint of Antioch, which has since been generally abandoned. But the ending could

that each *trapeza* represented a deposit bank through which certain specific funds were directed for the use of specific groups of *scrinia*.

What seems eventually to have happened is that, at some stage of the seventh or eighth century, the *officium* of the prefecture of the East had been divided up, and that the *genikē* and *idikē trapezai*, each with the group of *scrinia* to which it had formerly directed funds, had then been granted independent status as *sekreta*, the *sekreta tou genikou* and *tou eidikou*, under officials with an appropriately enhanced status. The same had presumably happened to the sub-department termed *ton stratiōtikon* which had then become the *sekreton tou stratiōtikou*.[170] Of the two remaining *sekreta*, the *sekreta tou sakelliou* and *tou vestiariou*, the former had presumably derived from the *sacellium*, a sub-department of the *sacrum cubiculum* known to have existed from the reign of Zeno onwards,[171] and the latter from the *sacrum vestiarum*, a sub-department of the *comitiva sacrarum largitionum*.[172] It has been suggested that the *vestiarion* had derived from another sub-department of the *sacrum cubiculum*, the *comitiva sacrae vestis*, known from the reign of Theodosius II onwards,[173] but this is very much less likely. In the first place, the *sacrum vestiarium* or *sacra vestis*, consisting of a *scrinium* with additional *officiales* and *deputati*, had formed the largest of all the sub-departments on the strength of the *officium* of the *comitiva sacrarum largitionum*,[174] and in the second, the minting of coin, a function known to have belonged to the *largitiones*, is also known to have belonged to the *vestiarion*, the master of the mint (*arkhōn tēs kharagēs*) being found on the strength of its *offikion*.[175]

The hypothetical derivations suggested above have at least three major considerations in their favour. Firstly, a derivation of this kind would have been very much in conformity with the known tendency of the prefecture to increase in power and influence. The prefecture, in other words, had eventually reached the point at which it was unwieldy as a single institution, and had consequently been broken down into smaller and more manageable units.[176] Secondly, several of the later *sekreta* fulfilled functions that had lain

indicate *th(ē)s(auroi)*, possibly indicating (unsystematically) the administrative source of the metal. In any case, it is interesting that the list should include Illyricum, but exclude Africa and Italy.

170 Stein, *Studien zur Geschichte des byzantinishchen Reiches*, pp. 149–50. As an awful warning of what can happen if this is not understood (see above, p. 410 n. 163), Guilland, 'Les logothètes, études sur l'histoire administrative de l'empire byzantin', p. 85, derives the following chronological succession: *comes rei privatae = eidikos = ho epi tōn oikeiakōn*. The *c.r.p.* seems in fact to have evolved into the *prōtovestiarios* who headed the *oikeiakon vestiarion* (see above, p. 199 n. 235); the *eidikon* had nothing to do with imperial (private) wealth, although it is not an uncommon fallacy that it did (see below, p. 433).

171 Jones, *Later Roman Empire* II, p. 567. Bury, *The Imperial Administrative System*, pp. 84–5.

172 *N.Dig.Occ.* XI.94. *N.Dig.Or.* XIII.28; ed. Seeck, pp. 153, 36.

173 Jones, *Later Roman Empire* II, p. 567.

174 *CJ* XII.23.7 (13, 15).

175 Philotheus, *Klētorologion*; ed. Oikonomides, p. 121. The mention by Constantine Porphyrogenitus (*De Caerimoniis* I (*Appendix*); Bonn edn, p. 502) of *vestomiliarēsia* being distributed in a triumph of Basil I also suggests that such coins were either produced, or stored, or both, in the *vestiarion*. I owe this latter reference to the kindness of Michael McCormick. See also below, p. 427 and n. 245.

176 Stein, *Studien zur Geschichte des byzantinischen Reiches*, p. 147.

within the competence of earlier and similarly named sub-departments. The *genikon*, for instance, was certainly responsible for the assessment and collection of land-tax (*dēmosios kanōn*), just as the prefecture certainly, and the *genikē trapeza* probably, had dealt with that of the *indictio*. The connection between the *vestiarion*, the *sacrum vestiarium*, and the minting of coin has already been mentioned. Thirdly, the officials who had headed the earlier fiscal institutions seem to disappear at much the same time as those who were to head the later ones appear. The last known mention of a prefect of the East occurs in 629,[177] that of a *comes sacrarum largitionum* in 605.[178] The *sakellarios* seems to have increased appreciably in significance during the first half of the seventh century,[179] and the first known mention of a *logothetēs* with enhanced status – appropriate to an independent *sekreton*, in this case possibly the *stratiōtikon* – occurs in 626.[180]

It is also noticeable at this same period that the systematic imposition of five-fold control-stamps (*sphragidai*) upon articles of silver plate – a practice associated with the *largitiones* from the reign of Anastasius onwards – begins to decline and show signs of disintegration.[181]

The changes in the structure of metropolitan fiscal administration described above were accompanied by parallel, but not necessarily exactly contemporaneous, ones in regional administration. It is the chronology and nature of these latter which has proved so controversial. Nevertheless it is the two sets of changes taken together which lend the administrative structure of the developed Byzantine state its distinctive character. For whereas the earlier structure had been based on a relatively small number of major metropolitan institutions (the two *comitivae* and, as it were only coincidentally, the eastern prefecture) and a comparatively large one of regional administrative tiers (prefectural, diocesan and provincial), the later was based on a larger number of metropolitan institutions (the five *sekreta*) and a single regional tier only: that of the theme (*thema*).

The creation or emergence of the theme as a territorial circumscription and administrative unit is, as mentioned above, the subject of controversy; and one to which it is not intended that this series of studies should contribute – or, at any rate, in more than the most basic and tentative of fashions. Nevertheless, it is worth noting, even if for the record only, that one school of thought, relying largely upon two entries in Theophanes' *Chronographia*, would place the creation of the theme as a territoral circumscription, and perhaps even as an administrative unit, as early as the years 621 and

[177] Heraclius, Novel XXV.10; Zepoi, *Ius Graeco-Romanum* I, p. 37: *tois endoxotatois...tōn anatolikōn hierōn praitōriōn hyparkhois*. All attempts to take the office later are implausible.

[178] *Chronicon Paschale*; ed. L. Dindorf (Bonn edn), p. 696: *Athanasios komēs largitiōnōn*.

[179] Bury, *The Imperial Administrative System in the Ninth Century*, pp. 84–5.

[180] *Chronicon Paschale*; Bonn edn, p. 721: *Theodosios ho endoxotatos patrikios kai logothetēs*.

[181] Dodd, *DOS* VII, pp. 31, 45.

622 – very much the kind of date which, as it happens, is also implied for the changes in metropolitan administration.[182]

The clear and consistent direction of these changes taken together was towards centralisation, and this was confirmed and reinforced by the limitations imposed upon the thematic tier of administration. For although the theme had, or came to acquire, territorial and administrative implications as well as purely military ones, it did not acquire an independent fiscal structure and existence. To be sure, it had its resident fiscal officials, such as the *prōtonotarios tou thematos*, who seems to have headed its civil administration and to have been particularly concerned with provisioning its military forces, and the *khartoularios tou thematos*, who seems to have been concerned with maintaining its military registers.[183] But although these officials recognised the authority of the *stratēgos*, the civil and military commander, within his theme, the former was also responsible to the *sakellion*, and the latter to the *stratiōtikon*.[184] Of the officials charged with control, calculation and collection of the main heads of taxation, and particularly the land-tax, the *epoptai thematōn*, the *exisōtai*, and the *dioikētai*, all except the last appear to have been sent out from the capital for the duration of particular missions only, and all were in any case also responsible to the *genikon*.[185]

The position is well epitomised by Leo VI in his *Taktika*:[186] 'It is on the one hand necessary that they [the *prōtonotarios, khartoularios*, etc.] should submit to the *stratēgos* in some matters, but it is on the other deemed safer that they should present the accounts (*logoi*) relating to the areas under their direction to Our Majesty [or presumably rather to the appropriate metropolitan *sekreton*], so that in this way We may learn of the condition and direction of Our civil and military administration.'

### B. *Mints: Continuity and disruption (602–27/8)*

It is against the background of these changes that various adjustments in the pattern of coin production taking place over the period *c*. 627–*c*. 630 should ultimately be seen.

The pattern of coin production as established by Diocletian, and as somewhat modified during the course of the fourth to sixth centuries, remained intact as late as the reign

[182] The notorious entries are Theophanes, *Chronographia*; ed. de Boor, I, pp. 302 (*Hērakleios...metēnegke ta strateumata tēs Eurōpēs epi tēn Asian kai dienoeito tē synergia tou theou kata Persidos khōrēsai*), 303 (*Enteuthen de epi tas tōn thematōn khōras aphikomenos synelege ta stratopeda kai prosetithai autois nean strateian*). It does not seem worthwhile listing here even the major items of the vast literature to which these entries have ultimately given rise. See, however, below, pp. 621–62.

[183] Oikonomides, *Les listes de préséance byzantines*, pp. 315 (*prōtonotarios*), 361, 364 (*khartoularios*).

[184] Philotheus, *Klētorologion*; ed. Oikonomides, pp. 121 (*prōtonotarioi*), 115 (*khartoularioi*).

[185] *Ibid.* pp. 113 (*epoptai*), 114 (*dioikētai*). For the *exisōtai*: H. Ahrweiler, 'Recherches sur l'administration de l'empire byzantin aux IX$^{e}$–XI$^{e}$ siècles', *Bulletin de Correspondance Hellénique* 84 (1960), p. 44, where the inclusion of *exisōtai* is plausible.

[186] Leo VI, *Taktika* IV.31; *PG* CVII, at col. 705.

of Phocas, towards the end of which it was temporarily disrupted by the revolt of the Heraclii (608–10). Copper coinage of Phocas is known from the regional mints of Thessalonica, Nicomedia, Cyzicus, Antioch, Alexandria(?), Carthage, Catania, Rome and Ravenna; gold, or gold and silver, from those of Thessalonica, Carthage, Catania and Ravenna.[187] The revolt of the Heraclii left traces of its progress in anomalous issues of copper from two mints presumably set up to cater for military needs, Alexandretta and Constantia(?) in Cyprus, and similar issues of gold from Alexandria.[188] With the successful conclusion of the revolt and the resultant accession of Heraclius, these anomalous features were, as had always previously happened in similar circumstances, speedily eliminated. (Map 35)

It has been supposed that the existence of a copper coinage dated to the ninth regnal year of Phocas (i.e. to Nov. 610–Nov. 611), probably from the mint of Cyzicus, possibly from that of Antioch, results from the abortive resistance put up by Comentiolus, the brother of Phocas, to the imposition of the Heraclian régime after 5 October 610. Comentiolus, based on Ancyra, seems briefly to have extended his control as far as Bithynia (although not, apparently, including Cyzicus), but there is no evidence whatsoever for his having controlled Antioch. Nor is there any good reason to believe that, had he struck coin, he would have done so in the name of the now deceased Phocas. Most probably, the date involved merely denotes confusion (possibly contemporary, possibly modern) between the numerals Ч (= 5) and ϛ (= 6), which form one element of it, but it is certainly possible that dies really had been prepared for an imminent ninth year and had been used in anticipation.[189]

The further, and very recently discovered, existence of a mint at Jerusalem, probably producing gold and certainly producing copper over the period *c.* 608–*c.* 615, almost certainly, in its earlier stages at least, reflects the appointment of Bonosus as *comes Orientis* by Phocas in 608. Originally appointed to put down civil disturbances in Antioch, he is subsequently found based on Caesarea (of Palestine) leading the abortive resistance to Heraclian forces in Palestine and Egypt. In its later stages, under Heraclian control, it probably reflects the equally abortive resistance to the invading Persians who took the

[187] Grierson, *DOC* II.1, under appropriate mint-headings. For Catania (gold), see: Hahn, *MIB* II, p. 78 ('Sicily'). The 'anomalous' mint of Carthagena (?), producing tremisses, should also not be forgotten (see above, p. 405 n. 148).

[188] Grierson, *DOC* II.1, pp. 207–8, 212–15. Morrisson (*BNC* I, p. 246) adds tremisses to Grierson's Alexandrian solidi – correctly. Hahn (*MIB* II, pp. 85–7) gives some of the Alexandrian gold (including the tremisses) to Cyprus, and the entirety of the Alexandrettan copper to Alexandria – both incorrectly. G. Rösch, 'Der Aufstand der Herakleioi gegen Phokas (608–610) im Spiegel numismatischer Quellen', *Jahrbuch der Österreichischen Byzantinistik* 28 (1979), pp. 51–62, adds little that is new.

[189] Grierson, *DOC* II.1, pp. 182–3, nos. 73–6 (and notes), where the obvious, and correct, conclusion (i.e. confusion or anticipation) is drawn. For the rest: W. E. Kaegi, 'New Evidence on the Early Reign of Heraclius', *Byzantinische Zeitschrift* 66 (1973), pp. 317–18; *idem*, 'Two Notes on Heraclius', *Revue des Études Byzantines* 37 (1979), p. 224.

city after a short siege in 614/15. The staff of the mint at Jerusalem was presumably derived from that of the mint of Antioch (the city being the headquarters of the *comes*) possibly by wholesale transfer. This, of course, would go far towards explaining both why the mint of Antioch never struck coin in the name of Heraclius, and why it was found necessary to set up a temporary mint at nearby Alexandretta during the revolt of the Heraclii.[190] (Pl. 16, 4–14)

The extraordinary vicissitudes that marked the reign of Heraclius himself in any case inevitably had repercussions upon the production of coinage. It seems probable that the setting up of a mint at Seleucia in Isauria in 615/16 for the production of copper was due to military needs, perhaps being causatively or functionally connected with the existence of an imperial factory (*fabrix*) – probably for the production of arms – there. Its transfer to Isaura itself in 617/18, and its suppression in the same, or in the following, year (618/19*), were in any case presumably due to enemy – i.e. Persian – activity.[191] The setting up of another mint at Constantia(?) in Cyprus in 626/7 for the production of copper was probably also due to military needs.[192] A military explanation for the setting up of these last two mints is also rendered particularly plausible by the report that Heraclius had a copper statue melted down and the proceeds sent off to the Pontus for the recruitment of an army.[193] (Pl. 16, 9, 15–16)

But production at even the more regular regional mints was interrupted: no coinage is known either for Nicomedia between 617/18 and 625/6, or for Cyzicus between 614/15 and 625/6.[194] No coinage is known for certain for Antioch after 609/10, although the temporary operation of nearby Alexandretta mentioned above may have slightly extended the region's supply.[195] Coinage is known for Alexandria, but that issued between *c.* 619 and *c.* 628 is wholly anomalous in character.[196] The explanation of these latter anomalies is again in the first two cases certainly, and in the other two probably, to be found in disruption or actual occupation by Persian forces. (Map 35)

In view of all this, the alternative proposition that the issue of base-metal coin in the north-eastern Mediterranean over the period 617/18–628/9 was a reasonably co-ordinated

* I owe knowledge of the so far unique coin (a follis) of this year, seen in the bazaar at Silifke, to Jim Russell.

190 M. F. Hendy and S. Bendall, 'Bonosus, *Comes Orientis*, and the Mints of Antioch and Jerusalem under Phocas and Heraclius' (in preparation). The gold solidi mainly involved have long been known, but attributed elsewhere: to Alexandria by Grierson (*DOC* II.1, pp. 332–4 (Heraclius)) and by Morrisson (*BNC* I, p. 236 (Phocas), p. 292 (Heraclius)); and to Cyprus by Hahn (*MIB* II, p. 77 (Phocas), III, pp. 89–90 (Heraclius)).

191 Grierson, *DOC* II.1, pp. 327–30. *Fabrix*: Zacos and Veglery, *Byzantine Lead Seals* I.2, p. 727, no. 1136: *tēs phabrikos Seleukias*.

192 Grierson, *DOC* II.1, pp. 330–1.

193 See above, p. 229 and n. 55.

194 Grierson, *DOC* II.1, pp. 231, 320, 325–6.

195 It may have needed to, if, as seems likely, the mint of Antioch had indeed been transferred to Jerusalem (see above, pp. 415–16 and n. 190).

196 Grierson, *DOC* II.1, pp. 336–7.

affair, commencing in Cyprus (610/11), and continuing at Seleucia (615–18), Isaura (618/19) and Antioch (618–26), and again in Cyprus (626–9), is an unrealistic and unacceptable one. The material on which it relies, including what are clearly barbarous and derivative copper folles, and an otherwise completely unknown Byzantine recovery of Antioch from the Persians, simply cannot stand up to detailed examination.[197]

### C. *Mints: The Heraclian reforms in the east (628/9)*

With the defeat of the Avar attack upon the capital in 626, the retreat of the Persians from Asia Minor, and their catastrophic defeats of 627 and 628, the restoration of the modified Diocletianic pattern of production was at least rendered possible. Indeed, such a restoration seems originally to have been intended, for coinage is once more known for both Nicomedia and Cyzicus in 625/6, and that issued by Alexandria lost its anomalous character immediately upon the imperial recovery of Egypt in 628.

Then, quite suddenly, between 628/9 and 629/30, this restoration was halted and the modified Diocletianic pattern of production then very largely dismantled. It may well be no coincidence that the year 627/8 was the first of a new indictional cycle.[198] The date, extent and limitations of the dismantling are best seen in a list of major fiscal units, regional mints, and their latest known coins (Table 12).[199]

Individual explanations for all or a number of the mint closures revealed by the list above can no doubt be produced: that Thessalonica had certainly long been isolated by Slavs and Avars;[200] that Nicomedia and Cyzicus, or their surrounding areas, or both, had probably been devastated by Persians;[201] that Antioch had certainly had its own internal disruptions;[202] and that Constantia(?), which had only recently been set up, had possibly fulfilled its military functions.[203]

All, or a number, of these explanations may indeed contain an element of truth, but they cannot nevertheless disguise the fact that the closures as a whole formed part of a conscious and consistent policy, and that that policy was an administratively based one. The former conclusion is derived from the programme of closures having been combined with the doubling of the weight standard of the metropolitan copper coinage, to be

197 The temptation to assign a coinage to Antioch after 609/10 has long proved irresistible, the attempt to prove regional co-ordination is recent: W. R. O. Hahn, 'Minting Activity in the Diocese of Oriens under Heraclius', *Numismatic Circular* 85 (1977), pp. 307–8 (with refs to previous works).

198 Grumel, *La chronologie*, p. 246.

199 The table is after Hendy, 'On the Administrative Basis of the Byzantine Coinage *c.* 400–*c.* 900 and the Reforms of Heraclius', p. 149, and is based on Grierson, *DOC* II.1, now slightly modified by Hahn, *MIB* II. Additional material may well come to light in future, but it is extremely unlikely to alter the general pattern. If the dates eventually stand exactly as in the table, they may be taken as suggesting that peripheral mints (Catania and Constantia) were affected first, and central ones just very slightly later.

200 See above, p. 79.

201 See above, p. 416.

202 See above, pp. 415–16.

203 See above, p. 416.

Table 12. *Major fiscal units, and the closure of mints, under Heraclius (Map 35)*

| Diocese or fiscal unit | | Mint | Latest known coins |
|---|---|---|---|
| Ppo. Italiae | Italia | Ravenna | → |
| | Urbs Roma | Rome | → |
| Ppo. Africae | Africa | Carthage | → |
| Com. S. Patrim. | Sicilia | Catania | 628/9 |
| Ppo. Illyrici | Macedonia | Thessalonica | 629/30 |
| Ppo. Orientis | Pontica | Nicomedia | 629/30(?) |
| | Asiana | Cyzicus | 629/30 |
| | Oriens | Antioch | 609/10 |
| | Aegyptus | Alexandria | → |
| Qu. Exercitus | Cyprus | Constantia(?) | 628/9 |

mentioned in the eighth chapter of this book,[204] and from the tightness of the chronology of the programme itself. The latter is derived from the consideration that, while all regional mints outside the exarchates of Africa and Italy were affected (Alexandria, in almost traditional fashion, being excepted), none within them was.

The crucial case is that of Sicilian Catania, the island having remained untouched by the disruptions of the preceding years, the mint having nevertheless been the only western one affected by the programme of closures. The reason for the latter is, of course, that the island and its mint lay outside African or Italian jurisdiction, coming rather under palatine administration.[205] The programme was, then, not only combined with other measures, but also abrupt in its application and administratively defined in its extent and limitations. Its immediate effect was to leave Constantinople as virtually the sole eastern source of coinage.

The dismantling of the eastern section of the modified Diocletianic pattern of coin production, with its still pronounced regional emphasis, between 628/9 and 629/30, therefore inevitably implied a radical change in the method by which coinage, and particularly copper coinage, was supplied to the regions. The chronology of this change, and the evolution of an alternative method of supply, are again best seen in the case of Sicily.

Three classes of what on good evidence appear to be Constantinopolitan folles, dated 629/30–630/1, 630/1–641, and 643/4, bear the large letters **SCL**$^{s}$ or **SC**$^{s}$ – both clearly forming abbreviations for **SICILIA** – either as a countermark or as an integral part of their design. It has been plausibly suggested that coins of the first class were manufactured at Constantinople, consigned in batches to Sicily, and countermarked there with dies made at Catania before being put into circulation; that those of the second were manufactured at Constantinople and countermarked there before being consigned to Sicily and put into

[204] See below, pp. 498–9, and Pl. 17,21. [205] See above, pp. 404–5, 406–9.

circulation; and that those of the third were manufactured at Constantinople specifically for use in Sicily, their design incorporating the countermarks of the other two classes, and that they were then consigned to the island and put into circulation.[206] The three classes therefore form a methodological progression in their manufacture and supply.

Now it is unlikely on general grounds that the countermarking of the first class of these Constantinopolitan folles took place appreciably later than 631, the latest date represented on its coins. Therefore, in a matter of at most three years, between 628 and 631, the supply of copper coinage to Sicily had changed from that by regional mint to that by consignment from the capital. (Pl. 18, 9–12)

A class of Constantinopolitan folles dated 639/40–640/1 bears the mint-mark **CON**$^{\Theta}$, and another datable to 666–8 bears the mint-mark **Θ**. In both cases the normal mint-mark **CON** has been replaced by one including or consisting of the letter **Θ**. It has been suggested that, in a manner similar to the consigned 'Sicilian' coins mentioned above, both classes were manufactured at Constantinople before being consigned to and put into circulation at Thessalonica.[207] Much the same has been suggested of certain other classes of roughly contemporary gold and silver coins bearing the letter **Θ** as a prominent additional feature.[208]

As it happens, the result of the alternative method of supply outlined above and exemplified in the consigned 'Sicilian' and 'Thessalonican' coins can itself be seen in a body of excavation material: that from Athens. There, as at most or all other excavated sites outside Constantinople, coins of the late seventh- and early eighth-century emperors are, with spasmodic exceptions, generally rare. The pattern is as listed in Table 13.

The abnormal feature of the list is to be found in the presence of a relatively high number of Constantinopolitan decanummia of Philippicus and Leo III: two of the spasmodic exceptions to the general rarity of late seventh- and early eighth-century coins mentioned above. The significance of this abnormality emerges on examination of the coins of Philippicus for, although the sixty-one pieces came from many different sections of the excavations, the imprint of only six obverse dies has been observed on thirty-one better preserved pieces. This quite extraordinary degree of concentration is explicable only on the supposition that the decanummia involved represent the remnant of a body of

206 Grierson, *DOC* II.1, pp. 355–6 (Class 2), 356–7 (Class 3), II.2, pp. 392, 399. For the revised attribution of the third class to Constans II rather than to Heraclonas, see: G. E. Bates, 'Constans II or Heraclonas?', *American Numismatic Society Museum Notes* 17 (1971), pp. 141–61. Hahn (*MIB* III, pp. 118–19) claims plausibly that certain examples of the second class were countermarked in Ravenna and consigned to Sicily, which would mean that the prefecture of Italy was also involved on the occasion, which is clearly interesting.

207 Grierson, *DOC* II.1, pp. 299, 305–6, II.2, p. 466.

208 Grierson, *DOC* II.1, p. 37. It may be suggested that, along the same lines, solidi of Heraclius and Constans II with a prominent X ending the reverse inscription were manufactured at Constantinople and consigned to Cherson. Hahn (*MIB* III, pp. 89, 126) tentatively attributes these coins to Cherson itself, which is implausible, as they do not in any other way appear very different from normal metropolitan pieces, and the explanation above would fit much better.

Table 13. *Copper coins from the Athenian excavations, 698–741 (after Thompson)*

| Emperor | 40 num. | 20 num. | 10 num. |
|---|---|---|---|
| Tiberius III (698–705) | 1 | — | — |
| Justinian II (second reign: 705–11) | 2 | 4 | — |
| Philippicus (711–13) | — | — | 61 |
| Anastasius II (713–15) | — | 4 | — |
| Theodosius III (715–17) | — | — | |
| Leo III (717–41) | — | — | 22 |

metropolitan coinage manufactured – or at least put by – specifically for use in Athens, transported without an appreciable admixture of extraneous coinage, and put into circulation there by whatever the current means were. The fact that the distribution-map shows a distinct concentration along the walls suggests that these means will have involved the military at some (probably early) stage.[209]

It cannot but be noticed that the point at which the changes in metropolitan and perhaps regional fiscal administration outlined at the beginning of this section seem to have occurred is very much the same as that at which the eastern section of the modified Diocletianic pattern of coin production was dismantled. The third decade of the seventh century seems to have been crucial for each of the elements involved, and the beginning of a new indictional cycle and the return of Heraclius to the capital in 629 after an absence of six years seem likely to have been of particular significance for the numismatic element. The shift of emphasis in fiscal administration and coin production, from a pattern retaining a still pronounced regional bias, to one exhibiting an even more pronounced degree of centralisation, was also identical in both cases.

The clear implication is, surely, that just as the creation of a particular administrative structure by Diocletian had been reflected in the pattern of contemporary coin production and supply, so the abandonment of that structure in favour of another by Heraclius was now also reflected in the coinage. The parallel is throughout too close and consistent to have resulted from mere coincidence, and can be ignored or denied only if it is deliberately mutilated by being forced into some partial and entirely meaningless chronological framework.[210] Its existence is indeed only logical: a phenomenon dependent above all upon the fact that it was one of the major fiscal institutions of the day that produced the coinage.

[209] M. Thompson, *The Athenian Agora* II, *Coins*, p. 71; *idem*, 'Some Unpublished Bronze Money of the Early Eighth Century', *Hesperia* 9 (1940), pp. 359–62, 363–9. For an explanation: below, pp. 659–62.

[210] See, for example: M. Fulford, 'Coin Circulation and Mint Activity in the Late Roman Empire: Some Economic Implications', *Archaeological Journal* 135 (1978), pp. 67–114 (attempting to prove, on the basis of archaeological material, that coinage in the fourth century was produced mainly as a response to the 'fluctuation of regional economies', fails to see that features of production, distribution and circulation,

## *D. Mints: Disintegration in the west (to 878)*

Despite the dismantling of the eastern section of the modified Diocletianic pattern of coin production, the western section, that contained within the exarchates of Africa and Italy, remained more or less intact throughout the reign of Heraclius: the mint of Carthage therefore continued to produce gold, silver and copper;[211] that of Ravenna the same;[212] and that of Rome copper only.[213]

The result was a clear distinction between the situation obtaining in the east, including the Balkans, and that in the west. This distinction was further emphasised when the Diocletianic pattern within Italy was itself radically altered during the reign of Constans II. Ravenna ceased to be the sole mint for precious metals and the volume of its products fell commensurably.[214] From then on Rome also struck in precious metals[215] and was joined by two newly created mints: Syracuse, which was presumably created subsequent to the despatch of the latest consigned 'Sicilian' folles in 643/4 and which struck in gold as well as copper;[216] and Naples, which was probably created after the appointment of the city's first duke, Basilius, in 661/2 and which also struck in gold and copper.[217] The earliest known gold positively attributable to Naples is that of Leontius but it is likely that earlier material will eventually be identified.[218]

A significant particular feature of these alterations is that for the first time Sicily was treated as an integral part of Italy for the production of coinage, and not as a dependency

are not necessarily identical). See also the ignorant remarks of G. L. Duncan in *Numismatic Chronicle* 21⁷ (1981), at p. 202 (review of King (ed.), *Imperial Revenue, Expenditure and Monetary Policy in the Fourth Century* A.D.), asserting without argument that any correlation between mint siting and the diocesan system is 'probably no more than a coincidence'; the assertion is so absurd as to be not worth challenging.

211 Grierson, *DOC* II.1, pp. 343–52.

212 *Ibid.* pp. 365–80.

213 *Ibid.* pp. 362–5. Hahn tentatively attributes gold to Rome or Alexandria (see above, p. 404 n. 137), and silver to the former (*MIB* III, p. 100), which is possible, but not persuasive.

214 Compare Grierson, *DOC* II.1, pp. 365–71 (Heraclius) and *idem*, II.2, pp. 506–8 (Constans II)

215 Grierson, *DOC* II.2, pp. 501–3.

216 *Ibid.* pp. 485–93. The volume of Syracusan gold is really quite extraordinarily large, right from the beginning, and not only while Constans himself was actually resident there (663–8). It may nevertheless well be that he was receiving funds (presumably in the form of bullion) from outside, for the fact that his assassin, the usurper Mezezius (668), issued solidi in Syracuse that differ in no appreciable way from the normal metropolitan style, but differ very clearly from the contemporary Syracusan one, renders it very probable that some metropolitan moneyers had been drafted from the capital to Syracuse. Presumably imperial and regional funds were kept distinct, metropolitan moneyers dealing with the former, Syracusan ones with the latter. Whether this instance is sufficient to prove a wholesale reversion to the travelling, or comitatensian, mint, of the preceding period, is quite unclear, as the circumstances were most extraordinary. See: W. R. O. Hahn, 'Mezezius in peccato suo interiit: Kritische Betrachtungen zu einem Neuling in der Münzreihe der byzantinischen Kaiser', *Jahrbuch der Österreichischen Byzantinistik* 29 (1980), pp. 61–70. Hahn's reservations as to the genuineness of these coins are understandable, but most probably misplaced. For an example, see below, Pl. 26, 8.

217 Grierson, *DOC* II.2, p. 500 (copper).

218 *Ibid.* p. 620. Hahn (*MIB* III, pp. 155, 169) now tentatively attributes gold to the mint under Constantine IV and Justinian II, which is not impossible.

of the palatine administration. Perhaps their most significant general feature is the direction that they took: one which was diametrically opposed to that taken by those which had occurred in the east, and which was therefore centrifugal not centripetal. There seems no doubt but that they reflected, and to a very real extent must have confirmed, the contemporary political and therefore presumably fiscal fragmentation of the Italian peninsula caused by its division between Byzantines and Lombards.[219]

In contrast to the situation in Italy, the pattern of coin production within the exarchate of Africa remained the same virtually up until the Arab conquest in 695/8. This contrast was no doubt due to the fact that, despite incessant Berber attacks from the interior tending to reduce Byzantine control to the coastal areas, and later Arab attacks from the east, the essential territorial integrity of the exarchate remained intact throughout.[220] Nevertheless, shortly before the Arab conquest, the mint of Carthage seems to have been moved to Sardinia – presumably to Cagliari, its capital – which had always been included within the reconstituted prefecture and exarchate. The precise stage at which this move occurred remains uncertain: Sardinian products become identifiable during the first reign of Justinian II, and a date of 692/3 has been suggested, although Carthaginian products may date as late as 695.[221] (Pl. 21, 10)

In view of the apparent complexity of the Italian pattern of production from the first half of the seventh century onwards, when compared with the African, it is perhaps worth repeating that this complexity was determined not by considerations of economic prosperity but by the necessities of political fragmentation. The contemporary products of Ravenna and Rome are consistently rare: they were presumably never issued more than spasmodically and in minimal quantities. The same holds good for the products of Naples and Sardinia. The products of Syracuse and Carthage are less rare, but gold from the former mint had tailed off markedly by the beginning of the eighth century, and that from the latter by the end of the seventh. The cause was probably the same in both cases, and is ultimately to be found in Arab attacks.

The mint of Ravenna continued production on up until the final disappearance of the exarchate itself as a result of its conquest by the Lombard king Aistulf (749–56) in 752. It then struck ephemeral issues in gold and copper in the name of its conqueror and closed.[222]

The mint of Rome seems never to have formally closed but rather to have drifted, in the numismatic sense at least, almost insensibly out of imperial control into papal. The preliminaries of this process are found as early as 595, for, in a letter of pope Gregory

219 Diehl, *Études sur l'administration byzantine dans l'exarchat de Ravenne*, pp. 23–31.

220 Diehl, *L'Afrique byzantine: histoire de la domination byzantine en Afrique* II, pp. 535–6, 580.

221 Grierson, *DOC* II.2, pp. 591–2. C. Morrisson, 'Le dernier solidus byzantin frappé à Carthage (695)', *Bulletin de la Société Française de Numismatique* 34 (1979), pp. 514–16; *idem*, *BNC* I, pp. 408–9 (folles dated 694/5).

222 Grierson, *DOC* III.1, pp. 297–8, 322–4.

I to the empress Constantina, he there already claims that, with regard to the daily expenses (*cotidianae expensae*) of the local military, he is effectively acting as imperial *sacellarius*.[223] In 640, the local military (*exercitus Romanus*), fearing that it was being defrauded by the pope of the salaries (*rogae*) supposedly sent by the emperor through his agency, sacked the Lateran Palace and laid hands on the riches of the church. The action seems to have had semi-official encouragement and approval.[224*] The first numismatic stage in the process seems implied in the noticeable tendency of its seventh-century gold products to bear privy marks involving, or surmounted by, a cross, a feature marking them out from the products of other Italian mints.[225] The second is indicated in the issue of a silver coin bearing an anonymous imperial bust as its obverse design and the letters GREO in monogram as its reverse. The persons involved have recently and convincingly been identified as emperor Leo III and pope Gregory II (715–31) or more probably Gregory III (731–41).[226] The third and final stage is to be seen in the issue of a silver penny, western in its physical dimensions, eastern in its design and execution, bearing a papal bust as its obverse design and a cross-on-steps as its reverse. The inscription leaves no doubt but that the pope involved is to be identified as Hadrian I (772–95).[227] (Pl. 27, 1–12)

The mint of Naples, the physical existence of which is known from 763 onwards from features such as open spaces or churches which are termed *ad monetam*,[228] seems to have drifted out of imperial control and into that of the increasingly independent local ruler, the duke, in a fashion similar to that of Rome, although the numismatic process is less clear. The latest emissions of the Neopolitan mint are probably to be found in certain solidi in the names of Nicephorus I and Stauracius, datable to the years 803–11, and in those of Theophilus, Michael II, and Constantine, datable to 829–42.[229] (Pl. 27, 13–17)

The mint of Syracuse continued production on up until the Arab conquest of the city, its latest emissions being semisses and tremisses in the name of Basil I and Constantine, datable to the years 868–79. It may have been supplemented occasionally by a mint at Catania, as it certainly was during the reign of Anastasius II, for an issue of copper folles. Two seals of Sicilian moneyers, one of John, *basilikos spatharios monētarios kai prōtonotarios*

* I owe these references to the kindness of Tom (T. S.) Brown.

223 Gregory I, *Epistolae* v.39; MGH, *Ep.* I, p. 328: ...*ita et in hac urbe in causis talibus eorum saccellarius ego sum*.

224 *Liber Pontificalis* LXXIII (Severinus); ed. Duchesne, I, p. 328. Noticeably, the imperial officials: *sigillaverunt omnem vestiarium ecclesiae seu cymilia episcopii*.

225 Grierson, *DOC* II.2, pp. 501–2 (Constans II), 560–2 (Constantine IV). Morrisson, *BNC* I, pp. 366–7 (Constans II), 391–2 (Constantine IV), 414 (Justinian II). See also Hahn, *MIB* III, under appropriate reigns.

226 Grierson, *DOC* III. 1, pp. 238, 278.

227 *Ibid.* pp. 89–91. *Corpus Nummorum Italicorum* XV.1, pp. 62–4.

228 E.g. B. Capasso, *Monumenta ad Neapolitani Ducatus Historiam Pertinentia* I, p. 262: *in platea que ad Moneta dicitur* (763).

229 Grierson, *DOC* III.1, pp. 361, 449–51.

*Sikelias*, the other of an anonymous *basilikos prōtospatharios kai monētarios Sikelias*, are known for the period (ninth century).[230] (Pl. 26, 7–21)

The mint of Sardinia seems still have been in operation as late as the reign of Leo III (717–41).[231]

Between the loss of Syracuse to the Arabs in 878 and that of the last of the Byzantine possessions in southern Italy to the Normans in 1071, the peninsula was presumably supplied (if it was formally supplied at all) with coinage from the capital.

## (v) *c.* 800–1081

The centralising reorganisation of the eastern fiscal administration, and therefore of coin production and supply, undertaken by Heraclius, ensured that for two centuries the mint of Constantinople remained the sole eastern source of coinage. The possible, and in any case short-lived, operation of a mint at the Crimean city of Bosporus or (less likely), Cherson in *c.* 654–9 for the production of copper half-folles (?) cannot be considered a definitive breach of this principle.[232] The existence of this metropolitan monopoly anticipated, and therefore did not itself originate in, but must have been confirmed and preserved by, the territorial losses of the seventh century. These resulted in the emergence of a much more compact, and therefore more conveniently administered, empire.

The first sign that this by then long-standing metropolitan monopoly had been definitively breached, with regard to the copper coinage at least, occurs during the joint reign of Michael II and Theophilus (821–9), and coincides, probably significantly, with an appreciable increase in the weight standard of the follis to be mentioned in the eighth chapter of this book.[233] The folleis of Michael II and Theophilus fall into two major groups, distinction between them depending upon the exercise of criteria such as style and execution. The one group is of near style and careful execution, the other somewhat rougher in both respects.[234] It seems probable that each group represents the activity of a separate mint, and that the neater represents that of the metropolitan mint, the rougher that of a regional one.

The metropolitan identification seems confirmed by a preliminary examination of the excavation material from the metropolitan church of St Polyeuctus (Saraçhane) where,

[230] Grierson, *DOC* III.2, p. 503 (Syracuse). N. Fairhead, 'A Catanian Follis of Anastasius II', *Numismatic Circular* 88 (1980), pp. 444–5 (Catania). Zacos and Veglery, *Byzantine Lead Seals* I.2, pp. 1148 no. 2057, 1415–16 no. 2630.

[231] Hahn, *MIB* III, pp. 205–6.

[232] Grierson, *DOC* II.1, pp. 38–9, II.2, p. 510. Hahn, *MIB* III, pp. 147–8, terms them folles and attributes them to Cherson. The point is not of major importance.

[233] See below, p. 503.

[234] D. M. Metcalf, 'The Folles of Michael II and of Theophilus before his Reform', *Hamburger Beiträge zur Numismatik* 21 (1967), pp. 25, 28–9 (nos 30–6). Neither Grierson nor Morrisson recognise the existence of this group, but if Metcalf's description is correct, then it ought to precede the similar group for Theophilus, which both recognise.

out of a total of seventeen identifiable specimens, all proved to be of the group of neat style and careful execution.* On the other hand, the precise identity of the regional mint, recognition of the very existence of which depends upon the application of general and subjective criteria (such as characteristic details of design, or style), and not upon explicit evidence (i.e. mint-marks) as it would have done during the later Roman and early Byzantine period, cannot now be determined absolutely.

However, the folleis of Theophilus' own reign (829–42) fall into two similar groups,[235] and it seems reasonable to suppose that they represent the same minting arrangement as had existed during the joint reign. In which case the evidence of regional excavation material will permit a greater, but by no means absolute, precision. For examination of the material from Corinth, where large numbers of these folleis occur, reveals that there the rougher group heavily outnumbers the neater, amounting to approximately two-thirds (102 out of 149) of the total of Theophilan pieces.[236] The position is duly reversed at St Polyeuctus, where, out of a total of twenty-seven identifiable specimens, all but one proved to be of the neater group. It therefore seems reasonable to conclude that, whatever the precise identity of the regional mint involved, that identity should be a European (rather than an Asian) one. On purely general grounds, and in the light of later events, it seems probable that the mint should be identified as Thessalonica.

The metropolitan folleis of Theophilus' reign were accompanied by what are clearly, despite a certain unevenness of weight, half-folleis. These are not uncommon, form a reasonable proportion of archaeological site-finds, and therefore represent an unique feature for the period.[237]

The rougher series of folleis (and, possibly, half-folleis) continues, sporadically, into the reigns of Basil I (867–86) and Leo VI (886–912),[238] and then apparently ceases. Under Basil, at least, it may have been accompanied by issues of fractional gold, along the lines of the Sicilian pattern.[239] It is therefore probably no coincidence that the Greek renegade

* To be published by the author in the final report of the excavations, under the editorship of their director, Professor Martin Harrison, of the University of Newcastle-upon-Tyne, and now in press.

235 Grierson, *DOC* III.1, pp. 413–15, 441.

236 D. M. Metcalf, 'The Reformed Folles of Theophilus: Their Styles and Localization', *American Numismatic Society Museum Notes* 14 (1968), p. 132 (Groups S, Z, H: of which Z seems the most clear-cut case). Subsequently, Metcalf ('Links between Stylistic Groups among the Reformed Folles of Theophilus', *Numismatic Circular* 84 (1976), pp. 6–7) has claimed groups S and Z to be very closely related, which is not improbable.

237 Grierson, *DOC* III.1, pp. 415, 438–9, 441 (pages in incorrect order).

238 Grierson, *DOC* III.2, pp. 479–80, 501–2 (Basil), 511, 518 (Leo VI) – both groups are classified as Constantinopolitan half-folleis. Morrisson, *BNC* II, pp. 547, 557, classifies both as regional folleis, and (*op. cit.* p. 547) adds a whole class of Basil's which Grierson (*op. cit.* pp. 493–4) has no hestitation in attributing to Constantinople. On the whole, Morrisson's case is the more logical and consistent, and it seems likely that Grierson's Constantinopolitan halves are in fact regional halves, and his Constantinopolitan follis a regional one.

239 Grierson, *DOC* III.2, pp. 479, 490–1 (classified as Constantinopolitan fractional gold). Again, Morrisson, *BNC* II, pp. 542–3, is inclined towards a regional attribution, but finally leaves them under Constantinople. Again, on the whole, it seems more consistent to class them with the folleis and halves.

Leo of Tripoli sacked Thessalonica in 904 and that the Bulgarian frontier was advanced to within twenty kilometers of the city subsequently.[240] Either of these developments on its own might have been responsible for any cessation in Thessalonican minting: both would have rendered it inevitable. (Pl. 26, 1–6)

At a date not far removed from that at which the first breach in the metropolitan monopoly of coin production occurred, a second also occurred. It has long been recognised that a series of roughly cast copper or base-metal coins, marked with the initials of the reigning emperor or emperors, and extending from the ninth into the tenth century, are to be considered as having emanated from the Byzantine possessions in the Crimea. The precise date at which this series commenced remains uncertain: the two earliest issues are generally reckoned to be that bearing the letter Π as its obverse design and X as its reverse, and that bearing the letters MB as its obverse design and X as its reverse.[241] The former set of letters is plausibly reckoned to stand for P(*olis*) Kh(*ersonos*), the latter either for M(*ikhael kai*) B(*asileios*), or M(*ikhael*) B(*asileus*), and (*Polis*) Kh(*ersonos*). The mint involved is therefore Cherson, and the earliest reign represented is that of Michael III, whether in its joint form with Basil (866–7) or its sole form (842–66). The most recent detailed treatments of these two issues reckons that with the initials of the mint alone to have preceded that with the initials of the mint and the emperor together, the initials of the emperor to stand for M(*ikhael*) B(*asileus*), and the series to have commenced in the fourth or fifth decade of the century. The series was terminated on the occupation of Cherson by Vladimir of Kiev in 989, and does not seem to have recommenced on the Byzantine recovery of the city in the following year.[242] (Pl. 27, 18–22)

The ninth- and tenth-century mints of Thessalonica (if such it be) and Cherson have two interesting and possibly significant features in common: the circumstances of their inception and their discontinuation. For each commenced production shortly after the city and surrounding area in which it stood had been elevated to the status of a theme. The precise date of the creation of the theme of Thessalonike remains uncertain, but the reigns of Nicephorus I (802–11) and Theophilus (829–42) have both been suggested, the former with somewhat more probability than the latter.[243] The theme of Cherson was created in or very shortly after 833.[244] Each was discontinued as a result of a local military disaster.

240 Refs: Ostrogorsky, *History of the Byzantine State*, pp. 257–8.

241 Grierson, *DOC* III.1, pp. 91–2 (mint), 469–70 (Michael III).

242 Grierson, *DOC* III.2, under appropriate reigns and mint-headings.

243 Ostrogorsky, *History of the Byzantine State*, p. 194. Toynbee, *Constantine Porphyrogenitus and his World*, p. 269, points out that it was in existence by 826, which would appear to be decisive.

244 Constantine Porphyrogenitus, *De Administrando Imperio* XLII; ed. Moravcsik and Jenkins, p. 185. *Continuation of Theophanes* III; Bonn edn, pp. 122–4. Both mention the preliminary mobilisation of Paphlagonian naval forces. See also: Toynbee, *Constantine Porphyrogenitus and his World*, p. 270. There are good reasons for doubting a recent attempt by Treadgold ('Notes on the Numbers and Organization

The administrative basis and significance of these two breaches of the metropolitan monopoly of coin production is difficult to assess. It has been suggested that the extension of the theme system, an undeniable feature of the ninth century, entailed the creation of a complex and parallel regional mint system – in a fashion similar to, and on much the same scale as, the parallel existing between the reigns of Diocletian and Heraclius – but this has not met with numismatic acceptance and is indeed administratively most unlikely. The *Klētorologion* of Philotheus[245] lists an *arkhōn tēs kharagēs* on the strength of the *offikion* of the *khartoularios tou vestiariou*, suggesting that only one *arkhōn* was operating in 899, or at least that no large number of such officials existed then, for thematic officials are commonly listed in the plural. Moreover, any suggestion along these lines fails to take into account the centralising emphasis of the contemporary pattern of fiscal administration which has already been mentioned. The later Roman and early Byzantine pattern of administration had favoured the existence of regional mints: that of the developed Byzantine administration can only have discouraged their existence. It is therefore understandable that an isolated or peripheral theme should have received a mint as a matter of convenience verging upon necessity, but most unlikely that themes should have received mints as a matter of recognised or even general practice.

With the discontinuation of the mints of Thessalonica and Cherson there was a reversion to the previously existing situation of a metropolitan monopoly. This was not permanently broken for a full half-century longer and until the reign of Constantine X (1059–67), although a further and minor breach seems already to have occurred during the latter part of the reign of Michael IV (1034–41), when the mint of Thessalonica was reopened briefly for the production of gold coinage. The immediate occasion of this reopening seems to have been the presence of Michael in or near the city during his military campaign of 1041 against Bulgarian rebels. Once the campaign had been brought to a conclusion the mint was closed, as had always previously been the case with mints created or reopened to perform specific and therefore temporary military functions.[246] Not long before, the emperor had also been staying at Thessalonica and, finding himself short of ready cash, had requested the loan of a kentenarion from archbishop Theophanes while gold was being conveyed from Constantinople. The request had effectively been refused, and the gold – apparently amounting to 10 kentenaria or 72,000 nomismata – had been lost when the ship carrying it had been

of the Ninth-century Byzantine Army', p. 278 and n. 32) to redate the creation to 839 (see below, p. 655 n. 442).

245 Philotheus, *Klētorologion*; ed. Oikonomides, p. 121. The fact that the *arkhōn* appears as such nowhere else in Philotheus' lists almost certainly means that elsewhere he appears under the synonym *khrys(o)epsētēs* who does not appear when the *arkhōn* does – see *ed.cit.* pp. 155 (*ho spatharios kai khrysoepsētēs*), 233 (*ho khrysepsētēs*). On both of these occasions he appears alongside the *zygostatēs*. The fact that in the Uspenski *Taktikon* (ed. Oikonomides, p. 61) only the *khrysepsētēs* appears, again alongside the *zygostatēs*, renders the point virtually certain. See also above, pp. 412–13 and n. 175.

246 Grierson, *DOC* III.2, pp. 721–2, 726. Hendy, 'Michael IV and Harold Hardrada', pp. 187–97.

wrecked. It may well have been this negative experience, as well as positive military convenience, that had suggested the reopening of the mint and the local production of gold coin.[247] (Pl. 28, 3)

During the reign of John I (969–76) the design of the copper follis had taken on the purely religious aspect (lacking, that is, an imperial portrait or inscription) to be mentioned in the eighth chapter of this book.[248] Folleis of this kind continued to be issued up until the coinage reform of Alexius I in 1092. During the reign of Constantine X they were joined by folleis bearing an imperial portrait or inscription that also continued to be issued up until 1092.[249] The two series, in other words, were issued at least more or less in parallel. Elaborate explanations have been put forward to account for this within the somewhat improbable context of a single mint: the metropolitan. That, for example, each issue bearing an imperial portrait or inscription was struck at the commencement of the appropriate reign and was then followed by an issue or issues bearing a religious design.[250] The implication is rather, surely, that the two series were issued wholly in parallel, but by different mints. The fact that at least one issue bearing a religious design (busts of Christ and the Virgin, Class G) is found both overstruck on, and overstruck by, an issue bearing an imperial design (a monogram of Romanus IV, 1068–71), can only be regarded as confirming such a conclusion.[251] The mint issuing the chronologically more extended series, the religious, was presumably the metropolitan, and although the identity of that producing the other series, the imperial, cannot yet be regarded as certain, the evidence once again suggests it to have been Thessalonica. This provisional identification is based on the fact that the mint of Thessalonica later, when its activity is better attested, produced copper tetartera similar in design to the earlier folleis[252] and that the brief usurpation of Nicephorus Basilacius – who is known to have held Thessalonica in 1077–8 – also seems to be represented among the earlier folleis.[253]

Finally, in the confusion of the political scene that marked much of the last quarter of the eleventh century, circumstances suddenly threw up an usurper, Nicephorus Melissenus, who held what remained of the Asian territories in 1080–1 before coming to terms with his European rival and relative Alexius Comnenus, and whose brief and partial tenure of power nevertheless saw the creation and operation of a mint that

[247] George Cedrenus, *Historianum Compendium*; Bonn edn, II, pp. 518–19, 526–7. See also above, pp. 204, 240.

[248] See above, p. 511.

[249] Grierson, *DOC* III.2, pp. 634–706 (Anonymous Folles, Classes A–N, of which L and M now have to be transferred to Trebizond – see below, pp. 437–8); pp. 774–8 (Constantine X), and under appropriate reigns and mint-headings up to and including Nicephorus III (i.e. to 1081). For the continuations up to the reform of Alexius I (i.e. to 1092): Hendy, *DOS* XII, pp. 74–6 (but the Constantinopolitan Third Coinage and the Thessalonican Type B should now be deleted: *DOC* IV).

[250] E.g. Thompson, *The Athenian Agora* II, *Coins*, p. 115.

[251] *Ibid.* p. 114.

[252] Hendy, *DOS* XII, pp. 88–9, 98–101.

[253] *Ibid.* pp. 78–9. *Contra* Grierson, *DOC* III.2, pp. 833–8. P. Grierson, 'Nicephorus Bryennius or Nicephorus Basilacius?', *Numismatic Circular* 84 (1976), pp. 2–3, still leaves the question unresolved.

produced at least an issue of fractions of the silver miliaresion in his name.[254] The mint was presumably Nicaea, which city seems to have acted as Nicephorus' headquarters; it represented a recognisable class that had, however, not been exemplified since the creation of the mints of Alexandretta, Constantia(?) and Jersusalem, during the revolt of the Heraclii in 608–10.

The fate of the regional *thesauri* that had existed during the later Roman and early Byzantine period is unknown. The *Klētorologion* of Philotheus[255] mentions certain officials termed *khartoularioi tōn arklōn* (i.e. 'of the chests') on the strength of the *offikion* of the *logothetēs tou genikou*. These officials seem to have been regional ones, and it has been suggested that they represent the former *praeopsiti thesaurorum*.[256] Certainly it seems reasonable to postulate the existence of a system of regional deposits, whether stationary or mobile, and it may have been something of the former kind that was involved when a Selçuk Turk named Karategin captured Sinope in *c.* 1085. According to Anna Comnena, who reports the incident,[257] Karategin thereby came into the possession of a considerable amount of gold and coin belonging to the imperial treasury (*khrysion hikanon kai khrēmata tōn basilikōn tamieiōn*). Similarly, although less specifically, when the Bulgarian khan Krum had captured Mesembria in 812, he had found there, besides stocks of weapons, a quantity of gold and silver (*khrysou te kai argyrou plēthos*).[258] On the other hand, it may have been something of the latter (that is, mobile) kind that was involved when the Bulgarians captured the salaries (*rhogai*) of the theme of Strymon, amounting to 1,100 lb gold, in 809,[259] and when the Arabs captured those of the theme of Armeniakon, amounting to 1,300 lb gold, near Euchaita, in 811.[260]

## (VI) 1081–1204

### A. *Fiscal administration*

The reign of Alexius I (1081–1118) in particular, and those of his successors John II (1118–43) and Manuel I (1143–80) to a lesser extent, represent, in the spheres of fiscal administration and coin production, the culmination of a series of changes extending back through the reign of Nicephorus III (1078–81) into those of Constantine X (1059–67) and Constantine IX (1042–55), and in a perhaps less conscious form even further.

Until the tenth century the basic unit of regional administration had been the theme

[254] Grierson, *DOC* III.2, pp. 839–40.

[255] Philotheus, *Klētorologion*; ed. Oikonomides, pp. 113 (*khartoularioi tōn arklōn*), 153 (*hoi spatharioi kai notarioi tōn arklōn tou genikou*).

[256] Bury, *The Imperial Administrative System in the Ninth Century*, p. 87.

[257] Anna Comnena, *Alexiad* VI.9.3–5; ed. Leib, II, pp. 64–6. See also below, p. 605 and n. 442.

[258] Theophanes, *Chronographia*; ed. de Boor, I, p. 499. See also below, pp. 654–5, 667–9.

[259] *Ibid.* pp. 484–5.

[260] *Ibid.* p. 489. *Continuation of Theophanes* I; Bonn edn, p. 11. See also above, pp. 183, 192.

in its classic form: an extensive territorial circumscription within which the *stratēgos* directly controlled military affairs and, in a somewhat less direct fashion, civil ones. The fact that the *stratēgos* controlled both almost inevitably meant that the boundaries within which each kind of jurisdiction was exercised were territorially coincident.[261] During the tenth century an increasing reliance upon the professional or tagmatic army, which was under centralised control, at the expense of the thematic army, which was under regional control, entailed a weakening in the military position of the *stratēgos* and a consequent enhancement in that of his civil subordinates. This eventually led to the complete independence of these civil officials and therefore to the removal of any inherent necessity for military and civil boundaries to coincide.[262] By the middle of the eleventh century this potential divergence had to a great extent been realised, and a system of regional administration, in which military and civil boundaries were in fact divergent, had formally emerged.

At the head of the basic unit of eleventh-century regional administration – a large territorial circumscription termed a theme but frequently consisting of several of the earlier units of the same name grouped together – stood a civil official termed a praetor or judge (i.e. *praitōr* or *kritēs*). This official, whose jurisdiction was both juridical and fiscal, seems to have originated in the earlier *praitōr* or *kritēs thematos*, one of the thematic officials who had gained independence from the *stratēgos*.[263] The following eleventh-century *praitores/kritai* are known for the European territories: for Dyrrhakhion, Bulgaria, Thessalonike–Strymon–Voleron (*Thettalia*), Hellas-Peloponnesos (*katōtika merē*), and Makedonia–Thrake.[264] Equivalents are known for the Asian territories, but their jurisdictional boundaries more frequently conformed to those of the earlier single themes and, where themes were nevertheless grouped together, this seems to have been done on a less definitive basis than was the case with European ones.[265]

It is, as it happens, neither Europe nor Asia that provides the classic example of the contemporary division of jurisdictions, but the island of Cyprus. There, as late as 1092, Alexius I appointed one Calliparius as judge and tax-assessor (*kritēs*. . . *kai exisōtēs*), while he appointed Eumathius Philocales as military governor (*doux/stratopedarkhēs*).[266]

It seems clear that, in however truncated and modified a form, this system survived on into the twelfth century in the European territories. The circumscriptions of Thessalonike–Strymon–Voleron, Hellas–Peloponnesos and Makedonia–Thrake can all be traced well into the second half of the century. Certainly that of Thessalonike–Strymon–Voleron appears both in the Veneto-Byzantine treaty of 1198, and in an Athonite document of 1199;[267] that of Hellas–Peloponnesos appears in the writings of

261 Ahrweiler, 'Recherches sur l'administration de l'empire byzantin aux IX^e^–XI^e^ siècles', p. 46.

262 *Ibid.* pp. 46–52.

263 *Ibid.* pp. 67–78.

264 *Ibid.* pp. 82–5.

265 *Ibid.* pp. 84–6.

266 Anna Comnena, *Alexiad* IX.2.4; ed. Leib, III, p. 164.

267 Tafel and Thomas, *Urkunden* I, p. 264. L. Petit and B. Korablev, *Actes de l'Athos* V, *Actes de Chilandar, première partie, actes grecs*, p. 13.

Michael Choniates as archbishop of Athens as well as elsewhere;[268] that of Makedonia–Thrake appears not only in chrysobulls of Michael VII and Nicephorus III, and in the taxation-reforms undertaken by Alexius I betwen 1105/6 and 1108/9, but also in the treaty of 1198.[269]

By the second half of the century, Hellas–Peloponnesos seems to have been under the direct control of the *megas doux* who also either himself bore the title of *praitōr* or who delegated it to another.[270] The coalescence of military and civil titles and functions revealed in this particular case seems to have been more general in this period, for Thessalonike–Strymon–Voleron seems also to have been governed by a *doux kai praktōr* whose title reveals his double competence.[271]

A huge, combined, circumscription, that of Makedonia–Thrake–Thessalonike–Strymon–Voleron, appears momentarily in 1102, when the *pansebastos sebastos* John Taronites functioned as its *praitōr kai anagrapheus*.[272] This, of course, was unprecedented, and it is tempting to connect it, however indirectly, with the various fiscal reassessments and taxation-reforms of the general period.[273]

On the other hand, Makedonia–Thrake, like Thessalonike–Strymon–Voleron, could also, on occasion at least, be divided into its component parts. George Mesopotamites was *doux* of Philippopolis (i.e. Makedonia alone) in 1092, obviously holding a military competence at least.[274] Nicetas Choniates mentions[275] both that a place (*topos*) called

[268] Ahrweiler, *Byzance et la mer*, pp. 275–9. Bon, *Le Péloponnèse byzantin*, pp. 95–8.

[269] Gautier, 'Le Diataxis de Michel Attaliate', pp. 103 (Michael VII), 111, 113 (Nicephorus III). Zepoi, *Ius Graeco-Romanum* I, p. 334 (Alexius). Tafel and Thomas, *Urkunden* I, pp. 267 (*Provintia Thrakis et Macedonie*), 269 (*Provincia Adrianupleos et Didimotichi* = Thrake; *Provincia Phylipupleos, Veroys, Moras et Archridij* = Makedonia). Clearly, the entry for Thrake–Makedonia refers to the lands of the former multiple theme, and this is then followed by a list of its current several subdivisions: what is significant for the present argument is that the larger unit still had in 1198 some kind of administrative status, even if it had meanwhile been subdivided.

[270] Ahrweiler, *Byzance et la mer*, p. 277.

[271] P. Lemerle, *Philippes et la Macédoine orientale*, pp. 157–8. Lemerle (pp. 161–8) observes that the multiple theme could be subdivided, but also (p. 168) that the theme appears in 1198 – one may guess for the same reasons as Makedonia–Thrake: the larger unit still possessed some kind of administrative status.

[272] F. I. Uspenskii, 'Mneniya i postanovleniya Konstantinopol'skikh' pomestnykh soborov' XI i XII vv. o razdache tserkovnykh imshchestv' (kharistikariĭ)', *Izvestiya Russkago Arkeologicheskago Instituta v Konstantinopole* 5 (1900), pp. 31, 42: *tou authentou mou tou pansebastou sebastou praitoros kai anagrapheōs Thrakēs kai Makedonias, Bolerou, Strymōnos kai Thessalonikēs, kyr Iōannou tou Tarōnitou*. . . .It is of course true that John Taronites was a near imperial relation (son of Michael Taronites and Maria Comnena, the eldest sister of Alexius I), and that as a matter of policy Alexius handed out ranks (such as *pansebastos sebastos*) to such relatives. But the nature of the actual office (*praitōr kai anagrapheus*) held by Taronites suggests that it involved a serious responsibility, and was no mere decoration. For Taronites: Gautier, 'Le synode des Blachernes (fin 1094), étude prosopographique', pp. 236–7.

[273] N. G. Svoronos, 'L'épibolè à l'époque des Comnènes', *Travaux et Mémoires* 3 (1968), p. 376 and n. 5, suggests that it may have been the intention of Alexius I in 1087/8 to order a fiscal reassessment of the whole empire, and although there is no absolutely decisive evidence, such is not implausible, given the immense amount of activity at this period. It is clear that the fiscal reassessments, taxation-reforms (above, pp. 235 and n. 86, 286), administrative reforms (below, pp. 432–4), and coinage-reform (below, pp. 513–17) form an impressive conjuncture.

[274] Anna Comnena, *Alexiad* VIII.9.7; ed. Leib, III, p. 155.

[275] Nicetas Choniates, *Historia*; ed. van Dieten, I, pp. 436 (*Neoutzikon*), 402 (*arkhē*).

Neoutzikon divided off the themes (*eparkhiai*) of Adrianos and Philippos (i.e. Adrianople and Philippopolis), implying that such a division was at least feasible, perhaps even normal, and that he himself was *doux* of Philippopolis in 1189, exercising its 'governance and registrary (*arkhē kai apographē*)', and therefore presumably holding a double competence – certainly he had military forces under his jurisdiction.

The evidence is thus not entirely consistent, but it does suggest that these combined circumscriptions did survive on into the later period, at least as formal and recognised phenomena, and that their governors might be either civil, or military, or even both, presumably as circumstances required or dictated. In any event, the three larger circumscriptions of Thessalonike–Strymon–Voleron, Hellas–Peloponnesos and Makedonia–Thrake included, perhaps significantly, the greater part of the most fertile or most developed – and therefore fiscally most productive – areas in the European territories.[276] They also involved the basic imperial territories which remained even after the losses of the late twelfth century.[277]

It seems equally clear that this system did not survive on into the twelfth century in the Asian territories, having been destroyed by the Selçuk invasions of the last quarter of the eleventh century. When, as a result of the efforts of the Comnenian emperors, the most fertile areas in those territories had been recovered from the Selçuks, and a degree of political stability restored to them, the system of regional administration that emerged was rather different from that still obtaining in its essentials in the European territories. In Asia a relatively large number of small-sized administrative units evolved, which units were also termed themes, and at the head of each of which there stood an official termed *doux kai anagrapheus* or similar. The two elements of this official's title denote his extensive competence, duke (*doux*) implying a military jurisdiction, registrar (*anagrapheus*) a fiscal one. In addition to which he possessed juridical powers. In some sense this twelfth-century system marked a reversion to the ninth- and tenth-century one for, despite the smallness of the later administrative unit, the extensive competence of its *doux* (which, amongst other things, implied the reunion of military and civil boundaries) resembled that of the earlier *stratēgos*.[278]

Besides these developments in regional administration, the eleventh and twelfth centuries saw a number of adjustments aimed at strengthening central control over the administration in general. Constantine IX, for instance, had probably created the post regularised by Alexius I under the title of *logothetēs tōn sekretōn* (i.e. 'of the bureaux'), which is first mentioned in 1081, and which is later found under the title of *megas logothetēs*, (i.e. 'grand logothete') to co-ordinate the activities of all the metropolitan bureaux. The latter emperor also created the post of *megas logariastēs* (i.e. 'grand accountant') *tōn sekretōn* or simply *megas logariastēs*, first mentioned in 1094, to co-ordinate the activities of the

[276] See above, pp. 21–5, 35–9, 44–54, 78–90. [277] See above, Map 19.

[278] Ahrweiler, *Byzance et la mer*, pp. 272–4.

metropolitan financial bureaux. Alongside this the emperor created the post of *megas logariastēs tōn euagōn sekretōn*, first mentioned in 1099, to co-ordinate the activities of the bureaux dealing with the imperal (private) properties. These last two were known as *ta dyo megala logariastata* or *logariastika sekreta* and clearly worked in parallel.[279]

It is still occasionally supposed[280] that these adjustments, particularly that involving the creation of the post of *megas logariastēs*, together with the near contemporary disappearance of the *eidikon* (after 1088), entailed the disappearance of the distinction between imperial (state) weath and imperial (private) wealth. Based largely upon a very general remark by Zonaras,[281] this is an untenable supposition: the existence of the two *megalōi logariastai* clearly contradicts it, and in any case, the *eidikon*, as descended from the *idikē trapeza* within the *praefectura orientis*, had little or nothing to do with imperial (private) wealth.[282]

The two main repositories of imperial wealth, the *vestiarion* proper (the repository of state wealth) and the *oikeiakon vestiarion* (the repository of private wealth) apparently also continued to exist.[283] It was apparently the former that was guarded by a military detachment of *exō vestiaritai*, and the latter, also termed *ta esō tameia*, that was guarded by a detachment of *esō vestiaritai*, in the late eleventh and the twelfth century.[284] It was presumably the former that was guarded by a detachment of Varangians towards the close of the twelfth century, and it was certainly the former that was also guarded by Varangians in the mid thirteenth century, when the distinction between imperial (state) wealth and imperial (private) wealth actually had disappeared.[285]

The creation of the various offices of co-ordination must nevertheless have reflected, and indeed may have entailed, the decline of the formerly independent financial *sekreta*, leading to the disappearance of the *sakellion* (after 1145), and the *stratiōtikon* (after 1088), as well as the *eidikon*, and to the continuing decline of the *genikon*. The last, signalised

279 *Logothetēs tōn sekretōn*: Ahrweiler, *Byzance et la mer*, pp. 200–2, and Oikonomides, 'L'évolution de l'organisation administrative de l'empire byzantin au XI^e siècle', pp. 131–3. *Megaloi logariastai*: Ahrweiler, *op. cit.* pp. 203–4, and Oikonomides, *op. cit.* pp. 140–1. For a magnificent example of the actual functioning – or rather later non-functioning – of these officials and their bureaux, see: P. Lemerle, 'Notes sur l'administration byzantine à la veille de la IV^e croisade, d'après deux documents inédits des archives de Lavra', *Revue des Études Byzantines* 19 (1961), pp. 258–72. See now also: Lemerle *et al.*, *Actes de Lavra* I, pp. 345–58.

280 E.g. Ahrweiler, *Byzance et la mer*, p. 203 (with refs to Dölger, *Finanzverwaltung*).

281 John Zonaras, *Annales* XVIII.29.22; Bonn edn, III, p. 766: *kai tois pragmasin oukh hōs koinois oud' hōs dēmosiois ekekhrēto kai heauton ouk oikonomon hēgēto toutōn, alla despotēn*. This is clearly a general comment, and merely means that Alexius did not pay too much attention to the distinction between private and public matters, not that he abolished the administrative distinction between imperial (private) and imperial (state) wealth.

282 See above, pp. 410–13, and my remarks in p. 410 n. 163. See also below, pp. 628–30.

283 Oikonomides, 'L'évolution de l'organisation administrative de l'empire byzantine au XI^e siècle', pp. 137–8.

284 *Ibid.* pp. 129–30 (*vestiaritai*). Nicetas Choniates, *Historia*; ed. van Dieten, I, p. 534 (*esō tameia*).

285 P. Karlin-Hayter, 'L'hétériarque: l'évolution de son rôle du *De Cerimoniis* au *Traité des Offices*', *Jahrbuch der Österreichischen Byzantinistik* 23 (1974), pp. 112–14 (twelfth century); see below, pp. 440, 442 and n. 319, 443 (thirteenth century).

by the dismantling of its headquarters, the building called the *Genikon*, under Isaac II, may also have occurred in the face of the increasing importance of the *sekreton* of the *epi tōn oikeiakōn*. This seems originally to have been a sub-department of the *genikon*, subsequently to have achieved independent status, and to have been concerned above all with the exploitation of lands that were proper to (i.e. *oikeiaka*), and owned by, the state.[286]

## *B. Mints*

It is in the light of these adjustments that, once again, certain roughly contemporaneous changes in the pattern of coin production should be seen.

On his accession in 1081, Alexius I inherited two main mints from his predecessors. One, the metropolitan, had never ceased producing both precious- and base-metal coin for any appreciable length of time, and need not be discussed here. The other, a regional one provisionally identified as Thessalonica in the preceding section of this chapter, had produced copper coin from the reign of Constantine X onwards.

Alexius' first several years, 1081–5, were spent in warding off a serious Norman invasion based on Epirus and northern and central Greece. Just as Thessalonica had been Michael IV's main military base in dealing with the Bulgarian rebellion of 1040–1 so it was now Alexius' in dealing with the Norman invasion. The military parallel produced a numismatic one: just as Michael's campaign had necessitated the production of a gold coinage at Thessalonica, so Alexius' now necessitated the production certainly of a gold and silver one, and probably a copper one, which was very similar in design to the earlier.[287] (Pls. 28, 3; 30, 2)

It was, however, only with the coinage reform in 1092, itself clearly and intimately associated with roughly contemporary political, fiscal and administrative developments, that the main lines of a more permanent Comnenian pattern of coin production began to emerge. The reform saw the operation of at least three, and possibly four, mints, one of which – producing the complete range of metals – was certainly the metropolitan, and another of which – producing the same range – was almost as certainly the Thessalonican. A further regional mint, and possibly two, seem to have been created specifically to implement the reform and, having performed that function, were then closed. Their identity remains uncertain but hoard evidence strongly suggests one – producing gold and billon only – to have been in the Thracian plain, and both Philippopolis (the capital of the theme of Makedonia) and Adrianople (the capital of that of Thrake) have been proposed as candidates. The hoard evidence, involving both gold and billon, clearly

[286] Oikonomides, 'L'évolution de l'organisation administrative de l'empire byzantin au XI$^{e}$ siècle', pp. 135–7 (disappearance of *sakellion*, *stratiōtikon* and *eidikon*). Nicetas Choniates, *Historia*; ed. van Dieten, I, p. 442: ...*lamprotatēn tou genikou oikodomēn katēdaphise*.

[287] Hendy, *DOS* XII, pp. 41–6 (Alexius); *idem*, 'Michael IV and Harold Hardrada', pp. 187–97 (Michael).

Table 14. *Balkan major fiscal units and mints*, c. *1092–1204* (*Map 36*)

| Fiscal unit | Mint | Date of operation |
|---|---|---|
| Thessalonike–Strymon–Voleron | Thessalonica | → |
| Hellas–Peloponnesos | Thebes(?) | *c.* 1092(?) – *c.* 1190(?) |
| Makedonia–Thrake | Philippopolis(?) | *c.* 1092(?) |

favours the former, but the question cannot be regarded as settled. The identity of the possible other – producing gold only – remains unknown.[288]

During the remainder of the reign of Alexius I and the reigns of John II and Manuel I, the Comnenian pattern of coin production crystallised. The metropolitan mint produced gold hyperpyra, electrum and billon trachea, and copper tetartera, all except the last, the circulation of which was confined virtually to the capital itself, in consistent bulk. The mint of Thessalonica produced gold hyperpyra and billon trachea on a rapidly dwindling scale, and copper tetartera and half-tetartera in consistent bulk. A further regional mint produced copper half-tetartera perhaps from the reign of Alexius, and certainly from that of Manuel, onwards. Its precise identity remains uncertain, but hoard evidence suggests it to have been in central or southern Greece, and Thebes (the probable capital of the earlier theme of Hellas), Athens, and Corinth (the capital of the earlier theme of Peloponnesos) have all been proposed as candidates. Thebes, which was certainly the capital of the later combined theme, must be considered as the most likely of the three.[289]

If the late eleventh- and twelfth-century main regional mints mentioned above, and identifiable with some reasonable degree of territorial exactitude, are listed along with the major units of fiscal administration in which they stood, the very tentative pattern emerges as in Table 14.

The main lines of this pattern, and in particular the distinction between coin-production and -supply in Thessalonike–Strymon–Voleron and Hellas–Peloponnesos (i.e. in what now approximates to modern Greece) on the one hand, and in Makedonia–Thrake (in what now approximates to southern Bulgaria) on the other, tend to be confirmed by

[288] Regional mints: Hendy, *DOS* XII, pp. 93–6, 343–4 (Gornoslav Hoard), 379 (Plovdiv [Boundardzhik] Hoard). Morrisson, *BNC* II, p. 671, who prefers Adrianople on the grounds of its supposedly greater administrative and military importance – but in fact Philippopolis was quite as important in both respects. The proposition of Metcalf (refs: *Coinage in South-eastern Europe 820–1396*, p. 107) that about half the reformed gold coinage of Alexius could have been struck at a central Greek mint, cannot be taken at all seriously, whether economically, administratively, or numismatically.

[289] For the products of the metropolis and Thessalonica, see: Hendy, *DOS* XII, under appropriate reigns and mint-headings. For the products of the central Greek mint, see: *ibid.* pp. 99–100 (Alexius I), 127–30 (Manuel I), 135 (Andronicus I). Morrisson, *BNC* II, p. 749 (Isaac II). For Thebes, see: Bon, *Le Péloponnèse byzantin*, p. 92. The metropolitan tetartera seem actually to have been of billon: see below, p. 515 and n. 334.

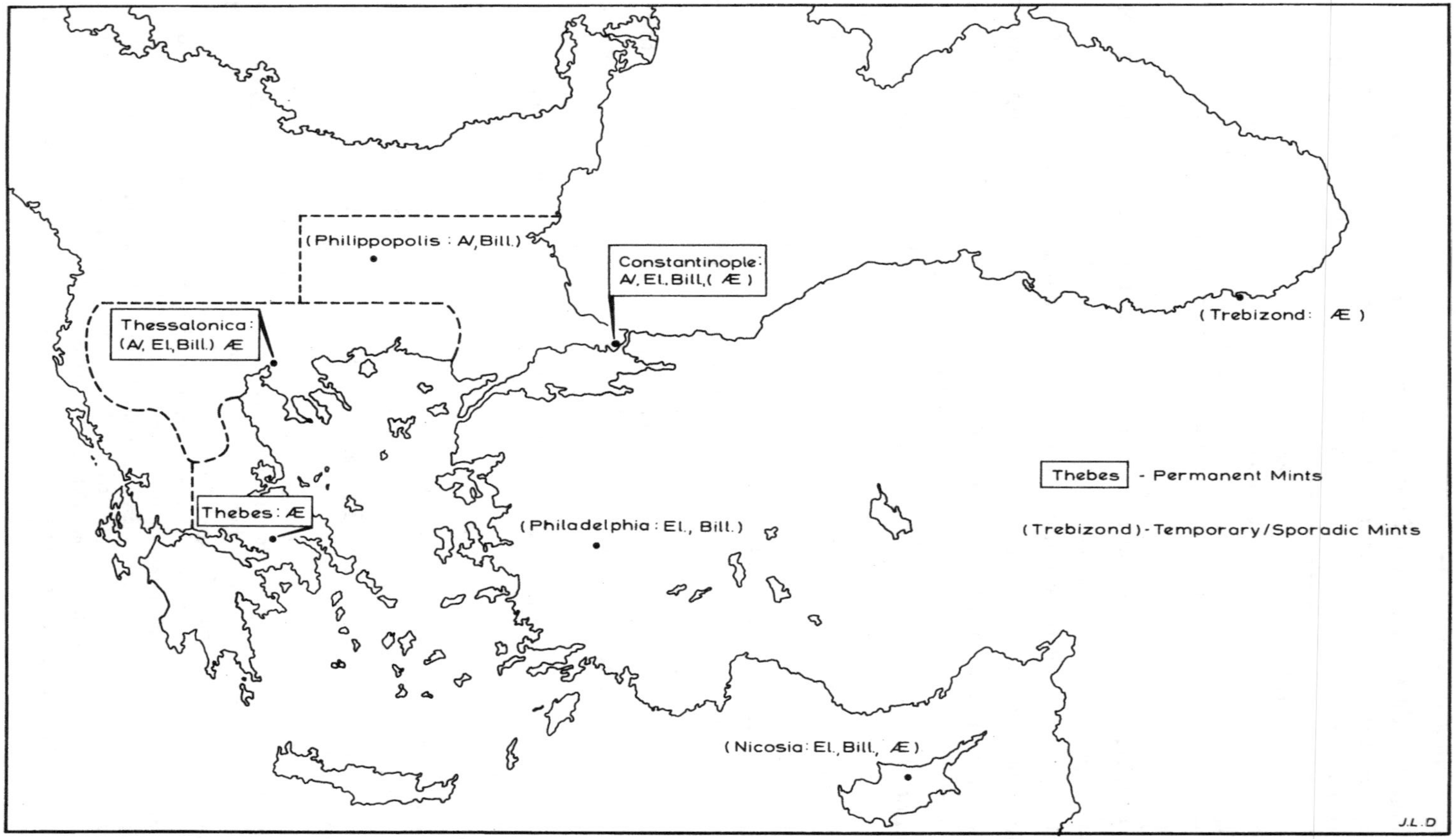


Map 36 The empire: Balkan multiple themes, and mints, *c.* 1092–1204

hoard evidence. The main base-metal product of the mint of Thessalonica was consistently the copper tetarteron and its half; the sole base-metal product of the mint of Thebes(?) was the copper half-tetarteron. The commonest twelfth-century hoard from modern Greece is still one consisting of that metal and those denominations: twelfth-century hoards of billon trachea are much less common and do not exceed what might be expected to have infiltrated from other areas in trade.[290] The sole base-metal product of the mint of Philippopolis(?) during its brief existence was the billon trachy, supply of which seems to have been undertaken subsequently from the capital. By far the commonest twelfth-century hoard from Bulgaria is still one consisting of that alloy and denomination: in fact hoards of copper tetartera or their halves, or both, simply do not occur.[291] The distinction is so marked and so consistent that it is not explicable by a supposed preference of 'Greeks' for tetartera and of 'Bulgarians' for trachea: it was a matter of production and supply, and therefore reflects administrative boundaries.[292]

The operation of the mint of Thessalonica can be traced throughout the twelfth and into the thirteenth century. That of Thebes(?) can be traced no further than the reign of Isaac II (1185–95) and, even if it had continued, it would have been interrupted, perhaps definitively, by the revolts of Manuel Camytzes in central Greece, and of Leo Sgouros in the Peloponnese, in 1201.[293] (Pl. 31, 15)

The implied connection between the existence of large European administrative units and a relative multiplicity of regional mints, even if only an unconscious one and based on administrative necessity or convenience, itself goes far towards explaining the lack of an equivalent system of mints in the Asian territories. For, as mentioned above, these Asian territories contrasted with the European in possessing smaller administrative units: in their case the necessity for, or convenience of, breaking the metropolitan monopoly of coin production and supply might well have been much less, and their officials' capacity to extract such a concession equally so.

It was, nevertheless, the Asian territories that were to throw up the last known examples before 1204 of mints being created outside the normal pattern, as a result of geographical remoteness or political separatism (i.e. revolt or usurpation) or both.

290 Hendy, *DOS* XII, p. 311, and 325–404 ('List of Hoards'). *Contra* I. Touratsoglou, 'Unpublished Byzantine Hoards of Billon Trachea from Greek Macedonia and Thrace', *Balkan Studies* 14 (1973), pp. 132–3, where this distinction is misunderstood or ignored.

291 This is confirmed by private correspondence with I. Iordanov of Shumen, who has even more recently than I worked on Bulgarian material of the period. The Assenovgrad Hoard (Hendy, *DOS* XII, pp. 326–7), which contained 5 tetartera out of a total of 180 coins, is scarcely an exception: the provenance is not too far from the Greek frontier, and the date of burial is late. As for Anatolia, the evidence is overwhelmingly that the metropolitan trachy alone circulated as a substantive subordinate denomination: one hoard of over 60 tetartera is reported to have come from southern Turkey – but this is, on the face of it, unlikely, and the denomination is absent from archaeological site-finds. See: M. D. O'Hara, 'Notes on Recent Byzantine Hoards', *Coin Hoards* 1 (1975), p. 68.

292 *Contra* C. Morrisson, in *Numismatic Chronicle* $9^7$ (1971), at p. 366 (review of Hendy, *DOS* XII).

293 Brand, *Byzantium Confronts the West*, pp. 133–4, 152–3.

At several stages of the late eleventh and early twelfth centuries, the city of Trebizond was the scene of contumacy or outright revolt against Alexius I and John II, on the part of successive members of the Gabras family, virtually hereditary dukes of Khaldia. Theodore Gabras between 1075 and 1098, Gregory Gabras (Taronites?) between *c.* 1103 and *c.* 1106, and Constantine Gabras between *c.* 1119 and *c.* 1140 were thus all at some stage, or stages, of their tenure of office semi-independent or entirely independent of the central government.[294] It is to these years, and to this situation, that the creation of a mint at Trebizond, and its issue of an entirely anomalous series of thirteen issues of copper folleis, have very recently been attributed.[295] The sequence consists of roughly manufactured coins, on an irregular standard of weight, most of which bear religious designs of some kind, including St Theodore and St Demetrius, and only a few of which bear the monogram or portrait of Alexius. It seems to have remained virtually unaffected by the coinage reforms of 1092, although the one issue that bears an actual portrait of Alexius also bears a religious design (a bust of Christ) that certainly derives from the first issues of the reformed coinage (1092 onwards), and probably dates to the brief tenure of the office of *doux* of Khaldia by the loyalist Dabatenus (1098–1103).[296] It is just possible that the city was also responsible for the production of two issues of billon trachea in the name of Isaac II, but this is much more uncertain.[297] (Pl. 31, 9)

In 1184 the island of Cyprus was the scene of a successful revolt against Andronicus I (1183–5). The rebel, and then usurper, one Isaac Comnenus, held the island as emperor until 1191 when he was dispossessed by Richard I of England during the course of the Third Crusade. Although no contemporary source mentions Isaac's issuing a coinage, the temptation to assume that he did so is of long standing, and a number of types, representing all the major denominations except the gold hyperpyron, have recently – and this time it is to be hoped definitively – been attributed to him.[298] Any doubt as to the Cypriot origin of this group of coins has since been dispelled by further provenances.[299]

In 1188–9 the city of Philadelphia was the scene of a brief and unsuccessful revolt and usurpation against Isaac II. Although the chronicler Nicetas Choniates reports that

[294] A. A. M. Bryer, 'A Byzantine Family: The Gabrades, *c.* 979–*c.* 1653', *University of Birmingham Historical Journal* 12 (1970), pp. 175–7.

[295] S. Bendall, 'The Mint of Trebizond under Alexius I and the Gabrades', *Numismatic Chronicle* 17⁷ (1977), pp. 126–36; *idem*, 'Some Further Notes on the Mint of Trebizond under Alexius I', *Numismatic Chronicle* 19⁷ (1979), p. 211; *idem*, 'A Follis of Alexius I of Trebizond', *Numismatic Circular* 89 (1981), p. 237. Hendy, *DOC* IV. See now also: S. Bendall, 'A New Twelfth-century Byzantine Coin from the Mint of Trebizond', *Numismatic Chronicle* 142 (1982), p. 163.

[296] Anna Comnena, *Alexiad* XII.7.1; ed. Leib, III, p. 75.

[297] S. Bendall, 'The Coinage of Trebizond under Isaac II (A.D. 1185–95), with a Note on an Unfinished Byzantine Die', *American Numismatic Society, Museum Notes* 24 (1979), pp. 213–17.

[298] Hendy, *DOS* XII, pp. 140–2, 148.

[299] The most significant of such provenances involves a hoard (Hendy, 'Seventeen Twelfth- and Thirteenth-century Byzantine Hoards', p. 69 (Larnaka Hoard)), but a number of other, single, provenances, are now known.

Theodore Mangaphas, the perpetrator, 'struck a silver nomisma and engraved his own name on it',[300] until very recently it had not been identified successfully.[301] The discovery of a billon trachy issued in the name of a ruler Theodore amongst the excavation material from the Stavropolis (Aphrodisias),* a city not far from Philadelphia and known to have been raided by Mangaphas, has since led to the identification of it, and a similar electrum or silver trachy, as the issue in question.[302] (Pl. 31, 7, 12–13 [Is.]; 8 [Th.])

## (VII) 1204–1453

### A. *Fiscal administration*

The conquest of Constantinople in 1204, during the course of the Fourth Crusade, finally shattered an administrative system which until then, whatever the undoubtedly vast extent of the changes involved, had possessed a continuous, if at some stages now very imperfectly perceived, line of development, stretching back into the ancient world. The period following the conquest to some extent resembles that following the reign of Phocas: it is possible to reconstruct the main lines of the administrative system as it stood at the end of each of these periods, but impossible to discern the details of its evolution.

The fundamental source of evidence bearing upon the administrative system of the final Byzantine period is without any doubt the treatise now commonly known as the *De Officiis* and for long incorrectly attributed to one George Codinus. The treatise lists the order of precedence and describes the services of the various officials of the court, and is in fact anonymous. It was written by someone familiar with such matters, and is to be dated to within a few years of 1350.[303]

All or most of those officials who had earlier dealt with the central administration of

* To be published by the author with the kind permission of the director of the excavations, Professor Kenan Erim, of the University of New York.

300 Nicetas Choniates, *Historia*; ed. van Dieten, I, p. 399.

301 Hendy, *DOS* XII (1969), p. 149.

302 See: Hendy, *DOC* IV, *contra* E. Pochitonov, 'La plus ancienne émission monétaire bulgare de l'époque du second royaume', *Byzantinoslavica* 31 (1970), pp. 54–63; *idem*, 'Théodore-Pierre Asène ou Théodore Mancaphas?', *Byzantinoslavica* 42 (1981), pp. 52–7. It appears that Pochitonov's first article, daring to attribute the billon issue in question to Theodore-Peter Asen (*c.* 1187), caused something of a storm in Bulgarian numismatic circles, a storm which manifested itself in a number of articles, by Gerassimov, Iouroukova and Iordanov, in the journal *Numizmatika*, contesting the attribution. I had myself, meanwhile, in the early seventies, and not least upon the evidence of the piece found at Aphrodisias, become convinced (and still am) that it represented the lost issue of Theodore Mangaphas. Iordanov also, without knowing of my evidence, came to the same conclusion (1976). All that Pochitonov has been able to show is that the issue in question is found in Bulgarian hoards – but that is not surprising, given their number and size, for even the rare Cypriot issues of Isaac Comnenus are also so found on occasion. The letter B that Pochitonov (implausibly) claims is sometimes Б̄ (for 'Bulgar') and sometimes B̄ (for 'Vlach' seems to me to be simply B̄ for 'basileus' – not customary usage on the coinage, but not really unexpected on the ill-designed and -struck issues of a provincial usurper.

303 Verpeaux, *Traité des offices*, pp. 25–40.

the empire are listed in the *De Officiis*. The *megas logothetēs* comes ninth in the order of precedence after the truly imperial dignities (*basileus-kaisar*), the *logothetēs tou genikou* fifteenth, the *logothetēs tōn oikeiakōn* thirty-sixth, the *megas logariastēs* thirty-seventh, and the *logothetēs tou stratiōtikou* forty-fourth.[304]

Even this list has its odd features. It is, for instance, not clear why the *logothetai tou genikou* and *tōn oikeiakōn* should outrank the *megas logariastēs*, although it may be expected that some forgotten personal enhancements, such as that arranged by Andronicus II for Theodore Metochites as *megas logothetēs* (ninth to fifth) in 1321, will have been responsible. In fact, the phenomenon seems to be of Lascarid origin.

It is, however, only when the service (*hypēresia*) rendered by each of these officials comes to be described that the full anomaly of the situation becomes evident. It is recorded that 'The *megas logothetēs* draws up laws and the chrysobulls sent out by the emperor to kings, sultans, and governors'; but also that 'The service of the *logothetēs tou genikou* is not known'; that 'The *logothetēs tōn oikeiakōn* similarly (has no service)'; that 'Nor has the *megas logariastēs* any service now'; and that 'The *logothetēs tou stratiōtikou* has no service'.[305] The only official of the central administration performing a definite fiscal service is the president (*prokathēmenos*) of the *vestiarion*, who comes fifty-eighth in the order of precedence, and of whom it is recorded that 'The *prokathēmenos tou vestiariou* heads the *vestiarion*, and also deals with sums entering and leaving, with revenues (*eisodoi*) and expenses (*exodoi*).'[306] He also apparently commanded the ship carrying the *vestiarion* itself when the emperor was engaged on a naval expedition.[307] That the *vestiarion* actually did accompany the emperor on military expeditions at this period seems confirmed by the fact that it was surely this, termed *to basilikon/koinon tamieion*, and containing gold and silver coin, special (i.e. ceremonial) garments (*peploi exalloi*), tunics (*stolai*) and belts (*zōnai*), pearls (*margara*) and precious stones (*lithoi*), that Michael VIII almost managed to lose, when ambushed by Mongols and Bulgars, in lower Thrace – evidently between Aenus and Ganus – in 1265.[308*]

The office of *prokathēmenos tou vestiariou* itself can be traced back at least as far as 1278, when the then *prokathēmenos*, Nicholas Panaretus, accompanied the *megas logothetēs* George Acropolites, and the *megas diermēneutēs* George Berrhoiotes, as lay representatives to the Council of Lyons. It is likely to have been considerably older, being quite probably a Nicaean innovation,[309] and its previous non-appearance is unsurprising in view of its low standing in the order of precedence.

* I owe this reference to the kindness of Paul Magdalino.

304 Anonymous, *De Officiis* I; ed. Verpeaux, pp. 137–8.

305 *Ibid.* III; ed. Verpeaux, pp. 174, 176, 182, 184.

306 *Ibid.* I, III; ed. Verpeaux, pp. 139, 186.

307 *Ibid.* III; ed. Verpeaux, p. 186.

308 George Pachymeres, *De Michaele et Andronico Palaeologis, De Mich.* III.25; Bonn edn, I, pp. 235–40.

309 *Ibid.* V.17; Bonn edn, I, p. 384 (Panaretus). *Contra* Angold, *A Byzantine Government in Exile*, p. 207 (proposing it to be an innovation of Michael VIII – but such an official would have been necessary much earlier given the structure of the Nicaean fiscal administration).

The precise significance of this situation, in which what had been offices with specific functions had become mere titles and ranks, the stages by which it came about and their chronology have all occasioned discussion. Much of this discussion has centred upon the *logothetēs tou genikou*, his office and its functions, and attempts have been made to prove him as having functioned effectively as a fiscal official until well into the fourteenth century.[310] These attempts nevertheless seem to miss the point: which is that in order to prove such a proposition, it would be necessary to demonstrate the logothete to have consistently acted in a fiscal capacity in virtue of his office alone, rather than to have done so on one occasion or another in virtue of his position as a senior court dignitary or favoured imperial advisor.

Very recently a more radical and – for the moment at least – more convincing proposition had been put forward. This takes as its premise the fact that the effective functioning of the officials mentioned above must have depended very considerably upon their heading *sekreta*, the bureaux through which much of their work will have been channelled, and indeed by which much of it will have been performed. In default of conclusive proof of the effective functioning of the officials themselves, equivalent evidence regarding that of their *sekreta* might be thought a sufficient substitute. But even this is not forthcoming. For with the conquest of 1204 the personnel of the *sekreta* will have been dispersed and their administrative records rendered unavailable, if not destroyed. Although study of the administrative system of the empire of Nicaea – that which necessarily provided the basis of the administrative system of the restored empire after the recovery of Constantinople in 1261 – does reveal the restoration of some form of regular juridical and fiscal administration as early as 1218, it also totally fails to reveal the restoration of the *sekreta* as part of that administration. It is difficult not to consider this combination of negative evidence as decisive proof against the effective functioning of most or all of the officials themselves.[311]

It seems quite clear that the administrative system of the empire of Nicaea was far less complex than that of the empire existing before 1204, lacking as it did the latter's bureaucratic structure, and that it was based rather upon the immediate imperial household (*oikos*), members of which frequently added the title *oikeios* (i.e. belonging to the household) to their other titles. It had, in other words, become much more concentrated and therefore dependent upon the person of the emperor.[312]

Significantly enough, the two officials whose names and titles are recorded in a document of 1218, incidentally revealing the restoration of administration, are John Strategopoulos, then *megas logothetēs*, and Nicholas Caloethus, then a secretary in the

[310] Refs: L.-P. Reybaud, *Le gouvernement et l'administration centrale de l'empire byzantin sous les premiers Paléologues (1258–1354)*, pp. 233–5.
[311] Angold, *A Byzantine Government in Exile*, pp. 147–50.
[312] *Ibid.* pp. 151–81.

imperial *vestiarion* (*en tō basilikō vestiariō grammatikos*).[313] The inclusion of a subordinate official of the *vestiarion* in the document not only anticipates the situation implied in the later *De Officiis*, where the *prokathēmenos tou vestiariou* is the only official of the central administration performing a definite fiscal service, but also accurately reflects the situation obtaining in the empire of Nicaea, where the *vestiarion* acted both as the sole repository of imperial wealth (which was a novel feature, but involved only an extension of its formerly shared rôle),[314] and as virtually the sole instrument of fiscal administration (which was a totally novel feature).[315] It is again difficult not to consider this combination of evidence as proof that a similar situation existed during the intervening period.

The explanation of the curiously low standing of the *prokathēmenos* may thus well be that, as he was not the head of an independent bureau (which no longer existed), he acted as little more than guardian of the imperial reserve, and, as a subordinate, accepted and disbursed payments to and from it, at the behest of whoever headed the administration as a whole, at any given time.

The fact that whereas, previously, it had been the *oikeiakon vestiarion*, the repository of imperial (private) wealth, that had accompanied the emperor on military campaigns and naval expeditions,[316] in 1265 it was the *koinon tamieion*, which can only have been the *vestiarion* proper, the repository of imperial (state) wealth, that accompanied Michael VIII,[317] and in the mid fourteenth century it was the *vestiarion* under the command of the *prokathēmenos* – again the *vestiarion* proper – that accompanied the emperor on naval expeditions,[318] demonstrates clearly enough that the former distinction between imperial private and state wealth had been abandoned. Again, this presumably occurred as a result of the conquest of 1204. Emperors, like John VI, who had been fabulously wealthy in their own right prior to their elevation, might well utilise that wealth in what they regarded as being the interests of the state subsequent to their elevation, but that is a very different matter.[319]

313 Miklosich and Müller, *Acta et Diplomata Graeca Medii Aevi* IV, pp. 290–5.

314 Shared, that is, with the various other *sekreta* such as the *oikeiakon vestiarion*, the *eidikon*, the *phylax*, and so on.

315 Angold, *A Byzantine Government in Exile*, pp. 204–10.

316 See above, pp. 275, 306–9.

317 See above, p. 440.

318 See above, p. 440.

319 See above, pp. 207–8 (John VI). *Contra* T. Miller, 'The Basilika and the Demosia: The Financial Offices of the Late Byzantine Empire', *Revue des Études Byzantines* 36 (1978), pp. 171–91. Miller argues that imperial (state) wealth – *ta dēmosia* – remained separate from imperial (private) wealth – *ta basilika* – but his argument will not hold. When Cantacuzene writes (Bonn edn, III, p. 80): *ek tōn dēmosiōn kai basilikōn*, he does not repeat the definite article and is clearly meaning that the two are the same (see above, p. 440), not that they are different. When he writes (Bonn edn, I, p. 338), of Apocaucus, that he took over: ...*tēn epi tou tōn basilikōn khrēmaton tamieiou, eti de kai tēn epi tōn eisprattontōn tous dēmosious phorous*..., he is merely acknowledging a distinction between the care of the repository and the care of the collecting apparatus. The fact that the treasury is 'imperial', but the taxes 'public', is of interest, but not of significance in this context. Again, when he writes (Bonn edn, II, p. 219), again of Apocaucus, but by this stage as *megas doux*, that the *tōn khrēmatōn prosodoi tōn koinōn* were directed by him, while (Bonn edn, II, p. 223) Cinnamus was *mystikos tōn basilikōn khrēmatōn tote tamiou*, the same distinction is operative. Miller's other case (Bonn

The presence of the *prokathēmenos*, and of the *vestiarion* itself, on at least major imperial expeditions, given the traditional attachment of the mint to the *vestiarion*, raises – at least as a theoretical or occasional possibility – the question of whether the mint might not also have accompanied such expeditions. This would obviously have represented a curious, and presumably quite unconscious, reversion to a much earlier practice.[320]

## *B. Mints*

The historian George Pachymeres records that, when Michael Palaeologus was created *megas doux* in 1258, he was also given access to the *basilikon tamieion* or imperial treasury. He continues, with obvious reference to this same treasury, that John III (1222–54) had collected and deposited a great sum of money at Magnesia (i.e. Manisa), a city beneath Mount Sipylus, and that John's son and successor Theodore II (1254–8) had also done the same at Astytzium (possibly the modern Kızkulesi), a town on the middle Scamander. He adds that the money at Magnesia was guarded by axe-bearing Celts, the normal description for members of the Varangian guard.[321]

It is generally accepted that the phrase *to basilikon tamieion* by this date is the equivalent of *to basilikon vestiarion*: the Nicaean *vestiarion* was therefore situated at Magnesia. Now this city lay in the economic heart of the empire of Nicaea, the area between the rivers Hermus and Maeander, and within easy reach of the administrative capital at Nymphaeum where it had been customary for the emperors to spend the autumn and winter since the conquest of 1204.[322] Astytzium, on the other hand, lay at the very edge of the Asian territories of the empire, and it seems reasonable to suppose the money deposited there to have been intended to cater for the European territories recovered by John III. It is also tempting to see in this distinction some relation to the functions of the two *domestikoi* of the eastern and western themes (*domestikoi tōn anatolikōn kai dysikōn thematōn*) mentioned by the *De Officiis* as having formerly been responsible for the public revenues (*dēmosia pragmata*) of those regions, but this is pure conjecture, for the evidence for these officials is confined to the late thirteenth and fourteenth centuries.[323]

edn, II, p. 99) is even less decisive, and mentions only that two persons were needed – or wanted – to direct finances, thus duplicating the situation in the chancery. All in all, the impression is gained that while a powerful court officer of the moment (Apocaucus) directed financial policy and the collecting apparatus, someone quite junior (Cinnamus) acted as guardian of the reserve (precisely as suggested above, p. 442).

320 See above, pp. 391–4, p. 421 n. 216. See also below, p. 446 n. 332.

321 George Pachymeres, *De Michaele et Andronico Palaeologis, De Mich.* I.23,25; Bonn edn, I, pp. 68, 71. For the modern site: Cook, *The Troad*, pp. 318–19.

322 See above, p. 116.

323 Anonymous, *De Officiis* I, III; ed. Verpeaux, pp. 139, 188. It is nevertheless clear that Theodore II was responsible not only for establishing the treasury at Astytzium, but also for closing (as it turned out, temporarily) the mint of Thessalonica, and for more tightly regulating the production of coin at the mint of Magnesia, all of which seems to betoken some concerted concern for financial matters, and it may quite well have been he who instituted the *domestikoi*. See: Hendy, *DOC* IV.

Given the situation of the Nicaean *vestiarion* at Magnesia, there are obvious administrative grounds for supposing the Nicaean mint to have been similarly situated. For the *vestiarion* (as implied above) had originated in the same *officium* as the mint, and had later given its name to the *sekreton* that included the mint.

On criteria of module, style and iconography, the coinage of Theodore I (1208–22) divides into two main groups, one of which seems to be generally later than the other and shows strong affinities with the coinage of Theodore's successor, John III. The two groups also seem to conform to rather different distribution patterns, the earlier occurring in reasonable but never relatively large proportions in European hoards, the later very rarely occurring in European hoards at all, but tending to occur in Asian hoards and site-finds, particularly in those from the area between the rivers Hermus and Maeander. The implication seems to be that at some stage of the reign of Theodore I the Nicaean mint was moved from Nicaea, within easy reach of the always potentially, sometimes actually, hostile Latins and Selçuks, to Magnesia, at the centre of the empire.

A general precondition of this move would have been Theodore's elimination of dynasts such as Theodore Mangaphas in Philadelphia, Manuel Mavrozomes in the Maeander valley, and Sabbas Asidenus in Sampson, near Miletus, and his consolidation of the same by his defeat of the Selçuk sultan Keyhusrev at Antioch-on-the-Maeander in 1211. The particular cause of the move, however, may have lain in the Latin campaigns which followed the Selçuk defeat and which led to Theodore's cession of a large part of north-western Asia Minor to the Latin emperor Henry in *c.* 1214.[324]

As it happens, the early date of this move, which might otherwise be expected to have been the work of John III, is supported by the evidence of the ecclesiastical historian Nicephorus Callistus Xanthopoulus. John (X) Camaterus, the last patriarch of Constantinople before the conquest of 1204, was appointed on 5 August 1198, and reigned until 26 May 1206, dying at Didymoteichum. According to Xanthopoulus, Michael (IV) Autoreianus, the first Byzantine patriarch after the conquest was appointed by Theodore on 20 March 1207 at Nicaea, and reigned until his death six years, five months and six days later. This should mean that he died in late August 1213. The patriarchal throne was then vacant for $10\frac{1}{2}$ months because of the emperor's absence in the region of Thrakesion (*eis to Thrakēsion*) and it was not until 28 September 1214 that Michael's successor Theodore (II) Eirenicus was appointed. Theodore reigned one year, four months and three days only. This should mean that he died in late January or early February 1216. The throne was then again vacant for some time because of the emperor's absence in the theme of Thrakesion (*en tō themati tōn Thrakēsiōn*) and it was not until 3 June 1216 that Eirenicus' successor, Maximus (II), was appointed.[325]

[324] Hendy, *DOS* XII, pp. 227, 232–5.

[325] Nicephorus Callistus Xanthopoulus, *Enarratio de Episcopis Byzantii*; ed. J.-P. Migne, in *PG* CXLVII, at col. 465. A. I. Papadopoulos-Kerameus, 'Theodoros Eirēnikos Patriarkhēs Oikoumenikos en Nikaia', *Byzantinische Zeitschrift* 10 (1901), pp. 182–92.

The chronology of virtually all the events of the period immediately following the conquest of 1204, let alone that of patriarchal appointments and deaths, has been the subject of much confusion and discussion. Even Xanthopoulus' evidence cited above is not without its obvious internal discrepancies: it is not at all clear, for example, if Autoreianus died in late August 1213, and the patriarchal throne was then vacant for 10½ months, why Eirenicus should not have been appointed until 28 September 1214. The latest, but not necessarily definitive, contribution to the discussion would indeed date the three post-conquest patriarchs mentioned above as follows: Michael IV, 20 March 1208–26 August 1214; Theodore II, 28 September 1214–31 January 1216; Maximus II, late June–late December 1216.[326] What is nevertheless significant is that, at least twice and possibly even three times, on the occasion of a patriarch dying in autumn or winter, Theodore should have been unable to appoint a successor until the following summer or autumn because he was in the region or theme of Thrakesion. The implication is clear: the custom according to which the emperor spent the autumn and winter in that theme, the *doux* of which was generally an *oikeios*, and in the centre of which Nymphaeum lay, had already been established by the early or middle years of Theodore's reign. This of course has no necessary bearing upon the identity of the actual builder of the palace at Nymphaeum, generally implied or reckoned by both contemporary and modern sources to be John III, although the city itself achieves a possibly significant earlier mention under Theodore,[327] but does at least lend a great deal of plausibility to the numismatic evidence for the early moving of the mint from Nicaea to Magnesia. And if the mint then, probably, the *vestiarion* too.

The existence and operation of mints at Constantinople and Thessalonica during the period of Latin occupation, 1204–61 for the former, 1204–24 for the latter, will be noted in the eighth chapter of this book.[328] The relation of these mints to the administrative system of their respective states remains unknown.

The existence and operation of a mint at Trebizond, at least from the reign of Andronicus I (1222–35) onwards, and of various other minor mints, such as Arta and Rhodes, will also be noted.[329] Evidence for the administrative system of the empire centred upon Trebizond is extremely meagre for the thirteenth century. It is, however, relatively plentiful for the fourteenth and fifteenth centuries, and here, as in the contemporary restored empire centred upon Constantinople, the *vestiarion* seems to have

[326] V. Laurent, 'La chronologie des patriarches de Constantinople au XIII$^{e}$ s. (1208–1309)', *Revue des Études Byzantines* 27 (1969), pp. 129–35, 150.

[327] Refs: Angold, *A Byzantine Government in Exile*, p. 63; see also above, p. 118. For the mention under Theodore: George Acropolites, *Historia* xv; ed. Heisenberg and Wirth, I, p. 27 (the emperor Henry encamps around Nymphaeum – *mekhri kai autou tou Nymphaiou tas skēnas ho Erēs epēxato* – and then returns). This might be taken as suggesting that Nymphaeum already possessed some significance, even if not yet a palatine one.

[328] See below, pp. 520–1.

[329] See below, pp. 522–3 (Trebizond), 523, 524 (Arta), 525 (Rhodes), 524–5 (Serbia), 519–20, 525 (Bulgaria).

acted both as the central repository of imperial wealth and as virtually the sole instrument of fiscal administration.[330]

After his recovery of Thessalonica from the Latins in 1224, Theodore Ducas, previously ruler of Epirus, used that city rather than Arta as his capital and therefore continued to utilise the mint there.[331] After his acquisition of Thessalonica from the Ducae in 1246, John III, the Nicaean emperor, in turn continued to utilise its mint as (with a brief but significant interruption by Theodore II) did both his Nicaean and Constantinopolitan successors.[332] For much of the final Byzantine period Thessalonica was therefore operating in parallel with Constantinople, producing billon trachea, and possibly even gold hyperpyra, in much the same way as it had done during the twelfth century. The administrative basis of this final period of operation remains unknown, unless it bore some relation to the functions of the *domestikos tōn dysikōn thematōn* of the *De Officiis*.[333] Its latest known, or at least identifiable, products, are datable to *c.* 1354–65, although one issue has been dated even later (1369–87).[334]

Subsequently, the only possible or probable candidate as an Anatolian mint is the city of Philadelphia, an isolated Byzantine enclave in Ottoman territory, surviving as such until 1390. It would thus have fallen into the class of mints tending to occur in peripheral or isolated regions of the empire as a matter of convenience or necessity. This identification, hinted at in documentary sources, and possibly even spelled out on silver and billon trachea of Michael VIII and on gold hyperpyra of Andronicus II with Michael IX, nevertheless remains conjectural.[335]

The only candidates that are at all plausible as Balkan mints (other than Thessalonica) are the cities of Adrianople and Didymoteichum, one of which may have been utilised

330 Bryer, 'The Society and Institutions of the Empire of Trebizond', I, pp. 340–51.

331 Hendy, *DOS* XII, pp. 268–72.

332 For John III and Theodore II: Hendy, *DOS* XII, pp. 290–3, 295. For Michael VIII and successors: S. Bendall and P. J. Donald, *The Billon Trachea of Michael VIII Palaeologos, 1258–1282*, pp. 23–34 (billon trachea only); *idem*, *The Later Palaeologan Coinage, 1282–1453*, pp. 198–263 (trachea); S. Bendall, 'A Thessalonican Hyperpyron of Andronicus II and Michael IX?', *Numismatic Circular* 89 (1981), p. 158 (gold hyperpyron). The attribution is provisional only, but certainly possible. If it were to prove definitive, it would be tempting to connect it somehow with Andronicus' Thessalonican stay of 1299/1300, and to take it as an indication that the mint actually did travel with the *vestiarion* on occasion (see above, p. 440). See now also: S. Bendall, 'Palaeologan Gold Coins from the Mint of Thessalonica', *Schweizer Münzblätter* 32 (1982), pp. 15–21, where what had been a provisional attribution is confidently extended to a whole body of material. The extension is not wholly convincing, particularly where the coins of Andronicus II alone are concerned.

333 See above, p. 443.

334 Bendall and Donald, *The Later Palaeologan Coinage, 1282–1453*, pp. 248–53 (Anna of Savoy), 254–5 (Manuel II as ruler in Thessalonica?),

335 See below, p. 527, Table 23: *Perperi di Filadelphe*. For the gold hyperpyra: Hendy, *DOS* XII, p. 252 (signum: Π/Φ). For the silver and billon trachea, Bendall and Donald, *The Billon Trachea of Michael VIII Palaeologos, 1258–1282*, pp. 12–20 nos C26–7 (signa: Λ/ΔΦ/Π/Ε, Φ/Α/Α/Φ – the 'A' looking very much like the late form of 'Δ', i.e. 'A'). I am informed by S. Bendall that a silver version of C27 exists in the Vienna Collection.

for a small issue of silver coin in the name of Matthew Asen-Cantacuzene, quasi-emperor, or emperor, in Thrace, during the period 1347–57.[336] (Pl. 35, 17)

Numismatic evidence indicates the metropolitan mint to have continued in operation until well into the reign of John VIII (1425–48).[337] Documentary evidence to be cited in the eighth chapter of this book indicates it to have been still in existence in 1436–9.[338] Finally, both numismatic and documentary evidence indicate it to have been used briefly for a final issue of coin on the very eve of the conquest of Constantinople by the Ottomans in 1453.[339] Few minor institutions have had so long and so nearly continuous a history.

336 P. Protonotarios, 'Une monnaie de l'empereur Matthieu Asen Cantacuzène (1354–1357)', *Revue Numismatique* 23[6] (1981), pp. 96–100. The specimen is, at the moment, unique, and is quite plausibly dated to 1354–6. It is quite possible that a further small issue of silver coin in the name of John (VI) Cantacuzene (Bendall and Donald, *The Later Palaeologan Coinage, 1282–1453*, pp. 150–1, no. 3) is also to be attributed to the same mint. The coins involved, very crude in style, have been dated to the period 1352–4. The only other possibility for both issues is, of course, the Cantacuzene fortress and treasury of Empythium (see above, p. 208).

337 See below, pp. 536–7, 542–3.

338 See below, p. 538 nn. 447–51.

339 See below, pp. 545–6.

# CHAPTER 8

# HISTORY

## (I) PROLEGOMENON

The monetary chaos that had marked the sole reign of Gallienus (260–8) and his immediate successors had been barely, if at all, alleviated by the modest measures of Aurelian (270–5) when Diocletian became emperor in 284. The standard components of the monetary system, the *denarius* which bore a laureate imperial portrait, and its inflationary and increasingly predominant double which is now generally termed the *antoninianus* and which bore a radiate portrait, survived the first half of the third century as coins of diminished but still easily recognisable silver content at about 45%. This content probably weakened further – perhaps to the region of 15% – by or during the joint reign of Valerian and Gallienus (253–60), but it was only during the sole reign of the latter that it collapsed to a mere 1%–2% or so. Both denominations meanwhile lost an appreciable proportion of their weight. The debasement and general depreciation of the silver coinage was accompanied, as might be expected, by a sharp increase in the amount issued: the total of *officinae* in established mints rose and new mints were created, flooding the empire with virtually worthless coin. This combination ensured the discontinuation of the subsidiary coinage of *sestertii*, *dupondii*, *asses* and *semisses*, in bronze and copper, when its issue at an intrinsic value equal or superior to that of the debased standard coinage was simply rendered uneconomic. The gold coinage, which had provided high-value multiples of the denarius, remained undebased and for that reason seems to have come to command a considerable premium. This in turn entailed its disappearance from circulation, and it was in any case by now issued sporadically, in small quantities, and at varying weights only, suggesting that it no longer bore any fixed relation to the standard coinage but was considered as bullion, each piece fetching whatever the market was currently prepared to pay. The traditional coinage system, with its complex range of denominations and relatively stable relationship between each, had thus effectively ceased to exist.[1]

[1] The secondary literature on the coinage of the period from Aurelian to Diocletian is vast and diffuse. The one factor which has acted as a fortunate control over the sheer quantity involved has been the recent

## (II) DIOCLETIAN TO ZENO (284–491)

### *A. Diocletian and reform*

It took some time for Diocletian (284–305), as the leading legislative and administrative force in his tetrarchic system of imperial rule, to turn his attention to a radical reconstruction of the coinage system: curiously enough almost exactly the same amount of time as Alexius I took, in somewhat similar circumstances, eight hundred years later.[2] The delay was in both cases doubtless due to the fact that a degree of political stability was essential for such a course of action even to be considered, let alone its success assured. Both reconstructions were also preceded or accompanied by administrative and other changes, again no doubt a significant coincidence.[3]

The restandardisation of the weight of the gold coin, at one sixtieth of a pound or about 5.3 g (and therefore occasionally marked with the Greek numeral Ξ), in *c.* 286, formed the prelude to a more dramatic phase of reconstruction in *c.* 294/6. This latter involved the introduction of a silver coin, apparently of high purity, at one ninety-sixth of a pound or about 3.2 g (and therefore occasionally marked with the Latin numerals **XCVI**); of a large coin consisting of some 10.0 g of billon (a low-grade copper/silver alloy), at a fineness of about 2%–3% silver; and of two smaller denominations, both seemingly consisting of copper only, the one with a radiate portrait weighing about 3.0 g, the other with a laureate portrait weighing about 1.3 g.[4] (Pls 4 and 6)

epigraphical discoveries at Aezani and Aphrodisias (see below), which have meant that much of the earlier literature has simply, and predictably, become redundant. As a collection of sources, Callu, *La politique monétaire des empereurs romains de 238 à 311* (1969), remains necessary, but should be used with care: as usual, the concentration of material is immense, but the use made of it is frequently uncritical and unconvincing. Two more recent and more concise treatments are: M. H. Crawford, 'Finance, Coinage and Money from the Severans to Constantine', in H. Temporini (ed.), *Aufstieg und Niedergang der römischen Welt* II, *Principat* 2 (1975), at pp. 560–93, and J. Lafaurie, 'Réformes monétaires d'Aurélien et de Dioclétien', *Revue Numismatique* $17^6$ (1975), pp. 73–138. For Diocletian, there is a useful list of the more recent principal literature in A. K. Bowman, 'The Economy of Egypt in the Earlier Fourth Century', in C. E. King (ed.), *Imperial Revenue, Expenditure and Monetary Policy in the Fourth Century A.D.* (1980), at p. 34 n. 5. In dealing with Diocletian's reform(s) of the coinage, I have not felt it necessary to indicate where and why I have disagreed with any or all of these treatments (or for that matter with any others): were I to have done so, the following section would have been even more large and complex than it already is.

[2] See below, pp. 513–17. [3] See above, p. 431 n. 273.

[4] For the nature of the reformed coinage system: Sutherland, *RIC* VI, pp. 93–4. The precise dating of the several elements of the reform remains uncertain: Sutherland (*op. cit.* p. 1 giving refs to previous and alternative views) proposed 294 as the date at which the reformed silver and billon were introduced, but this may well need modification. On the one hand, P. Bruun, 'The Successive Monetary Reforms of Diocletian', *American Numismatic Society Museum Notes* 24 (1979), p. 138, would place the introduction of the argenteus, in some mints at least, as early as 293. On the other, a possible redating of the Egyptian revolt of L. Domitius Domitianus – which has numismatic implications – from 296/7 to 297/8, would at least very strongly imply that the introduction of the billon nummus took place later than 294. See: J. D. Thomas, 'The Date of the Revolt of L. Domitius Domitianus', and A. Geissen, 'Numismatische Bemerkung zu dem Aufstand des L. Domitius Domitianus', both *Zeitschrift für Papyrologie und Epigraphik* 22 (1976), pp. 253–79 and 280–6 respectively. Neither the papyrological nor the numismatic evidence appears decisive, and I have adopted the equivocal 294/6 for the introduction of the nummus at least.

Two recent epigraphic discoveries have yielded striking new information concerning the denominational nomenclature and values of the reconstructed coinage. The discovery of a copy of Diocletian's *Edictum de Pretiis Venalium Rerum* of 301 that includes the virtually complete descriptions and prices of the precious metals finally occurred at Aezani in Phrygia Pacatiana. The relevant portion concerning gold reads:[5]

| | |
|---|---|
| *[De aur]o* | |
| *[Aur]i obruzae in regulis sive* | |
| *[in] solidis pondum unum* | Ð$\overline{\text{LXXII}}$ |
| *[Au]ri neti pondum unum* | Ð$\overline{\text{LXXII}}$ |

The equivalent Greek must read:

| | |
|---|---|
| *Peri khrysou* | |
| *Khrysou bryzēs en rhēgliois* | |
| *ē en holokottinois* | λ α′✱[$\overset{3}{\text{M}}$,β] |
| *Khrysou enēsmenou* | λ α′✱[$\overset{3}{\text{M}}$],β |

It is, in other words, quite clear that pure gold (*aurum obruza/khrysos bryzē*), whether in the form of ingots (*in regulis/en rhēgliois*), of coins (*in solidis/en holokottinois*), or of spun gold (*aurum netum/khrysos enēsmenos*),[6] was worth one and the same price by weight. This should finally dispose of the claim that the gold coinage was over-valued, or that its weight was made to fluctuate minutely in accordance with governmental monetary manipulations and policies.[7] It is also striking, although it was absolutely predictable, that the Diocletianic gold coin should already be termed a solidus, and that the term was therefore not introduced specifically to describe the later and lighter Constantinian gold coin.[8]

The Diocletianic solidus was, then, at one sixtieth of a pound of 72,000 denarii, worth a maximum of 1,200 denarii.

The relevant portion of the *Edictum de Pretiis* concerning silver reads:[9]

| | |
|---|---|
| *De argento hoc est pusula primi pondum I* | Ð$\overline{\text{VI}}$ |

The equivalent Greek must read:

| | |
|---|---|
| *Peri argyrou tout' estin m[...] pous[oula] prōtou* | λ α′✱,*s* |

[5] Diocletian, *Edictum de Pretiis Venalium Rerum* XXVIII.1–2; ed. M. Giacchero, pp. 206 (Latin), 207 (Greek). For the text of, and a commentary upon, the Aezani (Latin) text: M. H. Crawford and J. M. Reynolds, 'The Aezani Copy of the Prices Edict', *Zeitschrift für Papyrologie und Epigraphik* 34 (1979), pp. 176, 197 (with confirmation from the notorious Elatea text).

[6] *Aurum netum*: *ibid.* p. 197.

[7] See above, pp. 330 and nn. 81, 82, 337.

[8] See below, p. 466.

[9] Diocletian, *Edictum De Pretiis Venalium Rerum* XXVIII.9; ed. Giacchero, pp. 206 (Latin), 207 (Greek). For the Aezani text and commentary: Crawford and Reynolds, 'The Aezani Copy of the Prices Edict', pp. 177, 198.

The gold:silver ratio therefore stood at a perfectly traditional 1:12, also hinted at in an approximately contemporary papyrus source, and elsewhere, and the Diocletianic silver coin, at one ninety-sixth of a pound, should – other things being equal – have been worth 62.5 denarii. But other things were not equal. The discovery at Aphrodisias in Caria of what appears to have been an imperial letter separately accompanying the *Edictum de Pretiis*, and concerned with a revaluation of the current coinage introduces definite complications. For, in the text of the letter, a silver coin termed the argenteus (denarius or nummus being understood), which can really only be the Diocletianic silver coin, is tariffed at 100 denarii. This tariffing would give the silver pound an enhanced value of 9,600 denarii (against the text's 6,000 denarii).[10]

The forms of the entries for gold and silver in the *Edictum de Pretiis* give a clear implication as to what was happening. Gold is defined in terms of ingots, coins and spun gold, and given a single price; silver is defined in no such terms. Gold, in whatever form, is therefore being treated entirely as a commodity, silver only in its bullion form (i.e. ingots, etc.) is being so treated. Silver in bullion form was then indeed worth 6,000 denarii the pound, but silver in monetary form was indeed equally worth 9,600 the pound: the Diocletianic argenteus, worth 100 denarii, was therefore over-valued to the tune of some 60%. This is unexpected, and unexpectedly large, but by no means improbable, since to tolerate both gold and silver coins circulating at their bullion or near-bullion value is to invite complications, as their values inevitably fluctuate.[11]

The letter accompanying the *Edictum de Pretiis* is, however, concerned principally with the revaluation of the current coinage or, more probably, one or several denominations within the current coinage, and with the regulation of payments subsequently.

Immediately following the imperial entitulatures, the text of the letter commences:[12]

BICHARACTAMỊ[ ....*c.* 30....]ṆTIAỊỊ[....
QVAEINMAIORẸ[ ....*c.* 31....]RIORVM[....
ONFINVS[ ....*c.* 34....]C̣IASAP̣[....
ROMẠ[ ....*c.* 36....]AỊVRṾ[.....
TVOṚ ....*c.* 37....]P̣C̣OLI[.....
SIC̣[ ....*c.* 38....]ẠTTṾ[.....
]ẸVNIṾ[.....
]ẠTIONẠ[...

10 K. T. Erim, J. M. Reynolds and M. H. Crawford, 'Diocletian's Currency Reform; a New Inscription', *Journal of Roman Studies* 61 (1971), p. 173. For another example of a gold:silver ratio of 1:12 at this period, see above, p. 296 n. 208 (Aurelius Isidorus).

11 One may guess that this is what lies behind the relative plenty of the fourth-century silver coinage, and the scarcity of the fifth- and sixth-century one, in the east at least: the values of gold and silver had indeed fluctuated, but the state had not responded, in the end rendering it simply uneconomic to turn bullion silver into coin. Certainly, the sixth century sees the apex of silver plate. See below, pp. 465, 468, 480–2, 494.

12 Erim, Reynolds and Crawford, 'Diocletian's Currency Reform; a New Inscription', p. 172.

]ṾSTRIẠ[....
]ETDEỊ[.....
]EPREỊ[.....
]REM[

Now, the very first word, *bicharacta*, being a *hapax legomenon*, immediately raises problems. It clearly derives from a combination of the Latin prefix *bi* and the Greek verb *kharassein*, and it has been suggested[13] that the word, which is clearly a technical one, means 'twice stamped', and that it refers to the reconstructed coinage, created by a recoinage (i.e. a second stamping) of the old one. This is, of course, possible, but it is nevertheless unlikely. The prefix *bi* can certainly mean 'twice' (that is implying a notion of two elements in sequence), but it can also perfectly well mean 'doubly', 'two-fold', or 'in two manners' (that is implying a notion of two elements in parallel). The only comparable terms in this precise context are *dikharaktos*, *disignatum* and *dichoneutum*, all or several of which are themselves *hapakta*.[14] Nevertheless with the last of these terms firmer ground is reached, for it occurs in a law preserved in the *Codex Theodosianus*,[15] dated 371, which requires *aes dichoneutum* henceforth not only to be delivered to the *largitiones*, but even to be completely withdrawn from use and circulation (*de usu et conversatione*), so that no person shall be allowed to possess it publicly. The law concludes with an affirmation of capital punishment for melters of shaped bronze (*conflatores figurati aeris*) and counterfeiters of coinage (*adulteratores monetae*).[16] The term clearly derives from a combination of the Greek prefix *di* and the verb *kho(a)neuein*. Again, the prefix can mean 'twice' (i.e. in sequence) or 'doubly' (i.e. in parallel), and the term itself could therefore mean 'twice melted' or 'doubly melted' and so on.

Use of the term *bicharacta* is therefore datable to 301, and that of the term *dichoneutum* to 371. The two are certainly generically, and are quite possibly actually, related, both occurring in a strongly monetary context. The clear implication is that one is here in the presence of two technical terms describing the same thing, and that thing is the actual material, consisting of two elements, which through the processes of melting or stamping eventually became a coin. In other words an alloy, and in these cases almost certainly an alloy of copper and silver – that is, billon. Modern works[17] commonly term such an alloy as being of argentiferous leaded tin-bronze, or of argentiferous bronze, but in an ancient or mediaeval context there is little doubt that it was considered or treated as a copper-based binary one – containing copper to provide a body for the alloy, and

13 *Ibid.* p. 175.

14 Crawford, 'Finance, Coinage and Money from the Severans to Constantine', p. 581 n. 80.

15 *CTh.* XI.21.1. See below, pp. 472–3.

16 See above, pp. 322–4.

17 E.g. L. H. Cope, 'The Argentiferous Bronze Alloys of the Large Tetrarchic Folles of A.D. 294–307', *Numismatic Chronicle* 8⁷ (1968), pp. 131–4.

silver to provide an enhanced value for it. It is, for instance, in precisely such a fashion that a further law preserved in the *Codex Theodosianus*,[18] and dated 349, refers to metalworkers purifying the *maiorina* coin by separating off the silver from the copper.[19] The *maiorina* was the larger billon coin of the reformed coinage of 348.[20]

The letter accompanying the *Edictum de Pretiis* therefore commences with a reference to *bicharacta* (*moneta*), the large denomination in the reconstructed coinage consisting of some 10.0 g of billon alloy. Since the opening words of the very first sentence form a technical term, it is tempting to assume that they were immediately followed by an explanatory subordinate clause. *CTh.* XI.21.1 commences:[21] *Aes, quod dichoneutum vocatur*; *CTh.* IX.21.9 commences:[22] *Falsae monetae rei, quos vulgo paracharactas vocant*; and *CTh.* IX.23.1 terminates:[23] *Praeter pecunias, quas more solito maiorinas vel centenionales communes appelant*, in other words all open or close according to rather similar formulae. In this case, one is therefore tempted to supply, very tentatively, something along the following lines:

*BICHARACTA/MO*NETA/QVAM/APPELANT/PECVNIAM/SVBST*ANTIAM*
HABENTEM/EX/DVOBVS/METALLIS/FORMATAM/ET
*QVAE/IN/MAIOR*IBVS/NVMMIS/REPPERTA/EST...

In any case, it appears probable that these large billon coins are those that are only slightly later termed *nummi* or *noummoi* (*Italikoi*),[24] and that are possibly in this letter, and certainly in mid fourth-century texts, termed *maiores nummi* or *maiorinae*.[25]

As to the value of the billon nummus, it has been observed[26] that, on the basis of intrinsic value alone, it cannot have been tariffed at less than about one sixth of the bullion value of the argenteus (actually 10.85 d.:62.5 d.), the implication being that it, like the argenteus itself, stood somewhat higher, and was appreciably over-valued.

Now, in or about 301, that is at least approximately contemporaneously with the publication of the *Edictum de Pretiis* and the letter accompanying it, the silver content of the billon nummi from most or all of the eastern (i.e. Diocletianic) mints was distinctly hardened to somewhere in the region of 3%–4%.[27] At about the same time, a mark consisting of the Latin numerals **XXI** or **XX I** was placed upon the reverse of billon nummi

[18] *CTh.* IX.21.6. See below, p. 470.

[19] See also above, pp. 291–2, for a further law (*CTh.* IX.23.1) of the same period (356?) mentioning the melting down of coin.

[20] See below, pp. 470, 473, 474–5.

[21] See below, pp. 472–3.

[22] See above, p. 324.

[23] See above, pp. 291–2.

[24] Refs: Crawford, 'Finance, Coinage and Money from the Severans to Constantine', pp. 580–1 n. 80.

[25] It is of course quite conceivable that the letter actually read: *quae in maior(inis nummis repperta est)*. For the *maiorina*, see above, pp. 292–3, below, pp. 470, 472, 474–5.

[26] L. H. Cope, 'Diocletian's Price Edict and Second Coinage Reform in the Light of Recent Discoveries', *Numismatic Chronicle* 17⁷ (1977), pp. 22–3. These calculations are refined by Lafaurie, 'Réformes monétaires d'Aurélien et de Dioclétien', pp. 114–19.

[27] Cope, 'The Argentiferous Bronze Alloys of the Large Tetrarchic Folles of A.D. 294–307', pp. 126–9.

from the mints of Siscia and Alexandria (Pl. 6, 8).[28] There is little doubt but that this mark was intended to have some real significance, for it is noticeable that it is the diocesan mints of Siscia (Pannonia) and Alexandria (Aegyptus), within the territory allotted to Diocletian in the tetrarchic division of the empire, which abut directly on to the territory allotted to Maximian – Italia in the former case, Africa in the latter – that are involved.[29]

Although the silver content of the billon nummi from the western mints (those of Maximian) does not seem to have been hardened at this stage,[30] nevertheless coins from the mints of Trier, Aquileia, Ticinum and Rome (and later Siscia) discard the established reverse design of a personification of the Genius of the Roman People and the inscription: GENIO POPULI ROMANI (possibly the ROMẠ of the letter), in favour of a perhaps more impressive personification of Moneta and the inscription: SACRA MONET(*a*) AVGG(*ustorum*) ET CAESS(*arum*) NOSTR(*orum*), or near variant, at very much this stage (Pl. 6, 4).[31] It is difficult not to see in this last a parallel of some kind to the events in the east.

The mark **XXI** or **XX I** has been much discussed, although the recent epigraphical discoveries in particular have rendered a number of the explanations previously advanced totally redundant. Recently two major lines of possible explanation have been favoured: either that the mark represents a definition of metallic quantities or proportions present in the monetary alloy;[32] or that it represents a tariffing in terms of a smaller denomination.[33] Neither the suggestion that the mark signifies that there were present 20 obols of silver to 1 libra of bronze alloy, nor the suggestion that it signifies that the coin was worth 20 denarii, is entirely satisfactory in the light of the evidence as it stands at present, but it is at least probable that one of them is substantially correct.

A major, but not the only factor contributing to the doubtful status of both of the suggestions mentioned above lies in the reformed coinage of Aurelian and its continuation

[28] Sutherland, *RIC* VI, pp. 467 (Siscia), 665 (Alexandria).

[29] The connection between the mark XXI or XX I and the measures of 301 is challenged (for Siscia) by A. Jeločnik, 'The Alternation of Genio and Moneta Folles in the Siscia Mint', in *Proceedings of the 8th International Congress of Numismatics, New York–Washington September 1973*, at p. 325, but on grounds that are purely numismatic, and in any case relative and not absolute. It is, however, simply unlikely that a mark of this nature did not have some specific monetary reference, and as it is now known that the coinage underwent certainly a retariffing, and probably a metallic change, in 301, the very high probability is that there was a connection between mark and measures. Jeločnik's alternative explanation, that the Siscian mark is to be connected with Diocletian's passage through on his way to Rome in 303, rather alarmingly also ignores the mark's parallel appearance at Alexandria.

[30] Cope, 'The Argentiferous Bronze Alloys of the Large Tetrarchic Folles of A.D. 294–307', pp. 124–6.

[31] Sutherland, *RIC* VI, under appropriate mint-headings.

[32] E.g. Cope, 'The Argentiferous Bronze Alloys of the Large Tetrarchic Folles of A.D. 294–307', pp. 117–18 (XX obols of silver to I libra of bronze alloy base).

[33] E.g. Erim, Reynolds and Crawford, 'Diocletian's Currency Reform; a New Inscription', pp. 175–6 and n. 23 (XX I = 20 units [denarii]).

right up to the reformed coinage of Diocletian. For it too bears the mark **XXI** (or, less commonly, **XX**).

Now, whatever the marks **XXI/XX** on the coinage of Aurelian and his successors actually mean, and this has itself been much discussed,[34] there can be no reasonable doubt that that is what the marks **XXI/XX I** on the coinage of Diocletian in *c.* 301 also mean. It is in other words most improbable that such an obvious feature of the coinage for twenty years should be abandoned for a mere seven years or so (*c.* 294/6–*c.* 301), and then reappear with a fundamentally or even substantially different meaning. A further proposition, that the marks all represent twenty parts of bronze to one part of silver, and therefore denote an alloy consisting of roughly 95% bronze and 5% silver, is a simple one and – not least because of this – has much to recommend it.[35]

If the marks were to have defined a particular metal content, then, assuming that definition to have been adhered to, at least within reasonable limits, one should be entitled to expect that the coins on which they were superimposed would share a standard composition. The evidence that this was so in this case is not entirely satisfactory, but this may well result from the modern scientific assumption that it is possible to recover the precise composition of a large melt even of standard composition through the metallurgical examination of a single coin resulting from that melt, whereas it is quite clear that the examination of even different sections of a single coin by the same metallurgical method may lead to results differing quite appreciably.[36] All that can be said in this case is that the results, when understood within the limitations of the materials and methods used, do not preclude such a conclusion.[37]

If the marks were to have represented a tariffing in terms of a smaller denomination, then, in a Diocletianic context at least, there can be little doubt but that the denomination involved would have been the denarius. The mark **XX** would, in this case, simply have

[34] Refs: Callu, *La politique monétaire des empereurs romains de 238 à 311*, 325–8.

[35] Thus *contra* Crawford, 'Finance, Coinage and Money from the Severans to Constantine', p. 576 and n. 69 (Aurelian's mark XX I indicates a value of 20 asses, and, the long-standing tariffing of the denarius at 16 *asses* having been lost, and the original tariffing of 10 *asses* having been revived, the Aurelianic coin is therefore a double denarius: ingenious, but not convincing). For the interpretation XX I = 20 parts bronze to 1 part silver: Callu, *La politique monétaire des empereurs romains de 238 à 311*, p. 325 (amongst a list of other possibilities: the proposition was first made by Brambach in 1920). It should be noted that the fact that the mark must mean the same under Diocletian as it had under Aurelian, inevitably favours a metallurgical explanation, given the otherwise dissimilar nature of the coins involved. On the mark see, in the last instance: J. Lafaurie, 'La valeur des monnaies de billon en 300–302', *Bulletin de la Société Française de Numismatique* 37 (1982), pp. 142–4 (concludes that XX shows the coins to be $\frac{1}{20}$ [= 5%] of a notional coin of pure metal – essentially the same as proposed above. His further point, that the Diocletianic nummus was worth 10 d. remains unacceptable).

[36] E.g. the duplicate results in Cope, 'The Argentiferous Bronze Alloys of the Large Tetrarchic Folles of A.D. 294–307', pp. 124–9.

[37] *Ibid.* It is true that the silver percentages generally lie in the range 3–4% and rarely reach the range 4–5%, but it is not impossible that there is some factor, whether deriving from Roman technical practices, or from some metallurgical characteristic, that would explain this.

denoted a coin tariffed at 20 denarii, the mark **XXI** or **XX I** that there were 20 denarii in the one coin. But this must have been so whether under Aurelian or under Diocletian: the assertion that the one must have denoted a tariffing in asses (at 10 asses to the denarius!), the other a tariffing in denarii, while recognising the problems implied by the tariffing solution, merely escapes from them by inadequate special pleading.[38]

There is behind all this discussion the inconvenient fact that the only other tariffing specifically present in the text of the letter accompanying the *Edictum de Pretiis*, at least as it currently survives, is the incomplete one reading:[39]

TIQVINQVEDEN[ARI]ORVMPOTENTIAVIGE[ANT?]

Now, the natural restoration of this would undoubtedly be *viginti quinque denariorum potentia vigeant*, and as such could refer only to the billon nummus, in which case it would have been worth 25 denarii or one quarter of the argenteus. Based, however, on the *a priori* assumption that the billon nummus was worth 20 denarii (because of the mark **XXI/XX I**), it has been restored as (*nummi*) *radiati quinque denariorum potentia vigeant* or similar, in which case it could refer only to the copper radiate of about 3.0 g which would have been worth 5 denarii. Once again, this would seem to involve inadequate special pleading.[40]

The conclusion, based on such evidence as is currently available, which is admittedly inadequate and partial only, should therefore be that the billon nummus consisted of an alloy that was probably constructed in the proportions of twenty parts of bronze to one part of silver, therefore possessing a theoretical silver content of 5.0%, and that it was worth 25 denarii or one quarter of an argenteus, in 301. This tariffing would represent an over-valuation of over 100%, or not unexpectedly considerably in excess of that operating in the case of the (pure) argenteus.

The nomenclature and values of the two remaining denominations, the copper radiate of about 3.0 g, and the copper laureate of about 1.3 g, remain as difficult to define as those of the billon nummus. The radiate: laureate contrast in design traditionally denoted a double: single relationship, and this may well also be reflected in their weights. In this case there is no reason why they should not have been tariffed at 2 and 1 denarius, and thus have formed the successors of the antoninianus of the third century, and the denarius of the first and second centuries. This would, however, have represented the situation at the outset of Diocletian's reconstructed monetary system, in *c.* 294/6, and need not have represented that obtaining after 301.

The last qualification is necessary because it is clear that the letter accompanying the *Edictum de Pretiis* involved not simply a reiteration of pre-existing tariffs, but rather –

[38] See above, p. 455 n. 35.
[39] Erim, Reynolds and Crawford, 'Diocletian's Currency Reform; a New Inscription', p. 173.
[40] *Ibid.* pp. 175–6.

to some degree at least – a retariffing. This is clear from the statement that, from 1 September 301, any new debtors may hand over to the treasury (*fiscus*) the same (i.e. current) coinage (*pecunia*) at a doubled face-value (*geminata potentia*), and that the treasury, if the occasion demands it, should count out at the same rate (*pari condicione*).[41] Quite how far this doubling of face-values extended down through the denominational system remains to be discovered.

The fact that the letter commences with a reference to the billon nummus (*bicharacta moneta*) rather than with one to the gold solidus or the silver argenteus suggests that it was the main object of the revaluation. In fact it does not look as if the gold was formally affected at all: it is known that the government was compulsorily purchasing gold at 60,000 denarii the pound in early 300,[42] and the *Edictum de Pretiis* itself fixes a maximum of 72,000 denarii the pound in late 301.[43] There is simply no room for a doubling of value. If the gold was not affected, then it is most unlikely that the silver was – at least to the radical extent of doubling its value, although it is quite conceivable that its over-valuation was adjusted. What is quite clearly involved is, rather, a retariffing of the subordinate denominations: certainly the billon nummus, and probably the copper radiate and laureate.

The Diocletianic reconstructed coinage system, in its pre- and post-301 states, will thus have appeared as in Table 15. A number of matters are independently explained by this table. In the first place, that it is the subordinate denominations alone that suffer substantial alterations as a result of, or parallel to, the revaluation of 301. The silver-content of the billon nummus was appreciably hardened, and the marks **XXI** or **XX I** appeared in the east,[44] and the *Sacra Moneta* design and inscription appeared in the west.[45] The copper radiate and laureate ceased to be struck after 301, their places being taken by fractions of the nummus.[46] It is clear that, over the long term, being virtually entirely of copper, and having no significant admixture of silver, they could not plausibly be accommodated within the monetary system at doubled face-values, their over valuation having risen to an unacceptable degree. Nevertheless, over the short term, they must have been taken account of, and the possible occurrence of a denomination tarriffed at 4 (i.e *qu*]*attụ*[*or*) denarii in the letter accompanying the *Edictum de Pretiis*[47] suggests that doubled face-values of 4 and 2 denarii may well have been the temporary solution adopted for them. The follis, or standard purse, in its apparently original forms, consisted either of 12,500 denarii – which will have been either 125 silver argentei or 1,000 pre-301 billon nummi – or

41 *Ibid.* p. 173.

42 *P. Beatty Panop.* 2 ll. 215–16.

43 See above, p. 450.

44 See above, pp. 453–4.

45 See above, p. 454.

46 Sutherland, *RIC* VI, pp. 99–100.

47 Erim, Reynolds and Crawford, 'Diocletian's Currency Reform; a New Inscription', 172. On the other hand, this section of the inscription may simply be quoting the relation of the nummus to the argenteus – 25 : 100 = 1 : 4.

Table 15. *The coinage system under Diocletian (pre- and post-301)*

| Pre-301 | | Post-301 | |
|---|---|---|---|
| Gold solidus (max.) | 1,200 d. | Gold solidus (max.) | 1,200 d. |
| Silver argenteus | 100 d. | Silver argenteus | 100 d. |
| Billon nummus | $12\frac{1}{2}$ d. | Billon nummus | 25 d. |
| Copper radiate | 2 d. | Copper radiate | 4 d. |
| Copper laureate | 1 d. | Copper laureate | 2 d. |

of 250 denarii, equalling $2\frac{1}{2}$ silver coins (i.e. argentei) – which will have been 20 pre-reform billon nummi.[48]

Finally, it should be noted that the post-301 denominational table at least does not contradict the crude statistical analysis of prices in the *Edictum de Pretiis*, although it should in fact not be expected that the denominational structure should be so directly and clearly reflected in such an analysis, as is frequently supposed. In the case of wages, whether daily or piece-rate, the evidence for the existence of a 25 denarius piece (the common occurrence of rates of 25 or 50 d.) is in fact remarkably good. In that of prices in general, the evidence for the existence of a 4 denarius piece is even better.[49]

The *Edictum de Pretiis* and the accompanying imperial letter concerned with the revaluation of the current coinage are of course intimately connected, and it is as the sum of the two that Diocletian's fiscal concerns and measures in *c.* 301 should be seen.

The emperor's chief complaint, reiterated several times in the course of the proem to the *Edictum de Pretiis*, is of the universal existence and operation of a raging avarice (*avaritia desaeviens*), a desire of unrestrained madness (*cupido furoris imdomiti*) amounting to a religion (*velut quaedam religio*), and an unbridled passion for plundering (*effrenata livido rapiendi*). His sole specific instance of this insolence (*audacia*), however, is that wherever the common interest dictates the army (*exercitus*) be directed, not only to villages (*vici*) and to towns (*oppida*), but even to every road (*in omni itinere*), the profiteer (*sectio*) extorts prices for saleable goods (*pretia venalium rerum*) that are not simply four-fold or eight-fold but are such as to render the name of the price (*aestimatio*), and of the act, incapable of description by the human language. The result is that sometimes, through the sale of a single item (*distractione unius rei*), the soldier (*miles*) is deprived of his donative and salary (*donativum stipendiumque*), and that the entire contribution of the whole world (*omnis totius*

48 See above, pp. 451, 456–7.

49 E.g. L. H. Cope, 'Diocletian's Price Edict and its Associated Coinage Denominations', *Schweizer Münzblätter* 27 (1977), pp. 10–11. See also: E. Ruschenbusch, 'Diokletians Währungsreform vom 1.9. 301', *Zeitschrift für Papyrologie und Epigraphik* 26 (1977), p. 195–201.

*orbis collatio*) towards the support of the army falls to the detestable gains of robbers (*detestandis quaestibus diripientium*). The emperor's solution is to establish, not the prices of saleable goods, but a (maximal) limit (*modus*).[50]

The evident obsession with the wickedness of the world and the vulnerability of the army is, of course, much as might have been expected from an emperor of military origins, but it does reveal an attitude and reaction to events that, nevertheless, can easily be paralleled amongst the late Roman and Byzantine emperors. There is, in fact, good reason to believe that during the period 284–301 prices and salaries were continuing to rise: both the figures themselves[51] and the statement by Lactantius[52] that Diocletian, through various iniquities, caused an immensely high price level (*immensa caritas*), and then attempted to establish a law for the regulation of the prices of saleable goods (*lex pretiis venalium rerum*), are sufficient witnesses of that. On the other hand, because the emperor's own claim of a four-fold or eight-fold or even greater price rise cannot be substantiated over the relatively short period involved, it is commonly assumed that the claim is exaggerated. But Diocletian, although he mentions the operation of avarice not only over the years, or months, or days, but almost even over the hours and minutes themselves, says nothing specific of the time scale that he considers has brought this situation about. Were he to have had, say, the slightly longer period 268–301 in mind, the statement would have been perfectly reasonable. Over an even longer term, stretching back to the second century, prices had risen by twenty-five- or even fifty-fold, and stretching back to the principate by fifty- or even a hundred-fold.[53]

Two crucial papyrus sources, both concerned with military pay, suggest both the general background to, and the more particular aim of, the combination of edict and letter.

A letter from Aurelius Isidorus, *epitropos* of the Lower Thebaid, to Apollinarius, *stratēgos*, and the *apodektai*, of the Panopolite nome, dated 26 February 300,[54] mentions the payment of arrears to Leontius, *praepositus* of the *equites promoti* of the *Legio II Traiana* stationed at Tentyra. The following dates, sums and headings are involved:

| | | |
|---|---|---|
| 20 Nov. 299 (acc. Diocl.) | 2,500 d. | (*donation*) |
| 22 Dec. 299 (b'day Diocl.) | 2,500 d. | (*donation*) |
| 1 Jan. 300 (4-monthly pay) | 18,000 d. | (*stipendion*) |
| (Total) | 23,000 d. | |

[50] Diocletian, *Edictum de Pretiis Venalium Rerum, Proem*; ed. Giacchero, pp. 134–7.

[51] Callu, *La politique monétaire des empereurs romains de 238 à 311*, pp. 395–8 (prices), 399–400 (salaries).

[52] Lactantius, *De Mortibus Persecutorum* VII.6; ed. Moreau, I, p. 85.

[53] The principal figures and multipliers are given by Callu: *La politique monétaire des empereurs romains de 238 à 311*, pp. 401–7.

[54] *P. Beatty Panop.* 2 ll. 197–203.

A brief account slip, on behalf of an unnamed *praepositus*, and of uncertain (but definitely Constantinian) date,[55] reads:

> Account (*logos*) of the lord *praepositus*:
> for the *stipendion* of 1 September, 36,000 d.
> for the *donatiouon* of 25 July [acc. Const.], 2,500 d.
> total, 38,500 d.

Now, given that the two officers involved in these sources were of the same rank, that of *praepositus*, one source being dated immediately before 301, the other not too long after 301, it is clear that there is here, crystallised, the effects of Diocletian's combined measures of that year. The *donativum* of both officers is 2,500 d., while the *stipendium* of the earlier is 18,000 d. and that of the later is 36,000 d.: in other words, the later is precisely double the earlier. The implications of this seem obvious.

Two main possibilities arise as to the status and means of payment. Either the *donativum* was paid in precious-metal coin, which was not affected by the revaluation of 301, the sum therefore remaining the same, and the *stipendium* was paid in base-metal coin, the same number of pieces being handed over before and after 301, their doubled face-value leading to an effective doubling of the *stipendium* itself. Or both *donativum* and *stipendium* were paid in base-metal coin, but a distinction was drawn between the status of the *donativum* (theoretically a free-will payment), half the previous number of pieces being handed over after 301 so as to keep the sum the same, and that of the *stipendium* (an obligatory payment), the same number of pieces as previously being handed over after 301, again so as effectively to double the sum.

A decision as between these two main possibilities is difficult or impossible on the available evidence. It has been commonly assumed[56] that annual *donativa* (as opposed to accessional and quinquennial ones) were paid in base-metal coin, that is probably essentially in billon nummi, but this need not necessarily have been the case, as the sums were relatively small: for example, a *donativum* of 2,500 d. both pre- and immediately post-301 could have been handed over in the form of two solidi and one argenteus (2 × 1,200 d. + 100 d. = 2,500 d.). And while it would doubtless have been popular to hand over the same number of base-metal pieces, with a doubled face-value, after 301, it would have probably been most unpopular to hand over half the number of pieces, even with a doubled face-value, after that date. The fact that there is no obvious diminution in the production of base-metal coin at this period, at least as reflected in the number of *officinae* operating in the mints, may perhaps also be taken as favouring the first possibility.[57]

[55] *P. Oxy.* 1047.
[56] E.g. Jones, *Later Roman Empire* II, p. 623.
[57] Sutherland, *RIC* VI, pp. 37, 46, 57, 67.

In any case, it is now clear that Diocletian's specific concerns, evident in the proem to the edict, were indeed carried through in the measures that followed. Doubtless within a general context wider than the purely military, one of his specific aims was to restore to the military *stipendium* at least part of the purchasing power that it had lost over the few preceding years, possibly even the preceding thirty years. He attempted to achieve this aim through a combination of measures that were partly juridical, partly financial, and partly purely monetary: on the one hand to fix a maximum price-level, and on the other to harden the silver content of the main base-metal denomination, the billon nummus, to a degree that would permit it convincingly to hold a doubled face-value, meanwhile continuing to hand over the same number of pieces as previously where the *stipendium*, at least, was concerned, thereby (at least in theory) doubling the purchasing power of the *stipendium* itself.

This combination of measures of course failed. Diocletian himself forbade[58] those who possessed the commodities necessary to sustenance and employment (*species victui adque usui necessarias*) subsequently to think that they ought to be withdrawn (*subtrahendas*) from the market. Lactantius reports[59] that precisely that happened, and that no merchandise (*venale*) whatever appeared through fear; that an even higher price-level arose; and that the law was eventually abandoned.

The emperor was not necessarily well served even by his administrators, for at least one provincial governor (Fulvius Asticus of Phrygia [with Caria?]) characterised the maximal prices of the edict as 'just and established (*teimai dikaiai kai rhētai*)', which is precisely what Diocletian himself denied them to be – the process by which maxima become norms is perhaps better understood (but not necessarily better coped with) today.[60]

In the short term Diocletian's reconstructed coinage system proved remarkably successful. For over a decade the physical properties of all the denominations had remained substantially unaltered, despite their complexity when compared to those of the preceding period and although the values of some had undergone an early and drastic retariffing. In the medium term it proved much less so. With the abdication of Diocletian and Maximian in 305, and the political fragmentation that almost immediately followed, a whole section of the system – the subsidiary coinage – fell away, and absolute tariffing other than the most transitory became impossible. Nevertheless, in the longer term and more general sense, its influence proved decisive. Although as early as the reign of Claudius II (268–70) there had been an attempt to retrieve the gold coinage from the confusion

58 Diocletian, *Edictum de Pretiis Venalium Rerum, Proem*; ed. Giacchero, p. 137.

59 Lactantius, *De Mortibus Persecutorum* VII.7; ed. Moreau, I, p. 85.

60 M. H. Crawford and J. M. Reynolds, 'The Publication of the Prices Edict; a New Inscription from Aezani', *Journal of Roman Studies* 65 (1975), pp. 160–3. For Fulvius Asticus: *PLRE* I, p. 119. For Phrygia with Caria, see now: C. M. Roueché, 'Rome, Asia and Aphrodisias in the Third Century', *Journal of Roman Studies* 71 (1981), pp. 108–12.

of weight into which it had fallen, its success had been temporary and partial only and a multiplicity of standards characterised the succeeding period. The restandardisation of *c.* 286 marked the definitive re-establishment of the principle of a single major standard of weight, and although the particular standard adopted was soon superseded there was to be no regression from the principle itself. The Diocletianic silver coinage probably represented a metallic purity, and certainly represented a weight, that had not been seen since the reigns of Nero (57–68) and his immediate successors: although the single standard adopted was soon superseded in favour of several different ones, there was once again to be no systematic regression from the principle of stability and metallic purity.

### *B. Constantine and depreciation*

It was in the subsidiary coinage, as represented by the billon nummus, that the greatest weakness of the Diocletianic system lay. In 307 Constantine initiated a reduction in its weight, from about 10 g to somewhere between 6 and 7, in that portion of the west then under his control – Britain and Gaul. He was followed almost immediately by Maxentius in Italy and Africa and, after a slight delay, by Licinius in Pannonia, and by Galerius and Maximinus in the east.[61] In 310 Constantine initiated a second reduction, to somewhere between 4 and 5 g, and was again followed – this time with less promptitude and uniformity – by his colleagues.[62] The process continued after 312/13, when Constantine and Licinius achieved supremacy in west and east respectively, and after 324, when Constantine finally eliminated his colleague, the last survivor (other than himself) of the tetrarchic system of imperial rule. By 337, when Constantine died, the coin had been reduced to a mere 1.5 g or so – having meanwhile lost a large proportion of its already minimal silver content.[63] As the reduction in weight proceeded, it became probably less necessary, and certainly less convenient, to issue its fractions, and these (like those of the later follis) eventually dropped out of the coinage system altogether.[64] (Pl. 7)

The precise effects of this depreciation upon the value of the nummus and that of the gold pound as expressed in denarii remain uncertain: the question is moreover in all probability complicated by other factors. Coins from the mint of Lyons, under the control of Constantine, of the first reduction and datable to the years 308–9, bear the mark:[65] CI $\frac{\mathrm{H}}{\mathrm{S}}$ (Pl. 7, 1). This seems to incorporate the traditional abbreviation for the sestertius (HS). It must be supposed then that, despite the reduced weight of the coins, one hundred

61 Sutherland, *RIC* VI, pp. 100–1.

62 *Ibid.* pp. 101–3.

63 Bruun, *RIC* VII, pp. 9–10 and nn. 6–11 (weight standards); see below, pp. 464–5 and nn. 73–4 (silver-contents).

64 Sutherland, *RIC* VI, p. 100. Bruun, *RIC* VII, pp. 11, 47. See also above, p. 457.

65 Sutherland, *RIC* VI, pp. 263–5.

sestertii (i.e. twenty-five denarii) still went to make up each one of them. Constantine had thus not only initiated the reduction in weight but had maintained the tariff: if his colleagues imitated the reduction it seems likely that they also will have maintained the tariff.

Now, coins from the mint of Nicomedia, under the control of Galerius whose capital it was, of the first reduction and exactly coterminous with its existence at that mint (307–11), bear the mark **CMH** (Pl. 7, 2).[66] The 'C' will once more presumably be the Latin numeral for one hundred (sestertii); the '**MH**', assuming it to be numerical, can only be the Greek for forty-eight. It has been suggested that the Diocletianic nummus of about 10 g was struck at a theoretical figure of thirty-two to the pound.[67] If this was indeed the case, a coin of between 6 and 7 g (the first reduction) would of course be entirely appropriate to a figure of forty-eight to the pound.

Coins from the nearby mint of Cyzicus did not receive the mark until *c.* 308 perhaps by imitation from Nicomedia (Pl. 7, 3):[68] it seems to have persisted sporadically, perhaps by immobilisation of the reverse design with inscription: GENIO AVGVSTI, into a period when '**MH**' can hardly have remained appropriate.[69]

It might alternatively be supposed that at Nicomedia the whole mark '**CMH**' was removed when the '**MH**' part of it became inappropriate because of the continuing reductions in weight, while at Cyzicus the whole was retained because the '**C**' remained appropriate until the retariffing implied on the Licinian issues of 318–24 – when it finally disappeared. In any case, the '**C**' being not only a Latin notation but also involving the sestertius will probably have been strange to the east, whereas the '**MH**' being a Greek one and involving only a weight will presumably have been familiar. The superficially anomalous mixture of Latin and Greek notations used in the mark merely anticipated a phenomenon that later is so common as to be banal.[70]

Coins from the eastern mints, under the control of Licinius and datable to the years 321–4, bear the mark $\frac{\text{X}}{\text{IIP}}$ (= 12½, presumably denarii) (Pl. 7, 13–14).[71] Such a figure seems most likely to have resulted from halving twenty-five, in other words finally recognising, but only partly compensating for, what was by then a gross over-valuation of the nummus.

[66] *Ibid.* pp. 561–5.

[67] *Ibid.* p. 93.

[68] *Ibid.* p. 561.

[69] *Ibid.* p. 564.

[70] Crawford, 'Finance, Coinage and Money from the Severans to Constantine', at p. 588 n. 102, sees no way of interpreting the mark as one of value: but if the mark is split into its ethnic parts, **C** and **MH**, no difficulties arise.

[71] Bruun, *RIC* VII, pp. 536 n. 1,548 (Heraclea). The dating is Bruun's and objections have been raised to it (see, for example, below, n. 74), but it is not likely to be more than minimally out. The mark appears at all eastern mints. It is now clear that these issues have no silver in them at all, presumably as a consequence and sign of the devaluation: J.-N. Barrandon and C. Brenot, 'Analyse de monnaies de bronze (318–340) par activation neutronique à l'aide d'une source isotopique de californium 252', in *Les 'dévaluations' à Rome, époque républicaine et impériale (Rome, 13–15 novembre 1975)*, at p. 133 (nos 129–40: Iovi Conservatori).

The halving of the tariff in 321–4 seems to have achieved reference in several papyrus sources, notably *P.Ryl.* 607, *P.Oslo* 83 and *PSI* 965, of which the first is by far the most complete and informative:

Dionysius to Apion, greeting. The divine fortune of our lords [*sc.* the emperors] has decreed that the Italian coin (*to Italikon nomisma*) be reduced to half a nummus. Make haste, therefore, to spend all the Italian coinage (*argyrion*) that you have, and purchase on my behalf goods of every description (*eidē pantodapa*), at whatever price (*timē*) you find them. For this purpose I have despatched an *officialis* to you. But take notice that should you intend to indulge in any malpractices I shall not allow you to do so. I pray, my brother, that you may be long in health. (Verso): I received the letter from the *officialis* on 8 Pharmouthi.

The letter has been much discussed and widely dated, but there really is no good reason against, and there are in fact good reasons for, assuming the Licinian halving of the tariff to be the one referred to, and dating the letter to *c.* 321.[72]

The circumstances in which the letter was written and sent are in any case clear: someone (obviously an official) with inside or advance knowledge has heard of the imminent monetary retariffing or devaluation and is attempting to escape the consequences by moving into goods, presumably to hold and resell after the retariffing has been made public.

The nummus had not only suffered a drastic reduction in weight, but had also lost a large proportion of its silver content. The precise course of this latter phenomenon remains uncertain, but most western issues of the period *c.* 305–*c.* 328 seem only to contain between 1% and 2% silver, with only one or two issues dated 319/20 seeming to contain between 3% and 4% and possibly hinting at some temporary relief or reform.[73] Most issues of the period 313–40 again seem to contain between 1% and 3% silver, again with one or two issues dated 319/20 seeming to contain between 3% and 5%, according to alternative analytical procedures.[74]

Even the halving of the tariff in *c.* 321 which, like Diocletian's doubling of 301, was

[72] A. H. M. Jones, 'Inflation under the Roman Empire', *Economic History Review* 5 (1953), pp. 317–18. Crawford, 'Finance, Coinage and Money from the Severans to Constantine', at p. 589 and n. 105. The whole point about *P. Ryl.* 607 is that it very probably derives from the archive of one Theophanes, who was on the staff of the Prefect of Egypt in the second and third decades of the fourth century. Dionysius was possibly his father. This, of course, would explain the inside knowledge of the retariffing evident in the letter. It would also exclude any of the other datings, extending right back to Aurelian, that have been proposed for the letter.

[73] Cope, 'The Argentiferous Bronze Alloys of the Large Tetrarchic Folles of A.D. 294–307', pp. 124–7; *idem*, 'The Metallurgical Analysis of Roman Imperial Silver and *Aes* Coinage', in E. T. Hall and D. M. Metcalf (eds), *Methods of Chemical and Metallurgical Investigation of Ancient Coinage*, at pp. 34–41. J.-P. Callu, 'La circulation monétaire de 313 à 348', in H. A. Cahn and G. Le Rider (eds), *Proceedings of the 8th International Congress of Numismatics, New York–Washington September 1973*, at pp. 231–2.

[74] J.-N. Barrandon, J.-P. Callu and C. Brenot, 'The Analysis of Constantinian Coins (A.D. 313–40) by Non-destructive Californium 252 Activation Analysis', *Archaeometry* 19 (1977), pp. 173–86. A more comprehensive report is now also available: Barrandon and Brenot, 'Analyse de monnaies de bronze (318–340) par activation neutronique à l'aide d'une source isotopique de californium 252', pp. 123–44. It would in this respect also be interesting to know the silver content of the coins with the facing busts

almost certainly accompanied by legislation dictating that (in certain circumstances at least) the same number of pieces should be handed over as before, thus bringing about a purely notional reduction in some prices, can scarcely be termed deflationary in any but the most immediate sense. For a nummus that by then weighed only about 3 g and that contained a much reduced proportion of silver was still tariffed at the same as Diocletian's nummus of the period *c.* 294–301 which weighed about 10 g and had an intact proportion of silver.

The result of all this was inevitable: the price of gold began to rise in terms of denarii. Two early fourth-century sources put the value of the gold pound at 88,000 d. or more probably 110,000 d.[75] and at 100,000 d.[76] The pace then seems to have quickened: by 323 in the west it had reached over 430,000 d.;[77] and by 316/18 in the east it had also already reached over 430,000 d.[78] In 324, in the east, on the other hand, it seems to have stood at 313,000 d. only, perhaps thereby temporarily reflecting Licinius' devaluation of the nummus by half.[79]

The price of silver rose similarly: by the early fourth century the value of the silver pound stood at 8,000/8,328 d.[80] As the price of silver in bullion form rose, reducing the over-valuation of silver in monetary form, so it would have become less worthwhile to turn the one into the other, resulting in a virtual cessation of coining in silver.[81] On the other hand, silver seems to have weakened against gold, and during the fourth century the traditional gold:silver ratio still present in the *Edictum de Pretiis*,[82] that is 1:12, moved downwards and stabilised at what was to become the commonest early Byzantine ratio,[83] that is 1:14.4.

The reign of Constantine witnessed two further developments in the coinage system that were to be of long-term significance, both involving the precious-metal coinage.

of the two Licinii, struck at Nicomedia, Cyzicus and Antioch, and immediately preceding the coins with the mark $\frac{\text{X}}{\text{IIP}}$. See: P. Bastien, 'Coins with a Double Effigy issued by Licinius at Nicomedia, Cyzicus, and Antioch', *Numismatic Chronicle* 13⁷ (1973), pp. 87–97. Bastien dates the coins with the mark to 318–24.

75 *P. Ryl.* 616. See: J. R. Rea, '*P.S.I.* IV. 310 and Imperial Bullion Purchases', *Chronique d'Égypte* 49 (1974), p. 165, for a revision of the customary figure (88, 000 d.). There seems little point in worrying beyond a certain point about the precise or even close relative dating of these documents: the rates set may well have fluctuated not only with time but also with place, and indeed even with the kind of transaction involved.

76 *P. Oxy.* 2106.

77 *ILS* 9420 (Feltre Inscr.). The 'aurei' involved would by this date undoubtedly have been 'solidi' – i.e. not of $\frac{1}{60}$ but of $\frac{1}{72}$ lb. See below, p. 466.

78 *P. Oxy.* 3121.

79 *P. Oxy.* 1430. Licinius' devaluation would, of course, have meant, at least in theory, that whilst the same number of nummi would have been required to purchase a pound of gold, their face-value would have been halved, and one might thus expect to find an at least momentary drop in the price of gold in the east. Licinius, like Diocletian, presumably accompanied his monetary change with some kind of market price regulation.

80 *Sb.* 9253 (8,000 d.); *PSI* 310 (8,328 d.). On the latter: Rea, '*P.S.I.* IV.310 and Imperial Bullion Purchases', esp. pp. 169–74.

81 See below, pp. 466–7. The fact that the cessation of silver was universal seems to indicate that the cause was not simply Constantine's financial situation.

82 See above, p. 451 and n. 10.

83 See below, p. 481 Table 16.

Between 307 and 309, while his authority remained confined to Britain and Gaul, very little precious-metal coinage seems to have been issued from the mint of Trier, his capital, and such as was issued consisted of fractional pieces only.[84] It seems reasonable to equate this with financial exigence, particularly since it was at precisely this point that he began to manipulate the billon coinage in an inflationary direction. In 309 the issue of units (and their multiples) recommenced, but these were no longer related to the Diocletianic standard of one sixtieth of a pound: rather to what is recognisably a lower standard of one seventy-second of a pound or about 4.4 g.[85] (Coins from the mint of Antioch, datable to the years 336–7, actually bear the mark **LXXII**) (Pl. 5, 8).[86] The new coin, assuming the Diocletianic tariffing of gold to have survived, at least in theory, will have been worth a maximal 1,000 d., which probably also represented a slightly more convenient figure than the previous 1,200 d. for the purposes of reckoning.[87]

This standard, that of the classic *solidus* (*aureus* being understood), was not imitated by his colleagues and was introduced only as the extent of his territorial authority increased.[88] It is by no means certain that the term *solidus* itself originated with, or that its use was confined to, issues of the Constantinian standard, for certain coins from the mint of Antioch, under the control of Licinius, of the Diocletianic standard and datable to the years 317–19, bear the mark: **IS**/**IN** which – it is most plausibly suggested – stands for I S(*olidus*) INT(*eger*) (Pl. 5, 1).[89]

Nor is it at all certain that the term *aureus* was applied to issues of the Diocletianic standard only, for the Feltre inscription,[90] cut eleven years after Constantine's conquest of Italy and the introduction of the solidus there, still terms gold coins *aurei*. This should not be taken as implying that pre-Constantinian issues were intended: merely that the modern distinction between *aureus* and *solidus* is an artificial one, anticipating the latter's eventual supremacy. But it is above all ironical that, whatever its mathematical and practical convenience, a standard that was destined to dominate the late Roman and Byzantine worlds, and to last a millennium, should have originated in such squalid circumstances so early on in Constantine's career.[91]*

The issue of silver had virtually ceased everywhere by *c.* 310. It was recommenced in *c.* 320. But whereas the Diocletianic system had included only one basic denomination,

* The paragraphs above are as written before the discovery of the crucial fragments of the Aezani copy of the *Edictum de Pretiis*.

84 Sutherland, *RIC* VI, pp. 215–20.

85 *Ibid.* pp. 220–3. It seems that contemporary silver was debased (*ibid.* p. 224). It seems likely that only the acquisition of Maxentius' reserve (see above, p. 284 and n. 167) will have changed Constantine's financial situation.

86 Bruun, *RIC* VII, pp. 695–6.

87 See above, p. 450.

88 E.g. Arles, 313/17: Bruun, *RIC* VII, pp. 234, 244–5. Ticinum, 315: *ibid.* pp. 362–4.

89 *Ibid.* pp. 678–9.

90 See above, p. 465 and n. 77.

91 See now: Diocletian's *Edictum de Pretiis Venalium Rerum*, above, p. 450.

that weighing one ninety-sixth of a pound, the Constantinian seems to have included two: the Diocletianic, now revived, and a further, weighing one seventy-second of a pound – the same, that is, as the solidus.[92]

Much discussion has been wasted over the correct contemporary nomenclature of these two denominations: the Diocletianic is now frequently termed a *siliqua*, the Constantinian a *miliarensis*. Neither identification possesses any warrant other than modern convenience.

The monetary siliqua was primarily a weight, $\frac{1}{1728}$ lb, or one twenty-fourth that of a solidus, and secondarily an expression of value dependent upon and equivalent to that of a siliqua of gold. Because sums are found expressed in terms of so many solidi and so many siliquae it does not necessarily follow that the siliqua was a specific coin, although obviously a coin (and particularly a silver one) might have been struck to, and have held, that value on occasion: these sums (unless otherwise specified) might be made up with a combination of coins of any or all of the monetary metals.[93]

The miliarensis presents a problem of a different kind, for there is good evidence that the term did apply to a silver coin, or coins, and in its Greek form *miliarēsion* it undoubtedly did come to apply to the standard silver coin of Leo III and his successors. There is however no evidence that, except perhaps at its very inception when (according to a late gloss of composite origin and uncertain reliability) it may have applied to a coin worth the thousandth part of the gold pound (hence its origin, the figure itself is not improbable as an approximation: 72 × 14 = 1,008), the term applied to a coin with a particular value or weight standard. It seems much more probable that it rapidly acquired a generic meaning – if it had not done so from the first – and applied to silver coins in general. It is of course conceivable, even probable, that if on occasion only one basic silver denomination was being issued then the term would perforce acquire a temporary attachment to that denomination. It is nevertheless the definite impression of a generic meaning that is conveyed by quite early usage in sources other than the metrological – which give conflicting accounts of the term's origins.[94]

By 337, when Constantine died, the coinage system therefore consisted of the following major elements: the gold solidus, the two silver denominations, the depreciated remnant of the Diocletianic nummus.[95] (Pls 5, 7)

92 Bruun, *RIC* VII, p. 4.

93 The point was first made by Jones, and still stands; see, for example: A. H. M. Jones, 'Numismatics and History', in R. A. G. Carson (ed.), *Essays in Roman Coinage Presented to Harold Mattingly*, at p. 28 and n. 2. The equivalent point regarding the *miliarensis* is equally valid (*ibid.* at p. 28 and n. 1).

94 *Contra* J.-P. Callu, 'Les origines du "miliarensis": le témoignage de Dardanius', *Revue Numismatique* 22$^{6}$ (1980), pp. 120–30 (accepts without real question the equation *miliarensis* = $\frac{1}{72}$ lb, and proposes the Anastasian reform [498] as the origin of the equation 1 *miliarensis* = $\frac{1}{12}$ solidus). In any case, the latter equation actually goes back to Diocletian – see above, pp. 450, 451, and 458, Table 15.

95 See above, pp. 466 (solidus), 466–7 (silver), 462 (nummus).

### C. Constantius II and later attempts at base-metal stability

The gold coinage retained its precise form until late in the century, and even then underwent minor adjustment only. The fractions of the solidus had hitherto comprised the *semissis* (half), and the *tremissis* (third), actually a somewhat anomalous piece that seems to have weighed nine siliquae and therefore to have borne no simple fractional relationship to a unit of either one sixtieth or one seventy-second of a pound, but rather formed a sixteenth of an ounce. During the reign of Theodosius I (379–95) this piece was reduced in weight to eight siliquae and thus became a true third of the solidus.[96] (Pls 5, 7; 8, 10–11; 12, 13–18)

The silver coinage achieved great complexity in a whole series of parallel weight standards. To the two Constantinian, there were added, in 337 or soon after, two more – at one twenty-fourth and one sixtieth of a pound. Silver coins (*nummi argentei*) of this latter standard are mentioned in a law of 384, and their earlier existence is confirmed by certain examples of Constans (337–50) and Magnentius (750–3), from the mint of Aquileia, which bear the mark **LX**. To these four standards there was added a fifth, in *c.* 358, at what seems to be $\frac{1}{144}$ lb.[97] (Pl. 9, 1–11)

These standards were not necessarily all in use at any one time – but several generally were. Nor were those in current use necessarily the same everywhere – various differences, some undoubtedly reflecting political or administrative divisions, or both, are observable. It is the pieces of one sixtieth, one seventy-second, and particularly $\frac{1}{144}$ lb, that seem to have been issued most consistently. That of one twenty-fourth of a pound seems to have been discontinued after the reign of Magnentius, but reappears under Valentinian I (364–75) and Valens (364–78) and their colleagues and immediate successors; its reappearance is, however, brief and confined to the western and central mints of Trier, Arles, Rome, Siscia and Thessalonica.[98] That of $\frac{1}{144}$ lb virtually superseded that of one ninety-sixth of a pound, but the latter again reappears briefly under Valentinian and Valens; its large-scale reappearance is, however, confined to the eastern mints of Constantinople and Nicomedia.[99] Eventually, late in the reign of Theodosius or early in the reigns of Arcadius and Honorius, the standard of $\frac{1}{144}$ lb was itself virtually superseded by an even lighter one at what seems to be $\frac{1}{192}$ lb.[100] This, with its half at

96 Pearce, *RIC* IX, pp. 204, 205.

97 Kent, *RIC* VIII, pp. 57–9. The law is *CTh.* XV.9.1: see above, pp. 193–4. The mark LX: Kent, *op. cit.* pp. 320 (Constans), 328 (Magnentius).

98 See: Kent, *RIC* VIII; Pearce, *RIC* IX, under appropriate mint-headings. For a rough guide to the relative frequency of issue, see: Kent, *op. cit.* pp. 74–5, esp. the table on p. 74.

99 Pearce, *RIC* IX, p. xxviii.

100 *Ibid.* p. xxviii (described as a reduction in weight from *c.* 1.9 g to *c.* 1.3 g).

$\frac{1}{384}$ lb, continued into the fifth century, by which time issues of silver coinage had in any case become minimal.[101] (Pls 11, 19–22; 12, 19–22)

The billon coinage retained its outward form, although its silver content may have depreciated even further, until 348. In that year, which marked the eleventh centenary of the foundation of the City of Rome, the coinage underwent a virtually simultaneous and drastic reform in both east (under the control of Constantius II, 337–61) and west (under the control of Constans) where in fact it appears to have been initiated.[102]

A number of common principles – maintained to imperfect and differing degrees – can be seen underlying the structure and design of the reformed coinage. There were three denominations, represented by the largest coins at about $5\frac{1}{4}$ g, intermediate coins at about $4\frac{1}{4}$ g, and small coins at about $2\frac{1}{2}$ g.[103] The largest appear to have contained something of the order of 3.0% silver, the intermediate about 1.5% silver, and the small no deliberate silver at all.[104] This pattern followed the Diocletianic, according to which the largest coins of the subsidiary system also contained the most silver.[105] The reverse inscription – appropriate to the occasion – was standard, and read: FEL(*ix*?) TEMP(*orum*) REPARATIO. The imperial bust on the obverse of the largest coins demonstrated a regular tendency to be plain and facing right, that on the obverse of the intermediate to hold a globe and face left: clearly a deliberate distinction. This was reinforced in the west by the former coming to bear the mark A, the latter N, the meaning of neither of which is known. Each denomination had two reverse designs, each design tending to be confined to coins struck in the name of one emperor only.[106] (Pl. 9, 14–19)

Neither the absolute tariffing of these denominations nor their values relative to each other are known, although it seems a plausible enough supposition that the intermediate coin was worth half the largest. For despite its weight, which was well over half that of the largest, the intermediate coin appears to have contained a smaller proportion of silver.

The stability of this reformed coinage proved even more ephemeral than that of Diocletian's. By 352 the weight of the largest denomination had already fallen from about $5\frac{1}{4}$ g to about 4.3 g. At this stage coins from the mints of Aquileia and Siscia were marked **LXXI'**, presumably denoting a weight standard of one seventy-second of a pound.[107] By 354 there had been a further reduction to about $2\frac{1}{2}$ g, by 357 a further to about $2\frac{1}{4}$, and by 359 yet a further to a bare two.[108] Silver content had also fallen, by uncertain

[101] See below, p. 476, for Anastasius and the east, but the situation had long obtained there. In the west the situation was somewhat different, and both the Vandalic and Ostrogothic coinages (see below, pp. 479, 484–5) contained silver as a principal, or important, element.

[102] J. P. C. Kent, 'Fel. Temp. Reparatio', *Numismatic Chronicle* 7[7] (1967), pp. 83–90; *idem*, *RIC* VIII, p. 37.

[103] Kent, *RIC* VIII, pp. 34–6, 61.

[104] *Ibid.* p. 61.

[105] See above, p. 449.

[106] Kent, *RIC* VIII, p. 37.

[107] *Ibid.* pp. 64 (weight), 333 (Aquileia), 374 (Siscia).

[108] *Ibid.* p. 64.

stages, although coins of 351 already seem to average at about 1.3 % silver, implying that a decline in content anticipated that in weight.[109] As the largest denomination declined in weight so (as normally occurred) the intermediate and small ceased to be issued, and by 361, when Constantius died, the depreciated remnant of the largest was virtually the only coin in circulation.[110]

Two laws dealing specifically with the monetary affairs of the period are preserved in the *Codex Theodosianus*. *CTh*.IX.21.6 reads:

The same Augustus [Constantius] to Limenius, Praetorian Prefect

> We have learnt that many metalworkers (*flaturarii*) are purifying the *maiorina* coin (*maiorina pecunia*) no less criminally than frequently by separating off the silver from the copper. Therefore if anyone is caught in this operation from now on let him know that he is to suffer capital punishment, and indeed those who own the house or land that they are to be punished by the confiscation of their property to the *largitiones*: Our Clemency is naturally to be informed of their names.

Posted 12 February in the consulships of Limenius and Catullinus [349].

The relevant clauses of *CTh*.IX.23.1 read:

Emperor Constantius Augustus and Julian Caesar to Rufinus, Praetorian Prefect

> Whoever is found either melting down or transporting coins (*pecuniae*) to different regions in order to sell them, let him come under the sentence of sacrilege and suffer capital punishment...And if ships do by chance come with merchandise to whatever province then it shall be sold with all the customary freedom, with the exception of the coins which they call *maiorinae* or *centenionales communes* by usual custom or others which they [the merchants] know to be forbidden (*vetitae*).

Received 8 March at Constantina in the consulships of Constantius Augustus (for the eighth time) and Julian Caesar [356].

The original of the first was presumably either a law of Constans or a joint law of Constantius and Constans, for (Ulpius) Limenius to whom it was addressed was both praetorian prefect and prefect of the City of Rome in 349,[111] and whatever the undoubted anomalies of his origin and position therefore at least in theory under Constans' jurisdiction. Its terms show the *maiorina* to have been a billon coin and therefore, given its date, the name of the coin itself, and the additional information of *CTh*.IX.23.2, almost certainly identifiable as the largest of the reformed system of 348.[112]

The recipient, date and interpretation of the second have all been much discussed, but, whatever else, the most natural interpretation is that the *maiorina* and *centenionalis communis* are to be found in the largest and smallest coins respectively of the system of 348. A fuller treatment will, however, already have been found in the fifth chapter of this book.[113]

Meanwhile, towards the close of the usurpation of Magnentius and after his loss of Italy, a short-lived but possibly significant coinage 'reform' had taken place. Until 352/3

[109] *Ibid*. p. 64. [110] *Ibid*. p. 65. [111] *PLRE* I, p. 510 (Ulpius Limenius 2).
[112] See below, pp. 474–5. [113] See above, pp. 291–4.

the usurper had maintained his subsidiary coinage more or less in parallel with that of Constantius. It was then replaced by a large copper coin, the reverse design of which comprised a prominent Christogram, flanked by an alpha and omega, and the inscription: SALVS DD(*ominorum*) NN(*ostrorum*) AVG(*usti*) ET CAES(*aris*) or variant. This started out at a weight of about 8.3 g and then, doubtless because of the increasingly difficult political and financial situation also seen in Magnentius' issue of solidi that are light in weight, rapidly underwent two reductions, to about 6.7 g and then to about 4.5 g. At no time does it seem to have contained a significant admixture of silver. The coin failed to survive the emperor by whom it had been created.[114] (Pl. 10, 1)

It was in Gaul, the scene of Magnentius' 'reform', that the emperor Julian (361–3) had acted as Caesar for Constantius. The main element of Julian's own reform, which took place at the end of his short reign (363), was a large billon coin, the reverse design of which comprised the figure of a bull and the inscription: SECVRITAS REIPVB(*licae*). The design was as flagrantly pagan as Magnentius' was Christian, and seems to have caused the offence that was doubtless intended,[115] but this should not be allowed to disguise the fact that their weight standard was identical and that their dimensions were much the same. Both were of a strongly Diocletianic pattern, although Julian's coin – with its silver content of about 3% – bore the closer resemblance.[116] (Pl. 10, 2)

Alongside this large billon coin Julian also issued a small copper one, at just under 3 g. This, at a slightly reduced weight of about 2.4 g, was continued and came to provide the sole element of subsidiary coinage when the large coin, although issued by Jovian (363–4) with a less offensive reverse design, was discontinued almost immediately upon the accession of Valentinian I, presumably in 364/5.[117] (Pl. 10, 3)

As an accompaniment to the reform, there went a clear and decisive reduction in the number of *officinae* producing the coinage. This was less drastic in the case of the western and central mints up to and including Thessalonica, and more drastic – particularly in that of Constantinople (11 down to 4) and Antioch (15 down to 4) – in that of the eastern ones.[118]

The short usurpation of Julian's relative Procopius (365–6) had no effect upon these developments which exceeded the geographical and chronological limits of his power. His coinage is nevertheless of some interest, for its gold and main billon or copper issues (their precise composition remains unknown) revert uniformly to the reverse inscription: REPARATIO FEL TEMP. The main subsidiary coinage seems to have consisted of three denominations: a large coin at something over 11 g, an intermediate coin, and a small coin that apparently revived Julian's standard of just under 3 g. The large coins are known

[114] Kent, *RIC* VIII, pp. 43, 63–4.

[115] J. P. C. Kent, 'An Introduction to the Coinage of Julian the Apostate (A.D. 360–3)', *Numismatic Chronicle* 19[6] (1969), pp. 109–17; *idem*, *RIC* VIII, pp. 46–8, 65–6.

[116] See above, p. 449.

[117] Kent, *RIC* VIII, pp. 48, 66; Pearce, *RIC* IX, pp. xxx–xxxi.

[118] Kent, *RIC* VIII, pp. 47–8.

from the mints of Heraclea, Constantinople and Cyzicus; the intermediate from Cyzicus and Nicomedia; and the small from all four. It has been suggested that the large coins represent the quadruple of the small, the intermediate the double, ultimately providing a Julianic origin for the system as a whole. This is not improbable, but the influence of the reformed coinage of 348 should not be overlooked.[119]

As it happens, the subsequent fates of the Magnentian coinage and of the large Julianic-Valentinianic coins are both known, or can be deduced. The Magnentian coinage, as the product of a defeated usurper and however Christian its design, appears to have been demonetised, and is presumably amongst those appearing as 'forbidden' in the law of 356(?) that has already been mentioned.[120] The Procopian coinage, of similar status, presumably suffered a similar fate.[121]

The large Julianic-Valentinianic coins, possibly termed *nummi maiores* or *maiorinae*, like their Diocletianic and Constantian predecessors and their Gratianic successors,[122] also appear to have been demonetised, possibly by Theodosius I,[123] more probably by Valentinian I and Valens in the form of a law preserved in the *Codex Theodosianus*. *CTh*.XI.21.1 reads:

Emperors Valentinian [I] and Valens, Augusti, to Modestus, Praetorian Prefect

> The bronze (*aes*) which is called *dichoneutum*, not only shall be henceforth delivered to the *largitiones*, but even shall be entirely withdrawn from use and circulation (*de usu et conversatione*), and nobody shall be allowed to possess it publicly. And melters of shaped bronze (*conflatores figurati aeris*), and moreover counterfeiters of coinage (*adulteratores monetae*), shall be overtaken by capital punishment.

Given 7 April at Constantinople in the consulships of Gratian Augustus (for the second time) and Probus [371].

The law is certainly an eastern one, for (Domitius) Modestus was praetorian prefect in the East,[124] and Valens was indeed at Constantinople,[125] at this date.

The *aes dichoneutum* mentioned above is not specifically identified as a monetary metal, but the 'purifying' or melting of such metal had already been the subject of two laws of 349 and 356(?); the term *conversatio* in an undoubtedly monetary context and with the sense of 'circulation' occurs in a law of 395; and the melting of bronze and the counterfeiting of coin are so closely juxtaposed in this law of 371 that, despite the somewhat elliptical phraseology, the strong supposition is that the whole law is a monetary one.[126]

[119] Pearce, *RIC* IX, pp. 192–3 (Heraclea), 214, 215 (Constantinople), 240 (Cyzicus), 251, 252 (Nicomedia).

[120] See above, pp. 291–4, 470.

[121] See above, pp. 249–50.

[122] For an African inscription of 362/3 possibly mentioning *nummi maiores*: A. Chastagnol, 'Un nouveau document sur le majorina?', *Bulletin de la Société Française de Numismatique* 30 (1975), pp. 854–7. For Diocletian/Constantius: see above, pp. 451, 453 and n. 25, 470. For Gratian: see below, pp. 473–5.

[123] See above, p. 319.

[124] *PLRE* I, pp. 605–8 (Domitius Modestus 2).

[125] Seeck, *Regesten der Kaiser und Päpste*, p. 241.

[126] Melting: see above, pp. 291–2, 470. Circulation: see below, p. 474–5.

The question immediately rises as to the monetary identity of *aes dichoneutum*. There seems little doubt that *bicharacta, dichoneutum* and other such terms[127] refer essentially to the same thing, at least in a general way, and very probably in a particular one. *Aes dichoneutum* is therefore bronze which contains a second basic element, in this case doubtless silver, and is therefore to be identified as billon.

The latest billon coins to have been issued prior to this law are the large ones of Julian (mainly), of Jovian, and of Valentinian and Valens, which seem to have been terminated in 364/5.[128] The intention of the law was therefore to call in such survivors as were still in use and circulation in 371, and it may well have had a largely religious and iconographical basis.[129]

Whether the issue of the law of 371 is to be connected with that of a further one, possibly of the period 371–3, and preserved in the *Codex Justinianus*, remains uncertain. *CJ* XI.11.2 reads:

The same Augusti [Valentinian I and Valens] and Gratian Augustus to Julian, Praetorian Prefect
On account of the reduction (*pro imminutione*) that is being brought about in the exchange-rate (*aestimatio*) of the solidus, the price of all commodities (*species*) ought also to decrease.

(Sextius Rusticus) Iulianus was proconsul of Africa in 371–3, and it seems probable that, in the *Codex*, the abbreviation *pp.* or *ppo.* for *praefectus praetorio* results from a misreading of the *pa.* for *proconsul Africae*.[130]

What seems to have happened is that the value of the solidus had been reduced in terms of the subsidiary coinage, with the intention of effecting a corresponding reduction in the prices of other commodities. This latter had probably not been fulfilled, perhaps because the mercantile classes were aware that merely to maintain the current level of prices in terms of subsidiary coinage was automatically to enhance their margin of profits in terms of gold: a situation not without its more recent parallels, and one which the law was designed to terminate.

If the law addressed to Julian really is to be dated to the period 371–3, it is conceivable that, together with the one addressed to Modestus and dated 371, it forms a nexus, or the remains of a nexus, which had a bearing on some attempt at monetary adjustment or reconstruction of the time, and the details of which are probably now irrecoverable.

It was not until *c.* 379 that Gratian (375–83) and Valentinian II (375–92) in the west and Theodosius I in the east combined in what was effectively the last serious attempt to provide a subsidiary coinage beyond the simplest before the disintegration of the western half of the empire. To the small coin of 2.4 g that had provided the sole element

127 See above, p. 451–3.

128 See above, p. 471.

129 The pagan content of Julian's coin would clearly be unacceptable to the new régime, and there is a late report that Theodosius demonetised Julian's coinage, hinting at iconographical reasons: possibly a mistaken allusion to this present law (see above, p. 319).

130 *PLRE* I, p. 479 (Sextius Rusticus Iulianus 37).

of subsidiary coinage since the discontinuation of Julian's billon coin, there was added a larger one of about 5.25 g, and an even smaller one of something over 1.5 g. It seems a plausible enough supposition that these new coins represented the (at least approximate) double and half respectively of the already existing one. The reverse design adopted for the larger comprised the figure of an emperor raising a kneeling personification, and the inscription: REPARATIO REIPVB(*licae*). Now this, with the brief but possibly significant Procopian exception mentioned above, was the first time that the theme of *reparatio* had been taken up on the coinage since the disappearance of the series commencing with the reform of 348. The weight standard adopted for the larger coin of *c.* 379 also seems to have been identical with that of 348, and it is therefore difficult to avoid the conclusion that a considerable degree of conscious imitation existed on the later occasion. Whether Gratian and his colleagues went so far as to imitate the silver content of the earlier coin remains unknown, but does seem unlikely.[131] (Pl. 10, 4–8)

It is probable that the issue of the new coinage was again accompanied or followed by an adjustment in the relation of the solidus to the subsidiary coinage. Symmachus, writing as prefect of the City of Rome to Valentinian II in 384/5, mentions that 'the divine brother of your own divinity' (i.e. Gratian) had decided upon an exchange-rate that was then no longer viable, at least for the money-changers (*collectarii*).[132]

The system of coinage inaugurated in *c.* 379 remained intact somewhat longer in the east than it did in the west, where issues of the large coin had been discontinued permanently by 388. At much the same time issues of the intermediate had also become rare, the small being virtually the only survivor – and even that with its weight reduced from something over 1½ g to something over one only. This tendency had been confirmed by 402 by the western mints – Rome excepted – virtually ceasing to issue copper coin at all. Although production had eventually been resumed, the quantities involved were never to be more than minimal and the occasions sporadic – Rome again excepted.[133] (Pl. 11, 23–5)

It is against this background that the provisions of a further law preserved in the *Codex Theodosianus*[134] are to be understood:

Emperors Arcadius and Honorius Augusti to Dexter, Praetorian Prefect

> We command only the *centenionalis* coin (*centenionalis nummus*) to be handled in public circulation (*conversatio publica*), the making of larger coin (*maior pecunia*) having been discontinued. Therefore let no one dare exchange the *decargyrus* coin (*decargyrus nummus*) for another, knowing it to be forfeit to the treasury (*fiscus*) if found in public circulation.

Given 12 April at Milan in the consulships of Olybrius and Probinus [395].

[131] Pearce, *RIC* IX, p. xxxi.

[132] See above, pp. 250–1.

[133] Carson, Hill and Kent, *Late Roman Bronze Coinage A.D. 324–498*, under appropriate mint-headings. It is tempting to connect this virtual cessation of copper coinage with the final disappearance of the annual *stipendium et donativum* of the military, which could well have occurred at this stage: Jones, *Later Roman Empire* II, p. 624. For a seventh-century comparison, see below, pp. 640–5.

[134] *CTh.* IX.23.2.

The law itself is certainly a western one, for Honorius was in Milan and (Nummius Aemilianus) Dexter is known to have been praetorian prefect in Italy in 395.[135] By then neither the large nor the intermediate coin of *c.* 379 had been issued in the west for some years. The decargyrus, which according to the implication of the law was larger than the *centenionalis* and the issue of which had been discontinued, could therefore have been either of these. The fact that it was the large coin only that had been discontinued permanently (production of the intermediate having been resumed at Rome by 402 and at Aquileia by 408, together with the use of the terms *maior nummus* or *maiorina* in earlier contexts[136]) suggests, but does not prove, that this is the coin to be identified as the decargyrus. The *centenionalis*, in that case, could have been either the intermediate or the small coin. The fact that it is the intermediate alone that can be paralleled at all closely in the reformed coinage of 348 – which is also known to have had its *centenionalis*[137] – and in the coinage of the intervening period again suggests, but again does not prove, that this is the coin to be identified as the *centenionalis*. This would leave the small coin as its probable half. The issue cannot be satisfactorily resolved: the evidence as it stands is inadequate, and the granting of priority to different considerations would undoubtedly lead to different conclusions. It is quite possible that one of these coins, and most probably the large, was also termed a follis, the existence of which as a single coin is implied in prices of the early fifth century.[138]

In the east, issues of the large coin were discontinued by 400, although they were briefly revived by Theodosius II (408–50), Leo I (457–74) and Zeno (474–91). Their *reparatio* design and inscription had been abandoned for a new set by 383, and their weight standard had been reduced from about 5.25 g to about 4.7 g by 393. Issues of the intermediate coin were discontinued by 425, their weight standard having been reduced from about 2.4 g to about 1.7 g. This left the small coin, also reduced in weight from something over 1.5 g to something over one only, as the sole surviving element of subsidiary coinage. At this stage, the east had caught up with the west.[139] Some time later, probably during or just after the short usurpation of Basiliscus (475–6), the weight standard of the small coin was again reduced, to just over one half of one gramme only.[140] (Pl. 12, 23–8)

## (III) ANASTASIUS I TO THEODOSIUS III (491–717)

### *A. The Anastasian reform: Nature*

The Anastasian coinage reform had no discernible effect upon the denominational structure of either the gold or the now vestigial silver coinage, although it may have

135 *PLRE* I, p. 251 (Nummius Aemilianus Dexter 3).

136 See above, pp. 451, 453 and n. 25, 470, 472.

137 See above, pp. 291–4, 470.

138 See above, pp. 340–1 and n. 143.

139 J. D. MacIsaac, 'The Weight of the Late 4th and Early 5th Century Nummus (Æ 4)', *American Numismatic Society Museum Notes* 17 (1971), pp. 59–66.

140 Adelson and Kustas, *A Bronze Hoard of the Period of Zeno I*, pp. 23–39.

involved some further adjustment in the balance between the two. The gold fractional coinage of semisses and (particularly) tremisses had long demonstrated a tendency to increase in volume relative to the unit, the solidus. This tendency had at least been rendered possible, and may even have been encouraged, when the nine-siliqua piece, in becoming an eight-siliqua one under Theodosius I, also became a true third of the unit. It had almost certainly been encouraged by the drastic contraction of the silver coinage at the opening of the fifth century. A contraction of this kind and on this scale would have left a very large gap between the gold and copper denominations, and an expansion in the volume of gold fractions would have formed one obvious, if only partial, remedy to the problems that it created. The Anastasian reform, which if anything formalised the contraction of the silver coinage (subsequent issues cannot have exceeded the requirements of ceremonial), will thus merely have provided the final impetus to this tendency.

The efforts of Diocletian, Constantine and Theodosius had therefore resulted in the establishment of a stable and relatively flexible gold coinage. The efforts of the fourth-century emperors as regards the silver coinage are rather more difficult to evaluate, but their success was on the face of it a temporary and limited one only. The manifest failure of the period nevertheless lay in a complete inability to provide a stable and flexible subsidiary coinage in base metal. It was not a question of lack of effort: major attempts had been made in *c.* 294/6, 348, 363 and *c.* 379, but the first and last of these had each failed to survive two decades while the second and third had failed to last five years. It was the achievement of Anastasius (491–518) to remedy this defect, in large part at least. The measure by which this remedy was effected is described in no less than three contemporary or near contemporary sources – a commentary, perhaps, on the impression that it created at the time:

By means of the coins (*nummi*) called *Terentiani* by the Romans and *follares* by the Greeks, each being marked with its own name, the emperor Anastasius sold a [rate or form of] exchange (*commutationem distraxit*) that was pleasing to the people.

(Marcellinus Comes, *Chronicon*, s.a. 498; MGH, *AA*, XI, p. 95)

Now this same emperor [Anastasius] appointed the honorary consul John the Paphlagonian, called Caiaphas, to be *comes largitionum* in Constantinople. And he [John] made all the current small change (*kerma*), the *lepton*, into *follera*, and ordered them to be current throughout the Roman empire thereafter.

(John Malalas, *Chronographia* XVI; Bonn edn, p. 400)

And the emperor [Anastasius] issued a coinage of forty, twenty, ten, and five nummi.

(Anon., *Chronicle*; in Corpus Scriptorum Christianorum Orientalium, *Scriptores Syri* III.4 (2: *Versio*), at p. 115, s.a. 824 (=512/13))

The coins themselves show the reform to have been carried out in two main phases. The first (498) involved the introduction of copper coins marked with their name or value on their reverses: **M** (=40 nummi) weighing about 9 g; **K** (=20 nummi) weighing about 4.5 g; and I (= 10 nummi) weighing about 2.25 g. The second (512) involved doubling the weights of these denominations to about 18, 9 and 4.25 g respectively, and introducing another marked Є (= 5 nummi) weighing about 2.25 g – the same as the piece of 10 nummi during the first phase.[141] (Pl. 14)

It seems clear that Marcellinus is referring to the first phase of the reform, because it is generally agreed that *Terentiani* is a corruption of *terunciani*, coins weighing one third of an ounce or one thirty-sixth of a pound, which is very much what the pieces of 40 nummi (*folles*) of that phase do in fact weigh. It is probable that the anonymous Syriac source is referring to the second phase, for only then was the reform extended to the local mint of Antioch, and only then was the piece of 5 nummi introduced. Malalas, on the other hand, is in error in claiming the Anastasian reform to have entirely replaced the small coins characteristic of the preceding period: it is now clear that these coins continued to be issued, as single nummus pieces, up to and including the reign of Justinian I (527–65).[142]

The precise tariffing of the new follis against the solidus remains, as usual, uncertain. It is known from a novel of the (western) emperor Valentinian III (425–55), dated 445,[143] that the solidus was then not to be sold for less than 7,000 nummi when bought from a money-changer (*collectarius*) for 7,200. It does not follow that the eastern tariff was identical with the western, but they are not likely to have been seriously out of step.

It is also known from a reference in Procopius[144] that, at some point during the reign of Justinian, and before the death of his wife Theodora in 548, the money-changers (*argyramoiboi*) were ordered to reduce the rate at which they bought solidi from 210 folles (= 8,400 nummi) to 180 (= 7,200). The date and significance of this event have been disputed. It seems to be connected elsewhere with Peter Barsymes' tenure of the office of *comes sacrarum largitionum*. Two of the edicts of Justinian[145] mention a *comes* named Peter, the latter also stating that he had served twice in that office. The most plausible solution to the problem so far advanced is that when, in 538/9, the weight of the follis was raised from about 18 g to about 22 g, its tariffing against the solidus was accordingly reduced from 210 folles to 180, and that Peter Barsymes was therefore already in his first term of office.

Now, prior to 538/9 the weight of the follis had remained stable since the second phase of the Anastasian reform (512): it seems probable that its tariffing will have remained similarly stable at 210 to the solidus. The weight of the follis of the first phase of the

141 A. R. Bellinger, 'Byzantine Notes, 1: The Copper of Anastasius I', *American Numismatic Society Museum Notes* 12 (1966), pp. 84–7. D. M. Metcalf, *The Origins of the Anastasian Currency Reform*, pp. 87–90.

142 E.g. H. L. Adelson and G. L. Kustas, 'A Sixth Century Hoard of Minimi from the Western Peloponnese', *American Numismatic Society Museum Notes* 11 (1964), pp. 188–93. The point is now generally accepted.

143 Valentinian III, Novel XVI; see above, p. 365.

144 Procopius, *Historia Arcana* XXV.11–12; ed. Haury (Teubner), III, p. 155.

145 Justinian, Edicts VII.6 (542), XI (559).

reform (498) was, at about 9 g, approximately half that of the second: its tariffing is likely to have been approximately double, at 420 folles or 16,800 nummi.

The evidence therefore suggests the following sequence:

445 about 7,200 nummi to the solidus
498 about 16,800 nummi (420 folles)
512 8,400 nummi (210 folles)
538/9 7,200 nummi (180 folles)[146]

The large difference between 445 and 498 is likely to be accounted for – in large measure at least – by the reduction in the weight of the nummus under Basiliscus in 475–6.[147]

The so-called *Edict of Anastasius*, regulating the customary charges (*synētheiai*) made on shipping passing through the straits at Sestus–Abydus, in its repeated quotation of sums of 3 and 6 folleis, and of 1 keration (i.e. siliqua), pre-supposes the existence of some kind of duodecimal relationship between follis, keration and nomisma (i.e. solidus). The clear implication is that the keration then stood at more than 6 folleis, and therefore the nomisma at more than 144 folleis (5,760 nummi). The lowest possible tariffing will have been 1 keration = 7 folleis, the nomisma therefore standing at 168 folleis (=6,720 nummi), and the lowest plausible tariffing will have been 1 keration = 8 folleis, the nomisma therefore standing at 192 folleis (=7,680 nummi). Given the remaining uncertainties surrounding the inscription involved, however, it would be difficult to carry the argument further with any degree of plausibility.[148]

The success of the Anastasian reform may well have lain in the fact that a large coin of plain copper formed its basis, and not, as in the case of most earlier attempts at reform, an equivalent one of billon.[149] The latter was always liable to attack through the simple and not immediately traceable diminution of its silver content, whether by private and illegal initiatives, or by desperate governmental action.[150]

## B. *The Anastasian reform: Origins (the Vandals)*

The origins of the Anastasian reform have been much studied.[151] It seems clear that three bodies of numismatic material have to be taken into account: the copper coinages of Vandalic North Africa, Ostrogothic Italy, and the empire itself.

Such gold coinage as the Vandals may have issued during their occupation of North

[146] *Contra* Hahn, *MIB* I, pp. 23–7. See my remarks above, pp. 288–9 and n. 183.

[147] See above, p. 475.

[148] H. Grégoire, *Recueil des inscriptions grecques chrétiennes d'Asie Mineure*, pp. 4–5, no. 4; further refs in H. Antoniadis-Bibicou, *Recherches sur les douanes à Byzance, l'‘octava', le ‘kommerkion', et les commerciaires*, pp. 76–9, 241–5 (Appendix 1: ‘À propos de "l'édit" d'Anastase Ier').

[149] E.g. Diocletian (pp. 449, 453), Constantius II (pp. 469–70), Julian (p. 471).

[150] See above, pp. 462, 464 (Constantine), 469 (Constantius II); below, pp. 518–19 (Manuel I/Isaac II). For private initiatives, see above, pp. 470, 472.

[151] Bibliography (to 1967) in Metcalf, *The Origins of the Anastasian Currency Reforms*, pp. 103–5.

Africa (439–533) is likely to have been closely imitative of contemporary or near-contemporary imperial designs, and attributions have indeed been made to them on this basis, but almost certainly incorrectly.[152] Their silver coinage, or at least that struck in the name of the reigning king, commenced with Gunthamund (483–96) and continued with Trasamund (496–523), Hilderic (523–30), and Gelimer (530–4). It consisted of coins bearing the marks $\underset{C}{\overline{\mathbf{DN}}}$, $\overline{\mathbf{DN}}$ or $\underset{L}{\overline{\mathbf{DN}}}$, and $\underset{XXV}{\overline{\mathbf{DN}}}$ or **XXV** as their reverse designs. The first – apparently struck by Gunthamund alone – denoted a coin of one hundred (C) units, presumably denarii ($\overline{\mathbf{DN}}$), and weighed about 2 g (probably $\frac{1}{144}$ lb). The second denoted a coin of fifty (L) denarii, and weighed about 1 g until a point during the reign of Hilderic when it was raised to about $1\frac{1}{4}$ g (probably $\frac{1}{192}$ lb). The third denoted a coin of twenty-five (**XXV**) denarii and weighed about half a gramme until raised at the same time as its double to about 0.6 g.[153]

Alongside these silver coins there were issued two main series of copper coins, neither of which bore the name of the reigning king. One of these series consisted of four denominations, and was characterised by having a standing female personification as its obverse design, and the marks $\overline{\mathbf{NX}}\mathbf{LII}$, $\overline{\mathbf{NXXI}}$, $\overline{\mathbf{NXII}}$ and $\underset{IIII}{\overline{\mathbf{N}}}$ as its reverse designs. The first denomination, the reverse mark of which denoted a coin of forty-two (**XLII**) units, presumably nummi ($\overline{\mathbf{N}}$), weighed about 11 g. The other three, of 21, 12 and 4 nummi respectively, weighed approximately proportionally, their variation and rarity precluding the formulation of precise figures. The smallest denomination, that of 4 nummi, had what is apparently a royal bust holding a palm-branch rather than a standing personification as its obverse design, the former probably being more appropriate to a very small flan.[154] The other series consisted of three denominations and was characterised by having a standing male figure in military dress and the inscription: **KARTHAGO** as its obverse design, and a horse's head (an ancient Punic motif) surmounting the mark of value (**XLII XXI, XII**) as its reverse design.[155] The order in which these two series were issued remains uncertain, but since that with a standing personification seems the more complete, with four as opposed to three denominations, and is possibly a shade heavier than the other, it may have been the earlier.[156]

152 C. Morrisson, 'Les origines du monnayage vandale', in H. A. Cahn and G. Le Rider (eds), *Proceedings of the 8th International Congress of Numismatics, New York–Washington September 1973*, at pp. 461–2.

153 Wroth, *Catalogue of the Coins of the Vandals, Ostrogoths and Lombards... in the British Museum*, pp. 1–16 under approprite denominational headings.

154 *Ibid.* pp. 6–7 (under Huneric). The inclusion of the four-nummus piece within this series is not certain, but is very probable. Hahn, *MIB* I, p. 94, adds a single-nummus piece, but this is most implausible: it derives from his dating the series as a whole to the reign of Hilderic, and it breaks the otherwise anonymous nature of the series by bearing that king's name. It also has an anomalous reverse design: a cross.

155 Wroth, *Catalogue of the Coins of the Vandals, Ostrogoths and Lombards... in the British Museum*, pp. 3–4 (under Gaiseric).

156 This is now confirmed by F. M. Clover, 'Relations between North Africa and Italy, 476–500: Some Numismatic Evidence', in H. Temporini (ed.), *Aufstieg und Niedergang der römischen Welt* III (in press).

The reasoning behind the choice of such apparently inconvenient denominations as those of 42 and 21 nummi, and the relationship between the (probably notional) gold, silver and copper coinages, are both matters of some interest and significance.

The customary division of the gold solidus into 24 siliquae, the siliqua being at once a weight and an expression of value, meant that the subsidiary coinage – whether copper or silver – should, ideally at least, have borne some exact and relatively simple relationship – whether multiple or fractional – to that division. Even ideally this cannot have been easy. For instance, were the solidus to be valued at 12,000 nummi, then the siliqua would have been worth one twenty-fourth of that or 500 nummi. But one sixth of 500 is $83\frac{1}{3}$, one twelfth is $41\frac{2}{3}$, and one twenty-fourth is $20\frac{5}{6}$. It is with the last two of these complex figures that the reasoning behind the choice of denominations of 42 and 21 nummi becomes apparent: they represent no more than $41\frac{2}{3}$ and $20\frac{5}{6}$ rounded up to the next whole number.

This, in turn, implies that the Vandalic solidus must originally, or ideally, or both, have been valued at either 6,000 or 12,000 nummi. The evidence of the *Tablettes Albertini*, a collection of legal documents incised on wooden tablets and dated to the last three years of the reign of Gunthamund, demonstrates that while the ideal valuation may well have been 12,000 nummi, the actual one is likely to have been 350 folles which – assuming the coin of 42 nummi to have represented the follis – works out at 14,700 nummi, probably itself an approximation for 14,400 nummi.[157] This discrepancy should occasion no surprise, for the legislation of Valentinian III permitting the solidus to fluctuate in value between 7,000 and 7,200 nummi, and certain other comparable adjustments, have already been cited.[158]

Given an original valuation of the solidus at 12,000 nummi and therefore a siliqua of 500 nummi, the follis of 42 nummi representing the nearest possible to one twelfth of the latter, and its half of 21 nummi representing the nearest possible to one twenty-fourth, the question arises as to how the silver coinage, with its values expressed in terms of denarii, fitted into this scheme.

The price or equivalence of the silver pound in terms of gold during the later fourth, fifth and sixth centuries seems – according to most documentary sources – to have fluctuated inflexibly between four and (more commonly) five solidi, giving a gold: silver ratio of 1:18 and 1:14.4 respectively. The relevant sources are as in Table 16.[159]

157 Grierson, 'The *Tablettes Albertini* and the Value of the Solidus in the Fifth and Sixth Centuries A.D.', pp. 73–8. *Contra* Morrisson, 'Les origines du monnayage vandale', pp. 464–5, who concludes that the follis was a notional entity, going 1,400 to the solidus. See also below, p. 492 n. 207.

158 See above, pp. 477–8.

159 H. L. Adelson, 'Silver Currency and Values in the Early Byzantine Empire', in H. Ingholt (ed.), *Centennial Publication of the American Numismatic Society*, at pp. 1–26. J. Durliat, 'La valeur relative de l'or, de l'argent et du cuivre dans l'empire protobyzantin (IV$^{e}$–VII$^{e}$ siècle)', *Revue Numismatique* 22$^{6}$ (1980), pp. 138–54 – better for gold and silver than for copper.

Table 16. *Gold: silver ratios, 4th–6th c.*

| Source | Date | Ratio |
|---|---|---|
| *Sb*.6086 | '4th c.' | 1:18 |
| *P.Oslo* 162 | '4th c.' | 1:14.4 |
| *CTh*.XIII.2.1 | 397 | 1:14.4 |
| *CIL* V.8734 | '5th c.' | 1:15(?) |
| *CTh*.VIII.4.27 | 422 | 1:18 |
| *CJ* X.78.1 (=*CTh*.XIII.2.1) | 534 | 1:14.4 |
| John of Ephesus, *Eccl. Hist.* III.11 | 'by 578' | 1:18 |

The accessional donative to the military of five solidi and one pound of silver (called *augustiaticum*) that is recorded by Ammianus Marcellinus for Julian in 360,[160] and by Constantine Porphyrogenitus – probably via Peter the Patrician – for Leo I in 457,[161] for Leo II in 473,[162] for Anastasius I in 491,[163] and for Justin I in 518,[164] clearly represents the kind of ceremonial payment that may originally have indicated a current ratio of 1:14.4 without guaranteeing that it continued to do so. Indeed, when John of Ephesus reveals that, by the accession of Tiberius II (578–82), this donative had been replaced by one of nine solidi and no silver,[165] the probable implication is that a current ratio of 1:18 had thereby been acknowledged.

It is indeed highly likely that the precise amount of the basic *augustiaticum* should be taken back at least as far as the tetrarchy, and quite possibly even further. For five Diocletianic 'aurei', each at one sixtieth of a pound, and representing a maximal $5 \times 1{,}200$ d. $= 6{,}000$ d., would have been the exact equivalent of a pound of non-monetised silver (6,000 d.) at the then traditional gold: silver ratio of 1:12. This kind of half-and-half pattern is not uncommon in mediaeval payments.[166] It will, then, have been the introduction of the Constantinian 'solidus', at one seventy-second of a pound, and

160 Ammianus Marcellinus, *Rerum Gestarum Libri* XX.4.18; ed. Gardthausen, I, p. 205.

161 Constantine Porphyrogenitus, *De Caerimoniis* I.91; Bonn edn, p. 412.

162 *Ibid.* I.94; Bonn edn, p. 432 (the payment was made *kata to ethos*).

163 Constantine Porphyrogenitus, *De Caerimoniis* I.92; Bonn edn, pp. 423 (the payment was termed *augoustiatikon*), 425.

164 *Ibid.* I.93; Bonn edn, p. 429.

165 John of Ephesus, *Ecclesiastical History* III.11; trans. Smith, p. 186. Apparently Tiberius sent out 800 lb of gold to an army in the field against the Persians, which, at the rate of nine solidi, would give a total strength of 6,400 men.

166 See above, pp. 450–1. The five aurei would, of course, not have equalled a pound of monetised silver (9,600 d.), and this may go at least part of the way in explaining why the distinction between gold aurei and the silver pounds was first made. Nor, it should be noticed, did the emperor promise so many 'siliquae' or 'miliarenses'. That the payment of the silver half of the donative actually was made in bullion, at least on occasion, may be deduced from the survival of a number of ingots in the name of Magnentius, and of others with quinquennial figures on them – see: Painter, 'A Late-Roman Silver Ingot from Kent', pp. 86–91.

worth (a theoretical) 1,000 d., that ruptured this traditional symmetry. On the other hand, with the gold: silver ratio eventually rising to 1:14.4, five 'solidi' will once more have equalled a pound of silver.[167]

These were all, even so, clearly official (and inflexible) rates only, dependent upon the solidus as the standard coin, and variant market rates might occur for any number of temporary and local reasons. According to John Malalas,[168] Germanus was able to buy up silver at two or three nomismata the pound at Antioch in 540. But the city was by then under direct threat from the Sassanians, and the less valuable and portable of the precious metals might well have been at a discount at that stage.

The evidence of the Vandalic silver coinage, at least, seems curiously at variance with much of this, except perhaps with the oldest stratum of it. At a gold: silver ratio of 1:14.4 one half-siliqua in silver should have weighed about 1.3 g, and one quarter-siliqua about 0.7 g. These are very much the weights achieved by the heavier silver coins of Hilderic and his successors with the reverse designs $\underset{\llcorner}{\overline{\mathrm{DN}}}$ and $\underset{\mathrm{XXV}}{\overline{\mathrm{DN}}}$ respectively. At this period, then, one half-siliqua or 250 nummi was represented by a coin of fifty denarii, and one quarter-siliqua or 125 nummi by a coin of twenty-five denarii, five nummi going to make up one denarius. The solidus would thus have stood at 2,400 denarii. But what of the silver coin of Gunthamund with the reverse design $\underset{\mathrm{C}}{\overline{\mathrm{DN}}}$ and weighing about 2 g, and the proportionally lighter coins of Hilderic and his predecessors with the reverse designs $\underset{\llcorner}{\overline{\mathrm{DN}}}$ and $\underset{\mathrm{XXV}}{\overline{\mathrm{DN}}}$? These are entirely appropriate to a siliqua, half-siliqua and quarter-siliqua, respectively, at the comparatively high gold: silver ratio of 1:12 – the silver pound in other words equalling six solidi. The introduction of a gold: silver ratio of 1:14.4 (that then prevalent in the empire), and the abandonment of one of 1:12 (long abandoned in the empire), under Hilderic, may well reflect that king's known pro-Roman stance, deriving perhaps from his descent and upbringing.[169]

A monetary system consisting only of a copper coinage of 42 and 21 nummi and a silver coinage of 100 denarii (500 nummi), 50 denarii (250 nummi) and 25 denarii (125 nummi) would nevertheless have possessed one inherent and serious drawback: which is that since the copper coinage involved the fractions of a division – the siliqua – rounded upwards, and the silver coinage the division itself and its exact fractions, the former would not have multiplied out satisfactorily into the latter. Six folles at 42 nummi each, for example, totalled 252 and not 250 nummi.

This drawback could have been neutralised in two rather similar ways, and there is

[167] One may guess that not the least reason for the state's apparent inflexibility with regard to the gold: silver ratio (involving 4 and 5 solidi the pound only) will have been the preservation of a conveniently simple (but not necessarily market-based) rate for its donatives. In other words, although one can imagine an emperor promising either 4 or 5 solidi and a pound of silver, one cannot imagine him promising $4\frac{1}{3}$ or $4\frac{1}{2}$ solidi and a pound of silver.

[168] John Malalas, *Chronographia* XVIII; Bonn edn, p. 480.

[169] C. Courtois, *Les Vandales et l'Afrique*, pp. 267–9.

Table 17. *Vandalic silver: copper denominations (excl. 83 n.)*

| (100 d./500 n.) | (50 d./250 n.) | (25 d./125 n.) |
|---|---|---|
| 10 × 42 n. = 420 n. | 5 × 42 n. = 210 n. | 2 × 42 n. = 84 n. |
| 6 × 12 n. = 72 n. | 3 × 12 n. = 36 n. | 1 × 21 n. = 21 n. |
| 2 × 4 n. = 8 n. | 1 × 4 n. = 4 n. | 1 × 12 n. = 12 n. |
| Total 500 n. | Total 250 n. | 2 × 4 n. = 8 n. |
| | | Total 125 n. |

evidence that both were tried. In the first place, by providing additional and smaller copper denominations which singly and ideally formed exact fractions of the unit of 12,000 nummi, and in combination were also capable of forming fractions of its division rounded downwards, a mean (and hence an exact) relation between the copper and silver coinages might be obtained. It was this function that the copper pieces of 12 and 4 nummi were evidently intended to perform, for: 1 × 12 n. + 2 × 4 n. = 20 n. (*contra* 21 n. for $20\frac{5}{6}$ n.); 3 × 12 n. + 1 × 4 n. = 40 n. (*contra* 42 n. for $41\frac{2}{3}$); and so on. By dint of manipulation, calculations of the cumbersome type shown in Table 17 thus became feasible.

In the second place, much the same effect could be achieved with the provision of an additional and large copper denomination which was itself a fraction of the siliqua of 500 nummi rounded downwards. A denomination of this description does in fact exist, for certain sestertii and asses of the earlier – and particularly the Flavian – emperors are known with the figures LXXXIII and XLII respectively incised upon them[170] These were presumably coins that had either remained in circulation over the intervening period or, more likely, that had come to light after having been hoarded. Now, as mentioned above, one sixth of 500 is $83\frac{1}{3}$: the figure eighty-three incised on the sestertii therefore clearly represents that fraction rounded downwards to the nearest whole number. The fortunate result of this manoeuvre was that, by pairing coins representing fractions of the siliqua rounded downwards with equal numbers of those rounded upwards, calculations of the relatively simple type shown in Table 18 became possible. The sum of 83 nummi was itself attainable by the combination of one coin of 42 nummi, one of 21, one of 12, and two of 4.

It remains uncertain as to whether these incised coins were official or unofficial products,

[170] Wroth, *Catalogue of the Coins of the Vandals, Ostrogoths and Lombards...in the British Museum*, p. xviii. Grierson, 'The *Tablettes Albertini* and the Value of the Solidus in the Fifth and Sixth Centuries', pp. 77–8 and n. 27. See, in the last instance: C. Morrisson, 'The Re-use of Obsolete Coins: The Case of Roman Imperial Bronzes Revived in the Fifth Century', in C. N. L. Brooke, B. H. I. H. Stewart, J. G. Pollard and T. R. Volk (eds), *Studies in Numismatic Method Presented to Philip Grierson* (Cambridge, 1983), at pp. 95–111.

Table 18. *Vandalic silver: copper denominations (incl. 83 n.)*

| (100 d./500 n.) | (50 d./250 n.) | (25 d./125 n.) |
|---|---|---|
| 4 × 83 n. = 332 n. | 2 × 83 n. = 166 n. | 1 × 83 n. = 83 n. |
| 4 × 42 n. = 168 n. | 2 × 42 n. = 84 n. | 1 × 42 n. = 42 n. |
| Total 500 n. | Total 250 n. | Total 125 n. |

and even as to whether they preceded or succeeded the introduction of the more regular coinage. It is on the face of it likely that they were unofficial, and unlikely that, had the concept of a denomination so generally convenient as that of 83 nummi already existed when the regular coinage was introduced, it would not have been given physical realisation in that coinage.

### C. *The Anastasian reform: Origins (the Ostrogoths)*

The denominational structure of the Ostrogothic coinage is, mercifully, and most probably significantly, considerably simpler than that of the Vandalic. Not the least of the reasons for this is that the precious-metal elements of the former represent a more or less direct continuation of the coinage of the last western emperors, while those of the latter represent an entirely new departure. The precious-metal series commences with Theoderic (493–526), and continues with Athalaric (526–34), Theodahad (534–6), Witigis (536–40), Baduila (Totila) (541–52) and Theia (Teias) (552).[171]

The gold coinage of solidi, semisses and tremisses is closely imitative of contemporary or near-contemporary imperial designs, but possesses the occasional detail and a consistent style of its own. With an unique exception[172] it never bears a royal name, and only once – under Theoderic – bears the royal monogram.[173]

The silver coinage is of a more independent design, and although the obverse most frequently consists of an imperial bust and inscription, the reverse as frequently consists of an inscription including the royal name and title or of a royal monogram. There were two basic denominations, weighing about 1.3 and 0.7 g, although larger and smaller denominations are known, and the earlier coinage of Theoderic at least seems to have been struck to a somewhat different standard. These two denominations were continued

[171] Wroth, *Catalogue of the Coins of the Vandals, Ostrogoths and Lombards...in the British Museum*, pp. 43–97. For the mint-attributions: Kent, 'The Coinage of Theodoric in the Name of Anastasius', at pp. 67–74.

[172] The well-known medallion of Theoderic, weighing three solidi, and bearing his facing portrait and the inscription REXTHEODERICV SPIVSPRINCIS on the obverse, and a Victory with palm-branch and the inscription REXTHEODERICVSVICTORGENTIVM/COMOB on the reverse: Wroth, *Catalogue of the Coins of the Vandals, Ostrogoths and Lombards...in the British Museum*, p. 54.

[173] *Ibid.* p. 55 (nos 64–6).

by Justinian after his reconquest of Italy, and at that stage bore the Greek numerals **CN** (250) and **PKE** (125) as their respective reverse designs.[174] (Pl. 21, 22–3)

These latter numerals can only have referred to their value in denarii or nummi, and they will therefore have represented the equivalents in both weight and value of the later Vandalic coins of fifty and twenty-five denarii. The clear implication is that the solidus was then valued at 12,000 nummi in Italy, as opposed to 8,400/7,200 nummi at Constantinople, and that this represented a continuation of the Ostrogothic valuation. This accords well enough with the principles enunciated in the *Constitutio Pragmatica* of 554, by which Justinian regulated the affairs of Italy. The first clause of this constitution grants a more or less general recognition to the acts of Amalasuntha (as regent for Athalaric and wife of Theodahad) and to those of Athalaric and Theodahad themselves: those of Theoderic were presumably not questioned but are not specifically mentioned. The twentieth confirms the free currency of solidi of former emperors: once more presumably including, but not specifically mentioning, solid struck by the Ostrogothic kings in the name of the reigning emperor.[175]

Later in the reign of Justinian, the weight standard of the denomination marked **CN** was reduced to about 1 g, and that of the denomination marked **PKE** to about half a gramme. This may have resulted from a readjustment of the gold : silver ratio, but if so, the implied movement to a ratio of 1 : 12 represents a curious inversion of what had earlier happened in Vandalic North Africa.[176]

Cassiodorus, writing as *quaestor sacri palatii* under Theoderic in 507–11, remarks that the ancients 'wished the solidus to be of six thousand denarii', which by no means necessarily implies that it was so valued at the time of writing.[177] It is nevertheless perhaps worth remarking upon the existence of a gloss equating *dinoummia* with *denaria*.[178] This might be held to confirm the operation of a double tier of reckoning, by which the solidus was rated at either 12,000 nummi or 6,000 denarii (2 n. = 1 d.), in much the same way as it was rated by the Vandals at either 12,000 nummi or 2,400 denarii (5 n. = 1 d.). Proof of the operation of such a double tier may well lie in the existence of certain silver coins, issued by Theoderic, in the name of Anastasius, at Milan. These, weighing some 0.8 g, bear a reverse inscription incorporating the letters **CM**, the natural reading of which is 240. It has been observed, however, that although they are the approximate equivalents

174 Bellinger, *DOC* I, pp. 180–1 ('Heavy Group').

175 Justinian, *Constitutio Pragmatica* (*App.* vii), I, xx. See also above, p. 366.

176 Bellinger, *DOC* I, pp. 180–1 ('Light Group').

177 Cassiodorus, *Variae* I.10; MGH, *AA* XII, p. 19. *Sex milia denariorum solidum esse voluerunt* [*sc. veteres*]. . . . The statement might, on the face of it, be taken as merely an antiquarian reflection of the Greek division of talent and drachma (1 : 6,000), but the remaining evidence suggests that it was not, and that it represented a valid observation of the contemporary situation.

178 Pauly-Wissowa, *Real-Encyclopädie* III, p. 476, s.v. 'binio'; cf. *CJ* XI.29.1 (436), for a *dinummium vectigal* at Alexandria; see below, pp. 497–8 for the Egyptian notation.

in weight of Justinian's pieces marked **PKЄ**, they would then bear a notation approximately double Justinian's. The apparent contradiction would be neatly resolved if **CM** referred to nummi, which would mean 240 nummi = 120 denarii, much as on Justinian's pieces.[179]

The copper coinage of the last western emperors had consisted, as already mentioned, of the small nummi that then also predominated in the east. The issue of these coins, mainly from the mint of Rome, had been continued by Odovacer (476–93) and was in turn continued by his Ostrogothic successors. They tended, as in the east, to have an imperial and later a royal monogram as their reverse design.[180] At some uncertain stage they were supplemented by the issue, again from the mint of Rome, of three main series of multiple nummi, the common obverse design of which consisted of a helmeted head of Roma personified and the inscription: **INVICTA ROMA**. The first series comprised two denominations, of forty and twenty nummi, weighing on average something under 15 g and something over 7 g respectively. The reverse design consisted of a wolf suckling twins and the mark of value **XL** or **XX**, the former denomination also bearing the *officina* numbers one to five (**·I·** to **·IIIII·** or **·V·**).[181] The second series comprised one denomination only, of twenty nummi, weighing much the same as the corresponding coin of the first series. The reverse design consisted of a fig-tree flanked by two eagles, and the mark of value **·XX·**.[182] The third series also comprised one denomination only, of forty nummi, weighing something over 10 g. The reverse design consisted of an eagle, the mark of value **XL**, and the *officina* numbers one to five (**A–Є**).[183]

In the course of time this relatively simple pattern became overlaid with additional denominations, of ten and five (**X** and **V**) nummi, with differing obverse and reverse designs, including royal portraits or inscriptions or both, and with the operation of additional mints, Ravenna and Ticinum.[184]

It is noticeable that, although multiple nummi of forty and twenty nummi both represent exact fractions of the solidus of 12,000 nummi and (at least in combination) of its division, the siliqua of 500 nummi, they do not represent exact fractions, either

[179] Justinian's pieces would thus be worth CN (250) denarii or 500 nummi, and PKE (125) denarii or 250 nummi. The later pieces marked PK (see below, p. 487) would be worth 120 denarii or 240 nummi, that is the same as the Milanese coins. For these: Wroth, *Catalogue of the Coins of the Vandals, Ostrogoths and Lombards...in the British Museum*, p. 58, nos 80–1 (under Rome). For the apparent contradiction: Kent, 'The Coinage of Theodoric in the Names of Anastasius and Justin I', p. 71 (no. 18). Kent's dismissal of Hill's interpretation of CM as *C(aput) M(undi)* is surely justified. For the latest general position, see: J. P. C. Kent, 'The Italian Silver Coinage of Justinian I and his Successors', in S. Scheers (ed.), *Studia Paulo Naster Oblata* I, *Numismatica Antiqua*, at pp. 275–82.

[180] Wroth, *Coins of the Vandals, Ostrogoths and Lombards...in the British Museum*, pp. 45 (Odovacer), 51 (Theoderic), 66–7 (Athalaric), 74 (Theodahad), 89–90, 92–3, 94 (Baduila). See also: Hahn, *MIB* I, pp. 88–91, who adds Theia.

[181] Wroth, *Catalogue of the Coins of the Vandals, Ostrogoths and Lombards...in the British Museum*, pp. 104–5.

[182] *Ibid.* pp. 103–4.

[183] *Ibid.* pp. 102–3.

[184] *Ibid.* pp. 46–107 under appropriate reign- and mint-headings.

alone or in combination, of the silver coin of 125 denarii/250 nummi. In this, of course, they resemble their Vandalic counterparts. It must be supposed that the difference was at first made up by the continuing production of small nummi, although the subsequent introduction of pieces of ten and five nummi will in any case have neatly resolved the difficulty.

That the problem was nevertheless a real one seems confirmed by the introduction, after the Justinianic reconquest, of a silver coin weighing much the same as that of 125 denarii/250 nummi, issues of which it supplemented, but which bore the number **PK** (120), that is 120 denarii or 240 nummi, and thus represented the precise equivalent of six folles of forty nummi each.[185] (Pl. 21, 24)

The main question arising from any comparison between the Vandalic, Ostrogothic and imperial copper coinages is not which of the two 'barbarian' coinages provided the immediate inspiration for that of the Anastasian reform (it was unquestionably the Ostrogothic), but which of the barbarian coinages was the earlier. Which, in other words, provided the original inspiration for the follis of forty nummi or thereabouts?

The question is not an easy one to answer. It has been supposed that, because the values of the Vandalic silver denominations are expressed in denarii, those of the copper in nummi, and because the silver coinage bears the name of the reigning king, the copper not, the two cannot have been contemporaneous. The implication is that, because the regal silver coinage extends in a continuous series from Gunthamund to Gelimer, the copper coinage must have been the earlier.[186] Each of these considerations is fallacious, for it is clear that the denominational structure of the copper coinage – with its coins of 42, 21, 12 and 4 nummi – presupposes the existence of the silver coinage with its coins of one hundred, fifty and twenty-five denarii. The first copper coinage might therefore have been contemporaneous with the first silver, or might have succeeded it, but cannot have preceded it.

Now there exist certain Vandalic silver coins the obverse design of which consists of an imperial bust and a blundered inscription identifying it as that of Honorius who died in 423. Their reverse design consists of a standing female personification, and the inscription: **ANNO IIII K** or: **ANNO V K–K** presumably standing for K(*arthago*).[187] These 'imitative' dated coins, the style of which is very close indeed to that of the regal series proper commencing with Gunthamund, clearly precede the regal series. But by how much? It has been suggested that their dates represent the fourth and fifth regnal years of Huneric (i.e. 480/1, 481/2)[188] but this is based on the fallacious supposition that the copper coinage, and therefore any anomalous silver, must predate the reign of

185 Bellinger, *DOC* I, p. 182.

186 E.g. Wroth, *Catalogue of the Coins of the Vandals, Ostrogoths and Lombards...in the British Museum*, pp. xxii–xxiv (who gives the two series to Gaiseric and Huneric).

187 *Ibid.* p. 5 (under Huneric).

188 *Ibid.* p. xvi.

Gunthamund. Such a suggestion is not in itself an impossible one, but does fail to explain why no coins of Huneric's sixth to eighth regnal years (i.e. 482/3, 483/4, 484) have come to light or – given that the dated coins were followed by the regal series – why no coins in Huneric's name exist. It is surely more probable that the dated coins represent prototype issues of the appropriate years of Gunthamund himself (i.e. 487/8, 488/9), and that they were then more or less immediately followed by the developed regal series. Their attribution to the revolt of Gildo[189] remains totally unconvincing, if only because one of the principal features of that event was a rejection of the authority of Honorius, in whose name they were ostensibly struck, in favour of that of Arcadius.[190]

Two further considerations lend weight to this hypothesis. The *Tablettes Albertini*, dated 493–6, in mentioning solidi and folles as current coins, provide a useful *terminus ante quem* for the introduction of the latter. As mentioned above, there is reason to believe that the earliest folles were those with a standing female personification as their obverse design: significantly the same design as that on the reverse of the dated silver in question.[191]

There is thus a good *prima facie* case for supposing the earliest Vandalic coinage proper, both silver and copper, to have been introduced in 487/8. A more completely 'imitative' silver coinage, in the name of Honorius, and with a reverse design of Roma seated, but without a date, may well be even earlier, but how much earlier remains completely uncertain.[192]

The coinage crucial to the dating of the earliest Ostrogothic coins – or rather of the earliest Italian multiple nummi – is to be found not among the three main series from the Roman mint mentioned above, but in yet a further and rare group of folles. The obverse design of these coins consists of an imperial bust, the inscription **IMP**(*eratori*) **ZENO FELICISSIMO SEN**(*iore*) **AVG**(*usto*), or **IMP**(*erator*) **ZENO SEMPER AVG**(*ustus*), and the numeral **·IIII·** below the truncation of the bust. The reverse consists of a winged victory flanked by the letters **S** (*enatus*) **C** (*onsulto*), the mark of value **XL**, and the inscription **INVICTA ROMA**.[193] The longer obverse inscription incorporated what was basically

[189] C. Courtois, 'Le monnaies de Gildo', *Revue Numismatique* 16⁵ (1954), pp. 71–5.

[190] Claudian, *De Bello Gildonico*; MGH, *AA* x, pp. 54–73. Orosius, *Historiarum adversus Paganos Libri VII* VII.36; ed. K. Zangemeister (Teubner), pp. 286–8. Zosimus, *Historia Nova* V.11; ed. Mendelssohn (Teubner), pp. 228–9.

[191] That is, the *terminus* should stand as long as the folles involved are 'real' ones and not 'notional' ones, as suggested by Morrisson (see above, n. 157). The standing female personification also occurs on the regnal silver of Hilderic (Wroth, *Catalogue of the Coins of the Vandals, Ostrogoths and Lombards...in the British Museum*, pp. 13–14 (nos 3–7)), and it is this which leads Hahn (*MIB* I, p. 94) to attribute the two Vandal copper series to Hilderic and Gelimer respectively. The stylistic reason that he gives for his choice is worthless, given the differences in size between the silver and copper coinages, and there is no absolute reason to believe the essentially anonymous copper to have fallen into neatly defined regnal limitations in any case. It should in fact be noted that the two copper series do not fit well with the small regnal copper of the period.

[192] Wroth, *Catalogue of the Coins of the Vandals, Ostrogoths and Lombards...in the British Museum*, p. 2 (under Gaiseric).

[193] *Ibid.* pp. 100–1.

a tetrarchic formula, and the reverse type seems to have been based on what was probably a first-century design.[194]

It has long been customary to place these folles early in the reign of Zeno (474–91). Two arguments have been employed to this end. The first relies upon the existence of pieces of the issue purporting to have been struck not in the name of Zeno alone, but in the names of Zeno and a caesar named Leo jointly. If these pieces were genuine, this caesar could really be none other than the briefly reigning (476–7) and renamed (from Basiliscus) son of Zeno's *magister militum* Armatus. However, they are now generally admitted to have been misread or to have been altered by recutting in modern times.[195]

The second argument relies on the assumption that the numeral ·IIII· on the obverse of these folles represents a date: the fourth regnal year of Zeno (i.e. 477/8).[196] There is no way of proving or disproving this assumption in any absolute way, but it is implausible in itself (similar forms of numeral elsewhere definitely represent *officina* numbers), and in any case considerably less plausible than a third, and more recently advanced, argument.

This third argument takes note of the fact that the Zeno folles average at a weight of about 16 g or at a shade heavier than the first main series of Roman folles – that with a wolf and twins and the *officina* numbers ·I· to ·IIIII· on its reverse. The implication derived is that the Zeno folles, as the products of the fourth (·IIII·) *officina*, stand as a special issue at the head of the wolf and twins series.[197] It also notes that the obverse inscription of the Zeno folles proceeds anti-clockwise, facing outwards, and that this feature can be paralleled only on certain Roman or Milanese silver coins with the name of Anastasius (491–518), Zeno's successor, on the obverse, and the monogram of Theoderic together with the inscription **INVICTA ROMA** on the reverse.[198] The clear implication is that the Zeno folles should be placed right at the end of his reign and therefore that it is not Odovacer, but Theoderic, who should be considered as ultimately responsible for their production.[199] Such a dating in fact conforms well with what is known of the political situation of those years.

The main sources for the period are the anonymous *Excerpta Valesiana*[200] and Jordanes' *Getica*.[201] In 487 Theoderic, already king of the Ostrogoths, left Constantinople for the west apparently with the additional title of *magister militum* and *patricius*, a vague

[194] The formula was originally adopted for the retired augusti, Diocletian and Maximian (Sutherland, *RIC* VI, pp. 26–7).

[195] J. P. C. Kent, 'Zeno and Leo, the Most Noble Caesars', *Numismatic Chronicle* $19^{6}$ (1959), pp. 97–8.

[196] See Morrisson, 'Les origines du monnayage vandale', p. 470 (as one of two possibilities).

[197] Carson, Hill and Kent, *Late Roman Bronze Coinage, A.D. 324–498*, p. 44.

[198] Wroth, *Catalogue of the Coins of the Vandals, Ostrogoths and Lombards... in the British Museum*, pp. 57–8 (nos 74–82) = Kent, 'The Coinage of Theodoric in the Names of Anastasius and Justin I', pp. 70–1 (nos 17–19).

[199] Kent, 'Zeno and Leo, the Most Noble Caesars', p. 97.

[200] Anonymous, *Excerpta Valesiana* XLIX–LXIV; ed. J. Moreau and V. Velkov, pp. 14–19.

[201] Jordanes, *Getica* CCLXXXIX–CCXCV; MGH, *AA* V.1, pp. 132–4.

commendation to the Roman senate and people, and some kind of assurance of support and eventual position from Zeno. In 488 he arrived in Italy, defeated Odovacer, and eventually confined him to Ravenna. In 490, when already in control of Italy other than Ravenna, he sent Festus (who is termed *caput senatus*) to Constantinople, apparently requesting that he be made king over Italy. In 491 Zeno died and Festus, his request unanswered or refused by Anastasius the new emperor, returned to Italy. In 493, after Odovacer had been lured into surrender and murdered along with his remaining supporters, the Ostrogoths apparently acclaimed Theoderic as king over Italy without waiting for the permission of Anastasius. In 497, as a result of a further visit by Festus, Anastasius recognised Theoderic's kingship and returned to him the regalia (*ornamenta palatii*) that Odovacer had delivered to Zeno in 476.[202]

Between 488 and 491, and particularly in 490/1 while Theoderic was making his request to Zeno and awaiting a reply, there is every reason why the Roman senate (with which Theoderic already seems to have been on good terms) should have been allowed, encouraged, or ordered to issue multiple nummi both imitating and improving upon those already issued by the Vandals, and including amongst them a small group of folles in Zeno's name.

That this should be the sequence suggested by the external evidence should occasion no surprise, for it is above all the complex internal structure of the Vandalic coinage that conveys the impression of outright experiment and novel construction. To some extent this must have been rendered inevitable by Africa having possessed no regular imperial mint since the early fourth century, and therefore neither a competent personnel nor a tradition to make use of in constructing a coinage system. Nevertheless, even given that convenience and efficiency did not then rate the same priority as they do now, it is difficult to believe that, had the Roman senate been the first to produce the follis by its issue of coins of 40 and 20, then 10 and 5 nummi, the Vandalic authorities would subsequently have chosen to complicate the system by their issue of 42, 21, 12 and 4 nummi, only the last two of which bore a convenient and exact relationship to the gold solidus and none to the silver coinage representing its major sub-divisions.

It was therefore the Vandalic coinage (487/8) by way of the Ostrogothic (490/1) that provided the immediate source of inspiration for the imperial monetary reform of 498.

### D. *The Anastasian reform: Origins (the decargyrus nummus)*

Yet the possibility of a further source of inspiration should not be entirely excluded, for the issue of multiple nummi was not without a fairly recent precedent within the eastern

[202] A. H. M. Jones, 'The Constitutional Position of Odoacer and Theoderic', *Journal of Roman Studies* 52 (1962), pp. 126–30. M. McCormick, 'Odoacer, Emperor Zeno and the Rugian Victory Legation', *Byzantion* 47 (1977), pp. 212–22. See also above, p. 405 n. 147.

half of the empire itself. The existence of a rare group of such coins, struck in the names of Theodosius II, and of Leo I, his wife Aelia Verina, and his successor Zeno, was mentioned at the end of the preceding section of this chapter. The group in question comprises coins at an average weight of about 4.5 g with four reverse designs. The first of these designs, struck in the name of Theodosius, consists of the standing figures of two emperors holding a cross between them, and the inscription **CONCOR DIAAGV** (*sic*). The second and third, struck in the name of Leo, consist of the standing figure of the emperor trampling a captive underfoot and the inscriptions **VIRTUS EXRCITI** (*sic*) and **SALVS RPVRL(I)CA** (*sic*). The fourth, in the name of Verina, consists of the seated figure of a winged victory drawing a christogram on a shield resting on a column, and the inscription **SALVS REIPVBLICAE**. Zeno is represented by coins with much the same general reverse design as those of Leo, but with a hopelessly blundered inscription.[203] (Pl. 13, 1–4)

The precise chronological positions during the reigns of Theodosius, Leo and Zeno that these coins should occupy remains uncertain. The design used for Theodosius – implying as it probably does the existence of Valentinian III – suggests a date in the second half of his reign, and is presumably late. The commonest form of obverse inscription used for Leo – D(*ominus*) N(*oster*) LEO PERPET(*uus*) AVG(*ustus*) – again suggests a date late in his reign, and a connection with preparations for the disastrous expedition against the Vandals in 468 has been suggested,[204] although the fact that specimens, like those of Theodosius, display a marked tendency to emanate from the Crimea needs to be accounted for. In this latter connection, it is to be remarked that they were certainly not minted in Cherson (the mint-mark is in any case uniformly **CON**), and no local explanation so far provided seems satisfactory.[205]

It is nevertheless clear where the inspiration for their reverse designs and weight standard is to be found. The design of the pieces struck in the names of Leo and Zeno, and the *Virtus* inscriptions of the former, reproduce exactly the features of an issue in the names of Valentinian II, Theodosius I, Arcadius and Magnus Maximus (datable 383–*c.* 388), while the design and inscription of the pieces in the name of Verina reproduce those of an issue in the name of Aelia Flaccilla, the first wife of Theodosius I (datable 383–6). In the latter case, even the number of the *officina* to which production of the earlier issue was confined (**Є**) is reproduced on the later pieces (**E**) – presumably as an immobilisation. (It also appears on the *Virtus* but not the *Salus* pieces in the name of

203 Theodosius II: J. Sabatier, *Description générale des monnaies byzantines* I, p. 117, no. 23 (mint of Thessalonica). Leo I, Verina: J. Tolstoi, *Monnaies byzantines* I, pp. 126–7, nos 27–30 (Leo); 134, nos 57–8 (Verina). Zeno: P. Grierson, 'Three Unpublished Coins of Zeno', *Numismatic Chronicle* 8⁶ (1948), pp. 224–5.

204 Grierson, 'Three Unpublished Coins of Zeno', p. 225.

205 Refs: W. R. O. Hahn, 'The Numismatic History of Cherson in Early Byzantine Times – a Survey' (i), *Numismatic Circular* 86 (1978), p. 414; *idem*, 'The Numismatic History of Cherson in Early Byzantine Times – a Survey' (ii), *ibid.* p. 522.

Leo.) On the other hand, the weight standard of these earlier issues was not adopted for the latter pieces: rather, a somewhat reduced one that characterised issues in the name of Theodosius I, Arcadius and Honorius, from 393 onwards.[206] (Pl. 10, 7–8)

Now it was argued, at the conclusion of the preceding section of this chapter, that these fourth-century issues are to be identified with the decargyrus of *CTh*.IX.23.2. The term decargyrus itself, decked out in Latin form, nonetheless clearly derives from the Greek *deka*+*argyrion*, and is perhaps best translated as 'a piece of ten' – *argyrion* being used in its common sense of 'a piece of money' rather than that of 'a piece of silver'. It was thus even then a multiple of some kind, may also have been termed a follis, and in its fifth-century revived form can scarcely have been other than a multiple nummus.[207]

The point emphasised by these considerations is that, if it was possible for Constantinopolitan moneyers of *c.* 450 and later to have returned to the reverse designs and a weight standard of the late fourth century for their multiple nummus, then it should have been equally possible for those of 498 to have returned to the multiple nummus of *c.* 450 for a prototype of their follis. The follis of 498 was after all struck at about double the weight of the multiple nummus of *c.* 450, just as the follis of 512 was in turn struck at about double that of the follis of 498. This is not to assert the existence of such continuity in the point at issue: merely to emphasise the real possibility of its existence.

### *E. Later developments: The light-weight solidus*

The denominational structure of the gold coinage remained effectively stable throughout the period covered by this section, although – as mentioned at its commencement[208] – the Anastasian reform may itself have involved a further adjustment in balance between the gold and silver coinages (in favour of the former), and may also have provided a final impetus towards the full emergence of the fractional elements of this structure. From the reign of Justinian I to the first reign of Justinian II (685–95) issues of the traditional solidus weighing 24 siliquae were nevertheless accompanied by what appears to be a spasmodic series of solidi weighing somewhat less.

The purpose and significance of this series of light-weight solidi remain uncertain. Attempts to explain it with reference to external trade[209] have long since foundered. Attempts to explain it with detailed reference to supposedly frequent changes in the

[206] Pearce, *RIC* IX, p. xxxii.

[207] It is of course tempting to assume that, as the last large coin in general circulation, the *decargyrus nummus*/follis, when its production was discontinued and its circulation was prohibited, in 395, had nevertheless remained as a denomination of account, and as such a follis of 10 nummi. If this were so, then Morrisson's suggestion of a notional follis (see above, p. 480 n. 157) would be vindicated. On the other hand, her equation 1 sol = 1,400 folles would mean that the solidus was worth 1,400 × 10 = 14,000 nummi, which is more or less the figure arrived at by Grierson on different grounds (see above, p. 480 n. 157).

[208] See above, p. 476.

[209] See above, p. 262 (Adelson).

Table 19. *The light-weight solidus, 538/9–695* (Pl. 19, 1–13)

| Emperor | 20 sil. | 22 sil. | 23 sil. |
|---|---|---|---|
| Justinian I (527–65) | × | × | |
| Justin II (565–78) | × | × | |
| Justin II and Tiberius II (578) | | × | |
| Tiberius II (578–82) | | × | |
| Maurice Tiberius (582–602) | × | × | × |
| Phocas (602–10) | × | × | × |
| Heraclius (610–41) | × | × | × |
| Constans II (641–68) | × | | × |
| Constantine IV (668–85) | × | | |
| Justinian II (first reign: 685–95) | | × | |

gold:copper ratio[210] are very unlikely to prove more successful. This latter method not only begs the question of whether such changes really were that frequent (not only with regard to the metals themselves, but also with regard to the coinage), but also, in its rigid application, leads to the eventual evolution of a whole series of wildly accentuated ratios that cannot possibly be justified except on the grounds of an entirely circular logic. Attempts to explain it in terms of the increasingly unfavourable financial situation, and to draw parallels with another and later series and situation,[211] while less satisfyingly absolute and symmetrical, at least have the merit of being sufficiently flexible to permit an explanation of their use both within and without the empire.

The series appears to have commenced subsequent to 538/9, and to have consisted of three main sequences. The two most persistent of these consist of solidi bearing the reverse exergual marks **OBXX**, later **BOXX**, and **OB✱+✱**, later **OB+✱**, in place of the traditional **CONOB**. The first denotes a solidus weighing 20 siliquae, or about 3.6 g, and should doubtless be deciphered as **OB**(*ryzi*) **XX** (*siliquae*) or similar. The second denotes a solidus of $21\frac{1}{2}$ or, more probably, 22 siliquae, or about 4 g. The third sequence consists of solidi bearing a star in the field of the obverse and reverse designs, later the reverse exergual mark **BOΓK** instead. These two variants denote a solidus weighing 23 siliquae, or about 4.2 g, and the latter should doubtless be deciphered as **OB**(*ryzi*) **KΓ** (*siliquae*) or similar. The three sequences occur as in Table 19.[212]

[210] See above, pp. 288–9 and n. 183 (Hahn).

[211] M. F. Hendy, 'Light Weight Solidi, Tetartera, and the Book of the Prefect', *Byzantinische Zeitschrift* 65 (1972), pp. 57–80.

[212] After Hendy, 'Light Weight Solidi, Tetartera, and the Book of the Prefect', pp. 58–9. The entry for Justinian II has, however, been corrected: the light-weight solidus there is of 22 and not 23 siliquae. See: W. E. Metcalf, 'Three Seventh-century Byzantine Gold Hoards', *American Numismatic Society Museum Notes* 25 (1980), pp. 107–8.

### F. Later developments: The hexagram

The silver coinage retained its vestigial form throughout the sixth century in the east, although issues that must have amounted to a significant proportion of the local circulating medium continued to be produced in the west, in those areas (Africa and Italy) that had been reconquered from the Vandals and Ostrogoths.[213] (Pls 20, 22–4; 21, 1–4, 22–4; 22, 1–4)

Then, during the most inauspicious period of the reign of Heraclius, when the empire was under severe pressure from the Avars on the European side and the Persians on the Asian, a silver denomination of an entirely novel pattern was introduced. This new coin weighed about 6.75 g, the obverse design consisting of the seated figures of Heraclius and his eldest son Heraclius Constantine (Augustus from 613) together with the inscription **dd**(*omini*) **NN**(*ostri*) **hЄRACLIЧS ЄC hЄRA**(*clius*) **CONSC**(*antinus*), or variant. The reverse design consisted of a cross-on-steps and the all too appropriate inscription **dЄЧS AdIЧCA ROMANIS**, or variant.[214] (Pls 19, 14; 22, 4)

The introduction of the new coin is recorded by the *Chronicon Paschale*, under the year 615,[215] in the following terms:

In this year the silver hexagram coin (*nomisma hexagrammon argyroun*) was introduced by law (*apo nomou*); and during the same year official salaries (*basilikai rhogai*) were paid in it (*di'autou*), at half the former rate (*kata to hēmisy tēs arkhaiotētos*).

The hexagram, as its name denotes, weighed six *grammata* or *scripula* and thus one forty-eighth of a pound. Its value relative to the solidus is nowhere clearly stated, but hoards turn up in areas well outside the former Byzantine frontiers,[216] which suggests that its bullion- and face-values were not greatly discrepant, and in fact at a gold:silver ratio of 1:18 (that prevailing under Tiberius II) it would have been worth exactly one twelfth of a solidus.[217] Known references to payments of 8 and 3 hexagrams would then make good sense as representing sums of two-thirds and one-quarter, respectively, of a solidus.[218]

The coin's value to the follis is again nowhere clearly stated, but it has been suggested that the **XX** present on the reverse of an issue of light-weight hexagrams under Constantine IV represents a (reduced) value of 20 folles – in which case the full-weight coins would presumably have been valued at 24 folles, precociously, and however briefly, giving the classic equation of 1 solidus = 12 hexagrams = 288 folles.[219] (Pl. 19, 17)

Reservations have been expressed as to the reliability of the date given by the *Chronicon*

[213] See above, pp. 399–401 and Table 11.
[214] Grierson, *DOC* II.1, pp. 270–4.
[215] *Chronicon Paschale*; Bonn edn, 706.
[216] P. Yannopoulos, *L'hexagramme, un monnayage byzantin en argent du VII^e siècle*, pp. 102–8.
[217] See above, p. 481 and Table 16.
[218] Refs: Grierson, 'The Monetary Reforms of 'Abd al-Malik, their Metrological Basis and their Financial Repercussions', p. 262 n. 2.
[219] Grierson, *DOC* II.2, p. 536 (Class III(3)).

*Paschale* for the introduction of the hexagram[220] but, while demonstrating the general unreliability of at least some portions of the work's chronology, they fail to convince that this extends to the date in question – and *a fortiori* that the whole passage should be transferred to the year 626. Nor do they take sufficient account of the further evidence provided by Theophanes' *Chronographia*[221] which records that, in 622:

> Having taken the money of the holy churches in the form of a loan, pressed by difficulties, he [Heraclius] seized the *polykandēla* of the Great Church as well as other serviceable equipment and coined large numbers of *nomismata* and *miliarisia*.

Heraclius had done, in other words, much the same as a number of emperors were to do later, and had appropriated ecclesiastical wealth in order to turn it into the ready cash demanded by the extraordinary expenditure of a major crisis.[222]

In the ninth-century Latin version of the *Chronographia* by Anastasius, the Greek: *nomismata te kai miliarisia pampolla* is (quite properly) translated as: *nummi aurei et argentei plurimi*.[223] Now, if Heraclius struck large amounts of silver coin in 622, one is entitled to ask where they are to be found among the surviving numismatic material. The only plausible answer is amongst the earlier issues of hexagrams. The introduction of the hexagram could therefore have occurred in 615 (assuming the *Chronicon Paschale* to be correct), or contemporaneously with and as a result of the turning of ecclesiastical wealth into cash in 622 (assuming the *Chronicon* to be incorrect), but is most unlikely to have occurred as late as four years after that event, in 626.

The denomination was issued in considerable quantities by both Heraclius and Constans II, but these declined sharply towards the end of the reign of Constantine IV (*c*. 680?) and remained minimal for the rest of the period (Pl. 19, 15–17).[224] Late specimens, despite their metal and weight, tend to have been struck from obverse and even reverse dies originally intended for solidi: a tendency which seems to confirm their by then exceptional status (Pl. 19, 18–20).[225]

The causes behind the disappearance of the hexagram have attracted some discussion. Loss of metal through trade has been suggested, but fails to convince.[226] Inability to acquire metal through lack of access to trade routes has also been suggested, but equally fails to convince.[227] It is far less dramatic, but far more plausible, to suppose that an unrectified disequilibrium in the gold:silver ratio intervened, causing a lack of monetary metal, but not of bullion, just as it had in the fifth and sixth centuries.[228]

220 K. Eriksson, 'Revising a Date in the Chronicon Paschale', *Jahrbuch der Österreichischen Byzantinistik* 17 (1968), pp. 17–28; *idem*, 'The Cross on Steps and the Silver Hexagram', *ibid*. pp. 149–64.

221 Theophanes, *Chronographia*; ed. de Boor, I, p. 302–3.

222 See above, pp. 231–2.

223 Theophanes, *Chronographia*; ed. de Boor, II, p. 186.

224 Grierson, *DOC* II.2, pp. 534–6 (Constantine IV), 583 (Justinian II, first reign).

225 See n. 224 above (Justinian II) – all were struck from solidus dies.

226 See above, p. 278 (Grierson).

227 Yannopoulos, *L'hexagramme, un monnayage byzantin en argent du VIIe siècle*, pp. 66–9.

228 See above, p. 278 and n. 141.

### G. *Later developments: The follis and its fractions and variants*

The sixth century was, for the copper coinage, one of comparative stability. Between the second phase of the Anastasian reform (512) and the twelfth regnal year of Justinian I (538/9), the weight of the follis remained stable at about 18 g. During the twelfth regnal year it was raised to about 22 g, but this standard was only briefly held and was reduced to about 19 g during Justinian's sixteenth regnal year (542/3).[229] By way of several further reductions, each of minor proportions, it had reached about 11 g by the reign of Tiberius II, and then remained stable for the rest of the century.[230]

The only major change in the denominational structure of the copper coinage involved the introduction of a thirty-nummus piece (marked **XXX** and later **Λ**) during the reign of Tiberius II. (This use of Roman numerals to indicate the value of the copper denominations was a feature which quite naturally dominated the products of western mints, but which on occasion affected those of eastern mints too, and particularly under Tiberius II and Phocas.)[231] (Pl. 15, 4, 6–7)

The gradual decline in the weight of the follis during the period 542/3 to 609/10 was nevertheless paralleled in its fractions, with the result that the smallest of these tended to drop out of the monetary system as they became inconvenient to produce or handle.[232] The process is effectively illustrated in tabulating the finds of multiple nummi from the excavations at Athens, Corinth and Antioch (Table 20).[233]

An ingenious, if isolated, response to this process was provided by the mint of Cherson during the reign of Maurice Tiberius. Its earlier issues of that emperor consist of folles and half-folles with the customary marks **M** (=40) and **K** (=20), its later issues of equivalent coins with the marks **H** = (8) and **Δ** (=4). It had quite simply replaced a system of reckoning based upon the single nummus with one based upon five nummi, the pieces marked **H** equalling eight times five nummi and those marked **Δ** four times five nummi. The experiment was repeated under Heraclius, but then lapsed, having never been taken up elsewhere.[234] (Pl. 22, 16–17)

The existence of systems of reckoning that varied from the Constantinopolitan norm, and occasionally even the formal recognition of their existence in the localised issue of

[229] Nevertheless this rise in weight apparently had some particular effect on circulation, as it is noticeably these heavy issues of the period 538/9–542/3, that have been withdrawn from circulation by the early seventh century (see above, pp. 319–20 and n. 29). Clearly, it was one of the few occasions in Byzantine monetary history when the face-value of the copper coinage began to approach its bullion-value.

[230] Morrisson, *BNC* I, pp. 60–1 and table.

[231] Bellinger, *DOC* I, pp. 272–3 (30 num.), 272–6 (Tib. II, Constantinople), and under appropriate mint-headings. Grierson, *DOC* II.1, pp. 163–71 (Phocas, Constantinople), and under appropriate mint-headings.

[232] As with the tetrarchic *nummus* (see above, p. 462), and the Constantian *maiorina* (see above p. 469).

[233] After Grierson, 'Coinage and Money in the Byzantine Empire 498–*c.* 1090', p. 436, table 2.

[234] Bellinger, *DOC* I, pp. 373–4. Grierson, *DOC* II.1, p. 381.

Table 20. *The follis and its fractions: coins from the excavations at Athens, Corinth and Antioch, 491–668 (after Grierson)*

| Excavation | Value | Anastasius | Justin I | Justinian | Justin II | Tiberius II | Maurice Tiberius | Phocas | Heraclius | Constans II |
|---|---|---|---|---|---|---|---|---|---|---|
| Athens | M | 8 | 6 | 43 | 44 | 7 | 9 | 27 | 198 | 732 |
| | K | 2 | 1 | 23 | 127 | 11 | 17 | 21 | 31 | 37 |
| | I | 1 | — | 15 | — | — | — | 1 | — | — |
| | E | 20 | 6 | 16 | 35 | 1 | — | — | — | — |
| Corinth | M | 2 | 2 | 14 | 27 | 5 | 4 | 9 | 7 | 36 |
| | K | 1 | 2 | 10 | 53 | 9 | 6 | 9 | 2 | — |
| | I | — | — | 9 | 1 | 1 | — | — | — | — |
| | E | 2 | 5 | 5 | 4 | — | — | — | — | — |
| Antioch | M | 31 | 42 | 102 | 29 | 9 | 61 | 12 | 48 | 89 |
| | K | 2 | 6 | 47 | 43 | 15 | 48 | 7 | 3 | 1 |
| | I | 3 | 21 | 93 | 60 | 14 | 68 | 17 | — | — |
| | E | 523 | 831 | 108 | 55 | — | 1 | — | — | — |

copper coins marked with values varying from the Constantinopolitan, was not confined to Cherson. The case of Italy, which continued to use the Ostrogothic tariffing of the solidus at 12,000 nummi, has already been mentioned.[235] It may be suspected that something of the kind lay behind the brief issue of multiple nummi marked **IS** (=16), **I**(=10), **H** (=8), **Δ**(=4), **B** (=2), and **A**(=1), by the mint of Thessalonica under Justinian I (Pl. 20, 6–9).[236] But the most consistent use of such variant values was that made by the mint of Alexandria throughout the sixth and well into the seventh century. This mint, with a long tradition of monetary particularity, consistently issued multiple nummi marked **IB** (=12), occasionally pieces marked **S** (=6) and **Γ** (=3), and very rarely pieces marked **A** (=1).[237] On one occasion only, under Justinian I, it also issued a piece marked ΛΓ(=33) (Pl. 22, 10–15).[238] In its small module and thick fabric the denomination marked **IB** strikingly resembled the Alexandrian billon tetradrachm of the period preceding the Diocletianic reform, which may well not have been coincidental.

The precise implications of the Alexandrian denominational pattern for the system of reckoning prevalent in Egypt remains unclear. Several interesting possibilities do nevertheless arise. The fact that the main Alexandrian coin was one of twelve nummi suggests Vandalic Africa as a source of influence. The connection seems confirmed both by metallurgical evidence which shows the composition of Alexandrian coins to be related

235 See above, pp. 485–6.

236 Bellinger, *DOC* I, pp. 104–8. Hahn, *MIB* I, p. 68, adds the one-nummus piece.

237 Bellinger, *DOC* I, pp. 157–8 (Justinian 12 n., 6 n., 3 n.) and under appropriate reign- and mint-headings. The 6 n. piece appears more frequently than the 3 n. one. Hahn (*MIB* III, p. 114) adds the 1 n. piece for Heraclius.

238 Bellinger, *DOC* I, pp. 156–7.

to that of Carthaginian and western rather than eastern ones,[239] and by further examination of the denominational pattern. With regard to the latter, the crucial evidence is that of the extraordinary piece of 33 nummi, the rôle of which becomes clear in the light of the Vandalic precedents cited above:

$$12+6+3\text{n.} = 21\text{n.}$$
$$21+12\text{n.} = 33\text{n.}$$
$$33+6+3\text{n.} = 42\text{n.}$$

The first of these calculations, representing as it does merely the sum of the twelve-nummus piece and its commonest fractions, might well be passed off as coincidence were it not for the second and third – the latter of which again strongly suggest a solidus at least ideally tariffed at either 6,000 or 12,000 nummi. Now, as it happens, the one papyrus source of the period permitting the establishment of a definite relation between the gold and copper coinages directly equates 3 keratia (siliquae) with 36 folleis, one keration therefore equalling twelve folleis.[240] If the Egyptian follis was worth 40 nummi, like the Constantinopolitan, the contemporary solidus of 24 keratia will have been tariffed at 11,520 nummi; if – as seems more probable – it was worth 42 nummi, like the Vandalic, the solidus will have been tariffed at 12,086 nummi. (A purely notional follis of $41\frac{2}{3}$ nummi would have given a solidus tariffed at exactly 12,000 nummi.) The evidence is that of a single and apparently late (undated: 'seventh century') source, but is for all that very strong in the circumstances. In any case, that the Alexandrian twelve-nummus piece was equated with the forty-nummus piece prevalent elsewhere, at about this same period, seems clear from the presence, below the denomination mark **IB**, of the numeral **M**, on coins of the joint reign of Heraclius and Heraclius Constantine dated 632–41.[241] (Pl. 22, 13)

By contrast with the sixth century, the seventh was disastrous for the copper coinage. The follis held its weight at about 11 g until the sixth regnal year of Heraclius (615/16), then dropped to somewhere between 8 and 9 g. During the fifteenth year (624/5) it fell to something over 5 g and, despite a temporary rally during the twentieth and twenty-first years (629/30, 630/1), when it retained its former weight of about 11 g, remained there for the rest of the reign.[242] (Pl. 17, 20–2)

Much of this can be ascribed to, and even connected up with, the political events of Heraclius' reign. The first fall in weight, in 615/16, coincided with the Persian invasion of Asia Minor, the connection being confirmed by the quiescence of the Asian mints

[239] T. Padfield, 'Analysis of Byzantine Copper Coins by X-ray Methods', in E. T. Hall and D. M. Metcalf (eds), *Methods of Chemical and Metallurgical Investigation of Ancient Coinage*, at pp. 220–1. The trace metals particularly involved are tin, lead, and nickel, but several others show distinctions.

[240] *SPP* xx.218.

[241] Grierson, *DOC* II.1, p. 340.

[242] Grierson, *DOC* II.1, pp. 23 and table 3, 24 and n. 41.

(Cyzicus from 614/15, Nicomedia from 617/18).[243] The second fall in weight, in 624/5, coincided with the inconclusive middle of the emperor's campaign on the eastern borders and in Persian territory.[244] The temporary rally, in 629/30, 630/1, coincided with the emperor's final and decisive victory over the Persians and with an administrative reform in the production of copper coinage – the latter being a subject already dealt with more fully in the seventh chapter of this book.[245]

The reign of Heraclius' successor Constans II merely continued the situation. By then the half-follis was virtually the only fraction struck, but since even that rarely appears in the excavation of provincial sites it is unlikely to have amounted to a significant proportion of the circulating medium.[246] (Pl. 17, 23)

The reign of Constans' own successor Constantine IV saw, however, an interesting attempt at reform. A new follis of 40 nummi (marked **M**), weighing about 17 g, was introduced, and with it the full range of traditional fractions: thirty (**Λ**), twenty (**K**), ten (**I**) and five (**Є**) nummi. The series was clearly modelled on the Justinianic, in its obverse designs, a source of inspiration seen also in Constantine's acclamation as a New Justinian at the Sixth Ecumenical Council, and in his choice of a name for his son.[247] It also clearly involved a drastic retariffing of the whole coinage, for the coins of twenty and ten nummi bore not only the marks of value appropriate to them (**K** and **I**) but also the smaller marks **M** and **K**. The implication can only be that the new twenty-nummus piece was equivalent to the old forty, the new ten to the old twenty, and so on.[248] This is confirmed by the imposition of the countermark **K** upon folles of Constans II remaining in circulation in Cyprus.[249] The exchange-rate between copper and gold must also have undergone severe readjustment and the complete operation will thus have closely resembled that effected at the second phase of the Anastasian reform.[250] (Pl. 18, 1–5)

The reformed coinage of Constantine IV lasted the reign of that emperor more or less intact, and was then promptly abandoned. By the reign of Philippicus (711–13) the weight of the follis had fallen back to an average of about 3.5 g, remaining there until the end of the period covered by this section.[251] (Pl. 18, 6–8)

One further general feature of the copper coinage of the period seems worthy of note: from 538/9 onwards it had frequently been dated by the emperor's regnal year. The practice was extensive in the case of the follis, but much less so in that of its fractions,

243 See above, p. 416.

244 Stratos, *Byzantium in the Seventh Century* I, *602–634*, pp. 153–64.

245 See above, pp. 417–18.

246 See above, p. 496 and Table 20. Further excavation material (except metropolitan) merely confirms the point.

247 The reformed coinage also achieved a measure of general circulation: at least in the metropolis (see above, p. 425 n. (Saraçhane), below, p. 521 n. (Kalenderhane) and possibly Cyprus (coins from the Curium Basilica, to be published by the author in the final report of the excavations, under the editorship of their director (Peter (A. H. S.) Megaw)).

248 Grierson, *DOC* II.1, p. 28; II.2, pp. 519, 541–4.

249 Grierson, *DOC* II.1, pp. 57, 58.

250 See above, pp. 476–8.

251 Grierson, *DOC* II.1, p. 27 table 5.

doubtless to some extent for reasons of space. Its inception is customarily connected with the provisions of Novel XLVII of Justinian I, the first clause of which reads as follows:

> Therefore We command both whomsoever is concerned with administration, be it in legal affairs or be it wherever transactions are executed, and notaries who draw up whatever kind of document, whether in this Great City [i.e. Constantinople] or in other places that God has given Us to rule over, to begin documents after this fashion: with the year of the current Most Sacred Augustus and emperor; and after that to introduce the name of the consul for the year; and in the third place the indiction, the month, and the day.

The Novel was given on 31 August 537, obviously for the following indiction (1 September 537–31 August 538 = ind. 1): the earliest dated copper from Constantinople, Nicomedia and Cyzicus reads **ANNO XII** (April 538/April 539), that from Antioch and Carthage **ANNO XIII** (539/40). Instructions as to dating seem to have gone out from the *comitiva sacrarum largitionum* late in the twelfth regnal year: mints in the metropolitan region will have received them in that same year, those elsewhere not until the following year.[252]

The fact that the dating of the coinage was effectively (that is with rare and largely non-metropolitan exceptions only) confined to the copper denominations emphasises the essentially fiduciary nature of that coinage which therefore came within the scope of the Novel and needed the same kind of formulaic 'validation' as did a document.[253]

## (IV) LEO III TO NICEPHORUS III (717–1081)

### A. The Leontian reform: Nature

The Diocletianic reform – with Constantinian and Theodosian adjustments – had evolved a viable formula for the gold coinage; the Anastasian reform – despite recent setbacks that were to prove temporary only – had done the same for the copper; with the failure of the Heraclian hexagram it remained for the Leontian reform to do the same for the silver.

The instrument by which this last formula was achieved was a coin weighing something slightly in excess of 2 g (probably $\frac{1}{144}$ lb), the obverse design of which consisted solely of a five-line inscription **LЄOh/SCOhSꞆ/AhꞆIhЄЄ/CΘЄЧbA/SILIS·** (*Leōn kai Kōnstantine*

[252] Bellinger, *DOC* I, pp. 83–4 (Constantinople), 111–12 (Nicomedia), 124–5 (Cyzicus), 142 (Antioch), 164 (Carthage). The point is a nice example of the difficulties and slowness of communication: even Antioch is likely to have been effectively isolated from land-contact with the metropolis by the severity of the Anatolian winter, and the alternative, communication by sea, would have been unavailable – whether for Antioch or for Carthage – until the following spring.

[253] As I have already indicated on several occasions, I do not believe in the 'full-bodied', i.e. non-fiduciary, nature of the copper coinage. On the general question of fiduciary coinage in Byzantium: C. Morrisson, 'La monnaie fiduciaire à Byzance ou "vraie monnaie", "monnaie fiduciaire" et "fausse monnaie" à Byzance', *Bulletin de la Société Française de Numismatique* 34 (1979), pp. 612–16.

*ek Theou basileis*), the reverse design of a cross-on-steps and the inscription IhSЧS XPISTЧS hICA. The coin was thus issued during the reign of Leo III and Constantine V (i.e. between 720 and 741).[254] (Pl. 23, 13)

The miliaresion, as it undoubtedly was, or came to be called, with its thin flan, aniconic design and inscription, bears an obvious resemblance to the Arab dirhem as it emerged from the monetary reform of the Umaiyad caliph 'Abd al-Malik (685–705) in A.H.79 (= A.D. 698/9), and indeed it has been observed that a number of early miliaresia are overstruck on the clipped-down flans of Umaiyad and Abbasid dirhems.[255] The dirhem, then, influenced the miliaresion in much the same fashion as the solidus had earlier influenced the dinar – and particularly as the latter briefly emerged in A.H.74 (= A.D. 693/4).[256]

The new coin seems to have held something of a ceremonial status at first. It has been observed that, until the reign of Theophilus (829–42), issues occur in the names of pairs of emperors only: Leo III and Constantine V (720–41), Artavasdus and Nicephorus (742–3), Constantine V and Leo IV (751–75), Leo IV and Constantine VI (776–80), Constantine VI and Irene (780–97), Michael I and Theophylactus (811–13), Leo V and Constantine (813–20), Michael II and Theophilus (821–9), Theophilus and Constantine (830/1). The denomination is, for all that, consistently not uncommon, and it seems probable that when, in 829, Theophilus had it issued in his name alone, he was merely conferring upon it formal possession of a normal status that it had long held in reality.[257] (Pls 23, 14–17; 25, 4)

On at least one occasion and in very small quantities, half-miliaresia were also issued.[258] (Pl. 23, 21)

Theophilus' issue of miliaresia in his name alone was novel in a further respect, for it weighed over 3 g and thus represented an appreciable increase on the Leontian standard. Although the higher standard was on this occasion a temporary feature only, for his later

254 Grierson, *DOC* III.1, p. 63.

255 G. C. Miles, 'Byzantine Miliaresion and Arab Dirhem: Some Notes on their Relationship', *American Numismatic Society Museum Notes* 9 (1960), pp. 189–218. The alloy of the miliaresion, prior to the debasement of the eleventh century was, apparently with a few exceptions (the reign of Constantine V with Leo IV, 751–75, being notable in this respect), high, and in some cases probably as high as was technically feasible. From the reign of Basil I (867–86) onwards, it is even steadier and higher, moving from *c.* 90% to *c.* 95%. Coins of the earlier part of the period that are overstruck on Arabic dirhems have characteristically high silver-contents. See: A. A. Gordus and D. M. Metcalf, 'The Alloy of the Byzantine Miliaresion and the Question of the Reminting of Islamic Silver', *Hamburger Beiträge zur Numismatik* 24/6 (1970/2), pp. 9–36.

256 G. C. Miles, 'The Earliest Arab Gold Coinage', *American Numismatic Society Museum Notes* 13 (1967), pp. 205–29.

257 Grierson, *DOC* III.1, pp. 63–4. A very recent and plausible claim has been made that it was Michael II in 820/1 or 2, and not Theophilus in 829, who initiated miliaresia in the name of a single ruler. See: S. Bendall, 'Miliaresia of the Reign of Michael II, AD 820–822', *Numismatic Circular* 91 (1983), p. 44.

258 Grierson, *DOC* III.1, p. 253. This issue, of Leo III, known now from two specimens, both from the same dies, remains unique, but it is not impossible that others will turn up.

issues and those of Michael III (842–67) reverted to the Leontian, a higher one of about 3 g became permanent during the reign of Basil I (867–86).[259]

Just as the drastic contraction of the silver coinage at the opening of the fifth century seems to have encouraged the emergence of a gold fractional coinage, so the reappearance of a silver coinage under Leo III seems to have entailed its decline. The latest known *semisia* (semisses) and *trimisia* (tremisses)* are those of the joint reign of Basil I, Leo and Alexander (i.e. of the period 879–86),[260] although both the *Continuation of Theophanes*[261] and Symeon the Magister[262] report a substantial distribution of *argyria* (miliaresia) and trimisia to the poor during the reign of Romanus I Lecapenus (920–44). The consistent rarity of these coins from the reign of Leo III onwards nevertheless suggests that the ceremonial procession and distribution (*hypateia*) of: 'trimisia and semisia and new nomismata' reported by Theophanes' *Chronographia*[263] on the occasion of Constantine V's promotion of his sons Christopher and Nicephorus to the rank of caesar, and of Nicetas to that of *nobilissimus*, in 769, represented a far more typical expression of their use.

The Leontian reform was perhaps least successful with regard to the copper coinage for, although a brief attempt to reintroduce a comparatively heavy follis and appropriate fractions does seem to have been made, the effective result amounted to no more than a continuation of the existing unsatisfactory situation.[264]

It is in fact difficult to identify with any precision the point at which the copper coinage was stabilised, but this had occurred certainly by the reign of Leo IV (775–80) and possibly by the later part of the reign of Constantine V (741–75). By then the weight of the follis had been raised somewhat, to somewhere in excess of 5 g, and the quality of its production improved, as regards both fabric and design – the latter being executed in the neat flat style typical of the iconoclastic period.[265]

The improved copper coinage of Constantine V and Leo IV brought several previously apparent tendencies to their logical conclusion. In the first place they consisted of whole folleis only. The latest complete set of fractional coins marked with their value in *noummia* (nummi), K, I, Є, had been issued during the earlier part of the reign of Constantine V – and even then in apparently exiguous quantities.[266] Later fractional issues of the same

* It will be convenient to transfer from the Latin to the Greek terminology at this point, although a rigid distinction of this kind obviously lacks any historical basis.

259 *Ibid.* III.1, p. 65. D. M. Metcalf, 'The Antalya Hoard of Miliaresia of Basil I', *Numismatic Chronicle* 17[7] (1977), pp. 117–18.

260 Grierson, *DOC* III.1, p. 22. It should, however, be noted that both of the issues involved (*ibid.* III.2, pp. 490–1 (nos 5, 6)) may be the products of a regional mint – see above, p. 425 and n. 239.

261 *Continuation of Theophanes* VI; Bonn edn, p. 418. See also above, p. 196.

262 Symeon the Magister, *Annales*; Bonn edn, p. 743. See also above, p. 196.

263 Theophanes, *Chronographia*; ed. de Boor, I, pp. 443–4: *Kai outō proēlthon rhiptontes hoi basileis hypateian trimisia kai sēmisia kai nomismata kainourgia eōs tēs megalēs ekklēsias.* The ceremony noticeably took place at Easter (see above, pp. 196, 198). It is tempting to suppose that the adjective *kainourgia* refers to the whole nomismata only, and that old fractions were used, but this is not really justifiable.

264 Grierson, *DOC* III.1, pp. 68, 70.

265 *Ibid.* III.1, p. 70.

266 *Ibid.* III.1, pp. 294–5.

emperor consisted of minimal quantities of half-folleis, marked **K**, only; those of Leo IV consisted of coins at a weight appropriate to half-folleis, but marked **M** – the same, that is, as contemporary folleis.[267] The noummion had simply ceased to be used as an effective unit of reckoning, the half-follis being considered merely as a fraction of the follis and not as a multiple of the noummion, distinction between whole and half-follis presumably being made on the basis of size and weight alone.

The practice of dating the copper coinage by the regnal year of the emperor had lapsed even earlier. Leo III's issues were marked **XX**, then **ANN XX**, then **XXX NNN**. The first of these was an immobilisation from the first year of Justinian II's second reign (705–11); the second was a completely meaningless formula; the third was the same made symmetrical, the suggestion that it stood for **X**(*ristos*) **N**(*ika*) repeated it three times having little beyond antiquarian ingenuity to recommend it.[268] (Pl. 24, 1–8)

Subsequently – during the joint reign of Michael II and Theophilus – the weight standard of the follis was again increased, this time to somewhere between 7 and 8 g, and during the sole reign of the latter it also underwent a radical change of reverse design. The new pattern involved the disappearance of the meaningless Anastasian mark of value (**M**) and the immobilised Justinianic date (**XXX NNN**), and their replacement by a four-line inscription: **+ΘЄO/FILЄAVG/OVSϹЄSV/hICAS**.[269] Folleis of the new pattern were accompanied by a group of coins with the same general design but which weighed something under 4 g: there seems no doubt that these latter represented half-folleis, the first since Leo IV.[270] They failed, however, to achieve regular production.[271] (Pl. 25, 9–10, 15)

With the final stabilisation of the copper coinage the monetary system as a whole, having lost many of these features that had marked the late Roman and early Byzantine period, took on what is now generally considered to be its classic form and entered into a period of stability that, subject to various minor fluctuations, was to endure for almost three centuries. The three major denominations of the period were: the gold nomisma, the silver miliaresion and the copper follis.

### *B. The Leontian reform: Denominational relationships*

The denominational relationships between the miliaresion and the follis of the eighth to tenth centuries, and between both and the contemporary nomisma, remain uncertain, except for the last part of the period. Theophanes' *Chronographia*[272] records that the severe damage caused by an earthquake in 740 was repaired with the aid of a new tax, levied

[267] *Ibid.* III.1, p. 326. [268] *Ibid.* III.1, pp. 253–63.
[269] *Ibid.* III.1, p. 413. [270] *Ibid.* III.1, p. 415. See also above, p. 425 n. 237.
[271] Grierson, *DOC* III.2, p. 511. See also above, p. 425 n. 238.
[272] Theophanes, *Chronographia*; ed. de Boor, I, p. 412.

at the rate of one miliaresion per *holokotinos* (nomisma), and continues: 'and hence it became the custom to give the *dikerata* to the tax-collectors (*dioikētai*)'. While this in itself is clearly intended to explain the origin of the tax called *dikeraton*,[273] the implication also seems to be that the miliaresion was then already, as later, worth two keratia or one twelfth of a nomisma. It would thus have stood firmly at the centre of the Byzantine monetary tradition, its predecessors being the Diocletianic argenteus and the Heraclian hexagram, and its remote successor being the Palaeologan basilikon.[274]

Later evidence for the value of the miliaresion is more plentiful – and almost inevitably more confusing. A scholium on *The Book of the Prefect*,[275] the body of which is generally dated to the reign of Leo VI (886–912) although containing later material, mentions: 'For the whole nomisma is worth twelve miliaresia or twenty-four keratia'. The tariffing of the nomisma at twelve miliaresia is that also found in a section of the *De Caerimoniis* of Constantine VII (913–59)[276] – where, for instance, a series of payments amounting to 9 nomismata and 43 miliaresia is totalled as 12 nomismata and 7 miliaresia.

There is, on the other hand, a fair amount of evidence that this tariff did not prevail throughout the period and that an alternative and lower one also existed at some not easily definable stage. The accounts of the Cretan expedition of 949 reckon the price of some sails as 28 nomismata and 12 miliaresia, which seems to imply that the former was then worth more than twelve of the latter,[277] and an Italian document of 959 contains the precise equation: 'fourteen *miliarena* or a solidus of good gold'.[278] Finally, of two scholia on the *Basilika* – published early in the reign of Leo VI – the one[279] claims that the nomisma is worth 14 miliaresia, the other[280] that:

> ...Each of such silver coins (*argyria lepta*) is worth one and three-quarters keratia, and the follis one hundred and twenty-five such silver coins, which are worth two hundred and eighteen keratia and nine *nummoi* or, according to the reckoning which obtains at present (*nun*), one hundred and nine miliaresia and nine nummoi, becoming nine nomismata one miliaresion and nine nummoi in coined money (*en kharagmati*).

Now it is clear that the part of this scholium claiming the follis (purse) to be worth (originally to have contained) 125 silver coins has been lifted straight out of the fourth-century metrological writer Epiphanius.[281] This does not seem to have been the

[273] See above, pp. 238, 286–7.

[274] See above, pp. 450–1, 494; below p. 533–4.

[275] 'Leo VI', *To Eparkhikon Biblion* I.4; ed. Nicole, p. 16 n. 13.

[276] Constantine Porphyrogenitus, *De Caerimoniis* II.55; Bonn edn, pp. 799–800. The section involves the staff of the hippodrome, and the officials termed *ho argyros tou bestiou* and *ho argyros tōn stephanōn* therefore presumably have no connection with the *argyros* occasionally mentioned as being present at imperial ceremonies – see above, pp. 197–8 nn. 225, 227.

[277] Constantine Porphyrogenitus, *De Caerimoniis* II.45; Bonn edn, p. 675.

[278] *Codice Diplomatico Barese* I; ed. G. B. Nitto de Rossi and F. Nitti di Vito, no. 3, p. 6: *quattuordecim miliarenis aut solido de bono auro*.

[279] Hultsch (ed.), *Metrologicorum Scriptorum Reliquiae* I, p. 307.

[280] *Ibid.* I, pp. 308–9.

[281] See above, pp. 339–40.

case with the remainder, which also seems not to have been taken from any of the other surviving metrological sources, and it is in any case difficult to see how 'at present' can refer to any other time than the composition of the scholium as a whole – which must have been subsequent to the publication of the *Basilika*. A silver coin worth $1\frac{3}{4}$ keratia would have been tariffed at fourteen to the nomisma ($24 \div 1\frac{3}{4} = 13\frac{5}{7}$ or 14 to the nearest whole number). One hundred and twenty-five silver coins at $1\frac{3}{4}$ keratia each would have been worth $218\frac{3}{4}$ keratia. If, as in the scholium, three-quarters of a keration are equated with 9 nummoi then the whole keration would have been worth 12 nummoi, and the nomisma 288 ($24 \times 12$) nummoi. The *noummos* is, in other words, to be identified with the tenth-century follis (as will shortly be confirmed). The scholiast clearly used the term *noummos* to denote the follis (coin) to avoid confusion because, in quoting Epiphanius, he had already claimed the follis (purse) to be worth a large number of silver coins. When the scholium was composed, however, 218 keratia and 9 nummoi were worth 109 miliaresia and 9 nummoi, reckoning each miliaresion as worth 2 keratia rather than $1\frac{3}{4}$. The miliaresion would then have been tariffed at twelve to the nomisma ($24 \div 2 = 12$), a rate confirmed by the last equation of 109 miliaresia and 9 nummoi with 9 nomismata 1 miliaresion and 9 nummoi in coined money.

The available evidence therefore suggests that the miliaresion was worth one twelfth of a nomisma under Leo III; that it was lowered to one fourteenth of a nomisma at some uncertain stage, probably by 949 and certainly by 959; and that it was restored to its original value at some subsequent stage. The only alternative is to suppose that two different rates, one perhaps official the other unofficial, are represented.[282] Whether these fluctuations in value were related to the fluctuations in weight standard, and if so how, remains completely uncertain.

In any case, it is quite clear that the miliaresion was essentially a fiduciary coin, for a silver coin fluctuating at between 2 and 3 g in its weight can have held a bullion value of very approximately one twenty-fourth only of a gold nomisma, and not one twelfth or one fourteenth. It may well be that this was the secret of its success, for relatively minor fluctuations in the gold:silver ratio would then not have led to the emergence of quite severely inconvenient relationships between the gold and silver coinages, as they would have done in the case of most or even all of the earlier and later full-bodied silver coinages.[283] Nor would an insufficiently flexible official gold:silver ratio have led to the major fluctuations in the quantities in which silver bullion was turned into coin, as it had probably done previously.[284]

The one complicating factor is that a tradition in Suidas' *Lexicon*, which is generally

[282] See, for example: Grierson, *DOC* III.1, p. 67 n. 215, commenting on Bertelè's interpretation of the Italian document of 959 (above, p. 504 and n. 278).

[283] See, for example, the later basilikon – below, pp. 533–4. This happens to be the only case where such variant relationships are actually documented, but in other cases they are inherently probable.

[284] See above, pp. 451, 465 (argenteus), 494–5 (hexagram), 481 and Table 16 (gold:silver ratios).

Table 21. *The coinage system, eighth–eleventh c.*

| AV Nomisma | AR Miliaresion | (Keration) | Æ Follis |
|---|---|---|---|
| 1 | 12 | 24 | 288 |
| — | 1 | 2 | 24 |
| — | — | 1 | 12 |
| — | — | — | 1 |

dated to the tenth century, claims the miliaresion to be the tenth part of the nomisma (*Miliarēsion: to tou nomismatos dekaton*). This is otherwise unprecedented, is omitted in other traditions, and is therefore of suspect validity.[285]

As regards the tariffing of the copper coinage the situation is less complex, but this in all probability derives merely from the fact that less documentary evidence survives than in the case of the silver. A payment of 3 miliaresia and 20 folleis recorded in the *De Caerimoniis*[286] suggests that the miliaresion was worth more than 20 folleis. The scholium on *The Book of the Prefect* which has been quoted above provides an exact figure: 'It is necessary to know that one keration is twelve folleis or half a miliaresion'; or in other words that there were 24 folleis to a miliaresion and 288 to a nomisma.[287] The figure is confirmed by the scholium on the *Basilika* which has also been quoted and which terms the follis a *noummos*.[288] At the alternative rate of 14 miliaresia to a nomisma just over $20\frac{1}{2}$ folleis would have gone to make up a miliaresion – obviously an inconvenient figure. The point at which the prevailing figure originated remains uncertain, although if the reign of Constantine IV is discounted, then the joint reign of Michael II and Theophilus, when the weight of the follis was increased, forms a clear possibility.[289]

The Byzantine monetary system in what is now generally considered to be its classic form thus may be tabulated as in Table 21.

### C. *Later developments: The nomisma*

The long joint reign of the brothers Basil II and Constantine VIII (963–1025), the first part of which was spent under the tutelage of Nicephorus II Phocas (963–9) and John I Tzimiskes (969–76), proved crucial certainly to the gold and copper coinages and probably to the silver.

[285] Suidas, *Lexicon*; ed. A. Adler, III, p. 395, no. 1062: *Miliarēsion. To tou nomismatos dekaton*. See also: Grierson, *DOC* III.1, p. 19 and n. 43.

[286] Constantine Porphyrogenitus, *De Caerimoniis* II.53; Bonn edn, p. 786.

[287] See above, p. 504 and n. 275.

[288] See above, p. 504 and n. 280.

[289] See above, pp. 494 and n. 219 (Constantine IV), 503 (Michael II and Theophilus).

Nicephorus II is accused by the chroniclers George Cedrenus and John Zonaras (both of whom drew extensively, and on the whole accurately, upon John Scylitzes) of having introduced into circulation a light-weight gold coin called the *nomisma tetartēron*. The purpose and significance of this coin will, like that of the sixth-century light-weight solidus with which it appears to have been connected,[290] be held over for detailed discussion elsewhere, although its purpose seems to have been blatantly fiscal,[291] but it will be appropriate and convenient to describe its origin and physical characteristics now. Zonaras describes the creation of the tetarteron in the following terms:

Up until his [Nicephorus'] time the weight of every nomisma was equal to a *hexagion*: he created the tetarteron in diminishing the weight, and effected the collection of taxes (*eispraxeis*) in the heavy nomisma (*dia tou baryterou*) and payments and all expenses (*doseis kai panta ta analōmata*) in the mutilated one (*dia tou kekolobōmenou*). Moreover, although according to an old custom every nomisma (*statēr*) bearing the imperial portrait had the same value as that just struck by the reigning emperor, he ordered his own to be preferred. And why was this done? So that the merchants would ask for his nomisma only, and so that in this way he would draw a profit from all the exchanges (*allagia*) of nomisma that he effected.

(Bonn edn, III, p. 507; cf. Cedrenus, Bonn edn, II, p. 369)

The precise amount by which the tetarteron was lighter than the traditional standard nomisma (or *nomisma [hi]stamenon* as it now began to be termed in opposition to the tetarteron) is described in a further scholium, on one of the letters of John Tzetzes:[292]

Tetarteron: the histamenon having four quarters, he [Nicephorus] did not make three entire thirds, for with regard to the third the new nomisma was inferior to the histamenon by a twelfth.

The only feature of the tetarteron that seems to have been fundamentally misunderstood by Zonaras is that of using it for state expenditure while using the histamenon for revenue. Such a practice would have resulted in the gradual but complete withdrawal of the histamenon from circulation. This did not happen, and it is indeed probable that it was never intended to: the tetarteron, struck by Nicephorus II and by all but a few of his successors up to and including Nicephorus III Botaniates whose reign (1078–81) concludes this section of the chapter, was intended to and did circulate alongside of the histamenon. The third of the tetarteron was inferior to that of the histamenon by one twelfth: the creator of the tetarteron is therefore regarded as having subtracted $\frac{1}{36}$ (i.e. $\frac{1}{3}$ of $\frac{1}{12}$) from each third of the histamenon, making a total difference of $\frac{3}{36}$ or $\frac{1}{12}$ of its total weight. The tetarteron was thus a coin of 22 keratia, and will have been the equivalent of the sixth/seventh-century light-weight solidus with **OB+✱** as a distinguishing mark.[293]

290 Hendy, 'Light Weight Solidi, Tetartera, and The Book of the Prefect', p. 65.

291 *Ibid.* pp. 67–72.

292 John Tzetzes, *Epistolai*; ed. T. Pressel, p. 84 and n. 4.

293 H. Ahrweiler (-Glykatzi), 'Nouvelle hypothèse sur le tétartèron d'or et la politique monétaire de Nicéphore Phocas', *Zbornik Radova Vizantoloshkog Instituta* 8 (1963), pp. 6–8. See above, pp. 492–3. The persistent suggestion by Grierson (e.g. *DOC* III.1, pp. 37, 38) that the weight of the tetarteron was suggested by that of the dinar can only be regarded as fanciful.

Although the fact is unmentioned by either Zonaras or Cedrenus, the tetarteron was accompanied at some stage of its existence by a second light-weight gold coin termed the nomisma 'of two quarters' (*nomisma duo tetartōn*). The second coin is known from the text of *The Book of the Prefect* where members of several of the metropolitan guilds are forbidden to refuse: 'the genuine (*akibdelon, anotheuton*) nomisma tetarteron or duo tetartōn having the imperial imprint'.[294] It is also known, like the tetarteron, from a copper coin-weight bearing the inscription: **+/ΔV/O/TЄ/TAP/TѠN**.[295] Now this coin-weight weighs 3.95 g or somewhat more than that bearing the inscription: **+TE/TAP/TЄ/PON** and weighing 3.86 g.[296] Neither seems anywhere near absolutely accurate, for the tetarteron coin itself seems to weigh, on average, about 4 g.[297] Nevertheless, if they are relatively accurate, the 'duo tetartōn' may probably be identified with a brief issue of light-weight coins from the later part of the reign of Basil II and Constantine VIII which weighs, on average, about 4.20 g.[298] It would thus have been two quarters or half as light as the tetarteron and a coin of 23 keratia – and hence the equivalent of the sixth/seventh-century light-weight solidus with a double star or **BOΓK** as a distinguishing mark.[299]

The tetarteron was at first indistinguishable from the histamenon in metallic purity, design, module and fabric – in fact in all respects save weight. During the later part of the reign of Basil II and Constantine VIII it assumed a slightly smaller module and a correspondingly thicker fabric, while the histamenon assumed a slightly larger and thinner form: small differences in the design of each denomination accentuated this distinction. Finally, during the short sole reign of Constantine VIII (1025–8) the tetarteron and histamenon became iconographically completely distinct and remained so for the duration of their dual existence.[300] (Pl. 28, 1–9 and 10–17)

As far as is known, the metallic fineness of the metropolitan gold coinage had, up to this point, never been impaired in any long-term or systematic sense: such analyses as have been carried out, with brief and rare exceptions only, show a gold content of between

294 'Leo VI', *To Eparkhikon Biblion* IX.5, X.4, XI.9, XIII.2; ed. Nicole, pp. 40, 42–3, 54, 48.

295 Hendy, 'Light Weight Solidi, Tetartera, and The Book of the Prefect', pp. 79–80. This should probably be associated with a further coin-weight reading **+ΠA/ΛAIONO/ΛOTPA/XON/EΛA/ΦPON**, and weighing 3.90 g, Hendy, *loc. cit.*

296 *Ibid.* pp. 79–80.

297 Grierson, *DOC* III.1, pp. 31–3 and table 1.

298 Hendy, 'Light Weight Solidi, Tetartera, and the Book of the Prefect', pp. 72–3. Grierson, *DOC* III.1, pp. 33–5 and table 2.

299 See above, pp. 492–3. It should also be noted in this respect that the known provenances of such coins (the northern Dobrogea), together with one piece of documentary evidence (referring to Italy), suggests that the tetarteron/duo tetartōn may have been utilised mainly in peripheral regions of the empire (perhaps by way of military salaries?) in much the same way as the light-weight solidus tends to occur outside the empire (probably by way of tribute etc.), again favouring a connection between the two series. See: Grierson, *DOC* III.1, pp. 38–9 (tetarteron/duo tetartōn); above, pp. 262–3 (light-weight solidus).

300 *Ibid.* III.2, pp. 708–10.

22 and 24 carats fine – probably as high and consistent as the available technical processes were capable of producing, given the massive scale of the necessary operation.[301]

According to Cedrenus, Michael IV (1034–41) had been engaged in the money-changing profession before his elevation and had then indulged in debasement.[302] His coins as emperor vary between 24 carats and 19½, and it seems clear that however they are to be arranged – whether the purer coins are earlier in the sequence, the baser later, or (less likely) whether the baser coins occur over the whole sequence – a range of this width is to be accounted for only by a programme of official and conscious debasement.[303] Too little is known of the coinage of the two brief joint reigns succeeding that of Michael IV, those of Zoë and Michael V (1041–2), and of Zoë and Theodora (1042), to reveal their policies with regard to the metallic fineness of the gold coinage: it is indeed probable that no such coinage was produced in the names of Zoë or Michael or both.[304] The gold coinage of Constantine IX Monomachus (1042–55) ranges between a full 24 and 18 carats fine, the higher values belonging to the earlier issues and each change in value being paralleled by a change in design. Those of his successors, Theodora (1055–6), Michael VI Bringas (1056–7), Isaac I Comnenus (1057–9), Constantine X Ducas (1959–67), and Eudocia Macrembolitissa and her sons (1067), all seem to average at 18 carats fine: which plateau marks a period of comparative stability. The gold coinage of Romanus IV Diogenes (1067–71) ranges between 18 and 16 carats, that of Michael VII Ducas (1071–8) between 16 and 12 or 9 carats, and that of Nicephorus III Botaneiates (1078–81) averages at about 8 carats fine.[305] After the relatively restrained steps of Michael IV and Constantine IX, followed by the degree of stability achieved during the period 1055–*c.* 1070, the gold coinage had therefore lost approximately ten carats of fineness between *c.* 1070 and 1081.

301 Morrisson, 'La dévaluation de la monnaie byzantine au XI^e siècle: essai d'interprétation', pp. 32–5. The only apparent exception involves several issues of the middle of the reign of Basil II, which seem to show a fairly consistent reduced gold content of 20–21 carats: Morrisson, *op. cit.* p. 34; Grierson, *DOC* III.2, pp. 613–20 (Classes II–IV; 977–1005?). This, given that emperor's reputation for financial stringency and rectitude, and the size of his eventual reserve, is surprising, and possibly reflects temporary difficulties arising from his wars. At any rate, both the first and the last issues of the reign (the latter being from 1005? onwards), remain unaffected.

302 See above, p. 234 and n. 84.

303 The situation under Michael IV retains a degree of uncertainty: Grierson's measurements (of five examples) by specific gravity seem to demonstrate debasement, while Morrisson's measurements (of four examples) by neutron activation fail to confirm this. P. Grierson, 'Notes on the Fineness of the Byzantine Solidus', *Byzantinische Zeitschrift* 54 (1961), pp. 92–4; Morrisson, 'La dévaluation de la monnaie byzantine au XI^e siècle', p. 35. I would, on the other hand, confirm Grierson's claim that the variations in the colour of the Dumbarton Oaks specimens very strongly suggest substantial variations in fineness (Grierson, *op. cit.* p. 93; Morrisson, *op. cit.* p. 6 n. 15). If debasement is eventually confirmed, then it almost certainly follows that the purer coins are earlier, the less pure later.

304 Hendy, 'Michael IV and Harold Hardrada', pp. 188–9, followed by Grierson, *DOC* III, pp. 722, 727.

305 Morrisson, 'La dévaluation de la monnaie byzantine au XI^e siècle', pp. 36–40. These figures more or less confirm those arrived at earlier by P. Grierson, 'The Debasement of the Bezant in the Eleventh Century', *Byzantinische Zeitschrift* 47 (1954), pp. 392–3. Grierson's two articles on debasement form the basis of his *DOC* III.1, pp. 39–44 (E: 'The Debasement of the Nomisma'). The histamenon/trachy consistently appears somewhat less debased than the tetarteron.

Direct mention of debasement is surprisingly rare in contemporary literary sources: the fact emerges as much through allusion. Nicephorus Bryennius[306] and Zonaras[307] do admittedly both refer to it directly, but the latter only in the course of what appears to be a biased account of the monetary reforms of Alexius I. A passage in Michael Psellus' *Chronographia*,[308] in which the author describes the financial skill of Michael VII, notes that: 'He understood how the touchstone (*khrysitēs*) worked, and how many measures of pure material each of the pieces of stamped gold contained'; and Cecaumenus' *Stratēgikon*[309] alludes to a man claiming to possess a sufficient capital but not the particular issue of coin (*kharagē*) required for some purpose. The former clearly implies debasement, the latter very probably does. The total of material is, however, still not impressive.

Both histamenon and tetarteron were affected by the debasement, the latter perhaps somewhat more acutely than the former. During the reign of Michael IV the broad thin fabric of the histamenon had become even further accentuated and, at the same time, slightly convex: although the tetarteron does not seem to have been struck during that reign, pieces of succeeding reigns show its fabric to have remained as it was – small, thick and flat. Use of a convex fabric for the histamenon was by no means consistent at first and a brief and sudden reversion to a flat one was possible as late as the reigns of Theodora and Michael VI. Convexity was nevertheless predominant from the reign of Constantine IX onwards, and standard from that of Isaac I.[310] (Pl. 28, 3–9)

In contemporary Greek documents these convex coins are termed *histamena trakhea* or simply *trakhea*, with reference to their 'uneven' – as opposed to flat – shape.[311] In Latin documents they are termed *scifati*. This latter term was for long considered to have been derived from the Greek *skyphos*, with reference to the 'cup'-like fabric of the coin, but it has recently been suggested to have had its origin in the Arabic *shafah*, with reference rather to the prominent triple 'border' with which their designs are enclosed.[312] It is nonetheless probable that all consciousness of an Arabic derivation was soon lost and that, as a result of the false etymologies so dear to the Byzantines, the Greek one became preferred. The possible reasons for, or the significance of, the adoption of a convex fabric remain debated.[313]

306 See above, p. 235.

307 See below, pp. 516–17.

308 See above, p. 241.

309 Cecaumenus, *Stratēgikon* CXV; ed. Wassiliewsky and Jernstedt, p. 48. But the same passage goes on (p. 49) to mention 'adulterated and unstable nomismata (*ta kibdēla kai astata nomismata*)', which would seem to clinch the matter.

310 Grierson, *DOC* III.1, pp. 5–6.

311 Hendy, *DOS* XII, pp. 29–31.

312 P. Grierson, '*Nummi Scyphati*. The Story of a Misunderstanding', *Numismatic Chronicle* 11[7] (1971), pp. 253–60.

313 Grierson, *DOC* III.1, p. 6 – initiated to strengthen the broad thin fabric of the histamenon, then continued as a sign of debasement. C. Morrisson, 'La concavité des monnaies byzantines', *Bulletin de la Société Française de Numismatique* 30 (1975), pp. 786–8 – basically a strengthening device. Neither explanation is totally satisfactory by itself, as neither takes full account of the curious inconsistency of its early usage.

## *D. Later developments: The miliaresion and follis*

With the turn of the tenth century, issues of silver coinage seem to have become sporadic and their quantities minimal. Such silver as was issued during the eleventh century seems to have consisted largely of fractions of the miliaresion – the two-thirds and the third both having been identified – and the later issues are in any case considerably debased, like the gold.[314] To some extent this scarcity of silver probably reflected a more general phenomenon: the so-called 'silver famine' that afflicted the Muslim world from Asia to North Africa and Spain, as well as the Byzantine empire.[315] But to some extent it no doubt simply reflected the fact that the metal was increasingly being used as the main alloying metal for the debased gold coinage, a use that must have attracted and effectively immobilised large quantities of it. (Pl. 29, 1–6)

Under John I, the copper follis underwent a major change in design, the details of which are described by Scylitzes:

> He [John] ordered a figure of the Saviour to be engraved on the nomisma and follis (*obol*), which had not been done before. And on the other side there were engraved Roman letters reading more or less thus: 'Jesus Christ King of Kings' (*Iēsous Khristos Basileus Basileōn*). And the emperors kept this up afterwards.
>
> (John Scylitzes, *Synopsis Historiarum* XIX; ed. Thurn, p. 311)

The description is not an entirely accurate one. The figure of the Saviour does appear on both the nomisma and the follis of the reign, but is new on the latter only. The inscription does occur in a slightly abbreviated form: **+IhSЧS/XPISTЧS/bASILЄЧ/bASILЄ′** on the follis, but not on the nomisma, where the equivalent and traditional Latin formula: **+IhS/XIS/RЄX/RЄGNANTIhm** survives. The new pattern of follis, having a religious figure on the one side and a religious inscription on the other, in place of the imperial figure and inscription, was continued by John's successors with relatively minor alterations only.[316] (Pl. 29, 7–10)

[314] Grierson, *DOC* III.1, pp. 64–8. Morrisson, 'La dévaluation de la monnaie byzantine au XI$^{e}$ siècle', pp. 41–7. The course of debasement for silver is similar to, but not identical with, that for gold: a light and temporary debasement under Basil II, but then nothing further that is appreciable until Romanus IV, under whom the silver content fell from some 90% to some 70%. Coins of Michael VII oscillate between some 95% and some 70%; those of Nicephorus III, which are in any case much rarer, seem to do much the same. Again, as in the case of histamenon/trachy and tetarteron, the silver units seem somewhat less debased than their fractions. The heavy over-valuation of the miliaresion would have ensured that the relationship between it and the nomisma (12:1) need not have been affected during the period when it was essentially undebased while the nomisma was appreciably debased (i.e. from Michael IV to Romanus IV).

[315] Watson, 'Back to Gold – and Silver', pp. 2–5. It is to be doubted whether C. C. Patterson, 'Silver Stocks and Losses in Ancient and Medieval Times', *Economic History Review* 25$^{2}$ (1972), pp. 205–35, is, or can be made, relevant to this problem, at least in anything but the loosest possible way: the figures utilised at virtually all stages of the argument are hypothetical, not to say entirely imaginary.

[316] The passage is repeated, more or less word for word, by Cedrenus: *Historiarum Compendium*; Bonn edn, II, p. 414. See also: Grierson, *DOC* III.2, pp. 634–5 and n. 4, for the rejection of a proposed emendation to the text. For the coins: *ibid.* pp. 648–706 (but see above, pp. 428 n. 249).

With the introduction of the new pattern of follis, the weight standard of the denomination was also increased: at first to about 13 g, and then briefly to 18, after which it was reduced again to 13. It is tempting to regard this as an attempted response to the increasing scarcity of silver. Subsequently, however, a decline set in, resulting in a standard of 7 or 8 g that prevailed for the best part of the eleventh century. Towards the very end of the period a further decline brought the standard down to something above 5 g.[317]

Under Constantine X the issue of folleis having an imperial figure, or monogram, recommenced, and was continued by his successors, the coins being issued and circulating alongside of the later folleis having religious designs only.[318] (Pl. 29, 11–13)

The precise effect of such fluctuations – in metallic quality or weight or both – upon the monetary system remains uncertain. A late twelfth-century treatise on certain fiscal reforms of Alexius I, the *Palaia kai Nea Logarikē*, shows the equivalence 1 nomisma = 12 miliaresia = 288 folleis to have remained at least formally intact as late as the opening of the twelfth century.[319] Fluctuations in the metallic quality of the miliaresion and in the weight standard of the follis may indeed have had only a marginal effect upon the system of account, for both denominations were fiduciary in character. Those in the metallic quality of the standard denominations, the nomismata, must have been much more serious. It seems probable that with regard to the nomisma a hierarchical principle will have evolved, based on the old pure gold histamenon as a unit of account, the value of each new debased issue, once in circulation, being estimated against the old histamenon according to its intrinsic worth. A trachy of Nicephorus III, at a fineness of 8 carats, although paid out as a nomisma of full value, would for instance, once in circulation, have been counted as worth its eight keratia weight of pure gold, possibly plus the value of the silver going to make up the rest of the alloy. Sixteen keratia weight of silver being approximately equivalent in value to $1\frac{1}{2}$ keration, the total value of the trachy would then have been counted as worth $9\frac{1}{2}$ (i.e. $8+1\frac{1}{2}$) keratia, or 114 folleis.[320]

[317] *Ibid.* III.1, p. 71.

[318] *Ibid.* III.2, pp. 774–8 (Constantine X), 796–7 (Romanus IV), 818–20 (Michael VII), 831–2 (Nicephorus III). See also: *ibid.* p. 820 for what is an apparently unique half-follis of Michael VII, and pp. 836–8 for probable folleis of the usurper Nicephorus Basilacius (for which see also above, p. 428 n. 253).

[319] Zepoi, *Ius Graeco-Romanum* I, pp. 326: *Isteon, hoti 12 milliarēsia ē 12 argyra tō nomismati logariazontai eis to sekreton tou genikou· to gar milliarēsion anti argyrou logizetai, to de argyron anti milliaresiou*, 328: *Logariazein de 12 milliarēsia to nomismati ētoi to milliarēsion ekhein 24 folleis kata tēn palaian paradosin tou augoustou kaisaros....* These are only the two most specific references, and the whole treatise is in fact based on the equation. *The sekreton tou genikou* was responsible for the collection of the land-tax. The claim that the equation dated back to Augustus Caesar is of course incorrect.

[320] Hendy, *DOS* XII, p. 7.

## (v) ALEXIUS I TO ANDRONICUS III (1081–1341)

### *A. Alexius I: Nadir and reform*

Alexius I Comnenus (1081–1118) therefore inherited a badly debased gold coinage of histamena trachea and tetartera; a minimal and debased silver coinage, mainly of fractional miliaresia; and a copper coinage of folleis of reduced but still appreciable weight.[321]

During the first decade of the reign the coinage system of the preceding period finally disintegrated. 'Gold' trachea and tetartera struck towards the end of that decade consist of a greyish alloy in which there can have been little if any gold, but some silver, and much copper: it cannot have differed very much from that utilised for contemporary fractional miliaresia.[322] A sum of trachea of this description is indeed mentioned in a document of 1097 as being 'of imperfect quality (*tēs tetrēmmenēs poiotētos*)'.[323]

The Alexian coinage reform of 1092 attempted and achieved nothing less than a complete reconstruction of the coinage system on an entirely novel basis, making use of a series of regularly composed alloys rather than pure metals. If comparison is made with the past, only the Diocletianic reform had been on a similar scale, for those of Anastasius I and Leo III had involved single aspects of a pre-existing situation only. The reform possessed political, administrative and dynastic implications, and may well have been designed to operate formally from the first year of the new indictional cycle (1 Sept. 1092 = ind. 1).[324] (Pl. 30, 1–5 and 6–14)

The pre- and post-reform coinage, and therefore the date and outlines of the reform itself, have been distinguished in a systematic sense only comparatively recently. The

[321] See above, pp. 506–10 (gold), 511 (silver), 511–12 (copper).

[322] For the coins: Hendy, *DOS* XII, pp. 71–6, but for the follis see also above, p. 428 n. 249.

[323] Lemerle *et al.*, *Actes de Lavra* I, p. 277: ...*tou khrysiou diakharagmato(s) nomismata tessarakont(a) (kai) pent(e) trakhea st(au)rohagiodēmetr(a)t(a) tēs tetrēmmenēs poiot(ē)t(os)*.... The issue in question is clearly Hendy, *DOS* XII, pp. 71–2 (Thessalonica, Second Coinage), and confirms the attribution (the act involved was drawn up in Thessalonica). It was certainly of a vile alloy, essentially billon of a not very high quality.

[324] The date, 1092, is provided by the issue of coins of a recognisably reformed pattern in the names of the infant John II (obverse), and Alexius I and Irene Ducaena (reverse), which were surely meant to mark, and were probably meant to be used at, the coronation of John II in that year. The reform and coronation came after the worst political threats of the earlier part of the reign had been eliminated or stabilised. The coronation meant, by implication at least, that Alexius felt himself in a sufficiently powerful position to ignore, or at least to neutralise, the alienation of the powerful Ducas clan (it inevitably involved the relegation of the co-emperor Constantine, although of course John himself was half a Ducas). For the administrative implications, see above, pp. 432–4. Of the actual coronation issue, only the electrum, billon and lead/copper denominations are known, gold being absent and perhaps never struck (Hendy, *DOS* XII, pp. 84 (El.), 85 (Bill.); *idem*, *DOC* IV (Pb.)). The billon probably, and the lead/copper certainly, were the products of two mints, Constantinople and Thessalonica (Hendy, *DOC* IV). For the indiction: Grumel, *La chronologie*, p. 256. It may be suggested that whereas the coronation issue was designed for ceremonial/commemorative use in September 1092, the first regular issues (including gold) were designed for normal use immediately afterwards. For the documentary evidence for the new coinage: Hendy, *DOS* XII, p. 40.

reformed coinage comprised four major elements: a standard gold coin with a probable theoretical fineness of 20½ carats; an electrum (silver/gold alloy) coin with a fineness of between 5 and 6 carats; a billon coin with a silver content of between 6% and 7%; and a copper coin, together with its half.[325]

Of these, the gold, electrum and billon denominations all aimed at a weight standard appropriate to a histamenon nomisma, the first two generally achieving this aim, the third falling increasingly short.[326] All three were thus in theory capable of being described as histamena, although in practice only the billon was, mainly in Latin documents and under the form *stamina*.[327] All three were also of the convex fabric that had become common during the second half of the eleventh century, and were thus in theory liable to be termed trachea, although again in practice only the billon was, in Greek documents.[328] The gold was termed a *nomisma hyperpyron*, with obvious reference to its high gold content.[329] Both the electrum and billon seem officially to have been termed *aspra trakhea*, or 'white convex' coins, with reference to the colour of the alloys of which they were composed.[330] In practice in Greek documents the electrum seems to have been termed *to deuteron*, with a reference to the primacy of the hyperpyron, or *trikephalon*, with reference to the three 'heads' or figures – one on the obverse, two on the reverse – that frequently went to make up its designs.[331] In Latin documents it seems rather to have been termed *trimenus*, again after the three 'heads', or *manuelatus*, after the emperor Manuel I Comnenus, whose reign (1143–80) saw the production of large amounts of the coin. The billon, as mentioned above, seems generally to have been termed merely trachy, although on occasion, and in a vulgarising context, it is called stamenon.[332]

325 Hendy, *DOS* XII, pp. 10–11, 13 n. 3 (*AV* and El.), 21 and n. 18 (Bill.), 23–4 (Æ). For the electrum, see also: Hendy, *DOC* IV; and for the billon, see also: Hendy and Charles, 'The Production Techniques, Silver Content and Circulation History of the Twelfth-century Byzantine Trachy', p. 15, table 1 (John II 1st coinage–Manuel I 2nd coinage). The suggestion by Metcalf (*Coinage in South-eastern Europe, 820–1396*, p. 113) that the half-tetartera are in fact whole tetartera of 'reduced value', is on a par with his suggestion that the half-folleis of Theophilus are whole folleis on a reduced standard of weight, and similarly cannot be taken seriously.

326 See: Hendy, *DOS* XII, pp. 10–11 (*AV* and El.), pp. 412–20 (*AV*, El. and Bill.). It is clear that the billon fell short of the histamenon standard even at its inception (1092), but that it had declined even further in weight by the reign of Isaac II and Alexius III (i.e. 1185–1203).

327 Hendy, *DOS* XII, p. 28.

328 *Ibid.* XII, pp. 29–31.

329 *Ibid.* XII, pp. 34–7. C. Morrisson, 'Le nomisma hyperpère avant la réforme d'Alexis I Comnène', *Bulletin de la Société Française de Numismatique* 28 (1973), pp. 385–7, points out that use of the term antedated the reform of 1092, but this, while correct, is not particularly meaningful, as there is no doubt that its common usage postdates the reform, and moreover that it then applies to the coin of high gold-content.

330 Hendy, *DOS* XII, p. 31.

331 *Deuteron*: see above, p. 198. *Trikephalon*: Hendy, *DOS* XII, pp. 31–4.

332 Theodore Prodromos, *Carmina* III, l.341 (*dia deka stamena*), VI, l.34 (*dia stamenon*); ed. D.-C. Hesseling and H. Pernot, pp. 64, 74. See also IV, l.52 (*kai blakhikon stamenarean tyritsin* – a piece of Vlach cheese worth a stamenon); *ed cit.* p. 75. It seems clear that the term was utilised more commonly than one might otherwise have expected, but in the popular language, from where the Latins presumably picked it up.

The copper denomination, a small thick flat coin, was termed tetarteron, having taken over the nomenclature of the light-weight gold coin of the preceding period which it resembled in weight and fabric.[333] (Cf. Pls 28, 10–17; 30, 12–14)

As it happens, it would now appear that the first, very rare issues, of new tetartera, datable to 1092, and from the mints of both Constantinople and Thessalonica, are not of copper but of lead, and that the subsequent (and small-scale) issues from the Constantinopolitan mint were of billon, while those (large-scale) ones from Thessalonica and from a further regional mint, probably in central Greece, were of copper alone.[334] The lead issues were probably intended to signalise a sharp break with the precious-metal ones of the preceding period. It has also been suggested that the billon issues were produced for ceremonial distributions only, but this is contradicted by the administrative regularity of their production; by their quite common appearance in metropolitan archaeological excavations; and by their mention in quite normal contexts in contemporary written sources.[335]

The denominational relationships of the new system may best be tabulated as in Table 22.[336]

333 Hendy, *DOS* XII, pp. 28–9, but it is now clear that the coin weight (p. 29) is earlier, see above, p. 508 n. 295.

334 Lead: Hendy, *DOC* IV. Billon/copper: D. M. Metcalf, 'The Tetarteron in the Twelfth Century', *Numismatic Circular* 86 (1978), p. 574.

335 *Ibid.* p. 574. Although they do not seem to bear (at least with any regularity) the officina distinctions that characterise the other metropolitan denominations for much of the twelfth century, nevertheless during the long reigns of John II (1118–43) and Manuel I (1143–80), each issue of tetarteron balances off against a corresponding issue of hyperpyron, and electrum and billon trachy, suggesting that they were produced on much the same basis and as regularly as the others (Hendy, *DOC* IV). Their first appearance in the literary sources occurs in 1097, when, according to Fulcher of Chartres (*Historia Iherosolymitana* I.10; RHC, *Occ.* III.1, pp. 333–4), Alexius I: *iussit...de auro suo et argento atque palliis proceribus nostris dari; peditibus quoque distribui fecit de nummis suis aeneis, quos vocant tartarones.* The confusion between silver and copper in the case of a low grade billon coin is easy to parallel (see above, p. 302). It may be argued that even here they were being utilised in a ceremonial context, but if so, the scale seems likely to have been considerable. But they appear in quite reasonable numbers (even if still tending to be out-numbered by their Thessalonican copper equivalents) amongst the excavation materials from metropolitan sites like Saraçhane (see above, p. 425 n.) and Kalenderhane (see below, p. 521 n.). And they also appear twice, once specifically, once by implication, in contemporary Latin commercial documents: Tafel and Thomas, *Urkunden* I, p. 108 – *unum tetartero* (Rhaedestus, 1147); Müller, *Documenti sulle relazioni delle città toscane coll'Oriente Cristiano e coi Turchi – dimidium staminum* (Constantinople, 1162). The only way in which the latter sum could have been paid would have been in tetartera and/or their halves, although of course there is no guarantee that the coins involved would have been metropolitan billon ones rather than regional copper ones. Metcalf's use of the Pantocrator *typikon* to support his case is quite invalid: alms of the kind, and on the scale, mentioned, would necessarily have been paid in small coin, and if the tetarteron was available then it would make sense to use it. In short, the evidence suggests regular production, for a limited area of circulation, basically involving the capital and its environs. Ceremonial, in any specific sense, the coin was not. It is of course possible that the metropolitan tetarteron was worth $\frac{1}{288}$ hyperpyron, and the regional one $\frac{1}{288}$ electrum trachy, making the metropolitan tetarteron worth three regional ones, or $\frac{1}{96}$ trachy, and thus accounting for their variant metallic compositions. See also below, p. 588 and n. 159.

336 Based upon Hendy, *DOS* XII, p. 25, and *idem*, *DOC* IV, particularly for the tetarteron and half-tetarteron.

Table 22. *The coinage system*, c. *1092–1118*

| AV Hyperpyron 'perperus' | El. Aspron trakhy 'manuelatus' | (Keration) ('karatus') | Bill. Aspron trakhy 'staminum' | Æ Tetartēron 'tartaro' | Æ ½-tetartēron |
|---|---|---|---|---|---|
| 1 | 3 | 24 | 48 | 864 | 1,728 |
| — | 1 | 8 | 16 | 288 | 576 |
| — | — | 1 | 2 | 36 | 72 |
| — | — | — | 1 | 18 | 36 |
| — | — | — | — | 1 | 2 |
| | | | | | 1 |

Alexius' fiscal and monetary activities are summarised by Zonaras in the following unflattering terms:

This emperor [Alexius] finding the nomisma debased (*kekibdeleumenon*) by his predecessors struck a copper (*khalkeon*) one which he used for imperial expenditure (*eis ta tēs basileias analōmata*) while exacting tribute (*phoroi*) from the tax-payer in pure gold coins (*dia khrysinōn dokimōn*), but on some occasions in other gold coins of a worthless or half-gold kind (*di 'heterōn khrysinōn men kakeinōn all' hēmikhrysōn*), and sometimes even in copper coins (*dia tōn khalkeōn*). Because of a great lack of copper he converted folleis (*oboloi*) into nomismata, and also made some of the public works (I mean works in copper), that had been pulled down, into nomismata (*statēres*). And he also instituted new taxes (*dekatai*).

(Bonn edn, III, p. 738)

The precise application of these terms remains uncertain. Until the isolation of the Alexian coinage reform and its coinage, it was considered that they referred to a general situation of monetary debasement and confusion that was supposed to have characterised the late eleventh and twelfth century. They may indeed still be considered as referring to the ultimate stages of debasement that followed on from the severe financial crisis that is known to have dominated the earlier part of the reign.[337] Further consideration, however, suggests another interpretation, for if the evident hostility of the passage towards Alexius is laid aside, what remains forms an adequate and relatively complete description of the coinage reform of 1092 and the fiscal reforms that shortly followed it. Distinction is thus made between coins of 'pure' gold, of 'half-gold', and of 'copper'. 'Pure' gold would provide an acceptable description of the material used for the new hyperpyron, 'half-gold', a somewhat looser one of that used for the new electrum coin, and 'copper' an acceptable one of that used for the new billon coin. The conversion of folleis into nomismata then falls neatly into place as an attempt to account for the discontinuation of the follis in favour of the new billon coin and the copper tetarteron – and may well even be accurate in detail. As for the payment of taxes in 'pure' gold, 'half-gold', and

[337] As, not very plausibly, C. Morrisson, in *Numismatic Chronicle* 11[7] (1971), at pp. 359–60 (review of Hendy, *DOS* XII). For the correct dating of the passage, see now: Hendy, *DOC* IV.

'copper', coin, very much this kind of arrangement is envisaged in the fiscal measures embodied in the *Nea Logarikē* – which might itself well be described as a *nea dekatē*.[338]

The new coinage, despite its viability and long-term success, was nevertheless not immediately or entirely popular. Distrust seems to have concentrated upon the electrum denomination. Zonaras' description of the 'half-gold' coin as 'worthless' has already been noted, but other similar evidence exists. A scholium recorded in Du Cange[339] terms the *aspron trikephalon* an *apōleia*, that is a 'wasteful' or 'destructive', thing, and the western chronicler Arnold of Lübeck[340] somewhat misleadingly condemns the *manlat* as: 'One of the baser coins, which is neither completely gold nor completely copper, but consists as it were of a mixed and base material.' In the thirteenth century the electrum may have been termed *mokhthēron*, something 'wretched' or 'unsound', or even 'mixed' or 'muled', presumably with reference to its inferior value and composition.[341] The probable reason for this distrust is given by (the admittedly later) Nicholas Oresme:

> But it should be observed and laid down as a general rule that no alloy should be permitted except in the least precious metal used for small change. For instance, where the money consists of gold and silver, the gold should never be alloyed if it can be coined pure. The reason is that all such mixture is naturally suspect because the proportion of pure gold in it cannot readily be determined.
>
> (*De Moneta* III; ed. trans. Johnson, pp. 7–8)

By this criterion billon, which was used in coins of small value, was acceptable, while electrum, which was used in coins of still considerable value, was not.

## B. *The twelfth century: Temporary stability*

The twelfth century was, by and large, a period of monetary stability. The standard denomination of the new system, the gold hyperpyron of 24 keratia weight and value and $20\frac{1}{2}$ carats fine, remained unaltered throughout.[342]

338 In the *Nea Logarikē*, the *kharagma* was collected in the electrum trachy, and the *lepta psēphia* and *parakolouthēmata* were collected in the copper follis/tetarteron, at least in theory, but in the billon trachy in practice (see above, pp. 286–7). However, there seems not much doubt that if the *kharagma* had amounted to three electrum trachea (i.e. to $3 \times 4 = 12$ miliaresia), the tax-collector would have extracted one gold hyperpyron. The *Nea Logarikē* would almost certainly have been counted as a *nea dekatē*, for it sharply increased (effectively quadrupled) the tax-rate, in the *kharagma* one electrum trachy worth four miliaresia being collected instead of one miliaresion, and in the *parakolouthēmata* a somewhat lesser rate (Hendy, *DOS* XII, pp. 56–8).

339 C. Du Cange, *Glossarium ad Scriptores Medii et Infimae Graecitatis* II, col. 1605; *kai peri apōleias pragmatōn, dēlonoti asprōn, ē trikephalōn, kai tōn homoiōn.*

340 Arnold of Lubeck, *Chronica Slavorum* IV.12; MGH, *SS* XXI, p. 174; *Est autem manlat de viliori nummismate, qui nec totus sit aureus, nec totus cupreus, sed quasi de confusa et vili constat materia.*

341 Refs: Angold, *A Byzantine Government in Exile*, p. 107 n. 90 – a price is given as *eis hyperpyra tria kai mokhthēron hen.* Angold suggests the *mokhthēron* to be a billon trachy, but the scale of the payment involved indicates rather an electrum/silver one, and given the apparent unpopularity of the denomination the name is not impossible. It is of course quite possible that the term is simply being applied in its modern, casual sense, to a low-quality donkey, but a monetary sense of the kind suggested is not at all improbable.

342 Hendy, *DOS* XII, pp. 10–12 (Alexius I–Alexius III).

The electrum denomination, of 24 keratia weight, 8 keratia value, and between 5 and 6 carats fine, seems to have remained unaltered until the reign of Isaac II Angelus (1185–95) whom Nicetas Choniates reports[343] as having adulterated the silver coinage and struck a fraudulent nomisma. Electrum coins of this and the succeeding reign, that of Alexius III Comnenus (Angelus) (1195–1203), do indeed show a marked falling off from their previous standard and thus appear to confirm the chronicler's report.[344] Their value against the stable hyperpyron presumably then or later underwent adjustment, but the details of this remain uncertain, although the Florentine merchant Francesco Balducci Pegolotti estimates[345] the fineness of similar coins struck by the Lusignan kings of Cyprus at 'carati 4', which suggests that the modified Byzantine pieces may have gone four, or more probably six, to the hyperpyron, instead of three as previously.

The billon denomination was, according to a series of documentary sources, worth $\frac{1}{48}$ hyperpyron in 1136, $\frac{1}{120}$ hyperpyron in 1190, and $\frac{1}{184}$ hyperpyron in 1199.[346] Chemical analysis of a large number of these pieces shows their silver content to have declined from 6–7% under John II Comnenus (1118–43), to 4.5–6.0% under Manuel I, to 2.5–3.0% under Isaac II, and to 2–3% under Alexius III, thus accounting for their decline in value against the hyperpyron. The analysis also shows the billon to have been a fiduciary denomination, like the much earlier nummus, its bullion value nowhere near approaching its face-value.[347]

The pattern of hoards and their composition confirms the phenomenon, and frequently with surprising particularity.[348] Now, Choniates reports[349] that Manuel I put adulterated silver (*argyrion adokimon*) into the nomisma and thereby deceived the crusaders of 1147. Again, Odo of Deuil, the western chronicler of the Second Crusade, remarks[350] that the westerners almost invariably lost out on the exchange-rate between their *denier* and the Byzantine staminum which he describes as a copper coin (*cuprea moneta*). The evidence

343 Nicetas Choniates, *Historia*; ed. van Dieten, I, p. 444: *Alla kai to argyrion kibdēleusas adokimon to nomisma kekophe....*

344 Hendy, *DOS* XII, p. 12. Some specimens of Alexius' electrum coinage appear to the eye to contain very little, if any, gold, some silver, and quite a lot of copper.

345 Pegolotti, *La Pratica della Mercatura*; ed. Evans, p. 288.

346 Hendy, *DOS* XII, pp. 20–3.

347 Hendy and Charles, 'The Production Techniques, Silver Content and Circulation History of the Twelfth-century Byzantine Trachy', pp. 13–20. P. Grierson, 'The Date and Fineness of Byzantine "Neatly-clipped" Trachea', *Numismatic Circular* 83 (1975), p. 58. The coins involved in the latter article are ordinary trachea, later clipped down, to reduce their value, by the state: see above, p. 318 and n. 18. The two articles cited above are the only cases where highly reliable destructive ('wet') analysis has been utilised. For discrepant results, utilising other methods, refs: Metcalf, *Coinage in South-eastern Europe, 820–1396*, pp. 114–17 – but see above, p. 318 n. 18, below, p. 520 n. 359.

348 Hendy, *DOS* XII, pp. 158–161: coins of John II and of Manuel I up to and including his (undebased) Second Coinage very quickly dropped – or were taken – out of circulation, and with few exceptions only his (debased) Third and Fourth Coinages alone survived on into the succeeding reigns. *Ibid.* pp. 220–1: similarly, Manuel's debased coinages disappeared quite quickly from circulation once Isaac II and Alexius III, by debasing the coinage further, left even Manuel's debased pieces with a higher silver content.

349 Nicetas Choniates, *Historia*; ed. van Dieten, I, p. 67; *argyrion adokimon eis nomisma koptetai.*

350 Odo of Deuil, *De Profectione Ludovici VII in Orientem* III, IV; ed. Berry, pp. 40, 66.

of documentary sources, coins and hoards combined suggests that Choniates and Odo both had the billon denomination in mind, but that of the coins separately suggests that the former cannot have been correct in dating the decline in its silver content as early as 1147, barely four years after Manuel's succession: a date towards the middle of the reign seems more likely.[351]

The copper denominations, the tetarteron and its half, underwent only minor fluctuations of weight in the course of the century.[352] It is nevertheless noticeable that, as the value of the billon denomination declined, so the metropolitan production of tetartera, at least, also dropped off: coins of Isaac II are not uncommon, but those of Alexius III are decidedly so.[353] As is normal in the circumstances, production of the lower denomination simply became less necessary or convenient.[354] (Pl. 31)

### *C. The thirteenth century: The successor states*

The political disintegration that characterised the rule of the Angelus dynasty had thus already begun to find a counterpart, by way of complications to the relatively straightforward structure of the coinage, when Constantinople fell to the Fourth Crusade in 1204. These, however, are not to be compared with those following that event.

The fact that the *Partitio Romaniae* was only a partly successful operation had the effect of accentuating the number of states, Byzantine and Latin, that were established on territories which had formerly gone to make up the undivided empire. Of these states, several issued coinages to a great extent continuing the pattern of that of the Alexian reform. They had apparently, however, all been anticipated by the Asenid kingdom of Bulgaria which had established an independent existence during the late eighties of the century. The theoretical right of 'coining money in his own name (*cudendi monetam suo charactere insignitam*)' was sought by Kalojan (1197–1207) and granted by Innocent III in an exchange of letters in 1203/4.[355] But despite a recent and unconvincing attempt to attribute a named coinage to the even earlier Theodore/Peter Asen (1196–7),[356] the earliest coinage properly attributable to an Asenid tsar remains that in the name of Ivan

[351] Hendy, *DOC* IV: debased Third Coinage (First Phase) probably introduced in 1163.

[352] Hendy, *DOS* XII, pp. 109–10 (John II), 127–8 (Manuel I). See also *ibid.* pp. 413–20 (Alexius I–Alexius III).

[353] Alexius III's metropolitan type is much rarer than his Thessalonican one, and is known from three or four specimens only (Hendy, *DOS* XII, p. 152). One of these came from the metropolitan Kalenderhane excavations (see below, p. 521).

[354] As in the case of the Diocletianic nummus (above, p. 462), the Constantian maiorina (above, p. 469), and the Anastasian follis (above, p. 496). The virtual cessation of metropolitan production would, of course, be particularly readily understandable if the metropolitan billon tetarteron was worth $\frac{1}{288}$, and not $\frac{1}{864}$ hyperpyron (see above, p. 515 n. 335). Quite simply, as the value of the billon trachy fell towards $\frac{1}{184}$ hyperpyron in 1199 (see above, p. 518 n. 346), so it would have begun to approach that of the tetarteron, making the latter redundant.

[355] *Bullarium Privilegiorum ac Diplomatum Romanorum Pontificum Amplissima Collectio*; ed. C. Cocquelines, III.1, p. 107 (Innocent III, no. xxxviii): *Ad petitionem...publicam in regno tuo cudendi monetam tuo charactere insignitam, liberam tibi concedimus facultatem.*

[356] See above, p. 439 n. 302.

II Asen (1218–41).[357] The evidence of hoards nevertheless convincingly demonstrates it to have been preceded by a series of coins closely imitating the billon issues of Manuel I, Isaac II and Alexius III, and apparently appearing first in the Thracian plain during the last decade of the century.[358] The distinctions of organisational origin, hoard occurrence and style between these primarily Bulgarian imitations and their imperial originals are strikingly reinforced by considerations of metallic composition, the former consistently containing much less silver than the latter.[359] (Pl. 32, 14–16)

The probable coinages of two of the major Latin states that, as a result of the partition, temporarily replaced the Byzantine empire in Europe – the empire (1204–61) and the 'kingdom' of Thessalonica (1204–24) – have been distinguished only recently. Like the approximately contemporary Bulgarian coinage they were largely, but less closely, imitative of the billon issues of twelfth-century emperors, and are identifiable on the evidence of hoards;[360] like it they consistently contain much less silver than the originals.[361] (Pl. 32, 1–13)

357 See below, pp. 524–5.

358 Hendy, *DOS* XII, pp. 218–22; *idem*, *DOC* IV. *Contra* Metcalf, *Coinage in South-eastern Europe, 820–1396*, pp. 114–17. Metcalf's case, that these Bulgarian imitations are in fact imperial issues, struck at the same time as the coins they imitate, and put into circulation as an 'austerity' coinage, is constructed by way of a whole series of implausible arguments. It can only be said that it ignores (and can only exist through doing so) the massive burden of the numismatic evidence, is devoid of any historical support or likelihood, and – as in the case of his similar attempt involving the clipped trachea mentioned above – is ultimately a most wretched nonsense. One has only to wonder why, if the state was producing an 'austerity' coinage, it should choose to do so under two (or more) totally different guises, and then why it should have chosen to continue producing the more regular coinage at all, to glimpse the shoddy nature of the case. See above, p. 318 n. 18. Meanwhile, Touratsoglou, 'Unpublished Byzantine Hoards of Billon Trachea from Greek Macedonia and Thrace', pp. 140–1, attributes the series to Macedonia/Thrace/Constantinople pre- or post-1204, while M. Caramessini-Oekonomides, 'Contribution à l'étude de la circulation des monnaies byzantines en Grèce au XIII siècle', in *Actes du XV^e Congrès International d'Études Byzantines, Athènes, septembre 1976* II, *Art et Archéologie, Communications*, at pp. 123–4, is content to state categorically that they cannot be Bulgarian. Both Touratsoglou and Caramessini-Oekonomides accept the obvious date of the imitations (there is little else they can do, given the decisive nature of the material), but fail to see that because the imitations circulated widely (i.e. occur in Greece), a Bulgarian origin is not thereby disproved. The whole question shows distinct signs of becoming embroiled in Balkan numismatic nationalism. In fact, a more detailed examination of the hoard, geographical and historical evidence demonstrates quite decisively that the imitations are indeed Bulgarian.

359 Hendy and Charles, 'The Production Techniques, Silver Content and Circulation History of the Twelfth-century Byzantine Trachy', pp. 20–1. See also: Metcalf, 'Silver and Tin in the Byzantine Trachy Coinages, ca. 1160–1261', pp. 118 (§4, 'Manuel: reduced-value trachea' = Type A), 120 (§7, 'Isaac II: reduced-value trachea' = Type B), 123–4 (§10, 'Alexius III: reduced-value trachea' = Type C). The figures, within their limitations, are useful, but the particular classification and the general conclusions drawn may safely be disregarded.

360 Hendy, *DOS* XII, pp. 191–217. *Contra* the hysterical reaction of T. Bertelè, 'Moneta veneziana e moneta bizantina (secoli XII–XV)', in A. Pertusi (ed.), *Venezia e il Levante fino al secolo XV* I, *Storia-Diritto-Economia* 1, at pp. 93–104 (refusing but not refuting the identification), and the bizarre reaction of D. M. Metcalf, *Coinage in South-eastern Europe, 820–1396*, pp. 127–9 (transferring wholesale the later types (D–W) to the tsars of Bulgaria).

361 Hendy and Charles, 'The Production Techniques, Silver Content and Circulation History of the Twelfth-century Byzantine Trachy', pp. 20–1. See also: Metcalf, 'Silver and Tin in the Byzantine Trachy Coinages,

Documentary evidence for their existence and nature is sparse but suggestive. Choniates records,[362] of certain statues and other works standing in the hippodrome, that: 'The barbarians [i.e. crusaders of 1204] struck them into nomismata, great things being changed into small, and things accomplished at great expense exchanged for worthless small coins (*kermata*).' This would seem to confirm that at least some of the Latin coinage is to be found among the denominations of smaller value such as the billon or copper. A clause in the treaty of 1219 between Theodore I Comnenus-Lascaris (1208–22), emperor in Nicaea, and Giacomo Tiepolo, *podestà* of the Venetians in Romania, agrees[363] that: 'Neither my empire (*imperium*) nor your despotate (*dispotatus*) has the right to produce *yperperi*, or *manuelati*, or *stamena*, that are identical in design to those of the other party.' That an extraordinary clause of this kind should be considered necessary suggests that some such production of imitations had already taken place. Theodore's known coinage consists doubtfully of gold hyperpyra, but certainly of electrum manouelata and billon stamena, all in his own name:[364] it therefore seems improbable that he had also imitated any Latin coinage of Byzantine pattern that might have existed. The alternative is to suppose that the Venetians, or at any rate the Latins, had imitated Theodore's coinage. At least one such issue (theoretically in billon, actually in copper) has been identified,[365] in apparent confirmation of the imitative proclivities of the Latin moneyers. Pegolotti also mentions[366] *perperi latini* in his list of thirteenth- and fourteenth-century hyperpyra, and these again seem to be imitations, this time of the hyperpyron of John III Ducas (1222–54), emperor in Nicaea, produced in despite of the treaty of 1219.[367]

That the attribution of these billon coins, at least, to the Latin states is a valid one seems confirmed by their appearance in the excavation material from the metropolitan mosque of Kalenderhane, formerly a church and possibly dedicated to the Virgin *Kyriotissa*, where they tend to occur in close relation to the Latin chapel of Saint Francis of Assisi.* They also occur in excavation material from other metropolitan sites.[368]

* To be published by the author in the final report of the excavations, under the editorship of their directors, Professors Doğan Kuban of the Technical University, Istanbul, and Lee Striker, of the University of Pennsylvania.

---

ca. 1160–1261', pp. 126–7 (§18, 'Latin Emperors of Constantinople' = Types A–C), 127–8 (§19, 'Latin imitative coins attributed to Thessalonica'), 128–9 (§20, 'Types D–U: Constantinople or Bulgaria?'). Again, although the figures are useful, virtually everything else may be disregarded.

362 Nicetas Choniates, *Historia* (*De Signis Constantinopolitanis*); ed. van Dieten, I, p. 649. See: A. Cutler, 'The *De Signis* of Nicetas Choniates. A Reappraisal', *American Journal of Archaeology* 72 (1968), p. 116 (the article was published before the identification of the Latin coinage in question).

363 Tafel and Thomas, *Urkunden* II, p. 207. According to S. Brezeanu, 'Le premier traité économique entre Venise et Nicée', *Revue des Études Sud-Est Européennes* 12 (1974), pp. 143–6, the treaty of 1219 was a five-year renewal of one – probably at least very similar – concluded in 1214.

364 Hendy, *DOS* XII, pp. 227–36.

365 *Ibid.* XII, pp. 199 (smaller module, Type G).

366 See below, p. 527, Table 23.

367 Hendy, *DOS* XII, pp. 250, 253, 255.

368 Hendy, *DOC* IV (site in the precincts of the National Archaeological Museum. The coins were seen through the courtesy of the late Nezih Fıratlı).

The three major Byzantine states emerging from the events of 1204 all struck coinage, the rulers of each claiming the title and prerogative of an emperor of the Romans, given what they regarded as sufficient excuse, or the likelihood of their being able to maintain the claim against their rivals, or both.

The first of the emperors in Trebizond, the Grand Comneni (*Megaloi Komnēnoi*), to have issued a base-metal (copper) coinage in his own name seems to have been Andronicus I Comnenus-Gidon (1222–35).[369] A precious-metal (silver) coinage has customarily been attributed to his successor John I Comnenus-Axuch (1235–8), but this seems rather to fit more naturally at the head of the sequence attributable to John II (1280–97), leaving Manuel I (1238–63) as the originator of a coinage of that description.[370]

Manuel's earliest precious-metal coinage consists of convex silver coins with a seated figure of the Virgin as their obverse design, a standing figure of the emperor as their reverse. These are the presumptive descendants of the electrum coins of the Alexian reform. They were succeeded in turn by flat coins on which the standing figure of the patron saint of Trebizond, Eugenius, replaced the Virgin: this fabric and design then became standard. Weight seems to have been the same for both convex and flat coins, somewhere in the region of 2.9 g.[371] It bore no relation to any Byzantine standard and seems rather to have been derived ultimately from the Muslim dirhem, from which the contemporary *tram* of Cilician Armenia also appears to have been derived.[372] Metallic fineness was high, generally exceeding 95%.[373] Under John II the weight and fineness of the silver coin both declined slightly and continued to do so under his successors. By the reign of John IV (1429–58/60), the last emperor known to have issued coins, its weight

369 A. Veglery and A. Millas, 'Copper Coins of Andronicus I, Comnenus Gidon (1222–1235)', *Numismatic Circular* 85 (1977), pp. 487–8. The named coinage was apparently preceded by an imitative one along Bulgarian and Latin lines of much the same period: D. M. Metcalf and I. T. Roper, 'A Hoard of Copper Trachea of Andronicus I of Trebizond (1222–35)', *Numismatic Circular* 83 (1975), pp. 237–8. Veglery and Millas, *op. cit.* p. 488. S. Bendall, 'Andronicus I of Trebizond', *Numismatic Circular* 88 (1980), pp. 400–1. For the named copper coinage of John I: M. Kuršanskis, 'Une nouvelle monnaie de l'empire de Trébizonde', *Revue Numismatique* $14^6$ (1972), pp. 269–70.

370 E.g. Wroth, *Catalogue of the Coins of the Vandals, Ostrogoths and Lombards... in the British Museum*, pp. 232–5. O. Retowski, *Die Münzen der Komnenen von Trapezunt*, pp. 11–16. The transfer from John I to John II seems now generally agreed, but in default of a modern study of the series, the customary attribution still occasionally appears. See, meanwhile: M. Kuršanskis, 'L'usurpation de Théodora Grande Comnène', *Revue des Études Byzantines* 33 (1975), p. 202 and n. 61.

371 Wroth, *Catalogue of the Coins of the Vandals, Ostrogoths and Lombards... in the British Museum*, pp. lxxxiii, 236–56. Two small silver coins of Manuel, 13 mm only in diameter, and apparently weighing some 0.7 g, seem to be the sole survivors of a unique issue of quarter aspers: the 'half' and 'quarter' aspers traditionally attributed to the later Trapezuntine rulers are of course merely whole aspers on a much reduced standard of weight: M. Kuršanskis, 'Monnaies divisionnaires en argent de l'empire de Trébizonde', *Revue Numismatique* $19^6$ (1977), pp. 103–8.

372 Wroth, *Catalogue of the Coins of the Vandals, Ostrogoths and Lombards... in the British Museum*, p. lxxxv. P. Z. Bedoukian, *Coinage of Cilician Armenia*, p. 108. The Armenian silver coinage underwent a decline in weight and fineness that was similar to the Trapezuntine (Bedoukian, *op. cit.* pp. 108–25).

373 I owe the figures for fineness to the kindness of M. Kuršanskis, whose book (with A. A. M. Bryer), *Coinage and Money in the Byzantine Empire of Trebizond*, is in preparation.

had declined to under 1 g and its fineness to about a quarter.[374] Under Alexius II (1297–1330) the obverse and reverse designs were changed to figures of St Eugenius and the emperor on horseback. Although this motif seems likely to have been derived ultimately from a Muslim source, it is noticeable and perhaps significant that Alexius' Armenian near-contemporary, Levon II (1270–89), had also adopted it – himself probably from a Selçuk source and possibly via the bilingual (Selçuk and Armenian) coinage of his predecessor Hetoum I (1226–71).[375] (Pl. 33, 1–14)

The silver coins of the Trapezuntine emperors were termed *aspra*, because of the 'white' colour of their metal, and – in the fourteenth century at least – were also termed *Komnēnata* (*Cominiati* in Latin), after their issuers, to distinguish them from other aspra then current. The classic authority for the usage is no less than Alexius III who for instance, in a chrysobull dated 1374, inaugurated an annual grant of 'A thousand aspra of my own God-guarded issue (*theosyntēretou kharagēs*) that are called "Komnenata"'.[376]

The silver coinage had not only been anticipated, but was also accompanied throughout, by a convex copper one, the presumptive descendant of the billon of the Alexian reform. These copper coins seem to have lost weight more or less in parallel with the silver. Their contemporary nomenclature remains uncertain, but it is not improbable that they were termed trachea, like their predecessors.[377] (Pl. 33, 15–20)

The earliest coinage issued by the rulers of Epirus, subsequently emperors in Thessalonica, is currently represented by an issue attributable to Michael I Comnenus-Ducas (*c.* 1204–*c.* 1214) and presumably struck at Arta. The issue was continued without change in design by Theodore (*c.* 1214–30), probably during the period before his recovery of Thessalonica from the Latins in 1224, and with a change in design by Manuel (1230–7). It consists of convex electrum or silver coins and has been distinguished only very recently.[378]

With the recovery of Thessalonica, to which the centre of dynastic power then shifted, an almost complete range of Alexian denominations was issued: convex electrum or silver,

374 The general pattern of the decline in weight may be seen from Wroth's figures: *Catalogue of the Coins of the Vandals, Ostrogoths and Lombards... in the British Museum*, p. lxxxiv. On the other hand, more late material has now become available, and it is in any case clear that several of the later attributions will need revising: the details therefore remain uncertain. For the figures for fineness, see above, n. 373.

375 Bedoukian, *Coinage of Cilician Armenia*, pp. 227–35 (Hetoum-Kaikobad, Hetoum-Kaikhusrew), 290–307 (Levon).

376 Oikonomides, *Actes de Dionysiou*, no. 4, p. 61 (1374).

377 The term *trakhy/trakhion* certainly occurs in Trapezuntine documents (Kuršanskis and Bryer, *Coinage and Money in the Byzantine Empire of Trebizond*), referring to a subordinate denomination, just as it does in contemporary Byzantine documents (see below, p. 535 n. 433).

378 Hendy, *DOC* IV. Meanwhile: M. Caramessini-Oekonomides, 'Contribution à l'étude du monnayage de Michel II d'Épire', in *Actes du XIVe Congrès International des Études Byzantines, Bucarest, 6–12 septembre 1971* III, at pp. 187–90. See now, in the last instance: P. Protonotarios, 'Hē Nomismatokopia tou Vyzantinou Kratous tēs Ēpeirou (1204–1268)', *Ēpeirotika Khronika* 24 (1982), pp. 130–50, most of whose additional attributions and suggestions unfortunately cannot be taken seriously.

and billon coins, together with flat copper tetartera and their halves, the only exception being gold hyperpyra of which no issues are known. This range was continued, if somewhat less completely, by Manuel (1230–7) and John (1237–44). Both Theodore (probably after 1227/8) and John (before 1242) assumed the title of emperor, although Manuel appears to have remained content, or to have been constrained to remain content, with that of despot. (Pl. 34, 1–7)

Perhaps the most remarkable Thessalonican issue in the name of a ruler of the Comnenus-Ducas dynasty currently known is that recently distinguished as being in the joint names of John III, the Nicaean emperor, who had demoted John to the rank of despot in 1242, and had finally taken Thessalonica from his successor the despot Demetrius in 1246, and of Michael II Comnenus-Ducas, the ruler of Epirus. The issue is precisely datable to the year 1248/9, when a marriage-alliance between the two rulers was arranged. The design, representing John actually crowning Michael, is obviously intended to symbolise the resulting relationship of dominance and dependence, however theoretical and brief it may have been.[379] (Pl. 34, 5)

By 1246 the centre of dynastic power had in any case already shifted back to Arta, largely as a result of the defeat and capture of Theodore by the Bulgarian tsar Ivan II at Klokotnitsa in 1230. Michael II (*c.* 1231–*c.* 1268), who during the course of his career either claimed the title of despot or held it from the Nicaean and later the Constantinopolitan emperors, seems at first to have recognised the Thessalonican authority of Manuel, in whose name he may have issued a convex electrum or silver coin. At some subsequent stage, however, perhaps after the dynasty had ceased to control Thessalonica, he issued convex billon coins in his own name.[380]

A significant development of the period, although one that was perhaps least so in a purely monetary sense, was the sudden and brief issue of a range of Alexian denominations in the names of the tsars of Serbia and Bulgaria. Those in the name of Stephen Radoslav of Serbia (*c.* 1228–*c.* 1234) comprised convex electrum or silver, and billon coins. They entitle him: *rix ho Doukas*, a formula also known from his signature,

[379] Hendy, *DOS* XII, pp. 268–72 (Theodore), 274–7 (Manuel), 279–85 (John), 288–9 (Demetrius?), 290–3 (John III), 295 (Theodore II). Since the publication of *DOS* XII (1969), an appreciable number of new types have come to light and have been published in a number of articles in several different journals. The new types, with relevant bibliography, have been incorporated into, and will appear in, Hendy, *DOC* IV. The electrum/silver trachea of the series seem normally, to the eye, to be much debased with copper, but the billon does seem to retain a minimal silver content: Metcalf, 'Silver and Tin in the Byzantine Trachy Coinages', pp. 129–30. For the issue of John III and Michael II: M. F. Hendy and S. Bendall, 'A Billon Trachy of John Ducas, Emperor, and John Comnenus-Ducas, Despot (?)', *Revue Numismatique* $12^6$ (1970), pp. 143–8. T. Gerassimov, 'Medni Moneti na Ïoan III Vatatses e Epirskiya Despot Mikhail II', *Izvestiya na Arkheologicheskiya Institut* 34 (1974), pp. 319–21. The decision to leave the question mark in the title of the first article proved fortunate, as (inevitably) a fully legible specimen turned up shortly after its publication (although Gerassimov's photographs are not in themselves legible). For the precise dating of the issue: Hendy, *DOC* IV.

[380] Hendy, *DOS* XII, pp. 297–8; *idem*, *DOC* IV.

and presumably reflecting his descent from Euphrosyne Ducaena, the wife of Alexius III.[381] Those in the name of Ivan II of Bulgaria comprised gold hyperpyra and billon coins.[382] Both series were very heavily influenced by the contemporary Thessalonican one – to an extent suggesting either that the dies were produced in that city or, less likely, that they were produced locally by Thessalonican or Thessalonican trained staff.[383] Certainly the Serbian series was actually struck at Ras, where what are apparently remains of the mint have been discovered.[384]

Direct Thessalonican influence is visible in the Bulgarian coinage as late as the reign of Constantine Asen (Tich) (1257–77), the designs of whose billon issues imitated those of Thessalonican issues of John III and Theodore II Ducas-Lascaris (1254–8).[385]

Similar in monetary status to the two Slavonic series was that issued by the contemporary rulers of Rhodes, Leo (1232–?) and John (?–1248) Gabalas, who are known to have held the island in succession under the loose control of the Nicaean emperors. The series consists of small thin copper coins with a purely inscriptional design. Coins in the name of Leo entitle him: *kaisar ho Gabalas, ho doulos tou basileōs* (i.e. of John III). Those in the name of John entitle him: *ho Gabalas, ho authentēs tēs Rhodou.*[386]

It was, however, neither the emperors in Trebizond nor those in Thessalonica, still less the tsars of Serbia or Bulgaria or the rulers of Rhodes, who acted as the principal monetary heirs of the undivided empire, but the emperors in Nicaea. Their coinage is less complicated than those of their rivals, in that it is now denominationally more consistent and complete, suggesting that it was originally issued in larger quantities. Theodore I doubtfully issued gold, but certainly electrum or silver, and billon. His successors, John III, Theodore II and Michael VIII Palaeologus (1259–82), all issued a complete range of Alexian denominations: gold, electrum or silver, billon, and copper tetartera.[387] (Pls 34, 8–13; 35, 1–3)

381 Polemis, *The Doukai, a Contribution to Byzantine Prosopography*, p. 132, no. 102.

382 Hendy, *DOS* XII, pp. 296–7; *idem*, *DOC* IV.

383 The fact that some specimens of Stephen's billon coinage were struck with one engraved die only, the other being blank, suggests very strongly that the dies were supplied from Thessalonica and struck locally, and that when a die broke the local staff were unable to provide another. See below, n. 384.

384 M. Popović, 'La découverte d'un dépot de monnaie du roi Stéphane Radoslav dans la forteresse de Ras', in V. Kondić (ed.), *Frappe et ateliers monétaires dans l'antiquité et moyen âge*, at pp. 115–19. D. Gaj-Popović, 'Monnaie du roi Radoslav', in *ibid.* at pp. 121–32.

385 Hendy, *DOS* XII, p. 294 n. 1; *idem*, *DOC* IV.

386 G. Schlumberger, *Numismatique de l'Orient latin* I, pp. 215–16, 216–21 (other 'Rhodian' pieces, 1250–1309). Hendy, *DOS* XII, p. 296; *idem*, *DOC* IV.

387 Hendy, *DOS* XII, pp. 227–30 (Theodore I), 237–45 (John III), 256–60 (Theodore II), 261–3 (Michael VIII). Again, since the publication of *DOS* XII, an appreciable number of new types have come to light, and have been published in a number of articles, in several different journals. The new types, with the relevant bibliography, have been incorporated into and will appear in, Hendy, *DOC* IV. The first substantive electrum/silver type of Theodore I seems, to the eye, to retain some gold in its composition, but the second seems to contain silver only, and many of the issues of John III and his successors seem to be much debased with copper. Morrisson ('La Logarikè: réforme monétaire et réforme fiscale sous Alexis I^er^ Comnène',

### *D. 1261: The restored empire (decline of the hyperpyron)*

The recovery of Constantinople from the Latins by Michael VIII in 1261, and the substantial readjustments that must have followed that event, left little or no trace on the formal denominational structure of the coinage. The long reign of Andronicus II Palaeologus (1282–1328), in its several collegiate phases, marked on the other hand a decisive stage in the disintegration of the Alexian system.[388]

The gold coinage of the Nicaean emperors had been produced in what can only have been considerable quantities. Nicephorus Gregoras reports that the empire had been able to take advantage of famine conditions suffered by the neighbouring sultanate of Iconium by selling supplies in return for gold, silver and other precious materials. This, the predominant economic character of the empire, which seems to have been even more dependent upon its agriculture than was usual, and the skilful exploitation of the fiscal resources that it represented, may well have formed the main contributory factors behind the production of the only viable gold coinage of the period.[389]

Even so, the gold-content of the Nicaean hyperpyron was appreciably less than that of the Comnenian and Angelan, and the reigns of Michael VIII and Andronicus II saw it decline even further and with increasing speed. This debasement continued despite the latter's attempt at fiscal reform in *c.* 1321, which, according to Gregoras,[390] resulted in

p. 466 n. 29) gives readings of 4 carats fine for the first substantive type and of virtually pure silver for the second. The earlier billon of Theodore still seems to retain a minimal silver content: Metcalf, 'Silver and Tin in the Byzantine Trachy Coinages, ca. 1160–1261', pp. 124 (§13, 'Theodore I of Nicaea (1204–22): First coinage of the Nicaean mint: normal trachea'), 126 (§ 'Second coinage of the Nicaea mint'). The coins on p. 125 (14, 15) are Latin imitations.

388 Prior to the appearance of Grierson, *DOC* v, the Palaeologan period, like the fifth century, remains without an adequate modern comprehensive treatment. That is, as a catalogue, W. Wroth's *Catalogue of the Imperial Byzantine Coins in the British Museum* (II, pp. 608–43) of 1908 remains necessary, although now very seriously outmoded. The lack has been partially remedied by S. Bendall and P. J. Donald's *The Later Palaeologan Coinage, 1282–1453*, which is a useful handbook of coin-types, with basic references, and with modern mint-attributions, but which was never intended to have an extensive critical apparatus. For Michael VIII, the equivalent works are Bendall and Donald's *The Billon Trachea of Michael VIII Palaeologos, 1258–1282* and the same authors' 'The Silver Coinage of Michael VIII, AD 1258–1282', *Numismatic Circular* 90 (1982), pp. 121–4. A number of new coin-types have come to light since the publication of these works, and have been published in a number of smaller articles, which it is not proposed to list here. There is nevertheless a list of recent works (to 1977) on the Palaeologan period in T. Bertelè and C. Morrisson, *Numismatique byzantine*, at pp. 119–22. Finally, a 'Review Article', by C. Morrisson, of Bendall and Donald's two works, together with a concordance between them and *Numismatique byzantine*, is to be found in *Revue Numismatique* 21[6] (1979), pp. 256–65, and what is effectively another, by the same author, 'La numismatique des Paléologues: à propos de deux ouvrages récents', is to be found in *Revue des Études Byzantines* 39 (1981), pp. 319–23. A number of other quite major articles on Palaeologan monetary history or numismatics have been omitted from this list simply because they will be referred to frequently in the course of the succeeding sections of this chapter. See now also: S. Bendall, 'An Early Palaeologan Gold Hoard', *Numismatic Chronicle* 142 (1982), pp. 66–82.

389 Gregoras: see above, p. 283. Land: see above, pp. 117–22.

390 See above, p. 161.

Table 23. *The debasement of the hyperpyron (after Pachymeres and Pegolotti)*

| (Pachymeres) | | (Pegolotti) | | |
|---|---|---|---|---|
| Emperor | Fineness (carats) | Variety | Fineness (carats) | Date of issue |
| | | Perperi Latini | $16\frac{1}{2}$ | |
| | | Perperi comunali | $16\frac{3}{4}$ | |
| John III | 16 | Perperi buoni | | *c.* 1222–61 |
| | | Perperi d'un'altra ragione | | |
| | | Perperi d'un'altra ragione | | |
| Michael VIII | 15 | Perperi paglioloccati | $15\frac{1}{2}$ | *c.* 1261–82 |
| | | Perperi inginocchiati | 14 | 1282–95 |
| | | Perperi vecchi 3 santi | $13\frac{1}{2}$ | |
| Andronicus II | 14–12 | Perperi nuovi di rosa e di stella | $11\frac{3}{4}$ | 1295–? (post |
| (to *c.* 1308) | | Perperi di Filadelphe | 12 | *c.* 1308) |
| | | Perperi nuovi nuovi | 11 | |

one million nomismata (hyperpyra) reaching the imperial treasury (*to basilikon tameion*) annually. Its progress is described in some detail by George Pachymeres, writing in *c.* 1308:

And he [Andronicus II] debased the nomisma according to need (*dia tēn khreian*). For at first under John [III] Ducas the refined gold (*khrysos apephthos*) of nomismata amounted to two-thirds of their weight (*talantou*) [i.e. to sixteen carats], and this situation continued for some time. Then, under Michael [VIII], after the recovery of the City, because of the expenses (*doseis*) then necessary, not least with regard to the Italians, he [Michael] altered the reverse (*opisthen*) of the old designs by means of a representation of the City, and reduced the measure of gold (*to ek khrysou nomizomenon*) by a carat (*para keration*), so that it became fifteen [carats] compared with [a total of] twenty-four. Later, when he was succeeded, it amounted to fourteen [of gold] compared with ten [of alloy], and now the purity [of the gold coin] is said to be mixed by half [i.e. twelve of gold compared with twelve of alloy]...

(*De Michaele et Andronico Palaeologis, De Mich.*; Bonn edn, II, pp. 493–4)

Pachymeres' figures are confirmed to a remarkable degree by those of Pegolotti[391] given in a list of current perperi. The two sets are correlated in Table 23.[392]

An unpublished fourteenth-century mathematical treatise now in the library of Columbia University[393] mentions that '*perperi boctazati* [i.e. of John III] are of 17 carats', a reasonable approximation.*

* I owe this reference to the kindness of Philip Grierson.

391 Pegolotti, *La Pratica della Mercatura*; ed. Lane, pp. 288–9.

392 For the identification of Pegolotti's varieties: Hendy, *DOS* XII, pp. 250–4.

393 Ref. no. X511 A1 3.

The precise composition of the latest (*nuovi nuovi*) Palaeologan perperi is given by Pegolotti[394] as 11 carats gold, 6 carats silver, and 7 carats copper.

It is surely ironic, and – given the close political relationship known to have existed between John III and Frederick II of Hohenstaufen – possibly in some way significant that, as the gold-content of the hyperpyron was decreased from $20\frac{1}{2}$ to something over 16 carats, so the Sicilian *tari*, at $16\frac{1}{3}$ carats, was supplemented by the issue of the Hohenstaufen *augustalis*, at $20\frac{1}{2}$ carats – indeed, Pegolotti remarks that a mixture of John III's perperi makes good tari gold.[395]

The approximate range of contemporary debasement is confirmed in the mathematical writings of Nicholas Rhabdas, dated *c.* 1341, in which *exagia* (i.e. hyperpyra) of 21 and 15 carats of fine gold (*khrysiou katharou kokkia*) are both mentioned. Another, very similar, and approximately contemporary, treatise gives a number of reckonings between $21\frac{1}{2}$ and 11 carats. The upper limit seems a little extreme for the period, but the lower one is entirely realistic.[396]

The debasement of the hyperpyron during the second half of the thirteenth century and the first half of the fourteenth is also reflected in a number of other sources, Byzantine, western and others. In one of the most specific, a Genoese document of 1281 and therefore of the reign of Michael VIII, 50 iperperi are reckoned as equivalent to 47 old ones (*iperperi veteres*–) – a proportion almost exactly representing the known contemporary debasement from 16 to 15 carats.[397] The hyperpyron is also known to have been weakening against harder foreign currencies at this period. But while undeniably of significance in a general and collective sense, the detailed and isolated comparison of the hyperpyron with another currency is rarely of more than limited use in itself, for too little is known of the metallic composition of most currencies and of the legal and commercial factors and considerations operating when the documents containing such comparisons were drawn up.[398]

394 Pegolotti, *La Pratica della Mercatura*; ed. Evans, p. 40.

395 *Ibid.* p. 289 (of *perperi d'un' altra ragione*): *ma mescolate con queste l'altre due ragione sopradette rispondono come buono oro di terì, cioè a carati* $16\frac{2}{3}$ *d'oro fine per oncia.*

396 Tannery, 'Notice sur les deux lettres arithmétiques de Nicolas Rhabdas (texte grec et traduction)', p. 154. K. Vogel, *Ein byzantinisches Rechenbuch des frühen 14. Jahrhunderts*, i–iii (pp. 20, 22) – 11, 13, $13\frac{3}{4}$, $14\frac{1}{2}$, 15, $15\frac{1}{2}$, 18, $21\frac{1}{2}$ carats; lxxiv–lxxvii (pp. 96, 98, 100) – $12\frac{4}{5}$, 16, 18, 21 carats. The upper limit had not been reached in coinage since the eleventh century (even the Comnenian hyperpyron stood at $20\frac{1}{2}$ carats only), but the latest Palaeologan hyperpyron mentioned by Pegolotti stood at precisely 11 carats. See above, pp. 514, 517.

397 Brătianu, *Recherches sur Vicina et Cetatea Albă*, no. 7, p. 152: *iperperos quinquaginta auri de sagio implicatos in petiis quadraginta et septem iperperorum veterorum.* See: D. A. Zakythinos, *Crise monétaire et crise économique à Byzance du XIII^e^ au XV^e^ siècle*, p. 11 n. 1. Cf. A. Stussi (ed.), *Zibaldone da Canal, manoscritto mercantile del sec. XIV*, p. 67: *A Constantinopolli sì è perperi de do lege, l'una sì è perperi veii e lo perpero veio val lo saço s. XXXII a gss^i^. e l'alltra lega sì è perperi palliologati e val lo saço s. XXVIII, dir. IIII a gss^i^.*

398 Sources cited in Zakythinos, *Crise monétaire et crise économique à Byzance du XIII^e^ au XV^e^ siècle*, pp. 20–9, and in T. Bertelè, 'Moneta veneziana e moneta bizantina (secoli XII–XV)', at pp. 39–58. For an example of how even the stable gold hyperpyron of the twelfth century might appear differently against a variety of western currencies, see: Hendy, *DOS* XII, p. 14 n. 1. For an even better one of how the same hyperpyron

The widespread distrust and inconvenience which the monetary instability outlined above might cause is also well attested. In 1319, Andronicus II found himself obliged to ratify an agreement guaranteeing the city of Ioannina that: 'no other issue less than that at present current (*ouden heteron kharagma para to nun politeuomenon*)' would be put into circulation there.[399] But as early as 1253 William of Rubruck was able to record[400] of the Tartars in the Crimea that: 'When our servants offered them *ipperpera* they rubbed them with their fingers and held them to their noses to sense by smell whether they were copper (*utrum essent cuprum*).' The precise significance of this incident has been debated, but it is on the face of it unlikely that the Tartars were unable to tell pure gold from pure copper except by smell, and therefore likely that what they were doing was attempting to discover whether the gold hyperpyron contained copper as an alloy. This is not as improbable as it sounds, for copper has a distinctly sour smell that gold alone lacks. According to pseudo-Aristotle,[401] there was said to be among the Indians a copper so bright, clean and resistant to corrosion as to be indistinguishable from gold, and among Darius' drinking-cups many that could be distinguished as copper or gold only by means of the smell.* It is of course the case that the preponderant alloying material in contemporary hyperpyra was a substantial amount of copper, and not a minimal quantity of silver, as it had been under the Comneni and Angeli.[402]

Ibn Battuta, who had accompanied Maria Palaeologina, the natural daughter of Andronicus II and widow of the khan of the Kipchak Tartars, back to Constantinople in *c.* 1332, somewhat ungraciously notes[403] that subsequently: 'She sent for me and gave me three hundred dinars in their coinage (they call this *al-barbara*, and it is not good money)....' More significantly, in 1302, the Venetian government had found it necessary to write to Andronicus II on the subject of 'a defect found in the emperor's yperperi delivered by messer Ugolino Giustiniani'.[404] In 1310, it had stipulated that a payment

* I owe this reference to the kindness of Michael Crawford.

might fluctuate against even a single western currency (the Genoese denier), within a limited period (1156–91), see: M. Chiaudano, 'La moneta di Genova nel secolo XII', in *Studi in onore di Armando Sapori* I, at p. 211.

399 Miklosich and Müller, *Acta et Diplomata Graeca Medii Aevi* v, p. 82.

400 William of Rubruck, *Itinerarium*; ed. C. R. Beazley, p. 160: *Quum famuli nostri offerebant eis ipperpera, ipsi fricabant digitis, et ponebant ad nares, ut odore sentirent, utrum essent cuprum.*

401 Anonymous (Pseudo-Aristotle), *De Mirabilibus Auscultationibus* 834a (49); ed. W. S. Hett (Loeb), p. 256.

402 This is true even for the coinage of the Lascarid emperors, but for the Palaeologan ones there is documentary evidence (Pegolotti: see above, p. 528). For the Comneni and Angeli, see: Hendy, *DOS* XII, p. 13 n. 3 (a hyperpyron from the Gornoslav Hoard gave a reading of 75% *AV*, 23% *AR*, 1% *Æ*). For John III, see: T. Bertelè, 'Il titolo degli iperperi della zecca di Nicea', in *Proceedings of the XIIIth International Congress of Byzantine Studies, Oxford 5–10 September 1966*, at pp. 339–41 (a hyperpyron of John gave a reading of 75% *AV*, 16% *AR*, 9% prob. *Æ*).

403 Ibn Baṭṭūṭa, *Travels* VIII.444; ed. H. A. R. Gibb, II, p. 514.

404 G. Giomo, 'Le Rubriche dei Libri *Misti* del Senato perduti, trascritte', *Archivio Veneto* 18 (1879), p. 325.

from the same emperor be made in yperperi: 'of one and the same quality, that which is in use today (*unius et eiusdem qualitatis, que est ut utitur hodie*).[405] In 1315, the *Maggior Consiglio* had finally come to the following decisions:

> That three knowledgeable people be chosen by the lord Doge, the councillors, and the heads of department, to enquire into and thoroughly examine the fact that it seems to the lord Doge and the aforesaid officials that *bizanti* [hyperpyra], *turonensi* [coins of Tours], *unziae* [coins of Sicily], *quar*... [?], and other similar currencies, are in every respect now found in a much more diverse condition and in many other forms than they were before, to the prejudice and loss of the state and of individual people....
>
> (R. Cessi, *Problemi monetari veneziani*, no. 71, p. 68)

It is clear that the hyperpyron, for long a stable medium of exchange, had become – and justifiably so – a byword for the unreliability of its alloy. It has indeed been suggested[406] that it was already this that, in 1284, had finally decided the Venetian government to issue its own gold coin, the *ducatus* (ducat), more than thirty years after its rivals, Florence and Genoa. Certainly the unreliability of alloy is clearly reflected in the fourteenth-century Byzantine mathematical writings and treatises that have been mentioned above. Here, the hyperpyron is reckoned according to widely variant (and not always necessarily realistic) gold-contents in various exemplars, quite frequently being described as consisting of 'white gold (*argos khrysos*)'.[407]

As the quality of the alloy of the Palaeologan hyperpyron declined so, apparently, did the quantity in which it was issued. Pieces of the admittedly short joint reign of Andronicus II and Andronicus III (1325–8) are scarce, those of the reign of Andronicus III (1328–41) are definitely rare, and those of the joint reign of John V and John VI Cantacuzene (1347–53) are extremely so.[408] Pieces of the last mentioned joint reign are in fact the latest of traditional fabric and design now known, for those supposedly in the name of Manuel II (1391–1425) are crude forgeries.[409] (Pl. 35, 4–9)

### *E. 1261: The restored empire (introduction of the* basilikon *and* politikon*)*

The traditional electrum or silver coinage of the Nicaean emperors (its precise metallic development remains unknown[410]) had, except perhaps under Theodore I, and despite the large number of types involved, never been issued in more than exiguous quantities;

[405] *Diplomatarium Veneto-Levantinum, sive Acta et Diplomata Res Venetas Graecas atque Levantis Illustrantia a. 1300–1350*; ed. G. M. Thomas, no. xlvi, p. 84.

[406] Brătianu, *Études byzantines d'histoire économique et sociale*, p. 237.

[407] See above, p. 528 n. 396. *Argos khrysos*: Vogel, *Ein byzantinisches Rechenbuch des frühen 14. Jahrhunderts* LXXIV, p. 96: *Psēphos argou· Esti to exagion argou khrysou toutesti tōn 24 keratiōn 21*. See also *ibid.* p. 98.

[408] Bendall and Donald, *The Later Palaeologan Coinage, 1282–1453*, pp. 108–9 (Andronicus II/III), 116–17 (Andronicus III), 138–9 (John V/VI).

[409] On this, see in the last instance: T. Gerassimov, 'Des fausses hyperpères de Jean V et Manuel II Paléologue', *Byzantinobulgarica* 4 (1973), pp. 216–20.

[410] See above, pp. 525–6 n. 387.

that of Michael VIII after the recovery of the City seems to have been no greater in quantity and may well have been less; that of Andronicus II can only have been minimal.[411] It was replaced, during the joint reign of Andronicus II and Michael IX (1295–1320), by a silver coinage on the pattern of the Venetian grosso, having as its obverse design a seated figure of Christ with the inscription **KVPIЄ BOHΘЄI**, and as its reverse design the standing figures of the emperors holding a labarum between them with with the inscription **ANΔPONIKOC MIXAHΛ ΔЄCΠ** (*otai*) or **AVTOKPATOPЄC PωMAIωN**. The second of these reverse inscriptions is of some interest in itself, for the simultaneous use of the title *autokratōr* by more than one *basileus* had first occurred as recently as the joint reign of Michael VIII and Andronicus II (1272–82).[412] (Pl. 35, 12)

As it happens, a good deal is known of the new silver coinage from contemporary literary and documentary sources.[413] According to the Catalan historian Ramon Muntaner it was first issued in 1304, largely or entirely in connection with payments made to the Catalan mercenary *companya* then in imperial hire. Muntaner relates the circumstances in the following terms:

And when this peace was made, the *megaduch* [i.e. *megas doux*: Roger de Flor, the Catalan leader] requested that the emperor [Andronicus] distribute pay to the *companya*, and the emperor said that he would. And the emperor had coins struck after the manner of the Venetian ducat [in this case the grosso], which coins were worth eight *diners* of Barcelona. And he also had some made which were called *vincilions/vasilios* and which were not worth three *diners*, and he wished them to be current at the rate of those worth eight *diners*. And he ordered each to take horse, mule, provisions or other necessities from the Greeks and to pay in these coins.

(*Chronicle* CCX; ed. K. Lanz, p. 376)

And the *megaduch* refused to take these coins.

(*op. cit.* CCXI; *ed. cit.* p. 376)

And so the *cesar* [Roger de Flor, promoted from *megaduch*] took leave of the emperor, and the emperor gave him these bad coins with which to distribute pay. And the *cesar* took them...and so he came to Galipol with them, and began to distribute pay in them, and each paid his host in them.

(*op. cit.* CCXII; *ed. cit.* p. 378)

In his list of finenesses of silver coins of grosso type, Pegolotti mentions[414] what can only be Muntaner's two varieties under the headings: '*Basilei* of Romania made after the

[411] For Michael VIII: Bendall and Donald, 'The Silver Coinage of Michael VIII, A.D. 1258–1282', pp. 121–4. For Andronicus II, one example only is as yet known, but given the regular – if small-scale – production under Michael, and the hiatus between the accession of Andronicus and the introduction of the basilikon (i.e. 1282–95) it is not impossible that more will eventually appear.

[412] Verpeaux, *Traité des offices*, p. 27 n. 3.

[413] Cited by V. Laurent, in 'Le Basilikon, nouveau nom de monnaie sous Andronic II Paléologue', *Byzantinische Zeitschrift* 45 (1952), pp. 50–8.

[414] Pegolotti, *La Pratica della Mercatura*; ed. Evans, p. 290.

fashion of the Venetians (*fatti a modo di Viniziani*), at 11 oz. 8 d.', and 'The latest (*nuovi nuovi*) *basilei* of Romania at 5 oz. 12 d.'. The first of these finenesses is, as might be expected, closely comparable with that of the Venetian grosso at 11 oz. 14 d.[415] It is moreover confirmed by analyses, which give an average fineness of just over 920/1,000 or about 11 oz. 1 d.[416]

There are a number of minor discrepancies, but none is of sufficient moment to cast serious doubt upon the coincidence of identity between the coins of the two sources. Muntaner gives the impression that only the baser variety was termed *vasilio*, Pegolotti lists both varieties as *basilei*. Byzantine sources however, as will be seen below, neatly dispose of the problem by referring to the finer variety as *basilikon*. Muntaner gives the impression that production of both varieties began simultaneously, Pegolotti that the baser was also the later. Possibly neither is entirely correct: Muntaner's account is unsatisfactory in that it gives the finer variety no plausible rôle – both varieties were first issued simultaneously but only the baser was used to pay the Catalans and, through them, their hosts. Pegolotti may well have assumed, on the analogy of the hyperpyron, that the baser a coin the later it was. But what appear to be pieces of the finer variety, if of reduced weight, are known from reigns subsequent to the latest possible date for the redaction of his list. It therefore seems more likely that the baser variety represents a temporary issue within the main and finer series which numismatic evidence suggests to have been first issued in *c.* 1295.[417] Muntaner quotes the value of the baser variety at appreciably under half that of the finer, Pegolotti its fineness at only a little under half. Even assuming the former to be accurate, the two estimates are not entirely incompatible, however, for it is conceivable that public hostility was so great, immediately after its introduction, that its value was temporarily depressed below that of its actual silver-content.

Issues of the basilikon, the later on a reduced weight standard of just over 1 g, are known for most reigns of the first half of the fourteenth century, up to and including the joint reign of John V and Manuel II prior to the usurpation of Andronicus IV in 1376.[418] Rare examples of the half-basilikon are also known.[419] (Pl. 35, 13–18)

The basilikon was not, however, the only silver denomination of the period, for a further series of coins, much lighter than – perhaps only half the weight of – the contemporary basilikon, and composed of a much baser alloy, are known. The obverse design used for this series commonly comprises an equal-armed cross potent or pattée enclosed by a circular border and inscription, the latter on occasion imperial, but in most

[415] *Ibid.* p. 289.

[416] P. D. Whitting, 'Miliaresia of Andronicus II and Michael IX', *Numismatic Circular* 80 (1972), p. 270. See also: Bertelè, 'Moneta veneziana e moneta bizantina', p. 66, nos 43–4 (930, 915/1,000).

[417] P. Protonotarios, 'The Silver Coinage of the Joint Reign of Andronicus II and Michael IX (1295–1320)', *Numismatic Circular* 80 (1972), p. 452.

[418] Bendall and Donald, *The Later Palaeologan Coinage, 1282–1453*, pp. 184–5. The attribution is, however, tentative.

[419] *Ibid.* pp. 70, 106, 120, 144(?).

cases ΤΟ ΠΟΛΙΤΙΚΟΝ or simply ΠΟΛΙΤΙΚΟΝ. The reverse designs vary greatly, being on occasion an imperial figure, but in most cases a non-imperial motif, including that of a castle (*châtel*).[420] (Pl. 35, 19–20)

The nature and significance of the *politikon*, both in terms and coin, have been much discussed, but so far to little apparent effect.[421] The term *politikon*, applied to the nomisma (i.e. presumably to the hyperpyron), and with the clear sense of 'current', is known from a roughly contemporary, but otherwise entirely casual and uninformative incident (the discovery of a huge treasure-trove amongst the Turks), that is reported by Gregoras.[422]

The contemporary system of subsidiary coinage is described by Pegolotti:

> And one spends in minor transactions in the aforesaid places [i.e. Constantinople and Pera] a silver coin of which twelve go to the perpero, and this coin is of a fineness of.... And each of these said grossi is reckoned at eight *tornesi piccioli*.
>
> And one also spends another coin which is entirely of copper and which they call a stanmino, and the *tornese picciolo* is reckoned at four stanmini. But with such stanmini no payments are made except while in transit through Constantinople and its region, and then only for vegetables and small purchases.
>
> And one also spends Venetian silver grossi of Venice, and they are reckoned at 12½ or thirteen to the perpero according to whether silver is dear or cheap, and each of the said grossi of Venice is reckoned at eight *tornesi piccioli*, like the large grosso of the perpero mentioned above.
>
> (*La Pratica della Mercatura, ed. cit.* p. 40)

It seems clear that the silver grosso of Pegolotti's first paragraph, of which a traditional twelve went to the perpero/hyperpyron (as in the case of the argenteus, the hexagram and the miliaresion), should be identified with the same author's basileo/basilikon.[423] It seems equally clear that such a rate can only have been the official, and not a market and unofficial, one. This arises partly out of the fact that the Venetian grosso proper, with a slightly better alloy than the basilikon, is quoted as going 12½ or 13 to the hyperpyron – a rate which being outside Venetian jurisdiction can only have been an unofficial one.[424] These precise figures (12½ and 13 *argyrioi* to the hyperpyron) are repeated, presumably with reference to the Byzantine version, the basilikon, in the slightly later mathematical writings of Rhabdas. Again, another treatise gives variants.[425] But it also arises out of the fact that another and even lower rate than either of these survives. Muntaner, having remarked that Andronicus' finer variety of basilikon was worth 8 *diners* of Barcelona,

[420] *Ibid.* pp. 180–7.

[421] E.g. V. Laurent, '*To Politikon*. Monnaie divisionnaire de l'époque des Paléologues', *Cronică Numismatica şi Arheologică* 10 (1940), pp. 264–86.

[422] Nicephorus Gregoras, *Historia Byzantina* IX.10; Bonn edn, I, pp. 446–7.

[423] See above, pp. 531–2.

[424] See above, p. 532.

[425] Tannery, 'Notice sur les deux lettres arithmétiques de Nicolas Rhabdas', pp. 148–9: the figure of 12½ argyrioi to the hyperpyron is described (p. 148) as 'that obtaining now (*to prattomenon nun*)', showing silver to be dear then. Vogel, *Ein byzantinisches Rechenbuch des frühen 14. Jahrhunderts* XXI (p. 40): 9 and 7 to the hyperpyron – it is doubtful whether anything useful can be made out of these two figures.

then twice remarks[426] that the contemporary *perpre* was worth 10 *sous* or 120 of the same coin, implying a rate of 15 basilika to the hyperpyron. This figure is confirmed by a contemporary Greek source[427] where one third of 22 nomismata (i.e. hyperpyra) is equated with 7 nomismata and 5 aspra in basilika. It is also entirely compatible with that of 12½ or 13 to the hyperpyron for the Venetian grosso with its slightly better alloy.

The major problem presented by Pegolotti's description of the monetary system is the identity of his *tornese picciolo*. The silver grosso of his first paragraph has already been identified with the Palaeologan version of the Venetian coin with the same name. The copper stanmino of his second paragraph is clearly to be identified with the Palaeologan descendant of the Alexian convex billon coin, long termed staminum in western sources. The implication surely is that the *tornese* in question is also a coin of imperial mintage.

The *tornese picciolo* – so called to distinguish it from the larger *tornese grosso* – was in origin a silver denier of the French city of Tours (i.e. a *denier tournois*). It had been adopted, with appropriate adjustments in its inscriptions but no changes in its overall design, as the substantive coin of the Latin, largely French, states, established in central and southern Greece as a result of the Fourth Crusade. The two main mints of those states, Chiarenza (i.e. Glarentsa = Killini) in the principality of Achaia and Thebes in the duchy of Athens, had produced large quantities of the coin during the late thirteenth and early fourteenth centuries, although these had been severely reduced by the second quarter of the latter century. The coin had nevertheless by then achieved such a position in the monetary affairs of the Latin states that, in 1342/54, Venice was to find it expedient to supplement and eventually replace the depleted and much debased products of the Greek mints by introducing and exporting a *tornesello* of its own. Tornesi had, meanwhile, been produced briefly and in small quantities by even such Byzantine and semi-Byzantine rulers as John II Angelus-Comnenus, sebastocrator in Neopatras (1303–18), who significantly had been under the guardianship of Guy II de la Roche of Athens until 1308, and John Ducas (Orsini), despot in Arta (*c.* 1323–35).[428]

The obverse and reverse designs of the Greek tornesi were standard: an equal-armed cross potent or pattée enclosed by a circular border and inscription; a schematic representation of the *châtel tournois* and inscription. The latter was by no means an element essential to the denomination, for it was replaced by a winged lion of St Mark on the Venetian *tornesello*, and other similar instances might be quoted.[429] The former was the precise equivalent of the cross, border and inscription of the Palaeologan politikon described above. The fineness of the tornese of Chiarenza is given by Pegolotti as 2½ oz. to the pound, or somewhat less than the 3 oz. 12 d. of the French tournois, and its value

[426] Muntaner, *Chronicle* CCXVIII, CCXXI; ed. Lanz, pp. 385, 392.

[427] Cited in Laurent, 'Le Basilikon, nouveau nom de monnaie sous Andronic II Paléologue', p. 51.

[428] Schlumberger, *Numismatique de l'Orient latin* I, pp. 382–3 (Angelus), 374–5 (Orsini).

[429] *Ibid.* I, pp. 471–5.

as one twelfth of the Venetian grosso, or somewhat less than the one eighth grosso of the tornese in the list of Byzantine coins quoted above.[430] The only chemical analysis of a politikon yet performed gives a fineness of 250/1,000 or 3 oz. – well within the bracket provided by the Greek and French coins.[431] The fluorescence analysis of two similar pieces gives finenesses of 36% and 39% (av. 375/1,000) or some $4\frac{1}{2}$ oz., but this high reading is probably explicable by surface enrichment in the alloy of the coins involved.[432] The conclusion seems inevitable: the politikon was intended as a tornese and is to be identified with the coin of that name in the list.

### *F. 1261: The restored empire (remainder of the system)*

The value of the convex copper coins (Pegolotti's *stanmini* = *stamina*) would have stood at $\frac{1}{12} \times \frac{1}{8} \times \frac{1}{4} = \frac{1}{384}$ hyperpyron.[433] That of the flat copper coins remains unknown, but if it was the same as the Alexian tetarteron would have stood at $\frac{1}{864}$ hyperpyron.[434] Even the denomination's name is uncertain, although Rhabdas and the other treatise mention small sums in *assaria*.[435] (Pl. 36, 1–5)

The official coinage system of the first half of the fourteenth century would thus seem to have been as in Table 24.[436] The apparent symmetry and completeness of the table

[430] Pegolotti, *La Pratica della Mercatura*; ed. Evans, pp. 116–18.

[431] Bertelè and Morrisson, *Numismatique byzantine*, pp. 75–6.

[432] Bendall and Donald, *The Later Palaeologan Coinage, 1282–1453*, p. 30. See: Morrisson, 'Review Article', p. 264.

[433] The *trakhion* occurs in both Rhabdas and the other treatise already mentioned. In Rhabdas, seven sparrows (*strouthia*) eat nuts (*karya*) worth two trakhia in five days, demonstrating the trakhion to be a small coin. But $5+\frac{1}{2}+\frac{1}{26}$ keratia equal approximately $\frac{2}{3}$ trakhion. I had previously assumed (*DOS* XII, p. 19 n. 15) that the $5\frac{7}{13}$ keratia were the equivalent of $\frac{2}{3}$ trakhion, making for a trakhion of just over 8 keratia – obviously the former electrum trachy worth $\frac{1}{3}$ hyperpyron. Tannery assumes that it is the $\frac{1}{26}$ keration only that equals $\frac{2}{3}$ trakhion – and he may well be right, for that would make for a trakhion of around $\frac{1}{400}$ hyperpyron (Tannery, 'Notice sur les deux lettres arithmétiques de Nicolas Rhabdas', at pp. 144, 148, 189). In the other treatise, seven nuts cost two trakhia, and one pound of drink (*drosaton*) costs 360 trakhia (booze was clearly expensive), the latter suggesting that the trakhion stood at more than 360 to the hyperpyron (Vogel, *Ein byzantinisches Rechenbuch des frühen 14. Jahrhunderts* LII, p. 68, LXXXV, p. 104). These figures of 400 and 360 for the trakhion neatly bracket Pegolotti's figure of 384 for the stanmino, and it seems clear that the two are one and the same coin: again, as in the twelfth century, trakhion is used in literary texts and documents, whilst stamenon is picked up from the street by Latin merchants (see above, p. 514 n. 332). For an intervening document (1208) mentioning a sum in nomismata to be paid *dia trakhēon*: Miklosich and Müller, *Acta et Diplomata Graeca Medii Aevi* IV, p. 183.

[434] See above, p. 516 Table 22.

[435] Tannery, 'Notice sur les deux lettres arithmétiques de Nicolas Rhabdas', p. 148 (6, 30, 42 assaria). Vogel, *Ein byzantinisches Rechenbuch des frühen 14. Jahrhunderts* LI, p. 69 (4, 10, 120, 132, 252 assaria). It is doubtful whether anything useful can be made out of these figures, other than the not very helpful information that the assarion probably stood at more than 252 to the hyperpyron. The main point at issue is that the term assarion itself has an antiquarian flavour, and may well not have been the term commonly applied to the copper coin. On the other hand, the denominational terms otherwise used in the two treatises are not so hopelessly antiquarian as to be totally useless, and assarion may therefore pass, for the moment at least, as the literary/documentary term to be applied to the copper denomination.

[436] Based upon T. Bertelè, 'Lineamenti principali della numismatica bizantina', *Rivista Italiana di Numismatica* $12^5$ (1964), p. 92. (This article provided the basis of Bertelè and Morrisson, *Numismatique byzantine*.)

Table 24. *The coinage system*, c. *1300–50*

| AV Hyperpyron 'perpero' | AR Basilikon 'grosso' | Keration 'carato' | Bill. Politikon 'tornese' | Æ Trakhion 'stanmino' | Æ Tetartēron? assarion? |
|---|---|---|---|---|---|
| 1 | 12 | 24 | 96 | 384 | 864(?) |
| — | 1 | 2 | 8 | 32 | 72(?) |
| — | — | 1 | 4 | 16 | 36(?) |
| — | — | — | 1 | 4 | 9(?) |
| — | — | — | — | 1 | (?) |
| — | — | — | — | — | 1 |

should nevertheless not be allowed to disguise the fact that the monetary situation of the first half of the fourteenth century was one of general confusion and uncertainty. Nicephorus Gregoras relates[437] how an old friend of his, on returning to Constantinople by sea with ten gold nomismata – having spent all the rest – and thinking smaller coin (*leptotera merē tōn nomismatōn*) more appropriate to individual purchases, changed them immediately (*euthys ēllaxamēn*). The following day, having set out for the market dealers, he found his cash in hand so depreciated (*euron ekpeptōkos to en khersin ekeino moi kharagma*) that in the course of a single day the purchasing power (*posotēta*) of his ten nomismata had been reduced to only eight (*katabēnai mekhris oktō*). He was advised to spend whatever cash he had as quickly as possible on the necessities of life, for small change (*kerma*) fluctuated in value daily, and he was in danger of finding it worth nothing at all. The precise details and causes of what had happened remain obscure, but that instability was not confined to the gold coinage[438] and, rather, extended right down through the coinage system as a whole, seems abundantly clear.

## (VI) JOHN V TO CONSTANTINE XI (1341–1453)

### A. *Final stages: The transfer to silver (nature)*

Despite the impressive series of denominations that, in theory, went to make up the coinage system of the first half of the fourteenth century, John V, in fact, then, inherited an entirely ambivalent monetary situation on his emergence as sole emperor in 1354, and little or no coinage of the fabric and design typical of the first half of the century can be dated at all confidently to the subsequent period of his reign (1354–76, 1379–91).

At some still uncertain stage of the period as a whole, this series of denominations was

[437] Nicephorus Gregoras, *Historia Byzantina* XXV.27; Bonn edn, III, p. 52. See also: Zakythinos, *Crise monétaire et crise économique à Byzance du XIIe au XVe siècle*, pp. 114–15 (translation).

[438] See above, pp. 526–30.

replaced by another, the precious-metal element of which consisted of three denominations in high-quality silver (*c.* 950/1,000): a large piece weighing about $8\frac{1}{2}$ g; an intermediate weighing just under 4 g; and a small weighing just over one. Each of these pieces had a bust of Christ for its obverse design and an imperial bust for its reverse. In the case of the large, the imperial bust was enclosed by a border and a double circular inscription, the latter executed in large lettering and divided by a further border; in that of the intermediate it was enclosed by a border and a single inscription.[439] (Pl. 36, 6–16)

The precious-metal element was supported by a base-metal one consisting of two denominations in copper, the larger piece of which apparently weighed just over 2 g, the smaller about 0.75 g.[440] (Pl. 36, 17–20)

It was this series of denominations that lasted until the fall of the City to the Ottoman Turks in 1453, various minor adjustments to the metallic quality and weight standards of the silver pieces having meanwhile, for instance, reduced the metallic quality to *c.* 900/1,000, and the weight of the large piece to between 6 and 7 g.[441]

Because the formal structure of the traditional monetary system nevertheless evidently remained intact, it seems clear that the introduction of a coinage based not on the traditional gold, but rather on silver, will inevitably have entailed significant modifications to the way in which that system was expressed in terms of coinage.

The existence of one such modification, involving the consistent expression of the standard component of the monetary system, the hyperpyron, in terms of silver coinage, is confirmed by the evidence of documentary sources. The Florentine merchant Giovanni di Antonio da Uzzano, writing in *c.* 1440, remarks[442] that: 'The perpero is a silver coin (*moneta d'argento*), and thus the carato, and 24 carati make a perpero.' The Venetian merchant Giacomo Badoer, writing in 1436–9, mentions:[443] 'the use that I have made of these heavy perperi (*perperi grievi*), sold as silver (*per arzento*)'. Other mercantile documents of the period also mention the silver hyperpyron (*iperpero d'argento, iperperorum moneta argenti*, etc.), commencing with a group dated 1389–90 and witnessed by the notary Donato de Clavaro, and terminating with a similar group dated 1453 and witnessed by Lorenzo Calvi.[444]

439 It seems likely that the initial issues consisted of the large and small denominations alone, and that only later was the intermediate denomination introduced: Bendall and Donald, *The Later Palaeologan Coinage, 1282–1453*, pp. 154–7 (John V); 152–3 (Andronicus IV); 160–3 (Manuel II); 168–9 (John VII); 172–5 (John VIII); 176–7 (Constantine XI). For the quality of the metal: Bertelè, 'Moneta veneziana e moneta bizantina', p. 67 nos 56–67.

440 It seems likely that the initial issues consisted of both larger and smaller denominations, and that the later ones consisted of the smaller alone: Bendall and Donald, *The Later Palaeologan Coinage, 1282–1453*, pp. 152–3 (Andronicus IV, larger); 162–7 (Manuel II, both); 170–1 (John VII, both); 174–5 (John VIII, smaller).

441 *Ibid.* p. 160 (wt.), and Bertelè, 'Moneta veneziana e moneta bizantina', pp. 67–8, nos 68–75 (weight and met. quality).

442 Giovanni di Antonio da Uzzano, *La Pratica della Mercatura*; ed. G. F. Pagnini della Ventura, p. 135.

443 Giacomo Badoer, *Il Libro dei Conti*; ed. U. Dorini and T. Bertelè, p. 344.

444 Sources, mainly unpublished, cited in T. Bertelè, 'L'iperpero bizantino dal 1261 al 1453', *Rivista Italiana di Numismatica* $5^5$ (1957), p. 81; *idem*, 'Moneta veneziana e moneta bizantina', p. 25.

The method by which this modification was brought about can also be reconstructed, by means of an examination and comparison of certain entries in Badoer's account-books. On charta 48 of the manuscript[445] a sum described as consisting of 17 perperi grievi is entered in the final total as amounting to 17 perperi 7 carati; on charta 57[446] what is evidently the same sum, resulting in the same total, is described as consisting of $9\frac{1}{2}$ oz. $1\frac{1}{2}$ s. of stravati grievi at $22\frac{1}{2}$ perperi the pound, and as being 17 perperi by count. On charta 88[447] a sum described as consisting of 10 lb of stravati grievi at 22 perperi 15 carati the pound, and as being 223 perperi 6 carati by count, is entered in the final total as amounting to 226 perperi 6 carati; on charta 101[448] what is evidently the same sum, resulting in the same total, is described as consisting of 10 lb of silver of stravati at 22 perperi 15 carati the pound; on the same charta (101) the same sum, resulting in the same total, is again described as consisting of 10 lb of stravati grievi at 22 perperi 15 carati the pound; on charta 131[449] the same sum, resulting in the same total, is described as consisting of 224 perperi grievi at 22 perperi 15 carati the pound, and as weighing 10 lb. On charta 180[450] a sum described as consisting of 4 lb of stravati grievi at 22 perperi 15 carati the pound, and as being 89 perperi by count, is entered in the final total as amounting to 90 perperi 12 carati; on charta 186[451] what is evidently the same sum, described as consisting of 89 perperi grievi, weighing 4 lb, and at 22 perperi 15 carati the pound, is entered in the final total as amounting to 91 perperi 12 carati.[452] On charta 231[453] a sum described as consisting of silver is entered in the final total as amounting to 199 perperi 14 carati; on charta 249[454] what is evidently the same sum, resulting in the same total, is described as consisting of 8 lb 7 oz. 2 s. of stravati grievi at 23 perperi 4 carati the pound, and as being 194 perperi by count.

A number of interesting features are revealed by these entries. It is in the first place quite clear that the perpero of the day, whatever it was, and however it is to be identified amongst the surviving coins, was of silver and was also called a *stravato*. This coincidence of nomenclature has also been suspected[455] on the grounds of the hyperpyron possessing much the same exchange rate against the Ottoman asper (*aspro turchesco*), or *akçe*, as the *stavraton*. It is in the second place equally clear that there is regularly a discrepancy between sums described as consisting of perperi or stravati grievi, generally by count (*chontadi* or

[445] Badoer, *Il Libro dei Conti*; ed. Dorini and Bertelè, p. 97.

[446] *Ibid.* p. 114.

[447] *Ibid.* p. 179 (the entry mentions: *Critopulo da la zecha*).

[448] *Ibid.* p. 204 (again mentions: *Critopulo da la zecha*).

[449] *Ibid.* p. 265 (*Critopulo da la zecha*).

[450] *Ibid.* p. 362 (an entry above this mentions: *Chir Chostantin Critopulo per raxon del bancho...*).

[451] *Ibid.* p. 375 (the entry mentions: *chir Chostantin Critopulo dal bancho*).

[452] Note the discrepancy between the two totals: on charta 180 (p. 362) the total has been corrected from 91 perp. 12 car. to 90 perp. 12 car., but not on charta 186 (p. 375).

[453] Badoer, *Il Libro dei Conti*; ed. Dorini and Bertelè, p. 464.

[454] *Ibid.* p. 501.

[455] A. Cutler, 'The Stavraton: Evidence for an Elusive Byzantine Type', *American Numismatic Society Museum Notes* 11 (1964), pp. 237–44.

*a chonto*), and those – ostensibly the same – described simply as perperi and entered up in the final total. This discrepancy is well illustrated on charta 48[456] where 55½ perperi grievi by count are described as worth (*valse*) 56 perperi and entered as such in the final total. The phenomenon is repeated on charta 57.[457] Sums in perperi or stravati by count can have been composed only of actual coins, heavier than the average, and culled from the coin population as a whole for that reason. Sums in perperi entered up in the final total, and regularly reaching a somewhat higher figure than their equivalent in perperi or stravati grievi, will then have been calculated on the basis of an average overall weight.[458]

The most interesting of all these features, however, concerns the nature and identity of the contemporary hyperpyron. Uzzano's straightforward identification of the perpero as a silver coin lends the problem a deceptive air of simplicity: clearly the most straightforward solution would be to identify the perpero with the large silver coin that has already been described. But the problem is a rather more complex one than that. The entries quoted above give three rates for the perpero grievo: 22½ perperi the pound, 22 perperi 15 carati, and 23 perperi 4 carati. It seems clear that these rates can only be notional ones and that they refer to the number of coins struck from a pound weight of silver: at 22½ perperi the pound, 9½ oz. 1½ s. would indeed have yielded 17 perperi 7 carati; at 22 perperi 15 carati, 10 lb would have yielded 226 perperi 6 carati, and 4 lb would have yielded 90 perperi 12 carati; at 23 perperi 4 carati, 8 lb 7 oz. 2 s. would have yielded 199 perperi 14 carati.

It is when such notional rates are worked out in practice that complexities arise. It has been estimated[459] that, in the mid fourteenth century, the Byzantine pound was approximately equivalent to 304 g. Other calculations[460] would seem to suggest that this may be a little high, but the materials used (the average weight of coins, and so on) are less reliable, and it is probably better to retain the figure of 304 g. At 22½ perperi the pound the single perpero would have weighed about 13.5 g, at 22 perperi 15 carati about 13.4 g, and at 23 perperi 4 carati about 13.2 g. If the more generally accepted equivalence for the Byzantine pound is used, that of 324 g, then at 22½ perperi the pound the single perpero would have weighed about 14.4 g. In either case it would have weighed virtually double the lighter, and evidently later, large silver coins of about 7 g.

The clue as to what had happened lies in a consideration of the metallic relationship existing between the latest gold hyperpyron and the earliest large silver coin. According to Pegolotti[461] the latest gold perperi were of 11 carats fine. At an approximate weight of 4.2 g (304 g ÷ 72) such a hyperpyron would metallically have been worth about 1.9 g

456 Badoer, *Il Libro dei Conti*; ed. Dorini and Bertelè, p. 97.

457 *Ibid.* p. 114.

458 The ultimate problem involved, of course, is the difference between the actual and the theoretical weight of the coins involved. See also above, pp. 344–63.

459 Bertelè, 'I gioielli della corona bizantina', pp. 91–117.

460 Schilbach, *Byzantinische Metrologie*, p. 167.

461 See above, p. 528.

pure gold or about 17 g of silver (at a gold:silver ratio of 1:9). At the more generally accepted weight of 4.5 g (324 g ÷ 72) it would have been worth about 2.1 g pure gold or about 19 g silver. In either case it would have been worth virtually double the heavier, and evidently earlier, large silver coin of about 8.5 g. With the discontinuation of a gold coinage and the inception of a silver one, the hyperpyron had therefore simply ceased to be expressed by a single coin of the one metal and, at a virtually unaltered metallic value, had come to be expressed as the sum of two of the large coins of the other metal. To the extent that the denomination was no longer represented by any single coin it, like the rates used to define perperi grievi, had assumed a notional character.

It is just possible that, for a brief intervening period, the hyperpyron was expressed by a gold piece of which an unique specimen only now exists. This piece weighs 1.88 g and is of a high metallic purity (23½ carats). It has a standing figure of St John the Baptist, strongly reminiscent of that on the Florentine fiorino, as its obverse design, and a standing figure of John V as its reverse. There is, however, no conclusive reason for considering it to have been intended as a current coin, and it may even be a modern forgery.[462]

Although the name hyperpyron/perpero was applied to a notional denomination it seems clear that the equivalent stavraton/stravato, referring to a coin on which there was a cross, must have been applied originally to an actual and single coin, and only subsequently to the denomination made up of a number of these same coins. The presumption is that the name stavraton/stravato was applied originally to the large coin, but it is admittedly not immediately obvious how the name originated as a description. The most plausible origin is to be found in two crosses that precede the inner and outer circles of inscription on the reverse of what is apparently the earliest issue of John V. These crosses, coinciding above the imperial bust, might well have been considered a distinctive feature of the coin when first issued. That details of an order now apparently minute were then noticed and even studied is amply demonstrated by Pegolotti's description of the details of design and the mint *signa* on late thirteenth- and early fourteenth-century gold hyperpyra.[463]

If the large silver coin is indeed to be considered as representing one half of a notional hyperpyron then the intermediate and small coins in the same metal will, to judge from their weights, have represented one quarter and one sixteenth of an hyperpyron respectively. It seems clear that the last is to be identified with the *duchatelo* frequently mentioned in Badoer's accounts and itself probably identical with the *doukatopoulon* of a near-contemporary Byzantine account.[464] This equation is based not only upon the fact

[462] A. Blanchet, 'Les dernières monnaies d'or des empereurs de Byzance', *Revue Numismatique* 14⁴ (1910), pp. 81–3. See also: Gerassimov, 'Des fausses hyperpères de Jean V et Manuel II Paleólogue', pp. 214–16 (forgery). Bertelè, 'Moneta veneziana e moneta bizantina', pp. 139–41 (inclined to favour its authenticity, but doubtful about its nature).

[463] See above, p. 367 and n. 224.

[464] S. Kugeas, 'Notizbuch eines Beamten der Metropolis in Thessalonike aus dem Anfang des XV Jahrhunderts', *Byzantinische Zeitschrift* 23 (1914/19), p. 149. Stavrata nomismata also occur not infrequently in these accounts.

Table 25. *The coinage system, c. 1350–1453*

| Hyperpyron 'perpero' (notional) | AR Large stavraton 'stravato' | AR Intermediate | AR Small doukatopoulon 'duchatelo' | (Keration) ('carato') | Æ Large 'tornese' | Æ Small follis(?) 'folaro'(?) |
|---|---|---|---|---|---|---|
| 1 | 2 | 4 | 16 | 24 | 192 | 576 |
| — | 1 | 2 | 8 | 12 | 96 | 288 |
| — | — | 1 | 4 | 6 | 48 | 144 |
| — | — | — | 1 | $1\frac{1}{2}$ | 12 | 36 |
| — | — | — | — | 1 | 8 | 24 |
| — | — | — | — | — | 1 | 3 |
| — | — | — | — | — | — | 1 |

that it is the small coin alone that could be classed as a duchatelo, because of its resemblance to the Venetian *duchato* or grosso, but also upon the much more significant fact that the duchatelo is regularly tariffed at $1\frac{1}{2}$ carati, or one sixteenth of a perpero (occasionally a little more or a little less), in Badoer's accounts. The coin was thus by both weight and value a direct continuation of the depreciated basilikon of the immediately preceding period.[465]

Among other coins making a frequent appearance in Badoer's accounts is the tornese. Various kinds of tornese existed – Badoer himself mentions[466] Vlach tornesi (*tornexi vlachesci*) – but it is quite clear from the context that one kind was in common use and therefore that it was probably an imperial coin. The tornese by this time was, according to Badoer, who writes[467] of *rame in tornexi*, a copper coin, and an entry[468] in which a sum of 72 (6 × 12) tornesi is entered up as 9 carati thus puts its value at $\frac{1}{8}$ carato or $\frac{1}{192}$ perpero. The only imperial coin of the period conforming to these various requirements is the larger of the two copper denominations. Neither the name nor the value of the smaller is known with any degree of certainty, but an entry mentioning[469] '11 baskets of copper and 1 barrel of *folari*' might be held to imply that it was called a follis/folaro, and its weight is appropriate to a coin worth $\frac{1}{3}$ tornese or $\frac{1}{576}$ perpero. It would thus have held a traditional follis-relationship to the large silver coin in much the same way as the Alexian tetarteron had to the electrum trachy.[470]

The coinage system of the period would thus seem to have been as in Table 25.[471]

465 See above, pp. 532, 533–4.
466 Badoer, *Il Libro dei Conti*; ed. Dorini and Bertelè, p. 438.
467 *Ibid.* pp. 437, 438.
468 *Ibid.* p. 16.
469 *Ibid.* p. 645.
470 See above, p. 516 Table 22.
471 Based upon Bertelè, 'Lineamenti principali della numismatica bizantina', p. 93.

### B. *Final stages: The transfer to silver (chronology)*

The precise stage at which the new set of silver denominations was introduced remains uncertain, for the numismatic evidence is suggestive but in no way conclusive, while the documentary evidence is light in quantity but may nevertheless dictate a solution that is radically divergent from any hitherto based on the coins.

Certain of the heavier and therefore earlier large silver coins (along with some fractions) were issued in the name of an Andronicus, and current orthodoxy would identify the ruler involved as Andronicus IV, who briefly usurped the throne between 1376 and 1379, during the long sole reign of his father John V (1354–91). Indeed, the first suggestion[472] was that these silver coins stood at the head of the whole series, and that therefore it was Andronicus IV who was responsible for the reform which definitively transferred what was left of the Byzantine state from a gold-based currency to a silver-based one. This suggestion has been challenged, but the grip of orthodoxy has meant that the alternative – that the transfer was the work of John V himself – has never been regarded as much more than a theoretical possibility.[473]

Neither the historical nor the numismatic evidence will bear the weight of the case for Andronicus IV. In the first place, it is simply unlikely, without specific evidence which of course does not exist, that so brief an usurpation should have produced so radical a reform. And in the second place, a closer consideration of the probable chronological sequence of the series of issues of the large piece if anything lends support to the alternative case that it, at least, was already in existence in 1376, and therefore that it had been introduced by John V:

| | |
|---|---|
| John V, 1354–76 | |
| Outer inscr. | +Θ(εο)V ΧΑΡΙΤΙ ΒΑCΙΛЄVC ΤѠΝ ΡѠΜЄѠΝ |
| Inner inscr. | +ΙѠ(αννης)ΔЄCΠΟΤΙC Ο ΠΑΛЄΟΛΟΓΟC |
| Andronicus IV (1376–9) | |
| Outer inscr. | +ΑΝΔΡΟΝΙΚΟC ΔЄCΠΟΤΙC Ο ΠΑΛЄΟΛΟΓΟC |
| Inner inscr. | Θ(εο)V ΧΑΡΙΤΙ ΒΑCΙΛЄVC ΤѠΝ ΡѠΜЄѠΝ |
| John V, 1379–91 | |
| Outer inscr. | +ΙѠ(αννης) ΔЄCΠΟΤΙC Ο ΠΑΛЄΟΛΟΓΟC |
| Inner inscr. | Θ(εο)V ΧΑΡΙΤΙ ΒΑCΙΛЄVC ΤѠΝ ΡѠΜЄѠΝ |
| Manuel II (1391–1425) | |
| Outer inscr. | +ΜΑΝΟVΗΛ ΔЄCΠΟΤΙC Ο ΠΑΛЄΟΛΟΓΟC |
| Inner inscr. | Θ(εο)V ΧΑΡΙΤΙ ΑVΤΟΚΡΑΤΟΡ |

[472] Bertelè, 'L'iperpero bizantino dal 1261 al 1453', pp. 78–9.

[473] E.g. M. F. Hendy, in *Numismatic Chronicle* $9^7$ (1969), at p. x at back of volume (report of paper delivered 19.xi.68, pointing out the probability of John V between 1354 and 1376); Bertelè, 'Moneta veneziana e moneta bizantina', pp. 134–5 (rigidly orthodox line, reiterating Andronicus IV).

John VIII (1425–48)
Outer inscr. +IШANHC ΔЄCΠOTIC O ΠAΛЄOΛOΓOC
Inner inscr. Θ(εο)V XAPITI BACIΛЄVVC TШN PШMЄШN

(Pl. 36, 6–10)

The general accuracy of the sequence postulated above is confirmed by the fact that issues of John V prior to the usurpation of Andronicus IV are uniformly neat in style and careful in detailed execution as are, perhaps to a lesser degree, those of Andronicus himself. Issues of John subsequent to the usurpation of Andronicus exhibit a gradual deterioration in style and detail; those of Manuel II are uniformly slovenly in both respects, and those of John VIII are, in addition, reduced in weight.

The crucial section of the sequence is, however, that involving issues of John V and Andronicus IV. John's distinctive issue placed at the head of the sequence should surely belong there on three major counts: it is the only one on which the double inscription commences on the inner circle, the only one on which the eponymous cross consistently precedes the inscription on both the inner and outer circles, and the only one on which the imperial collar-piece is consistently depicted in a partial manner only, the triple-scalloped edge present on other issues being omitted. Were this issue to be placed elsewhere it would seriously disturb the continuity of the sequence.

It should therefore follow that the introduction of the large piece of the new series, and therefore probably of some or all of the smaller pieces, occurred before the usurpation of Andronicus IV in 1376. It would thus have been the work of John V. A solution along these lines has the merit of reducing, although perhaps not of entirely eliminating, the hiatus apparently intervening between the discontinuation of the old series and the introduction of the new.[474]

The documentary evidence as so far presented is, as already mentioned, slight. In 1381/2, plates of *istävrät* (i.e. stavrata) formed part of the wedding gifts for the future sultan Beyazıt I,[475] while in 1366/7, they, or apparently anything like them, fail to occur in the accounts of the military expedition then being conducted by Amadeus VI of Savoy.[476] This could be taken as proving that the stavraton existed in 1381/2, but not in 1366/7,[477] although it should be noted that, even if that were to have been the case, the rival claims of Andronicus IV and John V remain unsettled.

474 The coinage of the years 1354–76 is difficult to establish with any certainty: Bendall and Donald, *The Later Palaeologan Coinage, 1282–1453*, p. 130 (Period IV).

475 D. Theodoridis, 'Aus dem greichischen Lehngut in osmanischen', *Turcica* 7 (1975), pp. 36–8.

476 Bertelè, 'Moneta veneziana e moneta bizantina', pp. 123–34.

477 As regards the latter date: Bertelè, 'Moneta veneziana e moneta bizantina', p. 134. One ought to point out, however, that one of the major points of Bertelè's case, the continued use of gold hyperpyra in the period *c.* 1356–74, is in fact invalid. Doubtless, gold hyperpyra continued in use and circulation well after the introduction of the silver series, and the notional gold hyperpyron continued as the standard of the system in any case throughout.

But the stavraton did exist in 1366/7, for in the testamentary document of the *megas stratopedarkhēs* Demetrius Tzamblakon, which is datable to precisely that year, and which has already been mentioned,[478] there occur two very relevant references: one to donkeys and sheep to be sold 'for 500 silver hyperpyra (*hy[per]p[y]r[a] argyra pentak[osia]*)'; and the other to a sum of '2,000 silver hyperpyra (*hy[per]p[y]r[a] argyra khiliad[as] dyo*)'.[479]

Now, however these two references are translated, that is whether literally as 'silver hyperpyra' or whether loosely as 'hyperpyra in silver', the existence of the set of silver coins (and particularly of its large component) is either dictated or at least very strongly implied. Moreover, the clear implication is that such coins were already in normal circulation in the region of Serres–Christoupolis–Thessalonica, that to which the document pertains. This would, then, apparently settle the rival claims of Andronicus IV and John V in favour of the latter.

The situation is, however, still by no means resolved, and hard documentary evidence that has recently come to light (and is as yet unpublished) well demonstrates the appallingly unreliable nature of arguments based primarily on numismatic material, and only fleshed out with sparse documentary sources, however necessary such argumentation may on occasion be.

Two treaties between the Venetian dukes of Crete and the Türkmen emirs of Aydın form the documentation involved.* The treaty of 1337 mentions a customs-duty of two *stavrata*, and its renewal in 1353 gives as the apparent equivalent five *gigliati*. The two references taken together pre-suppose or very strongly imply, in 1337, the existence of a silver coin called a stavraton and weighing some 8 to 10 g. This can only be the heavier and earlier coin of the new set of silver denominations.[480]

Now, either the earlier of the two treaties involved, at least, is a later copy of an original, rendering the earlier monetary terminology in a later and more understandable form, which is apparently regarded as being unlikely, or else one has to envisage the basic monetary reform involving a transfer from gold to silver as being the work of neither Andronicus IV nor of John V, but rather of Andronicus III. The large silver coins issued in the name of an Andronicus would therefore again almost certainly belong not to Andronicus IV, as hitherto universally assumed, but to Andronicus III.

It must be pointed out, in favour of this rather dramatic re-interpretation of monetary events, that the signa appearing on the heavier and earlier silver coins of Andronicus and John are identical with, or very closely related to, some of those appearing on the latest gold coins of the preceding system – the hyperpyra of Andronicus II with Andronicus

* I owe the knowledge of these two references and their detailed implications to Elizabeth Zachariadou and Philip Grierson respectively.

478 See above, p. 212.

479 Theocharides, 'Eine Vermächtnisurkunde des Gross-Stratopedarchen Demetrios Tzamblakon', p. 490.

480 E. A. Zachariadou, 'Sept traités inédits entre Venise et les émirats d'Aydin et de Menteşe (1331–1407)', in *Studi Preottomani e Ottomani, Atti del Convegno di Napoli (24–26 settembre 1974)*, at pp. 229–40.

III, and of John V with John VI. This is not entirely conclusive as an argument, as signa appearing on hyperpyra of John III not infrequently reappear on hyperpyra of Michael VIII or of Andronicus II, at some considerable remove in time, but it is certainly suggestive.[481]

What may eventually emerge from all this is the precocious existence of a monetary reform, involving the transfer from gold to silver, introduced by Andronicus III, but temporarily abandoned either by that emperor or by John V. The reform would in any case presumably have been reintroduced by 1366/7 when, as noted above, the silver coins were already in circulation. Alternatively, it might be possible to suppose that the two systems co-existed for some, as yet undetermined and undeterminable, time. Only future research can tell. In any case, by the second half of the fourteenth century, the transfer from gold to silver was definitive.

The latest Byzantine coins known in any quantity are those in the name of John VIII, and indeed the Constantinopolitan mint seems certainly to have been active as late as the period 1436–9 for, among the Byzantines with whom Badoer did business, there comparatively frequently appears[482] a certain chir Chostantin Critopoulo, who is variously termed *da la zecha* or *dal bancho*, and who was therefore presumably an official of the mint, bank, or exchange. Coins are nevertheless known to have been struck as late as 1453, for no less than three contemporary or eye-witness accounts of the final siege of the City report that Constantine XI appropriated ecclesiastical property and had it melted down and struck into coin to pay the defenders on that occasion. The most specific and perhaps the most reliable of these accounts, that of Leonard of Chios, Archbishop of Mitylene, runs as follows:

> But the troubled emperor did not know what he was to do; he consulted his chief men; they advised that the citizens should not be disturbed through the exigencies of the occasion, but that recourse should be had to ecclesiastical property. He therefore ordered the holy vessels of God to be taken from the sacred churches, just as we have read the Romans to have done on account of the needs of the moment, to be melted down and struck into coin (*in pecuniam insigniri*), and to be given to the soldiers, the ditch-diggers, and the builders, who were concerned with their own interests, not those of the public, and who refused to work unless paid.
>
> (*Epistola de Expugnatione Constantinopolis* XXI; *PG* CLIX, col. 934)

The account[483] is confirmed by that of Nicolò Barbaro.[484]

[481] Some repetition at a considerable distance in time was probably inevitable: a number of the signa on the hyperpyra of John III consist of letters of the alphabet, clearly involving a basically annual sequence, and as the hyperpyra of Michael VIII and Andronicus II also involve letters one can only assume that the same régime was being followed. But more complex or multiple signa are also occasionally repeated. One can only hope that a fuller understanding and explanation of what was involved will derive from the publication of lists of, and commentaries upon, signa, in *DOC* IV and V.

[482] E.g. above, p. 538 nn. 447–51.

[483] See also: J. R. Jones, 'Literary Evidence for the Coinage of Constantine XI', *Numismatic Circular* 75 (1967), p. 97.

[484] Nicolò Barbaro, *Giornale dell' assedio di Costantinopoli 1453*; ed. E. Cornet, p. 66.

It is all too probable, however, that the whole episode was conducted in such haste and desperation that any surviving dies that came to hand were utilised, and thus that even if these coins were to be found many would not now be recognisable, for they would have been struck by dies, and have borne the names, of earlier emperors.

The sole surviving named coin of the last emperor is a unique quarter (notional) hyperpyron, or half (actual) hyperpyron.[485] A further specimen, happening not to include the imperial name, but having been struck from the same die, is also known.[486] These coins may, or may not, have been struck on the occasion mentioned above. (Pl. 36, 14)

### C. *Final stages: The transfer to silver (observations)*

It is frequently assumed that the debasement and disappearance of a Byzantine gold coinage during the first half of the fourteenth century was the direct result of the political and economic decadence of the empire, and that this debasement, resulting as it did in inconvenience and the loss of foreign confidence, led to the reintroduction of a western gold coinage.

Such an assumption provides a simple and convenient example of the connection between the economy of an ancient or mediaeval state and the coinage that is produced from it, and there is indeed sufficient evidence – Byzantine and western – to suggest a considerable degree of accuracy with regard both to the particular case and to the general phenomenon. It does nevertheless also involve a considerable degree of over-simplification with regard to the former, for when examined in the wider context of Mediterranean monetary history, it becomes clear that the disappearance of a Byzantine gold coinage and the emergence of a silver one conforms to a uniform pattern, involving on the one hand eastern states less obviously decadent than the empire, and on the other western countries less obviously emergent than the Italian mercantile cities.

It has in fact become clear that the Mediterranean was divided for most of the mediaeval period into two distinct monetary areas – the east and south, the west and north – and that although they were apparently pursuing diametrically opposed courses of monetary development, the causative factors behind these courses were in reality identical. Between the seventh and twelfth century the east largely relied on a gold-based coinage and the west on a silver-based one. Then, during the thirteenth and fourteenth centuries, a complete reversal occurred: the east turned to a largely silver-based coinage, the west to a gold-based one. There is considerable evidence for the large-scale export of gold to the west and for that of silver to the east during this same period, and there seems

485 S. Bendall, 'A Coin of Constantine XI', *Numismatic Circular* 82 (1974), pp. 188–9. Bendall and Donald, *The Later Palaeologan Coinage, 1282–1453*, pp. 176–7.

486 Private information from S. Bendall (Kunst und Münzen AG, Auction 12, 23.v.74, lot 904 – ascribed to Manuel II).

little doubt that the immediate cause behind the reversal which these exports reflected lay in the details of the gold:silver ratios prevalent in the two monetary areas. The fundamental cause remains less clear.[487]

The significance of these developments for Byzantine monetary history is obvious: during the second half of the thirteenth and the first half of the fourteenth century the gold coinage first faltered then disappeared; during the late thirteenth and the first half of the fourteenth century, with the joint reign of Andronicus II and Michael IX, a significant silver coinage was reintroduced, and during the second half of that century, with the sole reign of John V, that coinage definitively replaced the gold one. The decadence of the empire may well have been an important factor in these events: it was, however, not the only one, and it acted within limitations already imposed by factors with a much wider frame of reference.

APPENDIX

## THE SOMION/SOMMO

In the late thirteenth, fourteenth and fifteenth centuries, sums are occasionally found expressed in terms of a larger unit, the *somion*, which was clearly identical with, or rather a local variety of, the *sommo* or *summo* of contemporary Italian sources having the Black Sea littoral, or the Tartar empire to its northward and eastward, as their frame of reference. Pegolotti explains the nature of the *sommo* in two passages:

At Tana [Azov at the mouth of the Don] one spends silver sommi and aspri, and the sommo weighs 45 saggi [i.e. hexagia] of Tana, and they [the sommi] are of a fineness of 11 oz. 17 d. of silver to the pound. And if one brings silver to the mint at Tana, the mint coins each of the said sommi into 202 aspri; but although the mint coins a sommo into 202 aspri, if not...,[488] it pays back to the donor only 190 aspri, and the rest is retained [to be divided] between those who do the work and for the profit of the mint, so that 190 aspri are worth a sommo at Tana. These sommi are used in payment by weight, and take the form of bars (*verghe*) of silver of the aforesaid fineness; the bars are, however, not of equal weight, but one puts into one pan of the balance the bars of silver and into the other the poise of the sommi to be paid or received; and if there is less than the poise of a sommo one makes up the difference in aspri. And each sommo should weigh 45 saggi by the standard of Tana.

(*La Pratica della Mercatura*, *ed. cit.* p. 25)

[487] Watson, 'Back to Gold – and Silver', pp. 1–34.

[488] Probably $202\frac{1}{2}$ aspri in view of Badoer's evidence mentioned below.

Silver in pieces (*pezzi*) is sold at the aforesaid places [i.e. Constantinople and Pera] by the pound, and the greater part is made into sommi which are of a fineness of 11 oz. 17 d. to the pound, which sommi are taken to Gazera [the Crimea] and even to Gattaio [Cathay, China]; and the said sommi are bars of silver which are not of equal weight, but some weigh more and others less as they are melted, but one kind may weigh....

(*ed. cit.* pp. 40–1)

Although reckonings of 112 and 119½/120 aspri to the sommo at Caffa (Feodosiya) are preserved in Genoese private documents dated 1289/90,[489] the precise reckoning of 190 aspri to the sommo at Tana and in Gazaria is confirmed by an entry in a Venetian government document of the early fourteenth century.[490] That of 202½ aspri to the sommo at Chafa is found in Badoer.[491] It may well be that the discrepancy existing between the thirteenth-century reckonings of 112 and 119½/120 aspri to the sommo and the fourteenth- and fifteenth-century ones of 190 and 202/202½, offers at least an approximate indication of the extent to which the aspri involved had been reduced in weight, or metallic quality, or both.

Pegolotti elsewhere[492] reckons the sommo as weighing 8½ oz. Genoese, or 7 oz. Venetian minus two *grossi*: somewhat over 210 g. His contemporary, the Arabic traveller Ibn Battuta, describing his journey into the Tartar empire, reports as follows:

We made for the city of Ukak.... Between it and al-Sara [Sarai on the Volga], the sultan's capital, it is ten nights' march, and one day's march from this city are the mountains of the Rus.... In their country are silver mines, and from it are imported the *ṣawm*, that is, the ingots of silver and with which selling and buying are done in this land, each /*ṣawma* weighing five ounces [somewhat over 150 g].

(*Travels* VIII; trans. Gibb, II, pp. 498–9)

According to Uzzano,[493] a sommo: 'Is a weight of marked silver (*peso d'argento marchiato*)...and the said sommo is worth in Genoa 6 *fiorini* or a figure relative to the price of the silver, whether high or low.'

It seems clear that the sommo was primarily a silver ingot with an approximate weight standard, and secondarily a monetary unit of account. It seems equally clear that slightly variant weight standards existed locally. The *Libro di Mercatantie et Usanze de' Paesi*, a Florentine mercantile source datable to the mid fifteenth century, confirms[494] Pegolotti's description of the bar (*vergha*) form of the sommo, and gives[495] an approximately concordant assessment of its fineness (11 oz. 13 d.). The same source assumes[496] each of

[489] M. Balard, *Gênes et l'outre-mer* I, *Les actes de Caffa du notaire Lamberto di Sambuceto 1289–1290*, no. 177, pp. 100–1; no. 652, pp. 246–7; no. 885, p. 368.

[490] Giomo, 'Le Rubriche dei Libri *Misti* del Senato perduti, trascritte', p. 328.

[491] Badoer, *Il Libro dei Conti*; ed. Dorini and Bertelè, pp. 355, 422; cf. pp. 384, 493.

[492] Pegolotti, *La Pratica della Mercatura*; ed. Evans, pp. 23, 150.

[493] Uzzano, *La Pratica della Mercatura*; ed. Pagnini della Ventura, p. 134.

[494] *El Libro di Mercatantie et Usanze de'Paesi*; ed. F. Borlandi, pp. 58, 60.

[495] *Ibid.* p. 156.

[496] *Ibid.* pp. 30, 31, 58, 60, 61, 72.

the cities of Caffa, Tana, Saldadia (Sugdaia, Sudak), Sorghati (Solkhat, Staraya Krim) and Sarra (Sarai) to have possessed its own weight standard for the sommo, each standard except the last nevertheless consisting of 45 saggi, and each saggio of 24 charati. Most of the standards quoted seem to fall within the approximate range 200–205 g. The same source reckons[497] the sommo to have weighed 6/7 Venetian mark in Tribusonda, again approximately 205 g, and also to have consisted of 45 saggi, each of 24 charati.[498]

The circulation of precious metals, and particularly silver, in ingot, and particularly bar, form was a feature common to most of the areas that went to make up the Tartar empire and its dependent states, and was indeed traditional in many of them. There seems to have existed for instance a direct connection, amounting in all probability to identity, between the sommo of the Italian sources and the Russian *grivna*, the predecessor of the *roubl*. A connection of this kind is implied in a general fashion by a passage in Ibn Battuta's *Travels* which has been quoted above and which mentions the importation of ṣawm from the country of the Rus, but it is confirmed in a much more detailed fashion by further evidence.

The many hundreds of silver grivni found in Russia fall into two main groups: the one tending to a hexagonal form, dated to the eleventh to thirteenth centuries, and consistently weighing about 160 g; the other tending to a bar form, dated to the thirteenth to fifteenth centuries, and consistently weighing about 200 g. Both achieved widespread circulation, the first nevertheless being concentrated around Kiev, the second, commoner and even more widespread (examples having been found, for instance, in the Crimea and even in Romania), being concentrated around Novgorod.[499]

The weight of the first group is very much that of Ibn Battuta's ṣawma; the form and weight of the second are surely those of the sommo of the Italian sources. The case for this identity is further enhanced by the fact that when, during the second half of the fourteenth century, the Russian principalities resumed the issue of silver coin, the Moscow grivna or roubl was divided into 200 *dengi* (*denga* itself being derived from the Tartar *tamgha* or *tanga*),[500] a division closely comparable and connected with that of the sommo into 202($\frac{1}{2}$) aspri.[501] Significantly enough, in the circumstances, the word *som* means 'rouble' in the Ossetian language.[502]

The circulation of silver in ingot form was also of long standing in China, where the

497 *Ibid.* p. 64.

498 Schilbach, *Byzantinische Metrologie*, pp. 192–7. Bertelè, 'Moneta veneziana e moneta bizantina', pp. 105–22.

499 N. Bauer, 'Die Silber- und Goldbarren des russischen Mittelalters. Eine archäologische Studie', *Numismatische Zeitschrift* 22 (1929), pp. 77–120, 24 (1931), pp. 61–100. O. Iliescu, 'La monnaie génoise dans les pays roumains aux XIII$^e$–XV$^e$ siècles', in S. Pascu (ed.), *Colocviul Romàno-Italian 'Genovezii la Marea Neagră în secolele XIII–XIV', București 27–28 martie 1975*, at p. 165.

500 I. G. Spasski, *The Russian Monetary System, a Historico-Numismatic Survey*, pp. 102–3. C. M. Fraehn, *De Origine Vocabuli Rossici Den'gi*.

501 See above, pp. 547–8.

502 R. P. Blake, 'The Circulation of Silver in the Moslem East down to the Mongol Epoch', *Harvard Journal of Asiatic Studies* 2 (1937), pp. 315–16 n. 74.

standard unit was an ingot (*ting*) weighing 50 ounces (*liang*),[503] or considerably more than a sommo/grivna. Two standard ting, one datable to the Sung period, that preceding the Yuan or Tartar period and both based on an ounce of approximately 40 g, weigh, for instance, 2,070 and 2,060 g, or about ten times as much as the sommo/grivna.[504] Chinese influence has nevertheless been postulated to explain the existence of a minor group of grivni, of squat bar form but with a trough running the length of one side, dated to the fourteenth century, and again consistently weighing about 200 g. This group is found concentrated in the region of the lower and middle Volga and has therefore been attributed to the Tartars themselves.[505] In its possession of a trough on one side it resembles the Chinese sycee ingots.[506]

The standard ting, or at least an equivalent, is met with elsewhere in the Tartar empire besides China, however, for one or the other seems to have been termed *yastık* in Turkish, *balish* in Persian and *sükä* in the Tartar of the period.[507] The first two of these words both mean 'cushion', and the third means 'hatchet', neither description being inappropriate to the quadrangular and slightly concave-/convex-sided form of the ting itself, although equally neither would be appropriate to the bar form of the sommo/grivna. According to the Franciscan friar William of Rubruck,[508] who had been sent on a mission to the Tartars by Louis IX, the *iascot*, which he met with in Karakorum in 1253–4, was 'a piece of silver weighing ten marks'. Assuming the mark in question to have been the Parisian, the iascot will have weighed about 2,450 g; assuming it to have been the Tournois, it will have weighed about 2,250 g. Both figures are within the limits that might be expected from a round estimate of the weight of the ting. According to the Persian 'Ata-Malik Juvaini,[509] the historian of Chingis-Khan (1206–27) and his immediate successors, the balish was: 'worth fifty misquals [i.e. mithkals] of gold or silver, round about seventy-five rukni [i.e. of a ruler named Rukn ad din] dinars, the standard of which is two-thirds'. The precise meaning of this passage is not immediately clear, for no object is likely to have been worth the same weight in gold or silver indifferently. It seems more likely that the balish could consist of gold as well as of silver – a fact that Juvaini confirms elsewhere[510] – and that what is being described is the value of the commoner variety only, the silver, in terms of gold. The order of the weight of the balish is established by the fact that an old man could expect to carry one or two only,[511] and the more

503 L.-S. Yang, *Money and Credit in China, a Short History*, pp. 43–5. J. Cribb, 'An Historical Survey of the Precious Metal Currencies of China', *Numismatic Chronicle* 19[7] (1979), pp. 190–7, 198–209.

504 N. C. Chang, *An Inscribed Chinese Ingot of the 12th Century A.D.*, pp. 4, 8.

505 Bauer, 'Die Silber- und Goldbarren des russischen Mittelalters' (1931), pp. 91–4.

506 P. O. Sigler, *Sycee Silver.*

507 P. Pelliot, 'Le prétendu mot "iascot" chez Guillaume de Rubrouck', *T'oung Pao* 27 (1930), pp. 190–2; *idem*, *Notes sur l'histoire de la Horde d'Or*, pp. 8–9.

508 William of Rubruck, *Itinerarium*; trans. W. W. Rockhill, p. 156.

509 'Ata-Malik Juvaini, *The History of the World-Conqueror* I; trans. J. A. Boyle, I, p. 23.

510 *Ibid.* XXXII; trans. Boyle, I, p. 208.

511 *Ibid.* XXXII; trans. Boyle, I, p. 233.

precise weight is confirmed by the fact that about 2,000 g of silver might well have been worth fifty mithkals or 212.9 g (50 × 4.25) of gold.[512]

The existence of a sommo/grivna of about 200 g is known within an area stretching from the Black Sea and Russia to Urgench in Turkestan and to Hangzhou in China; that of a ting/yastık/balish/sükä of about 2,000 g is known within an area stretching from China to Karakorum in Mongolia and to Persia and to Armenia: an effective confirmation of the economic, or more probably fiscal, unity of the Tartar empire in its earlier stages.[513] It is nevertheless entirely ironical that the Russian rouble should derive ultimately from the Chinese ting, through the agency of the Tartars.

The origin and derivation of the word sommo/somion itself remain uncertain. The most plausible suggestion so far offered is that it derives from the Persian word *sīm* (Syriac *sīmā*), meaning 'silver', via Turkish, which could provide the required vowel shift from i to ö.[514]

512 Other versions and other authors seem to put the weight of the balish of gold or silver at five hundred mithkals or again at about 2,125 g; yet others refer to the *yastık* or *balish* (*chao*) or currency note with which the ingot was connected but with which it should not be confused (refs cited in M. Quatremère, *Histoire des Mongols de la Perse écrite en persan par Raschid-Eldin* I, pp. 320–1.

513 H. F. Schurmann, 'Mongolian Tributary Practices of the Thirteenth Century', *Harvard Journal of Asiatic Studies* 19 (1956), pp. 304–89.

514 Blake, 'The Circulation of Silver in the Moslem East down to the Mongol Epoch', pp. 315–16 n. 74.

# PRELIMINARY OBSERVATIONS, FUTURE DIRECTIONS

It is time to pause, and to consider, both what – if anything – has so far been achieved, and what yet remains to be done. It may at this stage be thought that a disproportionate amount of time, energy and space has been expended for the gain of remarkably little ground, in the form of the establishment and collation of a number of additional facts, and the elucidation of a few basic principles or patterns, only. This remains to be seen, but in any case it is to a certain extent inevitable, and in the nature of the matter. For it is, of course, exceedingly difficult indeed to recover the smallest and simplest principle or pattern from even an enormous number of raw historical facts, and this is the case when such facts are as plentiful as can be desired, let alone when they are nowhere near so. On the other hand such a recovery is perhaps one degree easier, and is certainly at least one degree surer, when using the widest possible spread of different classes of evidence, than when using one class only, as when recovering monetary principles or patterns from what is basically an accumulation of archaeological material, be that accumulation ever so large. For example, the limitations of, and dangers inherent in, the latter approach – that is, an overwhelming reliance upon the archaeological material, interpreted according to recently evolved modes of analysis of historical societies and economies, but also in apparently virtual or complete ignorance of the technological and organisational capacities and of the conceptual limitations imposed upon such a society and economy (whether these are established, or susceptible to conjecture only) – are apparent in, and have very seriously marred, an otherwise interesting and stimulating recent work on dark age economics.[1] In other words, despite the apparently limitless claims of the so-called New Archaeology, the conceptual limits involved, at least, are – and probably always will be – irrecoverable from such material and by such means alone.

What, therefore, has been attempted in the four sections and eight chapters above, and as stated at the beginning of this volume, is the identification of the principal dynamic factors operating behind, and the principal mechanisms operating within, the Byzantine

[1] R. Hodges, *Dark Age Economics. The Origins of Towns and Trade* A.D. *600–1000*.

monetary economy, recognising and incorporating the contemporary capacities and limitations involved, with the aim of assembling the elements necessary to the construction of a model against which the physical material, that is the archaeological evidence, may eventually be interpreted.

What therefore remains to be done, in the short term at least, is to make a number of general observations on the material so far assembled and interpreted; to pick up a number of points, most of which have already been mentioned but not yet pursued, and deal with them, however briefly; and then to move onto the longer term in summarising the present position and outlining the general directions in which it is hoped that future work will proceed, as well as bringing into focus a number of particular problems upon which it is hoped that such work will concentrate.

## (I) THE PROBLEM OF TRANSPORT AND TRADE

### A. Transport

The base-line chosen for the pyramidal form that the four sections above have taken was that of land and the basic geography of settlement and society. It should by now be abundantly clear, and if it is not then it will surely become so in future, that this base-line was chosen with some deliberation, for it is at this level that certain parameters which are likely to have impinged upon the nature and functioning of the monetary economy of an ancient or mediaeval – or indeed any pre-industrial – society tend to begin to be set. In the case of the Balkan and Anatolian peninsulas, whether as a relatively small part of the later Roman empire, or as virtually the whole of the developed Byzantine one, it was indeed here that they were so set. For their heavily accentuated physical structure dictated in each case certain distinct and inevitable secondary characteristics with regard to such phenomena as climate, natural vegetation and land-use, and these in turn, if they did not dictate, nevertheless strongly favoured, the emergence of very particular patterns of settlement and society that were not necessarily absolute, but that were even so heavily dominant, within quite sharply defined regions.

Of these last several interrelated factors enough has been said in the first two chapters, although it is worth emphasising that the processes and problems involved in the twin phenomenon of the erosion and deposition of the topsoil, which was also treated above, should be examined not simply in a Balkan and Anatolian context, but a general Mediterranean, and more particularly a Near-eastern, one. Here, considerable work has been carried out into the historical framework in an area stretching from northern Syria down into southern Israel and across to Jordan. The crude physical results of the process have been shown to be uniformly severe, and its impact upon agricultural potential equally so. Whether the explanation sometimes evolved – the indifference and ignorance of the

Muslim population – is entirely or even at all satisfactory remains much more doubtful: the phenomenon is visible to an equal degree in many areas which Muslim powers did not rule, or at least did not rule until quite late on.[2]

However, at least one other additional factor should be taken into account. It is clear that the climate and natural vegetation of the two regions have changed little in relatively recent historical times, although it has to be admitted that what are superficially marginal changes in the first can have quite severe effects on the second and vice versa. Nor have the most basic patterns of land-use changed fundamentally, although, for instance, it is quite conceivable that the ancient reliance upon the olive both as an element in diet and as an element in social ceremonial – for example lighting, and anointing at the baths and gymnasium – ensured that the olive was then cultivated in marginal (that is basically higher) areas that are today quite bereft of it. On the other hand, in Anatolia at least, a definite shift in the predominant forms of land-use is indeed visible: whereas cereal production, together with that of the olive and the vine where a marketable surplus was concerned, seems to have been characteristic of the coastal plain and river-valleys, and pastoral products seem to have been equally typical of the central plateau, now, with the advent of modern methods of transport and agriculture, the pattern as a whole has tended to shift one stage. That is, cereal production for a marketable surplus is now not untypical of the plateau, whereas the plain and valleys have been given over quite heavily to the cultivation of cash-crops such as tobacco, citrus fruits and cotton.[3]

There is no real doubt that one of the major factors – perhaps the single most important factor – permitting this shift has been the advent of modern modes and methods of transport: the introduction of the railways, which was a feature of the late nineteenth century, and which had a swift and dramatic effect; and that of petrol-driven vehicles which has obviously been a feature of the twentieth century. There is every evidence that, prior to this, the situation obtaining in the late Ottoman period with regard to the speed and costs of transport closely reflected that obtaining in the mediaeval and ancient periods, and there is complementary evidence that this situation provided one of the critical parameters impingeing not only upon the mediaeval and ancient patterns of land-use, but also, in all probability, upon those of the contemporary monetary economy as well.

Evidence for the precise costs of transport in the ancient and (eastern) mediaeval world are few and far between. What are perhaps the most precise occur in Diocletian's *Edictum*

[2] Refs: E. Ashtor, *A Social and Economic History of the Near East in the Middle Ages*, pp. 51–8 (Section d: Soil erosion and Near Eastern agriculture). On what is frequently the preliminary to erosion/deposition, see now: R. Meiggs, *Trees and Timber in the Mediterranean World*, pp. 371–403 (ch. 13, 'Deforestation'). On climatic change in the region, see in the last instance: J. L. Bintliff, 'Climatic Change, Archaeology and Quaternary Science in the Eastern Mediterranean Region', in A. F. Harding (ed.), *Climatic Change in Later Prehistory*, at pp. 150–8.

[3] See Map 8. See also: Tanoğlu *et al.*, *Türkiye Atlası*, maps 68, 75.

*de Pretiis Venalium Rerum* of 301, but even here the situation involves a considerable degree of uncertainty, for the *Edictum* itself was the product of atypical circumstances, was of not entirely certain geographical application, and was in any case intended to set maximal prices only.[4] In addition to which, one of the principal measures in which the relevant quantities are defined, the *castrensis modius*, retained until very recently a still undecided relationship to the normal Italian *modius* (1 : 1 or 1 : 2).[5] The general message is nonetheless clear: on the definitions that currently seem probable, the cost of transporting a 1,200 (Roman) pound wagon of wheat, at 20 denarii per (Roman) mile, amounted to approximately 55% of the value of the wheat for every 100 (Roman) miles. Transport costs by sea, river/canal and land seem to bear a very approximate relationship of 1 : 5 : 40 respectively. These figures and ratios seem at least roughly in line with more modern (western) ones.[6]

Whatever the precise figures and ratios, the effective results seem clear in Anatolia at least. Both Leo of Synnada (Şuhut) and John of Euchaita (Avkat) mention a distinct lack of wheat, oil, wine and timber in their regions, the former implying that such commodities could be imported from the coastal areas of Ionia/Lydia/Caria and Pamphylia.[7] This was doubtless the case for a metropolitan bishop and any economic peers that he might possess locally. Gregory of Nazianzus, in describing the similarly placed region of Caesarea (Kayseri), gives a very different impression: on the occasion of a severe famine, the city could not import what it needed, because it was not on the coast and was far inland.[8] This was doubtless equally the case for the generality of the population.

The reasoning clearly implied in the latter case is made even more nearly specific in the descriptions, by John Lydus and Procopius, of what happened after Anastasius had commuted taxation in kind for taxation in coin, and John the Cappadocian then abolished

[4] For the case that the *Edictum* was intended to apply to Diocletian's eastern half of the empire only, see the refs in: Duncan-Jones, *The Economy of the Roman Empire: Quantitative Studies*, p. 366. The case was always a weak one: it is on general principles unlikely that so early on, and particularly given Diocletian's own predominance, regulations of this nature would be so circumscribed, and the *Edictum* itself, in quoting prices for travel or transport between various cities, includes a number of journeys that are entirely within Maximian's western half. Now that it is clear that quite important monetary measures were also involved, the case is weakened even further (see above, pp. 451–8). It is, of course, true that the only surviving copies (with the exception of a single fragment from Sulmona in Italy) are eastern, and so are the only surviving references to it, but this accurately reflects the general balance of the evidence. Even in the eastern half, the survival of copies is patchy: there is no reason to believe that they were set up in stone in every province, let alone in every city. What is involved is probably a combination of the preferences of the various regional authorities, and the stronger epigraphical tradition of the eastern half of the empire.

[5] Duncan-Jones, *The Economy of the Roman Empire: Quantitative Studies*, pp. 366–9 (Appendix 17: Diocletian's Price Edict and the Cost of Transport). See now also: R. P. Duncan-Jones, 'The Size of the Modius Castrensis', *Zeitschrift für Papyrologie und Epigraphik* 21 (1976), pp. 53–62. Duncan-Jones' later figure (1 : 1½), if correct, means that the true percentages and proportions lie precisely half way between the earlier alternative figures given on his p. 368.

[6] Duncan-Jones, *The Economy of the Roman Empire: Quantitative Studies*, pp. 368–9.

[7] See above, pp. 138–42.

[8] See above, p. 296.

or pruned certain sections of the *cursus publicus*, even in Asiana, which included the fertile and productive western coastlands: land-owners who had previously sold off their surplus crops to the *cursus*, in return for coin with which to pay their taxes, could no longer do so because they were far removed from the sea/inland. Hitherto marketable crops subsequently remained rotting in their place.[9] Again, according to Procopius, when Peter Barsymes obtained grain for the City by means of compulsory purchase in Bithynia, Phrygia and Thrace, none of which regions was very far from the sea, and then forced the sellers to transport their products down to the coast, this was done only with great difficulty.[10]

All these descriptions and occasions clearly imply, to an extent that leaves no real doubt, the existence and operation of an acute problem regarding transport and its costs, in areas that were more than minimally remote from the coast or presumably from a navigable river. It is of interest, and perhaps of significance, that nowhere is the problem described absolutely unequivocally and in detail. This may of course be the result of the contemporary literary tradition, which tended to deprecate descriptions of too technical a nature and the use of technical terms, but it may well simply be that whereas some or even all of the individual elements of the problem were recognised, nevertheless they could not be integrated mentally or linguistically, or both, into a complete concept, involving cause and effect, with high costs rendering the transport of low-priced goods more than a short distance commercially unviable.

For actual figures and proportions, recourse necessarily has to be had to late nineteenth-century (that is basically pre-railway) reports of the Ottoman situation. Here, in *c.* 1890, it is recorded[11] of the *vilayet* of Sivas (Sebastea), that 1 *tonne* of grain, costing at most 40 (gold) francs at Sivas, and transported down to the coast via Tokat (Docea) and Amasya (Amasia), cost 140/160 francs on arrival at Samsun (Amisus). The distance covered, some 346 km along what appears to have been a Roman/Byzantine and Selçuk route (Maps 12, 24), therefore effectively tripled or quadrupled its price. Similarly, in *c.* 1895, it is recorded[12] of the *vilayet* of Kastamonu (Castamenon), that 1 *kilé* of wheat costing 40/45 *piastres* at Çankırı (Gangra), and transported to Kastamonu, cost 90/95 *piastres* on arrival. The distance covered, some 90 km as the crow flies, but actually some 132 km because of the intervening rough terrain (the Ilgaz Dağları), effectively doubled its price. It is remarked specifically in the first case, and implied in the second, that the process was very rarely gone through, except when grain of a very special quality, or presumably famine conditions elsewhere, were involved. But this presumably also benefited the large land-owner who might possess both the technical knowledge and the financial capacity for the production of special grains, and the facilities for long-distance transport.

[9] See above, pp. 294–6.

[10] See above, p. 51.

[11] Cuinet, *La Turquie d'Asie* I, p. 637.

[12] Cuinet, *La Turquie d'Asie* IV, p. 431.

The result was of course inevitable: of the *vilayet* of Ankara (Ancyra), in *c.* 1890, it is recorded that because of distance and the high costs of transport the crops were *condamnées à pourrir sur place* (a remarkable echo of Lydus and Procopius); and of the contemporary *sancaklar* of Kırşehir and Niğde (effectively Tyana), that because of the lack of outlets (*débouchés*) for the products of the soil, and because of the lack of routes and the means of communication (*défaut des voies et moyens de communications*), they were uncultivated and abandoned (Kırşehir), or producing minutely in comparison with local fertility (Niğde).[13]

The situation as regards livestock was of course somewhat different, as transport was, as it were, inbuilt. Mention has already been made[14] of the Marmara ports of Nicomedia and Pylae and, presumably, others as being the destinations of livestock of all kinds bound for the capital. It is quite possible that these were locally reared, although in the case of the flocks of sheep driven towards Nicomedia, the clear implication is that they were not.[15] But such livestock might well also travel very considerable distances: in the fourth and fifth centuries, a levy of pigs made on the middle and southern Italian provinces of Campania, Samnium and Lucania with Bruttium, to provide for the free distributions of pork at Rome, was driven on the trotter down from the provinces into the city, meanwhile losing some 15 or 20% of its weight – a factor which was duly accounted for in the calculation of the levy. The problems involved were the subject of complex legislation.[16] The levy was, of course, an official one, but there is no reason to suppose that a similar if somewhat smaller scale of distances could not be covered on a commercial basis, whether in the case of Rome or of Constantinople. It is in this connection, therefore, doubtless no coincidence that, in 1883 – that is at much the same time as the *sancak* of Kırşehir was recorded as lying uncultivated and abandoned – it was also recorded[17] that a huge flock of sheep was driven down from Kırşehir into Constantinople. The route involved, evidently a regular drovers' road, lay along the line Kırşehir–Aksaray (Colonia Archelais) – Sultanhan – Eskitul – Obruk–Zıvarık– Gözlu–Kolukısa–Karagöz–Ak Göl–Çeltik – Beypazarı – Torbalı. The distance recorded is well in excess of 600 km, and represents a great sweep south and west from Kırşehir, round the southern end of the Tuz Gölu, and then north and west, towards the Marmara. It thus includes, presumably intentionally, some of the most arid and deserted parts of the southern central plateau, and thus tends to avoid major routes, although it does involve one section that is particularly thickly studded with early Selçuk *hans*, and itself just possibly reflects a Roman/Byzantine route (Maps 12, 24).

Again, therefore, the general message is quite clear: grain produced as a surplus for

[13] Cuinet, *La Turquie d'Asie* I, pp. 259 (Ankara), 326–7 (Kırşehir), 837 (Niğde).

[14] See above, p. 55.

[15] See below, p. 563.

[16] Jones, *Later Roman Empire* II, pp. 702–4.

[17] Admiralty, *A Handbook of Asia Minor* III.2, p. 50.

anything other than local stockpiling, or the local market, had to be produced within a very short distance of the sea or of a navigable river; if it was not so produced, then transport costs soon rendered its distant marketing uneconomic.[18] So, even had grain been easily and widely grown on the Anatolian central plateau – and there is good reason to believe that wheat, at least, was not so grown – it could not have been traded over any great distance, and *a fortiori* it could not have been traded with the coast. Only in the case of famine was grain traded in this way, as for example in the (reverse) case of the severe thirteenth-century famine on the Selçuk-held plateau, which enriched the Byzantine-held periphery, and which involved grain as well as livestock. But this phenomenon was thought worthy of remark, it is quite exceptionally visible in the scale of the gold coinage of the emperor of the time, John III and even so it tells one nothing as to the nature and status of the Selçuk purchasers, who by the very nature of the case must have been of some appreciable wealth.[19]

What, then, of the other Mediterranean staples: the olive and the vine, and their products? In the first place, the first will not grow on the plateau at all, and the second will grow reasonably well in certain areas of it only, but in any case, the production of both is now very heavily concentrated on the periphery of the peninsula, particularly in the north-west and south-east.[20] Judging from the comments of Symeon Seth, Leo of Synnada and John of Euchaita, this was the case in the Byzantine period as well.[21] It is therefore impossible or very unlikely, respectively, that these commodities could have been produced in and traded from the plateau. And in any case, both seem to have been on the border-line of economic viability as regards long-distance trade by land, wine of special quality, or vintage, providing an obvious exception.[22]

The situation as described by Cecaumenus who, in a passage devoted to the fleet (*hē doxa tēs Rhōmanias!*), recognises the Cyclades, Cyprus and Crete, and both of the mainlands (i.e. those to either side of the Cyclades, the coastlands of Greece and Asia Minor), as sources of wheat (*sitos*), barley (*krithē*), pulse (*osprion*), cheese (*tyros*), wine (*oinos*), meat (*kreas*), olive-oil (*elaion*), considerable revenues (*nomismata polla*), and so on, is thus very different indeed.[23] (Cf. Map 13)

The only major commodities produced on a large scale, for a surplus involving extra-regional trade, that can be assigned to the central plateau throughout the period on general grounds thus involve livestock on the hoof and, presumably, non-perishable animal products. This is very much the verdict of the fourth-century *Expositio Totius Mundi et Gentium* which assigns to the inner Anatolian provinces men, animals, skins and

[18] See, for example: Rickman, *The Corn Supply of Ancient Rome*, pp. 15–16.

[19] See above, pp. 283, 256.

[20] See Map 8. See also: Tanoğlu *et al.*, *Türkiye Atlası*, Maps 68, 73.

[21] See above, pp. 138–42.

[22] Jones, *Later Roman Empire* II, p. 845. Rickman, *The Corn Supply of Ancient Rome*, p. 16.

[23] Cecaumenus, *Logos Nouthetētikos pros Basilea* CCLVII; ed. Wassiliewsky and Jernstedt, p. 102.

clothing (presumably woollen).[24] An imperial woollen mill (*gynaecium*) for the production of woollen fabrics and garments is indeed known for Caesarea, but this will not have been a commercial venture.[25]

Even here, however, the situation may well have been more complex, and economically less favourable to the plateau, than may at first sight appear. The only Anatolian woollen wares described in the *Edictum de Pretiis* by their points of origin are the *tapete Cappadocicum sive Ponticum* (*tapēs Kappadokikos ē Pontikos*), and the various objects described as *Laodiceni* (*Ladikēnoi*) or *Phrygiaci* (*Phrygiakoi*).[26] The Laodicea involved is clearly the Phrygian one (ad Lycum, Ladik, effectively Denizli). Now as it happens, the single most concentrated group of the classic Ottoman carpet manufacturies apparently producing for the market is that formed by Gördes (Gordium), Uşak, Kula and Ladik (Laodicea ad Lycum). The concentration involved very clearly centres upon Phrygia and the transitional land lying between the plain and the plateau.[27]

The underlying reason behind all this is equally clear: the area involved, the former Türkmen *kışla*,[28] is the first down from the plateau to which wool in crude form could be delivered, there to be processed and woven into fabrics, garments and rugs, and within – as regards transport – convenient and still relatively cheap reach of the coastal cities, from which they were eventually exported. It therefore effectively functioned as the narrow interface between two quite different major economic zones. Laodicea particularly, in this respect, may thus have had almost as continuous a functional history as Patras, with which it shares a number of features:[29] the *Edictum de Pretiis* in fact mentions a *biros Akhaïkos ētoi Phrygiakos kallistos* and a *birrhos Aphros ē Akhaïkos* as woollen wares, and both these could quite well have been the products of Patras.[30] As the *Notitia Dignitatum* does not give a full list of imperial factories and workshops for the east as it does for the west, it is impossible to be certain, but it would not be at all surprising if both Laodicea and Patras turned out to have been the site of *gynaecia*, and the latter also the site of a linen mill (*linyphia*) as well.

[24] See above, pp. 56–7. The fact that inner Anatolia exported men, or manpower, does not, of course, mean that it was heavily populated (see above, pp. 90–108). A similarly inhospitable and under-populated area, the Highlands of Scotland, has long provided the British army with recruits for some of its finest regiments. Nor should it be supposed that, with the loss of the plateau, the Byzantine army would have been totally deprived of such recruits: movement, although much slower, was then also much freer. See, for example, the 'narrator' in *Timarion*, who comes from Cappadocia, *ek tēs hyperoriou* – the idea is floated quite naturally, even if in this case in a fictional context: Anonymous, *Timarion*; ed. Romano, p. 53.

[25] Refs for Anatolian factories: Jones, *Later Roman Empire* II, p. 836.

[26] Diocletian, *Edictum de Pretiis Venalium Rerum* XIX, XXV; ed. Giacchero, I, pp. 174–9, 184–5. A clear potential complication arises from the existence of so many cities called Laodicea.

[27] Tanoğlu, *et al. Türkiye Atlası*, map 1/e. The ascription of particular kinds of carpets to these particular towns is very largely a traditional one, as is so often the case, but there need be no doubt of their deriving from the general area.

[28] See above, pp. 114–17, 122–3.

[29] See above, pp. 206–7. Patras, of course, is not simply on the coastal plain, but is actually on the coast – but most of its wool comes from the central Peloponnese.

[30] Diocletian, *Edictum de Pretiis Venalium Rerum* XIX.53, XXII.26; ed. Giacchero, I, pp. 176, 177, 182, 183.

It should perhaps also not be forgotten in this same respect that it was an imperial estate in geographically contiguous Lydia that produced packs and horse-cloths (presumably woollen ones) for the imperial baggage-train in the tenth century.[31]

What is particularly significant, however, is that if the pattern of delivery, production and transport suggested above was, even if not the only, then nevertheless the predominant, one, the plateau will once again have been deprived of the full economic advantage of what was one of its very few widely marketable products: it will, in other words, have been trading the raw materials only, and not the finished articles.

## B. *Trade*

Now, it seems clear that the basic provisioning of Constantinople with the staples of the Mediterranean diet (that is with wheat, wine and olive-oil, and with mutton and pork) on a commercial basis[32] was not only problematic for the state (a fact which even a cursory glance at *The Book of the Prefect* reveals), but also must have had a very considerable impact upon the economies of both Anatolia and the Balkans. But it seems equally clear that this impact must be understood within the basic parameters of an ancient or mediaeval economy, or indeed of any pre-industrial economy, and it is therefore in this respect, and in the appropriate circumstances, worthwhile utilising even quite late Ottoman evidence to complete the imperfect or fragmentary late Roman or Byzantine evidence.

It is by no means certain, but it does seem very probable, that this provisioning in fact provided the most important single causative factor behind purely commercial exchanges within the empire, or at least subsequent to the loss of the outlying eastern regions of Egypt, Palestine and Syria, and the western ones of Africa and the greater part of Italy, in the seventh century, and prior to the fall of the City to the Fourth Crusade in 1204.[33] Its previous fiscal impact with regard to wheat alone has already been noted when dealing with the sixth century.[34] The overwhelming predominance of Constantinople as a centre for the concentration of wealth, and for the consumption of produce, whether of commercially produced agricultural crops, or of fiscally produced taxation, was well recognised and neatly encapsulated by Michael Choniates – himself an interesting figure, born in Anatolia, educated secondarily and trained in the capital, and ending up as a metropolitan bishop in the Balkans – in a passage that has been quoted above.[35] This passage was clearly the product of some degree of bitterness, but its general tone is borne out by others that are the products of some degree of naïvety – the

[31] See above, p. 313.

[32] See above, pp. 46–54, 54–6. Jones, *Later Roman Empire* II, pp. 695–70. There is no evidence, after the sixth century for the existence of the institutionalised levies that had been an inheritance from Rome.

[33] For the economic/financial importance of Egypt, Palestine, and Syria: see above, pp. 168–71, 171–3; below pp. 613–18. For the relative unimportance of Africa and Italy: see above, pp. 164–8, 171–3.

[34] See above, p. 170 and Table 3.

[35] See above, pp. 51–2.

descriptions of Constantinople and its accumulated wealth by Benjamin of Tudela, Geoffrey of Villehardouin and Robert of Clari.[36]

The effect of this concentration of wealth and capacity for consumption is, as usual, likely to have been a very accentuated one. The predominant position of Constantinople, like the earlier one of Rome, is certain to have enhanced prices in the immediate hinterland quite considerably, and probably to the extent that normal patterns of production, profit and loss ceased to operate: it is thus quite likely that the sale of crops and livestock to the City that otherwise would have been utilised for local consumption, whether human or animal, was commonplace; and it is almost equally probable that a specialisation of production took place.[37] On the other hand, the full effect is likely to have been really quite limited, and confined to those regions either within very easy reach by land, or within relatively easy reach by sea – basically, Thrace, Bithynia and Mysia. The geographical situation of the capital, accessible from both the Bosphorus and (more immediately important) the Marmara, was obviously immensely more favourable in this respect than that of Rome.

Outside this immediate hinterland a clear distinction, based upon the relative speed and cost of transport, is likely to have made itself felt very sharply indeed. The evidence suggests that the islands – including even Cyprus and Crete – and the Aegean coastlands were well capable of providing, and did provide, the capital with its basic requirements in the way of cereals, wine and olive-oil.[38] The Black Sea coasts of Thrace and Pontus evidently participated, but, at least until the later period, are less well evidenced.[39] But the crucial requirement will have been proximity to the sea. With regard to livestock, the situation is likely to have been equally, but rather differently, acute, and it therefore seems worthwhile turning attention to the operation of two of the metropolitan guilds dealing with livestock and butchery, that is the general meat-dealers and butchers (*makelarioi*), and the pork-dealers and butchers (*khoiremporoi*), details of which are known from *The Book of the Prefect*.

The fifteenth chapter of *The Book of the Prefect* (*Peri tōn Makelariōn*)[40] forbids the *makelarioi* to buy pigs or to store pork, and requires them to sell their animals (*thremmata*) in the Strategium up until the first day of Lent, and their lambs (*arnai*) in the Forum Tauri from Easter until Pentecost. Two further regulations are of particular interest to the problems in hand. The *makelarioi* were required to travel out to the regions beyond

[36] Benjamin of Tudela, *Itinerary*; trans. Sharf, in *Byzantine Jewry from Justinian to the Fourth Crusade*, at pp. 134–6. Geoffrey of Villehardouin, *La conquête de Constantinople* CXXVIII, CLXXXV, CXCII, CCXLIX–CCLV; ed. Faral, I, pp. 130, 188, 194, II, pp. 50–60. Robert of Clari, *La conquête de Constantinople* LXXXI–XCVIII; ed. Lauer, pp. 80–95.

[37] Duncan-Jones, *The Economy of the Roman Empire: Quantitative Studies*, pp. 345–7 (Appendix 8, 'Prices at Rome').

[38] See above, n. 32 and Map 13.

[39] See above, pp. 38, 46–8, 49–50, 279 and n. 145.

[40] 'Leo VI', *To Eparkhikon Biblion*; ed. Nicole, pp. 50–1.

the Sangarius in order to meet those outside sheep-dealers driving their flocks towards Nicomedia and other such cities, so that the cheaper sale (*eunōtera hē prasis*) thus obtaining should accrue to the butchers (*tois sphattousin*), and not to the sellers (*mē tois emporois*). From the other side, the sheep-sellers (*probatemporoi*) were required to confine themselves to the (authorised) purchasers of animals (*tous exōnoumenous en tois thremmasi*), that is to the butchers, and to make their sales through them (*kai di'autōn tas emporeias poieitōsan*), not hindering those coming in from the country to the Queen City to make their sales (*mē kōlyontes tous mellontas eiserkhesthai khōritas kai apempolein en tē basileousē*).

The sixteenth chapter (*Peri tōn Khoiremporōn*)[41] requires all pork- purchasers, butchers and sellers (*exōnoumenoi kai sphattontes kai apempolountes*) to make their sales in the Forum Tauri, and forbids them – under threat of punishment – to travel outside the City to meet pig-sellers and make a sale, or even to use secretly some part of the City itself in order to do so. It also requires the heads of the guild (*prōtostatai*) to make it known to the Prefect whenever individuals from amongst the outside swineherds (*ek tōn exōthen khoiragelas*) arrive, so as to prevent them selling to middlemen (*metapratai* = re-sellers), rather than publicly (*koinōs*) in the Taurum; and it forbids pig-sellers to conceal their animals in an aristocratic household (*oikos arkhontikos*) so as to sell them secretly.

The two chapters are of some interest in themselves: it is, for example, surely dietarily significant that the *makelarioi*, who were presumably licensed to deal in all animals and meats other than the porcine, nevertheless seem to have dealt overwhelmingly in sheep and mutton. They also compare interestingly and significantly. It seems clear that the organisational norm common to both guilds is that shepherds and swineherds bring their animals from the surrounding countryside into the City itself, there to make their sales publicly (the state traditionally disapproved of, or discouraged, private exchanges), in particular places (the Strategium and the Forum Tauri), and on a carefully regulated profit margin.[42] An exception is nevertheless made in the case of what seem to be certain of the *makelarioi*, who are required actually to travel out beyond the Sangarius, in order to meet up there with incoming shepherds and their flocks. These shepherds are required to sell their animals to the *makelarioi* only, and not to hinder others coming in from the country to the capital to make their sales. The distinction surely is between those small flocks driven from the surrounding countryside into the City by local peasants, in very much the same fashion as still happens today, and those large flocks driven down from inner Anatolia and the plateau, in much the same way as was still happening in 1883. The point is in any case, and to a very approximate degree, inherently probable: the larger the flock involved, the greater the distance that is likely to have been involved, as the

[41] *Ibid.* pp. 51–2.

[42] *Ibid.* XV.2: *Hoi makelarioi tēn exōnēsin poiēsamenoi kata tēn poiotēta tōn zōōn kai tēn apempolēsin poieitōsan...to de loipon apempolōsi kata tēn exōnēsin. Idem,* XVI.2: *Hoi tous khoirous exōnoumenoi...kai epauxontes tas toutōn timas, typtomenoi kai koureuomenoi ekdiōkesthōsan.* The fixing of profit margins, elsewhere in the *Eparkhikon Biblion* explicit, is here at least strongly implied. See also below, p. 584.

smaller owner is not likely to have possessed the time or the resources necessary for long-distance travel that the larger owner or his agent is likely to have done. If the large flocks being driven towards the capital really had originated on the plateau, then their ultimate owners would presumably have been the great landed magnates who seem to have been concentrated there: certainly, their putative servants or agents behaved very much as might have been expected – apparently hindering the smaller and more local peasants who, in however insignificant a way, might have proved competitors.

The reason that a similar restriction was not imposed upon the *khoiremporoi* is simply that it was probably not needed. Herds of pigs on this huge scale could probably not have been assembled, and even if they were so assembled, they could probably not have been fed satisfactorily and driven that far: sheep are, as it were, 'esocentric' animals, tending to follow a leader, while pigs are 'exocentric', tending to scatter; sheep can graze extensively on poor pasture, while pigs need woodland if they are not to lose weight rapidly.

It is thus likely that the furthest that herds of pigs, and indeed most of the smaller flocks of sheep, would be brought in from, on a commercial basis, would be the nearer reaches of Paphlagonia, Galatia, Phrygia and the Mysian Highlands. Only the largest, and therefore the fewest, of the flocks of sheep would be brought in from inner Anatolia and the plateau.

Now, to the extent that trade, in the form of straightforward commodity-exchanges, traditionally provides the predominant motor for the distribution and circulation of coin, the exchanges involved in the basic provisioning of Constantinople, which – one has to assume, but quite plausibly – were heavily coin-based on the part of the purchasers, potentially could have provided a significant element in the distribution of coin to the regions. But in practice, it may be doubted whether the situation was quite so simple and so effective in this respect. Not all of the coins thus handed over to the sellers will, of course, have returned to the regions. The smallest sellers, whether of crops or livestock, are likely to have been local owners, and they are quite likely to have used some or all of their profits to purchase urban wares with which to return to their localities. In this respect, therefore, Constantinople will have been no different from fourth-century Antioch.[43] Over and above these local owners, the sellers, at least in the case of those bringing in agricultural produce from the coastlands of the Balkans and Anatolia and the islands, are, with increasing distance, increasingly likely to have been members of the mercantile classes, as in the case of the twelfth-century Venetian merchants trading mainly in Peloponnesian and Thessalian olive-oil and other such products.[44] These, if the balance of the customs dues in the Veneto-Byzantine treaty of 992 has been interpreted correctly, will have tended to purchase manufactured and luxury goods to take back to

[43] See above, p. 301.

[44] See above, p. 52; below, pp. 589, 591.

their regions, rather than return with large amounts of coin – which may well, indeed, in the particular case, have been illegal.[45] There remain the sellers bringing in sheep from inner Anatolia and the plateau (and, presumably, from the equivalent areas of the Balkans). Now, these flocks, which seem likely to have been large (they were one of the few forms of surplus which the inner regions could export, and they derived from an area characterised by large land-owning), will presumably have been driven down by their owners' servants or agents. It is therefore arguable that these latter will have been less likely to purchase extensively from the profit made from the sales, and more likely to have returned with the coin unspent to their regions of origin.[46] It is of course possible that this pattern was complicated or nullified by the intervening existence of a body of large middlemen who bought up surplus livestock on the plateau and drove them, or had them driven, down to the City. This is, however, unlikely: the influence of the state, and the structure of society, will not have encouraged the development of such a body, and in fact evidence which will be mentioned below clearly suggests that the direct delivery of a surplus was the norm.[47]

Is this last, therefore, the mechanism which effected the distribution of coin to inner Anatolia and the plateau, and ensured the existence and maintenance of a monetary economy in those regions? Given the physical structure and climate, and the pattern of settlement and society, in those areas, it seems wildly unlikely. It should not be forgotten that, as late as 1318, in somewhat similar circumstances, and in an island that is generally considered to have possessed a heavily monetised economy, certain areas of West Wales requested that the tax of one-fifteenth that had been imposed should be paid by them in kind rather than in coin, as they were 'never accustomed to have money in the Welshry'.[48] As pointed out above, it is only the largest land-owners who are likely to have had the time and resources to mount an expedition – for that was effectively what it was – on the scale required, and their rôle will therefore have been crucial. The ideology of the magnate class in this respect is perhaps best and most conveniently formulated by Cecaumenus (a Balkan magnate) in a section of his *Stratēgikon* entitled 'On being independent in one's household (*Peri tou en oikia idiazontos*)':

If you live independently in your household, and are without [other] occupation, concern yourself with the duties of the household, so that it may be well maintained, and do not neglect such

[45] See above, pp. 257–.60, 282–3.

[46] Unless, of course, the servants or agents handed in the profits involved to the owners' representatives in the City – most of the largest owners clearly kept up considerable metropolitan households.

[47] See below, p. 567.

[48] Ref: M. C. Prestwich, 'The Crown and the Currency. The Circulation of Money in Late Thirteenth and Early Fourteenth Century England', *Numismatic Chronicle* 142 (1982), p. 60. For a similar, and roughly contemporary, phenomenon, in upper Provence, see: G. Duby, *Rural Economy and Country Life in the Medieval West*, p. 131. Pastoral-based highlands, like central Anatolia, clearly tended to remain unmonetised, even by ancient and mediaeval standards.

things, for there is for you no means of life other than the working of the land (*to ergazesthai tēn gēn*). Make for yourself things that are self-working[49] (*poiēson seautō autourgias*): mills, workshops, gardens (*mylōnas kai ergastēria, kēpous*), and other such things as will give you an annual return (*karpous etēsiōs*), whether it be in rent or crop (*dia te paktou kai karpou*). Plant trees of all kinds, and reed-beds (*kalamōnas*), so that you may have a return without having a yearly worry, and thus have leisure. Get yourself livestock (*ktēnē*), such as plough-oxen (*boes arotēres*), and pigs (*khoiroi*), and sheep (*probata*), and such other animals as will breed yearly, increase and multiply. For these will furnish you with a plenty at table. And so you will rejoice at all these things: in the abundance of wheat (*sitou*), wine (*oinou*), and everything else, seed and livestock, edible and moveable. And if you lead this kind of life, do not relax and neglect it, otherwise everything will diminish.

(Cecaumenus, *Stratēgikon* LXXXVIII; ed. Wassiliewsky and Jernstedt, p. 36)

Cecaumenus then proceeds to warn against the consequences of the neglect that he has mentioned: one's servitors (*hypēretountes*) eat into one's profit (*kerdos*) and make themselves independent; in a time of famine (*khronos enantios kai aphorēsasēs tēs gēs*), one is found not to have a store of wheat and other grains (*enapotheton siton kai loipa spermata*) for the support of one's dependants (*eis diatrophēn tou laou*); if one wishes to buy something, not a nomisma is to be found (*oukh eurethēsetai...nomisma*).[50] All this, of course, is the ideology of self-sufficiency through diversification; the accumulation of every possible means of supply and wealth; and the gain and maintenance of control over dependants. It both has a conceptual history stretching back into antiquity,[51] and can be seen still being actualised in the descriptions of wealth which have been summarised or quoted above – in fact, Pacourianus' summary description of his properties bears a quite close resemblance to Cecaumenus' recommendations, both being, of course, approximately contemporary.[52] The possible argument that the former is formulaic and that the latter is theoretical, only, breaks down with the detailed descriptions, and the realisation that the ideology involved clearly and actually applied not only to those members of the magnate class residing on their estate (e.g. Boïlas), but also to those residing in the capital and at court (e.g. Cantacuzene).[53] What is also important, of course, is that the ideology never changed. The only potential difference is likely to have been that of size increasing flexibility: in other words, the resident owner of a single or a small number of estates might well maintain each as self-sufficient as possible, whereas the non-resident owner of a large number might equally have tended to favour specialisation, with single estates, or groups of estates, providing a single product or a restricted number of products, for his Constantinopolitan storehouses. There is no real evidence for or against this extra

[49] *Autourgia* is the nearest that Cecaumenus comes to naming the concept of self-sufficiency, as he never actually uses the term *autarkeia* – but the whole passage is nevertheless redolent of the latter.

[50] Cecaumenus, *Stratēgikon* LXXXIX; ed. Wassiliewsky and Jernstedt, p. 36.

[51] E.g. Duncan-Jones, *The Economy of the Roman Empire: Quantitative Studies*, pp. 37–8.

[52] See above, p. 213.

[53] See above, pp. 207–8, 211.

potential actually being exploited, although the very wide geographical spread of holdings notable in certain cases might be taken as suggesting that it was.[54]

In any case, given the ideological standpoint of the dominant class, and the clear indication that this ideology was actually implemented in as far as it was possible to do so, where self-sufficiency was concerned, a number of points follow.

In the first place, a whole stratum of economic life, which might otherwise have provided the pretext and occasion of exchange, simply did not exist, or was kept to a minimal significance. This, of course, is not to suggest that members of these classes had no knowledge of, or use for, coinage as a medium of exchange: Cecaumenus, for example, was perfectly familiar with both the use and misuse of coin, and with money-lending and interest, and the descriptions of wealth quoted or summarised above not infrequently mention its presence.[55] Nor is it to suggest that members of these classes did not regularly sell off the surplus produce of their estates: indeed it has already been suggested that inner-Anatolian magnates were selling off sheep for the provisioning of Constantinople. In addition, there survives a considerable amount of monastic documentation, involving the state grant of exemption from the *kommerkion* and other trade-based taxes to the monasteries concerned, for their own ships up to a defined number and capacity.[56] One of these grants, that to the Cosmosotira Monastery (1152) of twelve ships and a capacity of 4,000 *modioi*, derived from a grant originally made by Alexius I to his son, the *sebastokratōr* Isaac, for his estates grouped around Aenus at the mouth of the Maritsa (Map 19), and it seems certain that other members of the imperial clan and the court aristocracy, and possibly even members of other classes, possessed such exemption. Yet other individuals may well have possessed the ships, but not the exemption. It seems clear that one of the major uses made of these ships was, in the case of the monasteries, the direct sale of surplus produce, and probably, in the case of the *sebastokratōr* Isaac, both that and the direct Constantinopolitan provisioning of his household and accumulation of produce in his storehouses.[57] This latter is likely to have provided not the least of the reasons for twelfth-century appanages to have noticeably tended to be within convenient reach of the sea.[58] (Map 19)

It is, on the other hand, to suggest that the existence of this ideological principle will have meant that what, apart from the state itself, were economically the most powerful classes in the empire will deliberately have restricted their involvement in monetary affairs

54 See above, pp. 103, 202, 303.

55 E.g. see above, p. 356 (misuse of coin); see also: Cecaumenus, *Stratēgikon* XC (*peri danous kai tokous*), XCI (*peri hybrēs tou danistou*); ed. Wassiliewsky and Jernstedt, pp. 37–8.

56 For the useful list of such twelfth-century exemptions: Antoniadis-Bibicou, *Études d'histoire maritime de Byzance: à propos du 'thème des Caravisiens'*, pp. 132–3.

57 The most obvious example of such Constantinopolitan households/storehouses is that of Cantacuzene, but this – if it was in any way exceptional – was so only in size: clearly all other members of the imperial clan/court aristocracy will have possessed their own. See above, pp. 207–8.

58 The basic consideration being, of course, ease and cost of transport.

to the purchase of what they and their households, which could be enormous, needed or desired, but could otherwise not provide themselves with – obviously likely to have been overwhelmingly luxury and complex manufactured wares – and the accumulation of a necessary reserve. This latter will have varied in size, according to the institution or individual involved, but it is not likely to have been of very great size, relative to the overall accumulated wealth, or the rate of consumption, of a household, and it is not likely, because of its nature, to have formed a very 'active' body of coin. Indeed, it should be remembered that when the accumulation of the reserve held by the Monastery of Bachkovo reached a certain point (10 lb gold = 720 nomismata), the surplus was automatically liquidated – but in the form of the purchase of an estate, to be kept under monastic control.[59]

How far down through the social scale this ideological element extended remains currently a matter of uncertainty, but at no great depth it is likely to have become a matter not of ideology at all, but of absolute necessity for survival. It will have been far more immediately important for the moderately wealthy owner of a single estate of some size, and *a fortiori* for the peasant owner of a small-holding, to build up an accumulation of grain, wine, and oil or fat, and dried pulses, than one of nomismata or miliaresia. The one could tide him and his household over a difficult agricultural year – not an infrequent occurrence on the evidence of the sources – while the other, if he lived in the wrong area – inland, or in a place difficult of access – would do him no good at all, as the possession of a few gold and/or silver coins did not automatically guarantee him access to a ready market even in the best circumstances, and he could in any case probably not afford whatever was available in the worst. In addition, of course, it was precisely in such an area that coin would have been particularly difficult to come by, and it is likely that such coins as were actually acquired and as were not needed for the inevitable tax-collector or landlord would – as in the case of his social and economic superiors – have been accumulated rather than spent, and that if nevertheless they were spent, then the object of expenditure is equally likely to have been the occasional extra animal at the local *panēgyris*, or the even more occasional dowry, or some such relatively infrequent and major outlay. Precisely what a peasant in this kind of situation would or could have done with ninety-six copper folleis, received in return from the tax-collector as *strophē* or *anistrophē*, if he was unfortunate enough to be assessed (for example) at a *kharagma* of two gold nomismata for a tax-liability of $1\frac{2}{3}$ nomisma, remains entirely a matter of mystery and conjecture. Certainly, the evidence strongly suggests that neither the state in general, nor the tax-collector in particular, is likely to have worried overmuch.[60]

[59] See above, pp. 159–60.

[60] See above, pp. 286–7. The limited uses for, and desirability of, cash, are implied in the case of the ninth-century Paphlagonian peasant, Meletius, who sold off his surplus products (*ta khreiōdē*) at the local annual *panēgyris*, part in sale, part in exchange (*kai ta men pōlēsas, ta de antallaxas*), that is part for cash, part for necessities. Source quoted in Antoniadis-Bibicou, *Recherches sur les douanes à Byzance*, at pp. 247–8.

At least, the taxation reforms of Alexius I, the *Nea Logarikē*, in permitting the use of copper or billon coin for the payment of certain elements of the land-tax, the *lepta psēphia* and *parakolouthēmata*, instead of, as in the *Palaia Logarikē*, precious-metal only, will have eased the problem in that respect.[61]

In the second place, and possibly contingent upon the predominant ideology of the exploitation of the land, and the attainment of a self-sufficiency, both the state and the magnate classes inherently distrusted the mercantile ones, whose ideology and mode of operation was so alien, even antipathetic, to theirs. The state, whose administrators were rarely anything other than representative of the dominant class, or at least participants in their ideology, seems to have feared the potential power – whether economic or political – of the mercantile classes, and more particularly of the middlemen, whose position was perhaps the most alien of all, and whose potential was perhaps the greatest of all. As a consequence, and in as far as it was able, especially in the capital, where the contradictions between the two philosophies and modes of operation must have been most acute, obvious and dangerous, the state closely regulated the conditions under which the mercantile classes operated, amongst other things encouraging direct sales so as to discourage the existence of, and the necessity for, the middlemen.[62] The result was that these classes – concentrated, as so much of Byzantine civilisation and society was, upon the capital – remained economically necessary but, according to an on-going tradition, individually small in scale, and relatively devoid of influence.[63] The magnate classes, and in particular the military section of them, whose position was economically and (at least latently) politically pre-eminent, and whose ideology of self-sufficiency rendered the whole notion of a middleman redundant, even obnoxious, naturally enough seems to have preferred the direct sale of its surplus produce in any case.

Whether or not the state and the dominant class feared the mercantile classes economically and politically, they certainly despised them socially. In this respect, the terms of the legislation of the earlier emperors, on the one hand against the participation of the mercantile classes in administration, and their gaining of social status thereby, and on the other against the participation of the dominant class in trade, should be remembered.[64] So should the attitude of the emperor Theophilus when confronted with the mere possibility of being considered a *nauklēros*, an attitude which contrasts so beautifully with the clear and contemporary operation of the imperial *hypatos* and doge Giustiniano Partecipazio as an actual and habitual investor in overseas trading ventures.[65]

61 See above, p. 286.

62 On attitudes to the middleman, see above, p. 563.

63 See above, pp. 244–5. For the one period when they seem to have acquired political influence, see below, pp. 570–82.

64 See above, pp. 242–3.

65 See above, p. 247, and nn. 154, 155.

### C. *The abortive alliance (bureaucracy with commerce and artisanate, 1028–81)*

The crucial and determinant period for the nature and rôle of the Byzantine mercantile classes, and for their relationship with the state and the dominant class, seems to have been the middle and second half of the eleventh century. The period opened with the accession of Romanus III, who was apparently *eparkhos tēs poleōs*, in 1028, and subsequently with that of Michael IV, who was a former *argyramoibos*, in 1034. This was followed in its turn by the brief reign (1041–2) of Michael V, whose father had been a *kalaphatēs*. This nexus, partly function-, partly family-based, is unlikely to have been entirely coincidental, for it is clear that the metropolitan administration feared the regional magnates from the start, and it indeed set the scene for several decades.[66] What seems to have happened is that there gradually developed a conscious political division in the dominant class, with the military magnates/regional administrators on the one hand, and with the civil magnates/Constantinopolitan bureaucracy on the other. The division was in itself probably a reaction, however unconscious, against the policies of Basil II, who had managed to keep both factions under a strict and even despotic statist control at a time of unprecedented military and economic expansion: with his disappearance, and the relaxation of his policies in 1025, the two factions, suddenly freed from such artificial and anachronistic constraints, and long deprived of a share in the expansion in which they had participated, very soon became involved in a competition for supremacy.[67]

Because of the highly centralised administrative structure of the Byzantine state, which had been emphasised still further of late, the initial advantage in this competition was secured by the civil faction, that is by the Constantinopolitan bureaucracy, which with no great effort also appropriated to itself the dynastic loyalty towards the Macedonian dynasty, still formidable, particularly in the capital. The reign of Constantine IX is traditionally and correctly seen as being crucial: it was during his tenure of office (1042–55) that the military faction of the régime, thwarted and increasingly discriminated against by the metropolitan bureaucracy, began a belated attempt to realise the latent political power which it possessed. The attempt took the form of two serious revolts, both based upon the Balkans, by members of the military faction: George Maniaces (1043) and Leo Tornices (1047). Both, largely fortuitously, proved abortive, but that it had taken so long for such a reaction to manifest itself at all is in itself a comment upon the achievement of Basil II and the dominance of the capital.[68]

The brief succeeding reign, that of the only surviving member of the Macedonian dynasty, Theodora (1055–6), sustained by the dynastic loyalty and very little else,

[66] For the outlines of what follows, together with additional references: Vryonis, 'Byzantine Dēmokratia and the Guilds in the Eleventh Century', pp. 302–14. See now also: Lemerle, *Cinq études sur le XI^e siècle byzantin*, pp. 287–93.

[67] See above, pp. 136–8.

[68] For Tornices' rebellion, see above, p. 137.

provided a breathing-space, but that of her successor Michael VI (1056–7), who had formerly been an official of the bureau termed *stratiōtikon*, presumably *logothetēs*, and who was therefore securely identified with the civil faction, finally provoked the first successful military revolt, this time based upon Anatolia, for nearly a century. It seems clear that what actually provided the formal spark for the revolt was an uncompromisingly negative audience given to the senior military leaders by the emperor himself, on or about Easter Day (30 March) 1057.[69] According to Psellus,[70] the high-ranking military officers, and whoever had attained the rank of *stratēgos* and thus distinction, had come down into the City in the expectation of sharing in the generalised liberality of the régime. It is clear, and indeed directly affirmed, that they had come down to collect their annual *rhogai*, traditionally paid out in Holy Week – and, as it was the first such occasion of the reign, probably in the expectation of promotions and additional honours as well – and that it was this which provided a valid pretext for a general meeting which otherwise, in the highly-charged atmosphere of the time, would have reeked of treason.[71]

The successful revolt of Isaac Comnenus marked the triumph, however temporary it proved to be on this occasion, of the military faction of the dominant class, and in particular of its Anatolian section. It is clear from Psellus' account, the most complete and informed, if negatively slanted, that survives – for Psellus was a key member of the civil faction, who had managed to jettison Michael VI for Isaac I before jettisoning him for Constantine X – that the subsequent reign witnessed a marked reaction against a number of the policies adopted by the civil faction, and the complete reversal of others.[72]

One of the first things that Psellus reports of the reign of Isaac I is that, at what appears to have been some kind of audience with the senatorial order (*hē synklētikē taxis*), the emperor oppressed it with a fear that was not momentary (*deos ou ti brakhy tō synklētikō katalogō epeseisen*).[73] Attaliates also reports that Isaac cut off the gifts of *offikia* (*eita kai tas tōn offikiōn doseis autos perieteme prōtos*).[74] The combination, although not detailed, nevertheless represents the application of an unambiguous and consistent policy when placed in context.

It seems clear that, from the beginning of the second quarter of the eleventh century

69 Grumel, *La chronologie*, p. 255.

70 Michael Psellus, *Chronographia* VII.3; ed. Renauld, II, pp. 84–5. Cf. John Scylitzes, *Synopsis Historiarum*; ed. Thurn, p. 483.

71 George Cedrenus, *Historiarum Compendium*; Bonn edn, II, pp. 614–15: *Epei de ho kairos epestē tēs basilikēs philotimias, hēn dianemein etēsiōs kata ton kairon tou paskha pros tēn sygklēton eiōthasin hoi basileis, kai pantes eisēlthon hoi tou stratou hēgoumenoi kai genei kai andria ōnomasmenoi*. It was clearly at this stage that the episode involving Bryennius and Opsaras, and the payment of the troops of the theme of Anatolikon (see above, p. 191) took place, again confirming that both *stratēgoi* and *themata* were paid at this time of the year (see above, pp. 191–2).

72 On the sequence of great administrators, and on Psellus' somewhat ambivalent position within it, see: Lemerle, *Cinq études sur le XI^e siècle byzantin*, pp. 260–3.

73 Michael Psellus, *Chronographia* VII.47; ed. Renauld, II, pp. 112–13.

74 Michael Attaliates, *Historia*: Bonn edn, p. 61. See also above, pp. 228–9.

onwards, the population of Constantinople (variously described, but not infrequently termed *to dēmotikon plēthos*), and the members of the guilds (*syllogoi, hetaireiai, sōmateia, systēmata, banausoi*), more particularly their most senior members (*prostatai, prostateuontes, proestōtes, prōtostatai, primikērioi, exarkhoi*, etc.), had begun to play an increasingly significant rôle in political affairs.[75] The process was at first sporadic, and irregular, and is therefore very difficult to trace. It seems quite probable that the rise of the phenomenon was facilitated by the policies of Basil II, who did not need the vanquished rebel Bardas Sclerus to tell him to allow nobody in the armed forces to flourish overmuch (*kai mēdena tōn en strateiais ean pollōn euporein*),[76] who distrusted all his subjects,[77] and who surrounded himself with a body of picked men (*tina logada*), themselves not outstanding in intelligence (*oute tēn gnōmēn lamprōn*), nor remarkable for family (*oute mēn episēmōn to genos*), nor very much taught in letters (*oute ta es logous es to agan pepaideumenōn*), but to whom he entrusted imperial missives (*toutois kai tas basileious epistolas enekheirise*), and to whom he confided secret matters (*kai tōn aporrhētōn koinōnōn dietelei*).[78]

The creation of this picked body was to have significant consequences, for one of its members was almost certainly John the *orphanotrophos*, who was already powerful under Romanus III, who engineered the introduction of his brother Michael to the empress Zoë and was effectively head of the administration during Michael's reign, and who finally engineered the accession of his nephew Michael, first as caesar, then as junior emperor to Zoë. He is described by Psellus as a certain eunuch, who had been in the service of Romanus prior to his accession, who was of mean and contemptible status (*tēn men tykhēn phaulos kai katapeptōkōs*), but whom the emperor Basil had used very familiarly (*oikeiotata te ekhrēto*), and to whom he had confided secret matters (*kai ekoinōnei tōn aporrhētōn*), although not in a big way.[79]

The details of the two descriptions, the one of Basil's body of personal administrative assistants, the other of John's origins and early career, leave no real doubt as to the latter having belonged to the former: certainly he ran the administration in the same kind of ruthless, statist, fashion, as had his original mentor, specialising in state finances (*kai malista peri tas dēmosious syneisphoras oxytatos*).[80] What is clearly and interestingly indicated is that Basil had been prepared to seek his personal administrative assistants amongst the mercantile classes and the artisanate of the capital.[81] The eventual result was that the empire

[75] Refs: Vryonis, 'Byzantine Dēmokratia and the Guilds in the Eleventh Century', pp. 312–13.

[76] Michael Psellus, *Chronographia* I.28; ed. Renauld, I, p. 17.

[77] *Ibid.* I.29; ed. Renauld, I, p. 18.

[78] *Ibid.* I.30; ed. Renauld, I, p. 19.

[79] *Ibid.* III.18; ed. Renauld, I, pp. 44–5.

[80] *Ibid.* IV.12; ed. Renauld, I, p. 59.

[81] Clearly so as to counterbalance both the regional magnates and the traditional bureaucracy. The western comparison should not be taken too far, but all this does suggest a deliberate attempt to create something along the lines of a *ministerialis* class. Nothing could be further from the situation as it ended up under the Comneni; and even Psellus, who was himself of moderate birth only, is therefore predictably scathing of John's origins. See also below, p. 578, n. 106.

was, for a brief period (1034–42), ruled and administered by members of a family which originated at no great remove in precisely those classes.

When Michael V was deposed in 1042, it was not because of his origins – although they were remembered, and by implication used against him[82] – but because he had grossly misjudged his own position with regard to the formidable loyalty to the Macedonian dynasty still evidenced in the capital. In any case prior to, and in preparation for, his attempted deposition of Zoë he had found it politic to actively conciliate: 'The élite population of the City, and the crowd of the agora and the members of the craft-guilds (*ton d'apolekton tēs Poleōs kai hosoi tēs agoraiou tyrbēs ē tōn banausōn tekhnōn*)'. The attempt failed, and Michael was himself deposed by a rising seemingly largely planned and executed by 'those from the workshops (*hoi...epi tōn ergastēriōn*)', and 'the people of the agora (*to...agoraion genos*)' – that is, the membership of the guilds.[83]

The episode of 1042 represents the first occasion during the period in question on which the guilds and the artisanate are especially mentioned as having taken a significant and concerted part in major political events, but such action was to become increasingly common as the second half of the eleventh century proceeded. Although the reign of Constantine IX offers no specific mentions of such action, that of Michael VI provides a further crux.

Psellus commences his account of the reign of the latter emperor by remarking that to those who had just begun to exercise imperial office, it seemed necessary, for the establishment of their power, only to be acclaimed by the civil body (*to politikon genos*), as it was this alone with which they came into close contact. In reality, he continues, their security rested upon these three (i.e. the classic) foundations: the popular mass (*dēmotikō plēthei*), the senatorial order (*synklētikē taxei*), and the armed forces (*syntagmati stratiōtikō*); but for them, the third was the least of their cares, whilst it was upon the others that they lavished favours.[84]

It was this attitude that Michael exhibited, and actualised to an absurd degree: for he made excessive distributions of dignities (*ē prosēke tas tōn axiōmatōn dianemēseis pepoiēto*), not simply promoting from one grade to the next, but to up to five grades higher, and virtually on demand. And so his munificence was simply confusion (*kai ēn atekhnōs synkhysis to philotimon*).[85] Amongst the recipients of these dignities were, apparently, the ordinary citizens (*hoi politai*).[86] It was his refusal to extend this extraordinary munificence to the military that provided the formal spark for the rebellion that followed, although Psellus specifically remarks that from the first the rebels had wished to place the whole of the Roman empire under the military faction (*to stratiōtikon xympan to kratos Rhōmaiōn*

[82] George Cedrenus, *Historiarum Compendium*; Bonn edn, II, p. 537.

[83] Michael Psellus, *Chronographia* V.16, 25, 26; ed. Renauld, I, pp. 96, 102.

[84] *Ibid.* VII.1; ed. Renauld, II, p. 83.

[85] *Ibid.* VII.2; ed. Renauld, pp. 83–4.

[86] George Cedrenus, *Historiarum Compendium*; Bonn edn, II, p. 634. See also below, p. 574 and n. 90.

*hypopoiēsasthai*), to become the subjects of a general-emperor (*hypēkooi genesthai stratēgō autokratori*), and to terminate the civil succession to the empire (*kai tēn politikēn katalysai tēs basileias diadokhēn*), waiting only for the appearance of a candidate worthy of power (*eis arkhēn axiologōtatos*), who proved to be Isaac Comnenus.[87]

In the end, according to Psellus, it was certain seditious and turbulent individuals (*stasiōdeis andres kai tarakhōdeis*) who had infiltrated the senate (*tē synklētikē parentetrimmenous boulē*), who by creating confusion in the City, throwing the administration into disorder, and occupying the Great Church, effected the deposition of Michael.[88] The latter, up until the last moment, in negotiations with Isaac, had been claiming that he feared the popular mass and the senatorial order (*dedoika gar to te dēmotikon plēthos kai tēn synklētiken taxin*), which might not become party to the concessions that he was offering Isaac.[89]

Now although the precise identity of the seditious and turbulent individuals who had infiltrated the senate is nowhere stated by Psellus, there is not much doubt – in view of later developments – that they are to be identified as being amongst 'all of the most senior members of the guilds, and certain others of the humbler people (*hoi tōn hetaireiōn pantes arkhontes, kai tines alloi tōn aphanesterōn*)', who accompanied a group of *magistroi* and *patrikioi* to the Great Church, and who formed part of the gathering there (which also included the patriarch Michael Cerularius playing a typically ambivalent rôle), that decided upon and effected the deposition of Michael.[90] If this interpretation is correct, then it follows that some senior members of the guilds, at least, had gained entry into the senate by 1056–7.

There is in fact not much doubt but that, as is commonly the case, the situation goes back well into the reign of Constantine IX, of whom Psellus reports:

> Now there had been a scale of honour amongst the civil population (*taxin...tēs timēs en tō politikō dēmō*), and there had been imposed a rigid limit of promotion within it (*kai horou tinos epikeimenou ametathetou tēs anabaseōs*). But he [Constantine] demolished and removed this, and made virtually the whole of the population of the agora and the crowd eligible for the senate (*mikrou dein ton agoraion kai agyrtēn dēmon xympanta koinōnous tēs gerousias pepoiēke*). And it was not simply one or two who were so favoured, but forthwith, and at one fell swoop, everybody was transferred to a more splendid rank (*all' euthys apo mias phōnēs apantas eis tas hyperēphanous metenegkōn arkhas*).
>
> (Michael Psellus, *Chronographia* VI.29; ed. Renauld, I, p. 132)

Casual references in Psellus' minor works reveal that the emperor had decided no longer to rely on descent (*genealogia*) for the promotion of those forming the official body (*hoi en telei*), nor to rely on those of distinguished birth to fill the senate, public offices and other posts involving the law and administration (*tēn syglētikēn...boulēn kai ta tōn dēmosiōn arkheia kai hosa peri nomous te kai psēphismata*), but rather to rely on other considerations,

87 Michael Psellus, *Chronographia* VII.6; ed. Renauld, II, p. 86.

88 *Ibid.* VII.36; ed. Renauld, II, p. 106.

89 *Ibid.* VII.33; ed. Renauld, II, p. 104.

90 George Cedrenus, *Historiarum Compendium*; Bonn edn, II, pp. 634–7.

that is on those who provided satisfaction (*hoi eudokimoi*). A similar decision was made as regards the army, which may well have added to the discontent of the military magnates. It nevertheless seems clear that a formal distinction between the long-standing members of the senate, elected on the old grounds, and the more recent members, elected on the new, was preserved, for the latter are described as *astauroi te kai ablattoi* – that is, they were not permitted to wear decorations of crosses and borders upon their official tunics.[91]

It was therefore inevitable, given the ideological background of Isaac I, the manner of his accession, and the contemporary financial and political circumstances of the empire, that his reign should mark a sharp break with the policies not only of Michael VI, but also with those of a régime that had effectively been in power since 1025. Moreover, although brief in itself, the reign acts as a preview of the much longer one of his nephew, Alexius I, in at least one significant respect: the attitude taken towards the civil faction – that is, in this case, both the senate and the guilds.

The reign started well, with Isaac rewarding his supporters, and noticeably exhibiting generosity towards the public guilds (*dēmosioi syllogoi*). But once he had established his position, having appreciated the magnitude of the expenses of the state and of the salaries of the military (*to tōn analōmatōn tēs basileias kai tou opsōniou tōn stratiōtōn megethos*), and being aware of the great expense (*pollē dapanē*) of forthcoming wars,[92] the retrenchment of public finances became his overriding concern, leading him to extract what was owing from tax-payers, and to cancel and even claim back many of the generosities of preceding emperors, both where private individuals and monasteries were concerned, and even when protected by imperial chrysobull.[93] He seems to have demonstrated a particular hostility to the acts of his immediate predecessor, although if Psellus is accurate in his description of Michael's insensate munificence, it is difficult to see how this could have been avoided.[94] In any case, as mentioned above, he both caused fear in the senatorial order (which had been the chief beneficiary of imperial generosity for the last quarter-century), and cut off the gifts of *offikia*, a phrase probably indicating that he ceased to grant honorary membership of the various metropolitan and palatine *sekreta* to private individuals, thus entailing the state paying out annual *rhogai* to such members, but in return for no real service. It may well be that the guilds were chiefly affected by this latter measure, given the historic propensity of their members to seek such status-lending advancement.[95] In any case, according to Psellus, he began to be hated by the popular mass (*to dēmotikon plēthos*), and by a not inconsiderable portion of the army (*kai tōn stratiōtōn ouk oligon ti meros*), whose prosperity he had attacked.[96]

91 Refs: Lemerle, *Cinq études sur le XI^e^ siècle byzantin*, p. 290.

92 Michael Attaliates, *Historia*; Bonn edn, p. 60.

93 *Ibid.* p. 61.

94 Michael Psellus, *Chronographia* VII.60; ed. Renauld, II, p. 120.

95 See, for example, *argyropratai* and *trapezitai*: above, pp. 242–3, 244, 246; below, p. 584.

96 Michael Psellus, *Chronographia* VII.60; ed. Renauld, II, p. 120.

The premature – and still somewhat mysterious – abdication of Isaac in 1059 brought to the throne not a relative of Isaac, as might have been expected, but Constantine Ducas, who had previously held the high ranks of *vestarkhēs* and *proedros*, but whose actual earlier career remains obscure.[97] Constantine X began his reign with a dramatic gesture. It is clear that he favoured both the civil faction of the dominant class, and the mercantile classes and artisanate, and immediately upon his accession gathered together the metropolitan guilds (*ta sōmateia tēs poleōs*) and addressed them, subsequently honouring many of those from the agora and from the senate (*polloi tōn te tēs agoras kai tēs synklētou boulēs*),[98] promoting many of the senate and of the popular mass to higher grades of dignity (*pollous tōn tēs synklētou boulēs kai tou dēmōdous plēthous eis meizonas axiōmatōn bathmous proebibase*), and restoring personal honours (*tas oikeias timas*) to those from whom Isaac had taken them.[99]

The extraordinary nature of this gesture is further elaborated by Psellus:

> Then there began the putting into practice of his promises, and the performance of the two things that until then he had only proposed: the doing of good and the doing of justice. So, nobody of all those who came to him was unrecompensed – whether he was from amongst the dignitaries (*tōn en telei*), or from amongst those who were near to them in rank or far off from them, or even if he was from the guilds (*tōn banausōn*). Even the last gained a higher grade of dignity (*tous tōn axiōmatōn bathmous*), and moreover although up until then the citizen-body and the senatorial had remained separate (*kai diērēmenou teōs tou politikou genous kai tou synklētikou*), he removed the intervening barrier (*mesotoikhon*) and joined the two elements, thus transforming separation into unity.
>
> (Michael Psellus, *Chronographia* VII.15; ed. Renauld, II, p. 145)

Psellus is not entirely consistent in his accounts of the measures of Constantine IX and Constantine X, but what appears to have happened is that, whereas the former's preliminary measure created what was effectively an inferior class of senators, the latter's definitive one abolished the distinction between the two classes, and perhaps even extended senatorial eligibility. In any case, the measure finally abandoned an ideological position, and formally abrogated a consistent tradition, that had at least on occasion been the subject of legislation, stretching back into the later Roman period, and probably even further.[100] Moreover this, in combination with Constantine's clearly anti-military policies in other fields, can only further have weakened the position of the military faction, and indeed Psellus admits as much in mentioning that: 'with the dissolution of the military faction (*hoti tēs stratiōtikēs kataluomenēs meridos*)', enemy attacks became increasingly strong.[101]

[97] Polemis, *The Doukai, a Contribution to Byzantine Prosopography*, pp. 28–30 (no. 12).
[98] Michael Attaliates, *Historia*; Bonn edn, pp. 70–1.
[99] John Zonaras, *Annales* XVIII.8; Bonn edn, III, p. 674.
[100] See above, pp. 242–3.
[101] Michael Psellus, *Chronographia* VIII/Constantine Ducas 18; ed. Renauld, II, p. 146.

The next occasion on which the guilds and the populace are known specifically to have been involved in political action is the revolt which effected the desposition of Michael VII in favour of Nicephorus Botaniates, in 1078. The circumstances seem to have been remarkably similar to those obtaining during the revolt against Michael VI: first, a gathering in the Great Church, consisting of all the civil elements in the capital, including the patriarch and synod, picked members of the senate, the whole of the clergy, those of the agora, and the more prominent monks; then the acclamation of Nicephorus, an attack on the Great Palace, and the eventual capture and deposition of Michael.[102]

The sequel to these events was, apparently, even more dramatic than that which had followed the abdication of Isaac and the election of Constantine: Nicephorus III, who owed his entry into the City, and his position as emperor, to the several elements of the civil body, rewarded them handsomely. The scene is variously reported, at length and in detail, by several contemporary sources, emphasising its quite extraordinary nature. According to Attaliates, Nicephorus' munificence was: 'in dignities and in wholly admirable and magnificent honours, perpetual and constant; and in gifts and favours surpassing and overflowing (*to en axiōmasi kai timais peribleptois kai megaloprepesi diēnekes kai anendoton, kai to en dōrois kai kharismasi hyperpheron kai hyperekkhynomenon*)'. For the gift of a purse (*apodesmos*) of fifteen pounds (in weight) was a paltry thing; gifts of immoveable properties (*akinetai ktēseis*) were of one hundred pounds (in value), and sometimes twice or three times as much as that; and *offikia* of all kinds were poured out and lavished. Thus, imperial munificence was expressed in the gift not only of brilliant dignities (*perilamprois axiōmasi*), but also in that of *offikia*, estates (*agrois*), gold, and cast-off equipment (*aposkorakisei epēreiōn*), and everything that was desirable or useful. Nobody was refused anything, the church, particularly, being a beneficiary.[103] Attaliates then moves on to what was evidently the annual distribution of *rhogai*, held on Palm Sunday, 1 April 1078. The whole senate (*pasa...hē synklētos*), numbering thousands of men, had been convened, and all came forward, individually and by name, for great honours, being promoted by four or five grades, so that the *prōtovestiarios* told off by the emperor to receive the candidates and to call out the dignities was eventually overwhelmed and lost his voice.[104]

Bryennius, who is hostile to Nicephorus, is shorter and more scathing,[105] but Constantine Manasses, writing later, well after the establishment of the Comnenian dynasty, and therefore reflecting its social and political ideology, is the most splendidly savage of all:

> He [Nicephorus], mantled in garments glittering with gold, and dressed in gold-woven, pearl-bearing cloth, brilliant with purple-dyed blossoms and gold,...sat, raised up, on a silver-studded throne, adorning with dignities (*axiōmasi*) all who came forward: copper-smiths

[102] Michael Attaliates, *Historia*; Bonn edn, pp. 270–1.

[103] *Ibid.* pp. 273–4.

[104] *Ibid.* p. 275.

[105] See above, pp. 235–6.

(*khalkeis*), wood-cutters (*drytomous*), diggers (*skapheutas*), traders (*emporous*), farm-workers (*gaiomakhous*), boot-sellers (*krēpidopōlas*), rope-makers (*skhoinourgous*), fullers (*knapheis*), vineyard-workers (*ampelergatas*). He vulgarised the things that were precious, and defiled the things that were illustrious, in bringing down such glorious things to members of the guilds (*eis banausous*), which former emperors had given, as a reward for valour and for performing great deeds, and to those who were of blood (*ex aimatos*) and born of illustrious seed (*genous lamprosporou*).

(Constantine Manasses, *Breviarium Historiae*, 6701–10; Bonn edn, p. 285)

What, then, seems to have happened, during the course of the period in question, is that, with the death of Basil II in 1025, a power-vacuum occurred, and that after a brief intervening period of temporary arrangements, and by 1034, this had been filled by a eunuch former member of Basil's corps of low-born personal administrative assistants, utilising as a 'front' dynastic loyalty to the Macedonian dynasty, in combination with personnel from his own family, who naturally derived from the artisanate.[106] The 'flavour' of administration provided seems, as might have been expected, to have resembled that provided by Basil himself: that is statist, and reasonably indifferent with regard to sectional interest. This attempt at continuity in administration (with, at the same time, the implantation of a new dynasty) failed, and it was superseded from 1042 onwards by another pattern, this time combining dynastic loyalty and senatorial approval with extended personnel – that is, relying on a body that was inevitably overwhelmingly dominated by the court and by the civil administrations of the metropolitan *sekreta*, but in which the mercantile classes and the artisanate were for the first time represented.

Within a very few years of this change of emphasis, the military magnates of the regions made their first, and unsuccessful, counter-moves. The first, that of George Maniaces (1043), may be dismissed as the result of mere personal court-intrigue, but the second, that of Leo Tornices (1047), cannot be so dismissed, and Psellus' description of the rebel and his party amply demonstrates the hostility existing between the two factions of the

[106] Michael IV had previously been an *argyramoibos* (=*trapezitēs*): see above, p. 234. Michael V's father had been a ship-caulker (*kalaphatēs*): Michael Psellus, *Chronographia* IV.26; ed. Renauld, I, p. 69. Psellus, who does not actually utilise the technical term *kalaphatēs*, presumably as being too vulgar, is nevertheless very interesting, and typical, in his attitude to the father: he came from some God-forsaken hole at the back of beyond (*ēn gar ho patēr ek panerēmou tinos allēs eskhatias hōrēmonos*); he neither sowed nor planted (*gēn men oute speirōn oute phyteuōn*), for he was not in the slightest degree prosperous, and was not even a cattle-driver, goat-herd, or shepherd (*all'oude boukoliō epomenos ē poimniois epistatōn tōn ē agelaiokomōn*). Instead, he turned his attention to the sea (*epi de tēn thalattan trepsas ton noun*), but not for the purposes of trading or navigating (*oukh hōste emporeuesthai ē nautillesthai*), nor even for those of acting as a pilot for a fee (*misthos*). The man became something big in the ship-building line (*khrēma ti mega tē naupēgia*), but again, he did not cut or plane down the wood, nor was he involved in the construction (*ou dryotomōn oud' apoxeōn...oud' harmottōn...*), but rather he smeared with pitch what had already been constructed (*autos eu mala ta sympepēgmena tē pissē diekhrie*). The passage, of course, reveals more about Psellus' social attitudes than about the father's origins, but the hierarchically descending order of land-owning, sea-trading and manual-labouring, together with their various derivatives, is classic. Psellus, the metropolitan-born and -trained intellectual of 'bourgeois' origins, and reduced circumstances, is clearly reflecting the ideology of his social superiors but current associates: see below, pp. 584–6. See also above, p. 572, n. 81.

dominant class.[107] It is, in fact, quite remarkable that, between the accession of Constantine IX in 1042 and that of Alexius I in 1081, the sole occasion on which the military faction was able to impose its candidate upon the metropolis, and that candidate was able to impose distinctive and different policies upon the empire, is represented by the brief reign of Isaac I (1057–9), when an administration which was in immediate context reactionary, but which in the longer term might have proved relatively non-factional, seems to have obtained. This is, of course, not to claim that Isaac was the only emperor of the period who derived from the regional military. Of the two others, Romanus IV (1067–71) was married into the anti-military Ducas dynasty; was, although the effective, nevertheless technically not the senior emperor; and moreover was distracted by more immediately urgent matters than adjustments to the balance of the administration. Nicephorus III (1078–81) also seems, in his old age, to have been content to survive as long as possible without alterations to the administration.[108]

What, however, is significant of the period, and indeed unique in Byzantine history, is not merely the continuing conflict between the two factions of the dominant class, but also the clear emergence of a third element in the political structure, based upon the popular mass, and apparently headed by the members of the metropolitan guilds, the most senior of whom seemingly first infiltrated the senate as an exception, but then eventually, and quite contrary to tradition, were formally admitted into it as a norm.[109] More or less *pari passu* with this increase in social status, and doubtless causatively connected with it, went an increase in political power, with the popular mass, by way of the senior members of the guilds, taking part in the decision-making processes even where the election or deposition of emperors were concerned – and not simply informally and negatively as they had done on previous occasions, but to all appearances institutionally, as was perhaps the case with the deposition of Michael VI, and as was certainly the case (probably as a result of the measure of Constantine X mentioned above) with that of Michael VII. The populace, or at least the members of the guilds, seem also to have acquired certain military capacities and/or responsibilities in the defence of the City, although whether these were regular and institutionalised – that is, anything more than sporadic and informal only – remains uncertain.[110]

In any case, it is clear that the existence of the guilds as a separate and independently operating political entity was recognised by both factions of the dominant class. For the military, Cecaumenus offers the advice: 'Pay attention and be precise as to what goes on in the affairs of the City, so that nothing escapes you, but rather have agents on every

[107] See above, pp. 136–8.

[108] Nicephorus Bryennius, *Historiarum Libri IV*, anon.proem III. 25; ed. Gautier, pp. 55, 253.

[109] It may be doubted whether the earlier *argyropratai* who possessed what had theoretically been senatorial ranks were actually members of the senate: see above, p. 244.

[110] Refs: Vryonis, 'Byzantine Dēmokratia and the Guilds in the Eleventh Century', pp. 307, 308, 311. See also below, pp. 582–3.

side and everywhere in all the guilds, so that whenever something [*sc.* something political] is meditated, you learn of it.'[111]

To the civil faction, the operative centre of which was the metropolis itself, the popular mass and the guilds were, of course, even more immediately important, and it is clear that this faction, and the emperors who represented it, attempted to enter, and to a large degree succeeded in entering, into an alliance of political interest with them, and against what it regarded as the threat of the regional military. This alliance was procured, from the side of the emperor and the administration, by various measures which increased the wealth of all the metropolitan populace, and the social status of some. Unfortunately for the alliance, of course, there went, more or less *pari passu*, and undoubtedly connected with it, as Bryennius affirms directly, a financial crisis: at a time of decreasing public revenue, the state simply could not afford such increasing expenditure as was involved, and the contradiction eventually became so enhanced as to entail the dislocation of the financial structures of the state and the collapse of the monetary system.[112] Nor did the alliance hold consistently: Michael V, Michael VI and Michael VII were all deposed by bodies which included the popular mass and the members of the guilds, and it is clear from Psellus' account of the events of 1057 that the emperor, the administration, and most of the senior senators were – right up until the last moment – hoping to be able to come to some compromise arrangement with the rebel, but that they were simply pre-empted by the popular coup that effected the deposition of the emperor.[113]

Now, there seems little doubt, although it would be very difficult to prove from the textual evidence alone, that the increasing social and political rôle allotted to or assumed by the popular mass and the members of the guilds was itself a reflection of a corresponding increase in their economic base.[114] Nevertheless, two particular points, based on the textual evidence, very clearly suggest that such an increase was involved: the increasing political rôle of the urban population – interestingly enough combined with ecclesiastical involvement – was not confined to the metropolis; and a description of one instance of such an increased rôle, involving urban unrest, clearly suggests the underlying cause.[115]

In 1074, Isaac Comnenus, the elder brother of the future emperor Alexius and himself

111 Cecaumenus, *Stratēgikon* x; ed. Wassiliewsky and Jernstedt, p. 5.

112 See above, pp. 235–6.

113 Michael Psellus, *Chronographia* xv–xix, xxxiii; ed. Renauld, ii, pp. 91–4, 103–4. However ambivalent Psellus' position, and that of his companions, there is no good evidence that they were positively engaged in treason, and there is, rather, good evidence that they were taken by surprise by the coup.

114 It is nevertheless now clear that the prerequisite condition of a general expansion in the regional agricultural base was well under way by this date, and that it continued on into the twelfth century. This would have permitted, or even have encouraged, an appropriate degree of expansion in the urban economy, of which the Constantinopolitan was still clearly overwhelmingly the most lively and powerful. See: A. L. Harvey, 'The Growth of the Byzantine Rural Economy'.

115 For a textual commentary on, and further references to, what follows, see the footnotes to Nicephorus Bryennius, *Historiarum Libri IV* ii.28–9; ed. Gautier, pp. 200–6.

the future first *sebastokratōr*, was appointed *doux* of Antioch by the emperor Michael VII. Isaac found the affairs of the city so torn by civil strife (*kai tōn ekeise stasiasthentōn pragmatōn*) that the *magistros* Catacalon Tarchaneiotes, son of the recently deceased *doux* Joseph, had barely been able to control them. The city was divided into two: and one part had attached itself to the patriarch [Aemilianus[116]] and followed him faithfully, whilst the other favoured the chief citizens (*dikhē gar hē polis memeristo kai to men tō patriarkhē prosepoieito kai philiōs autō prosenēnekto, to de tous arkhontas etherapeuen*). Isaac had the patriarch removed from the city by a stratagem, and then exiled to Constantinople.[117] The patriarch's supporters (*hoi stasiastai*) rose: certain of those who had recently succeeded in advancing themselves, burning with envy, armed the masses against the dignitaries and the *doux* (*tōn gar arti prokoptein arxamenōn tines ekkauthentes hypo tou phthonou kata tōn en telei kai tou doukos to plēthos exōplisan*). Some blockaded the latter in the acropolis by closing off the entrances, whilst the remainder plundered the households of the chief citizens in the vicinity of the acropolis, seizing their wealth (*kai ton men eisō tēs akropoleōs sygkleisantes tas eisodous ephrouroun...hoi de loipoi pros tēn akropolin tas oikias tōn arkhontōn porthountes kai ta khrēmata diaprazontes*). Isaac, by now in a dangerous situation, reacted rapidly and ruthlessly, sending out messages into the surrounding cities for soldiers so as to reinforce his own, occupying the narrow streets (*stenōpa*) of the city, and arresting all who were found in them so as to prevent their regrouping. This being effected, there began a great slaughter of the Antiochene dissidents, and so the rising was utterly crushed (*Hou genomenou, synebē tōn Antiokheōn stasiastōn phonon polyn kai outō molis tēn stasin kateunasthēnai*).[118]

The details of this episode are, of course, and as usual, tantalisingly sparse and vague, although the mention of 'the growing agitation in the cities (*tas anaphyomenas tais polesi staseis*)' seems to imply that Antioch was not the only one affected.[119] The division in Antioch itself seems to have been between the *doux*, the dignitaries (*hoi en telei*) and the chief citizens (*hoi arkhontes*) on the one hand, and the mass (*plēthos*), led by 'those who had recently succeeded in advancing themselves', and who were 'burning with envy', on the other. It is difficult to see in the last anything other than some kind of emergent mercantile class and/or artisanate, which was as yet (unlike its metropolitan equivalent) deprived of social status and/or political power.

In 1078, Alexius Comnenus was himself asked by the then emperor Michael VII what line of action should be taken against the rising that had his deposition as its aim. Alexius

116 Clearly an interesting political and social figure: he was also present at, and played a leading part in, the later gathering in the Great Church that resulted in the deposition of Michael VII – Nicephorus Bryennius, *Historiarum Libri IV* III.18; ed. Gautier, p. 245: *anēr panourgos homou kai drastērios kai dēmon pros ataxian kinēsai eiper tis allos kai dynamenos kai boulomenos*. See also: Michael Attaliates, *Historia*; Bonn edn, p. 270 – *proexarkhontos toutois kai autou tou patriarkhou theoupoleōs megalēs Antiokheias 'te basilidi endiatribontos'*.

117 Nicephorus Bryennius, *Historiarum Libri IV* II.28; ed. Gautier, pp. 201–5.

118 *Ibid.* II.29; ed. Gautier, pp. 205, 207.

119 *Ibid.* II.29; ed. Gautier, p. 205.

replied that the greater part of the assembled mass was unwarlike, composed of members of the guilds, and would not stand the sight of fully-armed men prepared for battle (*Ephēse gar hōs tou synathroisthentos plēthous to pleiston apolemon te esti kai banauson kai ouk an hypostaien kathōplismenous andras idontes kai pros makhēn etoimous*). He therefore observed that it was necessary to arm the imperial Varangian guards, and to send them under a general against the rioters. The emperor demurred and, on being pressed by Alexius, reproached him for his savagery (*ōmotēs*) and announced his intention to abdicate.[120]

Both these incidents, that of 1074 and that of 1078, represented the reactions or proposed reactions of members of the military faction of the dominant class when confronted with urban disorder based on popular discontent with the prevalent social or political régime and led by members of the mercantile or artisan classes, and they compare interestingly with the reaction of the emperor himself, essentially a figure of the civil faction, when confronted with the same phenomenon. The military reactions also provide an interesting and significant insight into the course of the revolt of the Comneni in 1081, and the policies pursued during the subsequent reign of Alexius himself (to 1118).

### D. *The military reaction* (*Comnenian dominance, 1081–1204*)

It is quite clear that the actual decision to revolt was taken by the Comneni inside Constantinople itself, however long the possibility had been considered.[121] The first major action that they took, apart from sending their womenfolk into sanctuary, was to flee the City and make for their estates in Thrace, evidently somewhere in the region of Adrianople/Tzurulum.[122] This suggests that they had no great degree of support in the City itself, even if Anna reports that the mass (*plēthos*), which admired Alexius' audacity (*hormē*) and shrewdness (*agkhinoia*), composed a song (*asmation*) in his honour on the occasion.[123] Having collected their supporters and attracted a heterogeneous army, and having acclaimed Alexius emperor, they advanced on the City.[124] The then emperor, Nicephorus III, had meanwhile manned the walls, and whilst Alexius and the caesar John Ducas were reconnoitering them, the defenders jeered at the latter, calling him 'the abbot', and adding certain insolent and mocking words, again not suggesting any great popular enthusiasm.[125] The Comneni eventually penetrated the City by persuading not the native troops but the chief of the German mercenaries to betray a bastion on the outer wall to them. Anna mentions little of the defenders in the locality other than this,[126] but Zonaras revealingly mentions that the defenders of the inner wall included members of

[120] *Ibid.* III.20–1; ed. Gautier, pp. 247, 249.
[121] Anna Comnena, *Alexiad* II.3.1–4.9; ed. Leib, I, pp. 69–75.
[122] *Ibid.* II.5.1–6.10; ed. Leib, I, pp. 75–84.
[123] *Ibid.* II.4.9; ed. Leib, p. 75.
[124] *Ibid.* II.7.1–8.5; ed. Leib, I, pp. 84–90.
[125] *Ibid.* II.9.1–3; ed. Leib, I, pp. 90–1.
[126] *Ibid.* II.9.4–11.7; ed. Leib, I, pp. 91–8.

the general masses, or rather of the party from the agoras and the popular mass (*hoi pleiones adaeis ē mallon ex agoraiōn athroisthentes kai plēthyos dēmotidos*), who soon fled.[127] Again, Anna mentions little in detail of the looting and outrages that then followed,[128] whilst Zonaras mentions that the Comnenian military hauled down some members of the senatorial assembly from their mules, and stripped them of their clothes, leaving them half-naked and on foot in the middle of the streets (*kai hosois de tēs gerousias synēntōn, kataspōntes tōn hēmionōn autous, enious de ge kai apondyontes, en mesais tais agyiais eiōn hēmigymnous te kai pezous*).[129]

The quite definite impression is thus gained that, on the one hand, the urban population at least did not support the Comneni, and on the other, that the Comnenian party had a particular animus at least against the senatorial body. Again, Nicephorus, like Michael, not wishing there to be a civil war (Anna says that he 'pretended' not to want one – *eskhēmatizeto mē thelein emphylion genesthai polemon*), first attempted to make terms, and then, on the advice of the patriarch, abdicated.[130]

The party was, in more ways than one, over, and some forty years after the first major attempt by the military faction to wrest political power and control from the civil one, it had definitively succeeded. The reign that followed was, in many – even perhaps in most – respects, a highly successful one, particularly as regards foreign affairs and the recovery of the most valuable items of territory that had been lost; the re-establishment of internal political stability; the reorganisation of the military forces; the reconstruction of the fiscal administration and its mechanisms; and so on.[131] It cannot be disguised, however, that in some respects it was also a profoundly reactionary one – whether as regards culture, in the fields of intellectual enquiry and literature;[132] or whether as regards social structures, in the relations between the three main elements of which the existence has been noted above. Even in the fundamental reform of the coinage, undertaken in 1092/3, one might without difficulty detect the concept of a 'return to sound money'.[133]

Although the evidence is, as usual, sparse, there seems no doubt that Alexius was hostile to both the senate and the mercantile classes and artisanate, and that moreover this hostility was reflected in the policies that he actually implemented: his own ideological prejudices in this regard may well have been accentuated by the nature and events of his successful *coup d'état*. According to Zonaras, Alexius – like Isaac before him, for the two reigns, however disparate in length, betray a number of close similarities – cancelled many of his predecessor's acts. Lacking money at the commencement of his reign, he both cut

[127] John Zonaras, *Annales* XVIII.20; Bonn edn, III, p. 728.
[128] Anna Comnena, *Alexiad* II.10.4; ed. Leib, I, pp. 94–5.
[129] John Zonaras, *Annales* XVIII.20; Bonn edn, III, pp. 728–30.
[130] Anna Comnena, *Alexiad* II.11.7–12.6; ed. Leib, I, pp. 98–101.
[131] See above, pp. 108–31, 235 and n. 86.
[132] On this, see now: L. Clucas, *The Trial of John Italos and the Crisis of Intellectual Values in Byzantium in the Eleventh Century*, pp. 95–102.
[133] See above, pp. 513–17.

off the annual gifts (*etēsias doseis* = *rhogai*) that traditionally derived from dignities (*axiōmata*), which, in view of the policies of the preceding régime, would have hit precisely those classes mentioned above, and also confiscated the property of senators (*tōn synklētikōn ousias*).[134] Again, in summarising Alexius' qualities and policies, the same author remarks that he did not treat the senate with honour, nor did he place any trust in it, as was appropriate, but rather sought zealously to humiliate it (*kai tous tēs synklētou boulēs oute timēs hēs ekhrēn ēxiou oute pronian autōn etitheto kata to analogon, mallon mentoi kai espeuse tapeinōsai toutous*).[135]

A Novel of Alexius I, dated to a sixth indiction (and therefore 1082/3, 1097/8, or 1112/13),[136] concerns a court case between a certain Anna, wife of Michael Paidianites who was involved in business affairs (i.e. was a *pragmateutēs*), and Theophanes Pyrrhos and Leo Plakanos, the former of whom held the senatorial dignity of *anthypatos*, which earlier at least may have rated a considerable annual *rhoga* of 8 lb,[137] and both of whom were also involved in business affairs. The Novel, in other words, involves precisely that section of the mercantile classes that had benefited most from the measures of Constantine IX and Constantine X waiving the distinction between senate and guilds, and that largely thereby seems to have acquired institutionalised social status and political clout. Anna's two opponents, when required to take the oath, had demanded to do so in their households (*oikoi*), rather than in public (*dēmosia*), as they were senators (*synklētikoi*), a privilege which Anna contested as they were also involved in business affairs. The problem was therefore referred to the emperor. The whole Novel has something of the air of being a put-up job. But in any case, Alexius ruled that while it was right (*khreōn*) for senators to take the oath in their households, it was not so for those who were also formally enrolled in a guild (*tous mē eis systēma katagegrammenous*), it being subject to the prefect (*hypokeimenon tō eparkhō*), so as to preserve the greatness of the dignity (*alla to tou axiōmatos phylattontas megethos*). For (ordinary) individuals involved in business affairs, or wishing to be so involved, were not permitted to take the oath thus. Those who had chosen to enjoy the profit of business affairs (*to tēs pragmateias...kerdos*) were therefore to take the oath publicly, just as those did who did not enjoy the dignity (*kathaper tous mēdenos tetykhēkotas axiōmatos*).

In other words, Alexius, whilst not rescinding the measure of Constantine X (to whom, of course, he was related by marriage), nevertheless deprived it of what must have been one of its most desirable elements: the conferring of social status by means of the granting of outward privilege. He therefore reverted to the preliminary position adopted by Constantine IX.[138] The whole Novel is, in its way, and perhaps particularly in the phrases 'so as to preserve the greatness of the dignity' and 'the profit of business affairs', so very

[134] John Zonaras, *Annales* XVIII.20; Bonn edn, III, pp. 731, 733.

[135] *Ibid.* XVIII.29; Bonn edn, III, p. 766.

[136] Alexius I, Novel 'Peri tou tous systēmatikous kai pragmateutas mē oikoi omnyein', in Zepoi, *Ius Graeco-Romanum* I, at pp. 645–6. Grumel, *La chronologie*, p. 256.

[137] See above, p. 185, Table 4.

[138] See above, pp. 574–5.

similar to the much earlier 'so that in this way every honour and position of public service may be isolated from contagion'.[139] It is therefore redolent of the ideological standpoint of the regional-based military aristocracy, now triumphant, towards the urban milieu and, in this case, towards the mercantile classes: one of basic contempt. What is also interesting is the reference to the guilds being subject to the prefect, and this, together with the mention of *The Book of the Prefect* in Manuel's Novel LV of 1148,[140] clearly implies that they were still subject – or possibly even had been re-subjected – to the prefect and to his regulation, at least well on into the twelfth century, and therefore in theory at least probably right on up until 1204.

The only other major piece of evidence with regard to relations between the new régime and the urban milieu derives from Anna's account of the so-called Anemas conspiracy.[141] This latter seems to have been potentially one of the more dangerous, because broader-based than most, of the numerous conspiracies that threatened the life and position of Alexius. It was effectively headed by the four eponymous Anemas brothers, but was supported by others of the aristocracy (*heteroi tōn eugenōn*): the Antiochi, the so-called Exazeni, Constantine Ducas and Nicephorus Hyaleas; Nicetas Castamonites; Curticius; and George Basilacius. Such were those heading the military list (*tou stratiōtikou katalogou prōteuontes*). From the senate (*tēs de ge synklētou*) there was a certain John Solomon, who was of the foremost ranks of the senatorial body (*tēs synklētou logados ta prōta*), and because of his extraordinary wealth and illustrious birth (*dia ploutou periousian kai genous lamprotēta*), Michael Anemas had quite hypocritically offered him the throne if the conspiracy were successful. From the senatorial side there were also Sclerus and (Bardas) Xerus, who had recently filled the office of Prefect of the City.

Now, in the first place, Solomon is depicted – certainly in contrast to the military members of the conspiracy, and surely significantly – as a buffoon, small in stature and light in intelligence (*brakhytatos men ēn tēn hēlikian, kouphotatos de tēn gnōmēn*); falsely convinced of his expertise in Aristotelian and Platonic doctrines; naïve (*haplotēs*), and apparently given to promising future dignities (*axiōmata*) indiscriminately in order to attract support. This is, in other words, Anna and the stereotyped senator.[142]

In the second place, there is an apparent contradiction in the evidently widespread participation of members of both the military aristocracy and the senatorial order in the same conspiracy (although not unprecedented, and no matter that the former was attempting to use and dupe the latter).[143] The contradiction is, however, apparent only, and not actual, for two very good reasons, one general and one particular.

[139] See above, p. 242.

[140] See above, p. 258 and n. 5.

[141] Anna Comnena, *Alexiad* XII.5.4–6.9; ed. Leib, III, pp. 69–75.

[142] For Solomon, see also: Anna Comnena, *Alexiad* V.9.2; ed. Leib, II, p. 37 – interestingly enough, Solomon proves to have been a member of the Ducas/Italus circle, which will also not have endeared him to Anna. For this, see above, p. 583 and n. 132.

[143] See, for example, the abortive coup against Constantine X in 1059 – refs: Vryonis, 'Byzantine Dēmokratia and the Guilds in the Eleventh Century', pp. 310–11.

As to the general, Zonaras himself mentions[144] that Alexius did not treat all members of the military aristocracy equally well, and doubtless, by this stage of the reign, it had become apparent that only members of the imperial clan, based upon the Ducas–Comnenus alliance, together with a restricted number of other blood- or marriage-relationships, could expect the kind of quasi-imperial treatment that Zonaras[145] percipiently regards as characteristic of the new régime. Resentment might therefore well be expected consequent upon such a realisation.

As to the particular, the dating of the conspiracy is all-important. This is in fact difficult to effect, but *c.* 1106–7 has been suggested, and must be at least approximately correct.[146] It was precisely in the indictional year 1106/7 (= ind. 15)[147] that the fiscal reforms of Alexius, embodied in the *Nea Logarikē*, and involving a marked and universal increase in the rate of land taxation, should have begun to take effect:[148] this was therefore above all the time at which the interests and resentments of both the neglected military and the upper ranks of the senate, both of which must have been land-based, would have coincided.

It is not really known, and it is not discoverable within a short compass, what precisely the attitudes of the second and third emperors of the Comnenian dynasty, John and Manuel, towards the senate, and the guilds and popular mass, actually were. On the one hand, both had been brought up largely in the various metropolitan palaces where, as Psellus points out, they would have had some kind of contact at least with the various aspects and classes of the urban milieu, and one might therefore expect them to be somewhat less rigid than Alexius in this respect. On the other, as both Anna Comnena and Constantine Manasses were writing under Manuel, it is clear that the same ideological standpoint as prevailed under Alexius was then still flourishing, even if it were not actually prevalent. None of these bodies seems to have played more than a ceremonial rôle, whether political or otherwise, during the long period stretching from the accession of Alexius (1081) to the death of Manuel (1180), and the fact that quite shortly afterwards all reappear to a greater or lesser extent in the rôles that they are previously known to have occupied suggests that they were kept firmly under control during the period.

The reign of Andronicus I (1182/3–5) seems to have marked a watershed. It seems clear that he had decided and interesting views on precisely this kind of subject – probably as much in reaction to the views of his predecessors as anything else. The whole problem has, however, suffered from attempts to analyse it in the crude and now conceptually

[144] John Zonaras, *Annales* XVIII.29; Bonn edn, III, p. 767: *tois de loipois tōn eu gegonotōn oukh homoian enedeiknyto tēn proairesin.* As Zonaras has been dealing with the Comnenian relatives, the remainder of the military aristocracy is implied.

[145] *Ibid.* XVIII.21, 29; Bonn edn, III, pp. 731–3, 767.

[146] Dölger, *Regesten der Kaiserurkunden des oströmischen Reiches von 565–1453* I.2, p. 50. The doubts expressed on this date by P. Gautier ('Le synode des Blachernes (fin 1094). Étude prosopographique', pp. 224–5, n. 34) seem unjustified.

[147] Grumel, *La chronologie*, p. 256.

[148] Hendy, *DOS* XII, pp. 53, 55–6.

archaic terms of simple class-warfare, based upon modern conditions, and it is not proposed to re-examine it here.[149] The reign of Isaac II (1185–95) was initiated by a popular uprising against Andronicus, and it was therefore inevitable that, whatever Isaac's own ideological views were, the realities of the situation had changed fundamentally, and that his behaviour was dictated by them.[150]

It was towards the end of the reign of Andronicus, in an ambience dominated by the increasing unpopularity of the emperor, and by the taking of Thessalonica by the Normans and their subsequent advance upon the capital, that the senate, under Leo Monasteriotes, who was a judge (*kritēs tou bēlou*), and apparently also its president (*stoma tēs synklētou*), once more began to adopt a positive rôle.[151] Again, it was during the immediately succeeding period that it is remarked that those in the streets and agoras, money-changers, and linen-dealers, in other words members of the professional guilds, were purchasing such *axiōmata* as the rank of *sebastos*; that clothes-makers, stable-lads, brick-makers and blacksmiths were purchasing entry into the armed forces; and that one money-changer, Kalomodios, was thought worth fleecing by members of the court.[152] Finally, after a full century (1081–1181/2) during which no major outbreaks of urban violence are reported, there ensued a twenty-year period (1181/2–1204) during which a number of them are.[153] In other words, the distinct impression is gained that a process of development that had earlier been under way, and that had then been interrupted, was now being resumed.

It is frequently claimed that the metropolitan mercantile classes and artisanate of the twelfth century were in a state of economic depression, the cause generally assigned to that depression being competition from the Latins, that is in effect from the representatives of the Italian trading states of Venice, Genoa, and Pisa.[154] Even on a general plane this is implausible, for there is good reason to believe that the economic expansion that had marked the eleventh century had continued into, and may actually have reached its apogee in, the twelfth, and there is no good reason why Byzantine merchants and artisans should not have enjoyed the fruits of that expansion.[155] Moreover, on a more particular plane, whereas no good evidence has been adduced for the case for depression, there is such evidence for that for prosperity. In addition to the several western descriptions of

149 Refs: Brand, *Byzantium Confronts the West*, pp. 324–5 n. 18 (with particular reference to the work of Siuziumov).

150 Brand, *Byzantium Confronts the West*, pp. 70–3.

151 Nicetas Choniates, *Historia*; ed. van Dieten, 1, pp. 312–13.

152 See above, pp. 243 (purchase of *axiōmata*), 245 (Kalomodios). Nicetas Choniates, *Historia*; ed. van Dieten, 1, pp. 208–9. For the latest discussion of the last passage: P. Lemerle, *The Agrarian History of Byzantium from the Origins to the Twelfth Century. The Sources and Problems*, pp. 230–6.

153 Brand, *Byzantium Confronts the West*, pp. 83–4 (1187), 118 (1195), 121–2 (1197–1200), 122–4 (1201), 246–7, 248, 250 (1204).

154 E.g. Brand, *Byzantium Confronts the West*, pp. 6–7, 8–9.

155 Hendy, 'Byzantium 1081–1204: An Economic Reappraisal', pp. 31–52. See also: P. Tivchev, 'Sur les cités byzantines au XI^e–XII^e siècles', *Byzantinobulgarica* 1 (1962), pp. 145–82. Tivchev is concerned less with the metropolis than with the regions, but the same phenomenon is clearly evident there. His treatment is still the best available, being much less obsessed with 'Latin competition' and 'decline' than is usual.

metropolitan wealth and prosperity that have already been quoted,[156] there exist two more sources, this time Byzantine ones: the works of John Tzetzes, and – much more important – of Theodore Prodromos.

Tzetzes, in fact, merely remarks[157] amusingly on the immensely cosmopolitan nature of twelfth-century Constantinopolitan life, and mentions that he is able to speak (however formulaically, as it turns out) in seven languages, and then continues the theme by giving examples, transliterated into Greek, of the formulaic phrases that he knows in these languages – from the *dobra denē* of the Russian, through the *salamalek* of the Scythian (Pecheneg/Cuman), to the *bene benesti* of the Latin (Italian). The passages involved not only demonstrate the ethnic complexity of what basically must have been the commercial life of the metropolis, but also place the Latin element in its appropriate context – because of course, owing to the historical accident of documentary survival, one tends to receive a much over-accentuated impression of the Latin rôle in Byzantine commercial life.

Prodromos, as *Ptōkhoprodromos*,[158] is in the long run, and when properly analysed and commented upon, potentially capable of providing an equally amusing mine of information on twelfth-century Constantinopolitan life – whether on matters of imperial ideology, or on much more mundane ones of housing, clothing, diet, or trades and professions – and, moreover, is couched in a vulgarising language that is linguistically of the greatest interest. The work takes the form of four main poems, each involving the complaint of a stock character: the husband of a nagging wife who married beneath herself; the father of a family of thirteen; the run-of-the-mill young monk; and the scholar or secretary. Each is basically on the theme of the poverty of the particular character, and of the wealth of pretty well everybody else, and all represent an elaborate method of begging from Prodromos' patrons (the emperors John and Manuel, and a *sebastokratōr*).

The information, even solely as regards the themes that have been treated in the chapters preceding this, is enormous: gold hyperpyra, electrum trachea (*manoēlata*/*manolata*), billon trachea (*stamena*) and billon/copper tetartera (*tartera*) are all in normal circulation;[159] wine (*krasin*) comes from Varna, Ganos, Lesbos, Chios, Samos, Crete, and

[156] See above, pp. 561–2.

[157] Refs: Vryonis, 'Byzantine Dēmokratia and the Guilds in the Eleventh Century', pp. 291–2, n. 9.

[158] It is immaterial to the present case as to whether Prodromos himself was the author of these poems: all that matters is that there should be a later twelfth-century basis to them, and this, on the monetary – and other – evidence, there most certainly is. The following analyses are very preliminary ones only: variant mss give many other origins, and some, but by no means all, may represent much later accretions.

[159] Theodore Prodromos, *Carmina* III, IV; ed. Hesseling and Pernot, pp. 48–83; see III, p. 51 l. 75, IV, p. 74 l. 12 (*perpyra*/*hyperpyra*); III, p. 68 l. 407, IV, p. 74 l. 12 (*manoēlata*); III, p. 64 l. 341, IV, p. 75 ll. 51, 52, p. 77 l. 91 (*stamena*); IV, p. 76 l. 83, p. 77, l. 91 (*tartera*). This last should finally put paid to any notion that tetartera were not in normal circulation in the capital, and doubtless amongst them were metropolitan issues – see above, p. 515 and n. 335.

other uncertain places;[160] cheese (*tyrin*) comes from Vlachia (presumably Thessaly) and Crete, apparently in large part through the agency of the Venetians;[161] cherries (*kerasia*) come from Leucate;[162] cucumbers (*tetraggoura*) come from Pegae;[163] raisins come from Chios;[164] and so on.

Of more immediate interest in the present context, however, is Prodromos' enumeration of craftsmen (the *banausoi* of the preceding period), which is as follows:[165]

Gold cloth-maker (*tekhnitēs khrysorrhaptēs*)
Boot-maker (*tsaggarēs*)
Clothes-maker (*rhaptikēs*)
Baker (*magkipos*)[166]
Yoghourt-seller (*oxygalatas*)[167]
Dyer (*katablattas*)
Weigher (*sēkōtēs*)[168]
Embroiderer (*kentēklas*)
Pepper-grinder (*piperotriptas*)
Butcher (*makellarēs*)[169]
Sieve-maker (*koskinas*)

All of these, Prodromos describes as being vastly better-off than himself – a man of education – and makes his point largely by describing the various foods that they can afford and that, by implication, he cannot.

It is clear that the whole situation is outrageously 'camped-up' by Prodromos, and that the wealth of each craftsman and the foods and so on that he is therefore credited

[160] Theodore Prodromos, *Carmina* III; ed. Hesseling and Pernot, pp. 48–71 – see p. 55 l. 156 (*khiōtikon*); p. 59 l. 260 (*khiōtikon*); p. 60 l. 285 (*ganitikon, krētikon, samion* – other mss add *mitylēnaion*); p. 62 l. 312 (*khiōtikon*); p. 62 l. 313 (*barniōtikon*). That from Chios seems to be favourite. See also above, p. 51.

[161] *Ibid.* III, IV; ed. Hesseling and Pernot, pp. 48–83 – see III, p. 52 l. 98 (*krētikon*); III, p. 53 l. 109 (*epi tous benetikous*), III, p. 58 ll. 181, 182 (*krētikon, blakhikon*); IV, p. 75 l. 52 (*blakhikon*).

[162] *Ibid.* II; ed. Hesseling and Pernot, p. 44 l. 65b (*ek ton leukatēn*).

[163] *Ibid.* p. 44 l. 65c (*pēgatika*).

[164] *Ibid.* III; ed. Hesseling and Pernot, p. 60 l. 283 (*khiōtikas*). Something appears to have come from Kitros (*loc. cit.* – *kai apo to dia kitrou*), but it is unclear as to what it was. The port was, however, much frequented by Venetian merchants: Martin, 'Venice and the Byzantine Empire before the Fourth Crusade', p. 95.

[165] *Ibid.* IV; ed. Hesseling and Pernot, pp. 72–83 – p. 74 l. 23 (*tekh. khrys.*); p. 75 ll. 43, 45, p. 76 ll. 74, 79, 84 (*tsaggarēs*); p. 77 l. 90 (*rhaptikēs*); p. 77 l. 97 (*magkipos*); p. 77 l. 109 (*oxygalatas*); p. 78 l. 114 (*katablattas/sēkotēs*); p. 78 ll. 121, 124, 125, 127, 129 (*kentēklas/piperotriptas*); p. 82 ll. 232, 234 (*makellarēs*); p. 78 l. 130 (*koskinas*).

[166] For the guild: 'Leo VI', *To Eparkhikon Biblion* XVIII; ed. Nicole, pp. 53–5.

[167] This seems to be the most plausible general translation: the yoghourt-sellers, with yokes and pendant pans, still come into the City, mainly (so they claim) from Silivri, signalling their progress on their rounds by means of bells and cries. The fact that in this case the yoghourt is beaten, however, suggests that what is particularly involved is effectively *ayran*, the drink made with yoghourt beaten up to a froth in water.

[168] This, again, seems the most plausible translation. For the *zygostatai*, see above, pp. 317–18.

[169] For the guild: above, pp. 562–4.

as being able to afford and consume, cannot be taken – and were probably not intended to be taken – literally, but it is nevertheless unlikely that the author would have made so much of the point had the twelfth-century craftsmen not been at least moderately prosperous, and *a fortiori* had they formed a depressed class.

Now, if the analysis formulated above is anywhere near correct, it will mean that the metropolitan mercantile class and artisanate, after several centuries of apparent stability, but at a fairly low level in economic, political and social terms, then, between *c.* 1040 and 1081, reflecting the general economic expansion of the time, increasingly came to acquire both a certain degree of formal and a considerable degree of informal political power, and moreover a certain social status as well. In other words, they began to break out of the constraints hitherto imposed upon them by the prevailing ideology of the dominant class and by the mechanisms of the state. This period of development was brought to an abrupt end in 1081 with the reimposition of these constraints, and while there is some real evidence of subsequent prosperity, there is no evidence that the constraints were relaxed before *c.* 1181/2, when political circumstances permitted a resumption of the whole process. This resumed evolution will presumably itself have been shattered by the events of 1203/4, and by the imposition of an alien régime which was overwhelmingly dominated by a hostile mercantile state. For a full century, between 1081 and *c.* 1181/2, therefore, at precisely what otherwise might have been – and elsewhere (for example in the west) certainly was – a critical stage of their development, the urban classes were effectively held static, or at least were permitted to develop only within rigidly defined economic, political and social parameters.[170]

The Byzantine mercantile class and artisanate, of which the metropolitan element inevitably formed overwhelmingly the greater part, was thus not depressed or killed off by Latin competition, but simply never evolved beyond a certain point, not being permitted to do so by nature of the prevalent ideology of the dominant class, and by the existence and operation of such state mechanisms as were capable of imposing that same ideology.

### E. *The Latin investment (its size and rôle, 992–1204)*

The constricted nature of the Byzantine mercantile class at a critical stage of its evolution nevertheless may well have permitted and even favoured the penetration of the economy

[170] For a recent analysis of the development of the western economy, identifying the period *c.* 1050–1180 as one of critical preparatory growth, with a point of take-off being reached in *c.* 1180, see: G. Duby, *The Early Growth of the European Economy. Warriors and Peasants from the Seventh to the Twelfth Century*, pp. 157–270. Although it will not appeal to the parochialism of Byzantinists, there are nevertheless strong resemblances between the general course of eastern and western economic development: the crucial distinction is that, between *c.* 1080 and 1180, the further economic and social development of the Byzantine mercantile classes was politically blocked, and that by the time this blockage was removed, it was too late to recover lost ground.

by Latin merchants, and of course particularly by Venetian ones, this factor being in the long term possibly quite as important as the imperial concession of favourable rates for the *kommerkion*. Even so, there is little doubt that the nature of contemporary Latin penetration, and even more its actual scale and impact upon the economy as a whole, and the fiscal system in particular, has been much misunderstood and exaggerated.

To judge from the twelfth-century documentation, the predominant, though not the only, pattern of trade involved Latin – or at least Venetian – merchants importing into the empire, or picking up at their first major port of call within the empire, mainly primary products, whether agricultural or pastoral items such as oil or cheese, or raw materials such as timber or copper, but also extending to linen cloth. These were then transported to Constantinople and were there sold off as a contribution towards the essentially insatiable demands made by the provisioning of the capital.[171]

Any suggestion that the magnate classes particularly profited from this exchange, because they could unload their surplus products onto Latin merchants, and, therefore, that they were, for example, a major force behind the Veneto-Byzantine treaty of the early 1080s, is most implausible.[172] In the first place, as seen above, the magnate classes preferred to accumulate rather than to exchange, and when they did sell off their surplus they preferred to do so directly by means of their own agents and ships. In the second, the suggestion assumes, on behalf of the magnate classes, a modern awareness of the possibilities of commercial profit, and of the need to subordinate political considerations to economic ones; and on behalf of the Latin merchants, a commercial capacity to respond virtually immediately to such a policy; neither of which assumptions is remotely plausible in an ancient or mediaeval context. The overwhelming burden of the evidence is that Alexius granted the concessions involved in the treaty because of current or past naval aid given him by the Venetians against the Normans, as a matter of political necessity, and for no other reason whatsoever. It may well be, of course, that he found it far less difficult to grant such a privileged status to Venetians than he would have done to grant it to his own native mercantile class, but such a contradiction is common enough.

In any case, the distinct impression is gained that incoming cargoes, at least from the west, tended to be less valuable than outgoing ones, the difference being made up in precious metals, and the same pattern had already been implied in the case of Russian merchants in the tenth century.[173]

171 Martin, 'Venice and the Byzantine Empire before the Fourth Crusade', pp. 98–101. For cheese, see above, p. 589 and n. 161.

172 As for example most recently developed by A. R. Gadolin, in 'Alexis I Comnenus and the Venetian Trade Privileges. A New Interpretation', *Byzantion* 50 (1980), at pp. 440–4. The article is execrable. If there was an increase in trade between Byzantium and the west during the twelfth century, as indeed there almost certainly was, it will have been only partly as a result of this and other treaties, and will even in this respect have been fortuitous. See: Hendy, 'Byzantium 1081–1204: An Economic Reappraisal', pp. 39–41.

173 For the main western, Russian and Bulgarian references: Hendy, 'Byzantium 1081–1204: An Economic Reapppraisal', pp. 49–50.

Far more important from the point of view of this series of studies is the actual scale of the exchanges involved. This is commonly supposed to have been vast, but the figures that are available simply do not support the supposition.

In 992, the chrysobull issued by the emperors Basil II and Constantine VIII in favour of the Venetians noted that imperial *kommerkiarioi* based on the Dardanelles at Abydus were charging more than thirty solidi (*plus de 30 solidis*) on each Venetian ship (*navigio*) entering the straits. At the intercession of the doge and the people of Venice, the charge was henceforth reduced to two solidi on entering the straits, and moreover fifteen solidi on leaving, making a total of seventeen solidi in all.[174]

It is difficult to unravel the precise significance of all this, but it is tempting to suppose that the *kommerkiarioi* had previously been charging the Venetians the normal and full 10% *ad valorem* tax on each ship,[175] which would suggest that a ship entering the straits might have been carrying taxable goods to the value of some 300 solidi, probably representing an estimate on the high side, but quite possibly also excluding precious metals from taxation.[176] It is not known what the same ship leaving the straits would originally have been charged, and what the taxable goods carried would therefore have been worth, but if the same ratio of reduction (30:2) is applied, then the original charge would have been some 225 solidi and the worth of the taxable goods would therefore have been some 2,250 solidi. The total original gain to the imperial treasury would thus have amounted to some 255(30+225) solidi on each ship. The reduction of the gain from some 255 to 17 solidi in 992 would thus very strongly suggest that the total abandonment of the *kommerkion* in the early 1080s was not nearly as radical a measure as has hitherto been supposed. It should not, on the other hand, be supposed that the taxable goods of an individual merchant were worth some 300/2,250 solidi, as in many cases, and probably in the vast majority of them, each ship would have been carrying a number of merchants, representing an even greater number of investors, and this number could have been quite large.[177]

Now, to the extent that it could be argued, in the case of attempting to calculate the size of the imperial budget or of imperial income and expenditure, that what is involved is the mere playing of games with sets of totally hypothetical or unverifiable figures, so the same is arguable here: but equally, the same defence is valid – do the figures nevertheless reveal a reasonably consistent general pattern?

[174] See above, p. 282 and n. 161.

[175] Antoniadis-Bibicou, *Recherches sur les douanes à Byzance*, pp. 97–8. The assumption is made in the calculations that follow on below that the percentages for the *kommerkion* were applied both on entry and on exit. This seems to have been normal: *ibid.* pp. 110, 118–19.

[176] As specifically mentioned in the case of the Pisan treaty of 1111: see above, pp. 282–3.

[177] The literature on this subject, which has many ramifications, is vast, with a number of the points involved, particularly the legal ones, having been the subject of controversy. In addition, the situation in 992 may well have differed sensibly from that in 1171 and later. A still useful analysis of the Genoese situation, with regard to vessels and investments, is to be found in E. H. Byrne, *Genoese Shipping in the Twelfth and Thirteenth Centuries*, pp. 5–21.

On 12 March 1171, in response to the growing arrogance and disruptive behaviour of the Venetian quarter in Constantinople, and particularly the effecting of a provocative attack upon the newly re-established Genoese quarter, Manuel I had every available Venetian citizen within the empire arrested, imprisoned, and his property confiscated; few escaped.[178] The attack on the Genoese quarter seems to have taken place some time after August 1170 and, obviously, before March 1171, both provocation and response therefore occurring whilst the western merchants were port-bound, and over-wintering, in the City and in Romania.[179] The arrests and confiscations marked the temporary end of an almost continuously developing relationship that extended further back even than the treaties of the early 1080s and 992, and led to a breach which lasted at least until 1183, and which was not fully and formally healed until the treaties of 1187/9.[180]

As it happens, the terms of compensation agreed for the confiscations of 1171 are known both casually from Nicetas Choniates, and from the surviving copies of the treaties themselves, and had clearly been closely researched and officially registered. They involved the payment, by the Byzantine authorities, to individual Venetians who had suffered losses, of fifteen kentenaria. It is known from the rate at which an instalment of one kentenarion, forwarded by Andronicus I in 1185, was paid out, that the full extent of the losses had been some 48 kentenaria or 345,000 hyperpyra, the agreed compensation thus forming some $\frac{5}{16}$ of the total.[181]

According to the *Historia Ducum Veneticorum*, there were 20,000 Venetians in Romania in 1170, of whom 10,000 were actually caught in Constantinople in 1171.[182] These figures seem not wildly out of kilter with the few other estimates for westerners in Constantinople and the empire that are known,[183] but the fact that the theoretical average claim for

178 Refs: Brand, *Byzantium Confronts the West*, p. 318 n. 5.

179 G. W. Day, 'Genoese Involvement with Byzantium 1155–1204: A Diplomatic and Prosopographical Study', p. 46 n. 51. The necessary practice of over-wintering, navigation in the Mediterranean being suspended between November and March, and being still dangerous and therefore restricted between September and May, should never be forgotten – for the late Roman situation: Jones, *Later Roman Empire* II, p. 843.

180 Brand, *Byzantium Confronts the West*, pp. 195–9.

181 See above, p. 282, and nn. 157, 158. The rate at which the first instalment of one kentenarion was paid out in 1185 ($\frac{1}{2}$ ker. and $\frac{1}{2}$ den. (Ven.) per hyperpyron) agrees quite closely with that at which a later instalment of $2\frac{1}{2}$ kentenaria was paid out under Isaac ($1\frac{1}{10}$ ker. per hyperpyron).

182 Anonymous, *Historia Ducum Veneticorum*, s.a. 1171; ed. H. Simonsfeld, in MGH, *SS* XIV, at p. 78.

183 E.g., for 1182: William of Tyre, *Historia Rerum* XXII.12; RHC, *Occ.* I.2, p. 1084 (above 4,000). For 1203/4: Geoffrey of Villehardouin, *La conquête de Constantinople* CCV; ed. Faral, I, p. 210 (15,000). Bar Hebraeus, *Chronography*; ed. Budge, I, p. 358 (30,000). The figure of 60,000 given by Eustathius of Thessalonica for the second half of the century seems the most exaggerated of all: Hendy, 'Byzantium, 1081–1204: An Economic Reappraisal', p. 41 n. 2. Given the revised Venetian figure for 1171, that of the usually well-informed and reliable William of Tyre seems reasonable for 1182 (the otherwise predominant Venetians were absent on that occasion). This would suggest a total normal figure of somewhere not too much above 7,000 westerners in Constantinople in the seventies and eighties. This in turn means that Villehardouin's eye-witness figure of 15,000 in 1203/4, as it includes both merchants and dependants, a point which is explicitly stated, is not at all implausible (he, of all people, should have been an experienced judge of numbers). Bar Hebraeus' remark '...but on account of the great size of the city they were not conspicuous therein', puts the matter in its proper perspective, even if his own figure approximately doubles their true number. See also below, pp. 595, 596, 597 and n. 197.

compensation should therefore have been some 17 hyperpyra, whilst the actual average claim seems to have been some 60 hyperpyra,[184] suggests that they may have been appreciably exaggerated, at least as regards actual merchants, and that the true total figure may have been somewhere in the region of 6,000, and the Constantinopolitan one in that of 3,000.

It is, of course, exceedingly difficult to combine all these Venetian figures into a comprehensive pattern, but even if any of the relationships and conclusions arrived at are of the correct order only, they are likely to be informative. The total figure estimated for compensation, some 345,000 hyperpyra, represents not simply saleable commodities, but goods, cash, ships, houses and their furnishings, and other immoveable properties: in other words, the total investment. What the proportions were between goods and cash on the one hand, and ships and immoveable properties on the other, it is impossible to say, but for the sake of argument let it be supposed that the two were split more or less one-third in favour of the former, and two-thirds in favour of the latter, making some 115,000 hyperpyra in goods, and some 230,000 hyperpyra in ships and properties. At the full rate of the *kommerkion*, 10% on incoming and 10% on outgoing cargoes, 115,000 hyperpyra would have represented a theoretical gain to the imperial treasury of some 23,000 hyperpyra, but the actual figure would have been considerably less if incoming precious metals were excluded.[185] At the 992 figures, suggesting a full outgoing cargo of some 2,250 hyperpyra per ship (= 300 hyp. incoming goods and profit on their sale + imported precious metals and purchases from them), there would have been, in 1171, some fifty Venetian ships scattered throughout the empire, of which some twenty-five would have been in Constantinople and twenty-five elsewhere. Again, at the 992 figure, setting a *kommerkion* of 17 (2 + 15) hyperpyra per ship, the gain to the treasury would have been 850 hyperpyra only, confirming that the fiscal pass at least had already truly been sold in 992.[186] Finally, if the average claim for compensation, 60 hyperpyra, is divided in the same way as the global total of 345,000 hyperpyra ($\frac{1}{3}$ goods/$\frac{2}{3}$ ships and properties = 20/40 hyp.), and the former figure is taken as the average individual holding in goods and cash, then each ship might have held just over 110 merchants and their goods, while if the total figure is taken, then the complement falls to just under forty.[187]

The hypothetical nature of many of these figures, the possible sources of error, and even the internal inconsistencies between some of them, are evident and need no stressing,

184 Estimate derived from Metcalf, *Coinage in South-eastern Europe, 820–1396*, at p. 110.

185 See above, pp. 282–3, 592 n. 176. The proportion $\frac{1}{3}$:$\frac{2}{3}$ is of course a 'guesstimate' only, but is not entirely unsupported: in 1427, taxable wealth in Florence was distributed in the following fashion – moveable assets 29%, real property 53%, public debt 17%. See: D. Herlihy, 'The Distribution of Wealth in a Renaissance Community: Florence 1427', in P. Abrams and E. A. Wrigley (eds), *Towns in Societies. Essays in Economic History and Historical Sociology*, at p. 135.

186 See above, p. 282.

187 These are obviously intended as possible and very approximate maximal and minimal figures only, but their order, at least, is perfectly feasible.

although it may be noted that a more 'sophisticated' treatment would not necessarily render them more 'accurate'. As always, it is the general pattern which needs watching.

It is clear that the Venetian investment in the empire at this stage was by far in excess of that of Pisa and Genoa. This was partly because of their relatively late appearance on the scene (Pisa in 1111, Genoa in 1155–57/60); partly because of their lack of a 'special relationship' with the empire; and partly because their geographical locations dictated a different balance of commercial interests.

In 1162, the newly established Genoese quarter was attacked and sacked by a mob which seems to have consisted mainly of Pisans, but with some Venetian and even unofficial Greek backing. The Genoese community, numbering about 300, fled, leaving behind their goods. After a number of years of sporadic negotiation, the Genoese quarter was re-established in 1169/70, only to be again attacked and sacked, this time by a mob of Venetians. Again, an appreciable loss of goods occurred.[188]

In 1174/5, the Genoese ambassador to Constantinople, one Grimaldi, was given instructions to make the following claims for compensation:

| | |
|---|---|
| Loss of goods in 1162 | 29,443 hyp. |
| Loss of goods in 1170 | 5,674 hyp. |
| Loss of 6 ships in 1171 | 42,843 hyp. |
| Miscellaneous losses | 6,800 hyp. |
| Total | 84,760 hyp. |

Several of these sub-totals are themselves slightly discrepant internally, and the actual total claim made was 84,340 hyperpyra, but nothing more than the usual minor mediaeval inaccuracies, basically caused by the cumbersome system of notation, is involved.[189]

The claim for compensation for the 1162 sack, of which the detailed breakdown is known, has been made the subject of a number of calculations. In the first place, it has been suggested that the entire overseas investment of Genoa, in outgoing cash and goods, in the year 1161, amounted to some 300,000 hyperpyra, of which only some 13% involved Constantinople itself and Romania, the balance being overwhelmingly in favour of the former. This contrasts very interestingly with similar calculations made for Venice and its overseas investment.[190] In the second place, if the Genoese community really did

[188] Refs: Day, 'Genoese Involvement with Byzantium 1155–1204', pp. 18–19, 26.

[189] Day 'Genoese Involvement with Byzantium 1155–1204', p. 36. See also above, n. 189.

[190] Genoa: V. Slessarev, 'The Pound-value of Genoa's Maritime Trade in 1161', in D. Herlihy, R. S. Lopez, and V. Slessarev (eds), *Economy, Society, and Government in Medieval Italy. Essays in Memory of Robert L. Reynolds*, at p. 102 (£100,000[Gen.] = approx. 300,000 hyp.). Venice: Martin, 'Venice and the Byzantine Empire before the Fourth Crusade', pp. 95–6. The Genoese figures, even if only of the correct order, make nonsense of the size of official claims for losses in 1182 – see below, p. 596 and n. 196. For another run of Gen./Byz. figures (fluctuating between 0 and 19%), see: D. S. H. Abulafia, *The Two Italies. Economic Relations between the Norman Kingdom of Sicily and the Northern Communes*, pp. 99, 109, 111, 113, 119, 158, 161, 166, 174, 177, 182.

number about 300 in 1162, then the average per capita investment will have been somewhere in the region of 100 hyperpyra. On the other hand, it is known that the powerful Guercio family and its dependants, numbering something over thirteen individuals, accounted for roughly 30% of the total claim, and that as they had nearly all invested well above the average sum (most between 300 and 1,000 hyperpyra), the remainder must have invested well below it.[191] This is confirmed by the fact that the claim for compensation for the 1170/1 sack, of 5,674 hyperpyra, represented the investment of 85 individuals, representing an average of some 70 hyperpyra.[192] In the third place, although the number of ships involved is not known, the average value of five of the six ships lost in 1171 (the sixth on any reckoning must have been exceptionally valuable) was just under 4,000 hyperpyra and, assuming the figures involved all to represent cargo alone and not cargo and ship together, this might be taken as suggesting that the total claim for 1162 represented the contents of some seven or eight ships.[193] This, in turn, tallies with the small size of the single wharf or dock granted the Genoese in 1169/70.[194] Finally, at the full rate of the *kommerkion* (10% on incoming and 10% on outgoing cargoes) 29/30,000 hyperpyra would have represented a theoretical gain to the imperial treasury of some 6,000 hyperpyra, but at the privileged rate of 4% and 4% acquired by the Genoese it would have represented an actual gain of some 2,500 hyperpyra.[195]

In April 1182, the Genoese quarter, along with the Pisan, but of course not the vacant Venetian, one, was attacked and sacked by the urban mob: few escaped, the remainder losing not only their possessions but also generally their lives. After negotiations, the first round of which, in 1187, failed, probably because of the inflated nature of Genoese demands, the quarter was re-established in 1192. One of the demands, which the Genoese made in the second round of negotiations, but which they ultimately dropped, was for the payment by the Byzantine authorities, as compensation to Genoese who had suffered losses in 1182, of 228,000 hyperpyra.[196] Now, this figure makes sense, when compared

191 Day, 'Genoese Involvement with Byzantium 1155–1204', pp. 139–40. Cf. the part of the Guercii and their dependants in the communal loan of 1171: some 35% of the total – *ibid.* p. 141.

192 *Ibid.* p. 26.

193 *Ibid.* pp. 26, 46 n. 54. See also: Byrne, *Genoese Shipping in the Twelfth and Thirteenth Centuries*, pp. 22–4 (ch. 5, 'Cost and value of ships').

194 Day, 'Genoese Involvement with Byzantium 1155–1204', p. 26.

195 Antoniadis-Bibicou, *Recherches sur les douanes à Byzance*, p. 124. See also above, p. 592 and n. 175.

196 Refs: Day, 'Genoese Involvement with Byzantium 1155–1204', pp. 63–5. That the Genoese were capable of submitting grossly exaggerated claims seems clear – *ibid.* p. 27. See also above, p. 595 n. 190. It is worth noting at this point that, in the same year as the Genoese quarter was re-established (1192), Genoese pirates, in an attack on Rhodes, did 50,000 hyperpyra worth of damage to harbour property belonging to the *sebastokratōr* Alexius Angelus (the later Alexius III). It is interesting that whereas the property of hundreds or thousands of Genoese amounted to 228,000 hyp., the property of one *sebastokratōr* amounted to at least 50,000 hyp. Even if both the claims involved were exaggerated, as they very probably were, the comparison is an interesting one. Refs: Day, *op. cit.* pp. 67–9. See below, pp. 597–9. It is also interesting that Alexius seems to have been deriving a good deal of revenue from harbour-properties or revenues, some at least of which were the result of grants from his brother, Isaac II. See above, p. 88 and Map 19.

with the earlier Genoese, and both the Venetian, ones, only if it represents the full value not only of salable commodities, but that of goods, cash, ships, houses and their furnishings, and other immoveable properties. Again, what the proportions were between goods and cash, and ships and immoveable properties, it is impossible to say, but using the same as applied in the Venetian case (⅓ goods, ⅔ ships and properties), the result is 76,000 hyperpyra in the former, and 152,000 hyperpyra in the latter. At the full rate of the *kommerkion* (10% and 10%) 76,000 hyperpyra would have represented a theoretical gain to the imperial treasury of some 15,000 hyperpyra, but at the privileged rate of 4% and 4% it would have represented an actual gain of some 6,000 hyperpyra. Again, at the same average value of cargo as used above (4,000 hyperpyra), the claim for 1182 may have represented the contents of some twenty ships.

The size of the claim for compensation made by Pisa, in the negotiations leading up to the re-establishment of its quarter in 1191/2 and which – like the Venetians, but unlike the Genoese, one – was actually fulfilled, remains unknown. Nevertheless, given that the Pisan quarter was of rather longer standing than the Genoese, and that at least one set of figures suggests it to have been more populous than the latter – at least as matters stood in 1162 – let it be supposed that it stood more or less mid-way in total value between the Venetian and Genoese quarters.[197] This would give it a total value of some 286,000 hyperpyra. Again, using the same proportions as applied in the Venetian and Genoese cases (⅓:⅔), goods and cash would have amounted to some 95,000 hyperpyra. At the full rate of the *kommerkion*, 10% and 10%, 95,000 hyperpyra would have represented a theoretical gain to the imperial treasury of some 19,000 hyperpyra, but at the privileged rate of 4% and 4% it would have represented an actual gain of some 7,600 hyperpyra.[198]

In full recognition of all the possible sources of error in the figures quoted and evolved above, the following deductions and comparisons are nevertheless to be made. The total value of the Venetian investment in the empire, and of the Genoese and Pisan investments in Constantinople, in the period c. 1170–90, is likely to have stood somewhere in the very approximate order of 860,000 hyperpyra, at any given time. The grand total value of all three Italian investments in the empire as a whole, at this period, is therefore unlikely to have exceeded one million hyperpyra. This may sound very considerable, and indeed it is not entirely inconsiderable, but to put it in its proper context, as the combined product of thousands of merchants, and even more contributors, it may have been the equivalent of the total value of the fortunes of some half a dozen, perhaps even fewer, of the highest members of the Byzantine magnate classes.[199]

197 The Genoese quarter of some 300 members was attacked by Pisans numbering some 1,000: Day, 'Genoese Involvement in Byzantium 1155–1204', pp. 18–19. The fact that the Genoese figure for compensation was almost certainly grossly exaggerated, nevertheless means that the one evolved here for the Pisan is also to be regarded as very strongly maximal. This, of course, means that the figure evolved here for the total Italian investment is also appropriately maximal.

198 Antoniadis-Bibicou, *Recherches sur les douanes à Byzance*, p. 124. See also above, p. 592 and n. 175.

199 See above, pp. 203–6.

The point about the Latin communities in Constantinople was of course that they may have not been fabulously wealthy in themselves, but that the average wealth of their members, simply because they were largely merchants from outside, was inevitably greater than that of members of the much broader-based native population which surrounded them. In addition to this, the fact that such communities were topographically defined and therefore concentrated, lending them an enhanced political influence and power, and that their members were ethnically distinct in matters of language, dress and religion, and even in modes of behaviour (which on occasion attracted a fashionable imperial favour), all contributed to their widespread unpopularity. But in much of this, they resembled the Lombard, Hanseatic and Jewish communities of the mediaeval west, which were often equally unpopular, and equally unjustifiably so.

Utilising the figure of one million hyperpyra as representing the full extent of Italian investment in the empire, and the proportions $\frac{1}{3}:\frac{2}{3}$ as representing the relationship of goods and cash to ships and property, the theoretical gain to the imperial treasury would have been some 66,500 hyperpyra, at the full rate of *kommerkion* (10%+10%), but the actual figure would have been some 17,500 hyperpyra, because of the various privileged rates (0%+0%, 4%+4%), representing a loss to the treasury of some 49,000 hyperpyra. This is almost certainly a strongly maximal figure.[200]

It is worth noting, in this respect, that in 1191/2 the Ayyubid *khums* or trade-tax, levied at a theoretical rate of 20% (*khums* = fifth, clearly related to the Byzantine 10%+10%) but often at rates substantially above or below that rate on foreign (i.e. basically western) merchandise, is reckoned to have amounted to a total of 28,613 dinars at Alexandria, suggesting that the Byzantine figure may well be of the right order.[201]

The last Byzantine figure should again be placed in its appropriate context. In 1155/6, Manuel I is reckoned as having spent 2,160,000 hyperpyra on his Italian campaign; in 1158, the same emperor is reckoned to have spent 150,000 hyperpyra on the marriage of a favourite niece; in 1176 he is reckoned to have spent some 135,000 hyperpyra to procure peace from Kılıç Arslan II; and in 1170 he is reckoned to have spent 56,000 hyperpyra in an attempt to procure an agreement with the Genoese.[202] In 1185, on the deposition of Andronicus I, the urban mob is said to have found something in excess of 170,000 hyperpyra stored in the Great Palace; in 1185 and 1195, Isaac II is reckoned to have sent out 288,000 and 216,000 hyperpyra respectively to his armies on campaign; and in 1203, Alexius III fled the City with something in excess of 72,000 hyperpyra, again taken from the Great Palace.[203] At much the same time, the revenues of the island of Cyprus are said to have amounted to 50,000 hyperpyra *per annum*, and it is possible that

200 See the various points, involving the constituent items of the total figure, made above.

201 Rabie, *The Financial System of Egypt A.H. 564–741/A.D. 1169–1341*, pp. 90–2. This may mean that Benjamin of Tudela's lower estimate of 20,000 hyperpyra per annum for Constantinople in *c.* 1168 is on the low side, but is at least of the right order. See above, pp. 173–4.

202 See above, pp. 222, 265, 270.

203 See above, pp. 222, 225.

the revenues thought appropriate to an active *despotēs* amounted to the same annual sum.[204]

The figures for the total likely loss of revenue from the Italian trade, on the one hand, and for individual and occasional items of imperial revenue and expenditure and so on, on the other, are thus quite simply not on the same implicit scale, the latter implying the existence of a budget of a fundamentally different and vaster size, and this should not have been unexpected, for the very restrained scale of revenue from trade as a proportion of the total imperial budget has already been mentioned, and indeed will again be mentioned shortly.[205] Even reversing the proportions of goods and cash, and of ships and properties, held by the Italian communities, would not radically change the situation.

What one is seeing here, of course, are the surface financial distinctions reflecting the existence of two fundamentally different political and social structures, each with its own distinct set of dynamics and ideologies. On the one hand, there is the great territorial entity, as the empire still was, despite the truncation of its Anatolian holdings; in which the dominant class was overwhelmingly based on land, its exploitation, and the accumulation thereby of produce and – via the direct exchange of any surplus – of other forms of wealth; and in which this same class essentially despised trade, especially of an indirect kind, and moreover kept those who indulged in it, and made their living from it, under strict control and regulation – an attitude accentuated by the existence of an ever-present and overwhelming problem in the form of the provisioning of the capital. On the other hand, there is the geographically restricted, and therefore territorially small, entity of the Italian trading city, with a dominant class that physically could not be based on land alone, thereby being forced to hold quantities of cash which formed a relatively large proportion of its total wealth, and that in order to increase its wealth was forced to invest what it already possessed in trade of whatever kind, just like everybody else, and to a degree that was quite extraordinary in an ancient or mediaeval context. Again, on the one hand, there is an empire which relied on the taxation of land, and which on the proceeds of that taxation kept up a large standing army and a complex bureaucracy; and on the other, there is a city state which taxed trade, but which maintained a minimal state structure only, relying for its defence and government largely on the voluntary efforts of its own citizens.

These two structures were, of course, extreme in their differences, but it may be suggested that, in the east, the interrelated combination of tax-base and state superstructure, together with its appropriate ideology, lent sufficient strength for the empire to survive, however narrowly, the upheavals of the seventh and eighth centuries, but that having performed the office of preservation, and having developed the combination as far as it was possible to do so, those same strengths ensured that the empire was incapable of

[204] See above, pp. 173, 205.

[205] See above, pp. 157–8, below, pp. 613–18.

responding to the challenge of newly developing forms, whether internal or external. In the west, by contrast, the disbandment of the standing army, the largest single object of state expenditure, in the barbarian kingdoms, entailed the piecemeal but eventually complete disappearance of the land-tax, the largest single source of state revenue: as the latter was no longer absolutely necessary, it became, as it were, an item of largesse, in the form of the granting out of wholesale immunity from it, and in any case, with the gradual disintegration of the bureaucracy, it became increasingly sporadically and incompetently collected. The resultant loosening of demand upon the agricultural surplus, in liberating the latter for new and alternative uses, ultimately may well have formed a decisive factor in the transition from an ancient to a mediaeval society in the territorially-based states of the west.[206]

The quite basic point of all this is to be seen in two aspects: the general, and the particular. As to the former, it seems clear that the fundamental reasons for the 'decline' of Byzantium are to be sought not in such superficial and convenient external factors as Latin economic competition, for that was a symptom only, and was in any case incapable of the necessary impact, but, rather, deep within its own internal structures, whether of social form or of mental attitude. As to the latter, it seems equally clear that reasons for the 'decline' of its coinage are again not to be sought in terms of trade and, again, Latin competition and so on, but rather elsewhere, and in terms of the revenue and expenditure of the state, and of the mechanisms of military payment, the most important single factor in the state budget.[207] For the preceding chapters of this book have demonstrated quite uniformly and overwhelmingly that trade was not the basic dynamic behind the production of coinage in the late Roman and Byzantine empire, and now this section has equally clearly suggested that trade is unlikely to have been the basic mechanism in the primary distribution of coinage, and perhaps – even with Latin help – in its subsequent circulation.

It is in this context, and against this background, that statements such as: 'The economic preliminary, and the key, to the reform of the coinage carried out by Alexius I *c.* 1092 – and indeed to the whole pattern of monetary affairs in the twelfth century – was the chrysobull of May 1082 by which the emperor granted enormous trading privileges to the Venetians' are to be seen and assessed.[208] This statement, and others like it, derive from a thoroughly naïve and fundamentally misconceived view of the nature and rôle of the Byzantine coinage: in fact not only is it not correct, but it quite simply could never have been correct, and, to the contrary, the Veneto-Byzantine treaty of the early

[206] C. J. Wickham, 'The Other Transition: From the Ancient World to Feudalism', *Past and Present* 103 (1984), pp. 3–36. I owe a view of this article, prior to publication, to the kindness of the author.

[207] This, then, is Lemerle's 'société bloquée', but it is not his 'économie cassée', which the economy was not – it too was merely 'bloquée', the former necessarily entailing the latter. Lemerle, *Cinq études sur le XI^e siècle byzantin*, p. 309.

[208] Metcalf, *Coinage in South-eastern Europe, 820–1396*, p. 104.

1080s almost certainly had no more than the most marginal possible – and now quite unmeasurable – relation to, and impact upon, the history of the Byzantine coinage in the twelfth century.[209]

The one monetary area in which the treaty – and the Venetian and other Latin investments which it, and similar treaties, implied – may have had some appreciable and now visible impact, and indeed an entirely positive one, is the highly specific and localised one of monetary circulation in central and western Greece. If a list is drawn up, representing specific ports of call other than Constantinople, and based on twelfth-century Venetian documentation, it emerges that something like 60% of those documents involve the four centres of Corinth, Halmyrus, Thebes and Sparta, in that order of numerical significance.[210] Now, it has been noted above that the predominant pattern of Venetian (and presumably other Latin) trade seems to have involved the picking up of primary and basically agricultural produce at the first major port of call within the empire, and then its transportation to Constantinople.[211] One may guess that this trade achieved a greater impact even than the luxury one involving the silk stuffs produced at Corinth, Sparta and Thebes, and on Andros.[212] It therefore may well be that these merchants had an appreciable, and perhaps even definable, catalytic impact in the painfully slow process of setting up a new, or accentuating an old, cycle, whereby the peasantry of the region was encouraged, by the presence of a ready market, to produce a surplus that met not only the demands of the tax-collector and/or the landlord, but also regularly included an enhanced portion designed for the acquisition of a profit, of which coinage may well have formed at least a temporary part. Certainly, there are signs of a changing balance between town and countryside, in terms of the ownership of land, in precisely this region, and it may well be that this is one symptom of the establishment or accentuation of such a cycle.[213] But it would also be worth examining the archaeological record, including both hoards and site-finds, of the region, and comparing it with that of other regions, in this restrained light. But even here, the fiscal system is likely to have obtruded, for in this region the substantive minor denominations in circulation seem to have been the

[209] Attempts to connect variations in the silver-content of the billon trachy with the confiscations of 1171 are as futile as the connection attempted above: Metcalf, *Coinage in South-eastern Europe, 820–1396*, p. 111.

[210] Martin, 'Venice and the Byzantine Empire before the Fourth Crusade', p. 95. If Crete is added to nearby mainland Greece, as seems reasonable, then the proportion is over 60%.

[211] See above, p. 591.

[212] The silk industries of Corinth, Sparta and Thebes are of course well known (see for example above, pp. 51–2), that of Andros is mentioned by the pilgrim Saewulf: *deinde ad Andriam, ubi fiunt preciosa scindilia et samite, et alia pallia serico contexta – Relatio de Peregrinatione*; ed. Brownlow, p. 32.

[213] For the latest treatment (utilising the Theban cadaster), see: Lemerle, *The Agrarian History of Byzantium from the Origins to the Twelfth Century*, pp. 197–9. For the text: Svoronos, 'Le cadastre de Thèbes', pp. 11–19. One may nevertheless doubt that the large number of official ranks and dignities represented in the cadaster is really indicative of court ownership: most seem, in an eleventh-century context, to be of quite low standing, and many or all of these may simply represent the purchase of status by minor local worthies, thus aping the metropolitan fashion – see above, pp. 185–7, 571–87.

copper tetarteron and its half, whilst in other regions the equivalent denomination seems to have been the billon trachy[214] which, because of its still appreciable silver-content and value, was certainly much less lost but probably much more hoarded.[215] It would of course be possible to argue that the state deliberately produced small-value coins for already relatively highly monetised regions, whilst it produced higher-value ones for still relatively lightly monetised ones – or, alternatively, that it produced the former for regions with a relatively low price-structure, whilst it produced the latter for regions with a relatively high price-structure. But what is known of Byzantine monetary practices and policies does not suggest that such implied sophistication or sensitivity is either plausible or was even possible.

### (II) THE INTERVENTION OF THE STATE (ARMY AND *CURSUS PUBLICUS*)

It seems clear that if trade was at least neither the principal dynamic behind the production of coin, nor the principal mechanism behind its distribution, then an alternative structure must of necessity be found. In fact, the basic framework of such a structure has effectively already been established, with the isolation of clear evidence that the basic dynamic for the production of coin, throughout the history of the empire, or at least from the fourth to the fourteenth century, was the cyclical process involving the revenue and expenditure of the state, and operating within, and therefore being shaped by, the predominant pattern of the contemporary fiscal administration. The obvious clue as to the identity of one of the principal mechanisms, perhaps the principal mechanism, of distribution, is again the isolation of equally clear and consistent evidence that the factor which is likely to cause aberration from the predictable and normative pattern of production is nearly always an abnormal military situation – whether in the form of a straightforward military campaign, or in that of some still relatively short-lived emergency requiring or involving some kind of military reaction and/or solution. As there is good evidence that the military pay-roll provided quite decisively the principal item of the imperial budget, this should not be unexpected.

The whole question of the form and evolution of the military forces of the empire is a vast and complex one, and it is in no way intended that even a brief treatment should be attempted here, although the potentially decisive impact that the tight relationship between the demands of imperial finance and the pattern of military payment might have upon the production of coin, will in one particular and critical instance again be suggested below.[216]

[214] See above, pp. 434–7, Table 14 and Map 36.

[215] See above, pp. 514, 518. It seems clear that the billon trachy begins to appear in site-finds only as its silver-content decreases in the second half of the twelfth century – this pattern appears valid for both metropolitan and regional sites.

[216] See below, pp. 640–5, 659–62.

There remains one further state organ which, whilst, it may not have rivalled the military forces as regards its total impact upon the production and distribution of coin, may well nevertheless have had a relatively greater, and very probably did have a more uniform, impact upon distribution, and that is the institution of the *cursus publicus*, a factor that hitherto has been barely recognised at all in this rôle.

The *cursus publicus/dēmosios dromos* of the late Roman and early Byzantine period was under the jurisdiction of the praetorian prefects, and of their deputies, the diocesan vicars and provincial governors.[217] It was divided into two sections: the fast (*cursus velox/oxys dromos*); and the slow (*cursus clabularis/platys dromos*). The former consisted of horses (*veredi* = saddle-horses, and *parhippi* = pack-horses) and mules; the latter seemingly consisted of oxen only. The vehicles involved, drawn by mules in the case of the *cursus velox*, comprised light two-wheeled carts (*birotae*) which were drawn by three mules, and heavy four-wheeled ones (*raedae*) which were drawn by eight mules in summer and ten in winter. The oxen utilised in the case of the *cursus clabularis* drew even heavier carts (*angariae*), with two pairs forming the standard team.[218]

The maximum permissible loads were rigidly laid down: a *veredus* might carry 30 lb; a *birota* 200 lb; a *raeda* 1,000 lb; and an *angaria* 1,500 lb. The load for a *veredus* had been raised to 60 lb by the time of Justinian, and even then an interesting exception was made if what was being transported were the customary hundred-pound sacks in which it was necessary for gold (from taxation) to be carried by the grooms (*exceptis auri centenariis, quae necesse est ab hippocomis in solitis sacculis reportari*).[219] These sacks were presumably under seal – and therefore unable to be broken down into small amounts – as were still the *balantia* and *phaskōlia* later utilised for such purposes and mentioned by Anna Comnena and Nicetas Choniates.[220] The transport of precious metals by *raeda*, whether on the public or on a private account, was apparently one of the major functions of the *cursus velox*, which had its own series of set maximal loads.[221]

Despite an extensive and elaborate series of laws designed to regulate not only the size of loads, but also the normal daily rate of despatch of animals and carts, the nature of the whips or canes used to control the animals, and the granting out of warrants (*evectiones*) for the use of the post – confined in theory to officials but regularly usurped by private individuals who were influential enough – the animals were clearly heavily worked, and a quarter of them were replaced every year, implying an average working life of four years only.[222]

217 Basic prefectural jurisdiction is clear and incontrovertible: virtually all the laws of the chapter of the *Codex Theodosianus* dealing with the post (VIII.5: *De cursu publico*, *CJ* XII.50) are addressed to the prefects and their subordinates, and those that are not tend to deal with the misuse of *evectiones* by others (but see below, p. 608 and n. 240).

218 Jones, *Later Roman Empire* II, p. 830.

219 *CJ* XII.50.12.

220 See above, p. 227 (Anna). Nicetas Choniates, *Historia*; ed. van Dieten, I, p. 205.

221 Jones, *Later Roman Empire* II, pp. 830–1, III, pp. 275–6 n. 14.

222 *Ibid.* pp. 830–1, 832–3.

The normative regional representation of the *cursus* took the form of the post-station, which included two types, the larger being the rarer *mansio*, which included accommodation, and the smaller being the commoner *mutatio*, which in theory at least provided a change of animals only. The regular Greek term employed is *stathmos*, which as normally used at least is ambivalent. These *mansiones* and *mutationes* occurred at various distances along roads, depending mainly upon the nature of the terrain, the average distance nevertheless being some ten or eleven miles, *mansiones* being relatively more frequent than *mutationes* where cities were rare. According to Procopius, there were between five and eight *stathmoi* for each day's journey, presumably referring to urgent travel by horse.[223]

The number of such post-stations must have been vast, although the two major sources for the late Roman road-system, the *Itinerarium Antonini* and the *Tabula Peutingeriana*, apparently note cities and *mansiones* only, whilst the more restricted *Itinerarium Burdigalense* alone notes cities, *mansiones* and *mutationes*, and the last has already been quoted with reference to the number of cities and stations passed through in crossing the Balkan and Anatolian peninsulas.[224] (Cf. Maps 17, 24)

The physical size and extent of such *mansiones* and *mutationes* remain uncertain in detail, as any original distinction between the two seems to have soon become blurred, but a number of sites are known from archaeological excavations, mainly western ones, and although they can rarely be precisely identified, it is clear that they could be quite substantial affairs consisting of a number of buildings, often within an enclosure, and sometimes actually fortified and defended.[225] The number of animals involved also remains unclear, and in any case presumably varied with the importance of the route. But Procopius remarks that there were up to forty horses in each *stathmos*, and a law of 382 forbids a vicar on his travels to mobilise more than ten saddle-horses and thirty mules (*asini*), the latter therefore presumably drawing either ten *birotae* or – more likely – three *raedae*. On the other hand, a law of 378 had forbidden a post-station to forward more than five saddle-horses per day, except on direct imperial or very urgent official business, and had also forbidden the forwarding of more than one *raeda* of mules (*assium*).[226]

The number of personnel involved also remains unclear, but each post-station had, in addition to its head (*manceps*), a subordinate staff of farriers, cartwrights and veterinary surgeons, and each saddle- or pack-horse must have had its own groom (*hippocomus*), and every group of three mules also had its own (a *mulio*), clearly to attend each *birota*. All these must have had their own quarters, presumably on-site, as they were hereditary *servi*

223 Procopius, *Historia Arcana* XXX.3; ed. Haury and Wirth (Teubner), III, p. 181. Jones, *Later Roman Empire* II, pp. 831–2. R. Chevallier, *Roman Roads*, p. 186.

224 See above, pp. 73, 81, 99.

225 See, for example: Chevallier, *Roman Roads*, pp. 187–9.

226 Procopius, *Historia Arcana* XXX.4; ed. Haury and Wirth, III, p. 181. *CTh.* VIII.5.38 (382), VIII.5.35 (378).

*publici*, and in addition to these there must have been a substantial staff to service such official accommodation as was provided.[227]

The description by Gregory of Nazianzus of the *Mansio Sasima* which has already been quoted shows some at least of these post-stations – Sasima lay at the junction of three roads – to have had a certain vigour and size, and a varied social and economic composition, even if their population was largely a floating one. Some were in fact villages or even small towns, as was the *vicus* and *mansio* of Orcistus which lay at the junction of four roads, rather than simple stop-overs.[228] They also attracted additional official functions: each served as an official granary (*horrea*), and as a repository for standard weights and measures; they therefore presumably served as centres for tax-collection, and indeed Gregory mentions tax-collectors specifically in this respect.[229] They also, inevitably, attracted less official functions, as again implied by Gregory.

The *cursus publicus* was, then, a state organ not only of vast physical extent, but also probably second only to the army in its command of manpower and resources – certainly, it must have been superior in this respect to the civil bureaucracy. In one further significant respect also it will have been more comparable to the former than to the latter: that is, as a consumer of the agricultural surplus of the empire. The *servi publici* with whom the post-stations were manned will have received no salary, it is true, but they were necessarily in receipt of rations and clothing (*annonae et vestis*); the animals utilised will equally have needed fodder (*pabulum*); and the combined consumption capacities of men and animals will have been very considerable indeed.[230]

The evidence for the methods by which rations and fodder were levied and delivered is seemingly contradictory. It appears, from a law of 365, that fodder had hitherto been levied upon the provincial land-tax, abstracted and delivered on a virtually haphazard basis. From then on, it was to be levied upon each town (*oppidum*), with due regard to the length and difficulty of the journey involved (*pro longinquitate vel molestia itineris*), and at a particular and announced time (*certo ac denuntiato tempore*). The new system was to apply throughout the Italian provinces.[231]

According to John Lydus and Procopius, a very different system obtained in the sixth-century eastern provinces. Here, local land-owners actually sold their crops to the public post in return for coin, and it is at this point that the most significant aspect of the post with regard to the distribution of coin quite clearly and unambiguously emerges. For both authors report that the sale of crops to the post by inland land-owners enabled the latter to pay their taxes, which were levied in cash, and that when the post was abandoned as an economy measure these land-owners were ruined, for they could no longer sell their crops, as they were so far removed from the sea, and as the local military

227 Jones, *Later Roman Empire* II, pp. 832, 833. Chevallier, *Roman Roads*, p. 188.

228 Sasima: see above, p. 99. Orcistus: see above, p. 140.

229 See above, p. 99 and n. 83.

230 Jones, *Later Roman Empire* II, p. 833.

231 *CTh.* XI.1.9.

forces – evidently an important alternative consumer and purchaser – had also been removed from the area. By strong implication, the land-owners could no longer pay their taxes, and in any case simply let their crops rot in the ground.[232]

Now, what the authors are describing is an extremely tight and quite critical cycle, in which the state levied its taxes in coin, but could only expect payment in that form if it itself disbursed coin, as a consequence of its own consumption and therefore expenditure, within the same immediate geographical area. In diagrammatic form this extremely basic cycle may be rendered thus:

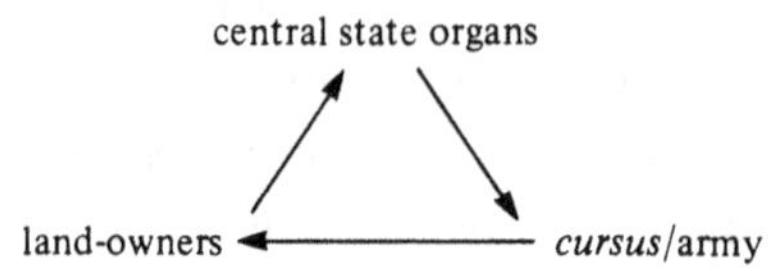


There is very considerable evidence that this monetary cycle obtained, with regard to the precious metals at least, or that where it did not obtain grave economic hardship and via this political disaffection resulted, from the fourth to the fourteenth century, over an area extending from Spain and Africa through the Balkans and Anatolia to the more easterly provinces such as Syria and Egypt. It was, in other words, consistent and predominant, and operated thus in all regions other than in those that were within economic reach of the sea or of a navigable river.[233]

Now, it would be absurd to deny that this cycle excluded trade, but it is nevertheless fair enough to point out that the trade involved was of a very particular and limited kind only. The one positive, if minor, advantage which the *cursus*, at least, will have extended to difficult areas is that the more remote or inland the area, the more necessary it will have been to provide an efficient service and protection to the users of the post by means of a rapid sequence of stations. The distributive impact of the post is thus likely to have been relatively greater in such areas. Moreover, the average distance between stations (some ten or eleven miles or sixteen or eighteen kilometres) will have been ideally geared to take advantage of the distance that a peasant and his loaded donkey could conveniently travel out and return in a single day, some six miles or ten kilometres, so that if a circle centred on a station and given a radius of some six miles or ten kilometres is taken as representing very approximately the area and distance involved, then very few points within that distance of the road will have been placed so as to render their owners or occupants unable conveniently to transport and to sell the surplus produce to at least one station of the post. The physical shape of such a 'monetary economy', the result of a primary and regular distributive cycle, would nevertheless have been extremely curious and accentuated, forming something like a series of small and contiguous or overlapping

[232] See above, pp. 294–6.

[233] See above, pp. 289–91, 291–3, 294–6, 296 and n. 208, 297, 298 and n. 213, 299.

nodes strung out along a line, rather like small beads on a necklace in three-dimensional form, with the occasional larger node or bead representing a town or city, which was of a sufficient size to possess an enhanced price-structure of its own, thus permitting the economic importation of an agricultural surplus from a rather larger area.[234]

Against all this, it should be pointed out that the trade involved was as it were 'imperfect' from a number of points of view, in that it was not entirely economic, or even necessarily entirely voluntary. The contrast with the private trade that was at least potential to the periphery, and which has been outlined above, is thus very considerable.[235] The presence or absence of the *cursus* was of course fortuitous, depending upon the needs of state communications. Moreover, as the repeated economies carried out upon it, in the east particularly under Leo and Justinian, show, the state was apparently unaware of the operation of the monetary cycle that its presence brought into being, or, if it was aware of the cycle, was nevertheless apparently quite unconcerned at the hardships consequent upon its termination. Again, from all that is known of the late Roman and Byzantine state, it seems very unlikely that the post will have paid out more than a bare minimum price for the products that it purchased, and it may well even be that the land-owners who sold their products to the post did so on otherwise uneconomic terms, in their desperation to obtain coin to pay their taxes. Indeed, later evidence suggests that the state, through the post, may well have resorted to compulsory purchase – the widespread *synonē* – to obtain the products that it needed.

This does not, of course, destroy the reality of the cycle, but it does once more emphasise the overwhelming dominance of the state in the economy, and does yet again warn against facile assumptions of straightforward 'trade' as being the main mechanism behind the distribution of coin, perhaps even in its circulation.

The economies of Leo and Justinian should have entailed the abolition of the *cursus clabularis* in the diocese of Oriens and in certain other regions (Leo), and a reduction in the number of stations to a single one per day's journey, that being furnished not with horses, but with a few asses (*oukh hippōn mentoi all'onōn oligōn*), virtually throughout, together with the abolition of both sections of the *cursus* in the diocese of Asiana (Justinian). There is evidence, however, that this did not happen, or that if it did the situation was at some subsequent stage at least partly rectified. For despite these economies, and the invasions which marked the seventh to ninth centuries – and the Arabs at least certainly seem to have used the existing road-system – the *dromos* survived both in Anatolia and the Balkans.[236]

The jurisdiction of the praetorian prefect and his subordinates over the post was

234 On the limitations of local trade in basics, even in larger towns and cities: Jones, *Later Roman Empire* II, pp. 844, 845.

235 See above, pp. 599, 561–2, 568–9.

236 Leo: *CJ* XII.50.22. Justinian: Procopius, *Historia Arcana* XXX.10; ed. Haury and Wirth, III, p. 182. John Lydus, *De Magistratibus* III.61; ed. Wuensch, p. 151. See also: Jones, *Later Roman Empire* II, pp. 833–4.

amongst those other important ones that were devolved upon independent bureaux probably during the seventh century.[237] In this case, direction of the post fell to the *logothetēs tou dromou* and his *sekreton*, the office first being met with in 760 but doubtless existing from much earlier.[238] A good deal of nonsense has been written on the *logothetēs*, his derivation, his status and his functions.[239] His derivation remains open to doubt.[240] His status in the imperial administration, which was high, *logothetai* being generally ranked as *magistroi* or *patrikioi* and being listed amongst the great officers of state; and his functions, which were considerable, having been seen as verging on the prime-ministerial or at least foreign-ministerial; resulted from nothing more mysterious than his heading an apparatus that – particularly after the truncation of the civil administration and its partial transfer to the military – was probably still second to that of the army itself only.[241]

The precise extent to which the regional sub-structure of the post survived remains uncertain: as is all too commonly the case, the more decorative central aspects of the office have been emphasised at the expense of the more mundane but much more

[237] See above, pp. 410–13.

[238] Oikonomides, *Les listes de préséance byzantines*, pp. 311–12. For the seals of the *logothetai* and their various subordinates, see now: V. Laurent, *Le corpus des sceaux de l'empire byzantin* II, *L'administration centrale*, pp. 195–261 (ch. 3, 'L'office du drome et son double service'). The rigid consignment of all seals mentioning the *dromos* only to the slow section of the post (*platys*), and the similar consignment of those mentioning the *oxys dromos* to its fast section, in this publication, leads to what is most probably a false distinction, including the continuing existence of two separate *logothetai*, two separate *offikia*, and two separate sets of subordinates. There is no other evidence for the existence of this distinction at such a late date, and the implications drawn from the assumption of its existence leave one unconvinced to say the least. If the evidence cited above (p. 607 and n. 236) is anywhere near correct, even if somewhat exaggerated, then there should have been no *platys dromos* at all, and a restricted *oxys dromos* only, at the later period. Without entirely excluding the possibility of a complete rectification of the situation after Justinian, it seems much more likely that the seals – whether they mention the *dromos* only or the *oxys dromos* – refer to one and the same institution and service, and that is to the surviving remnants of the *oxys dromos*. It is noticeable that the seals never mention the *platys dromos* specifically, and that the other sources never mention its characteristic oxen.

[239] For the latest major treatments, see: D. A. Miller, 'The Logothete of the Drome in the Middle Byzantine Period', *Byzantion* 36 (1966), pp. 438–70. Guilland, 'Les logothètes, études sur l'histoire administrative de l'empire byzantin', pp. 31–70 (§3: 'le logothète du drome'). See also: Oikonomides, *Les listes de préséance byzantines*, pp. 311–12.

[240] It has long been customary to derive the *logothetēs tou dromou* from the *curiosus cursus publici praesentalis* in the *officium* of the *magister officiorum*. See *N. Dig. Or.* XI.50; ed. Seeck, p. 33. John Lydus, *De Magistratibus* II.10; ed. Wuensch, p. 66. Bury, *The Imperial Administrative System in the Ninth Century*, p. 91. Such a direct derivation is, however, very doubtful. The *magister* had no direct jurisdiction over the *cursus* itself, the general organisation and operation of which fell to the prefects (see above, p. 603 and n. 217). The *magister* nevertheless, through the praesental *curiosus*, and the regional *curiosi* (*per omnes provincias* – *N. Dig. Or.* XI.51; ed. Seeck, p. 33), did exercise an inspectorate over the personnel of the *cursus* and was himself head of the *agentes in rebus* or couriers, also being responsible for the issuing of *evectiones* other than the prefectural (Jones, *Later Roman Empire* I, p. 369). This clearly gave him a powerful indirect position as regards the *cursus*. The post of *logothetēs tou dromou* thus represents an amalgamation of powers derived from both the prefects and the *magister*, rather than a straightforward derivation from one subordinate official or another.

[241] Status and functions: Miller, 'The Logothete of the Drome in the Middle Byzantine Period', pp. 462–8.

significant regional ones, and it is not the function of this book to recover more than the bare essentials of the latter.

The fact of regional survival is nevertheless clear. Michael Psellus, in mentioning the *dēmosios dromos*, seems to distinguish between *stathmoi* and *hippostaseis*, which may well represent a continuing distinction between *mansiones* and *mutationes*, and assumes the presence of horses, and of four baggage-animals (*hypozygia*), possibly mules, at each *stathmos*.[242] Ibn Ḥauḳal quotes at second hand a figure of 186 mail stages between Camacha and Constantinople via Charsianon, Nicomedia and Chalcedon, and another of 128 mail stages between Constantinople and Melitene via Ancyra. These figures are absurdly high. On the other hand, the more particular figures subsequently quoted, apparently at first hand, are much more reasonable: 10 stages between Camacha and Melitene; 20 stages between Melitene and Ancyra; 10 stages between Ancyra and Constantinople; that is, a total of 40 stages between Camacha and Constantinople.[243] Now, although Ibn Ḥauḳal's own figures are clearly rounded out, and the *Itinerarium Burdigalense* is none too trustworthy for precise figures, it may well be no coincidence that for the ten mail stages reckoned by the former for the journey between Ancyra and Constantinople, eleven *mansiones* are listed by the latter between Constantinople and Ancyra.[244] The near coincidence is certainly suggestive: the later figure would make sense on the assumption that Justinian's measures had involved the general abandonment of *mutationes*, but the retention of *mansiones*, which by no means does violence to Procopius' account. Further than this, however, it would be unwise to go. (Cf. Map 24)

In *c.* 904, the *koubikoularios* Samonas, the confidant of Leo VI, apparently in pretended flight from Constantinople to the Arab frontier, took the road 'with his own money and horses, hamstringing the public horses at each change (*allagē*)' – the latter so as to prevent pursuit. He was eventually prevented from crossing the Halys by the *droungarios* Nicephorus Caminas, and it thus seems clear that he had taken the road down along the line Nicaea–Malagina–Dorylaeum *en route* for Caesarea and the frontier.[245]

It is perhaps significant that Procopius' account of Justinian's economies excepts one road alone, that leading to Persia (*epi Persas*), from a reduction in the number of stations, and from being deprived of horses and confined to asses.[246] It is uncertain which road Procopius had in mind as having been excepted, but it is not at all unlikely that it was the road leading from the Marmara, through Malagina – where the imperial stables were later situated – and Dorylaeum, to Caesarea, and from there either eastwards towards

242 Michael Psellus, *Hermēneiai eis Koinolexias* III; ed. Sathas, in *Mesaiōnikē Bibliothēkē* V, at p. 532.

243 Ibn Ḥauḳal, *Liber Imaginis Terrae*; ed. Kramers, pp. 194–6.

244 Anonymous, *Itinerarium Burdigalense* 571–5; ed. Cuntz, pp. 91–2. This is, however, not counting *civitates* also as *mansiones*, which of course the *Itinerarium* does, and so makes 15 *mansiones*.

245 Refs: R. J. H. Jenkins, 'The "Flight" of Samonas', *Speculum* 23 (1948), pp. 217–18. See also: Miller, 'The Logothete of the Drome in the Middle Byzantine Period', p. 468 n. 1.

246 Procopius, *Historia Arcana* XXX.10; ed. Haury and Wirth, p. 182.

Melitene, or southwards over the Cilician Gates into Syria (Map 24). In which case, the accounts of Samonas' flight would confirm that the exception had proved permanent.

In any case, whatever the norm, there seems no doubt that other regional sections of the *dromos* also later possessed horses, although there is no certainty that they were used regularly, despite the obvious general likelihood that they were. This inference is to be drawn from Psellus' information mentioned above, and from Constantine Porphyrogenitus' information that the needs of the imperial baggage-train necessitated a levy of horses and mules made upon the *mētata* of Asia and Phrygia.[247]

The precise nature of the *mētaton* (also spelled *mitaton*) is something of a vexed question, and the term clearly had a number of meanings at this stage, all of which, however, were presumably in some way interrelated. A *mētaton*, according to *The Book of the Prefect*, was somewhere official that foreign merchants could lodge in whilst staying over in the capital, and in this sense it already had a long history.[248] It was also, however, as noted above, somewhere that could produce horses and mules in some numbers.[249] In this form, according to the *Klētorologion* of Philotheus, the *mētata* in general came (perhaps via the *praepositi gregum et stabulorum*[250]) under the *logothetēs tōn agelōn*, and were divided into two sections, those of Asia and of Phrygia, each coming under a *prōtonotarios*, and *dioikētai* and *episkeptētai*, the detailed division of responsibilities remaining uncertain.[251] But again, it was also something that Nicephorus Ouranus, whose best known post was that of *doux* of Antioch 999–*c.* 1006, and clearly speaking as a local land-owner, could describe as a strangulation (*agkhonē*), and ask a *kritēs tōn Thrakēsiōn* to act as a release from it (i.e. *hē tou mitatou tēs emēs agkhonēs, lysis*), additionally terming it an invasion, and a carrying off of forage, and an obligatory service (*tēn epagōgēn kai tēn pronomēn apagōn kai tēn douleian*).[252] Yet again, in a number of Athonite documents of much the same, and a somewhat later, period, monastic lands are exempted from the imposition of the *mētaton* (*epithesis mētatou*), and what must have been something very similar, the *aplēkton* (*diatrophē aplēktōn*).[253] The combination of Ouranus' description and the Athonite documents

247 See above, p. 311.

248 'Leo VI', *To Eparkhikon Biblion* v.5; ed. Nicole, p. 30: *Hoi...Syroi...outoi mē pleon tou trimēniaiou kairou en tois mitatois kathestatōsan....* Nicetas Choniates, *Historia*; ed. van Dieten, I, p. 553: *ho phēsi mitaton hē dēmōdēs dialektos.* For other refs: E. A. Sophocles, *Greek Lexicon of the Roman and Byzantine Periods*, p. 758, s.v. *mētaton*.

249 See above, p. 311.

250 These were members of the *officium* of the *comes rerum privatarum: N. Dig. Or.* XIV.6; ed. Seeck, p. 38.

251 Oikonomides, *Les listes de préséance byzantines*, pp. 338–9. For the seals of the *logothetai* and their various subordinates, see now: Laurent, *Le corpus des sceaux de l'empire byzantin* II, *L'administration centrale*, pp. 289–99 (ch. 5, 'Les troupeaux').

252 Nicephorus Ouranus, *Epistolai* XLII; ed. J. Darrouzès, in *Epistoliers byzantins du Xe siècle*, at pp. 241–2.

253 E.g. Lemerle *et al.*, *Actes de Lavra* I, pp. 110 (974?), 218 (1079), 243 (1082), 258 (1086), 198 (1060): *mētaton/epithesis mētatou*; 110 (974?), 198 (1060), 218 (1079), 243 (1082), 258 (1086), 218 (1079), 259 (1086): *aplēkton/diatrophē aplēktōn.* The two clearly belong certainly formulaically, and probably functionally, together.

clearly suggest that what was here involved was the compulsory requisitioning – presumably for low rates of compensation, effectively *synonē* – of supplies and so on for the military forces garrisoned, or more particularly lodged or encamped, in the vicinity.[254]

It is not easy to make entire sense of all this, and particularly where the term involves the levy of animals on the *mētata* of Asia and Phrygia: it is, in other words, difficult to see why, when the central and contemporary meaning of the term involves humans lodging somewhere, horses and mules should here be involved.

The answer to the problem arising may well lie in the territorial descriptions utilised: Asia and Phrygia. These are derived both from the *De Caerimoniis* and the *Klētorologion*, are confirmed by the evidence of seals, and are therefore not to be doubted as representing official usage.[255] Now, by the ninth and tenth centuries, descriptions of this kind are very rare in an official context, and one might well rather expect the very general geographical term Anatolia, or the much more specific thematic one Thrakesion, to have been used: Asia and Phrygia, on the other hand, point to a late Roman or early Byzantine origin, and therefore to provincial status. At that period certainly, and even later probably, the only state organ in which human lodgings and animal resources coincided, and in which therefore the *mētaton* would be readily understandable, was the *cursus publicus*, with its *mutationes* and *mansiones* (i.e. *mētata*), and its horses and mules. In view of the number of animals, and of the amount of professional expertise for their servicing, that are likely to have been required by the more important *mansiones*, it seems most unlikely that the only source of replacement for these animals was the regional levy that has been mentioned above, and that the expertise available was not also – eventually at least – channelled into stock-breeding so as to complement or accompany the levy. The *mētaton* then, in origin, will have been an occasional levy not on the regions, but on these stock-breeding establishments, and the variant meaning involving not lodgings as such, but animals from them, becomes readily understandable. That the *logothetēs tou dromou* should have had jurisdiction over the stations and – presumably – the currently used animals, whilst the *logothetēs ton agelōn* had jurisdiction over the stock-breeding aspect of the same establishments, should again occasion no surprise: indeed the subordinate organisation of their two *offikia* shows a strong resemblance, and there is even some evidence that the two offices could, at an early stage of their existence, be held in tandem.[256]

[254] See below, pp. 626–34, for a similar phenomenon – the transfer of meaning from something specific to a system or practice – with regard to the *apothēkē*.

[255] Constantine Porphyrogenitus, *De Caerimoniis* I, *Appendix*; Bonn edn, p. 458. Philotheus, *Klētorologion*; ed. Oikonomides, p. 117. Zacos and Veglery, *Byzantine Lead Seals* I.3, p. 1728, no. 3077 A (*prōtonotarios tou mētatou Asias*), p. 1747, no. 3115 (*episkeptitēs mētatou Phrygias*).

[256] *Offikia*: see n. 255 above (Phil. *Klēt.*). Offices held in tandem: Laurent, *Le corpus des sceaux de l'empire byzantin* II, *L'administration centrale*, pp. 198–9, no. 412 (*logothetēs tōn basilikōn agelōn kai tou dromou*) – the latter reading is superior to that of Zacos and Veglery, which is also referred to.

The *dēmosios dromos*, then, survived on as a major institution well into the developed Byzantine period, and seems then to have operated in much the same fashion as it had earlier. Precisely how the animals were later foddered remains uncertain. On the one hand, Psellus states: 'Now, as it [the post] is a public affair (*dēmosion...pragma*), the contribution (*synteleia*) involved is derived not from the private treasury (*tameion* = *oik. vestiarion*), nor from the public one (*prytaneion* = *dēm. vestiarion*), but rather it is the tax-return (*kēnsos*) that is involved, and in this way each community (*khōrion*) is assessed.' This seems to represent the method of direct extraction obtaining in fourth-century Italy. The same author also affirms that: 'Those who are subjected to this charge (*baros*) are under obligation for it alone, being discharged from other public duties (*leitourgia*).' The accuracy of this affirmation seems confirmed by the fact that Athonite documents mention on several occasions 'those who are exempt on account of the post (*exkoussatoi tou dromou*)',[257] and the Theban cadaster actually mentions units of land as: *hyper tou dromou...tou palaiou kinsou* – although the precise meaning of the formula remains uncertain.[258] On the other hand, compulsory purchase, the inevitable *synonē*, also seems a not implausible solution, as in the case of sixth-century Anatolia, and there is here perhaps yet another potential strand in the already complex problem of the *mētaton*. In this respect, it should be remembered that Nicephorus Ouranus' letter is addressed to a *kritēs tōn Thrakēsiōn*, that is of precisely the later theme which included both the earlier provinces of Asia and Phrygia. Ouranus does not specify whether the burden involved was caused by requisitioning for animals of the post, or for locally garrisoned military. The former is quite possible, but it should be noted that the theme was an ideal one for posting out military detachments for over-wintering in – the area was rich, and its climate clement, and it should be remembered in this respect that detachments of Varangians are recorded as over-wintering in the theme in 1034.[259] But if they did so over-winter, where should they do so but in stations of the public post?

In any case, it seems very likely that the nature and balance of the post as a major factor in the distribution of coin also continued, albeit possibly with a somewhat reduced impact because of its truncation under Leo and Justinian. But then the population amongst which it had to operate was also on a reduced scale, and so its relative impact may have remained much the same.

On the other hand, to what extent the *dromos* was re-established in the inner Balkans after their recovery in the eleventh century, and to what extent it survived in the peripheral area of Anatolia (where its impact in a distributive rôle will have been in any case relatively restrained) after the Comnenian stabilisation of the twelfth, remains quite

257 Michael Psellus, *Hermēneiai eis Koinolexias* III; ed. Sathas, in *Mesaiōnikē Bibliothēkē* V, at p. 533. *Exkoussatoi*: e.g. Lemerle *et al.*, *Actes de Lavra* I, p. 197; see also the remarks of Lemerle in *The Agrarian History of Byzantium from the Origins to the Twelfth Century*, at pp. 175–6.

258 Svoronos, 'Le cadastre de Thèbes', p. 12. See also pp. 133 n. 3, 143–4.

259 George Cedrenus, *Historiarum Compendium*; Bonn edn, II, pp. 508–9.

uncertain. Acropolites mentions[260] *stathmoi* on one of the roads leading through the Rhodope as late as the mid thirteenth century, but what these were, and how they were run, again remains completely uncertain.

### (III) A COMPARATIVE EXERCISE ON THE BUDGET

In the course of attempting to estimate the size of the Byzantine state budget, it has long been customary, or has at least been possible, to make some reference to the revenues of the Abbasid caliphate of the ninth century, which have been preserved in some detail. The reference is always accompanied by an admission that the Abbasid figures are in no close way comparable with any Byzantine ones, not least because the caliphate was territorially considerably larger than the empire – at least in its developed form – and many of the lands involved had never been included within either the late Roman or the Byzantine state. The point of the admission is, of course, quite proper and sound.[261]

There do nevertheless survive figures which, while considerably later, do also actually involve lands that had been included within the late Roman or Byzantine state, and that therefore provide not a basis for direct comparison, but still a series of comparable general patterns and proportions. The figures involved concern the Ottoman empire, whether as a unit or whether in its Egyptian section, and represent a whole spectrum of status, from the official record through to the more or less informed estimates of private individuals. The insights to be gained from these figures are extremely valuable, and particularly so given some of the perhaps more surprising conclusions reached above in dealing with the late Roman and Byzantine budgets.

The general proportions between items of revenue and expenditure present in the budget of Egypt during the Ottoman period are really quite extraordinarily stable over an extended period of time, and this, if nothing else, serves as a useful reminder of the effect of the virtually immutable parameters acting upon and constricting the structure of any pre-industrial state and society whether of the general area or not, and which are therefore to be found common to both the late Roman and Byzantine, and the Ottoman, budgets.

For example, taking the budgets for 1595/6 and 1797/8 as the early and late extremes, the following basic figures and proportions emerge:[262]

1595/6

Revs. from land-tax = 44,478,312 *para* = 76% fixed revs.
64% total revs.

[260] George Acropolites, *Historia* LIX; ed. Heisenberg and Wirth, I, p. 120: *tessaras de stathmous parēmeipsen ho stratos....*

[261] For this see, in the last instance: W. T. Treadgold, *The Byzantine State Finances in the Eighth and Ninth Centuries*, pp. 2–3, 64–5, 91–5.

[262] Figs from: S. J. Shaw, *The Financial and Administrative Organisation and Development of Ottoman Egypt 1517–1798*.

| | | |
|---|---|---|
| Revs. from urban *muqâta 'ât* | = 13,256,190 *para* = | 22% fixed revs.<br>20% total revs. |
| Exp. upon wages, salaries, pensions | = 31,636,672 *para* = | 65% total exp. |
| 1797/8 | | |
| Revs. from land-tax | = 75,212,389 *para* = | 65% fixed revs.<br>63% total revs. |
| Revs. from urban *muqâta 'ât* | = 17,391,415 *para* = | 15% fixed revs.<br>14% total revs. |
| Exp. upon wages, salaries pensions | = 53,111,117 *para* = | 62% total exp. |

The various balances are taken up by miscellaneous revenues, whether fixed or variable.

The principal point that immediately springs to the eye is, of course, the relative rôles played throughout by the revenues derived from the *harac* (land-tax) on the one hand (64%, 63% of total revenues), and by those derived from urban *muqâta 'ât* (tax-farms) on the other (20%, 14% of total revenues), unambiguously confirming the distinction between revenues based on land and agriculture, and those based on towns and trade, that has been posited above in a late Roman and Byzantine context. The secondary point is the proportion of the total revenue expended throughout on salaries and so on (65%, 62% of total revenues) falling neatly midway within the bracket 35%–55%–80% that has been posited above in a similar context.[263]

The earliest detailed budget for Ottoman Egypt so far made conveniently available is dated 1596/7, and presents a fascinating structure that is well worth entabulating in some detail:[264]

| | | |
|---|---|---|
| I. *Total revenues* | | *66,080,476 para* |
| Special arrears | 187,476 | |
| A. Land-tax | 40,780,691 | |
| B. Sale of treasury grains | 3,045,853 | |
| C. Customs-tax revenues | 5,450,579 | |
| D. Cairo *muqâta 'ât* | 5,681,288 | |
| E. Miscellaneous revenues | 10,934,589 | |
| II. *Total expenditures* | | *44,702,421 para* |
| A. Payments (*teslimat*) | 4,958,362 | |
| B. Salaries (*salyanat*) | 6,830,771 | (to principal officers) |

[263] See above, pp. 157–8, 162, 164, 172, 173–5, 205–6.

[264] Figs from: S. J. Shaw, *The Budget of Ottoman Egypt 1005–1006/1596–1597*, at p. 21.

| | | | |
|---|---|---|---|
| C. Wages (*mevacibat*) | | 26,557,591 | (to lesser officers, mainly mil.) |
| D. Deductions (*ihracat*) | | 2,833,500 | |
| E. Customary payments (*âdat*: pensions) | | 1,660,786 | |
| F. Purchases (*mubayaat*) | | 1,861,411 | |
| III. *Balance* | | | *21,378,055 para* |
| A. Deliveries | | 21,190,391 | |
| i) To the Holy Cities | (1,327,240) | | |
| ii) To Jerusalem | (35,320) | | |
| iii) To Istanbul | (19,827,831) | | |
| B. Left in the Egyptian treasury | | 187,664 | |
| IV. *Total customs-tax* | | | *9,065,266 para* |
| i) Alexandria, Rosetta, and dependencies | | 3,562,186 | |
| ii) Damietta | | 820,210 | |
| iii) Bulaq, Old Cairo, and dependencies | | 674,701 | |
| iv) Burullus and dependencies | | 393,482 | |
| (Sub-total) | | (5,450,579) | |
| v) Cairo | | 3,614,687 | |

It is, in the first place, of course, a salutary warning to have to recognise that the revenue of Egypt for 1596/7 might be described as amounting to either some 66 million *para* or some 1,650,000 gold pieces (from the point of view of the internal administration and involving the total gathered), or some 21 million *para* or some 535,000 gold pieces (from the point of view of the Istanbullu administration and involving the surplus forwarded).[265]

The same general patterns and proportions of revenue and expenditure as are present in the budgets of 1595/6 and 1797/8 are, as might be expected, also present in that of 1596/7. The land-tax accounts for 62% of the total revenue, and the customs-tax accounts for 8%. In fact these figures are crude ones only, and have to be refined by on the one hand consolidating the sale of treasury grains with the land-tax, from which they presumably ultimately derived, and by extracting the customs-tax element from the Cairene *muqâta 'ât* and consolidating it with the other customs-revenues. This raises the land-tax to 67% of the total revenue, and the customs-tax to 14%.

This latter figure compares well with the 5% or so calculated for the fifth- and sixth-

[265] See for instance above, p. 173.

century empire, which was territorially large and had extensive hinterlands, and the 20%–30% calculated for the fourteenth-century Byzantine and Trapezuntine empires, which were territorially small and effectively confined to littorals. One might indeed have expected Egypt to fall somewhat on the high side as regards customs-revenues, for apart from possessing a great Mediterranean port in Alexandria, in addition to the delta, the productive part of Egypt forms an extremely thin ribbon to either side of the Nile, and thus virtually the whole of productive Egypt is within easy reach of water transport.[266]

Other than this, 73% of total expenditure went on salaries and wages. The figures involved, giving a basic ratio of 7:27 for salaries (to the principal officers) and wages (to the lesser officers and so on), suggest that the multiplier of one-half employed above to calculate the effect of above-average pay and so on may well be more than ample.[267]

But perhaps the single most interesting and important fact emerging from the budget of 1596/7 is that no less than 33% of the total revenue was surplus to the needs of the local administration, and that of this virtually the whole (i.e. very nearly 500,000 gold pieces) was forwarded to Istanbul, leaving a minimal sum only in the Egyptian treasury. Egypt's fate, that of acting as a gigantic private estate, from which there were extracted surplus revenues sufficient to provide for the best part of the budget of an empire centred elsewhere, thus stretches from Alexander and Augustus, through Mehmed III, and beyond, to Napoleon.

The size of the budget of the earlier Ottoman empire as a whole is a much-vexed question, but perhaps not quite as vexed a one as that of the later Roman and Byzantine empire, for in the Ottoman case the material available is a good deal greater in quantity, and is a great deal better in quality: it already includes a number of items of contemporary official documentation that are of extraordinary importance, and it will doubtless include more as the vast resources of the Ottoman archives are further explored.[268]

Although earlier estimates and figures do exist, nevertheless for the picture as a whole, and as a unit against which to assess various other particular elements, recourse may for the moment be had to the estimates drawn up by Yunus Beg, the chief *dragoman* of the Ottoman court, and by Alviso Gritti, bastard of the doge of Venice, who was also a business-partner of Ibrahim the grand *vezir*, relating to the reign of Süleyman I (1520–66), and more particularly to the period 1530–7. The estimates therefore have some authority, and represent at least the considered and informed opinion of individuals who were in a good position to acquire official information if they considered it necessary. A not unimportant point is that the period involved was subsequent to the acquisition of the greater part of Anatolia by Mehmed II, and of Syria and Egypt by Selim I, the Ottoman

[266] See above, pp. 157–8.
[267] See above, pp. 166, 169.
[268] For one of these items, see below, p. 617, no. 271.

empire thus, in a strictly territorial sense, strongly resembling the late Roman empire in the east. The estimates (in Venetian ducats) are as follows:[269]

| | | |
|---|---|---|
| Land-tax | 1,300,000 | Anatolia and Greece (i.e. the Balkans) |
| | 700,000 | Syria |
| | 150,000 | Mesopotamia |
| | 1,600,000 | Egypt |
| Imperial farms, the islands, customs of Constantinople and Pera | 250,000 | |
| Total | 4,000,000 | |

The estimates are clearly partial ones only, and it has been suggested, on the basis of a modern – if now somewhat dated – analysis of Italian estimates of some twenty-five or thirty years later, that perhaps as much as an extra 2 million ducats ought to be allowed for revenues from mines, the salt monopoly, and so on. This suggestion may well be correct on general considerations, whilst being somewhat over-generous on particular ones, but there is no point in disputing something that is now essentially unquantifiable, and it is therefore best to accept it. The total revenue would therefore be very approximately 6 million ducats, the figure almost certainly nevertheless being a strongly maximal one.[270]

Now, there are a number of factors which may be taken as suggesting the accuracy or inaccuracy of a number of these individual estimates, but let it be supposed for the moment that the general pattern is nevertheless correct.[271]

On this supposition, the land-tax accounts for 94% of the total revenue if that total was 4 million ducats, and 63% if it was 6 million. The customs-tax (counting the entire

269 Figs from: A. H. Lybyer, *The Government of the Ottoman Empire in the Time of Suleiman the Magnificent*, at pp. 179–80, 273. It is worth noting that the 1,300,000 ducats for Anatolia and the Balkans compares well with the 600,000 for the Balkans alone in 1488/9, and that the 1,600,000 ducats for Egypt is close to the 1,650,000 for that country in 1596/7. See below, n. 271, and above, n. 264.

270 Lybyer, *The Government of the Ottoman Empire in the Time of Suleiman the Magnificent*, pp. 180–1.

271 Other estimates, of equal or lesser standing, are of course available, and these date from the 1430s through to the 1660s. A convenient list is to be found in Lybyer, *The Government of the Ottoman Empire in the Time of Suleiman the Magnificent*, at pp. 180–1, nn. 2, 3. A more recent treatment is to be found in F. Babinger, *Mehmed the Conqueror and his Time*, at pp. 450–8. Babinger (*op. cit.* p. 455) reckons state expenditure to have amounted to some 810,000 ducats, of which the army accounted for something in excess of 300,000, which is more or less in line with the late Roman and Byzantine evidence. The most recent treatment is that of S. Vryonis, 'Laonicus Chalcocondyles and the Ottoman Budget', *International Journal of Middle East Studies* 7 (1976), pp. 423–32. Chalcocondyles (Vryonis, *op. cit.* pp. 424, 426) reckons Mehmed's cash income as about 4 million ducats, of which the land-tax accounts for 900,000, the animal-tax for 300,000, and the trade-tax for 200,000, which is again more or less in line with the late Roman and Byzantine evidence. The official figures of the *harac* survey of 1488/9 (Vryonis, *op. cit.* pp. 429–30) give a ducat-equivalent of just over 600,000, but this sum is derived almost entirely from the Balkans – the tax was not (in theory, and as yet still in fact) levied upon Muslims, who were predominant in Anatolia. The Yunus Beg/Gritti figures nevertheless retain their potential importance because of the territorial similarity mentioned above.

250,000 ducats as for Constantinople and Pera, but necessarily omitting estimates for other ports and cities) amounts to 6% or 4% of the total revenue on the same basis. The first proportion evolved for the land-tax (94%) is, of course, very much like that calculated for the later Roman empire (95%),[272] although the second (63%) is just as like that calculated for Ottoman Egypt (64/63/67%).[273] The proportions evolved for the customs-tax (6/4%) actually bracket that calculated for the later Roman empire (5%).[274]

The proportions evolved for the individual territorial components are perhaps even more interesting. Egypt alone accounts for $\frac{2}{5}$ of the total revenue on a 4 million ducat-basis, and for $\frac{1}{4}$ on a 6 million one, but this latter is counting the land-tax only, and if the country is allotted an appropriate share of the 2 million difference, then its proportion in the second case of course remains stable. It is quite independently calculable that, in 1528, Egypt and Syria combined accounted for $\frac{1}{3}$ of the total Ottoman budget.[275] All this compares closely with the $\frac{3}{8}$ allowed Egypt as a fraction of the budget of the earlier prefecture of the East, and the $\frac{1}{3}$ allowed it if the prefecture of Illyricum is included.[276]

For all their manifest and immense crudities, and their manifold sources of possible error, the near coincidence of the two sets of proportions is almost uncanny, and although due allowance should obviously be made for sheer luck, the phenomenon nevertheless highlights something that is borne in more and more upon one the further one examines the history of the area: that is, as Fatih Sultan Mehmed himself was well aware, that the true heir of late Rome in the east, and of Byzantium, was the Ottoman empire. In this connection it might be noted that as late as the period 1862/3–1910/11, the *aşar* or tithe collected on the produce of the land, together with the (much smaller) *ağnam* or tax collected on animals, still formed easily the largest element in the Ottoman budget, the *gümrük* or customs-tax, although now appreciable, still coming well behind, and not only, it may be suspected, because of the foreign capitulations.[277]

It therefore follows that the more that is discovered on the subject of the budget and finances of the Ottoman state, particularly but in no way entirely with reference to the earlier period, and when these discoveries have been processed and appropriately interpreted, the greater the insight, even if confined to general patterns only, that will ultimately be gained into the budget and finances of its late Roman and Byzantine predecessor.

[272] See above, p. 157.
[273] See above, pp. 614, 615.
[274] See above, p. 157.
[275] H. Inalcık, *The Ottoman Empire. The Classical Age 1300–1600*, p. 128: the central government receives the surplus of the Egyptian budget, some 500,000 ducats annually, in cash; Egypt and Syria account for $\frac{1}{3}$ of the total budget in 1528.
[276] See above, pp. 171–2.
[277] S. J. Shaw, 'The Nineteenth-century Ottoman Tax Reforms and Revenue System', *International Journal of Middle East Studies* 6 (1975), pp. 428–30, 451 (table 1, total revenues), 452 (table 2, major sources of revenues), 452–3 (table 3, *aşar*), 453 (table 4, *ağnam*), 458 (table 9, *gümrük*).

## (IV) THE CONSEQUENCES FOR THE SEVENTH CENTURY[278]

### *A. Financial and military crisis*

The potential implications of all this are, of course, at once both evident and far-reaching.

That the seventh century must have witnessed an economic and financial crisis of fundamental proportions and long-standing nature in addition to a political one has barely been recognised, which is in itself a revealing commentary upon the state of the discipline: much energy has been expended rather, and in large measure fruitlessly, upon attempting to discover precisely when the first mention of a theme in its fully developed sense occurred, and upon other such dotty and antiquarian pursuits, which Byzantinists – much like the Byzantines before them – hold so dear.[279]

That this must nevertheless have been the case is quite clear and unambiguous, and arises out of even a quite cursory consideration of the changed balances between territory held, revenue extractable, and expenditure necessitated, that must have emerged and obtained during the late sixth century and the first half of the seventh.

At some stage of the late sixth century, the Danube frontier was breached, in an irrevocable way, by Avars and Slavs. Because of the paucity of the evidence involved, whether contemporary or later, the precise chronology and sequence of events remains uncertain, and the evident nature and scale of the phenomenon means that it is in any case likely to be quite unimportant: it is, in other words, time that the apparently interminable arguments as to precisely when the Slavs first attacked Thessalonica, or alternatively invaded the Peloponnese, were abandoned. For even if such problems were capable of 'definitive' solutions, the result would be of no great and wider significance: what is involved is clearly an increasing strain, leading to the progressive collapse and eventual swamping of a formal and traditionally hard-pressed system of defence on the one hand, and the largely hesitant and piecemeal penetration southwards of unorganised bands of prospective settlers on the other. It is entirely probable that at no particular date at all at the time did the irrevocable nature of what was happening occur to either side, and that any dates later evolved simply represent attempts to read back into the situation an organisation and unitary aspect which had never existed.[280]

[278] I should like to acknowledge the generosity of my friend and colleague John Haldon in acting as a helpful and uncomplaining 'sounding-board' in the production of this section, without, of course, committing him in any way to its findings and conclusions.

[279] The two most recent general works on the non-sequential history of the seventh century are: P. A. Yannopoulos, *La société profane dans l'empire byzantin des VIIe, VIIIe et IXe siècles*, and F. Winkelmann, H. Köpstein, H. Ditten and I. Rochow, *Byzanz im 7. Jahrhundert*. Their places of publication (Louvain and East Berlin, respectively) reflect their methodologies accurately enough, but even so and quite remarkably, neither more than barely mentions the possibility of a crisis in the state economy, despite its importance as a causative factor behind many of the changes witnessed by the seventh century.

[280] See above, pp. 78–81.

At any rate, it is clear that at least by the middle of the seventh century, and probably by a good deal earlier, the territorial situation very approximately represented in Map 16 had been brought into being: in the Balkans, the areas regularly held and administered by the imperial authorities were confined to isolated points, and thin and interrupted ribbons of land, on the peripheral littorals of the peninsula.

In contrast, the nature and sequence of events in the eastern provinces is far more clear-cut.

The first major Arab incursion into Palestine and Syria seems to have occurred in 633/4. In 634, the Byzantines were heavily defeated at Gabitha, and in 636 catastrophically so on the River Yarmuk. The collapse was swift and total. Aleppo, Damascus and Antioch all surrendered in 636/7, and the conquest of the remainder of Syria took place in 637/8. Edessa surrendered and the conquest of Mesopotamia took place in 639. Jerusalem surrendered in 638, most of Palestine in 640/3, and Alexandria in 642, representing the loss of all Egypt. Within a little less than a decade, therefore, and with minimal resistance only, the eastern provinces had been lost, and the empire, except in the north, had been confined to Anatolia behind the Taurus and Anti-Taurus Mountains.[281]

There remained to the empire: Anatolia behind the Taurus; the Aegean Islands together with Cyprus and Crete; and the peripheral remnants of the Balkans. There are good reasons for believing that Africa and Italy were effectively independent by this stage, and the latter was in any case fragmented between Byzantines and Lombards.[282]

Now, precisely how this pattern of territorial loss and retention worked out in terms of state finances, it is of course quite impossible to be certain, but approximate proportions can nevertheless be hazarded. It should be remembered that it has already been calculated that Egypt alone may have represented some $\frac{3}{8}$ of the budget of the eastern prefecture, or some $\frac{1}{3}$ of that of the combined eastern and Illyrian prefectures. It is therefore quite impossible that these territorial losses should have represented less than $\frac{1}{2}$ of the budget of the two prefectures, and it is quite probable that they represented considerably more. In fact, utilising the Ottoman model reflecting the situation during the reign of Süleyman; accepting the Balkans as providing $\frac{1}{2}$ of the combined figure for the Balkans and Anatolia; and accepting that the Balkans, Syria, Mesopotamia, and Egypt, had been completely lost; the proportion lost works out as representing some $\frac{3}{4}$ of the budget of the two prefectures. This may quite possibly form a 'worst-case' analysis, but even if it does, the result, and its implications, must have been truly shattering.[283]

It is with expenditure necessitated that the crucial problems and their implications emerge, and that it becomes necessary to intrude, however briefly and superficially, upon several of the major and still outstanding questions of Byzantine history. For at this stage, it is obviously necessary to enquire into the fate of what was consistently the largest single object of state expenditure: that is, the army.

281 Refs: Stratos, *Byzantium in the Seventh Century* II, *634–641*, pp. 50–116.

282 See above, pp. 406–9, 421–4.

283 See above, pp. 171–2, 616–18.

Fortunately, something of a consensus seems to be emerging, or indeed seems already to have emerged, on the subject of what is perhaps the greatest problem of all: the origins of the thematic armies of the developed Byzantine period.[284] It now seems generally accepted that the origins of the four original themes of Anatolia are to be found in the field armies of the sixth century and earlier. That is, that the origin of the thematic army of Anatolikon is to be found in the *exercitus orientalis*, that of Armeniakon in the *exercitus armenianus*, that of Thrakesion in the *exercitus thracianus*, and that of Opsikion in the *imperiale obsequium*, all of which are mentioned systematically, and for the first time together, in a letter of the emperor Justinian II to the pope Conon, in 687.[285] It seems equally generally accepted that the origins of the four original thematic *stratēgoi* are to be found in the *magistri militum utriusque militiae* who commanded those armies, the *m.m. Armeniae* having been added as late as the reign of Justinian, and the *m.m. praesentales* having commanded these armies in the immediate area of the capital, the court army or *obsequium*, and possibly in effect the partly ceremonial guards regiments as well.[286]

Even the basic step by which these former field armies and their commanders came to end up where they did in Anatolia, and thus to permit the commencement of the evolutionary processes involved, also seems agreed: as the imperial frontiers contracted or collapsed, so, eventually, and doubtless in varying states of completeness, and of order or disorder, the field armies retreated into the only major land-mass left to the empire: the Anatolian peninsula.[287] The date at which this step occurred is obviously dictated by that of the contraction or collapse of the individual frontiers. It seems clear that much of what remained of the *exercitus orientalis* must have retreated with Heraclius when he evacuated Syria in 636, and that the rest presumably accompanied the *dux* Theodore when he evacuated Alexandria in 642.[288] Similarly, the *exercitus armenianus* must have evacuated Armenia at the latest by 652/5 when the country under Theodore Rshtuni became tributary and effectively subject to the Arabs.[289] Each of these dates forms a *terminus ante quem* only, and the moves involved may well have occurred somewhat earlier. The dates at which the other two armies reached their eventual areas remains even less certain. The transfer of the *exercitus thracianus* to Anatolia has been the subject of highly-charged debate:

[284] This much-vexed problem continues to produce literature, but the latest general treatments are: Stratos, *Byzantium in the Seventh Century* I, *602–634*, pp. 266–82; Toynbee, *Constantine Porphyrogenitus and his World*, pp. 224–74; Lilie, *Die byzantinische Reaktion auf die Ausbreitung der Araber*, pp. 287–338. There is also a partial, but still quite wide-ranging discussion, with particular regard to the reign of Heraclius, in: J. F. Haldon, *Recruitment and Conscription in the Byzantine Army c. 550–950*, at pp. 28–40. For a useful discussion of the general background to the period 641–717: W. E. Kaegi, *Byzantine Military Unrest 471–843: An Interpretation*, at pp. 154–208.

[285] Mansi, *Sacrorum Conciliorum Nova et Amplissima Collectio* XI, col. 737: ... *exercitibus, tam ab a Deo conservando imperiali obsequio, quamque ab orientali [et] thraciano, similiter et ab armeniano....*

[286] Most recently and succinctly placed in focus by Toynbee, in *Constantine Porphyrogenitus and his World*, at pp. 224–30.

[287] *Ibid.* pp. 228–30.

[288] Stratos, *Byzantium in the Seventh Century* II, *634–641*, pp. 73–4, 108–14.

[289] *Ibid.* III, *642–668*, pp. 28–31.

as noted above, Theophanes records a transfer of the army in Europe to Asia as early as 621/2, but this step has been granted a permanence and significance out of all proportion to the vagueness of the terms involved.[290] The *obsequium* probably did not have to move at all: elements of the guards regiments such as *scholarii*, *domestici* and *protectores* are recorded as having long been conveniently stationed (whether garrisoned or billeted out) in cities of Hellespontus, Bithynia, Phrygia and Galatia from the reign of Justinian onwards, and it seems possible that the *excubitores* were also included on the basis of later evidence.[291] It would therefore be only natural for the praesental field armies to be stationed in the same area. In any case, it was clearly this last factor that ensured that whenever the Thracian army was moved into Anatolia, it moved not into the area directly abutting onto its former station, that is into the Marmara region, as might have been expected, but into one which was a good deal more southerly – quite simply, the obvious area was already occupied.

What one has to envisage, therefore, is the piecemeal withdrawal of these armies into Anatolia, either as the relevant frontier disintegrated and collapsed or simply became untenable, or else pre-emptively and somewhat in advance of this situation. Although it is tempting to speculate solely on the basis of such appallingly inadequate material as does exist, the precise dates and sequence of events are nevertheless probably ultimately irrecoverable. The one prediction that nevertheless does seem reasonable is that there should have been a crucial conjuncture of factors at some stage later in the reign of Heraclius or early in that of Constans II, or more precisely during the period *c.* 636–652/5, as the armies of the *magistri militum orientis* and *armeniae* arrived in those areas that subsequently became the themes of Anatolikon and Armeniakon. Beyond this, virtually everything is speculative, and therefore potentially a matter of controversy.

The question nevertheless does arise, as a matter of necessity, as to the military and organisational state of the armies involved at the moment of their arrival. There are several reasons for supposing that it was in fact less vestigial and chaotic than might otherwise perhaps be supposed.

In the first place, although the eastern and praesental armies, at least, must have been severely damaged by the double defeat in Syria, and by subsequent events, nevertheless for various reasons such events rarely have the absolute and catastrophic nature that is

[290] In the last instance: Haldon, *Recruitment and Conscription in the Byzantine Army*, pp. 29–39.

[291] Procopius, *Historia Arcana* XXIV.24–5; ed. Haury and Wirth, III, p. 151: *hoi domestikoi te kai protiktores... hoi de epi te Galatias ek palaiou kai khōriōn heterōn hidryntai*. Theophanes, *Chronographia*; ed. de Boor, I, p. 236: *skholarioi... en tē Nikomedeia kai Kiō kai Prousē kai Kyzikō kai Kotyaeiō kai Dorylaiō*. *Vita Sancti Theodori Syceotae* CI, ed. Festugière, p. 80: *domestikoi*(?) at Pessinus. XXV, XL, LXXVI, pp. 22, 40, 63: *protiktores* at Ancyra and Anastasiopolis. CLVI, CLIX, pp. 128, 133: *skholarioi* at Optatianae/Nicomedia. Only the *domestikoi*(?) at Pessinus (in Galatia Salutaris, later Anatolikon) infringe the pattern. For the *exkoubitores*: S. Vryonis, 'St. Ioannicius the Great (754–846) and the "Slavs" of Bithynia', *Byzantion* 31 (1961), pp. 245–8 – Joannicius, is enrolled as *exkoubitōr*, from Marycatus of Bithynia (nr Miletopolis, on the n. shore of Lake Apollonia) – this could well reflect earlier dispositions.

sometimes attributed to them, whether by contemporary or modern sources. It has been calculated, for example, that even in as catastrophic a sequence of events as the battle of Adrianople in 378 and the subsequent anti-Gothic campaigns, something like one-seventh only of the eastern *comitatus* was destroyed. Similarly, it has been calculated that even as a cumulative result of the fifth-century campaigns against Alaric and Radagaesus, the great invasions of Gaul, and the campaigns against virtually incessant usurpers, two-thirds of the western *comitatus* was destroyed.[292] These figures, while arrived at by way of necessarily very crude methods of reckoning, and therefore being at best very approximate only, nevertheless reveal a considerable capacity for survival even under continuously catastrophic conditions. The general point is confirmed by the fact that at no time during the period in immediate question did the state seemingly find it impossible to field an adequate army, whatever its record on the one hand, and granted that the area requiring defence – effectively Anatolia behind the Taurus – had been much reduced on the other.[293]

In the second place, it seems clear that the Anatolian areas into which the armies were withdrawn, and in which they were subsequently stationed (to utilise as neutral a term as possible), were defined virtually entirely in terms of late Roman and early Byzantine provincial boundaries. Where such boundaries were ignored, as in the case of Phrygia Salutaris, which was divided between the subsequent themes of Anatolikon and Opsikion, the reason seems to be clear. In this particular case, it has already been noted that elements of the guards regiments and probably of the *obsequium* had been stationed in its more northerly and Marmara-facing cities such as Dorylaeum and Cotyaeum as early as the sixth century. This will have meant that when the eastern army was moved back into Anatolia, this area will already have been occupied,[294] but that on the other hand, the narrow and waisted shape of Salutaris will have invited the division of the province at the point where the waist was narrowest, thus rendering its more southerly section available for the stationing of eastern troops (cf. Maps 25, 26). It has in fact long been recognised that the original themes of the developed Byzantine period territorially represented groups of late Roman and early Byzantine provinces,[295] and that when – as happened frequently – these themes were subsequently divided down into their constituent *tourmai* and so on, which were then given enhanced status as themes, the *tourmai*/themes still reflected, sometimes were even identical with, former provinces.[296]

The only major exception to this general pattern, in inner Anatolia at least, resulted from the creation or promotion of the theme of Kharsianon under Leo VI, and this

[292] Jones, *Later Roman Empire* III, p. 355.

[293] This is obviously only a very general point indeed, but a glance through the appropriate volumes of Stratos, *Byzantium in the Seventh Century* (I–III), demonstrates it well enough.

[294] See above, p. 622 and n. 291.

[295] See, for example: Gelzer, *Die Genesis der byzantinischen Themenverfassung*, pp. 127–30, cols 1, 2.

[296] *Ibid.* pp. 127–30, cols 1, 5.

involved the abstraction of several *tourmai*, *banda* and *topotērēsiai* from the themes of Armeniakon, Boukellarion and particularly Kappadokia, and their transfer to the new, or newly promoted, theme.[297] In what was clearly intended as a compensatory measure, several *banda* and *topotērēsiai* strung out along the main road from Dorylaeum to Colonia (Archelais) and Caesarea were abstracted from the themes of Anatolikon and Boukellarion and transferred to that of Kappadokia, thus accounting for the curious shape of the later theme of Kappadokia (cf. Maps 24–6). These compensatory additions were termed *ta Kommata*, having been 'cut off' from the other themes, thus demonstrating through their name the realisation that violence had been done to organisational norms.[298]

In any case, that the old provincial boundaries continued to retain a certain recognition and standing is evident not only from the appearance of specific provincial groupings in the *Notitiae Episcopatuum* and Conciliar Lists, but also from the occurrence of a similar phenomenon upon the seals of later *kommerkiarioi*. In this latter case, themes are on occasion specifically recognised as being composed of groups of provinces, and *kommerkiarioi* are, for example, known as being: 'of Colonia [nr Nicopolis] and of all the provinces (*eparkhiai*) of the Christ-loving Armeniakon [717/18]'; 'of the provinces of the Anatolikoi [732/3]'; 'of the command (*stratēgia*) of the Thrakēsioi [741/2]'; 'of the provinces of the God-guarded imperial Opsikion [745/6]'.[299] This small but crucial group

[297] Constantine Porphyrogenitus, *De Administrando Imperio* L; ed. Moravcsik and Jenkins, p. 237 – from Armeniakon: Komodromos and Tavia; from Boukellarion: Myriokephalon, Timios Stavros and Verinoupolis; from Kappadokia: Kasē, Nyssa and Kaisareia. It looks very much as if Constantine has inverted the units attributed to Armeniakon and Boukellarion. Constantine (*loc. cit.*) states that Kharsianon had formerly been a *tourma* of Armeniakon, and he certainly treats it as deriving from the latter in the *De Thematibus* (II; ed. Pertusi, p. 65). The statement is strictly and eponymically accurate, but the theme actually took its territorial base from the Cappadocian elements that were transferred to it, Caesarea may even have been its capital, and this is why it is counted as a derivative of Kappadokia/Anatolikon in Constantine's cycle of thematic *rhogai* – see below, pp. 648–9. For Kharsianon: Oikonomides, *Les listes de préséance byzantines*, p. 348. Toynbee, *Constantine Porphyrogenitus and his World*, p. 255.

[298] Constantine Porphyrogenitus, *De Administrando Imperio* L; ed. Moravcsik and Jenkins, p. 237 – from Boukellarion: Bareta, Balbadona, Aspona and Akarkous; from Anatolikon: Eudokias, Hagios Agapetos and Aphrazeia. Although Constantine gets his units right on this occasion, he still inverts the causative factors involved; it is clear that what is primarily involved is the creation or promotion of Kharsianon, and that what is secondarily only involved is the compensation of Kappadokia, whereas C's account commences with the latter and concludes with the former.

[299] Zacos and Veglery, *Byzantine Lead Seals* I.I, pp. 299–300, nos 222a/b (Armeniakon); p. 325, no. 245 (Anatolikon); p. 339, no. 261 (Thrakesion); p. 341, no. 263 (Opsikion). In the light of what is to emerge below (pp. 626–34, 654–62), it is worth noting that the seal of Thrakesion is of particular importance. In 742, marching through Opsikion on campaign against the Arabs, Constantine V was suddenly attacked by the rebel and usurper Artavasdus. In the resultant civil war, Constantine relied on Anatolikon and Thrakesion, and eventually defeated Artavasdus at Sardis, well inside the latter theme. The conclusion seems obvious: in 741/2 Thrakesion and part of Anatolikon if that is where Katō Hexapolis was (*op. cit.* pp. 337–8, no. 260a/b) had been mobilised, and Constantine was marching to pick up these troops at the *aplēkta* when he was attacked. The seal of Armeniakon may represent a mobilisation in reaction to the Arab siege of Constantinople and supporting or diversionary operations in 717/18; that mentioning Anatolikon may represent another in reaction to an Arab attack on Acroenum and Caesarea in 732; and that mentioning Opsikion may represent another on the occasion of Constantine's campaign against the Arabs in 746. Refs: Ostrogorsky, *History of the Byzantine State*, pp. 165–7, and Lilie, *Die byzantinische Reaktion auf die Ausbreitung der Araber*, pp. 128–33, 149.

of seals quite clearly shows the main and original themes at an early stage of their development, for the references are clearly still to people, that is to armies, but to armies which are nevertheless stationed in particular groups of provinces.[300]

Now what all this implies, of course, is that when the armies withdrew, or were withdrawn, into the Anatolian peninsula, they arrived not only in some appreciable numerical strength, but also in some appreciable degree of order. The latter deduction is to be derived from the fact that their subsequent stationing was carried out according to a reasoned (but not necessarily, of course, a pre-conceived) plan, in which current administrative norms were on the whole observed. The guards regiments and *obsequium*, as noted above, were already in some kind of occupation, and so the *exercitus thracianus* had to move south. The same factor dictated the division of Phrygia Salutaris at its accentuated waist, when the *exercitus orientalis* moved into the centre. It probably even dictated that it was on the boundary between Honorias and Paphlagonia (despite the Justinianic amalgamation of the two provinces[301]) that the *exercitus armenianus* stopped when it moved into the north and east.[302] (Maps 25, 26)

But what it also and in turn implies is that the state, having lost something of the order of three-quarters of its potential budget, would have had to continue financing an army which, whilst it may have suffered appreciable losses, nevertheless remained a considerable and coherent fighting-force, and which, when intact, had accounted for well over one-half of its actual budget. In an ancient or mediaeval context, and with the inevitable implication of an inelasticity of revenue, the financial strains involved must have been simply horrendous, and the question therefore ineluctably arises as to how the state continued to finance the army.[303]

The general tenor of financial exigence is quite clear. According to Cedrenus,[304] Heraclonas, in 641, distributed three solidi to each soldier: 'on account of (*hyper*) his brother [the deceased Heraclius Constantine]'. The circumstances are obscure, and the evidence contradictory, it being unclear, for example, whether the money involved derived from the sums left by Heraclius Constantine in order to secure the interests of his sons.[305] On the other hand, wherever the money derived from, the event is closely associated with either the accession of Heraclonas or the coronation of the young Constans II, and it therefore seems much more probable that it was intended to represent the traditional accessional donative or *augustaticum*. If it did indeed represent the donative,

300 The emphasis upon people – that is upon manpower – rather than upon land or places is a factor which will appear consistently in the remainder of this section, and forms an accurate reflection of the state's priorities at this stage. 301 See above, p. 178.

302 For the theme of Paphlagonia: below, p. 649 n. 414.

303 See above, pp. 158–9, 164, 171–2, 205–6, 237–42.

304 George Cedrenus, *Historiarum Compendium*; Bonn edn, I, p. 753. Stratos, *Byzantium in the Seventh Century* II, *634–641*, pp. 187, 217–18. Stratos seems as confused as the original sources.

305 See above, p. 222. For the chronology: H. K. Gallatin, 'A Study in Civil Government and Imperial Defense in the Seventh Century Byzantine State under Emperor Constans II (641–668)', pp. 148–9, and Stratos, *Byzantium in the Seventh Century* II, *634–641*, pp. 189–99, 217–18 (xxvi).

then the exigence is clear: the traditional donative was five solidi and one pound of silver or, as it had been effected as late as 578, nine solidi.[306] The Heraclian sum therefore represented only one-third of the former rate.[307]

## B. *The* apothēkē *and the* basilika kommerkia

In a more general sense, it is clearly at very much this stage that dated – or closely datable – seals of *kommerkiarioi* who are attached to, and clearly exercise jurisdiction over, various cities, and more particularly various groups of provinces and/or islands, quite suddenly become much more common. The formulaic titles involved vary: the earlier is commonly 'N.... *genikos kommerkiarios* of the *apothēkē* of M'; and the later is simply 'of the imperial *kommerkia* of M'.[308] A few such seals are known, bearing somewhat primitive and hesitant formulae, for several of the reigns from Justin II to Heraclius, but with the reign of Constans II, and more particularly with the years 654–9, the pace noticeably quickens and the spate becomes quite extraordinary, and from the seventies onwards the seals bear not only imperial figures but also indictional dates as well.[309]

The phenomenon has attracted a moderate amount of discursive discussion, but, one may suspect, insufficient integrated analysis, and it seems worthwhile attempting a very brief such analysis here.[310] Now, it is just possible that all that is represented is a simple change in fashion, with the use of such seals becoming generally more popular, but the

306 See above, p. 481.

307 See also the payment, by Heraclius himself, of official *rhogai* at one-half only of the former rate – above, p. 494.

308 Zacos and Veglery (*Byzantine Lead Seals*, I.I, pp. 135–6), elaborating upon earlier authors, make much of the change: it would perhaps be wiser to exercise caution. Much more significant is the obscure process by which the *gen. komm.* and *bas. komm.* evolved into the simple collector/collection of customs-taxes. The later *kommerkiarioi/abydikoi* were heavily concentrated upon the Peloponnese, Thessalonica, Cherson, and Chaldia, revealing a pattern of entry-ports, and they were of appreciably lower rank than their predecessors: Antoniadis-Bibicou, *Recherches sur les douanes à Byzance*, pp. 182–4, 232–8 (nos 75 onwards).

309 Zacos and Veglery, *Byzantine Lead Seals* I.I, pp. 212–14, 216–18 (nos 130, 130 bis, 132–5: to 654–9); p. 234 (no. 152: from 672/3 or 673/4).

310 The most recent analysis, a brief but perceptive one, is that of J. W. Nesbitt, in 'Double Names on Early Byzantine Lead Seals', *DOP* 31 (1977), pp. 115–17 and n. 20. Nesbitt, synthesising earlier treatments, proposes that (a) the *kommerkiarios* was always a tax – (i.e. customs –) collector; that (b) many seals bear on one side the imprint of burlap/sacking, suggesting that they were attached to sacks of merchandise; that (c) the *kommerkiarioi* were men of prominence, as attested by their ranks, and therefore ought in principle to be identifiable; and that (d) the general pattern of the phenomenon suggests that tax-farming by the indictional year was involved. All these propositions are accepted in what follows below, and it is only the origin, and the predominant nature and occasion, of the merchandise/trade/taxation, that is further defined. It ought to be observed, in this connection, that the high ranks and offices frequently held by the earlier *kommerkiarioi* suggests that what was involved was not simply trade of a general and strictly commercial nature, but something more specific and appropriate to their senior standing: they were in effect acting as quartermasters-general. For the (later) attachment of lead seals to precious stuffs, see: above, p. 258 (Liutprand); *The Russian Primary Chronicle, Laurentian Text*, trans. Cross and Sherbowitz-Wetzor, p. 75 (945: implied). For further refs, see: Antoniadis-Bibicou, *Recherches sur les douanes à Byzance*, pp. 164–7.

extraordinarily high proportion of such seals that are connected with the *apothēkē* and the *kommerkia* very strongly suggests that what is represented is a change in administrative forms and practices. It is clear that any suggestion that the seals were connected with, or reflected, the straightforward maintenance of or an increase in exchanges or trade, would be – given the disastrous nature of the times – the merest fantasy.[311] Indeed, it is precisely at this period that small change – the copper follis and its fractions – disappears definitively from Anatolian urban sites.[312] Rather, it is clear that they were connected with, or reflected, a drastic increase in the state regulation of exchanges or trade, and there is only one plausible reason for that: a desperate governmental search for economies or unexploited sources of revenue. It should be remembered that it was precisely and specifically in almost identical circumstances that the western government of Valentinian III had imposed the tax termed *siliquaticum* in 444/5. The novel involved[313] had quite simply and drastically dictated that all buying and selling, everywhere, should take place in a particular place and at a particular time, and that on every occasion of sale one-half siliqua in the solidus should be paid both by the buyer and by the seller, amounting to a tax of one twenty-fourth on every exchange.[314] The inevitably depressive consequences of the combination of the restrictions on the place and time of exchanges, and the tax upon them when they did occur, given the likely minimal returns involved, are a true measure of governmental despair.[315]

In origin, the *apothēkē* was clearly some kind of state warehouse, and several are known to have existed in important cities, such as Tyre and Alexandria, as early as the sixth century.[316] But it was equally clearly already more than a simple warehouse, as private

[311] As, for example, R. S. Lopez, 'The Role of Trade in the Economic Readjustment of Byzantium in the Seventh Century', *DOP* 13 (1959), p. 73 – the title of the article itself betrays the same general standpoint: but there was no such rôle in that century. [312] See below, pp. 640–5.

[313] Valentinian III, Novel xv (*De Siliquarum Exactionibus*).

[314] *Placuit itaque, ut omni venditione per solidum dimidia siliqua ab emptore, dimidia a venditore per omnem contractum aequaliter publico conferatur: in omnibus mobilibus inmobilibusque rebus venditiones tantum emptionesque dumtaxat tali condicione.... Iubemus enim et in oppidis et in regionibus certo loco ac tempore emendis atque vendendis rebus per honoratorum dispositionem nec non ordinum seu civium sub praesentia moderatoris provinciae manifesta definitione constitui.... Nulli itaque mercatori praeter hanc observationem nisi ad designata loca temporibus praestitutis ad negotiationis suae species distrahendas passim licebit accedere, uti certa ratio emendi atque vendendi ibi constare possit....* The lengthy provisions are indeed draconian. See also: Jones, *Later Roman Empire* I, p. 435, II, p. 826.

[315] *Ibid.* II, at p. 826, claims that the tax itself survived only in the very restricted area still under imperial control in 444/5, and this may indeed be true in the strict sense. It has been pointed out, however (P. H. Sawyer, 'Kings and Merchants', in P. H. Sawyer and I. N. Wood (eds), *Early Medieval Kingship*, at pp. 141–2), that the restrictive concepts embodied in the novel nevertheless had a wider and longer-term effect than Jones suspected. It is also worth noting that the payment of tax half by the buyer and half by the seller is equally typical of the Byzantine *kommerkion*: Antoniadis-Bibicou, *Recherches sur les douanes à Byzance*, pp. 112–13.

[316] For Tyre: Zacos and Veglery, *Byzantine Lead Seals* I.1, pp. 213–14 (no. 130 bis); see also Antoniadis-Bibicou, *Recherches sur les douanes à Byzance*, p. 159. For Alexandria: above, p. 246. For regional *apothecarii*: above, p. 242. See also for a (presumably) metropolitan *apothēkarios*: Nesbitt, 'Double Names on Early Byzantine Lead Seals', p. 118 n. 29.

merchants – *argyropratai* and presumably others – could have an agent in, or more probably attached to, such an *apothēkē*.[317] It is very probably to be connected with, and in that case was presumably the origin of, as the name of course suggests, *al-qaysāriyya/alcaicería*, an institution found in the Muslim world from Syria and Egypt to Spain, and generally involving the production and sale of luxury goods.[318] Private merchants could indeed purchase a 'house' or 'room' in the *qaysāriyya*, where they then did business, but the complex as a whole was run by the state either directly or through a tax-farmer, the *ṣāḥib al-sūq*, whose basic function was to collect state dues.[319] This was presumably a developed form of the institution, but is one that nevertheless possesses potentially valuable insights into its origins.

It may be guessed, and the process involved is in fact a little better than that, that the original function of the *apothēkē* was as a sales-point for the surplus products – and more particularly the luxury ones – of the late Roman and early Byzantine state factories: the *fabricae* (arms and armour-manufacturies), *gynaecia* (woollen-mills), *linyphia* (linen-mills), and *baphia* (dyeing-works).[320] It is known that the central *officium* at least, and probably the regional *thesauri* as well, of the *comitiva sacrarum largitionum* acted in a rather similar way, certainly working up bullion provided by private persons, and quite possibly even selling off (at an appropriate profit) pieces made out of bullion emanating from public institutions.[321]

Now, the *fabricae* in the east ended up under the control of the *magister officiorum*, and the remainder under that of the *comes sacrarum largitionum*.[322] But this control involved the plant, personnel and expertise only, and not the materials supplied or – presumably therefore – the finished products. The complete model is provided by the mint, which was controlled by the *comes largitionum*. The vast bulk of the precious metals supplied to the mint came in the form of bullion from the praetorian prefecture; it was then struck into coin by the mint; and it was finally returned whence it had come.[323] In the same

317 See above, p. 246.

318 Egypt and the Near East: Goitein, *A Mediterranean Society* I, *Economic Foundations*, pp. 191, 194, 365 – Tyre, noticeably, figures in the list. Spain: M. C. Quintanilla Raso, 'Notas sobre el comercio urbano en Córdoba durante la Baja Edad Media', in *Actas del I Congreso de Historia de Andalucía, Diciembre de 1976* I, *Andalucía Medieval*, at pp. 413–15, and J. H. Edwards, *Christian Córdoba. The City and its Region in the Late Middle Ages*, pp. 74, 85, 101–3. The Muslim and Christian *al-qaysāriyya/alcaicería* seems to have been devoted to the production and sale of luxury goods, and particularly those of precious stuffs, which was presumably a reflection of the primitive Byzantine form. I owe the Spanish references to the kindness of my friend and colleague, John Edwards.

319 Goitein, *A Mediterranean Society* I, *Economic Foundations*, p. 194. For the *ṣāḥib al-sūq* in Spain, see: P. Chalmeta Gendron, *El 'señor del zoco' en España: edades media y moderna, contribución al estudio de la historia del mercado*.

320 Jones, *Later Roman Empire* II, pp. 834–7. It is presumably no coincidence that Tyre, mentioned as the site of both an *apothēkē* and a *qaysāriyya*, possessed in *c.* 570 both a *gynaecea publica* and a *holosericum* or silk-weaving factory. Refs: W. Heyd, *Histoire du commerce du Levant au moyen-âge* I, p. 19 and n. 5.

321 Dodd, *Byzantine Silver Stamps*, pp. 23–35. See also above, p. 385 n. 51.

322 Jones, *Later Roman Empire* II, pp. 835, 836.

323 See above, pp. 388–91 and Table 10.

way, the *fabricae* were provided with the necessary raw materials by the prefecture, turned out a finished product, and presumably returned it.[324] The same pattern should clearly have operated in the case of the other state factories.[325] The prefecture, or one of its constituent organs, should therefore have become a vast agency for the provision of raw materials and the storage and supply of finished products. It may therefore be suggested that it is here that is to be found the origin of the *idikē trapeza* of the prefecture of the East, for its successor, the *idikon/eidikon*, was precisely a vast store of such objects – from raw metals to fine silk *himatia* – and it is clear that the ambivalence of the term *idikē* = special, as opposed to *genikē* = general, and *eidē* = things in kind or goods, was operative almost from the start.[326] The *idikon/eidikon* could also buy manufactured objects on the open market, and it could therefore probably also sell in the same way.[327] There is, in fact, some reason to believe that it could do so, whether via particular state institutions and officials, or the guilds, or both.[328]

This, then, was the Constantinopolitan nexus, but there is good reason to believe that there was by extension also a regional one.

The *epi tou eidikou* had amongst his subordinates the heads of the various imperial workshops (*arkhontes tōn ergodosiōn*), with the exception of the master of the mint (*arkhōn tēs kharagēs*, etc.).[329] What seems to have happened is that in the major administrative redistribution attendant upon the breaking up of the prefectural *officium*, the *idikē trapeza/idikon* had been given independent status and had not only retained the control over materials and finished products that it had previously possessed, but had also gained control over the institutions that used and produced them, and which had previously been under the *magister officiorum* and *comes largitionum*. Such a redistribution makes, after all, a good deal of organisational sense.[330] The *vestiarion*, however, had retained control over

[324] Jones, *Later Roman Empire* II, p. 835.

[325] *Ibid.* p. 837. In this case, however, procedure looks more varied, with the direct compulsory purchase of materials being at least used on occasion.

[326] For the *idikē trapeza*, see above, pp. 411–12. For the *eidikon*, see: Oikonomides, *Les listes de préséance byzantines*, pp. 316–17. See also: Constantine Porphyrogenitus, *De Caerimoniis* II.45; Bonn edn, pp. 671, 673–6, 677–8, for the huge quantities of supplies, arms, cash, and clothing, supplied by the *eidikon* for the Cretan expedition; and above, pp. 309–10 for the *eidikon*'s contribution to the imperial baggage-train. For the seals of the *eidikoi* and their various subordinates, see now: Laurent, *Le corpus des sceaux de l'empire byzantine* II, *L'administration centrale*, pp. 302–52 (ch. 7, '*L'eidikon*'). For what is perhaps the earliest seal of all (of a *basilikos idikos logos*), and the opposition *idikon/eidikon*, see: Zacos and Veglery, *Byzantine Lead Seals* I.1, p. 383, no. 320.

[327] See above, p. 310 and n.

[328] Laurent, *Le corpus des sceaux de l'empire byzantin* II, *L'administration centrale*, pp. 336–9 (*sērikopratai*, *holosērikopratai*, *vestiopratai*). For the guilds: 'Leo VI', *To Eparkhikon Biblion* IV (*vestiopratai*), V (*prandiopratai*), VI (*metaxopratai*), VII (*katartarioi*), VIII (*sērikarioi*), IX (*othōniopratai/mithaneis*); ed. Nicole, pp. 26–41. For the manufacture and sale of silk in general, see: R. S. Lopez, 'Silk Industry in the Byzantine Empire', *Speculum* 20 (1945), pp 1–42.

[329] Philotheus, *Klētorologion*; ed. Oikonomides, p. 123. See also above, n. 326.

[330] See above, pp. 410–13.

the mint, an understandable exception, that institution being too intimately connected with the immediate interests of the state.

The *ergodosia* subject to the *eidikon*, perhaps by way of a general director termed the *ergastēriarkhēs*, include the *blattion*, clearly involving the production of silk stuffs, and which perhaps had a separate sub-department (?) termed the *Zeuxippos*, which certainly produced them, as they still survive; the *khrysoklabon*, clearly involving the embroidery or sewing on of gold cloth onto ceremonial garments; and probably the *armamenton*, clearly involving the production or storage of arms.[331] A further *ergodosion*, the *khrysokheion*, may have been identical with the mint, which as noted above had remained subject to the *vestiarion*.[332]

Now, by collating a large number of datable seals, the official careers of a number of individuals, or pairs of partners, have been pieced together, and it has become clear that the offices held normally changed with the indictional year, resulting in some apparently bewildering sequences. For example, George, *patrikios*, and Theophylactus were *arkhontes tou blattiou* in 689–91; *genikoi kommerkiarioi* of the *apothēkē* of Asia and Caria, of that of Galatia II, of that of Isauria and Lycaonia, and that of Lazica, Trebizond and Cerasus, all in 691–3; *genikoi kommerkiarioi* of the *apothēkē* of Paphlagonia and Ionopolis in 692/3; *arkhontes tou blattiou* again in 705/6; and *genikoi kommerkiarioi* of the *apothēkē* of Hellespontus in 708/9.[333] It has also become clear that on occasion two apparently quite different offices could be held together, *genikos kommerkiarios* and *arkhōn tou blattiou* being the most popular combination.[334] This sequence and partnership, and this kind of combination, makes sense in one context only: that of tax-farming by the indictional (i.e. financial) year, presumably by way of the submission of competitive offers, and with actual collection being performed by agents.[335] This, as seen above, is also characteristic of the Syrian and Egyptian *qaysāriyya*. It may also have been a feature of the later Byzantine mint.[336]

What, then, was happening? It seems *prima facie* clear that the production of luxury

[331] Oikonomides, *Les listes de préséance byzantines*, p. 317, and Laurent, *Le corpus des sceaux de l'empire byzantin* II, *L'administration centrale*, pp. 325–46. For the production of arms, delivered to, and stored in, the *sacrum armamentum*, see: Justinian, Novel LXXXV (*De Armis; Basilidi Magistro Sacrorum Officiorum*; 539). The law forbids the production of arms anywhere other than in the state *fabricae*; forbids the sale of arms to private individuals; and mentions the delivery of arms to, and their storage in, not only the central *arrmamentum*, but also the *armamenta publica uniuscuiusque civitatis*.

[332] See above, p. 412, and p. 427 n. 245.

[333] For the general phenomenon, see: Zacos and Veglery, *Byzantine Lead Seals* I.1, pp. 143–61 (tables 1–16). For George and Theophylactus, see: *ibid.* pp. 150–1 (table 6²).

[334] *Ibid.* pp. 142–3.

[335] Nesbitt, 'Double Names on Early Byzantine Lead Seals', pp. 116–17.

[336] Bar Hebraeus, *Chronography*; ed. trans. Budge, I, p. 178: 'And the king of the Rhomaye [i.e. Basil II] was jealous of them. [i.e. the sons of Abu Imran], and he compelled them to strike royal darics [at their own expense] for one year: and they did so, and their wealth was not diminished'. See also above, p. 239. It is surely no coincidence that it is precisely at this date that it has been suggested that the coinage began to be marked by annual sets of *signa* (Grierson, *DOC* III.2, pp. 606, 644–7). How much further back the system can be traced remains an interesting problem. For the later annual sets of *signa*, see: Hendy, *DOC* IV.

goods, and particularly that of silk stuffs, by the state *ergodosia*; their distribution to the regions by not entirely certain means, and their sale there in the state *apothēkai*; and the collection of state taxation levied upon sales conducted within the warehouses – or customs-depots as they could equally well be termed – by the *kommerkiarioi*; were all intimately connected. It seems equally clear that the term *apothēkē* should be understood in a general sense, for some of the territorial circumscriptions involved were vast, and it is unlikely that a single building or complex only was involved: rather, a number may have been.[337] What was being granted, or rather farmed out, was the monopoly of sales of certain types of goods, and of tax-collection upon those sales, within particular and defined areas.

But is this sufficient? It does seem unlikely, on the face of it, that at a time of great crisis, and however desperate for economies and revenue the state should – to all appearances – drastically alter and/or regulate the provision of 'fancy goods' to the regions.

The real clue as to what was happening almost certainly lies in two casual references by Theophanes, taken in combination with a small but very particular and obviously related group of seals.

Theophanes records that, as a result of Justinian II's great but not entirely successful campaign of 688/9 in which he reached the region of Thessalonica, he took up a great crowd of Slavs and sent them to the region of Opsikion, by way of Abydus, and settled them there.[338] He also records that, some four years later (692/3), the same emperor picked out from the Slavs whom he had settled some 30,000 men, enlisted them, equipped them, and named a certain Neboulus as their leader. He then led them against the Arabs in the region of Sebastopolis. Neboulus, however, was bribed, and deserted to the enemy with 20,000 of his men. Justinian, in revenge, massacred the remainder, along with their wives and children, at Leucate, on the Gulf of Nicomedia.[339]

The seals involved, all dated to the eighth indiction (694/5), are as follows:[340]

*Geōrgiou, apo hypatōn/Asias Karias kai Lykias tōn andrapodōn*
*Geōrgiou, apo hypatōn/tōn andrapadōn tōn Sklab(o)ōn tēs Bithynōn eparkhias*
*Geōrgiou, apo hypatōn/apothēkēs tōn andrapodōn Phrygōn Saloutarias*
? ? ? */tōn andrapodōn tōn K...n I kai II Kappadokias*

[337] For example, Thrake, where both Mesembria/Develtus, and Hexamilium, at the opposite ends of the theme, may have been utilised: see below, pp. 654–5. For Armeniakon, where Sinope, Sebastopolis/Sebastea, Colonia, and Camacha, may all have been utilised: see below, p. 655 and n. 442.

[338] Theophanes, *Chronographia*; ed. de Boor, I, p. 364.

[339] *Ibid.* pp. 365–6. For Leucate, see also above, p. 589. For a discussion of this whole interlude, virtually the only recommendation for which is that it cites most of the relevant sources: Stratos, *Byzantium in the Seventh Century* v, *685–711*, pp. 11–18, 30–8. The two sections of the discussion are otherwise badly vitiated by chauvinist sentiment.

[340] Zacos and Veglery, *Byzantine Lead Seals* I.1, pp. 190–1 (table 33). Clearly to be connected with this group of seals is yet another contemporaneous one of George, for the Armeniakoi – precisely the region in which Sebastopolis lay: *ibid.* p. 164 (table 18/2).

That the two sets of material, both involving Slav prisoners of war (= *andrapoda*), must be related has long been recognised, and surely correctly so, but the nature of the relationship has been left virtually unexplored.

It is in the first place clear that there are here two absolute dates, and one perhaps less than absolute. The Thessalonican campaign is quite independently datable to the second indiction (= 688/9), and the seals are all unequivocally dated to the eighth indiction (= 694/5).[341] The Neboulus interlude and the massacre stand somewhat suspect: after all, even given the genuineness of the interlude, if Justinian really did massacre the remaining Slavs and their dependants in 692/3, then there ought to have been none, or at least no considerable numbers, left to be referred to by the seals in 694/5.[342] On the other hand, if Theophanes' date is definitely suspect, that his geographical location is faulty should occasion little surprise: the province of Bithynia and the northern half of that of Phrygia Salutaris were indeed both incorporated into the later theme of Opsikion, but the provinces of Asia, Caria and Lycia, and of the two Cappadocias, were all geographically well removed from metropolitan cognisance. The wider geographical spread is, nevertheless, extremely plausible, because it makes good strategic sense: the Cappadocias guard the entry into Anatolia, by way of the Cilician Gates; Bithynia and Phrygia Salutaris guard the other end of the same route, that is the approach to the capital; and Asia, Caria and Lycia form a coastal stretch increasingly exposed to Arab piracy and attacks. Justinian, then, was attempting to strengthen the defences of three critical, but increasingly battered and still threatened, areas. (Maps 24–6)

In any case, to retain both the Neboulus interlude and the massacre, and yet to resolve the evident contradiction of dates, it is clearly tempting, and would indeed be quite plausible, to move interlude and massacre either to 694/5 itself, or to even later, so that the Slavs could still be referred to in 694/5, while leaving open the possibility or probability of a contemporary or subsequent massacre.[343]

341 For the Thessalonican campaign, see the refs in Ostrogorsky, *History of the Byzantine State*, p. 130 and n. 2, and Grumel, *La chronologie*, p. 248. See also below, pp. 656–7.

342 See: Stratos, *Byzantium in the Seventh Century* v, *685–711*, at pp. 34–8. The piecing together of the sequence of events and of the precise chronology of this period forms an historical nightmare. In this particular case, neither sequence nor chronology is at all clear. A further complication arises from the fact that both the Byzantine and the Arab sources connect the outbreak of hostilities with the issue of dinars which were in some sense novel and offensive to the Byzantines. It seems very likely that there is here a reference to the issue of dinars bearing a standing figure of the caliph ʻAbd al-Malik, themselves heavily influenced by the contemporary imperial nomismata bearing a standing figure of Justinian. This is itself variously dated by the Arabic sources, and dates from 692/3 to 695/6 are given, or have been suggested, although 694/5 is the most popular. Be that as it may, the earliest dinars of the type in question now surviving are dated 693/4 (see above, p. 501). For an amusing (if somewhat fanciful) account of the whole interlude, involving papyrus, nomismata, and dinars, see the translation in Cipolla, *Money, Prices, and Civilization in the Mediterranean World*, pp. 16–20.

343 It may be suggested that the combined epigraphic, sigillographic, and numismatic, evidence provides the only 'hard' chronology for these events and years, and that it is around this nexus that the remaining

The variant nature of the formulae involved in the seals of this group has also occasioned some surprise, but probably should not have done so. It is just possible that the total omission of the conjunctive *kai* and the function *genikos kommerkiarios* on the reverse is significant, but it is probably merely a matter of the length of the full potential formula. The term *apothēkē*, and indeed the description *Sklaboi*, each appear once only, but again, it need not be doubted that their presence is understood on the remainder.[344]

Nevertheless, the larger question of just why the *apothēkē* should have been present or operative with respect to the Slav *andrapoda* captured in 688/9, and as far as can be seen with respect to them alone within the designated areas, and on that single occasion in 694/5 alone, inevitably bulks large. Why, in other words, should an institution or practice so far connected with the store and sale of 'fancy goods' be involved with Slav settlers at this stage: was it to sell silken and/or embroidered stuffs (i.e. *blattia*, and so on) to Slav womenfolk? The answer is, of course, that it was not at all to do that, but it was to provide and sell equipment and arms to the Slav menfolk as part and parcel of their enlistment. And here one would do well to recall the double nature of the *idikē trapeza*, and of its descendant, the *eidikon/idikon* and its dependencies, involving not only metropolitan *ergodosia*, but also regional *fabricae* and *gynaecia*, *linyphia* and *baphia*. The fate of the regional factories and mills remains unknown, but the survival of at least an otherwise unknown *phabrix Seleukeias* into the seventh century seems assured.[345]

Now, it is simply implausible that Justinian, in the taking, transporting and settling of his Slav prisoners of war, had no pre-conceived plan for them. Each of these aspects, particularly when involving the kind of scale that is uniformly evidenced in this case, involves major logistical problems, and it is very clear that in settling them where he did he already had a set – and by strong implication a military – end in mind.[346]

evidence should now be fitted. The basic chronology, on present showing, could thus go as follows (see also, below, pp. 655, 656–7):

| | |
|---|---|
| 687/8 | Preparations for Bulgarian campaign |
| 688/9 | Campaign and settlement of Slavs |
| 688/9 } 689/90 } | Issue of transitional Arab dinars (**IB/IΓ**) |
| 691 | Refusal of Arab tribute: evacuation of Cyprus |
| 692 | Issue of nomismata w. Christ |
| 693/4 | Issue of dinars w. standing caliph |
| 694/5 | Mobilisation of Slavs; Byz. campaign against Arabs; Justinian defeated and deposed. |

Stratos is extraordinarily and unconvincingly defensive concerning the alleged massacre, presumably because it might reflect ill on the Greeks with regard to the Slavs: everything else that is known of the savagery of Justinian, however, suggests that such a massacre is all too likely to have taken place.

344 Zacos and Veglery, *Byzantine Lead Seals* I.I, pp. 191, 266, 272.

345 See above, p. 416. Actually, given the known contents and competence of the *eidikon*, and therefore of the *apothēkē*, it is not necessary to exclude absolutely the provision and sale of 'fancy goods' along with more serious items: officers, at least, will have needed silk *skaramangia* and so on, and may well have purchased other stuffs for their womenfolk. But this was not the basic point of the exercise.

346 See also below, pp. 656–7.

Even the detailed chronology as emended supports this latter case. For, if Justinian was campaigning as far as Thessalonica in the indictional year 688/9, then it will have been during the traditional campaigning season, that is the spring and summer of 689. It would have been a major feat of logistical organisation, but a possible one, to get his prisoners of war – probably in bands, as they came in – across the straits via Abydus and, in large part at least, in place by the autumn of that same year. Five years later they – or a portion of the menfolk – were mobilised, that is enlisted, equipped, and put into the field. This, surely, implies the agreed grant of seed-corn and five years' immunity from taxation and/or military liability. The Slavs will thus have ploughed (or whatever) and planted in the autumn or winter of 689/90, and have cropped for the first time in the summer of 690; they will also have been permitted to enjoy the crops of the years 691–4, making five crops in all; then, at the first available subsequent opportunity, presumably in the winter or spring of 694/5, they will have been visited by, or made subject to, the *apothēkē*, involving the provision and purchase of arms and equipment, and in any case made ready for the campaigning season of 695. A similar process was contemporaneously also applied to the Armeniakoi, amongst whom, in the region of Sebastopolis, the projected campaign was to take place. The schedule involved is a tight, but a perfectly feasible and, given the varied nature of the direct and implied evidence, a very plausible, one.

The *apothēkē*, then, in this developed form, was probably neither a single building or complex, nor even a number of them, but a specific practice, involving the provision and sale of arms and equipment, and – inevitably – the charging of some unknown degree of taxation on the transaction. Once again, it should be noted, the trade involved was of an 'imperfect' kind. It may, of course, have involved something like a travelling warehouse, or static ones at the regional centres of mobilisation, the *adnoumia*,[347] but it was no longer simply that. This, of course, explains why, even when the territorial circumscription involved is a vast one, the seals of the *kommerkiarioi* always refer to the *apothēkē*, and never to the *apothēkai*, the full title apparently being *apothēkē tōn basilikōn kommerkiōn*. It also explains why the *apothēkē* can appertain to a particular group of people, like the Slav *andrapoda*, settled in particular but scattered regions, along with and amongst other sections of society which nevertheless appear to have remained unaffected. It has thus developed from being something specific and with a physical existence, to being a general system or practice as well – much like the *mētaton* or *aplēkton*.[348]

### C. *The general problem of the themes*

From this nexus of material, two most significant implications emerge: which are that, during the period 688/9–694/5, the Byzantine soldier was responsible for his own

[347] Ahrweiler, 'Recherches sur l'administration de l'empire byzantin aux IX$^{e}$–XI$^{e}$ siècles', pp. 8–9.
[348] For the *aplēkta* proper, see Map 24; for the derived form, see above, p. 610.

equipment and arms, and that, at least on occasion, he could be settled on land with the understood (if now undefinable) obligation of being subsequently liable for military service.[349] And here, quite suddenly, and ever so unwillingly, one finds oneself teetering on the brink of the precipice: for this, quite clearly, and in however nascent a state, is already the soldier of the developed Byzantine period, and so quite automatically one has involved oneself in the question of the origin and early nature of the themes.[350]

It is clear that there are, within this much-vexed problem, two major and quite distinct strands or processes involved: that by which the *magister militum* of the late Roman and early Byzantine period acquired formal jurisdiction over a defined territorial circumscription, thereby becoming the *stratēgos* of the developed Byzantine period; and that by which the soldiers under him, from being maintained and salaried and kept on a virtually permanent footing by the state, became in quite large part self-maintained, liable to periodic service only, and with the obligations involved deriving from the possession of land. The former, mercifully, is not immediately germane to the present series of studies, but the general model may well be supplied by the slightly earlier and rather similar process through which the *magistri militum* of Africa and Italy, because of the disturbed political and dislocated administrative circumstances of the sixth century, gradually acquired significance at the expense of their respective praetorian prefects, with their effective supremacy eventually being acknowledged and codified in the formation of the two exarchates.[351]

Just as there are two basic processes involved, so there are two basic approaches to the resolution of the problem: what one might call the 'catastrophist', which has also tended to place a heavy emphasis upon the personal qualities and capacities of the emperor Heraclius; and the 'gradualist', which term speaks for itself. The former, for long in the ascendant, has of late – and not least because of the understandable reaction that it eventually provoked – tended to give ground to the latter, and there is little doubt that this general shift is a healthy one, with the approach now favoured being potentially much the more fruitful. There is, however, a distinct danger, and there are actual signs currently, of its being erected into a received dogma, where nothing at all can happen, except piecemeal, and ever so gradually.

The situation seems dominated by dualities, for there are also two main elements in the problem of military developments: the provision and maintenance of equipment and arms; and the connection with the land.[352] It may be suggested that the former, at least, is now within sight of resolution. It has been cogently argued and demonstrated, quite

[349] The attachment of officials termed *kommerkiarioi* to the *apothēkē* surely implies not only the provision of arms, etc., but also their sale, and taxation on that sale: the military thus owned their arms. The Slav interlude implies land and a connection with service. These, then, are the two basic features of the military régime of the developed period.

[350] For the most recent general literature, see above, p. 621 n. 284.

[351] See above, pp. 406–9.

[352] For the most recent general literature, see: above, p. 621 n. 284

recently, that the ownership – that is the provision and maintenance – of horse, equipment and arms by the individual soldier is already assumed by *Ekloga* XVI.2, that is by 726/41, and that thereafter the assumption is consistent and uniform.[353] With the identification of the *apothēkē* as principally involving the provision and sale of equipment and arms to the military, this developed situation can now be taken back not only to 688/9–694/5 but, by strong implication, even further, because, as pointed out above, the seals of the *genikoi kommerkiarioi* who were responsible for this trade quite suddenly begin to become more common with the years 654–9. This suggests at least a *terminus ante quem* for the introduction of the system itself.[354]

The definition of two main elements as being involved in the immediate problem under discussion should not, however, disguise the fact that they are inevitably and intimately interrelated. For the provision and maintenance of horse, equipment and arms by the individual soldier is not only a significant change from the system obtaining in the late Roman and early Byzantine period, where the responsibility was undertaken by the state, but of itself dictates some kind of equivalent change in the general system of financing the soldier himself. In other words, the costs involved in such provision and maintenance, let alone anything else, should in no way be underestimated. At various points during the period stretching from the fourth to the sixth century, a military horse was reckoned as costing seven solidi, and the various items of a military uniform were reckoned as costing somewhat under six solidi.[355] The various items of arms and armour remain unknown as to costing, for these were produced not indirectly by levy – which reveals the occasional cost – but directly by the state *fabricae*, to which their production was indeed presumably confined.[356] On the other hand, it seems unlikely that they will have cost much, if anything, less than the horse or uniform, and it is therefore very probable that the initial cost of equipping a private soldier (and therefore of such a soldier later equipping himself) will have been somewhere in the region of twenty solidi. Indeed, later texts very strongly imply 18 or 18½ solidi to have been normal.[357] As to maintaining the same soldier, an annual adaerated *annona* worth four or five solidi was provided for his support, and a *capitus* worth four solidi was provided for that of his horse, if he rated one.[358] On occasion, at least, an additional provision was made for his household or dependants.[359]

Now, it is quite inconceivable that a financial burden of this weight could simply have been transferred from the state to the soldier, without some compensatory financial

353 Haldon, *Recruitment and Conscription in the Byzantine Army*, pp. 67–74.

354 See above, p. 626.

355 Jones, *Later Roman Empire* II, pp. 625–6.

356 See above, p. 630 n. 331 (Justinian, Novel LXXXV) – Justinian implies the confining of arms production to the *fabricae* to be a novelty, but it seems likely that the situation had long obtained in practice: there is, for example, as yet no apparent section on the price of arms in Diocletian's *Edictum de Pretiis Venalium Rerum*.

357 Refs: Lemerle, *The Agrarian History of Byzantium from the Origins to the Twelfth Century*, pp. 63 and n. 2, 123.

358 Jones, *Later Roman Empire* II, pp. 461, 630, 677; see also above, p. 166.

359 Jones, *Later Roman Empire* II, pp. 630–1.

mechanism being granted in return. The crucial question is, of course, the precise form that that compensation took. There is one form that it did not take, and could not have taken, and that is cash. The whole object of the transfer from state to soldier was clearly to remove a cash burden from one to the other (the state had actually handed out cash to the soldier so as to permit him to buy his horse and uniform), and in any case, as pointed out above, the state must have had, and did have, insufficient cash at precisely this stage.[360]

One is reluctant to wheel out the now classic phrase 'there is no alternative', and to attach it to land at this point in the discussion, but it is indeed difficult to see how the issue can any longer be avoided.

It may in the first place be suspected that some, at least, of the now common reluctance to accept an early 'settling' and 'landing' of the army, not necessarily overnight, but at least according to some system and over a relatively short period of time, is merely a reaction against the 'catastrophists' and the terms in which they for long tended to conduct the argument. If it is indeed part of such a reaction, then it should be recognised for what it is, and discarded. For in point of fact, of course, such a 'settling' and 'landing' was not at all without quite recent historical precedent, and a very general model may perhaps once again be had in the earlier west, where the barbarians had been in some sense 'settled' and 'landed', and, at least in Italy, Spain and Burgundy, according to some degree of system, and over a relatively short time-scale.[361]

The point is, of course, that there should have been plenty of land available. Whether, as seems likely, or not Anatolia had witnessed a drastic demographic decrease as a result of plague, civil disorder and foreign invasion, thus leaving quantities of private land unoccupied and/or ownerless, the state could have utilised for the purpose imperial land, that is the properties administered by the *res privata* and the *patrimonium*.[362] Not much is known of the quantities of imperial land available with direct reference to Anatolia, but there were extensive stretches of imperial estates in Pontus, Bithynia, Caria and Pamphylia, Phrygia Salutaris, and above all in Cappadocia, where it has been reckoned that the greater part of Cappadocia I was actually composed of such estates.[363] But in addition to these stretches, there were also scattered smaller holdings, which might well also have amounted to an appreciable proportion of the total of cultivable land. All in

360 See above, pp. 620, 625.

361 Jones, *Later Roman Empire* I, pp. 248–53. This traditionalist view of the land-settlement has recently been challenged: W. Goffart, *Barbarians and Romans A.D. 418–584. The Techniques of Accommodation.* Goffart argues that the institution of the barbarian *sors* in the west was neither a billeting, nor an expropriation, but a specific grant of state fiscal revenue – presumably something along the lines of the later Byzantine *pronoia* grant. The case is an interesting one, and clearly very relevant to the problem in hand, but it remains to be seen as to whether it wins partial or total accceptance.

362 See above, p. 371. n. 2.

363 Jones, *Later Roman Empire* I, p. 416, II, p. 713.

all, whether in larger or in smaller holdings, it may well be that the emperor owned something of the order of 15–18% of the total.[364]

And here the really quite extraordinary lack of recognisable imperial, or imperial-derived, estates in Anatolia in the twelfth century, compared with the proliferation of the same in the Balkans, ought perhaps to be remembered (Maps 19, 29). In Anatolia behind the Taurus and Anti-Taurus, where it has been argued that the great stretches of such earlier estates represented former royal lands, and which was never occupied in the long term by a foreign enemy, there are virtually no such later estates. It is by no means certain that this later lack was then of long standing, but the clear emphasis placed by the state upon converting recently-conquered land in eastern Anatolia into imperial *episkepseis* and *kouratōreia* in the tenth and eleventh centuries suggests a perceived need for the acquisition of more state land.[365] In the Balkans, where the periphery had been relatively heavily urbanised from an early period, and in which there had been no extensive stretches of earlier estates, but which was in large part nevertheless occupied in the long term by a foreign enemy, there is an abundance of later estates.[366] The contrast could be explained if, in Anatolia, the property of the *res privata* and the *patrimonium* had at some stage been granted away effectively in return for some kind of service, whether direct or indirect, and the state had subsequently, and in consequence, found it necessary, when recovering territory from the enemy, whether in eastern Anatolia or in the Balkans, to convert such territory into state land.

The recent arguments advanced in opposing the relatively formal and swift 'settling' and 'landing' of the army have tended to take two main directions. The first argument is that the later 'code-words' denoting estates carrying with them the obligation of military service, that is *stratiōtika ktēmata*, are found no earlier than the tenth century, with such estates becoming a matter of systematic legislation only with the undated Novel VIII of Constantine VII (i.e. of the period 945–59), which is devoted entirely to them. This complains that, with the passage of time (*kai epeidē tō khronō*) the position of the landed soldiers (*stratiōtai*) has deteriorated, and therefore what unwritten custom (*hē synētheia agraphōs*) in earlier times (*tois emprosthen khronois*) had instituted was now being codified.[367] The institution, or perhaps rather practice, is allowed to be taken back somewhat from this period, as indeed the wording of the novel itself dictates that it should be, and via various of the *taktika* and the hagiographical *vitae*, is given recognition in a primitive or even nascent form as early as 823/4. It is not allowed, however, to be taken back much further, and it is in any case deprived of basic significance in the formation and maintenance of the military forces of the empire.[368]

[364] There were smaller holdings even in the province of Asia: *ibid.* p. 414. For percentages: *ibid.* pp. 415–16 – Africa Proconsularis (18.5%), Byzacena (15%), Cyrrhus (16%).

[365] See above, pp. 104–6, 133–5, Map 29.

[366] See above, p. 89, Map 19.

[367] Refs: Lemerle, *The Agrarian History of Byzantium from the Origins to the Twelfth Century*, pp. 115–31 (novels), 131–54 (other docs).

[368] *Ibid.* pp. 149–50.

The second argument, which has already been alluded to, in a curious way, and quite unconsciously, complements the first, and in doing so extends back the potential antiquity of the system under discussion some considerable way. Although it too considers land as an important factor, it emphasises that the texts – whether of a formal or informal nature – concentrate rather upon the person of the soldier, his family and household, and his personal ownership of horse, equipment and arms. Again, via various hagiographical *vitae* and, more important, *Ekloga* XVI.2, it takes these elements back to 726/41, and by implication further. But, once more, although an early 'settling' of the army is readily acknowledged, a formal 'landing' is not permitted, and instead a preliminary billeting, in accordance with the known late Roman and early Byzantine regulations on the subject, is posited as an intermediate mechanism.[369]

Now, this is clearly not only not the place to attempt a detailed summary of the arguments, but it is also equally clearly not the place to attempt a detailed critique of them. All that should be said is that the one tends to emphasise the land factor, and makes little of the personal ownership of military paraphernalia, whilst the other tends to emphasise the ownership factor, and makes correspondingly less of land. But, as pointed out above, these two factors are intimately interrelated aspects of a single problem. The institution of the *apothēkē* takes back the ownership factor at least to the period 654–9, and both the ownership and the land factors very strongly appear to be already present in the episode involving the Slav *andrapoda* in the period 688/9–694/5. Unless a convincing intermediate and preliminary mechanism is provided, then the only plausible accompaniment to ownership is land. And in this respect it is worth pointing out that the provinces of Cappadocia I and II feature particularly prominently amongst the early (i.e. 654/9–694/5) seals of the *genikoi kommerkiarioi* of the *apothēkē*.[370] This, it is true, may be not simply that the region had been particularly heavily militarised through the granting out of state land, but also because it had now become particularly important strategically. The two considerations may thus, largely fortuitously, have gone together, and in this respect in turn it should be noted that the main nexus of these Cappodocian seals (687/8–694/5), or the later section of it at least, clearly coincides chronologically with the increasing tension and opening of actual warfare between Justinian II and 'Abd al-Malik. This must have led to repeated mobilisations, of which the episode involving the Slav *andrapoda* in 694/5 was only the final *dénouement*.[371]

To the contrary, however, it should be stressed that billeting, in itself, does not automatically provide such a convincing mechanism, begging quite as many questions as it answers. The late Roman and early Byzantine regulations on the subject say nothing

[369] Haldon, *Recruitment and Conscription in the Byzantine Army*, pp. 66–79.

[370] Zacos and Veglery, *Byzantine Lead Seals* I.1, pp. 178–9 (table 26). A useful comparative impression is to be gained from the descriptive listing on pp. 219–68 (nos 136–88).

[371] *Ibid.* pp. 178–9 (table 26); see also above, pp. 631–4.

of the implied permanent billeting of soldiers, or of the billeting of their households and dependants, or of the hosts being responsible – in whatever way, direct or indirect – for their military paraphernalia.[372]

## D. The evidence of the coinage

There is, in addition, a further and quite distinct strand in this question, that has been no more than briefly alluded to above. This involves the pattern of contemporary coin finds on Anatolian archaeological sites. Much stress has recently been placed upon this, in an uninformed and exaggerated way, as direct evidence for the end of antiquity and the beginning of the Byzantine middle ages. But what is perhaps the most significant feature of this pattern has been barely mentioned, and then almost as an afterthought. Emphasis is placed upon the number of hoards datable to *c.* 615, and the disappearance of single finds from sites at much the same time, reflecting the dislocating and disruptive effects of the Persian invasions. It is then observed that, with the restoration of more settled conditions later in the reign of Heraclius, there occur the beginnings of a minor recrudescence in site-finds, continuing into the reign of Constans II where it comes to an end, presumably reflecting renewed invasions, this time Arab ones. There then follow almost two centuries in which virtually no coins at all occur on Anatolian sites.[373] The balance of interest is almost certainly misguided.

Now, although individual variations to this pattern occur, they are relatively minor ones, and there is therefore no doubt that the general pattern itself is a valid and standard one, having been observed at all the major exacavations: Ancyra, Pergamum, Ephesus, Priene, Sardis, Aphrodisias and Anemurium.[374] It also occurs at Antioch, which demonstrates the phenomenon to be not only valid but widespread, for, of course, the city was at this stage not only not in Byzantine hands, but was not even under serious attack or even threat of attack from the Byzantines.[375]

[372] Jones, *Later Roman Empire* II, pp. 631–2.

[373] For the thesis in its most evolved form: Foss, 'The Persians in Asia Minor and the End of Antiquity', pp. 721–47. See also, however: A. P. Kazhdan, in *Byzantina* 9 (1977), at pp. 478–84 (review of Foss, *Byzantine and Turkish Sardis*), where a number of pertinent questions are asked by the original author of the general thesis of urban decline.

[374] For the basic refs: Hendy, 'Byzantium, 1081–1204: An Economic Reappraisal', p. 45 n. 4 (Sardis (old excavations), Pergamum (old excavations), Priene, Antioch). For Ancyra: C. Foss, 'Late Antique and Byzantine Ankara', *DOP* 31 (1977), p. 87 (Appendix 2, 'Coins from the Gymnasium at Çankırıkapı'). For Pergamum (new excavations): C. Morrisson, 'Provisional Inventory' (unpublished), 1980. For Ephesus: Foss, *Ephesus after Antiquity: a Late Antique, Byzantine and Turkish City*, pp. 197–8 (Appendix 7: 'Byzantine coins from Ephesus'). For Sardis (new excavations): Bates, *Byzantine Coins*, pp. 113–19. For Aphrodisias: M. F. Hendy, 'Provisional Inventory' (unpublished', 1975; see also above, p. 439 n. For Anemurium: J. Russell, 'Provisional Inventory' (unpublished), 1978. I owe the information from Pergamum and Anemurium to the kindness of Cécile Morrisson and Jim Russell respectively. The Sardis figures cited below are those from the new excavations.

[375] See above, p. 620. For the coins, see above, n. 374.

The relevant minor variation, which occurs at Pergamum, Sardis and Anemurium, involves the sheer quantity – whether absolute or relative – of material from the reign of Constans II. At both Pergamum and Sardis, this has been connected as a matter of general probability with fortress-building, and Ancyra has also been taken as suggesting much the same on similar grounds.[376]

Whatever the plausibility or accuracy of such an interpretation, what has not really been examined is the distribution of coins within the reign of Constans II itself, and here the relevance of the numismatic material to the wider question in hand very quickly becomes apparent. For, at Sardis, Aphrodisias and Anemurium at least, it is clear that a heavy concentration occurs within the first two-thirds of the reign, and that a minimal representation only marks the final third. At Sardis, the figures are 641–58, 81 coins, 658–68, 6 coins; at Aphrodisias, 641–58, 26 coins, 658–68, 0 coins; at Anemurium, 641–58, 98 coins, 658–68, 3 coins. At all three sites, as usual, subsequent reigns are represented vestigially only, if at all. Much the same general pattern seems evident at Pergamum, although there the evidence is necessarily much cruder and the particular pattern is somewhat less clear; it is, however, confirmed at Antioch. In both of these cases, subsequent reigns are again represented minimally.

It is therefore clear that it is very much at the same stage as the *apothēkē* system was getting under way, or at least is becoming evident through seals (654–9), that coin finds are ceasing to occur on Anatolian sites (658–68). It is difficult to avoid the conclusion that the one phenomenon was not only connected with, but was also actually causing, at least in part, the other.

One of the most striking examples of the probable causative connection between the military and the occurrence or non-occurrence of coins on archaeological sites at this period derives from the material from Sardis.[377] There, of the total of eighty-seven coins of Constans II, no less than forty-eight come from a single large, heavily-built room and its immediate environs, inside what were evidently the otherwise disused and probably ruined remains of one of the main public building complexes of the city-centre hard by, and in fact facing directly onto the main through-road, which itself, together with its associated smaller buildings (former shops), accounts for a further thirty coins. The well-removed acropolis, and the route from the city-centre up to it, account for a further small accumulation of $3 + 3 = 6$ coins, the whole accounting for no less than eighty-four out of the total of eighty-seven coins.

It is fairly clear that this extraordinarily accentuated geographical pattern has been influenced somewhat by the finding of the occasional small parcel of coins, but it is equally clear that it has not been fundamentally so influenced. It has been very plausibly suggested

[376] Foss, 'The Persians in Asia Minor and the End of Antiquity', pp. 742 (Pergamum), 737–8 (Sardis), 736 (Ancyra).

[377] Bates, *Byzantine Coins*, pp. 2–3, 113–19, Map 4 ('Building B Complex') at the end of vol.

that what it reflects is the barracking of a military detachment in the large room with, one may suppose, the duty of guarding – and possibly also repairing – the main road, again possibly utilising one or another of the small shops facing onto the road as a sentry-box.

But one must remember, of course, that this is very much the period of crisis, *c.* 636–652/5,[378] and if the interpretation above is correct, then it looks as if the remnants of the city may have received a refugee detachment of the *exercitus thracianus*.[379] What subsequently happened to the detachment remains entirely obscure, but it should be pointed out that the cessation of coinage on the site does not necessarily – of itself at least – denote the disappearance of the detachment. In any case, the overwhelming importance of the military factor in the production and distribution of coin will yet again have been emphasised.

It could well be that if not only a 'settling' but also a 'landing' of the field armies was taking place at about this time, then the process, which will presumably in principle have been initiated by a single legislative act, will nevertheless in practice not have been implemented uniformly, whether chronologically or geographically. It might well, for example, have been easier to find stretches of available land in the Cappadocias than in Lydia, and the process might therefore have been relatively speedy in the one, and more protracted – perhaps involving the preliminary but quite prolonged barracking of troops in semi-ruined cities – in the other. A cursory examination of the seals of the *genikoi kommerkiarioi* of the *apothēkē* suggests that there may actually be something in this, for there seems to be a strong northern and eastern balance in the earlier seals (i.e. those from 654/9 onwards), with such western provinces as Asia, Caria and Lycia, and so on, tending to appear from the last decade of the century onwards only.[380]

It nevertheless has to be faced that the detailed mechanisms behind all this are all too likely to be irrecoverable, and it would therefore be quite wrong, in attempting a reconstruction, to be too precise. But if the state was abandoning a system whereby it provided horse, uniform and equipment to its military, in the form of a cash grant, in favour of one whereby the responsibility was transferred to the military itself – even if the state continued to provide the administrative means of supply, via purchase from the *apothēkē* – then what it was doing in essence was exchanging a quite major cash-element in its finances for a non-cash one. For whatever the compensatory mechanisms provided, it is clear that they were not, and could not be, based on cash. If this changing pattern of operation obtained generally at this period, and the state was abandoning other major cash-items in its finances in favour of non-cash ones, as in at least one very major instance

[378] See above, pp. 620–2.

[379] See above, pp. 621–2.

[380] Zacos and Veglery, *Byzantine Lead Seals* I.I, pp. 162–91 (tables 17–33). Again a useful comparative impression is to be gained from the descriptive listing on pp. 219–68 (nos 136–88).

seems quite likely,[381] then the quite abrupt cessation of coin at most or all major archaeological sites in Anatolia becomes readily explicable. Although Justinian's novel regulating the administration of Africa might be taken as suggesting that gold alone was involved in military payments,[382] it is nevertheless clear that, at least by the seventh century, copper – which is basically what is in question here – was also a major factor in such payments. For not only does the episode involving Heraclius having had a statue melted down and sending the proceeds off to an army in the Pontus suggest as much, but it is also clear that the products of temporary mints set up during the Heraclian revolt, and those of similar mints set up during the Persian invasions and Heraclian campaigns, are very heavily concentrated upon copper – and these mints must have had a mainly military basis.[383]

What, then, one is witnessing at this juncture, the second half of the seventh century, is the state, in the face of a massive financial crisis, taking quite fundamental organisational and financial steps in order to ensure its survival, by way of transferring to its major object of expenditure a form of wealth which it still did possess (land or whatever), in place of a form which it no longer possessed in sufficient quantities to fulfil its previous obligations (cash). It did not thereby transfer from a 'monetary' to a 'natural' economy, simply because it had never possessed – and indeed never did possess – a monetary economy in any modern sense. The shift, however severe, was thus still one of degree, and not one of kind. Gold was still used, even for certain items of military expenditure, although such use was on a reduced scale: it was, however, still hoarded.[384] Copper, at least outside the capital, plainly became much scarcer, as the state no longer needed to produce it in any quantity, and the main mechanisms whereby it had been distributed had ceased to function: it by and large was not hoarded, and it is not found on archaeological sites. Moreover, the cities, which had made use of it subsequent to its primary distribution, show every sign of having needed it less in any case.[385]

381 That is, the payment of the annual adaerated *annonae* and *capitus*, and the transfer to land. As will be pointed out below, of the two main elements in the payment of the late Roman and early Byzantine military, the annual *annona*, etc., and the quinquennial/quadrennial *donativum*, the former disappears and only the latter survives. The former must, nevertheless, have been replaced (it provided the military with its basic subsistence, and indeed with more), and logic dictates that the replacement must have been land, whatever the precise mechanisms.

382 See above, pp. 165–7.

383 See above, pp. 229 and n. 55, 415–17.

384 It was still used in the devolved form of quinquennial/quadrennial donative (=*rhogai*) in Anatolia, at least: see below, pp. 648–9. It was still hoarded: see for example above, p. 342 (the Lagbe Hoard, but others of the period are known).

385 General pattern (Anatolia): see above, pp. 640–1. Exception (Balkans): see above, pp. 419–20 and Table 13, below, pp. 659–62. Cities: Foss, 'The Persians in Asia Minor and the End of Antiquity', pp. 744–7 (summary). See also Foss's detailed treatments of Sardis and Ephesus. It is in no way intended that this brief treatment should diverge from the general findings of that author (urban decline and demographic regression): merely that his causative factors should be re-examined and questioned, and his utilisation of the numismatic evidence at least refined.

The disappearance of coin from Anatolian archaeological sites therefore has nothing directly to do with the end of antiquity and the beginning of the Byzantine middle ages, although the two phenomena are clearly not entirely unconnected: if Anatolia had been in a better economic and social situation than it clearly was in the mid seventh century, then the state might not have had – or indeed have been able – to take such radical steps as it did. Nevertheless it was, as always, state and army that provided the primary dynamics behind the change involved, and not features of, or factors in, the general economic and social situation.

As regards land, what the state in its collective and organic sense (for these things occurred at a time of imperial minority and youth) must have dreaded above all at this stage was the disintegration and eventual disappearance of its army, through the lack of the accustomed means of payment. It is this, of course, that explains why early references to the military – whether legal or hagiographical – are uniformly in terms of the individual soldier and his paraphernalia, of his household and dependants, and of his periodic obligations to the state. In this, they resemble the early thematic seals mentioned above.[386] It was trained manpower, not land, that in the immediate sense mattered. It was only with the relaxation of outside pressures; the move from a defensive to an offensive posture; and the inevitable complications deriving from inheritance, and the incessant but in no way new depredations of the powerful; that the state eventually in the tenth century turned to legislation and codification. The case for land is therefore admittedly circumstantial but is nevertheless compelling.

It may be suggested that, paradoxically, the state, either by granting out land to the military, or by at the very least making land available to it, however necessary the action may have been, and however successful it may have been in resolving the crisis involved, was at the same time sowing the seeds of its own eventual destruction. For, to the late Roman and early Byzantine *potentes/dynatoi* already well established in the inner regions of Anatolia, and representing a basically civil phenomenon, there was now added a new, large and wholly military element.[387] One may guess that it was the fusion of these two factors – great land-owning in combination with the militarisation of society – that resulted in the magnate class that was, in the Comneni, eventually to take over the state.[388] Once again, if a general model is to be sought, it may well be found in the west, where the pre-existing Gallo-Roman senatorial families almost insensibly fused with the

386 See above, p. 624.

387 See above, pp. 103–4 and Map 26.

388 See above, pp. 100–3, 136–8 and Map 25. It is frequently argued that the period of Persian and Arab invasions was responsible for the decline of great land-owning. There is actually no really hard evidence for this whatsoever, and nor is it inherently probable: at periods of disturbance – but not, admittedly, permanent hostile occupation – it is precisely the great land-owner, with scattered estates, who is able to survive, and indeed to maintain the capital necessary to buy up small and concentrated, but temporarily ruined, parcels of land. The relationship been land-owner and dependant/tenant may well have undergone change, but that, of course, is a very different matter.

emergent Germanic nobility, eventually becoming virtually indistinguishable from it, and, far from being displaced by the Carolingian régime, as sometimes thought, soon became even if not instrumental in, then beneficiaries of, its disintegration.[389]

As regards coinage, it was in the ninth century that the situation again began to change – and then doubtless not because of a 'resurgence of trade' or some similar romanticised concept, but rather because of the extension of formal administrative control over outlying areas, particularly in the Balkans, combined with concomitant changes in the imposition and/or general pattern of taxation. It may be posited that both of these aspects were the responsibility of Nicephorus I (802–11), whose administrative and financial interests and expertise are immediately recognisable, even if they are now derived through grotesquely biased sources. It was, it may therefore be guessed, the fruits of this combination which Theophilus (829–42) inherited and perhaps even accentuated – but did not initiate.

## E. *The survival of substructures of military payment*

Despite all these radical changes, there remained visible, as late as the tenth century, an underlying structure and pattern, in matters of finance and the military, that was unmistakeably still late Roman and early Byzantine, and it is to this vestigial stratum that attention and comparative examination should now be turned, as it sheds significant light upon the situation earlier obtaining.

It has been stressed, in this series of studies, repeatedly and probably *ad nauseam*, that the chief financial institution of the late Roman and early Byzantine period was the *praefectura praetorio*. Prior to the events of the seventh century there were two senior prefectures in the area under discussion, together with a junior third. The two senior were the prefecture of Illyricum and the prefecture of the East, the junior was the *quaestura exercitus*, established by Justinian in 536/7. The prefecture of Illyricum, which consisted of the two dioceses of Macedonia and Dacia, met up territorially with the prefecture of the East, which consisted of the five dioceses of Thrace, Asiana, Pontica, Oriens and Aegyptus, at the borders of the dioceses of Macedonia (prov. Macedonia I) and of Thrace (prov. Rhodope).[390] The actual border was formed by the River Nestos. The *quaestura*, carved out of the prefecture of the East, consisted of the Danubian provinces of Moesia II and Scythia, the middle provinces of the (Aegean) Islands and Caria, and the southerly and further insular province of Cyprus.[391]

[389] See, for example: K. F. Werner, 'Important Noble Families in the Kingdom of Charlemagne – A Prosopographical Study of the Relationship between King and Nobility in the Early Middle Ages', in T. Reuter (ed.), *The Medieval Nobility*, at pp. 137–202.

[390] See above, pp. 398–9; Jones, *Later Roman Empire*, Map 6 ('The Empire in the last years of Justinian').

[391] See above, p. 404: Jones, *Later Roman Empire*, Map 6.

What gave the prefectures, and evidently the *quaestura* as well, their financial clout was that each was responsible for the calculation and collection of the annual general levy, the *indictio*, within its constituent dioceses and provinces, the whole forming the basic budget of the state.[392] In the *indictio*, the military ration-allowances (*annonae*) and fodder-allowances (*capitus*) will have formed the largest single item.[393] These *annonae* and *capitus*, originally both calculated and collected in kind, were by the sixth century at least largely adaerated according to customary rates: the *annona* for four or five solidi, the *capitus* for four.[394] Justinian's novel regulating the administration of Africa might be taken as suggesting that gold alone was involved in this adaeration, but the seventh-century evidence mentioned above indicates that copper also was.[395] At any rate, the payment of adaerated *annonae* and *capitus* for the military in Illyricum will have been dealt with through the *trapeza* of the prefecture at Thessalonica; that for the military in the East through its *trapeza(i)* in Constantinople; and that for the military in the *quaestura* through its own *trapeza* which was almost certainly also in the capital, given the derivation and composition of the *quaestura* itself, and the known residence of the *quaestor* there on occasion.[396]

Although the annual adaerated *annona* and *capitus* provided the basic pay of the military (they were clearly more than subsistence allowances), this was not the only source of payment, for the accessional and quinquennial *donativa*, both called *augustaticum*, also formed part of the regular military income.[397] The *donativa* were in theory the responsibility of the *comitiva sacrarum largitionum*, but in actual practice assessment of the relevant taxes perhaps, and their collection certainly, were undertaken through the prefecture and its subordinate tiers of administration, the dioceses and provinces.[398] The accessional donative is known to have been a basic five solidi and one pound of silver, or nine solidi, and the quinquennial donative a basic five solidi.[399]

It seems clear that payment of accessional and quinquennial *donativa* was frequently somewhat late, and also that when an imperial college was involved, one kind of donative might be 'consolidated' with another, and the timing involved thereby altered.[400] Procopius claims that Justinian allowed the quinquennial donative to lapse, not having paid it once in a reign of thirty-two years (in 550), but this seems unlikely as regards the field armies, although it may have been true of the *limitanei*, whom Justinian does seem to have downgraded in status.[401] Certainly the accessional donative survived as late

392 See above, pp. 371–2, 398–9.

393 This follows logically from the military forming the largest single item in the budget as a whole: see above, pp. 158–9, 164, 172, 205–6.

394 See above, pp. 165–7, 294–5.

395 See above, pp. 415–17, and n. 383.

396 See above, p. 404; Justinian, in Novel LXI, explicitly states: *si ipse in hac regia urbe verseris...sin autem ipse in Scythia et Mysia commoreris...*

397 See above, pp. 177, 188, 481.

398 See above, p. 372.

399 See above, n. 397.

400 See above, pp. 187–9.

401 See above, pp. 166–7, 176–7.

as 578, and probably as late as 641.[402] The claim is therefore probably a Procopian exaggeration, although it would not be surprising, in view of the financial strains evident towards the end of the reign, if payment had become even more irregular than previously.

There is, however, one further and more significant element of potential confusion as regards the quinquennial donative: which is that, although clearly related to the quinquennial cycle of *lustra*, and although specifically described as being of five-yearly incidence by both Zachariah of Mitylene and by Procopius,[403] it is also by strong implication (the incidence of the connected *collatio lustralis/khrysargyron*) referred to as being of four-yearly incidence by both Joshua the Stylite and by Zosimus.[404]

It is, of course, the case that the first pair of sources is describing actual payments to the military, whilst the second is describing the levying of taxation clearly intended to fund such payments, but it is on the face of it odd that two obviously and closely related phenomena should be so seriously out of kilter. The answer in fact seems to be that the *vota*, of which the *donativa* were an integral part, were celebrated and undertaken from the commencement of the final year of the current quinquennium. The payments will thus have taken place at a time that could be described as the completion of four years or as the commencement of five years. For example, Arcadius, created Augustus in January 383, celebrated his *quinquennalia* in January 387. And so on – at least in theory.[405]

The precise extent to which this double system of annual adaerated *annonae* and *capitus* in combination with accessional and quinquennial *donativa* survived on into the seventh century and later remains uncertain, although it seems clear that it was already on the verge of disintegration in the last part of the sixth century. Maurice had clearly had plans for drastic alterations to the main system of payment, including perhaps a reduction in actual pay, and certainly a reduction in the cash element in it, but it was fear of precisely this kind of alteration that caused his downfall, and it seems unlikely that it had been implemented, or if it had been implemented that the situation was not restored by Maurice's successor Phocas.[406] In any case, as noted above, the accessional donative remains intact as late as 578, and is probably to be seen in vestigial form as late as 641. Presumably, attempts were made to preserve the traditional system, but with time they became increasingly irregular and unrealistic.[407]

402 See above, pp. 481, 625–6.

403 See above, p. 189, and Procopius, *Historia Arcana* XXIV.28; ed. Haury and Wirth, III, p. 151.

404 See above, p. 174, and Zosimus, *Historia Nova* II.38; ed. Mendelssohn, p. 96.

405 See above, pp. 188–9.

406 Jones, *Later Roman Empire* II, pp. 670–1. Haldon, *Recruitment and Conscription in the Byzantine Army*, pp. 23–4, 69 and n. 123.

407 Quinquennial donative: see above, n. 401. Accessional donative: see above, n. 402. For rather later accessional donatives, which do not seem to have possessed the massive institutionalised nature of the earlier ones, see above, pp. 198–9. The recent discovery that African gold minting under Tiberius and Maurice, as measured by the quantity of dies used, exhibits clear four-/five-year indictional peaks, very strongly suggests that the quinquennial system of donatives was still operative there and then: C. Morrisson, 'Estimation du volume du émissions de solidi de Tibère et Maurice à Carthage (578–602)', *Pact* 5 (1981), pp. 267–84.

The later situation, as revealed by Constantine Porphyrogenitus, is a good deal clearer, or is capable of clarification, at least in its major features.

According to Constantine,[408] the old pattern (*to palaion typos*) of payment had involved the themes receiving their pay (*rhoga*) in annual groups of three, according to a four-yearly cycle (i.e. *kata tessara etē*), on the following basis:

| | | | | | |
|---|---|---|---|---|---|
| Year 1: | Anatolikon | (1) | Year 3: | Kharsianon | (7) |
| | Armeniakon | (2) | | Koloneia | (8) |
| | Thrakesion | (3) | | Paphlagonia | (9) |
| Year 2: | Opsikion | (4) | Year 4: | Thrake | (10) |
| | Boukellarion | (5) | | Makedonia | (11) |
| | Kappadokia | (6) | | Khaldia | (12) |

As the cycle was completed with time, so it began over again.

Now, the date to which Constantine is referring in mentioning the old pattern remains unspecified, but the list of themes exactly reproduces the composition and order of the list of thematic *stratēgoi* in the *Klētorologion* of Philotheus (899), and it may therefore be assumed that the cycle as presented by Constantine was operative in *c.* 900, that is during the reign of Leo VI.[409]

The cycle is nevertheless clearly an 'evolved' form, and must have been preceded by a 'primitive' form, or, more likely, by both an 'intermediate' and a 'primitive' form. This, or these, may be represented on the following basis:

| | | | | | |
|---|---|---|---|---|---|
| Year 1: | Anatolikon | (1) | < | Kappadokia | (6) |
| | | | | Kharsianon | (7) |
| Year 2: | Armeniakon | (2) | < | Koloneia | (8) |
| | | | | Paphlagonia | (9) |
| | | | | Khaldia | (12) |
| Year 3: | Thrakesion | (3) | < | Thrake | (10) |
| | | | | Makedonia | (11) |
| Year 4: | Opsikion | (4) | — | Boukellarion | (5) |

The 'primitive' form of the cycle will have been that in which Anatolikon (1), Armeniakon (2), Thrakesion (3), and Opsikion (4) were paid in quadrennial rotation. The 'intermediate' form will have been that in which the same were paid in quadrennial rotation, but each along with its evolving geographical and administrative derivatives (5–12). For it is clear that, with two major exceptions (Boukellarion and Khaldia) only, the original themes dictate the subsequent order of precedence in the 'evolved' cycle.

408 See above, p. 184 and n. 150.

409 See above, p. 184 and n. 152. The numerical order given both above and below is simply that of relative precedence, and not that of absolute precedence in the relevant lists.

The reasoning behind the two exceptions remains uncertain: the enhanced precedence of Boukellarion (5) might be explicable if (as indeed seems to have been the case) it were the first to have been split off from the four original themes of the cycle; the debased precedence of Khaldia (12) is presumably explicable on the grounds of its restricted, Pontus-facing, geographical nature, and its *stratēgos* taking half of his *rhoga* from the local *kommerkion* tax.[410] In any case, both features are already present in the Uspenski *Taktikon* (842/3).[411] Other than this, it is worth noting that Kharsianon goes with Anatolikon, from which it was largely – but not entirely – derived,[412] and that Thrake and Makedonia go with Thrakesion, from which they were only distantly derived.[413] That said, the general pattern is incontrovertible.[414]

The fundamental question arising from all this is clearly that of how far back the 'primitive' form of the cycle can be taken. The answer is, of course, that by its very nature it must go back into the first half of the eighth century at least, and that there is no reason against, and every reason for, taking it back to the original field armies involved in the evolution of the Anatolian thematic system itself – right back, that is, into the seventh century. For it seems clear that the quadrennial cycle of later *rhogai* is none other than a highly devolved form of the quadrennial/quinquennial cycle of earlier *donativa*.[415]

This devolution has absolutely no major piece of evidence against it. On the positive side, it is easy to imagine how the state, strapped as it was for cash, might eventually have found it easier to pay its donative to one field army every year, rather than to all the field armies every four years. Indeed, at a time of political and military disruption, and of financial exigence, it might simply have been more prudent to keep one army reasonably content every year.

Quite how the order of precedence within the cycle was decided upon remains uncertain. The *Notitia Dignitatum* gives the order as: *magistri militum praesentales I/II*; *m.m.*

410 Boukellarion: Oikonomides, *Les listes de préséance byzantines*, p. 348 (767/8). As pointed out by Treadgold ('Notes on the Numbers and Organization of the Ninth-century Byzantine Army', pp. 286–7), until 815/20 there were only five themes in Anatolia, still implying the existence of Boukellarion alone as a derivative theme; it was only between 815/20 and 826, with the addition of Paphlagonia, that thematic numbers really began to increase. On Khaldia, see, in the last instance: Treadgold, *op. cit.* p. 280.

411 *Uspenski Taktikon*; ed. Oikonomides, p. 49.

412 See above, pp. 623–4, and Map 25.

413 See, in the last instance: Lilie, '"Thrakien" und "Thrakesion"', pp. 7–47.

414 Amongst other things, the 'intermediate' cycle nicely confirms Treadgold's contention ('Notes on the Numbers and Organization of the Ninth-century Byzantine Army', pp. 286–7 (§vi: 'Where did the Theme of Paphlagonia come from?')), that Paphlagonia derived from Armeniakon, and not from Boukellarion.

415 The one really appreciable difference between the two cycles involves the actual scale of payment: the quinquennial/quadrennial cycle seems at least to have involved the flat-rate payment of five solidi, although even here, some of the items of massive plate marked with *vota* figures suggests higher payments for some; the later cycle seems to have involved payment varying with length of service. See above, pp. 177, 182. There is, however, ample time available for the necessary evolution from the one to the other scale.

*per Orientem*; and *m.m. per Thracias*.[416] This seems borne out by Justinian II's letter of 687: *obsequium, orientalis, thracianus,* and *armenianus*.[417] Neither bears an obvious relationship to the later order. It may eventually have been a matter of simple strategic location: Anatolikon and Armeniakon were out on the Anatolian frontier, probably in that order of exposure; Thrakesion and Opsikion were nearer and less exposed, but with the former being more exposed than the latter.[418]

On the rather more negative side, if this devolution is accepted, then it will mean that the *rhogai* of the later period were not only paid, but also reckoned, quadrennially, and that the sums given for thematic *rhogai* captured by the enemy in the ninth century were quadrennial, and not annual, ones.[419] The Arabic sources give the impression that *rhogai* were reckoned annually, but paid periodically and apparently on variant cycles.[420] The former is on the whole unlikely, and if this devolution is accepted is simply not the case. The latter is again unlikely, but may represent a tendency towards some irregularity of, or lateness in, payment, much like that which has already been noted above. Far more likely, as an explanation, however, is an incompleteness of knowledge that is frequently apparent in Arabic sources: certainly there is no historical need to postulate experimentation with variant cycles on the part of the Byzantines, and to do so would be to grant the Arabic evidence a status higher than it warrants.

It should be noted as significant, in this cycle, that mention is confined to the original Anatolian themes and to their territorial derivatives: that is, effectively to the field armies of the former prefecture of the East, and to no others. There is, in other words, no reference to anything that might have derived from the prefecture of Illyricum or from the *quaestura exercitus*. The point is nicely made by the inclusion in the cycle of the themes of Thrake and Makedonia, the former unitary first having given rise to the derivative second in *c.* 800. Now, the westernmost theme of the Anatolian cycle is Makedonia, and this met up with the easternmost theme of the Balkan group, the theme of Strymon, at the River Nestos – which is precisely where the former dioceses of Thrace (prefecture of the East) and Macedonia (prefecture of Illyricum) had met up.[421]

The point is again neatly confirmed by the composition of Constantine's list[422] of *rhogai* paid to thematic *stratēgoi* under Leo VI. The list of *rhogai* and *stratēgoi* follows the order of the preceding quadrennial cycle exactly, except that it places Koloneia (previously 8) last, after Khaldia (previously 12). The reason for this exception remains unclear: Koloneia does not appear to be quite the latest creation in the cycle, as it first appears as a theme

[416] *N. Dig. Or.* v–viii; ed. Seeck, pp. 11–26.

[417] See above, p. 621. The *exercitus armenianus*, as derived from the *orientalis*, would naturally rank lowest.

[418] I owe this suggestion to the kindness of John Haldon. It should be noted that the later order of precedence more or less reflects the sequence in which the *apothēkē* spreads. See above, p. 642.

[419] See above, pp. 183, 429.

[420] See above, p. 182.

[421] Oikonomides, *Les listes de préséance byzantines*, p. 349. Constantine Porphyrogenitus, *De Thematibus* 3; ed. Pertusi, pp. 88–9, 163–4, 167.

[422] See above, p. 184, and n. 151.

in 863, whereas Kharsianon was still a *kleisoura* in that year.[423] But, in any case, Constantine continues with his list of *rhogai* and *stratēgoi*, including later thematic creations on the expanding Anatolian frontier, and also the *kleisourai* most of which later themselves become themes. He then gives a 'naval' group, to which attention must shortly be turned, and concludes by remarking that 'the *stratēgoi* of the west do not receive a *rhoga*, as they take their own customary fees from their own themes on an annual basis'. He then gives a list of the western *stratēgoi*, and, sure enough, the easternmost of them is that of Strymon, whose theme abuts onto Makedonia, which is included in the cycle.

It therefore follows that the original four Anatolian themes, together with their subsequent territorial derivatives, including Thrake/Makedonia, operated according to a very particular pattern of payment that both is recognisably a very devolved form of the old quadrennial/quinquennial system, and also that is based territorially upon the old prefecture of the East. Their soldiers were paid by quadrennial cycle, and their *stratēgoi* were paid, presumably annually, and both from Constantinopolitan funds. The lands of the old prefecture of Illyricum fell under a different régime: their soldiers were paid, possibly annually and possibly from local funds; their *stratēgoi* were paid, certainly annually, and certainly from local funds. There is here a very clear distinction that must go back into the late Roman and early Byzantine period, when the *exercitus illyrianus* (to put it into Justinian II's phraseology) would have been paid their annual adaerated *annonae* and *capitus* via the prefectural *arca/trapeza* in Thessalonica, from funds levied upon the prefectural *indictio*. The precise course of events subsequently will remain obscure, although a very general suggestion will shortly be made, but the *exercitus illyrianus* itself presumably ceased to exist, or at least as a unitary and organised force, for it very noticeably does not achieve a mention in Justinian's letter, whereas the several eastern armies, and even the African and Italian ones, all do.[424]

What, then, of the 'naval' group of themes alluded to above? It is composed of three themes: Kibyrrhaioton, Samos and Aigaion Pelagos. Their *stratēgoi* each receive a *rhoga* of 10 lb, putting them on the one hand below the lowest of the regular Anatolian *stratēgoi* (20 lb), but, as still by implication paid out of Constantinopolitan funds, distinguishing them on the other from the Balkan *stratēgoi*.[425] All these are mentioned in the *Klētorologion* of Philotheus (899) but, in the precise format, Kibyrrhaioton only occurs in the *Uspenski Taktikon* (842/3), where however a *drouggarios tou Aigaiopelagous* and a *drouggarios tou Kolpou* (presumably = *tēs Samou*) do appear.[426] Kibyrrhaioton itself however appears much earlier, in 698, as a drungariate, for Theophanes and Nicephorus both report, albeit

[423] Oikonomides, *Les listes de préséance byzantines*, pp. 348–9.

[424] See above, pp. 78–81, 621, and Maps 15, 16.

[425] See above, p. 184 and nn. 150, 151.

[426] Philotheus, *Klētorologion*; ed. Oikonomides, p. 139. *Uspenski Taktikon, ed. cit.* pp. 49, 53. Treadgold ('Notes on the Numbers and Organization of the Ninth-century Byzantine Army', p. 278) would prefer to see the *dr. tou Kolpou* as attached to the Gulf of Attalia/Pamphylia, but the interpretation adopted above seems the more probable.

variantly, that Tiberius III (Apsimar) was previously *drouggarios*, and the most likely reading is that he was *drouggarios* of the Kibyrrhaioton commanding at Corycus (or Coracaesium).[427] That all three themes had originally been drungariates is indeed directly affirmed by Leo VI.[428]

Quite what had happened, as usual, remains obscure in its details, but the most convincing reconstruction is that these three drungariates at least – for others put in a fleeting appearance – had previously formed subordinate parts of the unitary command of the fleet, headed by the *stratēgos tōn Karabōn/stratigos caravisianorum*, that is known to have existed from some stage after the middle of the seventh century through to the first quarter of the eighth. It has been conjectured that this command was instituted by Constans II (or less likely by Constantine IV) and was based on Samos, but that it was disbanded and fragmented into its constituent drungariates between 710/11 and 732, therefore by Leo III, and possibly subsequent to, and as a consequence of, the failure of the second great siege of Constantinople by the Arabs in 717/18.[429]

It should be noted, in passing, that references to the command of the fleet involve not simply the ships (*karaboi*) themselves, but even more commonly their complements, the *karabisianōn stratiōtai*, or *plōïzomenoi*, doubtless marines, and that in this respect they confirm the contemporary emphasis upon manpower rather than upon land (or ships) that has been observed above with regard to the themes.[430]

The main question arising, however, is whether Constans II (assuming that it was he), in instituting the command, acted *ab initio*, or whether he utilised a pre-existing structure as a base. The question can be answered only on the grounds of general likelihood, but it must be observed that the basic structure of the command looks very suspiciously indeed like an expanded version of that of the middle section of the *quaestura exercitus*.

The middle section of the *quaestura* consisted, as observed above, of the (Aegean) Islands and Caria, that is, of both insular and terran components. There is also absolutely no doubt that the *quaestura* must have been very much a navally-based concern, as its three sections were so widely disparate, and even the Danubian section, on a navigable stretch of the river, was doubtless supplied mainly by ship. The full Greek title of the *quaestura* seems to have been the *arkhē tōn nēsōn kai tōn epi skythias te kai mysias stratiōtikōn tagmatōn*,

[427] Refs: Antoniadis-Bibicou, *Études d'histoire maritime de Byzance*, p. 85 and n. 2. The readings are: *eis Kourikiōtas hyparkhonta* (Theophanes); *stratou arkhonta tōn Kourikiōtōn* (Nicephorus). The Corycus involved is unlikely to be that near Seleucia/Silifke, which is too far to the east, and a very minor Corycus on the Gulf of Attalia has therefore instead been suggested. Coracaesium/Calonorus, known as a port from ancient to Selçuk times (in the latter case as Alanya), and specifically mentioned as such in the tenth century, seems a possible alternative. See: Toynbee, *Constantine Porphyrogenitus and his World*, p. 259 and n. 7; above, p. 58 and n. 111.

[428] Leo VI, *Taktika* XIX.24; ed. Migne in *PG* CVII, at col. 997: *kai hoi tōn allōn thematōn plōïmoi stratēgoi drouggarioi ekalounto pote tois anō khronois.*

[429] Antoniadis-Bibicou, *Études d'histoire maritime de Byzance*, pp. 63–89. The suggestion that the command was instituted not by Constans II but by Constantine IV (Ahrweiler, *Byzance et la mer*, pp. 22–3) is less attractive.

[430] See above, pp. 624, 644.

or more briefly the *arkhē tōn nēsōn*.[431] This *arkhē* seems to have been intact, and functioning as intended, as late as the reign of Tiberius II (i.e. in 575/8), but its Danubian section, at least, cannot have remained in that condition for very much longer, that is not much further than, say, the downfall of Maurice in 602. The turn of its southerly section, the island of Cyprus, would have come in 654 with the fall of that island to the Arabs. This would have left only the Aegean components.[432]

The possible derivation of the *stratēgia tōn karabōn* from the *arkhē tōn nēsōn* has been recognised for some time, but the matter has not been seen as capable of direct proof, and nor indeed is it.[433] The case is based on two main planks: the similarity of function, and the similarity of terminology. The former has already been alluded to above. As regards the latter, it has been pointed out that the *Vita Theophanis* mentions that Isaac, Theophanes' father, who died in 780, had been in command of the *aigaiopelagētōn arkhē*, phraseology which strongly resembles that of the *arkhē tōn nēsōn*.[434] It does in fact seem quite probable that Constans, in instituting the *stratēgia tōn karabōn*, took the old circumscription of the (Aegean) Islands, then part of the only surviving section of the *quaestura*, added a certain degree of coastal jurisdiction to it,[435] and placed the *stratēgos* over the whole, with responsibility for the fleet and its personnel. The derivation would thus not be direct – the fate of the actual office of *quaestor exercitus* remains unknown – but it would be indirect, in that the surviving section of the one formed the main jurisdictional, perhaps even territorial basis, of the other.

That the *stratēgoi* of the 'naval' group of themes should rank well below those of the Anatolian cycle, and even below most of those of the Balkan group, and yet still take their *rhogai* from Constantinople, rather than from local funds, would therefore be readily understandable: basically, if somewhat indirectly, they still represented the old account of the *arkhē tōn nēsōn*, with its *trapeza* in the capital.

What one has here, therefore, in distinguishing the differing patterns of payment obtaining amongst the three separate groupings of *themata* and their *stratēgoi*, are financial and military sub-structures that have survived from the late Roman and early Byzantine period. That this should be the case should be the occasion of little surprise, for it is

431 Tiberius II, Novel 'Peri kouphismōn dēmosiōn' (575); ed. Zepoi, in *Ius Graeco-Romanum* I, at p. 18. Menander Protector, *Fragmenta* XLVIII; ed. Müller, VI, p. 252 (578). See also above, p. 411 n. 169 (Justin II).

432 For 575/8: see above, n. 431. For 654: Stratos, *Byzantium in the Seventh Century* III, *642–668*, pp. 44–5. There had been an earlier attack in 649, which had been destructive, but the Arabs had speedily withdrawn – *ibid.* pp. 39–41.

433 See, for example: Toynbee, *Constantine Porphyrogenitus and his World*, pp. 235–6 (with refs).

434 *Vita Theophanis;* ed. C. de Boor, pp. 28, 30. See also: Antoniadis-Bibicou, *Études d'histoire maritime de Byzance*, pp. 96–7.

435 *Ibid.* pp. 63–98 (the jurisdiction was over ships and men, rather than over territory as such; the last came with the creation of the theme of Kibyrrhaioton proper between 710/11 and 732; it involved transferring land from Anatolikon and Thrakesion).

precisely such sub-structures that might have been expected to survive, tenaciously, and however disguised, whilst the superstructure had nevertheless changed quite dramatically.[436]

## *F. The* apothēkē *and the* kommerkia *again*

And finally, it is necessary to revert briefly to the *apothēkē*, for it seems clear that much the same distinctions as have been noted above are to be seen there, too.

It has already been observed, in a general fashion, that the *apothēkē* system seems to have been applied first in northern and eastern Anatolia, and only later to the western part.[437] It is clear, however, that when the western part does appear, it does so along with one part of the Balkans only – and this part, as might have been expected, involves Thrace. The *apothēkē* of Mesembria appears regularly from 690/1 onwards, later becoming the imperial *kommerkia* of Mesembria, then of Mesembria and Thrake, and finally simply of Thrake.[438] In this respect, it should be remembered that when, in 812, khan Krum took Mesembria, he found there manufactured wares for all kinds of purposes such as are to do with the administration of man's affairs (*peplēsmenēn pantōn tōn opheilontōn pros katoikēsin anthrōpōn pareinai pragmatōn*), but including thirty-six copper siphons together with the Greek fire to go with them, and a quantity of gold and silver.[439] What he had found, of course, was the physical *apothēkē Mesembrias*, and it may be no coincidence that a very late seal of the imperial *kommerkia* of Thrake is quite probably dated 810/11.[440] There are hints that Develtus, and Hexamilium at the other end of the

436 Another, quite extraordinary, survival of such a sub-structure, is to be found with reference to Mesopotamia: it is known that the late Roman and early Byzantine *dux Mesopotamiae* was paid his *annonae* and *capitus* from the *dōdekatē* collected by the local *kommerkiarios*; it is also known that the later Byzantine *stratēgos Mesopotamias* took the whole of his *rhoga* from the proceeds of the local *kommerkion*. Refs: Antoniadis-Bibicou, *Recherches sur les douanes à Byzance*, pp. 87, 159. For the seal of a *stratēgos* of Mesopotamia, noticeably similar in format to that of a *kommerkiarios*, see: Zacos and Veglery, *Byzantine Lead Seals* I.1, pp. 361–2, no. 284 (810/11 or 825/6).

437 See above, p. 642.

438 Zacos and Veglery, *Byzantine Lead Seals* I.1, pp. 182–4 (table 30: Mesembria/Mesembria and Thrake), 188–9 (table 32: Thrake). The authors point out (*op. cit.* p. 138) that in the later period (751–833), the only regions and cities specifically mentioned on the dated seals of the *basilika kommerkia* are Thrake and Makedonia, and Thessalonica, Adrianople, Hexamilium, and Develtus. This is again nothing to do with trade as such, but is doubtless much to do with the pressing military danger from the Bulgars and Slavs that marked the years 756–815/16. Indeed, a number of concentrations of these later seals seem to match up with identifiable military occasions: Thessalonica in 783/4 is probably to be connected with Stauracius' expedition of 783/4 (he certainly used Thessalonica as a base); Thrake in 785/6, 787/8, looks suspiciously like preparations for the Bulgarian war beginning in 789; Thrake in 800/1(?), 801/2, 802/3, is possibly to be connected with the Slav rebellions in Greece and the Peloponnese at that period; Thrake and Makedonia in 820/1 and Adrianople in 822/3 are likely to be connected with the rebellion of Thomas the Slav in 821–3. Refs: *op. cit.* pp. 189, 196–7, 201, and Ostrogorsky, *History of the Byzantine State*, pp. 182, 192, 204–5. Conversely, the virtual cessation of specifically Anatolian seals after 745/6 doubtless reflects the easing of military pressure by the Arabs, resulting from the civil war of 747–50, the replacement of the Umayyads by the Abbasids, the transfer of the caliphate from Damascus to Iraq, and the foundation of Baghdad in 762. Again, the phenomenon is nothing to do with trade as such. Refs: Zacos and Veglery, *op. cit.* pp. 195–7 (table 34: The imperial commercia).

439 See above, p. 429.

440 Zacos and Veglery, *Byzantine Lead Seals* I.1, pp. 357–8, nos 281 a/b/c.

theme, may have on occasion acted in a similar way to Mesembria.[441] It would incidentally also be of great interest to know whether Sinope, as well as Sebastopolis/Sebastea, Colonia and Camacha, had acted in the same way for the theme of Armeniakon, as Mesembria and so on had acted for the theme of Thrake.[442] What is, however, of interest and significance, is that the inclusion of Mesembria/Thrake as a norm, forming the only such early Balkan inclusion, completes the Anatolian cycle of themes.

It is to the contrary clear that the *apothēkē* system was not so applied to the remainder of the Balkans until a date well into the eighth century. The first possible 'normative' appearance of Thessalonica occurs in 712/13, but it does not appear again until 723/4, although this latter appearance is followed by a spate.[443] Similarly, Hellas first appears in 698/9, but again it does not appear again until 736/7, although again this latter appearance is followed by a spate.[444]

The exceptional early appearance of Hellas in 698/9 is an interesting one. The date at which the *stratēgia* of Hellas[445] was created remains uncertain. The army is not included in Justinian II's letter of 687, and it therefore seems clear that it was not then a theme.[446] Theophanes records[447] that, in 695, Justinian nominated Leontius, *patrikios* and former *stratēgos* of the Anatolikoi, as *stratēgos* of Hellas. The clear implication is that he wanted him out of the way. Leontius promptly mounted a *coup d'état* and had Justinian deposed. The nuances behind these manoeuvres are, of course, uncertain, but it does look as if the *stratēgia* of Hellas was an undesirable post, and it may even be that Leontius was intended to be its first occupant – with all the inconveniences that this would have entailed. In any event, the exceptional appearance of the *apothēkē* of Hellas in 698/9 may well be connected with the creation of the *stratēgia* either shortly before 695 or shortly after that date, Leontius clearly being a frustrated appointment. One may wonder whether the slight delay does not represent a deliberate administrative feature.[448]

441 *Ibid.* pp. 347–8, no. 270 (751–75: *Thrakē kai Hexamilion*); 362–3, no. 285 (829–42: *Develtos*).

442 Sinope: see above, p. 429. Sebastopolis/Sebastea: Zacos and Veglery, *Byzantine Lead Seals* 1.1, pp. 232–3, nos 150 a/b. Colonia and Camacha: *ibid.* pp. 295–6, no. 219. Cerasus and Trapezus should probably also be added: *ibid.* pp. 245–6 (no. 164), 258–9 (nos 178, 179). For a seal of Leo, *koumerkiarios* of Sinope of the Euxine Pontus (832/3 or 847/8), see: *ibid.* 1.3, p. 1646, no. 2894. If, as seems likely, 832/3 is correct, then there is here a clear connection with the establishment of the theme of Cherson (to which city Sinope was closely related) in *c.* 833 – see above, p. 426 and n. 244. Interestingly, Sinope seems to have co-ordinated with Develtus for the occasion – see: *ibid.* 1.1, pp. 362–3, nos 285 a/b (832/3).

443 *Ibid.* pp. 185–7 (table 31).

444 *Ibid.* pp. 174–5 (table 24).

445 Oikonomides, *Les listes de préséance byzantines*, p. 351. For a longer discussion: Toynbee, *Constantine Porphyrogenitus and his World*, pp. 265–6. For the term *stratēgia Hellados*: Zacos and Veglery, *Byzantine Lead Seals* 1.1, pp. 331–2, no. 254 (738/9).

446 Toynbee, *Constantine Porphyrogenitus and his World*, p. 265.

447 Theophanes, *Chronographia*; ed. de Boor, 1, pp. 368–9. Stratos, *Byzantium in the Seventh Century* v, *685–711*, pp. 70–4.

448 That is, that a short period of administrative measures involving the setting up of a thematic structure (whatever that was, at this date), was followed by a mobilisation along Anatolian lines. Whether the delay was for the same reason as suggested above (p. 634) for the Slav *andrapoda* remains much more doubtful. doubtful.

The point of all this is that, although future discoveries may alter the pattern somewhat, the early application of the *apothēkē* system to Thrake, contrasting with its late application to the remainder of the Balkans (that is, to Thessalonike and Hellas), clearly echoes the distinction found earlier in relation to the prefectures of the East and of Illyricum, and also found later in relation to the Anatolian cycle and the Balkan group of themes. The distinction is therefore a continuing and a valid one.

It is, however, in turning to the Aegean islands that the most fruitful sigillographic and historical nexus of all emerges. It is in general observable that the *apothēkē* system was applied to the islands more or less along with western Anatolia and Thrace, and well before it was applied at all regularly to the Balkans.[449] Again, of course, this intermediate position may well be derived from the *quaestura exercitus*, and almost certainly is reflected in the similar position to be seen later in the 'naval' group of *stratēgoi*.

The particular group of five seals involved is as follows:[450]

1. *Kosma stratēlatou kai genikou kommerkiariou apothēkēs (t)ōn(?) ky(kladōn)(?)* 687/8, 688/9
2. ...*kai genikou kommerkiariou apothēkēs tō(n) kykladō(n) (n)ēsō(n)* 696/7
3. ...*apo eparkhōn kai genikou kommerkiariou apothēkēs tou ai(gaiou) pel(agous)* 711–13
4. *Iōannou apo eparkhōn kai genikou kommerkiariou apothēkēs tou aigeou (p)elagou(s)* 713/14
5. *Anastasiou hypatou basilikou balnitoros kai genikou kommerkiariou apo(th)ēkēs asias k(ar)ias tōn n(ēs)ōn holō(n) (kai hel)lēs(pontou)* 721/2

It has been observed above that it was in 688/9 that Justinian II mounted his campaign which reached the region of Thessalonica, took Slav captives, and settled them in the region of Opsikion and other Anatolian areas. It has also been observed that a good deal of forethought and logistical arrangement would have been necessary for the campaign.

According to Theophanes,[451] in 687/8, Justinian, after a successful operation in eastern Anatolia having ramifications as far south as Syria/Lebanon and as far north as Armenia, transferred *ta kaballarika themata* to Thrace, wishing to capture the Bulgars and the Sklavinias. This was clearly done in preparation for his campaign in the following year, the cavalry presumably over-wintering in Thrace in 688/9. In 687/8 the *apothēkē* appears in Cilicia I and II, Cappadocia I and II, and in Armenia I.[452] In 688/9 it appears in Constantinople and Helenopontus; in 689/90, 690/1, in Cappadocia I and II, Lycaonia and Pisidia; and in 689/90 in Lazica, Cerasus and Trebizond.[453] Now, not all of these

[449] Zacos and Veglery, *Byzantine Lead Seals* 1.1, pp. 162–89 (tables 17–32).

[450] Refs: 1: *ibid.* pp. 244–5 (no. 163); 2: *ibid.* p. 274 (no. 196); 3: *ibid.* pp. 286–7 (no. 211); 4: *ibid.* pp. 288–9 (no. 213); 5: *ibid.* pp. 306–7 (no. 226).

[451] Theophanes, *Chronographia*; ed. de Boor, 1, pp. 363, 364. Stratos, *Byzantium in the Seventh Century* v, *685–711*, p. 11.

[452] Zacos and Veglery, *Byzantine Lead Seals* 1.1, pp. 241 (no. 159: Cilicia I/II), 242 (no. 160: Cappadocia I/II), 244 (no. 162: Armenia I).

[453] *Ibid.* 1.1, p. 170 (table 21: Constantinople); 1.3, p. 1593 (no. 2762: Helenopontus); 1.1, pp. 247 (no. 166: Capp. I/II, Lycaonia, Pisidia), 245–6 (no. 164: Lazica, Cerasus, Trebizond).

mobilisations were necessarily to do with preparations for, and involvement with, the campaign of 688/9, but it is evident that some or most must have been. This is all the more so as they were basically the responsibility of two men: Julian (Cilicia I and II, and Helenopontus); and Cosmas (Cappadocia I and II, and Lazica, etc.).

Preparations for, and involvement with, the campaign of 688/9 were not, however, confined to Anatolia, for it is in 687/8, 688/9, that the *apothēkē* apparently appears in the Cyclades, as in the first seal listed above. Not only that, but in 688/9, 689/90, it also appears in Crete.[454] The mobilisation in the Cyclades was the responsibility of Cosmas, that in Crete was the responsibility of Julian. The case thus resembles that of the Slav *andrapoda* and George.[455]

Justinian, advancing along the classic Egnatian route between the Rhodope and the sea, was, of course, needing supply and support from the fleet. The whole expedition was, in fact, an extremely well-prepared and co-ordinated one.

According to Theophanes,[456] in 696/7, Leontius, in response to the news of the fall of Carthage to the Arabs (probably in 695),[457] sent the *patrikios* John with the whole of the Roman fleet (*meta pantōn tōn Rhōmaiïkōn plōïmatōn*) to Africa, where it briefly recovered Carthage and a certain amount of territory outside. In 696/7 the *apothēkē* appears in the Cyclades, as in the second seal listed above, and also in Sicily – an extremely rare and presumably significant occurrence. The only directly comparable seals involve the *apothēkē* appearing in Phrygia Pacatiana and Lydia, and in Cilicia, quite possibly representing a hurried mobilisation of coastally-oriented forces to provide the fleet with a military backing – noticeably, both were again the responsibility of one man, Cyriacus.[458]

According to Theophanes,[459] towards the end of his short reign Anastasius II, hearing that the Arabs had despatched a fleet from Alexandria to Phoenix in the Lycian Peninsula for the cutting of timber, prepared a detachment of fast ships from the metropolitan fleet (*ek tou oikeiou stolou ta eudroma skaphē*), mobilised the forces of the Opsikion (*taxatous ek tou Opsikiou thematos*), obviously to provide the fleet with military backing, and sent them – probably reinforced by detachments of the regional fleet – to Rhodes, under John, who was a deacon of the Great Church, who was nick-named 'little father John', who

454 Cyclades: see above, n. 450 (no. 1). Crete: Zacos and Veglery, *Byzantine Lead Seals* I.1 (table 5: Julian).

455 That is, a large number of regions being the responsibility of a single person, or of a very restricted number of persons.

456 Theophanes, *Chronographia*; ed. de Boor, I, p. 370.

457 In fact, Theophanes lumps the whole and quite complex and lengthy sequence of events under the year 698/9, but the generally accepted date for the fall of Carthage is 695, in which case the fleet would presumably have been sent in 696/7, the final evacuation of Carthage by the Byzantines occurring in 698. The chronology is, as usual, open to question, the sources being contradictory: Stratos, *Byzantium in the Seventh Century* V, *685–711*, pp. 78–84. Stratos effectively discards the non-Byzantine evidence (which is admittedly confused), but is much mistaken in doing so.

458 Zacos and Veglery, *Byzantine Lead Seals* I.1, p. 155 (table 9: Cyriacus). Sicily: *ibid.* pp. 274–5 (no. 197).

459 Theophanes, *Chronographia*; ed. de Boor, I, pp. 385–6. Antoniadis-Bibicou, *Études d'histoire maritime de Byzance*, p. 82.

was at that time *logothetēs tou genikou*, and who was named *stratēgos kai kephalē* for the occasion. The expedition was intended as a pre-emptive strike, to deprive the Arabs of access to or possession of the much-needed wood. Once on Rhodes, however, the troops rebelled, killed John, and began to return home. At Adramyttium, on the edge of their own theme, they found a local man, Theodosius, who was in charge of the collection of revenue, and acclaimed him emperor. Theodosius promptly fled, but was found, and was forced to accept the acclamation. The rebels were joined by the whole of the Opsikion theme and by the local Gothograeci and advanced on Chrysopolis, from where they conducted operations against the capital. This civil war lasted six months, and only then did the rebels gain entry into the City, depose Anastasius, and impose Theodosius.

This interlude has been summarised in such detail only because it is of potential significance to the subject in hand. Theophanes, who is not a little confused at this stage, reports the whole under the year 714/15, and – partly in consequence – it is generally agreed that Anastasius was replaced by Theodosius in mid or late 715. So much has to be accommodated within that year that the suspicion inevitably arises that the fleet and troops had over-wintered in Rhodes, but had actually been sent in 714. Be that as it may, it is surely no coincidence that in 713/14 the *apothēkē* appears in the Aegean Sea, as in the fourth seal listed above. Moreover, in the same year, it appears in Constantinople itself.[460] In both cases, the man involved is one John, *apo eparkhōn*. John's apparent career in this kind of position is an interesting one. Apart from the two cases just cited, it has been conjectured that he was responsible for the *apothēkē* of the Aegean Sea at an uncertain date under Philippicus (i.e. between 711 and 713).[461] His only other known appearance is as joint *arkhōn tou blattiou*, again in 713/14, along with one Peter, who was a deacon.[462]

So: on the one hand there is Theophanes' John, who was a deacon, and also *logothetēs tou genikou*, who was sent with part of the metropolitan and regional fleets from Constantinople to Rhodes in 714/15, and who was killed there by rebels; and on the other hand there is a sigillographic John, *apo eparkhōn*, who was *genikos kommerkiarios* of the *apothēkē* of both Constantinople and of the Aegean Sea in 713/14, who does not seem to appear later, or at least not with the same dignity, and who is also combined with a Peter, who was a deacon. There is, moreover, one earlier case where the offices of *logothetēs tou stratiōtikou* and *genikos kommerkiarios* are combined, and also two later cases where the offices of *logothetēs tou genikou* and *genikos kommerkiarios* are combined. The name John is, of course, one of the commonest, but the conclusion is nevertheless irresistible: in this case, the two Johns are in fact one and the same.[463]

460 Zacos and Veglery *Byzantine Lead Seals* I.I, p. 289 (no. 213 bis).

461 *Ibid.* p. 157 (table 12: John).

462 *Ibid.* I.I, p. 290 (nos 214 a/b).

463 It is of course possible that John *apo eparkhōn* active up to 713/14 is identical with John *apo eparkhōn* of *c.* 720–9, and even with John *hypatos* of 720/1–730/1, but, given the interruptions, it does on the whole seem more likely that different individuals are involved. For the two last, see: Zacos and Veglery, *Byzantine Lead Seals* I.I, pp. 317–18, no. 238; p. 160, table 14. For the combinations of offices: *ibid.* p. 143. It should

And here the sigillographic, the archaeological and numismatic, and the administrative materials all begin to meet up. At some stage of the short reign of Philippicus (711–13), the *apothēkē* appears in the Aegean Sea, as in the third seal listed above. The precise date of its appearance unfortunately remains uncertain, as the indictional date is not visible on the seal, but if its appearance is to be connected with a similar appearance at Constantinople, and with another (the earliest) at Thessalonica, then the date would be 712/13.[464] Although its appearance cannot be linked with specific events, as it can be on other occasions, this should not in principle be a matter of surprise, given the sporadic and sketchy nature of the available evidence. And it should also be stressed that many, perhaps most, of the mobilisations revealed by the seals were probably purely routine ones, which would in any case go unnoticed by the sources. Early in the reign of Leo III, in 721/2, the *apothēkē* again appeared in Asia, Caria, the whole of the Islands, and Hellespontus, as in the fifth seal listed above. Again, its appearance cannot be linked with specific events, but in the same year it appears elsewhere, and as both the Aegean and the other occasion are the responsibility of one man, Anastasius, the two may be connected.[465]

Now, in tracing and analysing above the sweeping changes in the system of supplying coin to the regions that took place under Heraclius, there has already been occasion to remark upon the extraordinarily accentuated pattern of coin occurrence in the body of excavation material from Athens. Coinage of the late seventh and early eighth centuries is generally very rare at Athens, as it is elsewhere, but there are two groups of copper coin that quite drastically break the prevalent dearth, and these are a group of 61 decanummia of Philippicus and another of 22 decanummia of Leo III (Table 13). The rarity of the two issues involved is emphasised by the fact that they are known virtually only from the Athenian material. It has been observed that the very tight composition of the coins of Philippicus demonstrates them to have formed part of a body of coin quite specifically transported from Constantinople and injected into the circulating medium at Athens, and it has been suggested on quite independent grounds that the military was closely involved in its handling. The same mechanisms presumably operated in the case of the coins of Leo. Coins of the first group include pieces of Philippicus' second regnal year, and so the injection must have taken place in 712/13 – that is in precisely the same year as postulated for the appearance of the *apothēkē* in the Aegean Sea. Coins of the second group are also closely datable: they must have been struck

also be noticed that by 715/16 Theopemptus had seemingly replaced John as *gen. log.*: *ibid.* pp. 296–7, no. 220. The point does not, of course, affect the definition of what the *apothēkē* actually was, and that has been outlined above.

464 *Ibid.* p. 286 (no. 210). See also above, p. 655 and n. 443.

465 Zacos and Veglery, *Byzantine Lead Seals* I.1, p. 307 (no. 227) – the reading given for this seal, including the letters...*lle*..., perhaps again suggests Helespontus (rather than Helenopontus, as tentatively proposed), perhaps in a different combination.

between Leo's accession on 25 March 717 and his co-option of Constantine V on 25 March 720.[466] The appearance of the *apothēkē* in the whole of the Islands is dated to between 1 September 721 and 31 August 722. This disappointing but rather slight discrepancy is happily an apparent one only, for there is absolutely no difficulty at all in supposing that Leo's coins had meanwhile been lodged in the *vestiarion* – or in this case more likely the *eidikon* – for eighteen months or so, before being transported and disbursed.

What, then, was going on? It is, of course, quite conceivable that in both of the above cases there is an as yet missing seal of the *apothēkē* of Hellas or some similar circumscription which would obviously have included Athens, but on the whole it seems unlikely, and it is in any case probably unnecessary to postulate their existence. For although Athens is clearly not on an island, it is within easy reach of a number of them, and moreover it is within a few miles of the (Aegean) sea. It is known that the *stratēgos tōn karabōn*, during the short existence of the unitary office, had under his jurisdiction the bases of the provincial detachments of the fleet, not only on the various islands but also on the several stretches of mainland coast – Caria, Lycia and Pamphylia, which later became the theme of Kibyrrhaioton, being only the most obvious example – and the combined evidence therefore very clearly suggests that Athens/Piraeus was one such base.[467] The point is obviously inherently probable: the combined theme of Hellas-Peloponnesos was, in the twelfth century, still under the particular command of the *megas doux*, who was in command of the fleet.[468] The terms 'the Aegean Sea', and 'the whole of the Islands', employed on the seals of 712/13(?) and 720/1 are in effect probably synonymous: it must have been very difficult to describe satisfactorily the mobilisation of a command which included so many territorially disparate bases, in so many different *stratēgiai*. Probably, only when a very specific partial term such as 'the Cyclades' (as used in 713/14) occurs should a definite partial mobilisation be understood.

Athens, then, was being mobilised, and presumably as part of the *stratēgia tōn karabōn*, or at least as part of one of its constituent administrative components. Other ports, such as nearby Argos, may have been subject to a similar régime, and it should not be forgotten that it was on the nearby island of Ceos that Theophilus, *stratigos Caravisianorum*, met the pope Constantine I in 710/11.[469]

466 Philippicus: see above, pp. 419–20. Leo: Grierson, *DOC* III.1, pp. 232–3 (Class 1). See now: P. Grierson, 'A New Early Follis Type of Leo III (718)', *Numismatic Chronicle* 14[7] (1974), pp. 75–7. The position of the new type remains uncertain: it may be the earliest, or it may be a short-lived intermediate one, within the issue of Class 1.

467 Antoniadis-Bibicou, *Études d'histoire maritime de Byzance*, pp. 72–3: the 'primitive' bases involved will be those grouped under the later themes of Kivyrrhaioton, Samos and Aigaion Pelagos. Athens is just off the map, but the inclusion of Anatolian terran bases pre-supposes the existence of Balkan ones. On this, see below, and Ahrweiler, *Byzance et la mer*, pp. 32–3, 62–6, 71–92: most or all of these had presumably been part of the *stratēgia tōn karabōn*.

468 See above, p. 431.

469 *Liber Pontificalis* XC (Constantinus); ed. Duchesne, I, p. 390: *coniungentes in insula quae dicitus Caea, occurrit Theophilus patricius et stratigos Caravisianorum*. Co-ordination between terran and insular components of the local *stratēgiai* is implied by Theophanes' report that, in April 727, the *Helladikoi te kai hoi tōn Kykladōn*

A number of questions nevertheless immediately arise. Why were there only two consequential injections of coin into Athens – or at least only two that are now recognisable? A preliminary solution to the question may lie in the fact that coin was injected into the city on two out of the three occasions of the period on which there seems to have been a general mobilisation of the Aegean/Islands, and it is possible that the third, on the occasion of Anastasius' intended pre-emptive attack, was simply rather more specific – it should be remembered that he seems to have mobilised only the fastest ships of the Constantinopolitan fleet – and therefore that it omitted Athens.

In any case, the size of the two injections of coin into Athens must have been relatively small, and their impact was clearly very localised: neither, for example, is at all traceable at Corinth, which was probably the capital of the *stratēgia* of Hellas at this stage.[470] On the other hand, it is at Corinth, the administrative centre, that the number of coins from the excavations begins to increase quite rapidly from the first quarter of the ninth century onwards, while it is at Athens that the increase comes both later and slower.[471]

What is important is that, if one accepts the concentration of coins of Constans II at Athens as being in some way related to the presence of that emperor, his court and administration, and his army, in 662/3, on his way westwards to Italy and Sicily, then, with the identification of these two smaller bodies of coin as being related to the mobilisation of the Aegean/Islands, in 712/13 and 721/2, it follows that the only three occasions on which there was an at all appreciable injection of currency into the area during the period *c.* 650–850, all occurred as the direct result of a particular state intervention.[472] Once again, the rôle of the state and its organs, as a direct distributary mechanism behind the coinage, is seen to be supreme.

*nēsōn* made a sudden but unsuccessful naval attack on Constantinople. The same author reports that, later in the same year (the end of June onwards), the Arabs conducted a serious siege of Nicaea. It is tempting to connect these two events with the contemporary activities of Theophanes, who was *patrikios*, *prōtospatharios*, and *genikos logothetēs*, and who was responsible for the *apothēkē* of Thessalonica, of Constantinople, of Hellespontus and Lydia, and of Bithynia and Phrygia Salutaris and Pacatiana, all in 727/8. Thessalonica could have been mobilised to 'pacify' Hellas and the Cyclades, and it should be noted that all the remaining provinces focus upon Nicaea. Refs: Theophanes, *Chronographia*; ed. de Boor, I, pp. 405–6. Zacos and Veglery, *Byzantine Lead Seals* I.I, p. 317, no. 237 (Thess.); p. 314, no. 234 (Cpl.); p. 316, no. 236 (Hellesp.); p. 315, no. 235 (Bith.). See also: *ibid.* p. 161 (table 16: Theophanes); above, p. 657 n. 455; and Map 26.

470 Toynbee, *Constantine Porphyrogenitus and his World*, p. 263.

471 Figs: Metcalf, *Coinage in South-eastern Europe, 820–1396*, p. 37.

472 For ref. and comments: Grierson, *DOC* II.2, p. 404 and n. 12 (Asclepaion Hoard). It may well be that not only gold, but also copper was involved: Charanis observes that (noticeably echoing the Anatolian evidence) the vast bulk of the coins of Constans II found at Athens (812 out of 817) date between 641 and 662/3 – P. Charanis, 'The Significance of Coins as Evidence for the History of Athens and Corinth in the Seventh and Eighth Centuries', *Historia* 4 (1955), pp. 164–7. Although one has a number of reservations about the use of the numismatic material in this article, the particular point seems reasonable, and it is indeed noticeable that the proportions of coins of Heraclius, Constans II and Constantine IV, as between Athens (7:30:2) and Corinth (1:3:0), might well be taken as a further indication of the significance of the imperial presence in the formation of the Athenian circulating medium.

There is, however, an apparent contradiction to be resolved: it has been argued that, in the case of Anatolia, the advent of the *apothēkē* and all that it represents was responsible for the disappearance of coin – or at least copper coin – whilst, in that of the Balkans – or at least the Aegean/Islands – it is being argued that it was responsible in however sporadic and ephemeral a way for the appearance of coin. It should, however, be remembered that it has also been argued that there was a fundamental difference in the pattern of payment as between the three distinct groups of themes: the Anatolian, the Balkan, and the 'naval'. The contradiction would be neatly resolved if it were to be assumed that the difference in the supply of coin was the direct consequence of an equivalent difference in the method of payment. It is quite possible – even probable – that in the case of Anatolia, the state had not only 'settled' the military, but in a quite short space of time had also 'landed' it. In this case, the military would, as indeed suggested above, have become responsible for its own mounting and equipping. Such a relatively swift 'landing', at least, is unlikely to have taken place in the Aegean/Islands, and *a fortiori* in the Balkan mainland – there simply would have been insufficient land, whether imperial or deserted private, available for the purpose. In Anatolia, therefore, the annual adaerated *annonae* and *capitus* had been abandoned and only the quinquennial/quadrennial donative, in however modified a form, retained; whereas in the Aegean/Islands and the Balkans, it may well have been that some other arrangement, involving sporadic and vestigial monetary payments, survived or evolved. The problem is clearly incapable of definite resolution, but all the evidence of this series of studies suggests that it is only this kind of explanation that is in the long run likely to prove a viable one.

## (v) FUTURE DIRECTIONS

And so, however faintly, and however fitfully, the basic structure of the Byzantine monetary economy begins to slide into focus. The structure itself proves to be of a somewhat strange, but surely not of an entirely unexpected, shape. Any issue that arises as to its viability should concern not the strangeness of the overall shape, but the internal consistency of the individual dynamics and mechanisms that go to make up the collective whole. And here is what is perhaps the strongest argument in favour of its viability, for the dynamics and mechanisms involved do indeed possess an internal consistency.

The fundamental dynamic behind the production of coin throughout the late Roman and Byzantine period – or at least right up until the thirteenth and fourteenth centuries – was the need of the state to provide for itself a standard medium for the collection of its revenue and the disbursement of its expenditure. The needs of the private sector of the economy, and any desire it might have had for the provision of a stable and conveniently available medium of exchange, were of secondary consideration only. The presence or absence of a quite strict balance between state revenue and expenditure was a critical factor in the monetary economy: if the state built into its budget an appreciable surplus and allowed the results of that surplus to accumulate, then coin quickly became scarce and commodity-prices fell noticeably; if the state ran a deficit of more than a minimal kind, then it could either finance that deficit from any reserve that it might have, or, if it had no such reserve, it could resort – in the short term – to a restricted number of crude and desperate measures, but at still quite short a remove it would have to reflect the deficit in its coinage, that is to debase it. Floating a loan or loans to cover such a deficit was, in any systematic sense, simply not an available option.

In order to maximise, so it hoped, the potential supply of the precious metals that it particularly demanded, the state, again until quite late on in its history, forbade the export of such metals by private individuals, whilst encouraging their import, but it was always prepared to ignore the logic of its own rulings when it considered it necessary or desirable to provide subsidies, tributes or bribes to foreign powers, or to dazzle enemies or potential enemies, or friends or potential friends. Indeed, the profusion of its wealth, only partly metallic, and the apparently careless generosity with which it gave that wealth away, formed a cardinal principle of its foreign policy.

Within, the state produced its coinage according to a geographical balance that very heavily and inflexibly reflected the pattern of the fiscal administration of the day: if that administration was a relatively decentralised one, then the number of mints at work was likely to be appropriately large, although always within the prevalent administrative context; if that administration was a relatively centralised one, then the only mint of any importance at all was likely to be Constantinople. The one clear non-administrative factor that was always likely to negate this tight relationship was the needs of the state's main object of expenditure, that is, those of its military forces, whether such needs were short-term, resulting from perhaps a specific campaign, or long-term, resulting from perhaps the permanent garrisoning of frontier-troops. Again, the needs or desires of the private sector do not seem to have been considered at all in the pattern of coin-supply: the existence of a relatively dense population, and of a relatively complex and lively economy, to which the services of a local mint might well have been welcome or advantageous, was no guarantee at all of the provision of such services. Indeed, at at least one period of the empire's history, it was precisely such regions that did not have the services of such mints – simply because they did not also tend to need a strong military presence.

The perceived needs of the state dictated not only where and when coin was produced, but even what kind of coin was produced. The state issued its precious-metal coinage, as noted above, to serve as a medium of revenue and expenditure. It produced its base-metal one, mostly but not entirely, of copper, basically to fuel the speed of the very restricted cycle by way of the operation of which the precious-metal coinage passed through its hands. Otherwise, it tended to discriminate against its own base coinage, accepting it in taxation only where absolutely necessary, and even then off-loading it onto the public as quickly as possible.

The needs of the state were supreme, not only as the basic dynamic behind the production of coin, but also, via its own constituent organs, and in this respect particularly via the military and the public post, as the primary mechanism behind the distribution of coin. That this should have been the case results from two main considerations. First: because the dominant class, which both possessed a relatively high proportion of the total amount of available wealth, and also generally provided the personnel through which the state was ruled and administered, feared and despised the mercantile classes, it – except for one brief and abortive moment in the eleventh century – closely supervised their operations and their gains, maintaining on the one hand the simplest possible structure of exchange, and dictating on the other through the control of purchase (and sale) prices the eventual profit margin. Second: because the interiors of the two great peninsulas that provided the empire with its territorial base were not – given the vast dominance of agriculture – easily exploitable, whether as a matter of production itself, or whether as a matter of the economic transport and disposal of any surplus production, household or local consumption overwhelmingly prevailed, except, of course, where the state intervened as an alternative purchaser and consumer. Only at the periphery of the peninsulas did these latter restraints cease to operate, and there the predominant factor behind exchange is likely to have been the provisioning of Constantinople, which as an economic force should never be underestimated, but which was also particularly easily controllable and was in fact particularly rigorously controlled. The combination of these two main factors ensured that the Byzantine mercantile classes remained relatively small in scale and underdeveloped in nature, and therefore that their potential as a catalyst for exchange, and as a consequent distributory and circulatory mechanism behind the coinage, remained feeble. The situation was compounded by the economic rôle of the dominant class, which, when it sold off the surplus agricultural produce of its estates, preferred an almost direct sale to the consumer, thereby virtually obviating the need for middle-men within the process.

With the production and distribution of coin being overwhelmingly dominated by the needs of the state; with the ideology of the dominant class being hostile to the development of the mercantile classes; with the existence of state mechanisms capable of imposing that ideology, and moreover being used to do so; and with the structure and nature of the territorial base being largely unfavourable to the evolution of widespread and complex systems of exchange; the circulation of coinage must throughout have been of a relatively specialised and superficial nature, being predominantly a matter of taxation and of accumulation as a store of wealth. Only towards the peripheries of the two peninsulas will some of these conditions have been relaxed sufficiently so as to provide the potential for an appreciable degree of development.

It is, then, within these perhaps somewhat forbidding general parameters that future work, including the more detailed interpretations of the physical evidence, will proceed. It will be necessary to isolate the various elements of continuity, discontinuity and development, for within the set parameters even the last is of course not at all precluded – and even in matters of production, distribution and circulation. For example, it seems very probable that, in effect, for much of the late Roman and Byzantine period, only metal obtained by the state through its various procedures was worked up into coin by the mint(s), whilst by the end of the twelfth century probably, and by the thirteenth and fourteenth centuries certainly, metal provided by private individuals was also commonly being so worked up. Again, the precise balance between primary and secondary mechanisms of distribution will have fluctuated: at one period, *c.* 650–850, the state seems to have provided virtually the only such mechanism, whilst by the thirteenth and fourteenth centuries the state itself, together with its institutional bodies, its administrative structures, and its financial mechanisms, had been first partly destroyed by the decisive catastrophe of 1204, and then its remnant had been further subverted by the inherited and all-pervasive clan-structure of the Palaeologi and their related families. Yet again, as the territorial base of the state began to contract definitively, in Anatolia as a consequence of the defeat of 1071, and in the Balkans as a consequence of the emergence of the Slav kingdoms in the 1180s, so a definite shift towards the peripheries of the peninsulas will have occurred, and it was of course there that several of the constricting factors affecting circulation were relaxed. All in all, one may guess that it was only towards the end of the twelfth century, and more particularly in the thirteenth and fourteenth centuries, that the Byzantine coinage began to be produced and distributed, and to circulate overall, along the recognisable lines of those of the feudal states of the west – or in other words, just as the latter were evolving into something beyond that.

And yet, the monetary history, and more particularly the monetary behaviour, of the coinages of those mediaeval western states should in no way be ignored as a possible source of information as to how the coinage of the late Roman and Byzantine empire actually worked. In many, even most, ways, those coinages and their behaviour are better – that is closer – documented than the Byzantine one, even if over a much shorter period of time. For example, a recent synthetic analysis of previous work on the rôle of the crown in the circulation of coinage in late thirteenth- and early fourteenth-century England that has been alluded to above brings to light a number of possible insights into how the relationship between state and circulation may have worked out in Byzantium.[473] The situation was one in which the financial problems of the crown in mounting and maintaining major wars were paramount; in which the private export of coin was generally forbidden; in which coinage was nevertheless physically scarce and commodity-

[473] Prestwich, 'The Crown and the Currency', pp. 51–65.

prices were therefore low; in which governmental expenditure might be equivalent to some 30% of the total money-supply; in which – however exceptionally – the government might have some 25% of that supply in reserve; in which individuals were forced to dig into their reserves to pay their taxes; and in which at least one admittedly remote part of the kingdom was as yet apparently totally unmonetised. All these are particular points, but none of them is totally unfamiliar or has gone unmentioned in this series of studies: the structure that, together, they represent may well have borne a generic similarity to that obtaining in the late Roman and Byzantine empire at one or more stages of its long history. In other words, although particular features might vary, the general structure, dictated as it was by a number of common positive factors and negative parameters, might well have been much the same. Moreover, a systematic comparative exercise carried out on one (or more) of the better known monetary economies of the west, on the one hand, and on the Byzantine monetary economy, on the other, might very well – just as did the similar exercise undertaken above on the Ottoman and Byzantine budgets – yield extremely useful information, in illuminating more fully features that are known from the Byzantine material only partially. The widest possible trawl should be made in the acquisition of such information, and, as mentioned at the beginning of this book, even historically recent or present-day economies that were or are in essence pre-industrial may well repay examination. What is needed is a model, even if a flexible and composite one.

Much, then, remains to be done. For example, there are still a number of features of metropolitan production that are of interest, and that still require further analysis, and it is not impossible that they will be found to be related to features of the financial administration. Price-structures have deliberately gone unmentioned above, and although – because of the extremely limited amount of geographical and chronological evidence – it remains questionable as to whether much more than the little that has already been done on this problem can further and with use be done, nevertheless the possibility should at least be examined. Some detailed exploration should be carried out into the workings of money and exchange in a local economy, to see to what extent it reflected the wider economy, and to what it remained peculiar. One may suspect that here both the earlier Egyptian, and the later monastic, documentation may prove to be fruitful on the one hand, and that the use of comparative evidence may prove to be not only invaluable, but even necessary, on the other. And lastly, and only lastly, the archaeological material – in its widest sense, that is including coins derived both from controlled excavation and from casual finding – should be examined in its own right, and not merely as an adjunct to other aspects of the monetary economy.

And finally, if this series of studies has sought to demonstrate anything at all, it is surely that not only is the Byzantine monetary economy not simply to be identified with the coins alone, but it is not even to be identified with the coinage in a slightly wider sense and padded out with a modicum of mainly secondary historical material and sporadic references to trade and traders. It is, of course, a multi-faceted structure, and the product of a whole series of interrelated and interacting factors, extending down through administration, society and economy into the land itself. None of these factors should be neglected or ignored, and indeed, in positing the existence or operation of any one factor, the likely influence of results on the other related factors should always be appreciated or anticipated. In other words, the monetary economy should also be looked at as an organic whole. It is after all as methodologically unsatisfactory for the numismatist, in discussing Byzantine monetary policies, to be totally unaware of the conceptual possibilities available or perhaps more importantly not available to the administration and society that supposedly introduced and implemented them, as it is for the historian, in discussing whether or not the Byzantine army received grants of land at some stage, to be totally unaware of the range of alternative forms and processes of military payment, or even of the existence of a need on the part of the state to move from one form to another: in other words, at this point, the two kinds of ignorance meet up –

> 'And yet, when all is said and done, I suppose things do move on...'
>
> (Cavafy)

## ADDENDUM

### *The* 'Apothēkē', *Thrake, and the Origins of Leo III*

Since the completion of the text above, a further significant nexus of material has fallen into place, and seems worth placing on record.

It has been observed above (pp. 654–5) that the *apothēkē* of Mesembria/Thrake begins a long series of appearances in 690/1, that is during the first reign of Justinian II (685–95), thereby completing the Anatolian cycle of themes.

Now, Theophanes records (*Chronographia*; ed. de Boor, I, p. 391) that the emperor Leo III derived originally from Germanicea in Syria (*ek tēs Germanikeōn katagomenos*...), a derivation supported strongly by the oriental sources (latest discussion: S. Gero, *Byzantine Iconoclasm During the Reign of Leo III, with Particular Reference to the Oriental Sources* [Louvain, 1973], pp. 1–31). Theophanes then remarks that Leo had been resettled with his parents in Mesembria in Thrace (*syn tois goneusi metoikizetai en Mes. tēs Thrak.*) by Justinian II during his first reign. An alternative tradition, apparently originating with the apocryphal, but early, *Sancti Joannis Damasceni, Epistola ad Theophilum Imperatorem*

(*PG* xcv, col. 357), has a certain *patrikios* Masisinnius/Sisinnius, who was then exercising the governorship of the command of the Anatolikoi (*tis tōn Anatolikōn stratēgias tēn hēgemonian periekhōn*), going the rounds of his area enlisting soldiers (*stratologiais tēn khōran peripoleuōn*), and amongst others enlisting Leo (*kai Leōn... stratologētheis*), who was a handsome and well-built young man (*neaniskos*), and who provided himself with a living working as an artisan (*banausos tēn epistēmēn ex autēs tēn zōēn porizomenos*).

The two traditions as to Leo's early career, perhaps because they are apparently discrepant, have been suspected or ignored (see, in the last instance, Gero, *Byzantine Iconoclasm during the Reign of Leo III*, suspecting the Thracian episode (pp. 28–31), and ignoring the Sisinnius one). In fact, they are not only compatible, but also fit perfectly the known historical context. The household (parents and young adult son at least), and others besides, had been subjected to Justinian's known policy of the transfer and resettlement of populations already alluded to above (pp. 631–4), and had been transferred from Germanicea in Syria to Mesembria in Thrace, through the agency of a *stratēgos tōn Anatolikōn*. The significant points are that it was only during the period 681–94/5 – that is, virtually coterminous with Justinian's first reign (685–95) – that the Byzantines were in control of Germanicea (Gero, *Byzantine Iconoclasm during the Reign of Leo III*, pp. 27–8), and that the official responsible for the application of such a policy would indeed have been a *stratēgos tōn Anatolikōn*. Moreover, there is at least one *patrikios* Sisinnius certainly known for the general period (he was killed in 719 – Theophanes, *Chronographia*; ed. de Boor, I, p. 400), and others are probably attested sigillographically (Zacos and Veglery, *Byzantine Lead Seals*, I.3, p. 1855). There is also, of course, the Sisinnius, *stratēgos tōn karabōn*, operating in the Aegean and at Thessalonica at a date most recently placed *c.* 682–4 – even nearer the period in question (Lemerle, *Les plus anciens recueils des miracles de saint Démétrius*, II, pp. 154–62).

The family, then, having been resettled in Thrace, presumably on land, was made responsible for the provision of a soldier – Leo. Again, the policy is a known one (above, pp. 634–40). The *apothēkē*, connected above (pp. 626–34, 654–62) with the provision and sale of arms and equipment to the military, duly appears at Mesembria in 690/1.

According to Theophanes (*loc. cit.*), Leo precipitated his advancement by offering 500 sheep – there is no mention of Leo himself acting as a shepherd, but the sheep were presumably from the family lands – to Justinian, as the latter was returning through Thrace in order to dethrone Tiberius III and so inaugurate his second reign, that is in 705. In gratitude, Justinian created Leo a *spatharios* and made him a close friend (*gnēsion philon*). Subsequently, Justinian sent Leo to the Caucasus, where he was involved in a long series of diplomatic and military manoeuvres that are reported in detail by Theophanes, arriving back in Constantinople under Anastasius II (713–15) who made him *stratēgos tōn Anatolikōn*, a post which he still held in 716/17 when the events which brought him to the throne began (Theophanes, *Chronographia*; ed. de Boor, I, pp. 391–5). According to the apocryphal *Epistola ad Theophilum Imperatorem* (*loc. cit.*), on enlistment Leo rose fast and high, was created *spatharios* by Theodosius III (715–17), and was sent with 120 *dromones* to western parts (Campania, Amalfi and Naples), arriving back in Constantinople in time to receive the throne from Theodosius on his abdication in 717.

There is no doubt at all that the two traditions for Leo's career subsequent to his transfer, resettlement and enlistment present problems, but these are no greater than any others of the same period, and should not be allowed to discredit the whole. In general, Theophanes should be preferred, because his account of the Caucasian expedition, and indeed of the events leading up to the accession of Leo in 717, are so lengthy and detailed as to have aroused the suspicion that it derives from an eye-witness account (for an analysis based on this understanding, A. R. Santoro, 'Byzantium and the Arabs during the Isaurian Period 717–802 A.D.' (Ph.D. Thesis, Rutgers, New Brunswick, N.J., 1978), pp. 83–118).

There remains the possibility that the apocryphal *Epistola*'s brief claim for a western expedition is basically correct, but that it is mistaken in its chronology and in any case failed to achieve a mention in Theophanes' *Chronographia*. There is in fact one section of Leo's career where such an expedition would fit quite well: Theophanes jumps quite suddenly from Justinian's creation of Leo as *spatharios*, presumably in 705, to an account of the Caucasian expedition, but it is unlikely – however momentous that was – that it lasted over the full period 705–713/15 when Leo returned to Constantinople. Room therefore exists for Leo having been involved in, or having led, a naval expedition to Italy, sometime during the period 705–11, and there was indeed sufficient pretext for mounting such an expedition: in 703/4, Gisulf I of Benevento had attacked Campania; in 710, the pope Constantine, on his outward journey to Constantinople, met the patrician and exarch John Rizocopus at Naples, and in 711 on his return journey landed at Gaeta – both cities being of course in Campania. The apocryphal *Epistola* therefore certainly has a plausible general focus, but it has to be admitted that no specific event can now be identified as lying behind its claim (refs: Stratos, *Byzantium in the Seventh Century*, v, pp. 100–1, 133–5).

# BIBLIOGRAPHIES

The following are not intended to form an exhaustive bibliography of the subject as a whole. Only those works that have been utilised in such a direct way as to be cited in the footnotes above have been included and, similarly, only such book-reviews as have been cited extensively in their own right.

A Primary sources (Greek)
B Primary sources (Latin)
C Primary sources (Syriac)
D Primary sources (Arabic/Persian)
E Primary sources (other languages)
F Papyri
G *Vitae/Acta Sanctorum*
H Major collections of sources; books or articles publishing, or principally and directly based upon, particular sources; etc.
I Secondary sources

## A. PRIMARY SOURCES (GREEK)

*Basilika*; ed. H. J. Scheltema, N. van der Wal and D. Holwerda, *Basilicorum Libri LX* A.I-, *Textus* B.I-, *Scholia* (Groningen/Jakarta, 1955/3– ). Now completely replaces the Heimbach edn which, on a number of occasions, I have nevertheless been forced to use.

Acropolites, George, *Historia*; ed. A. Heisenberg and P. Wirth, in *Georgii Acropolitae Opera* (2 vols, Teubner, Stuttgart, 1978).

Agathias of Myrina, *Historiarum Libri V*; ed. R. Keydell (Berlin, 1967) (=CFHB II).

Anonymous, *De Re Militari*; ed. R. Vári (*Incerti Scriptoris Byzantini Saeculi X: Liber de Re Militari*) (Teubner, Leipzig, 1901).

Anonymous, *Peri Stratēgikēs*; ed. H. Köchly and W. Rüstow, in *Griechische Kriegsschriftsteller* II (Leipzig, 1855), at pp. 42–209.

Anonymous (Pseudo-Aristotle), *De Mirabilibus Auscultationibus*; ed. W. S. Hett (*Aristotle, Minor Works*) (Loeb, London, 1936).

Anonymous (Pseudo-Codinus), *De Officiis*; ed. J. Verpeaux (*Pseudo-Kodinos, Traité des offices*) (Paris, 1966) (=Le Monde Byzantin I).

Anonymous (Pseudo-Lucian), *Timarion*; ed. R. Romano (Naples, 1974) (=Collana di Studi e Testi II).

Athanasius, *Apologia ad Constantium Imperatorem*; ed. J.-P. Migne, in *PG* xxv (Paris, 1884), at cols 596–641.
Attaliates, Michael, *Historia*; ed. I. Bekker (Bonn, 1853) (CSHB).
Bryennius, Nicephorus, *Historiarum Libri IV*; ed. P. Gautier (Brussels, 1975) (=CFHB IX).
Cabasilas, Nicholas, *Logos kata Tokizontōn*; ed. J.-P. Migne, in *PG* CL (Paris, 1865), at cols 728–49.
Candidus, *Fragmenta*; ed. K. Müller, in *FHG* IV (Paris, 1851), at pp. 135–7.
Cantacuzene, John (VI), *Historiarum Libri IV*; ed. L. Schopen and B. G. Niebuhr (3 vols, Bonn, 1828 (I), 1831 (II), 1832 (III)) (CSHB).
Cecaumenus, *Logos Nouthetētikos pros Basilea*; ed. B. Wassiliewsky and V. Jernstedt (St Petersburg, 1896; rep. Amsterdam, 1965).
— *Stratēgikon*; ed. B. Wassiliewsky and J. Jernstedt (Petersburg, 1896; rep. Amsterdam, 1965).
Cedrenus, George, *Historiarum Compendium*; ed. I. Bekker (2 vols, Bonn, 1838, 1839) (CSHB).
Choniates, Michael, *Epistolai*; ed. S. Lampros in *Mikhaēl Akominatou tou Khōniatou ta Sōzomena* (2 vols, rep. Groningen, 1968).
Choniates, Nicetas, *Epanagnōstikon eis ton Patriarkhēn kai tēn Synodon*; ed. K. N. Sathas in *Mesaiōnikē Bibliothēkē* I, at pp. 77–84 (Arabic numerotation).
— *Historia*; ed. J.-L. van Dieten (2 vols, I (text), II (indices), both Berlin/New York, 1975 (=CFHB XI.1, 2)).
*Chronicon Paschale*; ed. L. Dindorf (2 vols, Bonn, 1832) (CSHB).
Cinnamus, John, *Epitome*; ed. A. Meineke (Bonn, 1836) (CSHB).
Comnena, Anna, *Alexiad*; ed. B. Leib (3 vols, Paris, 1937 (I), 1943 (II), 1945 (III)).
Constantine (VII) Porphyrogenitus, *De Administrando Imperio*; ed. G. Moravcsik and R. J. H. Jenkins (rev. edn, Washington, D.C., 1967) (=CFHB I).
— *De Caerimoniis (Aulae Byzantinae)*; ed. J. Reiske (Bonn, 1829) (CSHB).
— *De Caerimoniis*; ed. A. Vogt (4 vols, all Paris, 1935 (I: text and commentary), 1939 (II: text), 1940 (II: commentary)).
— *De Thematibus*; ed. A. Pertusi (Vatican City, 1952) (=Studi e Testi, CLX).
*Continuation of Theophanes* ('Theophanes Continuatus'); ed. I. Bekker (Bonn, 1838) (CSHB).
Cosmas Indicopleustes, *Christian Topography*; ed. E. O. Winstedt (*The Christian Topography of Cosmas Indicopleustes*) (Cambridge, 1909).
Cydones, Demetrius, *Ad Ioannem Palaeologum Oratio*; ed. R.-J. Loenertz (*Démétrius Cydones, Correspondance*) (Vatican City, 1956) (=Studi e Testi CLXXXVI).
— *Epistulae*; ed. R.-J. Loenertz (*Démétrius Cydones, Correspondance*) (Vatican City, 1956) (=Studi e Testi CLXXXVI).
*Digenes Akrites*; ed. I. N. Mavrogordato (Oxford, 1956).
Epiphanius, *De Mensuris et Ponderibus*; ed. J. E. Dean (*Epiphanius' Treatise on Weights and Measures, the Syriac Version*) (Chicago, 1935) (=Studies in Ancient Oriental Civilization XI).
Eustathius of Thessalonica, *De Capta Thessalonica Liber*; ed. S. Kyriakidis (*La Espugnazione di Tessalonica*) (Palermo, 1961) (=Istituto Siciliano di Studi Bizantini e Neoellenici, Testi e Monumenti, Testi V).
— *De Emendenda Vita Monachica*; G. L. F. Tafel, in *Eustathii Metropolitae Thessalonicensis Opuscula* (Frankfurt-am-Main, 1832), at pp. 214–67.
— *Orationes*; ed. W. Regel and N. Novossadsky, in W. Regel, *Fontes Rerum Byzantinarum Sumptibus Academiae Caesareae Scientiarum* I.1 (Petrograd, 1892), at pp. 1–131.

Evagrius, *Ecclesiastical History*; ed. J. Bidez and L. Parmentier (*The Ecclesiastical History of Evagrius with the Scholia*) (London, 1898).

Genesius, Joseph, *Regum Libri IV*; ed. A. Lesmueller-Werner and H. Thurn (Berlin/New York, 1978) (=CFHB XIV).

Gregoras, Nicephorus, *Historia Byzantina*; ed. L. Schopen (3 vols, Bonn, 1829 (I), 1830 (II), 1855 (III)) (CSHB).

Gregory of Nazianzen, *Orationes*; ed. J.-P. Migne, in *PG* XXXV (Paris, 1886), at cols 396–1252, XXXVI (Paris, 1886), at cols 12–664.

Harmenopoulus, Constantine, *Hexabiblos*; ed. G. E. Heimbach (*Const. Harmenopouli Manuale Legum sive Hexabiblos*) (Leipzig, 1851).

John of Antioch, *Fragmenta*; ed. K. Müller in *FHG* IV (Paris, 1851), at pp. 535–622.

John Lydus, *De Magistratibus Populi Romani Libri III*; ed. R. Wuensch (Teubner, Stuttgart, 1967).

— *Liber de Mensibus*; ed. R. Wuensch (Teubner, Leipzig, 1898).

John Malalas, *Chronographia*; ed. L. Dindorf (Bonn, 1831) (CSHB).

Julian (Fl. Cl. Julianus), *Orationes*; ed. W. C. Wright (*The Works of the Emperor Julian*) (3 vols, Loeb, London/New York, 1913 (I, II), 1923 (III)).

Leo the Deacon, *Historia*; ed. C. B. Hase (Bonn, 1828) (CSHB).

Leo Grammaticus, *Chronographia*; ed. I. Bekker (Bonn, 1842) (CSHB).

Leo VI, *Taktika*; ed. J.-P. Migne in *PG* CVII (Paris, 1863), at cols 669–1120.

'Leo VI', *To Eparkhikon Biblion*; ed. J. Nicole (rep. Variorum, London, 1970).

Leo of Synnada, *Epistolai*; ed. J. Darrouzès, in *Epistoliers byzantins du X^e siècle* (Paris, 1960), III, at pp. 165–210 (=Archives de l'Orient Chrétien VI).

Leonard of Chios, *Epistola de Expugnatione Constantinopolis*; ed. J.-P. Migne, in *PG* CLIX (Paris, 1866), at cols 923–44.

Libanius, *Orationes*; ed. R. Foerster (4 vols, Teubner, Leipzig, 1903 (I.1, 2), 1904 (II), 1906 (III), 1908 (IV)).

Malchus (of Philadelphia), *Fragmenta*; ed. K. Müller, in *FHG* IV (Paris, 1851), at pp. 111–32.

Manasses, Constantine, *Breviarium Historiae*; ed. I. Bekker (Bonn, 1837) (CSHB).

Mauropus, John, *Opera*; ed. P. de Lagarde, in *Abhandlung der königlichen Gesellschaft der Wissenschaften zu Göttingen* XXVIII (1882).

Menander Protector, *Fragmenta*; ed. K. Müller, in *FHG* IV (Paris, 1851), at pp. 200–69.

Michael the Rhetor, *Oratio ad Manuelem Imperatorem*; ed. W. V. E. Regel, in *Fontes Rerum Byzantinarum* I (St Petersburg, 1892), at pp. 165–82.

Nicephorus (patriarch), *Breviarium*; ed. I. Bekker (Bonn, 1837) (CSHB).

Nicholas Mysticus, *Epistolae*; ed. R. J. H. Jenkins and L. G. Westerink (*Nicholas I, Patriarch of Constantinople, Letters*) (Washington, D.C., 1973) (=DOT II).

Olympiodorus of Thebes, *Fragmenta*; ed. K. Müller, in *FHG* IV (Paris, 1851), at pp. 57–68.

Ouranus, Nicephorus, *Epistolai*; ed. J. Darrouzès, in *Epistoliers byzantins du X^e siècle* (Paris, 1960), V, at pp. 217–48.

Pachymeres, George, *De Michaele et Andronico Palaeologis*; ed. I. Bekker (2 vols, Bonn, 1835) (CSHB).

Pausanias, *Description of Greece*; ed. W. H. S. Jones (5 vols, Loeb, London/New York, 1918 (I), 1926 (II), 1933 (III), 1935 (IV, V)).

Philotheus, *Klēterologion*; ed. N. Oikonomides, in *Les listes de préséance byzantines de IX^e et X^3 siècles* (Paris, 1972), at pp. 65–235.

Plato, *Critias*; ed. R. G. Bury in *Plato* VII (Loeb, London/New York, 1929), at pp. 255–307.

Plethon, George Gemistus, *Orationes*; ed. J.-P. Migne, in *PG* CLX (Paris, 1866), at cols 321–65.

Priscus of Panium, *Fragmenta*; ed. K. Müller in *FHG* IV (Paris, 1851), at pp. 69–110.

Procopius of Caesarea, *De Aedificiis Libri VI*; ed. J. Haury and G. Wirth, in *Procopius Caesariensis Opera Omnia* IV (Teubner, Leipzig, 1964).

— *De Bello Gothico*; ed. J. Haury and G. Wirth, in *Procopii Caesariensis Opera Omnia* II (Teubner, Leipzig, 1963).

— *De Bello Vandalico*; ed. J. Haury and G. Wirth, in *Procopii Caesariensis Opera Omnia* I (Teubner, Leipzig, 1963), at pp. 305–552.

— *Historia Arcana*; ed. J. Haury and G. Wirth, in *Procopii Caesariensis Opera Omnia* III (Teubner, Leipzig, 1963).

Prodromos, Theodore, *Carmina*; ed. D.-C. Hesseling and H. Pernot (*Poèmes prodromiques en grec vulgaire*) (Amsterdam, 1910).

Psellus, Michael, *Chronographia*; ed. E. Renauld (2 vols, Paris, 1926 (I), 1928 (II); both rep. 1967).

— *Dikastikē Apophasis*; ed. K. N. Sathas, in *Mesaiōnikē Bibliothēkē* V, at pp. 197–212.

— *Hermēneiai eis Koinolexias*; ed. K. N. Sathas, in *Mesaiōnikē Bibliothēkē* V, at pp. 525–43.

— *Peri Geōrgikōn*; ed. J.-F. Boissonade, in *Anecdota Graeca* I (Paris, 1829; rep. Hildesheim, 1962), at pp. 242–7.

— *Synopsis tōn Nomōn*; ed. J.-P. Migne, in *PG* CXXII (Paris, 1889), at cols 925–74.

*Scriptores Originum Constantinopolitanarum*; ed. T. Preger (2 vols, Teubner, Leipzig, 1901 (I), 1907 (II)).

Scutariotes, Theodore, *Synopsis Khronikē*; ed. K. N. Sathas in *Mesaiōnikē Bibliothēkē* VII (as *Anonymou Synopsis Khronikē*).

Scylitzes, John, *Synopsis Historiarum*; ed. H. Thurn (Berlin/New York, 1973) (= CFHB V).

'Scylitzes, John' (*Scylitzes Continuatus*); ed. I. Bekker (Bonn, 1839) (CSHB). Printed as a continuation of George Cedrenus, *Historiarum Compendium* II, at pp. 639–744.

Seth, Symeon, *Syntagma de Alimentorum Facultatibus*; ed. B. Langkavel (Teubner, Leipzig, 1868).

Sozomen, *Historia Ecclesiastica*; ed. J.-P. Migne, in *PG* LXVII (Paris, 1864), at cols 844–1630.

Strabo, *Geography*; ed. H. L. Jones (8 vols, Loeb, London/New York, 1917 (I), 1923 (II), 1924 (III), 1927 (IV), 1928 (V), 1929 (VI), 1930 (VII), 1932 (VIII)).

Suidas, *Lexicon*, ed. A. Adler, III, K-O (Teubner, Leipzig, 1933).

Symeon the Magister, *Annales*; ed. I. Bekker (Bonn, 1838) (CSHB).

Synesius, *Epistolai*; ed. J.-P. Migne, in *PG* LXVI (Paris, 1864), at cols 1321–1560.

Theodoret of Cyrrhus, *Epistolai*; ed. Y. Azéma (*Theodoret de Cyr, Correspondance*), I (Paris, 1955) (= Sources Chrétiennes XL).

Theophanes, *Chronographia*; ed. C. de Boor (2 vols, I (Greek text), II (Latin translation by Anastasius, etc.), both Leipzig (I: 1883, II: 1885)).

Theophylact Simocatta, *Historiae*; ed. C. de Boor and P. Wirth (Teubner, Stuttgart, 1972).

Thomas Magistros, *Peri Basileias*; ed. J.-P. Migne, in *PG* CXLV (Paris, 1865), at cols 448–96.

Tzetzes, John, *Epistolai*; ed. T. Pressel (Tübingen, 1851; rep. Amsterdam, 1964).

Xanthopoulus, Nicephorus Callistus, *Enarratio de Episcopis Byzantii*; ed. J.-P. Migne, in *PG* CXLVII (Paris, 1865), at cols 450–68.

Zonaras, John, *Annales*; ed. T. Büttner-Wobst (3 vols, Bonn, 1841 (I), 1844 (II), 1897 (III)) (CSHB).

Zosimus, *Historia Nova*; ed. L. Mendelssohn (Teubner, Leipzig, 1887).

## B. PRIMARY SOURCES (LATIN)

*Codex Theodosianus*; ed. T. Mommsen, P. M. Meyer, P. Krueger, *Theodosiari Libri XVI cum Constitutionibus Sirmondianis* (3rd edn, 3 vols, all Berlin, 1962: I.I, *Prolegomena*; I.2, *Textus cum Apparatu*; II, *Leges, Novellae ad Theodosianum Pertinentes*).

*Codex Justinianus*; ed. P. Krueger, T. Mommsen, T. Schoell and G. Kroll, *Corpus Iuris Civilis* (3 vols, all Berlin, 1954: I, *Institutiones, Digesta*; II, *Codex Justinianus*; III, *Novellae*).

Adam of Bremen, *Gesta Hammaburgensis Ecclesiae Pontificum*; MGH, *SS* VII, pp. 267–389.

Agnellus, *Liber Pontificalis Ecclesiae Ravennatis*; MGH, *SRLang.* pp. 265–391.

Albert of Aix, *Historia Hierosolymitana*; RHC, *Occ.* IV (Paris, 1879), pp. 265–713.

Ammianus Marcellinus, *Historia*; ed. V. Gardthausen (2 vols, Teubner, Leipzig, 1874 (I), 1875 (II)).

*Annales Herbipolenses*; MGH, *SS* XVI (Hanover, 1859/Leipzig, 1925), pp. 1–12.

*Annales Palidenses*; MGH, *SS* XVI (Hanover, 1859/Leipzig, 1925), pp. 48–98.

Anonymous, *Continuatio Havniensis Prosperi*; MGH, *AA* IX (= *Chron. Min. Saec. IV–VII* I) (Berlin, 1892), pp. 298–339.

Anonymous, *De Rebus Bellicis*; ed. R. Ireland (Oxford, 1979) (= British Archaeological Reports, International Series LXIII.2 (*De Rebus Bellicis: The Text*)).

Anonymous, *Epistola de Morte Friderici Imperatoris*; MGH, *SRG:NS* V, pp. 173–8.

Anonymous, *Excerpta Valesiana*; ed. J. Moreau and V. Velkov (Teubner, Leipzig, 1968).

Anonymous, *Expositio Totius Mundi et Gentium*; ed. J. Rougé (Paris, 1966).

Anonymous, *Gesta Francorum et Aliorum Hierosolimitanorum*; ed. R. Hill (London, 1962).

Anonymous, *Historia Ducum Veneticorum*; ed. H. Simonsfeld, MGH, *SS* XIV (Hanover, 1883), pp. 69–89.

Anonymous ('Ansbert'), *Historia de Expeditione Friderici Imperatoris*; MGH, *SRG:NS* V (Berlin, 1928), pp. 1–115.

Anonymous, *Historia Peregrinorum*; MGH, *SRG:NS* V (Berlin, 1928), pp. 116–72.

Anonymous, *Itinerarium Burdigalense*; ed. O. Cuntz, in *Itineraria Romana* (Teubner, Leipzig, 1929), at pp. 86–102.

Arnold of Lübeck, *Chronica Slavorum*; MGH, *SS* XXI (Hanover, 1869/Leipzig, 1925), pp. 100–250.

Augustine of Hippo, *De Civitate Dei*; ed. J.-P. Migne, in *PL* XLI (Paris, 1900).

— *Sermones*; ed. J.-P. Migne in *PL* XXXVIII (Paris, 1865).

Aurelius Victor (Sextus), *Liber de Caesaribus*; ed. F. Pichlmayr and R. Gruendel (Teubner, Leipzig, 1966).

Avitus of Vienne, *Epistulae*; MGH, *AA* VI.2 (Berlin, 1883), pp. 35–103.

Benedict of Peterborough, *Gesta Regis Henrici Secundi* (*The Chronicle of the Reigns of Henry II and Richard I, A.D. 1169–1192; Known Commonly under the Name of Benedict of Peterborough*), ed. W. Stubbs, in *Rerum Britannicarum Medii Aevi Scriptores* (2 vols, London, 1867).

Cassian, John, *Collationes*; ed. E. Pichery (3 vols, Paris, 1955 (I), 1958 (II), 1959 (III)) (= Sources Chrétiennes XLII, LIV, LXIV).

Cassiodorus (Fl. Mag. Aur. Cass. Senator), *Variarum Libri XII*; MGH, *AA* XII (Berlin, 1894).

Claudian(us), Claudius, *De Bello Gildonico*; MGH, *AA* X (Berlin, 1892), pp. 54–73.

Corippus, Flavius Cresconius, *In Laudem Iustini Augusti Minoris Libri IV*; ed. Averil Cameron (London, 1976).

Diocletian, *Edictum de Pretiis Venalium Rerum*; ed. M. Giacchero (*Edictum Diocletiani et*

*Collegarum de Pretiis Rerum Venalium* I, *Edictum*) (Genoa, 1974) (=Pubblicazioni dell' Istituto di Storia Antica e Scienze Ausiliarie dell' Università di Genova VIII).

Fredegar, *Chronicarum Libri IV*; MGH, *SRMerov.* II (Berlin, 1888).

Fulcher of Chartres, *Historia Iherosolymitana Gesta Francorum Iherusalem Peregrinantium ab Anno Domini MXCV usque ad Annum MCXXVII*; RHC, *Occ.* III.1 (Paris, 1867), pp. 311–485.

Gregory I (pope), *Epistolae*; MGH, *Ep.* I, II (2nd edn, Berlin, 1957).

Gregory of Tours, *Historia Francorum*; MGH, *SRMerov.* I (2nd edn, 3 fasc., Berlin, 1937 (I.1), 1942 (I.2), 1951 (I.3)).

Isidore of Seville, *Etymologiarum sive Originum Libri XX*; ed. W. M. Lindsay (2 vols, Oxford, 1911).

John of Brompton, *Chronicon*; ed. R. Twysden, in *Historiae Anglicanae Scriptores X* I (London, 1652), at cols 721–1284.

Jordanes, *Getica*; MGH, *AA* V.1 (Berlin, 1882), pp. 53–138.

Lactantius (L. Caecilius Firmianus), *De Mortibus Persecutorum*; ed. J. Moreau (*De la mort des persécuteurs*) (2 vols, text and commentary, Paris, 1954) (=Sources Chrétiennes XXXIX).

*Liber Pontificalis* I (Peter-Hadrian I); ed. L. Duchesne (2nd edn, Paris, 1955).

Liutprand of Cremona, *Legatio Constantinopolitana*; ed. J. Becker (*Die Werke Liudprands von Cremona*) (Hanover/Leipzig, 1915), at pp. 175–212.

Marcellinus Comes, *Chronicon*; MGH, *AA* XI (=*Chron. Min. Saec. IV–VII* II) (Berlin, 1894), pp. 37–109.

Martin I (pope), *Epistulae*; ed. J.-P. Migne in *PL* LXXXVII (Paris, 1863), at cols 119–204.

Obert, *Oberti Cancellarii Annales, a. 1164–1173*; MGH, *SS* XVIII, pp. 56–96.

Odo of Deuil, *De Profectione Ludovici VII in Orientem*; ed. V. G. Berry (New York, 1948) (=Records of Civilization, Sources and Studies).

Oresme, Nicholas, *De Moneta*; ed. C. Johnson (*The De Moneta of Nicholas Oresme and English Mint Documents*) (London, 1956).

Orosius, Paulus, *Historiarum adversus Paganos, Libri VII*; ed. K. Zangemeister (Teubner, Leipzig, 1889).

Otto of Freising, *Gesta Friderici Imperatoris*; ed. G. Waitz (3rd edn, Hanover/Leipzig, 1912), pp. 1–161.

Pacatus, Latinius Drepanius, *Panegyricus Theodosio Augusto Dictus*; in E. Galletier (ed.), *Panégyriques Latins* II (*XI–XII*) (Paris, 1955), at pp. 47–117.

Paul the Deacon, *Historia Langobardorum*; MGH, *SRLang.* (Berlin, 1878), pp. 12–187.

Pelagius II (pope), *Epistolae et Decreta*; ed. J.-P. Migne, in *PL* LXXII (Paris, 1878), at cols 703–60.

Pliny (Caius Plinius Secundus), *Natural History*; ed. H. Rackham, II (*Libri III–VII*) (Loeb, Cambridge, Mass./London, 1942).

Raymond of Aguilers, *Historia Francorum qui Ceperunt Iherusalem*; RHC, *Occ.* III (Paris, 1866), pp. 231–309.

Roger of Hoveden, *Chronica*; ed. W. Stubbs (4 vols, London, 1868 (I), 1869 (II), 1870 (III), 1871 (IV) (Rerum Britannicarum Medii Aevi Scriptores).

Saewulf, *Relatio de Peregrinatione ad Hierosolymam et Terram Sanctam*; ed. trans. W. R. B. Brownlow (London, 1896) (in Palestine Pilgrims' Text Society IV (1897)).

Sidonius (C. Sollius Apollinaris), *Epistulae*; ed. P. Mohr (Teubner, Leipzig, 1895).

Symmachus, Quintus Aurelius, *Epistulae*; MGH, *AA* VI.1 (Berlin, 1883), pp. 1–278.

— *Relationes*; MGH, *AA* VI.1 (Berlin, 1883), pp. 279–317.

William of Rubruck, *Itinerarium*; ed. C. R. Beazley (*The Texts and Versions of John de Plano Carpini and William de Rubruquis*) (Hakluyt, London, 1903).

— *Itinerarium*; trans. W. W. Rockhill (*The Journey of William of Rubruck to the Eastern Parts of the World, 1253–55*) (Hakluyt, London, 1900).

William of Tyre, *Historia Rerum in Partibus Transmarinis Gestarum a Tempore Successorum Mahumeth usque ad Annum Domini MCLXXXIV*; RHC, *Occ.* I. 1,2 (Paris, 1844). The continuators to be found in II.1,2 (Paris, 1859).

## C. PRIMARY SOURCES (SYRIAC)

Anon, *Chronicle*; in Corpus Scriptorum Christianorum Orientalium, *Scriptores Syri* III.4 (2: *Versio*), at pp. 114–16.

Bar Hebraeus, *Chronography*; ed. trans. E. A. T. W. Budge (*The Chronography of Gregory Abû'l Faraj...commonly known as Bar Hebraeus*) (2 vols, London, 1932, I (English translation), II (Syriac texts)).

John of Ephesus, *Ecclesiastical History*; trans. R. P. Smith (*The Third Part of the Ecclesiastical History of John Bishop of Ephesus now First Translated from the Original Syriac*) (Oxford, 1860).

Joshua the Stylite, *Chronicle*; ed. trans. W. Wright (*The Chronicle of Joshua the Stylite, Composed in Syriac A.D. 507*) (Cambridge, 1882).

Michael the Syrian, *Chronicle*; ed. trans. J.-B. Chabot (*Chronique de Michel le Syrien, patriarche jacobite d'Antioche (1166–1199)*) (3 vols, Paris, 1899 (I), 1901 (II), 1905 (III)).

Zachariah of Mitylene, *Chronicle*; ed. F. J. Hamilton and E. W. Brooks (*The Syriac Chronicle known as that of Zachariah of Mitylene*) (London, 1899).

## D. PRIMARY SOURCES (ARABIC)

Ibn Baṭṭūṭa, *Travels*; ed. H. A. R. Gibb (*The Travels of Ibn Baṭṭuṭa A.D. 1325–1354*) (3 vols, Cambridge, 1958 (I), 1962 (II), 1971 (III)) (=The Hakluyt Society, 2nd Series, nos CX, CXVII, CXLI).

Edrisi, *Geography*; trans. P. A. Jaubert (*Géographie d'Edrisi traduite de l'arabe en français*) (2 vols, Paris, 1836 (I), 1840 (II)) (Recueil de Voyages et de Mémoires, Publié par la Société de Géographie V, VI).

Ibn Ḥauḳal, *Liber Imaginis Terrae*; ed. J. H. Kramers (2 parts, Amsterdam, 1938/9) (=Bibliotheca Geographorum Arabicorum II.1, 2).

Juvaini, 'Ala-ad-Din 'Ata-Malik, *The History of the World-Conqueror*; ed. J. A. Boyle (2 vols, Manchester, 1958).

Ibn al-Zubair, *Kitāb al Dhakā'ir wa al-Tuḥaf*; ed. M. Ḥamīdallāh (Kuwait, 1959) (=The Arab Heritage I).

## E. PRIMARY SOURCES (OTHER LANGUAGES)

Badoer, Giacomo, *Il Libro dei Conti*; ed. U. Dorini and T. Bertelè (*Il Libro dei Conti di Giacomo Badoer (Costantinopoli 1436–1440)*) (Rome, 1956) (=Il Nuovo Ramusio III).

Barbaro, Nicolò, *Giornale dell'assedio di Costantinopoli 1453*; ed. E. Cornet (Vienna, 1856).

Benjamin of Tudela, *Itinerary*; trans. A. Sharf, in *Byzantine Jewry from Justinian to the Fourth Crusade* (London, 1971), at pp. 134–6.

Daniel (abbot), *Pilgrimage in the Holy Land*; trans. C. W. Wilson (London, 1895) (in Palestine Pilgrims' Text Society IV (1897)).

Geoffrey of Villehardouin, *La conquête de Constantinople*; ed. E. Faral (2 vols, Paris, 1938, 1939).

*El Libro di Mercatantie et Usanze de'Paesi*; ed. F. Borlandi (Turin, 1936) (=Documenti e Studi per la Storia del Commercio e del Diritto Commerciale Italiano VII).

Muntaner, Ramon, *Chronicle*; ed. K. Lanz (*Chronik des edlen en Ramon Muntaner*) (Stuttgart, 1844) (=Bibliothek des literarischen Vereins in Stuttgart VIII).

Pegolotti, Francesco Balducci, *La Pratica della Mercatura*; ed. A. Evans (Cambridge, Mass., 1936) (=The Mediaeval Academy of America, Publication no. XXIV).

Robert of Clari, *La conquête de Constantinople*; ed. P. Lauer (Paris, 1924; rep. 1974) (=Les Classiques Français du Moyen Age XL).

*The Russian Primary Chronicle*; trans. S. H. Cross and O. P. Sherbowitz-Wetzor (*The Russian Primary Chronicle, Laurentian Text*) (Cambridge, Mass., 1953) (=The Mediaeval Academy of America, Publication no. LX).

Sturluson, Snorri, *Heimskringla: The Saga of Harald Sigurtharson*; trans. L. M. Hollander (*Heimskringla, History of the Kings of Norway*) (Austin, 1964), at pp. 577–663.

Uzzano, Giovanni di Antonio da, *La Pratica della Mercatura*; ed. G. F. Pagnini della Ventura (Florence 1766) (=Della decima e di varie altre gravezze imposte dal Comune di Firenze, della moneta e della mercatura de' Fiorentini fino al secolo XVI, IV).

Zibaldone da Canal; ed. A. Stussi (*Zibaldone da Canal, manoscritto mercantile del sec. XIV*) (Venice, 1967) (=Fonti per la Storia di Venezia V.1).

### F. PAPYRI

*O. Strass.* P. Viereck, *Griechische und griechisch-demotische Ostraka der Universitäts- und Landesbibliothek zu Strassburg im Elsass* I (Berlin, 1923).

*P. Apollonos Ano* R. Rémondon, *Papyrus grecs d'Apollônos Anô* (Cairo, 1953) (=Ministère de l'Éducation Nationale, Documents de Fouilles de l'Institut Français d'Archéologie Orientale du Caire XIX).

*P. Beatty Panop.* T. C. Skeat, *Papyri from Panopolis in the Chester Beatty Library, Dublin* (Dublin, 1964) (=Chester Beatty Monographs X).

*P. Cairo* J. Maspero, *Papyrus grecs d'époque byzantine* (3 vols, rep. Osnabrück/Milan, 1973) (=Catalogue Général des Antiquités Égyptiennes du Musée du Caire I (nos 67001–67124, 1911), II (nos 67125–67278, 1913), III (nos 67279–67359, 1916)).

*P. Cair. Isidor.* A. E. R. Boak and H. C. Youtie, *The Archive of Aurelius Isidorus in the Egyptian Museum, Cairo, and the University of Michigan* (Ann Arbor, 1960).

*P. Fay.* B. P. Grenfell, A. S. Hunt and D. G. Hogarth, *Fayûm Towns and their Papyri* (London, 1900).

*P. Flor.* D. Comparetti and G. Vitelli, *Papiri Greco-Egizzi* I, *Papiri Fiorentini. Documenti pubblici e privati dell'età romana e bizantina* (Milan, 1906).

*P. Klein. Form.* C. Wessely, *Studien zur Palaeographie und Papyruskunde* (=*SPP* III, VIII) (Leipzig, 1904, 1908).

*P. Lips.* L.Mitteis, *Griechische Urkunden der Papyrussammlung zu Leipzig* (Leipzig, 1906).
*P. Lond.* F. G. Kenyon, H. I. Bell and T. C. Skeat, *Greek Papyri in the British Museum* (London, 1893– ).
*P. Michael.* D. S. Crawford, *Papyri Michaelidae* (Aberdeen, 1955).
*P. Ness.* C. J. Kraemer, *Excavations at Nessana* III, *Non-literary Papyri* (Princeton, 1958).
*P. Oslo.* S. Eitrem and L. Amundsen, *Papyri Osloenses* (Oslo, 1925– ).
*P. Oxy.* B. P. Grenfell, A. S. Hunt *et al.*, *The Oxyrhynchus Papyri* (London, 1898– ).
*P. Ryl.* A. S. Hunt, J. de M. Johnson, V. Martin, C. H. Roberts and E. G. Turner, *Catalogue of the Greek Papyri in the John Rylands Library, Manchester* (Manchester, 1911– ).
*PSI Papiri greci e latini* (Pubblicazioni della Società Italiana per la ricerca dei papiri greci e latini in Egitto), ed. G. Vitelli *et al.* (Florence, 1912– ).
*Sb. Sammelbuch griechischen Urkunden aus Aegypten*, ed. F. Preisigke, F. Bilabel and E. Kiessling (1915– ).
*SPP* C. Wessely, *Studien zur Palaeographie und Papyruskunde* (Leipzig, 1901– ).
See also 'H', under: Day, J., and Keyes, C. W.; Marini, G.; Shelton, J. C.; Tjäder, J.-O.

## G. VITAE/ACTA SANCTORUM

*Vita Sancti Eligii*; MGH, *SRMerov.* IV (Hanover/Leipzig, 1902), pp. 634–761.
*Vita Sancti Gregorii Magni* (by Paul the Deacon); ed. J.-P. Migne, in *PL* LXXV (Paris, 1902), at cols 41–242.
*Vita Sancti Ioannis Eleemosynarii*; ed. H. Gelzer (*Leontios' von Neapolis Leben des Heiligen Johannes des Barmherzigen Erzbischofs von Alexandrien*) (Freiburg/Leipzig, 1893) (= Sammlung ausgewählter kirchen- und dogmengeschichtlicher Quellenschriften V).
*Vita Sancti Lucae Stylitae*; ed. A. Vogt, in *Analecta Bollandiana* 28 (1909), at pp. 5–56.
*Acta Sancti Marcelli*; ed. H. Delehaye, in *Analecta Bollandiana* 41 (1923), at pp. 257–87.
*Vita Sanctae Melaniae Junioris*; ed. H. Delehaye, in *Analecta Bollandiana* 8 (1889), at pp. 16–63 (Latin), and in *AB* 22 (1903), at pp. 5–50.
*Vita Sanctae Olympiadis*; ed. H. Delehaye, in *Analecta Bollandiana* 15 (1896), at pp. 400–23, and in *AB* 16 (1897), at pp. 44–51.
*Vita Sancti Philareti*; ed. M.-H. Fourmy and M. Leroy, in *Byzantion* 9 (1934), at pp. 85–170.
*Vita Sancti Phocae*; ed. K. van der Vorst, in *Analecta Bollandiana* 30 (1911), at pp. 252–95.
*Vita Sancti Porphyrii Gazae*; ed. H. Grégoire and M.-A. Kugener (*Marc de diacre, Vie de Porphyrie, évêque de Gaza*) (Paris, 1930).
*Vita Sancti Sabae*; ed. E. Schwartz (*Kyrillos von Skythopolis*) (Leipzig, 1939) (= Texte und Untersuchungen zur Geschichte der altchristlichen Literatur XLIX.2).
*Vita Theodori Castrensis*; ed. E. W. Brooks ('John of Ephesus: Lives of the Eastern Saints') in *PO* XIX, at pp. 200–6.
*Vita Sancti Theodori Syceotae*; ed. A.-J. Festugière, *Vie de Théodore de Sykéôn* (Brussels, 1970) (= Subsidia Hagiographica XLVIII).
*Vita Sancti Theophanis*; ed. C. de Boor, in *Theophanis Chronographia* II (Leipzig, 1885), at pp. 3–30.
*Vita Willibaldi Episcopi Eichstetensis*; MGH, *SS* XV.1 (Hanover, 1887).

### H. MAJOR COLLECTIONS OF SOURCES; BOOKS OR ARTICLES PUBLISHING, OR PRINCIPALLY AND DIRECTLY BASED UPON, PARTICULAR SOURCES; ETC.

*L'Année Épigraphique*

Ashburner, W., 'The Farmer's Law', *Journal of Hellenic Studies* 30 (1910), pp. 85–108.

Balard, M., *Gênes et l'outre-mer* I, *Les actes de Caffa du notaire Lamberto di Sambuceto 1289–1290* (Paris/The Hague, 1973) (=École Pratique des Hautes Études, Sorbonne, VIe Section, Documents et Recherches XII).

Bompaire, J., *Actes de Xéropotamou* (2 parts, text and plates, Paris, 1964) (=Archives de l'Athos III).

*Bullarium Privilegiorum ac Diplomatum Romanorum Pontificum Amplissima Collectio*; ed. C. Cocquelines, III.1 (Rome, 1740).

Capasso, B., *Monumenta ad Neapolitani Ducatus Historiam Pertinentia* (2 vols, Naples, 1881 (I.1), 1885 (II.1), 1892 (II.2)).

Carile, A., 'Partitio Terrarum Imperii Romanie', *Studi Veneziani* 7 (1965), pp. 125–305.

Chastagnol, A., 'Un nouveau document sur le majorina?', *Bulletin de la Société Française de Numismatique* 30 (1975), pp. 854–7.

Clugnet, L. (ed.), 'L'orfèvre Andronicus et son épouse Athanasie', in 'Vie et récits de l'abbé Daniel, de Scété (VIe siècle) (Suite) (I)', in *Revue de l'Orient Chrétien* 5 (1900), at pp. 370–87.

*Codice Diplomatico Barese* I; ed. G. B. Nitto de Rossi and F. Nitti di Vito (*Cod. Dipl. Bar., Le Pergamene del Duomo di Bari*) (Bari, 1897).

Darrouzès, J., 'Listes épiscopales du concile de Nicée (787)', *Revue des Études Byzantines* 33 (1975), pp. 5–76.

— 'Listes synodales et notitiae', *Revue des Études Byzantines* 28 (1970), pp. 57–96.

Day, J., and Keyes, C. W., *Tax Documents from Theadelphia, Papyri of the Second Century A.D.* (New York, 1956) (=Columbia Papyri, Greek Series V).

Delehaye, H., 'Constantini Acropolitae, hagiographi byzantini, epistularum manipulus', *Analecta Bollandiana* 51 (1933), pp. 263–84.

Diehl, E., *Inscriptiones Latinae Christianae Veteres* (2nd edn, 4 vols, Berlin, 1961 ((I–III), 1967 (IV)).

Forsyth, J. H., 'The Byzantine-Arab Chronicle (938–1034) of Yaḥya b. Saʿīd al-Anṭākī', (Ph.D. thesis, Michigan, 1977).

Gautier, P., 'La Diataxis de Michel Attaliate', *Revue des Études Byzantines* 39 (1981), pp. 5–143.

— 'Le typikon du Christ Sauveur Pantocrator', *Revue des Études Byzantines* 32 (1974), pp. 1–145.

Giomo, G., 'Le Rubriche dei Libri *Misti* del Senato perduti, trascritte', *Archivio Veneto* 18 (1879), pp. 315–38.

Grégoire, H., *Recueil des inscriptions grecques chrétiennes d'Asie Mineure* (Paris, 1922).

Heisenberg, A., *Nikolaos Mesarites: die Palastrevolution des Johannes Komnenos* (Würzburg, 1907) (=Programm k. Alten Gymnasiums zu Würzburg für das Studienjahr 1906/1907).

Hultsch, F., *Metrologicorum Scriptorum Reliquiae* (2 vols, I: *Quo Scriptores Graeci Continentur*, II: *Quo Scriptores Romani et Indices Continentur*, Teubner, Leipzig, 1864, 1866).

*Inscriptiones Latinae Selectae*; ed. H. Dessau (3 vols, Berlin, 1892 (I), 1902 (II.1), 1906 (II.2), 1914 (III.1), 1916 (III.2)).
*Inscriptions of Roman Tripolitania*; ed. J. M. Reynolds and J. B. Ward Perkins (Rome/London, 1952).
Iverites, I., 'Ek tou arkheiou tēs en Hagio Orei Hieras Monēs tōn Ivērōn: Vyzantinai diathēkai', *Orthodoxia* 60 (Dec. 1930), pp. 613–18.
— 'Ek tou arkheiou tēs en Hagio Orei Hieras Monēs tōn Ivērōn: Vyzantinai diathēkai (synekheia)', *Orthodoxia* 66 (June 1931), pp. 364–71.
Kugeas, S., 'Notizbuch eines Beamten der Metropolis in Thessalonike aus dem Anfang des XV Jahrhunderts', *Byzantinische Zeitschrift* 23 (1914/19), pp. 143–63.
Lappa-Zizikas, E., 'Un chrysobulle inconnu en faveur du monastère des Saints-Anargyres de Kosmidion', *Travaux et Mémoires* 8 (1981), pp. 255–68.
*Laterculus Veronensis*; ed. O. Seeck (*Notitia Dignitatum accedunt Notitia Urbis Constantinopolitanae et Laterculi Provinciarum*) (Berlin, 1876).
Lefort, J., *Actes d'Esphigménou* (2 parts, text and plates, Paris, 1973) (= Archives de l'Athos VI).
*Leges Burgundionum*; MGH, *Leges* II.1 (Hanover, 1892).
Lemerle, P., *Actes de Kutlumus* (2 parts, text and plates, Paris, 1946) (= Archives de l'Athos II).
Lemerle, P., Guillou, A., and Svoronos, N., *Actes de Lavra* I, *Des origines à 1204* (2 parts, text and plates, Paris, 1970) (= Archives de l'Athos v).
Loenertz, R.-J., 'La chronique brève de 1352, texte, traduction et commentaire, deuxième partie: de 1328 à 1341', *Orientalia Christiana Periodica* 30 (1964), pp. 39–64.
Mansi, G. D., *Sacrorum Conciliorum Nova et Amplissima Collectio* XI, XII, XIII, XVI, XVII (all rep. Graz, 1960).
Marini, G., *I Papyri Diplomatici* (Rome, 1805).
Miklosich, F., and Müller, J. (eds), *Acta et Diplomata Graeca Medii Aevi Sacra et Profana* VI (Vienna, 1890).
Morozzo della Rocca, R., and Lombardo, A., *Documenti del commercio veneziano nei secoli XI–XIII* (2 vols, Turin, 1940) (= Documenti e Studi per la Storia del Commercio e del Diritto Commerciale Italiano XIX, XX).
Müller, J., *Documenti sulle relationi delle città toscane coll'Oriente Christiano e coi Turchi, fino all'anno MDXXXI* (Florence, 1879) (= Documenti degli Archivi Toscani).
Noailles, P., and Dain, A., *Les novelles de Léon VI le Sage* (Paris, 1944).
*Notitia Dignitatum*; ed. O. Seeck (*Notitia Dignitatum accedunt Notitia Urbis Constantinopolitanae et Laterculi Provinciarum*) (Berlin, 1876).
Oikonomides, N., *Actes de Dionysiou* (2 parts, text and plates, Paris, 1968) (= Archives de l'Athos IV).
— *Les listes de préséance byzantines des IXe et Xe siècles* (Paris, 1972).
Papachryssanthou, D., *Actes du Prôtaton* (2 parts, text and plates, Paris, 1975) (= Archives de l'Athos VII).
Papadopoulos-Kerameus, A. I., *Noctes Petropolitanae, Sbornik vizantiĭskikh tekstov XII–XIII vekov* (St Petersburg, 1913).
Petit, L., 'Le Monastère de Notre-Dame de Pitié en Macédoine', *Izvestiya Russkago Arkheologicheskago Instituta v Konstantinopole* 6 (1900–1), pp. 1–153.
— 'Typikon de Grégoire Pacourianos pour le monastère de Pétritzos (Bačkovo) en Bulgarie', *Vizantiĭskiĭ Vremennik* 11 (1904), Supp. 1, pp. i–xxxii, 1–63.

— 'Typikon du monastère de la Kosmosotira près d'Aenos (1152)', *Izvestiya Russkago Arkheologicheskago Instituta v Konstantinopole* 13 (1908), pp. 17–77.

Petit, L., and Korablev, B., *Actes de l'Athos* v, *Actes de Chilandar, première partie, actes grecs* (St Petersburg, 1911) (=Vizantiĭskiĭ Vremennik 17 (1910) Supp. 1).

Petrides, S., 'Jean Apokaukos, lettres et autres documents inédits', *Izvestiya Russkago Arkheologicheskago Instituta v Konstantinopole* 14 (1909), pp. 69–100.

Sathas, K. N., *Mesaiōnikē Bibliothēkē* (7 vols, Venice/Paris, 1872 (I, III), 1873 (II), 1874 (IV), 1876 (V), 1877 (VI), 1894 (VII)).

Schreiner, P., 'Zwei unedierte Praktika aus der zweiten Hälfte des 14.Jahrhunderts', *Jahrbuch der Österreichischen Byzantinistik* 19 (1970), pp. 33–49.

Shelton, J. C., *A Tax List from Karanis (P. Cair. Mich. 359)* (2 vols, Bonn, 1975 (I: text), 1977 (II: commentary and indexes)) (=Papyrologische Texte und Abhandlungen XVII, XVIII).

Starr, J., *The Jews in the Byzantine Empire, 641–1204* (Athens, 1939, rep. 1969) (=Texte und Forschungen zur Byzantinisch-Neugriechischen Philologie XXX).

*Supplementum Epigraphicum Graecum* IX (Leyden, 1944).

Tafel, G. L. F., and Thomas, G. M. (eds), *Urkunden zur älteren Handels- und Staatsgeschichte der Republik Venedig* (3 vols, all Vienna; I (*814–1205*), II (*1205–55*) 1856, III (*1256–99*) 1857) (=Fontes Rerum Austriacarum XII–XIV).

Tannery, P., 'Notice sur les deux lettres arithmétiques de Nicolas Rhabdas (texte grec et traduction)', in *Mémoires Scientifiques* IV, *Sciences exactes chez les byzantins* (Paris/Toulouse, 1920), at pp. 61–198.

Theocharides, G. I., 'Eine Vermächtnisurkunde des Gross-Stratopedarchen Demetrios Tzamblakon', in P. Wirth (ed.), *Polychronion: Festschrift Franz Dölger zum 75. Geburtstag* (Heidelberg, 1966), at pp. 486–95.

Thomas, G. M. (ed.), *Diplomatarium Veneto-Levantinum, sive Acta et Diplomata Res Venetas Graecas atque Levantis Illustrantia a. 1300–1350* (Venice, 1880).

Thompson, E. A., *A Roman Reformer and Inventor, being a New Text of the Treatise* De Rebus Bellicis (Oxford, 1952).

Tjäder, J.-O., *Die nichtliterarischen lateinischen Papyri Italiens aus der Zeit 445–700* I, *Papyri 1–28* (Lund, 1955).

Vogel, K., *Ein byzantinisches Rechenbuch des frühen 14. Jahrhunderts, Text, Übersetzung und Kommentar* (Vienna, 1968) (=Wiener Byzantinische Studien VI).

Zachariadou, E. A., 'Sept traités inédits entre Venise et les émirats d'Aydin et de Menteşe (1331–1407)', in *Studi Preottomani e Ottomani, Atti del Convegno di Napoli (24–26 settembre 1974)* (Naples, 1976), at pp. 229–40.

Zepos, I. and P., *Ius Graeco-Romanum* (8 vols, Athens, 1931).

## I. SECONDARY SOURCES

Abulafia, D. S. H., *The Two Italies. Economic Relations between the Norman Kingdom of Sicily and the Northern Communes* (Cambridge, 1977).

Adelson, H. L., *Light Weight Solidi and Byzantine Trade during the Sixth and Seventh Centuries* (New York, 1957) (=American Numismatic Society, Numismatic Notes and Monographs CXXXVIII).

— 'The Monetary Deterioration in the Fifth Century', in A. Kindler (ed.), *International Numismatic Convention, Jerusalem 27–31 December 1963, The Patterns of Monetary Development in Phoenicia and Palestine in Antiquity, Proceedings* (Jerusalem, 1967), at pp. 262–82.
— 'Silver Currency and Values in the Early Byzantine Empire', in H. Ingholt (ed.), *Centennial Publication of the American Numismatic Society* (New York, 1958), at pp. 1–26.
Adelson, H. L., and Kustas, G. L., *A Bronze Hoard of the Period of Zeno I* (New York, 1962) (= American Numismatic Society, Numismatic Notes and Monographs CXLVIII).
— 'A Sixth Century Hoard of Minimi from the Western Peloponnese', *American Numismatic Society Museum Notes* 11 (1964), pp. 159–205.
Admiralty (Naval Staff, Intelligence Division), *I.D. 1114: A Handbook of Macedonia and Surrounding Territories* (London, 1916).
— *I.D. 1129: A Handbook of Turkey in Europe* (London, 1917).
— *I.D. 1155: A Handbook of Bulgaria* (London, 1917).
— *I.D. 1204: A Handbook of Roumania* (London, 1918).
— *C.B. 847 A: A Handbook of Asia Minor* I, *General* (London, 1919).
— *C.B. 847 B: A Handbook of Asia Minor* II, *Western Asia Minor* (London, 1919).
— *C.B. 847 C(2): A Handbook of Asia Minor* III.2, *The Central Plateau West of the Kyzyl Irmak* (London, 1919).
— *C.B. 847 D 2: A Handbook of Asia Minor* IV.2, *Cilicia, Antitaurus, and North Syria* (London, 1919).
Adontz, N., and Grégoire, H., 'Nicéphore au col roide', *Byzantion* 8 (1933), pp. 203–12.
Ahrweiler, H., *Byzance et la mer: la marine de guerre, la politique, et les institutions maritimes de byzance aux VIIe–XVe siècles* (Paris, 1966) (= Bibliothèque Byzantine, Études V).
— 'Choma-Aggélokastron', *Revue des Études Byzantines* 24 (1966) (= Mélanges Venance Grumel I), pp. 278–33.
— 'Les forteresses construites en Asie Mineure face à l'invasion seldjoucide', in *Akten des XI. internationalen Byzantinistenkongresses, München 1958* (Munich, 1960), at pp. 182–9.
— 'L'histoire et la géographie de la région de Smyrne entre les deux occupations turques (1081–1317) particulièrement au XIIIe siècle', *Travaux et Mémoires* 1 (1965), pp. 1–204.
— 'Nouvelle hypothèse sur le tétartèron d'or et la politique monétaire de Nicéphore Phocas', *Zbornik Radova Vizantoloshkog Instituta* 8 (1963), pp. 1–9.
— 'La politique agraire des empereurs de Nicée', *Byzantion* 28 (1958), pp. 51–66.
— 'Recherches sur l'administration de l'empire byzantin aux IXe–XIe siècles', *Bulletin de Correspondance Hellénique* 84 (1960), pp. 1–111.
Alföldi, M. R., *Die constantinische Goldprägung: Untersuchungen zu ihrer Bedeutung für Kaiserpolitik und Hofkunst* (Mainz, 1963).
Andréadès, A. M., 'De la monnaie et de la puissance d'achat des métaux précieux dans l'empire byzantin', *Byzantion* 1 (1924), pp. 75–115.
— 'Le montant du budget de l'empire byzantin', *Revue des Études Grecques* 34 (1921), pp. 20–56.
Angold, M. J., *A Byzantine Government in Exile, Government and Society under the Laskarids of Nicaea (1204–1261)* (Oxford, 1974).
Antoniadis-Bibicou, H., *Études d'histoire maritime de Byzance: à propos du 'thème des Caravisiens'* (Paris, 1966).
— *Recherches sur les douanes à Byzance, l''octava', le 'kommerkion' et les commerciaires* (Paris, 1963) (= Cahiers des Annales XX).

— 'Démographie, salaires et prix à Byzance au XI^e siècle', *Annales (Ec. Soc. Civ.)* 27 (1972), pp. 215–46.

Artuk, I. and C., *Istanbul Arkeoloji Müzeleri Teşşhirdeki İslâmî Sikkeler Kataloğu* (2 vols, Istanbul, 1970 (I), 1974 (II)).

Asdracha, C., *La région des Rhodopes aux XIII^e et XIV^e siècles: étude de géographie historique* (Athens, 1976) (= Texte und Forschungen zur Byzantinisch-Neugriechischen Philologie XLIX).

Ashtor, E., *A Social and Economic History of the Near East in the Middle Ages* (London, 1976).

Astruc, C., 'L'inventaire dressé en septembre 1200 du trésor et de la bibliothèque de Patmos, édition diplomatique', *Travaux et Mémoires* 8 (1981), pp. 15–30.

Avdev, S., 'Secheni li ca perperi vuv Varna i Mesembriya prez XIV vek', *Numizmatika* 3 (1979), pp. 7–14.

Avramea, A. P., *Hē Vyzantinē Thessalia mekhri tou 1204: Symbolē eis tēn Historikēn Geōgraphian* (Athens, 1974).

Babelon, E., 'La trouvaille de Helleville (Manche) en 1780', *Revue Numismatique* 10⁴ (1906), pp. 160–89.

Babinger, F., *Mehmed the Conqueror and his Time* (Princeton, 1978) (= Bollinger Series XCVI).

Balard, M., 'L'activité économique des ports du bas-Danube au XIV^e siècle', *Travaux et Mémoires* 8 (1981) (= Hommage à M. Paul Lemerle), pp. 35–43.

Baratte, F., 'Quelques remarques à propos des lingots d'or et d'argent du bas-empire', in V. Kondić (ed.), *Frappe et ateliers monétaires dans l'antiquité et moyen âge* (Belgrade, 1976) (= Actes du Symposium du 30 janvier au 1 février dans la Musée Nationale de Belgrade), at pp. 63–71.

Barker, J. W., *Manuel II Palaeologus (1391–1425): A Study in Late Byzantine Statesmanship* (New Brunswick, N.J., 1969).

Barone, N., 'La cedola per l'imposta ordinata dal Re Carlo I d'Angiò nel 1276 per la circolazione della nuova moneta di denari in Terra d'Otranto', in *Studi di Storia Napoletana in Onore di Michelangelo Schipa* (Naples, 1926), at pp. 127–39.

Barrandon, J.-N., and Brenot, C., 'Analyse de monnaies de bronze (318–340) par activation neutronique à l'aide d'une source isotopique de californium 252', in *Les 'dévaluations' à Rome, époque républicaine et impériale (Rome, 13–15 novembre 1975)* (Rome, 1978) (= Collection de l'École Française de Rome XXXVII), at pp. 123–44.

Barrandon, J.-N., Callu, J.-P., and Brenot, C., 'The Analysis of Constantinian Coins (A.D. 313–40) by Non-destructive Californium 252 Activation Analysis', *Archaeometry* 19 (1977), pp. 173–86.

Bastien, P., 'Coins with a Double Effigy issued by Licinius at Nicomedia, Cyzicus, and Antioch', *Numismatic Chronicle* 13⁷ (1973), pp. 87–97.

— 'The Iantinum Mint', *American Numismatic Society Museum Notes* 25 (1980), pp. 77–85.

Bates, G. E., *Byzantine Coins* (Cambridge, Mass., 1971) (= Archaeological Exploration of Sardis, Monograph I).

— 'Constans II or Heraclonas: An Analysis of the Constantinopolitan Folles of Constans II', *American Numismatic Society Museum Notes* 17 (1971), pp. 141–61.

Bauer, N., 'Die Silber- und Goldbarren des russischen Mittelalters. Eine archäologische Studie', *Numismatische Zeitschrift* 22 (1929), pp. 77–120, 24 (1931), pp. 61–100.

Beaujard, B., and Huvelin, H., 'À propos de l'atelier monétaire rouennais de Carausius', *Bulletin de la Société Française de Numismatique* 33 (1978), pp. 360–7.

Bedoukian, P. Z., *Coinage of Cilician Armenia* (New York, 1962) (=American Numismatic Society, Numismatic Notes and Monographs CXLVII).

Bell, H. W., *Sardis* XI, *Coins* (I: *1910–1914*) (Leiden, 1916).

Bellinger, A. R., *Catalogue of the Byzantine Coins in the Dumbarton Oaks Collection and in the Whittemore Collection* I, *Anastasius I to Maurice, 491–602* (Washington, D.C., 1966).

— 'Byzantine Notes', *American Numismatic Society Museum Notes* 12 (1966), pp. 83–124.

Bendall, S., 'Andronicus I of Trebizond', *Numismatic Circular* 88 (1980), pp. 400–1.

— 'The Coinage of Trebizond under Isaac II (A.D. 1185–95), with a Note on an Unfinished Byzantine Die', *American Numismatic Society Museum Notes* 24 (1979), pp. 213–17.

— 'A Coin of Constantine XI', *Numismatic Circular* 82 (1974), pp. 188–9.

— 'An Early Palaeologan Gold Hoard', *Numismatic Chronicle* 142 (1982), pp. 66–82.

— 'A Follis of Alexius I of Trebizond', *Numismatic Circular* 89 (1981), p. 237.

— 'Miliaresia of the Reign of Michael II, A.D. 820–822', *Numismatic Circular* 91 (1983), p. 44.

— 'The Mint of Trebizond under Alexius I and the Gabrades', *Numismatic Chronicle* $17^7$ (1977), pp. 126–36.

— 'A New Twelfth-century Byzantine Coin from the Mint of Trebizond', *Numismatic Chronicle* 142 (1982), p. 163.

— 'Palaeologan Gold Coins from the Mint of Thessalonica', *Schweizer Münzblätter* 32 (1982), pp. 15–21.

— 'Some Further Notes on the Mint of Trebizond under Alexius I', *Numismatic Chronicle* $19^7$ (1979), p. 211.

— 'A Thessalonican Hyperpyron of Andronicus II and Michael IX?', *Numismatic Circular* 89 (1981), p. 158.

Bendall, S., and Donald, P. J., *The Billon Trachea of Michael VIII Palaeologos, 1258–1282* (London, 1974).

— *The Later Palaeologan Coinage, 1282–1453* (London, 1979).

— 'The Silver Coinage of Michael VIII, A.D. 1258–1282', *Numismatic Circular* 90 (1982), pp. 121–4.

Bendall, S., and Sellwood, D., 'The Method of Striking Scyphate Coins using two Obverse Dies', *Numismatic Chronicle* $18^7$ (1978), pp. 93–104.

Bertelè, T., 'I gioielli della corona bizantina dati in pegno alla Repubblica veneta nel sec. XIV e Mastino II della Scala', in *Studi in Onore Amintore Fanfani* II, *Medioevo* (Milan, 1962), at pp. 89–117.

— 'L'iperpero bizantino dal 1261 al 1453', *Rivista Italiana di Numismatica* $5^5$ (1957), pp. 70–89.

— 'Lineamenti principali della numismatica bizantina', *Rivista Italiana di Numismatica* $12^5$ (1964), pp. 33–118.

— 'Moneta veneziana e moneta bizantina (secoli XII–XV)', in A. Pertusi (ed.), *Venezia e il Levante fino al secolo XV* I, *Storia-Diritto-Economia* I (2 parts: I.I, I.2, Florence, 1973), at pp. 3–146.

— 'Il titolo degli iperperi della zecca di Nicea', in *Proceedings of the XIIIth International Congress of Byzantine Studies, Oxford 5–10 September 1966* (London/New York/Toronto, 1967), at pp. 339–41.

Bertelè, T., and Morrisson, C., *Numismatique byzantine, suivie de deux études inédites sur les monnaies des Paléologues* (Wetteren, 1978).

Beschaouch, A., 'La mosaïque de chasse à l'amphithéâtre découverte à Smirat en Tunisie', *Comptes Rendus de l'Académie des Inscriptions et Belles-Lettres* (1966), pp. 134–57.

Bidez, J., 'Amiens, ville natale de l'empereur Magnence', *Revue des Études Anciennes* 27 (1925), pp. 312–18.

Bintliff, J. L., 'Climatic Change, Archaeology and Quarternary Science in the Eastern Mediterranean Region', in A. F. Harding (ed.), *Climatic Change in Later Prehistory* (Edinburgh, 1982), at pp. 143–61.

Blake, R. P., 'The Circulation of Silver in the Moslem East down to the Mongol Epoch', *Harvard Journal of Asiatic Studies* 2 (1937), pp. 291–328.

Blanchet, A., 'Les dernières monnaies d'or des empereurs de Byzance', *Revue Numismatique* $14^4$ (1910), pp. 78–90.

Bogaert, R., *Banques et banquiers dans les cités grecques* (Leyden, 1968).

Bon, A., *Le Peloponnèse byzantin jusqu'en 1204* (Paris, 1951) (=Bibliothèque Byzantine, Études I).

Boni, G., 'Roma: nuove scoperte nella città e nel suburbio', *Notizie degli Scavi* (1899), pp. 325–33.

Bowman, A. K., 'The Economy of Egypt in the Earlier Fourth Century', in C. E. King (ed.), *Imperial Revenue, Expenditure and Monetary Policy in the Fourth Century A.D.* (Oxford, 1980) (=British Archaeological Reports, International Series LXXVI), at pp. 23–40.

Brand, C. M., *Byzantium Confronts the West 1180–1204* (Cambridge, Mass., 1968).

— *Deeds of John and Manuel Comnenus* (New York, 1976) (trans. of, and brief comm. on, John Cinnamus' *Epitome*).

— 'Two Byzantine Treatises on Taxation', *Traditio* 25 (1969), pp. 35–60.

Brătianu, G. I., *Études byzantines d'histoire économique et sociale* (Paris, 1938).

— *Recherches sur Vicina et Cetatea Albă* (Bucharest, 1935).

Brenot, C., 'Un bronze de Zénon de l'atelier d'Antioche', *Bulletin de la Société Française de Numismatique* 23 (1968), pp. 323–4.

Brezeanu, S., 'Le premier traité économique entre Venise et Nicée', *Revue des Études Sud-Est Européennes* 12 (1974), pp. 143–6.

Brice, W. C., 'The Turkish Colonization of Anatolia', *Bulletin of the John Rylands Library Manchester* 38 (1955–6), pp. 18–44.

Broughton, T. R. S., 'Roman Asia Minor', in T. Frank (ed.), *An Economic Survey of Ancient Rome* IV, *Africa, Syria, Greece, Asia Minor* (Baltimore, 1938), at pp. 499–916.

Browning, R., 'Literacy in the Byzantine World', *Byzantine and Modern Greek Studies* 4 (1978) (=Essays Presented to Sir Steven Runciman), pp. 39–54.

— 'The Riot of A.D. 387 in Antioch: The Role of the Theatrical Claques in the Later Empire', *Journal of Roman Studies* 42 (1952), pp. 13–20.

Bruun, P. M., *The Roman Imperial Coinage* VII, *Constantine and Licinius, A.D. 313–337* (London, 1966).

— 'A Law Concerning Tax Payment in Gold and the Constantinian Solidus', in *Congresso internazionale di Numismatica, Roma 11–16 settembre 1961* II, *Atti* (Rome, 1965), at pp. 387–98.

— 'The Successive Monetary Reforms of Diocletian', *American Numismatic Society Museum Notes* 24 (1979), pp. 129–48.

Bryer, A. A. M., 'The Society and Institutions of the Empire of Trebizond' (Ph.D. thesis, Oxford, 1967).

— 'A Byzantine Family: The Gabrades, *c.* 979–*c.* 1653', *University of Birmingham Historical Journal* 12 (1970), pp. 164–87.

— 'The Estates of the Empire of Trebizond: Evidence for their Resources, Products, Agriculture, Ownership and Location', *Arkheion Pontou* 35 (1978) (= *Maurē Thalassa*), pp. 370–477.

— 'Greeks and Türkmens: The Pontic Exception', *DOP* 29 (1975), pp. 113–48 (with fold-out at end).

Bury, J. B., *History of the Eastern Roman Empire from the Fall of Irene to the Accession of Basil I (802–867)* (London, 1912).

— *The Imperial Administrative System in the Ninth Century, with a Revised Text of the Kletorologion of Philotheos* (London, 1911) (= The British Academy, Supplemental Papers I).

Byrne, E. H., *Genoese Shipping in the Twelfth and Thirteenth Centuries* (Cambridge, Mass., 1930) (= Monographs of the Mediaeval Academy of America I).

Cahen, C., *Pre-Ottoman Turkey: A General Survey of the Material and Spiritual Culture and History c. 1071–1330* (London, 1968).

— *Turcobyzantina et Oriens Christianus* (Variorum, London, 1974).

— 'La campagne de Mantzikert d'après les sources musulmanes', *Byzantion* 9 (1934), pp. 613–42.

Callu, J.-P., *La politique monétaire des empereurs romains de 238 à 311* (Paris, 1969) (= Bibliothèque des Écoles Françaises d'Athènes et de Rome CCXIV).

— 'La circulation monétaire de 313 à 348', in H. A. Cahn and G. Le Rider (eds), *Proceedings of the 8th International Congress of Numismatics, New York–Washington September 1973* (Paris/Basel, 1976) (= Association Internationale des Numismates Professionels, Publication IV), at pp. 227–42.

— 'Dénombrement et pesée: le sou théodosien', *Bulletin de la Société Française de Numismatique* 34 (1979), pp. 611–12.

— '"Follis Singularis" (à propos d'une inscription de Ghirza, Tripolitaine)', *Mélanges de l'École Française de Rome* 71 (1959), pp. 321–37.

— 'Les origines du "miliarensis": le témoignage de Dardanius', *Revue Numismatique* $22^{6}$ (1980), pp. 120–30.

— '"Pensa" et "Follis" sur une inscription d'Afrique', *Antiquités Africaines* 15 (1980) (= Hommages à Jean Lassus II), pp. 273–83.

— 'Rôle et distribution des éspèces de bronze de 348 à 392', in C. E. King (ed.), *Imperial Revenue, Expenditure and Monetary Policy in the Fourth Century A.D.* (Oxford, 1980) (= British Archaeological Reports, International Series LXXVI), at pp. 41–93. Repeated, in English, at pp. 95–124.

— 'Sozomène, v.15 et la corporation des monétaires', *Bulletin de la Société Française de Numismatique* 27 (1972), pp. 271–3.

Cameron, Alan, 'The Date of the Anonymous *De Rebus Bellicis*', in M. W. C. Hassall (ed.), *De Rebus Bellicis* (Oxford, 1979) (= British Archaeological Reports, International Series LXIII), at pp. 1–7.

Cameron, Alan, and Schauer, D., 'The Last Consul: Basilius and his Diptych', *Journal of Roman Studies* 72 (1982), pp. 126–45.

Canard, M., *Histoire de la dynastie des H'amdanides de Jazīra et de Syrie* I (Algiers, 1951) (= Publications de la Faculté des Lettres d'Alger, 2nd series, vol. XXI).

— 'Les sources arabes de l'histoire byzantine aux confins des X$^{e}$ et XI$^{e}$ siècles', *Revue des Études Byzantines* 19 (1961) (= Mélanges Raymond Janin), pp. 283–314.

Caramessini-Oekonomides, M., 'Contribution à l'étude de la circulation des monnaies byzantines en Grèce au XIII$^{e}$ siècle', in *Actes du XV$^{e}$ Congrès International d'Études Byzantines, Athènes, septembre 1976*, II, *Art et Archéologie, Communications* (Athens, 1981), at pp. 121–8.

— 'Contribution à l'étude du monnayage de Michel II d'Épire', in *Actes du XIV$^{e}$ Congrès International des Études Byzantines, Bucarest, 6–12 septembre, 1971* (Bucharest, 1976), at pp. 187–90.

Carrié, J.-M., 'Le rôle économique de l'armée dans l'Égypte romaine', in *Armées et fiscalité dans le monde antique, Paris, 14–16 octobre, 1976* (Paris, 1977) (= Colloques Nationaux du Centre National de la Recherche Scientifique CMXXXVI), at pp. 373–93.

Carson, R. A. G., 'The Sequence-marks on the Coinage of Carausius and Allectus', in R. A. G. Carson (ed.), *Mints, Dies and Currency: Essays dedicated to the Memory of Albert Baldwin* (London, 1971), at pp. 57–65.

Carson, R. A. G., Hill, P. V., and Kent, J. P. C., *Late Roman Bronze Coinage, A.D. 324–498* (London, 1960).

Casey, P. J., 'Carausius and Allectus – Rulers in Gaul?', *Britannia* 8 (1977), pp. 283–301.

— 'Magnus Maximus in Britain', in *idem* (ed.), *The End of Roman Britain: Papers arising from a Conference, Durham 1978* (Oxford, 1979) (= British Archaeological Reports, British Series LXXI), at pp. 66–79.

Cessi, R., *Problemi Monetari Veneziani (fino atutto il sec. XIV)* (Padua, 1937).

Chalmeta Gendron, P., *El 'señor del zoco' en España: edades media y moderna, contribución al estudio de la historia del mercado* (Madrid, 1973).

Chang, N. C., *An Inscribed Chinese Ingot of the 12th Century A.D.* (New York, 1944) (= American Numismatic Society, Numismatic Notes and Monographs CIII).

Chaput, E., *Phrygie: exploration archéologique* I, *Géologie et géographie physique* (Paris, 1941).

Charanis, P., 'The Significance of Coins as Evidence for the History of Athens and Corinth in the Seventh and Eighth Centuries', *Historia* 4 (1955), pp. 163–72.

Chastagnol, A., *La préfecture urbaine à Rome sous le bas-empire* (Paris, 1960) (= Publications de la Faculté des Lettres et Sciences Humaines d'Alger XXXIV).

— 'L'administration du diocèse italien au bas-empire', *Historia* 12 (1963), pp. 348–79.

Chevallier, R., *Roman Roads* (London, 1976).

Chiaudano, M., 'La moneta di Genova nel secolo XII', in *Studi in onore di Armando Sapori* I (Milan, 1957), at pp. 187–214.

Christol, M., 'Effort de guerre et ateliers monétaires de la périphérie au III$^{e}$ s. ap. J.-C.: l'atelier de Cologne sous Valérien et Gallien', in *Armées et fiscalité dans le monde antique, Paris, 14–16 octobre, 1976* (Paris, 1977) (= Colloques Nationaux du Centre National de la Recherche Scientifique CMXXXVI), at pp. 235–77.

Chrysostomides, J., 'Venetian Commercial Privileges under the Palaeologi', *Studi Veneziani* 12 (1970), pp. 267–356.

Cipolla, C. M., *Money, Prices and Civilization in the Mediterranean World, Fifth to Seventeenth Century* (Princeton, 1956).

— 'Currency Depreciation in Medieval Europe', *Economic History Review* 15$^{2}$ (1962/3), pp. 413–22.

Clover, F. M., 'Relations between North Africa and Italy, 476–500: Some Numismatic Evidence', in H. Temporini (ed.), *Aufstieg und Niedergang der römischen Welt* III (in press).

Clucas, L., *The Trial of John Italos and the Crisis of Intellectual Values in Byzantium in the Eleventh Century* (Munich, 1981) (=Miscellanea Byzantina Monacensia XXVI).

Committee for the World Atlas of Agriculture (ed.), *The World Atlas of Agriculture* (5 vols, of which I: *Europe, U.S.S.R., Asia Minor*, IV: *Africa*, and (separate): *Land Utilisation Maps and Relief Maps*, are germane. All Novara, 1969 (I and Maps), 1976 (IV)).

Constantelos, D., *Byzantine Philanthropy and Social Welfare* (New Brunswick, N.J., 1968).

Cook, J. M., *The Troad, an Archaeological and Topographical Study* (Oxford, 1973).

Cope, L. H., 'The Argentiferous Bronze Alloys of the Large Tetrarchic Folles of A.D. 294–307', *Numismatic Chronicle* $8^7$ (1968), pp. 115–49.

— 'The Chemical Composition of a Tetradrachm of Probus with a Reverse Type illustrating Codex Theodosianus XII, VII, I', *Numismatic Chronicle* $15^7$ (1975), pp. 187–90.

— 'Die-module Measurements, and the Sequence of Constantine's Reformed Folles Issues of Spring A.D. 310 and of early A.D. 313', *Schweizer Münzblätter* 77 (1970), pp. 46–61.

— 'Diocletian's Price Edict and its Associated Coinage Denominations', *Schweizer Münzblätter* 27 (1977), pp. 7–12.

— 'Diocletian's Price Edict and Second Coinage Reform in the Light of Recent Discoveries', *Numismatic Chronicle* $17^7$ (1977), pp. 220–6.

— 'The Metallurgical Analysis of Roman Imperial Silver and *Aes* Coinage', in E. T. Hall and D. M. Metcalf (eds), *Methods of Chemical and Metallurgical Investigation of Ancient Coinage* (London, 1972) (=Royal Numismatic Society, Special Publication VII), at pp. 3–47.

*Corpus Nummorum Italicorum* XV.1, *Roma dalla caduta dell'impero d'occidente al 1572* (Rome, 1934).

Courtois, C., *Les Vandales et l'Afrique* (Paris, 1955).

— 'Les monnaies de Gildo', *Revue Numismatique* $16^5$ (1954), pp. 71–5.

Crawford, M. H., 'Finance, Coinage and Money from the Severans to Constantine', in H. Temporini (ed.), *Aufstieg und Niedergang der römischen Welt* II, *Principat* 2 (Berlin/New York, 1975), at pp. 560–93.

Crawford, M. H., and Reynolds, J. M., 'The Aezani Copy of the Prices Edict', *Zeitschrift für Papyrologie und Epigraphik* 34 (1979), pp. 163–210.

— 'The Publication of the Prices Edict: A New Inscription from Aezani', *Journal of Roman Studies* 65 (1975), pp. 160–3.

Cribb, J., 'An Historical Survey of the Precious Metal Currencies of China', *Numismatic Chronicle* $19^7$ (1979), pp. 185–209.

Croke, B., 'Anatolius and Nomus: Envoys to Attila', *Byzantinoslavica* 42 (1981), pp. 159–70.

— 'The Date of the "Anastasian Long Wall" in Thrace', *Greek, Roman, and Byzantine Studies* 23 (1982), pp. 59–78.

Cuinet, V., *La Turquie d'Asie, géographie administrative, statistique descriptive et raisonnée, de chaque province de l'Asie-Mineure* (4 vols, Paris, 1890 (I), 1892 (II), 1894 (III), 1895 (IV)).

Curzon, R., *Armenia: A Year at Erzeroom, and on the Frontiers of Russia, Turkey, and Persia* (London, 1854).

Cutler, A., 'The De Signis of Nicetas Choniates. A Reappraisal', *American Journal of Archaeology* 72 (1968), pp. 113–18.

— 'The Stavraton: Evidence for an Elusive Byzantine Type', *American Numismatic Society Museum Notes* 11 (1964), pp. 237–44.

Dagron, G., and Morrisson, C., 'Le *Kentènarion* dans les sources byzantines', *Revue Numismatique* $17^6$ (1975), pp. 145–62.

Dain, A., 'Le partage du butin de guerre d'après les traités juridiques et militaires', in *Actes du VI<sup>e</sup> Congrès International d'Études Byzantines, Paris, 27 juillet–2 août 1948* I (Paris, 1950), at pp. 347–54.

Davidescu, D., Stancu, M., and Papacostea, C., 'Rumania', in Committee for the World Atlas of Agriculture (ed.), *The World Atlas of Agriculture* I (Novara, 1969), at pp. 343–67.

Day, G. W., 'Genoese Involvement with Byzantium 1155–1204: A Diplomatic and Prosopographical Study' (Ph.D. thesis, Urbana, 1978).

Deichmann, F. W., 'Giuliano Argentario', *Felix Ravenna* $5^3$ (56) (1951), pp. 5–26.

Delmaire, R., 'La caisse des largesses sacrées et l'armée au bas-empire', in *Armées et fiscalité dans le monde antique, Paris, 14–16 octobre, 1976* (Paris, 1977) (= Colloques Nationaux du Centre National de la Recherche Scientifique CMXXXVI), at pp. 311–30.

Demougeot, E., 'À propos des solidi gallici du V$^e$ siècle après J.-C.', *Bulletin de la Société Française de Numismatique* 38 (1983), pp. 269–70.

Dennis, G. T., 'Nicholas Cabasilas Chamaëtos and his Discourse on Abuses committed by Authorities against Sacred Things', *Byzantine Studies/Études Byzantines* 5 (1978), pp. 80–7.

Der Nersessian, S., 'The Armenian Chronicle of the Constable Smpad or of the "Royal Historian"', *DOP* 13 (1959), pp. 141–68.

Dewdney, J. C., *Turkey* (London, 1971).

Diaconu, P., 'Păcuiul lui Soare – Vicina', *Byzantina* 8 (1976), pp. 407–47.

Diehl, C., *L'Afrique byzantine: histoire de la domination byzantine en Afrique (533–709)* (2 vols, Paris, 1896).

— *Études sur l'administration byzantine dans l'exarchat de Ravenne (568–751)* (Paris, 1888) (= Bibliothèque des Écoles Françaises d'Athènes et de Rome LIII).

— 'Une crise monétaire au VI$^e$ siècle', *Revue des Études Grecques* 32 (1919), pp. 158–66.

Djurić, I., 'Poroditsa Phoka', *Zbornik Radova Vizantoloshkog Instituta* 17 (1976), pp. 189–296.

Dodd, E. C., *Byzantine Silver Stamps, with an Excursus on the Comes Sacrarum Largitionum by J. P. C. Kent* (Washington, D.C., 1961) (= *DOS* VII).

Dölger, F., *Beiträge zur Geschichte der byzantinischen Finanzverwaltung besonders des 10. und 11. Jahrhunderts* (Leipzig, 1927) (= Byzantinisches Archiv IX).

— *Regesten der Kaiserurkunden des oströmischen Reiches von 565–1453* I.1 (*565–1025*), I.2 (*1025–1204*), I.3 (*1204–1282*), I.4 (*1282–1341*), I.5 (*1341–1453*) (Munich/Berlin, 1924 (1), 1925 (2), 1932 (3), 1960 (4), 1965 (5)).

Downey, G., 'Procopius on Antioch: A Study of Method in the "De Aedificiis"', *Byzantion* 14 (1939), pp. 361–78.

Dragonas, C., and Olympitis, N., 'Greece', in Committee for the World Atlas of Agriculture (ed.), *The World Atlas of Agriculture* I (Novara, 1969), at pp. 191–207.

Duby, G., *The Early Growth of the European Economy, Warriors and Peasants from the Seventh to the Twelfth Century* (London, 1974).

— *Rural Economy and Country Life in the Medieval West* (London, 1968).

Du Cange, C., *Glossarium ad Scriptores Mediae et Infimae Graecitatis* (2 vols, Lyons, 1688; rep. Bratislava, 1891).

Dürr, N., *Catalogue de la Collection Lucien Naville, au Cabinet de Numismatique du Musée d'Art et d'Histoire de Genève* (Geneva, 1974) (first printed in *Genava* 12 (1964)).

Duichev, I., 'La chronique byzantine de l'an 811', *Travaux et Mémoires* I (1965), pp. 205–54.

Duncan-Jones, R. P., *The Economy of the Roman Empire: Quantitative Studies* (Cambridge, 1974).

— 'Pay and Numbers in Diocletian's Army', *Chiron* 8 (1978), pp. 541–60.

— 'The Size of the Modius Castrensis', *Zeitschrift für Papyrologie und Epigraphik* 21 (1976), pp. 53–62.

Durliat, J., 'La valeur relative de l'or, de l'argent et du cuivre dans l'empire protobyzantin (IVe–VIIe siècle)' *Revue Numismatique* 22[6] (1980), pp. 138–54.

Dvornik, F., *Byzantine Missions among the Slavs: SS. Constantine-Cyril and Methodius* (New Brunswick, N.J., 1970).

— *The Photian Schism: History and Legend* (Cambridge, 1948).

Ebcioğlu, İ., 'İzmit Definesi', *Istanbul Arkeoloji Müzeleri Yıllığı* 13–14 (1966–7), pp. 166–74.

Eberhard, W., 'Nomads and Farmers in Southeastern Turkey, Problems of Settlement', *Oriens* 6 (1935), pp. 32–49.

Edwards, J. H., *Christian Córdoba. The City and its Region in the Late Middle Ages* (Cambridge, 1982).

Eickhoff, E., *Friedrich Barbarossa im Orient: Kreuzzug und Tod Friedrichs I* (Tubingen, 1977) (= Istanbuler Mitteilungen, Beiheft XVII).

Erdmann, K. and H., *Das Anatolische Karavansaray des 13. Jahrhunderts* (I: *Katalog-Text, Katalog-Abbildungen* (Berlin, 1961); II: *Baubeschreibung. Die Ornamente* (Berlin, 1976)) (= Istanbuler Forschungen XXI, XXXI).

Eriksson, K., 'The Cross on Steps and the Silver Hexagram', *Jahrbuch der Österreichischen Byzantinistik* 17 (1968), pp. 149–64.

— 'Revising a Date in the Chronicon Paschale', *Jahrbuch der Österreichischen Byzantinistik* 17 (1968), pp. 17–28.

Erim, K. T., Reynolds, J. M., and Crawford, M. H., 'Diocletian's Currency Reform; a New Inscription', *Journal of Roman Studies* 61 (1971), pp. 171–7.

Evert-Kappesowa, H., 'Une grande propriété fonçière du VIIIe s. à Byzance', *Byzantinoslavica* 24 (1963), pp. 32–40.

Fagerlie, J. M., *Late Roman and Byzantine Solidi found in Sweden and Denmark* (New York, 1967) (= American Numismatic Society, Numismatic Notes and Monographs CLVII).

Fahmy, A. M., *Muslim Sea-Power in the Eastern Mediterranean from the Seventh to the Tenth Century A.D. (Studies in Naval Organisation)* (2nd edn, Cairo, 1966).

Fairhead, N., 'A Catanian Follis of Anastasius II', *Numismatic Circular* 88 (1980), pp. 444–5.

Farag, W. A., 'Byzantium and its Muslim Neighbours during the Reign of Basil II (976–1025)' (Ph.D. thesis, Birmingham, 1979).

Favaretti, G., 'Albania', in Committee for the World Atlas of Agriculture (ed.), *The World Atlas of Agriculture* I (Novara, 1969), at pp. 21–6.

Finley, M. I., *The Ancient Economy* (London, 1973).

Foss, C., *Byzantine and Turkish Sardis* (Cambridge, Mass./London, 1976) (= Archaeological Exploration of Sardis IV).

— *Ephesus after Antiquity: A Late Antique, Byzantine and Turkish City* (Cambridge, 1979).

— 'Late Antique and Byzantine Ankara', *DOP* 31 (1977), pp. 27–87.

— 'Late Byzantine Fortifications in Lydia', *Jahrbuch der Österreichischen Byzantinistik* 28 (1979), pp. 297–320.

— 'The Persians in Asia Minor and the End of Antiquity', *English Historical Review* 90 (1975), pp. 721–47.

Fraehn, C. M., *De Origine Vocabuli Rossici Den'gi'* (Kazan, 1815).

Frances, E., 'La disparition des corporations byzantines', in *Actes du XII^e Congrès International d'Études Byzantines, Ochrid, 10–16 septembre, 1961* II (Belgrade, 1964), at pp. 93–101.

Frayn, J. M., *Subsistence Farming in Roman Italy* (London, 1979).

French, D., *Roman Roads and Milestones of Asia Minor* I, *The Pilgrim's Road* (Oxford, 1981) (= British Archaeological Reports, International Series CV/British Institute of Archaeology at Ankara, Monograph III).

Fulford, M., 'Coin Circulation and Mint Activity in the Late Roman Empire: Some Economic Implications', *Archaeological Journal* 135 (1978), pp. 67–114.

Gadolin, A. R., 'Alexis I Comnenus and the Venetian Trade Privileges. A New Interpretation', *Byzantion* 50 (1980), pp. 439–46.

Gaj-Popović, D., 'Monnaie du roi Radoslav', in V. Kondić (ed.), *Frappe et ateliers monétaires dans l'antiquité et moyen âge* (Belgrade, 1976) (= Actes du Symposium du 30 janvier au 1 février dans le Musée Nationale de Belgrade), at pp. 121–32.

Gallatin, H. K., 'A Study in Civil Government and Imperial Defense in the Seventh Century Byzantine State under Emperor Constans II (641–668)' (Ph.D. thesis, Urbana, 1972).

Ganshof, F.-L., 'Robert le Frison et Alexis Comnène', *Byzantion* 31 (1961), pp. 57–74.

Gara, A., *Prosdiagraphomena e circolazione monetaria: aspetti dell'organizzazione fiscale in rapporto alla politica monetaria dell' Egitto Romano* (Milan, 1976) (= Testi e Documenti per lo Studio dell' Antichità LVI).

Gautier, P., 'Le synode des Blachernes (fin 1094), étude prosopographique', *Revue des Études Byzantines* 29 (1971), pp. 213–84.

Geissen, A., 'Numismatische Bemerkung zu dem Aufstand des L. Domitius Domitianus', *Zeitschrift für Papyrologie und Epigraphik* 22 (1976), pp. 280–6.

Gelzer, H., *Die Genesis der byzantinischen Themenverfassung* (Leipzig, 1899, rep. Amsterdam, 1966).

Gentili, G. V., *La villa Erculia di Piazza Armerina: i mosaici figurati* (Milan, 1959).

Gerassimov, T., 'Byzantinische Goldmünzen mit Graphiten', *Byzantinobulgarica* 5 (1978), pp. 123–46.

— 'Des fausses hyperpères de Jean V et Manuel II Paléologue', *Byzantinobulgarica* 4 (1973), pp. 213–20.

— 'Medni Moneti na Ïoan III Vatatses e Epirskiya Despot Mikhail II', *Izvestiya na Arkheologicheskiya Institut* 34 (1974), pp. 319–21.

Goffart, W., *Barbarians and Romans, A.D. 418–584. The Techniques of Accommodation* (Princeton, 1980).

Goitein, S. D., *Letters of Medieval Jewish Traders* (Princeton, 1973).

— *A Mediterranean Society, the Jewish Communities of the Arab World as Portrayed in the Documents of the Cairo Geniza* I, *Economic Foundations* (Berkeley/Los Angeles, 1967).

— 'A Letter from Seleucia (Cilicia) dated 21 July 1137', *Speculum* 39 (1964), pp. 298–303.

Gordus, A. A., and Metcalf, D. M., 'The Alloy of the Byzantine Miliaresion and the Question of the Reminting of Islamic Silver', *Hamburger Beiträge zur Numismatik* 24/6 (1970/2), pp. 9–36.

Goubert, P., 'L'administration de l'Espagne byzantine I, les gouverneurs de l'Espagne byzantine', (*Revue des*) *Études Byzantines* 3 (1945), pp. 127–42.

— 'Administration de l'Espagne byzantine II (suite), les provinces, les capitales, les villes, les diocèses', (*Revue des*) *Études Byzantines* 4 (1964), pp. 70–110.

Grégoire, H., 'Notes épigraphiques', *Byzantion* 8 (1933), pp. 49–88.
— 'Notes de géographie byzantine', *Byzantion* 10 (1935), pp. 251–6.
Grierson, P., *Catalogue of the Byzantine Coins in the Dumbarton Oaks Collection and in the Whittemore Collection* II, *Phocas to Theodosius III, 602–717* (2 vols: II.1, *Phocas and Heraclius (602–641)*; II.2, *Heraclius Constantine to Theodosius III (641–717)*; both Washington, D.C., 1968).
— *Catalogue of the Byzantine Coins in the Dumbarton Oaks Collection and in the Whittemore Collection* III, *Leo III to Nicephorus III, 717–1081* (2 vols: III.1, *Leo III to Michael III (717–867)*; III.2, *Basil I to Nicephorus III (867–1081)*; both Washington, D.C., 1973).
— The President's Address, Session 1962–3, 'Coin Wear and the Frequency Table', in *Numismatic Chronicle* 3[7] (1963), at pp. i–xvi (at end of vol.).
— The President's Address, Session 1963–4, 'Weight and Coinage', in *Numismatic Chronicle* 4[7] (1964), at pp. i–xvii (at end of vol.).
— 'Coinage and Money in the Byzantine Empire, 498–*c.* 1090', in *Settimane di studio del Centro italiano di studi sull'alto medioevo* VIII, *Moneta e scambi nell'alto medioevo (21–27 aprile 1960)* (Spoleto, 1960). Also separately printed.
— 'Commerce in the Dark Ages: A Critique of the Evidence', *Transactions of the Royal Historical Society* 9[5] (1959), pp. 123–40.
— 'The Date and Fineness of Byzantine "Neatly-clipped" Trachea', *Numismatic Circular* 83 (1975), p. 58.
— 'The Debasement of the Bezant in the Eleventh Century', *Byzantinische Zeitschrift* 47 (1954), pp. 379–94.
— 'Harold Hardrada and Byzantine Coin Types in Denmark', *Byzantinische Forschungen* I (1966) (=*Polychordia: Festschrift Franz Dölger zum 75. Geburtstag*), pp. 124–38.
— 'The Monetary Reforms of 'Abd al-Malik, their Metrological Basis and their Financial Repercussions', *Journal of the Economic and Social History of the Orient* 3 (1960), pp. 241–64.
— 'The Monetary Reforms of Anastasius and their Economic Consequences', in A. Kindler (ed.), *International Numismatic Convention, Jerusalem 27–31 December 1963, The Patterns of Monetary Development in Phoenicia and Palestine in Antiquity, Proceedings* (Jerusalem, 1967), at pp. 283–302.
— 'A New Early Follis Type of Leo III (718)', *Numismatic Chronicle* 14[7] (1974), pp. 75–7.
— 'Nicephorus Bryennius or Nicephorus Basilacius?', *Numismatic Circular* 84 (1976), pp. 2–3.
— 'Notes on the Fineness of the Byzantine Solidus', *Byzantinische Zeitschrift* 54 (1961), pp. 91–7.
— '*Nummi Scyphati*. The Story of a Misunderstanding', *Numismatic Chronicle* 11[7] (1971), pp. 253–60.
— 'The Roman Law of Counterfeiting', in R. A. G. Carson and C. H. V. Sutherland (eds), *Essays in Roman Coinage Presented to Harold Mattingly* (Oxford, 1956), at pp. 240–61.
— 'The *Tablettes Albertini* and the Value of the *Solidus* in the Fifth and Sixth Centuries A.D.', *Journal of Roman Studies* 49 (1959), pp. 73–80.
— 'Three Unpublished Coins of Zeno', *Numismatic Chronicle* 8[6] (1948), pp. 223–6.
— 'Two Byzantine Coin Hoards of the Seventh and Eighth Centuries at Dumbarton Oaks', *DOP* 19 (1965), pp. 207–28.
Grumel, V., *Traité d'études byzantines* I, *La chronologie* (Paris, 1958).
Guey, J., 'Code théodosien XII, 7, 1 (19 juillet 325): Le "surhaussement" du Solidus; balance

et technique d'une pesée fiscale', *Bulletin de la Société Française de Numismatique* 34 (1979), pp. 610–11.

Guilland, R., 'Un compte-rendu du procès par Psellos', *Byzantinoslavica* 20 (1959), pp. 205–30.

— 'Les eunuques dans l'empire byzantin', *(Revue des) Études Byzantines* I (1943), pp. 197–238.

— 'Les logothetès, études sur l'histoire administrative de l'empire byzantin', *Revue des Études Byzantines* 29 (1971), pp. 5–115.

— 'Sur quelques termes du *Livre des Cérémonies* de Constantin VII Porphyrogénète', *Revue des Études Grecques* 62 (1949), pp. 328–50.

Guillou, A., *Régionalisme et indépendance dans l'empire byzantin au VII^e siècle: l'exemple de l'exarchat et de la pentapole d'Italie* (Rome, 1969) (= Istituto Storico Italiano per il Medio Evo, Studi Storici LXXV–LXXVI).

Hahn, W. R. O., *Moneta Imperii Byzantini* I, *Von Anastasius I. bis Justinianus I. (491–565)*; II, *Von Justinus II bis Phocas (565–610)*; III, *Von Heraclius bis Leo III./Alleinregierung (610–720)* (Vienna, 1973, 1975, 1981) (= Österreichische Akademie der Wissenschaften, phil.-hist. Klasse, Denkschriften CIX, CXIX, CXLVIII).

— 'Mezezius in peccato suo interiit: Kritische Betrachtungen zu einem Neuling in der Münzreihe der byzantinischen Kaiser', *Jahrbuch der Österreichischen Byzantinistik* 29 (1980), pp. 61–70.

— 'Minting Activity in the Diocese of Oriens under Heraclius', *Numismatic Circular* 85 (1977), pp. 307–8.

— 'More about the Minor Byzantine Gold Mints from Tiberius II to Heraclius', *Numismatic Circular* 87 (1979), pp. 552–5.

— 'New Light on the Thessalonican *Moneta Auri* in the Second Half of the Sixth Century', *Numismatic Chronicle* 21⁷ (1981), pp. 178–82.

— 'The Numismatic History of Cherson in Early Byzantine Times – a Survey' (I), *Numismatic Circular* 86 (1978), pp. 414–15.

— 'The Numismatic History of Cherson in Early Byzantine Times – a Survey' (II), *Numismatic Circular* 86 (1978), pp. 521–2.

— 'Regensburger Denare mit dem Bildniss Kaiser Heinrich IV. im byzantinischen Stil als Schlussmünzen in nordischen Schatzfunden', im R. Zeitler (ed.), *Les pays du nord et Byzance (Scandinavie et Byzance), Actes du colloque nordique et international de byzantinologie tenu à Upsal 20–22 avril 1979* (Uppsala, 1981), at pp. 117–24.

Haldon, J. F., *Byzantine Praetorians: An Administrative, Institutional and Social Survey of the Opsikion and Tagmata, c. 580–900* (Bonn, 1984) (= Poikila Byzantina III).

— *Recruitment and Conscription in the Byzantine Army c. 550–950. A Study on the Origins of the Stratiotika Ktemata* (Vienna, 1979) (= Österreichische Akademie der Wissenschaften, phil.-hist. Klasse CCCLVII).

— 'Kudāma ibn Dj'afar and the Garrison of Constantinople', *Byzantion* 48 (1978), pp. 78–90.

Haldon, J. F., and Kennedy, H., 'The Arab–Byzantine Frontier in the Eighth and Ninth Centuries: Military Organisation and Society in the Borderlands', *Zbornik Radova Vizantoloshkog Instituta* 19 (1980), pp. 79–116.

Hammond, N. G. L., *Epirus. The Geography, the Ancient Remains, the History and the Topography of Epirus and Adjacent Areas* (Oxford, 1967).

— *A History of Macedonia* I, *Historical Geography and Prehistory* (Oxford, 1972).

Hannestad, K., 'Les relations de Byzance avec la Transcaucasie et l'Asie centrale aux 5$^{e}$ et 6$^{e}$ siècles', *Byzantion* 25–7 (1955–7), pp. 421–56.

Harris, J., 'A Gold Hoard from Corinth', *American Journal of Archaeology* 43 (1939), pp. 268–77.

Harvey, A. L., 'The Growth of the Byzantine Rural Economy' (Ph.D. thesis, Birmingham, 1983).

Heichelheim, F., *Wirtschaftliche Schwankungen der Zeit von Alexander bis Augustus* (Jena, 1930).

Heisenberg, A., *Aus der Geschichte und Literatur der Palaiologenzeit* (Munich, 1920) (= *Sitzungsberichte der Bayerischen Akademie der Wissenschaften (philos.-philolog. u. hist. Klasse)* x).

Hendy, M. F., *Catalogue of the Byzantine Coins in the Dumbarton Oaks Collection and in the Whittemore Collection* IV, *Alexius I to Michael VIII, 1081–1261* (Washington, D.C., in progress).

— *Coinage and Money in the Byzantine Empire 1081–1261* (Washington, D.C., 1969) (= *DOS* XII).

— 'On the Administrative Basis of the Byzantine Coinage *c.* 400–*c.* 900 and the Reforms of Heraclius', *University of Birmingham Historical Journal* 12 (1970), pp. 129–54.

— 'Aspects of Coin Production and Fiscal Administration in the Late Roman and Early Byzantine Period', *Numismatic Chronicle* 12$^{7}$ (1972), pp. 117–39.

— 'Byzantium 1081–1204: An Economic Reappraisal', *Transactions of the Royal Historical Society* 20$^{5}$ (1970), pp. 31–52.

— 'The Gornoslav Hoard, the Emperor Frederick I, and the Monastery of Bachkovo', in C. N. L. Brooke, J. G. Pollard, B. H. I. H. Stewart and T. R. Volk (eds), *Studies in Numismatic Method: Essays Presented to Philip Grierson* (Cambridge, 1983), at pp. 179–91.

— 'Light Weight Solidi, Tetartera, and The Book of the Prefect', *Byzantinische Zeitschrift* 65 (1972), pp. 57–80.

— 'Michael IV and Harold Hardrada', *Numismatic Chronicle* 10$^{7}$ (1970), pp. 187–97.

— 'Mint and Fiscal Administration under Diocletian, his Colleagues, and his Successors, A.D. 305–24', *Journal of Roman Studies* 62 (1972), pp. 75–82.

— 'Seventeenth Twelfth- and Thirteenth-century Byzantine Hoards', *Coin Hoards* 6 (1981), pp. 61–72.

Hendy, M. F., and Bendall, S., 'A Billon Trachy of John Ducas, Emperor, and John Comnenus-Ducas, Despot(?)', *Revue Numismatique* 12$^{6}$ (1970), pp. 143–8.

Hendy, M. F., and Charles, J. A., 'The Production Techniques, Silver Content and Circulation History of the Twelfth-century Byzantine Trachy', *Archaeometry* 12 (1970), pp. 13–21.

Herlihy, D., 'The Distribution of Wealth in a Renaissance Community: Florence 1427', in P. Abrams and E. A. Wrigley (eds), *Towns in Societies. Essays in Economic History and Historical Sociology* (Cambridge, 1978), at pp. 131–57.

Herrin, J., 'Aspects of the Process of Hellenization in the Early Middle Ages', *The Annual of the British School of Archaeology at Athens* 68 (1973), pp. 113–26.

— 'Realities of Byzantine Provincial Government: Hellas and Peloponnesos, 1180–1205', *DOP* 29 (1975), pp. 253–86.

Heyd, W., *Histoire du commerce du Levant au moyen-âge* (2 vols, 2$^{me}$ réimpression, Leipzig, 1936).

Hill, G., *A History of Cyprus* I, *To the Conquest by Richard Lion Heart* (Cambridge, 1940).

Hillman, G., 'Agricultural Productivity and Past Population Potential at Aşvan', *Anatolian Studies* 23 (1973), pp. 225–40.
— 'Agricultural Resources and Settlement in the Aşvan Region', *Anatolian Studies* 23 (1973), pp. 217–24.
— 'Crop Husbandry and Food Production: Modern Basis for the Interpretation of Plant Remains', *Anatolian Studies* 23 (1973), pp. 241–4.
Hodges, R., *Dark Age Economics. The Origins of Towns and Trade A.D. 600–1000* (London, 1982).
Hoffman, J., *Rudimente von Territorialstaaten im byzantinischen Reich (1071–1210): Untersuchungen über Unabhängigkeitsbestrebungen und ihr Verhältnis zu Kaiser und Reich* (Munich, 1977) (= Miscellanea Byzantina Monacensia XVII).
Honigmann, E., 'Un itinéraire arabe à travers le Pont', *Annuaire de l'Institut de Philologie et d'Histoire Orientales et Slaves* 4 (1936) (= Mélanges Franz Cumont), pp. 261–71.
Hopkins, K., *Conquerors and Slaves* (Cambridge, 1978) (= Sociological Studies in Roman History I).
— 'Rules of Evidence', *Journal of Roman Studies* 68 (1978), pp. 180–6 (review of F. Millar, *The Emperor in the Roman World (31 B.C.–A.D. 377)* (London, 1977)).
Iliescu, O., 'La monnaie génoise dans les pays roumains aux XIII$^{e}$–XV$^{e}$ siècles', in S. Pascu (ed.), *Colocviul Româno-Italian 'Genovezii la Marea Neagră în secolele XIII–XIV', Bucureşti 27–28 martie 1975* (Bucharest, 1977) (= Bibliotheca Historica Romaniae, Studii LVII), at pp. 155–71.
— 'Le montant du tribut payé par Byzance à l'empire ottoman en 1379 et 1424', *Revue des Études Sud-est Européennes* 9 (1971), pp. 427–32.
— 'Nouvelles informations relatives aux lingots romains d'or trouvés en Transylvanie', *Revue des Études Sud-est Européennes* 3 (1965), pp. 269–81.
İnalcık, H., *The Ottoman Empire. The Classical Age 1300–1600* (London, 1973).
Janin, R., *Constantinople byzantine, développement urbain et répertoire topographique* (2nd edn, Paris, 1964) (= Archives de l'Orient Chrétien IV.A).
— *La géographie ecclésiastique de l'empire byzantin* I.3, *Le siège de Constantinople et le patriarcat œcuménique: les églises et les monastères* (Paris, 1953).
Jasny, N., *The Wheats of Classical Antiquity* (Baltimore, 1944) (= The Johns Hopkins University Studies in Historical and Political Science LXII.3).
Jeločnik, A., 'The Alternation of Genio and Moneta Folles in the Siscia Mint', in H. A. Cahn and G. Le Rider (eds), *Proceedings of the 8th International Congress of Numismatics, New York–Washington September 1973* (Paris/Basel, 1976) (= Association Internationale des Numismates Professionels, Publication IV), at pp. 315–32.
Jenkins, R. J. H., 'The Bronze Athena at Byzantium', *Journal of Hellenic Studies* 67 (1947), pp. 31–3.
— 'The "Flight" of Samonas', *Speculum* 23 (1948), pp. 217–35.
Johnson, A. C., and West, L. C., *Byzantine Egypt: Economic Studies* (Princeton, 1949).
— *Currency in Roman and Byzantine Egypt* (Princeton, 1944).
Jones, A. H. M., *Cities of the Eastern Roman Provinces* (2nd edn, Oxford, 1971).
— *The Greek City from Alexander to Justinian* (Oxford, 1940).
— *The Later Roman Empire 284–602: A Social, Economic and Administrative Survey* (2 vols and separate maps, Oxford, 1964).
— 'The Date and Value of the Verona List', *Journal of Roman Studies* 44 (1954), pp. 21–9.
— 'Inflation under the Roman Empire', *Economic History Review* 5$^{2}$ (1953), pp. 293–318.

— 'Numismatics and History', in R. A. G. Carson (ed.), *Essays in Roman Coinage Presented to Harold Mattingly* (Oxford, 1956), at pp. 13–33.
— 'The Origin and Early History of the Follis', *Journal of Roman Studies* 49 (1959), pp. 34–8.
— 'The Constitutional Position of Odoacer and Theoderic', *Journal of Roman Studies* 52 (1962), pp. 126–30.
Jones, A. H. M., Martindale, J. R., and Morris, J., *The Prosopography of the Later Roman Empire* I: *260–395*, II: *395–527* (Cambridge, 1971 (I), 1980 (II)).
Jones, J. R., 'Literary Evidence for the Coinage of Constantine XI', *Numismatic Circular* 75 (1967), p. 97.
Kaegi, W. E., *Byzantine Military Unrest 471–843: An Interpretation* (Amsterdam, 1981).
— 'New Evidence on the Early Reign of Heraclius', *Byzantinische Zeitschrift* 66 (1973), pp. 308–30.
— 'Regionalism in the Balkan Armies of the Byzantine Empire', in *Actes du IIe Congrès International des Études du Sud-est Européen (Athens, 7–13 mai 1970)* II: *Histoire* (Athens, 1972), at pp. 397–405.
— 'Two Notes on Heraclius', *Revue des Études Byzantines* 37 (1979), pp. 221–7.
— 'Two Studies in the Continuity of Late Roman and Byzantine Military Institutions', *Byzantinische Forschungen* 8 (1982), pp. 87–113.
Kapamadji, N., and Morrisson, C., 'Trachéa d'electrum légers de Jean II et Manuel Ier Comnène', *Bulletin de la Société Française de Numismatique* 27 (1972), pp. 163–6.
Karlin-Hayter, P., 'L'hétériarque: l'évolution de son rôle du *De Ceremoniis* au *Traité des Offices*', *Jahrbuch der Österreichischen Byzantinistik* 23 (1974), pp. 101–43.
— 'Notes sur les archives de Patmos comme source pour la démographie et l'économie de l'île', *Byzantinische Forschungen* 5 (1977), pp. 189–215.
Kazhdan, A. P., *Sotsial'n'ĭi Sostav Gospodstvuiushchego Klassa Vizantĭi XI–XII vv.* (Moscow, 1974).
Kent, J. P. C., *The Roman Imperial Coinage* VIII, *The Family of Constantine I, A.D. 337–364* (London, 1981).
— 'The Coinage of Theodoric in the Names of Anastasius and Justin I', in R. A. G. Carson (ed.), *Mints, Dies and Currency; Essays dedicated to the Memory of Albert Baldwin* (London, 1971), at pp. 67–74.
— 'Fel. Temp. Reparatio', *Numismatic Chronicle* 7[7] (1967), pp. 83–90.
— 'Gold Coinage in the Later Roman Empire', in R. A. G. Carson and C. H. V. Sutherland (eds), *Essays in Roman Coinage Presented to Harold Mattingly* (Oxford, 1956), at pp. 190–204.
— 'Gold Standards of the Merovingian Coinage, A.D. 580–700', in E. T. Hall and D. M. Metcalf (eds), *Methods of Chemical and Metallurgical Investigation of Ancient Coinage* (London, 1972) (=Royal Numismatic Society, Special Publication VIII), at pp. 69–74.
— 'An Introduction to the Coinage of Julian the Apostate (A.D. 360–3)', *Numismatic Chronicle* 19[6] (1959), pp. 109–17.
— 'The Italian Silver Coinage of Justinian I and his Successors', in S. Scheers (ed.), *Studia Paulo Naster Oblata* I, *Numismatica Antiqua* (Louvain, 1982) (=Orientalia Lovaniensia Analecta XII), at pp. 275–82.
— 'Julius Nepos and the Fall of the Western Empire', in *Corolla Memoriae Erich Swoboda Dedicata* (Graz/Cologne, 1966) (=Römische Forschungen in Niederösterreich V), at pp. 146–50.
— 'Zeno and Leo, the Most Noble Caesars', *Numismatic Chronicle* 19[6] (1959), pp. 93–8.

King, C. E., 'The *Sacrae Largitiones*: Revenues, Expenditure, and the Production of Coin', in C. E. King (ed.), *Imperial Revenue, Expenditure, and Monetary Policy, in the Fourth Century A.D.* (Oxford, 1980) (=British Archaeological Reports, International Series LXXVI), at pp. 141–73.

— 'A Hoard of Clipped Siliquae in the Preston Museum', *Numismatic Chronicle* 21⁷ (1981), pp. 40–64.

Kolars, J. F., *Tradition, Season and Change in a Turkish Village* (Ph.D. thesis, University of Chicago. Dept of Geography Research Paper no. 82, Chicago, 1963).

Kraus, F. F., *Die Münzen Odovacers und des Ostgotenreiches in Italien* (Halle (Saale), 1928) (=Münzstudien v).

Kuršanskis, M., 'Monnaies divisionnaires en argent de l'empire de Trébizonde', *Revue Numismatique* $19^6$ (1977), pp. 103–8.

— 'Une nouvelle monnaie de l'empire de Trébizonde', *Revue Numismatique* $14^6$ (1972), pp. 269–70.

— 'L'usurpation de Théodora Grande Comnène', *Revue des Études Byzantines* 33 (1975), pp. 187–210.

— Lafaurie, J., 'Eligius monetarius', *Revue Numismatique* $19^6$ (1977), pp. 111–51.

— 'Monnaies décriées dans le second appendice de la Lex Burgundionum', *Bulletin de la Société Française de Numismatique* 31 (1976), pp. 73–5.

— 'Réformes monétaires d'Aurélien et de Dioclétien', *Revue Numismatique* $17^6$ (1975), pp. 73–138.

— 'La valeur des monnaies de billon en 300–302', *Bulletin de la Société Française de Numismatique* 37 (1982), pp. 142–4.

Laiou-Thomadakis, A. E., *Constantinople and the Latins: The Foreign Policy of Andronicus II, 1282–1328* (Cambridge, Mass., 1972).

— *Peasant Society in the Late Byzantine Empire, a Social and Demographic Study* (Princeton, 1977).

— 'The Byzantine Economy in the Mediterranean Trade System; Thirteenth–Fifteenth Centuries', *DOP* 34/5 (1980/1), pp. 177–222.

Lallemand, J., *L'administration civile d'Égypte de l'avènement de Dioclétien à la création du diocèse (284–382)* (Brussels, 1964) (=Académie Royale des Lettres, Classe des Lettres, Mémoires, 2nd series, LVII.2).

— 'Sou d'or de Zénon frappé à Thessalonique', *Bulletin du Cercle d'Études Numismatiques* 1 (1964), pp. 49–51.

Larsen, J. A. O., 'Roman Greece', in T. Frank (ed.), *An Economic Survey of Ancient Rome* IV, *Africa, Syria, Greece, Asia Minor* (Baltimore, 1938), at pp. 259–498.

Laurent, V., *Le corpus des sceaux de l'empire byzantin* II, *L'administration centrale* (Paris, 1981).

— *Le corpus des sceaux de l'empire byzantin* V, *L'église* (one volume in three separately bound parts, also with separately bound plates: V.1 (nos 1–1013), V.2 (nos 1014–1627), V.3 (nos 1628–2027) – all Paris, V.1 (1963), V.2 (1965), V.3 (1972), Plates (1965).

— 'Le Basilikon, nouveau nom de monnaie sous Andronic II Paléologue', *Byzantinische Zeitschrift* 45 (1952), pp. 50–8.

— 'Bulletin de numismatique byzantine (1940–49)', *Revue des Études Byzantines* 9 (1951), pp. 192–251.

— 'La chronologie des patriarches de Constantinople au XIIIe s. (1208–1309)', *Revue des Études Byzantines* 27 (1969), pp. 129–50.

— '*To Politikon*. Monnaie divisionnaire de l'époque des Paléologues', *Cronică Numismatica şi Arheologică* 10 (1940), pp. 264–86.

Le Gentilhomme, P., 'Le monnayage et la circulation monétaire dans les royaumes barbares en occident (V^e^–VIII^e^ siècle)', *Revue Numismatique* $7^5$ (1943), pp. 45–112.

Lemerle, P., *The Agrarian History of Byzantium from the Origins to the Twelfth Century. The Sources and Problems* (Galway, 1979).

— *Cinq études sur le XI^e^ siècle byzantin* (Paris, 1977).

— *Philippes et la Macédoine orientale à l'époque chrétienne et byzantine: recherches d'histoire et d'archéologie* (2 vols, text and album, Paris, 1945) (= Bibliothèques des Écoles Françaises d'Athènes et de Rome CLVIII).

— *Les plus anciens recueils des miracles de saint Démétrius et la pénétration des slaves dans les Balkans* II, *Commentaire* (Paris, 1981).

— 'La Chronique improprement dite de Monemvasie: le contexte historique et légendaire', *Revue des Études Byzantines* 21 (1963), pp. 5–49.

— 'La composition et la chronologie des deux premiers livres des *miracula S. Demetrii*', *Byzantinische Zeitschrift* 46 (1953), pp. 349–61.

— 'Notes sur l'administration byzantine à la veille de la IV^e^ croisade, d'après deux documents inédits des archives de Lavra', *Revue des Études Byzantines* 19 (1961) (= Mélanges Raymond Janin), pp. 258–72.

— '"Rhoga" et rente d'état aux X^e^–XI^e^ siècles', *Revue des Études Byzantines* 25 (1967) (= Mélanges Venance Grumel II), pp. 77–100.

Leyser, K., 'The Tenth Century in Byzantine–Western Relationships', in D. Baker (ed.), *Relations between East and West in the Middle Ages* (Edinburgh, 1973), at pp. 29–63.

Liebeschuetz, J. H. W. G., *Antioch: City and Imperial Administration in the Later Roman Empire* (Oxford, 1972).

Lilie, R.-J., *Die byzantinische Reaktion auf die Ausbreitung der Araber: Studien zur Strukturwandlung des byzantinischen Staates im 7. und 8. Jhdt.* (Munich, 1976) (= Miscellanea Byzantina Monacensia XXII).

— 'Die Schlacht von Myriokephalon (1176): Auswirkungen auf das byzantinische Reich im ausgehenden 12. Jahrhundert', *Revue des Études Byzantines* 35 (1977), pp. 257–75.

— '"Thrakien" und "Thrakesion". Zur byzantinischen Provinzorganisation am Ende des 7. Jahrhunderts,' *Jahrbuch der Österreichischen Byzantinistik* 26 (1977), pp. 7–47.

Lombard, M., 'Un problème cartographié: le bois dans la Méditerranée musulmane (VII^e^–XI^e^ siècles)', *Annales (Ec. Soc. Civ.)* 14 (1959), pp. 234–54.

Lopez, R. S., 'Byzantine Law in the Seventh Century, and its Reception by the Germans and Arabs', *Byzantion* 16 (1942/3), pp. 445–61.

— 'Harmenopoulos and the Downfall of the Bezant', in *Tomos Kōnstantinou Harmenopoulou* (Thessalonica, 1952) (= *Panepistēmion Thessalonikēs, Epistemonikē Epetēris* VI), at pp. 111–25.

— 'The Role of Trade in the Economic Readjustment of Byzantium in the Seventh Century', *DOP* 13 (1959), pp. 67–85.

— 'Silk Industry in the Byzantine Empire', *Speculum* 20 (1945), pp. 1–42.

Lopez, R. S., and Raymond, I. W., *Medieval Trade in the Mediterranean World: Illustrative Documents, Translated with Documents and Notes* (New York, 1955) (= Records of Civilization, Sources and Studies LII).

Loriot, F., 'Les aurei de Dioclétien et Maximien à la marque IAN', *Bulletin de la Société Française de Numismatique* 36 (1981), pp. 88–92.

Lybyer, A. H., *The Government of the Ottoman Empire in the Time of Suleiman the Magnificent* (Cambridge, Mass., 1913) (Harvard Historical Studies XVIII).

McCormick, M., 'Odoacer, Emperor Zeno and the Rugian Victory Legation', *Byzantion* 47 (1977), pp. 212–22.

MacIsaac, J. D., 'The Weight of the Late 4th and Early 5th Century Nummus (Æ 4)', *American Numismatic Society Museum Notes* 17 (1971), pp. 59–66.

MacMullen, R., 'The Emperor's Largesses', *Latomus* 21 (1962), pp. 159–66.

— 'How Big was the Roman Imperial Army?', *Klio* 62 (1980), pp. 451–60.

Magie, D., *Roman Rule in Asia Minor to the End of the Third Century after Christ* (2 vols, I (Text), II (Notes), Princeton, N.J., 1950).

Malz, G., 'The Date of Justinian's Edict XIII', *Byzantion* 16 (1942/3), pp. 135–41.

Manfroni, C., *Storia della Marina Italiana dalle Invasioni Barbariche al Trattato di Ninfeo (Anni di c. 440–1261)* (Livorno, 1899).

Mango, C. A., *Byzantium: The Empire of New Rome* (London, 1980).

— *Materials for the Study of the Mosaics of St. Sophia at Istanbul* (Washington, D.C., 1962) (= *DOS* VIII).

Maricq, A., 'Noms de monnaies ou noms de vases dans la "Nov. Just." 102, 2?', *Byzantion* 20 (1950), pp. 317–26.

Martin, M. E., 'Venice and the Byzantine Empire before the Fourth Crusade' (M.A. thesis, University of Birmingham, 1973).

— 'The First Venetians in the Black Sea', *Arkheion Pontou* 35 (1978) (*Maurē Thalassa*), pp. 111–22.

Matschke, K.-P., 'Situation, Organisation, und Aktion der Fischer von Konstantinopel und Umgebung in der byzantinischen Spätzeit', *Byzantinobulgarica* 6 (1980), pp. 281–98.

Matthews, J. F., *Western Aristocracies and Imperial Court A.D. 364–425* (Oxford, 1975).

Meiggs, R., *Trees and Timber in the Mediterranean World* (Oxford, 1982).

Meredith, D., 'Annius Plocamus: Two Inscriptions from the Berenice Road', *Journal of Roman Studies* 43 (1953), pp. 38–40.

Metcalf, D. M., *Coinage in South-eastern Europe, 820–1396* (London, 1979) (= Royal Numismatic Society, Special Publications no. XI).

— *The Copper Coinage of Thessalonica under Justinian I* (Vienna, 1976) (= Österreichische Akademie der Wissenschaften, phil.-hist. Klasse, Denkschriften CXXVII).

— *The Origins of the Anastasian Currency Reform* (Amsterdam, 1969).

— 'The Antalya Hoard of Miliaresia of Basil I', *Numismatic Chronicle* $17^7$ (1977), pp. 113–25.

— 'The Folles of Michael II and of Theophilus before his Reform', *Hamburger Beiträge zur Numismatik* 21 (1967), pp. 21–34.

— 'Links between Stylistic Groups among the Reformed Folles of Theophilus', *Numismatic Circular* 84 (1976), pp. 6–7.

— 'The Reformed Folles of Theophilus: Their Styles and Localization', *American Numismatic Society Museum Notes* 14 (1968), pp. 121–53.

— 'Silver and Tin in the Byzantine Trachy Coinages, ca. 1160–1261', *Revue Belge de Numismatique* 123 (1977), pp. 107–31.

— 'The Tetarteron in the Twelfth Century', *Numismatic Circular* 86 (1978), p. 574.
Metcalf, D. M., and Roper, I. T., 'A Hoard of Copper Trachea of Andronicus I of Trebizond (1222–35)', *Numismatic Circular* 83 (1975), pp. 237–8.
Metcalf, D. M., and Schweizer, F., 'Milliprobe Analyses of some Visigothic, Suevic, and other Gold Coins of the Early Middle Ages', *Archaemotry* 12 (1970), pp. 173–88.
Metcalf, W. E., 'Three Seventh-century Byzantine Gold Hoards', *American Numismatic Society Museum Notes* 25 (1980), pp. 87–108.
Michon, E., 'Le "modius" de Ponte Puñide (Espagne)', *Mémoires de la Société Nationale des Antiquaires de France* $4^8$ (1914), pp. 214–312.
Miles, G. C., 'Byzantine Miliaresion and Arab Dirhem: Some Notes on their Relationship', *American Numismatic Society Museum Notes* 9 (1960), pp. 189–218.
— 'The Earliest Arab Gold Coinage', *American Numismatic Society Museum Notes* 13 (1967), pp. 205–29.
Milivoievic, M., and Roglić, J., 'Yugoslavia', in Committee for the World Atlas of Agriculture (ed.), *The World Atlas of Agriculture* I (Novara, 1969), at pp. 512–27.
Miller, F., 'The *Privata* from Diocletian to Heraclius: Documentary Evidence', in C. E. King (ed.), *Imperial Revenue, Expenditure and Monetary Policy in the Fourth Century A.D.* (Oxford, 1980) (= British Archaeological Reports, International Series LXXVI), at pp. 125–40.
Miller, D. A., 'The Logothete of the Drome in the Middle Byzantine Period', *Byzantion* 36 (1966) (= Mémorial Henri Grégoire), pp. 438–70.
Miller, E., 'Fragment inédit de Nicétas Choniate relatif à un fait numismatique', *Revue Numismatique* $11^2$ (1866), pp. 3–12.
Miller, T., 'The Basilika and the Demosia: The Financial Offices of the Late Byzantine Empire', *Revue des Études Byzantines* 36 (1978), pp. 171–91.
Milne, J. G., *Catalogue of Alexandrian Coins* (Oxford, 1971).
— 'The Currency of Egypt under the Romans to the Time of Diocletian', *Annals of Archaeology and Anthropology* 7 (1914–16), pp. 51–66.
Morris, R., 'The Powerful and the Poor in Tenth-century Byzantium: Law and Reality', *Past and Present* 73 (Nov. 1976), pp. 3–27.
Morrisson, C., *Catalogue des monnaies byzantines de la Bibliothèque Nationale*; I: *d'Anastase 1^er^ à Justinien II (491–711)*; II: *de Philippicus à Alexis III (711–1204)* (both Paris, 1970).
— 'La concavité des monnaies byzantines', *Bulletin de la Société Française de Numismatique* 30 (1975), pp. 786–8.
— 'Découverte de trésors à l'époque byzantine et monnaies inconnues: les *pentalaimia*', *Bulletin de la Société Française de Numismatique* 37 (1982), pp. 150–2.
— 'La découverte des trésors à l'époque byzantine: théorie et pratique de l'*euresis thesaurou*', *Travaux et Mémoires* 8 (1981) (= Hommage à M. Paul Lemerle), pp. 321–43.
— 'Le dernier solidus byzantin frappé à Carthage (695)', *Bulletin de la Société Française de Numismatique* 34 (1979), pp. 514–16.
— 'La dévaluation de la monnaie byzantine au XI^e^ siècle: essai d'interprétation', *Travaux et Mémoires* 6 (1976), pp. 3–48.
— 'Estimation du volume des émissions de solidi de Tibère et Maurice à Carthage (578–602)', *Pact* 5 (1981), pp. 267–84.
— 'La Logarikè: réforme monétaire et réforme fiscale sous Alexis I^er^ Comnène', *Travaux et Mémoires* 7 (1979), 419–64.

— 'La monnaie fiduciaire à Byzance ou "vraie monnaie", "monnaie fiduciaire" et "fausse monnaie" à Byzance', *Bulletin de la Société Française de Numismatique* 34 (1979), pp. 612–16.

— 'Le nomisma hyperpère avant la réforme d'Alexis I Comnène', *Bulletin de la Société Française de Numismatique* 28 (1973), pp. 385–7.

— 'Numismatique byzantine', in École Pratique des Hautes Études, IVe Section, *Annuaire* (1974/5), at pp. 455–62.

— 'La numismatique des Paléologues: à propos de deux ouvrages récents', *Revue des Études Byzantines* 39 (1981), pp. 319–23.

— 'Les origines du monnayage vandale', in H. A. Cahn and G. Le Rider (eds), *Proceedings of the 8th International Congress of Numismatics, New York–Washington September 1973* (Paris/Basel, 1976) (= Association Internationale des Numismates Professionels, Publication no. IV), at pp. 461–72.

— 'The Re-use of Obsolete Coins: The Case of Roman Imperial Bronzes Revived in the Fifth Century', in C. N. L. Brooke, B. H. I. H. Stewart, J. G. Pollard and T. R. Volk, (eds) *Studies in Numismatic Method Presented to Philip Grierson* (Cambridge, 1983), at pp. 95–111.

— 'Review Article', in *Revue Numismatique* $21^6$ (1979), pp. 256–65 (review of Bendall and Donald's *The Billon Trachea of Michael VIII Palaeologos, 1258–1282* and the same authors' *The Later Palaeologan Coinage, 1282–1453*, together with a concordance between those works and Bertelè and Morrisson's *Numismatique byzantine*).

— 'Le rôle des Varanges dans la transmission de la monnaie byzantine en Scandinavie', in R. Zeitler (ed.), *Les pays du nord et Byzance (Scandinavie et Byzance, Actes du colloque nordique et internationale de byzantinologie tenu à Upsal 20–22 avril 1979)* (Uppsala, 1981), at pp. 131–40.

Mülâyim, Z. Gökalp, 'Turkey', in Committee for the World Atlas of Agriculture (ed.), *The World Atlas of Agriculture* I (Novara, 1969), at pp. 423–37.

Nesbitt, J. W., 'Mechanisms of Agricultural Production on Estates of the Byzantine Praktika' (Ph.D. thesis, Wisconsin, 1972).

— 'Double Names on Early Byzantine Lead Seals', *DOP* 31 (1977), pp. 111–21.

— 'The Life of St. Philaretos (702–792) and its Significance for Byzantine Agriculture', *The Greek Orthodox Theological Review* 14.2 (1969), pp. 150–8.

— 'The Rate of March of Crusading Armies in Europe: A Study and Computation', *Traditio* 19 (1963), pp. 167–81.

Newell, E. T., *The Byzantine Hoard of Lagbe* (New York, 1945) (= American Numismatic Society, Numismatic Notes and Monographs, CV).

Noonan, T. S., 'The Circulation of Byzantine Coins in Kievan Rus', *Byzantine Studies/Études Byzantines* 7 (1980), pp. 143–81.

Obolensky, D., 'Byzantine Frontier Zones and Cultural Exchanges', *XIV[e] Congrès International des Études Byzantines, Bucarest 6–12 septembre 1971, Rapports* II, pp. 91–101.

Oddy, W. A., 'The *Moneta Genavensis* of the *Lex Burgundionum*', *Revue Numismatique* $22^6$ (1980), pp. 131–5.

O'Hara, M. D., 'Notes on Recent Byzantine Hoards', *Coin Hoards* I (1975), pp. 67–8.

Oikonomides, N., *Hommes d'affaires grecs et latins à Constantinople (XIIIe–XVe siècles)* (Montreal/Paris, 1979) (= Conference Albert-le-Grand, 1977).

— 'La décomposition de l'empire byzantin à la veille de 1204 et les origines de l'empire de Nicée: à propos de la "Partitio Romaniae"', *XV[e] Congrès International d'Études Byzantines*,

*Athènes 1976, Rapports et Co-rapports* I, *Histoire* (*1: Forces centrifuges et centripètes dans le monde byzantin entre 1071 et 1261*), pp. 1–28.

— 'L'évolution de l'organisation administrative de l'empire byzantin au XIe siècle (1025–1118)', *Travaux et Mémoires* 6 (1976), pp. 125–52.

— 'L'organisation de la frontière orientale de Byzance aux Xe–XIe siècles et le taktikon de l'Escorial', *XIVe Congrès International des Études Byzantines, Bucarest 6–12 septembre 1971, Rapports* II, pp. 73–90.

— 'A propos des armées des premiers Paléologues et des compagnies de soldats', *Travaux et Mémoires* 8 (1981), pp. 353–71.

— 'St George of Mangana, Maria Skleraina, and the "Malyj Sion" of Novgorod', *DOP* 34/5 (1980/1), pp. 239–46.

Oliver, J. H., 'Achaia, Greece, and Laconia', *Greek, Roman and Byzantine Studies* 21 (1980), pp. 75–81.

Ostrogorsky, G., *History of the Byzantine State* (2nd English edn, Oxford, 1968).

— *Pour l'histoire de la féodalité byzantine* (Brussels, 1954) (=Corpus Bruxellense Historiae Byzantinae, Subsidia I).

— 'Byzantine Cities in the Early Middle Ages', *DOP* 13 (1959), pp. 45–66.

Padfield, T., 'Analysis of Byzantine Copper Coins by X-ray Methods', in E. T. Hall and D. M. Metcalf (eds), *Methods of Chemical and Metallurgical Investigation of Ancient Coinage* (London, 1972) (=Royal Numismatic Society, Special Publication VIII), at pp. 219–34.

Painter, K. S., 'A Late-Roman Silver Ingot from Kent', *Antiquaries Journal* 52 (1972), pp. 84–92.

Papadopoulos-Kerameus, A. I., 'Theodoros Eirēnikos Patriarkhēs Oikoumenikos en Nikaia', *Byzantinische Zeitschrift* 10 (1901), pp. 182–92.

Patlagean, E., *Pauvreté économique et pauvreté sociale à Byzance 4e–7e siècles* (Paris/The Hague, 1977) (=Civilisations et Sociétés XLVIII).

Patterson, C. C., 'Silver Stocks and Losses in Ancient and Mediaeval Times', *Economic History Review* $25^2$ (1972), pp. 205–35.

Pauly, Wissowa, Kroll *et al.* (eds), *Real-Encyclopädie der classischen Altertumswissenschaft* II (Stuttgart, 1896).

Payne, S., 'Kill-off Patterns in Sheep and Goats: The Mandibles from Aşvan Kale', *Anatolian Studies* 23 (1973), pp. 281–303.

Pearce, J. W. E., *The Roman Imperial Coinage* IX, *Valentinian I–Theodosius I* (London, 1951).

— 'Notes on the Terling and other Silver Hoards found in Britain', *Numismatic Chronicle* $13^5$ (1933), pp. 170–81.

Péchoux, P.-Y., and Sivignon, M., *Les Balkans* (Paris, 1971) (=Magellan: La Géographie et ses Problèmes XVI).

Pellat, C., 'Ǧāḥiẓiana I, le *Kitāb al-Tabaṣṣur bi-l-tiǧāra* attribué à Gahiz', *Arabica* I (1954), pp. 153–65.

Pelliot, P., *Notes sur l'histoire de la Horde d'Or suivies de quelques noms turcs d'hommes et de peuples finissant en 'ar'* (=Oeuvres Posthumes de Paul Pelliot II, Paris, 1949).

— 'Le prétendu mot "iascot" chez Guillaume de Rubrouck', *T'oung Pao* 27 (1930), pp. 190–2.

Pflaum, H.-G., 'Un procurateur de la monnaie de Thessalonique', *Bulletin de la Société Française de Numismatique* 27 (1972), pp. 315–16.

Pierce, R. H., 'Notes on Obols and Agios in Demotic Papyri', *Journal of Egyptian Archaeology* 51 (1965), pp. 155–9.

de Planhol, X., *Les fondements géographiques de l'histoire de l'islam* (Paris, 1968).

— *De le plaine pamphylienne aux lacs pisidiens, nomadisme et vie paysanne* (Paris, 1958) (= Bibliothèque Archéologique et Historique de l'Institut Français d'Archéologie d'Istanbul III).

Pochitonov, E., 'La plus ancienne émission monétaire bulgare de l'époque du second royaume', *Byzantinoslavica* 31 (1970), pp. 54–63.

— 'Théodore-Pierre Asène ou Théodore Mancaphas?', *Byzantinoslavica* 42 (1981), pp. 52–7.

Polemis, D. I., *The Doukai, a Contribution to Byzantine Prosopography* (London, 1968) (= University of London Historical Studies XXII).

Popović, M., 'La découverte d'un dépot de monnaie du roi Stéphane Radoslav dans la forteresse de Ras', in V. Kondić (ed.), *Frappe et ateliers monétaires dans l'antiquité et moyen âge* (Belgrade, 1976), at pp. 115–19.

Prestwich, M. C., 'The Crown and the Currency. The Circulation of Money in Late Thirteenth and Early Fourteenth Century England', *Numismatic Chronicle* 142 (1982), pp. 51–65.

Protonotarios, P., 'Une monnaie de l'empereur Matthieu Asen Cantacuzène (1354–1357)', *Revue Numismatique* $23^6$ (1981), pp. 96–100.

— 'Hē Nomismatokopia tou Vyzantinou Kratous tēs Ēpeirou (1204–1268)', *Ēpeirōtika Khronika* 24 (1982), pp. 130–50.

— 'The Silver Coinage of the Joint Reign of Andronicus II and Michael IX (1295–1320)', *Numismatic Circular* 80 (1972), pp. 452–3.

Quatremère, M., *Histoire des Mongols de la Perse écrite en persan par Raschid-Eldin* I (Paris, 1836).

Quintanilla Raso, M. C., 'Notas sobre el comercio urbano en Córdoba durante la Baja Edad Media', in *Actas del I Congreso de Historia de Andalucía, Diciembre de 1976* I, *Andalucía Medieval* (Cordoba, 1978), at pp. 413–22.

Rabie, H., *The Financial System of Egypt, A.H. 564–741/A.D. 1169–1341* (London, 1972) (= London Oriental Series XXV).

Radojčić, B., 'La région de la Dendra de la Serbie au XII$^{e}$ siècle', *Balkan Studies* 11 (1970), pp. 249–60.

Ramsay, W. M., *The Cities and Bishoprics of Phrygia* (2 vols, Oxford, 1895 (I.1: *The Lycos Valley and South-western Phrygia*), 1897 (I.2: *West and West-central Phrygia*)).

— *The Historical Geography of Asia Minor* (London, 1890) (= Royal Geographical Society, Supplementary Papers IV).

— 'Pisidia and the Lycaonian Frontier', *Annual of the British School at Athens* 9 (1902/3), pp. 243–73.

Ramsay, W. M. (ed.), *Studies in the History and Art of the Eastern Provinces of the Roman Empire* (Aberdeen, 1906).

Raybaud, L.-P., *Le gouvernement et l'administration centrale de l'empire byzantin sous les premiers Paléologues (1258–1354)* (Paris, 1968).

Rea, J. R., '*P.S.I.* IV.310 and Imperial Bullion Purchases', *Chronique d'Égypte* 49 (1974), pp. 163–74.

Reece, R. M., 'The Anonymous: A Numismatic Commentary', in M. W. C. Hassall (ed.),

*De Rebus Bellicis* (Oxford, 1979) (=British Archaeological Reports, International Series LXIII), at pp. 59–66.

Rémondon, R., 'L'édit XIII de Justinien a-t-il été promulgué en 539?', *Chronique d'Égypte* 30/59 (1955), pp. 112–21.

Retowski, O., *Die Münzen der Komnenen von Trapezunt* (Moscow, 1910/11, rep. Brunswick, 1974).

Rickman, G. E., *The Corn Supply of Ancient Rome* (Oxford, 1980).

Robert, L., *A travers l'Asie Mineure: poètes et prosateurs, monnaies grecques, voyageurs et géographie* (Paris, 1980) (=Bibliothèque des Écoles Françaises d'Athènes et de Rome CCXXXIX).

— 'Inscriptions grecques de Sidè en Pamphylie (époque impériale et bas-empire)', *Revue de Philologie* 31[3] (1957), pp. 15–53.

— 'Les Kordakia de Nicée, le combustible de Synnada, et les poissons-scies. Sur des lettres d'un métropolite de Phrygie au Xe siècle. Philologie et réalités I', *Journal des Savants* (1961), pp. 97–166.

Rösch, G., 'Der Aufstand der Herakleioi gegen Phokas (608–610) im Spiegel numismatischer Quellen', *Jahrbuch der Österreichischen Byzantinistik* 28 (1979), pp. 51–62.

Ross, M. C., *Catalogue of the Byzantine and Early Mediaeval Antiquities in the Dumbarton Oaks Collection* II, *Jewelry, Enamels, and Art of the Migration Period* (Washington, D.C., 1965).

Rott, H., *Kleinasiatische Denkmäler aus Pisidien, Pamphylien, Kappodokien, und Lykien* (Leipzig, 1908) (=Studien über christliche Denkmäler, n.s. V/VI).

Roueché, C. M., 'Rome, Asia and Aphrodisias in the Third Century', *Journal of Roman Studies* 71 (1981), pp. 103–20.

Ruggini, L., 'A proposito del *follis* nel IV secolo', *Atti della Accademia Nazionale dei Lincei, Rendiconti* 16[8] (1961), pp. 306–19.

Runciman, S., *A History of the First Bulgarian Empire* (London, 1930).

— *The Sicilian Vespers, a History of the Mediterranean World in the Later Thirteenth Century* (Cambridge, 1958).

— 'The Widow Danelis', in K. Varvaressos (ed.), *Études dédiées à la mémoire d'André M. Andréadès* (Athens, 1940), at pp. 425–31.

Ruschenbusch, E., 'Diokletians Währungsreform vom 1.9.301', *Zeitschrift für Papyrologie und Epigraphik* 26 (1977), pp. 193–210.

Sabatier, J., *Description générale des monnaies byzantines, frappées sous les empereurs d'orient depuis Arcadius jusqu'à la prise de Constantinople par Mahomet II* (2 vols, Paris/London, 1862).

Salama, P., 'Recherches numismatiques sur l'usurpateur africain L. Domitius Alexander (Atelier de Carthage, 308–10)', in H. A. Cahn and G. Le Rider (eds), *Actes du 8ème Congrès International de Numismatique, New York–Washington, septembre 1973* (Paris/Basel, 1976), at pp. 365–9.

— 'Les trésors maxentiens de Tripolitaine', *Libya Antiqua* 3–4 (1966–7), pp. 21–7.

Sawyer, P. H., 'Kings and Merchants', in P. H. Sawyer and I. N. Wood (eds), *Early Medieval Kingship* (Leeds, 1977).

Schilbach, E., *Byzantinische Metrologie* (Munich, 1970) (=Byzantinisches Handbuch IV).

Schlumberger, G., *Numismatique de l'Orient latin* (2 vols, text and plates, Paris 1878, rep. Graz 1954).

— *Sigillographie de l'empire byzantin* (Paris, 1884).

Schuman, V. B., 'The Basis of Accounting Practices in the Karanis Tax Rolls', *Aegyptus* 32 (1952), pp. 241–52.
Schurmann, H. F., 'Mongolian Tributary Practices of the Thirteenth Century', *Harvard Journal of Asiatic Studies* 19 (1956), pp. 304–89.
Seeck, O., *Regesten der Kaiser und Päpste für die Jahre 311 bis 476 n. Chr.: Vorarbeit zu einer Prosopographie der christlichen Kaiserzeit* (Stuttgart, 1919).
Segrè, A., 'Essays on Byzantine Economic History, I, The *Annona Civica* and the *Annona Militaris*', *Byzantion* 16(1) (1942/3), pp. 393–444.
Seibt, W., *Die byzantinischen Bleisiegel in Österreich* I, *Kaiserhof* (Vienna, 1978) (= Veröffentlichungen der Kommission für Byzantinistik II.1).
— 'Über das Verhältnis von *kēnarios* bzw. *domestikos tēs trapezēs* zu den anderen Funktionären der *basilikē trapeza* in mittelbyzantinischer Zeit', *Byzantinische Zeitschrift* 72 (1979), pp. 34–8.
Semple, E. C., *The Geography of the Mediterranean Region, its Relation to Ancient History* (London, 1932).
Shaban, M. A., *Islamic History, a New Interpretation* I (*A.D. 600–750*), II (*A.D. 750–1055*) (Cambridge, 1971 (I), 1976 (II)).
Shaw, S. J., *The Budget of Ottoman Egypt 1005–1006/1596–1597* (The Hague/Paris, 1968).
— *The Financial and Administrative Organisation and Development of Ottoman Egypt 1517–1798* (Princeton, 1962) (= Princeton Oriental Studies XIX).
— 'The Nineteenth-century Ottoman Tax Reforms and Revenue System', *International Journal of Middle East Studies* 6 (1975), pp. 421–59.
Ševčenko, I., 'The Inscription of Justin II's time on the Mevlevihane (Rhesion) Gate at Istanbul', *Zbornik Radova Vizantoloshkog Instituta* 12 (1970), pp. 1–8.
— 'Nicolas Cabasilas' "Anti-zealot" Discourse: A Reinterpretation', *DOP* 11 (1957), pp. 79–171.
— 'Society and Intellectual Life in the Fourteenth Century', *XIV^e^ Congrès International des Études Byzantines, Bucarest 6–12 septembre 1971, Rapports* I, pp. 7–30.
Sigler, P. O., *Sycee Silver* (New York, 1943) (= American Numismatic Society, Numismatic Notes and Monographs XCIX).
Slessarev, V., 'The Pound-value of Genoa's Maritime Trade in 1161', in D. Herlihy, R. S. Lopez and V. Slessarev (eds), *Economy, Society, and Government in Medieval Italy Essays in Memory of Robert L. Reynolds* (Kent, 1969), at pp. 95–111.
Sophocles, E. A., *Greek Lexicon of the Roman and Byzantine Periods (from B.C. 146 to A.D. 1100)* (Cambridge, Mass./Leipzig, 1914, rep. Hildesheim/New York, 1975).
Sorlin, I., 'Bulletin byzantino-slave: publications soviétiques sur le XI^e^ siècle', *Travaux et Mémoires* 6 (1976), pp. 367–98.
Spaer, A., 'The Rafah Hoard: Byzantine Sixth-century Folles', *Numismatic Chronicle* 18^7^ (1978), pp. 66–70.
Spasski, I. G., *The Russian Monetary System, a Historico-Numismatic Survey* (trans. Z. I. Gorishina, rev. L. S. Forrer, Amsterdam, 1967).
Sperber, D., *Roman Palestine 200–400, Money and Prices* (Ramat-Gan, 1974).
Stavrakas, S., 'The Byzantine Provincial Elite: A Study in Social Relationships during the Ninth and Tenth Centuries' (Ph.D. thesis, Chicago, 1978).
Stefan, F., *Die Münzstätte Sirmium unter den Ostgoten und Gepiden. Ein Beitrag zur Geschichte des germanischen Münzwesens in der Zeit der Völkerwanderung* (Halle (Saale), 1925).

Stein, E., *Histoire du bas-empire* (2 vols., Paris/Brussels, 1949 (II: *476–565*), 1959 (I.1.2: *284–476*); both rep. Amsterdam, 1968).

— *Studien zur Geschichte des byzantinischen Reiches, vornehmlich unter den Kaisern Justinus II u. Tiberius Constantinus* (Stuttgart, 1919).

— Review of A. Andréadès' article 'Le montant du budget de l'empire byzantin' (1921), in *Byzantinische Zeitschrift* 24 (1923/4), at pp. 377–87.

— 'Untersuchungen zum Staatsrecht des Bas-Empire', *Zeitschrift der Savigny-Stiftung für Rechtsgeschichte, Romanistische Abteilung* 41 (1920), pp. 195–251.

Stern, S. M., 'An Embassy of the Byzantine Emperor to the Fatimid Caliph Al-Mu'izz', *Byzantion* 20 (1950), pp. 239–58.

Stratos, A. N., *Byzantium in the Seventh Century* (5 vols, all Amsterdam, 1968 (I: *602–634*), 1972 (II: *634–641*), 1975 (III: *642–668*), 1978 (IV: *668–685*), 1980 (V: *Justinian II, Leontius and Tiberius, 685–711*)).

Sutherland, C. H. V., *The Roman Imperial Coinage* VI, *From Diocletian's Reform* (*A.D. 294*) *to the Death of Maximinus* (*A.D. 313*) (London, 1967).

Svoronos, N. G., 'L'épibolè à l'époque des Comnènes', *Travaux et Mémoires* 3 (1968), pp. 375–95.

— 'Notes sur l'origine et la date du code rural', *Travaux et Mémoires* 8 (1981), pp. 487–500.

— 'Recherches sur le cadastre byzantin et la fiscalité aux XIe et XIIe siècles: le cadastre de Thèbes', *Bulletin de Correspondance Hellénique* 83 (1959), pp. 1–145.

— 'Remarques sur les structures économiques de l'empire byzantin au XIe siècle', *Travaux et Mémoires* 6 (1976), pp. 49–67.

Tanoğlu, A., Erinç, S., and Tümertekin, E., *Türkiye Atlası* (Istanbul, *c.* 1961) (=Istanbul Üniversitesi Edebiyat Fakültesi Yayınları no. 903).

Teall, J. L., 'The Byzantine Agricultural Tradition', *DOP* 25 (1971), pp. 33–59.

— 'The Grain Supply of the Byzantine Empire, 330–1025', *DOP* 13 (1959), pp. 87–139.

Texier, C. F. M., *Asie Mineure: description géographique, historique et archéologique des provinces et des villes de la chersonnèse d'Asie* (Paris, 1862) (=L'univers: histoire et description de tous les peuples).

Theodoridis, D., 'Aus dem griechischen Lehngut in osmanischen', *Turcica* 7 (1975), pp. 32–49.

Thiriet, F., *La Romanie vénitienne au moyen âge: Le développement et l'exploitation du domaine colonial vénitien (XIIe–XVe siècles)* (Paris, 1959).

Thomas, J. D., 'The Date of the Revolt of L. Domitius Domitianus', *Zeitschrift für Papyrologie und Epigraphik* 22 (1976), pp. 253–79.

Thompson, E. A., *The Goths in Spain* (Oxford, 1969).

Thompson, M., *The Athenian Agora* II, *Coins from the Roman through the Venetian Period* (Princeton, 1954).

— 'Some Unpublished Bronze Money of the Early Eighth Century', *Hesperia* 9 (1940), pp. 358–80.

Tivchev, P., 'Sur les cités byzantines au XIe–XIIe siècles', *Byzantinobulgarica* 1 (1962), pp. 145–82.

Tivchev, P., and Tsankova-Petkova, G., 'Au sujet des relations féodales dans les territoires bulgares sous la domination byzantine à la fin du XIe et pendant la première moitié du XIIe siècle', *Byzantinobulgarica* 2 (1966), pp. 107–25.

Tolstoi, J. (I. I.), *Monnaies byzantines* (3 vols in 9 fascicules, St Petersburg, 1912–14).

Tomaschek, W., *Zur historischen Topographie von Kleinasien im Mittelalter* I, *Die Küstengebiete und die Wege der Kreuzfahrer* (Vienna, 1891) (=Sitzungsberichte der kais. Akademie der Wissenschaften in Wien (phil.-hist. Klasse) CXXIV.8).

Tondo, L., 'Il *De Rebus Bellicis* e la politica monetaria', *Rivista Italiana di Numismatica* 23⁶ (78) (1976), pp. 201–7.

Touratsoglou, I., 'Unpublished Byzantine Hoards of Billon Trachea from Greek Macedonia and Thrace', *Balkan Studies* 14 (1973), pp. 131–66.

Toynbee, A. J., *Constantine Porphyrogenitus and his World* (London, 1973).

Treadgold, W. T., *The Byzantine State Finances in the Eighth and Ninth Centuries* (Boulder, 1982) (=East European Monographs CXXI (Byz. Ser. II)).

— 'Notes on the Numbers and Organization of the Ninth-Century Byzantine Army', *Greek, Roman and Byzantine Studies* 21 (1980), pp. 269–88.

Tůma, O., 'The Dating of Alexius's Chrysobull to the Venetians: 1082, 1084, or 1092?', *Byzantinoslavica* 42 (1981), pp. 171–85.

Turtledove, H. N., 'The Immediate Successors of Justinian: A Study of the Persian Problem and of Continuity and Change in Internal Secular Affairs in the Later Roman Empire during the Reigns of Justin II and Tiberius II Constantine (A.D. 565–582)' (Ph.D. thesis, UCLA, Los Angeles, 1977).

Ulrich-Bansa, O., *Moneta Mediolanensis (352–498)* (Venice, 1949).

Unwin, A. H., *Goat-Grazing and Forestry in Cyprus* (London, *c.* 1928).

Uspenskii, F. I., 'Mneniya i postanovleniya Konstantinopol' skikh' pomestnykh soborov' XI i XII vv.o razdache tserkovnykh imshchestv (*kharistikarii*)', *Izvestiya Russkago Arkheologicheskago Instituta v Konstantinople* 5 (1900), pp. 1–48.

Vandersleyen, C., *Chronologie des préfets d'Égypte de 284 à 395* (Brussels, 1962) (=Collection Latomus LV).

Vasiliev, A. A., *Byzance et les Arabes* (2 vols, Brussels, 1935 (I: *820–67*), 1968 (II.1: *867–959*), 1950 (II.2: *867–959*), *Extraits des sources arabes*)). Also 3rd vol. (Brussels, 1935: E. Honigmann, *Die Ostgrenze des byzantinischen Reiches*).

— *The Goths in the Crimea* (Cambridge, Mass., 1936) (=Monographs of the Mediaeval Academy of America XI).

— 'Manuel Comnenus and Henry Plantagenet', *Byzantinische Zeitschrift* 29 (1929/30), pp. 233–44.

Vavilov, N. I., *The Origin, Variation, Immunity, and Breeding of Cultivated Plants* (New York, 1951) (Chronica Botanica XIII.1/6).

— *World Resources of Cereals, Leguminous Seed Crops and Flax, and their Utilization in Plant Breeding* (Moscow, 1957).

Veglery, A., and Millas, A., 'Copper Coins of Andronicus I, Comnenus Gidon (1222–1235)', *Numismatic Circular* 85 (1977), pp. 487–8.

Vita-Finzi, C., *The Mediterranean Valleys, Geological Changes in Historical Times* (Cambridge, 1969).

Vryonis, S., *The Decline of Medieval Hellenism in Asia Minor and the Process of Islamization from the Eleventh through the Fifteenth Century* (Berkeley/Los Angeles/London, 1971).

— 'The Internal History of Byzantium during the "Time of Troubles" (1057–81)' (Ph.D. thesis, Harvard University, Cambridge, Mass., 1956).

— 'An Attic Hoard of Byzantine Gold Coins (668–741) from the Thomas Whittemore

Collection, and the Numismatic Evidence for the Urban History of Byzantium', *Zbornik Radova Vizantoloshkog Instituta* 8.1 (1963) (= Mélanges Georges Ostrogorsky 1), pp. 291–300.
— 'Byzantine Dēmokratia and the Guilds in the Eleventh Century', *DOP* 17 (1963), pp. 287–314.
— 'Byzantium: The Social Basis of Decline in the Eleventh Century', *Greek, Roman, and Byzantine Studies* 2 (1959), pp. 159–75.
— 'The Evolution of Slavic Society and the Slavic Invasions in Greece: The First Major Slavic Attack on Thessaloniki, A.D. 597', *Hesperia* 50 (1981), pp. 378–90.
— 'Laonicus Chalcocondyles and the Ottoman Budget', *International Journal of Middle East Studies* 7 (1976), pp. 423–32.
— 'Nomadization and Islamization in Asia Minor', *DOP* 29 (1975), pp. 41–71.
— 'Review Essay' (of M. W. Weithmann, *Die Slavische Bevölkerung auf der Griechischen Halbinsel*) in *Balkan Studies* 22 (1981), at pp. 405–39.
— 'St. Ioannicius the Great (754–846) and the "Slavs" of Bithynia', *Byzantion* 31 (1961), pp. 245–8.
— 'Two Numismatic Items from the Thomas Whittemore Collection', *Byzantinische Forschungen* 3 (1968), pp. 229–34.
Wagstaff, M., 'Physical Geography and Settlements (Aşvan Project)', *Anatolian Studies* 23 (1973), pp. 197–215.
Walker, D. R., 'A Copper Coinage for Leontius I', *Numismatic Circular* 75 (1967), pp. 264–5.
Warmington, E. H., *The Commerce between the Roman Empire and India* (2nd edn, London/Dublin/New York, 1974).
Watson, A. M., 'Back to Gold – and Silver', *Economic History Review* $20^2$ (1967), pp. 1–34.
Webb, P. H., *The Roman Imperial Coinage* v.1 (London, 1927).
— *The Roman Imperial Coinage* v.2 (London, 1933).
Weithmann, M. W., *Die Slavische Bevölkerung auf der Griechischen Halbinsel: Ein Beitrag zur Historischen Ethnographie Südosteuropas* (Munich, 1978) (= Beiträge zur Kenntnis Südosteuropas und des Nahen Orients XXXI).
Werner, K. F., 'Important Noble Families in the Kingdom of Charlemagne – A Prosopographical Study of the Relationship between King and Nobility in the Early Middle Ages', in T. Reuter (ed.), *The Medieval Nobility. Studies on the Ruling Classes of France and Germany from the Sixth to the Twelfth Century* (Amsterdam/New York/Oxford, 1978/9) (= Europe in the Middle Ages, Selected Studies XIV), at pp. 137–202.
White, K. D., *Roman Farming* (London, 1970) (Aspects of Greek and Roman Life).
Whittaker, C. R., 'Inflation and the Economy in the Fourth Century A.D.', in C. E. King (ed.), *Imperial Revenue, Expenditure and Monetary Policy in the Fourth Century A.D.* (Oxford, 1980) (= British Archaeological Reports, International Series LXXVI), at pp. 1–22.
Whitting, P. D., 'Miliaresia of Andronicus II and Michael IX', *Numismatic Circular* 80 (1972), pp. 270–4.
— 'A Seventh-century Hoard at Carthage', *Numismatic Chronicle* $6^7$ (1966), pp. 225–33.
Wickham, C. J., 'The Other Transition: From the Ancient World to Feudalism', *Past and Present* 103 (1984), pp. 3–36.
Wilkes, J. J., *Dalmatia* (London, 1969) (History of the Provinces of the Roman Empire).

Willcox, G. H., 'A History of Deforestation as indicated by Charcoal Analysis of Four Sites in Eastern Anatolia', *Anatolian Studies* 24 (1974), pp. 117–33.

Winkelmann, F., Köpstein, H., Ditten, H., and Rochow, I., *Byzanz im 7. Jahrhundert. Untersuchungen zur Herausbildung des Feudalismus* (Berlin, 1978) (= Berliner Byzantinistische Arbeiten XLVIII).

Wirth, P., 'Das Ende der römisch-byzantinischen Goldwährung', *Jahrbuch für Numismatik und Geldgeschichte* 25 (1975), pp. 113–22.

Wittek, P., 'Von der byzantinischen zur türkischen Toponymie', *Byzantion* 10 (1935), pp. 11–64.

Wolff, R. L., 'Mortgage and Redemption of an Emperor's Son: Castile and the Latin Empire of Constantinople', *Speculum* 29 (1954), pp. 45–84.

Wroth, W., *Catalogue of the Coins of the Vandals, Ostrogoths and Lombards, and of the Empires of Thessalonica, Nicaea and Trebizond in the British Museum* (London, 1911).

Yang, L.-S., *Money and Credit in China, a Short History* (Cambridge, Mass., 1952) (= Harvard – Yenching Institute, Monograph Series XII).

Yannopoulos, P. A., *L'hexagramme, un monnayage byzantin en argent du VIIe siècle* (Louvain, 1978) (= Publications d'Histoire de l'Art et d'Archéologie de l'Université Catholique de Louvain XI – Numismatica Lovanensia III).

— *La société profane dans l'empire byzantin des VIIe, VIIIe et IXe siècles* (Louvain, 1975) (= Université de Louvain, Recueil de Travaux d'Histoire et de Philologie 6[6]).

Youroukova, I., 'L'activité de l'atelier d'orfèvre a Niš au IVe s. à la lumière d'une nouvelle trouvaille en Bulgarie', in V. Kondić (ed.), *Frappe et ateliers monétaires dans l'antiquité et moyen âge* (Belgrade, 1976), at pp. 73–8.

Youtie, H. C., 'A Problem in Graeco-Roman Bookkeeping', *Zeitschrift für Papyrologie und Epigraphik* 15 (1974), pp. 117–41.

Zacos, G., and Veglery, A., *Byzantine Lead Seals* (one volume in three separately bound parts, also with separately bound plates: I.1 (nos 1–1095), I.2 (nos 1096–2671A), I.3 (nos 2672–3231, and indexes), all Basel, 1972).

Zahariev, I., Jordanov, T., and Raichev, B., 'Bulgaria', in Committee for the World Atlas of Agriculture (ed.), *The World Atlas of Agriculture* I (Novara, 1969), at pp. 57–69.

Zakythinos, D. A., *Crise monétaire et crise économique à Byzance du XIIIe au XVe siècle* (Athens, 1948).

# KEY TO PLATES

The overwhelming bulk of the coins in the plates below derive from the collections of the Barber Institute of Fine Arts, Birmingham, and the Dumbarton Oaks Center for Byzantine Studies, Washington, D.C., and the author offers all due thanks to the authorities of those institutions for the provision of photographic facilities and for permission to illustrate the results. The remainder of the coins derive from various other public, and from private, collections, and the author would particularly like to thank those private collectors who over the years have so generously placed photographs of their own material at his disposal.

With regard to the Dumbarton Oaks specimens in particular, and to the coinages of the twelfth and thirteenth centuries in general, an attempt has been made – wherever possible if without great loss of quality – to illustrate specimens that do not appear in the plates of *DOC* I–IV, or of *DOS* XII. In a number of cases, and for varying reasons, whether because of the rarity of the issues involved or because of the lack of available photographic time, this attempt has not been carried through, but it has nevertheless been constantly kept in mind with the aim of contributing to the provision of as large a pool of illustrated material as is reasonably possible.

In the Key below, the author has utilised for the purpose of standard reference the relevant volumes (VI–IX) of *RIC* for the late Roman coinage, and those (I–IV) of *DOC* for the Byzantine one. For coins not listed in *DOC* I have utilised the appropriate volumes (I–III) of *MIB*. In the case of the Byzantine coinage, where an already published DO specimen has been illustrated, the individual reference stands alone; where a non-DO specimen has been illustrated, the reference is to the whole variety or class. Where a coin type or variety mentioned in *DOC* but not represented in the collection at the time of publication (denoted there by a bracketed reference) has subsequently been acquired, the reference is accompanied by an asterisk. For the late Roman base-metal coinage from Arcadius/Honorius to Zeno (i.e. 395–491), R. A. G. Carson *et al.*, *Late Roman Bronze Coinage A.D. 324–498* (*LRBC* in the lists below) has been utilised; for the whole coinage of the empire of Trebizond, O. Retowski, *Die Münzen der Komnenen von Trapezunt* (Ret. below) has been utilised; and for the coinage of the Byzantine empire itself from Michael

VIII to Constantine XI (i.e. 1261–1453), the two works by S. Bendall and P. J. Donald mentioned in the Bibliography above (*TMP* and *LPC* below) have been utilised. This leaves the late Roman precious-metal coinage from Arcadius/Honorius to Zeno without standard reference, and it has been deliberately left so, rather than employ the now grossly outmoded works of Cohen and Sabatier and the rare one of Tolstoi: non-specialists will probably not require a reference, and specialists know all too well how to go about finding one in those works. Nevertheless, where such a coin, or a series of coins (for example Thessalonican solidi), has been mentioned specifically in the text above and has also been given a reference in a footnote, it has duly been given an appropriate page- and footnote-reference in the Key below.

I have throughout attempted to impart as accurate as possible an impression of the general denominational- and mint-structure of the coinage, but whilst doing so I have not thought it necessary to eschew the use of rare types and denominations.

The abbreviations below have been utilised with regard to collections or coins:

| | |
|---|---|
| B | Barber Institute of Fine Arts, Birmingham |
| DO | Dumbarton Oaks Center for Byzantine Studies, Washington, D.C. |
| | |
| ANS | American Numismatic Society, New York |
| BE | Bank of England, London |
| BM | British Museum, London |
| BN | Bibliothèque Nationale, Paris |
| MG | Musée d'Art et d'Histoire de Genève, Geneva |
| ML | Musée du Louvre, Paris |
| MM | Metropolitan Museum, New York |
| PC | private collection |
| T | in trade |

The traditional symbols have been utilised with regard to the metal-content of the coins both in the Key below and in the Plates themselves: AV = gold; El = electrum (gold + silver); AR = silver; B = billon (silver + copper); Æ = copper; Pb = lead.

In the case of the regnal attributions in the Key below, only the obverse or 'heads' side of the coins involved has normally been considered: at a number of periods the imperial figures represented spill over onto the reverse or 'tails' side, but to give a complete collegiate listing in these cases would simply be unwieldy.

PLATE I

| | | | | | | |
|---|---|---|---|---|---|---|
| 1 | Constantine I | Siscia | AV | 20.06 | DO | *RIC* 208 |
| 2 | Constantine I | Constantinople | AV | 13.48 | DO | *RIC* 87 |
| 3 | Constantius II | Antioch | AV | 20.05 | DO | *RIC* 158 |
| 4 | Constantius II (Caes.) | Constantinople | AV | 5.42 | DO | *RIC* 105 |
| 5 | Constans I | Siscia | AR | 12.43 | DO | *RIC* 148 |
| 6 | Constantine I | Siscia | AR | 13.17 | DO | *RIC* 259 |
| 7 | Constantius II | Thessalonica | AR | 14.64 | DO | *RIC* 78 |

PLATE 2

| | | | | | | |
|---|---|---|---|---|---|---|
| 1 | Constans I | Siscia | AR | 13.44 | DO | *RIC* 41 |
| 2 | Constantius II | Thessalonica | AR | 12.88 | DO | *RIC* 79 |
| 3 | Constantius II | Thessalonica | AV | 8.97 | DO | *RIC* 143 |
| 4 | Theodosius II | Constantinople | AV | | DO | – |
| 5 | Valens | Trier | AV | 8.92 | DO | *RIC* cf. 36a/b |
| 6 | Justin I | Constantinople | AR | 12.40 | DO | *MIB* N7 |
| 7 | Justinian I | Constantinople | AV | (4/5 sol.) | ML | *MIB* 2 |
| 8 | Maurice Tiberius | Constantinople | AV | (6 sol.) | MM | *DOC* (1) |

PLATE 3

| | | | | | | |
|---|---|---|---|---|---|---|
| 1 | Constantine I | Sirmium | AV | | DO | *RIC* – |
| 2 | Constantius II (Caes.) | Trier | AV | 9.00 | DO | *RIC* 468 |
| 3 | Constantius II | Arles | AV | 6.68 | DO | *RIC* [illegible] |
| 4 | Theodosius II | Constantinople | AV | 5.35 | DO | – |
| 5 | Leo I | Constantinople | AV | 5.33 | DO | – |
| 6 | Anastasius I | Constantinople | AV | 5.34 | DO | *DOC* 1 |
| 7 | Julian | Constantinople(?) | Æ (Ex.) | 3.98 | MG | above, p. 333, n. 102 |
| 8 | Arcadius, Honorius and Theod. II | Cpl. John, c.s.l.–c.404 | Æ (Ex.) | 4.12 | MG | above, p. 333, n. 102 |
| 9 | Valens, Gratian and Valentinian II | Sirmium | AV | 520.00 | BE | above, pp. 385, 388, and n. 51 |
| 10 | Valens, Gratian and Valentinian II | Sirmium | AV | | BM | above, pp. 385, 388, and n. 51 |

## PLATE 4

| No. | Ruler | Mint | Metal | Weight | Collection | Reference |
|---|---|---|---|---|---|---|
| 1 | Galerius (Caes.) | Antioch | AV | 27.00 | DO | *RIC* 2 |
| 2 | Maximian | Trier | AV | 5.12 | DO | *RIC* 43 |
| 3 | Maximian | Alexandria | AV | 5.35 | DO | *RIC* 3 |
| 4 | Constantius I (Caes.) | Antioch | AV | 5.36 | DO | *RIC* 24 |
| 5 | Galerius (Caes.) | Antioch | AV | 5.29 | DO | *RIC* 10 |
| 6 | Maximinus (Caes.) | Nicomedia | AV | 5.43 | DO | *RIC* 43 |
| 7 | Galeria Valeria | Thessalonica | AV | 5.26 | DO | *RIC* 29 |
| 8 | Licinius I | Antioch | AV | 5.61 | DO | *RIC* 3 |
| 9 | Constantine I | Serdica | AV | 5.26 | DO | *RIC* 4 |
| 10 | Licinius I | Nicomedia | AV | 5.28 (pierced) | DO | *RIC* 41 |
| 11 | Galerius (Caes.) | Ticinum | AR | 3.09 | DO | *RIC* 21b |
| 12 | Diocletian | Carthage | AR | 3.28 | DO | *RIC* 15a |
| 13 | Diocletian | Nicomedia | AR | 3.36 | DO | *RIC* 25a |
| 14 | Constantine I (Caes.) | Trier | AR | 2.94 | DO | *RIC* 638 |
| 15 | Constantine I | Trier | AR | 1.71 | B | *RIC* 828 |
| 16 | Maximian | Rome | AR | 2.99 | DO | *RIC* 192 |
| 17 | Maxentius | Rome | AR | 3.36 | DO | *RIC* 187 |

## PLATE 5

| No. | Ruler | Mint | Metal | Weight | Collection | Reference |
|---|---|---|---|---|---|---|
| 1 | Licinius I | Antioch | AV | $\frac{1}{60}$ lb | T | *RIC* 23 |
| 2 | Constantine I | Trier | AV | $\frac{1}{72}$ lb, 4.46 | DO | *RIC* 815 |
| 3 | Constantine I | Ticinum | AV | 4.42 | DO | *RIC* 26 |
| 4 | Constantine I | Rome | AV | 4.62 | DO | *RIC* p. 688 |
| 5 | Constantine I | Thessalonica | AV | 4.44 | DO | *RIC* 18 |
| 6 | Constantine I | Nicomedia | AV | 4.31 | DO | *RIC* 70 |
| 7 | Constantine I | Constantinople | AV | 1.52 | DO | *RIC* 117 |
| 8 | Constantine I | Antioch | AV | 4.45 | DO | *RIC* 98 |
| 9 | Fausta | Thessalonica | AV | 4.56 | DO | *RIC* 137 |
| 10 | Crispus (Caes.) | Cyzicus | AV | 4.47 | DO | *RIC* 20 |
| 11 | Constantine II (Caes.) | Antioch | AV | 4.38 | DO | *RIC* 47 |
| 12 | Constantius II (Caes.) | Constantinople | AV | 4.34 | DO | *RIC* 115 |
| 13 | Delmatius (Caes.) | Constantinople | AV | 4.25 | DO | *RIC* 113 |

| | | | | | |
|---|---|---|---|---|---|
| 14 Constantine I | Siscia | AR | 3.05 | DO | *RIC* 229 |
| 15 Constantine I, Crispus and Constantine II (Caess.) | Sirmium | AR | 4.25 | DO | *RIC* 14 |
| 16 Constantine II (Caes.) | Thessalonica | AR | 3.05 | DO | *RIC* 194 |

PLATE 6

| | | | | | |
|---|---|---|---|---|---|
| 1 Diocletian | London | B | 7.40 | PC | *RIC* 1a |
| 2 Constantine I (Caes.) | Lyons | B | 10.65 | B | *RIC* 190b |
| 3 Constantius I (Caes.) | Ticinum | B | 10.40 | B | *RIC* 32a |
| 4 Maximian | Aquileia | B | 8.21 | B | *RIC* 31b |
| 5 Constantine I (Caes.) | Aquileia | B | 10.51 | DO | *RIC* 111 |
| 6 Maximian | Carthage | B | 9.51 | DO | *RIC* 25b |
| 7 Dom. Domitianus | Alexandria | B | 7.71 | PC | *RIC* 20 |
| 8 Constantius I (Caes.) | Alexandria | B | 9.89 | B | *RIC* 33a |
| 9 Diocletian | Cyzicus | Æ | 3.04 | B | *RIC* 16a |
| 10 Maximian | Cyzicus | Æ | 2.80 | B | *RIC* 16b |
| 11 Severus II | Alexandria | Æ | 3.13 | B | *RIC* 84 |
| 12 Diocletian | Alexandria | Æ | 1.54 | PC | – |

PLATE 7

| | | | | | |
|---|---|---|---|---|---|
| 1 Constantine I | Lyons | B | 6.18 | PC | *RIC* 302 (Mart.) |
| 2 Maximinus | Nicomedia | B | 6.41 | B | *RIC* 66c |
| 3 Constantine I | Cyzicus | B | 6.12 | B | *RIC* 77b |
| 4 Maxentius | Aquileia | B | 4.79 | DO | *RIC* 113 |
| 5 Dom. Alexander | Carthage | B | | BM | *RIC* 70 |
| 6 Maxentius | Ostia | B | 6.75 | B | *RIC* 35 |
| 7 Licinius I | Siscia | B | 6.93 | DO | *RIC* 198b/207b |
| 8 Licinius I | Arles | B | 3.99 | DO | *RIC* 61 |
| 9 Constantine I | Siscia | B | 3.54 | DO | *RIC* 233c |
| 10 Constantine I | Thessalonica | B | 3.76 | DO | *RIC* 61b |
| 11 Licinius II (Caes.) | Trier | B | 3.57 | B | *RIC* 256 |
| 12 Licinius I | Trier | B | 3.87 | B | *RIC* 259 |

| | | | | | |
|---|---|---|---|---|---|
| 13 Crispus (Caes.) | Alexandria | B | 3.29 | B | *RIC* 29 |
| 14 Licinius II (Caes.) | Alexandria | B | 3.49 | DO | *RIC* 30 |
| 15 Constantine I | Arles | B | 2.95 | DO | *RIC* 318 |
| 16 Constantine I | Heraclea | B | 2.46 | DO | *RIC* 121 |
| 17 Hannibalian | Constantinople | B | 1.56 | DO | *RIC* 146/7 |
| 18 Constantius II | Antioch | B | 1.99 | DO | *RIC* 61 |
| 19 Constans I | Alexandria | B | 1.94 | DO | *RIC* 21 |

PLATE 8

| | | | | | |
|---|---|---|---|---|---|
| 1 Constans I | Trier | AV | 4.57 | DO | *RIC* 129 |
| 2 Constantius II | Nicomedia | AV | 4.42 | DO | *RIC* 33 |
| 3 Constantius II | Nicomedia | AV | 4.60 | DO | *RIC* 74 |
| 4 Const. Gallus (Caes.) | Nicomedia | AV | 4.72 | DO | *RIC* 75 |
| 5 Julian (Caes.) | Arles | AV | 4.40 | DO | *RIC* 239 |
| 6 Magnentius | Aquileia | AV | 4.32 | DO | *RIC* 134 |
| 7 Decentius (Caes.) | Trier | AV | 3.96 | DO | *RIC* 293 |
| 8 Julian | Antioch | AV | 4.15 | DO | *RIC* 206 |
| 9 Procopius | Cyzicus | AV | 4.40 | DO | *RIC* 1 |
| 10 Constantius II | Aquileia | AV | 2.26 | DO | *RIC* 8 |
| 11 Constantius II | Rome | AV | 1.59 | B | *RIC* 300 |
| 12 Jovian | Constantinople | AV | 4.42 | DO | *RIC* 169 |
| 13 Valentinian I | Antioch | AV | 4.35 | DO | *RIC* 20d |
| 14 Valens | Trier | AV | 4.46 | DO | *RIC* 17e |
| 15 Valentinian II | Trier | AV | 4.46 | DO | *RIC* 49c(2) |
| 16 Gratian | Sirmium | AV | 4.45 | DO | *RIC* 9a |
| 17 Magnus Maximus | London | AV | | BM | *RIC* 2b |
| 18 Theodosius I | Milan | AV | 4.51 | DO | *RIC* 8b(1) |
| 19 Eugenius | Lyons | AV | 4.46 | DO | *RIC* 45 |
| 20 Theodosius I | Sirmium | AV | 4.45 | B | *RIC* 15a |

PLATE 9

| | | | | | |
|---|---|---|---|---|---|
| 1 Constans I | Siscia | AR | 4.10 | DO | *RIC* 158 |
| 2 Constans I | Thessalonica | AR | 3.20 | DO | *RIC* 98 |
| 3 Constantius II | Sirmium | AR | 2.91 | DO | *RIC* 17 |
| 4 Constantius II | Constantinople | AR | 3.36 | DO | *RIC* 102 |
| 5 Const. Gallus (Caes.) | Lyons | AR | 3.57 | DO | *RIC* 182 |

| | | | | | |
|---|---|---|---|---|---|
| 6 | Valens | Trier | AR | 4.08 | DO | *RIC* 26b(2)/42a(1) |
| 7 | Valens | Rome | AR | 4.42 | DO | *RIC* 8b(4) |
| 8 | Jovian | Nicomedia | AR | 1.97 | DO | *RIC* 127 |
| 9 | Valentinian I | Antioch | AR | 2.14 | DO | *RIC* 33a(1) |
| 10 | Magnus Maximus | Milan | AR | 1.89 | DO | *RIC* 19a |
| 11 | Fl. Victor | Milan | AR | 1.80 | DO | *RIC* 19b |
| 12 | Constantius II | Rome | B | 4.08 | B | *RIC* 128 |
| 13 | Constantius II | Alexandria | B | 6.54 | B | *RIC* 72 |
| 14 | Constans I | Lyons | B | 3.49 | B | *RIC* 84 |
| 15 | Constans I | Aquileia | B | 3.67 | B | *RIC* 103 |
| 16 | Constantius II | Antioch | B | 7.02 | B | *RIC* 125 |
| 17 | Constans I | Trier | B | 2.76 | B | *RIC* 228 |
| 18 | Nepotian | Rome | B | | BM | *RIC* 202 |
| 19 | Vetranio | Thessalonica | B | 4.53 | DO | *RIC* 132 |

PLATE 10

| | | | | | | |
|---|---|---|---|---|---|---|
| 1 | Magnentius | Amiens | B/Æ | 8.55 | T | *RIC* 34 |
| 2 | Julian | Antioch | B | 9.36 | B | *RIC* 216 |
| 3 | Jovian | Thessalonica | B/Æ | 8.18 | DO | *RIC* 235 |
| 4 | Gratian | Aquileia | Æ | 5.00 | DO | *RIC* 30a(2) |
| 5 | Theodosius I | Antioch | Æ | 5.46 | DO | *RIC* 42e(2) |
| 6 | Magnus Maximus | Arles | Æ | 5.48 | DO | *RIC* 26a(1–3) |
| 7 | Theodosius I | Alexandria | Æ | 4.72 | B | *RIC* 18b |
| 8 | Aelia Flaccilla | Constantinople | Æ | 4.65 | DO | *RIC* 55 (5) |
| 9 | Honorius | Aquileia | AV | 4.41 | DO | – |
| 10 | Constantius III | Ravenna | AV | 4.55 | DO | – |
| 11 | Galla Placidia | Ravenna | AV | 4.47 | DO | – |
| 12 | Constantine III | Arles | AV | 4.49 | DO | – |
| 13 | Jovinus | Lyons | AV | 4.29 | DO | – |
| 14 | Priscus Attalus | Rome | AV | 4.43 | DO | – |
| 15 | Johannes | Ravenna | AV | 4.45 | DO | – |
| 16 | Galla Placidia | Ravenna | AV | 1.45 | DO | – |
| 17 | Johannes | Ravenna | AV | 1.41 | DO | – |

PLATE 11

| | | | | | | |
|---|---|---|---|---|---|---|
| 1 | Valentinian III | Rome | AV | 4.48 | DO | – |
| 2 | Justa Grata Honoria | Ravenna | AV | 4.48 | DO | – |
| 3 | Licinia Eudoxia | Ravenna | AV | 4.49 | DO | – |
| 4 | Petronius Maximus | Rome | AV | 4.43 | DO | – |

| | | | | | |
|---|---|---|---|---|---|
| 5 Avitus | Arles | AV | 4.38 | DO | – |
| 6 Majorian | Arles | AV | 4.47 | DO | – |
| 7 Libius Severus | Milan | AV | 4.40 | DO | – |
| 8 Anthemius | Milan | AV | 4.30 | DO | – |
| 9 Aelia Euphemia | Ravenna | AV | 4.48 | DO | – |
| 10 Glycerius | Ravenna | AV | 4.35 | DO | – |
| 11 Julius Nepos (1) | Arles | AV | 4.35 | DO | – |
| 12 Romulus Augustus | Ravenna | AV | 4.42 | DO | – |
| 13 Julius Nepos (2) | Milan | AV | 4.28 | DO | – |
| 14 Libius Severus | Rome | AV | 2.17 | DO | – |
| 15 Anthemius | Ravenna | AV | 2.19 | DO | – |
| 16 Justa Grata Honoria | Ravenna | AV | 1.38 | DO | – |
| 17 Romulus Augustus | Milan | AV | 1.46 | DO | – |
| 18 Julius Nepos (2) | Milan | AV | 1.46 | DO | – |
| 19 Galla Placidia | Rome | AR | 1.87 | DO | – |
| 20 Galla Placidia | Ravenna | AR | 0.98 | DO | – |
| 21 Libius Severus | Rome | AR | 0.95 | DO | – |
| 22 Julius Nepos (1) | Ravenna | AR | 2.07 | DO | – |
| 23 Majorian | Ravenna | Æ | 1.47 | DO | *LRBC* – |
| 24 Libius Severus | Rome | Æ | 0.90 | B | *LRBC* 871 |
| 25 Anthemius | Rome | Æ | 1.53 | DO | *LRBC* 874 |

PLATE 12

| | | | | | |
|---|---|---|---|---|---|
| 1 Arcadius | Constantinople | AV | 4.47 | DO | – |
| 2 Aelia Eudoxia | Constantinople | AV | 4.49 | DO | – |
| 3 Theodosius II | Constantinople | AV | 4.37 | DO | – |
| 4 Theodosius II | Constantinople | AV | 4.48 | DO | – |
| 5 Aelia Pulcheria | Constantinople | AV | 4.32 | DO | – |
| 6 Aelia Eudocia | Constantinople | AV | 4.47 | DO | – |
| 7 Marcian | Constantinople | AV | 4.49 | DO | – |
| 8 Leo I | Constantinople | AV | 4.46 | DO | – |
| 9 Aelia Verina | Constantinople | AV | | DO | – |
| 10 Leo II and Zeno | Constantinople | AV | 4.47 | DO | – |
| 11 Basiliscus and Marcus | Constantinople | AV | 4.46 | DO | – |
| 12 Zeno | Antioch | AV | | BM | – |
| 13 Theodosius II | Constantinople | AV | 2.22 | DO | – |
| 14 Marcian | Constantinople | AV | 2.22 | DO | – |
| 15 Leo I | Constantinople | AV | 2.23 | DO | – |

| | | | | | |
|---|---|---|---|---|---|
| 16 Arcadius | Constantinople | AV | 1.49 | DO | – |
| 17 Aelia Pulcheria | Constantinople | AV | 1.48 | DO | – |
| 18 Zeno | Constantinople | AV | 1.49 | DO | – |
| 19 Arcadius | Constantinople | AR | 1.98 | DO | – |
| 20 Theodosius II | Constantinople | AR | 1.22 | DO | – |
| 21 Aelia Pulcheria | Constantinople | AR | 1.69 | DO | – |
| 22 Zeno | Constantinople | AR | 1.96 | DO | – |
| 23 Theodosius II | Constantinople | Æ | 1.33 | DO | *LRBC* 2245–6 |
| 24 Theodosius II | Alexandria | Æ | 0.99 | DO | *LRBC* – |
| 25 Marcian | Constantinople | Æ | 1.12 | DO | *LRBC* 2250 |
| 26 Marcian | Nicomedia | Æ | 1.55 | DO | *LRBC* 2464 |
| 27 Leo I | Constantinople | Æ | 1.36 | DO | *LRBC* 2262–4 |
| 28 Zeno | Constantinople | Æ | 1.05 | DO | *LRBC* 2279 |

PLATE 13

| | | | | | |
|---|---|---|---|---|---|
| 1 Leo I | Constantinople | Æ | 3.67 | B | above, p. 491, n. 203 |
| 2 Leo I | Constantinople | Æ | 3.75 | DO | above, p. 491, n. 203 |
| 3 Aelia Verina | Constantinople | Æ | 5.94 | DO | above, p. 491, n. 203 |
| 4 Zeno | Constantinople | Æ | 5.39 | DO | above, p. 491, n. 203 |
| 5 Anastasius I | Constantinople | AV | 4.48 | B | *DOC* 7a–j |
| 6 Justin I | Constantinople | AV | 4.49 | DO | *DOC* 2e |
| 7 Justin I and Justinian I | Constantinople | AV | 4.31 | B | *DOC* 1a–(c) |
| 8 Justinian I | Carthage | AV | 4.31 | B | *DOC* 277a.1–e.3 |
| 9 Justin II | Constantinople | AV | 4.41 | DO | *DOC* 4f |
| 10 Anastasius I | Constantinople | AV | 4.37 | PC | *DOC* – |
| 11 Tiberius II, Constantine | Constantinople | AV | 4.40 | DO | *DOC* 2 |
| 12 Maurice Tiberius | Constantinople | AV | 4.45 | DO | *DOC* 2a |
| 13 Phocas | Constantinople | AV | 4.37 | DO | *DOC* 3.1 |
| 14 Anastasius I | Constantinople | AV | 2.13 | DO | *DOC* 8.1 |
| 15 Tiberius II, Constantine | Constantinople | AV | 2.19 | DO | *DOC* 5 |
| 16 Phocas | Constantinople | AV | 2.15 | DO | *DOC* 15 |
| 17 Anastasius | Constantinople | AV | 1.48 | B | *DOC* 10a.1–16 |
| 18 Justinian I | Constantinople | AV | 1.22 | DO | *DOC* 19.10 |
| 19 Maurice Tiberius | Constantinople | AV | 1.50 | DO | *DOC* 14.1 |
| 20 Justinian I | Constantinople | AR | 4.29 | DO | *DOC* 21.1 |
| 21 Maurice Tiberius | Constantinople | AR | 2.17 | DO | *MIB* 55 |

PLATE 14

| | | | | | |
|---|---|---|---|---|---|
| 1 Anastasius I | Constantinople | Æ | 9.35 | DO | *DOC* 16a.2 |
| 2 Anastasius I | Nicomedia | Æ | 4.71 | DO | *DOC* 36.5 |
| 3 Anastasius I | Nicomedia | Æ | 1.71 | B | *DOC* 38.1–3 |
| 4 Anastasius I | Constantinople | Æ | 18.39 | B | *DOC* 23f.1–10 |
| 5 Justin I | Thessalonica | Æ | 15.15 | B | *DOC* 23.1–3 |
| 6 Justin I | Antioch | Æ | 14.36 | B | *DOC* 48a–(b) |
| 7 Justinian I | Antioch | Æ | 16.98 | B | *DOC* 206a.1–d.5 |
| 8 Justin I and Justinian I | Antioch | Æ | 15.94 | B | *DOC* (14) |
| 9 Justinian I | Rome | Æ | 9.97 | B | *DOC* 321a.1–3 |
| 10 Anastasius I | Constantinople | Æ | 8.67 | B | *DOC* 24a.1–g.2 |
| 11 Justinian I | Constantinople | Æ | 4.09 | DO | *DOC* 34.5 |
| 12 Anastasius I | Constantinople | Æ | 1.87 | B | *DOC* 26a.1–d.3 |
| 13 Justin I | Antioch | Æ | 1.24 | DO | *DOC* 56c.bis* |

PLATE 15

| | | | | | |
|---|---|---|---|---|---|
| 1 Justinian I | Constantinople | Æ | 17.76 | B | *DOC* 39a.1–e |
| 2 Tiberius II, Constantine | Cyzicus | Æ | 17.38 | B | *DOC* 35a–b.2 |
| 3 Maurice Tiberius | Antioch | Æ | 12.34 | B | *DOC* 159b.1–c.3 |
| 4 Tiberius II, Constantine | Constantinople | Æ | 11.54 | DO | *DOC* 15b.3 |
| 5 Justinian I | Cyzicus | Æ | 9.23 | B | *DOC* cf. 187a–188 |
| 6 Tiberius II, Constantine | Constantinople | Æ | 7.59 | DO | *DOC* 17b.2 |
| 7 Phocas | Nicomedia | Æ | 5.14 | DO | *DOC* 64a |
| 8 Justinian I | Antioch | Æ | 4.40 | B | *DOC* cf. 252, (253) |
| 9 Justin II | Constantinople | Æ | 3.86 | DO | *DOC* 59.4 |
| 10 Justinian I | Constantinople | Æ | 3.65 | DO | *DOC* 96a.1 |
| 11 Justin II | Constantinople | Æ | 1.81 | DO | *DOC* 60c.3 |

PLATE 16

| | | | | | |
|---|---|---|---|---|---|
| 1 Heraclii ('Interrregnum') | Carthage | AV | 4.42 | B | *DOC* (3) |
| 2 Heraclii ('Interregnum') | Carthage | AR | 0.71 | B | *DOC* (4) |

| | | | | | |
|---|---|---|---|---|---|
| 3 Heraclii ('Interregnum') | Carthage | Æ | 3.51 | DO | *DOC* 8.2 |
| 4 Heraclii ('Interregnum') | Alexandria | AV | 4.47 | DO | *DOC* 10.2 |
| 5 Heraclii ('Interregnum') | Alexandria | AV | 4.41 | DO | *DOC* 13 |
| 6 Heraclii ('Interregnum') | Alexandretta | Æ | 7.90 | B | *DOC* (15), 16 |
| 7 Heraclii ('Interregnum') | Alexandretta | Æ | 4.16 | DO | *DOC* p. 214, n. 16 |
| 8 Heraclii ('Interregnum') | Cyprus | Æ | | T | *DOC* (18) |
| 9 Heraclius, Hera. Const. and Martina | Cyprus | Æ | 6.37 | B | *DOC* 184a.1–185 bis |
| 10 Phocas | Jerusalem | AV | | BM | *MIB* 30 ('Cyprus') |
| 11 Heraclius | Jerusalem | AV | 4.48 | B | *DOC* 186 ('Alexandria') |
| 12 Heraclius and Hera. Const. | Jerusalem | AV | 4.52 | B | *DOC* 187c.1-3 ('Alexandria') |
| 13 Heraclius | Jerusalem | Æ | | PC | *MIB* x 27–8, and p. 110 |
| 14 Heraclius | Jerusalem | Æ | | PC | *MIB* x 27–8, and p. 110 |
| 15 Heraclius | Seleucia | Æ | 10.64 | B | *DOC* 179–(180b) |
| 16 Heraclius | Isaura | Æ | 9.88 | B | *DOC* (183) |

PLATE 17

| | | | | | |
|---|---|---|---|---|---|
| 1 Heraclius | Constantinople | AV | 4.42 | DO | *DOC* 1b.2 |
| 2 Heraclius, Hera. Const. and Heraclonas | Constantinople | AV | 4.33 | B | *DOC* $39^{2}$a, b |
| 3 Constans II | Constantinople | AV | 4.43 | DO | *DOC* 3.1 |
| 4 Constans II | Constantinople | AV | 4.42 | DO | *DOC* 41.c |
| 5 Constantine IV | Constantinople | AV | 4.40 | DO | *DOC* 6c.2 |
| 6 Justinian II (1) | Constantinople | AV | 4.49 | DO | *DOC* 1b |
| 7 Justinian II (1) | Constantinople | AV | 4.41 | DO | *DOC* 7e.2 |
| 8 Leontius | Constantinople | AV | 4.31 | DO | *DOC* 1a.3 |
| 9 Tiberius III, Apsimar | Constantinople | AV | 4.35 | DO | *DOC* 1b |
| 10 Justinian II (2) and Tiberius | Constantinople | AV | 4.27 | DO | *DOC* 2a.10 |

| | | | | | | |
|---|---|---|---|---|---|---|
| 11 | Philippicus | Constantinople | AV | 4.43 | DO | *DOC* 1b. |
| 12 | Anastasius II, Artemius | Constantinople | AV | 4.47 | DO | *DOC* 2a.1 |
| 13 | Theodosius III | Constantinople | AV | 4.43 | DO | *DOC* 1b.2 |
| 14 | Constans II | Constantinople | AV | 2.22 | B | *DOC* 44.1–5 |
| 15 | Constans II | Constantinople | AV | 1.58 | B | *DOC* 45.1–6 |
| 16 | Leontius | Constantinople | AV | 1.97 | DO | *DOC* 3.4 |
| 17 | Anastasius II, Artemius | Constantinople | AV | 1.37 | DO | *DOC* 5.1 |
| 18 | Justinian II (2) and Tiberius | Constantinople | AV | 2.15 | B | *DOC* 4a |
| 19 | Justinian II (2) and Tiberius | Constantinople | AV | 1.40 | B | *DOC* 6b.1–4 |
| 20 | Heraclius | Cyzicus | Æ | 11.34 | DO | *DOC* 169a.9 |
| 21 | Heraclius and Hera. Const. | Constantinople | Æ | 10.90 | B | *DOC* 105a.1–d.2 |
| 22 | Heraclius, Hera. Const. and Heraclonas | Constantinople | Æ | 4.74 | DO | *DOC* 125d.3 |
| 23 | Constans II | Constantinople | Æ | 1.49 | DO | *DOC* 93a.2 |

PLATE 18

| | | | | | | |
|---|---|---|---|---|---|---|
| 1 | Constantine IV | Constantinople | Æ | 17.31 | B | *DOC* 28a–e.4 |
| 2 | Constantine IV | Constantinople | Æ | 12.33 | DO | *DOC* 34 |
| 3 | Constantine IV | Constantinople | Æ | 7.36 | ANS | *DOC* 37.1–9 |
| 4 | Constantine IV | Constantinople | Æ | 4.30 | B | *DOC* 38.1–9 |
| 5 | Constantine IV | Constantinople | Æ | 2.25 | DO | *DOC* 40.3 |
| 6 | Leontius | Constantinople | Æ | 7.85 | DO | *DOC* 5a |
| 7 | Tiberius III, Apsimar | Constantinople | Æ | 5.39 | DO | *DOC* 8b.1 |
| 8 | Philippicus | Constantinople | Æ | 3.54 | DO | *DOC* 10 |
| 9 | 'Heraclius' | 'Sicily' | Æ | 17.79 | B | *DOC* 241a.1–e |
| 10 | 'Heraclius and Hera. Const.' | Constantinople 'Sicily' | Æ | 9.60 | DO | *DOC* 242b.3 |
| 11 | 'Heraclius and Hera. Const.' | Constantinople 'Sicily' | Æ | 10.04 | DO | *DOC* 243.1 |
| 12 | Constans II | Constantinople | Æ | 4.76 | B | *DOC* (9a)–f |

PLATE 19

| | | | | | | |
|---|---|---|---|---|---|---|
| 1 | Justinian I | Constantinople | AV | 3.74 | B | *DOC* 10, 11 |
| 2 | Justin II | Constantinople | AV | 3.72 | B | *DOC* (9)–(11) |

| | | | | | | |
|---|---|---|---|---|---|---|
| 3 | Maurice Tiberius | Constantinople | AV | 3.70 | B | *MIB* 14[1,2] |
| 4 | Justinian I | Constantinople | AV | 4.10 | B | *DOC* (16) |
| 5 | Justin II | Constantinople | AV | 4.05 | B | *DOC* 138 ('Antioch') |
| 6 | Justin II and Tiberius II, Constantine | Constantinople | AV | | BM | *DOC* (1), (2) ('Antioch') |
| 7 | Tiberius II, Constantine | Constantinople | AV | 4.05 | B | *DOC* 38.1, 2 ('Antioch') |
| 8 | Tiberius II, Constantine | Ravenna | AV | 4.01 | B | *DOC* (63) |
| 9 | Maurice Tiberius | Constantinople | AV | 3.96 | B | *DOC* 8 |
| 10 | Phocas | Constantinople | AV | 4.02 | B | *DOC* (8a)–(c) |
| 11 | Heraclius, Hera. Const. and Heraclonas | Constantinople | AV | 4.06 | B | *DOC* (46) |
| 12 | Constans II | Constantinople | AV | 4.26 | B | *DOC* (22a)–(f) |
| 13 | Constans II | Constantinople | AV | 4.28 | B | *DOC* (24a)–(d) |
| 14 | Heraclius and Hera. Const. | Constantinople | AR | 6.49 | B | *DOC* 61.1–4 |
| 15 | Constans II | Constantinople | AR | 6.42 | B | *DOC* 50.1–12 |
| 16 | Constantine IV | Constantinople | AR | 6.85 | DO | *DOC* 23.1 |
| 17 | Constantine IV | Constantinople | AR | 5.60 | DO | *DOC* 27.2 |
| 18 | Justinian II (1) | Constantinople | AR | 6.41 | DO | *DOC* 17 |
| 19 | Tiberius III, Apsimar | Constantinople | AR | 6.07 | DO | *DOC* 6 |
| 20 | Philippicus | Constantinople | AR | 6.29 | B | *DOC* (8) |

PLATE 20

| | | | | | | |
|---|---|---|---|---|---|---|
| 1 | Theodosius II | Thessalonica | AV | 4.44 | DO | above, p. 398, n. 117 |
| 2 | Leo I | Thessalonica | AV | 4.37 | DO | above, p. 398, n. 117 |
| 3 | Zeno | Thessalonica | AV | 4.39 | B | above, p. 398, n. 117 |
| 4 | Zeno | Thessalonica | AV | 4.48 | DO | above, p. 398, n. 117 |
| 5 | Anastasius I | Thessalonica | AV | 4.46 | B | *DOC* 27 |
| 6 | Justinian I | Thessalonica | Æ | 7.45 | B | *DOC* 98d.1–6 |
| 7 | Justinian I | Thessalonica | Æ | 3.92 | DO | *DOC* 100a.1 |
| 8 | Justinian I | Thessalonica | Æ | 1.45 | DO | *DOC* 101 |
| 9 | Justinian I | Thessalonica | Æ | 1.51 | DO | *DOC* 102.1 |
| 10 | Justin II | Thessalonica | Æ | 4.79 | DO | *DOC* 63.4 |

| | | | | | | |
|---|---|---|---|---|---|---|
| 11 | Maurice Tiberius | Thessalonica | Æ | 6.26 | DO | *DOC* 82.1 |
| 12 | Phocas and Leontia | Thessalonica | Æ | 4.74 | DO | *DOC* 51.6 |
| 13 | Phocas | Thessalonica | Æ | 10.89 | DO | *DOC* 47.2 |
| 14 | Justinian I | Carthage ('Africa') | AV | 4.36 | BN | *MIB* 26 |
| 15 | Justinian I | Carthage | AV | 4.48 | DO | *DOC* 277b |
| 16 | Tiberius II, Constantine | Carthage | AV | 4.44 | B | *MIB* 14 |
| 17 | Maurice Tiberius | Carthage | AV | 4.49 | B | *DOC* 226 |
| 18 | Phocas | Carthage | AV | 4.50 | B | *MIB* 32[1] |
| 19 | Heraclius and Hera. Const. | Carthage | AV | 4.48 | B | *DOC* (217) |
| 20 | Constans II and Constantine IV | Carthage | AV | 4.30 | B | *DOC* (122) |
| 21 | Constantine IV | Carthage | AV | 4.18 | B | *DOC* cf. 48 |
| 22 | Justinian II (1) | Carthage | AV | 4.41 | DO | *DOC* 28 |
| 23 | Maurice Tiberius | Carthage | AR | 0.90 | DO | *DOC* 240.1, 2* |
| 24 | Theodosius (s. of Maur. Tib.) | Carthage | AR | 1.40 | B | *DOC* (307, 8) |

PLATE 21

| | | | | | | |
|---|---|---|---|---|---|---|
| 1 | Theodosius (s. of Maur. Tib.) | Carthage | AR | 0.68 | DO | *DOC* 306* |
| 2 | Heraclius | Carthage | AR | 0.72 | DO | *DOC* 231* |
| 3 | Heraclius | Carthage | AR | 0.68 | DO | *DOC* 233.5 |
| 4 | Constans II | Carthage | AR | 0.48 | B | *DOC* 132.1–3 |
| 5 | Justinian I | Carthage | Æ | 22.98 | DO | *DOC* 293.2 |
| 6 | Justin II and Sophia | Carthage | Æ | 18.58 | DO | *DOC* 198.1 |
| 7 | Justinian II (1) | Carthage | Æ | 3.78 | DO | *DOC* 29* |
| 8 | Phocas | Carthage | Æ | 6.54 | DO | *DOC* 116.5 |
| 9 | Constans II | Carthage | Æ | 4.26 | B | *DOC* 138.1–10 |
| 10 | Tiberius III, Apsimar | Sardinia | AV | 4.35 | B | *DOC* 15 |
| 11 | Justinian I | Rome | AV | 4.46 | DO | *DOC* 319* |
| 12 | Justinian I | Ravenna | AV | 4.44 | DO | *DOC* 333a |
| 13 | Justin II | Ravenna | AV | 4.42 | B | *DOC* 210a–(c) |
| 14 | Maurice Tiberius | Ravenna | AV | 4.48 | B | *DOC* 285a.1–(e) |
| 15 | Phocas | Ravenna | AV | 4.48 | B | *DOC* 124a, (b) |
| 16 | Heraclius and Hera. Const. | Ravenna | AV | 4.51 | B | *DOC* 271a–(d) |
| 17 | Constans II | Ravenna | AV | 4.39 | DO | *DOC* 200 |

| | | | | | |
|---|---|---|---|---|---|
| 18 Justin II | Ravenna | AV | 1.45 | DO | *DOC* 212 |
| 19 Tiberius II, Constantine | Ravenna | AV | 1.50 | B | *DOC* 64.1, 2 |
| 20 Heraclius | Ravenna | AV | 1.46 | B | *DOC* (276) |
| 21 Constans II | Ravenna | AV | 1.45 | B | *DOC* (201), 2 |
| 22 Justinian I | Ravenna | AR | 1.05 | B | *DOC* 334d.1–(g) |
| 23 Justinian I | Ravenna | AR | 0.50 | DO | *DOC* 335c |
| 24 Justinian I | Rome | AR | 0.71 | DO | *DOC* 336.1 ('Ravenna') |

PLATE 22

| | | | | | |
|---|---|---|---|---|---|
| 1 Justin II | Ravenna | AR | 0.74 | B | *DOC* 213a–b.2 |
| 2 Phocas | Ravenna | AR | 0.41 | DO | *DOC* 130a.2 |
| 3 Heraclius | Ravenna | AR | 0.37 | B | *DOC* 281.1–4 |
| 4 Heraclius and Hera. Const. | Ravenna | AR | 7.00 | DO | *DOC* 277.1 |
| 5 Justinian I | Ravenna | Æ | 8.85 | DO | *DOC* 342.1 |
| 6 Heraclius, Hera. Const. and Martina | Ravenna | Æ | 8.08 | B | *DOC* (290) |
| 7 Constantine IV | Ravenna | Æ | 3.66 | DO | *DOC* 91 |
| 8 Maurice Tiberius | Ravenna | Æ | 2.73 | DO | *DOC* cf. 291* |
| 9 Justin II | Alexandria | AV | | BM | *DOC* (187) |
| 10 Justinian I | Alexandria | Æ | 13.52 | B | *DOC* 273. 1–4 |
| 11 Justin II | Alexandria | Æ | 4.36 | B | *DOC* 188.1–5 |
| 12 Maurice Tiberius | Alexandria | Æ | 3.97 | B | *DOC* 213.1–11 |
| 13 Heraclius, Hera. Const. and Heraclonas | Alexandria | Æ | 7.63 | B | *DOC* 197.1–6 |
| 14 Heraclius | Alexandria | Æ | 2.47 | B | *DOC* 198.1–14 |
| 15 Heraclius | Alexandria | Æ | 2.81 | B | *DOC* 201.1, 2 |
| 16 Maurice Tiberius and Constantina | Cherson | Æ | 13.37 | B | *DOC* 299.1–300.3 |
| 17 Maurice Tiberius and Constantina | Cherson | Æ | 5.03 | DO | *DOC* 301 |
| 18 Justinian I | Spain | AV | 1.50 | BM | *DOC* (376) |
| 19 Heraclius | Spain | AV | 1.38 | DO | *DOC* 312 |
| 20 Justinian I | Salona | Æ | 5.85 | DO | *DOC* 358.2 |
| 21 Maurice Tiberius | Catania | Æ | 2.84 | B | *DOC* (265) |
| 22 Heraclius | Catania | Æ | 4.08 | DO | *DOC* 251.1 |

PLATE 23

| | | | | | | |
|---|---|---|---|---|---|---|
| 1 | Leo III | Constantinople | AV | 4.42 | DO | *DOC* 1b |
| 2 | Leo III and Constantine V | Constantinople | AV | 4.44 | DO | *DOC* 4a.2 |
| 3 | Artavasdus | Constantinople | AV | 4.45 | DO | *DOC* 2a |
| 4 | Constantine V | Constantinople | AV | 4.43 | DO | *DOC* 1c |
| 5 | Constantine V and Leo IV | Constantinople | AV | 4.45 | DO | *DOC* 2c.3 |
| 6 | Leo IV and Const. VI | Constantinople | AV | 4.35 | DO | *DOC* 1b.5 |
| 7 | Const. VI and Irene | Constantinople | AV | 4.42 | DO | *DOC* 1.3 |
| 8 | Irene | Constantinople | AV | 4.39 | DO | *DOC* 1a.4 |
| 9 | Nicephorus I | Constantinople | AV | 4.45 | DO | *DOC* 2a.4 |
| 10 | Michael I | Constantinople | AV | 4.38 | DO | *DOC* 1a.4 |
| 11 | Leo V | Constantinople | AV | 4.44 | DO | *DOC* 2a.2 |
| 12 | Michael II | Constantinople | AV | 4.43 | DO | *DOC* 1 |
| 13 | Leo III and Const. V | Constantinople | AR | 2.10 | B | *DOC* 22b.1–3 |
| 14 | Leo IV and Const. VI | Constantinople | AR | 2.19 | DO | *DOC* 3.1 |
| 15 | Const. VI and Irene | Constantinople | AR | 1.66 | DO | *DOC* 4a.7 |
| 16 | Michael I and Theophylact | Constantinople | AR | 2.03 | B | *DOC* 3.1–6 |
| 17 | Leo V and Const. | Constantinople | AR | 2.09 | DO | *DOC* 4.3 |
| 18 | Leo III | Constantinople | AV | 2.17 | DO | *DOC* 8 |
| 19 | Artavasdus | Constantinople | AV | 2.20 | DO | *DOC* 4 |
| 20 | Leo III and Const. V | Constantinople | AV | 1.32 | DO | *DOC* 18a.3 |
| 21 | Leo III and Const. V | Constantinople | AR | 0.85 | DO | *DOC* 23 |

PLATE 24

| | | | | | | |
|---|---|---|---|---|---|---|
| 1 | Leo III | Constantinople | Æ | 7.49 | DO | *DOC* 24 |
| 2 | Leo III | Constantinople | Æ | 2.40 | DO | *DOC* 25 |
| 3 | Leo III | Constantinople | Æ | 7.60 | B | *DOC* 29a–d.3 |
| 4 | Leo III | Constantinople | Æ | 2.28 | DO | *DOC* 33.2 |
| 5 | Leo III and Const. V | Constantinople | Æ | 6.20 | DO | *DOC* 38a.1 |

| | | | | | | |
|---|---|---|---|---|---|---|
| 6 | Leo III and Const. V | Constantinople | Æ | 1.97 | DO | *DOC* 41b |
| 7 | Leo IV and Const. VI | Constantinople | Æ | 5.01 | DO | *DOC* 4.5 |
| 8 | Leo IV and Const. VI | Constantinople | Æ | 2.24 | DO | *DOC* 5.5 |
| 9 | Michael II | Constantinople | Æ | 5.30 | B | *DOC* 7.1–4 |
| 10 | Theophilus | Constantinople | AV | 4.49 | DO | *DOC* 1a.1–(d) |
| 11 | Theophilus, Theodora and Thecla | Constantinople | AV | 4.41 | DO | *DOC* 4 |
| 12 | Theophilus | Constantinople | AV | 4.45 | DO | *DOC* 5 |
| 13 | Theodora | Constantinople | AV | 4.49 | DO | *DOC* 1a.1 |
| 14 | Michael III | Constantinople | AV | 4.45 | DO | *DOC* 3.1 |
| 15 | Basil I | Constantinople | AV | 4.38 | DO | *DOC* 1 |
| 16 | Leo VI | Constantinople | AV | 4.37 | DO | *DOC* 1b.1 |
| 17 | Leo VI and Const. VII | Constantinople | AV | 4.43 | DO | *DOC* 2.1 |
| 18 | Alexander | Constantinople | AV | 4.48 | DO | *DOC* 2.1 |
| 19 | Const. VII and Zoë | Constantinople | AV | 4.42 | DO | *DOC* 2.1 |

PLATE 25

| | | | | | | |
|---|---|---|---|---|---|---|
| 1 | Constantine VII and Romanus I | Constantinople | AV | 4.40 | DO | *DOC* 10.2 |
| 2 | Constantine VII | Constantinople | AV | 4.47 | DO | *DOC* 13a.1 |
| 3 | Romanus II | Constantinople | AV | 4.38 | DO | *DOC* 2 |
| 4 | Michael II and Theophilus | Constantinople | AR | 2.04 | B | *DOC* 6.1–11 |
| 5 | Theophilus and Michael III | Constantinople | AR | 2.11 | B | *DOC* 12.1–6 |
| 6 | Basil I and Constantine | Constantinople | AR | 2.80 | B | *DOC* 7.1–20 |
| 7 | Romanus I, Const. VII, Stephen and Const. | Constantinople | AR | 2.67 | B | *DOC* 20.1–16 |
| 8 | John I | Constantinople | AR | 2.79 | B | *DOC* 7b.1–6 |
| 9 | Michael II and Theophilus | Constantinople | Æ | 8.68 | B | *DOC* 9.1–10 |
| 10 | Theophilus | Constantinople | Æ | 7.86 | B | *DOC* 15a.1–17 |
| 11 | Michael III and Basil I | Constantinople | Æ | 7.00 | B | *DOC* 8.1–7 |

| | | | | | |
|---|---|---|---|---|---|
| 12 Basil I, Const. and Leo VI | Constantinople | Æ | 7.37 | B | *DOC* 10d.1–3 |
| 13 Leo VI | Constantinople | Æ | 9.30 | B | *DOC* 5.1–8 |
| 14 Nicephorus II | Constantinople | Æ | 8.94 | B | *DOC* 8.1–10 |
| 15 Theophilus | Constantinople | Æ | 4.34 | DO | *DOC* 16b.3 |

PLATE 26

| | | | | | |
|---|---|---|---|---|---|
| 1 Michael II and Theophilus | Thessalonica(?) | Æ | 7.17 | DO | *DOC* 10.10 ('Constantinople') |
| 2 Theophilus | Thessalonica(?) | Æ | 6.17 | DO | *DOC* 17.4 |
| 3 Basil I and Constantine | Thessalonica(?) | Æ | 5.07 | DO | *DOC* 8a.2 ('Constantinople') |
| 4 Basil I | Thessalonica(?) | Æ | 4.39 | B | *DOC* 13a.1–4 ('Constantinople') |
| 5 Leo VI and Alexander | Thessalonica(?) | Æ | 3.52 | DO | *DOC* 7a.2 ('Constantinople') |
| 6 Basil I | A/ | Æ | 1.46 | DO | *DOC* 6 |
| 7 Constans II and Constantine IV | Syracuse | A/ | 4.37 | B | *DOC* (156a)–(d) |
| 8 Mezezius | 'Syracuse' | A/ | 4.49 | B | above, p. 421, n. 216 |
| 9 Justinian II | Syracuse | A/ | 4.16 | DO | *DOC* 43* |
| 10 Leo III | Syracuse | A/ | 3.93 | DO | *DOC* 44 |
| 11 Michael I | Syracuse | A/ | 3.82 | DO | *DOC* 4 |
| 12 Theophilus | Syracuse | A/ | 3.87 | B | *DOC* 24.1–3 |
| 13 Constantine V | Syracuse | A/ | 1.86 | DO | *DOC* 16.1 |
| 14 Basil I | Syracuse | 'A/' | 1.06 | DO | *DOC* 14a |
| 15 Constans II | Syracuse | A/ | 1.53 | B | *DOC* 171a–f |
| 16 Philippicus | Syracuse | A/ | 1.25 | DO | *DOC* 18* |
| 17 Constans II | Syracuse | Æ | 4.83 | DO | *DOC* 177a.2 |
| 18 Constantine IV | Syracuse | Æ | 4.77 | DO | *DOC* 61.4 |
| 19 Leo V and Const. | Syracuse | Æ | 3.91 | DO | *DOC* 19a.8 |
| 20 Theophilus | Syracuse | Æ | 3.66 | DO | *DOC* 30.2 |
| 21 Michael III | Syracuse | Æ | 3.19 | DO | *DOC* 12.3 |

PLATE 27

| | | | | | |
|---|---|---|---|---|---|
| 1 Constans II | Rome | A/ | 4.35 | B | *MIB* 113 |
| 2 Constantine IV | Rome | A/ | 4.31 | B | *MIB* – |

| | | | | | | |
|---|---|---|---|---|---|---|
| 3 | Tiberius III | Rome | AV | 4.22 | DO | *MIB* 57 |
| 4 | Leo III | Rome | AV | 4.19 | B | *DOC* cf. (66)–74 |
| 5 | Constantine V and Leo IV | Rome | 'AV' | 2.84 | DO | *DOC* 27 |
| 6 | Constans II | Rome | AV | 1.45 | DO | *DOC* 190* |
| 7 | Constantine V | Rome | AV | 1.47 | B | *DOC* 38 |
| 8 | Leo IV | Rome | AV | 1.30 | DO | *DOC* 10 |
| 9 | Constans II | Rome | Æ | 3.41 | DO | *DOC* 194.4 |
| 10 | Leontius | Rome | Æ | 0.97 | DO | *DOC* 25.2 |
| 11 | Leo III | Rome | AR | 0.32 | DO | *DOC* 92 |
| 12 | Constantine IV | Rome | Æ | 2.14 | DO | *DOC* 82.2 |
| 13 | Leo III | Naples | AV | 4.00 | DO | *DOC* 60 |
| 14 | Nicephorus I | Naples | AV | 4.11 | DO | *DOC* 12 |
| 15 | Theophilus | Naples | AV | 4.17 | DO | *DOC* 31c.2 |
| 16 | Theophilus and Constantine | Naples | AV | 4.18 | DO | *DOC* 33a.2 |
| 17 | Constans II | Naples | Æ | 2.84 | DO | *DOC* 186.1 |
| 18 | Michael III | Cherson | Æ/Pb | 2.22 | DO | *DOC* 15.1 |
| 19 | Basil I | Cherson | Æ/Pb | 2.61 | DO | *DOC* 20a.9 |
| 20 | Leo VI | Cherson | Æ/Pb | 2.57 | DO | *DOC* 9.3 |
| 21 | Constantine VII and Romanus I | Cherson | Æ/Pb | 3.69 | DO | *DOC* 38.2 |
| 22 | John I | Cherson | Æ/Pb | 3.10 | DO | *DOC* 8.2 |

PLATE 28

| | | | | | | |
|---|---|---|---|---|---|---|
| 1 | Basil II and Constantine VIII | Constantinople | AV | 4.42 | B | *DOC* 6a.1–11 |
| 2 | Romanus III | Constantinople | AV | 4.41 | B | *DOC* 1b.1–10 |
| 3 | Michael IV | Thessalonica | AV | 4.38 | ANS | *DOC* 2 |
| 4 | Constantine IX | Constantinople | AV | 4.36 | B | *DOC* 4a.1–3 |
| 5 | Theodora | Constantinople | AV | 4.46 | B | *DOC* 1a.1–11 |
| 6 | Michael VI | Constantinople | AV | 4.36 | B | *DOC* 1b.1–3 |
| 7 | Eudocia with Michael VII and Constantius | Constantinople | AV | 4.33 | B | *DOC* 1.1–6 |
| 8 | Michael VII | Constantinople | AV | 4.34 | B | *DOC* 2d.1–22 |
| 9 | Nicephorus III | Constantinople | 'AV' | 4.30 | B | *DOC* 3b.1–16 |
| 10 | Basil II and Constantine VIII | Constantinople | AV | 4.23 | B | *DOC* 15b.1–4 |
| 11 | Constantine VIII | Constantinople | AV | 4.08 | B | *DOC* 4.1, 2 |
| 12 | Theodora | Constantinople | AV | 4.01 | B | *DOC* 2.1–14 |
| 13 | Michael VI | Constantinople | AV | 4.01 | B | *DOC* 2.1–4 |
| 14 | Isaac I | Constantinople | AV | 3.99 | B | *DOC* 3.1–3 |

| | | | | | | |
|---|---|---|---|---|---|---|
| 15 | Constantine X | Constantinople | AV | 4.07 | B | *DOC* 3a.1–4 |
| 16 | Romanus IV and Eudocia | Constantinople | AV | 4.04 | DO | *DOC* 3.5 |
| 17 | Nicephorus III | Constantinople | 'AV' | 4.03 | B | *DOC* 5b–(d) |

PLATE 29

| | | | | | | |
|---|---|---|---|---|---|---|
| 1 | Basil I and Constantine VIII | Constantinople | AR | 2.59 | B | *DOC* 20a–e |
| 2 | Constantine IX | Constantinople | AR | 2.76 | B | *DOC* 7a.1–7 |
| 3 | Theodora | Constantinople | AR | 1.64 | B | *DOC* 3 |
| 4 | Constantine X | Constantinople | AR | 1.66 | DO | *DOC* 6b.1 |
| 5 | Michael VII and Maria | Constantinople | AR | 2.06 | DO | *DOC* 6c |
| 6 | Romanus IV | Constantinople | AR | 0.72 | DO | *DOC* 7.3 |
| 7 | Anonymous 'A2' | Constantinople | Æ | 12.52 | B | *DOC* A2.36.1–3 |
| 8 | Anonymous 'C' | Constantinople | Æ | 9.25 | B | *DOC* C.1–48 |
| 9 | Anonymous 'D' | Constantinople | Æ | 8.76 | DO | *DOC* D.14 |
| 10 | Anonymous 'G' | Constantinople | Æ | 12.01 | B | *DOC* G.1–28 |
| 11 | Constantine X and Eudocia | Constantinople | Æ | 9.09 | B | *DOC* 8.1–32 |
| 12 | Romanus IV | Constantinople | Æ | 6.76 | DO | *DOC* 8.12 |
| 13 | Nicephorus III | Constantinople | Æ | 5.55 | DO | *DOC* 9.13 |

PLATE 30

| | | | | | | |
|---|---|---|---|---|---|---|
| 1 | Alexius I | Constantinople | 'AV' | 4.30 | PC | *DOC* 2a.1–(c.3) |
| 2 | Alexius I | Thessalonica | 'AV' | 4.18 | PC | *DOC* 5a.1–3 |
| 3 | Alexius I | Constantinople | 'AV' | 3.92 | DO | *DOC* 6c.21 |
| 4 | Anonymous 'K' | Constantinople | Æ | 6.50 | DO | *DOC* K.8 |
| 5 | Alexius I | Thessalonica(?) | Æ | 4.14 | B | *DOC* 19.1–7 |
| 6 | Alexius I | Constantinople | AV | 4.43 | B | *DOC* 20g.1–22 |
| 7 | Alexius I | Thessalonica | AV | | ANS | *DOC* 20.l |
| 8 | Alexius I | Constantinople | El | 4.13 | B | *DOC* 22.1–(3) |
| 9 | Alexius I | Thessalonica | El | | PC | *DOC* 23a.1–(c) |
| 10 | Alexius I, Irene and John II | Thessalonica | B | 3.75 | B | *DOC* 27 |
| 11 | Alexius I | Thessalonica | B | 4.01 | B | *DOC* 28 |
| 12 | Alexius I, Irene and John II | Constantinople | Pb | | PC | *DOC* 32.1–6 |
| 13 | Alexius I | Constantinople | Æ | 3.66 | DO | *DOC* 33.13 |
| 14 | Alexius I | Thessalonica | Æ | 2.30 | B | *DOC* 44.1, 2 |

PLATE 31

| | | | | | | |
|---|---|---|---|---|---|---|
| 1 | Manuel I | Constantinople | AV | 4.44 | B | *DOC* 1d.1–5 |
| 2 | Alexius III | Constantinople | AV | 4.38 | B | *DOC* 1a.1–4 |
| 3 | Andronicus I | Constantinople | El | 3.20 | B | *DOC* 2a.1–3 |
| 4 | Isaac II | Constantinople | El | 2.89 | DO | *DOC* 2a.12 |
| 5 | John II | Thessalonica | B | 4.73 | B | *DOC* 11.1–5 |
| 6 | Manuel I | Constantinople | B | 4.35 | B | *DOC* 13a.1–5 |
| 7 | Isaac Comnenus | 'Cyprus' | B | | PC | *DOC* (4) |
| 8 | Theodore Mancaphas | Philadelphia | B | | PC | *DOC* (2.1–4) |
| 9 | Anonymous | Trebizond | Æ | | PC | above, p. 438, n. 295 |
| 10 | John II | Thessalonica | Æ | | PC | *DOC* (15) |
| 11 | Manuel I | Thessalonica | Æ | 4.47 | B | *DOC* 18.1–23 |
| 12 | Isaac Comnenus | 'Cyprus' | Æ | 2.67 | DO | *DOC* 7 bis |
| 13 | Isaac Comnenus | 'Cyprus' | Æ | | PC | *DOC* (text) |
| 14 | Manuel I | Thessalonica | Æ | 3.15 | B | *DOC* 20.1–12 |
| 15 | Isaac II | Greek Mint | Æ | 1.36 | B | *DOC* (6) |
| 16 | Alexius III | Constantinople | Æ | | PC | *DOC* 6 |

PLATE 32

| | | | | | | |
|---|---|---|---|---|---|---|
| 1 | Latin Imitative | Constantinople | B | 3.55 | DO(Hd.) | *DOC* 1.1–14 |
| 2 | Latin Imitative | Constantinople | B | 3.17 | B | *DOC* 2.1–10 |
| 3 | Latin Imitative | Constantinople | B | 4.39 | B | *DOC* 4.1–10 |
| 4 | Latin Imitative | Constantinople | B | | PC | *DOC* 23.1–11 |
| 5 | Latin Imitative | Thessalonica | B | 2.80 | B | *DOC* 24.1–6 |
| 6 | Latin Imitative | Thessalonica | B | 3.75 | B | *DOC* 26.1–8 |
| 7 | Latin Imitative | Morea(?) | B | 2.25 | DO(Hd.) | *DOC* 30.1–22 |
| 8 | Latin Imitative | Morea(?) | B | 1.56 | DO(Hd.) | *DOC* 31.1–4 |
| 9 | Latin Imitative | Morea(?) | B | 1.95 | DO(Hd.) | *DOC* 32.1–3 |
| 10 | Latin Imitative | Morea(?) | B | 1.76 | DO(Hd.) | *DOC* 33.1–5 |
| 11 | Latin Imitative | Morea(?) | B | 1.26 | DO(Hd.) | *DOC* 34.1–3 |
| 12 | Latin Imitative | Morea(?) | B | 1.31 | DO(Hd.) | *DOC* 35.1–3 |
| 13 | Latin Imitative | Morea(?) | B | 1.59 | DO(Hd.) | *DOC* 36a.–c.2 |
| 14 | Bulgarian Imitative | ? | B | 3.09 | DO | *DOC* 1a.18 |
| 15 | Bulgarian Imitative | ? | B | 2.97 | DO | *DOC* 2.11 |
| 16 | Bulgarian Imitative | ? | B | 2.39 | DO | *DOC* 3a.1 |

PLATE 33

| | | | | | |
|---|---|---|---|---|---|
| 1 Manuel I | Trebizond | AR | | BN | Ret. pp. 24–5 |
| 2 Manuel I | Trebizond | AR | 2.98 | B | Ret. pp. 26–65 |
| 3 John II(1) | Trebizond | AR | 2.90 | B | Ret. pp. 11–16 ('John I') |
| 4 Theodora | Trebizond | AR | 2.94 | B | Ret. pp. 132–3 |
| 5 John II(2) | Trebizond | AR | 3.05 | B | Ret. pp. 84–104 |
| 6 John II and Alexius II | Trebizond | AR | 2.52 | DO | Ret. p. 130 |
| 7 Alexius II | Trebizond | AR | 2.17 | B | Ret. pp. 136–46 |
| 8 Andronicus III | Trebizond | AR | 2.08 | T | Ret. p. 148 |
| 9 Manuel II | Trebizond | AR | 1.97 | T | Ret. – |
| 10 Basil | Trebizond | AR | 2.11 | B | Ret. pp. 151–2 |
| 11 Michael(2) | Trebizond | AR | 1.35 | B | Ret. pp. 158–9 |
| 12 Alexius III | Trebizond | AR | 1.70 | B | Ret. pp. 163–9 |
| 13 Manuel III | Trebizond | AR | 1.03 | B | Ret. pp. 173–6 |
| 14 Alexius IV | Trebizond | AR | 0.86 | DO | Ret. pp. 179–83 |
| 15 John I | Trebizond | Æ | | PC | above p. 522, n. 369 |
| 16 George | Trebizond | Æ | 1.90 | B | Ret. – |
| 17 John II and Alexius II | Trebizond | Æ | 2.47 | B | Ret. p. 131 |
| 18 Alexius III | Trebizond | Æ | 1.13 | DO | Ret. p. 171, no. 51 |
| 19 Alexius III | Trebizond | Æ | 1.10 | DO | Ret. p. 171, no. 47 |
| 20 Alexius III | Trebizond | Æ | 1.69 | DO | Ret. p. 171, no. 48 |

PLATE 34

| | | | | | |
|---|---|---|---|---|---|
| 1 Theodore Ducas | Thessalonica | B | 3.80 | PC | *DOC* 5a.1–d.2 |
| 2 Manuel Ducas | Thessalonica | B | | PC | *DOC* (3a.1)–c.3 |
| 3 John Ducas | Thessalonica | B | 2.08 | B | *DOC* 2.1–(3) |
| 4 John III | Thessalonica | B | | ANS | *DOC* 3.1–7 |
| 5 John III and Michael II Ducas | Thessalonica | B | | PC | *DOC* (1.1) |
| 6 Theodore Ducas | Thessalonica | Æ | 3.67 | B | *DOC* 12.1–(6) |
| 7 Theodore Ducas | Thessalonica | Æ | 1.97 | DO | *DOC* 15b.3 |
| 8 John III | Magnesia | AV | 4.27 | B | *DOC* 6b.1–9 |
| 9 Theodore II | Magnesia | AV | | PC | *DOC* (2a) |
| 10 Theodore I | Magnesia | AR | 4.27 | B | *DOC* 4.1–8 |
| 11 John III | Magnesia | AR | | PC | *DOC* (text) |
| 12 Theodore I | Nicaea | B | 3.89 | B | *DOC* 5a.1–8 |
| 13 John III | Magnesia | B | 2.67 | DO | *DOC* 48c |

PLATE 35

| | | | | | | |
|---|---|---|---|---|---|---|
| 1 | Theodore II | Magnesia | B | 2.55 | B | *DOC* 10a.1–(b) |
| 2 | John III | Magnesia | Æ | 1.62 | B | *DOC* 58.1–12 |
| 3 | Michael VIII | Magnesia | Æ | 1.77 | B | *DOC* 6.1, 2 |
| 4 | Michael VIII | Constantinople | AV | 4.06 | B | – |
| 5 | Andronicus II and Michael IX | Constantinople | AV | 4.20 | DO | *LPC* p. 62, no. 1 |
| 6 | Andronicus II | Constantinople | AV | 3.66 | B | *LPC* p. 34, no. 1 |
| 7 | Andronicus II and III | Constantinople | AV | 4.10 | B | *LPC* p. 108, no. 1 |
| 8 | Anna and John V | Constantinople | AV | 4.14 | B | *LPC* p. 116, no. 1 |
| 9 | John V and VI | Constantinople | AV | 4.25 | B | *LPC* p. 138, no. 1 |
| 10 | Michael VIII | Constantinople | AR | 2.20 | PC | above, p. 526, n. 388 |
| 11 | Michael VIII | Constantinople | AR | 2.76 | B | above, p. 526, n. 388 |
| 12 | Andronicus II and Michael IX | Constantinople | AR | 2.13 | B | *LPC* p. 88, no. 35 |
| 13 | Andronicus III | Constantinople | AR | 1.46 | B | *LPC* p. 118, no. 4 |
| 14 | Anna and John V | Constantinople | AR | 1.13 | B | *LPC* p. 132, nos 1, 2 |
| 15 | John VI | Constantinople | AR | 1.02 | DO | *LPC* p. 148, no. 1 |
| 16 | John VI | Constantinople | AR | 0.82 | DO | *LPC* p. 148, no. 2 |
| 17 | Matthew Asen-Cantacuzene | Didymotichum(?) | AR | | PC | above, p. 447, n. 336 |
| 18 | Andronicus II and Michael IX | Constantinople | AR | 1.09 | DO | *LPC* p. 70, no. 11 |
| 19 | Andronicus II | Constantinople | B | 0.77 | DO | *LPC* p. 36, no. 4 |
| 20 | Anonymous | Constantinople | B | 0.61 | B | *LPC* p. 184, no. 7 |

PLATE 36

| | | | | | | |
|---|---|---|---|---|---|---|
| 1 | Michael VIII | Thessalonica | B | 2.70 | B | *TMP* p. 25, no. 4 |
| 2 | Andronicus III | Constantinople | B | 4.12 | B | *LPC* p. 122, no. 9 |
| 3 | Andronicus III | Constantinople | Æ | 2.30 | B | *LPC* p. 126, no. 12 |
| 4 | Andronicus II and Michael IX | Constantinople | Æ | 1.80 | B | *LPC* p. 84, no. 29 |
| 5 | Anna and John V | Thessalonica | Æ | 2.24 | DO | *LPC* p. 246, no. 2 |
| 6 | John V(1) | Constantinople | AR | 8.64 | B | *LPC* cf. p. 154, no. 2 |
| 7 | Andronicus IV | Constantinople | AR | 7.84 | B | *LPC* p. 152, no. 1 |
| 8 | John V(2) | Constantinople | AR | 8.40 | B | *LPC* p. 154, no. 2 |
| 9 | Manuel II | Constantinople | AR | 7.15 | B | *LPC* p. 160, no. 1 |

| | | | | | |
|---|---|---|---|---|---|
| 10 John VIII | Constantinople | Æ | 6.89 | B | *LPC* p. 172, no. 1 |
| 11 Manuel II | Constantinople | Æ | 3.65 | B | *LPC* p. 160, no. 2 |
| 12 John V | Constantinople | Æ | 4.03 | DO | *LPC* p. 168, no. 1 |
| 13 John VIII | Constantinople | Æ | 3.45 | B | *LPC* p. 172, no. 2 |
| 14 Constantine XI | Constantinople | Æ | 2.89 | PC | *LPC* p. 176, no. 1 |
| 15 John V(2) | Constantinople | Æ | 1.00 | B | *LPC* p. 154, no. 3 |
| 16 Manuel II | Constantinople | Æ | 0.82 | DO | *LPC* p. 162, no. 5 |
| 17 Manuel II | Constantinople | Æ | 2.35 | DO | *LPC* p. 164, no. 7 |
| 18 Andronicus IV | Constantinople | Æ | 2.09 | DO | *LPC* p. 152, no. 3 |
| 19 Manuel II | Constantinople | Æ | 0.78 | B | *LPC* p. 166, no. 12 |
| 20 Manuel II | Constantinople | Æ | 0.74 | DO | *LPC* p. 166, no. 11 |

1 The imperial largesse: AV, AR ceremonial coins/medallions (1).

2 The imperial largesse: AV, AR ceremonial coins/medallions (2).

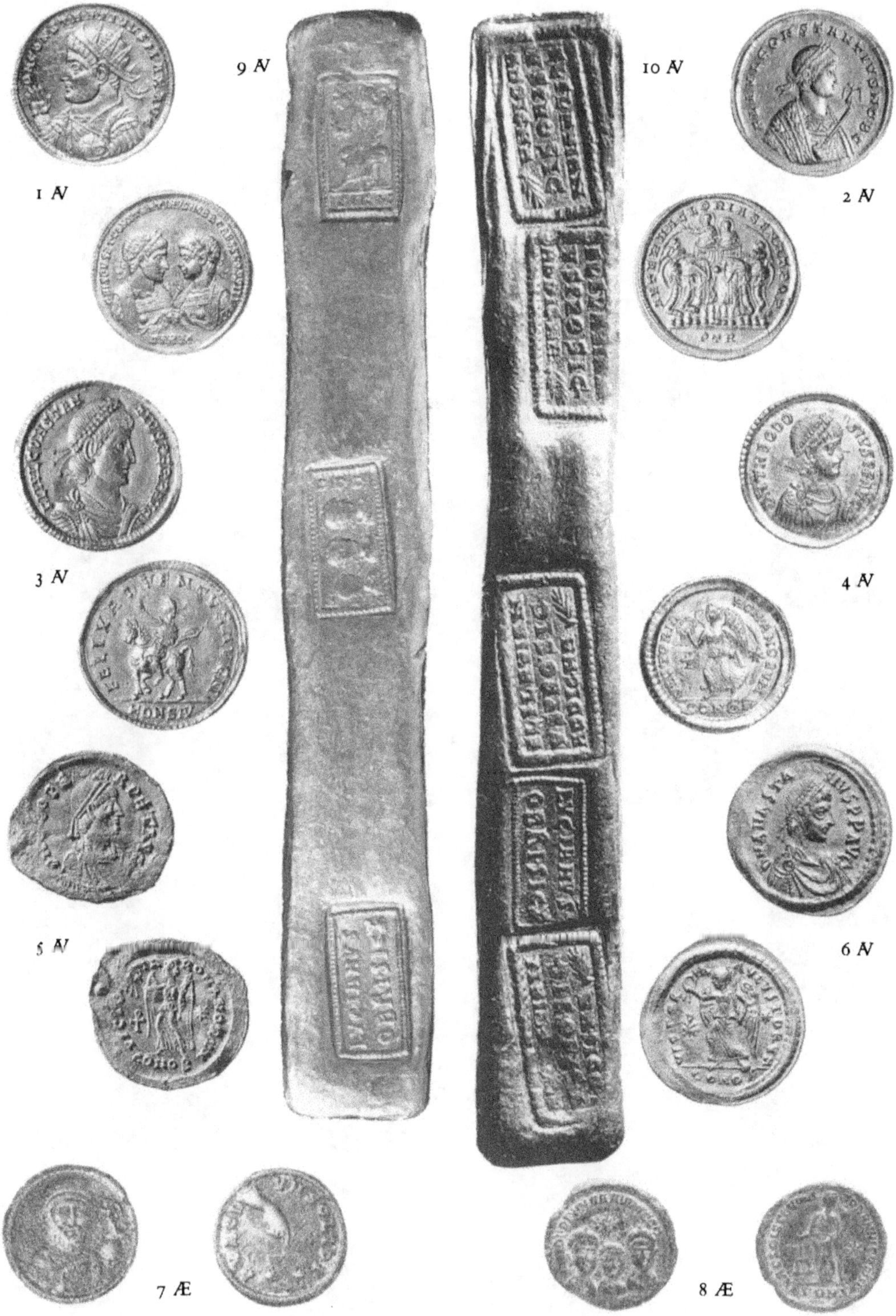


3 The imperial largesse: AV ceremonial coins/medallions (3) (**1**–**6**); Æ hexagia (**7**: Julian, **8**: Arcadius, Honorius and Theodosius II); AV ingots (Valens, Gratian and Valentinian II) (**9**–**10**).

4 Diocletian, colleagues and successors (1): AV, AR, *c.* 294/6–321/2.

5 Constantine, colleagues and family: AV, AR, *c.* 310–336/7.

6 Diocletian, colleagues and successors (2): B, Æ, *c.* 294/6–307.

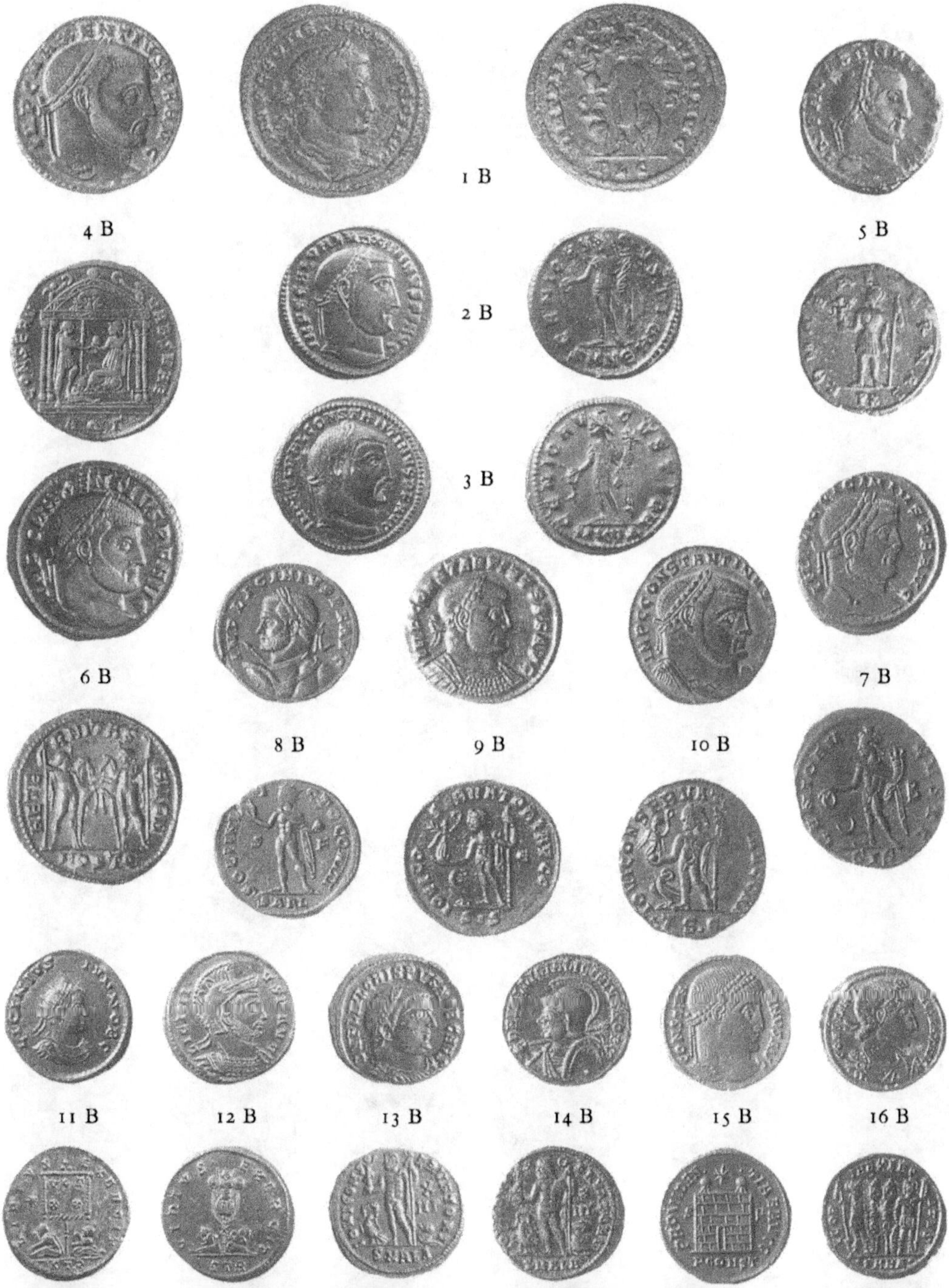


7 Constantine, colleagues and successors: B, *c.* 308/9–348.

8 The sons of Constantine to Theodosius I: AV, *c.* 342/3–395.

9 The sons of Constantine to Magnus Maximus: AR, *c.* 340/50–388 (**1–11**). *Fel. Temp. Reparatio*: B, Æ, *c.* 348–350 (**12–19**).

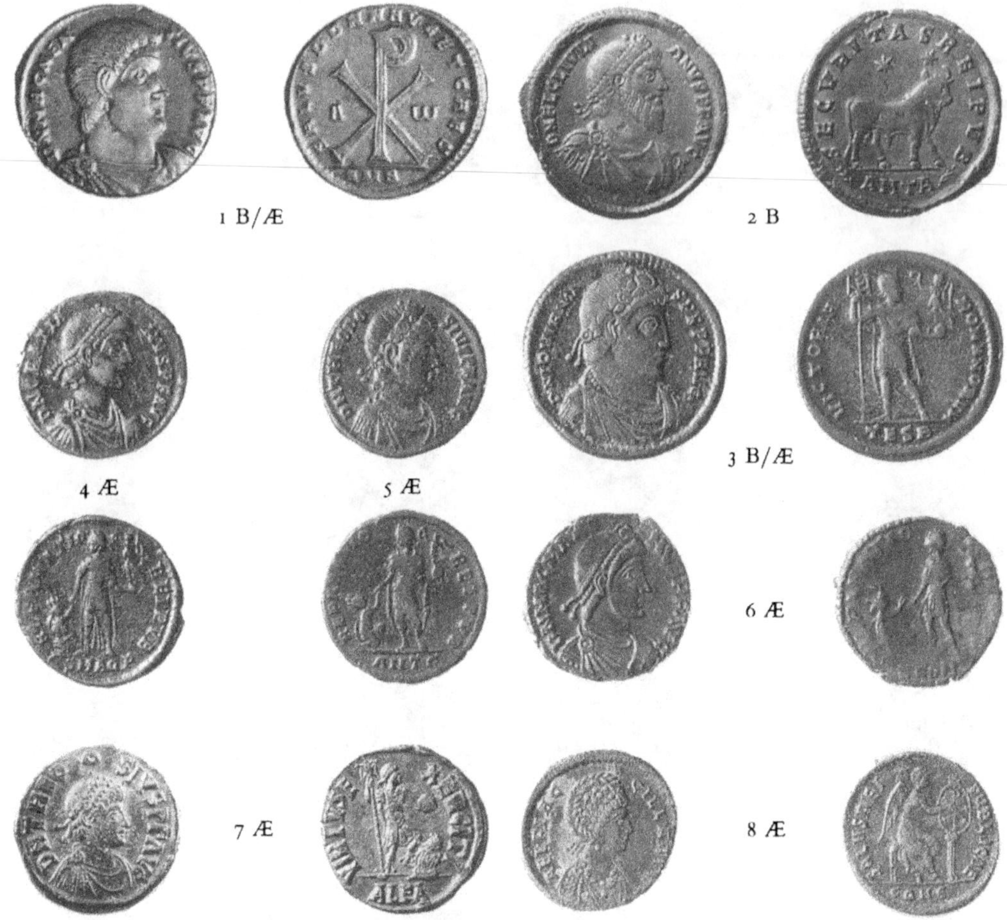


10 Magnentius to Gratian and colleagues: B/Æ 1/2, *c.* 352–388 (**1–8**). The west, Honorius to Johannes: AV, *c.* 395–425 (**9–17**).

11 The west, Valentinian III to Julius Nepos: AV, AR, Æ, *c.* 425–480.

12 The east, Arcadius to Zeno: AV, AR, Æ, *c.* 395–491.

13 The multiple nummus, Leo I and Zeno: Æ, *c.* 457–491 (**1–4**). Anastasius to Phocas: AV, AR, *c.* 491–602 (**5–21**).

14 Anastasius to Justinian: Æ, *c.* 498–538/9.

15 Justinian to Phocas: Æ, *c.* 538/9–602.

16 The Heraclian Revolt and the Persian Wars: Anomalous issues and temporary mints, *c.* 608–628/9.

17 Heraclius to Justinian II (1): AV, *c.* 610–711 (**1–19**); Æ, *c.* 610–668 (**20–3**).

18 Heraclius to Justinian II (2): Æ, *c.* 668–711 (**1–8**). The centralisation of production: Æ, 'Sicily', *c.* 629/30–643/4 (**9–12**).

19 Justinian I to Justinian II: AV light-weight solidi, *c.* 538–668 (**1–13**); AR hexagrammata, *c.* 615–713 (**14–20**).

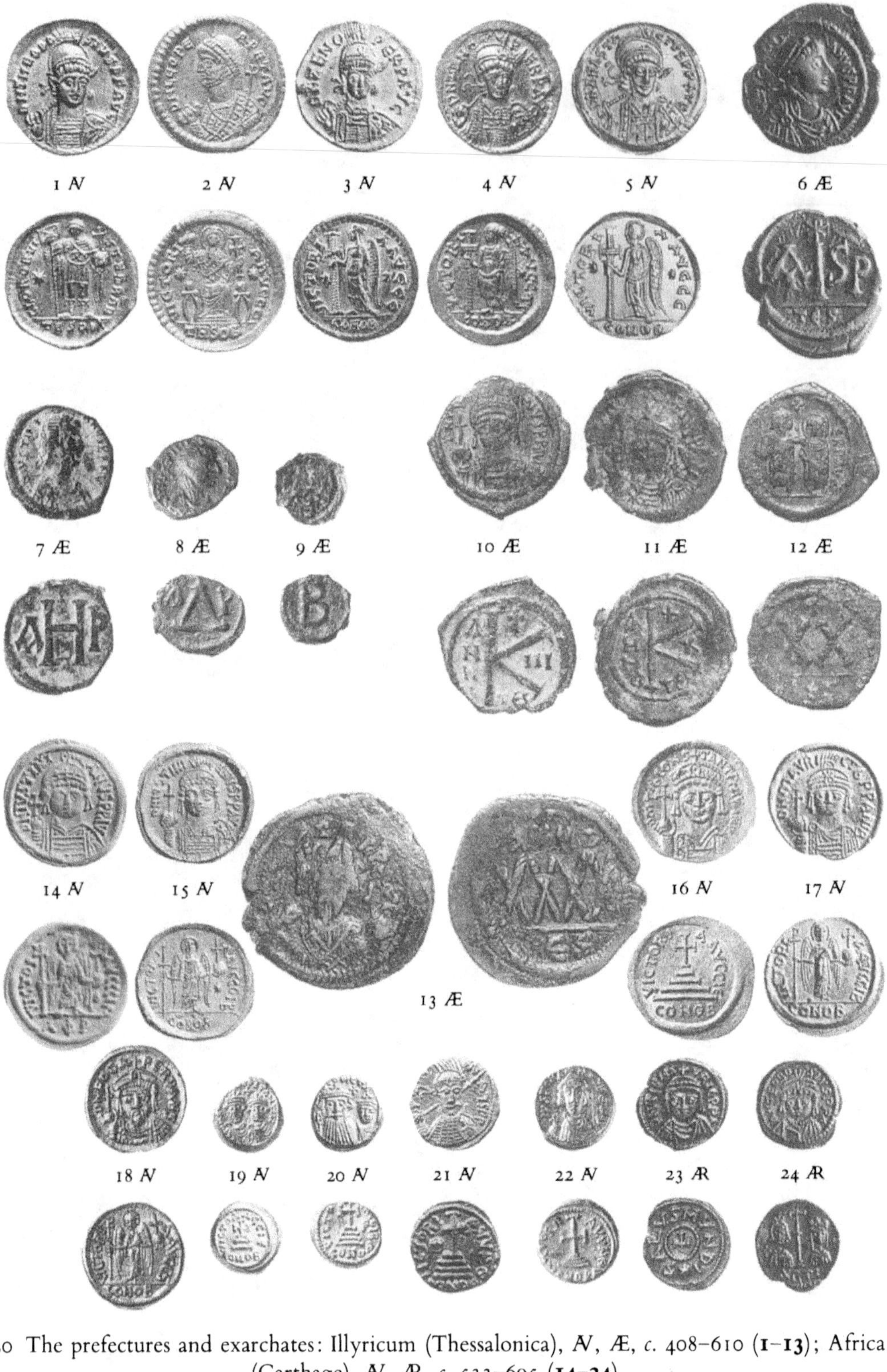


20 The prefectures and exarchates: Illyricum (Thessalonica), AV, Æ, *c.* 408–610 (**1–13**); Africa (Carthage), AV, AR, *c.* 533–695 (**14–24**).

21 The prefectures and exarchates: Africa (Carthage, Sardinia) (2), AV, AR, Æ, *c.* 533–705 (**1–10**); Italy (Rome, Ravenna), AV, AR, *c.* 535–578 (**11–24**).

22 The prefectures and exarchates: Italy (Ravenna) (2), AR, Æ, *c.* 540–685 (**1–8**). Anomalous mints and denominations: Alexandria, AV, Æ (**9–15**); Cherson, Æ (**16, 17**); Spain (Carthagena?), AV (**18, 19**); Dalmatia (Salona?), Æ (**20**); Sicily (Catania), Æ (**21, 22**).

23 Leo III to Michael II (1): AV, *c.* 717–829 (**1–12**, **18–20**); AR, *c.* 717–820 (**13–17**, **21**).

24 Leo III to Michael II (2): Æ, *c.* 717–829 (**1–9**). Theophilus to Constantine VII and Zoë: AV, *c.* 829–919 (**10–19**).

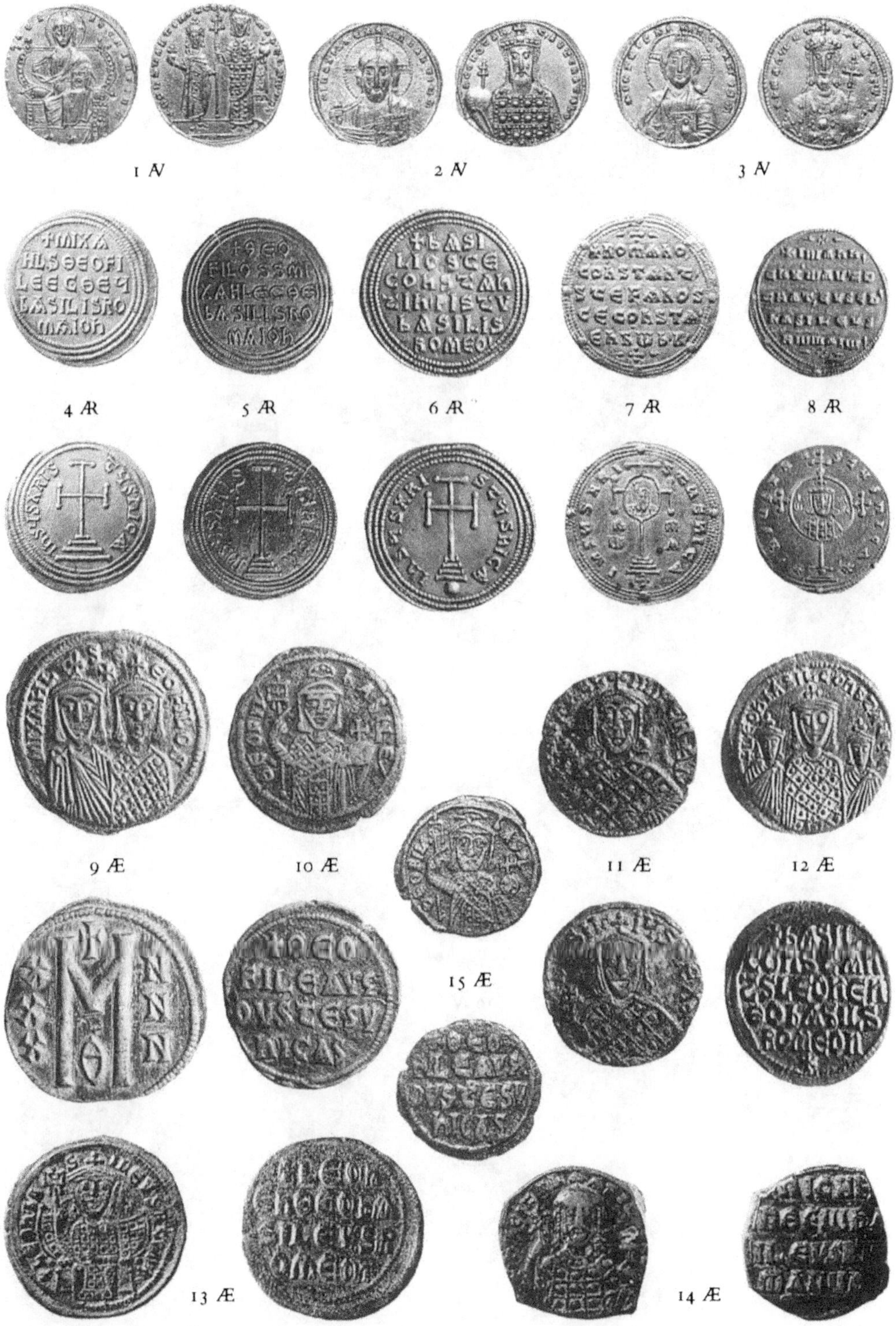


25 Constantine VII and Romanus I to Romanus II: AV, *c.* 920–963 (**1–3**). Michael II to John I: AR, *c.* 820–976 (**4–8**). Michael II to Nicephorus II: Æ, *c.* 820–969 (**9–14**).

26 Regional and peripheral mints, Constans II to John I (1): Thessalonica (?), AV, Æ, *c.* 820–886 (**1–6**); Sicily (Syracuse), AV, Æ, *c.* 641–867 (**7–21**).

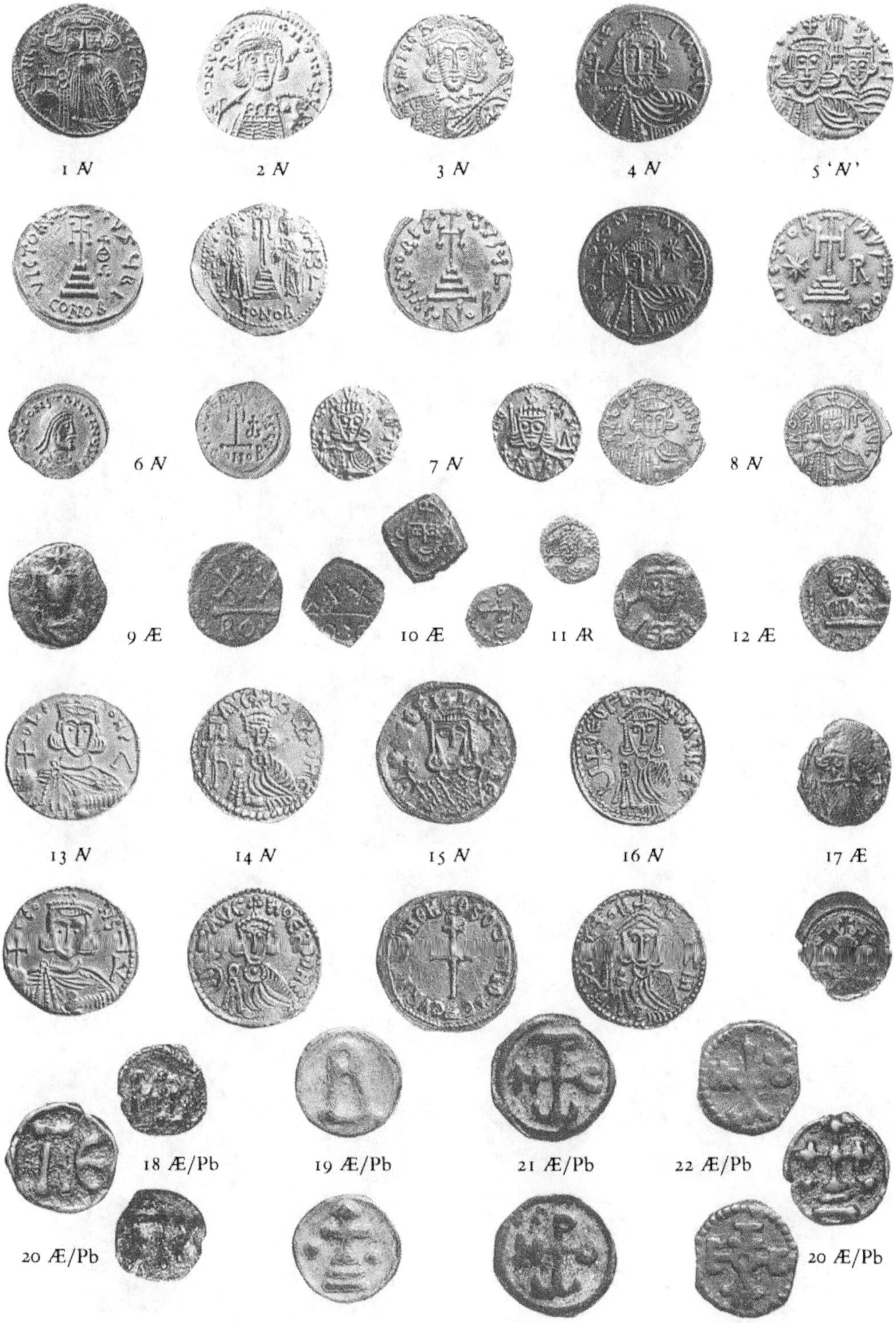


27 Regional and peripheral mints, Constans II to John I (2): Rome, AV, AR, Æ, *c.* 641–775 (**1–12**); Naples, AV, Æ, *c.* 641–842 (**13–17**); Cherson, Æ/Pb, *c.* 842–976 (**18–22**).

1 AV 2 AV 3 AV 4 AV 5 AV

6 AV 7 AV 8 AV 9 'AV'

10 AV 11 AV 12 AV 13 AV 14 AV 15 AV

16 AV 17 'AV'

28 Basil II to Nicephorus III (*c.* 976–1081) (1): AV histamena/trachea (**1–9**); AV tetartera (**10–17**).

29 Basil II to Nicephorus III (*c.* 976–1081) (2): Æ miliaresia and fractions (**1–6**); Æ folleis (**7–13**).

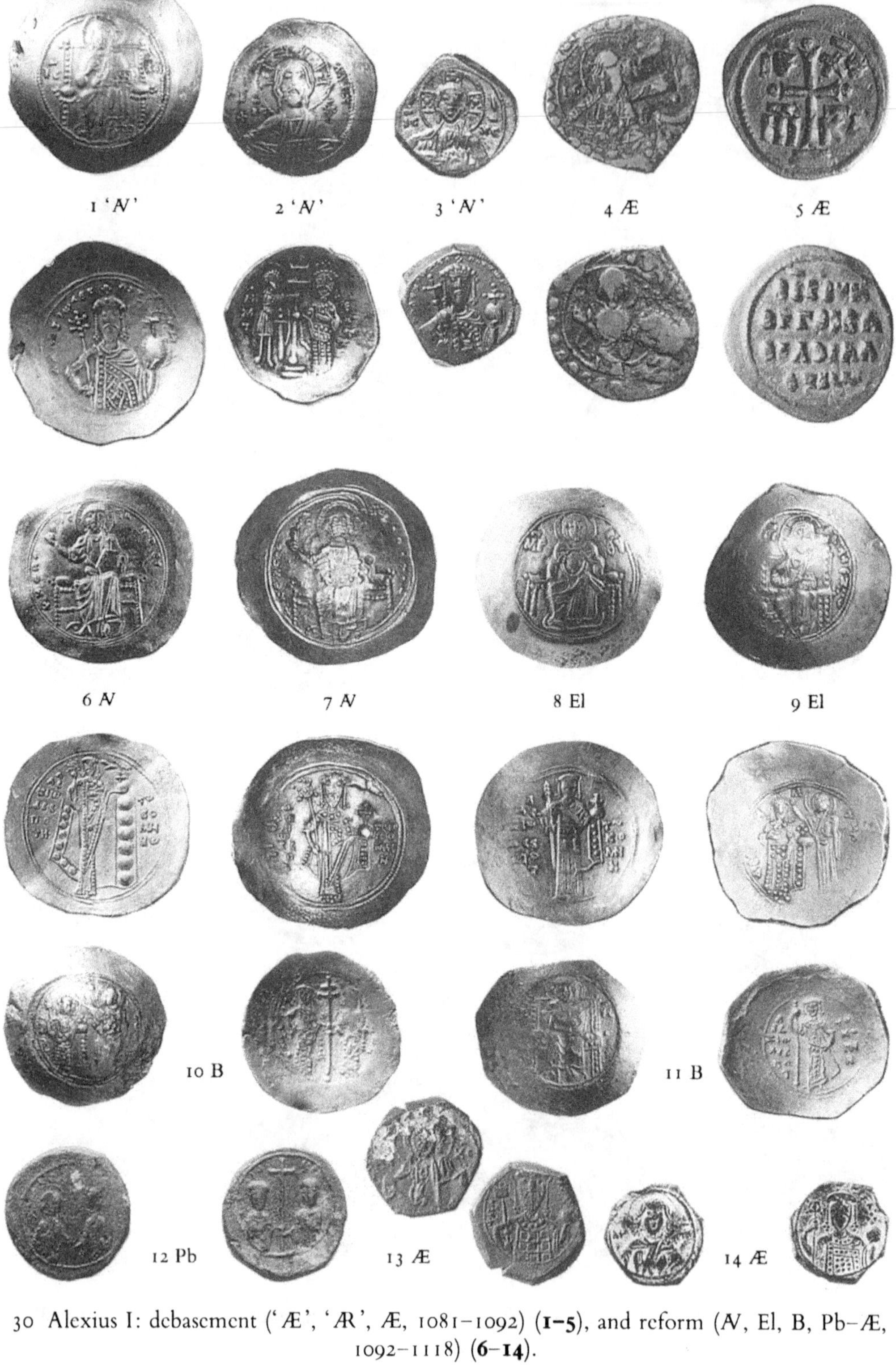


30 Alexius I: debasement ('Æ', 'AR', Æ, 1081–1092) (**1–5**), and reform (AV, El, B, Pb–Æ, 1092–1118) (**6–14**).

31 John II to Alexius III: AV, El, B, Æ, *c.* 1118–1203.

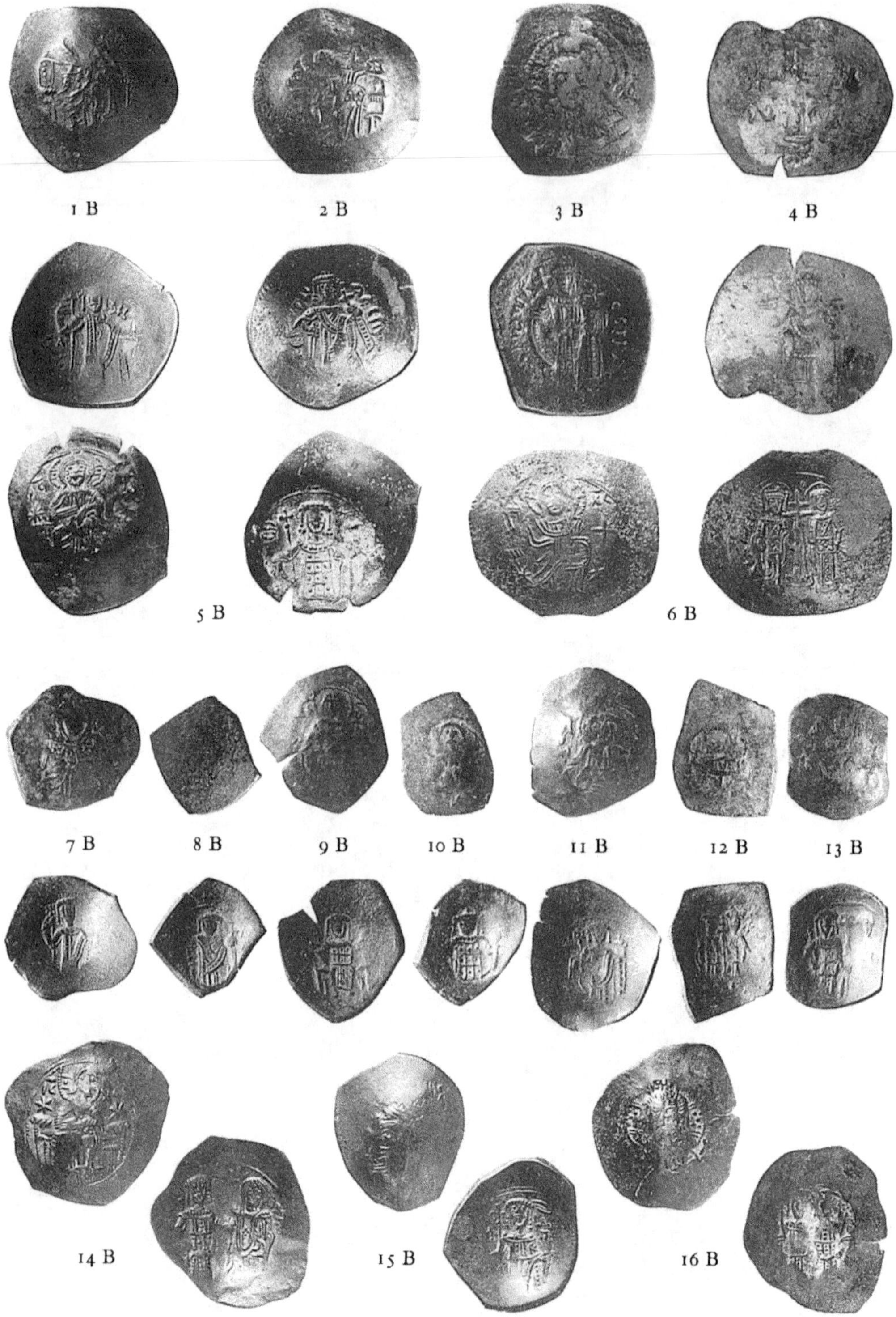

1 B 2 B 3 B 4 B

5 B 6 B

7 B 8 B 9 B 10 B 11 B 12 B 13 B

14 B 15 B 16 B

32 The successor states (1): The Latins in Constantinople, *c.* 1204–1261 (**1–4**); in Thessalonica, *c.* 1204–1224 (**5, 6**); in Greece (?), *c.* 1210–1240 (**7–13**). The Bulgarians, *c.* 1195–1215 (**14–16**).

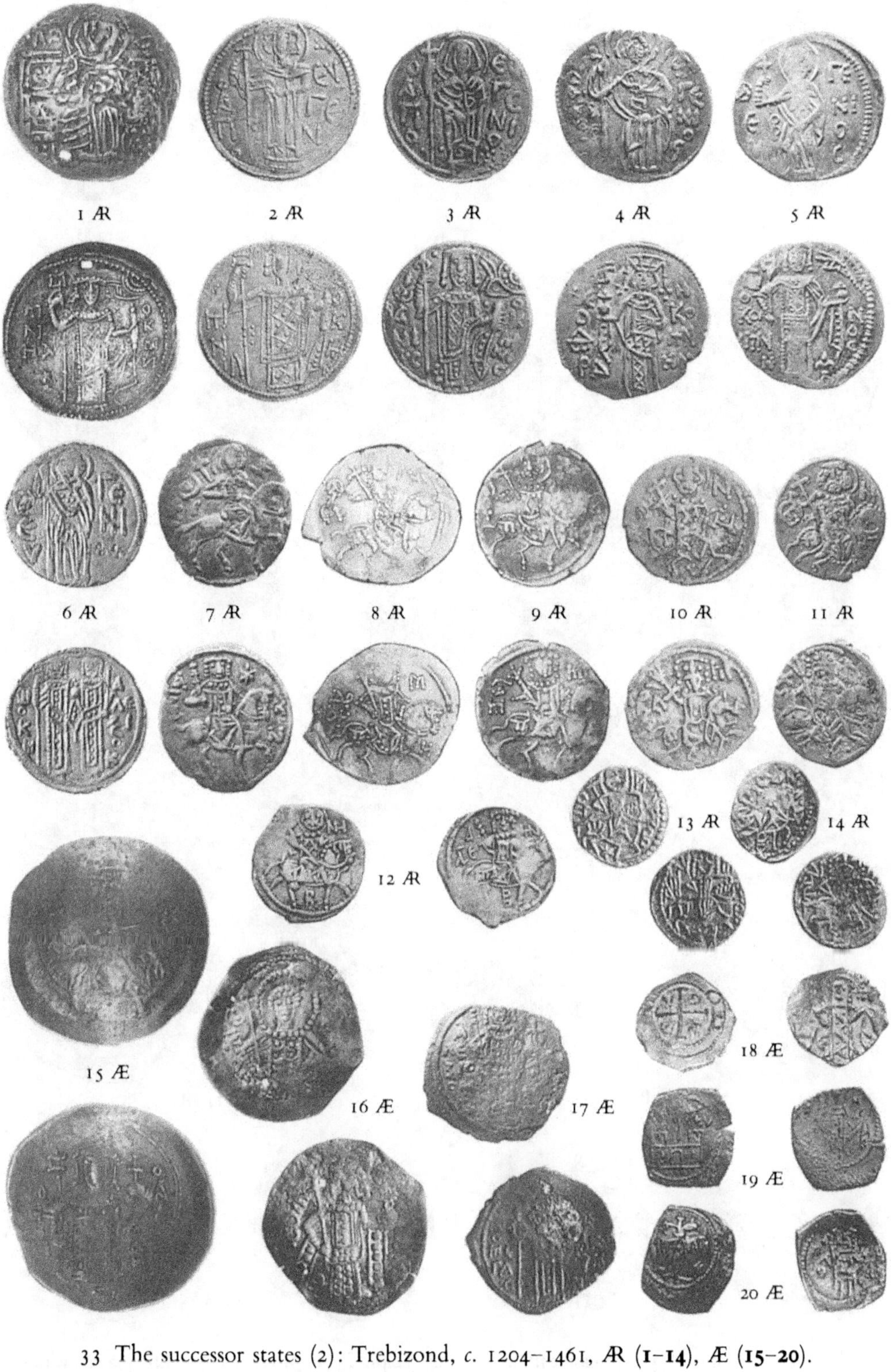

33 The successor states (2): Trebizond, *c.* 1204–1461, AR (**1–14**), Æ (**15–20**).

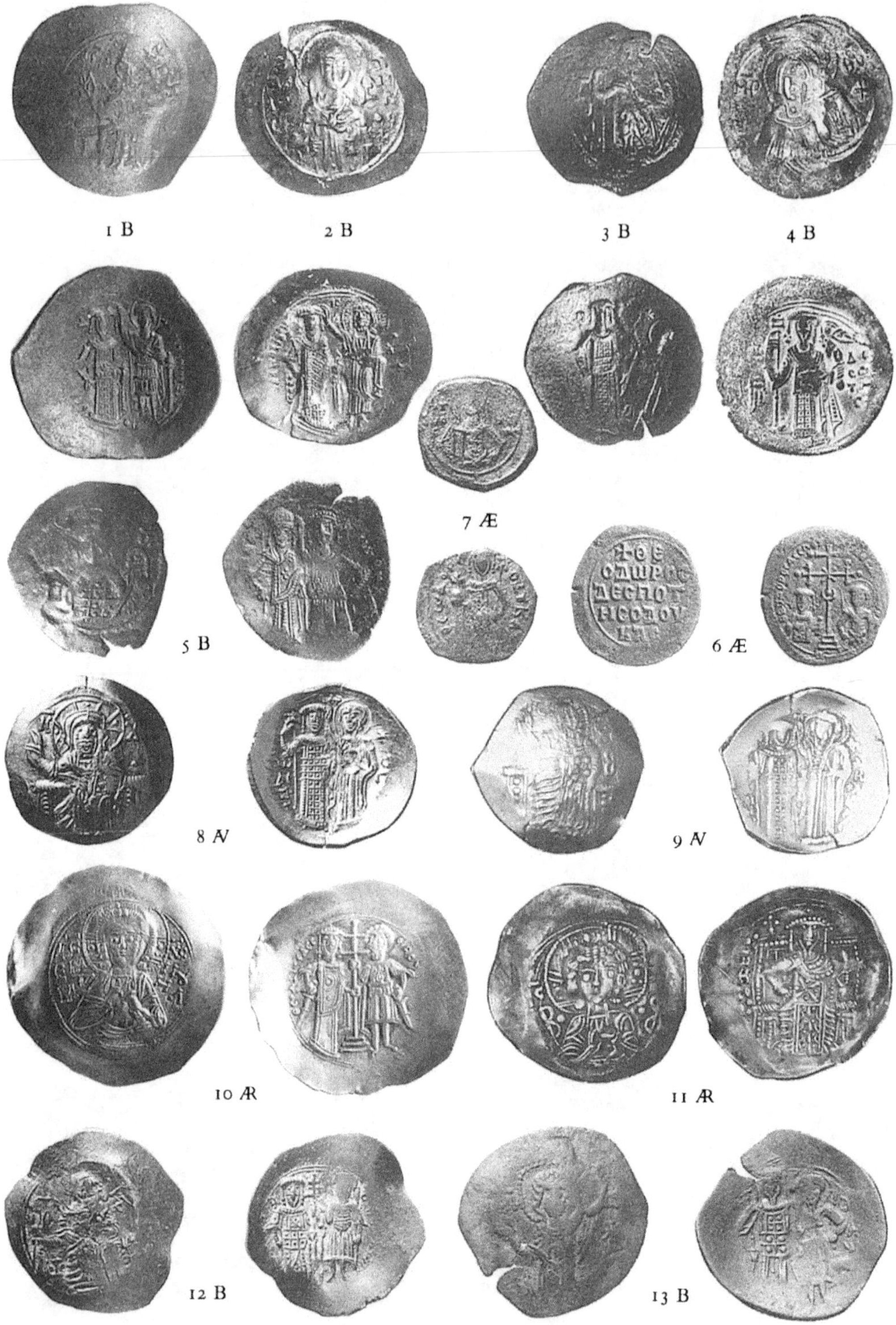


34 The successor states (3): Thessalonica, *c.* 1224–1248, B (**1–5**), Æ (**6, 7**); Nicaea/Magnesia, *c.* 1205–1261, AV (**8, 9**), AR (**10, 11**), B (**12, 13**).

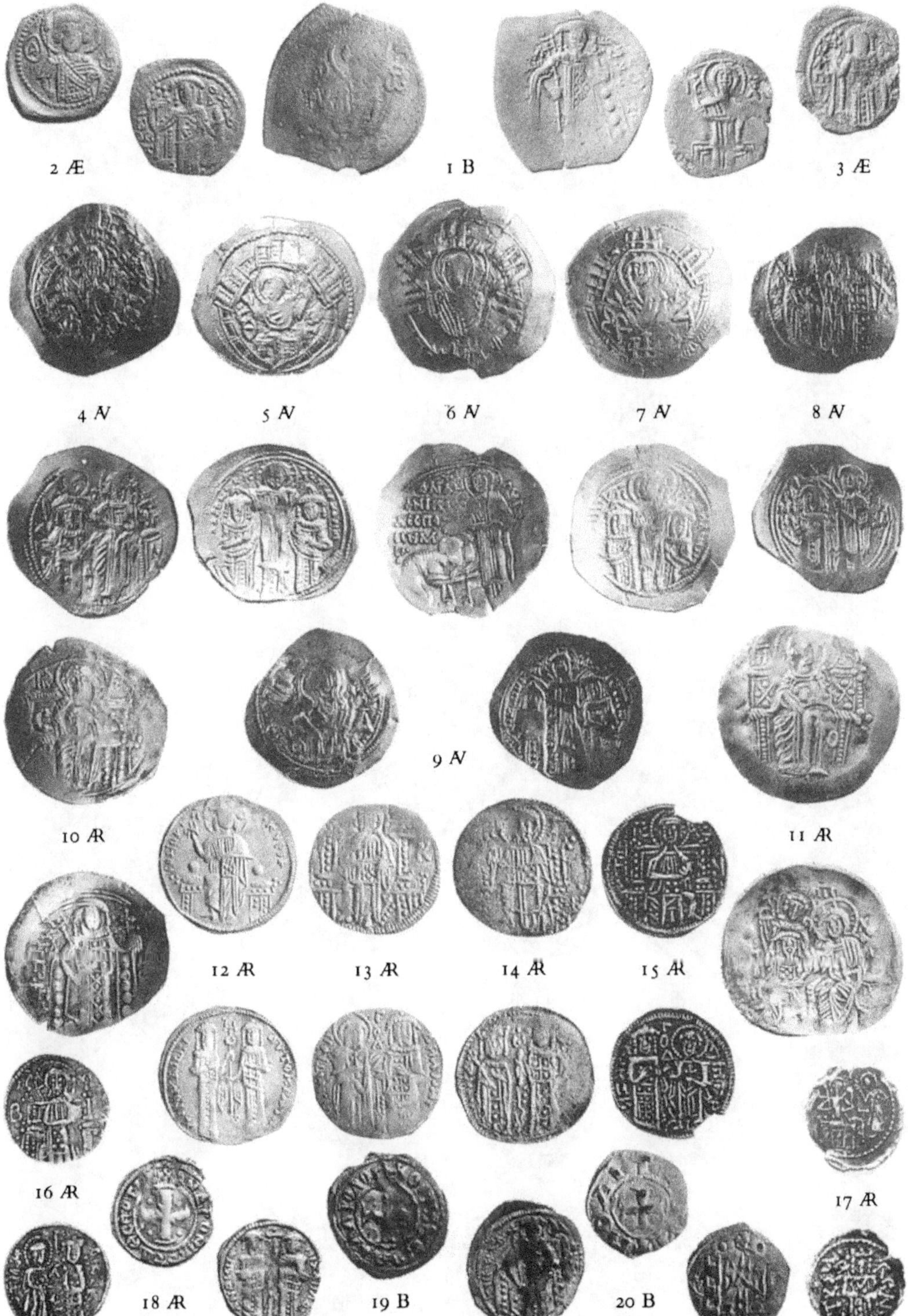


35 The successor states (4): Nicaea/Magnesia, *c.* 1205–1261, B (**1**), Æ (**2, 3**). The restored empire, *c.* 1261–1357 (1): AV (**4–9**), AR (**10–18**), B (**19, 20**).

36 The restored empire, *c.* 1261–1365 (2): B (**1**, **2**), Æ (**3–5**). The transition to silver, *c.* 1360?–1453: Æ (**6–16**), Æ (**17–20**).

# INDEXES

## 1. AUTHORS AND COMPILATIONS (ANCIENT AND MEDIAEVAL)

## 2. AUTHORS, EDITORS AND COMPILATIONS (MODERN)

## 3. PLACES (ANCIENT AND MEDIAEVAL)

## 4. PEOPLE (ANCIENT AND MEDIAEVAL)

other than authors or compilers, for whom see INDEX 1: AUTHORS

## 5A. IMPERIAL INSTITUTIONS, OFFICES AND RANKS

## 5B. TECHNICAL TERMS AND UNUSUAL WORDS

## 6. GENERAL

For EU product safety concerns, contact us at Calle de José Abascal, 56–1°,
28003 Madrid, Spain or eugpsr@cambridge.org.

www.ingramcontent.com/pod-product-compliance
Lightning Source LLC
LaVergne TN
LVHW081958200926
848481LV00010B/2766
* 9 7 8 0 5 2 1 0 8 8 5 2 7 *